TO THE STUDENT: Three helpful supplemental study aids for this textbook are available:

☐ *Student Guide* by Dudley W. Curry contains, for each chapter in this textbook, a detailed review of key ideas plus practice test questions and problems with solutions.

☐ *Working Papers* by Dudley W. Curry provide partially filled in problem data and column headings for important in-text problems.

☐ *Practice Set* (Chimes, Inc.) by Dudley W. Curry comprises a simulated case covering all the steps in the accounting cycle, tying together the fundamentals of bookkeeping and accounting, and including partially filled in working papers.

Introduction to
FINANCIAL
ACCOUNTING

PRENTICE-HALL SERIES IN ACCOUNTING

Charles T. Horngren, Editor

3rd Edition

Introduction to
FINANCIAL
ACCOUNTING

Charles T. Horngren
Stanford University

Gary L. Sundem
University of Washington–Seattle

Prentice-Hall, Inc., Englewood Cliffs, New Jersey 07632

Library of Congress Cataloging-in-Publication Data

Horngren, Charles T. (date)
  Introduction to financial accounting.

  (Prentice-Hall series in accounting)
  Bibliography: p.
  Includes index.
  1. Accounting.   I. Sundem, Gary L.   II. Title.
III. Series.
HF5635.H813   1987   657   86-25310
ISBN 0-13-483264-7

Editorial/production supervision: Barbara Grasso
Interior and cover design: Jayne Conte
Cover photo: Seattle, Washington. F. P. G. International
Manufacturing buyer: Ray Keating

Printed in the United States of America

10 9 8 7 6 5 4 3 2 1

ISBN 0-13-483264-7   01

Prentice-Hall International (UK) Limited, *London*
Prentice-Hall of Australia Pty. Limited, *Sydney*
Prentice-Hall Canada Inc., *Toronto*
Prentice-Hall Hispanoamericana, S.A., *Mexico*
Prentice-Hall of India Private Limited, *New Delhi*
Prentice-Hall of Japan, Inc., *Tokyo*
Prentice-Hall of Southeast Asia Pte. Ltd., *Singapore*
Editora Prentice-Hall do Brasil, Ltda., *Rio de Janeiro*

To Professor Dudley W. Curry

Charles T. Horngren is the Edmund W. Littlefield Professor of Accounting at Stanford University. A graduate of Marquette University, he received his MBA from Harvard University and his Ph.D. from the University of Chicago. He is also the recipient of honorary doctorates from Marquette University and De Paul University.

A Certified Public Accountant, Horngren served on the Accounting Principles Board for six years, the Financial Accounting Standards Board Advisory Council for five years, and the Council of the American Institute of Certified Public Accountants for three years. He is currently serving as a trustee of the Financial Accounting Foundation.

A member of the American Accounting Association, Horngren has been its President and its Director of Research. He received the Outstanding Accounting Educator Award in 1973 when the association initiated an annual series of such awards.

The California Certified Public Accountants Foundation gave Horngren its Faculty Excellence Award in 1975 and its Distinguished Professor Award in 1983. He is the first person to have received both awards.

In 1985 the American Institute of Certified Public Accountants presented its first Outstanding Educator Award to Horngren.

Professor Horngren is also a member of the National Association of Accountants, where he was on its research planning committee for three years. He was a member of the Board of Regents, Institute of Certified Management Accountants, which administers the Certified Management Accountant examinations.

Horngren is the co-author (with Gary L. Sundem) of the companion volume *Introduction to Management Accounting,* Seventh Edition, 1987. He is also the co-author (with George Foster) of *Cost Accounting: A Managerial Emphasis,* Sixth Edition, 1987.

Charles T. Horngren is the Consulting Editor for the Prentice-Hall Series in Accounting.

Gary L. Sundem is Professor of Accounting at the University of Washington, Seattle. He received his B.A. degree from Carleton College and his MBA and Ph.D. degrees from Stanford University.

Professor Sundem served as Editor of *The Accounting Review,* 1982–86. His other American Accounting Association positions have included membership on the Executive Committee, Chair of the Planning Committee for the Association's 1981 annual meeting, and Director of the AAA Doctoral Consortium.

A member of the National Association of Accountants, Sundem is past president of the Seattle chapter. He has served on NAA's Committee on Academic Relations and is currently on the national Board of Directors.

Professor Sundem has had numerous publications in accounting and finance journals, including *The Accounting Review, Journal of Accounting Research,* and *Journal of Finance.* He received an award for the most notable contribution to accounting literature in 1978. He has made presentations at over fifty universities in the United States and abroad.

Sundem was chairman of the University of Washington's department of accounting in 1978–82. He has been a consultant to industry and government.

CONTENTS

☐ PART TWO Some Major Elements of Financial Accounting

6 SALES, RECEIVABLES, PURCHASES, AND COST OF GOODS SOLD 210

7 VALUING INVENTORIES AND MEASURING GROSS PROFIT 267

8   INTERNAL CONTROL, CASH, AND SPECIAL JOURNALS 314

9   LONG-LIVED ASSETS AND DEPRECIATION 372

10 LIABILITIES AND INTEREST 421

11 STOCKHOLDERS' EQUITY AND THE INCOME STATEMENT 480

15 STATEMENT OF CHANGES IN FINANCIAL POSITION 670

16 FINANCIAL STATEMENTS: CONCEPTUAL FRAMEWORK AND INTERPRETATION 715

☐ **PART ONE Income, Conceptual Framework, and Acceptance**

☐ **PART TWO Analysis of Financial Statements**

☐ PART FOUR Appendixes

PREFACE

Introduction to Financial Accounting is the first member of a matched pair of books that provides full coverage of the essentials of financial and managerial accounting. The second book is *Introduction to Management Accounting*. In combination, the pair can be used throughout two semesters or three quarters of introductory accounting.

Introduction to Financial Accounting is a textbook for introductory accounting courses that presuppose no prior knowledge of accounting. It deals with important topics that all students of management should study. Our goals have been to choose *relevant* subject matter and to present it *clearly* and *flexibly*. The book is oriented to the user of financial statements, but it gives ample attention to the needs of potential accounting practitioners.

Because financial accounting is so pervasive, an understanding of its uses and limitations is valuable whether the student eventually becomes a company president, a sales manager, a professional accountant, a hospital administrator or a politician. In particular, knowledge of accounting for business is worthwhile because all of us relate to companies in one or more of the following ways: investors, managers, customers, creditors, government regulators, observers, or critics.

A philosopher once said, "You have to know what something *is* before you know what it *is used for*. When you know what it is used for, then you can decide what changes deserve serious thought." *Introduction to Financial Accounting* describes the most widely used accounting theory and practice. Emphasis is on *what accounting is* rather than *what it should be*. After all, beginning students must know what accounting today is really like before they can make judgments as to what changes in practice are desirable. Ample consideration is given to proposed changes in accounting throughout the book (especially in Chapter 14 on inflation and in Chapter 16 on the conceptual framework), but the thrust is toward understanding generally accepted theory and practice.

This text stresses underlying concepts, but it makes them concrete with profuse illustrations, many taken from corporate annual reports. Moreover, accounting procedures such as transaction analysis, journalizing, and posting are given abundant consideration. In this way, the reader obtains a thorough grasp of the fundamentals of accounting. The study of concepts develops understanding of procedures, and the study of procedures enriches understanding of concepts. A major objective is to equip students with enough fundamental concepts and terminology so that they can comprehend a typical corporate annual report.

Flexibility has been a driving force in writing this book. Are you among the many instructors who favor solidifying the fundamentals by using lots of journal entries, T-accounts, work sheets, and special journals? Then see Chapters 3, 4, and 5, including their appendixes, and the appendixes to Chapters 6, 8, and 15. Are you among the other instructors who favor downplaying the details and emphasizing concepts? Then consider skipping some of the material just cited, in whole or in part.

The flexibility of the book is illustrated by the heavy use of chapter appendixes. They give the instructor latitude in picking and choosing among various topics. In short, greater depth and breadth are available, depending on the preferences of the teacher. Moreover, parts of the bodies of some chapters can be omitted if desired. Prime candidates for exclusion can be found in Chapters 6–16. Examples are the following topics: any materials in Chapter 6, other than the valuation of accounts receivable, and the presentation of consolidated statements in Chapter 12.

A major feature is the use of the fundamental accounting equation as a central thread throughout the book for explaining new concepts and analyzing transactions. For example, consider the presentations in Chapter 9 on plant assets, Chapter 10 on bonds, Chapter 12 on intercompany investments, Chapter 13 on interperiod income tax allocation, and Chapter 15 on the statement of changes in financial position. Such presentations give instructors immense latitude. They can use journal entries, or T-accounts, or the balance sheet equation format *exclusively,* if desired.

Additional features of this book include attempts to spark the reader's curiosity from the outset by:

1. Introducing financial statements of actual companies in Chapter 1.
2. Integrating a few financial ratios in an appendix to Chapter 2, a few more in Chapter 4, a few more in Chapter 7, and so on, rather than relegating all such matters of interpretation of financial statements to the rear of the book.
3. Introducing simple income tax aspects in Chapter 4 rather than later. Income taxes are not only important, they stimulate reader interest.
4. Providing a solid conceptual foundation in the first two chapters before covering the mechanics of journals, ledgers, and related procedural matters in Chapter 3.
5. Using a minimum of technical detail to introduce relatively complicated subjects and allowing chapter appendixes to examine the subjects in more depth. Examples are LIFO-FIFO in Chapter 7, compound interest in Chapter 10, changing prices in Chapter 14, and the statement of changes in financial position in Chapter 15.
6. Using published financial information as a basis for sections of assignment material in each chapter.
7. Presenting a set of learning objectives at the beginning of each chapter.

ALTERNATIVE WAYS OF USING THIS BOOK

Texts are fundamentally teaching instruments. Teaching is highly personal and heavily influenced by the backgrounds and interests of assorted students in miscellaneous settings. To satisfy this audience, a book must be a pliable tool, not a straitjacket.

In our opinion, the first eleven chapters plus Chapter 15 (Statement of Changes in Financial Position) provide the foundation for the field of financial accounting. These twelve chapters may be amplified by assigning other chapters in a variety of sequences that do not disrupt the readers' flow of thought. The most obvious candidates for insertion are:

☐ Chapters 1, 2, 3, 4, 5, 6, 7, 8, 9, 10, 11 and any of 12–16.

```
          ↑        ↑
         8*       14
         15       15
         16       16
```
* The appendix on special journals

Chapter 8 deals with internal controls, cash, and special journals. The chapter appendix (special journals) may be assigned anytime after Chapter 5.

Chapter 15 may be assigned after Chapter 9 (or even after Chapter 5); it is placed near the end of this book because the statement of changes in financial position is an excellent vehicle for reviewing all the fundamentals of financial accounting.

ASSIGNMENT MATERIAL

As always, careful choices among the wide variety of assignment material in each chapter will slant the course toward various combinations of breadth and depth, theory and procedures, simplicity and complexity.

The assignment material contains sections called Understanding Published Financial Reports, which have exercises or problems that use information presented in actual corporate annual reports or news stories. In this way, some major points in the chapter will be underscored by "real world" illustrations. Most of the annual reports used are relatively recent.

Special review assignment material is contained in Chapters 5 and 16. In addition, some assignments in Chapters 12–16 tend to crystallize previous work. The review assignment material for Chapter 16 is especially noteworthy. It uses corporate annual reports as a basis for review of all parts of the course. These cases or problems provide a splendid test of the student's overall comprehension. Their successful solution enhances a student's confidence enormously, especially because he or she is dealing with real companies' financial statements.

The front of the solutions manual contains several alternate detailed assignment schedules and ample additional suggestions to teachers regarding how best to use this book.

CHANGES IN THIS EDITION

Users of the second edition gave the assignment material high marks regarding quality, quantity, and range. They especially liked the references in the text and the assignment materials to actual companies. The third edition enhances the latter feature because it spurs student interest and enthusiasm.

We have devoted enormous attention to the assignment material for each chapter. The beginning of the Chapter 1 Assignment Material explains the format and the various ways of using the material. If they desire, instructors may select materials from the Understanding Published Financial Reports subgroups exclusively throughout a course and cover all the essentials of financial accounting. For example, instructors may assign relatively simple, straightforward homework in the Fundamental Assignment Material section by using only the subgroup called Understanding Published Financial Reports. These exercises demonstrate how a course in introductory accounting can stick to essentials even while using real-life numbers and organizations.

The most noteworthy change is the switching of the contents of chapters 3 and 4. That is, journals, ledgers, debits, and credits are now introduced in Chapter 3; adjusting entries are introduced in Chapter 4.

The explanation of adjustments is essentially the same as before. The balance sheet equation provides the dominant conceptual framework. However, journal entries accompany each presentation of an adjustment.

All chapters were thoroughly rewritten and updated. Consider the following examples of assorted changes and new features:

a. Clearer definitions of assets, liabilities, and owners' equity.
b. Earlier presentation of concepts of realization and matching; later presentation of dividends. Simplified comparison of accrual basis and cash basis.
c. Journal entries introduced earlier, not delayed until after a full explanation of T-Accounts.
d. New sections on data processing, the effects of computers, and electronic spreadsheets.
e. New sections on accumulated depreciation, the effects of errors, and coping with incomplete records.
f. Updating to include recent FASB Statements and the Internal Revenue Code of 1986.
g. Many new problems, both easy and difficult, using recent annual reports.
h. Page references for vocabulary words at the ends of chapters and in the glossary.

SUPPLEMENTS FOR THE INSTRUCTOR

Solutions Manual—prepared by Horngren and Sundem, includes suggestions for how to tailor the text material to your course needs, and solutions to all in-text assignment material and the practice set.

Instructor's Resource Outline—prepared by Jonathan Schiff, provides a complete teaching outline for the course with objectives, lecture discussions, problem and example selections, sources for additional materials, and a correlation of the *Solutions Manual* to the text.

Test Bank—prepared by Duane Milano, offers over 1500 true/false and multiple-choice questions, exercises, and problems with a wide range of rigor; available with *Prentice-Hall's Telephone Test Preparation Service.*

Acetate Transparencies—features an increased number of transparencies of selected problems and key exhibits from the text. Free upon adoption.

Prentice-Hall's Telephone Test Preparation Service and Floppy Disk Testing Service—Contact your local sales representative for further details.

Gradebook/Class Record File Software—helps instructors to keep class records, compute class statistics, average grades, print graphs, sort by student name or grade, and more. Disks are available for Apple and IBM. Free upon adoption.

SUPPLEMENTS FOR THE STUDENT

Student Guide—prepared by Dudley W. Curry, gives a brief survey and a detailed summary of the text to assist study as well as a comprehensive set of self-test and practice exercises for each chapter with solutions.

Working Papers—provides partially filled in problem data and column headings for appropriate in-text problems.

Practice Set (Chimes Inc.)—prepared by Dudley W. Curry, comprises a simulated case covering all steps in the Accounting Cycle, tying together the fundamentals of bookkeeping and accounting, and including partially filled in working papers.

Applications in Financial Accounting Using The Twin^{TM}*/Lotus*^{R}*1–2–3*^{R}—prepared by Ali A. Peyvandi and Wayne D. Robertson, this supplement leads students from a level of little or no experience in computers to a level where they can solve accounting problems using The Twin^{TM} and Lotus^R 1-2-3^R. This complete supplement also includes a computer disk (for IBM PC computers and compatibles) that contains many partially completed problems and ample space for students to place all their assignments.

ACKNOWLEDGMENTS

Introduction to Financial Accounting is dedicated to Dudley W. Curry, an emeritus professor at Southern Methodist University, where he won several awards for outstanding teaching. His work on this book has earned our highest praise and deepest gratitude. He read every word, improved many, added some, harmed none. He provided invaluable ideas and bountiful constructive criticism, and prepared the following supplementary aids: student guide, working papers, and the practice set.

We appreciate the help of Duane Milano, who prepared an expanded test bank.

We are also especially grateful to Jonathan Schiff for his review of the manuscript and his preparation of Instructor's Resource Outlines.

The following professors supplied helpful reviews and comments: Philip R. Brown, Wayne S. Boutell, M. Robert Carver, Jr., Paul K. Chaney, Roger H. Chope, James R. Davis, William P. Enderlein, Clarence E. Fries, Patricia A. Frishkoff, Al Hartgraves, David E. Hoffman, Merle W. Hopkins, Joseph Icerman, Eugene A. Imhoff, Jr., Badr Ismail, A. J. Johnson, Naida Kaen, D. L. Kleepsie, Kathleen T. McGahran, Trini Melcher, Curtis Norton, Nancy O. Tang, Arthur L. Thomas, and Torben Thomsen.

Our appreciation extends to our present and former colleagues. In particular, James M. Patell has been generous in allowing us to use some of his case materials.

Elsie Young has our special appreciation for her cheerful and skillful typing and related help. Valerie Amphlett and Ali Salama have our gratitude for ably performing assorted editorial chores. Barbara Pearson deserves special recognition for her flawless typing of the solutions manual.

Finally, our thanks to Julie Warner, Barbara Grasso, Jayne Conte, Marie Lines, Nancy McDermott, and Bob McGee at Prentice-Hall.

Comments from users are welcome.

Charles T. Horngren
Gary L. Sundem

Chapter 1

ENTITIES AND
BALANCE SHEETS

LEARNING OBJECTIVES

Learning objectives will be found at the beginning of each chapter. They specify some of the important knowledge and skills you should have after completing your study of the chapter and your solving of the assignment material.

1. Define and give an example of an **asset**, a **liability**, and **owner's equity**, which are the three major elements of a balance sheet

2. Define **transaction**

3. Define **accounting entity** and describe how we determine whether a transaction is a personal transaction or one that affects the accounting entity only

4. Specify the effects of typical transactions on an entity's financial position

5. Explain the advantages and disadvantages of each form of business organization—proprietorships, partnerships, and corporations

6. Describe the major differences in accounting for proprietorships and corporations

NATURE OF ACCOUNTING

Accounting is an important subject. This opinion is widely shared, as shown by eleven hundred responses to a questionnaire sent to professors and managers by the American Assembly of Collegiate Schools of Business. Here are the top three courses ranked in terms of how much time and effort should be spent by students on each one of them:

	RANKED BY MANAGERS	RANKED BY PROFESSORS
Accounting	1	2
Finance	2	3
Economics	3	1

□ Decisions and Accounting

Do you make decisions that have a financial impact? Your answer is undoubtedly yes. Regardless of your roles in life (for example, manager, politician, investor, head of household, student), you will find a knowledge of accounting helpful. The major purpose of this book is to help you feel comfortable with financial information. Individuals who are uncomfortable are often severely handicapped in a variety of situations.

"Comfortable" means knowing the vocabulary and what financial statements mean and do not mean. Knowing what financial statements do *not* communicate is just as important as knowing what they do communicate. Accounting has been called the "language of business." It might better be called the "language of financial decisions." In any event, the degree of comfort being aimed at might be compared to living in a foreign country. The better you can speak the language, the more comfortable you will be; and you will be much more able to manage all aspects of living there than if you know no foreign words or only a few foreign words. You will be more likely to make intelligent decisions.

In brief, a beginning accounting student must learn a language. Accounting is the major means of communicating about the financial impact of an organization's activities. Learning includes becoming familiar with a vocabulary and developing an ability to construct, understand, and use financial statements.

□ Applicability to Nonprofit Organizations

This book is aimed at a variety of readers, including students who aspire to become either managers or professional accountants. The major focus is on profit-seeking organizations. However, the fundamental ideas also apply to nonprofit (that is, not-for-profit) organizations. Moreover, all managers typically have personal investments in profit-seeking organizations or must interact with businesses in some way.

Managers and accountants in various settings such as hospitals, universities, and government agencies have much in common with their counterparts in profit-seeking organizations. There is money to be raised and spent. There are budgets to be prepared and control systems to be designed and implemented. There is an obligation to use resources wisely. If used intelligently, accounting contributes to efficient operations. The strengthening of the accounting system was a mandatory condition imposed by the federal government in saving New York City from bankruptcy.

The overlap of government and business is everywhere. Government administrators and politicians are much better equipped to deal inside and outside their organizations if they understand accounting. For example, a knowledge of accounting is crucial for decisions regarding research contracts, defense contracts, and loan guarantees. Keep in mind that decisions about loan guarantees have been made with respect to tiny businesses (for instance, through the Small Business Administration) as well as large businesses such as Lockheed and Chrysler.

□ Scope of Accounting

Accounting is a broad subject. Do not confuse it with bookkeeping. Arithmetic is a small part of the broad discipline of mathematics; bookkeeping is a small part of the broad discipline of accounting. Accountants design their systems after considering the types of information desired by managers and other users. Bookkeepers and computers then perform the more routine tasks of following detailed procedures established by accountants.

Managers, investors, and other interested groups usually want the answers to two important questions about an organization: How well did it do during a given period? and Where does the organization stand on a given day? The accountant answers these questions with two major financial statements—an income statement and a balance sheet. To obtain these statements, accountants analyze, record, quantify, accumulate, summarize, classify, report, and interpret the numerous events and their financial effects on the organization.

Accounting helps decision making by showing where and when money has been spent and commitments have been made, by evaluating performance, and by indicating the financial implications of choosing one plan versus another. Some type of accounting is an essential ingredient to the smooth functioning of almost all organizations, cultures, and economies.

Consider some fundamental relationships:

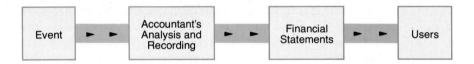

Here are some examples of users and the decisions they must make:

USERS	DECISIONS
Managers of organizations	Where to expand or reduce operations? How did subordinates perform? Whom to reward?
Lenders of money	Grant a loan? Which lending terms to specify?
Suppliers of goods and services	Extend credit? How much? How long?
Shareholders of organizations	Increase or reduce investment?
Income tax authorities	Is taxable income measured properly?
U.S. Securities and Exchange Commission	Do the financial statements of a publicly held corporation conform to requirements of securities laws?

OVERALL ROLE OF ACCOUNTING

☐ Financial and Management Accounting

The financial statements discussed in this book are common to all areas of accounting. "Financial accounting" is often distinguished from "management accounting." The major distinction between them is their use by two different classes of decision makers. The field of **financial accounting** serves *external* decision makers, such as stockholders, suppliers, banks, and governmental agencies. **Management accounting** serves *internal* decision makers, such as top executives, department heads, college deans, hospital administrators, and people at other management levels *within* an organization.[1]

The more that managers know about accounting, the better they are able to plan and control their organization and its subunits. In dealing with both inside and outside parties, managers are handicapped if their comprehension of accounting is sketchy or confused. So the learning of accounting is almost always a wise investment, no matter what the manager's specialty. Moreover, managers' performance and rewards often hinge on how accounting

---

[1] For a book-length presentation of the field, see *Introduction to Management Accounting* (Englewood Cliffs, N.J.: Prentice-Hall, 1987), the companion volume to this textbook.

measurements are made. Therefore managers have a natural self-interest in learning about accounting.

☐ Employers of Accountants

The accounting profession can be classified in many ways. A major classification is **public accounting** and **private accounting**. "Public" accountants are those whose services are offered to the general public on a fee basis. Such services include auditing, income taxes, and management consulting. "Private" accountants are all the rest. They consist of not only those individuals who work for businesses but also those who work for government agencies, including the Internal Revenue Service.

In the accompanying diagram, the solid arrows indicate how accountants often move from public accounting firms to positions in business or government. Obviously, these movements can occur at any level or in any direction.

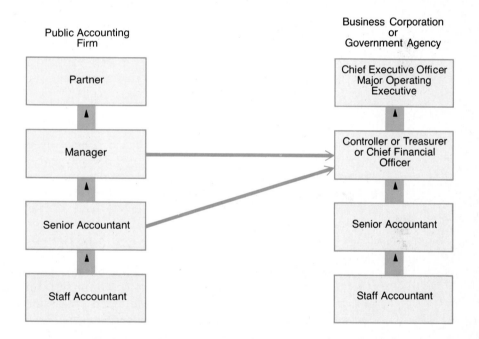

Accounting cuts across all management functions, including purchasing, manufacturing, wholesaling, retailing, and a variety of marketing and transportation activities. It provides an excellent opportunity for gaining broad knowledge. Senior accountants or controllers in a corporation are sometimes picked as production or marketing executives. Why? Because they may have impressed other executives as having acquired general management skills. A number of recent surveys have indicated that more chief executive officers began their careers in an accounting position than in marketing, production, engineering, or any other area.

ROLE OF AUDITING

☐ Managers and Credibility

Various forms of organization are explored more deeply later in this chapter. Financial statements are the ultimate responsibility of the managers who are entrusted with the resources under their command. In proprietorships, the owner is often also the top manager. In partnerships, top management may be shared. In corporations, the ultimate responsibility is delegated by stockholders to the board of directors, as indicated in the accompanying diagram.

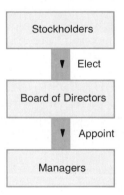

Frequently, the chairman of the board is also the top manager and the major shareholder. For example, for over thirty years Henry Ford II was the major stockholder, the chairman of the board, and the chief executive officer (CEO) of the Ford Motor Company. Nevertheless, ownership is often widely dispersed, the chairman also serves as a corporate officer, and the chief executive officer may be president.[2] Indeed, sometimes the chief executive officer is strictly a professional manager with no ownership position whatsoever.

Long ago stockholders and creditors such as banks wanted some third-party assurance about the reliability of the financial information being supplied by the managers. The public accounting profession arose to serve this function of adding credibility to financial reporting.

A **certified public accountant** (CPA) in the United States earns this designation by a combination of education, qualifying experience, and the passing of a three-and-one-half-day written national examination. The examination is administered and graded by a national organization, the American Institute of Certified Public Accountants (AICPA). The institute is the principal professional association in the private sector that regulates the quality of the public accounting profession. Other English-speaking nations have simi-

---

[2] Conference Board, *Who Is Top Management?* surveyed four hundred chief executives. In about 50% of the companies, the CEO is the chariman of the board of directors. In 30%, the CEO is the president of the corporation. In virtually all other companies, it is chairman, president, and CEO all rolled into one person.

lar arrangements but use the term *chartered accountant* (CA) instead of certified public accountant.

The CPA examination covers four major topical areas: auditing, accounting theory, business law, and accounting practice. The last is a series of accounting problems divided into two long parts covering a wide variety of topics, including income taxes, cost accounting, and accounting for nonprofit institutions.

Thus, even though the AICPA prepares and grades the CPA examination on a national basis, the individual states have their own regulations concerning the qualifications for taking and passing the examination and for earning the right to practice as a CPA. These regulations are determined and enforced by state boards of accountancy.[3]

☐ Independent Opinion

The financial statements of publicly held corporations and many other corporations are subject to independent audits by CPAs that form the basis for a professional accounting firm's opinion. This **independent opinion** typically includes key phrasing, as illustrated by the following opinion rendered by a large CPA firm, Coopers & Lybrand, regarding H. J. Heinz Company, the maker of catsup and other products:

☐ In our opinion, the aforementioned consolidated financial statements present fairly the financial position of H. J. Heinz Company and consolidated subsidiaries as of May 1, 1986 and May 2, 1985, and the results of their operations and the changes in their financial position for each of the three years in the period ended May 1, 1986, in conformity with generally accepted accounting principles applied on a consistent basis.

Coopers & Lybrand

Pittsburgh, Pennsylvania
June 24, 1986

This book will explore the meaning of such key phrases as "present fairly" and "generally accepted accounting principles." For now, reflect on the fact that the accounting firm must conduct an audit before it can render the above opinion. An **audit** is an in-depth examination that is made in accordance with generally accepted auditing standards (which have been developed primarily by the AICPA). This examination includes miscellaneous tests of the accounting records, internal control systems, and other auditing procedures as deemed necessary. The examination leads to the accountant's independent opinion. This opinion (sometimes called *certificate*) is the accountant's stamp of approval on *management's* financial statements.

---

[3] The Certificate in Management Accounting (CMA) is the internal accountant's counterpart to the CPA. The major objective of the CMA is to establish management accounting as a distinct profession. Information can be obtained from the Institute of Certified Management Accountants, P.O. Box 405, Montvale, N.J., 07645–0405.

The sizes of accounting firms vary. There are small proprietorships, where auditing may represent as little as 10% or less of annual billings. *Billings* are the total amounts charged to clients for services rendered to them. The bulk of the work of these firms is income taxes and "write-up" work (the actual bookkeeping services for clients who are not equipped to do their own accounting).

There are also gigantic firms that have over two thousand partners with offices located throughout the world. Such enormous firms are necessary because their clients are also enormous. For instance, Price Waterhouse, a large CPA firm, has reported that its annual audit of one client takes the equivalent of seventy-two accountants working a full year. Another client has three hundred separate corporate entities in forty foreign countries that must ultimately be consolidated into a set of overall financial statements. Most publicly held corporations in the United States are audited by these large firms. The eight largest American accounting firms are (in alphabetical order):

Arthur Andersen & Co.	Ernst & Whinney
Arthur Young & Company	Peat Marwick
Coopers & Lybrand	Price Waterhouse & Co.
Deloitte Haskins & Sells	Touche Ross & Company

About 12% of the three hundred thousand U.S. CPAs are employed by these **Big Eight** firms.[4] However, of the largest twenty-six hundred companies listed on the U.S. stock exchanges, 85% are clients of the Big Eight. Some of these accounting firms have annual billings in excess of a billion dollars. As much as 70% of the billings is attributable to auditing services. The top partners in big accounting firms are compensated on about the same scale as their corporate counterparts.

THE BALANCE SHEET

The beginning of this book has provided a glimpse of the entire field of accounting, including the important role of auditing. Basically, accounting provides information for a wide variety of decisions. At this point, we turn to what the accountant does. As you read on, you will become familiar with the underlying theory and concepts of accounting—gradually, chapter by chapter, rather than in one enormous gulp in Chapter 1. By working with concrete situations, you are more likely to get a solid grasp of the uses and limitations of accounting. The final chapter provides a review and knitting together of the various topics in this book.

---

[4] These eight large accounting firms tend to receive more publicity than other firms. However, please remember that there are thousands of other able accounting firms, varying in size from sole practitioners to huge international partnerships.

☐ Assets, Liabilities, and Owners' Equity

Suppose George Smith has had previous experience in the bicycle business but is now a salaried employee of a local company. He has decided to "go independent," that is, to quit his job and open a large bicycle shop. Smith has heard about the troubles of new businesses that lack money. So he raised plenty. Two friends, Alex Handl and Susan Eastman, each invest $40,000 in his business, and Smith invests $320,000. Thus the total investment by the owners is $400,000. Then Smith, acting for the business (which is called Biwheels Company), borrows $100,000 from a local bank for business purposes. An opening balance sheet of this new enterprise follows:

BIWHEELS COMPANY
Balance Sheet
December 31, 19X1[5]

ASSETS		LIABILITIES AND OWNERS' EQUITY	
Cash	$500,000	Liabilities (note payable)	$100,000
		Owners' equity	400,000
Total assets	$500,000	Total liabilities and owners' equity	$500,000

Balance sheet is a widely used term. It is not as descriptive as its newer substitute terms: **statement of financial position** or **statement of financial condition**. But old terms die hard, so *balance sheet* will be used in this book. Besides, the term constantly reminds us of a powerful device, the accountant's balance sheet equation:

$$\text{Assets} = \text{Liabilities} + \text{Owners' equity}$$

☐ Definitions of Major Balance Sheet Items

The balance sheet is a photograph of financial status at an instant of time. It has two counterbalancing sections, as the equation indicates. Key introductory definitions follow:

Assets are economic resources that are expected to benefit future cash inflows or help reduce future cash outflows. Examples are cash, inventories, and equipment.

Liabilities are economic obligations of the organization to outsiders. An example is a debt to a bank. The usual evidence of this debt is a promissory note that states the terms of payment. Accountants use **note payable** to describe the existence of such a promissory note. Another example of a liability is an **account payable** that results from a purchase of goods or services on credit.

---

[5] Throughout this book, years will usually be designated 19X1, 19X2, 19X3, etc.

Owners' equity is the residual interest in (that is, remaining claim against) the organization's assets after deducting liabilities. At the inception of a business, the owners' equity is measured by the total amounts invested by the owners.

The right side of the balance sheet equation represents outsider and owner "claims against" the total assets shown on the left side. Many accountants prefer to think of the right side as "interests in" or "sources of" the total assets. The residual or "leftover" nature of owners' equity is often emphasized by reexpressing the balance sheet equation as follows:

$$\text{Owners' Equity} = \text{Assets} - \text{Liabilities}$$

☐ Effects of Transactions

A **transaction** is any event that affects the financial position and requires recording. Some examples will clarify this definition. The first Biwheels transaction was the investment by the owners. The second transaction was the bank loan. Consider a third transaction, the acquisition of bicycles from a manufacturer for $150,000 cash on January 2, 19X2. A new balance sheet could be prepared. It would have the same heading, except that the date would be January 2:

ASSETS		LIABILITIES AND OWNERS' EQUITY	
Cash	$350,000	Liabilities	
Merchandise		(note payable)	$100,000
inventory	150,000	Owners' equity	400,000
		Total liabilities	
Total assets	$500,000	and owners' equity	$500,000

Think of each transaction's impact on the balance sheet equation:

		ASSETS	=	LIABILITIES AND OWNERS' EQUITY	
TRANSACTION	Cash	+ Merchandise Inventory	= Note Payable	+ Owners' Equity	
(1) 12/31/19X1	+400,000		=	+400,000	
(2) 12/31/19X1	+100,000		= +100,000		
(3) 1/2/19X2	−150,000	+150,000	=		
Balances, 1/2/19X2	350,000 +	150,000	= 100,000 +	400,000	

From the start, note that after each transaction the total assets must always equal the total liabilities and owners' equity. That is, the equality of the balance sheet equation cannot (and should not) be destroyed by any transaction.

EXHIBIT 1-1 *(Place a clip on this page for easy reference.)*

BIWHEELS COMPANY
Analysis of Transactions for December 31, 19X1–January 12, 19X2 (in dollars)

DESCRIPTION OF TRANSACTION	Cash	ASSETS + Accounts Receivable +	Merchandise Inventory +	Store Equipment =	= LIABILITIES + OWNERS' EQUITY Note Payable +	Accounts Payable +	Owners' Equity
(1) Initial investment	+400,000				=		+400,000
(2) Loan from bank	+100,000				= +100,000		
(3) Acquire inventory for cash	−150,000		+150,000		=		
(4) Acquire Inventory on credit			+ 10,000		=	+10,000	
(5) Acquire store equipment for cash plus credit	− 4,000			+15,000 =		+11,000	
(6) Sale of equipment		+1,000		− 1,000 =			
(7) Return of bicycles acquired on January 3			− 800		=	− 800	
(8) Payments to creditors	− 4,000				=	− 4,000	
(9) Collections from debtors	+ 700	− 700					
Balance, January 12, 19X2	342,700 +	300 +	159,200 +	14,000 =	100,000 +	16,200 +	400,000
			516,200		=	516,200	

In the third transaction, the form of the assets changed because cash decreased and a new asset, the inventory of merchandise for sale, was recorded. But the total amount of assets is unchanged. Moreover, the right-side items are completely unchanged.

If desired, Biwheels could prepare a new balance sheet after each transaction. Obviously, such a practice is awkward and unnecessary. Therefore, balance sheets are rarely produced more often than once a month.

☐ **Illustrative Transactions**

Exhibit 1–1 shows how a series of transactions may be analyzed using the balance sheet equation. The transactions are numbered for easy reference. Please examine how the first three transactions, which were discussed earlier, are analyzed in Exhibit 1–1. (For your convenience in referring to it later, you may wish to put a paper clip on the exhibit.)

Consider how each of the following additional transactions might be analyzed:

4. Jan. 3. Biwheels buys bicycles for $10,000 from a manufacturer who is eager for business. Payment does not have to be made for thirty days.

5. Jan. 4. Biwheels acquires assorted store equipment for a total of $15,000. A cash down payment of $4,000 is made. The remaining balance must be paid in sixty days.

6. Jan. 5. Biwheels sells a store showcase to a business neighbor after Smith decides he dislikes it. Its selling price, $1,000, happens to be exactly equal to its cost. The neighbor agrees to pay within thirty days.

7. Jan. 6. Biwheels returns some bicycles (which had been acquired on January 3 for $800) to the manufacturer for full credit (an $800 reduction of the amount that Biwheels owes the manufacturer).

8. Jan. 10. Biwheels pays $4,000 to the manufacturer described in transaction 4.

9. Jan. 12. Biwheels collects $700 of the $1,000 owed by the business neighbor for transaction 6.

To check your comprehension, use the format in Exhibit 1–1 to analyze each transaction. Try to do your own analysis of each transaction before looking at the entries shown for it in the exhibit. For example, you could cover the numerical entries with a sheet of paper or a ruler and then proceed through each transaction, one by one.

☐ Explanations of Transactions

4. PURCHASES ON CREDIT. The vast bulk of purchases (and sales) throughout the world are conducted on a *credit* basis rather than on a *cash* basis. This "buy now, pay later" attitude is particularly prevalent in dealings among manufacturers, wholesalers, and retailers. Indeed, the extension of credit seems to be a major lubricant of the world's economies. Thus, unless evidence indicates that customers may not pay their debts, cash is not expected until a later date. Furthermore, an "authorized signature" of the buyer is usually sufficient; no formal promissory note is necessary. This practice is known as buying (or selling) on **open account**; the debt is shown on the buyer's balance sheet as an account payable. As Exhibit 1–1 shows for this merchandise purchase on account, the inventory (asset) of Biwheels is increased and an account payable (liability) is created in an amount of $10,000.

5. PURCHASE FOR CASH PLUS CREDIT. This is the first illustration of a *compound* effect in the sense that more than two balance sheet items are affected simultaneously. Store equipment is increased by the full amount of its cost regardless of whether payment is made in full now, in full later, or partially now and partially later. Therefore Biwheels' Store Equipment (asset) is increased by $15,000, Cash (asset) is decreased by $4,000, and Accounts Payable (liability) is increased by $11,000.

6. SALE ON CREDIT. This transaction is similar to a purchase on credit, except that Biwheels is now the seller. Accounts Receivable (asset) of $1,000 is created and Store Equipment (asset) is decreased by $1,000. We are purposely avoiding transactions that result in profits or losses until the next chapter. Instead we are concentrating on elementary changes in the balance sheet equation.

7. RETURN OF BICYCLES TO SUPPLIER. When a company returns merchandise to its suppliers for credit, its inventory is reduced and its liabilities are reduced.

In this instance, the amount of the decrease on each side of the equation is $800.

8. PAYMENTS TO CREDITORS. A *creditor* is one to whom money is owed. The manufacturer is an example of a creditor. This payment reduces Biwheels' assets (Cash) and its liabilities (Accounts Payable) by $4,000.

9. COLLECTIONS FROM DEBTORS. A *debtor* is one who owes money. Here the business neighbor is the debtor and Biwheels is the creditor. This collection increases one of Biwheels' assets (Cash) and decreases another asset (Accounts Receivable) by $700.

An **account** is a summary of the changes in a particular asset or liability or owners' equity. A cumulative total may be drawn at *any* date for each *account* in Exhibit 1–1. The following balance sheet uses the totals at the bottom of Exhibit 1–1. Observe that a balance sheet represents the financial impact of an accumulation of transactions to a specific point in time.

BIWHEELS COMPANY
Balance Sheet
January 12, 19X2

ASSETS		LIABILITIES AND OWNERS' EQUITY	
Cash	$342,700	Note payable	$100,000
Accounts receivable	300	Accounts payable	16,200
Merchandise			
inventory	159,200	Total liabilities	$116,200
Store equipment	14,000	Owners' equity	400,000
Total	$516,200	Total	$516,200

TRANSACTIONS AND ENTITIES

☐ Accounting Transactions

The accounting process focuses on transactions as they affect an organization. As you know, many events may affect a company—including wars, elections, and general economic booms or depressions. However, the accountant recognizes only specified types of events as being worthy of formal recording as *accounting transactions*.

Consider an illustration. Suppose the president of Exxon is killed in an airplane crash, and the company carries no life insurance. The accountant would not record this event. Suppose further that an employee embezzles $1,000 in cash from Exxon, is discovered the same day, and the company carries no employee theft insurance. The accountant would record this event.

The death of the president may have considerably more economic or financial significance than the embezzlement. But the monetary effect is hard to measure in any objective way. The accountant is concerned about measuring the impact of events in some systematic, reliable manner. Through the years, many concepts, conventions, and rules have been developed regarding what events should be recorded as *accounting transactions* and how their financial impact should be measured. We will introduce these major concepts gradually over the next few chapters.

☐ Business and Personal Entities

The first basic concept in accounting has supreme importance—the **entity**. An entity is a specific area of accountability, a center of attention, a clear-cut boundary for reporting. The entity concept is important because accounting usually focuses on how to measure the financial impact of events as they affect a particular entity. An example of an entity is the General Motors Corporation, a huge entity that encompasses many smaller entities such as the Chevrolet Division and the Buick Division. In turn, Chevrolet encompasses many smaller entities such as a Michigan assembly plant and an Ohio assembly plant.

The key point here is that the entity concept helps the accountant relate events to a sharply defined area of accountability. For example, *business* entities should not be confused with *personal* entities. A purchase of groceries for merchandise inventory is an accounting transaction for a grocery store (the business entity), but the store owner's purchase of a diamond necklace with a personal check is not (the personal entity).

TYPES OF OWNERSHIP

☐ Proprietorships, Partnerships, and Corporations

Entities take many forms. Owners must decide whether their businesses should be organized as sole proprietorships, partnerships, or corporations. A **proprietorship** is a separate organization with a single owner. Most often the owner is also the manager. Therefore proprietorships tend to be small retail establishments and individual professional businesses such as those of dentists, physicians, and attorneys. From an *accounting* viewpoint, each proprietorship is an individual entity that is separate and distinct from the proprietor.

A **partnership** is a special form of organization that joins two or more individuals together as co-owners. Many retail establishments, as well as dentists, physicians, attorneys, and accountants, conduct their activities as partnerships. Indeed, partnerships can sometimes be gigantic. For instance, the largest accounting firms have more than one thousand partners. Again, from an *accounting* viewpoint, each partnership is an individual entity that is separate from the personal activities of each partner.

Corporations are organizations created by individual state laws. The owners are identified as stockholders or shareholders. Many states allow having only one stockholder; other states require at least two stockholders. Individuals form a corporation by applying to the state for approval of the company's *articles of incorporation*. When approved, the corporation becomes a *legal* entity, an "artificial person" that conducts its business completely apart from its owners. The corporation is also, of course, an *accounting* entity.

□ Advantages of Corporations

The corporate form of organization has many advantages. Perhaps its most notable feature is the **limited liability** of owners, which means that corporate creditors (such as banks or suppliers) ordinarily have claims against the corporate assets only. Therefore if a corporation drifts into financial trouble, its creditors cannot look for repayment beyond the corporate entity. That is, generally the owners' personal assets are not subject to the creditors' grasp. In contrast, the owners of proprietorships and partnerships typically have *unlimited liability*, which means that business creditors can look for repayment beyond the business entity's assets to the owners' personal assets. For example, if Biwheels were a partnership, *each* partner would bear a personal liability for full payment of the $100,000 bank loan.

Other advantages of the corporation include the ease of transfer of ownership, ease of raising ownership capital, and continuity of existence. The corporation usually issues **capital stock certificates** (often called simply **stock certificates**) as formal evidence of ownership shares. These shares may be sold and resold among present and potential owners. Moreover, ownership capital may be solicited from hundreds or thousands of potential stockholders. Furthermore, the corporation has an indefinite life in the sense that it continues even if its ownership changes. In contrast, proprietorships and partnerships officially terminate upon the death or complete withdrawal by an owner.

The income tax effects of the form of ownership may vary significantly. For example, a corporation is taxed as a separate entity (as a corporation). But no income taxes are levied on a proprietorship (as a proprietorship) or on a partnership (as a partnership). Instead, the income earned by proprietorships and partnerships is attributed to the owners as personal taxpayers. In short, the income tax laws regard corporations as being taxable entities, but proprietorships or partnerships as not being taxable entities. Whether the corporation provides tax advantages heavily depends on the personal tax situations of the owners. (See Chapter 13, Appendix B, for more discussion.)

Regardless of the economic and legal advantages or disadvantages of the corporate form, some small-business owners incorporate simply for prestige. That is, they feel more important if they can refer to "my corporation" and if they can refer to themselves as "chairman of the board" or "president" instead of "business owner" or "partner."

In terms of numbers of entities, there are fewer corporations than there are proprietorships or partnerships. However, the corporation has far more economic significance. Corporations conduct a sheer money volume of business that dwarfs the volume of other forms of organization. Moreover, almost every reader of this book interacts with, owes money to, or invests in corporations. For these reasons, this book emphasizes the corporate entity.

☐ Financial Presentations of Owners' Equity

The basic accounting concepts that underlie the owners' equity are unchanged regardless of whether the organization is a proprietorship, a partnership, or a corporation. However, owners' equities for proprietorships and partnerships are often identified as **capital**. In contrast, owners' equity for a corporation is usually called **stockholders' equity** or **shareholders' equity**. Examine the possibilities for Biwheels that are shown in the accompanying table.

OWNER'S EQUITY FOR A PROPRIETORSHIP (Assume George Smith is the sole owner)	
George Smith, capital	$400,000

OWNERS' EQUITY FOR A PARTNERSHIP	
George Smith, capital	$320,000
Alex Handl, capital	40,000
Susan Eastman, capital	40,000
Total partners' capital	$400,000

OWNERS' EQUITY FOR A CORPORATION	
Stockholders' equity:	
Paid-in capital:	
Capital stock, 10,000 shares issued at par value of $10 per share	$100,000
Paid-in capital in excess of par value of capital stock	300,000
Total paid-in capital	$400,000

The presentations for the proprietorship and the partnership are self-explanatory. However, the corporation deserves comment. The capital investments in a corporation by its owners at the inception of business and subsequently are often called **paid-in capital** or **contributed capital**. In turn, as the table shows, paid-in capital is usually reported in two major parts.

Stock certificates typically have some printed nominal dollar amount that is required by most states. This amount is determined by the board of directors and is usually called **par value** or **stated value**.

In our example, 10,000 shares have been issued for $40 per share. The par value is $10 per share, and the **paid-in capital in excess of par value** is $30 per share. As an outgrowth of these state laws, the total ownership claim of $400,000 arising from the investment is thus split between two equity claims, one for $100,000 "capital stock, at par" and one for $300,000 "paid-in capital in excess of par" or "contributed capital in excess of par" or "additional paid-in capital."

For our purposes here, the technical details and history of par or stated values are unimportant. Chapter 11 explores these details. In any event, in most states it is illegal to issue shares unless their par value is fully paid in. As a result, the par or stated values are usually set far below the full market price of the shares upon issuance. For example, consider the following excerpts from recent actual corporate balance sheets.

Occidental Petroleum Corporation

Common shares, $.20 par value; authorized 100 million shares; issued 68,057,086 shares	$ 13,611,000
Additional paid-in capital	798,695,000

Note the extremely small amount of par value in comparison with the additional paid-in capital. This illustrates the insignificance of "par value" in today's business world.

Cluett Peabody and Company (makers of Arrow shirts)

Shareholders' Equity:	
Common stock	$ 9,773,000
Paid-in surplus	36,193,000

The term *paid-in surplus* is an outdated synonym for *additional paid-in capital*.

Clark Equipment Company

Capital stock common—authorized 20,000,000 shares $7.50 par value—outstanding 13,686,131 shares (includes capital in excess of par value)	$151,850,000

This presentation does not split the paid-in capital into two lines. Inasmuch as par value is small and has little significance, this approach is praiseworthy.

In summary, all of the above corporate presentations can be described accurately with a simple term, *total paid-in capital* (which will be distinguished from other ownership equity arising from profitable operations). Par value has been described here, not because of its economic significance, but because it is so often actually reported on published balance sheets.

The preceding excerpts use slightly different terms to describe capital stock: *common shares*, *common stock*, and *capital stock common*. Sometimes there is more than one type of capital stock issued by a corporation (as explained in Chapter 11). But there is always **common stock**, which represents the "residual" ownership.

Common shareholders bear the most risk of all investors, but they also are entitled to unlimited rewards. In a few instances, the rewards become astronomical. For example, suppose a person invested $1,250 for 100 shares of the initial public offering of Winnebago Industries, Inc., in January 1966. By maintaining this investment and then selling the shares in mid-1972, that person would have received $1.5 million. Since then, however, the energy situation and other factors have caused the market value per share to plummet from $49 to less than $2 and then soar to $20 in 1986.

SOME ACTUAL BALANCE SHEETS

To become more familiar with the balance sheet and its equation, consider the following excerpts from some actual recent financial reports. The terms vary among organizations, but the essential balance sheet equation does not.

BankAmerica Corporation (in thousands)

ASSETS		LIABILITIES AND STOCKHOLDERS' EQUITY	
Cash	$ 7,649,266	Deposits	$ 94,047,703
U.S. government and		Other liabilities	18,513,288
other securities	15,911,503	Total liabilities	$112,560,991
Loans receivable	84,043,461	Stockholders' equity	5,118,511
Premises and equipment	2,367,152		
Other assets	7,708,120	Total liabilities and	
Total assets	$117,679,502	stockholders' equity	$117,679,502

This balance sheet illustrates how banks gather and use money. Over 70% of the total assets are in the form of investments in loans, and about 80% of the total liabilities and stockholders' equity are in the form of deposits, the major liability. That is, these financial institutions are in the business of raising funds from depositors and, in turn, lending those funds to businesses, homeowners and others. The stockholders' equity is usually tiny in comparison with the deposits (only 5% in this case).

What BankAmerica accounts would be affected if you deposited $1,000? Cash would rise by $1,000 and the liability, Deposits, would rise by the same amount. Why are deposits listed as liabilities? Because BankAmerica owes these amounts to depositors. They are depositors' claims on the assets of Bank-America.

Peat Marwick (a large public accounting firm):

ASSETS		LIABILITIES AND CAPITAL	
Cash	$ 49,467,000	Notes payable	$ 6,281,000
Receivables and		Accounts payable and	
related assets	115,471,000	related liabilities	46,561,000
Investments	2,651,000	Long-term liabilities	8,636,000
Furniture and		Total liabilities	$ 61,478,000
equipment	26,473,000	Partners' capital	137,891,000
Other assets	5,307,000	Total liabilities	
Total assets	$199,369,000	and capital	$199,369,000

This CPA firm is one of the largest partnerships in the world. It has about 6,000 partners and 60,000 employees. In a two-person partnership, the owners' equity section might show two separate capital accounts, one for Partner A and one for Partner B. However, when there are many partners, their ownership interests are summarized as Partners' Capital.

What accounts would be affected if a partner retired and withdrew $300,000? Cash and Partners' Capital would each decline by $300,000.

Pacific Gas and Electric Company

ASSETS		CAPITALIZATION AND LIABILITIES	
Plant in service	$13,344,788,000	Stockholders' equity	$ 7,130,997,000
Other assets	3,982,345,000	Long-term debt	6,143,070,000
		Other liabilities	4,053,066,000
		Total capitalization	
Total assets	$17,327,133,000	and other liabilities	$17,327,133,000

Note the placement of the accounts on the balance sheet of this public utility. Most companies show Cash as their first asset and show Stockholders' Equity after liabilities. However, many utilities traditionally follow the method used by Pacific Gas and Electric. The emphasis is on long-term assets, stockholders' equity, and long-term debt.

The basic balance sheet equation still holds regardless of how its elements are shuffled:

Assets = Liabilities + Owners' equity
Assets = Owners' equity + Liabilities
Assets − Liabilities = Owners' equity
Assets − Owners' equity = Liabilities

Long-term debt is debt due beyond one year. What Pacific Gas and Electric accounts would be affected if the company borrowed $5 million on a ten-year note? Other Assets (cash) and Long-Term Debt would each rise by $5 million.

United States Government September 30, 1985 (issued by the Secretary of the Treasury; all amounts are in billions):

ASSETS		LIABILITIES AND DEFICIT	
Cash	$ 72.8	Accounts payable	$ 161.5
Receivables	301.4	Borrowings from the	
Inventories	151.4	public	1,299.5
Property and equipment	312.1	Pensions payable	3,181.8
Other assets	99.6	Other liabilities	93.8
		Total liabilities	$4,736.6
		Fiscal deficit	(3,799.3)
		Total liabilities and	
Total assets	$937.3	deficit	$ 937.3

This balance sheet gives a sobering picture of the financial position of the United States. Note that "Owners' Equity" evaporates and becomes negative ("Fiscal Deficit") when liabilities exceed assets.

What accounts would be affected when the U.S. Treasury issues treasury notes of $10 billion? Cash and Borrowings would each rise by $10 billion.

SUMMARY

Financial statements are major sources of information for decision making by managers, creditors, and owners. Employers of accountants include profit-seeking and non-profit organizations. Public accounting firms provide independent auditing services that add credibility to financial reports.

The balance sheet provides a photograph of the financial position of an organization at any instant. That is, it answers the basic question, Where are we?

The basic accounting equation is Assets = Liabilities + Owners' Equity. The amounts in the equation are affected by a host of transactions, which are events that require recording.

The entity is an extremely important accounting concept. Entities may take different forms, including proprietorships, partnerships, and corporations. There are also entities within entities. For example, the University of California contains various schools and departments within schools. The department is an accounting entity nested within the school, which is a larger entity nested within the university.

This chapter has introduced a conceptual framework of accounting that is by far the most widely followed throughout the world. Where do we go from here? Chapters 2 through 5 describe the framework more fully, emphasizing how income is measured and using the balance sheet equation as a primary tool for analysis. Then succeeding chapters probe various topics in more depth.

SUMMARY PROBLEMS FOR YOUR REVIEW

☐ Problem One

Review Exhibit 1–1 (p. 11). Analyze the following additional transactions of Biwheels Company. Begin with the balances shown for January 12, 19X2, in Exhibit 1–1. Prepare an ending balance sheet for Biwheels Company (say, on January 16 after these additional transacitons).

    i. Biwheels pays $10,000 on the bank loan (ignore interest).

    ii. Smith buys furniture for his home for $5,000 using his family charge account at Macy's.

    iii. Biwheels buys merchandise inventory for $50,000. Half of the amount is paid in cash, and half is owed on open account.

    iv. Biwheels collects $200 more from its business debtor.

☐ Problem Two

"If I purchase 100 shares of the outstanding stock of General Motors Corporation (or Biwheels Company), I invest my money directly in that corporation. General Motors must record that event." Do you agree? Explain.

☐ Problem Three

"The same individual can be an owner, an employee, and a creditor of a corporation." Do you agree? Explain.

☐ Solution to Problem One

See Exhibits 1–2 and 1–3. Note that transaction ii is ignored because it is wholly personal. However, visualize how Smith's personal balance sheet would be affected. His assets, Home Furniture, would rise by $5,000 and his liabilities, Accounts Payable, would also rise by $5,000.

EXHIBIT 1–2

BIWHEELS COMPANY
Analysis of Additional January Transactions

DESCRIPTION OF TRANSACTION	Cash +	Accounts Receivable +	Merchandise Inventory +	Store Equipment =	Note Payable +	Accounts Payable +	Owners' Equity
	ASSETS			=	LIABILITIES + OWNERS' EQUITY		
Balance, January 12, 19X2	342,700 +	300 +	159,200 +	14,000 =	100,000 +	16,200 +	400,000
(i) Payment on bank loan	− 10,000			=	− 10,000		
(ii) Personal; no effect							
(iii) Acquire inventory, half for cash	− 25,000		+ 50,000	=		+25,000	
(iv) Collection of receivable	+ 200	−200		=			
Balance, January 16	307,900 +	100 +	209,200 +	14,000 =	90,000 +	41,200 +	400,000
	531,200			=	531,200		

EXHIBIT 1–3

BIWHEELS COMPANY
Balance Sheet
January 16, 19X2

ASSETS		LIABILITIES AND OWNERS' EQUITY	
		Liabilities:	
Cash	$307,900	Note payable	$ 90,000
Accounts receivable	100	Accounts payable	41,200
Merchandise inventory	209,200	Total liabilities	$131,200
Store equipment	14,000	Owners' equity	400,000
		Total liabilities	
Total assets	$531,200	and owners' equity	$531,200

☐ Solution to Problem Two

Money is invested directly in a corporation when the entity originally issues the stock. For example, 100,000 shares of stock may be issued at $80 per share, bringing in $8 million to the corporation. This is a transaction between the corporation and the stockholders. It affects the corporate financial position:

Cash	$8,000,000	Stockholders' equity	$8,000,000

In turn, 100 shares of that stock may be sold by an original stockholder (Dan Marino) to another individual (John Elway) for $130 per share. This is a private transaction; no cash is received by the corporation. Of course, the corporation records the fact that 100 shares originally owned by Marino are now owned by Elway, but the corporate financial position is unchanged. Accounting focuses on the business entity; the private dealings of the owners have no direct effect on the financial position of the entity and hence are unrecorded except for detailed records of the owners' identities.

In summary, Elway invests his money in the shares of the corporation when he buys them from Marino. However, individual dealings in shares already issued and held by stockholders have no direct effect on the financial position of the corporation.

☐ Solution to Problem Three

As a separate entity, the corporation enters contracts, hires employees, buys buildings, and conducts other business. In particular, note that the chairman of the board, the president, the other officers, and all the workers are employees of the corporation. Thus Katherine Graham could own some of the capital stock of a corporation and also be an employee. Moreover, money owed to employees for wages and salaries is a liability of a corporation. So the same person can simultaneously be an owner, an employee, and a creditor of a corporation. Similarly, consider an employee of a telephone company who is a stockholder of the company. She could be receiving telephone services from the same company and thus also be both a *customer* and a *debtor* of the company.

HIGHLIGHTS TO REMEMBER

A "Highlights to Remember" section is at the end of each chapter. These sections briefly recapitulate some key ideas, suggestions, comments, or terms that might otherwise be overlooked or misunderstood.

1. *Balance sheet* is a widely used term, but it is not as descriptive as its newer substitute terms: *statement of financial position* or *statement of financial condition*.

2. An *entity* is a specific area of accountability, a boundary for reporting.

3. The transactions of a personal entity should not be mingled with those of a business entity.

4. The ownership equity of a corporation is usually called *stockholders' equity*. It initially takes the form of *common stock* at par or stated value plus *additional paid-in capital*.

5. The buyer of, say, 100 shares of stock almost always acquires the shares through the open marketplace. The seller of the 100 shares is some other shareholder, *not* the corporation itself. In other words, shares are issued en masse by a corporation at its inception and perhaps every few years thereafter. Once the shares are outstanding, the trading occurs between the individual shareholders and not between the corporation and any individual shareholder.

ACCOUNTING VOCABULARY

An "Accounting Vocabulary" section will immediately follow the "Highlights to Remember" section in each chapter. Vocabulary is an extremely important and often troublesome phase of the learning process. A fuzzy understanding of terms will hamper the learning of concepts and the ability to solve accounting problems.

Before proceeding to the assignment material or to the next chapter, be sure you understand the following words or terms. Their meaning is explained in the chapter and also in the glossary at the end of this book:

Account, p. *13* Accounts Payable, *9* Assets, *9* Audit, *7* Balance Sheet, *9* Big Eight, *8* Capital, *16* Capital Stock Certificate, *15* Certified Public Accountant, *6* Common Stock, *18* Contributed Capital, *16* Corporation, *14* Entity, *14* Financial Accounting, *4* Independent Opinion, *7* Liabilities, *9* Limited Liability, *15* Management Accounting, *4* Notes Payable, *9* Open Account, *12* Owners' Equity, *10* Paid-in Capital, *16* Paid-in Capital in Excess of Par Value, *16* Partnership, *14* Par Value, *16* Private Accounting, *5* Proprietorship, *14* Public Accounting, *5* Shareholders' Equity, *16* Stated Value, *16* Statement of Financial Condition, *9* Statement of Financial Position, *9* Stock Certificate, *15* Stockholders' Equity, *16* Transaction, *10*

Formulate good habits now. Check your understanding of these words or terms as a routine part of your study. Years ago you were urged to brush your teeth daily. The brushing habit is a good investment of your time. Similarly, the habit of checking your accounting vocabulary, chapter by chapter, is a good investment of your time.

ASSIGNMENT MATERIAL

The assignment material for each chapter is usually divided as follows:

Fundamental assignment material
  General coverage
  Understanding published financial reports
Additional assignment material
  General coverage
  Understanding published financial reports

The *fundamental assignment material* consists of relatively straightforward material aimed at conveying the essential concepts and techniques of the particular chapter. These assignments provide a solid introduction to the major concepts of the chapter. They closely follow the chapter presentations with an absolute minimum of new twists.

The *additional assignment material* contains some problems that are specifically identified as substitutes for ones in the fundamental material, plus some problems that spur the reader to do some original thinking.

The *general coverage* subgroups contain the conventional types of textbook assignment materials.

The *understanding published financial reports* subgroups focus on real-life situations. This use of actual companies and news events enhances the student's interest in accounting. Indeed, the most elementary concepts can be learned just as easily by relating them to real companies rather than artificial companies.

The *understanding published financial reports* subgroups also underscore a major objective of this book: to increase the reader's ability to read, understand, and use published financial reports and news articles. In later chapters, this group provides a principal means of reviewing not only the immediate chapter but also the previous chapters. Thus the group is a major way of both testing the reader's cumulative grasp of the subject and enhancing self-confidence.

FUNDAMENTAL ASSIGNMENT MATERIAL

☐ General Coverage

1–1. **ANALYSIS OF TRANSACTIONS.** (Alternates are 1–2, 1–3, 1–18, and 1–19.) Use the format of Exhibit 1–1 (p. 11) to analyze the following transactions for April of Span Cleaners. Then prepare a balance sheet as of April 30, 19X1. Span was founded on April 1.

  a. Issued 1,000 shares of $1 par common stock for cash, $50,000.
  b. Issued 1,200 shares of $1 par common stock for equipment, $60,000.
  c. Borrowed cash, signing a note payable for $30,000.
  d. Purchased equipment for cash, $20,000.
  e. Purchased office furniture on account, $10,000.
  f. Disbursed cash on account (to reduce the account payable), $4,000.
  g. Sold equipment on account at cost, $8,000.
  h. Discovered that the most prominent competitor in the area was bankrupt and was closing its doors on April 30.
  i. Collected cash on account, $3,000. See transaction g.

1–2. ANALYSIS OF TRANSACTIONS. (Alternates are 1–1, 1–3, 1–18, and 1–19.) H. J. Heinz Company is a well-known seller of catsup and other food products. Condensed items from its balance sheet, April 30, 1985, follow (in thousands):

ASSETS		LIABILITIES AND STOCKHOLDERS' EQUITY	
Cash	$ 19,398	Notes payable	$ 189,742
Accounts receivable	333,463	Accounts payable	282,145
Inventories	708,389	Other liabilities	771,433
Property and		Stockholders' equity	1,230,454
other assets	1,412,524		
Total	$2,473,774	Total	$2,473,774

Required:

Use a format similar to Exhibit 1–1 (p. 11) to analyze the following transactions for the first two days of May. Then prepare a balance sheet as of May 2, 1985:

1. Issued 1,000 shares of common stock to employees for cash, $18. (Dollar amounts are in thousands.)
2. Issued 1,500 shares of common stock for the acquisition of special equipment from a supplier, $27.
3. Borrowed cash, signing a note payable for $100.
4. Purchased equipment for cash, $125.
5. Purchased inventories on account, $90.
6. Disbursed cash on account (to reduce the accounts payable), $354.
7. Sold display equipment to a retailer on account at cost, $14.
8. Collected cash on account, $84.

1–3. ANALYSIS OF TRANSACTIONS. (Alternates are 1–1, 1–2, 1–18, and 1–19.) General Foods Corporation is a huge processor and marketer of foods and beverages. Among its well-known brands are Maxwell House coffee, Jell-O, and Post breakfast cereals. Its condensed items from a recent March 31 balance sheet follow (in thousands):

ASSETS		LIABILITIES AND STOCKHOLDERS' EQUITY	
Cash	$ 163,104	Notes payable	$ 344,832
Receivables	899,752	Accounts payable	280,238
Inventories	1,191,250	Other liabilities	1,609,841
Land, buildings,		Stockholders' equity	1,625,826
equipment	1,606,631		
Total	$3,860,737	Total	$3,860,737

Consider the following transactions that occurred during the first three days of April (in thousands of dollars):

1. Inventories were acquired for cash, $100.
2. Inventories were acquired on open account, $200.
3. Unsatisfactory coffee beans acquired an open account in March were returned for full credit, $40.
4. Equipment of $120 was acquired for a cash down payment of $30 plus a six-month promissory note of $90.
5. To encourage wider displays, special store equipment was sold on account to Chicago area stores for $400. The equipment had cost $400 in the preceding month. (This was an exception

to typical practice. Ordinarily, such equipment was retained by General Foods, lent to selected stores, and moved from location to location in accordance with particular marketing strategies.)

6. Robert Redford and Barbra Streisand codirected and coproduced a movie. As a favor to a General Foods executive, they agreed to display Maxwell House coffee and Post Toasties on a breakfast table in a prominent scene. No fee was paid by General Foods.

7. Cash was disbursed on account (to reduce accounts payable), $170.

8. Collected cash on account, $180.

9. Borrowed cash from a bank, $500.

10. Sold additional common stock for cash to new investors, $900.

11. The president of the company sold 5,000 shares of his personal holdings of General Foods stock through his stockbroker.

Required:

1. Using a format similar to Exhibit 1–1 (p. 11), prepare an analysis showing the effects of the April transactions on the financial position of General Foods.
2. Prepare a balance sheet, April 3.

ADDITIONAL ASSIGNMENT MATERIAL

☐ **General Coverage**

1–4. Give three examples of users of financial statements.

1–5. Give three examples of decisions that are likely to be influenced by financial statements.

1–6. Briefly distinguish between *financial accounting* and *management accounting*.

1–7. Give four examples of accounting entities.

1–8. Give two synonyms for *balance sheet*.

1–9. Explain the difference between a *note payable* and an *account payable*.

1–10. Give two synonyms for *owners' equity*.

1–11. Explain the meaning of *limited liability*.

1–12. Why does this book emphasize the corporation rather than the proprietorship or the partnership?

1–13. "The idea of par value is insignificant." Explain.

1–14. Distinguish between CPA, CA, CMA, CEO, and AICPA.

1–15. **DESCRIBING UNDERLYING TRANSACTIONS.** The balances of each item in Cryptic Company's accounting equation are given below for August 31 and for each of the next eight business days. State briefly what you think took place on each of these eight days, assuming that only one transaction occurred each day.

	CASH	ACCOUNTS RECEIVABLE	LAND	EQUIPMENT	ACCOUNTS PAYABLE	OWNERS' EQUITY
Aug. 31	$3,000	$7,000	$ 9,000	$ 8,000	$ 6,000	$21,000
Sept. 1	4,000	6,000	9,000	8,000	6,000	21,000
2	4,000	6,000	9,000	10,000	8,000	21,000
3	1,000	6,000	9,000	10,000	8,000	18,000
4	2,000	9,000	5,000	10,000	8,000	18,000
5	2,000	9,000	10,000	10,000	8,000	23,000
8	1,500	9,000	10,000	10,000	7,500	23,000
9	1,000	9,000	10,000	13,000	10,000	23,000
10	1,000	9,000	10,000	12,700	9,700	23,000

1–16. PREPARE BALANCE SHEET. (Alternate is 1–17.) Roark Corporation's balance sheet at June 29, 19X1, contained only the following items (arranged here in random order):

Paid-in capital	$198,000	Machinery and equipment	$ 20,000
Notes payable	20,000	Furniture and fixtures	8,000
Cash	8,000	Notes receivable	10,000
Accounts receivable	10,000	Accounts payable	12,000
Merchandise inventory	30,000	Building	230,000
Land	46,000	Long-term debt payable	132,000

On the following day, June 30, these transactions and events occurred:

1. Purchased machinery and equipment for $14,000, paying $3,000 in cash and signing a ninety-day note for the balance.
2. Paid $2,000 on accounts payable.
3. Sold on account some land that was not needed for $6,000, which was the Roark Corporation's acquisition cost of the land.
4. The remaining land was valued at $250,000 by professional appraisers.
5. Issued capital stock as payment for $20,000 of the long-term debt.

Required:

Prepare in good form a balance sheet for June 30, 19X1, showing supporting computations for all new amounts.

1–17. PREPARE BALANCE SHEET. (Alternate is 1–16.) Cone Corporation's balance sheet at August 30, 19X1, contained only the following items (arranged here in random order):

Cash	$ 5,000	Accounts payable	$ 4,000
Notes payable	10,000	Furniture and fixtures	3,000
Merchandise inventory	40,000	Long-term debt payable	12,000
Paid-in capital	78,000	Building	20,000
Land	6,000	Notes receivable	2,000
Accounts receivable	13,000	Machinery and equipment	15,000

On August 31, 19X1, these transactions and events took place:

1. Purchased merchandise on account, $2,500.
2. Sold at cost for $1,000 cash some furniture that was not needed.
3. Issued additional capital stock for machinery and equipment valued at $12,000.
4. Purchased land for $25,000, of which $5,000 was paid in cash, the remaining being represented by a five-year note (long-term debt).
5. The building was valued by professional appraisers at $45,000.

Required:

Prepare in good form a balance sheet for August 31, 19X1, showing supporting computations for all new amounts.

1–18. ANALYSIS OF TRANSACTIONS. (Alternates are 1–1, 1–2, 1–3, and 1–19.) Consider the following January transactions:

1. ABC Corporation is formed on January 1, 19X1, by three private investors, Hughes, Hestor, and Edam. ABC will be a wholesale distributor of kitchen appliances. Each investor is issued 30,000 shares of common stock ($1 par value) for $10 cash per share.
2. Merchandise inventory of $290,000 is acquired for cash.
3. Merchandise inventory of $100,000 is acquired on open account.
4. Unsatisfactory merchandise that cost $9,000 in transaction 3 is returned for full credit.

5. Equipment of $50,000 is acquired for a cash down payment of $12,000 plus a three-month promissory note of $38,000.
6. As a favor, ABC sells equipment of $3,000 to a business neighbor on open account. The equipment had cost $3,000.
7. ABC pays $30,000 on the account described in transaction 3.
8. ABC collects $1,000 from the business neighbor. See transaction 6.
9. ABC buys merchandise inventory of $150,000. One-third of the amount is paid in cash and two-thirds is owed on open account.
10. Hughes sells half of his common stock to Wedford for $14 per share.

Required:

1. Using a format like Exhibit 1–1 (p. 11), prepare an analysis showing the effects of January transactions on the financial position of ABC Corporation. Use two stockholders' equity accounts: Capital Stock (at par) and Additional Paid-in Capital.
2. Prepare a balance sheet, January 31, 19X1.

1–19. **ANALYSIS OF TRANSACTIONS.** (Alternates are 1–1, 1–2, 1–3, and 1–18.) You began a business as a wholesaler of shoes. The following events have occurred:

1. On March 1, 19X1, you invested $100,000 cash in your new sole proprietorship, which you call Apex Distributors.
2. Acquired $10,000 inventory for cash.
3. Acquired $5,000 inventory on open account.
4. Acquired equipment for $13,000 in exchange for a $3,000 cash down payment and a $10,000 promissory note.
5. Two retail shoe stores, which you had hoped would be prime customers, disclosed that they were bankrupt.
6. You take shoes home for your family. The shoes were carried in Apex inventory at $500. (Regard this as a borrowing by you from Apex Distributors.)
7. Shoes that cost $1,000 in transaction 2 were of the wrong style. You returned them and obtained a full cash refund.
8. Shoes that cost $1,000 in transaction 3 were of the wrong color. You returned them and obtained shoes of the correct color in exchange.
9. Shoes that cost $400 in transaction 3 had an unacceptable quality. You returned them and obtained full credit on your account.
10. Paid $3,000 on promissory note.
11. You use your personal cash savings of $2,000 to acquire some equipment for Apex. You consider this as an additional investment in your business.
12. Paid $1,000 on open account.
13. Two shoe manufacturers who are suppliers for Apex announced a 6% rise in prices, effective in thirty days.
14. You use your personal cash savings of $3,000 to acquire a new sofa for your family.
15. You exchange equipment that cost $3,000 in transaction 4 with another wholesaler. However, the equipment received, which is almost new, is smaller and is worth only $1,200. Therefore the other wholesaler also agrees to pay you $800 in cash now and an additional $1,000 in cash in sixty days. (No gain or loss is recognized on this transaction.)

Required:

1. Using Exhibit 1–1 (p. 11) as a guide, prepare an analysis of Apex transactions for March. Confine your analysis to the effects on the financial position of Apex Distributors.
2. Prepare a balance sheet for Apex, March 31, 19X1.

1–20. **PREPARE BALANCE SHEET.** Lisa Angelo is a realtor. She buys and sells properties on her own account, and she also earns commissions as a real estate agent for buyers and sellers. Her business was organized on November 24, 19X1, as a sole proprietorship. Angelo also owns her own personal residence. Consider the following on November 30, 19X1:

1. Angelo owes $100,000 on a mortgage on some undeveloped land, which was acquired by her business for a total price of $160,000.
2. Angelo had spent $15,000 cash for a Century 21 real estate franchise. Century 21 is a national affiliation of independent real estate brokers. This franchise is an asset.
3. Angelo owes $120,000 on a personal mortage on her residence, which was acquired on November 20, 19X1, for a total price of $170,000.
4. Angelo owes $1,800 on a personal charge account with Bloomingdale's Department Store.
5. On November 28, Angelo hired David Goldstein as her first employee. He was to begin work on December 1. Angelo was pleased because Goldstein was one of the best real estate salesmen in the area. On November 29, Goldstein was killed in an automobile accident.
6. Business furniture of $17,000 was acquired on November 25 for $6,000 on open account plus $11,000 of business cash. On November 26, Angelo sold a $1,000 business chair for $1,000 to her next-door business neighbor on open account.
7. Angelo's balance at November 30 in her business checking account after all transactions was $14,500.

Required: | Prepare a balance sheet as of November 30, 19X1, for Lisa Angelo, realtor.

1–21. **PERSONAL AND PROFESSIONAL ENTITIES.** J. Galvez, a recent graduate of a school of medicine, was penniless on December 25, 19X1.

1. On December 26, Galvez inherited an enormous sum of money.
2. On December 27, she placed $90,000 in a business checking account for her unincorporated practice of medicine.
3. On December 28, she purchased a home for a down payment of $100,000 plus a home mortgage payable of $300,000.
4. On December 28, Galvez agreed to rent a medical office. She provided a $1,000 cash damage deposit (from her business cash), which will be fully refundable when she vacates the premises. This deposit is a business asset. Rental payments are to be made in advance on the first business day of each month. (The first payment of $700 is not to be made until January 2, 19X2.)
5. On December 28, Galvez purchased medical equipment for $5,000 business cash plus an $11,000 promissory note due in ninety days.
6. On December 28, she also purchased medical supplies for $1,000 on open account.
7. On December 28, Galvez purchased medical office furniture for $4,000 of business cash.
8. On December 29, Galvez hired a medical assistant-receptionist for $380 per week. He was to report to work on January 2.
9. On December 30, Galvez lent $2,000 of business cash in return for a one-year note from G. Holden, a local candy store owner. Holden had indicated that she would spread the news about the new physician.

Required: | 1. Use the format demonstrated in Exhibit 1–1 (p. 11) to analyze the transactions of J. Galvez, physician. To avoid crowding, put your numbers in thousands of dollars. Do not restrict yourself to the account titles in Exhibit 1–1.
2. Prepare a balance sheet as of December 31, 19X1.

☐ **Understanding Published Financial Reports**

1–22. **EFFECTS ON BALANCE SHEETS.** Refer to the balance sheets of the actual companies cited in the chapter, pages 18–19.

For each of the following transactions, indicate the amount of change for each account affected. Also indicate the direction of the change, increase or decrease. Use specific account titles.

1. BankAmerica lends $100,000 to Joan Kessler on a home mortgage note.
2. Isabel Garcia deposits $1,000 in a savings account in one of the branch offices of BankAmerica.

3. The U.S. government acquires some nuclear aircraft carriers for (a) $5 billion cash or (b) issuance of U.S. Savings Bonds. Answer 3a, and then 3b.
4. Peat Marwick pays a retiring partner a lump sum of $200,000 cash for the withdrawal of the partner's ownership equity.
5. Peat Marwick admits a new partner in exchange for a cash payment of $15,000 plus a promissory note (due within a year) of $20,000.
6. Pacific Gas and Electric buys an additional plant for (a) $50 million cash or (b) $10 million cash plus a $40 million, 25-year mortgage note payable. Answer 6a, and then 6b.
7. Pacific Gas and Electric receives an advance deposit of $100 from a subscriber in a student dormitory. The $100 is completely refundable when service is terminated at the end of the school year.

1–23. **U.S. TRANSACTIONS.** Show how the balance sheet of the U.S. government (which is illustrated on page 20) will be affected by the events below. Indicate the amounts and the accounts affected.

1. The Department of the Interior pays $10 million cash to Boise Cascade Corporation for some forests that will be converted into a national park.
2. The Department of Defense purchases and accepts immediate delivery of $3 million of weapons from Lockheed Corporation. Terms are $1 million in cash with the remainder to be paid within ninety days.
3. The Internal Revenue Service collects $1 billion in income taxes receivable from General Electric Corporation.
4. The Social Security Administration pays $1 billion in April to pensioners.
5. The president is assassinated.
6. The Soviet Union decides to pay a World War II debt and gives the United States $1 billion cash.
7. The Soviet Union invades China.
8. The U.S. Treasury sells a new government bond issue of $10 billion. (A bond is a long-term payable.)
9. The General Services Administration buys $10 million of trucks for cash from Chrysler Corporation.
10. The Department of the Interior buys $1 million of trucks for cash from the General Services Administration.

1–24. **BALANCE SHEET EFFECTS.**

1. Citibank showed the following items (among others) on its balance sheet at December 31, 19X1:

Cash	$ 947,000,000
Total deposits	6,383,000,000

Suppose you made a deposit of $1,000 in Citibank. How would each of the bank's assets and liabilities be affected? How would each of your personal assets and liabilities be affected? Be specific regarding the accounts affected.
2. Suppose a savings and loan association makes an $800,000 loan to a local hospital for remodeling. What would be the effect on each of the association's assets and other accounts immediately after the loan was made? Be specific.
3. Suppose you borrowed $10,000 from the Household Finance Company on a personal loan. How would such a transaction affect each of your personal assets and liabilities?

1–25. **PRESENTING PAID-IN CAPITAL.** Consider excerpts from two balance sheets:

Occidental Petroleum Corporation

Common shares, $.20 par value; authorized 100 million shares; issued 68,057,086 shares	$ 13,611,000
Additional paid-in capital	798,695,000

Clark Equipment

Capital stock common—$7.50 par value—outstanding 13,686,131 shares (includes capital in excess of par value)	$151,850,000

1. How would the presentation of Occidental's stockholders' equity accounts be affected if one million more shares were issued for $50 cash per share?
2. How would the presentation of Clark Equipment's stockholders' equity accounts be affected if one million more shares were issued for $50 cash per share? Be specific.

1–26. **PRESENTING PAID-IN CAPITAL.** Honeywell, Inc., maker of thermostats and a variety of complex control systems, presented the following in its balance sheet of January 1, 1986:

Common stock—$1.50 par value, 47,422,792 shares issued and outstanding	?
Additional paid-in capital	675,700,000

What amount should be shown on the common stock line? What was the average price per share paid by the original investors for the Honeywell common stock? How do your answers compare with the $72 market price of the stock on January 2, 1986? Comment briefly.

1–27. **PREPARE BALANCE SHEET.** (Alternate is 1–28.) General Motors Corporation (GM) is the world's largest manufacturer of automobiles. GM's recent annual report included the following balance sheet items (in millions of dollars):

U.S. government and other securities	$ 8,100
Properties	19,402
Accounts payable	4,744
Inventories	7,360
Capital stock	788
Cash	?
Total stockholders' equity	?
Long-term debt	2,417
Total assets	52,145
Loans payable	3,086
Accounts receivable	7,358
Other assets	9,458
Additional stockholders' equity	23,426
Other liabilities	17,684

Required:

Prepare a condensed balance sheet, including amounts for

1. Cash. What do you think of its relative size?
2. Total stockholders' equity.
3. Total liabilities.

1–28. **STOCKHOLDERS' EQUITY.** (Alternate is 1–27.) Honeywell Inc. is a manufacturer of systems for automation and control. The home thermostat is one of its products. Its balance sheet, January 1, 1986, contained the following (in millions):

Long-term debt	$ 641.6
Cash	(1)
Total shareholders' equity	(2)
Total liabilities	(3)
Accounts receivable	1,138.8
Common stock	71.1
Inventories	1,035.6
Accounts payable	261.6
Properties	1,580.5
Additional shareholders' equity	2,495.8
Other assets	782.2
Other liabilities	1,563.6
Total assets	5,033.7

Required:

Prepare a condensed balance sheet, including amounts for

1. Cash. What do you think of its relative size?
2. Total shareholders' equity.
3. Total liabilities.

Chapter 2

THE INCOME STATEMENT:
THE ACCRUAL BASIS

LEARNING OBJECTIVES

After studying this chapter, you should be able to

1. Define and explain **revenues**, **expenses**, **net income, dividends**, and **retained income**
2. Distinguish between **dividends** and **expense, unexpired costs** and **expired costs**, and the **cash** and **accrual** bases of accounting
3. Use the expanded balance sheet equation for analyzing some typical transactions of an entity and for constructing a set of financial statements
4. Explain what is meant by **generally accepted accounting principles** (GAAP) and by the three principles described in this chapter: **realization**, **matching and cost recovery**, and **stable monetary unit**
5. Compute and explain four popular ratios relating to the earnings, dividends, and market prices of the common stock of corporations (Appendix 2)

What is income? How is it measured? These questions have been the subject of perpetual debate among accountants, economists, managers, investors, politicians, and others. We now consider income-producing activities and how the accountant portrays them.

THE RUDIMENTS OF INCOME

☐ Various Meanings

Almost all of us have a reason for learning about how accountants measure income. For example, we want to know how we are doing as individuals, as corporations, as hospitals, or as universities. Even nonprofit institutions use a concept of income as a way of determining how much they can afford to spend to accomplish their objectives. Investors use a concept of income to measure their successes and failures and to compare the performance of their existing and potential holdings. Indeed, income is the primary way of evaluating the economic performance of people, corporations, other entities, and economies as a whole.

At first glance, income seems like a straightforward concept. Most persons think of income as being what is reported on individual tax returns. However, individuals who have filed any but the simplest income tax returns will quickly testify that the concept of taxable income frequently drives calm, intelligent, honest taxpayers to the brink of madness. The problems of measuring income are seldom simple.

The general idea of income has been expressed in several ways, including a net increase in "wealth" or "capital" or "general purchasing power" or "financial resources" or "command over goods and services." Most people may agree with such abstract descriptions, but fierce arguments have occurred regarding how to measure the income of a *specific* individual or entity for a *specific* time period.

Politicians may assail an industry or company for ill-gotten profits; in turn, executives will complain that the accounting measurements of income are faulty. These disputes will never be fully resolved. Still, accountants are usually in the center of the arguments. Most controversies in accounting deal with how income is to be measured. The issues are usually extremely important in the minds of the disputants, whose livelihood or measures of accomplishment are frequently affected. Examples of these parties include managers, tax collectors, hospital administrators, economists, and attorneys.

This chapter *introduces* the subject of income measurement. Income will then receive ample attention throughout the rest of this book.

☐ Operating Cycle

Most organizations exist to satisfy a desire for some type of goods or services. Whether they are profit seeking or not, they typically follow a similar, somewhat rhythmic, pattern of economic activity. An **operating cycle** (also called a *cash cycle* or *earnings cycle*) is the time span during which cash is used to acquire goods and services, which in turn are sold to customers, who in turn pay for their purchases with cash. Consider the following example. A retail business usually engages in some version of the operating cycle in order to earn profits:

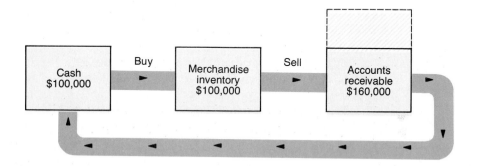

The box for Accounts Receivable (amounts owed to the business by customers) is larger than the other two boxes because the objective is to sell goods at a price higher than the acquisition cost. Retailers and nearly all other businesses buy goods and services and perform acts (such as placing them in a convenient location or changing their form) that merit selling prices that yield an expected profit. The total amount of profit earned during a particular period depends on the excess of selling prices over costs of the goods and additional expenses and on the speed of the operating cycle.

☐ Revenues and Expenses

Consider the Biwheels illustration presented in Chapter 1. Recall that Exhibit 1–1, which is reproduced here, summarizes nine transactions. Suppose a tenth transaction is a summary of sales for the entire month of January amounting to $160,000 on open account. The cost to Biwheels of the inventory sold is $100,000. Note that this and other transactions illustrated here are indeed *summarized* transactions. For example, all the sales will not take place at once, nor will purchases of inventory, collections from customers, or disbursements to suppliers. A vast number of repetitive transactions occur in practice, and specialized data-collection techniques are used to measure their effects on the entity.

How should transaction 10 be analyzed? Basically, this transaction has two phases, a *revenue phase* (10a) and an *expense phase* (10b) (dollar signs omitted):

DESCRIPTION OF TRANSACTION		ASSETS =		LIABILITIES AND OWNERS' EQUITY
Balances, January 12, 19X2		516,200 =		516,200
(10a) Sales on account (inflow of assets)	Accounts receivable,	+160,000 =	Owners' equity,	+160,000
(10b) Cost of inventory sold (outflow of assets)	Inventory,	−100,000 =	Owners' equity,	−100,000
Balances, January 31, 19X2		576,200 =		576,200

Transaction 10a illustrates the accounting for *revenue*. **Revenues** are generally gross increases in assets from delivering goods or services to customers.

Transaction 10b illustrates the accounting for an expense. **Expenses** are generally gross decreases in assets from delivering goods or services.

Transactions 10a and 10b also illustrate the fundamental meaning of **profits** or **earnings** or **income**, which can simply be defined as the excess of revenues over expenses.

Transaction 10 is also analyzed in Exhibit 2–1, which merely continues Exhibit 1–1 (where the form of organization was not specified). However, a

EXHIBIT 1–1

BIWHEELS COMPANY
Analysis of Transactions For December 31, 19X1–January 12, 19X2 (in dollars)

DESCRIPTION OF TRANSACTION	Cash	+ Accounts Receivable +	Merchandise Inventory +	Store Equipment =	Note Payable +	Accounts Payable +	Owners' Equity
		ASSETS			= LIABILITIES + OWNERS' EQUITY		
(1) Initial investment	+400,000			=			+400,000
(2) Loan from bank	+100,000			=	+100,000		
(3) Acquire inventory for cash	−150,000		+150,000	=			
(4) Acquire inventory on credit			+ 10,000	=		+10,000	
(5) Acquire store equipment for cash plus credit	− 4,000			+15,000 =		+11,000	
(6) Sales of equipment		+1,000		− 1,000 =			
(7) Return of bicycles acquired on January 3			− 800	=		− 800	
(8) Payments to creditors	− 4,000			=		− 4,000	
(9) Collections from debtors	+ 700	− 700		=			
Balance, January 12, 19X2	342,700 +	300 +	159,200 +	14,000 =	100,000 +	16,200 +	400,000
		516,200			=	516,200	

EXHIBIT 2–1 *(Place a clip on this page for easy reference.)*

BIWHEELS COMPANY
Analysis of Transactions for January 19X2 (in dollars)

DESCRIPTION OF TRANSACTION	ASSETS					=	LIABILITIES + OWNERS' EQUITY			
							Liabilities		Stockholders' Equity	
	Cash	+ Accounts Receivable	+ Merchandise Inventory	+ Prepaid Rent	+ Store Equipment	=	Note Payable	+ Accounts Payable	+ Paid-in Capital	+ Retained Income
(1)–(9) See Exhibit 1–1 Balance, January 12, 19X2	342,700 +	300 +	159,200	+	14,000	=	100,000 +	16,200	+ 400,000	
(10a) Sales on open account (inflow of assets)		+160,000				=				+160,000 (revenue)
(10b) Cost of inventory sold (outflow of assets)			–100,000			=				–100,000 (increase expense)
(11) Pay rent in advance	– 6,000			+6,000		=				
(12) Recognize expiration of rental services				–2,000		=				– 2,000 (increase expense)
(13) Recognize expiration of equipment services (depreciation)					– 100	=				– 100 (increase expense)
Balance, January 31, 19X2	336,700 +	160,300 +	59,200 +	4,000 +	13,900	=	100,000 +	16,200	+ 400,000 +	57,900
			574,100					574,100		

37

corporate organization is now assumed. The owners' equity has two parts: paid-in capital (or contributed capital) and retained income. Paid-in capital denotes the total amount of capital paid in (or contributed) by the "common" shareholders. (There are no other classes of shareholders in this company.) **Retained income**, to be discussed more completely later, is additional owners' equity generated by profits.

As the Retained Income column in Exhibit 2–1 shows, increases in revenues increase stockholders' equity. In contrast, increases in expenses decrease stockholders' equity. So expenses are negative stockholders' equity accounts. The relationships just depicted can also be illustrated as follows:

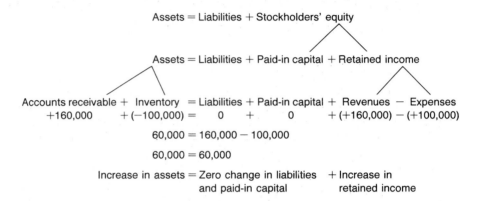

Transaction 10 is the $160,000 sale on open account of inventory that had cost $100,000. Two things happen simultaneously: an inflow of assets in the form of accounts receivable (10a) in exchange for an outflow of assets in the form of inventory (10b). Liabilities are completely unaffected, so owners' equity rises by $160,000 − $100,000, or $60,000.

☐ Realization

Ponder the operating cycle in Exhibit 1–1. Transactions 3 and 4 were purchases of merchandise inventory. They were steps toward the ultimate goal—the earning of a profit. But by themselves purchases earn no profit; remember that owners' equity was unaffected by the inventory acquisitions in transactions 3 and 4. That is, no profit is realized until a sale is actually made to customers.

Accountants use several measurement conventions (often called *principles*). A major convention is a **realization** test for determining whether revenue should be recognized as being earned during a given period. To be realized, revenue must ordinarily meet three criteria:

1. The goods or services must be fully rendered. That is, the earning process must be virtually complete. The usual evidence is full delivery to customers.
2. An exchange of resources between two independent parties must occur. The usual evidence is a market transaction whereby the buyer pays or promises to pay cash and the seller delivers merchandise or services.

3. The collectibility of any noncash asset received from the buyer must be reasonably assured. The usual evidence is the customer's record as a credit risk.

☐ Matching and Cost Recovery

Matching is a favorite buzzword in accounting. The convention of matching is the linking of accomplishments or revenues with the related efforts or expenses. The revenues realized in a particular period (measured by the selling prices of goods and services delivered to customers) minus the related expenses (measured by the cost of goods and services used) is the income for the period. In short, matching is a short description of how to measure income.

The heart of recognizing expense is the **cost recovery** concept. That is, assets such as inventories are carried forward as assets because their costs are expected to be recovered in the form of cash inflows (or reduced cash outflows) in future periods. At the end of each period, the accountant (especially the outside auditor at the end of each year) carefully examines the evidence to determine whether these assets—these prepaid costs—should be carried forward to future periods or written off as an expense of the current period.

☐ Prepaid Rent

To focus on the matching concept, assume that there are only two expenses other than the cost of goods sold: rent expense and depreciation expense. (Interest expense on the bank loan will be considered separately in a later chapter.)

Transaction 11 is the payment of store rent of $6,000 covering January, February, and March of 19X2. Rent is $2,000 per month, payable quarterly in advance. (For simplicity regarding the dates in Chapter 1, assume that this initial payment was made on January 16, although ordinarily it would have been made on January 2.)

The rent disbursement is made to acquire the right to use store facilities for the next three months. The $6,000 measures the *future* benefit from these services, so the asset *Prepaid Rent* is created (see Exhibit 2–1). Assets are defined as economic resources. They are not confined to tangible items that you can see or touch, such as cash or inventory. Assets also include the intangible legal rights to future services, such as the use of facilities.

Transaction 12 recognizes that one-third of the rental services have expired, so the asset is reduced and stockholders' equity is also reduced by $2,000 as rent expense for January. This recognition of rent *expense* means that $2,000 of the asset, Prepaid Rent, has been "used up" (or has flowed out of the entity) in the conduct of operations during January.

Prepaid rent of $4,000 is carried forward as an asset as of January 31 because the accountant was virtually certain that it represented a future benefit. Why? Because without the prepayment, cash outflows of $2,000 each would have to be made for February and March. So the presence of the prepayment is a benefit in the sense that future cash outflows will be reduced by $4,000. Furthermore, future revenues (sales) are expected to be high enough to ensure the recovery of the $4,000.

☐ Depreciation

Transaction 13 recognizes that the store equipment is really a bundle of services that will have a limited useful life. Therefore accountants usually predict the length of the useful life, predict the ultimate disposal value, and allocate the *cost* of the equipment to the years of its useful life in some systematic way. This process is called the recording of **depreciation** expense; it applies to physical assets such as buildings, equipment, furniture, and fixtures owned by the entity. Land is not subject to depreciation.

The most popular depreciation method is the *straight-line method*. Suppose the predicted life of the equipment is ten years, and the estimated terminal disposal value is $2,000:

$$\text{Straight-line depreciation} = \frac{\text{Original cost} - \text{Estimated terminal disposal value}}{\text{Years of useful life}}$$

$$= \frac{\$14,000 - \$2,000}{10}$$

$$= \$1,200 \text{ per year, or } \$100 \text{ per month}$$

More will be said about depreciation in Chapter 5. But no matter how much is said, the general concept of expense should be clear by now. The purchases and uses of goods and services (for example, inventories, rent, equipment) ordinarily consist of two basic steps: (a) the *acquisition* of the *assets* (transactions 3, 4, 5, and 11) and (b) the *expiration* of the assets as *expenses* (transactions 10b, 12, and 13). When these assets expire, the total assets and owners' equity are decreased. When sales to customers bring new assets to the business, its total assets and owners' equity are increased. Expense accounts are basically deductions from stockholders' equity. Similarly, revenue accounts are basically additions to stockholders' equity.

☐ The Income Statement

Exhibit 2–1 is extremely important because it provides an overview of the entire accounting process. We have already seen how a balance sheet may be prepared through the use of such an exhibit. Similarly, an income statement may be prepared by analyzing the *changes* in owners' equity, as Exhibit 2–2 demonstrates. An **income statement** is a report of all revenues and expenses pertaining to a specific time period.

The income statement is also called the **statement of income, operating statement**, **statement of operations**, **results of operations**, **statement of earnings**, and **statement of revenues and expenses**. For many years the most popular name for this statement was statement of profit *and* loss, often termed the **P & L statement**. Such a label is justifiably fading into oblivion. After all, the ultimate result is either a profit *or* a loss.

The terms *income*, *earnings*, and *profits* are often used interchangeably. Indeed, many companies will use net *income* on their income statements but will refer to retained income as retained *earnings*. The term *net income* (or *net profit*) is the world-famous "bottom line"—the remainder after *all* ex-

EXHIBIT 2–2

BIWHEELS COMPANY
Income Statement
For the Month Ended January 31, 19X2

Sales (revenues)		$160,000
Deduct expenses:		
Cost of goods sold	$100,000	
Rent	2,000	
Depreciation	100	
Total expenses		102,100
Net income		$ 57,900

penses (including income taxes, which are illustrated later) have been deducted from revenue.

The term *earnings* is becoming increasingly popular because it has a preferable image. *Earnings* apparently implies compensation for honest toil, whereas *income* or *profit* evidently inspires cartoonists to portray managers as greedy, evil-looking individuals.

The term **cost of sales** is a synonym for **cost of goods sold**. Both terms mean the entity's original acquisition cost of the inventory that *was sold to customers during the reporting period*.

Relationship Between Balance Sheet and Income Statement

The income statement measures the operating performance of the corporation by relating its accomplishments (revenues from customers) and its efforts (cost of goods sold and other expenses). It measures performance for *a span of time*, whether it be a month, a quarter, or longer. Therefore the income statement must always indicate the exact period covered. The above example was for the month ended January 31, 19X2. Recall that the balance sheet shows the financial position at an *instant of time*, and therefore the balance sheet must always indicate the exact date.

The income statement is the major link between two balance sheets:

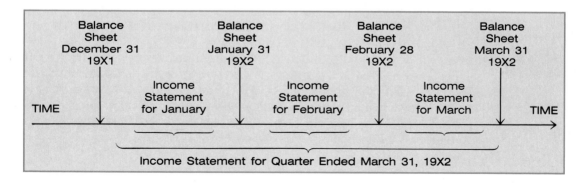

Remember that the balance sheet provides a snapshot, a photograph at an *instant* of time; in contrast, the income statement provides a moving picture for a *span* of time.

As Exhibit 2–1 shows, the accountant records increases (revenues of $160,000) and decreases (expenses of $102,100) in owners' equity. At the end of a given period, these items are summarized and explained in the form of an income statement, as Exhibit 2–2 illustrates. The net income ($57,900) is then added to Retained Income, which appears in the balance sheet as an element of owners' equity and which, for successful companies, often accumulates to vast amounts over many years as the major part of the shareholders' residual claim against total assets.

□ Analytical Power of the Balance Sheet Equation

As you study Exhibits 1–1 and 2–1, the following points should clarify the way in which accountants use the fundamental balance sheet equation as their framework for analyzing and reporting the effects of transactions:

$$\text{Assets (A)} = \text{Liabilities (L)} + \text{Stockholders' equity (SE)} \tag{1}$$

SE equals the original ownership claim plus the increase in ownership claim due to profitable operations. That is, SE equals the claim arising from paid-in capital plus the claim arising from retained income. Therefore

$$\text{Assets} = \text{Liabilities} + \text{Paid-in capital} + \text{Retained income} \tag{2}$$

But, in our illustration, Retained Income equals Revenue minus Expenses. Therefore

$$\text{Assets} = \text{Liabilities} + \text{Paid-in capital} + \text{Revenue} - \text{Expenses} \tag{3}$$

Revenue and expense accounts are nothing more than subdivisions of stockholders' equity—temporary stockholders' equity accounts, as it were. Their purpose is to summarize the volume of sales and the various expenses so that management is kept informed of the reasons for the numerous increases and decreases in stockholders' equity in the course of ordinary operations. In this way comparisons can be made, standards or goals can be set, and control can be better exercised.

The entire accounting system is based on the simple balance sheet equation. As you know, equations in general have enormous analytical potential because they permit dual algebraic manipulations. The equation is always kept in balance because of the duality feature.

Exhibits 1–1 and 2–1 illustrate the dual nature of the accountant's analysis. For each transaction, the equation is always kept in balance. If the items affected are confined to one side of the equation, you will find that the total amount added is equal to the total amount subtracted on that side. If the items affected are on both sides, then equal amounts are simultaneously added or subtracted on each side.

The striking feature of the balance sheet equation is its universal applicability. No transaction has even been conceived, no matter how simple or complex, that cannot be analyzed via the equation. The top technical partners in the world's largest professional accounting firms, when confronted with the most intricate transactions of multinational companies, will inevitably discuss and think about their analyses in terms of the balance sheet equation and its major components: assets, liabilities, and owners' equity (including the explanations of changes in owners' equity that must often take the form of revenues and expenses).

☐ Measurement of Expenses: Assets Expire

Transactions 10b, 12, and 13 recognize the cost of merchandise sold and the expiration of services acquired. They demonstrate how assets can be viewed as bundles of economic services awaiting future use or expiration. It is helpful to think of assets, other than cash and receivables, as prepaid or stored costs (for example, inventories or equipment) that are carried forward to future periods rather than immediately charged against revenue:

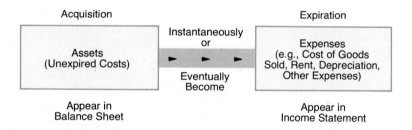

Expenses are used-up assets. Thus, assets are unexpired costs held back from the expense stream and carried in the balance sheet to await expiration in future periods.

The analysis of the inventory, rent, and depreciation transactions in Exhibit 2–1 maintains this distinction of acquisition and expiration. The unexpired costs of inventory, prepaid rent, and equipment are assets until they are used up and become expenses.

Services are often acquired and used almost instanteously. Examples are advertising services, miscellaneous supplies, and sales salaries and commissions. Conceptually, these costs should, at least momentarily, be viewed as assets upon acquisition before being written off as expenses. For example, suppose there was an extra transaction in Exhibit 2–1 whereby newspaper advertising was acquired for $1,000 cash. To abide by the acquisition-expiration sequence, the transaction could be analyzed in two phases:

TRANSACTION	ASSETS			= LIABILITIES +	STOCKHOLDERS' EQUITY	
	Cash	Other + Assets +	Unexpired Advertising =		Paid-in Capital +	Retained Income
Extra (a)	−1,000		+1,000 =			
Extra (b)			−1,000 =			−1,000 (expense)

As a matter of practice, however, many services are acquired and used up so quickly that accountants do not bother recording an asset such as Unexpired Advertising or Prepaid Rent for them. Instead a shortcut is usually taken when goods and services are to be routinely consumed in the period of their purchase:

TRANSACTION	Cash	+ Other Assets =	Liabilities +	Paid-in Capital +	Retained Income
Extra (a) and (b) together	−1,000		=		−1,000 (expense)

Making the entry in two steps instead of one is cumbersome from a practical bookkeeping viewpoint. However, the two steps underscore a *crucial concept*. We want an orderly way of thinking about what the manager does. The manager acquires goods and services, not expenses per se. These goods and services become expenses as they are used in obtaining revenue.

Some of the most difficult issues in accounting center on *when* an unexpired cost expires and becomes an expense. For example, some accountants believe that research and development costs should be accounted for as unexpired costs (and shown on balance sheets among the assets as "Deferred Research and Development Costs") and written off to expense in some systematic manner over a period of years. But the regulators of financial accounting in the United States have ruled that such costs have vague future benefits that are difficult to measure reliably and thus have required writing them off as expenses immediately. In cases such as this, research costs are not found on balance sheets.

ACCRUAL BASIS AND CASH BASIS

☐ **Efforts and Accomplishments**

The process of determining income and financial position is anchored to the **accrual basis** of accounting, as distinguished from the **cash basis**. In accrual accounting, the impact of transactions on financial position and performance is recognized on the accounting records in the time periods when services are rendered or used instead of when cash is received or disbursed. That is, revenue is recognized as it is *earned*, and expenses are recognized as they are *incurred*—not when cash changes hands.

Transaction 10a in Exhibit 2–1, page 37, shows an example of the accrual basis. Revenue is recognized when sales are made on credit, not when cash is received. Similarly, transactions 10b, 12, and 13 (for cost of goods sold, rent, and depreciation) show that expenses are recognized as efforts are expended or services used to obtain the revenue (regardless of when cash is disbursed). Therefore income is often affected by measurements of noncash resources and obligations. The accrual basis is the principal conceptual framework for relating accomplishments (revenues) with efforts (expenses).

If the *cash basis* of accounting were used instead of the accrual basis, *revenue and expense recognition would depend solely on the timing of various cash receipts and disbursements*. Our Biwheels example for January would show zero revenue because no cash was collected from customers. Similarly, rent expense would be $6,000 (the cash disbursed for rent) rather than the $2,000 rent applicable to January. A cash measurement of net income or net loss is obviously ridiculous in this case, and it could mislead those unacquainted with the fundamentals of accounting.

Ponder the rent example. Under the cash basis, January must bear expenses for the entire quarter's rent of $6,000 merely because cash outflows occurred then. In contrast, the accrual basis measures performance more sharply by allocating the rental expense to the operations of the three months that *benefited from the use* of the facilities. In this way, the economic performance of each month will be comparable. Most accountants maintain that it is nonsense to say that January's rent expense was $6,000 and February's and March's was zero.

□ **Pause for Reflection**

If you have never studied accounting before, or if you studied it long ago, do not proceed further until you have solved the following problem. There are no shortcuts. Pushing a pencil is an absolute necessity for becoming comfortable with accounting concepts. The cost-benefit test will easily be met; your gain in knowledge will exceed your investment of time.

Please do the work on your own. In particular, do not ask for help from professional accountants or advanced accounting students if they introduce any new terms beyond those already covered. For example, the technical terms *debits*, *credits*, and *ledger accounts* will only confuse, not clarify, at this stage. Instead, scrutinize Exhibits 1–1 and 2–1. Note how each transaction affects the balance sheet equation. Then solve the review problem that follows.

SUMMARY PROBLEM FOR YOUR REVIEW

□ **Problem One**

Biwheels' transactions for January were analyzed in Exhibits 1–1 and 2–1. The balance sheet, January 31, 19X2, is:

BIWHEELS COMPANY
Balance Sheet
January 31, 19X2

ASSETS		LIABILITIES AND STOCKHOLDERS' EQUITY		
		Liabilities:		
Cash	$336,700	Note payable		$100,000
Accounts receivable	160,300	Accounts payable		16,200
Merchandise		Total liabilities		$116,200
inventory	59,200	Stockholder's equity:		
Prepaid rent	4,000	Paid-in capital	$400,000	
Store equipment	13,900	Retained income	57,900	
		Total stockholders' equity		457,900
		Total liabilities and		
Total assets	$574,100	stockholders' equity		$574,100

The following series of transactions occurred during February:

(14) Collection of accounts receivable, $130,000.
(15) Payments of accounts payable, $15,000.
(16) Acquisitions of inventory on open account, $80,000, and for cash, $10,000.
(17) Merchandise carried in inventory at a cost of $110,000 was sold on open account for $125,000 and for cash for $51,000.
(18) Recognition of rent expense for February.
(19) Recognition of depreciation expense for February.

Required:

1. Prepare an analysis of transactions, employing the equation approach demonstrated in Exhibit 2–1.
2. Prepare a balance sheet as of February 28, 19X2, and an income statement for the month of February.

☐ Solution to Problem One

1. *Analysis of transactions*. The answer is in Exhibit 2–3. All transactions are straightforward extensions or repetitions of the January transactions.

2. *Preparation of financial statements*. Exhibits 2–4 and 2–5 contain the balance sheet and the income statement, which have been described earlier.

EXHIBIT 2-3

BIWHEELS COMPANY
Analysis of Transactions for February 19X2 (in dollars)

DESCRIPTION OF TRANSACTION	Cash	+ Accounts Receivable	+ Merchandise Inventory	+ Prepaid Rent	+ Store Equipment	=	Notes Payable	+ Accounts Payable	+ Paid-in Capital	+ Retained Income
									Liabilities	**Stockholders' Equity**
Balance, January 31, 19X2	336,700 +	160,300 +	59,200 +	4,000 +	13,900	=	100,000 +	16,200 +	400,000 +	57,900
(14) Collection of accounts receivable	+130,000	−130,000								
(15) Payments of accounts payable	− 15,000					=		−15,000		
(16) Acquisitions of inventory on open account and for cash	− 10,000		+ 90,000			=		+80,000		
(17a) Sales on open account and for cash	+ 51,000	+125,000				=				+176,000 (increase revenue)
(17b) Cost of inventory sold			−110,000			=				−110,000 (increase expense)
(18) Recognize expiration of rental services				−2,000		=				− 2,000 (increase expense)
(19) Recognize expiration of equipment services (depreciation)					− 100	=				− 100 (increase expense)
Balance, February 28, 19X2	492,700 +	155,300 +	39,200 +	2,000 +	13,800	=	100,000 +	81,200 +	400,000 +	121,800

703,000 = 703,000

EXHIBIT 2–4

BIWHEELS COMPANY
Balance Sheet February 28, 19X2

ASSETS			LIABILITIES AND STOCKHOLDERS' EQUITY		
			Liabilities:		
Cash	$492,700		Notes payable	$100,000	
Accounts receivable	155,300		Accounts payable	81,200	$181,200
Merchandise					
inventory	39,200		Stockholders' equity:		
Prepaid rent	2,000		Paid-in capital	$400,000	
Store equipment	13,800		Retained income	121,800	521,800
Total	$703,000		Total		$703,000

EXHIBIT 2–5

BIWHEELS COMPANY
Income Statement
For the Month Ended February 28, 19X2

Sales		$176,000
Deduct expenses:		
Cost of goods sold	$110,000	
Rent	2,000	
Depreciation	100	112,100
Net income		$ 63,900

DIVIDENDS AND RETAINED INCOME

☐ Dividends Are Not Expenses

Extending our Biwheels illustration, we now assume an additional transaction in February. On February 28, cash dividends of $50,000 are declared by the board of directors and disbursed to stockholders. The accountant would analyze this transaction (20) as follows:

	ASSETS = LIABILITIES	+ STOCKHOLDERS' EQUITY
	Cash	Retained Income
(20) Declaration and payment of cash dividends	−50,000 =	−50,000

As transaction 20 shows, cash dividends are not expenses like rent and depreciation. They should not be deducted from revenues because dividends are not directly related to the generation of sales or the conduct of operations. Generally, **dividends** are distributions of cash to stockholders that reduce retained income. The ability to pay dividends is fundamentally caused by profitable operations. Retained income increases as profits accumulate, and it decreases as dividends occur.

The entire right-hand side of the balance sheet can be thought of as claims against the total assets. The liabilities are the claims of creditors. The stockholders' equity represents the residual claims of owners arising out of their initial investment (paid-in capital) and subsequent profitable operations (retained income). *Retained income* is also called **retained earnings**, **undistributed earnings**, or **reinvested earnings**.

As a successful company grows, this account can soar enormously if dividends are not paid. Retained income can easily be the largest stockholders' equity account.

Statement of Retained Income

Exhibit 2–6 shows a new financial statement, the **statement of retained income**. The statement merely lists the beginning balance (in this case, January 31), followed by a description of any major changes (in this case, net income and dividends), and the ending balance (February 28).

EXHIBIT 2–6

BIWHEELS COMPANY
Statement of Retained Income
For the Month Ended February 28, 19X2

Retained income, January 31, 19X2	$ 57,900
Net income for February	63,900
Total	$121,800
Dividends declared	50,000
Retained income, February 28, 19X2	$ 71,800

Frequently, the statement of retained income is added on to the bottom of the income statement. If so, the combined statements are called a *statement of income and retained income*. For example, Exhibits 2–5 and 2–6 could be combined and retitled and would appear as shown in Exhibit 2–7.

Customs of Presentation

Exhibits 2–6 and 2–7 illustrate some customs that accountants follow when they prepare all their financial statements. To save space and unnecessary repetition, accountants often place a subtotal on the right side of the final number in a column, as is illustrated by the $112,100 in Exhibit 2–7:

EXHIBIT 2–7

BIWHEELS COMPANY
Statement of Income and Retained Income
For the Month Ended February 28, 19X2

Sales		$176,000
Deduct expenses:		
Cost of goods sold	$110,000	
Rent	2,000	
Depreciation	100	112,100
Net income		$ 63,900*
Retained income, January 31, 19X2		57,900
Total		$121,800
Dividends declared		50,000
Retained income, February 28, 19X2		$ 71,800

* Note how the income statement ends here. The $63,900 simultaneously becomes the initial item on the statement of retained income portion of this combined statement.

Deduct expenses:		
Cost of goods sold	$110,000	
Rent	2,000	
Depreciation	100	112,100

Under this arrangement the expenses caption is used only once. As an alternative, accountants sometimes use the caption twice, as a first line to describe the classification and then on a separate additional final line to describe the subtotal of the classification. In our example, the final line would be: Total expenses $112,100.

Dollar signs are customarily used at the beginning and end of each column of dollar amounts and for each subtotal or total within the column. However, many accountants will use a dollar sign only with the beginning number in a column and with the final number in the same column. For example, these accountants would not use a dollar sign with the $63,900 and the $121,800 in Exhibit 2–7. Double-underscores (double rulings) are typically used to denote final numbers.

☐ **Retained Income and Cash**

Retained income is not a pot of cash that is awaiting distribution to stockholders. Consider the following illustration:

Step 1. Assume an opening balance sheet of:

Cash	$100	Paid-in capital	$100

Step 2. Purchase inventory for $50 cash. The balance sheet now reads:

Cash	$ 50	Paid-in capital	$100
Inventory	50		
Total assets	$100		

Steps 1 and 2 demonstrate a fundamental point. Owners' equity is an undivided claim against the total assets (in the aggregate). For example, half the shareholders do not have a specific claim on cash, and the other half do not have a specific claim on inventory. Instead all the shareholders have an undivided claim against (or, if you prefer, an undivided interest in) all the assets.

Step 3. Now sell the inventory for $80, which produces a retained income of $80 − $50 = $30:

Cash	$130	Paid-in capital	$100
		Retained income	30
		Total owners' equity	$130

At this stage, the retained income might be reflected by a $30 increase in cash. But the $30 in retained income connotes only a *general* claim against *total assets*. This can be clarified by the transaction that follows.

Step 4. Purchase inventory and equipment, in the amounts of $60 and $50, respectively. Now:

Cash	$ 20	Paid-in capital	$100
Inventory	60	Retained income	30
Equipment	50		
Total assets	$130	Total owners' equity	$130

Where is the $30 in retained income reflected? Is it reflected in Cash, in Inventory, or in Equipment? The answer is indeterminate. This example helps to explain the nature of the Retained Income account. It is a *claim*, not a pot of gold. Retained income is increased by profitable operations, but the cash inflow from sales is an increment in assets (see Step 3). When the cash inflow takes place, management will use the cash, most often to buy more inventory or equipment (Step 4). Retained income (and also paid-in capital) is a *general* claim against, or *undivided* interest in, *total* assets, *not* a specific claim against cash or against any other particular asset. Do not confuse the assets themselves with the claims against the assets.

THE INCOME STATEMENT: THE ACCRUAL BASIS

☐ Misconceptions About Dividends

As previously stated, dividends are distributions of assets that reduce owner-ship claims. The cash assets that are distributed typically arose from profitable operations. Thus dividends or withdrawals are often spoken of as "distributions of profits" or "distributions of retained income." Dividends are often errone-ously described as being "paid out of retained income." In reality, cash divi-dends are distributions of assets that reduce a portion of the ownership claim. The distribution is made possible by profitable operations.

The amount of cash dividends declared by the board of directors of a company depends on many factors. For example, the amount of a dividend often is some fraction of net income, but dividends are not necessarily tied to current net income. Although profitable operations and the existence of a balance in Retained Income are generally essential, dividend policy is also influenced by the company's cash position and future needs for cash to pay debts or to purchase additional assets. Dividends are also influenced by whether the company is committed to a stable dividend policy or to a policy that normally ties dividends to fluctuations in net income. Under a stable policy, dividends may be paid consistently even if a company encounters a few years of little or no net income. (More is said about dividends in Chapter 11.)

Incidentally, the terms **liquidation** and *to liquidate* are often encoun-tered in the world of accounting. Depending on the specific situation, *liquida-tion* means payment of a debt, or the conversion of assets into cash, or the complete sale of assets and settlement of claims when an entity is terminated. Thus an entity is sometimes described as being "highly liquid" when it has a vast amount of cash in relation to its other assets or its debts. Then liabilities are more likely to be paid, that is, liquidated.

☐ Steps in Paying Dividends

As shown earlier, the effect of the declaration and payment of a dividend is as follows:

	ASSETS = LIABILITIES +	STOCKHOLDERS' EQUITY
	Cash	Retained Income
(20) Declaration and payment of cash dividends	−50,000 =	−50,000

Entry 20 telescoped the declaration and payment together as if every-thing had occurred on the same day. Corporations usually approach dividend matters in steps. The board of directors declares a dividend on one date (decla-ration date) payable to stockholders of record as of a second date (record date) and actually pays the dividend on a third date (payment date).

The *Wall Street Journal* lists dividends as follows:

COMPANY	PERIOD	AMT.	PAYABLE DATE	RECORD DATE
Colgate-Palmolive Co.	Q*	$.34	5–15	4–25
Dow Chemical Co.	Q	.45	4–30	3–31

* Q indicates that the dividend is typically declared quarterly.

Such dividend actions entail two accounting transactions. First, the *declaration* affects the corporation's financial position because the shareholders also become creditors for the amount (only) of the legally declared dividend. Second, the resulting liability is reduced only when the cash is disbursed. Consequently, entry 20 would be subdivided into two phases:

	ASSETS	=	LIABILITIES	+	STOCKHOLDERS' EQUITY
	Cash	=	Dividends Payable	+	Retained Income
(20a) Date of declaration		=	+50,000		−50,000
(20b) Date of payment	−50,000	=	−50,000		
The net effect is eventually the same as in 20 above	−50,000	=	0		−50,000

Although the ultimate effect is the same as that shown originally in transaction 20, a balance sheet prepared *between* the date of declaration and the date of payment must show dividends payable as a *liability*. Note too that although a corporation may be expected to pay dividends, no legal liability occurs until a board of directors formally declares a dividend.

NONPROFIT ORGANIZATIONS

The examples in this chapter have focused on profit-seeking organizations, but balance sheets and income statements are also used by not-for-profit organizations. For example, hospitals and universities have income statements, although they are called statements of *revenue and expense*. The "bottom line" is frequently called "excess of revenue over expense" or "net financial result" rather than "net income."

The basic concepts of assets, liabilities, revenue, expense, and operating statements are applicable to all organizations, whether they be utilities, symphony orchestras, private, public, American, Asian, and so forth. However, some nonprofit organizations have been slow to adopt some ideas that are widely used in progressive companies. For example, in many governmental organizations the accrual basis of accounting has not yet supplanted the cash basis. This has hampered the evaluation of the performance of such organizations. A recent annual report of the New York Metropolitan Museum of Art stated: "As the Museum's financial operations have begun to resemble in complexity those of a corporation, it has become necessary to make certain changes in our accounting . . . operating results are reported on an accrual rather than the previously followed cash basis. Thus, revenue and expenses are recorded in the proper time period."

An article in *Forbes* commented:

☐   Shoddy, misleading accounting has not been the cause of our cities' problems but it has prevented us from finding solutions. Or even looking for solutions until it's too late. Chicago's schools, for example, suddenly found themselves unable to pay their teachers. Had the books been kept like any decent corporation's, that could never have happened. The most basic difference is in the common use of cash accounting rather than the accrual method that nearly all businesses use.

GENERALLY ACCEPTED ACCOUNTING PRINCIPLES

This section continues our study of some accounting principles. So far, the accrual basis and the concepts of realization and matching have been discussed.

☐ **"Principles" Is a Misnomer**

The auditor's opinion, which was introduced in Chapter 1 and which usually appears at the end of annual reports prepared for stockholders and other external users, is often mistakenly relied on as an infallible guarantee of financial truth. Somehow accounting is considered an exact science, perhaps because of the aura of precision that financial statements seemingly possess. But accounting is more art than science. The financial reports may appear accurate because of their neatly integrated numbers, but they are the result of a complex measurement process that rests on a huge bundle of assumptions and conventions called **generally accepted accounting principles (GAAP)**.

What are these generally accepted accounting principles? This technical term covers much territory. It includes both broad concepts or guidelines and detailed practices. It includes all conventions, rules, and procedures that together make up accepted accounting practice at any given time.

Accounting principles become "generally accepted" by agreement. Such agreement is not influenced solely by formal logical analysis. Experience, custom, usage, and practical necessity contribute to the set of principles. Accordingly, it might be better to call them conventions, because "principles" connotes that they are the product of airtight logic.

☐ **FASB, APB, and SEC**

Every technical area seems to have regulatory bodies or professional associations whose names are often abbreviated. Accounting is no exception.

American generally accepted accounting principles have been most heavily influenced by the **Financial Accounting Standards Board (FASB)** and its predecessor body, the **Accounting Principles Board (APB)**. The FASB consists of seven qualified individuals who work full time. The board is supported by a large staff and an annual $12 million budget.

The FASB is an independent creature of the private sector and is financially supported by various professional accounting associations (such as the leading organization of auditors, the American Institute of Certified Public Accountants, also known as the **AICPA**).

The FASB was established in 1973 as the replacement for the APB. The APB consisted of a group of eighteen accountants (mostly partners in large accounting firms) who worked part time. The APB issued a series of thirty-one *Opinions* during 1962–73, many of which are still the "accounting law of the land." Many of these **APB Opinions** and **FASB Statements** will be referred to in succeeding chapters of this book.

The U.S. Congress has designated the **Securities and Exchange Commission (SEC)** as holding the ultimate responsibility for authorizing the generally accepted accounting principles for companies whose stock is held by the general investing public. However, the SEC has informally delegated much rule-making power to the FASB. This public sector–private sector authority relationship can be sketched as follows:

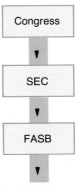

Issues pronouncements on various accounting issues. These pronouncements govern the preparation of typical financial statements.

Reconsider the three-tiered structure above. Note that Congress can overrule both the SEC and the FASB, and the SEC can overrule the FASB. Such undermining of the FASB occurs rarely, but pressure is exerted on all three tiers by corporations if they think an impending pronouncement is "wrong." Hence the setting of accounting principles is a complex process involving heavy interactions among the affected parties: public regulators (Congress and SEC), private regulators (FASB), companies, the public accounting profession, representatives of investors, and other interested groups.

In sum, the public body (the SEC) has informally delegated much rule-making power regarding accounting theory and practice to the private bodies (the APB and FASB). These boards have rendered a series of pronouncements on various accounting issues. Certified public accountants issue opinions concerning the fairness of corporate financial statements prepared for external use. These auditors must see that corporate statements do not depart from these pronouncements.

☐ **Stable Monetary Unit**

The monetary unit (called the dollar in the United States, Canada, Australia, New Zealand, and elsewhere) is the principal means for measuring assets and equities. It is the common denominator for quantifying the effects of a wide variety of transactions. Accountants record, classify, summarize, and report in terms of the monetary unit.

Such measurement assumes that the principal counter—the dollar—is an unchanging yardstick. Yet we all know that a 1988 dollar does not have the same purchasing power as a 1978 or 1968 dollar. Therefore accounting statements that include different dollars must be interpreted and compared with full consciousness of the limitations of the basic measurement unit.

SUMMARY

An underlying structure of concepts, techniques, and conventions provides a basis for accounting practice. This structure is typically referred to as a set of generally accepted accounting principles (GAAP). This chapter has focused on how accountants measure income (the excess of revenue over expense) on the accrual basis. The essence of the accrual basis is the so-called matching process whereby revenues and expenses are assigned to a particular period for which a measurement of income is desired.

Revenues (accomplishments) are assigned to the period in which they are *realized* (earned). Expenses (efforts) are assigned to a period in which the pertinent goods and services are either *used* or appear to have no future benefit. The *cost recovery* concept helps determine whether resources such as inventories, prepayments, and equipment should be carried forward to future periods as assets or written off to the current period as expenses.

SUMMARY PROBLEM FOR YOUR REVIEW

☐ **Problem Two (The first problem appeared earlier in the chapter, page 45.)**

The following are samples of the interpretations and remarks frequently encountered with regard to financial statements. Do you agree or disagree with these observations? Explain fully.

1. "Sales show the cash coming in from customers, and the various expenses show the cash going out for goods and services. The difference is net income."

2. Consider the following accounts of Delta, a leading U.S. airline:

Common stock, par value $3.00 per share, 39,761,154 shares outstanding	$ 119,283,000
Additional paid-in capital	80,088,000
Retained earnings	849,536,000
Total stockholders' equity	$1,048,907,000

A shareholder commented, "Why can't that big airline pay higher wages and dividends too? It can use its hundreds of millions of dollars of retained earnings to do so."

3. "The total Delta stockholders' equity measures the amount that the shareholders would get today if the corporation were liquidated."

☐ Solution to Problem Two

1. Cash receipts and disbursements are not the fundamental basis for the accounting recognition of revenues and expenses. Credit, not cash, lubricates the economy. Therefore, if services or goods have been delivered to a customer, a legal claim to cash in the form of a receivable is deemed sufficient justification for recognizing revenue. Similarly, if services or goods have been used up, a legal obligation in the form of a payable is justification for recognizing expense.

This approach to the measurement of net income is known as the accrual method. Revenue is recognized as it is earned by (a) goods or services rendered, (b) an exchange in a market transaction, and (c) the assurance of the collectibility of the asset received. Expenses are recognized when goods or services are used up in the obtaining of revenue (or when such goods or services cannot justifiably be carried forward as an asset because they have no potential future benefit). The expenses and losses are deducted from the revenue, and the result of this matching process is net income, the net increase in stockholders' equity from the conduct of operations.

2. As the chapter indicated, retained earnings is not cash. It is a stockholders' equity account that represents the accumulated increase in ownership claims due to profitable operations. This claim or interest may be partially liquidated by the payment of cash dividends, but a growing company will reinvest cash in sustaining the added investments in receivables, inventories, plant, equipment, and other assets so necessary for expansion. As a result, the ownership claims measured by retained earnings may become "permanent" in the sense that, as a practical matter, they will never be liquidated as long as the company remains a going concern.

This linking of retained earnings and cash is only one example of fallacious interpretation. As a general rule, there is no direct relationship between the individual items on the two sides of the balance sheet. For example, Delta's cash was less than $46 million on the balance sheet date when its retained earnings exceeded $800 million.

3. Stockholders' equity is a difference, the excess of assets over liabilities. If the assets were carried in the accounting records at their liquidating value today, and the liabilities were carried at the exact amounts needed for their extinguishment, the remark would be true. But such valuations would be coincidental because assets are customarily carried at *historical cost* expressed in an unchanging monetary unit. Intervening changes in markets and general price levels in inflationary times may mean that the assets are woefully understated. Investors may make a critical error if they think that balance sheets indicate current values.

Furthermore, the "market values" for publicly owned shares are usually determined by daily trading conducted in the financial marketplaces such as the New York Stock Exchange. These values are affected by numerous factors, including the *expectations* of (a) price appreciation and (b) cash flows in the form of dividends. The focus is on the future; the present and the past are examined as clues to what may be forthcoming. Therefore the present stockholders' equity is usually of only incidental concern.

For example, the above stockholders' equity was $1,048,907,000 ÷ 39,761,154 shares, or $26 per share. During that year, a year of low profits, Delta's market price per common share fluctuated between $22 and $36.

HIGHLIGHTS TO REMEMBER

1. Other than cash and receivables, assets may be regarded as unexpired, prepaid, or stored costs (for example, inventory or equipment) that are carried forward to future periods rather than being immediately offset against revenue as expenses of the current period.

2. Revenues and expenses are components of stockholders' equity. Revenues increase stockholders' equity; expenses decrease stockholders' equity.

3. Dividends are not expenses.

4. Among the synonyms for *income statement* are *statement of income*, *statement of operations*, *results of operations*, *statement of earnings*, *statement of revenues and expenses*, and *profit and loss statement*.

5. *Income*, *earnings*, and *profits* are synonyms.

6. *Cost of goods sold* and *cost of sales* are synonyms.

7. If you have had little or no exposure to accounting, you should at least solve the "Summary Problems for Your Review" before proceeding to the next chapter. To read about basic accounting concepts is not enough. Work some problems too—the more, the better. Cramming at the end of a few more chapters is definitely not recommended. Accounting is a cumulative subject. The foundation is laid in these initial four chapters.

8. In accrual accounting, an expense is seldom accompanied by an immediate cash disbursement. That is, *expense* should not be confused with the term *cash disbursement*.

9. In accrual accounting, revenue is seldom accompanied by an immediate cash receipt. That is, *revenue* should not be confused with the term *cash receipt*.

ACCOUNTING VOCABULARY

Accounting Principles Board (APB), p. 55   Accrual Basis, *44*   AICPA, *55*   APB Opinions, *55*   Cash Basis, *44*   Cost of Goods Sold, *41*   Cost of Sales, *41*   Cost Recovery, *39*   Depreciation, *40*   Dividends, *49*   Earnings, *36*   Expense, *36*   Financial Accounting Standards Board (FASB), *55*   FASB Statements, *55*   Generally Accepted Accounting Principles (GAAP), *54*   Income, *36*   Income Statement, *40*   Liquidation, *52*   Matching, *39*   Operating Cycle, *35*   Operating Statement, *40*   Profits, *36*   P & L Statement, *40*   Realization, *38*   Reinvested Earnings, *49*   Results of Operations, *40*   Retained Earnings, *49*   Retained Income, *38*   Revenue, *36*   Securities and Exchange Commission (SEC), *55*   Statement of Retained Income, *49*   Statement of Revenues and Expenses, *40*   Undistributed Earnings, *49*

APPENDIX 2: FOUR POPULAR FINANCIAL RATIOS

To underscore how financial statements are used, this book will gradually introduce you to various financial ratios. Because stock market prices are quoted on a per-share basis, many ratios are expressed per share (and after income taxes).

A financial ratio is computed by dividing one number by another. For a set of complex financial statements, literally hundreds of ratios can be computed if desired. Every analyst has a set of favorite ratios, but one is so popular that it dwarfs all others: earnings per share of common stock (EPS).

In its *Statement on Objectives*, the Financial Accounting Standards Board, which is described in this chapter, stressed that the main focus of financial reporting is on earnings. The income statement and its accompanying earnings per share are paramount to many users of financial reports, so accounting authorities have specified how various items therein must be displayed.

The accounting regulators have promulgated the requirement that EPS data appear on the face of the income statement of publicly held corporations. This is the only instance where a financial ratio is required as a part of the body of financial statements.

Earnings Per Share (EPS)

When the owners' equity is relatively simple, the computation of EPS is straightforward. For example, consider a recent annual report of PepsiCo Corporation, the well-known beverage and food company. The bottom of its income statement showed:

Net income	$212,547,000
Net income per share of common stock	$2.25

The earnings per share (called *net income per share* by PepsiCo) was calculated as follows:

$$\text{EPS} = \frac{\text{Net income}}{\text{Average number of shares outstanding}}$$

$$\text{EPS} = \frac{\$212,547,000}{94,462,222} = \$2.25$$

The PepsiCo's computation is relatively simple because the company has only one type of capital stock, little fluctuation of shares outstanding throughout the year, and no unusual items affecting the computation of net income. EPS calculations can become more difficult when the last complications arise. See Chapter 11 for further discussion.

Price-Earnings Ratio (P-E)

Another popular ratio is the price-earnings (P-E) ratio:

$$\text{P-E} = \frac{\text{Market price per share of common stock}}{\text{Earnings per share of common stock}}$$

The numerator is typically today's market price; the denominator, the EPS for the most recent twelve months. Thus the P-E ratio varies throughout a given year, depending on the fluctuations in the stock price. For example, PepsiCo's P-E ratio would be:

	USING HIGHEST MARKET PRICE DURING FOURTH QUARTER	USING LOWEST MARKET PRICE DURING FOURTH QUARTER
P-E =	$\dfrac{\$38}{\$2.25}$	$\dfrac{\$34}{\$2.25}$
P-E =	16.9	15.1

P-E ratios are rarely carried out to any decimal places when published in the business press. The P-E ratio is sometimes called the *earnings multiple*. It measures how much the investing public is willing to pay for the company's prospects for earnings. Note especially that the P-E ratio is a consensus of the marketplace. This earnings multiplier may differ considerably for two companies within the same industry. It may also change for the same company through the years. Glamour stocks often have astronomical ratios. In general, a high P-E ratio indicates that investors predict that the company's net income will grow at a fast rate.

☐ Dividend-Yield Ratio

Individual investors are usually interested in the profitability of their personal investments in common stock. That profitability takes two forms: cash dividends and market-price appreciation of the stock. Two popular ratios are the *dividend-yield ratio* (the current dividend per share divided by the current market price of the stock) and the price-earnings ratio (just discussed). The *dividend-yield ratio* (or *dividend-yield percentage*), also simply called *dividend yield*, is computed as follows:

$$\text{Dividend yield} = \frac{\text{Cash dividends per share}}{\text{Market price per share}}$$

PepsiCo would show:

	USING HIGHEST MARKET PRICE DURING FOURTH QUARTER	USING LOWEST MARKET PRICE DURING FOURTH QUARTER
Dividend yield =	$\dfrac{\$1.665}{\$38}$	$\dfrac{\$1.665}{\$34}$
Dividend yield =	4.4%	4.9%

When published in the business press, dividend yields are ordinarily carried to one decimal place. Dividend ratios may be of particular importance to those investors in common stock who seek regular cash returns on their investments. For example, an investor who favored high current returns would not buy stock in growth companies. Growth companies have conservative dividend policies because they are using most of their profit-generated resources to help finance expansion of their operations.

Market prices at which stocks are traded in organized marketplaces, such as the New York Stock Exchange, are quoted in the daily newspapers. The dividend yields are also published, as measured by annual disbursements based on the last quarterly dividends.

Consider the following stock quotations for PepsiCo regarding trading of January 9, 1986:

52 WEEKS HIGH	LOW	STOCK	DIV.	YLD. %	P-E RATIO	SALES 100s	HIGH	LOW	CLOSE	NET CHG.
75⅜	40⅝	PepsiCo	1.78	2.5	12	4,622	71¼	70	70½	−1½

Reading from left to right, the highest price at which PepsiCo common stock was traded in the preceding fifty-two weeks was $75.375 per share; the lowest price, $40.625. The current dividend rate for twelve months is $1.78 per share, producing a yield of 2.5% based on the day's closing price of the stock. The P-E ratio is 12, also based on the closing price. Total sales for the day were 462,200 shares. The highest price at which the stock was traded was $71.25 per share; the lowest, $70. The closing price was that of the last trade for the day, $70.50, which was $1.50 lower than the preceding day's last trade.

Keep in mind that transactions in publicly traded stock are between *individual investors* in the stock, not between the *corporation* and the individuals. Thus a "typical trade" results in the selling of, say, 100 shares of PepsiCo stock held by Ms. Johnson in Minneapolis to Ms. Davis in Atlanta for $7,050 cash. Both of these parties would ordinarily transact the trade through their respective stockbrokers, who represent individual shareholders. PepsiCo Corporation would not be directly affected by the trade except that its records of shareholders would show the 100 shares now held by Davis and not held by Johnson.

☐ Dividend-Payout Ratio

Although not routinely published, the dividend-payout ratio also receives much attention from analysts. Consider McDonald's, the well-known fast-food chain. The formula for its payout computation is given below, followed by McDonald's ratio, using figures from a recent annual report:

$$\text{Dividend-payout ratio} = \frac{\text{Common dividends per share}}{\text{Earnings per share}}$$

$$\text{Dividend-payout ratio} = \frac{\$.76}{\$4.39} = 17.3\%$$

Clearly, McDonald's fits into the category of a low-payment company. As long as McDonald's continues its worldwide expansion, a minimal payout can be anticipated. In contrast, companies without exceptional growth tend to pay a higher percentage of their earnings as dividends. Public utilities will ordinarily have a payout ratio of 60% to 70%. For instance, Pacific Gas and Electric Company paid dividends amounting to 64.5% of 1985 earnings.

Financial ratios are also covered in Chapters 4, 7, 8, 10, 11, and especially 16.

FUNDAMENTAL ASSIGNMENT MATERIAL

☐ General Coverage

2–1. **BALANCE SHEET EQUATION.** (Alternates are 2–4 and 2–5.) Find the unknowns (in thousands), showing computations to support your answers. Consider each case independently:

	CASE		
	1	2	3
Assets, beginning of period	$ 80	$ C	$ G
Assets, end of period	90	290	F
Liabilities, beginning of period	C	100	95
Liabilities, end of period	G	G	85
Paid-in capital, beginning of period	10	20	E
Paid-in capital, end of period	F	F	75
Retained income, beginning of period	25	70	90
Retained income, end of period	E	E	100
Revenues	100	D	300
Expenses	85	180	260
Net income	D	30	C
Dividends	–0–	10	D
Additional investment by stockholders	–0–	40	25

2–2. ANALYSIS OF TRANSACTIONS, PREPARATION OF STATEMENTS. (Alternates are 2–6, 2–8, 2–28, and 2–36.) The Dorian Company was incorporated on March 1, 19X1. Dorian had six holders of common stock. Alice Dorian, who was the president and chief executive officer, held 60% of the shares. The company rented space in department stores and specialized in selling costume jewelry. Dorian's first venture was in the Goliath Department Store.

The following events occurred during March.

1. The company was incorporated. Common stockholders invested $80,000 cash.
2. Purchased merchandise inventory for cash, $50,000.
3. Purchased merchandise inventory on open account, $10,000.
4. Merchandise carried in inventory at a cost of $35,000 was sold for cash for $20,000 and on open account for $60,000, a grand total of $80,000. Dorian (not Goliath) carries and collects these accounts receivable.
5. Collection of the above accounts receivable, $12,000.
6. Payments of accounts payable, $6,000. See transaction 3.
7. Special display equipment and fixtures were acquired on March 1 for $21,000. Their expected useful life was twenty-one months with no terminal scrap value. Straight-line depreciation was adopted. This equipment was removable. Dorian paid $5,000 as a down payment and signed a promissory note for $16,000.
8. On March 1, Dorian signed a rental agreement with Goliath. The agreement called for a flat $3,000 per month, payable quarterly in advance. Therefore Dorian paid $9,000 cash on March 1.
9. The rental agreement also called for a payment of 10% of all sales. This payment was in addition to the flat $3,000 per month. In this way, Goliath would share in any success of the venture and be compensated for general services such as cleaning and utilities. This payment was to be made in cash on the last day of each month as soon as the sales for the month were tabulated. Therefore Dorian made the payment on March 31.
10. Wages, salaries, and sales commissions were all paid in cash for all earnings by employees. The amount was $32,000.
11. Depreciation expense was recognized. See transaction 7.
12. The expiration of an appropriate amount of prepaid rental services was recognized. See transaction 8.

Required:

1. Prepare an analysis of Dorian Company's transactions, employing the equation approach demonstrated in Exhibit 2–1 (p. 37). Show all amounts in thousands.
2. Prepare a balance sheet as of March 31, 19X1, and an income statement for the month of March. Ignore income taxes.
3. Given these sparse facts, analyze Dorian's performance for March and its financial position as of March 31, 19X1.

2–3. CASH BASIS VERSUS ACCRUAL BASIS. Refer to the preceding problem. If Dorian Company measured income on the cash basis, what revenue would be reported for March? Which basis (accrual or cash) provides a better measure of revenue? Why?

□ **Understanding Published Financial Reports**

2–4. BALANCE SHEET EQUATION. (Alternates are 2–1 and 2–5.) Albertson's, Inc., is a large supermarket chain located in the southern and western United States. Its actual terminology and actual data for a recent fiscal year follow (in thousands):

Assets, beginning of period	$ 632,793
Assets, end of period	709,847
Liabilities, beginning of period	A
Liabilities, end of period	E
Paid-in capital, beginning of period	42,216
Paid-in capital, end of period	D
Retained earnings, beginning of period	160,598
Retained earnings, end of period	C
Sales and other revenues	3,489,345
Cost of sales, and all other expenses	3,440,867
Net earnings	B
Dividends	13,083
Additional investment by stockholders	583

Required: | Find the unknowns (in thousands), showing computations to support your answers.

2–5. BALANCE SHEET EQUATION. (Alternates are 2–1 and 2–4.) General Foods Corporation is a large processor and marketer of food products, including Maxwell House Coffee, Jell-O, Birds Eye, and Oscar Mayer brands. Its actual terminology and actual data (in millions of dollars) follow for a recent fiscal year:

Cost and expenses	B
Net earnings	$ 200
Dividends	109
Additional investments by stockholders	1
Assets, beginning of period	3,130
Assets, end of period	E
Liabilities, beginning of period	A
Liabilities, end of period	2,158
Paid-in capital, beginning of period	148
Paid-in capital, end of period	D
Retained earnings, beginning of period	1,463
Retained earnings, end of period	C
Revenues	8,411

Required: | Find the unknowns (in millions), showing computations to support your answers.

2–6. ANALYSIS OF TRANSACTIONS, PREPARATION OF STATEMENTS. (Alternates are 2–2 and 2–8.) Wm. Wrigley Jr. Company manufactures and sells chewing gum. The company's actual condensed balance sheet data for a recent December 31 follow (in millions):

Cash	$ 48	Notes and accounts payable	$ 27
Receivables	53	Dividends payable	2
Inventories	84	Other liabilities	44
Prepaid expenses	7	Paid-in capital	18
Property, plant, and equipment	126	Retained earnings	227
Total	$318	Total	$318

The following summarizes some major transactions during January (in millions):

1. Gum carried in inventory at a cost of $30 was sold for cash of $20 and on open account of $42, a grand total of $62.
2. Collection of receivables, $50.
3. Depreciation expense of $3 was recognized.
4. Selling and administrative expenses of $24 were paid in cash.
5. Prepaid expenses of $1 expired in January. These included fire insurance premiums paid in the previous year that applied to future months.

6. The December 31 liability for dividends was paid in cash on January 25.
7. On January 30, the company declared a $1 dividend, which will be paid on February 25.

Required:

1. Prepare an analysis of Wrigley's transactions, employing the equation approach demonstrated in Exhibit 2–1 (p. 37). Show all amounts in millions. (For simplicity, only a few major transactions are illustrated here.)
2. Prepare a statement of earnings and also a statement of retained earnings for the month ended January 31. Also prepare a balance sheet, January 31. Ignore income taxes.

2–7. CASH BASIS VERSUS ACCRUAL BASIS. Refer to the preceding problem. If Wrigley measured income on the cash basis, what revenue would be reported for January? Which basis (accrual or cash) provides a better measure of revenue? Why?

2–8. ANALYSIS OF TRANSACTIONS, PREPARATION OF STATEMENTS. (Alternates are 2–2 and 2–6.) Ohio Mattress Company manufactures and sells Sealy-brand bedding. The company's actual condensed balance sheet data for a recent December 31 follow (in millions):

Cash	$ 9	Accounts payable	$ 2
Accounts receivable	8	Other liabilities	7
Inventories	7	Paid-in capital	6
Prepaid expenses	1		
Property, plant, and equipment	20	Retained earnings	30
Total	$45	Total	$45

The following summarizes some major transactions during January (in millions):

1. Mattresses carried in inventory at a cost of $3 were sold for cash of $2 and on open account of $5, a grand total of $7.
2. Acquired inventory on account, $5.
3. Collected receivables, $3.
4. On January 2, used $3 cash to prepay some rent and insurance for the entire year.
5. Payments on accounts payable (for inventories), $2.
6. Paid selling and administrative expenses in cash, $1.
7. The $1 of prepaid expenses, December 31, for rent and insurance expired in January.
8. Depreciation expense of $1 was recognized for January.

Required:

1. Prepare an analysis of Ohio's transactions, employing the equation approach demonstrated in Exhibit 2–1 (p. 37). Show all amounts in millions. (For simplicity, only a few major transactions are illustrated here.)
2. Prepare a statement of earnings for the month ended January 31 and a balance sheet, January 31. Ignore income taxes.

2–9. CASH BASIS VERSUS ACCRUAL BASIS. Refer to the preceding problem.
If Ohio Mattress measured income on the cash basis, what revenue would be reported for January? Which basis (accrual or cash) provides a better measure of revenue? Why?

ADDITIONAL ASSIGNMENT MATERIAL

☐ General Coverage

2–10. Give two synonyms for *income statement*.
2–11. "Expenses are assets that have been used up." Explain.
2–12. "The manager acquires goods and services, not expenses per se." Explain.

2–13. What are the three tests of realization?

2–14. Give two synonyms for *net income*.

2–15. "Expenses are negative stockholders' equity accounts." Explain.

2–16. "Depreciation is a process of allocation, not valuation." Do you agree? Explain.

2–17. "Cash dividends are not expenses." Explain.

2–18. Give two synonyms for *retained income*.

2–19. "Retained income is not a pot of gold." Explain.

2–20. What is the meaning of a *general claim*?

2–21. What are the major defects of the cash basis?

2–22. "The heart of recognizing expense is the cost recovery concept." Explain.

2–23. "Changes in the purchasing power of the dollar hurt the credibility of financial statements." Do you agree? Explain.

2–24. Distinguish between GAAP, FASB, and APB.

2–25. "The SEC has informally delegated much rule-making power to the FASB." Explain.

2–26. **SYNONYMS AND ANTONYMS.** Consider the following terms: (1) reinvested earnings, (2) unexpired costs, (3) expenses, (4) net earnings, (5) prepaid expenses, (6) stored costs, (7) statement of earnings, (8) used-up costs, (9) net profits, (10) net income, (11) revenues, (12) retained income, (13) sales, (14) statement of financial condition, (15) statement of income, (16) statement of financial position, (17) retained earnings, (18) statement of operations, (19) cost of goods sold, (20) undistributed earnings, and (21) cost of sales.

Required:

Group the items that have similar meanings. Name the groups. Answer by indicating the numbered items that belong in each group.

2–27. **FUNDAMENTAL REVENUE AND EXPENSE.** The Thomas Company was formed on April 1, 19X1, when some stockholders invested $100,000 cash in the company. During the first week, $75,000 cash was spent for merchandise inventory (women's clothing). During the remainder of the month, total sales reached $82,000, of which $50,000 was on open account. The cost of the inventory sold was $48,000. For simplicity, assume that no other transactions occurred except that on April 29 the Thomas Company acquired $15,000 additional inventory on open account.

Required:

1. Using the balance sheet equation approach (as illustrated in Exhibit 2–1, page 37), analyze all transactions for April. Show all amounts in thousands.
2. Prepare a balance sheet, April 30, 19X1.
3. Prepare two income statements for April, side by side. The first should use the accrual basis of accounting, and the second the cash basis. Which basis provides a more informative measure of economic performance? Why?

2–28. **ACCOUNTING FOR PREPAYMENTS.** (Alternate is 2–2.) The Rowley Company, a wholesaler of stereo equipment, began business on June 1, 19X1. The following summarized transactions occurred during June:

1. Rowley's stockholders contributed $300,000 in cash in exchange for their common stock.
2. On June 1, Rowley signed a one-year lease on a warehouse, paying $96,000 cash in advance for occupancy of twelve months.
3. On June 1, Rowley acquired warehouse equipment for $140,000, A cash down payment of $60,000 was made and a note payable was signed for the balance.
4. On June 1, Rowley paid $12,000 cash for a twelve-month insurance policy covering fire, casualty, and related risks.
5. Rowley acquired assorted merchandise for $50,000 cash.
6. Rowley acquired assorted merchandise for $260,000 on open account.

7. Total sales were $290,000, of which $50,000 were for cash.
8. Cost of inventory sold was $245,000.
9. Rent expense was recognized for the month of June.
10. Depreciation expense was recognized for the month. The warehouse equipment was expected to have a five-year useful life with an estimated terminal salvage value of $20,000.
11. Insurance expense was recognized for the month.
12. Collected $40,000 from credit customers.
13. Disbursed $100,000 to trade creditors.

For simplicity, ignore all other possible expenses.

Required:

1. Using the balance sheet equation format (as illustrated in Exhibit 2–1, page 37), prepare an analysis of each transaction. Show all amounts in thousands. What do transactions 8–11 illustrate about the theory of assets and expenses? (Use a Prepaid Insurance account, which is not illustrated in Exhibit 2–1.)
2. Prepare an income statement for June on the accrual basis.
3. Prepare a balance sheet, June 30, 19X1.

2–29. **COMPARISON OF CASH BASIS VERSUS ACCRUAL BASIS.** Refer to the preceding problem. If Rowley Company measured income on the cash basis, what revenue would be reported for June? Which basis (accrual or cash) provides a better measure of revenue? Why?

2–30. **NATURE OF RETAINED INCOME.** This is an exercise on the relationships between assets, liabilities, and ownership equities. The numbers are small, but the underlying concepts are large.

1. Assume an opening balance sheet of:

Cash	$1,000	Paid-in capital	$1,000

2. Purchase inventory for $600 cash. Prepare a balance sheet. A heading is unnecessary in this and subsequent requirements.
3. Sell the entire inventory for $850 cash. Prepare a balance sheet. Where is the retained income in terms of relationships within the balance sheet? That is, what is the meaning of the retained income? Explain in your own words.
4. Buy inventory for $400 cash and equipment for $700 cash. Prepare a balance sheet. Where is the retained income in terms of relationships within the balance sheet? That is, what is the meaning of the retained income? Explain in your own words.
5. Buy inventory for $300 on open account. Prepare a balance sheet. Where is the retained income and account payable in terms of the relationships within the balance sheet? That is, what is the meaning of the account payable and the retained income? Explain in your own words.

2–31. **ASSET ACQUISITION AND EXPIRATION.** The Constance Company had the following transactions:

a. Paid $12,000 cash for rent for the next six months.
b. Paid $1,000 for stationery and wrapping supplies.
c. Paid $3,000 cash for an advertisement in the *Wall Street Journal*.
d. Paid $10,000 cash for a training program for employees.

Required:

1. To see the theory of asset acquisition–asset expiration, for each transaction show the effects on the balance sheet equation in two phases: acquisition and expiration at the end of the month of acquisition. Show all amounts in thousands.
2. For the same transactions, show how a shortcut analysis of each transaction is conducted when goods or services are to be routinely consumed (or substantially consumed) in the period of their purchase. Show all amounts in thousands.

2–32. FIND UNKNOWNS. The following data pertain to the Bunce Corporation. Total assets at January 1, 19X1, were $100,000; at December 31, 19X1, $120,000. During 19X1, sales were $200,000, cash dividends were $4,000, and operating expenses (exclusive of cost of goods sold) were $50,000. Total liabilities at December 31, 19X1, were $55,000; at January 1, 19X1, $40,000. There was no additional capital paid in during 19X1.

Required: (These need not be computed in any particular order.)

1. Net income for 19X1.
2. Cost of goods sold for 19X1.
3. Stockholders' equity, January 1, 19X1.

2–33. INCOME STATEMENT. A statement of an automobile dealer follows:

MARVEL CARS, INC.
Statement of Profit and Loss
December 31, 19X3

Revenues:		
Sales	$1,000,000	
Increase in market value of		
land and building	200,000	$1,200,000
Deduct expenses:		
Advertising	$ 100,000	
Sales commissions	50,000	
Utilities	20,000	
Wages	150,000	
Dividends	100,000	
Cost of cars purchased	700,000	1,120,000
Net profit		$ 80,000

Required: List and describe any shortcomings of this statement.

2–34. ADDITIONAL REVIEW OF CHAPTER ILLUSTRATIONS. Use the format demonstrated in Exhibit 2–1 (p. 37), including the balances of January 12, 19X2. However, assume that the following transactions 10 through 13 occurred instead of those in Exhibit 2–1:

10. Sales for January were $200,000, one-fourth being for cash and three-fourths on open account. The cost to Biwheels of the inventory sold was $120,000.
11. Rent is $3,000 per month. A year's rent was paid in advance in early January.
12. The expiration of rental services for the month of January was recognized.
13. Suppose the predicted life of the store equipment is six years, and the estimated disposal value is $3,200. The amount of depreciation for January was recognized.

Consider an additional transaction (call it transaction EX). On January 31, cash dividends of $40,000 were declared and disbursed.

Required:
1. Prepare an analysis of Biwheels Company's transactions, using the approach demonstrated in Exhibit 2–1.
2. Prepare an income statement and a statement of retained income for January. Also prepare a balance sheet as of January 31, 19X2.

2–35. PREPARE FINANCIAL STATEMENTS. The items appearing in a set of financial statements for Completion Corporation are listed below in random order. These statements were prepared by the company's sales manager at the end of the second year of company operations, December 31, 19X2.

Accounts payable	$ 21,000	Retained income:	
Paid-in capital	120,000	January 1, 19X2	$ 6,400
Fixtures and equipment	30,800	December 31, 19X2	19,000
Cost of goods sold	110,000	Office supplies on hand	2,100
Salary expense	54,300	Notes payable	10,000
Prepaid fire insurance	2,300	Merchandise inventory	93,100
Accounts receivable	33,200	Rent expense	12,000
Notes receivable	6,000	Sales	198,000
Utilities expenses	2,900	Advertising expense	6,200
Net income	12,600	Cash	2,500

You are satisfied that the statements in which these items appear are correct except for several matters that were ignored by the sales manager. The following information should have been entered on the books and reflected in the financial statements:

a. About $1,300 of the office supplies reported to be "on hand" have actually been consumed in 19X2 operations.
b. Of the amount shown for prepaid fire insurance, $900 has expired during 19X2.
c. Depreciation of fixtures and equipment for 19X2 amounts to $1,200.
d. Cash dividends of $5,000 were declared late in December 19X2 by the board of directors. These dividends are not to be paid until January 19X3.

Required:

Prepare in good form the following corrected financial statements, ignoring income taxes:

1. Income statement for 19X2
2. Statement of retained income for 19X2
3. Balance sheet at December 31, 19X2

It is not necessary to prepare a columnar analysis of the transaction effects on each of the elements of the accounting equation.

2–36. TRANSACTION ANALYSIS AND FINANCIAL STATEMENTS. (Alternate is 2–2.) Consider the following balance sheet of a wholesaler of lighting fixtures:

HUTTON LIGHTING COMPANY
Balance Sheet
December 31, 19X1

ASSETS		LIABILITIES AND STOCKHOLDERS' EQUITY		
		Liabilities:		
Cash	$ 100,000	Accounts payable		$ 700,000
Accounts receivable	400,000	Stockholders' equity:		
Merchandise inventory	800,000	Paid-in capital	$160,000	
Prepaid rent	40,000	Retained income	570,000	
		Total stockholders'		
Equipment	90,000	equity		730,000
Total	$1,430,000	Total		$1,430,000

The following is a summary of transactions that occurred during 19X2:

a. Acquisitions of inventory on open account, $1 million.
b. Sales on open account, $1.5 million; and for cash, $100,000.
c. Merchandise carried in inventory at a cost of $1.1 million was sold as described in b.

d. The warehouse twelve-month lease was renewed on September 1, 19X2. However, the rent was increased to $84,000 for the year commencing September 1. The entire rent was paid in cash in advance.

e. The warehouse equipment shown in the balance sheet had been purchased on July 1, 19X1, for $110,000. It was expected to have a five-year useful life and a terminal salvage value of $10,000.

f. Collections on accounts receivable, $1.25 million.

g. Wages for 19X2 were paid in full in cash, $200,000.

h. Miscellaneous expenses for 19X2 were paid in full in cash, $80,000.

i. Payments on accounts payable, $900,000.

j. Cash dividends for 19X2 were paid in full in December, $100,000.

Required:

1. Prepare an analysis of transactions, employing the equation approach demonstrated in Exhibit 2–1 (p. 37). Show the amounts in thousands of dollars.
2. Prepare a balance sheet, statement of income, and statement of retained income. Also prepare a combined statement of income and retained income.
3. Reconsider transaction *j*. Suppose the dividends were declared on December 15, payable on January 31, 19X3, to shareholders of record on January 20. Indicate which accounts and financial statements in requirement 2 would be changed and by how much. Be complete and specific.

☐ Understanding Published Financial Reports

2–37. SPECIAL MEANINGS OF TERMS. A 1986 news story described the disappointing sales of a new model car, the Nova. An auto dealer said: "Even if the Nova is a little slow to move out of dealerships, it is more of a plus than a minus. . . . We're now selling 14 more cars per month than before. That's revenue. That's the bottom line."

Required:

| Is the dealer confused about accounting terms? Explain.

2–38. TWO SIDES OF A TRANSACTION. For each of the following transactions, show the effects on the entities involved. As was illustrated in the chapter, use the A = L + OE equation to demonstrate the effects. Also name each amount affected, show the dollar amounts, and indicate whether the effects are increases or decreases.

Illustration. The Massachusetts General Hospital collects $1,000 from the Blue Cross Health Care Plan.

Entity	Cash	Receivables	Trucks	=	Payables	+ OE
Hospital	+1,000	−1,000		=		
Blue Cross	−1,000			=	−1,000	

1. Borrowing of $100,000 on a home mortgage from Fidelity Savings by Evan Porteus.
2. Payment of $10,000 principal on the above mortgage. Ignore interest.
3. Purchase of a two-year subscription to *Time* magazine for $80 cash by Charles Bonini.
4. Purchase of trucks by the U.S. Postal Service for $10 million cash from the U.S. General Services Administration. The trucks were carried in the accounts at $10 million by the Services Administration.
5. Purchase for $100,000 cash of U.S. government bonds by Lockheed Corporation.
6. Cash deposits of $10 on the returnable bottles sold by Safeway Stores to a retail customer, Herbert Simon.
7. Collections on open account of $100 by Sears store from a retail customer, Kenneth Arrow.
8. Purchase of traveler's checks of $1,000 from American Express Company by Michael Harrison.

9. Cash deposit of $500 in a checking account in BankAmerica by David Kreps.
10. Purchase of a United Airlines "super-saver" airline ticket for $500 cash by Robert Wilson on June 15. The trip will be taken on September 10.

2–39. Traveler's Checks. The American Express Company had $4 billion of traveler's checks outstanding on December 31, 1985. Each May, Citibank of New York conducts a special sale of its traveler's checks whereby up to $5,000 of its checks can be purchased for a flat fee of $2 instead of the usual commission percentage.

Required:

When a company issues $1,000 of its traveler's checks, how are its assets and liabilities affected? Describe how profits might be made in the traveler's checks business.

2–40. Earnings and Dividend Ratios. Study Appendix 2. Procter & Gamble's brand names include Tide, Crest, Jif, and Prell. The company's 1985 annual report showed earnings of $635 million. Cash dividends per share were $2.60. Procter & Gamble had 167,105,260 average number of common shares outstanding. No other type of stock was outstanding. The market price of the stock at the end of the year was $70 per share.

Required:

Compute (1) earnings per share, (2) price-earnings ratio, (3) dividend yield, and (4) dividend-payout ratio.

2–41. Earnings and Dividend Ratios. Study Appendix 2. Chevron Corporation is one of the largest oil companies in the world. The company's revenue in 1985 was $30 billion. Net income was $1,534,000,000. EPS was $4.48. The company's common stock is the only type of shares outstanding.

Required:

1. Compute the average number of common shares outstanding during the year.
2. The dividend-payout ratio was 54%. What was the amount of dividends per share?
3. The average market price of the stock for the year was $35 per share. Compute (a) dividend yield and (b) price-earnings ratio.

2–42. Financial Ratios. Study Appendix 2. Following is a list of several well-known companies and selected financial data included in a letter sent by a stock brokerage firm to some of its clients:

| | PER-SHARE DATA | | | RATIOS AND PERCENTAGES | | |
COMPANY	Price	Earnings	Dividends	Price-Earnings	Dividend Yield	Dividend-Payout
Bethlehem Steel	$22	$1.80	$—	$—	—%	90%
B. F. Goodrich	20	—	1.56	—	—	80
Gulf & Western	—	2.75	0.75	5.5	—	—
Inland Steel	22	—	2.00	22.0	9.1	—
Texaco	30	6.50	—	—	10.0	—
U.S. Steel	24	3.50	2.00	—	—	—
Wells Fargo	—	—	1.92	—	8.3	36

The missing figures for this schedule can be computed from the data given.

Required:

1. Compute the missing figures and identify the company with
   (a) The highest dividend yield
   (b) The highest dividend-payout percentage
   (c) The lowest market price relative to earnings

2. Assume that you know nothing about any of these companies other than the data given and the computations you have made from the data. Which company would you choose as

(*a*) The most attractive investment? Why?

(*b*) The least attractive investment? Why?

2–43. **NONPROFIT OPERATING STATEMENT.** Examine the accompanying statement of the Stanford Faculty Club. Identify the Stanford classifications and terms that would not be used by a profit-seeking hotel and restaurant. Suggest terms that the profit-seeking entity would use instead.

STANFORD FACULTY CLUB
Statement of Income and Expenses
For Fiscal Year 1985–86

Food Service:			
Sales		$435,128	
Expenses:			
Food	$167,088		
Labor	272,849		
Operating costs	30,535	470,472	
Deficit			$ (35,344)
Bar:			
Sales		$ 90,549	
Expenses:			
Cost of liquor	$ 29,302		
Labor	5,591		
Operating costs	6,125	41,018	
Surplus			49,531
Hotel:			
Sales		$ 33,771	
Expenses		23,803	
Surplus			9,968
Surplus from operations			$ 24,155
General income (members' dues, room fees, etc.)			95,546
General administration and operating expenses			(134,347)
Deficit before university subsidy			$ (14,646)
University subsidy			30,000
Net surplus after university subsidy			$ 15,354

2–44. **NET INCOME AND RETAINED EARNINGS.** John Wiley & Sons, Inc., is a book publisher. Like most companies, Wiley heavily condenses the data in its annual report. Wiley's 1985 data (in thousands) included interest expense, $2,810; cash dividends, $4,510; income before income taxes, $8,652; net sales, $198,119; cost of sales, $85,092; retained earnings at the beginning of year, $59,996; provision for income taxes, $1,547; and operating and administrative expenses, $101,565.

Required:

Wiley presents a single "statement of income and retained earnings." Using the above data, reconstruct Wiley's statement for the year. Regarding the presentation of income taxes, include the following: income before income taxes, provision for income taxes, and net income.

2–45. **NET INCOME AND RETAINED INCOME.** McDonald's Corporation is a well-known fast-foods restaurant company. The following data are from a recent annual report (in thousands):

McDonald's Corporation

Retained earnings, end of year	$2,499,448	Dividends paid	$ 80,327
Revenues	3,760,860	General, administrative, and selling expenses	419,432
Interest expense	140,766	Depreciation	199,311
Income tax expense	349,200	Retained earnings, beginning of year	2,146,736
Food and paper expense	1,012,111	Other operating expenses	507,002
Wages and salaries	607,253		
Rent	92,746		

Required:

1. Prepare the following for the year:

   (a) Income statement. The final three lines of the income statement were labeled as income before provision for income taxes, provision for income taxes, and net income.

   (b) Statement of retained income.
2. Comment briefly on the relative size of the cash dividend.

2–46. **EARNINGS STATEMENT, RETAINED EARNINGS.** The Procter & Gamble Company has many well-known products. Examples are Tide, Crest, Jif, and Prell. The following is an exact reproduction of the terms and amounts in the financial statements contained in its 1985 annual report (in millions):

Net sales and other income	$13,745	Retained earnings at beginning of year	$4,879
Cash	19	Cost of products sold	9,099
Interest expense	165	Dividends to shareholders	444
Income taxes	369	Marketing, administrative, and other expenses	3,477
Accounts payable—Trade	981		

Required:

Choose the relevant data and prepare (1) the income statement for the year and (2) the statement of retained income for the year. The final three lines of the income statement were labeled as earnings before income taxes, income taxes, and net earnings.

2–47. **THE CASE OF THE PRESIDENT'S WEALTH.** This is a classic case in accounting. From the *Chicago Tribune*, August 20, 1964:

☐ Accountants acting on President Johnson's orders today reported his family wealth totaled $3,484,098.

☐ The statement of capital, arrived at through conservative procedures of evaluation, contrasted with a recent estimate published by *Life* magazine, which put the total at 14 million dollars.

☐ The family fortune, which is held in trust while the Johnsons are in the White House, was set forth in terms of book values. The figures represent original cost rather than current market values on what the holdings would be worth if sold now.

☐ Announced by the White House press office, but turned over to reporters by a national accounting firm at their Washington branch office, the financial statement apparently was intended to still a flow of quasi-official and unofficial estimates of the Johnson fortune. . . .

☐ The report apportions the capital among the family, with $378,081 credited to the President; $2,126,298 to his wife Claudia T., who uses the name Lady Bird; $490,141 to their daughter Lynda Bird; and $489,578 to their daughter Luci Baines.

☐ The statement said the family holdings—under the names of the President, his wife, and his two daughters, Lynda Bird and Luci Baines—had increased from $737,730 on January 1, 1954, a year after Johnson became Democratic leader of the Senate, to $3,484,098 on July 31 this year, a gain of $2,746,368. . . .

☐ A covering letter addressed to Johnson said the statement was made "in conformity with generally accepted accounting principles applied on a consistent basis."

☐ By far the largest part of the fortune was listed as the Johnsons' interest in the Texas Broadcasting Corporation, carried on the books as worth $2,543,838.

☐ The accountants stated that this valuation was arrived at on the basis of the cost of the stock when the Johnsons bought control of the debt-ridden radio station between 1943 and 1947, plus accumulated earnings ploughed back as equity, less 25 percent capital gains tax.[1]

Editorial, *Chicago Tribune*, August 22, 1964:

☐ An accounting firm acting on Mr. Johnson's instructions and employing what it termed "generally accepted auditing standards" has released a statement putting the current worth of the Lyndon Johnson family at a little less than 3½ million dollars. . . .

☐ Dean Burch, chairman of the Republican National Committee, has remarked that the method used to list the Johnson assets was comparable to placing the value of Manhattan Island at $24, the price at which it was purchased from the Indians. The Johnson accounting firm conceded that its report was "not intended to indicate the values that might be realized if the investment were sold."

☐ In fact, it would be interesting to observe the response of the Johnson family

---

[1] You need not be concerned about the details of this method of accounting until you study Chapter 12. In brief, when an investor holds a large enough stake in a corporation, such investment is accounted for at its acquisition cost plus the investor's pro rata share of the investee's net income (or net loss) minus the investor's share of dividends. For example, suppose the Texas Broadcasting Corporation earned $100,000 in a given year and that Johnson owned 100% of the corporation. In this situation, the Johnson financial statements would show an increase in Interest in Texas Broadcasting Corp. of $100,000 less the $25,000 income tax that would become payable upon disposition of the investment. (Today's accountants would prefer to increase the Investment account by the full $100,000 and the liabilities by $25,000. See the Carter financial statements.)

if a syndicate of investors were to offer to take Texas Broadcasting off the family's hands at double the publicly reported worth of the operation. . . .

Required:

1. Evaluate the criticisms, making special reference to fundamental accounting concepts or "principles."
2. The financial statements of President and Mrs. Carter are shown in an accompanying exhibit. Do you prefer the approach taken by the Carter statements as compared with the Johnson statements? Explain.

Perry, Chambliss, Sheppard and Thompson
Certified Public Accountants
Americus, Georgia

JAMES EARL CARTER, JR. AND ROSALYNN CARTER
STATEMENT OF ASSETS AND LIABILITIES
DECEMBER 31, 1977
(UNAUDITED)

ASSETS

	Cost Basis	Estimated Current Value
Cash	$204,979.04	$204,979.04
Cash Value of Life Insurance	45,506.88	45,506.88
U.S. Savings Bonds, Series E	1,425.00	1,550.94
Loan Receivable	50,000.00	50,000.00
Overpayment of 1977 Income Taxes	51,121.27	51,121.27
Personal Assets Trust—Note 3	151,097.87	557,717.11
Residence, Plains, Georgia	45,000.00	54,090.00
Lot in Plains, Georgia	1,100.00	3,155.00
Automobile	4,550.75	2,737.50
Total Assets	$554,780.81	$970,857.74

LIABILITIES

	Cost Basis	Estimated Current Value
Miscellaneous Accounts Payable, Estimated	$ 1,500.00	$ 1,500.00
Provision for Possible Income Taxes on Unrealized Asset Appreciation—Note 4	–0–	174,000.00
Total Liabilities	$ 1,500.00	$175,500.00
Excess of Assets Over Liabilities	$553,280.81	$795,357.74

NOTE 1: Estimated market values of real estate are 100% of the fair market values as determined by county tax assessors except as to certain assets held in the personal assets trust, which are stated at book value.

NOTE 2: This statement excludes campaign fund assets and liabilities.

NOTE 3: The interest in Carter's Warehouse partnership, the capital stock of Carter's Farms, Inc., the remainder interest in certain real estate and securities and a commercial lot in Plains, Georgia, were transferred to a personal assets trust in January, 1977. The primary purpose of the trust is to isolate the President from those of his assets which are most likely to be affected by actions of the federal government. The President was responsible as a general partner for obligations of the partnership before his partnership interest was transferred to the trust. The transfer to the trust did not affect such responsibility.

NOTE 4: If the market values of the assets were realized, income taxes would be payable at an uncertain rate. A provision for such income taxes has been made at rates in effect for 1977.

NOTE 5: The amounts in the accompanying statements are based principally upon the accrual basis method of accounting.

Chapter 3

THE RECORDING PROCESS: JOURNALS AND LEDGERS

LEARNING OBJECTIVES

After studying this chapter, you should be able to:

1. Analyze transactions in the form of debits and credits and with the help of a general ledger
2. Prepare journal entries and post them to the general ledger
3. Check the accuracy of your work by preparing a trial balance
4. Use a trial balance to prepare an income statement
5. Explain the meaning of going concern, objectivity, materiality, and cost-benefit

Chapters 1 and 2 concentrated on the accountant's *overall conceptual approach* to reporting on the economic activities of an organization. This chapter introduces the actual data-processing framework used in practice for recording and accumulating the financial effects of voluminous transactions. We concentrate on *specific procedures and techniques* instead of new accounting concepts.

DOUBLE-ENTRY SYSTEM AND LEDGER ACCOUNTS

☐ **The Account**

To begin, consider how the accountant would record the Biwheels transactions that were introduced in Chapter 1. Recall their effects on the elements of the balance sheet equation:

	A		= L	+ SE
	Cash	Merchandise Inventory	Note Payable	Paid-in Capital
(1) Initial investment by owners	+400,000		=	+400,000
(2) Loan from bank	+100,000		= +100,000	
(3) Acquire inventory for cash	−150,000	+150,000	=	

This balance sheet equation approach emphasizes the concepts, but it can obviously become unwieldy if there are many accounts and numerous transactions. You can readily see that changes in the balance sheet equation can occur many times daily. In large businesses, such as a department store, hundreds or thousands of repetitive transactions occur hourly. In practice, *ledgers* must be used to keep track of how these multitudes of transactions affect each particular asset, liability, revenue, and expense account. A **ledger** contains a group of related accounts kept up to date in a systematic manner. The ledger may be in the form of a bound record book, a loose-leaf set of pages, a set of machine account cards, or some kind of electronic storage element such as magnetic tape or disk. The ledger accounts used here are simplified versions of those used in practice. They are called **T-accounts** because they take the form of the capital letter T. The above transactions would be shown in T-accounts as follows:

Assets		=	Liabilities + Stockholders' Equity	

Cash

Increases		Decreases	
(1)	400,000	(3)	150,000
(2)	100,000		

Note Payable

Decreases		Increases	
		(2)	100,000

Inventory

Increases		Decreases	
(3)	150,000		

Paid-in Capital

Decreases		Increases	
		(1)	400,000

The above entries were made in accordance with the rules of a **double-entry system,** so named because at least two accounts are always affected by each transaction. Asset accounts have left-side balances. They are increased by entries on the left side and decreased by entries on the right side.

Liabilities and owners' equity accounts have right-side balances. They are increased by entries on the right side and decreased by entries on the left side. Consider each entry:

1. Transaction: Initial investment by owners, $400,000 cash.
    Analysis: The asset **Cash** is increased.
                The stockholders' equity **Paid-in Capital** is increased.
    Entry:

Cash

(1)	400,000		

Paid-in Capital

		(1)	400,000

2. Transaction: Loan from bank, $100,000.
    Analysis: The asset **Cash** is increased.
                The liability **Note Payable** is increased.
    Entry:

Cash

(1)	400,000		
(2)	100,000		

Note Payable

		(2)	100,000

3. Transaction: Acquired inventory for cash, $150,000.
    Analysis: The asset **Cash** is decreased.
                The asset **Merchandise Inventory** is increased.
    Entry:

Cash

(1)	400,000	(3)	150,000
(2)	100,000		

Merchandise Inventory

(3)	150,000		

Each T-account summarizes the changes in a particular asset, liability, or stockholders' equity. Each transaction is keyed in some way, such as by the numbering used in this illustration or by the date or both. This keying helps the rechecking (auditing) process by aiding the tracing of transactions to original sources. A **balance** is the difference between the total left-side and right-side amounts in an account at any particular time. Accounts exist to keep an up-to-date summary of the changes in specific assets and equities. Financial statements can be prepared at any instant if the accounts are up to date. The necessary information is tabulated in the accounts. For example, the balance sheet after the first three transactions would contain the following accounts:

ASSETS		LIABILITIES + OWNERS' EQUITY	
Cash	$350,000	Liabilities:	
Merchandise		Note payable	$100,000
Inventory	150,000	Stockholders' equity:	
		Paid-in capital	400,000
Total	$500,000	Total	$500,000

☐ The Strange Debit-Credit Language

You have just seen that the double-entry system features entries on left sides or right sides of each account. Accountants use special words, **debit** and **credit**, to denote how to analyze a transaction. For instance, suppose a CPA were asked how to analyze and record transaction 1. She would say, "That's easy. Debit Cash and credit Paid-in Capital." By so doing, she enters $400,000 on the *left* side of Cash and $400,000 on the *right* side of Paid-in Capital. In short, *debit* means left and *credit* means *right*. The word **charge** is often used instead of *debit*, but no single word is used as a synonym for *credit*.

Beginners in the study of accounting are frequently confused by the words *debit* and *credit*. Perhaps the best way to minimize confusion is to ask what words would be used as substitutes? *Left* would be used instead of debit, and *right* would be used instead of credit.

The words *debit* and *credit* have a Latin origin. They were used centuries ago when double-entry bookkeeping was introduced by Pacioli, an Italian monk. Even though *left* and *right* are more descriptive words, *debit* and *credit* are too deeply entrenched to avoid.

Debit and *credit* are used as verbs, adjectives, and nouns. "Debit $1,000 to cash and credit $1,000 to accounts receivable" are examples of uses as verbs, meaning that $1,000 should be placed on the left side of the Cash account and on the right side of the Accounts Receivable account. Similarly, if "a debit is made to cash" or "cash has a debit balance of $12,000," the word *debit* is a noun or an adjective that describes the status of a particular account. Thus *debit* and *credit* are short words packed with meaning.

In our everyday conversation we sometimes use the words *debit* and *credit* in a general sense that may completely diverge from their technical accounting uses. For instance, we may give praise by saying, "She deserves plenty of credit for her good deed," or we may give criticism by saying, "That misplay is a debit on his ledger." When you study accounting, forget these general uses and misuses of the words. Merely think right or left—that is, right side or left side.

Consider how the words *debit* and *credit* appear on your bank statement or your Visa or MasterCard statement of your account. For example, a *credit balance* in your checking account means that the bank owes you money. That is, a right-side (credit) balance in the *bank's* record of your account indicates a liability of the bank to you.

USING THE JOURNAL AND THE LEDGER

☐ Steps in Recording

To emphasize analysis (an activity of the brain rather than of the pen or computer), the effects of transactions (1)–(3) were entered directly in the ledger. In actual practice, the accountant uses other records in addition to ledger accounts. The steps in recording are:

1. The recording steps begin when the transaction is substantiated by **source documents**. These are supporting original records of any transaction; they are memorandums of what happened. Examples of source documents include sales slips or invoices, check stubs, purchase orders, receiving reports, cash receipt slips, minutes of the board of directors, and other authorizing memorandums.
2. An analysis of the transaction is placed in a **book of original entry**, which is a formal chronological record of the effects of the entity's transactions on the balances in pertinent accounts. The most common example of a book of original entry is the **general journal**.

☐ The Journal Entry

A **journal entry** is an analysis of the effects of a transaction on the accounts, usually accompanied by an explanation. The accounts to be debited and credited are identified. For example, the top part of Exhibit 3–1 shows how the opening three entries for Biwheels would be "journalized."

The conventional form of the general journal includes the following:

1. The date and number of the entry are placed near the left margin.
2. In the space for the description, the title of the account or accounts to be *debited* (charged) are placed flush left. The title of the account or accounts to be *credited* are indented in a consistent way, but only for two or three letter spaces.
3. The amounts are placed in the debit-credit *money columns*. No dollar signs are used.
4. The journal entry is not complete without the narrative explanation, which is sometimes brief and sometimes exhaustive. The length of the explanation de-

EXHIBIT 3–1

Journal Entries

GENERAL JOURNAL

Date	Entry No.	Accounts and Explanation	Post Ref.	Debit	Credit
19X1					
12/31	1	Cash	100	400,000	
		Paid-in capital	300		400,000
		Capital stock issued to Smith,			
		Handl and Eastman.			
12/31	2	Cash	100	100,000	
		Note payable	202		100,000
		Borrowed at 9% interest on a			
		one-year note.			
19X2					
1/2	3	Merchandise inventory	130	150,000	
		Cash	100		150,000
		Acquired inventory for cash.			

GENERAL LEDGER

Cash   Account No. 100

Date	Explanation	Journ. Ref.	Debit	Date	Explanation	Journ. Ref.	Credit
19X1				19X2			
12/31	(often blank because			1/2		3	150,000
	the explanation is						
	already in the journal)	1	400,000				
12/31		2	100,000				

Merchandise Inventory   Account No. 130

Date	Explanation	Journ. Ref.	Debit	Date	Explanation	Journ. Ref.	Credit
19X2							
1/2		3	150,000				

EXHIBIT 3–1 (continued)

Note Payable   Account No. 202

Date	Explanation	Journ. Ref.	Debit	Date	Explanation	Journ. Ref.	Credit
				19X1			
				12/31		2	100,000

Paid-in Capital   Account No. 300

Date	Explanation	Journ. Ref.	Debit	Date	Explanation	Journ. Ref.	Credit
				19X1			
				12/31		1	400,000

pends on the complexity of the transaction and how extensively the details are to be carried in supporting files of documents.

5. The explanation is often placed flush left and aligned with the debit entry, although practice varies. The important point is consistency so that all explanations will be vertically aligned.

6. To avoid a blurry mess, a space is skipped between each journal entry.

☐ Posting to the Ledger

Posting is the transferring of amounts from the journal to the appropriate accounts in the ledger. To demonstrate, consider entry 3 for Biwheels. Exhibit 3–1 shows how the credit to cash is posted.

The sample of the general ledger in Exhibit 3–1 is in the form of elaborate T-accounts; that is, debits are on the left side and credits on the right side.

Note how cross-referencing occurs. The date is traced to the ledger, and the journal entry number is placed in the reference column. The completion of the posting is signified by inserting the account number in the reference column of the journal. (A blank reference column for an entry in the journal would indicate that the entry has not yet been posted to the ledger account.) The process of numbering or otherwise specifically identifying each journal entry and each posting is known as the **keying of entries**. This facilitates auditing and finding and correcting errors. Always key your entries.

☐ Running Balance Column

Exhibit 3–2 shows a popular account format that provides a running balance. There are three money columns: debit, credit, and balance. The running balance feature is easily achieved by electronic computers or accounting machines.

EXHIBIT 3–2

Ledger Account with Running Balance Column

Cash Account No. 100

Date	Explanation	Journ. Ref.	Debit	Credit	Balance
19X1					
12/31	(often blank because the explanation is	1	400,000		400,000
12/31	already in the journal)	2	100,000		500,000
19X2					
1/2		3		150,000	350,000

Above all, note that the same postings to Cash (or any other pertinent accounts) are made regardless of the account format used: T-account (Exhibit 3–1) or running balance (Exhibit 3–2).

☐ **Chart of Accounts**

Organizations have a **chart of accounts**, which is normally a numbered or coded list describing all account titles. These numbers are used as references, as Exhibit 3–1 demonstrates. Each account described in the journal should have an identifying number in the post ref. column. The following is the chart of accounts for Biwheels:

ACCOUNT NUMBER		ACCOUNT NUMBER	
100	Cash	300	Paid-in capital
120	Accounts receivable	400	Retained income
		500	Sales
130	Merchandise inventory	600	Cost of goods sold
		601	Rent expense
140	Prepaid rent	602	Depreciation expense
170	Store equipment		
202	Note payable		
203	Accounts payable		

Although an outsider may not know what the code means, accounting employees become so familiar with the code that they think, talk, and write in terms of account numbers instead of account names. Thus an outside auditor may find entry 3, the acquisition of Merchandise Inventory (Account #130) for Cash (Account #100), journalized as follows:

	MONEY COLUMNS	
19X2	dr.	cr.
Jan. 2 # 130	150,000	
# 100		150,000

This journal entry is the employee's shorthand. Its brevity and lack of explanation would hamper any outsider's understanding of the transaction, but the entry's meaning would be clear to anyone within the organization.

ADDITIONAL TRANSACTIONS

As we have seen, the transaction is analyzed mentally, then journalized, and then posted to the ledger. Therefore we now prepare journal entries for transactions 4 through 13 as a continuation of the journal entries 1 through 3 already appearing in Exhibit 3–1.

4. Transaction: Acquired inventory on credit, $10,000.
   Analysis: The asset **Merchandise Inventory** is increased.
   The liability **Accounts Payable** is increased.
   Entry: In the journal (explanation omitted):

   Merchandise inventory   10,000
      Accounts payable   10,000

   Post to the ledger (postings are indicated by circled amounts):

Merchandise Inventory*		Accounts Payable	
(3)	150,000	(4)	10,000
(4)	10,000		

* Also often called Inventory of Merchandise, or if it is the only type of inventory account, it is simply called Inventory.

5. Transaction: Acquired store equipment for $4,000 cash plus $11,000 trade credit.
   Analysis: The asset **Cash** is decreased.
   The asset **Store Equipment** is increased.
   The liability **Accounts Payable** is increased.
   Entry: In the journal:

   Store equipment   15,000
      Cash   4,000
      Accounts payable   11,000

   Post to the ledger:

Cash				Accounts Payable	
(1)	400,000	(3)	150,000	(4)	10,000
(2)	100,000	(5)	4,000	(5)	11,000

Store Equipment	
(5)	15,000

Entry 5 is called a **compound entry**, which means that more than two accounts are affected by a single entry. In contrast, a **simple entry** affects only two accounts. Whether simple or compound, as entry 5 shows, the net effect is *always* to keep the accounting equation in balance:

$$\text{Assets} = \text{Liabilities} + \text{Stockholders' equity}$$
$$+15{,}000 - 4{,}000 = +11{,}000$$

A helpful hint: When analyzing a transaction, initially pinpoint the effects (if any) on cash. Did cash increase or decrease? Then think of the effects on other accounts. In this way, you get off to the right start. Usually, it is much easier to identify the effects of a transaction on cash than to identify the effects on other accounts.

6. Transaction: Sold showcase to neighbor for $1,000 on open account.
Analysis: The asset **Accounts Receivable** is increased.
The asset **Store Equipment** is decreased.
Entry: In the journal:

Accounts receivable	1,000	
Store equipment		1,000

Post to the ledger:

Accounts Receivable

(6) 1,000	

Store Equipment

(5) 15,000	(6) 1,000

One asset goes up, but another asset goes down. No liability or owners' equity account is affected.

7. Transaction: Returned inventory to supplier for full credit, $800.
Analysis: The asset **Merchandise Inventory** is decreased.
The liability **Accounts Payable** is decreased.
Entry: In the journal:

Accounts payable	800	
Merchandise inventory		800

Post to the ledger:

Merchandise Inventory			Accounts Payable		
(3) 150,000	(7) 800	(7) 800	(4) 10,000		
(4) 10,000			(5) 11,000		

8. Transaction: Paid cash to creditors, $4,000.
Analysis: The asset **Cash** is decreased.
The liability **Accounts Payable** is decreased.
Entry: In the journal:

Accounts payable	4,000	
Cash		4,000

Post to the ledger:

	Cash					Accounts Payable			
(1)	400,000	(3)	150,000	(7)	800	(4)	10,000
(2)	100,000	(5)	4,000	(8)	4,000	(5)	11,000
		(8)	4,000				

9. Transaction: Collected cash from debtors, $700.

Analysis: The asset **Cash** is increased.
The asset **Accounts Receivable** is decreased.

Entry: In the journal:

Cash	700	
Accounts receivable		700

Post to the ledger:

	Cash		
(1)	400,000	(3)	150,000
(2)	100,000	(5)	4,000
(9)	700	(8)	4,000

	Accounts Receivable		
(6)	1,000	(9)	700

REVENUE AND EXPENSE TRANSACTIONS

Revenue and expense transactions deserve special attention because their relation to the balance sheet equation is usually the most difficult to understand. Focus on the equation:

$$\text{Assets} = \text{Liabilities} + \text{Stockholders' equity} \tag{1}$$
$$\text{Assets} = \text{Liabilities} + \text{Paid-in capital} + \text{Retained income} \tag{2}$$

If we ignore dividends at this stage, Retained Income is merely the accumulated revenue less expenses. Therefore the T-accounts can be shown as follows:

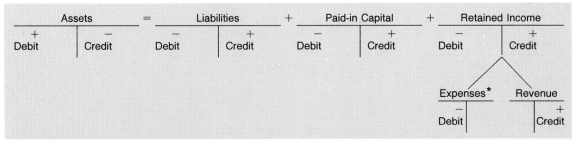

* Be careful here. Although entries on the left side of this account *increase* expenses, their effect on the balance sheet equation is to *decrease* Income. The negative sign denotes this decrease in Stockholders' Equity.

Revenue and expense accounts are really "little" stockholders' equity accounts. *That is, they are primarily a part of stockholders' equity*. Their *net* effects are periodically summarized as one number, net income, which increases retained income.

Retained income is a balance sheet account, whereas revenue and expense accounts record the *changes* between balance sheet dates in the stockholders' equity attributable to operations. Thus these revenues and expenses are shown in the income statement.

Consider each entry in detail:

10a. Transaction: Sales on credit, $160,000.

Analysis: The asset **Accounts Receivable** is increased.
The stockholders' equity **Sales** is increased.

Entry: In the journal:

Accounts receivable	160,000	
Sales		160,000

Post to the ledger:

Accounts Receivable				Sales		
(6)	1,000	(9)	700		(10a)	160,000
(10a)	160,000					

10b. Transaction: Cost of merchandise inventory sold, $100,000.

Analysis: The asset **Merchandise Inventory** is decreased.
The stockholders' equity is decreased by creating a negative stockholders' equity account, **Cost of Goods Sold.**

Entry: In the journal:

Cost of goods sold	100,000	
Merchandise inventory		100,000

Post to the ledger:

Merchandise Inventory				Cost of Goods Sold	
(3)	150,000	(7)	800	(10b)	100,000
(4)	10,000	(10b)	100,000		

Before proceeding, reflect on the logic. Expenses *decrease* stockholders' equity. They are offsets to the normal right-side balances of stockholders' equity accounts. Therefore *increases* in expenses are *decreases* in stockholders' equity. For Cost of Goods Sold of $100,000, the following logic applies:

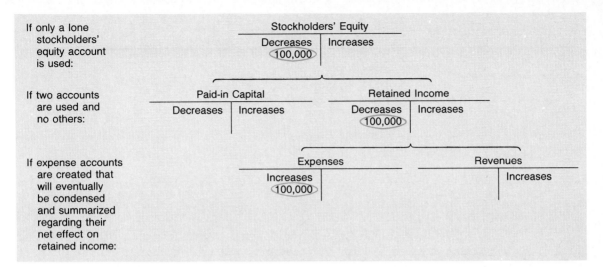

If only a lone stockholders' equity account is used:			

There is no contradiction here. Expenses are negative stockholders' equity accounts. An *increase* in a negative account (such as increasing Cost of Goods Sold by $100,000) has the ultimate effect of *decreasing* stockholders' equity.

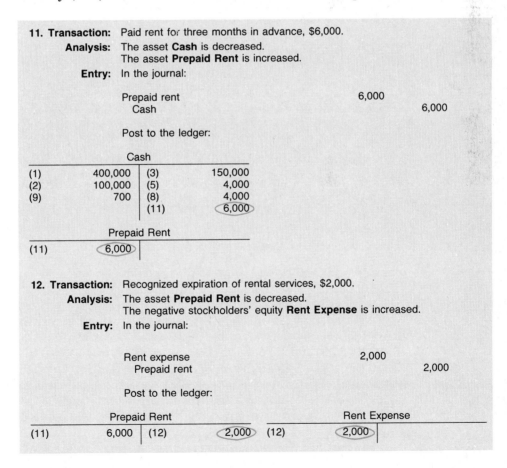

11. Transaction: Paid rent for three months in advance, $6,000.

Analysis: The asset **Cash** is decreased.
The asset **Prepaid Rent** is increased.

Entry: In the journal:

Prepaid rent   6,000
   Cash   6,000

Post to the ledger:

Cash

(1)	400,000	(3)	150,000
(2)	100,000	(5)	4,000
(9)	700	(8)	4,000
		(11)	6,000

Prepaid Rent

(11)	6,000	

12. Transaction: Recognized expiration of rental services, $2,000.

Analysis: The asset **Prepaid Rent** is decreased.
The negative stockholders' equity **Rent Expense** is increased.

Entry: In the journal:

Rent expense   2,000
   Prepaid rent   2,000

Post to the ledger:

Prepaid Rent				Rent Expense	
(11)	6,000	(12)	2,000	(12)	2,000

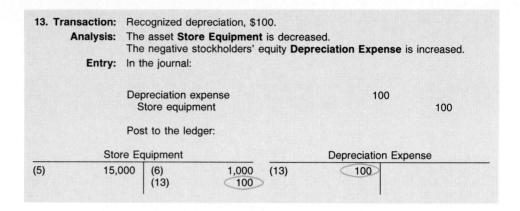

13. Transaction: Recognized depreciation, $100.
   Analysis: The asset **Store Equipment** is decreased.
   The negative stockholders' equity **Depreciation Expense** is increased.
      Entry: In the journal:

Depreciation expense	100	
Store equipment		100

Post to the ledger:

Store Equipment				Depreciation Expense	
(5)	15,000	(6)	1,000	(13)	100
		(13)	100		

Exhibit 3–3 shows the formal journal entries for transactions 4–13. The Posting Reference (Post. Ref.) column used the numbers from the chart of accounts, which are also shown on each account in the ledger.

DEBITS = CREDITS

Recall the balance sheet equation:

$$A = L + \text{Stockholders' equity} \tag{1}$$
$$A = L + \text{Paid-in capital} + \text{Retained income} \tag{2}$$

Assume no dividends:

$$A = L + \text{Paid-in capital} + \text{Revenue} - \text{Expenses} \tag{3}$$

The accountant often talks about the entries in a technical way:

$$\text{transposing: } A + \text{Expenses} = L + \text{Paid-in capital} + \text{Revenue} \tag{4}$$

Finally,

$$\text{Left} = \text{Right}$$
$$\text{Debit} = \text{Credit}$$

Debit means one thing and one thing only—"left side" (not "bad," "something coming," etc.). *Credit* means one thing and one thing only—"right side" (not "good," "something owed," etc.).

For example, if you asked an accountant what entry to make for transaction 10b, the answer would be, "I would debit (or charge) Cost of Goods Sold for $100,000; and I would credit Merchandise Inventory for $100,000." Note that the total dollar amount of the debits (entries on the left side of the account(s) affected) will *always* equal the total dollar amount of the credits (entries on the right side of the account(s) affected) because the whole accounting system is based on an equation. The symmetry and power of this analytical debit-credit technique is indeed impressive.

Assets are traditionally carried as left-side balances. Why do assets and

EXHIBIT 3–3

Journal

Date	Entry No.	Accounts and Explanation	Post Ref.	Debit	Credit
19X2	4	Merchandise inventory	130	10,000	
		Accounts payable	203		10,000
		Acquired inventory on credit.			
	5	Store equipment	170	15,000	
		Cash	100		4,000
		Accounts payable	203		11,000
		Acquired store equipment for cash plus credit. (This is an example of a *compound journal entry*, whereby more than two accounts are affected by the same transaction.)			
	6	Accounts receivable	120	1,000	
		Store equipment	170		1,000
		Sold store equipment to business neighbor.			
	7	Accounts payable	203	800	
		Merchandise inventory	130		800
		Returned some bicycles to supplier.			
	8	Accounts payable	203	4,000	
		Cash	100		4,000
		Payments to creditors.			
	9	Cash	100	700	
		Accounts receivable	120		700
		Collections from debtors.			
	10a	Accounts receivable	120	160,000	
		Sales	500		160,000
		Sales to customers on credit.			
	10b	Cost of goods sold	600	100,000	
		Merchandise inventory	130		100,000
		To record the cost of inventory sold.			
	11	Prepaid rent	140	6,000	
		Cash	100		6,000
		Payment of rent in advance.			
	12	Rent expense	601	2,000	
		Prepaid rent	140		2,000
		Recognize expiration of rental service.			
	13	Depreciation expense	602	100	
		Store equipment	170		100
		Recognize depreciation for January.			

expenses both carry debit balances? They carry left-side balances for different reasons. *Expenses* are temporary stockholders' equity accounts; they are negative equity accounts. Decreases in stockholders' equity are entered on the left side of the accounts because they offset the normal (i.e., right-side) stockholders' equity balances. Because expenses decrease stockholders' equity, they are carried as left-side balances.

Debits are often abbreviated as *dr.*, and credits are often abbreviated as *cr.*

To recapitulate:

Assets = Liabilities + Owners' equity

Assets		=	Liabilities		+	Owners' Equity	
+	−		−	+		−	+
Increase	Decrease		Decrease	Increase		Decrease	Increase
Debit	Credit		Debit	Credit		Debit	Credit
Left	Right		Left	Right		Left	Right

Because revenues increase owners' equity, they are recorded as credits. Because expenses decrease owners' equity, they are recorded as debits. Normal balances are:

Assets	Debit	
Liabilities		Credit
Owners' equity		Credit
Revenues		Credit
Expenses	Debit	

GENERAL LEDGER AND TRIAL BALANCE

☐ **General Ledger and Presenting of Balances**

The **general ledger** is the record that contains the group of accounts that supports the amounts shown in the major financial statements. Exhibit 3–4 shows the Biwheels general ledger in T-account form. Pause and examine the postings in the general ledger. (It is customary *not* to use dollar signs in either the journal or the ledger. Note too that negative numbers are never used in the journal or the ledger.)

The account balance may be kept as a running balance, or it may be updated from time to time as desired. There are many acceptable techniques for updating. Accountants' preferences vary. The double horizontal lines in Exhibit 3–4 mean that all postings above the double lines are summarized as a single balance immediately below the double lines. Therefore all amounts above the double underscores should be ignored for purposes of computing the next updated balance.

The accounts without double underscores in Exhibit 3–4 contain a lone number. This number automatically serves also as the ending balance. For

EXHIBIT 3-4

General Ledger of Biwheels Company

Transactions contained in this illustration:
1. Initial investment
2. Loan from bank
3. Acquired merchandise inventory for cash
4. Acquired merchandise inventory on credit
5. Acquired store equipment for cash plus credit
6. Sales of equipment on credit
7. Return of merchandise inventory for credit
8. Payments to creditors
9. Collections from debtors
10a. Sales on credit
10b. Cost of merchandise inventory sold
11. Pay rent in advance
12. Recognize expiration of rental services
13. Recognize depreciation

ASSETS
(Increases on left, decreases on right)

LIABILITIES AND STOCKHOLDERS' EQUITY
(Decreases on left, increases on right)

Cash — Account No. 100

(1)	400,000	(3)	150,000
(2)	100,000	(5)	4,000
(9)	700	(8)	4,000
		(11)	6,000

1/31 Bal.
336,700

Note Payable 202

| | | (2) | 100,000 |

Paid-in Capital 300

| | | (1) | 400,000 |

Accounts Receivable 120

| (6) | 1,000 | (9) | 700 |
| (10a) | 160,000 | | |

1/31 Bal.
160,300

Accounts Payable 203

| (7) | 800 | (4) | 10,000 |
| (8) | 4,000 | (5) | 11,000 |

1/31 Bal.
16,200

Retained Income 400

| | | 1/31 Bal. | |
| | | | 57,900 |

Expense and Revenue Accounts

Merchandise Inventory 130

| (3) | 150,000 | (7) | 800 |
| (4) | 10,000 | (10b) | 100,000 |

1/31 Bal
59,200

Cost of Goods Sold 600

| (10b) | 100,000 | | |

Sales 500

| | | (10a) | 160,000 |

Prepaid Rent 140

| (11) | 6,000 | (12) | 2,000 |

1/31 Bal.
4,000

Rent Expense 601

| (12) | 2,000 | | |

Store Equipment 170

| (5) | 15,000 | (6) | 1,000 |
| | | (13) | 100 |

1/31 Bal.
13,900

Depreciation Expense 602

| (13) | 100 | | |

* The details of the revenue and expense accounts appear in the income statement. Their net effect is then transferred to a single account, Retained Income, in the balance sheet. The procedures for accomplishing this transfer, called closing the books, are explained in Chapter 5.

Note: An ending balance is shown on the side of the account with the larger total.

example, the Note Payable entry of $100,000 also serves as the ending balance for trial balance purposes.

☐ **Trial Balance**

A **trial balance** is a list of all accounts with their balances. Its purpose is twofold: (a) to help check on accuracy of posting by proving whether the total debits equal the total credits, and (b) to establish a convenient summary of balances in all accounts for the preparation of formal financial statements.

A trial balance may be taken at any time the accounts are up to date, for example, on January 2, 19X2, after the first three transactions of Biwheels:

BIWHEELS COMPANY
Trial Balance
January 2, 19X2

	BALANCE	
ACCOUNT TITLES	Debit	Credit
Cash	$350,000	
Merchandise Inventory	150,000	
Note payable		$100,000
Paid-in capital		400,000
Total	$500,000	$500,000

Obviously, the trial balance becomes more detailed (and more essential) when there are many more accounts. The word "trial" was well chosen; the list is prepared as a *test* or *check* before proceeding further.

Exhibit 3–5 is the trial balance of the general ledger of Exhibit 3–4. In particular, note that Retained Income has no balance here. Instead all the revenue and expense accounts are listed. As Exhibit 3–4 indicates, when the formal balance sheet is prepared, the retained income would summarize the net effect of the revenue and expense accounts on stockholders' equity.

The trial balance assures the accountant that the debits and credits are equal. It is also the springboard for the preparation of the balance sheet and the income statement. The income statement accounts are summarized later as a single number, net income, which then becomes Retained Income in the formal balance sheet.

The trial balance helps alert the accountant to possible errors. However, a trial balance may balance even when there are recording errors. For example, a $10,000 cash receipt on account may erroneously be recorded as $1,000. Then both Cash and Accounts Receivable would be in error by offsetting amounts of $9,000. Another example would be the recording of a $10,000 cash receipt on account as a credit to Sales rather than as a reduction of Accounts Receivable. Sales would be overstated and Accounts Receivable overstated by $10,000. Nevertheless, the trial balance would still show total debits equal to total credits.

EXHIBIT 3–5

BIWHEELS COMPANY
Trial Balance
January 31, 19X2

	DEBITS	CREDITS
Cash	$336,700	
Accounts receivable	160,300	
Merchandise inventory	59,200	
Prepaid rent	4,000	
Store equipment	13,900	
Note payable		$100,000
Accounts payable		16,200
Paid-in capital		400,000
Retained income		—
Sales		160,000
Cost of goods sold	100,000	
Rent expense	2,000	
Depreciation expense	100	
Total	$676,200	$676,200

SUBSIDIARY LEDGERS

The general ledger is usually supported by various **subsidiary ledgers**, which provide details for several accounts in the general ledger. For instance, an accounts receivable subsidiary ledger (which is illustrated in Chapter 6) would contain a separate account for each credit customer. The accounts receivable balance that appears in the Sears balance sheet is in a single account in the Sears general ledger. However, that lone balance is buttressed by detailed individual accounts receivable with millions of credit customers. You can readily visualize how some accounts in general ledgers might have subsidiary ledgers, which in turn are supported by sub-subsidiary ledgers, and so on. Thus a subsidiary accounts receivable ledger might be subdivided alphabetically into Customers A–D, E–H, and so forth, or by customer account numbers.

ANALYTICAL USE BY ACCOUNTANTS

Professional accountants frequently think about complicated transactions in terms of how they would be analyzed in a journal or in T-accounts. That is, accountants use these bookkeeping devices as models of the organization. Accountants often ask one another, "How would you journalize that transaction?" or "How would the T-accounts be affected?" In short, accountants have found that they can think straighter if they force themselves to visualize the transaction in terms of the balance sheet equation and debits and credits.

DATA PROCESSING AND COMPUTERS

Data processing is a general term that usually means the totality of the procedures used to record, analyze, store, and report on chosen activities. An accounting system is a data-processing system. For instructional ease, most introductory accounting textbooks (including this one) focus on manual (pen and ink) methods of data processing. Of course, almost all organizations use mechanical aids (for example, a simple cash register) and electronic aids (for example, massive computer systems for billing for telephone services).

The physical forms of journals and ledgers have changed significantly. The data may be kept on tape or disks or some other form of computer record. Nevertheless, whatever their form, journals and ledgers remain as the backbone of accounting systems.

Entries in journals and ledgers by pen or pencil are efficient ways to learn the accounting cycle. However, each transaction can be journalized by entering the appropriate account numbers and amounts into a computer. The computer then does the posting to the ledger. If managers desire, they can have a new balance sheet each day.

The microcomputer has enabled small organizations to process data more efficiently than ever. When you check out at a pharmacy or clothing store, the cash register often does more than just record a sale. It may also record a decrease in inventory. It may activate an order to a supplier if the inventory level is low. If a sale is on credit, the machine may check a customer's credit limit, update the accounts receivable, and eventually prepare monthly statements for mailing to the customer.

The magnitude of the data-processing task is illustrated by the Amoco Oil Company, which changed its method of recording credit sales. A new "transaction recorder" device records the carbon-copy impressions of every transaction on a one-inch-deep line on special log sheets inside the recorder. The sheets are scanned by the Amoco computer, and the data are later reproduced on the customer's monthly statement of account.

With the old system, Amoco had received 650,000 separate sales slips daily. Each slip was being handled fourteen times. The new system reduces the incoming paper load by 90% and eliminates all but one handling.

MORE ON GENERALLY ACCEPTED ACCOUNTING PRINCIPLES

Basic concepts of accounting theory are too vast to consume in one gulp, so they are being introduced gradually as we proceed. Previous chapters discussed some basic concepts of accounting, such as entity, realization, matching and cost recovery, and stable monetary unit. We now consider four other major ideas that are part of the body of generally accepted accounting principles: going concern, objectivity, materiality, and cost-benefit.

Continuity or the Going Concern Convention

The **continuity** or **going concern convention** is the assumption that in all ordinary situations an entity persists indefinitely. This notion implies that existing *resources*, such as plant assets, *will be used* to fulfill the general purposes of a continuing entity *rather than sold* in tomorrow's real estate or equipment markets. It also implies that existing liabilities will be paid at maturity in an orderly manner.

Suppose some old specialized equipment has a depreciated cost (that is, original cost less accumulated depreciation) of $10,000, a replacement cost of $12,000, and a realizable value of $7,000 on the used-equipment market. The continuity convention is often cited as the justification for adhering to acquisition cost (or acquisition cost less depreciation, $10,000 in this example) as the primary basis for valuing assets such as inventories, land, buildings, and equipment. Some critics of these accounting practices believe that such valuations are not as informative as their replacement cost ($12,000) or their realizable values upon liquidation ($7,000). Defenders of using $10,000 as an appropriate asset valuation argue that a going concern will generally use the asset as originally intended. Therefore the recorded cost (the acquisition cost less depreciation) is the preferable basis for accountability and evaluation of performance. Hence other values are not germane because replacement or disposal will not occur en masse as of the balance sheet date.

The opposite view to this going concern or continuity convention is an immediate-liquidation assumption whereby all items on a balance sheet are valued at the amounts appropriate if the entity were to be liquidated in piecemeal fashion within a few days or months. This liquidation approach to valuation is usually used only when the entity is in severe, near-bankrupt straits.

Objectivity or Verifiability

Users want assurance that the numbers in the financial statements are not fabricated by management or by accountants in an attempt to mislead or to falsify the financial position and performance. Consequently, accountants seek and prize **objectivity** or **verifiability** as one of their principal strengths and regard it as an essential characteristic of measurement. Objectivity results in accuracy that is supported by convincing evidence that can be verified by independent accountants. It is a relative rather than an absolute concept. Some measurements can be extremely objective (such as cash in a cash register) in the sense that the same measurement would be produced by each of a dozen CPAs. But there are gradations of objectivity. A dozen CPAs are less likely to arrive at the same balances for receivables, inventories, plant and equipment, and miscellaneous assets. Yet they strive for measurement rules that will produce results that are subject to independent check. That is why accountants are generally satisfied with existing tests of realization; requiring actual exchanges of goods and services between the entity and another party before revenue is realized helps ensure verifiability.

Many critics of existing accounting practices want to trade objectivity (verifiability) for what they conceive as more relevant or valid information. For example, the accounting literature is peppered with suggestions that accounting should attempt to measure "economic income," even though objectivity may be lessened. This particular suggestion often involves introducing asset valuations at replacement costs when these are higher than historical costs. The accounting profession has generally rejected these suggestions, even when reliable replacement price quotations are available, because no evidence short of a bona fide sale is regarded as sufficient to justify income recognition. However, inflation during the 1970s and 1980s has led to experimentation with the use of replacement costs and other versions of current values for external purposes. (See Chapter 14 for a fuller discussion.)

□ Materiality

Because accounting is a practical art, the practitioner often tempers accounting reports by applying judgments about materiality. The **materiality convention** is a characteristic attaching to a statement, fact, or item that, if omitted or misstated, would tend to mislead the user of the financial statements under consideration.

Many outlays that should theoretically be recorded as assets are immediately written off as expenses because of their lack of significance. For example, many corporations have a rule that requires the immediate write-off to expense of all outlays under a specified minimum of, say, $100, regardless of the useful life of the asset acquired. In such a case, coat hangers may be acquired and may last indefinitely, but they may never appear in the balance sheet as assets. The resulting $100 understatement of assets and stockholders' equity would be too trivial to worry about.

When is an item material? There will probably never be a universal clear-cut answer. What is trivial to General Motors may be material to Joe's Tavern. A working rule is that an item is material if its proper accounting would probably affect the decision of a knowledgeable user. In sum, materiality is an important convention. But it is difficult to use anything other than prudent judgment to tell whether an item is material.

□ Cost-Benefit

Accounting systems vary in complexity from the minimum crude records kept to satisfy governmental authorities to the sophisticated budgeting and feedback schemes that are at the heart of management planning and controlling. The **cost-benefit criterion** means that as a system is changed, its expected additional benefits should exceed its expected additional costs. Often the benefits are difficult to measure, but this criterion at least implicitly underlies the decisions about the design of accounting systems. Sometimes the reluctance to adopt suggestions for new ways of measuring financial position and performance is because of inertia. More often it is because the apparent benefits do not exceed the obvious costs of gathering and interpreting the information.

Accounting is commonly misunderstood as being a precise discipline that produces exact measurements of a company's financial position and performance. As a result, many individuals regard accountants as little more than mechanical tabulators who grind out financial reports after processing an imposing amount of detail in accordance with stringent predetermined rules. Although accountants take methodical steps with masses of data, their rules of measurement allow much room for judgment. Managers and accountants who exercise this judgment have more influence on financial reporting than is commonly believed. These judgments are guided by the basic concepts, techniques, and conventions called generally accepted accounting principles (GAAP). Examples of the latter include the basic concepts just discussed. Their meaning will become clearer as these concepts are applied in future chapters.

SUMMARY PROBLEMS FOR YOUR REVIEW

☐ Problem One

Do you agree with the following statements? Explain.

1. To charge an account means to credit it.
2. One person's debit is another person's credit.
3. A charge account may be credited.
4. My credit is my most valuable asset.
5. She has more credits than debits.
6. When I give credit, I debit my customer's account.

☐ Solution to Problem One

Remember that in accounting, *debit* means left side and *credit* means right side.

1. No. *Charge* and *debit* and *left side* are synonyms.
2. Yes, in certain situations. The clearest example is probably the sale of merchandise on open account. The buyer's account payable would have a credit (right) balance, and the seller's account receivable would have a debit (left) balance.
3. Yes. When collections are received, Accounts Receivable are credited (right).
4. It depends. In technical accounting terms, asset balances are debits, not credits. Of course, the word *credit* also has some general, nontechnical meanings. As used in this statement, "my credit" refers to "my ability to borrow," not which side of a balance sheet is affected. "My ability to borrow" may indeed be a valuable right, but the accountant does not recognize that ability (as such) as an asset to be measured and reported in the balance sheet. When borrowing occurs, the borrower's assets are increased (debited, increased on the left side) and the liabilities are increased (credited, increased on the right side).
5. No. From a technical accounting standpoint, the total debits (left) must always equal the total credits (right). As used here in a general sense, the statement could be translated: She has more positive characteristics than negative.
6. Yes. Accounts Receivable is debited (left). "Give credit" in this context means that the corresponding account payable on the customer's accounting records will be increased (credited, right).

The trial balance of Perez Used Auto Co. on March 31, 19X1, follows:

| | BALANCE | |
ACCOUNT TITLE	Debit	Credit
Cash	$ 10,000	
Accounts receivable	20,000	
Automobile inventory	100,000	
Accounts payable		$ 3,000
Notes payable		70,000
Perez, owner's equity		57,000
Total	$130,000	$130,000

The Perez business entity is not incorporated; it is a proprietorship. The account, Perez, Owner's Equity, is used here; in practice, it is often called Perez, Capital.

Perez rented operating space and equipment on a month-to-month basis. During April, the business had the following summarized transactions:

a. Perez invested an additional $20,000 cash in the business.
b. Collected $10,000 on accounts receivable.
c. Paid $2,000 on accounts payable.
d. Sold autos for $120,000 cash.
e. Cost of autos sold was $70,000.
f. Replenished inventory for $60,000 cash.
g. Paid rent expense in cash, $14,000.
h. Paid utilities in cash, $1,000.
i. Paid selling expense in cash, $30,000.
j. Paid interest expense in cash, $1,000.

Required:

1. Open the following T-accounts in the general ledger: cash, accounts receivable, automobile inventory, accounts payable, notes payable, Perez, owner's equity, sales, cost of goods sold, rent expense, utilities expense, selling expense, and interest expense. Enter the March 31 balances in the appropriate accounts.
2. Journalize transactions (a)–(j) and post the entries to the ledger. Key entries by transaction letter.
3. Prepare the trial balance at April 30, 19X1.
4. Prepare an income statement for April. Ignore income taxes.

☐ **Solution to Problem Two**

The solutions to requirements 1 through 4 are in Exhibits 3–6 through 3–9. The opening balances are placed in the appropriate accounts in Exhibit 3–7; the journal entries are prepared in Exhibit 3–6 and posted to the ledger in Exhibit 3–7; a trial balance is prepared in Exhibit 3–8; and the income statement is shown in Exhibit 3–9.

SUMMARY

The accountant's recording process concentrates on the journal and the general ledger. The journal provides a chronological record of transactions, whereas the general ledger provides a dated summary of the effects of the transactions on all accounts, account by account.

EXHIBIT 3–6

PEREZ USED AUTO CO.
General Journal

ENTRY	ACCOUNTS AND EXPLANATION	POST REF.*	DEBIT	CREDIT
a.	Cash	✓	20,000	
	Perez, owner's equity	✓		20,000
	Investment in business by Perez.			
b.	Cash	✓	10,000	
	Accounts receivable	✓		10,000
	Collected cash on accounts.			
c.	Accounts payable	✓	2,000	
	Cash	✓		2,000
	Disbursed cash on accounts owed to others.			
d.	Cash	✓	120,000	
	Sales	✓		120,000
	Sales for cash.			
e.	Cost of goods sold	✓	70,000	
	Automobile inventory	✓		70,000
	Cost of inventory that was sold to customers.			
f.	Automobile inventory	✓	60,000	
	Cash	✓		60,000
	Replenished inventory.			
g.	Rent expense	✓	14,000	
	Cash	✓		14,000
	Paid April rent.			
h.	Utilities expense	✓	1,000	
	Cash	✓		1,000
	Paid April utilities.			
i.	Selling expense	✓	30,000	
	Cash	✓		30,000
	Paid April selling expenses.			
j.	Interest expense	✓	1,000	
	Cash	✓		1,000
	Paid April interest expense.			

* Ordinarily, account numbers are used to denote specific posting references. Otherwise check marks are used.

EXHIBIT 3–7

PEREZ USED AUTO CO.
General Ledger

Cash			
Bal.*	10,000	(c)	2,000
(a)	20,000	(f)	60,000
(b)	10,000	(g)	14,000
(d)	120,000	(h)	1,000
	160,000	(i)	30,000
		(j)	1,000
			108,000†
Bal.	52,000		

Accounts Receivable			
Bal.*	20,000	(b)	10,000
Bal.	10,000		

Automobile Inventory			
Bal.*	100,000	(e)	70,000
(f)	60,000		
Bal.	90,000		

Accounts Payable			
(c)	2,000	Bal.*	3,000
		Bal.	1,000

Notes Payable			
		Bal.*	70,000

Cost of Goods Sold		
(e)	70,000	

Selling Expenses		
(i)	30,000	

Utilities Expense		
(h)	1,000	

Perez, Owner's Equity			
		Bal.*	57,000
		(a)	20,000
		Bal.	77,000

Sales		
	(d)	120,000

Rent Expense		
(g)	14,000	

Interest Expense		
(j)	1,000	

* Balances denoted with an asterisk are as of March 31; balances without asterisks are as of April 30. Lone numbers in any accounts also serve as ending balances.

† Subtotals are included in the Cash account. They are not an essential part of T-accounts. However, when an account contains many postings, subtotals ease the checking of arithmetic.

EXHIBIT 3–8

PEREZ USED AUTO CO.
Trial Balance
April 30, 19X1

	BALANCE	
ACCOUNT TITLE	Debit	Credit
Cash	$ 52,000	
Accounts receivable	10,000	
Automobile inventory	90,000	
Accounts payable		$ 1,000
Notes payable		70,000
Perez, owner's equity		77,000
Sales		120,000
Cost of goods sold	70,000	
Rent expense	14,000	
Utilities expense	1,000	
Selling expense	30,000	
Interest expense	1,000	
Total	$268,000	$268,000

EXHIBIT 3–9

PEREZ USED AUTO CO.
Income Statement
For the Month Ended April 30, 19X1

Sales		$120,000
Deduct expenses:		
Cost of goods sold	$70,000	
Rent expense	14,000	
Utilities expense	1,000	
Selling expense	30,000	
Interest expense	1,000	116,000
Net income		$ 4,000

Accounting can be learned without journals. The general ledger is really the major backup for financial statements. Nevertheless, the journal entry is a convenient, simple way of presenting an analysis of a transaction. Consequently, journal entries are popular teaching devices and provide an easy basis for discussion among students, teachers, and professional accountants.

HIGHLIGHTS TO REMEMBER

1. Concentrate on relating journals and ledgers to changes in the balance sheet equation.
2. Students tend to be puzzled by the fact that both assets and expenses normally have debit balances. Expenses have debit balances because they are reductions in stockholders' equity. In other words, expenses are a negative component of stockholders' equity.
3. There is no shortcut to learning debits and credits. Learning occurs by solving homework problems. Whether such homework is satisfying depends largely on your approach. Before you prepare journal entries, think hard about the relationships between the accounts. The mechanics of the journal and the ledger then become much easier to understand.
4. All accountants, including your authors, will testify that fewer aspects of accounting are more maddening than trial balances that fail to balance. Such failures are inevitably the result of some careless or rushed journalizing or posting. Use deliberate care. Avoid short-cuts. Much more time is invested in trying to find an error after it has been made than is invested in exercising care in the first place. Moreover, trying to find one's error is seldom fun.

ACCOUNTING VOCABULARY

Balance, p. 78 Book of Original Entry, 79 Charge, 78 Chart of Accounts, 82 Compound Entry, 84 Continuity Convention, 95 Cost-Benefit Criterion, 96 Credit, 78 Data Processing, 94 Debit, 78 Double-Entry System, 77 General Journal, 79 General Ledger, 90 Going Concern Convention, 95 Journal Entry, 79 Keying of Entries, 81 Ledger, 76 Materiality, 96 Objectivity, 95 Posting, 81 Simple Entry, 84 Source Document, 79 Subsidiary Ledger, 93 T-account, 76 Trial Balance, 92 Verifiability, 95.

FUNDAMENTAL ASSIGNMENT MATERIAL

□ General Coverage

3-1. JOURNAL, LEDGER, TRIAL BALANCE. (Alternates are 3-2, 3-3, and 3-29 through 3-34.) The trial balance of O'Toole and Goldberg's Appliance Co. on December 31, 19X1, follows:

| ACCOUNT TITLE | BALANCE | |
	Debit	Credit
Cash	$ 20,000	
Accounts receivable	30,000	
Merchandise inventory	120,000	
Accounts payable		$ 35,000
Notes payable		80,000
Paid-in capital		29,000
Retained income		26,000
Total	$170,000	$170,000

Operating space and equipment are rented on a month-to-month basis. A summary of January transactions follows:

a. Paid $18,000 on accounts payable.
b. Collected $23,000 on accounts receivable.
c. Sold appliances for $70,000 cash and $30,000 on open account.
d. Cost of appliances sold was $60,000.
e. Replenished inventory for $63,000 on open account.
f. Paid selling expense in cash, $30,000.
g. Paid rent expense in cash, $5,000.
h. Paid interest expense in cash, $1,000.

Required:

1. Open the appropriate T-accounts in the general ledger. In addition to the seven accounts listed in the trial balance of December 31, open accounts for Sales, Cost of Goods Sold, Selling Expense, Rent Expense, and Interest Expense. Enter the December 31 balances in the accounts.
2. Journalize transactions (a)–(h). Post the entries to the ledger, keying by transaction letter.
3. Prepare a trial balance, January 31, 19X2.

□ Understanding Published Financial Reports

3-2. TRANSACTION ANALYSIS, TRIAL BALANCE. (Alternates are 3-1, 3-3, and 3-29 through 3-34.) Kellogg Company's major product line is ready-to-eat breakfast cereals. Examine the accompanying condensed trial balance, which is based on Kellogg's annual report and actual terminology.

KELLOGG COMPANY
Trial Balance
December 31, 1986
(in millions)

Cash	$ 163.7	
Accounts receivable	158.9	
Inventories	231.2	
Prepaid expenses	28.4	
Property and equipment, net	658.4	
Other assets	38.5	
Accounts payable		$ 104.5
Other liabilities		364.3
Paid-in capital		48.7
Retained earnings		761.6
Total	$1,279.1	$1,279.1

Consider the following assumed partial summary of transactions for 1987 (in millions):

a. Acquired inventories for $1,600 on open account.
b. Solid inventories that cost $1,500 for $2,400 on open account.
c. Collected $2,300 on open account.
d. Disbursed $1,550 on open accounts payable.
e. Paid cash of $300 for advertising expenses. (Debit Operating Expenses.)
f. Paid rents and insurance premiums in cash in advance, $20. (Debit Prepaid Expenses.)
g. Prepaid expenses expired, $18. (Debit Operating Expenses.)
h. Other liabilities paid in cash, $110.
i. Interest expense of $13 was paid in cash. (Debit Interest Expense.)
j. Depreciation of $50 was recognized. (Debit Operating Expenses.)

Required:

1. Record the transactions in the journal.
2. Enter beginning balances in T-accounts. Post the journal entries to the T-accounts. Key your entries with the transaction letters used here.
3. Prepare a trial balance, December 31, 1987.

3–3. **TRANSACTION ANALYSIS, TRIAL BALANCE.** (Alternates are 3–1, 3–2, and 3–29 through 3–34.) McDonald's Corporation is a well-known fast-foods restaurant company. Examine the accompanying condensed trial balance, which is based on McDonald's annual report and actual terminology.

McDONALD'S CORPORATION
Trial Balance
December 31, 1986
(in millions)

Cash	$ 40	
Accounts and notes receivable	76	
Inventories	23	
Prepaid expenses	37	
Property and equipment, net	2,497	
Other assets	226	
Notes and accounts payable		$ 141
Other liabilities		1,388
Paid-in capital		81
Retained earnings		1,289
Total	$2,899	$2,899

Consider the following assumed partial summary of transactions for 1987 (in millions):

a. Revenues in cash, company-owned restaurants, $2,000.
b. Revenues, on open account from franchised restaurants, $600.
c. Inventories acquired on open account, $727.
d. Cost of the inventories sold, $720.
e. Depreciation, $226. (Debit Depreciation Expense.)
f. Paid rents and insurance premiums in cash in advance, $42. (Debit Prepaid Expenses.)
g. Prepaid expenses expired, $37. (Debit Operating Expenses.)
h. Paid other liabilities, $148.
i. Cash collections on receivables, $590.
j. Cash disbursements on notes and accounts payable, $747.
k. Interest expense in cash, $100.
l. Other expenses in cash, mostly payroll and advertising, $1,510. (Debit Operating Expenses.)

Required:

1. Record the transactions in the journal.
2. Enter beginning balances in T-accounts. Post the journal entries to the T-accounts. Key your entries with the transaction letters used here.
3. Prepare a trial balance, December 31, 1987.

ADDITIONAL ASSIGNMENT MATERIAL

☐ General Coverage

3–4. "Increases in cash and stockholders' equity are shown on the right side of their respective accounts." Do you agree? Explain.

3–5. "Revenue and expense accounts are really little stockholders' equity accounts." Explain.

3–6. "As dividends are declared, they are frequently debited to Retained Income. If used, a separate Dividends Declared account should have a debit balance." Do you agree? Explain.

3–7. "Double entry means that amounts are shown in the journal and the ledger." Do you agree? Explain.

3–8. "*Debit* and *credit* are used as verbs, adjectives, or nouns." Give examples of how *debit* may be used in these three meanings.

3–9. "A trial balance assumes that the amounts in the financial statements are correct." Do you agree? Explain.

3–10. Give two examples of subsidiary ledgers.

3–11. "There can be no more than two subsidiary ledgers. Otherwise the double-entry system cannot be maintained." Do you agree? Explain.

3–12. Name three source documents for transactions.

3–13. "The ledger is the major book of original entry because it is more essential than the journal." Do you agree? Explain.

3–14. "This idea implies that existing equipment will be *used* rather than *sold* in tomorrow's equipment markets." What is the name of this idea?

3–15. "A dozen CPAs are likely to produce the same measurement if this idea is applied." What idea is being described?

3–16. "What is trivial to General Motors may be significant to Joe's Tavern." What idea is being described?

3–17. **DEBITS AND CREDITS.** For each of the following accounts, indicate whether it normally possesses a debit or a credit balance. Use *DR* or *CR*:

1. Accounts payable	6. Depreciation expense
2. Accounts receivable	7. Dividends payable
3. Supplies expense	8. Paid-in capital
4. Supplies inventory	9. Subscription revenue
5. Retained income	10. Sales

3–18. DEBITS AND CREDITS. Determine for the following transactions whether the account *named in parentheses* is to be debited or credited.

1. Sold merchandise (Merchandise Inventory), $1,000.
2. Paid Johnson Associates $3,000 owed them (Accounts Payable).
3. Bought merchandise on account (Merchandise Inventory), $2,000.
4. Received cash from customers on accounts due (Accounts Receivable), $1,000.
5. Bought merchandise on open account (Accounts Payable), $5,000.
6. Borrowed money from a bank (Notes Payable), $10,000.

3–19. DEBITS AND CREDITS. For the following transactions, indicate whether the accounts *in parentheses* are to be debited or credited. Use *DR* or *CR*:

1. A county government received property taxes (Tax Revenue).
2. A three-year fire insurance policy was acquired (Prepaid Expenses).
3. Wages were paid to employees (Wages Expense).
4. A newsstand sold magazines (Sales Revenue).
5. Merchandise was sold on credit (Accounts Receivable).
6. Dividends were declared and paid in cash (Retained Income).

3–20. TRUE OR FALSE. Use *T* or *F* to indicate whether each of the following statements is true or false:

1. In general, entries on the right side of asset accounts represent decreases in the account balances.
2. Increases in liability and revenue accounts should be recorded on the left side of the accounts.
3. Decreases in retained income are recorded as debits.
4. In general, all credit entries are recorded on the right side of accounts and represent decreases in the account balances.
5. Both increases in assets and decreases in liabilities are recorded on the debit sides of accounts.
6. In some cases, increases in account balances are recorded on the right sides of accounts.
7. Cash collections of accounts receivable should be recorded as debits to Cash and credits to Accounts Receivable.
8. Credit purchases of equipment should be debited to Equipment and charged to Accounts Payable.
9. Repayments of bank loans should be charged to Notes Payable and credited to Cash.
10. Asset debits should be on the left and liability debits should be on the right.
11. Inventory purchases on account should be credited to Accounts Payable and debited to an expense account.

3–21. MATCHING TRANSACTIONS OF ACCOUNTS. Listed here are a series of accounts that are numbered for identification. On page 106 at the right are columns in which you are to write the identification numbers of the accounts affected by the transactions described. The same account may be used in several answers. Answer all; omit none.

1. Cash	7. Notes payable
2. Accounts receivable	8. Paid-in capital
3. Inventory	9. Retained earnings
4. Equipment	10. Sales
5. Prepaid insurance	11. Cost of goods sold
6. Accounts payable	12. Operating expenses

	DEBIT	CREDIT
(a) Purchased new equipment for cash plus a short-term note.	4	1, 7
(b) Paid cash for salaries and wages for work done during the current fiscal period.		
(c) Made sales on credit. Inventory is accounted for as each sale is made.		
(d) Collected cash from customers on account.		
(e) Paid some old trade bills with cash.		
(f) Purchased three-year insurance policy on credit.		
(g) Sold for cash some old equipment at cost.		
(h) Paid off note owed to bank.		
(i) Paid cash for inventory that arrived today.		
(j) Bought regular merchandise on credit.		
(k) In order to secure additional funds, 400 new shares of common stock were sold for cash.		
(l) Some insurance premiums have expired.		
(m) Paid cash for ad in today's *Chicago Tribune*.		
(n) Recorded the entry for depreciation on equipment for the current fiscal period.		

3–22. JOURNALIZING AND POSTING. (Alternate is 3–23.) Prepare journal entries and post to T-accounts for the following transactions of Chris Olsen, Realtor:

a. Acquired office supplies of $1,000 on open account. Use a Supplies Inventory account.
b. Sold a house and collected a $10,000 commission on the sale. Use a Commissions Revenue account.
c. Paid cash of $700 to a local newspaper for current advertisements.
d. Paid $800 for a previous credit purchase of a desk.
e. Recorded office supplies used of $200.

3–23. JOURNALIZING AND POSTING. (Alternate is 3–22.) Prepare journal entries and post to T-accounts for the following transactions of Maria Delgado's Gourmet Foods Company:

a. Collections on accounts, $6,000.
b. Cash sales, $12,000.
c. Paid cash for wages, $3,000.
d. Acquired inventory on open account, $5,000.
e. Paid cash for janitorial services, $400.

3–24. RECONSTRUCT JOURNAL ENTRIES. (Alternate is 3–25.) Reconstruct the journal entries (omit explanations) that resulted in the postings to the following T-accounts:

Cash				Accounts Payable				Paid-in Capital		
(a)	50,000	(e)	30,000	(e)	30,000	(b)	90,000		(a)	50,000

Accounts Receivable		
(c)	100,000	

Inventory				Cost of Goods Sold			Sales		
(b)	90,000	(d)	55,000	(d)	55,000			(c)	100,000

3–25. RECONSTRUCT JOURNAL ENTRIES. (Alternate is 3–24.) Reconstruct the journal entries (omit explanations) that resulted in the postings to the following T-accounts of a consulting firm:

Cash				Equipment			Revenue from Fees	
(a)	60,000	(b)	1,000	(c)	15,000		(d)	80,000
		(c)	5,000					

Accounts Receivable		Note Payable				Supplies Used	
(d)	80,000		(c)	10,000			

Supplies Inventory			Paid-in Capital			Supplies Used	
(b)	1,000	(e)	300	(a)	60,000	(e)	300

3–26. ACCOUNT NUMBERS, JOURNAL, LEDGER, TRIAL BALANCE. Journalize and post the entries required by the following transactions. Prepare a trial balance, January 3, 19X3. Ignore interest. Use dates, posting references, and the following account numbers:

Cash	100	Paid-in capital	140
Accounts receivable	101	Retained income	150
Equipment	111	Revenues	200
Accounts payable	120	Expenses	300–301, etc.
Note payable	130		

January 1, 19X3. The Dryden Laundry and Cleaning Company was formed with $100,000 cash upon the issuance of common stock.

January 2. Equipment was acquired for $75,000. A cash down payment of $25,000 was made. In addition, a note for $50,000 was signed.

January 3. Sales on credit to a local hotel, $1,200.

January 3. Supplies acquired (and used) on open account, $200.

January 3. Wages paid in cash, $600.

3–27. ACCOUNT NUMBERS, T-ACCOUNTS, AND TRANSACTION ANALYSIS. Consider the following (in thousands):

GOODHUE STATIONERY SUPPLIERS
Trial Balance
December 31, 19X5

ACCOUNT NUMBER	ACCOUNT TITLES	BALANCE	
		Debit	Credit
10	Cash	$ 50	
20	Accounts receivable	110	
21	Note receivable	100	
30	Inventory	120	
40	Prepaid insurance	12	
70	Equipment	90	
80	Accounts payable		$ 130
100	Paid-in capital		60
110	Retained income		172
130	Sales		900
150	Cost of goods sold	500	
160	Wages expense	200	
170	Miscellaneous expense	80	
		$1,262	$1,262

The following information had not been considered before preparing the trial balance:

1. The note receivable is a 12% note signed by a major customer. It is a three-month note dated November 1, 19X5. Interest earned during November and December was collected at 4 P.M. on December 31. The interest rate is 12% per year.
2. The Prepaid Insurance account reflects a one-year fire insurance policy acquired for cash on August 1, 19X5.
3. Depreciation for 19X5 was $15,000.
4. Wages of $11,000 were paid in cash at 5 P.M. on December 31.

Required:

1. Enter the December 31 balances in a general ledger. Number the accounts. Allow room for additional T-accounts.
2. Prepare the journal entries prompted by the additional information. Show amounts in thousands.
3. Post the journal entries to the ledger. Key your postings. Create logical new account numbers as necessary.
4. Prepare a new trial balance. December 31, 19X5.

3–28. **TRIAL BALANCE ERRORS.** Consider the accompanying Gambrel trial balance (in thousands of dollars):

GAMBREL AUTO PARTS STORE
Trial Balance
For the Year Ended December 31, 19X7

Cash	$ 10	
Equipment	20	
Accounts payable	42	
Accounts receivable	15	
Prepaid insurance	1	
Prepaid rent		$ 4
Inventory	129	
Paid-in capital		12
Retained income		5
Cost of goods sold	600	
Wages expense	100	
Miscellaneous expenses	80	
Advertising expense		30
Sales		890
Note payable	40	
	$1,037	$941

Required:

List and describe all the errors in the above trial balance. Be specific. Based on the available data, prepare a corrected trial balance.

3–29. **JOURNAL, LEDGER, AND TRIAL BALANCE.** Hardware Unlimited is a retailer. The entity's balance sheet had the following balances on March 31, 19X1:

Cash	$ 42,000	
Accounts receivable	90,000	
Inventory	10,000	
Prepaid rent	2,000	
Accounts payable		$ 25,000
Paid-in capital		100,000
Retained income		19,000
	$144,000	$144,000

Following is a summary of the transactions that occurred during April:

    a. Collections of accounts receivable, $88,000.
    b. Payments of accounts payable, $24,000.
    c. Acquisitions of inventory on open account, $80,000.
    d. Merchandise carried in inventory at a cost of $70,000 was sold on open account for $85,000.
    e. Recognition of rent expense for April, $1,000.
    f. Wages paid in cash for April, $8,000.
    g. Cash dividends declared and disbursed to stockholders on April 29, $18,000.

Required:

    1. Prepare journal entries (in thousands of dollars).
    2. Enter beginning balances in T-accounts. Post the journal entries to T-accounts. Use the transaction letters to key your postings.
    3. Prepare a trial balance, April 30, 19X1.

    3–30. **FINANCIAL STATEMENTS.** Refer to the preceding problem. Prepare a balance sheet as of April 30, 19X1, and an income statement for the month of April. Prepare a statement of retained income. Prepare the income statement first.

    3–31. **JOURNAL, LEDGER, TRIAL BALANCE.** Joan Hansen owned and managed a corporation that operated as a retail shoe store. The accompanying trial balance existed on March 1, 19X2, the beginning of a fiscal year.

HANSEN SHOE STORE
Trial Balance
March 1, 19X2

Cash	$ 2,300	
Accounts receivable	25,000	
Merchandise inventory	78,000	
Prepaid rent	4,000	
Store equipment	15,000	
Accounts payable		$ 45,000
Paid-in capital		30,000
Retained income		49,300
	$124,300	$124,300

Summarized transactions for March were:

    1. Acquisitions of merchandise inventory on account, $49,000.
    2. Sales for cash, $39,300.
    3. Payments to creditors, $34,000.
    4. Sales on account, $33,000.
    5. Advertising in newspapers, paid in cash, $3,000.
    6. Cost of goods sold, $40,000.
    7. Collections on account, $29,000.
    8. Miscellaneous expenses paid in cash, $8,000.
    9. Wages paid in cash, $9,000.
    10. Entry for rent expense (Rent was paid quarterly in advance, $6,000 per quarter. Payments were due on February 1, May 1, August 1, and November 1.)
    11. Depreciation of store equipment, $250.

Required:

    1. Enter the March 1 balances in a general ledger.
    2. Prepare journal entries for each transaction.
    3. Post the journal entries to the ledger. Key your postings.
    4. Prepare a trial balance, March 31, 19X2.

3–32. JOURNAL, LEDGER, TRIAL BALANCE. Three women who had been college classmates have decided to pool a variety of work experiences by opening a women's clothing store. The business has been incorporated as Sartorial Choice, Inc. The following transactions occurred during April:

1. On April 1, 19X1, each woman invested $11,000 in cash in exchange for 1,000 shares of stock each.
2. The corporation quickly acquired $50,000 in inventory, half of which had to be paid for in cash. The other half was acquired on open accounts that were payable after thirty days.
3. A store was rented for $500 monthly. A lease was signed for one year on April 1. The first two months' rent were paid in advance. Other payments were to be made on the second of each month. An entry was also made for April rent expense. Make two entries, 3a and 3b.
4. Advertising during April was purchased on open account for $3,000 from a newspaper owned by one of the stockholders. Additional advertising services of $6,000 were acquired for cash. Make two entries, 4a and 4b.
5. Sales were $65,000. The average markup above the cost of the merchandise was two-thirds of cost (not two-thirds of sales revenue). Eighty percent of the sales were on open account. Make two entries, 5a and 5b.
6. Wages and salaries incurred in April and paid in cash amounted to $11,000.
7. Miscellaneous services paid for in cash were $1,410.
8. On April 1, fixtures and equipment were purchased for $6,000 with a down payment of $1,000 plus a $5,000 note payable in one year.
9. See transaction 8 and pay interest of $40 on April 30.
10. See transaction 8 and make the April 30 entry for depreciation expense on a straight-line basis. The estimated life of the fixtures and equipment is ten years with no expected terminal scrap value.

Required:

1. Journalize all transactions for April.
2. Post the entries to the ledger, keying your postings by transaction number.
3. Prepare a trial balance, April 30, 19X1.

3–33. JOURNALIZING, POSTING, TRIAL BALANCE. Fertile Ground Company, a retailer of garden supplies and equipment, had the accompanying balance sheet accounts, December 31, 19X3:

ASSETS		LIABILITIES AND STOCKHOLDERS' EQUITY	
Cash	$ 20,000	Accounts payable*	$110,000
Accounts receivable	40,000	Paid-in capital	50,000
Inventory	150,000	Retained income	90,000
Prepaid rent	4,000		
Store equipment	36,000		
Total	$250,000	Total	$250,000

* For merchandise only.

Following is a summary of transactions that occurred during 19X4:

a. Purchases of merchandise inventory on open account, $500,000.
b. Sales, all on credit, $790,000.
c. Cost of merchandise sold to customers, $440,000.
d. On June 1, 19X4, borrowed $80,000 from a supplier. The note is payable at the end of 19X8. Interest is payable yearly on December 31 at a rate of 15% per annum.
e. Disbursed $23,000 for the rent of the store. Add to Prepaid Rent.
f. Disbursed $165,000 for wages through November.

g. Disbursed $76,000 for miscellaneous expenses such as utilities, advertising, and legal help. (Combined here to save space. Debit Miscellaneous expenses.)

h. On July 1, 19X4, lent $20,000 to the office manager. He signed a note that will mature on July 1, 19X5, together with interest at 10% per annum. Interest for 19X4 is due on December 31, 19X4.

i. Collections on accounts receivable, $690,000.

j. Payments on accounts payable, $480,000.

The following entries were made at December 31, 19X4:

k. Previous rent payments applicable to 19X5 amounted to $3,000.

l. Depreciation for 19X4 was $6,000.

m. Wages earned by employees during December were paid on December 31, $5,000.

n. Interest on the loan from the supplier was disbursed.

o. Interest on the loan made to the office manager was received.

Required:

1. Prepare journal entries in thousands of dollars.
2. Post the entries to the ledger, keying your postings by transaction letter.
3. Prepare a trial balance, December 31, 19X4.

3–34. **TRANSACTION ANALYSIS, TRIAL BALANCE.** Television Repair Service, Incorporated, had the accompanying trial balance on January 1, 19X2.

TELEVISION REPAIR SERVICE, INC.
Trial Balance
January 1, 19X2

Cash	$ 4,000	
Accounts receivable	5,000	
Parts inventory	2,000	
Prepaid rent	2,000	
Trucks	15,000	
Equipment	3,000	
Accounts payable		$ 1,800
Paid-in capital		17,000
Retained income		12,200
Total	$31,000	$31,000

During January, the following summarized transactions occurred:

Jan. 2 Collected accounts receivable, $3,000.

3 Rendered services to customers for cash, $2,200 ($700 collected for parts, $1,500 for labor). Use two accounts, Parts Revenue and Labor Revenue.

3 Cost of parts used for services rendered, $300.

7 Paid legal expenses, $400 cash.

9 Acquired parts on open account, $900.

11 Paid cash for wages, $1,100.

13 Paid cash for truck repairs, $500.

15 Paid cash for utilities, $300.

19 Billed hotel for services, $4,000 ($1,200 for parts and $2,800 for labor).

19 Cost of parts used for services rendered, $500.

24 Paid cash for wages, $1,300.

27 Paid cash on accounts payable, $1,400.

31 Rent expense for January, $1,000 (credit Prepaid Rent).

31 Depreciation for January: trucks, $600; equipment, $200.

31 Paid cash to local gas station for gasoline for trucks for January, $300.

31 Paid cash for wages, $900.

1. Enter the January 1 balances in T-accounts. Leave room for additional accounts.
2. Record the transactions in the journal.
3. Post the journal entries to the T-accounts. Key your entries by date. (Note how keying by date is not as precise as by transaction number or letter. Why? Because there is usually more than one transaction on any given date.)
4. Prepare a trial balance, January 31, 19X2.

☐ Understanding Published Financial Reports

3–35. RECONSTRUCTING JOURNAL ENTRIES, POSTING. H. J. Heinz Company has many food products, including catsup, Ore-Ida, Star-Kist, and Weight Watchers brands. The Heinz balance sheet at the end of its 1986 fiscal year included (in thousands):

Cash	$ 19,398
Receivables	343,865
Prepaid expenses	57,155
Land	22,645
Accounts payable	282,145

Consider the following assumed transactions that occurred immediately subsequent to the balance sheet date. Dollars are in thousands:

a. Collections from customers	$100,000
b. Purchase of land for cash	2,000
c. Purchase of insurance policies on account	1,200
d. Disbursements to trade creditors	95,000

Required:

1. Enter the five account balances in T-accounts.
2. Journalize each transaction.
3. Post the journal entries to T-accounts. Key each posting by transaction letter.

3–36. RECONSTRUCTING JOURNAL ENTRIES, POSTING. (Alternate is 3–37.) House of Fabrics, Inc., is the largest home sewing retailer in the United States. It has 760 stores. A partial income statement for its 1986 fiscal year showed the following actual numbers and nomenclature (in thousands):

Sales		$278,256
Cost of sales	$133,726	
Store and operating expenses	94,758	
Warehouse and administrative expenses	26,686	
Interest expense	1,281	256,451
Income before income taxes		$ 21,805

Required:

1. Prepare five summary journal entries for the given data. Omit explanations. For simplicity, assume that all transactions (except for cost of sales) were for cash.
2. Post to a ledger for all affected accounts. Key your postings by transaction letter.

3–37. RECONSTRUCTING JOURNAL ENTRIES, POSTING. (Alternate is 3–36.) Procter & Gamble has many popular products, including Tide, Crest, and Jif. A partial income statement for its 1986 fiscal year showed the following actual numbers, nomenclature, and format (in millions):

Income:	
Net sales	$13,552
Interest and other income	193
	13,745
Costs and expenses:	
Cost of products sold	9,099
Marketing, administrative, and	
other expenses	3,477
Interest expense	165
	12,741
Earnings before income taxes	$ 1,004

Required:

1. Prepare five summary journal entries for the given data. Omit explanations. For simplicity, assume that all transactions (except for cost of products sold) were for cash.
2. Post to a ledger for all affected accounts. Key your postings by transaction letter.
3. The company uses *income* as a heading for the first part of its income statement. Suggest a more descriptive term. Why is it more descriptive?

Chapter 4

ACCOUNTING ADJUSTMENTS

AND FINANCIAL STATEMENT

PREPARATION

LEARNING OBJECTIVES

After studying this chapter, you should be able to:

1. Make adjustments for the expiration of unexpired costs, the realization (earning) of unearned revenues, the accrual of unrecorded expenses, and the accrual of unrecorded revenues
2. Prepare an elementary classified balance sheet and explain the major relationships therein
3. Show the major differences between single-step and multiple-step income statements
4. Distinguish between common terms used to describe items in the income statement

This chapter covers three major topics: (1) accounting adjustments, (2) classified balance sheets, and (3) various formats of the income statement.

ADJUSTMENTS TO THE ACCOUNTS

The preceding chapter demonstrated the various steps in recording:

Transactions ▶ Documentation ▶ Journal ▶ Ledger ▶ Trial Balance ▶ Statements

These steps have a final aim: financial statements prepared on the accrual basis of accounting.

The arguments on behalf of the accrual basis instead of the cash basis of accounting are in Chapter 2 (p. 45). In short, the accrual basis provides more precise measures of economic performance (income statement) and financial position (balance sheet). To obtain satisfactory precision, the accountant uses **adjustments** at the end of each reporting period. *Adjustments* (also called **adjusting entries**, *adjusting the books*, and *adjusting the accounts*) can be defined as the key final process (before the computation of ending account balances) of assigning the financial effects of transactions to the appropriate time periods. Thus adjustments are made at periodic intervals, that is, when the financial statements are about to be prepared.

Earlier a *transaction* was defined as any economic event that should be recorded by the accountant. Note that this definition is *not* confined to market transactions, which are actual exchanges of goods and services between the entity and another party. For instance, the losses of assets from fire or theft are also transactions even though no market exchange occurs.

Adjustments are a special category of transactions. The principal adjustments can be classified into four types:

I. Expiration of unexpired costs
II. Realization (earning) of unearned revenues
III. Accrual of unrecorded expenses
IV. Accrual of unrecorded revenues

As we will see, all of these adjustments have an important common characteristic. They record **implicit transactions**, in contrast to the **explicit transactions** that trigger nearly all day-to-day routine entries.

To illustrate, entries for credit sales, credit purchases, cash received on account, and cash disbursed on account are supported by explicit evidence.

This evidence is usually in the form of miscellaneous source documents (for example, sales slips, purchase invoices, employee payroll checks).

On the other hand, adjustments for depreciation expense and expiration of prepaid rent are prepared from special schedules or memorandums. Adjustments recognize "implicit" events (like the passage of time) that are temporarily ignored in day-to-day recording procedures.

Adjustments provide a more complete and accurate measure of efforts, accomplishments, and financial position. They are an essential part of accrual accounting because they improve the matching of revenues and expenses. In contrast, a strictly defined cash basis of accounting uses no adjustments.

I. EXPIRATION OF UNEXPIRED COSTS

Assets frequently expire because of the passage of time. This type of adjustment was illustrated in the preceding chapter by the recognition of monthly depreciation expense and rent expense. Because we have already described this important adjustment, we will not dwell on it here. Other examples of adjusting for asset expirations include the write-offs to expense of such assets as Office Supplies Inventory, Advertising Supplies Inventory, and Prepaid Fire Insurance.

II. REALIZATION (EARNING) OF UNEARNED REVENUES

Sometimes it is easier to see how accountants analyze transactions by visualizing the financial positions of both parties to a contract. Recall the Biwheels' January advance payment of $6,000 for three months' rent. Compare the financial impact on Biwheels Company with the impact on the owner of the property, who received the rental payment:

	OWNER OF PROPERTY (LANDLORD, LESSOR)			BIWHEELS COMPANY (TENANT, LESSEE)		
	A =	L +	SE	A	= L +	SE
	Cash	Unearned Rent Revenue	Rent Revenue	Cash	Prepaid Rent	Rent Expense
(a) Explicit transaction (advance payment of three months' rent)	+6,000 =	+6,000		−6,000	+6,000 =	
(b) January adjustment (for one month's rent)	=	−2,000	+2,000		−2,000 =	−2,000
(c) February adjustment (for one month's rent)	=	−2,000	+2,000		−2,000 =	−2,000
(d) March adjustment (for one month's rent)	=	−2,000	+2,000		−2,000 =	−2,000

The adjusting journal entries for (a) and (b) follow:

OWNER (LANDLORD)			TENANT (BIWHEELS CO.)		
(a) Cash	6,000		Prepaid rent	6,000	
Unearned rent revenue		6,000	Cash		6,000
(b) Unearned rent revenue	2,000		Rent expense	2,000	
Rent revenue		2,000	Prepaid rent		2,000

Entries for (c) and (d) would be the same as for (b).

You are already familiar with the Biwheels analysis. The $2,000 monthly entries for Biwheels are examples of the first type of adjustments, the expiration of unexpired costs.

Study the transactions from the viewpoint of the owner of the rental property. The first transaction recognizes **unearned revenue**, which is revenue received or recorded before it is earned. Unearned revenue is also called **deferred revenue** or **deferred credit**, which is a *liability* because the lessor is obligated to deliver the rental services (or to refund the money if the services are not delivered). Sometimes this account is called Rent Collected in Advance, but it is an unearned revenue type of liability account no matter what its label. That is, it is revenue collected in advance that has not been earned as yet.

Adjustments I and II (p. 116) are really mirror images of each other. If one party to a contract has a prepaid expense, the other has an unearned revenue. A similar analysis could be conducted for, say, a three-year fire insurance policy or a three-year magazine subscription. The buyer recognizes a prepaid expense (asset) and uses adjustments to spread the initial cost to expense over the useful life of the services. In turn, the seller, such as a magazine publisher, must initially recognize its liability, Unearned Subscription Revenue. For example, the publisher of *Time* magazine showed a balance of over $200 million as of December 31, 1986, calling it Unearned Portion of Paid Subscriptions. The unearned revenue is then systematically recognized as *earned* revenue when magazines are delivered throughout the life of the subscription. The following diagrams show that explicit cash transactions in such situations are initially recognized as balance sheet items and are later transformed into income statement items via periodic adjustments:

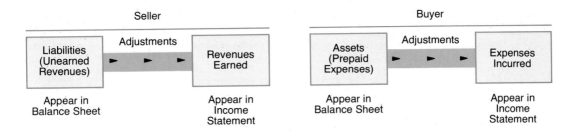

Other examples of unearned revenues are advances from customers who have paid for goods or services to be delivered at a future date. For instance, airlines often require advance payments for special-fare tickets.

Unearned revenue is sometimes called **unearned income** or **deferred income**, but revenue is a more accurate description than income because the latter is, strictly speaking, a difference or "what's left over" after deducting appropriate expenses from revenue. When unearned revenue becomes earned, the expenses matched with the revenue are also recognized. Income is only the amount by which the earned revenue exceeds the related cost of goods or services delivered to customers.

III. ACCRUAL OF UNRECORDED EXPENSES

Accrue means the accumulation of a receivable or payable during a given period even though no explicit transaction occurs. Examples of accruals are the wages of employees for partial payroll periods and the interest on borrowed money before the interest payment date. The receivables or payables grow as the clock ticks or as some services are continuously acquired and used, so they are said to accrue (accumulate).

It is awkward and unnecessary to make hourly, daily, or even weekly formal recordings in the accounts for many accruals. Consequently, adjustments are made to bring each expense (and corresponding liability) account up to date just before the formal financial statements are prepared.

☐ **Accounting for Payment of Wages**

Consider wages. Most companies pay their employees at predetermined times. Here is a sample calendar for January:

			JANUARY			
S	M	T	W	T	F	S
	1	2	3	4	5	6
7	8	9	10	11	12	13
14	15	16	17	18	19	20
21	22	23	24	25	26	27
28	29	30	31			

Suppose Biwheels pays its employees each Friday for services rendered during that week. For example, wages paid on January 26 would be compensation for the week ended January 26. The cumulative total wages paid on the Fridays during January were $20,000, or $5,000 per five-day workweek. Although day-to-day and week-to-week procedures may differ from entity to entity, a popular way to account for wages expense is the shortcut procedure described in Chapter 2 for goods and services that are routinely consumed in the period of their purchase:

	ASSETS (A)	=	LIABILITIES (L)	+	STOCKHOLDERS' EQUITY (SE)
	Cash				Wages Expense
(a) Routine entry for explicit transactions	−20,000	=			−20,000

☐ Accounting for Accrual of Wages

In addition to the $20,000 already paid, Biwheels owes $3,000 for employee services rendered during the last three days of January. The employees will not be paid for these services until February 2. No matter how simple or complex a set of accounting procedures may be in a particular entity, periodic adjustments ensure that the financial statements adhere to accrual accounting. The tabulation below repeats entry *a* for convenience and then adds entry *b*:

	A	=	L	+	SE
			Accrued		
			Wages		Wages
	Cash		Payable		Expense
(a) Routine entry for explicit transactions	−20,000 =				−20,000
(b) Adjustment for implicit transaction, the accrual of unrecorded wages		=	+3,000		− 3,000
Total effects	−20,000 =		+3,000		−23,000

The journal entries (a) and (b) would be:

(a)	Wages expense	20,000	
	Cash		20,000
(b)	Wages expense	3,000	
	Accrued wages payable		3,000

Entry *b* is the first example in this book of the impact of the analytical shortcut that bypasses the asset account and produces an expense that is offset by an increase in a liability.[1]

☐ Accrual of Interest

Other examples of accrued expenses include sales commissions, property taxes, income taxes, and interest on borrowed money. Interest is rent paid for the use of money, just as rent is paid for the use of buildings or automobiles. The interest accumulates (accrues) as time unfolds, regardless of when the actual cash for interest is paid.

Incidentally, distinguish between the return *on* investment (for example, interest on a loan) and the return *of* investment (for example, *principal* of a loan). For example, suppose a loan of $100 is payable at the end of one

---

[1] Conceptually, entries *a* and *b* could each be subdivided into the asset acquisition–asset expiration sequence, but this two-step sequence is not generally used in practice for such expenses that represent the immediate consumption of services.

year at 12% interest. The total payment of $112 would consist of the return *on* investment (interest) of $12 plus the return *of* investment (principal) of $100.

Recall that Biwheels borrowed $100,000 on December 31, 19X1. Assume that the principal and interest on the one-year loan are payable on December 31, 19X2. The interest rate is 9%. (Unless stated otherwise, quoted interest rates typically imply an interest rate *per year*.)

Ponder the theory of asset acquisition and expiration as applied to a bank loan. Biwheels has had the benefit of a $100,000 bank loan for one month. As of January 31, Biwheels owes the bank for these services (the use of money); the amount is $\frac{1}{12} \times .09 \times \$100,000 = \$750$. These money services of $750 have been acquired *and* used up (just like employee services) because Biwheels has had the loan for one month. Therefore the shortcut approach is usually taken; the adjustment is recorded in a fashion similar to the adjustment for accrued wages:

	A =	L	+	SE
		Accrued Interest Payable		Interest Expense
Adjustment for January interest not yet paid	=	+750		−750

IV. ACCRUAL OF UNRECORDED REVENUES

The accrual of unrecorded revenues is the mirror image of the accrual of unrecorded expenses. The adjustments show the realization of revenues that have been earned but not yet shown in the accounts. Consider the bank that has lent the money to Biwheels. As of January 31, the bank has earned $750 on the loan. The following tabulation shows the mirror-image effect:

	BANK, AS A LENDER				BIWHEELS, AS A BORROWER			
	A	= L +	SE		A =	L	+	SE
	Accrued Interest Receivable		Interest Revenue			Accrued Interest Payable		Interest Expense
January interest	+750	=	+750		=	+750		−750

The adjusting journal entries are:

LENDER			BORROWER		
Accrued interest receivable	750		Interest expense	750	
Interest revenue		750	Accrued interest payable		750

Other examples of accrued revenues and receivables include "unbilled" fees. For example, attorneys, public accountants, physicians, and advertising agencies may earn hourly fees during a particular month but not send out bills to their clients until the completion of an entire contract or engagement. Under the accrual basis of accounting, such earnings should be attributed to the month when earned rather than later. Suppose an attorney had rendered $10,000 of services during January that would not be billed until March 31. Before the attorney's financial statements could be prepared for January, an adjustment for previously unrecorded revenues would be necessary:

	A	= L +	SE
	Accrued (Unbilled) Fees Receivable		Fee Revenue
Adjustment for fees earned	+10,000	=	+10,000

CASH LEADS AND LAGS

Cash flows (that is, cash receipts and disbursements) may lead or lag the recognition of revenue and expense. Recall that the first two types of adjustments were usually made *subsequent* to the cash flows. For example, the cash received or disbursed for rent had an *initial* impact on the balance sheet. The adjustment process was used to show the *later* impact on the income statements.

The third and fourth types of adjustments are made *before* the related cash flows. The income statement is affected *before* the cash receipts and disbursements occur. Exhibit 4–1 summarizes these relationships and under-

Four Major Types of Accounting Adjustments Before Preparation of Financial Statements

	EXPENSE	REVENUE
Payment precedes recognition of expense or revenue	I. Expiration of unexpired cost. *Illustration*: The write-off of prepaid rent as rent expense.	II. Realization (earning) of unearned revenues. *Illustration*: The mirror image of type I, whereby the landlord recognizes rent revenue and decreases unearned rent revenue (rent collected in advance).
Recognition of expense or revenue precedes payment	III. Accrual of unrecorded expenses. *Illustration*: Wage expense for wages earned by employees but not yet paid.	IV. Accrual of unrecorded revenues. *Illustration*: Interest revenue earned but not yet collected by a financial institution.

scores the basic distinctions between the cash basis and the accrual basis of accounting. Study the exhibit in conjunction with the following diagrams:

I. Entails computing the portion of an asset used up as expense in the current reporting period:

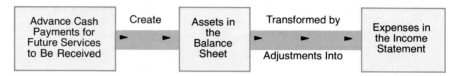

II. Entails computing the portion of advance payment previously received that has been earned (realized) in the current reporting period by performing a service or delivering goods to a customer:

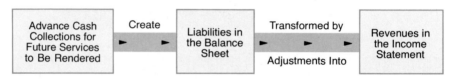

III. Entails computing the amount owed for goods and services rendered *for* the entity by outside parties such as suppliers and employees. Therefore the entity has an expense not previously recognized and a liability in the form of a legal obligation to pay:

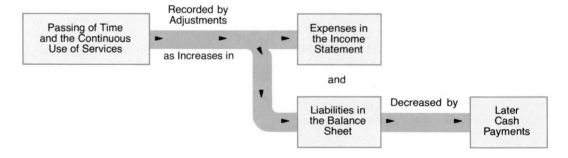

IV. Entails computing the amount owed by customers or clients for goods and services rendered by the entity. Therefore the entity has revenue not previously recognized and an asset in the form of a legal right to collect:

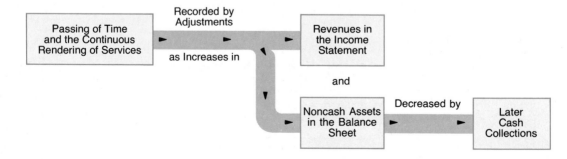

SUMMARY PROBLEM FOR YOUR REVIEW

☐ **Problem One**

Chan Co. is a retailer of stereo equipment. Chan has been in business one month. The company's trial balance, January 31, 19X2, has the following accounts:

Cash	$ 71,700	
Accounts receivable	160,300	
Note receivable	40,000	
Merchandise inventory	250,200	
Prepaid rent	15,000	
Store equipment	114,900	
Note payable		$100,000
Accounts payable		117,100
Unearned rent revenue		3,000
Paid-in capital		400,000
Sales		160,000
Cost of goods sold	100,000	
Wages expense	28,000	
Total	$780,100	$780,100

Consider the following adjustments on January 31:

a. January depreciation, $1,000.

b. On January 2, rent of $15,000 was paid in advance for the first quarter of 19X2. Adjust for January rent.

c. Wages earned by employees during January but not paid as of January 31 were $3,750.

d. Chan borrowed $100,000 from the bank on January 1. This explicit transaction was recorded when the business began. The principal and 9% interest are to be paid one year later (January 1, 19X3). However, an adjustment is necessary now for the interest expense of $750 for January.

e. On January 1, a cash loan of $40,000 was made to a local supplier. The promissory note stated that the loan is to be repaid one year later (January 1, 19X3), together with interest at 12% per annum. On January 31, an adjustment is needed to recognize the interest earned on the note receivable.

f. On January 15, a nearby corporation paid $3,000 cash to Chan Co. as an advance rental for Chan's storage space and equipment to be used temporarily from January 15 to April 15 (three months). On January 31, an adjustment is needed to recognize the rent revenue earned for one-half month.

g. Adjustment. Income tax expense was accrued on January income at a rate of 50% of income before taxes. (Income taxes are discussed later in this chapter, but prepare the adjustment now. Debit Income Tax Expense for $11,200 and credit Accrued Income Taxes Payable.)

Required:

1. Enter the trial balance amounts in the general ledger. Set up the following new asset account: Accrued Interest Receivable. Set up the following new liability accounts: Accrued Wages Payable, Accrued Interest Payable, and Accrued Income Taxes Payable. Set up the following new expense and revenue accounts: Depreciation Expense, Rent Expense, Interest Expense, Interest Revenue, Rent Revenue, and Income Tax Expense.
2. Journalize transactions (a)–(g) and post the entries to the ledger. Key entries by transaction letter.
3. Prepare a trial balance as of January 31, 19X2.

☐ Solution to Problem One

The solutions to requirements 1 through 3 are in Exhibits 4–2, 4–3, and 4–4, respectively. Accountants often refer to the final trial balance, Exhibit 4–4, as the adjusted trial balance. Why? Because all the necessary adjustments have been made, and the trial balance provides the data directly for the formal financial statements.

EXHIBIT 4–2

CHAN CO.
Journal Entries

(a)	Depreciation expense	1,000	
	Store equipment		1,000
	Depreciation for January.		
(b)	Rent expense	5,000	
	Prepaid rent		5,000
	Rent expense for January.		
(c)	Wages expense	3,750	
	Accrued wages payable		3,750
	Wages earned but not paid.		
(d)	Interest expense	750	
	Accrued interest payable		750
	Interest for January.		
(e)	Accrued interest receivable	400	
	Interest revenue		400
	Interest earned for January: 12% × $40,000 × 1/12 = $400.		
(f)	Unearned rent revenue	500	
	Rent revenue		500
	Rent earned for January. Rent per month is $3,000 ÷ 3 = $1,000; for one-half month, $500.		
(g)	Income tax expense	11,200	
	Accrued income taxes payable		11,200
	Income tax on January income.		

EXHIBIT 4–3

CHAN CO.
General Ledger

ASSETS	LIABILITIES + STOCKHOLDERS' EQUITY
(Increases left, decreases right)	(Decreases left, increases right)

Cash

Bal.	71,700	

Note Payable

		Bal.	100,000

Paid-in Capital

		Bal.	400,000

Accounts Receivable

Bal.	160,300	

Accounts Payable

		Bal.	117,100

Sales

		Bal.	160,000

Note Receivable

Bal.	40,000	

Unearned Rent Revenue

(f)	500	Bal.	3,000
		Bal.	2,500

Cost of Goods Sold

Bal.	100,000	

Merchandise Inventory

Bal.	250,200	

Accrued Wages Payable

		(c)	3,750

Wages Expense

Bal.	28,000	
(c)	3,750	
Bal	31,750	

Prepaid Rent

Bal.	15,000	(b)	5,000
Bal.	10,000		

Accrued Interest Payable

		(d)	750

Depreciation Expense

(a)	1,000	

Store Equipment

Bal.	114,900	(a)	1,000
Bal.	113,900		

Accrued Income Taxes Payable

		(g)	11,200

Rent Expense

(b)	5,000	

Accrued Interest Receivable

(e)	400	

Interest Expense

(d)	750	

Interest Revenue

		(e)	400

Rent Revenue

		(f)	500

Income Tax Expense

(g)	11,200	

EXHIBIT 4–4

CHAN CO.
Adjusted Trial Balance
January 31, 19X2

| ACCOUNT TITLE | BALANCE | |
	Debit	Credit
Cash	$ 71,700	
Accounts receivable	160,300	
Note receivable	40,000	
Merchandise inventory	250,200	
Prepaid rent	10,000	
Store equipment	113,900	
Accrued interest receivable	400	
Note payable		$100,000
Accounts payable		117,100
Unearned rent revenue		2,500
Accrued wages payable		3,750
Accrued interest payable		750
Accrued income taxes payable		11,200
Paid-in capital		400,000
Sales		160,000
Cost of goods sold	100,000	
Wages expense	31,750	
Depreciation expense	1,000	
Rent expense	5,000	
Interest expense	750	
Interest revenue		400
Rent revenue		500
Income tax expense	11,200	
Total	$796,200	$796,200

CLASSIFIED BALANCE SHEET

☐ **Current Assets and Liabilities**

There are now enough items to justify the preparation of a **classified balance sheet** for Chan Co., as in Exhibit 4–5. A balance sheet is *classified* when its items are grouped into various subcategories. You can readily imagine many more categories than are shown in Exhibit 4–5. At this stage, concentrate on the *current assets* and *current liabilities*. **Current assets** are cash plus assets that are expected to be converted to cash or sold or consumed during the next twelve months or within the normal operating cycle if longer than a year. Similarly, **current liabilities** are those liabilities that fall due within the coming year or within the normal operating cycle if longer than a year. **Working capital** is the excess of current assets over current liabilities.

Exhibit 4–5 shows only one long-term asset, Store Equipment, and no long-term liabilities. However, most balance sheets contain several long-term assets and at least one type of long-term debt.

The stockholders' equity is now $400,000 plus January net income of $11,200, or $411,200. Of course, the $11,200 does not appear as a separate

EXHIBIT 4–5

CHAN CO.
Balance Sheet
January 31, 19X2

ASSETS		LIABILITIES AND OWNERS' EQUITY		
Current assets:		Current liabilities:		
Cash	$ 71,700	Note payable	$100,000	
Accounts receivable	160,300	Accounts payable	117,100	
Note receivable	40,000	Unearned rent		
Accrued interest		revenue	2,500	
receivable	400	Accrued wages		
Merchandise		payable	3,750	
inventory	250,200	Accrued interest		
Prepaid rent	10,000	payable	750	
Total current		Accrued income		
assets	$532,600	taxes payable	11,200	
		Total current		
		liabilities		$235,300
Long-term asset:		Stockholders' equity:		
Store equipment	113,900	Paid-in capital	$400,000	
		Retained income	11,200	411,200
Total	$646,500	Total		$646,500

number in the trial balance. Instead the $11,200 is the net effect of all the balances in the revenue and expense accounts. The balance sheet condenses the $11,200 effect as retained income. (The next chapter will explain the journal entries necessary to achieve this effect.)

☐ Current Ratio

Users of balance sheets often worry about **solvency determination**. This is the assessment of the likelihood of an entity's ability to meet its financial obligations as they become due. Classifications of current assets and current liabilities can help assess solvency.

The **current ratio** (also called the **working capital ratio**) is widely used as a part of solvency determination. Chan's current ratio is

$$\text{Current ratio} = \frac{\text{Current assets}}{\text{Current liabilities}} = \frac{\$532,600}{\$235,300} = 2.3$$

Other things being equal, the higher the current ratio, the more assurance the creditor has about being paid in full and on time. Short-term creditors might use the current ratio to help gauge whether Chan is in a good position to pay current debts on time. The analyst will compare these measures through time and with similar companies and will make judgments accordingly.

In particular, the creditors look at the level of cash. However, ratios and similar measures have limitations, so creditors usually want some budget (prediction) of cash receipts and disbursements. For instance, does Chan have plenty of cash in relation to short-term liabilities? Whether cash is too high or too low really depends on the predictions of operating requirements over the coming months. Intelligent cash management would call for trying to invest any temporary excess cash to generate additional income.

☐ Formats of Balance Sheets

The particular form and detail of financial statements vary among companies. Consider the exact reproduction of the balance sheet of Hawaiian Airlines as shown in Exhibit 4–6. The format, indentation, and classifications are those actually presented. Note that no separate captions are used for noncurrent items. Many accountants would prefer to use captions such as *long-term assets* and *long-term liabilities*, respectively, to parallel the captions for *current assets* and *current liabilities*. Other accountants prefer not to use such captions when there are only one or two items within a specific class.

The Current Portion of Long-Term Debt is that part due within the coming year. The Air Traffic Liability is unearned revenue. It represents air-

EXHIBIT 4–6

HAWAIIAN AIRLINES, INC.
Condensed Balance Sheet (in thousands)
March 31, 1986

ASSETS	
Current Assets:	
Cash	$ 24,541
Accounts receivable	13,485
Inventories	2,305
Prepaid expenses and other current assets	3,453
Total current assets	43,784
Property and Equipment—less accumulated depreciation of $51,659	98,726
Other Assets	13,877
Total	$156,387

LIABILITIES AND STOCKHOLDERS' EQUITY	
Current Liabilities:	
Current portion of long-term debt	$ 6,710
Accounts payable	18,325
Accrued liabilities	6,541
Air traffic liability	13,518
Total current liabilities	45,094
Long-Term Debt	90,716
Other Liabilities	6,437
Stockholders' Equity:	
Common stock	5,752
Capital in excess of par value	4,709
Retained earnings	3,679
Total stockholders' equity	14,140
Total	$156,387

fares collected in advance from customers for services to be rendered. Note that the current liabilities exceed the current assets. Many airlines have continuing difficulties in generating enough cash to meet their obligations.

More is said about classifications and the analysis of the balance sheet in succeeding chapters, especially Chapter 16.

INCOME STATEMENT

We now continue the discussion of the income statement.

☐ Single- and Multiple-Step Statements

Most investors are vitally concerned about the company's ability to produce long-run earnings and dividends. In this regard, income statements are much more important than balance sheets.

Given the Chan Co. trial balance presented in Exhibit 4–4 (p. 126), consider the income statement shown in Exhibit 4–7, Part A. The statement there is called a **single-step income statement** because it merely groups all revenues together (sales plus interest and rent revenues) and then lists and deducts all expenses together without drawing any intermediate subtotals.

Another major form of income statement is the **multiple-step** statement. It contains one or more subtotals that often highlight significant relationships. For example, Exhibit 4–7, Part B, shows a **gross profit** figure (also called **gross margin**). *Gross profit* is defined as the excess of sales revenue over the cost of the inventory that was sold.

The next section of the multiple-step statement usually contains a group of recurring expenses that are often labeled as operating expenses because

EXHIBIT 4–7, PART A *Single-Step Income Statement*

CHAN CO.
Income Statement
For the Month Ended January 31, 19X2

Sales	$160,000	
Rent revenue	500	
Interest revenue	400	
Total sales and other revenues		$160,900
Expenses:		
Cost of goods sold	$100,000	
Wages	31,750	
Depreciation	1,000	
Rent	5,000	
Interest	750	
Income taxes	11,200	
Total expenses		149,700
Net income		$ 11,200

EXHIBIT 4–7, PART B *Multiple-Step Income Statement*

CHAN CO.
Income Statement
For the Month Ended January 31, 19X2

Sales		$160,000
Cost of goods sold		100,000
Gross profit		$ 60,000
Operating expenses:		
Wages	$ 31,750	
Depreciation	1,000	
Rent	5,000	37,750
Operating income		$ 22,250
Other revenue and expense:		
Rent revenue	$ 500	
Interest revenue	400	
Total other revenue	$ 900	
Deduct: Interest expense	750	150
Income before income taxes		$ 22,400
Income taxes (at 50%)		11,200
Net income		$ 11,200

they pertain to the firm's routine, ongoing operations. Examples are wages, rent, depreciation, and various other expenses such as telephone, heat, and advertising. These operating expenses are deducted from the gross profit to obtain **operating income**, which is also called **operating profit**. Of course, cost of goods sold could also be viewed as an operating expense because it is also deducted from sales revenue to obtain "operating income." However, because of its size and importance, it is usually deducted separately from sales revenue, as shown here.

The next grouping is usually called *other revenue and expense* (or *other income* or *other expense* or *nonoperating items* or some similar catchall title). These are not directly related to the mainstream of a firm's operations. The revenues are usually minor in relation to the revenues shown at the top of the income statement. The expenses are also minor, with one likely exception, interest expense.

Because interest expense is usually a result of *financial* rather than *operating* decisions, it appears as a separate item after operating income. In this way, comparisons of operating income between years and between companies are facilitated. Some companies make heavy use of debt, which causes high interest expenses, whereas other companies incur little debt and low interest expenses. The distinction between operating aspects and financial aspects can be illustrated by a news story about a faltering airline:

☐   The cost problems of Air Florida have essentially been *financial-cost* problems. In terms of basic *operating costs* of the airline, it is quite competitive. . . . Over the period 1977–1982, its fleet and route structure expanded, and its debt ballooned. [emphasis supplied]

In its ultimate sense, **profitability evaluation** is the assessment of the likelihood of a particular rate of return on an investment. Comparisons through time and within and among industries are used as a basis for predictions and decisions. Consider three of the most popular ratios for measuring profitability:

1. A multiple-step statement is often useful to a retailer in choosing a pricing strategy and in judging its results. Of particular interest is the **gross profit percentage**, or **gross margin percentage**, which is defined as gross profit divided by sales. The Chan gross profit percentage for January was

$$\text{Gross profit percentage} = \text{Gross profit} \div \text{Sales}$$
$$= \$60,000 \div \$160,000$$
$$= 37.5\%$$

These relationships can also be presented as follows:

	AMOUNT	PERCENTAGE
Sales	$160,000	100.0%
Cost of goods sold	100,000	62.5
Gross profit	$ 60,000	37.5

2. Obviously, the ratios of various expenses to sales will be carefully followed by managers from month to month. Users of financial statements are particularly concerned about the relationship of net income, the famous "bottom line," to two basic amounts. One of these is the sales figure:

$$\text{Return on sales} = \text{Net income} \div \text{Sales}$$
$$= \$11,200 \div \$160,000$$
$$= 7\%$$

3. Another basic amount with which net income is often compared is invested capital (as measured by average stockholders' equity). This ratio is widely regarded as the ultimate measure of overall accomplishment:

$$\text{Return on stockholders' equity} = \text{Net income} \div \text{Average stockholders' equity}$$
$$= 11,200 \div \tfrac{1}{2} \ (\text{January 1 balance, \$400,000} + \text{January 31}$$
$$\text{balance, \$411,200})$$
$$= \$11,200 \div \$405,600$$
$$= 2.8\% \ (\text{for one month})$$

These ratios are being introduced at this early stage because they are so widely encountered. The 37.5% gross profit is relatively low as compared with the usual 40% to 45% for the retail stereo industry. However, Chan has maintained excellent expense control because its 7% return on sales and its 33.6% return on stockholders' equity (an annual rate of $2.8 \times 12 = 33.6\%$)

are higher than the 6% and 18% annual returns usually earned by the industry.[2]

Statistical studies have shown that *profitability evaluation ratios* have higher power than *solvency determination ratios* (such as the current ratio) for predicting performance regarding *both* income and solvency.[3]

Later chapters study the uses and limitations of these and other ratios. For example, Chapter 6 explores the analytical role of gross profit percentages, and Chapter 16 reviews the most widely used ratios.

☐ Accrual of Income Taxes

Income taxes are worldwide, although rates and details differ from country to country and state to state. Corporations in the United States are subject to federal and state corporate income taxes. Tax rates are progressive; taxable income over $100,000 is taxed at the maximum rate. The rates are changed almost yearly by either the U.S. Congress or the state legislatures or both. For many corporations, the federal-plus-state income tax rates hover around 50%.

Various labels are used for income taxes on the income statement: *income tax expense*, *provision for income taxes*, and just plain *income taxes* are found most frequently. About 85% of publicly held companies show federal income taxes as a separate last item just before net income. In contrast, the other 15% list federal income taxes along with other operating expenses such as wages, as is shown in the Occidental Petroleum statement in the next section of this chapter. A recent IBM annual report contains the format adopted by the vast majority of companies:

Earnings before income taxes	$5,092,414,000
Provision for income taxes	2,373,000,000
Net earnings	$2,719,414,000

Income tax expenses are accrued each month (not just once a year) as income before income taxes is generated. A popular synonym for income before income taxes is **pretax income**. The amount of the accrual for income taxes obviously depends on the amount of pretax income.

---

[2] Of course, returns on investments in partnerships are also computed. Consider this letter from the managing partner of the Fresno Ramada Inn: "In the Annual Report that was recently mailed, we found a typographical error in the discussion of operations which referred to a return of '$375,000 per $1,000 Partnership Capital Unit.' The Motel is a good investment, but not that good. It should have read '$375.00 per $1,000 Partnership Capital Units.' We apologize for the error."

[3] For an excellent presentation of the modern thinking in this area, see George Foster, *Financial Statement Analysis*, 2nd ed. (Englewood Cliffs, N.J.: Prentice-Hall, 1986).

ILLUSTRATIONS OF INCOME STATEMENTS

This section demonstrates how various entities may use assorted terminology and formats for their individual statements of income. Note throughout that extremely condensed income statement information is provided in published reports (as opposed to the detail that is shown for internal users). All the income statements below cover a *fiscal year*, which may not coincide with a calendar year. A **fiscal year** is defined as the year established for accounting purposes for the preparation of annual reports. To save space, the separate lines indicating the years are omitted; however, the particular titles of the statements are shown.

from Cluett

Cluett, Peabody & Co. (makers of Arrow Shirts)
STATEMENT OF INCOME AND RETAINED EARNINGS

REVENUES:	
Sales	$589,389,000
Royalty income (from use of Sanforization process)	8,816,000
Other income	134,000
Total revenue	$598,339,000
COSTS AND EXPENSES:	
Cost of sales and royalty related expenses	$448,121,000
Selling, general and administrative expenses	109,742,000
Interest expense	4,561,000
Total costs and expenses	$562,424,000
Income before income taxes	$ 35,915,000
Income taxes	16,642,000
Net income	$ 19,273,000
Retained earnings, January 1	120,966,000
Subtotal	$140,239,000
Cash dividends declared	6,024,000
Retained earnings, December 31	$134,215,000

Cluett, Peabody uses a combined statement of income and retained earnings. Its income statement uses a *single-step* format, *as do most corporate external reports*. In general, a single-step income statement merely groups all revenues together and all expenses together without drawing subtotals within revenue and expense categories.

Accountants use the label *net* to denote that some amounts have been deducted in computing the final result. In a statement of income, the term *net* is not ordinarily used to describe any subtotals of income that precede the final net income number. For example, the Cluett, Peabody statement shows "*income* before income taxes," not "*net income* before income taxes."

The term "costs and expenses" is sometimes found instead of just "expenses." "Expenses" would be an adequate description. Why? Because the "costs" listed on the income statement are "expired costs," such as "cost of sales," and thus are really expenses of the current period.

Although Cluett, Peabody uses a single-step income statement, note where income taxes appear. Most companies follow this practice of showing income taxes as a separate item immediately above net income (regardless of the grouping of the other items on the income statement).

Also note the inconsistent use of the terms *income* and *earnings* (a frequent occurrence). That is, net *income* is used in one place, but retained *earnings* in another place. Such usage is common. However, to be completely consistent, retained *income* should be paired with net *income*, and retained *earnings* should be paired with net *earnings*.

Occidental Petroleum Corporation
STATEMENT OF OPERATIONS

REVENUES:		
Net sales		$6,017,517,000
Interest and other income		62,214,000
Total revenues		$6,079,731,000
EXPENSES:		
Cost of sales	$4,706,095,000	
Selling, general and administrative and other operating expenses	373,234,000	
Provision for domestic and foreign income, franchise and other taxes	677,720,000	
Interest expense	95,762,000	
Other expenses	9,008,000	
Total expenses		5,861,819,000
Net income		$ 217,912,000

Note that Occidental uses the title *statement of operations*. It also uses an extreme version of the single-step income statement. That is, its tabulation of expenses lists cost of sales; selling, general, and administrative expenses; income taxes; and interest expense in almost indiscriminate fashion in the sense that income taxes are placed in the midst of its expenses rather than just before the presentation of the net income line.

SRI International
STATEMENT OF REVENUE, COSTS, AND EXPENSES

Project revenue	$113,878,000
Costs and expenses, predominately salaries and wages (detailed)	112,032,000
Net excess of revenue over costs and expenses	$ 1,846,000

SRI International, a nonprofit organization that does consulting services, also has a bottom line in its statement of operations. However, instead of using terms like "net income" or "net profit," these organizations tend to use "net operating result" or the lengthy but more descriptive term shown here. SRI International is not subject to income taxes.

BankAmerica Corporation
STATEMENT OF INCOME (dollar amounts in thousands)

Interest revenue	$12,078,816
Interest expense	8,874,179
Interest revenue less interest expense	3,204,637
Noninterest revenue	1,457,801
Personnel expense	2,156,495
Other expense	2,052,844
Income before income taxes	453,099
Provision for income taxes	107,574
Net income	$ 345,525

BankAmerica Corporation provides a typical income statement for banks and savings institutions. They raise money from one major source (depositors) and then invest it (largely in the form of loans). Their net income (net earnings) depends on the spread between their "borrowing rate," which must be paid to depositors, and their "lending rate," which is earned on their loans and investments.

The format of the BankAmerica statement could be confusing. Why? BankAmerica merely lists noninterest revenue, personnel expense, and other expense as though each should be added to the $3,204,637 figure. However, the $453,099 income before income taxes is computed by *adding* the noninterest revenue of $1,457,801 to the $3,204,637 and *deducting* the personnel expense and other expense. Showing additional subtotals would be an improvement.

SUMMARY

At the end of each accounting period, adjustments must be made so that financial statements can be presented on a full-fledged accrual basis. The major adjustments are for (1) the expiration of unexpired costs, (2) the realization (earning) of unearned revenues, (3) the accrual of unrecorded expenses, and (4) the accrual of unrecorded revenues.

Classified balance sheets divide various items into subcategories. For example, assets and liabilities are separated into current and long-term.

Income statements usually appear in single-step, condensed form in published annual reports and in multiple-step, detailed form in the reports used within an organization.

SUMMARY PROBLEMS FOR YOUR REVIEW

The first problem appeared earlier in the chapter, page 123.

☐ Problem Two

Time Incorporated is a diversified company best known for such magazines as *Time*, *Sports Illustrated*, *People*, and *Fortune*. The company had the following transactions (among others) during the year 19X1:

1. Equipment was acquired on August 1 for $48,000. It has a useful life of four years and no expected terminal salvage value. Depreciation will be accounted for by the straight-line method.
2. A three-year fire insurance policy was purchased on March 31 for $3,600 cash. (Prepaid Insurance was increased and Cash was decreased.)
3. In a special campaign to raise money from Beverly Hills subscribers, Time sold some two-year subscriptions for *People* on November 1 for $24,000 cash. (Cash was increased and Unearned Subscription Revenue was increased.) Magazines were delivered to these subscribers in November and December.
4. Wages earned by employees but unpaid on December 31 were $28,000.
5. On May 1, Time had lent $100,000 cash to a building contractor on a one-year note with 15% interest payable at maturity.

Required:

For the year ended December 31, 19X1, prepare all adjustments called for by the above transactions. Assume that appropriate entries were routinely made for the explicit transactions described above. However, no adjustments have been made before December 31. For each adjustment, prepare an analysis in the same format used when the adjustment process was explained in the chapter. Also prepare a journal entry for each adjustment. Omit explanations.

☐ Solution to Problem Two

	A	=	L	+	SE
	Equipment				Depreciation Expense
1. Depreciation is: $48,000 ÷ 48 = $1,000 per month, or $5,000 for the five months from August 1 to December 31.	−5,000	=			−5,000

Journal entry:

Depreciation expense	5,000	
Equipment		5,000

	A	=	L	+	SE
	Prepaid Insurance				Insurance Expense
2. Insurance expense is: $3,600 ÷ 36 = $100 per month, or $900 for the nine months from March 31 to December 31.	−900	=			−900

Journal entry:

Insurance expense	900	
Prepaid insurance		900

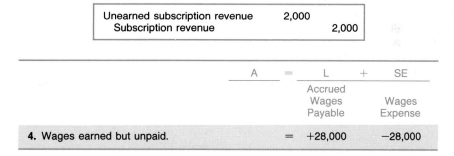

	A	=	L	+	SE
			Unearned Subscription Revenue		Subscription Revenue
3. Subscription revenue is: $24,000 ÷ 24 = $1,000 per month, or $2,000 for the two months of November and December.		=	−2,000		+2,000

Journal entry:

Unearned subscription revenue	2,000	
Subscription revenue		2,000

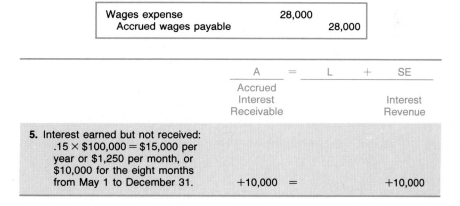

	A	=	L	+	SE
			Accrued Wages Payable		Wages Expense
4. Wages earned but unpaid.		=	+28,000		−28,000

Journal entry:

Wages expense	28,000	
Accrued wages payable		28,000

	A	=	L	+	SE
	Accrued Interest Receivable				Interest Revenue
5. Interest earned but not received: .15 × $100,000 = $15,000 per year or $1,250 per month, or $10,000 for the eight months from May 1 to December 31.	+10,000	=			+10,000

Journal entry:

Accrued interest receivable	10,000	
Interest revenue		10,000

□ Problem Three

Refer to the preceding problem. Assume that the other parties to the transactions used the accrual basis of accounting. For adjustments 2 and 5, prepare an analysis in the same format for the insurance company and the building contractor, respectively. Also prepare a journal entry for each adjustment. Omit explanations.

□ Solution to Problem Three

	A	=	L	+	SE
			Unearned Insurance Revenue		Insurance Revenue
2. Insurance premiums earned		=	−900		+900

Journal entry:

Unearned insurance revenue	900	
Insurance revenue		900

	A	=	L	+	SE
			Accrued Interest Payable		Interest Expense
5. Interest expense for eight months		=	+10,000		−10,000

Journal entry:

Interest expense	10,000	
Accrued interest payable		10,000

HIGHLIGHTS TO REMEMBER

1. Frequently, accounting adjustments are clarified when they are seen as mirror images by looking at both sides of the adjustment simultaneously. For example, (a) the expiration of unexpired costs (the tenant's rent expense) is accompanied by (b) the earning of unearned revenues (the landlord's rent revenue).
2. Similarly, (a) the accrual of unrecorded expenses (a borrower's interest expense) is accompanied by (b) the accrual of unrecorded revenues (a lender's interest revenue).
3. Income tax expense is usually accrued monthly (based on pretax income for the month), regardless of when cash is disbursed. Income tax expense usually appears just before the net income line on the income statement.
4. Interest expense is typically classified separately from operating expenses.

ACCOUNTING VOCABULARY

Accrue, p. 118 Adjusting Entries, 115 Adjustments, 115 Classified Balance Sheet, 126 Current Assets, 126 Current Liabilities, 126 Current Ratio, 127 Deferred Credit, 117 Deferred Income, 118 Deferred Revenue, 117 Explicit Transactions, 115 Fiscal Year, 133 Gross Margin, 129 Gross Margin Percentage, 131 Gross Profit, 129 Gross Profit Percentage, 131 Implicit Transactions, 115 Multiple-Step Income Statement, 129 Operating Income, 130 Operating Profit, 130 Pretax Income, 132 Profitability Evaluation, 131 Single-Step Income Statement, 129 Solvency Determination, 127 Unearned Income, 118 Unearned Revenue, 117 Working Capital, 126 Working Capital Ratio, 127.

FUNDAMENTAL ASSIGNMENT MATERIAL

□ **General Coverage**

4–1. **ADJUSTING ENTRIES.** (Alternates are 4–3, 4–4, and 4–26.) Mia Rinaldi, certified public accountant, had the following transactions (among others) during 19X2:

a. For accurate measurement of performance and position, Rinaldi uses the accrual basis of accounting. On August 1, Rinaldi acquired office supplies for $2,000. Office Supplies Inventory was increased and Cash was decreased by $2,000 on Rinaldi's books. On December 31, Rinaldi's inventory was $800.
b. On September 1, a client gave Rinaldi a retainer fee of $36,000 cash for monthly services to be rendered over the following twelve months. Rinaldi increased Cash and Unearned Fee Revenue.
c. Rinaldi accepted a $10,000 note receivable from a client on October 1 for tax services. The note plus interest of 12% per year were due in six months. Rinaldi increased Note Receivable and Fee Revenue for $10,000.
d. As of December 31, Rinaldi had not recorded $500 of unpaid wages earned by her secretary during late December.

Required:

For the year ended December 31, 19X2, prepare all adjustments called for by the above transactions. Assume that appropriate entries were routinely made for the explicit transactions described above. However, no adjustments have been made before December 31. For each adjustment, prepare an analysis in the same format used when the adjustment process was explained in the chapter. Also prepare the adjusting journal entry.

4–2. **MULTIPLE-STEP INCOME STATEMENT.** (Alternate is 4–5). From the following data, prepare a multiple-step income statement for the Martin Company for the fiscal year ended May 31, 19X5 (in thousands except for percentage). *Hint*: see page 130.

Interest expense	$ 72	Cost of goods sold	$550
Rent expense	50	Depreciation	30
Sales	950	Rent revenue	10
Interest revenue	12	Wages	200
Income tax rate	40%		

☐ Understanding Published Financial Reports

4–3. **FOUR MAJOR ADJUSTMENTS.** (Alternates are 4–1, 4–4, and 4–26.) The Goodyear Tire and Rubber Company included the following items in its January 31, 1986, balance sheet (in millions):

Prepaid expenses (a current asset)	$ 54
Domestic and foreign taxes (a current liability)	290

Required:

Analyze the impact of the following transactions on the financial position of Goodyear. Prepare your analysis in the same format used when the adjustment process was explained in the chapter. Also show adjusting journal entries.

1. On January 31, an adjustment of $1 million was made for the rentals of various retail outlets that had originally increased Prepaid Expenses but had expired.
2. During December 1985, Goodyear sold tires for $1 million cash to Consolidated Freightways, but delivery was not made until January 28. Unearned Revenue had been increased in December. No other adjustments had been made since. Prepare the adjustment on January 31.
3. Goodyear had lent cash to several of its independent retail dealers. As of January 31, the dealers owed $2 million of interest that had been unrecorded.
4. On January 31, Goodyear increased its accrual of federal income taxes by $17 million.

4–4. **FOUR MAJOR ADJUSTMENTS.** (Alternates are 4–1, 4–3, and 4–26.) Delta Airlines had the following items in its balance sheet, June 30, 1986, the end of the fiscal year:

Maintenance and operating supplies	$ 35,197,000
Prepaid expenses and other current assets	30,969,000
Air traffic liability	297,633,000
Accrued income taxes	13,007,000

A footnote stated: "Passenger ticket sales are recorded as revenue when the transportation is used. The value of unused tickets is included in current liabilities in the financial statements." The title of this current liability is Air Traffic Liability. The income statement included:

Passenger revenues	$3,963,610,000
Income taxes provided	102,625,000

Required:

Analyze the impact of the following assumed transactions on the financial position of Delta. Prepare your analysis in the same format used when the adjustment process was explained in the chapter. Also show adjusting journal entries.

1. Rented a sales office in a BankAmerica office building for one year, beginning June 1, 1986, for $12,000 cash.
2. On June 30, 1986, an adjustment was made for the rent in requirement 1.
3. Sold two charter flights to Texas Instruments for $90,000 each. Cash of $180,000 was received in advance on May 20, 1986. The flights were for transporting marketing personnel to two business conventions in New York.
4. As the financial statements were being prepared on June 30, accountants for both Delta and Texas Instruments independently noted that the first charter flight had occurred in late June. The second would occur in early August. An adjustment was made on June 30.
5. Delta had lent $2 million to Boeing. Interest of $160,000 was accrued on June 30.
6. Additional federal income taxes of $100,000 were accrued on June 30.

4–5. **BUDWEISER FINANCIAL STATEMENTS.** (Alternate is 4–2.) Anheuser-Busch (maker of Budweiser beer) is the largest beer producer in the United States. Some financial data from an annual report were (in millions):

Anheuser-Busch, Inc.

Interest expense	$ 32	Cash dividends declared	?
Sales	3,847	Net income	$ 217
Gross profit	872	Retained earnings:	
Operating income	357	Beginning of year	929
Marketing, administrative,		End of year	1,095
and research expenses	?	Provision for income taxes	
Cost of products sold	?	(income tax expense)	108

Required:

1. Prepare a combined multiple-step statement of income and retained earnings for the year ended December 31, 1986. *Hint:* see page 130.
2. Compute the percentage of gross profit on sales and the percentage of net income on sales.
3. The average stockholders' equity for the year was $1,119 million. What was the percentage of net income on average stockholders' equity?

ADDITIONAL ASSIGNMENT MATERIAL

☐ General Coverage

4–6. Give two examples of an explicit transaction.
4–7. Give two examples of an implicit transaction.
4–8. Give two synonyms for *deferred revenue*.

4–9. Explain the difference between *incur* and *accrue*.

4–10. "Accountants often use routine shortcuts when they record expenses." Explain, giving an illustration.

4–11. Distinguish between the return *on* investment and the return *of* investment.

4–12. "The accrual of previously unrecorded revenues is the mirror image of the accrual of previously unrecorded expenses." Explain, using an illustration.

4–13. Explain the difference between a *single-step* and a *multiple-step* income statement.

4–14. Why does interest expense appear below operating income on a multiple-step income statement?

4–15. Name three popular ratios for measuring profitability.

4–16. Give a popular synonym for *income before income taxes*.

4–17. Give a synonym for *income tax expense*.

4–18. Explain why income tax expense is usually the final deduction on both single-step and multiple-step income statements.

4–19. **TRUE OR FALSE.** Use *T* or *F* to indicate whether each of the following statements is true or false.

1. The cash balance is the best evidence of stockholders' equity.
2. From a single balance sheet you can find stockholders' equity for a period of time but not for a specific day.
3. It is not possible to determine change in the condition of a business from a single balance sheet.
4. Retained Earnings should be accounted for as a current asset item.
5. Cash should be classified as a stockholders' equity item.
6. Machinery used in the business should be recorded as a noncurrent asset item.

4–20. **TENANT AND LANDLORD.** The Iglehart Company, a retail hardware store, pays quarterly rent on its store at the beginning of each quarter. The rent per quarter is $9,000. The owner of the building in which the store is located is the Rouse Corporation.

Required:

Using the balance sheet equation format, analyze the effects of the following on the tenant's and the landlord's financial position:

1. Iglehart pays $9,000 rent on July 1.
2. Adjustment for July.
3. Adjustment for August.
4. Adjustment for September. Also prepare the journal entry.

4–21. **CUSTOMER AND AIRLINE.** The Levitz Furniture Company decided to hold a managers' meeting in Hawaii in February. To take advantage of special fares, Levitz purchased airline tickets in advance from United Airlines at a total cost of $90,000. These were acquired on December 1 for cash.

Required:

Using the balance sheet equation format, analyze the impact of the December payment and the February travel on the financial position of both Levitz and United. Also prepare journal entries for February.

4–22. **ACCRUALS OF WAGES.** Consider the following calendar:

APRIL
S	M	T	W	T	F	S
		1	2	3	4	5
6	7	8	9	10	11	12
13	14	15	16	17	18	19
20	21	22	23	24	25	26
27	28	29	30			

The Ace Department Store commenced business on April 1. It is open every day except Sunday. Its total payroll for all employees is $10,000 per day. Payments are made each Tuesday for the preceding week's work through Saturday.

Required:

Using the balance sheet equation format, analyze the financial impact on Ace of the following:

1. Disbursements for wages on April 8, 15, 22, and 29.
2. Adjustment for wages on April 30. Also prepare the journal entry.

4–23. **PLACEMENT OF INTEREST IN INCOME STATEMENT.** Two companies have the following balance sheets as of December 31, 19X2:

COMPANY A

Cash	$100,000	Note payable*	$200,000
Other assets	300,000	Stockholders' equity	200,000
Total	$400,000	Total	$400,000

* 12% interest.

COMPANY B

Cash	$100,000	Stockholders' equity	$400,000
Other assets	300,000		
Total	$400,000		

In 19X3, each company had sales of $900,000 and expenses (excluding interest) of $800,000. Ignore income taxes.

Required:

Did each company earn the same net income? The same operating income? Explain, showing computations of operating income and net income.

4–24. **IDENTIFICATION OF TRANSACTIONS.** Correlation Corporation's financial position is represented by the nine balances shown on the first line of the following schedule (in thousands of dollars). Assume that a single transaction took place for each of the following lines, and describe what you think happened, using one short sentence for each line.

	CASH	ACCOUNTS RECEIVABLE	INVENTORY	EQUIPMENT	ACCOUNTS PAYABLE	ACCRUED WAGES PAYABLE	UNEARNED RENT REVENUE	PAID-IN CAPITAL	RETAINED INCOME
Bal.	14	32	54	0	29	0	0	50	21
(1)	24	32	54	0	29	0	0	60	21
(2)	24	32	54	20	29	0	0	80	21
(3)	24	32	66	20	41	0	0	80	21
(4a)	24	47	66	20	41	0	0	80	36
(4b)	24	47	58	20	41	0	0	80	28
(5)	30	41	58	20	41	0	0	80	28
(6)	10	41	58	20	21	0	0	80	28
(7)	14	41	58	20	21	0	4	80	28
(8)	14	41	58	20	21	2	4	80	26
(9)	14	41	58	19	21	2	4	80	25
(10)	14	41	58	19	21	2	3	80	26

4–25. EFFECTS ON BALANCE SHEET EQUATION. Following is a list of effects of accounting transactions on the basic accounting equation: Assets equal Liabilities plus Stockholders' Equity.

a. Increase in assets, increase in liabilities
b. Increase in assets, decrease in liabilities
c. Increase in assets, increase in stockholders' equity
d. Increase in assets, decrease in assets
e. Decrease in assets, decrease in liabilities
f. Increase in liabilities, decrease in stockholders' equity
g. Decrease in assets, increase in liabilities
h. Decrease in liabilities, increase in stockholders' equity
i. Decrease in assets, decrease in stockholders' equity
j. None of these

Which of the above relationships defines the accounting effect of each of the following?

1. The adjusting entry to record accrued salaries.
2. The adjusting entry to record accrued interest receivable.
3. The collection of interest previously accrued.
4. The settlement of an account payable by the issuance of a note payable.
5. The earning of income previously collected. Unearned Revenue was increased when collection was made in advance.
6. The recognition of an expense that had been paid for previously. A "prepaid" account was increased upon payment.
7. The adjusting entry to recognize periodic depreciation.

4–26. FOUR MAJOR ADJUSTMENTS. (Alternates are 4–1, 4–3, and 4–4.) Maria Aparicio, an attorney, had the following transactions (among others) during 19X2, her initial year in practicing law:

a. On August 1, Aparicio leased office space for one year. The landlord (lessor) insisted on full payment in advance. Prepaid Rent was increased and Cash was decreased by $12,000 on Aparicio's books. Similarly, the landlord increased Cash and increased Unearned Rent Revenue.
b. On October 1, Aparicio received a retainer fee of $24,000 cash for services to be rendered to her client, a local trucking company, over the succeeding twelve months. Aparicio increased Cash and Unearned Fee Revenue. The trucking company increased Prepaid Expenses and decreased Cash.
c. As of December 31, Aparicio had not recorded $300 of unpaid wages earned by her secretary during late December.
d. During November and December, Aparicio rendered services to another client, a utility company. She had intended to bill the company for $3,200 services through December 31, but she decided to delay formal billing until late January when the case would probably be settled.

Required:

1. For the year ended December 31, 19X2, prepare all adjustments called for by the above transactions. Assume that appropriate entries were routinely made for the explicit transactions described above. However, no adjustments have been made before December 31. For each adjustment, prepare an analysis in the same format used when the adjustment process was explained in the chapter. Prepare two adjustments for each transaction, one for Aparicio and one for the other party to the transaction. In part *c*, assume that the secretary uses the accrual basis for his personal entity.
2. For each transaction, prepare the journal entries for Maria Aparicio *and* the other entities involved.

4–27. ACCOUNTING FOR DUES. (Alternates are 4–28 and 4–29.) The Vasquez Athletic Club provided the following data from its comparative balance sheets:

	DECEMBER 31	
	19X2	19X1
Dues receivable	$30,000	$25,000
Unearned dues revenue	—	10,000

The income statement for 19X2, which was prepared on the accrual basis, showed dues revenue earned of $240,000.

Required:

Prepare journal entries and post to T-accounts for the following:

1. Billing of $25,000 of dues in 19X1. Billing occurs after dues have been earned. However, dues collected in advance are not billed.
2. Collections of $10,000 of unearned dues in advance during the final week of 19X1.
3. Billing of dues revenue during 19X2.
4. Collection of dues receivable in 19X2.
5. Earning of dues collected in advance.

4–28. **ACCOUNTING FOR SUBSCRIPTIONS.** (Alternate is 4–27.) A magazine company collects subscriptions in advance of delivery of its magazines. However, many magazines are delivered to magazine distributors (for newsstand sales), and these distributors are billed and pay later. The subscription revenue earned for the month of December on the accrual basis was $210,000. Other pertinent data were:

	DECEMBER	
	31	1
Unearned subscription revenue	$170,000	$120,000
Subscriptions receivable	7,000	9,000

Required:

Reconstruct the entries for December. Prepare journal entries and post to T-accounts for the following:

1. Collections of unearned subscription revenue of $120,000 prior to December 1.
2. Billing of subscriptions receivable (a) of $9,000 prior to December 1, and (b) of $80,000 during December. (Credit Revenue Earned.)
3. Collections of cash during December and any other entries that are indicated by the given data.

4–29. **RENTAL MANAGEMENT.** (Alternates are 4–27 and 4–28.) A real estate company's operations frequently include the management of various properties and collections of rents. Most rentals are paid in advance, some for two or more months at a time. Some are billed and payment is received at the end of the rental period or later. Consider the following data for December (in thousands):

Rent revenue earned, accrual basis	?
Rent collections during December:	
In advance and unearned	2,750
On receivables	250

Pertinent balances were:

	DEC. 31	NOV. 30
Unearned rental revenue	$2,000	$200
Rent receivable	700	300

Required:

Post the November 30 balances to the unearned rental revenue and rent receivable T-accounts. Then journalize and post the appropriate entries for December:

1. Rent collections.
2. Any adjustments or other entries indicated in order to obtain December 31 balances as given.
3. What is the amount of the rent revenue earned on the accrual basis?

4–30. **FINANCIAL STATEMENTS AND ADJUSTMENTS.** Connection Distributors, Inc., has just completed its third year of business, 19X3. A set of financial statements was prepared by the principal stockholder's eldest child, a college student who is beginning the third week of an accounting course. Following is a list (in no systematic order) of the items appearing in the student's balance sheet, income statement, and statement of retained income:

Accounts receivable	$175,100	Merchandise inventory	$201,900
Note receivable	36,000	Cost of goods sold	590,000
Cash	87,300	Unearned rent revenue	4,800
Paid-in capital	600,000	Insurance expense	2,500
Building	280,000	Unexpired insurance	2,300
Land	169,200	Accounts payable	52,500
Sales	936,800	Interest expense	600
Salary expense	124,300	Telephone expense	2,900
Retained income:		Notes payable	20,000
December 31, 19X2	164,000	Net income	110,500
December 31, 19X3	274,500	Miscellaneous expense	4,400
Advertising expense	98,300	Maintenance expense	3,300

Assume that the statements in which these items appear are current and complete except for the following matters not taken into consideration by the student:

a. Salaries of $5,200 have been earned by employees for the last half of December 19X3. Payment by the company will be made on the next payday, January 2, 19X4.
b. Interest at 10% per annum on the note receivable has accrued for two months and is expected to be collected by the company when the note is due on January 31, 19X4.
c. Part of the building owned by the company was rented to a tenant on November 1, 19X3, for six months, payable in advance. This rent was collected in cash and is represented by the item labeled Unearned Rent Revenue.
d. Depreciation on the building for 19X3 is $6,100.
e. Cash dividends of $60,000 were declared in December 19X3, payable in January 19X4.
f. Income tax at 50% applies to 19X3, all of which is to be paid in the early part of 19X4.

Required:

Prepare the following corrected financial statements:

1. Multiple-step income statement for 19X3.
2. Statement of retained income for 19X3.
3. Classified balance sheet at December 31, 19X3. (Show appropriate support for the dollar amounts you compute.)

4–31. **MIRROR SIDE OF ADJUSTMENTS.** Problem 4–3 described some Goodyear adjustments. Repeat the requirements for each adjustment as it would be made by (1) landlords, (2) Consolidated Freightways, (3) retail dealers, and (4) U.S. government.

4–32. **MIRROR SIDE OF ADJUSTMENTS.** Problem 4–4 described some Delta Airlines adjustments. Repeat the requirements for each adjustment as it would be made by (1) BankAmerica, (2) BankAmerica, (3) Texas Instruments, (4) Texas Instruments, (5) Boeing, and (6) U.S. government.

4–33. **EFFECTS OF INTEREST ON LENDERS AND BORROWERS.** Sears lent Riegal Paint Manufacturing Company $900,000 on March 1, 19X1. The loan plus interest of 12% is payable on March 1, 19X2.

Required:

1. Using the balance sheet equation format, prepare an analysis of the impact of the transactions on both Sears's and Riegal's financial position on March 1, 19X1. Show the summary adjustment on December 31, 19X1, for the period March 1–December 31.
2. Prepare adjusting journal entries for Sears and Riegal.

4–34. **ACCRUED VACATION PAY.** Delta Airlines had the following as a current liability on its balance sheet, June 30, 1986:

Accrued vacation pay	$74,754

Under the accrual basis of accounting, vacation pay is ordinarily accrued throughout the year as workers are regularly paid. For example, suppose a Delta baggage handler earns $600 per week for fifty weeks and also gets paid $1,200 for two weeks' vacation. Accrual accounting requires that the obligation for the $1,200 be recognized as it is earned rather than when the payment is disbursed. Thus, in each of the fifty weeks Delta would recognize a wage expense (or vacation pay expense) of $1,200 ÷ 50 = $24.

Required:

1. Prepare the weekly Delta adjusting journal entry called for by the $24 example.
2. Prepare the entry for the $1,200 payment of vacation pay.

4–35. **JOURNAL ENTRIES AND POSTING.** General Foods Corporation is a processor and marketer of many food products, including Maxwell House coffee, Jell-O, and Birds Eye frozen foods. The company's balance sheets included (in thousands):

	MARCH 31	
	1986	1985
Prepaid expenses	$57,468	$35,911
Accrued income taxes	76,479	89,151

During the fiscal year ended March 31, 1986, $100 million cash was disbursed and charged to Prepaid Expenses. Similarly, $196 million was disbursed for income taxes and charged to Accrued Income Taxes.

Required:

1. Assume that the Prepaid Expenses account relates to outlays for miscellaneous operating expenses (for example, supplies, insurance, and short-term rentals). Prepare summary journal entries for (a) the disbursements and (b) the expenses for fiscal 1986. Post the entries to the T-accounts.

2. Assume that there were no other accounts related to income taxes. Prepare summary journal entries for (a) the disbursements and (b) the expenses for fiscal 1986. Post the entries to T-accounts.

4–36. ADVANCE SERVICE CONTRACTS. Savin Corporation, a manufacturer in the office copier industry, showed the following balance sheet accounts:

	APRIL 30	
	19X2	19X1
Deferred income, principally service contracts (Note 1)	$6,354,893	$4,062,580

Note 1 stated: "The Company bills customers in advance for service contracts. Advance service contract billings are deferred and reflected in income ratably over the term of the contract."

Required:

1. Prepare summary journal entries for the creation in 19X1 and subsequent earning in 19X2 of the deferred income of $4,062,580. Use the following accounts: Accounts Receivable, Deferred Income, and Income from Service Contracts.
2. Post the journal entries to T-accounts.
3. A one-year service contract was billed to the Mount Sinai Hospital on January 1, 19X2, for $1,200. The full amount was collected on February 15. Prepare all pertinent journal entries through February 28, 19X2. ("Ratably" means an equal amount per month.)

4–37. JOURNAL ENTRIES AND ADJUSTMENTS. Portland General Electric Company is a public utility in Oregon. An annual report included the following footnote:

☐ Revenues—Revenues have been recorded as customers' meters were read, principally on a cycle basis throughout each month. This resulted in revenue being earned but not billed at the end of an accounting period. The changes in unbilled revenues from year to year were generally not significant. Due to the accelerating increase in rate levels and costs, the disparity between billed revenues and costs increased significantly. Accordingly, effective January 1 of this year, the Company changed to a method of accounting to accrue the amount of estimated unbilled revenues for services provided to the month end to more closely match revenues and costs.

The income statements showed:

	19X2	19X1
Operating revenues	$303,678,000	$253,073,000
Operating income	83,239,000	73,127,000

The balance sheet showed as part of current assets (amounts in thousands):

	DECEMBER 31	
	19X2	19X1
Receivables, customer accounts	$22,477,000	$19,176,000
Estimated unbilled revenues	20,209,000	—

1. Prepare the adjusting journal entry for (a) the unbilled revenues at the end of 19X2 and (b) the eventual billing and collection of the unbilled revenues. Ignore income taxes.
2. Which of the accounts shown above would have been affected if the company had not adopted the new policy? Give the name of each account and the amount of the effect. Ignore income taxes.

4–38. **POSTAL SERVICE ACCOUNTING.** The U.S. Postal Service is a separate federal entity created by the Postal Reform Act. The Postal Service financial statements are audited by an independent accounting firm. Its current liabilities for a given year included:

Prepaid permit mail and box rentals	$329,355,000
Estimated prepaid postage—Note 1	770,000,000

Note 1 stated: "Estimated prepaid postage represents the estimated revenue collected prior to the end of the year for which services will be subsequently rendered."

The Postal Service's statement of operations showed "operating revenue" of $19,133,041,000.

The current assets included "Receivables, U.S. Government," of $126,890,000.

1. Provide alternative descriptions for the two accounts.
2. A large retailer, Sears, has rented boxes in thousands of post offices to accelerate receipts from customers. Suppose $1 million of those rentals that were prepaid by Sears had expired as of September 30. Journalize a $1 million adjustment for expired rentals on the accounts of the Postal Service and Sears.
3. Many mail-order retailers prepay postage. In addition, millions of citizens buy rolls of postage stamps for later use. Note 1 describes how the Postal Service recognizes such prepayments. Suppose in a given year that Sears used $2 million of its prepaid postage that had not been adjusted for. Journalize a $2 million adjustment on the accounts of the Postal Service and Sears.
4. The Postal Service's statement of operations included the following as a separate addition to its operating revenue:

Operating appropriations (for revenue forgone for certain classes of mail)	$789,108,000

A footnote stated that the Postal Reform Act authorizes "to be appropriated each year a sum determined by the Postal Service to be equal to revenue forgone by it in providing certain mail services to the U.S. Government at free or reduced rates." Journalize the effects on the accounts of the Postal Service of an adjustment as of September 30 that increases appropriations by $10 million. Also journalize the effects on the accounts of the U.S. government. For simplicity, assume that no cash had changed hands as yet regarding these appropriations.

4–39. **UTILITY FINANCIAL STATEMENTS.** Portland General Electric Company is a public utility in Oregon. A recent annual report included (in thousands of dollars):

Portland General Electric Company

Operating revenues	$303,678	Retained earnings, beginning	
Purchased power	76,911	of year	$102,823
Interest charges	48,838	Administrative and other	
Other income	14,383	expense	33,914
Depreciation	31,587	Taxes other than income	
Transmission and		taxes	24,280
distribution	11,672	Production of power	23,794
Maintenance and repairs	13,313	Taxes on income	4,968
		Retained earnings, end	
		of year	94,918
		Dividends declared	?

Required:

| Prepare (1) a statement of income and (2) a statement of retained earnings.

4–40. **SAFEWAY FINANCIAL STATEMENTS.** Safeway Stores is the largest food retailer in the United States. An annual report contained the following data:

Safeway Stores

Interest expense	$ 72,831,000	Cost of sales	$ 9,829,071,000
Provision for income		Cash dividends paid	59,924,000
taxes (income tax		Operating and	
expense)	130,600,000	administrative	
Sales	12,550,569,000	expenses	2,371,949,000
		Retained earnings,	
		end of year	830,189,000

Required:

1. Prepare a combined multiple-step statement of income and retained earnings for the year.
2. Compute the percentage of gross profit on sales and the percentage of net income on sales.
3. The average stockholders' equity for the year was about $900 million. What was the percentage of net income on average stockholders' equity?
4. Why might stockholders want to invest in a company with such a consistently low percentage of net income to sales?

4–41. **FOOD COMPANY FINANCIAL STATEMENTS.** CPC International has annual sales that rank the company among the hundred largest U.S.-based industrial corporations and the ten largest food companies. Branded grocery products make up 58% of the company's sales: Hellmann's, Best Foods, Skippy, Mazola, Karo, and so forth. An annual report included the data shown below (in millions of dollars). Unless otherwise specified, the balance sheet amounts are the balances at the end of the year.

Net sales	$4,343	Cash	$ 30
Long-term debt	282	Cost of sales	3,112
Plants and properties	1,182	Financing costs	99
Selling, administrative		Accounts payable	184
and general expenses	495	Loans and notes payable	205
Inventories:		Temporary investments	
Beginning of year	636	(a current asset)	51
End of year	560	Provision for income taxes	146
Marketing and other expenses	273	Cash dividends declared	92
Retained earnings at		Prepaid expenses	15
beginning of year	950	Other assets	151
Notes and accounts receivable	473	Income taxes payable	85
Accrued expenses payable	210	Other noncurrent	
Dividends payable	23	liabilities	238
Paid-in capital	159		

Required:

1. Prepare a combined multiple-step statement of income and retained earnings.
2. Prepare a classified balance sheet.
3. The average stockholders' equity for the year was about $1,171 million. What was the percentage of net income on average stockholders' equity?
4. Compute (a) gross profit percentage and (b) percentage of net income to sales.
5. Optional: Why might stockholders want to invest in a company with such a consistently low percentage of net income to sales?

4–42. **PROFESSIONAL FOOTBALL INCOME.** Examine the accompanying condensed income statement of the Green Bay Packers Inc.

GREEN BAY PACKERS INC.
Income Statement
For the Year Ended March 31, 1986

Income:		
Regular season:		
Net receipts from home games	$ 3,223,803	
Out-of-town games	2,288,967	
Television and radio programs	14,322,244	$19,835,014
Preseason:		
Net receipts from preseason games	1,356,751	
Television and radio programs	355,032	1,711,783
Miscellaneous:		
Club allocation of league receipts	784,988	
Other income	511,516	1,296,504
Total income		22,843,301
Expenses:		
Salaries and other season expenses	16,243,729	
Training expense	725,079	
Overhead expense	4,744,336	
Severance pay	656,250	22,369,394
Income from operations		473,907
Interest income		1,203,281
Income before taxes		1,677,188
Provision for income taxes		167,000
Net income		$ 1,510,188

1. Do you agree with the choice of terms in this statement? If not, suggest where a preferable label should be used.
2. Is this a single-step income statement? If not, which items would you shift to prepare a single-step statement?
3. Identify the major factors that affect the Packers' net income.

Chapter 5

ACCOUNTING CYCLE: RECORDING AND FORMAL PRESENTATION

LEARNING OBJECTIVES

After studying this chapter, you should be able to:

1. Explain the differences among three forms of the balance sheet: account form, report form, and working capital form
2. Explain the accounting cycle
3. Explain the nature of accumulated depreciation and entries therefor
4. Prepare closing entries for pertinent accounts
5. Use a work sheet to prepare adjustments, financial statements, and closing entries (Appendix 5A)
6. Prepare adjustments when alternative recording methods are used for the related originating transactions (Appendix 5B)

This chapter begins with a set of financial statements. It then shows in detail how this set—the accountant's and the manager's formal financial reports—has been produced. Thus our focus is on the final output of the accounting cycle *and* on the recording process rather than solely on the recording process.

Our illustrative company is the Oxley Company, a retailer of nursery products for lawns and gardens. To keep the data manageable for instructional purposes, many simplifying assumptions are made. Nevertheless, this illustration provides an opportunity to review the previous chapters, to see how assorted concepts tie together, to visualize the magnitude of the accounting information system, and to learn more about the techniques of recording and accumulating data.

FORMS OF FINANCIAL STATEMENTS

☐ **Report Form**

Exhibits 5–1, 5–2, and 5–3 display Oxley's balance sheet, income statement, and statement of retained income, respectively. Exhibit 5–1 presents a classified balance sheet in **report form** (assets at top) in contrast to the **account form** (assets at left) that has previously been illustrated.

Exhibit 5–1 also presents **comparative balance sheets**. Comparative financial statements present data for two or more reporting periods. The columnar format of Exhibit 5–1 is usually favored. Note too that the most recent data are usually (but not always) shown first; in a series of years, for instance, the oldest data would appear last.

The only strange account in Exhibit 5–1 is *Accumulated Depreciation*, which will be explained later in this chapter.

☐ **Working Capital Form**

The manner of presentation of a balance sheet is a matter of form rather than substance. Indeed, some companies use a **working capital form**, whereby the current assets are listed first and the current liabilities are deducted, to show working capital explicitly in the balance sheet. For example, the working-capital form of presentation of the data in Exhibit 5–1 would be shown as follows (in millions):

	DECEMBER 31	
	19X2	19X1
Current assets (detailed)	$290	$202
Deduct: Current liabilities (detailed)	219	101
Working capital (also called net current assets)	$ 71	$101
Other assets (detailed)	368	408
Total assets less current liabilities	$439	$509
Deduct: Long-term liabilities (detailed).	40	120
Net assets	$399	$389
Stockholders' equity (detailed)	$399	$389

A user who is comfortable with accounting is not unduly disturbed by the "geography" of where the current liabilities are placed or whether a total is drawn for all assets in the conventional manner. Knowledgeable readers can cope with any form if they know the substance being portrayed. In this regard, note that the working-capital form draws a total for **net assets**, which by definition are total assets less total liabilities and must therefore be equal to the total stockholders' equity:

$$\text{thus if} \quad A = L + SE$$
$$\text{then} \quad A - L = SE$$

THE ACCOUNTING CYCLE

☐ **Various Steps Taken**

The preparation of the finished financial statements is the final stage in what is often called the **accounting cycle**: the various steps in the total processing of accounting data. Pause and study Exhibit 5–4, which shows the principal steps.

The steps in the accounting cycle can be enumerated more fully than shown in Exhibit 5–4. For example, the accountant frequently uses a work sheet (explained in a chapter appendix) to cope with the task of preparing the formal financial statements. Moreover, the cycle shown here is for a year, but it could occur monthly, quarterly, or for any other period as desired.

Consider the Oxley balance sheet for December 31, 19X1, as the start of our illustration of the accounting cycle. The following Oxley transactions, which are condensed here, occurred during 19X2 (amounts are in thousands):

a. Acquired merchandise inventory on account, $359.
b. Delivered merchandise to customers who had previously paid $5 in full in advance.
c. Sales of merchandise (all on account and excluding transaction b) during 19X2 were $994.
d. The cost of merchandise sold (including that in transaction b) during 19X2 was $399.
e. Cash collected on account was $969.

EXHIBIT 5–1 *(Place a clip on this page for easy reference.)*

OXLEY COMPANY
Balance Sheet (in thousands)

ASSETS	DECEMBER 31 19X2	DECEMBER 31 19X1
Current assets:		
Cash	$150	$ 57
Accounts receivable	95	70
Accrued interest receivable	15	15
Inventory of merchandise	20	60
Prepaid rent	10	—
Total current assets	$290	$202
Long-term assets*		
Long-term note receivable	288	288

	DECEMBER 31 19X2	DECEMBER 31 19X1
Equipment, at original cost	$200	$200
Deduct: Accumulated depreciation	120	80
Equipment, net	80	120
Total assets	$658	$610

LIABILITIES AND STOCKHOLDERS' EQUITY

	19X2	19X1
Current liabilities:		
Accounts payable	$ 90	$ 65
Accrued wages payable	24	10
Accrued income taxes payable	16	12
Accrued interest payable	9	9
Unearned sales revenue	—	5
Note payable, current portion	80	—
Total current liabilities	$219	$101
Long-term note payable	40	120
Total liabilities	$259	$221
Stockholders' equity:		
Paid-in capital†	$102	$102
Retained income	297	287
Total stockholders' equity	$399	$389
Total liabilities and stockholders' equity	$658	$610

* This caption is frequently omitted. Instead the long-term note receivable, the equipment, and other categories are merely listed as separate items following the current assets.

† Details are often shown in a supplementary statement or in footnotes. In this case, there are 200,000 common shares outstanding: $.25 par per share, or 200,000 × $.25 = $50,000. Additional paid-in capital is $52,000.

EXHIBIT 5–2

OXLEY COMPANY
Statement of Income
(in thousands except earnings per share)

	FOR THE YEAR ENDED DECEMBER 31, 19X2		FOR THE YEAR ENDED DECEMBER 31, 19X1	
Sales		$999		$800
Cost of goods sold		399		336
Gross profit (or gross margin)		$600		$464
Operating expenses:				
Wages	$214		$150	
Rent	120		120	
Miscellaneous	100		50	
Depreciation	40	474	40	360
Operating income (or operating profit)		$126		$104
Other revenue and expense:				
Interest revenue	$ 36		$ 36	
Deduct: Interest expense	12	24	12	24
Income before income taxes		$150		$128
Income tax expense		60		48
Net income		$ 90		$ 80
Earnings per common share*		$ .45		$ .40

* Dividends per share, $.40 and $.20, respectively. For publicly held companies, there is a requirement to show earnings per share on the face of the income statement, but it is not necessary to show dividends per share. Calculations of earnings per share: $90,000 ÷ 200,000 = $.45, and $80,000 ÷ 200,000 = $.40.

EXHIBIT 5–3

OXLEY COMPANY
Statement of Retained Income
(in thousands)

	FOR THE YEAR ENDED DECEMBER 31	
	19X2	19X1
Retained income, beginning of year	$287	$247
Add: Net income	90	80
Total	$377	$327
Deduct: Dividends declared	80	40
Retained income, end of year	$297	$287

EXHIBIT 5–4

Steps in Accounting Cycle

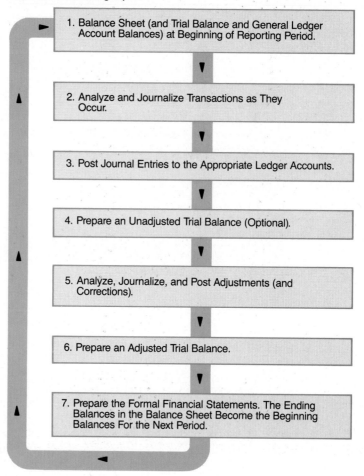

1. Balance Sheet (and Trial Balance and General Ledger Account Balances) at Beginning of Reporting Period.

2. Analyze and Journalize Transactions as They Occur.

3. Post Journal Entries to the Appropriate Ledger Accounts.

4. Prepare an Unadjusted Trial Balance (Optional).

5. Analyze, Journalize, and Post Adjustments (and Corrections).

6. Prepare an Adjusted Trial Balance.

7. Prepare the Formal Financial Statements. The Ending Balances in the Balance Sheet Become the Beginning Balances For the Next Period.

f. The note receivable was from a key industrial customer. The $288 principal is payable on August 1, 19X4. Interest of 12.5% per annum is collected each August 1 (to be computed).

Cash was disbursed as follows for

g. Accounts payable, $334.

h. Wages, $200, including the $10 accrued in December 31, 19X1.

i. Income taxes, $56, including the $12 accrued on December 31, 19X1.

j. Interest on note payable, including the $9 accrued on December 31, 19X1. Interest of 10% per annum on the $120 principal is paid each March 31 (to be computed).

k. Rent, $130 for 13 months, which was debited to Prepaid Rent.

l. Miscellaneous expenses, $100.

m. Dividends, $80. A separate account called Dividends Declared was created. For simplicity, assume that declaration and payment occurred on the same day.

No interim statements were prepared, so no adjusting entries were made until December 31, 19X2, when the following were recognized:

n. Accrual of interest receivable (to be computed).

o. The disbursements for rent included $10 paid on December 31, 19X2, pertaining to the month of January 19X3.

p. Accrual of wages payable, $24.

q. Accrual of interest payable (to be computed).

r. Depreciation for 19X2, $40.

s. Two-thirds of the principal of the note payable is transferred to Note Payable, Current Portion, because two-thirds is due March 31, 19X3. The other third is payable on March 31, 19X5.

t. Accrual of income taxes payable. The total income tax expense for 19X2 is 40% of the income before income taxes (to be computed).

Required:

I. Prepare a general ledger in T-account form, entering the account balances of December 31, 19X1. Provide space for additional accounts.

II. Analyze and journalize all transactions for 19X2, including the year-end adjustments.

III. Post the entries in II to the T-accounts.

IV. Prepare an adjusted trial balance as of December 31, 19X2. If it fails to balance, check to see that all items were posted to the correct sides of the accounts.

V. Prepare a multistep income statement for 19X2.

VI. Prepare a statement of retained income for 19X2.

VII. Prepare a comparative classified balance sheet for December 31, 19X1 and 19X2.

VIII. Journalize and post the entries necessary to "close the books" for 19X2.

You are *urged* to try to solve requirements I–IV on your own before examining the solution. The general ledger (Parts I and III) is illustrated in Exhibit 5–6. The general journal (Part II) is illustrated in Exhibit 5–5. Note how the accounts are numbered. Posting and journalizing are keyed to facilitate cross-checking. The trial balance (Part IV) is illustrated in Exhibit 5–7.

Parts V through VII were illustrated in the preceding sections of this chapter: Exhibits 5–1, 5–2, and 5–3. Part VIII is described in the section entitled "Closing the Accounts."

☐ Detailed Explanation of Parts I, II, and III

Parts I, II, and III are covered in their entirety in Exhibits 5–5 and 5–6. Therefore many readers will find the following detailed step-by-step explanation (on pages 164 through 170) unnecessary. However, other readers prefer this transaction-by-transaction analysis. Why? Because it strengthens understanding by reviewing some fundamental concepts and procedures.

EXHIBIT 5–5

Journal Entries

Date	Entry No.	Accounts and Explanation	Post. Ref.	Debit	Credit
				(in thousands of dollars)	
19X2					
Dates	a	Inventory of merchandise	130	359	
are		Accounts payable	200		359
varied		Acquired inventory on account			
and					
are	b	Unearned sales revenue	237	5	
not		Sales	320		5
entered		Delivery of merchandise to customers who had paid			
in		in advance			
this	c	Accounts receivable	110	994	
illus-		Sales	320		994
tration,		Sales on account			
except					
for	d	Cost of goods sold	340	399	
Dec. 31		Inventory of merchandise	130		399
		To record the cost of inventory sold			
	e	Cash	100	969	
		Accounts receivable	110		969
		Collections from customers			
	f	Cash	100	36	
		Accrued interest receivable	111		15
		Interest revenue	330		21
		Collection of interest (12.5% of $288 = $36)			
	g	Accounts payable	200	334	
		Cash	100		334
		Payments to creditors			
	h	Accrued wages payable	210	10	
		Wages expense	350	190	
		Cash	100		200
		Payments of wages			
	i	Accrued income taxes payable	220	12	
		Income tax expense	395	44	
		Cash	100		56
		Payments of income taxes			
	j	Accrued interest payable	230	9	
		Interest expense	380	3	
		Cash	100		12
		Payment of interest (10% of $120)			
	k	Prepaid rent	140	130	
		Cash	100		130
		Disbursements for rent			

EXHIBIT 5–5 (continued)

Date	Entry No.	Accounts and Explanation	Post. Ref.	Debit	Credit
				(in thousands of dollars)	
19X2					
	l	Miscellaneous expenses	364	100	
		Cash	100		100
		Disbursements for miscellaneous expense items such as utilities, repairs, etc.			
	m	Dividends declared	310A	80	
		Cash	100		80
		Declaration and payment of dividends			
		Year-End Adjusting Entries			
Dec. 31	n	Accrued interest receivable	111	15	
		Interest revenue	330		15
		Accrual of interest for five months at 12.5% on $288: (12.5%) ($288) (5/12) = $15			
Dec. 31	o	Rent expense	360	120	
		Prepaid rent	140		120
		To record 19X2 rent expense at $10 per month. (Note that this leaves a $10 debit balance in Prepaid Rent for January, 19X3.)			
Dec. 31	p	Wages expense	350	24	
		Accrued wages payable	210		24
		To recognize wages accrued but unpaid at Decem-ber 31, 19X2			
Dec. 31	q	Interest expense	380	9	
		Accrued interest payable	230		9
		Accrual of interest for nine months at 10% on $120: (10%) ($120) (9/12) = 9			
Dec. 31	r	Depreciation expense	370	40	
		Accumulated depreciation, equipment	170A		40
		To record depreciation for 19X2. (The text explains this entry in more depth.)			
Dec. 31	s	Long-term note payable	280	80	
		Note payable, current	240		80
		To reclassify $80 as a current liability			
Dec. 31	t	Income tax expense	395	16	
		Accrued income tax payable	220		16
		To record the income tax expense, which is 40% of the income before income taxes, or .40 × $150 = $60. (Of this amount, $44 has already been paid and charged to expense in entry i, leaving $16 of expense accrued but not paid.)			

EXHIBIT 5-6

GENERAL LEDGER of OXLEY COMPANY

ASSETS
(Increases left, decreases right)

Cash — Account No. 100

Bal.* 57	(g) 334
(e) 969	(h) 200
(f) 36	(i) 56
	(j) 12
	(k) 130
	(l) 100
	(m) 80
	912
1,062	
† 150	

Accounts Receivable 110

* 70	(c) 95
(e) 994	
†	969

Accrued Interest Receivable 111

* 15	(f) 15
(n) 15	
†	15

LIABILITIES + STOCKHOLDERS' EQUITY
(Decreases left, increases right)

Accounts Payable 200

(g) 334	* 65
	(a) 359
	† 90

Accrued Interest Payable 230

(j) 9	* 9
	(q) 9
	† 9

Long-Term Note Payable 280

(s) 80	* 120
	† 40

Paid-in Capital 300

*	* 102
	† 102

Accrued Wages Payable 210

(h) 10	* 10
	(p) 24
	† 24

Unearned Sales Revenue 237

(b) 5	* 5
	† 0

Dividends Declared 310A

(m) 80	

Accrued Income Taxes Payable 220

(i) 12	* 12
	(t) 16
	† 16

Note Payable, Current Portion 240

	* 80
	(s) 80
	† 80

Retained Income 310

	* 310
	† 287

Inventory of Merchandise 130

*	60	(d) 399
(a)	359	
†	20	

Cost of Goods Sold 340

(d)	399

Wages Expense 350

(h)	190
(p)	24

Sales 320

(b)	5
(c)	994

Prepaid Rent 140

(k)	130	(o) 120
†	10	

Rent Expense 360

(o)	120

Miscellaneous Expense 364

(l)	100

Interest Revenue 330

(f)	21
(n)	15

Long-Term Note Receivable 160

*	288
†	288

Interest Expense 380

(j)	3
(q)	9

Income Tax Expense 395

(l)	44
(t)	16

Equipment 170

*	200
†	200

Accumulated Depreciation, Equipment 170A

*	80
(r)	40
†	120

Depreciation Expense 370

(r)	40

* All amounts denoted with an asterisk are balances, December 31, 19X1.

† Balances drawn and carried forward to below the double underlines, December 31, 19X2.

163

EXHIBIT 5–7

OXLEY COMPANY
Adjusted Trial Balance
December 31, 19X2 (in thousands)

Cash	$ 150	
Accounts receivable	95	
Accrued interest receivable	15	
Inventory of merchandise	20	
Prepaid rent	10	
Long-term note receivable	288	
Equipment	200	
Accumulated depreciation, equipment		$ 120
Accounts payable		90
Accrued wages payable		24
Accrued income taxes payable		16
Accrued interest payable		9
Note payable, current portion		80
Long-term note payable		40
Paid-in capital		102
Retained income, December 31, 19X1		287
Dividends declared	80	
Sales		999
Interest revenue		36
Cost of goods sold	399	
Wages expense	214	
Rent expense	120	
Miscellaneous expense	100	
Depreciation expense	40	
Interest expense	12	
Income tax expense	60	
	$1,803	$1,803

DETAILED ANALYSIS OF TRANSACTIONS

a. Transaction: Acquired merchandise inventory on account, $359.

Analysis: The asset **Inventory of Merchandise** is increased.
The liability **Accounts Payable** is increased.

Entry: In the journal (explanation omitted):

Inventory of merchandise	359	
Accounts payable		359

Post to the ledger (postings are indicated by the circled amounts):

Inventory of Merchandise*			Accounts Payable	
Bal.	60		Bal.	65
(a)	359		(a)	359

* Also often called Merchandise Inventory, or if it is the only type of inventory account, it is simply called Inventory.

b. Transaction: Delivered merchandise to customers who had previously paid $5.

    Analysis: The liability **Unearned Sales Revenue** is decreased.
        The stockholders' equity **Sales** is increased.

      Entry: In the journal:

Unearned sales revenue	5	
Sales		5

Post to the ledger:

Unearned Sales Revenue				Sales		
(b)	5	Bal.	5		(b)	5

---

c. Transaction: Sales of merchandise on account, $994.

    Analysis: The asset **Accounts Receivable** is increased.
        The stockholders' equity **Sales** is increased.

      Entry: In the journal:

Accounts receivable	994	
Sales		994

Post to the ledger:

Accounts Receivable			Sales		
Bal.	70		(b)		5
(c)	994		(c)		994

---

d. Transaction: The cost of merchandise sold, $399.

    Analysis: The Asset **Inventory of Merchandise** is decreased.
        The negative stockholders' equity **Cost of Goods Sold** is increased.

        Recall that all expense accounts are reductions in stockholders' equity; thus expense accounts can properly be regarded as negative stockholders' equity.

      Entry: In the journal:

Cost of goods sold	399	
Inventory of merchandise		399

Post to the ledger:

Inventory of Merchandise				Cost of Goods Sold		
Bal.	60	(d)	399	(d)	399	
(a)	359					

---

e. Transaction: Cash collected on account from customers, $969.

    Analysis: The asset **Cash** is increased.
        The asset **Accounts Receivable** is decreased.

      Entry: In the journal:

Cash	969	
Accounts receivable		969

Post to the ledger:

Cash			Accounts Receivable		
Bal.	57		Bal.	70	(e)	969
(e)	969		(c)	994		

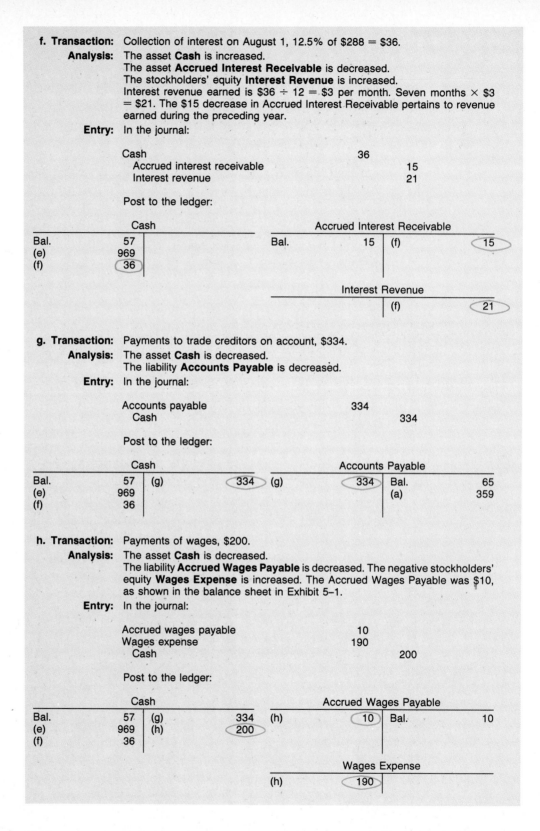

f. Transaction: Collection of interest on August 1, 12.5% of $288 = $36.

Analysis: The asset **Cash** is increased.
The asset **Accrued Interest Receivable** is decreased.
The stockholders' equity **Interest Revenue** is increased.
Interest revenue earned is $36 ÷ 12 = $3 per month. Seven months × $3 = $21. The $15 decrease in Accrued Interest Receivable pertains to revenue earned during the preceding year.

Entry: In the journal:

Cash	36	
Accrued interest receivable		15
Interest revenue		21

Post to the ledger:

Cash				Accrued Interest Receivable			
Bal.	57			Bal.	15	(f)	15
(e)	969						
(f)	36						

Interest Revenue			
		(f)	21

g. Transaction: Payments to trade creditors on account, $334.

Analysis: The asset **Cash** is decreased.
The liability **Accounts Payable** is decreased.

Entry: In the journal:

Accounts payable	334	
Cash		334

Post to the ledger:

Cash				Accounts Payable			
Bal.	57	(g)	334	(g)	334	Bal.	65
(e)	969					(a)	359
(f)	36						

h. Transaction: Payments of wages, $200.

Analysis: The asset **Cash** is decreased.
The liability **Accrued Wages Payable** is decreased. The negative stockholders' equity **Wages Expense** is increased. The Accrued Wages Payable was $10, as shown in the balance sheet in Exhibit 5–1.

Entry: In the journal:

Accrued wages payable	10	
Wages expense	190	
Cash		200

Post to the ledger:

Cash				Accrued Wages Payable			
Bal.	57	(g)	334	(h)	10	Bal.	10
(e)	969	(h)	200				
(f)	36						

Wages Expense			
(h)	190		

i. Transaction: Payments of income taxes, $56.

Analysis: The asset **Cash** is decreased.
The liability **Accrued Income Taxes Payable** is decreased.
The negative stockholders' equity **Income Tax Expense** is increased. The payable was $12, as shown in the balance sheet in Exhibit 5–1.

Entry: In the journal:

Accrued income taxes payable	12	
Income tax expense	44	
Cash		56

Post to the ledger:

Cash					Accrued Income Taxes Payable		
Bal.	57	(g)	334	(i)	12	Bal.	12
(e)	969	(h)	200				
(f)	36	(i)	56				

		Income Tax Expense	
(i)		44	

j. Transaction: Payment of interest on March 31, 10% of $120 = $12.

Analysis: The asset **Cash** is decreased.
The liability **Accrued Interest Payable** is decreased. The negative stockholders' equity **Interest Expense** is increased. Interest expense is $12 ÷ 12 = $1 per month; three months × $1 = $3. The $9 decrease in Accrued Interest Payable pertains to interest expense during the preceding year.

Entry: In the journal:

Accrued interest payable	9	
Interest expense	3	
Cash		12

Post to the ledger:

Cash					Accrued Interest Payable		
Bal.	57	(g)	334	(j)	9	Bal.	9
(e)	969	(h)	200				
(f)	36	(i)	56				
		(j)	12				

		Interest Expense	
(j)		3	

k. Transaction: Payment of rent, $130.

Analysis: The asset **Cash** is decreased.
The asset **Prepaid Rent** is increased.

Entry: In the journal:

Prepaid rent	130	
Cash		130

Post to the ledger:

Cash					Prepaid Rent	
Bal.	57	(g)	334	(k)	130	
(e)	969	(h)	200			
(f)	36	(i)	56			
		(j)	12			
		(k)	130			

l. Transaction: Payment of miscellaneous expenses, $100.

Analysis: The asset **Cash** is decreased.

The negative stockholders' equity **Miscellaneous Expense** is increased.

Entry: In the journal:

Miscellaneous expense	100	
Cash		100

Post to the ledger:

Cash					Miscellaneous Expense	
Bal.	57	(g)	334	(l)	100	
(e)	969	(h)	200			
(f)	36	(i)	56			
		(j)	12			
		(k)	130			
		(l)	100			

m. Transaction: Dividends declared and paid, $80.

Analysis: The asset **Cash** is decreased.

The negative stockholders' equity **Dividends Declared** (an offsetting account to Retained Income) is increased.

Entry: In the journal:

Dividends declared	80	
Cash		80

Post to the ledger:

Cash					Dividends Declared	
Bal.	57	(g)	334	(m)	80	
(e)	969	(h)	200			
(f)	36	(i)	56			
		(j)	12			
		(k)	130			
		(l)	100			
		(m)	80			

n. Transaction: Accrual of interest receivable for 5 months $\times$ $3 = $15.

Analysis: The asset **Accrued Interest Receivable** is increased.

The stockholders' equity **Interest Revenue** is increased.

Entry: In the journal:

Accrued interest receivable	15	
Interest revenue		15

Post to the ledger:

Accrued Interest Receivable					Interest Revenue	
Bal.	15	(f)	15		(f)	21
(n)	15				(n)	15

o. Transaction: Recognition of rent expense.

Analysis: All prepaid rent has expired except for $10 for the month of January 19X3.

The asset **Prepaid Rent** is decreased.

The negative stockholders' equity **Rent Expense** is increased.

Entry: In the journal:

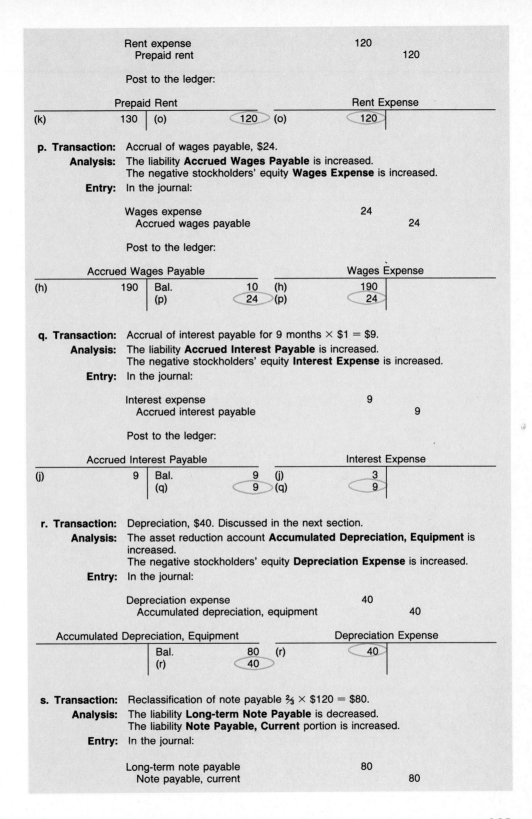

| | Rent expense | 120 | |
| | Prepaid rent | | 120 |

Post to the ledger:

Prepaid Rent				Rent Expense		
(k)	130	(o)	120	(o)	120	

p. Transaction: Accrual of wages payable, $24.
   Analysis: The liability **Accrued Wages Payable** is increased.
   The negative stockholders' equity **Wages Expense** is increased.
   Entry: In the journal:

| | Wages expense | 24 | |
| | Accrued wages payable | | 24 |

Post to the ledger:

Accrued Wages Payable				Wages Expense		
(h)	190	Bal.	10	(h)	190	
		(p)	24	(p)	24	

q. Transaction: Accrual of interest payable for 9 months $\times$ \$1 = \$9.
   Analysis: The liability **Accrued Interest Payable** is increased.
   The negative stockholders' equity **Interest Expense** is increased.
   Entry: In the journal:

| | Interest expense | 9 | |
| | Accrued interest payable | | 9 |

Post to the ledger:

Accrued Interest Payable				Interest Expense		
(j)	9	Bal.	9	(j)	3	
		(q)	9	(q)	9	

r. Transaction: Depreciation, $40. Discussed in the next section.
   Analysis: The asset reduction account **Accumulated Depreciation, Equipment** is increased.
   The negative stockholders' equity **Depreciation Expense** is increased.
   Entry: In the journal:

| | Depreciation expense | 40 | |
| | Accumulated depreciation, equipment | | 40 |

Accumulated Depreciation, Equipment				Depreciation Expense		
		Bal.	80	(r)	40	
		(r)	40			

s. Transaction: Reclassification of note payable $\frac{2}{3} \times$ \$120 = \$80.
   Analysis: The liability **Long-term Note Payable** is decreased.
   The liability **Note Payable, Current** portion is increased.
   Entry: In the journal:

| | Long-term note payable | 80 | |
| | Note payable, current | | 80 |

Post to the ledger:

Long-term Note Payable				Note Payable, Current		
(s)	80	Bal.	120	(s)		80

t. Transaction: Income tax expense for the year. Income before taxes must be computed and then 40% thereof recognized as expense (.40 × $150 = $60). Moreover, the accrued liability must be accurate. Therefore, because $44 has already been paid for the current year and charged to expense (see Transaction i), the amount remaining ($60 − $44 = $16) must be charged to expense.

Analysis: The liability **Accrued Income Taxes Payable** is increased.
The negative stockholders' equity **Income Tax Expense** is increased.

Entry: In the journal:

Income tax expense	16	
Accrued income taxes payable		16

Accrued Income Taxes Payable				Income Tax Expense	
(i)	12	Bal.	12	(i)	44
		(t)	16	(t)	16

NEW ACCOUNTS AND TRANSACTION ANALYSIS

The new features in Exhibits 5–5 and 5–6 deserve explanation, notably the use of Accumulated Depreciation and the entries in 19X2 that are the aftermath of the year-end adjustments of 19X1.

☐ **Nature of Accumulated Depreciation**

Equipment and similar long-lived assets are initially recorded at *cost*. The major difficulties of measurement center on the choice of a pattern of depreciation—that is, the allocation of the original cost to the particular periods that benefit from the use of the assets.

Accountants often stress that depreciation is a process of *allocation of the orginal cost* of acquisition: It is not a process of valuation in the ordinary sense of the term. The usual balance sheet presentation does *not* show replacement cost, resale value, or the price changes since acquisition. The accounting for the latter is discussed in Chapter 14.

The amount of original cost to be allocated over the total useful life of the asset as depreciation is the difference between the total acquisition cost and the estimated **residual value**. The latter is the predicted value from disposal of a long-lived asset at the end of its useful life. Synonyms for residual value are **terminal value** and **disposal value**. The depreciation allocation to each year may be made on the basis of time or service. The estimate of useful life, which is an important factor in determining the yearly allocation of depreciation, is influenced by estimates of physical wear and tear, technological change, and economic obsolescence. Therefore the useful life is usually less than the physical life.

EXHIBIT 5–8

Straight-Line Depreciation
(in thousands)

	BALANCE AT END OF YEAR				
	1	2	3	4	5
Equipment (at original acquisition cost)	$200	$200	$200	$200	$200
Less:Accumulated depreciation (the portion of original cost that has already been charged to operations as expense)	40	80	120	160	200
Book value (the portion of original cost that will be charged to future operations as expense)	$160	$120	$ 80	$ 40	$ 0

For example, suppose all the equipment in Exhibit 5–1 had been acquired simultaneously for $200,000. Its residual value is zero, and its estimated useful life is five years. Exhibit 5–8 shows how the asset would be displayed in the balance sheet if a straight-line method of depreciation were used.[1] The annual depreciation expense that would appear on the income statement would be

$$\frac{\text{Original cost} - \text{Estimated residual value}}{\text{Years of useful life}}$$

or

$$\frac{\$200,000 - \$0}{5} = \$40,000 \text{ per year}$$

When the account *Accumulated Depreciation* is used, the balance sheet equation is affected as follows when depreciation is recognized (denoted as transaction r, in thousands of dollars):

Transaction: Recognition of depreciation, $40,000

Analysis: The asset reduction account **Accumulated Depreciation, Equipment** is increased. The negative stockholders' equity account **Depreciation Expense** is increased.

Entry: In the journal:

Depreciation expense	40	
Accumulated depreciation, equipment		40

Post to the ledger:

Accumulated Depreciation, Equipment		Depreciation Expense	
Bal.	80	(r) 40	
(r)	40		

---

[1] Other patterns of depreciation are discussed in Chapter 9.

Accumulated Depreciation Is Contra Account

The balance sheet in Exhibit 5–1 distinguishes between the store equipment's original cost, $200,000, and its **accumulated depreciation** or **allowance for depreciation**. As the name implies, *accumulated depreciation* is the cumulative sum of all depreciation recognized since the date of acquisition of the particular assets described. The original cost is an objective measurement. In contrast, the measurement of depreciation is affected by predictions of useful lives and residual values.

Accountants have customarily preserved the record of the original cost of plant assets in a separate account. *Accumulated depreciation* was described as an *asset reduction* account in our illustrative analysis and corresponding journal entry. A more popular term is **contra asset**. As used by accountants, *contra* means an offset to, deduction from, or reduction of a companion or an associated amount. Therefore a **contra account** or **offset account** is a separate but related account that offsets a companion account.

count has two distinguishing features: (1) it always has a companion account, and (2) it has the opposite balance of the companion account. In our illustration, the relationships on December 31, 19X2, are:

Asset:	Equipment	$200,000
Contra asset:	Accumulated depreciation, equipment	120,000
Net asset:	Book value	$ 80,000

The **book value** or **net book value** or **carrying amount** or **carrying value** is defined as the balance of an account shown on the books, net of any contra accounts. In our example, the book value is $80,000, the original acquisition cost less the contra account for accumulated depreciation.

Depreciation Is Not Cash

Accumulated depreciation is the part of an asset that has been used up. It is not a pool of cash set aside to replace the asset. Professor William A. Paton once compared depreciation to a boy's eating a jelly-filled doughnut (the original cost, $200,000). The boy is so eager to taste the jelly that he licks it and creates a hole in the center of the doughnut (the depreciation in Year 1). He continues his attack on the doughnut, and the hole enlarges. The hole is the accumulated depreciation, the total amount eaten. The book value or carrying amount of the asset, the part remaining, diminishes as the hole gradually becomes larger throughout the useful life of the doughnut. At the end of its fourth year of useful life, the book value consists of the original doughnut ($200,000) less its gaping hole ($160,000), leaving a crumbly $40,000.

If you remember that accumulated depreciation is like a hole in a doughnut, you will be less likely to fall into the trap of those who think that accumulated depreciation is a sum of cash being accumulated for the replacement of plant assets. **Fund** is defined as a specific amount of cash or investment in securities earmarked for a special purpose. If a company decides to accumulate specific cash for the replacement of assets, such cash is an asset that should be labeled as a *cash fund for replacement of assets*. Holiday Inns, Inc., has had such a fund, calling it a capital construction fund. Such funds are quite rare because most companies can earn better returns by investing any available cash in ordinary operations rather than in special funds. Typically, companies will use or acquire cash for the replacement and expansion of plant assets only as specific needs arise.

☐ Disposal of Equipment

To illustrate more completely the nature of a contra account, consider what happens to accumulated depreciation upon disposal of equipment. Assume that half the equipment is sold near the end of December of the fourth year of its life for $25,000. Assume straight-line depreciation, a five-year life for all the equipment, and zero residual value. The required journal entry would be as follows:

Cash	25	
Accumulated depreciation, equipment	80	
Equipment		100
Gain on sale of equipment		5
To record sale of equipment. The accumulated depreciation at the end of four years would be $4 \times (100 \div 5) = \$80$. The gain is $5 ($25 − the $20 book value).		

The gain would appear as "other income" in the income statement. Note that the disposal of the equipment requires the removal of its carrying amount or book value, which appears in *two* accounts, not one. Therefore *both* the Accumulated Depreciation account and the Equipment account are affected when dispositions occur.

The T-accounts after the sale would show:

Equipment				Accumulated Depreciation, Equipment			
Bal.	200	Sale	100	Sale	80	Bal.	160*

* $4 \times (\$200 \div 5) = \$160$.

The lesson here is that depreciable assets are accounted for with two accounts rather than one. Consequently, when such assets are sold or scrapped, both accounts must be reduced. If the analogy helps clarity, think of the Equipment account as the original dough in the doughnut and its Accumulated Depreciation as the hole in the doughnut. When the doughnut is sold, both the dough and the hole are disposed of simultaneously.

□ Aftermath of Adjustments

Entries for interest, wages, income taxes, and other accruals (for example, see *f*, *h*, *i*, and *j*) have a common theme: Beware of the transactions that relate to the adjustments of the preceding period. The explicit subsequent transaction involves a cash inflow or outflow. Part of each cash flow in this example relates to the accrual made at the end of 19X1. Why be concerned? Because failure to remember the accruals may result in double-counting of expenses (or revenues). A common error, for instance, would be to recognize the entire $12,000 disbursement for interest in entry *j* as an expense of 19X2, whereas $9,000 was already recognized as an expense in 19X1 and is properly charged in entry *j* to the liability account *Accrued Interest Payable*.

□ Dividends Declared

The overall approach to accounting for cash dividends was explained in Chapter 2, page 48. Some companies debit Retained Income directly when their boards of directors declare dividends. Other companies prefer to use a separate "temporary" stockholders' equity account (Dividends Declared or simply Dividends) to compile the dividends, which tend to be declared quarterly by publicly held corporations. The Oxley Corporation follows the latter approach.

CLOSING THE ACCOUNTS

□ Transferring and Summarizing

Accountants often use the term **closing the books** to refer to the final step taken at the end of a *given* year to facilitate the recording of the *next* year's transactions. The step is called **closing**, but *transferring and summarizing* or *clearing* are better labels. Why? Because all balances in the "temporary" stockholders' equity accounts (prime examples are revenues and expenses) are summarized and transferred to a "permanent" stockholders' equity account, Retained Income. **Closing entries** have the effect of clearing, transferring, or summarizing revenue and expense accounts. When the closing entries are completed, the current revenue and expense accounts have zero balances. Closing is a clerical procedure. It is devoid of any new accounting theory. Its purpose is to set the revenue and expense meters back to zero so that those accounts can be used afresh in the new year. For instance, without the closing process the sales account of a business like Shell Oil would continue to cumulate revenue, so that the balance would be the sum of many years of sales rather than only one year of sales.

Exhibit 5–9 shows the general effects of the closing (transferring) process, using numbers from our illustration. How does the debit-credit process accomplish this summarizing and transferring?

STEP 1. An Income Summary account, which has a life of one day (or an instant) is often created. As Exhibit 5–9 indicates, the Income Summary account is a convenience. However, it is not absolutely necessary; many accountants prefer to accomplish the entire closing process by a single (massive) compound entry to Retained Income.

EXHIBIT 5–9

General Effects of Closing the Accounts
(Data are from Exhibit 5–6, p. 162)

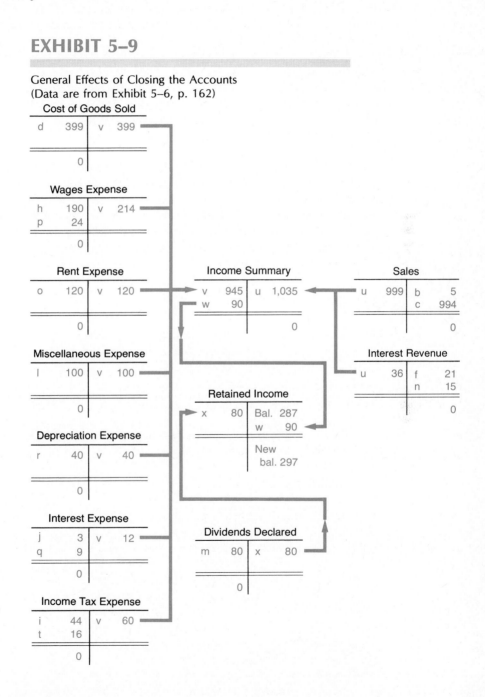

STEP 2. The credit balances of the revenue accounts are debited in entry u in Exhibit 5–9. The balances in Sales and Interest Revenue are now zero. They have been "closed." Their meters are back to zero, but their amounts have not vanished. Instead the amounts now rest in aggregate form as a credit in Income Summary.

STEP 3. The debit balances of the expense accounts are credited, as shown in entry v. Their individual amounts also now reside in aggregate form as a debit in Income Summary.

STEP 4. The net income is computed and transferred from Income Summary to its "permanent" home, Retained Income, as shown in entry w.

STEP 5. The Dividends Declared account is then closed directly to Retained Income, as shown in entry x. Note that the Income Summary account is *not* used for closing the Dividends account. Why? Because dividends are not expenses and do not affect net income.

At the end of Step 5, the Retained Income account has been brought up to date. The books (the journal and ledger) are now ready for a new year. Exhibit 5–9 presents zero balances for all affected accounts except for Retained Income. In practice, these zero balances are not specifically shown. They appear in Exhibit 5–9 and in the following detailed explanations to emphasize the fundamental purpose of the closing process—setting the revenue and expense meters back to zero.

☐ Detailed Explanation of Closing

The following entries and explanations provide a more detailed description of the closing process that has been summarized in Exhibit 5–9:

u. Transaction: Clerical procedure of transferring the ending balances of revenue accounts to the Income Summary account.

Analysis: The stockholders' equity accounts **Sales** and **Interest Revenue** are decreased. The stockholders' equity account **Income Summary** is increased.

Entry: In the journal:

Sales	999	
Interest revenue	36	
Income summary		1,035

To close the revenue accounts by transferring their ending balances to Income Summary.

Post to the ledger:

Sales					Income Summary		
(u)	999	(b)	5			(u)	1,035
		(c)	994				
			0				

Interest Revenue			
(u)	36	(f)	21
		(n)	15
			0

v. Transaction: Clerical procedure of transferring the ending balances of expense accounts to the Income Summary account.

Analysis: The negative stockholders' equity accounts **Cost of Goods Sold, Wages Expense**, etc., are decreased. The stockholders' equity account **Income Summary** is decreased.

Entry: In the journal:

Income summary	945	
Cost of goods sold		399
Wages expense		214
Rent expense		120
Miscellaneous expense		100
Depreciation expense		40
Interest expense		12
Income tax expense		60

To close the expense accounts by transferring their ending balances to Income Summary.

Post to the ledger:

Cost of Goods Sold

(d)	399	(v)	399
	0		

Income Summary

(v)	945	(u)	1,035

Rent Expense

(o)	120	(v)	120
	0		

Wages Expense

(h)	190	(v)	214
(p)	24		
	0		

Depreciation Expense

(r)	40	(v)	40
	0		

Miscellaneous Expense

(l)	100	(v)	100
	0		

Interest Expense

(j)	3	(v)	12
(q)	9		
	0		

Income Tax Expense

(i)	44	(v)	60
(t)	16		
	0		

w. Transaction: Clerical procedure of transferring the ending balance of Income Summary account to the Retained Income account.

Analysis: The stockholders' equity account **Income Summary** is decreased. The stockholders' equity account **Retained Income** is increased.

Entry: In the journal:

Income summary	90	
Retained income		90

To close Income Summary by transferring net income to Retained Income.

Post to the ledger:

Income Summary

(v)	945	(u)	1,035
(w)	90		
			0

Retained Income

		Bal.	287
		(w)	90

x. Transaction: Clerical procedure of transferring the ending balance of Dividends Declared to the Retained Income account.

Analysis: The negative stockholders' equity account **Dividends Declared** is decreased. The stockholders' equity account **Retained Income** is decreased.

Entry: In the journal:

Retained Income	80	
Dividends declared		80
To close Dividends Declared by transferring the ending balance to Retained Income.		

Post to the ledger:

Dividends Declared				Retained Income		
(m)	80	(x)	80	(x)	80	Bal. 287
						(w) 90
	0					Bal. 297

☐ **Terminology of Types of Accounts**

Accounts that are subjected to periodic closing are frequently called **temporary** (also called **nominal**) accounts, as distinguished from **permanent** (also called **real**) accounts. The temporary (nominal) accounts are the revenues, expenses, and dividends declared. They are all really subparts of ownership equity. They are created to provide a detailed explanation for the changes in retained income from period to period. They are the ingredients of the income statement and the statement of retained income.

In contrast, the permanent (real) accounts are the balance sheet accounts. The word *permanent* may be misleading. After all, the balances of permanent (real) accounts fluctuate. Moreover, some permanent accounts come and go. For example, unearned sales revenue appears on Oxley's balance sheet of December 31, 19X1, but not December 31, 19X2.

COMPUTERS AND THE ACCOUNTING CYCLE

Professionally prepared computer programs (called *software*) can do all the steps in the accounting cycle except generate the numbers for initial journal entries and for many adjusting entries.

The details of computer systems are beyond the scope of this book. However, their presence has made many time-honored manual accounting methods obsolete. For example, the entire "closing the books" process, including the use of Income Summary accounts, becomes obsolete when computers merely remove the old balances in revenue and expense accounts and automatically transfer the resulting net income to a Retained Income account. Furthermore, an ordinary journal is unnecessary if a computer can indefinitely store the effects of accounting transactions in its memory and print an analysis of any transaction upon command.

So-called spread sheet computer programs are widely used. They provide accountants with a trial balance on an "electronic" work sheet. Any adjustments or corrections are entered into a computer, which automatically changes the trial balance and the resulting financial statements. As you can imagine, accountants save considerable time. For a short description of an electronic work sheet, see page 187.

EFFECTS OF ERRORS

☐ Major Types of Errors

Accountants' errors affect a variety of items, including revenues and expenses for a given period. Some errors are counterbalanced by offsetting errors in the ordinary bookkeeping process in the next period. Such errors misstate net income in both periods; they also affect the balance sheet of the first period but not the second.

For example, the omission of $1,000 of accrued wages payable would (a) overstate pretax income and understate year-end liabilities by $1,000 for the first year, and (b) understate income by $1,000 and have no effect on year-end liabilities for the second year. Note that the retained income balance at the end of the second year would be correct (ignoring income tax considerations). The *total* of the two incorrect pretax incomes would be identical with the total of the two correct pretax incomes.

Some errors are not counterbalanced in the ordinary bookkeeping process. Until specific correcting entries are made, all subsequent balance sheets will be in error.

For example, overlooking a depreciation expense of $2,000 in *one year only* (a) would overstate pretax income, assets, and retained income by $2,000 in that year, and (b) would continue to overstate assets and retained earnings on successive balance sheets for the life of the fixed asset. But observe that pretax income for each subsequent year would not be affected unless the same error is committed again.

An analysis such as the following is often helpful (figures assumed):

| | Pretax Income | | | Accumulated Depreciation, December 31, |
	19X1	19X2	19X3	19X3
Corrections:				
Omission of accrued salaries, December 31, 19X1	$ (1,000)*	$ 1,000		
Omission of depreciation expense, 19X1	(2,000)			$2,000
Total corrections	$ (3,000)	$ 1,000	—	$2,000
Book balances (assumed)	13,000	16,000	11,000	3,500
Corrected balances	$10,000	$17,000	$11,000	$5,500

* Negative amounts are in parentheses.

☐ Correcting Entries

When errors are discovered, correcting (as distinguished from correct) entries are often necessary. Consider the following examples:

1. A repair expense is erroneously debited to Equipment on December 27. The error is discovered on December 31:

ERRONEOUS ENTRY, 12/27			CORRECTING ENTRY, 12/31		
Equipment	500		Repair expense	500	
Cash		500	Equipment		500

The correcting entry shows a credit to Equipment to cancel or offset the erroneous debit to Equipment. Moreover, the entry debits Repair Expense correctly.

2. A collection on account is erroneously credited to Sales on November 2. The error is discovered on November 28:

ERRONEOUS ENTRY, 11/2			CORRECTING ENTRY, 11/28		
Cash	3,000		Sales	3,000	
Sales		3,000	Accounts receivable		3,000

INCOMPLETE RECORDS

Accountants must sometimes construct financial statements from incomplete data. For example, documents may be stolen, destroyed, or lost. Moreover, many instructors believe that students reinforce their understanding of underlying concepts by solving problems that contain a variety of disorganized and fragmentary data.

T-accounts help organize an accountant's thinking and aid the discovery of unknown amounts. For example, suppose the proprietor of a local sports shop asks you to prepare an income statement for 19X2. She provides the following accurate but incomplete information:

List of customers who owe money:	
December 31, 19X1	$ 4,000
December 31, 19X2	6,000
Cash receipts from customers during 19X2, appropriately credited to customers' accounts	280,000

You want to compute revenue (sales) on the accrual basis. Assume that all sales were made on account. Shortcuts may be available, but the following steps demonstrate a general approach to the reconstruction of incomplete accounts:

STEP 1: Enter all known items into the key T-account. Knowledge of the usual components of such an account is essential:

Accounts Receivable			
Bal. 12/31/X1	4,000	Collections	280,000
Sales	S		
Total debits	(4,000 + S)	Total credits	280,000
Bal. 12/31/X2	6,000		

STEP 2: Find the unknown. Simple arithmetic will often suffice; however, the following solution illustrates the algebraic nature of the relationships in an asset T-account:

$$\text{Total debits} - \text{Total credits} = \text{Balance}$$
$$(4,000 + S) - 280,000 = 6,000$$
$$S = 6,000 + 280,000 - 4,000$$
$$S = 282,000$$

Obviously, the analyses become more complicated if more entries have affected a particular account. Nevertheless, the key idea is to fill in the account with all known debits, credits, and balances. Then solve for the unknown.

SUMMARY

Comparative and classified financial statements help readers detect changes in key account balances and ratios. The substance of statements is unaffected by the assorted forms of their presentation.

The accounting cycle refers to the recording process that leads from the beginning to the ending financial statements. Closing the accounts is a clerical procedure that aids the periodic compilation of revenues and expenses and the start of a new accounting cycle.

The steps in the accounting cycle can be enumerated in different ways. For example:

1. Begin with the general ledger balances at the start of the reporting period.
2. Analyze and journalize transactions as they occur.
3. Post journal entries to the appropriate ledger accounts.
4. Prepare an unadjusted trial balance (optional).
5. Analyze, journalize, and post adjustments and corrections.
6. Prepare an adjusted trial balance.
7. Prepare the formal financial statements.
8. Prepare closing journal entries and post them so that the ledger is ready for the new accounting cycle.

SUMMARY PROBLEMS FOR YOUR REVIEW

☐ Problem One

Review the transactions for the Oxley Company during 19X2. Suppose that wages expense accrued but unpaid at the end of 19X2 were $34 instead of $24. What numbers would be changed on the income statement for 19X2 and on the balance sheet, December 31, 19X2? What would be the new numbers? The financial statements are on pages 156–157.

☐ Solution to Problem One

	FOR THE YEAR ENDED DECEMBER 31, 19X2	
INCOME STATEMENT ACCOUNTS	As in Exhibit 5–2	Revised
Wages expense	$214	$224
Income before income taxes	150	140
Income tax expense (at 40%)	60	56
Net income	90	84

	DECEMBER 31, 19X2	
BALANCE SHEET ACCOUNTS	As in Exhibit 5–1	Revised
Accrued wages payable	$ 24	$ 34
Accrued income taxes payable	16	12
Retained income	297	291

Note the final effects. Retained income would be decreased by $6, and total liabilities would be increased by a net of $6. Accrued wages increase by $10, but accrued income taxes decrease by $4 (40% of the $10 decrease in income before taxes).

☐ Problem Two

The balance sheet of Holiday Inns showed Accrued Interest of $18,558,000 under current liabilities, January 1, 1986. Interest payments of $98 million were disbursed during 1986. Prepare the journal entry that summarizes those disbursements.

☐ Solution to Problem Two

Accrued interest	18,558,000	
Interest expense	79,442,000	
Cash		98,000,000
To record disbursements for interest; interest expense is $98,000,000 − $18,558,000, or $79,442,000.		

The nomenclature used here illustrates why beginners in accounting should be alert to how the account description is used by a particular entity. That is, the term *Accrued*

Interest is basically unclear. Does it mean *receivable* or *payable*? The answer is obvious in the annual report of Holiday Inns because the account is classified as a current liability. But some other company may use the same term, *Accrued Interest*, to describe a receivable. Hence, for clarity this textbook generally uses *accrued interest receivable* or *accrued interest payable* rather than *accrued interest* alone.

HIGHLIGHTS TO REMEMBER

1. *Accumulated depreciation*, which is often called *allowance for depreciation*, is widely misunderstood. It *is* the cumulative sum of all depreciation already recognized since the date of acquisition of the particular assets described. It *is not* a sum of cash being compiled for the replacement of plant assets.
2. In the basic financial statements, depreciation *is* a process of *allocation of the original cost* of acquisition. It *is not* an attempt at valuation at replacement cost or resale value.
3. Dividends Declared is a separate account that offsets Retained Income. Dividends are not expenses.
4. Beginners in accounting often err by ignoring the effects on the current period of adjustments that were made at the end of the preceding period.

ACCOUNTING VOCABULARY

Account Form, p. *154* Accounting Cycle, *155* Accumulated Depreciation, *172* Allowance for Depreciation, *172* Book Value, *172* Carrying Amount, *172* Carrying Value, *172* Closing, *174* Closing Entries, *174* Closing the Books, *174* Comparative Balance Sheets, *154* Contra Account, *172* Contra Asset, *172* Disposal Value, *170* Fund, *173* Net Assets, *155* Net Book Value, *172* Nominal Accounts, *178* Offset Account, *172* Permanent Accounts, *178* Real Accounts, *178* Report Form, *154* Residual Value, *170* Reversing Entries, *191* Temporary Accounts, *178* Terminal Value, *170* Working-Capital Form, *154* Working Paper, *183* Work Sheet, *183*

APPENDIX 5A: THE WORK SHEET

☐ **Purpose of Work Sheet**

The body of this chapter described the rudiments of the accounting cycle. This appendix explores the cycle in more detail by explaining a favorite tool of the accountant. The **work sheet** (also called a **working paper**) is a columnar approach to moving from a trial balance to the finished financial statements. It provides an orderly means for (a) preparing adjusting entries, (b) computing net income, (c) preparing the formal financial statements, and (d) closing the books.

Although a work sheet is not essential to obtaining financial statements, it is a valuable informal device for bringing everything together in a single place, especially when there are numerous accounts and year-end adjustments. It helps assure the accountant that potential errors and overlooked adjustments will be discovered.

For learning purposes, the work sheet is usually prepared with a pencil. However, as already mentioned, accountants typically use the electronic spreadsheets or work sheets discussed at the end of this appendix.

☐ Steps in Preparation

Because the work sheet is an informal tool, there is no unique way of preparing it. However, a typical work sheet is illustrated in Exhibit 5–10. A step-by-step description of its preparation follows.

1. In the body of the chapter we focused on an adjusted trial balance, which was prepared *after* the adjusting entries had been made. Frequently, however, the accountant initially prepares an "unadjusted" trial balance as the first pair of columns in the work sheet. Then adjustments are entered in the second pair of columns. This provides a systematic and convenient way of reviewing the unadjusted trial balance together with the adjustments to make sure that nothing is overlooked.

The numbers in the first pair of columns come from the balances in the general ledger in Exhibit 5–6 *after* the last entry for the period's transactions (entry *m*) but *before* the first entry for the end-of-period adjustments (entry *n*). This preparation of the unadjusted trial balance provides a check on the general accuracy of the ledger *before* adjustments are entered. Thus it provides an early chance to catch errors. The frequent use of self-checks as detailed work proceeds may seem unnecessary. Nevertheless, as students and practicing accountants will testify, time is inevitably saved in doing the complete job. Few accounting tasks are more maddening than trying to trace an error discovered at a final stage back through a maze of interrelated journal entries and ledgers.

Concentrate on the first pair of columns, the Unadjusted Trial Balance. Many accounts are listed in their appropriate locations even though they have zero balances. Why? Because through experience the accountant knows that such accounts are almost always affected by the adjustment process. Listing all the accounts can help avoid overlooking required adjustments. Inasmuch as the work sheet is an informal document, some accountants prefer first to list only the accounts with balances and later to list the additional accounts (below the $1,699 total in this illustration) when adjustments are made.

2. The second pair of columns is used for preparing the adjusting entries *n* through *t*. These columns are also totaled as a check on accuracy.

3. After the adjustments have been made, the third pair of columns represents the net effects of the first pair plus the second pair. That is, the unadjusted trial balance plus the adjustments equals the adjusted trial balance. Note how check after check is built into the work sheet.

4. The fourth pair of columns provides an income statement; the fifth pair, a statement of retained income; the sixth pair, a balance sheet. By tracing the numbers in those columns to the formal statements in Exhibits 5–1, 5–2, and 5–3, you can readily see how a work sheet can aid the preparation of the formal statements, especially when there are numerous accounts and adjustments.

The Income Statement columns are sometimes used as the primary place for computing income before taxes and (in simple cases) the income tax expense for the year. That is why the subtotals are drawn as shown. When the net income has finally been computed, the amount is transferred to the fifth pair of columns for the statement of retained income. Again, as in every pair, the columns are totaled to check accuracy.

The Income Statement and the Retained Income columns often guide the preparation of closing entries. Note how the Income Statement columns contain all the details necessary for the closing process; indeed, you can visualize the pair as a detailed Income Summary T-account used for closing. Similarly, the Retained Income columns can be visualized as the Retained Income T-account.

The final step is to move the ending balance of Retained Income from the fifth pair of columns to the sixth pair, the Balance Sheet columns.

EXHIBIT 5-10

OXLEY COMPANY
Work Sheet
For the Year Ended December 31, 19X2

Account Titles (in thousands of dollars)	Unadjusted Trial Balance Debit	Unadjusted Trial Balance Credit	Adjustments Debit	Adjustments Credit	Adjusted Trial Balance Debit	Adjusted Trial Balance Credit	Income Statement Debit	Income Statement Credit	Statement of Retained Income Debit	Statement of Retained Income Credit	Balance Sheet Debit	Balance Sheet Credit
Cash	150				150						150	
Accounts receivable	95				95						95	
Accrued interest receivable			(n) 15		15						15	
Inventory of merchandise	20				20						20	
Prepaid rent	130			(o) 120	10						10	
Long-term note receivable	288				288						288	
Equipment	200				200						200	
Accumulated depreciation, equipment		80		(R) 40		120						120
Accounts payable		90				90						90
Accrued wages payable				(p) 24		24						24
Accrued income taxes payable				(t) 16		16						16
Accrued interest payable				(q) 9		9						9
Note payable—current portion				(s) 80		80						80
Long-term note payable		120	(s) 80			40						40
Paid-in capital		102				102						102
Retained income, December 31, 19X1		287				287				287		
Dividends declared	80				80				80			
Sales		999				999		999				
Interest revenue		21		(n) 15		36		36				
Cost of goods sold	399				399		399					
Wages expense	190		(p) 24		214		214					
Rent expense			(o) 120		120		120					
Miscellaneous expense	100				100		100					
Depreciation expense			(R) 40		40		40					
Interest expense	3		(q) 9		12		12					
	1699	1699					885	1035				
Income tax expense	44		(t) 16		60		60					
			304	304	1803	1803	1035	1035				
Net income							90			90		
							1035	1035	80	377		
Retained income, December 31, 19X2									297			297
									377	377	778	778

(n) Accrual of interest receivable, $15   (o) Rent expense, $120   (p) Accrual of wages, $24   (q) Accrual of interest payable, $9   (r) Depreciation expense, $40
(s) Reclassification of note, $80   (t) Income tax expense, .40 × $150 income before income taxes, .40 × $150 income before income taxes = $60. Adjustment for accrued portion is $16.

185

The detailed sequence for the fourth, fifth, and sixth pairs of columns follows:

a. Add each of the two Income Statement columns and calculate the difference, as follows:

Credit column total (revenues)	$1,035
Debit column total (expenses)	885
Income before income taxes	$ 150

b. Compute the income tax expense, which is .40 × $150 = $60. Extend the $60 on the Income Tax Expense line as a debit in the Income Statement columns. Net income amounts to $150 − $60 = $90.

c. Add "net income" to the list of account titles. Place the $90 amount in the Income Statement debit column and in the Statement of Retained Income credit column. Note that this is akin to the closing journal entry that transfers net income from the Income Statement Summary to Retained Income.

d. Add each of the two Income Statement columns to see that the totals are equal.

e. Add the two Statement of Retained Income columns and calculate the difference, as follows:

Credit column total (beginning balance of retained income plus net income for the period)	$377
Debit column total (dividends declared)	80
Retained earnings balance, December 31, 19X2	$297

f. Add "retained income, December 31, 19X2," to the list of account titles. Place the $297 amount in the Statement of Retained Income debit column and in the Balance Sheet credit column.

g. Add each of the two Statement of Retained Income columns to see that the totals are equal.

h. Add each of the two Balance Sheet columns to see that the totals are equal. When they are equal, the accountant is ready to prepare the formal statements. When they are not equal, the accountant seldom smiles. He or she faces the labors of rechecking the preceding steps in reverse order.

☐ Flexibility of Uses

Ponder the work sheet in its entirety. It is a clever means of summarizing masses of interrelated data. Obviously, the work sheet in Exhibit 5–10 is tiny in comparison with some work sheets used to prepare the financial statements of huge corporations that have many subdivisions. Work sheets are flexible. Many more sets of columns may be added. On the other hand, Exhibit 5–10 could be cut to six columns instead of twelve by using parentheses instead of separate columns for the credits.

Accountants often use the work sheet as the principal means of preparing monthly and quarterly financial statements. Adjustments may be necessary for preparing these interim statements, but the accountant may not wish to enter adjustments formally in the journal and ledger each month. For example, suppose the work sheet in Exhibit 5–10 were for the month of January 19X2. Adjustments might be entered on the work sheet in the same manner, but no adjusting entries would be made in the journals and ledgers. In this way, formal interim financial statements can be prepared without the books being cluttered by the elaborate adjusting and closing entries.

☐ Detailed Accounting Cycle

The body of this chapter described the major steps of the accounting cycle. The appendix described the work sheet. Earlier chapters described other features of the cycle. The detailed steps of the accounting cycle when a work sheet is used are summarized below.

1. Begin with the balance sheet (and general ledger balances) at the start of the reporting period.
2. Analyze and journalize transactions as they occur.
3. Post journal entries to the appropriate ledger accounts.
4. Prepare an unadjusted trial balance on a work sheet.
5. Complete the work sheet.
6. Prepare the formal financial statements.
7. Using the work sheet as a guide:
   a. Journalize and post the adjusting entries.
   b. Journalize and post the closing entries.
8. Use the ledger to prepare an after-closing, or postclosing, trial balance. This serves as a double-check to ensure that the ledger is ready for the new accounting cycle. The balances in the after-closing trial balance (which is not shown here) should be identical to those in the Balance Sheet columns of the work sheet.

☐ Electronic Spreadsheet

The general procedure for electronic spreadsheets as applied to the accountant's typical work sheet follows:

1. List the accounts.
2. Enter the trial balance amount of each account as shown in the first two amount columns of Exhibit 5–10, page 185.
3. Enter the adjustment amounts. The adjustment amount for Accrued Interest Receivable belongs in line 3, column 3.
4. Write the equation to calculate each income statement amount. For example, Interest Revenue's final credit balance is $36, as follows:

Trial balance amount, a credit	$21
− Debit adjustments	0
+ Credit adjustments	15
= Income statement amount, a credit	$36

The spreadsheet is programmed to place $36 on line 19 in columns 6 and 8 of the work sheet.

5. Write the equation to calculate each balance sheet amount. For example, Prepaid Rent's final debit balance is:

Trial balance amount, a debit	$130
+ Debit adjustments	0
− Credit adjustments	−120
= Balance sheet amount, a debit	$ 10

The spreadsheet is programmed to place $10 on line 5 in columns 5 and 11 of the work sheet.

Major advantages of the electronic spreadsheet include the following:

1. The format is stored and can be used repeatedly. This avoids laborious writing of column heads and account titles.
2. Revisions of the basic format are easy.
3. Mathematical computations and placements of each account are achieved via computer. Speed and accuracy are maximized. Drudgery is minimized.
4. "What if" analysis is easily conducted. For example, suppose a manager desired to know the effects of various contemplated expense or revenue transactions on the income statement and balance sheet. Electronic spreadsheets can answer such questions instantly.

APPENDIX 5B: VARIETY IN DATA PROCESSING AND JOURNALIZING

This appendix stresses that there are many appropriate data-processing paths to the same objectives. The focus should be on the final product, not on whether one path is theoretically better than other paths. For example, should we use manual or computer methods? Should we use one pattern of journal entries or another? The answers to the questions of data-processing alternatives are inherently tied to the *overall* costs and benefits of the possible competing systems in a *specific* organization. What is good for General Motors is probably not good for Sophia's Pizza House, and vice versa.

□ **Variety in Recording Assets**

Oxley Company's entries for rent (see entries *k* and *o* reproduced below from our chapter illustration) exemplify how accountants might adopt different patterns for journalizing:

ENTRY	AS IN CHAPTER: ALL ASSET NOW; RECOGNIZE EXPENSE LATER		FIRST ALTERNATIVE: FORESEE ULTIMATE EFFECTS NOW; NO ADJUSTMENT LATER		SECOND ALTERNATIVE: ALL EXPENSE NOW; RECOGNIZE ASSET LATER	
k Cash payment	Prepaid rent 130 Cash	130	Rent expense 120 Prepaid rent 10 Cash	130	Rent expense 130 Cash	130
o End-of-period adjustment	Rent expense 120 Prepaid rent	120	No entry		Prepaid rent 10 Rent expense	10

Is one choice better than another? All produce the same final account balances. However, from a strict theory point of view, the first-column method is superior because of its straightforward recognition that all acquisitions of goods and services are assets that expire and become expenses later. Under the first-column method, entry *k* regards all acquisitions as assets, and entry *o* writes off the prepayments that have expired. Good theory often also makes good practice. For example, it is often easier to review asset accounts to determine what should be expensed than it is to review expense accounts to determine what should not have been expensed.

The alternative in the middle column foresees the fact that Prepaid Rent will be $10 at the end of the year and anticipates the year-end adjustment in compound fashion, as entry *k* indicates. In practice, this pattern of entries is seldom found because it requires too much analytical time when each cash disbursement occurs.

The alternative in the third column is the direct opposite of the first column and is frequently encountered in practice. The pattern is to record as expenses such items as rent (or insurance premiums or office supplies) when cash is disbursed (or when a liability such as accounts payable is created) upon their acquisition, as entry *k* illustrates. Adjustments such as entry *o* are made at the end of the reporting period to reduce the expenses that would otherwise be overstated and to increase the assets for the appropriate amount of prepayments.

From an economical data-processing point of view, any of the three alternatives might be acceptable. The accountant should choose the one that is easiest to record. By far the most important point here is that any of the alternatives, properly applied, will lead to the same answers—the correct expense and the correct ending asset balance.

☐ Variety in Recording Liabilities

As in the recording of assets, many varieties of the recording of liabilities are acceptable, provided that they result in the proper ending balances for the expense and liability accounts for any particular time in question. Consider the entries for income taxes:

ENTRY	AS IN CHAPTER: PAY OLD LIABILITY AND RECOGNIZE EXPENSE; RECOGNIZE MORE EXPENSE LATER			FIRST ALTERNATIVE: PAY LIABILITY NOW; RECOGNIZE EXPENSE LATER			SECOND ALTERNATIVE: RECOGNIZE EXPENSE NOW; ADJUST TO GET CORRECT BALANCES LATER		
i Cash payment	Accrued income taxes payable	12		Accrued income taxes payable	56		Income tax expense	56	
	Income tax expense	44		Cash		56	Cash		56
	Cash		56						
t End-of-period adjustment	Income tax expense	16		Income tax expense	60		Income tax expense	4	
	Accrued income taxes payable		16	Accrued income taxes payable		60	Accrued income taxes payable		4

The chapter entries *i* and *t* followed the most theoretically defensible position. Entry *i* recognized that $12 of the $56 disbursement pertained to the liability carried over from the preceding period. Entry *t* recognized that the year-end liability arising from the current period was $16.

In contrast, the alternatives in the other two columns are often found. In the middle column, the pattern results in a *temporary* debit balance in Accrued Income Taxes Payable, which normally has a credit balance. The U.S. government does not want to wait until after the end of the year to get its income taxes. Interim payments of estimated income taxes must be made and are frequently debited to the liability account (entry *i*) even before any income tax expense is computed and credited to the liability account (entry *t*). The accrued liability account will now show the same $16 balance as in the preceding method: $12 − $56 + $60 = $16.

The alternative in the third column contrasts sharply with that of the middle column, but the final account balances are the same. As entry *i* indicates, all disbursements are regarded as expenses. At year-end (entry *t*), the accrued liability account is adjusted so that an accurate amount is shown: $12 + $4 = $16.

☐ Temporarily Incorrect Balances

The major lesson of this appendix deserves emphasis. For sensible reasons governing day-to-day recording procedures, accountants may routinely debit expense for the *full amount* (or credit revenue or credit asset or debit liability accounts) when cash changes

EXHIBIT 5-11

Reversing Entries

	WITHOUT REVERSING ENTRIES: THE PATTERN ILLUSTRATED IN CHAPTER	WITH REVERSING ENTRIES
Adjustment, December 31, 19X2 Entry p as in chapter.	Wages expense .... 24 Accrued wages payable 24	Wages expense .... 24 Accrued wages payable 24
Books closed for 19X2 (Entries would be identical and therefore are not shown here.)		
Reversal January 2, 19X3.	None	Accrued wages payable .... 24 Wages expense 24
Disbursements during 19X3 (assume a total of 210).	Accrued wages payable .... 24 Wages expense .... 186 Cash 210	Wages expense .... 210 Cash 210
Postings during 19X3.	Accrued Wages Payable Bal. 24	24 Wages Expense 186	186	Accrued Wages Payable 24	Bal. 24 Wages Expense 210	24 210

190

hands. This may result in temporarily incorrect balances in a number of accounts throughout a reporting period. However, the accountant is aware that such a condition is commonplace. Consequently, many adjustments become necessary for legitimate data-processing reasons. Their aim is to achieve the correct balances for the reporting period.

The justification for such "full amount" approaches centers on costs and benefits. On a day-to-day basis, an accountant or a clerk or a computer does not have to be concerned with remembering whether routine cash flows really affect past accruals. Instead all receipts or disbursements are handled in *identical fashion* throughout the year. To the extent that such routines (used by, say, a computer or a lower-level clerk) cause temporary errors in accruals, the year-end adjustments (prepared by, say, a higher-level accountant) produce the necessary corrections.

☐ Reversing Entries

Reversing entries are sometimes used to cope with the proper accounting for accruals. As the name implies, *reversing entries* switch back all debits and credits made in a related preceding adjusting entry. To illustrate their effect, compare the pattern of journal entries illustrated in the chapter with the pattern of reversing entries that would be employed, as shown in Exhibit 5–11. The adjustments (and the closing entries, not shown) would be identical whether reversing entries are used or not. The differences occur only for the routine journalizing during the following year, 19X3, as Exhibit 5–11 demonstrates.

Some accountants favor using reversing entries because they or their clerks or their computers do not have to be concerned with whether a later routine cash disbursement (or receipt) applies to any accrued liabilities (or assets) that were recognized at the end of the preceding period. So reversing entries are creatures of practical data processing. They have no theoretical merit, and their use is diminishing.

FUNDAMENTAL ASSIGNMENT MATERIAL

☐ General Coverage

5–1. JOURNAL ENTRIES FOR DEPRECIATION. (Alternatives are 5–4 and 5–5.) On January 1, 19X1, the Morales Company acquired some conveyor equipment for $550,000. The equipment had an expected useful life of ten years and an expected terminal scrap value of $50,000. Straight-line depreciation was used.

Required:

1. Prepare the journal entry that would be made annually for depreciation.
2. Some of the equipment with an original cost of $66,000 on January 1, 19X1, and an expected terminal scrap value of $6,000 was sold for $45,000 cash on December 31, 19X3. Prepare the journal entry for the sale.
3. Refer to requirement 2. Suppose the equipment had been sold for $49,000 cash instead of $45,000. Prepare the journal entry for the sale.

5–2. EFFECTS OF ADJUSTMENTS OF PRECEDING PERIOD. (Alternates are 5–6 and 5–7.) The Berti Company had the following balances as of December 31, 19X1:

Accrued interest receivable	$130,000
Accrued wages payable	200,000
Unearned sales revenue	100,000

During early 19X2, cash was collected for interest of $220,000. Cash was disbursed for wages of $900,000. Total sales of $700,000 included $100,000 of deliveries to all customers who had made advance payments during 19X1.

Required: | Prepare the journal entries for the 19X2 transactions described.

5–3. **CLOSING ENTRIES.** (Alternates are 5–8, 5–9, 5–24, and 5–25.) After posting the following balances to T-accounts, journalize and post the entries required to close the books (in thousands):

Retained income		Wages expense	$300
(before closing entries)	$200	Miscellaneous	
Sales	900	expenses	35
Interest revenue	20	Income tax expense	20
Cost of goods sold	500	Dividends declared	30

What is the balance in Retained Income after closing entries?

☐ Understanding Published Financial Reports

5–4. **JOURNAL ENTRIES FOR DEPRECIATION.** (Alternates are 5–1 and 5–5.) Alaska Airlines' balance sheet, January 1, 1986, included the following:

Flight equipment and other equipment	$199,694,000
Less accumulated depreciation	61,611,000
Book value	$138,083,000

Assume that on January 2, 1986, some new baggage-handling equipment was acquired for $954,000 cash. The equipment had an expected useful life of five years and an expected terminal scrap value of $54,000. Straight-line depreciation was used.

Required: | 1. Prepare the journal entry that would be made annually for depreciation on the new equipment.
2. Suppose some of the equipment with an original cost of $106,000 on January 2, 1986, and an expected terminal scrap value of $6,000 was sold for $75,000 cash two years later. Prepare the journal entry for the sale.
3. Refer to requirement 2. Suppose the equipment had been sold for $60,000 cash instead of $75,000. Prepare the journal entry for the sale.

5–5. **JOURNAL ENTRIES FOR DEPRECIATION.** (Alternates are 5–1 and 5–4.) The Coca-Cola Company balance sheet, January 1, 1986, included the following:

Property, plant and equipment	$2,632,290,000
Less allowances for depreciation	1,009,715,000
Book value	$1,622,575,000

Note that the company uses "allowances for" rather than "accumulated" depreciation. Assume that on January 2, 1986, some new bottling equipment was acquired for $880,000 cash. The equipment had an expected useful life of five years and an expected terminal scrap value of $80,000. Straight-line depreciation was used.

1. Prepare the journal entry that would be made annually for depreciation.
2. Suppose some of the equipment with an original cost of $55,000 on January 2, 1986, and an expected terminal scrap value of $5,000 was sold for $28,000 cash two years later. Prepare the journal entry for the sale.
3. Refer to requirement 2. Suppose the equipment had been sold for $43,000 cash instead of $28,000. Prepare the journal entry for the sale.

5–6. EFFECTS OF ADJUSTMENTS OF PRECEDING PERIOD. (Alternates are 5–2 and 5–7.) The New York Times Company showed the following actual balances and descriptions in its balance sheet, January 1, 1986:

Current liabilities:	
Payrolls	$40,054,000
Unexpired subscriptions	40,621,000

The company also showed Interest Receivable of $342,000.

During early 1986, assume the following: $842,000 was collected for interest; cash of $98,054,000 was disbursed for payrolls; and deliveries of $33,621,000 were made of the company's publications that had been subscribed to and fully collected before 1986.

Prepare the journal entries for the 1986 transactions.

5–7. EFFECTS OF ADJUSTMENTS OF PRECEDING PERIOD. (Alternates are 5–2 and 5–6.) The Times Mirror Company engages principally in publishing, notably the *Los Angeles Times*, *Dallas Times Herald*, *Denver Post*, *Newsday*, *Sporting News*, *Golf*, and *Popular Science*. Its annual report included the following balances, January 1, 1986:

Interest receivable	$ 2,841,000
Employees' compensation payable	62,417,000
Unearned income	48,162,000

Assume that during early 1986, cash of $4,841,000 was collected for interest. Cash of $99,417,000 was disbursed for employees' compensation. Deliveries of $28,162,000 were made of magazines and newspapers that had been subscribed to and fully collected during 1986.

Prepare the journal entries for the 1986 transactions.

5–8. CLOSING ENTRIES. (Alternates are 5–3, 5–9, 5–24, and 5–25.) Albertson's, Inc., is a prominent supermarket chain located in the southern and western United States. The actual balances and descriptions that follow pertain to a recent year and are in millions of dollars:

Sales		Federal and state taxes on	
and other revenue	$3,489	income	$ 40
Cost of sales	2,719	Cash dividends	13
Operating and		Retained earnings, beginning	
administrative expenses	682	of year	161

After posting the balances to T-accounts, journalize and post the entries required to close the books. What is the balance in Retained Earnings after closing entries?

5–9. **CLOSING ENTRIES.** (Alternates are 5–3, 5–8, 5–24, and 5–25.) Hershey Foods Corporation has many well-known products, including Hershey's and Reese's candies. The accompanying actual balances and descriptions pertain to a recent year and are in millions of dollars.

Retained earnings,		Selling, administrative, and	
beginning of year	$ 345	general expenses	$268
Net sales	1,451	Interest expense	13
Cost of sales	1,016	Provision for income taxes	75
		Cash dividends	26

Required:

After posting the balances to T-accounts, journalize and post the entries required to close the books. What is the balance in Retained Earnings after closing entries?

ADDITIONAL ASSIGNMENT MATERIAL

☐ **General Coverage**

5–10. Distinguish between the *report form*, *account form*, and *working-capital form* of balance sheet.

5–11. "Net assets are always equal to stockholders' equity." Do you agree? Explain.

5–12. "Depreciation is not a process of valuation in the ordinary sense of the term." Explain.

5–13. Why are separate cash funds for replacement of plant assets rare?

5–14. "A contra asset is a liability." Do you agree? Explain.

5–15. "Closing the books might better be called clearing the nominal accounts." Do you agree? Explain.

5–16. "The word *permanent* to describe real accounts is misleading." Explain.

5–17. Appendix 5A. Why are work sheets used?

5–18. Appendix 5B. "Variety in recording accounting transactions is unacceptable diversity." Do you agree? Explain.

5–19. Appendix 5B. "Liabilities can have temporary debit balances." Explain.

5–20. Appendix 5B. "Reversing entries are designed for the correction of errors." Do you agree? Explain.

5–21. **JOURNALIZE, POST, AND PREPARE TRIAL BALANCE.** Consider the accompanying Itami trial balance.

ITAMI ENGINEERING CONSULTANTS, INC.
Trial Balance
June 28, 19X5
(in thousands)

	DEBIT	CREDIT
Cash	$ 21	
Accounts receivable	110	
Unbilled client receivables	—	
Prepaid trade association dues	6	
Prepaid insurance	3	
Equipment	59	
Accumulated depreciation, equipment		$ 8
Accounts payable		16
Note payable		80
Accrued interest payable (on note)		5
Dividends payable		10
Accrued wages payable		—
Accrued income taxes payable		—
Unearned fee revenue		—
Paid-in capital		50
Retained income		21
Dividends declared	10	
Fee revenue		840
Rent expense	24	
Wages expense	400	
Depreciation expense	—	
Miscellaneous expenses	362	
Interest expense	5	
Income tax expense	30	
Total	$1,030	$1,030

The following additional information pertains to June 29 and 30, which is the end of Itami's fiscal year (amounts in thousands):

  a. Billed clients for $15.
  b. Paid the liability for dividends.
  c. Unbilled revenue as of June 30, based on time logged on various client projects, was $60. (Debit Unbilled Client Receivables.)
  d. Half the prepaid association dues had expired. (Debit Miscellaneous Expenses.)
  e. Wages incurred but unpaid, $9.
  f. One-third of the prepaid insurance had expired. (Debit Miscellaneous Expenses.)
  g. The note is payable on July 31. It is a 15%, seven-month note. Principal and interest are payable at maturity.
  h. Depreciation expense for the fiscal year is $10.
  i. Received $14 cash advance from a client for services to be rendered after June 30.
  j. Income tax rate was 35%.

Required:

  1. After posting the above balances to T-accounts, analyze and journalize all entries arising from the above information.
  2. Post the journal entries to T-accounts. Use check marks as posting references in the journal.
  3. Prepare an adjusted trial balance, June 30, 19X5.

5–22. **ADJUSTMENTS AND CLOSING.** Consider the accompanying Johnson trial balance.

JOHNSON COMPANY
Unadjusted Trial Balance
December 31, 19X2
(in thousands of dollars)

	DEBIT	CREDIT
Cash	$ 20	
Accounts receivable	100	
Notes receivable	50	
Merchandise inventory	120	
Prepaid rent	12	
Equipment	90	
Accumulated depreciation, equipment		$ 20
Accounts payable		130
Paid-in capital		100
Retained income		67
Sales		880
Cost of goods sold	460	
Wages expense	200	
Miscellaneous expenses	120	
Income tax expense	25	
Total	$1,197	$1,197

The following additional information is not reflected in the trial balance (amounts are in thousands):

a. Interest accrued on notes receivable, $5.

b. Depreciation, $10.

c. Wages accrued but unpaid, $6.

d. Utilities accrued but unpaid, $4 (charge Miscellaneous Expenses).

e. Rent expired, $5.

f. Dividend declared but unpaid, $12. Use a Dividends Declared account, which is really just an offset to Retained Income.

g. A cash receipt of $2 from a credit customer was credited erroneously to Accounts Payable, so a correction must be made.

h. Additional income tax expense must be accrued. The income tax rate is 40% of pretax income. Compute the additional tax after computing the effects of the above adjustments to revenue and expense accounts.

Required:

1. After posting the above balances to T-accounts, analyze and journalize all entries arising from the descriptions in *a* through *h* above. Use new accounts as necessary.
2. Post your journal entries to T-accounts. Use check marks as posting references in the journal.
3. Prepare an adjusted trial balance, December 31, 19X2. Allow space for four columns, placing your numbers for this requirement in the first pair of columns.
4. Prepare and post the closing journal entries to T-accounts. Key the entries as *i, j*, etc.
5. Prepare a postclosing trial balance by placing the appropriate numbers in the second pair of columns in your answer to requirement 3 above.

5–23. **PREPARE FINANCIAL STATEMENTS.**   Consider the accompanying Sauceda trial balance.

SAUCEDA RETAILERS, INC.
Adjusted Trial Balance
December 31, 19X5
(in thousands)

	DEBIT	CREDIT
Accounts payable		$ 70
Accounts receivable	$ 90	
Accrued income taxes payable		10
Accrued interest payable (due annually)		4
Accrued wages payable		20
Accumulated depreciation, building		70
Accumulated depreciation, equipment		47
Building	120	
Cash	49	
Cost of goods sold	498	
Dividends declared	11	
Equipment	60	
Income tax expense	20	
Interest expense	6	
Inventory	120	
Long-term note payable (due in 19X8)		50
Other operating expenses	110	
Paid-in capital		110
Prepaid insurance	2	
Retained income		35
Sales		970
Wages expense	300	
Total	$1,386	$1,386

Required:

1. Prepare a multiple-step income statement.
2. Prepare a statement of retained income.
3. Prepare a classified balance sheet.
4. Compute the working capital and the current ratio.

5–24. **CLOSING ENTRIES.** (Alternates are 5–3, 5–8, 5–9, and 5–25.) Sauceda Retailers, Inc., had the following accounts included in an adjusted trial balance, December 31, 19X5 (in thousands):

Cost of goods sold	$498	Interest		Sales	$970
Dividends declared	11	expense	$ 6	Wages	
Income tax expense	20	Other		expense	300
		operating			
		expenses	110		

Required:

After posting the above balances to T-accounts, journalize and post the entries to close the books. What is the balance in Retained Income after closing?

5–25. **CLOSING ENTRIES.** (Alternates are 5–3, 5–8, 5–9, and 5–24.) Itami Engineering Consultants, Inc., had the following accounts included in an adjusted trial balance, June 30, 19X5 (in thousands):

Retained income	$ 21	Rent expense	$ 24	Miscellaneous	
Dividends		Wages expense	409	expenses	$366
declared	10	Depreciation		Interest expense	6
Fee revenue	915	expense	10	Income tax	
				expense	35

Required: After posting the above balances to T-accounts, journalize and post the entries necessary to close the books. Number your entries as 1, 2, etc.

What is the balance in Retained Income after closing?

5–26. CLOSING THE ACCOUNTS. The following accounts show their final balances before closing and their closing entries (in thousands). Prepare the closing journal entries that were evidently made.

Cost of Goods Sold		Dividends Declared		Other Revenues	
500	500	70	70	40	40

Income Summary		Sales		Retained Income	
840	940	900	900	70	600
100					100

Other Expenses	
340	340

What is the balance in Retained Income after closing?

5–27. WORK SHEET. Appendix 5A. An unadjusted trial balance for Hartman Sporting Goods is on the accompanying work sheet. The following additional information is available.

a. Wages earned but unpaid, $2,000.

b. Adjustment for prepaid rent. Rent was paid quarterly in advance, $9,000 per quarter. Payments were due on January 1, April 1, July 1, and October 1.

c. The store equipment originally cost $16,800 on February 1, 19X1. It is being depreciated on a straight-line basis over seven years with zero expected terminal value.

d. The note payable is based on a one-year loan of $20,000. The note is dated November 1, 19X1. Principal plus 15% interest is payable at maturity.

e. Income taxes are to be accrued. The applicable income tax rate is 30%.

Required: Enter the adjustments and complete the work sheet.

5–28. WORK SHEET. Appendix 5A. Refer to Problem 5–21. Prepare a complete work sheet, including pairs of columns for unadjusted trial balance, adjustments and other entries, adjusted trial balance, income statement, statement of retained income, and balance sheet.

5–29. WORK SHEET. Study Appendix 5A. Refer to Problem 5–22. Prepare a complete work sheet, including pairs of columns for unadjusted trial balance, adjustments and other entries, adjusted trial balance, income statement, statement of retained income, and balance sheet for Johnson Company. If you did not solve Problem 5–22, prepare closing journal entries now.

5–30. ALTERNATIVE ANALYSES OF TRANSACTIONS. (Alternate is 5–31.) Study Appendix 5B. Consider the following balances, December 31, 19X1:

Accrued interest receivable	$10,000
Prepaid rent	6,000
Accrued wages payable	16,000

Exhibit for Assignment 5-27

HARTMAN SPORTING GOODS
Work Sheet
For the Month Ended February 28, 19X2

Account Title	Unadjusted Trial Balance Debit	Unadjusted Trial Balance Credit	Adjustments Debit	Adjustments Credit	Adjusted Trial Balance Debit	Adjusted Trial Balance Credit	Income Statement Debit	Income Statement Credit	Statement of Retained Income Debit	Statement of Retained Income Credit	Balance Sheet Debit	Balance Sheet Credit
Cash	26800											
Accounts receivable	36600											
Merchandise inventory	110000											
Prepaid rent	6000											
Store equipment	16800											
Accumulated depreciation, equip.		2400										
Accounts payable		62000										
Note payable		20000										
Accrued interest payable		750										
Paid-in capital		50000										
Retained income		45850										
Sales		93200										
Cost of goods sold	50000											
Advertising expense	4000											
Wages expense	1000											
Miscellaneous expenses	1000											
	270600	270600										

During 19X2, $30,000 cash was received for interest for one year on a long-term note of $200,000. Interest was due yearly on September 1. In addition, half the principal of the note was paid on September 1, 19X2.

During 19X2, cash disbursements of $39,000 were made for rent. The rent was payable $9,000 quarterly in advance on March 1, June 1, September 1, and December 1. The rent was raised to $12,000 quarterly beginning December 1, 19X2.

During 19X2, $800,000 was disbursed for wages. The ending balance of accrued wages payable, December 31, 19X2, was $25,000.

Required:

| In responding to the requirement for journal entries, use the following format:

	REQUIREMENT 1		REQUIREMENT 2	
EXPLANATION OF ENTRY	(in thousands of dollars)			
Summary cash receipts or disbursements	Journal entry		Journal entry	
End-of-period adjustments	Journal entry		Journal entry	
Example: Paid insurance of $40,000	Prepaid insurance Cash	40 40	Insurance expense Cash	40 40
Adjustment so that ending balance of prepaid insurance is $30,000	Insurance expense Prepaid insurance	10 10	Prepaid insurance Cash	30 30

1. Assume that the accounting system provides for the appropriate portions of the above cash collections and cash disbursements to be applied to any balances of accruals and prepayments carried over from the preceding period. Given the above data, prepare summary journal entries, including the adjusting entries, for 19X2. Post the entries to T-accounts. Do not prepare the entry for the repayment of the principal on the note.
2. Assume that the accounting system regards all the above cash collections and cash disbursements as revenues or expenses. Adjustments are then made at the end of each year to recognize the appropriate accruals and prepayments. Given the above data, prepare summary journal entries, including the adjusting entries for 19X2. Post the entries to T-accounts.
3. Which set of data-processing procedures do you prefer, those in requirement 1 or those in requirement 2? Explain.

5–31. **ALTERNATIVE ANALYSES OF TRANSACTIONS.** (Alternate is 5–30.) Study Appendix 5B. Consider the following balances, December 31, 19X1 (in thousands of dollars):

Accrued interest receivable	$16
Prepaid fire insurance	3
Accrued wages payable	8

The accounting system provides for cash collections of interest to be credited first to any existing accrued interest receivable carried over from the preceding period. Cash collections for interest during 19X2 were $24. Label this as entry f.

The accounting system for wages is to debit any existing accrued payables first and debit any remainder of the disbursement to expense. Cash disbursements for wages during 19X2 were $193. Label this as entry i.

Prepayments of expenses are routinely debited to asset accounts. A cash disbursement for a three-year insurance policy, effective September 1, 19X2, was $36. Label this as entry l.

1. Prepare T-accounts for Accrued Interest Receivable, Interest Revenue, Prepaid Fire Insurance, Insurance Expense, Accrued Wages Payable, and Wages Expense. Post the opening balances therein, December 31, 19X1. Journalize and post the above entries f, i, and l to the appropriate accounts. (At the same time, you may wish to use a Cash T-account to complete the postings. However, the Cash T-account is not required for purposes of this problem.)

2. The following correct balances were applicable at the end of 19X2:

Accrued interest receivable	$ 8
Prepaid fire insurance	?
Accrued wages payable	15

Journalize and post the adjusting entries, December 31, 19X2. Label them as o, p, and s. Assume that the prepaid insurance of December 31, 19X1, expired during 19X2.

3. Assume the same data as in requirements 1 and 2. However, suppose the following summarized journal entries had been made during 19X2:

ENTRY	ACCOUNTS AND EXPLANATION	POST REF.	DEBIT (in thousands of dollars)	CREDIT (in thousands of dollars)
f	Cash	✓	24	
	Interest revenue	✓		24
	Collection of interest.			
i	Wages expense	✓	193	
	Cash	✓		193
	Payments of wages.			
l	Insurance expense	✓	36	
	Cash	✓		36
	Payment of insurance.			

Given the above entries f, i, and l, prepare the adjusting journal entries o, p, and s, December 31, 19X2. Post the entries to a new set of T-accounts having the same opening balances given in the first paragraph of this problem. How do the ending balances in the accounts affected by the adjustments compare with the ending balances in the same accounts in requirement 2?

4. Which set of data-processing procedures do you prefer for interest, wages, and insurance, those in requirements 1 and 2 or those in requirement 3? Explain.

SPECIAL REVIEW MATERIAL

The problems in this special collection cover Chapters 1 through 5 in their entirety, with particular emphasis on relating the cash and accrual bases. Problem 5–32 is the most comprehensive.

Problems 5–38 through 5–40 focus on the reconstruction of economic events from incomplete data. They often require solving for unknown data from scattered known data. The use of T-accounts or the balance sheet equation is helpful.

5–32. **ACCOUNTING CYCLE.** This is a comprehensive review of Chapters 1 through 5. Diaz Lumber, a retail corporation, had the following postclosing trial balance, December 31, 19X1 (in thousands of dollars):

ACCOUNT NUMBER	NAME OF ACCOUNT	DR.	CR.
10	Cash	21	
20	Accounts receivable	100	
34	Notes receivable, current	100	
35	Accrued interest receivable	16	
40	Merchandise inventory	160	
52	Prepaid fire insurance	3	
62	Notes receivable, long-term	100	
74	Equipment	110	
74A	Accumulated depreciation, equipment		66
100	Accounts payable		90
111	Accrued wages payable		8
123	Accrued income taxes payable		4
137	Unearned sales revenue		10
200	Paid-in capital		110
230	Retained income		322
		610	610

The following summarized transactions (in thousands of dollars) occurred during 19X2:

a. Merchandise inventory purchased on open account was $520.

b. Total sales were $890, of which 80% were on credit.

c. The sales in *b* were exclusive of the deliveries of goods to customers who had paid in advance as of December 31, 19X1. All of those goods ordered in advance were indeed delivered during 19X2.

d. The cost of goods sold for 19X2, including those in *c*, was $440.

e. Collections from credit customers were $682.

f. The notes receivable are from a major supplier of lumber. Interest for twelve months on all notes was collected on May 1. The rate is 12% per annum. The accounting system provides for cash collections of interest to be credited first to any existing accrued interest receivable carried over from the preceding period.

g. The principal of the current notes receivable was collected on May 1, 19X2. The principal of the remaining notes is payable on May 1, 19X3 (see entry *q*). Transaction *t* also affects cash receipts.

Cash disbursements were:

h. To trade creditors, $500.

i. To employees for wages, $193. The accounting system for wages is to debit any existing accrued payables first and debit any remainder of a disbursement to expense.

j. For miscellaneous expenses such as store rents, advertising, utilities, and supplies, which were all paid in cash, $189. (These items are combined here to reduce the detailed recording of items that are basically accounted for alike.)

k. For new equipment acquired on July 1, 19X2, $74.

l. To the insurance company for a new three-year fire insurance policy effective September 1, 19X2, $36 (rates had increased). Prepayments of expenses are routinely debited to asset accounts.

m. To the federal and state governments for income taxes, $19. Income tax expense was debited for $15 of the $19. (For your general information, most businesses must pay income taxes regularly throughout the year.)

n. The board of directors declared cash dividends of $26 on December 15 to stockholders of record, January 5, and to be paid on January 21, 19X3. (Note that this is not a cash disbursement until payment has been made.) Debit Dividends Declared, which is really just an offset to Retained Income.

The following adjustments were made on December 31, 19X2:

o. For interest on notes receivable.
p. For insurance. The prepaid insurance of December 31, 19X1, had expired too.
q. For reclassification of the notes receivable.
r. For depreciation. Depreciation on old equipment in 19X1 was $22. All depreciation is straight-line. The old equipment is being depreciated over five years with no residual value. The new equipment is being depreciated over four years with a residual value of $10. One-half year's depreciation was taken on the new equipment in 19X2.
s. Wages earned but unpaid, December 31, 19X2, $15.
t. As of December 31, 19X2, customers had made a total of $7 in advance cash payments for "layaway" plans and for merchandise not yet in stock. These payments were exclusive of any other transactions described above. This is an explicit transaction rather than an adjustment. (Recall that in Chapter 4 adjustments were described as relating to *implicit* transactions.)
u. Total income tax expense for 19X2 is $20, computed as 40% of pretax income of $50. (Note that part of the 19X2 tax expense has already been recorded and paid, as indicated in transaction *m*.)

Required:

1. After posting the opening balances to T-accounts, analyze and journalize all transactions, including adjustments, for 19X2.
2. Post all journal entries to T-accounts. Be painstaking as you post. Use the given account numbers as posting references. For accounts not in the trial balance of December 31, 19X1, use check marks as posting references instead.
3. Prepare a trial balance, December 31, 19X2.
4. Prepare a multistep income statement for 19X2.
5. Prepare a statement of retained income for 19X2.
6. Prepare classified comparative balance sheets for December 31, 19X1 and 19X2. Classify the prepaid insurance, December 31, 19X2, as a current asset even though a portion thereof might justifiably be classified as a long-term asset.
7. Journalize and post the entries necessary to "close the books" for 19X2.

5–33. **WORK SHEET.** Study Appendix 5A. Refer to the preceding problem. Examine the accompanying unadjusted trial balance that includes the results of transactions *a* through *n* (and also *t*) (in thousands).

Required:

1. Prepare a twelve-column work sheet, using the unadjusted trial balance as the first pair of columns. Add pairs of columns for adjustments, adjusted trial balance, income statement, statement of retained income, and balance sheet. When entering the unadjusted trial balance on the work sheet, allow space for new accounts as follows: two spaces after Accounts Receivable, two spaces after Accounts Payable, and three spaces between Miscellaneous Expenses and Income Tax Expense.
2. Enter the adjustments for transactions *o* through *u*. The effects of transaction *t* are already contained in the unadjusted trial balance.
3. Complete the work sheet. Check the accuracy of your work by comparing the work sheet results with the formal financial statements prepared in the solution to Problem 5–32.

ACCOUNT TITLE	DEBIT	CREDIT
Cash	$ 1	
Accounts receivable	130	
Merchandise inventory	240	
Prepaid fire insurance	39	
Notes receivable, long-term portion	100	
Equipment	184	
Accumulated depreciation, equipment		$ 66
Accounts payable		110
Dividends payable		26
Unearned sales revenue		7
Paid-in capital		110
Retained income		322
Dividends declared	26	
Sales		900
Interest revenue		8
Cost of goods sold	440	
Wages expense	185	
Miscellaneous expense	189	
Income tax expense	15	
Total	$1,549	$1,549

5–34. **EFFECTS OF ERROR.** The bookkeeper of a certain firm, the Dark Co., included the cost of a new motor truck, purchased on December 30 for $16,000 to be paid in January, as an operating expense instead of as an addition to the proper asset account. What was the effect of this error ("no effect," "overstated," or "understated"?—use symbols n, o, or u, respectively) on:

1. Operating expenses for the year ended December 31	_____
2. Profit from operations for the year	_____
3. Retained earnings as of December 31 after the books are closed	_____
4. Total liabilities as of December 31	_____
5. Total assets as of December 31	_____

5–35. **EFFECTS OF ERRORS.** What will be the effect—understated (u), overstated (o), or no effect (n)—upon the income of the present and future periods if:

	PERIOD	
	19X1	19X2
1. Prepaid items like rent have been paid (in late 19X1) through half of 19X2 but not adjusted at the end of 19X1. The payments have been debited to Prepaid Rent. They were written off in mid-19X2.	_____	_____
2. Accrued wages payable have not been recognized at the end of 19X1.	_____	_____
3. Revenue has been collected in advance, but earned amounts have not been recognized at the end of 19X1. Instead all revenue was recognized as earned in 19X2.	_____	_____
4. Revenue for services rendered has been earned, but the unbilled amounts have not been recognized at the end of 19X1.	_____	_____

In all cases assume that amounts carried over into 19X2 would affect 19X2 operations via the routine accounting entries of 19X2.

5–36. **EFFECTS OF ERRORS.** Assume a going concern and analyze the effect of the following errors on the net profit figures for 19X1 and 19X2. Choose one of three answers: understated (u), overstated (o), or no effect (n). Problem a has been answered as an illustration.

    a. EXAMPLE: Failure to adjust at end of 19X1 for sales salaries accrued. 19X1: o; 19X2: u. (*Explanation*: In 19X1, expenses would be understated and profits overstated. This error would carry forward so that expenses in 19X2 would be overstated and profits understated.)

    b. Failure to adjust at end of 19X1 for interest earned but not received on notes receivable.

    c. Omission of Depreciation on Office Machines in 19X1 only. Correct depreciation was taken in 19X2.

    d. Machinery, cost price $500, bought in 19X1, was not entered in the books until paid for in 19X2. Ignore depreciation; answer in terms of the specific error described.

    e. Failure to adjust for the following at end of 19X2: Physical count of office supplies on hand, $100. Office Supplies, an asset account, was charged for purchases of supplies and had an unadjusted balance of $300.

    f. Three months' rent, collected in advance in December 19X1, for the first quarter of 19X2 was credited directly to Rent Earned in 19X1. No adjustment was made for the unearned rent at the end of 19X1.

5–37. **EFFECTS OF ADJUSTMENTS AND CORRECTIONS.** (Appendix 5B is helpful regarding some items.) Listed below are a series of accounts which are numbered for identification. All accounts needed to answer the parts of this question are included. Prepare an answer sheet with columns in which you are to write the identification numbers of the accounts affected by your answers. The same account may be used in several answers.

1. Cash	16. Accrued wages and salaries
2. Accounts receivable	payable
3. Notes receivable	17. Accrued interest payable
4. Inventory	18. Unearned subscription revenue
5. Accrued interest receivable	19. Capital stock
6. Accrued rent receivable	20. Sales
7. Fuel on hand	21. Fuel expense
8. Unexpired rent	22. Salaries and wages
9. Unexpired insurance	23. Insurance expense
10. Unexpired repairs and	24. Repairs and maintenance
maintenance	expense
11. Land	25. Rent expense
12. Buildings	26. Rent revenue
13. Machinery and equipment	27. Subscription revenue
14. Accounts payable	28. Interest revenue
15. Notes payable	29. Interest expense

Required:

Prepare any necessary adjusting or correcting entries called for by the following situations, *which were discovered at the end of the calendar year*. With respect to each situation, assume that no entries have been made regarding the situation other than those specifically described (i.e., no monthly adjustments have been made during the year). *Consider each situation separately*. These transactions were not necessarily conducted by one business firm. Amounts are in thousands of dollars. *Illustration*: Purchased new equipment for $100 cash, plus a $300 short-term note. The bookkeeper failed to record the transaction. The answer would appear as follows:

	ACCOUNT		AMOUNT	
	debit	credit	debit	credit
Illustration	13	1 & 15	400	100 & 300
a.	__	____	__	____
b.	__	____	__	____
c.	__	____	__	____
etc.	__	____	__	____

a. A business made several purchases of fuel oil. Some purchases ($800) were debited to Fuel Expense, while others ($1,100) were charged to an asset account. An oil gauge revealed $400 of fuel on hand at the end of the year. There was no fuel on hand at the beginning of the year.

b. On April 1, a business took out a fire insurance policy. The policy was for two years and the premium paid was $400. It was debited to Insurance Expense on April 1.

c. On December 1, $400 was paid in advance to the landlord for four months' rent. The tenant debited Unexpired Rent for $400 on December 1. What adjustment is necessary on December 31 on the tenant's books?

d. Machinery is repaired and maintained by an outside maintenance company on an annual fee basis, payable in advance. The $240 fee was paid in advance on September 1 and charged to Repairs and Maintenance Expense. What adjustment is necessary on December 31?

e. On November 16, $800 of machinery was purchased. $200 cash was paid down and a ninety-day, 5% note payable was signed for the balance. The November 16 transaction was properly recorded. Prepare the adjustment for the interest.

f. A publisher sells subscriptions to magazines. Customers pay in advance. Receipts are originally credited to Unearned Subscription Revenue. On August 1, many one-year subscriptions were collected and recorded, amounting to $12,000.

g. On December 30, certain merchandise was purchased for $1,000 on open account. The bookkeeper debited Machinery and Equipment and credited Accounts Payable for $1,000. Prepare a correcting entry.

h. A 120-day, 7%, $7,500 cash loan was made to a customer on November 1. The November 1 transaction was recorded correctly.

i. A $300 purchase of equipment on December 5 was erroneously debited to Accounts Payable. The credit was correctly made to Cash.

5–38. MEASURING INCOME ON CASH AND ACCRUAL BASES. Following are the summarized transactions of Dr. Cristina Faragher, a dentist, for 19X7, her first year in practice:

1. Acquired equipment and furniture for $50,000. Its expected useful life is five years. Straight-line depreciation will be used. Assume no salvage value.

2. Fees collected, $80,000. These fees included $2,000 paid in advance by some patients on December 31, 19X7.

3. Rent is paid at the rate of $500 monthly, payable on the twenty-fifth of each month for the following month. Total disbursements during 19X7 for rent were $6,500.

4. Fees billed but uncollected, December 31, 19X7, $15,000.

5. Utilities expense paid in cash, $600. Additional utility bills unpaid at December 31, 19X7, $100.

6. Salaries expense of dental assistant and secretary, $16,000 paid in cash. In addition, $1,000 was earned but unpaid on December 31, 19X7.

Dr. Faragher may elect either the cash basis or accrual basis of measuring income for income tax purposes, provided that she uses it consistently in subsequent years. Under either alternative, the original cost of the equipment and furniture must be written off over its five-year useful life rather than being regarded as a lump-sum expense in the first year.

Required:

1. Prepare a comparative income statement on both the cash and accrual bases, using one column for each basis.
2. Which basis do you prefer as a measure of Dr. Faragher's performance? Why? What is the justification for the government's allowing the use of the cash basis for income tax purposes?

5-39. **RECONSTRUCTION OF TRANSACTIONS.** The Jankowski Athletic Club presented the following statements at the end of 19X6:

Comparative Balance Sheets

	DECEMBER 31	
	19X6	19X5
Cash	$ 9,170	$ 1,100
Dues receivable	3,000	2,500
Investments	3,000	8,000
Furniture and fixtures	900	500
Accumulated depreciation on furniture and fixtures	(100)	—
Accrued interest receivable	200	100
Supplies	250	100
Total	$16,420	$12,300
Accounts payable (supplies only)	$ 1,300	$ 1,500
Notes payable	50	300
Accrued general expenses	450	400
Dues received in advance	—	100
Members' equity	14,620	10,000
Total	$16,420	$12,300

Supplemental Information:

Dues revenue for the year	$8,000
Cash collected during 19X6 for interest	600
Cash payments during 19X6 for supply purchases	1,850
Loss on the sale of investments	1,000

All purchases of supplies were on account. There were no dividends or other distributions to members.

Required:

Compute the following amounts:

1. Cash received in 19X6 for dues.
2. Interest revenue for 19X6.
3. Cash received from sale of investments. Even though accounting for investments has not been covered so far in the text, think how gains or losses might be accounted for. The approach is similar to the sale of equipment, which is illustrated in this chapter.
4. Supplies used (supplies expense) for 19X6.
5. Cash paid during 19X6 for general expenses. General expenses are all expenses other than supplies and depreciation.

5–40. JOURNAL ENTRIES. Cincinnati Bell, Inc., has provided communications services, mainly telephone services, in parts of Ohio, Kentucky, and Indiana. Its total operating revenues for a recent year were $275,733,000. Its balance sheets showed:

	END OF YEAR	BEGINNING OF YEAR
Advance billing and customers' deposits	$4,941,000	$4,085,000

To save space, annual reports often combine accounts. In this instance, Advance Billing is really one account, an unearned revenue account. For example, customers typically are billed for their basic monthly phone charges in advance of the service rendered.

Customers' Deposits is another account. For example, a new customer may be required to make a security deposit of $300. When the customer terminates the service, the deposit is usually returned in cash.

Required:

1. Prepare a summary journal entry to show how the $4,085,000 was initially recorded.
2. During the year, additional amounts of advance billings and deposits amounted to $14 million. Moreover, $2 million of customers' deposits was returned in cash to customers. Prepare summary journal entries for these events.
3. At the end of the year, prepare any necessary adjusting journal entry to obtain the balance given for the year.
4. Post all the above entries to T-accounts. (Use Cash or Accounts Receivable, Advance Billings and Customer Deposits, and Operating Revenues.)

5–41. FINANCIAL STATEMENTS. NL Industries, Inc., has widespread operations in petroleum services to the oil industry and in the manufacture of chemicals. A recent annual report included the items listed below (in millions of dollars). The balance sheet items included here are the amounts at December 31, unless otherwise indicated.

Property, plant, and equipment, original cost	$1,362
Accumulated depreciation	466
Net sales	2,536
Interest expense	65
Bank loans payable	32
Retained earnings, beginning of year	762
Common stock	50
Cost of goods sold	1,469
Provision for income taxes	194
Income taxes payable	108
Long-term debt	499
Additional paid-in capital	145
Selling, general, and administrative expenses	492
Dividends declared	59
Inventories	394
Prepaid expenses	12
Accounts payable	119
Accounts receivable	460
Accrued liabilities	209
Other liabilities (noncurrent)	117
Cash and equivalents	27
Other assets (noncurrent)	509

1. Prepare a combined multiple-step statement of income and retained earnings.
2. Prepare the classified balance sheet as of the end of the year.
3. Compute the working capital and the current ratio.

5–42. SUMMARIZED CORPORATE ANNUAL REPORT. Inspect an annual report of a publicly held corporation. (Your instructor will give more specific instructions regarding how to obtain access to such reports at your school.) Read the report. The report will contain many details not covered in your study to date. Nevertheless, you will see the general picture portrayed by the balance sheet, income statement, and other statements. Complete the following:

1. Name of company
2. Location of corporate headquarters
3. Principal products or services
4. Main geographic area of activity
5. Name and title of chief executive officer (CEO)
6. Ending date of latest operating year reported
7. Indicate the terms (if any) used instead of (a) balance sheet, (b) income statement, (c) retained income, (d) stockholders' equity, (e) revenues, (f) expenses
8. Total assets
9. Total liabilities
10. Total stockholders' equity
11. Total revenues (you may need to compute this)
12. Total expenses (you may need to compute this)
13. Net income (see above and subtract item 12 from item 11, then check the result with reported net income)
14. Total cash dividends declared
15. Earnings per share of common stock (EPS)
16. Annual dividends per share of common stock
17. Market in which stock is traded (see *Wall Street Journal* or local newspapers)
18. Latest market price of common (see *Wall Street Journal* or local newspapers)
19. Price-earnings ratio (compute or see *Wall Street Journal* or local newspapers)
20. Dividend yield (compute or see *Wall Street Journal* or local newspapers)
21. Dividend-payout ratio (you may need to compute this)
22. Name of independent public accountants
23. Did they certify that all amounts were correct? If not, what did they say? (Do not simply copy the actual wording; be brief.)
24. Total number of shareholders*
25. Total number of employees*
26. Total number of shares of common stock outstanding
27. Common stockholders' equity per share* (book value per share)
28. Comparative statistics (financial and operating data) were reported for how many years?
29. Give very briefly your general impression of this report (for example, quality, scope, usefulness, format, readability, interest to you, etc.)

---

* May not be reported by the corporation. If not reported, write "not available."

Chapter 6

SALES, RECEIVABLES, PURCHASES, AND COST OF GOODS SOLD

LEARNING OBJECTIVES

After studying this chapter, you should be able to

1. Compute gross profit rates and explain why they are important to managers and shareholders

2. Explain how to account for sales and purchase returns, allowances, and discounts, particularly for management use

3. Explain how accounts receivable are valued via the specific write-off method and the allowance method of accounting for uncollectible accounts

4. Identify the items included in the cost of merchandise acquired

5. Explain and illustrate the difference between perpetual and periodic inventory systems

6. Explain popular ways to estimate bad debt expense under the allowance method: (a) percentage of sales, (b) aging of accounts, and (c) percentage of ending accounts receivable (Appendix 6A)

7. Explain how trade discounts and cash discounts are analyzed for management use (Appendix 6B)

8. Show in detail how perpetual and periodic inventory systems affect unadjusted trial balances and work sheets (Appendix 6C)

TOPICAL COVERAGE OF TWO CHAPTERS

Accounting is commonly misunderstood as being a precise discipline that produces exact measurements of a company's financial position and performance. As a result, many individuals regard accountants as little more than mechanical tabulators who grind out financial reports after processing an imposing amount of detail in accordance with stringent predetermined rules. However, although accountants do take methodical steps with masses of data, their rules of measurement allow much room for judgment. Managers and accountants who exercise this judgment have more influence on financial reporting than is commonly believed.

The measurements of sales revenue and cost of goods sold are important areas affected by choices among accounting alternatives. This and the next chapter are a two-part package. Together they explain the calculation and meaning of *gross profit*. This chapter considers

1. Why gross profit is an important measure
2. What effects merchandise returns, allowances, and cash discounts have on revenue
3. How to account for credit sales and accounts receivable
4. What accounting procedures are used for perpetual and periodic inventory systems

The next chapter compares different methods of valuing inventories and discusses the impact of market prices on accounting for inventories.

IMPORTANCE OF GROSS PROFIT

As you already know from page 129, the difference between sales revenue and the cost of inventories sold is the *gross profit* or *gross margin*. Managers and investors are intensely interested in this margin and in its changes. Gross profit must exceed all operating expenses to produce a net income.

The approach here pertains to any entity that sells goods. However, we focus mostly on retailers and wholesalers. The accounting becomes more complicated for manufacturers because they use three major types of inventories: materials, work in process, and finished goods. Such coverage is beyond the scope of this discussion.[1]

---

[1] For a discussion of inventories in a manufacturing company, see *Introduction to Management Accounting*, the companion to this textbook.

Gross Profit Percentage

Gross profit is often expressed as a percentage of sales. Consider a typical Safeway grocery store:

	AMOUNT	PERCENTAGE
Sales	$1,000,000	100%
Cost of goods sold (also called cost of sales)	800,000	80
Gross profit (also called gross margin)	$ 200,000	20%

Investors and managers closely watch the gross profit percentage. It provides clues about the causes of changes in profit, as we see in the next sections.

Reports to Shareholders

Investors are often concerned about gross profits. Consider an example based on a quarterly report to shareholders of Superscope, Inc., a real-life manufacturer and distributor of stereophonic equipment that encountered rocky times. The following condensed income statement was presented for a three-month period (thousands omitted):

	CURRENT YEAR	PREVIOUS YEAR
Net sales	$40,000	$40,200
Costs and expenses:		
Cost of sales	33,100	28,200
Selling, general and administrative	11,200	9,900
Interest	2,000	1,200
Income (loss) before income tax provision (benefit)	(6,300)	900
Income tax provision (benefit)	(3,000)	200
Net income (loss)	$ (3,300)	$ 700

Although the statement does not show the amount of gross profit, the gross profit percentages can readily be computed as ($40,000 − $33,100) ÷ $40,000 and as ($40,200 − $28,200) ÷ $40,200, or 17% and 30%, respectively. To show how seriously these percentages are considered, the chairman's letter to shareholders began as follows:

☐ I shall attempt herein to provide you with a candid analysis of the Company's present condition, the steps we have instituted to overcome current adversities, and the potential which we believe can, in due course, be realized by the Company's realistic and positive determination to regain profitability.

☐ In the second quarter the Company's gross profit margins decreased to 17.2 percent compared to 30 percent in the corresponding quarter of a year ago. For the first six months gross profit margins were 21.8 percent, down from 31.2 percent for the corresponding period of a year ago.

☐ Essentially, the gross profits and consequential operating losses in the second quarter, as reflected in the condensed financial statements appearing in this report, resulted from lower than anticipated sales volume and from the following second quarter factors: liquidation of our entire citizens band inventory; increases in dealer cash discounts and sales incentive expenses; gross margin reductions resulting from sales of slow moving models at less than normal prices; and markdown of slow moving inventory on hand to a realistic net realizable market value.

☐ Gross Profit Tests

Auditors, including those from the Internal Revenue Service (IRS), use the gross profit percentage to satisfy themselves about the accuracy of records. For example, the IRS compiles gross profit percentages by types of retail establishment. If a company shows an unusually low percentage compared with similar companies, IRS auditors may suspect that the taxpayer has failed to record all cash sales. Similarly, managers watch changes in gross profit percentages to judge operating profitability and to monitor how well employee theft and shoplifting are being controlled.

Suppose an internal revenue agent, a manager, or an outside auditor had gathered the following data for a particular jewelry company for the past three years (in millions):

	19X3	19X2	19X1
Net sales	$350	$300	$300
Cost of goods sold	210	150	150
Gross profit	$140	$150	$150
Gross profit percentage	40%	50%	50%

This illustrates a **gross profit test** whereby the percentages are compared to detect any phenomenon worth investigating. Obviously, the decline in the percentage might be attributable to many factors. Possible explanations include the following:

1. Competition has intensified, resulting in intensive price wars that reduced selling prices.
2. The mix of goods sold has shifted so that, for instance, the $350 million of sales in 19X3 is composed of relatively more products bearing lower gross margins (e.g., more costume jewelry bearing low margins and less diamond jewelry bearing high margins).
3. Shoplifting or embezzling has soared out of control. For example, a manager may be pocketing and not recording cash sales of $70 million. After all, sales

in 19X3 would have been $420 million if the past 50% margin had been maintained.[2]

MERCHANDISE RETURNS AND ALLOWANCES

Every business sells merchandise that may be returned. The customer may be unhappy with the product for many reasons, including color, size, style, quality, and a simple changing of the mind. The supplier (vendor) calls these **sales returns**; the customer calls them **purchase returns**. Such merchandise returns are minor for manufacturers and wholesalers but are major for retail department stores. For instance, returns of 12% of gross sales are not abnormal for stores like Marshall Field's or Macy's.

Every business also sells products that may lead to subsequent reductions of the selling price (the original price previously agreed upon). The customer may not return the goods in question. For example, a customer may complain about scratches on a household appliance or about buying a toaster for $40 on Wednesday and seeing the same item for sale in the same store or elsewhere for $35 on Thursday. Such complaints are often settled by the seller's granting a **sales allowance**; the buyer receives a **purchase allowance**.

Managers of retail stores typically use two accounts for sales transactions: (1) *Sales* (which records gross sales as they occur), and (2) *Sales Returns and Allowances* (which compiles those two closely related sales reductions in a single account). Managers want such a separate record so they can watch changes in the level of returns and allowances. For instance, a change in the percentage of returns in fashion merchandise may give early signals about changes in customer tastes. Similarly, a buyer of fashion or fad merchandise may want to keep track of purchase returns to help assess the quality of products and services of various suppliers.

Consider an example of how to account for sales and sales returns and allowances. Suppose a J. C. Penney's Department Store has $900,000 gross sales on credit and $80,000 sales returns and allowances. The analysis of transactions would show:

	A	= L +	SE
Sales on credit	+900,000 [Increase Accounts Receivable]	=	+900,000 [Increase Sales]
Returns and allowances	−80,000 [Decrease Accounts Receivable]	=	−80,000 [Increase Sales Returns and Allowances]

The income statement would begin:

---

[2] Gross profit tests are applied in retailing to help control inventory shortages. This *retail method* of inventory control is explained in Chapter 8.

Gross sales	$900,000
Deduct: Sales returns and allowances	80,000
Net sales	$820,000

or

Sales, net of $80,000 returns and allowances	$820,000

The journal entries (without explanations) are:

Accounts receivable	900,000	
Sales		900,000
Sales returns and allowances	80,000	
Accounts receivable		80,000

DISCOUNTS FROM SELLING PRICES

There are two major types of sales discounts: *trade* and *cash*. **Trade discounts** begin with some gross selling price and apply one or more reductions thereto in accordance with management policies. These discounts are price concessions or ways of quoting the actual prices that are charged to various customers. Appendix 6B discusses trade discounts, including their management implications (such as discounts for bulk sales).

□ **Cash Discounts**

In contrast to trade discounts, **cash discounts** are rewards for prompt payment. They are rarely given to retail customers, and their use is decreasing among manufacturers and wholesalers. Consider an example. A manufacturer sells furniture to a retailer such as K Mart for $30,000. Terms are stated on the sales invoice as 2/10, n/60. This means that the retailer may remit $30,000 less a cash discount of .02 × $30,000, or $30,000 − $600 = $29,400, if payment is made within ten days after the invoice date. Otherwise the full $30,000 is due in sixty days.[3]

The cash discount is offered to entice prompt payment, which reduces the manufacturer's need to invest in Accounts Receivable. Early collection

---

[3] Terms may be quoted in various ways. For example

n/30 means the full billed price is due on the thirtieth day after the invoice date.

1/5, n/30 means payment less a 1% cash discount must be made within five days of the invoice date; otherwise the full billed price is due in thirty days after the invoice date.

15 E.O.M. means the full price is due within fifteen days after the end of the month of sale. Thus, if the invoice is dated December 20, payment is due January 15.

also reduces the risk of bad debts. On the other hand, the granting of favorable credit terms with attractive cash discounts is a way to compete with other sellers. That is, if one competitor grants such terms, other competitors tend to do likewise.

Should cash discounts be taken by purchasers? The answer is usually yes, but this depends on the relative costs of interest. Suppose K Mart decides not to pay for sixty days. It has the use of $29,400 for an extra fifty days $(60 - 10)$ for an "interest" payment of $600. Based on a 365-day year, that is an effective interest rate of approximately:

$$\frac{\$600}{\$29,400} = 2.04\% \text{ for 50 days, or } 14.9\% \text{ for 365 days}$$
(which is 2.04% multiplied by 7.3 periods of 50 days each)

Most well-managed companies, such as K Mart, can usually obtain funds for less than 14.9% per annum, so their accounting systems are designed to take advantage of all cash discounts automatically. However, some retailers have trouble getting loans or other financing at interest rates lower than the annual rates implied by the cash discount terms offered by their suppliers.

☐ Accounting for Cash Discounts

Cash discounts are essentially reductions of sales prices. The vast bulk of discounts offered are indeed taken. Consequently, a detailed income statement will often contain:[4]

Gross sales		xxx
Deduct:		
Sales returns and allowances	x	
Cash discounts on sales	x	xxx
Net sales		xxx

The important feature of the presentation is the fact that returns, allowances, and discounts are offsets to gross sales. Management may design an accounting system to use one account, Sales, or several accounts, as shown above. If only one account is used, all returns, allowances, and cash discounts would be direct decreases to the sales account. If a separate account is used for cash discounts on sales, the following analysis is made, using the numbers in our example:

---

[4] Reports to shareholders offer highly summarized figures. A typical example is Gulf & Western Industries, a large conglomerate. Its 1985 income statement began "Net sales . . . $1,667.2 million." In many countries outside the United States, the word *turnover* is used as a synonym for *sales*. For instance, in Denmark, Gulf & Western's performance would be described as a "turnover of $1,667.2 million."

	A	= L +	SE
1. Sell at terms of 2/10,n/60	+30,000 [Increase Accounts Receivable]	=	+30,000 [Increase Sales]
2. Either collect $29,400 ($30,000 less 2%)	+29,400 [Increase Cash]		−600 [Increase Cash Discounts on Sales]
	−30,000 [Decrease Accounts Receivable]	=	
or collect $30,000	+30,000 [Increase Cash]		
	−30,000 [Decrease Accounts Receivable]	=	(no effect)

The journal entries follow:

1.	Accounts receivable	30,000	
	Sales		30,000
2.	Cash	29,400	
	Cash discounts on sales	600	
	Accounts receivable		30,000
or			
	Cash	30,000	
	Accounts receivable		30,000

An alternative approach to accounting for cash discounts, called the "net" method, is described in Appendix 6B.

☐ Bank Cards

Many retailers accept bank cards such as VISA or MasterCard (or similar cards, such as American Express, Carte Blanche, or Diner's Club). Retailers do so for two major reasons: (a) to obtain credit customers who would otherwise shop elsewhere, and (b) to get cash immediately rather than wait for customers to pay in due course.

Retailers can deposit VISA slips in their bank accounts daily (just like cash). But this service costs money (usually from 3% to 5% of gross sales).[5] Thus sales of $10,000 could result in cash of only $10,000 − .03($10,000), or $10,000 − $300, or $9,700. The $300 amount could be separately tabulated for management control purposes:

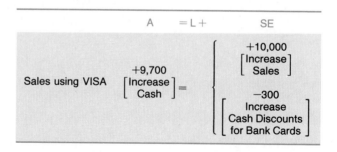

The journal entry follows:

Cash	9,700	
Cash discounts for bank cards	300	
Sales		10,000

CREDIT SALES AND ACCOUNTS RECEIVABLE

An entity's **accounts receivable** (sometimes called **trade receivables**) are amounts owed to the entity by its customers as a result of delivering goods or services and of extending credit in the ordinary course of business. Accounts receivable should be distinguished from deposits, accruals, notes, and other assets not arising out of everyday sales. Moreover, the amounts included as accounts receivable should be collectible in accordance with the company's usual terms of sale.

☐ Realization of Revenue

Chapter 2 (p. 38) describes the basic accounting concept of realization. Under *cash-basis accounting*, realization (earning) of revenue occurs simply when cash is collected for sales of goods or services. Under *accrual-basis accounting*, however, realization (earning) of revenue requires a three-pronged test. Goods or services must be (a) delivered to customers (b) in exchange for an asset (such as an account receivable) that (c) is virtually assured of being converted soon into cash.

How should accountants measure revenue? Ordinarily, by approximating the "net realizable value" of the asset inflow from the customer. That is,

---

[5] Large-volume retailers bear less cost as a percentage of sales. For example, J. C. Penney pays 4.3 cents per transaction plus 1.08% of the gross sales using bank cards.

the revenue is the present cash equivalent value of the asset received. Obviously, if a cash sale is made, the value of the asset is the cash inflow. If a credit sale is made, the value of the asset is often recorded on the same basis as a cash sale. However, the realizable value of a credit sale is not really the same as a cash sale. For example, some credit customers may never pay.

Uncollectible Accounts

Granting credit entails costs and benefits. One *cost* is the possibility that some credit customers will never pay. Another is the cost of administration and collection. The *benefit* is the boost in sales and profit that would otherwise be lost if credit were not extended. That is, many potential customers would not buy if credit were unavailable. The accountant often labels the major cost as "bad debt expenses" and the benefit as the additional gross profit on credit sales.

The extent of nonpayment of debts varies from industry to industry. It depends on the credit risks that managers are willing to accept. For instance, many small retail establishments will accept a higher level of risk than large stores such as Sears. Accompanying the risks are corresponding collection expenses.

The problem of uncollectible accounts is especially difficult in the health-care field. Some hospitals and physicians hire a collection agency for a fee based on collections attained, whereas others do not delegate this pursuit of delinquent debtors. For example, the Bayfront Medical Center of St. Petersburg, Florida, suffered bad debts equal to 21% of gross revenue. Management decided to collect its own delinquent accounts receivable instead of paying fees to a collection agency. The management problem here is also one of weighing costs and benefits. Will the reduction in collection fee expense exceed the reduction in collections of revenue?

Measuring Bad Debts: Specific Write-Off Method

The measurement of income becomes complicated because some debtors are either unable or unwilling to pay their debts. Such "**bad debts**" are also called "uncollectible accounts" or "doubtful accounts."

Suppose a retailer has credit sales of $100,000 (one thousand customers averaging $100 each) near the end of 19X1 and predicts on the basis of experience that $2,000 will never be collected (but cannot identify the *specific* customers who will not pay).

How should we account for this situation? There are two basic ways. First, consider the **specific write-off method** (also called **specific charge-off method**). Assume that during the second year, 19X2, the retailer identifies customers who are expected to never pay $2,000 that they owe from sales of 19X1. See the analysis below:

	A	= L +	SE

Specific Write-off Method

19X1 Sales	+100,000 [Increase Accounts Receivable]	=	+100,000 [Increase Sales]
19X2 Write-off	−2,000 [Decrease Accounts Receivable]	=	−2,000 [Increase Bad Debts Expense]

The *specific write-off* method is straightforward and easy to understand. All sales are assumed to be fully collectible until proved otherwise. For example, the balance sheet of December 31, 19X1, would show an asset:

Accounts receivable	$100,000

When the chances of collection from specific customers become dim, the amounts in the *particular accounts* are written down and some sort of selling expense (frequently called *bad debts expense* or *uncollectible accounts expense*) is recognized.

The specific write-off method has justifiably been criticized because it fails to apply the matching principle of accrual accounting. That is, the cause of the bad debts expense was the making of the sale. Accrual accounting maintains that the bad debts expense really relates to the period of sale rather than the period of actual write-off. In this example, the specific write-off method produces two wrongs. In 19X1, the $100,000 amount for assets and revenue is overstated by $2,000 because only $98,000 is actually expected to be collected. In 19X2, expenses are correspondingly overstated by $2,000. The $2,000 of bad debts expense should be recognized in 19X1, not 19X2, because it was caused by 19X1 sales. Otherwise 19X1 income is overstated by $2,000, and 19X2 income is understated by $2,000.

The principal arguments in favor of the specific write-off method are based on cost-benefit and materiality. The method is simple. Moreover, no great error in measurement occurs if amounts of bad debts are small or do not vary considerably from year to year.

□ Measuring Bad Debts: Allowance Method

The **allowance method** uses estimates and a contra asset (deduction from receivables) account, often called **allowance for uncollectible accounts, allowance for bad debts**, or **allowance for doubtful accounts**. A summary of its effects on the balance sheet equation follows:

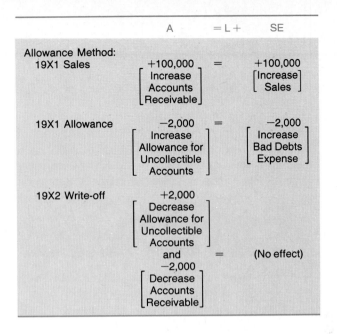

	A	= L +	SE
Allowance Method:			
19X1 Sales	+100,000 [Increase Accounts Receivable]	=	+100,000 [Increase Sales]
19X1 Allowance	−2,000 [Increase Allowance for Uncollectible Accounts]	=	−2,000 [Increase Bad Debts Expense]
19X2 Write-off	+2,000 [Decrease Allowance for Uncollectible Accounts] and −2,000 [Decrease Accounts Receivable]	=	(No effect)

The *allowance method* (also called the **reserve method**) would result in the following presentation in the balance sheet, December 31, 19X1:[6]

Accounts receivable	$100,000
Less: Allowance for uncollectible accounts	2,000
Net accounts receivable	$ 98,000

or

Accounts receivable, $100,000 less $2,000 allowance for uncollectible accounts	$ 98,000

or, as Ashton-Tate, producer of dBASE III and other computer software, reported (in thousands):

[6] Wyle Laboratories, a large electronics manufacturer, uses the term "reserves" instead of "allowances" in its annual report. Banks call their "allowances" *loan loss reserves*, which are offset against their total loans receivable from customers. During the 1980s, a nationwide rash of bad loans caused much concern about the adequacy of these reserves.

	JANUARY 31	
	1985	1984
Trade accounts receivable, less allowance for doubtful accounts of $1,555 and $941, respectively	$12,702	$8,457

Exhibit 6–1 summarizes the journal entries for the specific write-off method and the allowance method. The principal argument in favor of the allowance method is its superiority in measuring accrual accounting income in any given year. That is, the realization concept demands that income *earned in 19X1* be $100,000 *less* the $2,000 that is estimated never to be collected.

□ Applying the Allowance Method

A contra asset account is created under the allowance method because of the inability to write down a specific account at the time bad debts expense is recognized. In our example, at the end of 19X1 the retailer has, say, $70,000 in Accounts Receivable. Based on past experience, a bad debts expense is recognized at a rate of 2% of total credit sales, or .02 × $100,000, or $2,000.

Visualize the relationship between the general ledger item *Accounts Receivable* and its supporting detail (which is a form of supporting ledger, called a *subsidiary ledger*) on December 31, 19X1:

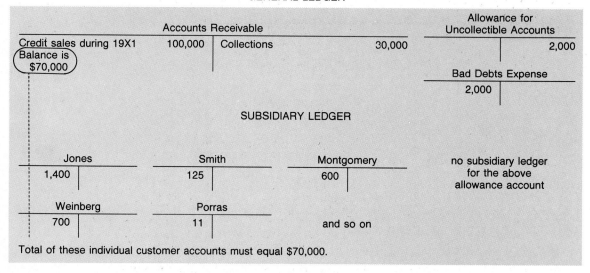

In 19X2, the Jones and Montgomery accounts become past due. After exhausting all practical means of collection, the retailer judges the accounts to be uncollectible. The following write-off entries would be made:

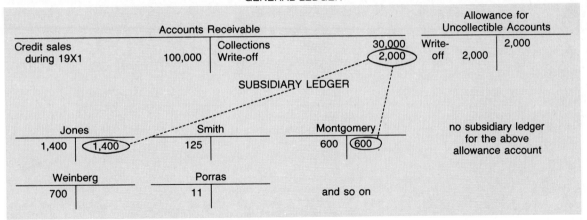

GENERAL LEDGER

Convince yourself that the ultimate write-off has no effect on total assets:

	BEFORE WRITE-OFF	AFTER WRITE-OFF
Accounts receivable	$70,000	$68,000
Allowance for uncollectible accounts	2,000	—
Book value (net realizable value)	$68,000	$68,000

☐ Bad Debt Recoveries

The allowance method is based on approximations. A few accounts will be written off as uncollectible, but then collection occurs at a later date. When such **bad debt recoveries** occur, the write-off should be reversed, and the

EXHIBIT 6-1

Journal Entries for Bad Debts

	1. SPECIFIC WRITE-OFF METHOD			2. ALLOWANCE METHOD		
19X1 Sales	Accounts receivable Sales	100,000	100,000	Accounts receivable Sales	100,000	100,000
19X1 Allowances	No entry			Bad debts expense Allowance for uncollectible accounts	2,000	2,000
19X2 Write-off	Bad debts expense Accounts receivable	2,000	2,000	Allowance for uncollectible accounts Accounts receivable	2,000	2,000

collection handled as a normal receipt on account. In this way, the customer is more likely to restore his or her otherwise poor credit rating with the company.

In our example, assume that Montgomery's account for $600 is written off in February 19X2 and collected in October 19X2. The appropriate journal entries are:

Feb. 19X2	Allowance for bad debts	600	
	Accounts receivable		600
	To write off uncollectible account		
	of Montgomery, a specific customer.		
Oct. 19X2	Accounts receivable	600	
	Allowance for bad debts		600
	To reverse February 19X2 write-off		
	of account of Montgomery.		
	Cash	600	
	Accounts receivable		600
	Collection on account		

For additional discussion of the problems of estimating bad debts and related matters, see Appendix 6A.

PERPETUAL AND PERIODIC INVENTORIES

The key to calculating the cost of goods sold is accounting for inventory. The remainder of the chapter explains two methods of keeping inventory records, perpetual and periodic inventory systems. The next chapter continues the discussion of inventories.

☐ General Comparison

There are two fundamental ways of keeping inventory records for merchandise: perpetual and periodic. The **perpetual inventory system** (which has been assumed in this textbook until now) keeps a running, continuous record that tracks inventories and the cost of goods sold on a day-to-day basis. Such a record facilitates managerial control and the preparation of interim financial statements. However, physical inventory counts should be taken at least once a year to check on the accuracy of the clerical records.

Previous chapters have described sales as two-phased transactions:

	A	= L +	SE
a. Sale	+ (Increase Accounts Receivable)	= +	(Increase Sales Revenue)
b. Cost of inventory sold	− (Decrease Inventory)	= −	(Increase Cost of Goods Sold)

The second phase illustrates the perpetual inventory system, which simultaneously attributes a specific cost to the inventory delivered to customers in the first phase.

The **periodic inventory system**, on the other hand, does *not* involve a day-to-day record of inventories or of the cost of goods sold. Instead the cost of goods sold and an updated inventory balance are computed only at the end of an accounting period, when a physical count of inventory is taken. The cost of the goods purchased is accumulated by recording the individual purchase transactions throughout any given reporting period, such as a year. The accountant computes the cost of goods sold by subtracting the ending inventories (determined by physical count) from the sum of the opening inventory and purchases. Exhibit 6–2 compares the perpetual and periodic inventory systems.

EXHIBIT 6–2

Inventory Systems

PERIODIC SYSTEM		PERPETUAL SYSTEM	
Beginning inventories		Cost of goods sold (kept	
(by physical count)	xxx	on a day-to-day basis	
Add: Purchases	xxx	rather than being de-	
Cost of goods available		termined periodi-	
for sale	xxx	cally)*	xxx
Less: Ending inventories			
(by physical count)	xxx		
Cost of goods sold	xxx		

* Such a condensed figure does not preclude the presentation of a supplementary schedule similar to that on the left.

As Exhibit 6–2 implies, the cost of goods sold under the perpetual system is computed instantaneously as goods are sold, whereas under the periodic system, the computation is delayed:

$$\underbrace{\text{Beginning inventory} + \text{Purchases}}_{\text{Amount available for sale}} - \underbrace{\text{Ending inventory}}_{- \text{Amount left over}} = \underbrace{\text{Cost of good sold}}_{= \text{Amount sold}}$$

The periodic system computes cost of goods sold as a *residual amount*. First, the beginning inventory is added to the purchases to obtain the total cost of goods available for sale. Then the ending inventory is counted, and its cost is deducted from the cost of goods available for sale to obtain the cost of goods sold.

Under the periodic inventory system, the gross margin for monthly and quarterly statements must usually be estimated (often based on past percentage relationships). Why? Because a physical inventory count is costly and therefore seldom taken more than once a year. Consequently, a gross margin percentage is typically applied to the current month's or quarter's sales. *Gross margin percentage* is defined as gross margin divided by sales.

☐ Physical Inventory

Good inventory control procedures require a physical count of inventory at least annually in both periodic and perpetual inventory systems. Such a count is necessary for calculating the cost of goods sold in a periodic inventory system. However, it can be just as important in a perpetual system, providing a check on the accuracy of the inventory records. Suppose the physical count differs from the perpetual inventory amount. For example, the following result might be obtained:

Perpetual inventory record:	Part 1F68X	142 units @ $20	$2,840
Physical count:	Part 1F68X	125 units @ $20	$2,500

Seventeen units (142 units − 125 units) have disappeared without being charged as cost of goods sold. Accountants call this *inventory shrinkage*, and it will be discussed in detail on pages 333–335 of Chapter 8. The journal entry to adjust inventory from $2,840 to $2,500 is

Inventory shrinkage	340	
Merchandise inventory		340
To adjust the ending inventory		
to its balance per physical count.		

☐ Which to Choose?

Whether a perpetual or a periodic system is desirable depends on the relative costs and benefits of each. Perpetual systems are becoming more popular because they increase management's control over operations and because their data-processing costs have dropped substantially. Computers and optical scanning equipment have become more versatile and less costly.

Small businesses tend to favor the periodic inventory system. As businesses grow and become more complex, perpetual inventory systems are installed. Many unhappy surprises can be avoided if managers keep a closer watch on inventories than periodic systems ordinarily provide.

In summary, the perpetual system is more accurate but more costly. The periodic system is less accurate, especially for monthly or quarterly statements. It is less costly because there is no day-to-day data processing regarding cost of goods sold. However, if theft or the accumulation of obsolete merchandise is likely, periodic systems often prove to be more expensive in the long run.

COST OF MERCHANDISE ACQUIRED

☐ Difficulties of Measuring Cost

The cost of merchandise acquired eventually becomes part of the cost of goods sold in the gross profit section of the income statement. What items constitute the cost of incoming merchandise? To be more specific, does cost include all or part of the following: invoice price, transportation charges, trade and cash discounts, cost of handling and placing in stock, storage, purchasing department, receiving department, and other indirect charges? In practice, accountants usually regard only the invoice price plus the directly identifiable transportation charges less any offsetting discounts as the cost of merchandise. The other costs are classified as administrative or operating expenses; they are placed below the gross profit line in an income statement.

The accounting for *purchase* returns, purchase allowances, and cash discounts on purchases is just the opposite of their sales counterparts. Using the periodic inventory system, suppose gross purchases were $960,000 and purchase returns and allowances were $75,000. The summary journal entries would be:

Purchases	960,000	
Accounts payable		960,000
Accounts payable	75,000	
Purchase returns and allowances		75,000

Suppose also that cash discounts of $5,000 were taken upon payment of the remaining $960,000 − $75,000 = $885,000 of payables. The summary journal entry would be:

Accounts payable	885,000	
Cash discounts on purchases		5,000
Cash		880,000

The accounts *Cash Discounts on Purchases* and *Purchase Returns and Allowances* are deducted from Purchases in calculating cost of goods sold.

☐ Inward Transportation

The major cost of transporting merchandise is typically the freight charges from the shipping point of the seller to the receiving point of the buyer. When the seller bears this cost, the terms are stated on the sales invoice as F.O.B. destination. When the buyer bears this cost, the terms are stated as F.O.B. shipping point. **F.O.B.** means "free on board."

In theory, any transportation costs borne by the buyer should be added to the cost of the inventory acquired. In practice, several different items are typically ordered and shipped simultaneously. Therefore it is often difficult to allocate freight costs among the items. In addition, management may want to compile freight costs separately to see how they compare with regard to periods and modes of transportation. Consequently, accountants frequently use a separate transportation cost account, labeled as Freight In, Transportation In, Inbound Transportation, or Inward Transportation.

Freight in (or **inward transportation**) appears in the purchases section of an income statement as an additional cost of the goods acquired during the period. On the other hand, **freight out** represents the costs borne by the *seller* and is shown as a "shipping expense," which is a form of selling expense. Thus Freight In affects the gross profit section of an income statement, but Freight Out does not and should therefore appear below the gross profit line. A detailed gross profit section often is arranged as follows (figures in thousands are assumed):

Gross sales			$1,740
Deduct: Sales returns and allowances		$ 70	
Cash discounts on sales		100	170
Net sales			$1,570
Deduct: Cost of goods sold:			
Merchandise inventory, December 31, 19X1		$100	
Purchases (gross)	$960		
Deduct: Purchase returns and allowances	$75		
Cash discounts on purchases	5	80	
Net purchases		$880	
Add: Inward transportation		30	
Total cost of merchandise acquired		910	
Cost of goods available for sale		$1,010	
Deduct: Merchandise inventory,			
December 31, 19X2		140	
Cost of goods sold			870
Gross profit or gross margin			$ 700

ACCOUNTING PROCEDURES FOR PERIODIC INVENTORY SYSTEMS

☐ **Details of Cost of Goods Sold Section**

Exhibit 6–3 provides a detailed cost of goods sold section of an income statement for 19X2. The balance in merchandise inventory at the beginning of 19X2 (December 31, 19X1) was $100,000. A summary of transactions for 19X2 follows:

a. Purchases	$990,000
b. Purchase returns and allowances	$ 80,000

The physical count of the ending inventory for 19X2 led to a cost valuation of $140,000. Note how these figures are used to compute the $870,000 cost of goods sold:

$$\frac{\text{Beginning}}{\text{inventory}} + \text{Net purchases} - \frac{\text{Ending}}{\text{inventory}} = \frac{\text{Cost of}}{\text{goods sold}}$$

$$\$100,000 + \$910,000 - \$140,000 = \$870,000$$

$$\underbrace{\qquad\qquad}_{\substack{\text{Cost of goods} \\ \text{available for sale}}} - \frac{\text{Cost of goods}}{\text{left over}} = \frac{\text{Cost of}}{\text{goods sold}}$$

$$\$1,010,000 - \$140,000 = \$870,000$$

EXHIBIT 6–3

Gross Profit Section of Income Statement for 19X2 (in thousands)

	PERPETUAL		PERIODIC	
Sales (assumed)	$1,570			$1,570
Deduct cost of goods sold:				
Merchandise inventory,				
December 31, 19X1			$ 100	
Add: Purchases		$990		
Deduct: Purchase returns and allowances		80		
Net purchases			910	
Cost of goods available for sale			$1,010	
Deduct: Merchandise Inventory,				
December 31, 19X2			140	
Cost of goods sold	870*			870
Gross profit or gross margin	$ 700			$ 700

* As Exhibit 6–4 shows, the records are kept so that no separate accounts exist for Purchases, Purchase Returns and Allowances, and similar accounts. Nevertheless, the Inventory account could be analyzed if desired to present the same details revealed on the right by the periodic method.

Exhibit 6–4 compares the balance sheet effects of the perpetual and periodic inventory systems. The analysis is confined to the relevant accounts. For simplicity, the opening balance sheet consists solely of Inventory and Accounts Payable; furthermore, no cash is paid on accounts throughout the year.

As Exhibit 6–4 shows, the perpetual system entails directly increasing the Inventory account by the $990,000 purchases and decreasing it by the $870,000 cost of goods sold. The Cost of Goods Sold account would be increased daily as sales are made. In a nutshell, these entries should be familiar. The only new aspect here is the accounting for the purchase returns, allowances, and cash discounts (if any). These directly reduce the Inventory account, as the $80,000 purchase return illustrates. The only closing entry at the end of the period is the transfer of cost of goods sold to income summary.

Before proceeding, reflect on the perpetual system in Exhibit 6–4.

The periodic system is called "periodic" because neither the Cost of Goods Sold nor the Inventory accounts are computed on a daily basis. Moreover,

EXHIBIT 6–4

Comparative Analysis of Purchase Transactions (in thousands of dollars)

	A			= L +		SE
PERIODIC SYSTEM	Inventory	Purchases	Purchase Returns and Allowances	Accounts Payable		
Balance, 12/31/X1	+100			= +100		
a. Gross purchases		+990		= +990		
b. Returns and allowances			−80	= −80		
c. As goods are sold (no entry)						
Closing the accounts at end of period:						
d1. Transfer to cost of goods sold	−100	−990	+80	=	−1,010	[Increase Cost of Goods Sold]
d2. Recognize ending inventory	+140			=	+140	[Decrease Cost of Goods Sold]
d3. Transfer cost of goods sold to income summary				=	+870	[Decrease Cost of Goods Sold]
					−870	[Decrease Income Summary]
Ending balances, 12/31/X2	+140	0	0	= +1,010	−870	
PERPETUAL SYSTEM						
Balance, 12/31/X1	+100			= +100		
a. Gross purchases	+990			= +990		
b. Returns and allowances	−80			= −80		
c. As goods are sold	−870			=	−870	[Increase Cost of Goods Sold]
Closing the accounts at end of period:						
d1. } No entry						
d2. }						
d3. Transfer cost of goods sold to income summary				=	+870	[Decrease Cost of Goods Sold]
					−870	[Decrease Income Summary]
Ending balances, 12/31/X2	+140			= +1,010	−870	

Purchases and Purchase Returns and Allowances are accounted for separately, as entries *a* and *b* indicate. Entries *d*1 and *d*2 in Exhibit 6–4 show the eventual periodic calculation of cost of goods sold.

The periodic system may seem awkward when compared with the perpetual system. The beginning inventory and cost of goods sold are untouched until the end of the period. However, the periodic system avoids the costly process of calculating the cost of goods sold for each sale.

Entry *d*1 transfers the beginning inventory balance, purchases, and purchase returns and allowances, totaling $1,010,000, to cost of goods sold. This provides the cost of goods available for sale, the first step in calculating cost of goods sold.

Next, the ending inventory is physically counted and its cost is computed. Entry $d2$ recognizes the $140,000 ending inventory and reduces the $1,010,000 cost of goods available for sale by $140,000 to obtain a final cost of goods sold of $870,000. All of these details can be shown in the cost of goods sold section of the income statement. However, published income statements usually include only a single cost of goods sold number.

☐ Journal Entries

The journal entries for the perpetual and periodic records follow, using the foregoing data:

	PERPETUAL RECORDS			PERIODIC RECORDS		

a. Gross purchases:	Inventory
	    Accounts payable
		990	990	Purchases
				    Accounts payable
					990	990

b. Returns and allowances:	Accounts payable
	    Inventory
		80	80	Accounts payable
				    Purchase returns
				      and allowances
					80	80

c. As goods are sold:	Cost of goods sold Inventory	870	870	No entry		

d. At the end of the accounting period:	d1.
	d2. } No entry
				d1. Cost of goods sold
				    Purchase returns
				      and allowances
				    Purchases
				    Inventory
					1,010
					
					80
						
						990
						100

				d2. Inventory Cost of goods sold	140	140

The cost of goods sold would be closed to income summary under either method:

d3. Income summary	870	
Cost of goods sold		870

Exhibit 6–5 shows the postings of the above journal entries. Note that the periodic method produces the same final balances in Inventory and Income Summary as the perpetual method. However, as entries $d1$ and $d2$ demonstrate, the cost of goods sold is computed at the end of the year; consequently, the related journal entries and postings are made then.

EXHIBIT 6–5

General Ledger

PERPETUAL INVENTORY		PERIODIC INVENTORY

PERPETUAL INVENTORY

Accounts Payable

(b)	80	*	100
		(a)	990

Inventory

*	100	(b)	80
(a)	990	(c)	870

Cost of Goods Sold

(c)	870	(d3)	870

Income Summary

(d3)	870	

PERIODIC INVENTORY

Accounts Payable

(b)	80	*	100
		(a)	990

Inventory

*	100	(d1)	100
(d2)	140		

Cost of Goods Sold

(d1)	1,010	(d2)	140
		(d3)	870

Income Summary

(d3)	870	

Purchases

(a)	990	(d1)	990

Purchase Returns and Allowances

(d1)	80	(b)	80

* Balance in thousands of dollars, December 31, 19X1.

SUMMARY

Most organizations use the allowance method for measuring bad debts. The allowance method provides a better linking of cause (credit sales) and effect (bad debts) than the direct write-off method.

Returns, allowances, and discounts are deductions from the sales or purchases to which they pertain. The extent of individual recordkeeping for these items depends on their materiality and their usefulness to the managers in particular organizations.

Perpetual inventory records may be kept for units only or for both units and dollars. Periodic inventory records are less detailed, although separate accounts are usually kept for purchases, purchase returns and allowances, and cash discounts on purchases. The journal entries for cost of goods sold in the periodic system are made at the end of the accounting period. Such entries in a perpetual system are made continuously.

SUMMARY PROBLEMS FOR YOUR REVIEW

☐ Problem One

Following are some accounts taken from the trial balance of the Ace Department Store, December 31, 19X5. Prepare a detailed income statement for 19X5. All amounts are in thousands.

Office salaries	$ 38	Cash discounts on sales	$ 1
Sales salaries and commissions	200	Purchase returns and allowances	10
Depreciation expense, trucks and store fixtures	10	Office supplies used	3
Purchases	431	Income tax expense	30
Sales returns and allowances	50	Rent expense, selling space	40
Delivery expenses (akin to freight out)	30	Cash discounts on purchases	2
Unearned sales revenue	7	Depreciation expense, office equipment	1
Allowance for bad debts	12	Advertising expense	30
Inventory, December 31, 19X4	270	Freight in	25
Rent expense, office space	6	Bad debts expense	10
		Miscellaneous expense	6
		Sales	1,039

The amount of inventory on hand, December 31, 19X5, determined by a physical count, was $200.

☐ **Solution to Problem One**

The detailed income statement is in Exhibit 6–6. Note the classification of operating expenses into a selling category and a general and administrative category. The list of accounts in the problem contained two items that belong in a balance sheet rather than an income statement, the Unearned Sales Revenue (a liability) and the Allowance for Bad Debts (an offset to Accounts Receivable).

EXHIBIT 6–6

ACE DEPARTMENT STORE
Income Statement
For the Year Ended December 31, 19X5
(in thousands)

Revenues:			
Gross sales			$1,039
Less: Sales returns and allowances		$ 50	
Cash discounts on sales		1	51
Net sales			$ 988
Cost of goods sold:			
Inventory, December 31, 19X4		$270	
Add: Gross purchases	$431		
Less: Purchase returns and allowances	$10		
Cash discounts on purchases	2	12	
Net purchases		$419	
Add: Freight in		25	
Cost of merchandise acquired		444	
Cost of goods available for sale		$714	
Deduct: Inventory, December 31, 19X5		200	
Cost of goods sold			514
Gross profit from sales			$ 474
Operating expenses:			
Selling expenses:			
Sales salaries and commissions		$200	
Rent expense, selling space		40	
Advertising expense		30	
Depreciation expense, trucks and store fixtures		10	
Bad debts expense		10	
Delivery expenses		30	
Total selling expenses		$320	

Exhibit 6 (continued)

General and administrative expenses:			
Office salaries	$ 38		
Rent expense, office space	6		
Depreciation expense, office equipment	1		
Office supplies used	3		
Miscellaneous expense	6		
Total general and administrative expenses		54	
Total operating expenses			374
Income before income tax			$ 100
Income tax expense			30
Net income			$ 70

The delivery expenses and the bad debts expense are shown under selling expenses. Some accountants prefer to show the bad debts expense as an offset to gross sales.

☐ Problem Two

H. J. Heinz Company sells many popular food products, including its best-selling Heinz ketchup. Its balance sheet showed the following (in millions):

	MAY 1	
	1985	1984
Receivables:	343	307
Less allowance for doubtful accounts	10	12
	$333	$295

Required:

Suppose a large grocery chain that owed Heinz $2 million announced bankruptcy on May 2, 1985. Heinz decided that chances for collection were virtually zero. The account was immediately written off. Show the balances as of May 2, 1985, after the write-off. Explain the effect of the write-off on income for May 1985.

☐ Solution to Problem Two

Receivables ($343 − $2)	$341
Less allowance for doubtful accounts	8
	$333

The write-off will not affect the *net* carrying amount of the receivables, which is still $333 million. Moreover, the income for May 1985 will be unaffected. Why? Because the estimated expense has already been recognized in prior periods. Under the allowance method, net assets and income are affected when the estimation process occurs, not when the write-off actually happens.

HIGHLIGHTS TO REMEMBER

The allowance method of accounting for bad debts recognizes an expense before the specific bad account is identified and written off.

The terms *net sales* and *net purchases* represent gross amounts less offsetting amounts for returns, allowances, and cash discounts.

Inward transportation is typically regarded as an addition to the purchase cost of merchandise acquired.

The mechanics of a periodic inventory system may seem cumbersome, but the aims are the same as those of the perpetual inventory system: to compute the proper cost of goods sold for the period in question and the proper ending inventory.

ACCOUNTING VOCABULARY

Accounts Receivable, p. *218* Aging of Accounts, *237* Allowance for Bad Debts, *220* Allowance for Doubtful Accounts, *220* Allowance for Uncollectibles, *220* Allowance Method, *220* Average Collection Period, *238* Bad Debt Recoveries, *223* Bad Debts, *219* Cash Discounts, *215* F.O.B., *227* Freight in, *228* Freight out, *228* Gross Profit Test, *213* Inward Transportation, *228* Periodic Inventory System, *225* Perpetual Inventory System, *224* Purchase Allowances, *214* Purchase Returns, *214* Reserve Method, *221* Sales Allowances, *214* Sales Returns, *214* Specific Charge-off Method, *219* Specific Write-off Method, *219* Trade Discounts, *215* Trade Receivables, *218*

APPENDIX 6A: MORE ON ACCOUNTS RECEIVABLE AND BAD DEBTS

ESTIMATING UNCOLLECTIBLES

This chapter includes a section on accounting for bad debts. The allowance method was cited as being more consistent with accrual accounting than the specific write-off method. We now explore the allowance method in more detail. To refresh your memory, please review the chapter presentation on pages 220–224 before proceeding here.

The net amount of Accounts Receivable is supposed to equal the net realizable value of the asset. Therefore, if the Allowance for Bad Debts is too high, the net asset is understated; if too low, the net asset is overstated. The general tendency is to be conservative, which means that the allowance is usually overstated.

Under the allowance method, there are three popular ways to estimate the bad debts expense for a particular year: (1) percentage of sales, (2) percentage of ending accounts receivable, and (3) aging of accounts. The percentage of sales method is used in the example on page 222. Based on past experience, bad debts expense is recognized at a percentage rate of total credit sales (or of total sales if the proportions of cash and credit sales are little changed through the years). This percentage may be altered from year to year, depending on the amount in the Allowance for Bad Debts that is carried over from one year to the next. Bad debts expense is debited and the allowance account is credited.

The main weakness of the percentage of sales method is that it ignores the most current information about receivables, the actual collection experience for the year. The other two methods incorporate this information by basing the allowance on the end-of-the-year accounts receivable balance rather than on the entire year's sales.

PERCENTAGE OF ENDING ACCOUNTS RECEIVABLE

Auditors of the Internal Revenue Service favor the percentage of ending accounts receivable method as a reasonable approach for applying the accrual method of accounting to bad debts. The additions to the Allowance for Bad Debts are calculated to achieve a desired balance in the Allowance account. Consider the following:

| | ACCOUNTS RECEIVABLE AT END OF YEAR | BAD DEBT EXPERIENCE | |
		Deemed Uncollectible and Written Off	Recoveries
19X1	$100,000	$ 3,800	$ 300
19X2	80,000	2,700	250
19X3	90,000	2,700	150
19X4	110,000	4,600	500
19X5	120,000	6,000	400
19X6	112,000	2,400	200
Six-year total	$612,000	$22,200	$1,800
Average (divide by 6)	$102,000	$ 3,700	$ 300

The 19X6 addition to the Allowance for Bad Debts would be computed as follows:

1. Determine the average net losses as a percentage of the average ending balance of Accounts Receivable: Average net bad debt losses would be $3,700 less $300 average recoveries, or $3,400. Divide $3,400 by $102,000 to obtain 3.333%.
2. Apply the percentage to the ending Accounts Receivable balance to determine the balance that should be in the Allowance account at the end of the year: 3.333% × $112,000 receivables at the end of 19X6 is $3,733.
3. Prepare an adjusting entry to bring the Allowance to the appropriate amount. Suppose the books show a $600 balance at the end of 19X6. Then the bad debts expense for 19X6 is $3,733 − $600, or $3,133. The journal entry would be:

Bad debts expense	3,133	
Allowance for bad debts		3,133
To bring the Allowance to the level justified by bad debt experience during the past six years.		

The *percentage of accounts receivable method* differs from the percentage of sales method in two ways: (1) the percentage is based on the ending accounts receivable balance rather than on sales, and (2) the dollar amount calculated is the appropriate *ending balance* in the allowance account, not the amount added to the account for the year.

AGING OF ACCOUNTS

Aging of accounts is an analysis of the elements of individual accounts receivable according to the time elapsed since the dates of billing. Aging is done for management control purposes as well as for financial-reporting purposes. Like the percentage of ending accounts receivable method, the aging method estimates the appropriate *ending balance* in the allowance account. Computer technology facilitates the regular aging of accounts for credit managers. In this way, managers can easily detect the accounts that deserve follow-up for collection purposes. For example, a $112,000 balance in Accounts Receivable on December 31, 19X6, might be aged as follows:

NAME	TOTAL	1–30 DAYS	31–60 DAYS	61–90 DAYS	OVER 90 DAYS
Oxwall Tools	$ 20,000	$20,000			
Chicago Castings	10,000	10,000			
Estee	20,000	15,000	$ 5,000		
Sarasota Pipe	22,000		12,000	$10,000	
Ceilcote	4,000			3,000	$1,000
Other accounts (each detailed)	36,000	24,000	8,000	2,000	2,000
Total	$112,000	$69,000	$25,000	$15,000	$3,000
Bad debt percentages		0.1%	1%	5%	90%
Bad debt allowance to be provided	$ 3,769	$ 69	$ 250	$ 750	$2,700

Experience with the aging schedule may lead to its being used as the primary basis for estimating bad debts. The accounts with the oldest outstanding balances should have already been subject to extra collection efforts. As the tabulation indicates, the outlook for ultimate collection is less optimistic as the age of the account balance increases. Experience leads to the percentages illustrated. In this case, fully 90% of the balances older than ninety days are not expected to be collected.

The outside auditors examine the aging schedule to assess the net realizable value of the accounts. It is foolhardy to rely solely on some overall percentage. In particular, this year's proportion of the accounts receivable in the over-ninety-days category is compared with the proportion in previous years.

Auditors do not like surprises. Percentages based on past experience may not provide an appropriate allowance for bad debts when a big customer has suddenly slowed payments. For example, is Sarasota Pipe's $22,000 balance heading for the over-ninety-days category? Is Sarasota Pipe heading for bankruptcy? These are specific questions that the credit manager and the auditors should ask (rather than blindly using past percentages).

Another advantage of the aging schedule is that credit managers can make particular judgments about the quality of their customers. For instance, suppose Oxwall Tools bought plenty of merchandise but habitually was a "slow-pay" customer. Aging schedules always showed substantial balances in the 61–90 and over-90-day columns. Should the credit manager crack down on Oxwall? Many companies tolerate slow-paying customers (especially if they are big customers) as a way of competing. If so, the over-ninety-days schedule would have to be divided between those slow payers who are tolerated for legitimate competitive reasons and those who are likely dead-beats.

AVERAGE COLLECTION PERIOD

The average age of accounts receivable is a key financial ratio. It is often called the *average collection period* and is defined as follows:

$$\text{Average collection period} = \frac{\text{Average accounts receivable}}{\text{Sales on account}} \times 365$$

In our example, suppose that sales on account (or credit sales) in 19X6 were $1 million:

$$\text{Average collection period} = \frac{\frac{1}{2}\,(\$120,000 + \$112,000)}{\$1,000,000} \times 365$$
$$= 42.3 \text{ days}$$

Credit managers, bank loan officers, and auditors follow changes in this ratio and compare it with the entity's credit terms. Of course, the lengthening of collection periods is usually not a welcome signal, although it is sometimes the result of a deliberate loosening of credit terms in order to attract more sales.

Another way of computing the average collection period follows:

$$\text{One day's sales on account} = \frac{\text{Sales on account for the year}}{365 \text{ days}}$$
$$= \$1,000,000 \div 365$$
$$= \$2,740$$
$$\text{Average collection period} = \frac{\text{Average accounts receivable}}{\text{One day's sales on account}}$$
$$= \frac{\frac{1}{2}\,(\$120,000 + \$112,000)}{\$2,740}$$
$$= \$116,000 \div \$2,740$$
$$= 42.3 \text{ days}$$

APPENDIX 6B: MORE ON DISCOUNTS

This appendix discusses trade discounts, management analysis of discounts, and the net method of accounting for cash discounts.

☐ Trade Discounts

Various industries use assorted ways of determining the particular selling price for different types of sales transactions. A popular way is the *trade discount*, which reduces the gross selling price by some percentage. For example, as many customers of so-called discount retail catalog merchandisers know, the "full" retail price is listed together with some codes or instructions that show the "discounted" selling price. Consider the following from Best Products Company's *Buyer's Book*:

620157BL*9446* . . . $144.95

The numbers after the letters indicate the $94.46 price paid by Best's customers, whereas the $144.95 is the comparable full retail price. The initial numbers plus the letters form a catalog number that identifies the specific merchandise.

Some wholesalers' catalogs will show a retail price less a series of discounts that might apply under various conditions, such as the number bought. For instance, Inmac, a computer accessories company, lists:

Maxell Flexible Disks

ORDER NO.	DESCRIPTION	PRICE PER DISK SOLD IN BOXES OF 10		
		10	20–50	60–100
8953	3½" SSDD	$4.45	$3.95	$3.60
8971	5¼" SSDD	2.65	2.40	2.15
8972	5¼" DSDD	3.55	3.20	2.90
8973	5¼" DS High Density	7.40	6.70	5.95
8974	8" SSDDIBM 2305830	4.60	4.15	3.75

Accounting reports to shareholders ordinarily show only the sales after deducting these trade discounts. Accounting reports to managers usually show these trade discounts only if deemed informative for evaluating performance. For instance, some automobile dealers will develop elaborate accounting systems for monitoring their sales performance.

Consider an example. Suppose a dealer has a car for sale for $12,000 list price and grants a discount of $1,000 from list price in a cash sale. To evaluate the effects and levels of discounts from period to period, the dealer may wish to record the sale at the list price of $12,000 and the discount in a separate offsetting account called Discounts from List Price. An income statement might show:

Sales at list price	$12,000
Discounts from list price	1,000
Net sales	$11,000

The trade-in of an old car complicates matters. Suppose a customer traded in her used car. The dealer should attribute a "cash-equivalent" price (say $4,000) to the used car. That is, the car should be added to the dealer's inventory at what it would have cost the dealer had he bought it outright for cash.

Of course, the salesman may tell the customer that she is being given a generous trade-in allowance of $5,000 for her car. But the trade-in allowances commonly quoted by dealers ($5,000 in this case) invariably consist of two major parts: trade discount off list price ($1,000) and a cash-equivalent wholesale price for the used car ($4,000).

The foregoing transactions are analyzed as follows:

	A	= L +	SE
Cash sale	+11,000 [Increase Cash]	=	+12,000 [Increase Sales at List Price] −1,000 [Increase Discounts from List Price]
Trade-in plus cash	+7,000 [Increase Cash] +4,000 [Increase Inventory of Used Cars]	=	+12,000 [Increase Sales at List Price] −1,000 [Increase Discounts from List Price]

The pertinent journal entries (without explanations) would be:

Cash	11,000	
Discounts from list price	1,000	
Sales		12,000

Cash	7,000	
Discounts from list price	1,000	
Inventory of used cars	4,000	
Sales		12,000

Some auto dealers would not bother recording the discounts from list price. If so, only one account, Sales (net), would be kept; it would be increased by $11,000 in the above transactions. Note that accounting systems and data processing can be designed in differing ways, depending on the preferences of the users of the detailed reports. For external reports to shareholders and others, highly condensed figures suffice, such as net sales alone.

Another example of management's focus on discounts is in public accounting firms. A specific partner usually has responsibility for billing and collecting fees from clients. The aim is to collect the regular billing rates per hour. For example, the firm's regular billing rate for some partners might be $100 per hour. The partner's skill at billing and collection is judged by his or her relative success at "realization." In this setting, *realization* is defined as the actual amount collected in relation to the target amount.

For instance, if the actual amount collected for a partner's time is $60 per hour instead of $100 (because of client resistance or hard bargaining), the realization rate is 60%. The accounts might be designed to show:

Fees earned at regular rates	$100
Allowances or discounts granted	40
Fees realized	$ 60

☐ Net Method of Accounting For Cash Discounts

The method of accounting for discounts as described in the chapter is known as the "gross" method. Critics claim that the "net" method is better. Reconsider the example in the chapter. Recall that $30,000 of sales were made at terms 2/10, n/60. The net method would work as follows:

	A	= L +	SE
1. Sell at terms of 2/10, n/60	+29,400 [Increase Accounts Receivable]	=	+29,400 [Increase Sales]
2. Either collect $29,400	+29,400 [Increase Cash] −29,400 [Decrease Accounts Receivable]	=	0
or collect $30,000	+30,000 [Increase Cash] −29,400 [Decrease Accounts Receivable]	=	+600 [Increase Revenue from Forfeited Cash Discounts]

The journal entries follow:

| 1. Accounts receivable | 29,400 | |
| Sales | | 29,400 |

2. Cash	29,400	
Accounts receivable		29,400
or		
Cash	30,000	
Revenue from forfeited cash discounts		600
Accounts receivable		29,400

The "net" method would initially record the Accounts Receivable and Sales at $29,400, the net realizable value of the receivable. No cash discounts would be recorded except when a customer pays $30,000 instead of $29,400. The extra $600 would be regarded as "revenue from forfeited cash discounts," which is similar to "interest revenue."

The net method has appeal from a management point of view. Why? Because it automatically pinpoints those customers who are *not* taking advantage of cash discounts. Such information may provide early warnings about customers who may become high credit risks.

The net method has intrinsic merit, but it is seldom used. Why? Because industry custom and data-processing convenience have led to the recording of all sales invoices at their stated amounts before cash discounts. After all, most invoices do *not* offer a cash discount, and accounting systems are designed primarily for these ordinary transactions.

☐ Estimation of Returns, Allowances, and Cash Discounts

If sales returns, allowances, and cash discounts *are material in amount*, an allowance method similar to that for uncollectible accounts should be used. Adjustments are typically made at the end of the accounting period for estimated amounts of returns, allowances, and cash discounts attributable to current operations. Otherwise sales are recognized in one period, and the related actual returns, allowances, and discounts are recognized in a later period. Under the accrual basis of accounting, all of these related items should be recognized in the period of sale.

To illustrate the accrual basis, suppose sales of $100,000 are made on December 31 on terms of 3/10, n/30. Past experience has demonstrated that virtually 100% of the customers will take advantage of the cash discount. Compare the following summary journal entries:

	CORRECT APPLICATION OF ACCRUAL BASIS			INCORRECT APPLICATION OF ACCRUAL BASIS		
Dec. 31	Accounts receivable	100,000		Accounts receivable	100,000	
	Sales		100,000	Sales		100,000
Dec. 31	Cash discounts on sales	3,000		No entry		
	Allowance for cash					
	discounts on sales		3,000			
Jan. 1–10	Cash	97,000		Cash	97,000	
	Allowance for cash			Cash discounts on sales	3,000	
	discounts on sales	3,000		Accounts receivable		100,000
	Accounts receivable		100,000			

	CORRECT BALANCE SHEET PRESENTATION		INCORRECT BALANCE SHEET PRESENTATION	
Dec. 31	Accounts receivable	$100,000	Accounts receivable	$100,000
	Deduct: Allowance for discounts	3,000		
	Accounts receivable, net	$ 97,000		

The income statement would show higher cash discounts and lower operating income of $3,000 under the correct application of the accrual basis.

Incidentally, note how the net method of accounting for cash discounts would "automatically" provide a correct application. Why? Because the original sale would be recorded at $97,000.

Most companies do not refine their accrual basis of accounting to the extent illustrated in this example. Instead they omit year-end estimates for sales returns, allowances, and discounts. This cruder approach is typically justified on the basis of lack of materiality of the dollar amounts. That is, the refinement would insignificantly affect the financial results. Nevertheless, outside auditors test for materiality and sometimes require a company to change its accounting policy. Consider the comments in an annual report of Topps Chewing Gum, makers of bubble gum, baseball cards, and candy:

☐ Topps changed its accounting for sales returns by accruing estimated sales returns in the years the related sales are recognized. Prior to the change, Topps followed the practice of recording sales returns when received.

APPENDIX 6C: ACCOUNTING CYCLE FOR PERIODIC AND PERPETUAL INVENTORIES

This appendix shows how accounting data are processed under both periodic and perpetual inventory systems. The data regarding inventories are the same as those used on pages 228–232 of the chapter—inventories: beginning, $100,000; ending, $140,000; purchases, $990,000; purchase returns and allowances, $80,000. This appendix adds more data and provides an overall review of the data-processing aspects of Chapters 5 and 6.

☐ **Problem**

Gomez Radio Stores sells radios and related equipment. Exhibit 6–7 shows how the Gomez unadjusted trial balances would appear under two different inventory systems as of December 31, 19X2 (in thousands of dollars).

EXHIBIT 6–7

GOMEZ RADIO STORES
Unadjusted Trial Balance
December 31, 19X2

	PERPETUAL INVENTORY		PERIODIC INVENTORY	
	Debit	Credit	Debit	Credit
Cash	900		900	
Accounts receivable	180		180	
Allowance for uncollectible accounts				
Merchandise inventory	140*		100†	
Equipment	300		300	
Accumulated depreciation, equipment		100		100
Accounts payable		1,010		1,010
Accrued income taxes payable				
Paid-in capital		100		100
Retained income		110		110
Sales		1,640		1,640
Sales returns and allowances	70		70	
Cost of goods sold	870			
Purchases			990	
Purchase returns and allowances				80
Various expenses (summarized here)	500		500	
Bad debts expense				
Income tax expense				
	2,960	2,960	3,040	3,040

* Balance, December 31, 19X2.
† Balance, December 31, 19X1.

Required:

1. Prepare two work sheets, one for the perpetual inventory system and one for the periodic inventory system. Enter the pertinent unadjusted trial balance in the first pair of columns for each work sheet. Enter the amounts in thousands of dollars.
2. The unadjusted trial balances given here are probably misnamed. A more descriptive title would be "partially adjusted" trial balances. We assume that all necessary entries (for example, depreciation) have already been made except for the three following (labeled j, k, and l for later reference):
   j. Bad debts expense should be recognized. Past experience indicates that a provision should be made of 1% of the year's credit sales of $1 million.
   k. The cost of the ending inventory was $140,000.
   l. Income tax expense was recognized at a rate of 30% of pretax income.
   Enter any necessary entries in the adjustment columns. Then complete the work sheet. To show the flexibility of the work sheet, omit the columns for the adjusted trial balance.
3. Prepare formal income statements, using a format for the gross profit section that is similar to that of Exhibit 6–3.
4. Prepare the adjusting journal entries, using the worksheets as a guide. Show adjacent sets of entries for the perpetual and periodic systems.
5. Prepare the closing journal entries, using the work sheets as a guide. Show adjacent sets of entries for the perpetual and periodic systems.

The solutions to the above requirements are shown sequentially in Exhibits 6–8 through 6–11.

EXHIBIT 6–8

GOMEZ RADIO STORES
Work Sheet (Perpetual Inventory System)
For the Year Ended December 31, 19X2 (in thousands of dollars)

Account Titles	Unadjusted Trial Balance Debit	Unadjusted Trial Balance Credit	Adjustments Debit	Adjustments Credit	Income Statement Debit	Income Statement Credit	Statement of Retained Income Debit	Statement of Retained Income Credit	Balance Sheet Debit	Balance Sheet Credit
Cash	900								900	
Accounts receivable	180								180	
Allowance for uncollectible accounts				(j) 10						10
Merchandise inventory	140								140	
Equipment	300								300	
Accumulated depreciation—equipment		100								100
Accounts payable		1010								1010
Accrued income taxes payable				(l) 57						57
Paid-in capital		100								100
Retained income		110						110		
Sales		1640				1640				
Sales returns and allowances	70				70					
Cost of goods sold	870				870					
Various expenses (summarized here)	500				500					
	2960	2960								
Bad debts expense			(j) 10		10					
Income tax expense			(l) 57		57					
			67	67	1450	1640				
Net income					133			133		
					1640	1640				
Retained income, December 31, 19X2							243	243	1520	243
							243	243	1520	1520

j: Bad debts estimated, .01 × $1,000,000 = $10,000.   k. Not applicable.
l. Income tax expense, .30 ($1640 − $1450) = .30 × $190 income before income taxes, or $57.

EXHIBIT 6-9

GOMEZ RADIO STORES
Work Sheet (Periodic Inventory System)
For the Year Ended December 31, 19X2 (in thousands of dollars)

Account Titles	Unadjusted Trial Balance Debit	Unadjusted Trial Balance Credit	Adjustments Debit	Adjustments Credit	Income Statement Debit	Income Statement Credit	Statement of Retained Income Debit	Statement of Retained Income Credit	Balance Sheet Debit	Balance Sheet Credit
Cash	900								900	
Accounts receivable	180								180	
Allowance for uncollectible accounts				(j) 10						10
Merchandise inventory, December 31, 19X1	100				100					
Equipment	300								300	
Accumulated depreciation—equipment		100								100
Accounts payable		1010								1010
Accrued income taxes payable				(l) 57						57
Paid-in capital		100								100
Retained income		110						110		
Sales		1640				1640				
Sales returns and allowances	70				70					
Purchases	990				990					
Purchase returns and allowances		80				80				
Various expenses (summarized here)	500				500					
	3040	3040								
Bad debts expense			(j) 10		10					
Merchandise inventory, December 31, 19X2						140			140	
Income tax expense			(l) 57		57					
			67	67	1670	1860				
Net income					133			133		
					1860	1860				
Retained income, December 31, 19X2							243			243
							243	243	1520	1520

j. Bad debts estimated, .01 × $1,000,000 = $10,000. k. See text for thorough explanation of how ending inventory is accounted for. l. Income tax expense, .30 ($1,860 − $1,670) = .30 × $190 income before income taxes, or $57.

The work sheet for the perpetual inventory system (Exhibit 6–8) has the same format as that introduced in Chapter 5. The general format for the periodic inventory system is similar except for the items shaded in Exhibits 6–8 and 6–9. The purpose for the differences is to include all details of cost of goods sold in the income statement. The worksheet for the periodic system (Exhibit 6–9) has two inventory lines rather than one and includes lines for purchases and purchase returns and allowances instead of a line for cost of goods sold. The beginning inventory (December 31, 19X1) remains untouched in the ledger throughout 19X2. It appears as a debit in the unadjusted trial balance, and it is also placed in the income statement debit column. Of course, in the formal income statement it is added to net purchases to obtain the cost of goods available for sale. (The *beginning* inventory does not belong in the section for the ending balance sheet.)

The ending inventory (December 31, 19X2) is not in the unadjusted trial balance. Mechanically, it can be placed on the work sheet in various ways. A popular way is shown in Exhibit 6–9 where the ending balance is a separate line item below the totals of the unadjusted trial balance.

The ending inventory amount is shown in two places: the income statement credit column and the balance sheet debit column. The $140,000 is a credit in the income statement section because it is deducted from the cost of goods available for sale to obtain the cost of goods sold. The $140,000 is a debit in the balance sheet section because it represents an asset on the ending balance sheet.

Entries in the income statement columns of the four shaded lines of Exhibit 6–9 provide the cost of goods sold: beginning inventory + purchases − purchase returns

EXHIBIT 6–10

GOMEZ RADIO STORES
Income Statement
For the Year Ended December 31, 19X2
(in thousands of dollars)

	PERPETUAL SYSTEM		PERIODIC SYSTEM
Gross sales	$1,640		$1,640
Deduct: Sales returns and allowances	70		70
Net sales	$1,570		$1,570
Deduct: Cost of goods sold			
Merchandise inventory, December 31, 19X1		$100	
Gross purchases		$990	
Deduct: Purchase returns and allowances		80	
Net purchases			910
Cost of goods available for sale			$1,010
Deduct: Merchandise inventory, December 31, 19X2			140
Cost of goods sold	870		870
Gross profit	$ 700		$ 700
Operating expenses:			
Bad debts expense	$ 10		$ 10
Various expenses	500		500
Total operating expenses	$ 510		$ 510
Income before income taxes	$ 190		$ 190
Income tax expense	57		57
Net income	$ 133		$ 133

and allowances − ending inventory = $100,000 + $990,000 − $80,000 − $140,000 = $870,000.

□ Comparison of Journal Entries

The formal income statement is shown in Exhibit 6–10. Exhibit 6–11 represents the adjusting and closing journal entries in response to requirements 4 and 5. All entries are identical for the perpetual and periodic systems except for summarizing the cost of goods sold (see entries *n1* and *n2*).

Under the perpetual system, the cost of goods sold is accumulated on a continuous basis throughout the year. As sales are made, Cost of Goods Sold is debited and Inven-

EXHIBIT 6–11

GOMEZ RADIO STORES
Adjusting and Closing Journal Entries
For the Year Ended December 31, 19X2

	PERPETUAL INVENTORY SYSTEM		PERIODIC INVENTORY SYSTEM	
4. Adjusting journal entries:				
j. Bad debts:	Bad debts expense	10	Bad debts expense	10
	Allowance for uncollectible accounts	10	Allowance for uncollectible accounts	10
k. Ending inventory:	Not applicable		See closing entries below	
l. Income tax expense:	Income tax expense	57	Income tax expense	57
	Accrued income taxes payable	57	Accrued income taxes payable	57
5. Closing journal entries:				
m. Revenue accounts:	Sales	1,640	Sales	1,640
	Sales returns and allowances	70	Sales returns and allowances	70
	Income summary	1,570	Income summary	1,570
n. Expense accounts:	Income summary	1,437	n1. Cost of goods sold	870
	Cost of goods sold	870	Purchase returns and allowances	80
	Various expenses	500	Merchandise inventory	140
	Bad debts expense	10	Purchases	990
	Income tax expense	57	Merchandise inventory	100
			n2. Income summary	1,437
			Cost of goods sold	870
			Various expenses	500
			Bad debts expense	10
			Income tax expense	57

tory is credited. Under the periodic system, the cost of goods sold is computed at the end of the year. The closing entries highlight this aspect of the periodic method.

In practice, entries under the periodic system vary considerably. No matter what the entries, the ending inventory and the cost of goods sold must be $140 and $870, respectively. Many accountants would use one compound entry as entry n. Note how such an entry directly lists each entry in the income statement columns of the work sheet. There is no explicit listing of the cost of goods sold:

Income summary	1,437	
Merchandise inventory	140	
Purchase returns and allowances	80	
Merchandise inventory		100
Purchases		990
Various expenses		500
Bad debts expense		10
Income tax expense		57

FUNDAMENTAL ASSIGNMENT MATERIAL

☐ **General Coverage**

6–1. **UNCOLLECTIBLE ACCOUNTS.** (Alternates are 6–3 and 6–4.) During 19X2, the Freeland Paint Store had sales of $600,000, of which $450,000 was on credit. Freeland expects that 2% of the credit sales will never be collected, although no accounts are written off until ten assorted steps are taken to attain collection. The ten steps require a minimum of fourteen months.

Assume that during 19X3, specific customers are identified who are never expected to pay $9,000 that they owe from the sales of 19X2.

Required:

Show the impact on the balance sheet equation of the above transactions in 19X2 and 19X3 under (1) the specific write-off method and (2) the allowance method. Which method do you prefer? Why?

6–2. **DETAILED INCOME STATEMENT.** (Alternates are 6–5 and 6–6.) Following are accounts taken from the adjusted trial balance of the Johnson Building Supply Company, December 31, 19X5. The company uses the periodic inventory system. Prepare a detailed income statement for 19X5. All amounts are in thousands:

Freight in	$ 50	Sales salaries and	
Miscellaneous expenses	12	commissions	$160
Sales	1,080	Inventory, December 31, 19X4	300
Bad debts expense	8	Allowance for bad debts	14
Cash discounts on purchases	15	Rent expense, office space	10
Inventory, December 31, 19X5	325	Gross purchases	500
Office salaries	60	Depreciation expense, office	
Rent expense, selling space	90	equipment	2
Income tax expense	44	Cash discounts on sales	10
Sales returns and allowances	50	Advertising expense	40
Office supplies used	4	Purchase returns and	
Depreciation expense, trucks		allowances	40
and store fixtures	30	Delivery expense	20

6–3. UNCOLLECTIBLE ACCOUNTS. (Alternates are 6–1 and 6–4.) Dart & Kraft, Inc., has many well-known brands. Examples are Kraft, Tupperware, Duracell, West Bend, and Sealtest. Its balance sheet, December 28, 1985, included the following data (in millions of dollars):

Accounts and notes receivable	$1,064.0
Less—Allowance for doubtful accounts and notes	(37.5)
	$1,026.5

Required:

1. The company used the allowance method for accounting for bad debts. Suppose the company added $36 million to the allowance during 1985. Write-offs of uncollectible accounts were $31.1 million. Show (a) the impact on the balance sheet equation of these transactions and (b) the journal entries.
2. Suppose Dart & Kraft had used the specific write-off method for accounting for bad debts. Using the same information as in requirement 1, show (a) the impact on the balance sheet equation and (b) the journal entry.
3. How would the Dart & Kraft balance sheet amounts shown above have been affected if the specific write-off method had been used up to that date? Be specific.

6–4. UNCOLLECTIBLE ACCOUNTS. (Alternates are 6–1 and 6–3.) Exxon Corporation is the world's largest producer of oil and gas. Its balance sheet included the following actual presentation:

	DECEMBER 31	
	1983	1984
	(Millions of Dollars)	
Notes and accounts receivable, less estimated doubtful accounts	$7,900	$7,366

(Unlike most corporations, Exxon presents its most recent financial statement in the final column of a comparative presentation.)

Required:

1. Footnote 2 to Exxon's financial statements read: "Estimated doubtful notes and accounts receivable were $171 million at the end of 1983 and $165 million at the end of 1984." Suppose that during 1984 Exxon added $145 million to its allowance for estimated doubtful accounts. Write-offs of uncollectible accounts were $151 million. Show (a) the impact on the balance sheet equation of these transactions and (b) the journal entries.
2. Assume that Exxon had used the specific write-off method for accounting for bad debts. Using the same information as in requirement 1, show (a) the impact on the balance sheet equation and (b) the journal entry.
3. How would the Exxon balance sheet amounts have been affected if the specific write-off method had been used? Be specific.

6–5. DETAILED INCOME STATEMENT. (Alternates are 6–2 and 6–6.) The Ohio Mattress Co. makes Sealy mattresses. Its annual report had the following actual descriptions and data for the year ended November 30, 1985 (in thousands):

Net sales	$267,321
Cost of goods sold	182,247
Gross profit	85,074
Selling, general and administrative expenses	66,218
Operating profit	18,856

Consider the following additional data, in thousands (inventories and allowances for doubtful accounts are actual; remaining data are assumed):

Inventory:		Allowances for doubtful accounts:	
November 30, 1985	$35,542	November 30, 1985	$ 1,960
November 30, 1984	30,602	November 30, 1984	852
Cash discounts on purchases	1,200	Advertising expense	6,000
Depreciation expense, office		Delivery expense	6,700
equipment	2,873	Cash discounts on sales	1,600
Bad debts expense	1,900	Inward transportation	2,590
Sales returns and allowances	3,200	Sales salaries and	
Miscellaneous general expenses	2,420	commissions	27,100
Purchase returns and allowances	2,800	Administrative salaries	15,425
Depreciation expense, trucks		Gross purchases	188,597
and selling space	3,800		

Required:

| Prepare a detailed multistep income statement that ends with operating profit.

6–6. **DETAILED INCOME STATEMENT.** (Alternates are 6–2 and 6–5.) Hartmarx Corporation is a clothing company with many brands of apparel, including Hart, Schaffner, & Marx. The company's annual report contained the following actual data for the year ended November 30, 1985 (in thousands):

Net sales	$1,109,537
Cost of goods sold	641,246
Selling, administrative and occupancy expenses	391,079
Operating profit	77,212

The balance sheets included the following actual data (in thousands of dollars):

	NOVEMBER 30	
	1985	1984
Allowance for doubtful accounts	$ 9,810	$ 9,794
Inventories	310,944	306,140

Consider the following additional assumed data (in thousands of dollars):

Bad debts expense	$ 5,400	Freight in	$32,000
Gross purchases	642,050	Advertising expense	29,000
Cash discounts on sales	10,000	Sales returns and allowances	35,000
Sales salaries and compensation	180,000	Depreciation expense	26,000
Purchase returns and allowances	24,000	Cash discounts on purchases	4,000
Freight out	52,000	Rent expense	15,000
		Miscellaneous expenses	83,679

Required: | Prepare a detailed multistep income statement that ends with operating profit. You need not subclassify the selling, administrative, and occupancy expenses into three separate categories.

ADDITIONAL ASSIGNMENT MATERIAL

☐ General Coverage

6–7. "A gross profit test is a computation of the minimum price permitted by federal law." Do you agree? Explain.

6–8. Suppose a company's gross profit declines. What are some possible causes for the decline?

6–9. Distinguish between *cash discounts* and *trade discounts*.

6–10. "Trade discounts should not be recorded by the accountant." Do you agree? Explain.

6–11. "As a help to management control, the net method of accounting for discounts is better than the gross method." Do you agree? Explain.

6–12. "Retailers who accept VISA or MasterCharge are foolish because they do not receive the full price for merchandise they sell." Comment.

6–13. The El Camino Hospital uses the allowance method in accounting for bad debts. A journal entry was made for writing off the accounts of Jane Jensen, Eunice Belmont, and Samuel Maze:

Bad debts expense	14,321	
Accounts receivable		14,321

Do you agree with this entry? If not, show the correct entry and the correcting entry.

6–14. Distinguish among the following: *reserve method*, *allowance method*, *specific write-off method*, and *specific charge-off method*.

6–15. "The Allowance for Bad Debts account has no subsidiary ledger, but the Accounts Receivable account does." Explain.

6–16. Distinguish between *F.O.B. destination* and *F.O.B. shipping point*.

6–17. "Freight out should be classified as a direct offset to sales, not as an expense." Do you agree? Explain.

6–18. Distinguish between the *perpetual* and *periodic* inventory systems.

6–19. How can a credit balance arise in an Accounts Receivable subsidiary ledger? How should it be accounted for?

6–20. "Under the allowance method, there are three popular ways to estimate the bad debts expense for a particular year." Name the three.

6–21. What is meant by "aging of accounts"?

6–22. Describe why a write-off of a bad debt should be reversed if collection occurs at a later date.

6–23. What is the relationship between the average collection period and the average age of accounts receivable?

6–24. **BAD DEBTS.** Prepare all journal entries regarding the following data. Consider the following balances of the Rochester Clinic on December 31, 19X1: Receivables from Patients, $165,000; and Allowance for Doubtful Receivables, $40,000. During 19X2, total billings to individual patients, excluding the billings to third-party payers such as Blue Cross and Medicare, were $2 million. Past experience indicated that

15% of such individual billings would ultimately be uncollectible. Write-offs of receivables during 19X2 were $270,000.

6–25. BAD DEBT ALLOWANCE. Kim Oriental Groceries had sales of $950,000 during 19X2, including $300,000 of sales on credit. Balances on December 31, 19X1, were: Accounts Receivable, $35,000; and Allowance for Bad Debts, $5,000. Data for 19X2: Collections on accounts receivable were $270,000. Bad debts expense was estimated at 2% of credit sales, as in previous years. Write-offs of bad debts during 19X2 were $7,000.

Required:

1. Prepare journal entries regarding the above information for 19X2.
2. Show the ending balances of the balance sheet accounts, December 31, 19X2.
3. Based on the given data, what questions seem worth raising with Sung Kim, the president of the store?

6–26. BAD DEBT RECOVERIES. Waterhouse Building Supplies has many accounts receivable. The Waterhouse balance sheet, December 31, 19X1, showed: Accounts Receivable, $800,000; and Allowance for Uncollectible Accounts, $36,000. In early 19X2, write-offs of customer accounts of $15,000 were made. In late 19X2, a customer, whose $3,000 debt had been written off earlier, won a $1 million lottery. She immediately remitted $3,000 to Waterhouse. The company welcomed her money and her return to a high credit standing. Prepare the journal entries for the $15,000 write-off in early 19X2 and the $3,000 receipt in late 19X2.

6–27. SUBSIDIARY LEDGER. A new furniture store makes credit sales of $300,000 in 19X4 to fifty customers: Ricks, $3,000; Vogel, $2,000; Parker, $4,000; others, $291,000. Total collections during 19X4 were $200,000 including $3,000 from Parker, but nothing was collected from Ricks or Vogel. At the end of 19X4 an allowance for uncollectible accounts was provided of 4% of credit sales.

Required:

1. Set up appropriate general ledger accounts plus a subsidiary ledger for Accounts Receivable. The subsidiary ledger should consist of three individual accounts plus a fourth account called *Others*. Post the entries for 19X4. Prepare a statement of the ending balances of the individual accounts receivable to show that they reconcile with the general ledger account.
2. On March 24, 19X5, the Ricks and Vogel accounts are written off. Post the entries.

6–28. SALES RETURNS AND DISCOUNTS. Family Clothing Wholesalers had gross sales of $700,000 during the month of February. Sales returns and allowances were $20,000. Cash discounts granted were $50,000.

Required:

Prepare an analysis of the impact of these transactions on the balance sheet equation. Also prepare a detailed presentation of the revenue section of the income statement.

6–29. CASH DISCOUNT TRANSACTIONS. Zoom Photo Equipment Wholesalers sells at terms of 1/10, n/30. It sold equipment to Brooks Retailers for $50,000 on open account on January 10. Payment (net of cash discount) was received on January 19. Using the balance sheet equation framework, analyze the two transactions for Zoom.

6–30. ENTRIES FOR CASH DISCOUNTS AND RETURNS ON SALES. Lake City Furniture is a wholesale dealer that sells on credit terms of 2/10, n/30. Consider the following transactions:

Mar. 9 Sales on credit to Riordan Store, $14,000.
Mar. 11 Sales on credit to Suburban Furniture, $12,000.
Mar. 18 Collected from Riordan Store.
Mar. 26 Accepted the return of furniture from Suburban Furniture, $2,000.

Apr. 10 Collected from Suburban Furniture.

Apr. 12 Riordan returned some defective furniture that she had acquired on March 9 for $500. Lake City issued a cash refund immediately.

Required:

Prepare journal entries for these transactions. Omit explanations. Assume that the full appropriate amounts were exchanged.

6–31. ENTRIES FOR PURCHASE TRANSACTIONS. The Zweig Company is a Swiss wholesaler of small giftware. Its unit of currency is the Swiss franc (Sfr.). Zweig uses a periodic inventory system. Prepare journal entries for the following summarized transactions (omit explanations):

Aug. 2. Purchased merchandise, Sfr. 300,000, terms 2/10, n/45.

Aug. 3. Paid cash for freight in, Sfr. 10,000.

Aug. 7. Zweig complained about some defects in the merchandise acquired on August 2. The supplier hand-delivered a credit memo granting an allowance of Sfr. 20,000.

Aug. 11. Cash disbursement to settle purchase of August 2.

6–32. TWO SIDES OF DISCOUNT TRANSACTIONS. (Alternate is 6–34.) Valley Medical, a wholesaler of hospital supplies, sells to hospitals on credit terms of 1/10, n/30. Consider the following transactions:

May 3 Sold goods for $8,000 to Orange County Hospital.

May 8 Sold goods for $30,000 to Mount Sinai Hospital.

May 10 Orange County Hospital returned $2,000 of the goods of May 3.

May 12 Received cash from Orange County Hospital in settlement of May transactions.

June 6 Received cash from Mount Sinai Hospital in settlement of May 8 transaction.

Required:

Prepare journal entries (omit explanations) in parallel columns for the buyer and the seller for each of the above transactions. Assume that periodic inventory systems are in use.

6–33. NET DISCOUNT METHOD. (Alternate is 6–35.) Study Appendix 6B. Refer to the preceding problem. Repeat the requirements, using the net discount method.

6–34. TWO SIDES OF DISCOUNT TRANSACTIONS. (Alternate is 6–32.) Prepare journal entries (omit explanations) in parallel columns for the buyer and the seller for each of the following transactions. Assume that periodic inventory systems are in use.

1. Merchandise was sold for $60,000 on credit, terms 2/20, n/60.
2. Merchandise of $3,900 was returned as defective.
3. The buyer complained that the remaining merchandise was not the color ordered. The seller gave a credit allowance of $5,100.
4. The buyer paid the appropriate amount of cash to eliminate half of the remaining balance within the 20-day discount period.
5. The buyer paid the remaining balance 60 days after the date of the original invoice.

6–35. NET DISCOUNT METHOD. (Alternate is 6–33.) Study Appendix 6B. Refer to the preceding problem. Repeat the requirements, using the net discount method.

6–36. RECORDING SALES BY AUTO DEALERS. Study Appendix 6B. Snead Autos maintains an elaborate accounting system for monitoring the performance of its sales personnel. Using the A = L + SE equation, show the impact of the following transaction on the entity: A new car is sold that has a list price of $20,000. An old car is traded in and cash is paid for the difference between the trade-in allowance of $6,000 and the list price. The car that was traded in was equivalent to others that could have been acquired at wholesale auctions for $4,200. Prepare a compound journal entry for Snead.

6–37. GROSS OR NET DISCOUNT TRANSACTIONS. Study Appendix 6B. Zoom Photo Equipment Wholesalers sells at terms of 1/10, n/30. It sold equipment to Rivers

Bros. for $80,000 on open account on January 28. Payment (net of cash discount) was received on February 5.

Required:

Using the equation framework:

1. Analyze the two transactions for Zoom using the (a) "gross" method and (b) "net" method of accounting for discounts.
2. Repeat the analysis of the collection in requirement 1, but assume that payment was not received until February 26 when $80,000 cash was received.
3. Which method do you prefer? Why?
4. Prepare all journal entries for requirements 1 and 2. Omit explanations.

6–38. **CREDIT TERMS, DISCOUNTS, AND ANNUAL INTEREST RATES.** As the struggling owner of a new 24-hour convenience store, you suffer from a habitual shortage of cash. Yesterday the following invoices arrived:

VENDOR	FACE AMOUNT	TERMS
Farmers' Produce	$ 450	n/30
Rose Exterminators	90	EOM
Top Meat Supply	500	n/10, EOM
Jabbar Fisheries	850	1/10, n/30
Garcia Equipment	2,000	2/10, n/30

Required:

1. Write out the exact meaning of each of the terms.
2. You can borrow cash from the local bank at an annual interest rate of 16%. Should you borrow to take advantage of the cash discounts offered by the two vendors? Why? Show computations. For interest rate computations, assume a 360-day year.

6–39. **ACCOUNTING FOR CREDIT CARDS.** The Milgrom Shoe Store has extended credit to customers on open account. Its average experience for each of the past three years has been:

	CASH	CREDIT	TOTAL
Sales	$500,000	$200,000	$700,000
Bad debts expense	—	4,000	4,000
Administrative expense	—	2,000	2,000

Milgrom is considering whether to accept bank cards (e.g., VISA, Mastercard). She has resisted because she does not want to bear the cost of the service, which would be 5% of gross sales.

The representative of VISA claims that the availability of bank cards would have increased overall sales by at least 10%. However, regardless of the level of sales the new mix of the sales would be 50% bank card and 50% cash.

Required:

1. How would a bank card sale of $100 affect the accounting equation? Where would the discount appear on the income statement?
2. Should Milgrom adopt the bank card if sales do not increase? Base your answer solely on the sparse facts given here.
3. Repeat requirement 2, but assume that total sales would increase 10%.

6–40. TRADE-INS VERSUS DISCOUNTS. Many states base their sales tax on gross sales less any discount. Trade-in allowances are not discounts, so they are not deducted from the sales price for sales tax purposes.

Suppose Sven Gustafson had decided to trade in his old car for a new one with a list price of $20,000. He will pay cash of $12,000 plus sales tax. If he had not traded in a car, the dealer would have offered a discount of 15% of the list price. The sales tax is 8%.

Required: How much of the $8,000 price reduction should be called a discount? How much a trade in? Mr. Gustafson wants to pay as little sales tax as legally possible.

6–41. LATE PAYMENT FEES. Johnson and Flora, a law firm, has been plagued by slow payments from clients. During 19X1, the firm instituted the following credit policy: 1/10, n/30, but add 2% of the invoice for each thirty days or part thereof after the due date.

Invoices dated September 30, 19X1, were billed to clients for $100,000. The appropriate amount of cash was collected for 20% of that amount within the first ten days. Another 50% was collected within the next twenty days. Another 10% of the original billing was paid within the following thirty days. Payments included the appropriate "late charge." No other payments had been received by December 31, the end of the fiscal year. (The "due date" was October 30.)

Required: Prepare all the journal entries required by the above data. Ignore the question of bad debts; that is, assume that all receivables will ultimately be collected.

6–42. ENTRIES FOR PERIODIC AND PERPETUAL SYSTEMS. Schaefer Co. has an inventory of $200,000, December 31, 19X1. Data for 19X2 follow:

Gross purchases	$800,000
Cost of goods sold	810,000
Inventory, December 31, 19X2	150,000
Purchase returns and allowances	40,000

Using the data, prepare a comparative analysis of the entries for a perpetual and a periodic inventory system. Present your comparison as it affects the balance sheet equation. Also present comparative journal entries.

6–43. ENTRIES FOR PURCHASE TRANSACTIONS. Fernandez Importers uses a periodic inventory system. Prepare journal entries for the following summarized transactions for 19X2 (omit explanations). For simplicity, assume that the beginning and ending balances in accounts payable were zero.

1. Purchases (all using trade credit), $740,000
2. Purchase returns and allowances, $70,000
3. Freight in, $82,000 paid in cash
4. Cash discounts on purchases, $14,800

6–44. CLOSING ENTRIES, PERIODIC INVENTORY SYSTEM. Refer to the data in the preceding problem. Inventories were: December 31, 19X1, $81,000; December 31, 19X2, $95,000. Sales were $1,300,000. Prepare the closing journal entries, December 31. 19X2. Omit explanations.

6–45. CLOSING ENTRIES, PERIODIC INVENTORY SYSTEM. Consider the following data taken from the adjusted trial balance of the Marquis Company, December 31, 19X1 (in millions):

Purchases	$100	Sales	$222
Sales returns and allowances	14	Purchase returns and	
Freight in	9	allowances	5
Cash discounts on purchases	2	Cash discounts on sales	7
Inventory (beginning of year)	25	Other expenses	80

Required: Prepare the closing journal entries. The ending inventory was $30 million. Show postings to T-accounts for Income Summary and Retained Income.

6–46. GROSS PROFIT SECTION. Given the following, prepare a detailed gross profit section for Handy Hardware Wholesalers for the year ended December 31, 19X8 (in thousands):

Cash discounts on sales	$ 4	Cash discounts on purchases	$ 3
Purchase returns and		Sales returns and allowances	18
allowances	25	Gross purchases	600
Merchandise inventory,		Merchandise inventory,	
December 31, 19X8	172	December 31, 19X7	140
Freight in	60	Gross profit	328

6–47. GROSS MARGIN SECTION. The Alabama Furniture Exchange had the following data for the year ended December 31, 19X2 (in thousands):

Inventory, December 31, 19X2	$ 530	Cash discounts on sales	$ 6
Sales for cash	300	Gross purchases	1,150
Sales for credit	1,300	Freight out	120
Sales returns and allowances	194	Bad debts expense	30
Inventory, December 31, 19X1	100	Sales personnel compensation	220
Freight in	110	Purchase returns and allowances	50
Cash discounts on purchases	10		

Required: Prepare the gross margin section of a multiple-step income statement. Compute the "gross margin percentage."

6–48. RECONSTRUCTION OF RECORDS. On February 7, 19X2, a tornado caused heavy damage to the Omaha Record Store. All the merchandise was destroyed. Some accounting data are missing. In conjunction with an insurance investigation, you have been asked to estimate the cost of the inventory destroyed. The following data are available:

Cash discounts on purchases	$ 1,000	Inventory, December 31, 19X1	$17,000
Gross sales	210,000	Purchase returns and allowances	4,000
Sales returns and allowances	10,000	Inward transportation	2,000
Gross purchases	161,000	Gross margin percentage on net	
Accounts receivable, December 31, 19X1	14,000	sales	45%

6–49. COST OF INVENTORY DESTROYED BY FIRE. R. Kelly requires an estimate of the cost of merchandise lost by fire on March 7. Merchandise inventory on January 1 was $40,000. Purchases since January 1 were $35,000; freight in, $3,000; purchase returns and allowances, $2,000. Sales are made at a gross profit of 25% of *sales* and totaled $42,000 up to March 7. What was the cost of the merchandise destroyed?

6–50. GROSS PROFIT COMPUTATIONS AND INVENTORY COSTS. On January 15, 19X4, P. Warner valued his inventory at cost, $18,000. His statements are based on the calendar year, so you find it necessary to establish an inventory figure as of January 1, 19X4. You find that from January 2 to January 15, sales were $60,000; sales returns, $1,500; goods purchased and placed in stock, $54,000; goods removed from stock and returned to vendors, $2,000; freight in, $500. Calculate the inventory cost as of January 1, assuming that goods are marked to sell at 30% above cost.

6–51. PERCENTAGE OF SALES AND PERCENTAGE OF ENDING ACCOUNTS RECEIVABLE. The Tartabull Company had credit sales of $3 million during 19X7. Most customers paid promptly (within 30 days), but a few took longer; an average of 1.2% of credit sales were never paid. On December 31, 19X7, accounts receivable were $200,000. The Allowance for Bad Debts account, before any recognition of 19X7 bad debts, had a $1,000 credit balance.

Tartabull produces and sells playground equipment and other outdoor children's toys. Most of the sales (about 80%) come in the period of March through August; the other 20% is spread almost evenly over the other six months. Over the last six years, an average of 15% of the December 31 accounts receivable has not been collected.

Required:

1. Suppose Tartabull Company uses the percentage of sales method to calculate an allowance for bad debts. Present the accounts receivable and allowance accounts as they should appear on the December 31, 19X7, balance sheet. Give the journal entry required to recognize the bad debts expense for 19X7.
2. Repeat requirement 1 except assume that the Tartabull Company uses the percentage of ending accounts receivable method.
3. Which method do you prefer? Why?

6–52. AGING OF ACCOUNTS. Study Appendix 6A. DeBroeck Company prepared the following analysis of Accounts Receivable, February 28, 19X1:

NAME OF CUSTOMER	TOTAL	REMARKS
Northwest Nurseries	$ 14,000	50% over 90 days 50% 61–90 days
Levine Landscaping	8,000	75% 31–60 days, 25% under 30 days
Sun Mountain Supply	10,000	60% 61–90 days, 40% 31–60 days
Hurley Tree Farm	15,000	all under 30 days
Tseng Florists	5,000	20% 61–90 days, 80% 1–30 days
Other accounts (each detailed)	60,000	50% 1–30 days, 30% 31–60 days, 15% 61–90 days, 5% over 90 days
Total	$112,000	

Required:

Prepare an aging schedule, classifying ages into four categories: 1–30 days, 31–60 days, 61–90 days, and over 90 days. Assume that the prospective bad debt percentages for each category are 0.2%, 0.8%, 10%, and 80%, respectively. What is the desired balance in Allowance for Uncollectible Accounts?

6–53. PERCENTAGE OF ENDING ACCOUNTS RECEIVABLE. Study Appendix 6A. Consider the following data for the Valenzuela Company:

	ACCOUNTS RECEIVABLE AT END OF YEAR	BAD DEBT EXPERIENCE	
		Deemed Uncollectible and Written Off	Recoveries
19X3	$220,000	$ 8,000	$600
19X4	170,000	5,600	400
19X5	180,000	6,100	300
19X6	230,000	9,000	900
19X7	250,000	11,300	800
19X8	210,000	5,000	600

Required: The unadjusted balance in Allowance for Uncollectible Accounts at December 31, 19X8, is $300. Using the percentage of ending accounts receivable method, prepare an adjusting entry to bring the Allowance to the appropriate amount at December 31, 19X8.

6–54. **ESTIMATING ALLOWANCE FOR UNCOLLECTIBLE ACCOUNTS.** Study Appendix 6A. Fujita Company has made an analysis of its sales and accounts receivable for the past five years. Assume that all accounts written off in a year relate to sales of the preceding year and were part of the accounts receivable at the end of that year. That is, no account is written off before the end of the year of the sale, and all accounts remaining unpaid are written off before the end of the year following the sale. The analysis showed:

	SALES	ENDING ACCOUNTS RECEIVABLE	BAD DEBTS WRITTEN OFF DURING THE YEAR
19X1	$650,000	$ 90,000	$12,000
19X2	750,000	97,000	12,500
19X3	750,000	103,000	14,000
19X4	850,000	110,000	16,500
19X5	850,000	110,000	17,000

The balance in Allowance for Uncollectible Accounts on December 31, 19X4, was $16,000.

Required:
1. Determine the bad debts expense for 19X5 and the balance of the Allowance for Uncollectible Accounts for December 31, 19X5, using the percentage of sales method.
2. Repeat requirement 1 using the percentage of ending accounts receivable method.

6–55. **BAD DEBT RECOVERIES.** Study Appendix 6A. The Acme Department Store uses the allowance method for accounting for bad debts. Assume that on February 26, 19X1, G. Howe's account is written off in the amount of $630 after several attempts to collect from him. On September 26, 19X1, Howe, filled with remorse and cash, pays his debt in full.

Required:
1. Prepare the journal entry of February 26.
2. Show two ways to journalize the transaction of September 26.

6–56. **AVERAGE COLLECTION PERIOD.** Study Appendix 6A. Consider the following:

	19X3	19X2	19X1
Sales	$4,500,000	$6,000,000	$4,800,000

	DECEMBER 31		
	19X3	19X2	19X1
Accounts receivable	$370,000	$460,000	$360,000

Eighty percent of the sales are on account.

Required:

Compute the average collection period for each of the years 19X2 and 19X3. Comment on the results.

6–57. WORK SHEETS FOR PERIODIC AND PERPETUAL INVENTORIES. Study Appendix 6C. Adrian Company sells sporting goods. Exhibit 6–12 shows how the Adrian unadjusted trial balances would appear under two different inventory systems as of December 31, 19X2 (in thousands of dollars).

Required:

1. Prepare two work sheets, one for the perpetual inventory system and one for the periodic inventory system. Enter the pertinent unadjusted trial balance in

EXHIBIT 6–12

ADRIAN COMPANY
Unadjusted Trial Balance
December 31, 19X2
(in thousands of dollars)

	PERPETUAL INVENTORY		PERIODIC INVENTORY	
	Debit	Credit	Debit	Credit
Cash	200		200	
Accounts receivable	370		370	
Allowance for uncollectible accounts				
Merchandise inventory	500*		300†	
Equipment	400		400	
Accumulated depreciation, equipment		100		100
Accounts payable		400		400
Accrued income taxes payable				
Paid-in capital		100		100
Retained income		470		470
Sales		2,300		2,300
Sales returns and allowances	100		100	
Cost of goods sold	1,400			
Purchases			1,690	
Purchase returns and allowances				90
All other expenses (summarized here)	400		400	
Bad debts expense				
Income tax expense				
	3,370	3,370	3,460	3,460

* Balance, December 31, 19X2.

† Balance, December 31, 19X1.

the first set of columns for each work sheet. Enter the amounts in thousands of dollars.

2. The unadjusted trial balances given here are probably misnamed. A more descriptive title would be "partially adjusted" trial balances. Assume that all necessary adjustments (for example, depreciation) have already been entered except for (labeled *j*, *k*, and *l* for later reference):

j. Bad debts expense should be recognized. Past experience indicates that a provision should be made of 2% of the year's credit sales of $1 million.

k. The cost of the ending inventory was $500,000.

l. Income tax expense was recognized at a rate of 40%.

Enter any necessary adjustments in the adjustment columns. Then complete the work sheet. To show the flexibility of the work sheet, omit the columns for the adjusted trial balance.

3. Prepare formal income statements in a format similar to that in Exhibit 6–3.

4. Prepare the adjusting journal entries, using the work sheets as a guide. Show adjacent sets of entries for the perpetual and periodic systems.

5. Prepare the closing journal entries, using the work sheets as a guide. Show adjacent sets of entries for the perpetual and periodic systems.

6–58. **REVIEW OF CHAPTERS 1–6. ADJUSTING AND CORRECTING ENTRIES.** Examine the accompanying Unadjusted Trial Balance as of December 31, 19X2.

MANTLE CLOAK COMPANY
Unadjusted Trial Balance
December 31, 19X2

ACCOUNT NUMBER		
1. Cash	$ 5,000	
2. Note receivable	1,000	
3. Accounts receivable	10,300	
4. Allowance for bad debts		$ 300
5. Inventory balance, as of January 1, 19X2	20,000	
6. Unexpired insurance	600	
7. Office supplies on hand		
8. Unexpired rent		
9. Equipment	4,000	
10. Accumulated depreciation, equipment		500
11. Accounts payable		10,000
12. Long-term 5% mortgage payable		3,000
13. Accrued interest payable		
14. Accrued wages payable		
15. Mantle capital		18,500
16. Sales		120,000
17. Sales returns	1,000	
18. Cash discounts on sales	1,000	
19. Purchases	71,000	
20. Purchase returns		1,000
21. Wages	22,000	
22. Rent and heat	10,000	
23. Bad debts expense		
24. Other operating expenses	7,000	
25. Supplies expense	400	
26. Insurance expense		
27. Depreciation		
28. Interest expense		
	$153,300	$153,300

For each of the following items 1 through 12 prepare the necessary entries. Select only from the accounts listed in the Trial Balance. The same account may be used in several answers. Answer by using account *numbers* and indicating the dollar amounts of debits and credits. For example, item 1 would call for a debit to Cash (1) for $100, a debit to Equipment (9) for $300, and a credit to Mantle Capital (15) for $400. (*Note*: The accounts that carry no balances are listed in the table for your convenience in making adjustments. All accounts needed to answer the questions are included.)

1. On December 30, the owner invested $100 in cash plus equipment valued at $300. The bookkeeper has not recorded the transaction.
2. It is estimated that the Allowance for Bad Debts should be *increased* by an amount equal to 0.5% of 19X2 gross sales.
3. A correct entry was made, early in December, for $1,000 worth of goods sold to a customer on open account. The customer returned these goods on December 29. The bookkeeper has made no entry for the latter transaction, although a credit memo was issued, December 31.
4. Unexpired insurance was $450 on December 31, 19X2.
5. The interest on the mortgage is payable yearly on January 2. (Adjust for a *full year's* interest. Do not refine the arithmetic for one or two days' interest.)
6. There was a $1,000 payroll robbery on December 15. Wages had been debited for $1,000 and Cash credited for $1,000 for the original payroll. A substitute payroll was made up on December 16, Wages again debited for $1,000, and Cash again credited for $1,000. However, the loss was covered by insurance. On December 20, the insurance company remitted $1,000, and the Mantle bookkeeper debited Cash and credited Sales.
7. The equipment cost is being allocated to operations on the basis of an estimated useful life of twenty years and no residual value.
8. Mantle withdrew $500 in cash on December 31. The bookkeeper has not recorded the transaction.
9. A $500 rental charge for January 19X3 was paid in cash to the DiMaggio Realty Company on December 31. The Mantle Company bookkeeper did not record the transaction.
10. Wages of salesclerks earned, but not paid, amount to $100.
11. A physical count of the office supplies revealed that there is a balance of $300 on hand as of December 31, 19X2.
12. On December 20, a customer paid the Mantle Company $980 for a $1,000 invoice, deducting a 2% discount. The bookkeeper made the appropriate entries. On December 30, Mr. Mantle discovered that the customer should have paid the full $1,000 because the discount period had expired on December 17. He sent the customer another invoice for the extra $20. The bookkeeper has not recorded the latter transaction.

☐ Understanding Published Financial Reports

6-59. **STUDENT LOANS.** The 1985 annual report of the University of Washington includes information about its receivables from student loans in a footnote to the financial statements (in thousands):

	1984		1985	
Student Loans:				
Federal programs	$29,738		$29,599	
Less—allowances	4,920	$24,818	3,910	$25,689
University funds	$ 3,487		$ 3,735	
Less—allowances	420	3,067	340	3,395
Total, net		$27,885		$29,084

1. Compare the quality of the loans under federal programs with the quality of those using university funds. Compare the quality of the loans outstanding at the end of 1985 with the quality of those outstanding at the end of 1984.
2. Using the balance sheet equation format, show which University of Washington accounts would be affected by new student tuition loans of $200,000 from university funds. Ignore allowances for bad debts.
3. Using the allowance method, show which accounts would be affected by an allowance for bad debts of an appropriate percentage of the $200,000. Choose a percentage. Also show the effects if a student loan of $1,400 is subsequently written off.

6–60. BANK CARDS. VISA and MasterCard are used to pay for a large percentage of retail purchases. The financial arrangements are similar for both bank cards. A news story said:

☐ If a cardholder charges a pair of $60 shoes, for instance, the merchant deposits the sales draft with his bank, which immediately credits $60 less a small transaction fee (usually 2 percent of the sale) to the merchant's account. The bank that issued the customer his card then pays the shoe merchant's bank $60 less a 1.5 percent transaction fee, allowing the merchant's bank a .5 percent profit on the transaction.

1. Prepare the journal entry for the sale by the merchant.
2. Prepare the journal entries for the merchant's bank regarding (a) the merchant's deposit and (b) the collection from the second bank.
3. Prepare the journal entry for the second bank (the bank that issued the credit card).
4. The national losses from bad debts for bank cards are about 1.8% of the total billings to cardholders. If so, how can the banks justify providing this service if their revenue from processing is typically 1.5% to 2.0%?

6–61. HOSPITAL BAD DEBTS. Hospital Corporation of America is a health-care company that operates over 400 hospitals and other medical facilities. A recent annual report showed the beginning of the company's income statement as follows (in thousands):

Operating revenues	$4,177,971
Less provision for contractual adjustments and doubtful accounts	679,327
Net revenues	$3,498,644

1. Prepare a reasonable footnote to accompany the above presentation. What do you think is the purpose of contractual allowances?
2. Prepare the summary journal entries for the $4,177,971 and the $679,327.

6–62. DISCOUNTS AND DOUBTFUL ITEMS. Scott Paper Company includes the following in its annual report (in thousands):

	JANUARY 1	
	1986	1985
Customer receivables	$331,028	$297,508
Reserves for discounts and doubtful items	(15,409)	(16,797)
	315,619	280,711

Required:

1. What is the most common substitute term for *reserve* in the context of accounting for receivables?
2. Compute the ratio of the reserves for discounts and doubtful items to gross accounts receivable for each of the two dates. What are some possible reasons for the change in this ratio?
3. Assume that all discounts are cash discounts, not trade discounts. Why does the reserve for cash discounts exist? Prepare a journal entry to create a reserve for discounts of $5,409,000. Prepare the journal entry that would ordinarily reduce the reserve for discounts.

6–63. ILLEGAL PAYMENT. The Internal Revenue Code does not permit taxpayers to deduct bribes, kickbacks, and other illegal payments as business expenses.

A wholesaler violated state law by secretly selling liquor at a discount to certain retailers. The specific discounts were agreed upon before each sale and rebated at a later date. The IRS deemed them nondeductible business expenses. The wholesaler took the case to court.

Required:

As an attorney, what arguments would you submit in court on behalf of the wholesaler?

6–64. RECONSTRUCTION OF TRANSACTIONS. Consider the following actual account descriptions and balances of La-Z-Boy Chair Company, maker of the popular La-Z-Boy chairs and other furniture:

	APRIL 28	
	1985	1984
Receivables, less allowances of $2,445,000 in 1985 and $2,300,000 in 1984 for doubtful accounts	$89,722,121	$77,256,571
Inventories	27,935,706	26,104,801

Required:

1. Suppose that for the fiscal year ended April 28, 1985, La-Z-Boy had a bad debts expense of $2,750,000. Compute the amount of bad debts written off during the year.
2. The income statement for the fiscal year included the item "cost of sales" of $191,312,763. Compute the net cost of the acquisitions of inventory for the fiscal year.

6–65. RECONSTRUCTION OF TRANSACTIONS. Ralston Purina Company has many well-known products, including Purina Dog Chow, Ry-Krisp, and Jack in the Box restaurants. Consider the following account descriptions and balances (in millions):

	SEPTEMBER 30	
	1985	1984
Receivables, less allowance for doubtful accounts	$259.9	$276.5
Inventories	359.4	359.4

Required:

1. Suppose that during the fiscal year ended September 30, 1985, Ralston Purina had bad debts expense of $12 million. The balances in Allowances for Doubtful Accounts were $13 million on September 30, 1984, and $14 million on September 30, 1985. Compute the amount of accounts receivable written off during the 1985 fiscal year.

2. The purchases of inventories during the 1985 fiscal year were $3,708.4 million. The income statement had an item "cost of products sold." Compute its amount.

6–66. NONPROFIT FINANCIAL REPORTS, BAD DEBTS. Following is the condensed partial statement of SRI International, a nonprofit corporation that offers an array of consulting services:

SRI INTERNATIONAL
Statement of Revenue, Cost and Expenses For the Year Ended December 31, 19X6

Project revenue	$113,878,000
Project costs	64,116,000
Excess of revenue over costs	$ 49,762,000
Expenses (detailed and including a separate line, Uncollectible Project Revenue, of $2,845)	48,278,000
Excess of revenue over costs and expenses from operations	$ 1,484,000

The balance sheet showed:

	DECEMBER 31	
	19X6	19X5
Receivables (less allowance for uncollectible accounts, $1,958,000, 19X6; and $518,000, 19X5)	21,514,000	20,068,000

A footnote stated:

☐ Project revenue comprises direct costs and related overhead and fee. Revenue is recorded as costs are incurred. Provision for uncollectible project revenue is based on past experience and review of receivables as to collectibility.

Required:

1. Are bad debts accounted for on the specific charge-off or allowance basis? Explain. Compare the collectibility of the accounts at the end of 19X5 and 19X6. Why might collectibility differ at the end of each year?
2. Examine the descriptions used by SRI International. What terms might be used instead by a profit-seeking enterprise?

6–67. ALLOWANCE FOR LOAN LOSSES. During 1982, Penn Square Bank, one of the largest lenders to the energy industry in the southwestern United States, was closed by regulatory authorities.

At the end of 1980, Penn Square had an allowance for loan losses of $1.4 million; at the end of 1981, $6.3 million. By June 30, 1982, the overseers of the bank's liquidation had written off $50.0 million of the bank's loans as uncollectible.

Required:

1. Prepare the journal entry for the $50 million write-off. Assume that no other entries regarding bad debts had been made during 1982.
2. As an outside auditor, or as the president of the bank, what evidence would you have sought near the end of 1981 to satisfy yourself that the allowance for loan losses was sufficient?

6–68. BAD DEBTS AND CASINOS. Study Appendix 6A. Metro-Goldwyn-Mayer, Inc. (MGM) conducts extensive hotel and gaming operations. A footnote in its 1984 annual report showed (in thousands):

Metro-Goldwyn-Mayer, Inc.

Allowances for uncollectible gaming receivables are provided to reduce gaming receivables and revenues to amounts anticipated to be collected. Gaming receivables and the related allowances were as follows (in thousands):

	1984	1983
Gaming receivables	$6,949	$6,945
Allowances for uncollectibles	2,214	2,904
Receivables charged against allowances during period, net of recoveries	2,294	6,934

1. Prepare the ratios of allowances for uncollectibles to gaming receivables for both dates. (The footnote does not disclose the specific dates. However, the first two items apply to August 31, 1984 and 1983, respectively. The third item pertains to the fiscal years 1984 and 1983.)
2. What other title could be used for "Receivables charged against allowances during period"?
3. How do you think these ratios compare with those of other industries? Would these ratios differ markedly among various casino companies? Why?

6–69. **BAD DEBT RECOVERIES.** See the preceding problem. Assume that bad debt recoveries by MGM during the year were $400,000. Prepare all summary journal entries affecting the Allowances for Uncollectibles for the fiscal year 1984. Also show the Allowance T-account.

6–70. **RETURNABLE DIAMONDS.** Norton Company is the world's largest producer of abrasive products and a leading supplier of industrial diamond products. Its annual report for 1984 contained the following account that related to its sale of diamond bits for petroleum drilling and mining:

Unrealized gross earnings on returnable diamonds	$8,674,000

Required:

1. Name the financial statement and the specific classification therein of the above account. Suppose the above unrealized amount related to $52 million of gross sales of the product. Show the effect on the balance sheet equation of the sale. Also prepare the pertinent journal entry.
2. Suppose Norton Company sells diamond bits amounting to $100,000 to the Shell Oil Company. Later Shell receives a $14,000 credit for the unconsumed usable diamond content of the salvaged bits returned. Show the effect of the return on Norton's balance sheet equation. Also prepare the pertinent journal entry for the return.

6–71. **SHIPPING EXPENSES AND DISCOUNTS.** The 1984 income statement of Kimberly-Clark Corporation, maker of Kleenex, Huggies, and other products using absorbent fibers, shows the following gross profit (in millions):

Net sales	$3,616
Cost of products sold	2,320
Distribution expense	152
Gross profit	$1,144

1. Does the "Distribution expense" refer to freight in or freight out for Kimberly-Clark?
2. Suppose that on March 1, 19X6, Kimberly-Clark bought $1 million of paper with terms 2/10, n/30, F.O.B. shipping point. Shipping costs were $42,000. The total amount due was paid on March 7. The paper was sold on credit for $1.3 million on March 25 with terms 2/20, n/30, F.O.B. destination. Shipping costs were $30,000, which was paid immediately. The customer paid on April 16. Prepare journal entries for these two transactions. Assume a perpetual inventory system.

6–72. **ALLOWANCE AND PROVISION FOR DOUBTFUL ACCOUNTS.** Study Appendix 6A. Allied Stores is one of the country's largest retailing companies, owning department stores such as The Bon and Jordan Marsh and specialty stores such as Brooks Brothers and Bonwit Teller. The following footnote was in Allied's annual report:

Accounts Receivable—Customers

	FEBRUARY 2, 1985	JANUARY 28, 1984
Revolving credit accounts	$ 905,322	$835,921
Installment accounts	100,929	79,854
Other accounts	8,633	11,993
	1,014,884	927,768
Less allowance for doubtful accounts	19,072	16,094
	$ 995,812	$911,674

Management described receivables as follows:

☐ Net customer receivables increased $84 million over the prior year balance due to increased charge sales. The percent of sales made on credit was 67.7% of total sales in the year ended February 2, 1985, compared with 65.6% and 63.8% in 1984 and 1983, respectively. The quality and estimated collectibility of accounts receivable have remained strong. The allowance for doubtful accounts was 1.88% of customer receivables at year end, versus 1.73% in 1984 and 1.74% in 1983. The net provision for doubtful accounts in dollars and as a percent of credit sales was as follows: 1985—$24.5 million (.85%); 1984—$19.2 million (.74%); 1983—$17.8 million (.81%).

1. Management's description referred to an *allowance* for doubtful accounts and a *provision* for doubtful accounts. How does an *allowance* differ from a *provision*?
2. Management refers to a *net* provision. The provision amount is *net* of what? That is, what was subtracted from a gross provision to yield a net provision?
3. What were total credit sales for fiscal 1985?
4. Assume that there were no bad debt recoveries in 1985. What amount of accounts receivable was written off as uncollectible in 1985?

Chapter 7

VALUING INVENTORIES AND MEASURING GROSS PROFIT

LEARNING OBJECTIVES

After studying this chapter, you should be able to

1. Explain the differences between various inventory methods and their effects on the measurements of assets and net income
2. Show the effects of inventory errors on measurements of financial performance and position
3. Explain the uses of the gross profit equation and inventory turnover measures
4. Explain the meaning and impact of the liquidation of LIFO inventories and the presence of LIFO reserves (Appendix 7A)
5. Explain the effects of various accounting methods on perpetual inventory systems (Appendix 7B)

This chapter describes how different inventory methods affect financial statements, shows what effect market prices have on accounting for inventories, and explains the relationship between gross profit and inventories.

INVENTORIES AND THE ACCRUAL BASIS

The presence of inventories underscores the desirability of accrual accounting. Indeed, the Internal Revenue Service insists that taxpayers with merchandise inventories for resale must use the accrual rather than the cash basis of accounting in determining the cost of goods sold expense. That is, taxpayers are not allowed tax deductions for the mere purchase of inventory, whether for cash or credit. Exhibit 7–1 displays a central aspect of accrual accounting as the measurement of inventory (an asset) and the cost of goods sold (an expense). The central idea is straightforward. Inventories on hand represent future benefits, and inventories no longer on hand should not be listed as assets.

EXHIBIT 7–1

Merchandising Company (Retailer or Wholesaler)

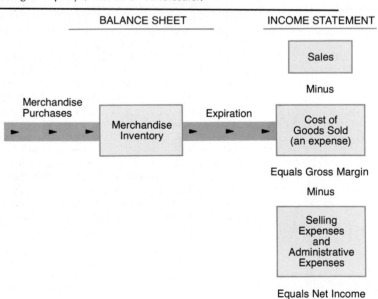

There are two major steps in accounting for inventories. First, obtain a *physical count*. Second, obtain a *cost valuation*. The physical count is an imposing, time-consuming, and expensive process that sometimes requires a complete stoppage of normal business. For instance, you have probably seen "closed for inventory taking" signs either in departments or in entire businesses. Frequently, the process is conducted on staggered dates and by resorting to statistical sampling procedures. In any case, the inventories in corporate annual reports are not based merely on accounting records alone. The external auditors must assure themselves that accurate up-to-date physical counting has occurred.

PRINCIPAL INVENTORY METHODS

☐ Four Major Methods

Each period, accountants must divide the costs of merchandise acquired between cost of goods sold and cost of items remaining in ending inventory. Various inventory methods accomplish this division. If unit prices and costs did not fluctuate, all inventory methods would show identical results. But prices change, and these changes raise central issues regarding cost of goods sold (income measurement) and inventories (asset measurement). Four principal inventory methods have been generally accepted in the United States: specific identification, weighted average, FIFO, and LIFO. Each will be explained and compared.

As a preview of the remainder of this chapter, consider the following simple example of the choices facing management. A new vendor of a cola drink at the fairgrounds began the week with no inventory. He bought one can on Monday for 30 cents; a second can on Tuesday for 40 cents; and a third can on Wednesday for 56 cents. He then sold one can on Thursday for 90 cents. What was his gross profit? His ending inventory? Answer these questions in your own mind before reading on.

Part I of Exhibit 7–2 provides a quick glimpse of the nature of the generally accepted methods. Their underlying assumptions will be explained shortly. As you can readily see, the vendor's choice of an inventory method can often significantly affect gross profit (and hence net income) and ending inventory valuation for balance sheet purposes.

1. **SPECIFIC IDENTIFICATION** (COLUMN 1). This method concentrates on the *physical* linking of the *particular* items sold. If the vendor reached for the Monday can instead of the Wednesday can, the *same inventory method* would show different results. Thus Part I of Exhibit 7–2 indicates that gross profit for operations of Monday through Thursday could be 60¢, 50¢, or 34¢, depending on the particular can handed to the customer. Obviously, this method permits great latitude for measuring results in any given period. The next three methods do not trace the actual physical flow of goods except by coincidence.

2. **FIRST-IN, FIRST-OUT (FIFO)** (COLUMN 2). This method assumes that the stock acquired earliest is sold (used up) first. Thus the Monday unit is deemed to have been sold regardless of the actual physical unit delivered. In times of

EXHIBIT 7–2

Comparison of Inventory Methods for Cola Vendor (all monetary amounts are in cents)

Part I
Income Statement for the Period Monday through Thursday

	(1) SPECIFIC IDENTIFICATION			(2) FIFO	(3) LIFO	(4) WEIGHTED AVERAGE
	(1A)	(1B)	(1C)			
Sales	90	90	90	90	90	90
Deduct cost of goods sold:						
1 30¢ (Monday) unit	30			30		
1 40¢ (Tuesday) unit		40				
1 56¢ (Wednesday) unit			56		56	
1 weighted-average unit [(30 + 40 + 56) ÷ 3 = 42]						42
Gross profit for Monday through Thursday	60	50	34	60	34	48
Computation of cost of goods sold:						
Beginning inventory	0	0	0	0	0	0
Add purchases, 3 units:						
(30 + 40 + 56)	126	126	126	126	126	126
Cost of goods available for sale	126	126	126	126	126	126
Less ending inventory, 2 units:						
40 + 56	96			96		
30 + 56		86				
30 + 40			70		70	
2 × 42						84
Cost of goods sold, Monday through Thursday	30	40	56	30	56	42

Part II
Income Statements for Friday Only and for Monday through Friday

	(1A)	(1B)	(1C)	(2) FIFO	(3) LIFO	(4) WEIGHTED AVERAGE
Sales, 2 units @ 90	180	180	180	180	180	180
Cost of goods sold (Thursday ending inventory from above)	96	86	70	96	70	84
Gross profit, Friday only	84	94	110	84	110	96
Gross profit, Monday through Thursday (from above)	60	50	34	60	34	48
Gross profit, Monday through Friday	144	144	144	144	144	144

rising prices, FIFO usually shows the largest gross profit (60¢ in Part I of Exhibit 7–2).

3. **LAST-IN, FIRST-OUT (LIFO)** (COLUMN 3). This method assumes that the stock acquired most recently is sold (used up) first. Thus the Wednesday unit is deemed to have been sold regardless of the actual physical unit delivered. In times of rising prices, LIFO generally shows the lowest gross profit (34¢ in Part I of Exhibit 7–2).

4. **WEIGHTED-AVERAGE COST** (COLUMN 4). This method assumes that all items available for sale during the period are best represented by a weighted-average cost. Exhibit 7–2 shows the calculations. The weighted-average method usually

produces a gross profit somewhere between that obtained under FIFO and LIFO (48¢ as compared with 60¢ and 34¢ in Part I of Exhibit 7–2).

□ Inventories and Matching

Part I of Exhibit 7–2 indicates why theoretical and practical disputes easily arise regarding the "best" inventory method. As Exhibit 7–3 demonstrates, the four inventory methods have four separate cost-flow assumptions. When identical goods are purchased at different times and at different prices, accountants face a "matching" problem. The choice of an inventory method is an attempt to adhere to the basic concept of matching and cost recovery, which was introduced in Chapter 2. The difficulty is not with "matching" as an *abstract* idea; instead disputes arise regarding how to *apply* it. Thus more than one inventory method has evolved, and the four methods illustrated in Exhibits 7–2 and 7–3 have all become accepted as part of the body of generally accepted accounting principles.

EXHIBIT 7–3

Diagram of Inventory Methods (Data are from Exhibit 7–2; monetary amounts are in cents)

Beginning inventory	+	Merchandise purchases	=	Cost of goods available for sale
0	+	126	=	126

Cost of goods available for sale	−	Cost of goods sold	=	Ending inventory	
1 @ 30 1 @ 40 1 @ 56 126	−	30 or 40 or 56	=	96 or 86 or 70	Specific identification
	−	30	=	96	FIFO
	−	56	=	70	LIFO
	−	42	=	84	Weighted average

□ The Consistency Convention

Inventory methods have chainlike effects because the ending asset balance for one reporting period becomes the beginning asset balance for the succeeding reporting period. Suppose the vendor sells his remaining inventory on Friday and goes into a more attractive business. Part II of Exhibit 7–2 shows that the *cumulative* gross profit over the life of an entity will be the same under all inventory methods. However, *individual* reporting periods can be dramatically affected. For example, income based on FIFO is higher than income based on LIFO for Monday through Thursday, but not for Friday only.

The major distinction among inventory methods is timing: *When* should the cost of inventories be released from being an asset to become an expense? The remainder of this chapter will explore the various suggested answers to this question.

As we proceed, keep in mind that a chosen inventory method must be used consistently from year to year. Although switches from one inventory method to another may occur occasionally (most notably from FIFO to LIFO), they are relatively rare events in the life of an entity. **Consistency** is such a prized convention in accounting that outside auditors' independent opinions must include wording such as the following: "The accompanying financial statements present fairly . . . in conformity with generally accepted accounting principles applied on a basis *consistent with that of the preceding year*." If a change was made, the audit opinion must mention that change.

The differences between LIFO and FIFO can be substantial. Furthermore, a company does not necessarily use one inventory method for all its products. To illustrate, General Mills, maker of Wheaties, Cheerios, and other food products, stated in a footnote in its annual report:

General Mills, Inc.

The components of year-end inventories are as follows (in millions):

May 26	1985	1984
Valued at LIFO	$170.4	$262.6
Valued primarily at FIFO	207.3	399.1
Total Inventories	$377.7	$661.7

If the FIFO method of inventory accounting had been used in place of LIFO, inventories would have been $47.5 million and $79.7 million higher than reported at May 26, 1985 and 1984, respectively.

LIFO is the most popular inventory method for large U.S. companies. Over two-thirds of the companies use LIFO for at least some of their inventories. Over 60% use FIFO, and 40% use weighted average for a portion of their inventories. Less than 10% use any other method, including specific identification. Over half of the companies use more than one inventory method.

☐ Specific Identification

An obvious way to account for inventory is through *specific identification* via physical observation or the labeling of items in stock with individual numbers or codes. Such an approach is easy and economically justifiable for relatively expensive merchandise like custom artwork and diamond jewelry. However, most organizations have vast segments of inventories that are too numerous and insufficiently valuable per unit to warrant such individualized attention.

As Exhibit 7–2 shows, specific identification requires the linkage of individual inventory items with the exact purchase costs of each unit. In the past, this tracing might have been simple if the item was a Cadillac or a Lincoln, but not if the item was a toothbrush or a jar of peanut butter.

Of course, in this computer age it is becoming economically feasible to track more and more inventory in this manner. Nevertheless, the computerized inventory systems are most often used to help management plan and control the *physical* levels of various inventories. These systems rarely attempt to use specific identification to trace individual *costs* to individual items such as boxes of cereal or jars of coffee. In sum, the specific identification method continues to be largely confined to expensive individualized merchandise.

To the extent that accountants and managers believe that sales and cost of goods sold should reflect the *physical flow* of goods, specific identification is the most attractive inventory method. Its major drawback in many cases is its expense. Moreover, many critics claim that income measurement's first concern should not be with *physical* flows but with the *economic* flows (to be explained momentarily).

Exhibit 7–2 also demonstrates how the specific identification method can measure three different gross profits with the same set of facts. Thus, unlike FIFO or LIFO, specific identification may permit management to manipulate income and inventory values by filling a sales order from a number of physically equivalent items bearing various inventory cost prices.

☐ **FIFO, LIFO, Weighted Average**

As briefly explained earlier, FIFO assumes for costing purposes that the units acquired latest are still on hand. The earliest costs are considered to be the cost of goods sold. In contrast, LIFO assumes that the units acquired earliest are still on hand. Thus the most recent, or last, inventory costs are considered to be the cost of goods sold. The attempt is to match the most current costs against current revenue (sales).[1]

As Part I of Exhibit 7–2 indicates, LIFO usually results in the reporting of less income than FIFO when prices are rising.[2] Why? Because the recent, *higher* costs become the cost of goods sold. Suppose prices are falling. The most recent costs are then *lower*, so LIFO reports higher income than FIFO. As might be expected, the weighted-average method generally produces results that lie between the extremes of FIFO and LIFO.

Ponder the calculation of a *weighted* average. *Weighted* average should be used to give appropriate consideration to quantities. The average is com-

---

[1] Professor George Sorter refers to LISH–FISH instead of FIFO–LIFO. LISH is FIFO because "last in is still here," and FISH is LIFO because "first in is still here."

[2] An exception can occur when inventories are seriously depleted. See Appendix 7A and the gross profit for Friday only in Exhbit 7–2.

puted by dividing the *total* cost of the beginning inventory plus purchases, by the *total* number of units in those two classes. Suppose our cola vendor had bought two cans rather than one on Monday at 30¢ each:

Weighted average = Cost of goods available for sale ÷ Units available for sale
Weighted average = [(2 × 30¢) + (1 × 40¢) + (1 × 56¢)] ÷ 4
= 156¢ ÷ 4
= 39¢

☐ Essence of FIFO

Accountants and managers tend to develop strong feelings regarding the comparative merits of FIFO and LIFO. Adherents of FIFO maintain that it is the most practical way to describe what operating managers actually do. That is, most managers deliberately attempt to move their merchandise on a first-in, first-out basis. This approach avoids spoilage, obsolescence, and the like. Thus the inventory flow assumption underlying FIFO corresponds most closely with the actual physical flows of inventory items in most businesses. Furthermore, the asset balance for inventories is a close approximation of the "actual" dollars invested, because the inventory is carried at the most recent purchase prices paid. Such prices are not likely to differ much from current prices at the balance sheet date. Consequently, its proponents maintain that FIFO properly meets the objectives of both the income statement and the balance sheet.

☐ Essence of LIFO

Adherents of LIFO are usually critical of FIFO because of the latter's effects on income when prices are rising. They claim that FIFO-based income is deceiving in the sense that some of the corresponding increase in net assets is merely an "inventory profit." That is, an "inventory profit" is fictitious because for a going concern, part of it is needed for replenishing the inventory. Consequently, it is not profit in the layperson's sense of the term; it does not indicate an amount that is entirely available to pay dividends. For instance, consider our cola vendor:

	FIFO	LIFO
Sales, one unit on Thursday	90¢	90¢
Cost of goods sold	30	56
Gross profit	60¢	34¢

The proponent of LIFO would claim that FIFO "overstates" profits (the "inventory profit") by 60¢ − 34¢ = 26¢. Suppose replacement prices stay at 56¢. The vendor will need 30¢ + 26¢ = 56¢, not merely the 30¢ reported as FIFO cost of goods sold, to replace the unit sold. In commenting on reporting profits in general, a *Newsweek* article said:

☐ But inventory profits also played a significant role. In an inflationary world, parts acquired for inventory tend to appreciate in value by the time they are used in the manufacturing process. The company then reflects the difference in its selling price—and takes an "inventory profit." It must restock at the new, higher cost, of course, but as long as the inflation continues, so does the inventory-profit process.

Advocates of LIFO also stress that in times of rising prices, there may be greater pressure from stockholders to pay unjustified higher cash dividends under FIFO than LIFO. In the above example, the payment of a cash dividend of 60¢ by a vendor using FIFO would result in his not having enough cash to replenish his inventory. He would have only 90¢ − 60¢ = 30¢. In contrast, LIFO would be more likely to conserve cash to the extent that less cash dividends would be paid if less income is reported. The vendor would have 90¢ − 34¢ = 56¢ available for replenishing inventory (if he paid a cash dividend of 34¢, ignoring the effects of other expenses).

☐ Criticisms of LIFO

Critics of LIFO point to absurd balance sheet valuations. Under LIFO, older and older prices, and hence less-useful inventory values, are reported, especially if physical stocks grow through the years. In contrast, under FIFO, the balance sheet tends to contain current prices and values. LIFO companies can offset this criticism to some extent by disclosing FIFO inventory values in a footnote to the financial statement. For example, see the General Mills annual report footnote on page 272.

Another criticism of LIFO is that, unlike FIFO, it permits management to influence immediate net income by the *timing of purchases*. For instance, if prices are rising and a company desires, for income tax or other reasons, to report less income in a given year, managers may be inclined to buy a large amount of inventory near the end of the year, that is, to accelerate the replacement of inventory that would normally not occur until early in the next year.

Consider an example. Suppose in our illustration that acquisition prices had increased from 56¢ on Wednesday to 61¢ on Thursday, the day of the sale of the one unit. Suppose that one more unit was acquired on Thursday for 61¢. How would net income be affected under FIFO? Under LIFO?

There would be no effect on cost of goods sold or gross profit under FIFO, although the balance sheet would show ending inventory as 61¢ higher. In contrast, LIFO would show a 5¢ higher cost of goods sold and a 5¢ lower gross profit:

	LIFO	
	As in Exhibit 7–2	If One More Unit Acquired
Sales	90¢	90¢
Cost of goods sold	56¢	61¢
Gross profit	34¢	29¢
Ending inventory:		
First layer, Monday	30¢	30¢
Second layer, Tuesday	40¢	40¢
Third layer, Wednesday		56¢
	70¢	126¢

Thus a 34¢ gross profit may be transformed into a 29¢ gross profit merely because of a change in the timing and amount of merchandise *acquired*, not because of any change in *sales*.

The second part of the above tabulation uses the word *layer*. As the term implies, a **LIFO layer** (also called **LIFO increment** or **LIFO pool**) is an identifiable addition to inventory. As a company grows, the LIFO layers tend to pile on one another as the years go by. Thus many LIFO companies will show inventories that may have ancient layers (going back to 1940 in some instances). The reported LIFO values may therefore be far below what FIFO values might otherwise show.

□ Importance of Income Taxes

The accounting literature is full of fancy theoretical arguments that support LIFO. For example, some accountants maintain that LIFO shows the "real" impact of inflation on cost of goods sold more clearly than FIFO. But there is one—and only one— dominant reason why more and more U.S. companies have adopted LIFO. *Income taxes!* LIFO is acceptable for income tax purposes. Furthermore, the Internal Revenue Code requires that if LIFO is used for income tax purposes, it must also be used for financial reporting purposes. If prices persistently rise, and if inventory quantities are maintained so that LIFO layers bearing "old" prices are not used up, current taxable income will be less under LIFO than FIFO. Consequently, income taxes will be postponed. Intelligent financial managers would therefore be tempted to adopt LIFO. Indeed, some observers maintain that executives are guilty of serious mismanagement by not adopting LIFO when FIFO produces significantly higher taxable income.

The 1985 annual report of Becton, Dickinson and Company indicated that its "change to the LIFO method of accounting for substantially all of the domestic inventories, whereby the most current costs are charged against current revenues for both financial reporting and income tax purposes, resulted in improved cash flow due to lower income taxes paid." Management often faces some significant choices between accounting methods. The impact of these choices on the cash position can be enormous.

□ Tyranny of Reported Earnings

The accrual accounting model has survived many tests through time. It is here to stay. Nevertheless, as useful as it is for evaluating performance, its limitations should never be overlooked. For example, net income (or earnings per share) is *only one* measure of performance. Even though this "bottom line" is important, it is sometimes overemphasized in the minds of management. It may lead to decisions that boost current reported net income but may not be in the best long-run interests of the stockholders. Thus managers may slash advertising, maintenance, and research expenses to bolster 19X7 earnings. But such "economy measures" can produce some unfavorable results: reduction in share of the customer market, poorer condition of equipment, and lack of new products, all of which may have devastating effects on earnings in 19X8, 19X9, and thereafter.

Similarly, managers may be reluctant to switch to LIFO from FIFO because reported income will be less. There is widespread but mistaken belief that the stock market can be fooled by the reported net income numbers. In the long run, the wealth of the shareholders is usually enhanced by decisions that postpone income tax disbursements even though reported net income may be lower. A senior officer of Chase Manhattan Bank has observed:

☐ The standard accounting model too often is misleading. Despite growing aware-ness of inflation's impact, for example, many big companies still account for inventories on a first in, first out basis, under which it's assumed that the oldest goods in inventory are sold first, thus reducing the *reported* cost of goods and maximizing *reported* earnings. But unfortunately FIFO also results in real higher taxes and less actual cash retained in the corporate till. It's a strange way of doing business and suggests that the investor who puts much faith in "earnings-per-share multiples" may be doing so at considerable risk.[3]

The following table summarizes the choices faced by many top managers:

INVENTORY METHOD	ACTUAL CASH POSITION	REPORTED NET INCOME
FIFO	Lower	Higher
LIFO	Higher	Lower

As the quotation suggests, the dilemma should usually be solved in favor of LIFO. The company would then be better able to meet the dividend expecta-tions of stockholders or of other demands. Why? Because the company will have a better cash position despite lower reported net income.

REPLACEMENT COST METHOD

All inventory methods described thus far have been *historical cost* methods as distinguished from a method based on **replacement cost**. The latter method, which is sometimes also called **next-in, first-out (NIFO)**, has strong advocates. However, replacement cost is *not* currently acceptable in the *basic* financial statements for corporate annual reporting or income tax reporting. Still, almost two thousand U.S. companies having either (1) inventories and net fixed assets amounting to more than $125 million or (2) total assets amount-ing to more than $1 billion *must* provide *supplementary* disclosure in share-holder reports of the "current cost" (which is often replacement cost) amounts of inventory and operating income.

Suppose that our vendor in Exhibit 7–2 used the replacement cost

---

[3] Joel M. Stern, "Annual Reports and Stock Prices," *Wall Street Journal*, January 29, 1979, p. 20.

method, and that the replacement cost of inventories was 61¢ per can on Thursday. Gross profit for Monday through Thursday would be:

	REPLACEMENT COST	LIFO	FIFO
Sales, one unit on Thursday	90¢	90¢	90¢
Cost of goods sold	61	56	30
Gross profit	29¢	34¢	60¢

The proponents of replacement cost would claim that both LIFO and FIFO overstate profits in times of rising prices. The vendor needs 61¢ to replenish his inventory. His going concern could not maintain the same level of operations if it paid cash dividends in an amount equal to net income under *either* LIFO or FIFO. For example, the payment of dividends guided by the reported profits of the LIFO method would leave only 56¢ for replenishment, not the necessary 61¢.

The supporters of the replacement cost method maintain that it gives managers and owners a better idea of whether dividends are justified in light of a company's continuing operating requirements. Supporters also want income tax laws revised. Why? They claim that it is unfair to have an income tax levied on the "fictitious" or "illusory" profits shown by the generally accepted inventory methods. Chapter 14 explores the replacement cost method in greater depth.

LOWER OF COST OR MARKET

☐ The Conservatism Convention

Conservatism has been a hallmark of accounting. In a technical sense, **conservatism** means selecting the method of measurement that yields the gloomiest immediate results. This attitude is reflected in such working rules as "Anticipate no gains, but provide for all possible losses," and "If in doubt, write it off."

Accountants have traditionally regarded the historical costs of acquiring an asset as the ceiling for its valuation. Assets may be written up only upon an exchange, but they may be written down without an exchange. For example, consider *lower-of-cost-or-market* procedures. Inventories are written down when replacement costs decline, but they are never written up when replacement costs increase.

Conservatism has been criticized as being inherently inconsistent. If replacement market prices are sufficiently objective and verifiable to justify write-downs, why aren't they just as valid for write-ups? Furthermore, the critics maintain, conservatism is not a fundamental concept. Accounting reports should try to present the most accurate picture feasible—neither too high nor too low. Accountants defend their attitude by saying that erring

in the direction of conservatism would usually have less-severe economic consequences than erring in the direction of overstating assets and net income.

Conservatism that leads to understating net income in one period also
creates an overstatement of net income in a future period. For example, if
a $100 inventory is written down to $80, net income is reduced by $20 in
the period of the write-down but *increased* by $20 in the period the inventory
is sold.

☐ **Role of Replacement Cost**

A prime example of conservatism is the **lower-of-cost-or-market** method
(LCM), which is the superimposition of a market-price test on an inventory
cost method. That is, the current market price is compared with cost (derived
by specific identification, FIFO, and so forth), and the lower of the two is
selected as the basis for the valuation of goods at a specific inventory date.
The annual report of ITT Corporation states: "Inventories are valued generally
at the lower of cost (first-in, first-out) or market . . . counts of inventories
are made at least annually."

Market generally means the *current replacement cost* or its equivalent.
It ordinarily does *not* mean the ultimate selling price to customers. Consider
the following facts. A company has 100 units in its ending FIFO inventory
on December 31, 19X1. Its gross profit for 19X1 has been tentatively computed
as follows:

Sales	$2,180
Cost of goods available for sale	$1,980
Ending inventory, at cost of 100 units	790
Cost of goods sold	$1,190
Gross profit	$ 990

There has been a sudden decline in market prices during the final week of
December to $4 per unit. If the lower market price is indicative of lower
ultimate sales prices, an inventory write-down of $790 − (100 × $4), or $390,
is in order. The required journal entry (without explanation) is:

Loss on write-down of inventories	390	
Merchandise inventory		390

Therefore reported income for 19X1 would be lowered by $390:

	BEFORE $390 WRITE-DOWN	AFTER $390 WRITE-DOWN	DIFFERENCE
Sales	$2,180	$2,180	
Cost of goods available	$1,980	$1,980	
Ending inventory	790	400	−$390
Cost of goods sold	$1,190	$1,580	+$390
Gross profit	$ 990	$ 600	−$390

The theory states that of the $790 cost, $390 is considered to have expired during 19X1 because the cost cannot be justifiably carried forward to the future as an asset measure. Furthermore, the decision to purchase was made during 19X1, but unfortunate fluctuations occurred in the replacement market during the same period. These declines in prices caused the inventory to lose some value, some revenue-producing power. On the other hand, if *selling prices* also are not likely to fall, the revenue-producing power of the inventory will be maintained and no write-down would be justified.

In sum, if predicted selling prices will be *unaffected* by the fact that current replacement costs are below the carrying cost of the inventory, do nothing. If predicted selling prices will be lower, use replacement cost.

If a write-down occurs, the new $400 valuation is what is left of the original cost of the inventory. In other words, the new market price becomes, for accounting purposes, the remaining unexpired cost of the inventory. Thus, if replacement prices rise to $8 per unit in January 19X2, no restoration of the December write-down will be permitted. In short, the lower-of-cost-or-market method would regard the $4 cost as of December 31 as the "new cost" of the inventory. Historical cost is the ceiling for valuation under generally accepted accounting principles.

☐ Conservatism in Action

Compared with a strict cost method, the lower-of-cost-or-market method reports less net income in the period of decline in market value of the inventory and more net income in the period of sale. More generally, cumulative net income (the sum of all net income amounts from the inception of the firm to the present date) is never lower and is usually higher under the strict cost method. Exhibit 7–4 underscores this point. Suppose our example company goes out of business in early 19X2. That is, no more units are acquired. There are no sales in 19X2 except for the disposal of the inventory in question at $8 per unit (100 × $8 = $800). Neither combined gross profit nor combined net income for the two periods will be affected by the LCM method, as the bottom of Exhibit 7–4 reveals.

This example shows that conservatism can be a double-edged sword in the sense that net income in a current year will be hurt by a write-down of inventory (or any asset) and in a future year will be helped by the amount of the write-down. As Exhibit 7–4 illustrates, 19X2 income is higher by the $390 write-down of 19X1.

A full-blown lower-of-cost-or-market method is rarely encountered in practice. Why? Because it is expensive to get the correct replacement costs of hundreds or thousands of different products in inventory. Still, auditors definitely feel that the costs of inventories should be fully recoverable from future revenues. Therefore auditors inevitably make market-price tests of a representative sample of the ending inventories. In particular, auditors want to write down the subclasses of inventory that are obsolete, shopworn, or otherwise of only nominal value.

EXHIBIT 7–4

Effects of Lower-of-Cost-or-Market

	COST METHOD		LOWER-OF-COST-OR-MARKET METHOD	
	19X1	19X2	19X1	19X2
Sales	$2,180	$800	$2,180	$800
Cost of goods available	$1,980	$790	$1,980	$400
Ending inventory	790	—	400*	—
Cost of goods sold	$1,190	$790	$1,580	$400
Gross profit	$ 990	$ 10	$ 600	$400

Combined gross profit for two years:
Cost method:
  $990 + $10 = $1,000
Lower-of-cost-or-market method:
  $600 + $400 = $1,000

* The inventory is shown here after being written down by $390, from $790 to $400. For internal purposes, many accountants prefer to show the write-down separately, presenting a gross profit before write-down of inventory, the write-down, and a gross profit after write-down. The journal entry would be:

Loss on write-down of inventory	390	
Inventory		390
To write down inventory from $790 cost to $400 market value.		

EFFECTS OF INVENTORY ERRORS

The identification of inventory errors and their effects is a popular way (a) to test understanding and develop perspective regarding the nature and role of inventories in relation to income statements and balance sheets and (b) to show the interrelationships of financial statements for two or more reporting periods. Inventory errors can arise from many sources. Examples are wrong physical counts (possibly because goods that are in receiving or shipping areas instead of the inventory stockroom were omitted when physical counts are made) and clerical errors.

An undiscovered inventory error usually affects two reporting periods. It is counterbalanced by the ordinary accounting process in the next period. That is, the error affects income by identical offsetting amounts; it also affects the balance sheet at the end of the first period but not at the end of the second. For example, suppose ending inventory in 19X7 is understated by $10,000 because of errors in physical count. The year's cost of goods sold would be overstated, pretax income understated, assets understated, and retained income understated. For the moment, ignore income taxes:

	A	= L +		SE	
	Inventory			Retained Income	
Effects of error	$10,000 understated	=		$10,000 understated because cost of goods sold is overstated and net income is understated	

Again, thinking in terms of effects on the balance sheet equation is helpful. A useful generalization is: If ending inventory is understated, retained income is understated. Similarly, if ending inventory is overstated, retained income is overstated.

Now consider also the effects of income taxes, using a 40% tax rate:

	A	=	L	+	SE
	Inventory		Income Tax Liability		Retained Income
Effects of error	$10,000 understated	=	$4,000 understated	+	$6,000 understated*

* Cost of goods sold overstated	$10,000
Pretax income understated	$10,000
Income taxes understated	4,000
Net income, which is included in ending retained income, understated	$ 6,000

The above effects are not particularly easy to understand unless a complete illustration is studied. Consider the complete income statements (all numbers are in thousands and are assumed):

19X7	CORRECT REPORTING		INCORRECT REPORTING*		EFFECTS OF ERRORS
Sales		$980		$980	
Deduct: Cost of goods sold:					
Beginning inventory	$100		$100		
Purchases	500		500		
Cost of goods available for sale	$600		$600		
Deduct: Ending inventory	70		60		Understated by $10
Cost of goods sold		530		540	Overstated by $10
Gross profit		$450		$440	Understated by $10
Other expenses		250		250	
Income before income taxes		$200		$190	Understated by $10
Income tax expense at 40%		80		76	Understated by $4
Net income		$120		$114	Understated by $6
Ending balance sheet items:					
Inventory		$ 70		$ 60	Understated by $10
Retained income includes current net income of		120		114	Understated by $6
Income tax liability†		80		76	Understated by $4

* Because of error in ending inventory.

† For simplicity, assume that the entire income tax expense for the year will not be paid until the succeeding year. Therefore the ending liability will equal the income tax expense.

Think about the effects of the uncorrected error on the following year, 19X8. The beginning inventory will be $60,000 rather than the correct $70,000. Therefore *all* the errors in 19X7 will be offset by counterbalancing errors in 19X8. Thus the retained income at the end of 19X8 would show a cumulative effect of zero. This is because the net income in 19X7 would be understated by $6,000, but the net income in 19X8 would be overstated by $6,000.

The point not to overlook is that the ending inventory of one period is also the beginning inventory of the succeeding period. Assume that the operations during 19X8 are a duplication of those of 19X7 except that the ending inventory is correctly counted as $40,000. Note the role of the error in the beginning inventory:

19X8	CORRECT REPORTING		INCORRECT REPORTING*		EFFECTS OF ERRORS
Sales		$980		$980	
Deduct: Cost of goods sold:					
Beginning inventory	$ 70		$ 60		Understated by $10
Purchases	500		500		
Cost of goods available for sale	$570		$560		Understated by $10
Deduct: Ending inventory	40		40		
Cost of goods sold		530		520	Understated by $10
Gross profit		$450		$460	Overstated by $10
Other expenses		250		250	
Income before income taxes		$200		$210	Overstated by $10
Income tax expense at 40%		80		84	Overstated by $4
Net income		$120		$126	Overstated by $6
Ending balance sheet items:					
Inventory		$ 40		$ 40	Correct
Retained income includes:					
Net income of previous year		120		114⎤	Counterbalanced and
Net income of current year		120		126⎦	thus now correct
Income tax liability:					
End of previous year		80		76⎤	Counterbalanced and
End of current year		80		84⎦	thus now correct†

* Because of error in beginning inventory.

† The $84 really consists of the $4 that pertains to income of the previous year plus $80 that pertains to income of the current year.

GROSS PROFIT AND INVENTORIES

☐ Gross Profit Equations

A thorough understanding of the relationships among inventory, cost of goods sold, and gross profit aids managers, investors, and anyone else who wishes to assess a company's performance. Suppose a manager of a K Mart store wants to prepare a monthly income statement without incurring the expense of a physical inventory count. The manager can estimate gross profit (based on past experience) and calculate both cost of goods sold and ending inventory.

The conventional presentation of gross profit for a K Mart store (in thousands) is:

SYMBOL			
S	Net sales		$10,000 (100%)
	Deduct cost of goods sold:		
BI	Beginning inventory	$1,300	
P	Add net purchases	8,200	
CGA	Cost of goods available for sale	$9,500	
EI	Deduct ending inventory	2,300	
CGS	Cost of goods sold (also called cost of sales)		7,200
GP	Gross profit (also called gross margin and sometimes called gross profit margin)		$ 2,800 (28%)

The basic relationship can be stated algebraically:

$$\text{Net sales} - \text{Cost of goods sold} = \text{Gross profit}$$
$$S \quad - \quad CGS \quad = \quad GP$$

and

$$\text{Cost of goods sold} = \text{Beginning inventory} + \text{Net purchases} - \text{Ending inventory}$$
$$CGS = \quad BI \quad + \quad P \quad - \quad EI$$

The ending inventory is customarily measured at the close of each reporting period. However, the actual amount of the ending inventory for monthly and quarterly financial statements frequently is not known because it is too costly to obtain a physical count. In such cases, the gross profit relationships are often used to estimate the ending inventory figure.

For example, in our illustration, assume that past sales have usually resulted in a gross profit percentage of 28%. (Unless otherwise stated, any gross profit percentage given is based on *net sales*, not cost.)[4] Then the accountant would estimate gross profit to be .28 × $10,000, or $2,800. Using the above equations, the ending inventory could have been estimated:

$$S - CGS = GP$$
$$\$10,000 - CGS = \$2,800$$
$$CGS = \$7,200$$

and

$$CGS = BI + P - EI$$
$$\$7,200 = \$1,300 + \$8,200 - EI$$
$$EI = \$1,300 + \$8,200 - \$7,200$$
$$EI = \$2,300$$

---

[4] As a general rule, when dealing with percentages in any situation, it is wise to ask, What is the base? That is, which item represents 100%? On an income statement, net sales is invariably the base.

Retailers often use a well-known strategy to increase profits. They lower prices and yet hope to increase their gross profits by selling their inventories more quickly, replenishing, selling again, and so forth. Managers speak of improving their **inventory turnover**, which is defined as cost of goods sold divided by the average inventory held during a given period. Average inventory is usually the beginning inventory and ending inventory divided by 2. Using our assumed K Mart data, the average inventory would be ($1,300 + $2,300) ÷ 2 = $1,800. The inventory turnover would be computed as follows:

$$\text{Turnover} = \text{Cost of goods sold} \div \text{Average inventory}$$
$$= \$7,200 \div \$1,800 = 4$$

How could K Mart have improved its total gross profit? Maybe the store could not change the amount of its investment in inventory but could sell the inventory more quickly by cutting selling prices.

Suppose our data pertained to operations for January. Perhaps lowering prices by 10% could have resulted in selling inventory twice as quickly. This means that inventory costing $1,800 and sold for $2,500 would now be sold for $2,500 less 10%, or $2,250. The lower prices would cause a doubling of the physical quantity sold. Inventory turnover would increase from 4 to 8. Total gross profit for January would have been $3,600 instead of the given $2,800:

		AMOUNT	%
Sales	$2,500 × 4 turnovers =	$10,000	100%
Cost of goods sold	1,800 × 4 turnovers =	7,200	72
Gross profit	$ 700 × 4 turnovers =	$ 2,800	28%
Sales	$2,250 × 8 turnovers =	$18,000	100%
Cost of goods sold	1,800 × 8 turnovers =	14,400	80
Gross profit	$ 450 × 8 turnovers =	$ 3,600	20%

The above example demonstrates, all other things being equal, that the quicker the turnover, the greater the total gross profit obtained. Each time the inventory is sold, it is said to have been turned over. Obviously, for any given investment in inventory, and a given rate of gross profit, the quicker the turnover, the higher the rate of return on investment. Again we see how accounting measurements can help in the evaluation of performance and in making decisions.

SUMMARY

Four major inventory methods are in use: specific identification, weighted average, FIFO, and LIFO. When prices are rising, less income is generally shown by LIFO than FIFO.

LIFO is popular in the United States because it offers income tax advantages that become most pronounced during times of steady or rising inventories combined with rising prices. Note that even when inventories are declining, *cumulative* taxable income is always less under LIFO than FIFO because the inventory valuation is less and the cumulative cost of goods sold is higher.

The lower-of-cost-or-market method requires a write-down of inventory to its replacement cost if purchase prices fall and selling prices are also likely to fall.

SUMMARY PROBLEMS FOR YOUR REVIEW

☐ **Problem One**

Examine Exhibit 7–5. The company uses the periodic inventory system. Using these facts, prepare a columnar comparison of income statements for the year ended December 31, 19X2. Compare the FIFO, LIFO, and weighted-average inventory methods. Assume that other expenses are $1,000. The income tax rate is 40%.

EXHIBIT 7–5

Facts for Summary Problem One

	IN	OUT	BALANCE
December 31, 19X1			200 @ $5 = $1,000
January 25	170 @ $6 = $1,020		
January 29		150*	
May 28	190 @ $7 = $1,330		
June 7		230*	
November 20	150 @ $8 = $1,200		
December 15		100*	
Total	510 $3,550	480	
December 31, 19X2			230 @ ?

* Selling prices were $9, $11, and $13, respectively:

150 @ $ 9 = $1,350	
230 @ $11 = $2,530	
100 @ $13 = $1,300	
Total sales 480 $5,180	

Summary of costs to account for:

Beginning inventory	$1,000
Purchases	3,550
Cost of goods available for sale	$4,550

☐ **Solution to Problem One**

See Exhibit 7–6.

☐ **Problem Two**

"When prices are rising, FIFO results in fool's profits because more resources are needed to maintain operations than previously." Do you agree? Explain.

☐ **Solution to Problem Two**

The merit of this position depends on the concept of income favored. LIFO gives a better measure of "distributable" income than FIFO. Recall the cola example in the chapter. The gross profit under FIFO was sixty cents and under LIFO was thirty-

EXHIBIT 7-6

Comparison of Inventory Methods
For the Year Ended December 31, 19X2

		FIFO	LIFO	WEIGHTED AVERAGE
Sales, 480 units		$5,180	$5,180	$5,180
Deduct cost of goods sold:				
Beginning inventory, 200 @ $5		$1,000	$1,000	$1,000
Purchases, 510 units (from Exhibit 7–5)*		3,550	3,550	3,550
Available for sale, 710 units†		$4,550	$4,550	$4,550
Ending inventory, 230 units:‡				
150 @ $8	$1,200			
80 @ $7	560	1,760		
or				
200 @ $5	$1,000			
30 @ $6	180		1,180	
or				
230 @ $6.408				1,474
Cost of goods sold, 480 units		2,790	3,370	3,076
Gross profit		$2,390	$1,810	$2,104
Other expenses		1,000	1,000	1,000
Income before income taxes		$1,390	$810	$1,104
Income taxes at 40%		556	324	442
Net income		$834	$486	$662

* Always equal across all three methods.

† These amounts will not be equal in general across the three methods because beginning inventories will generally be different. They are equal here only because beginning inventories were assumed to be equal.

‡ Under FIFO, the ending inventory is composed of the last purchases plus the second-last purchases, and so forth, until the costs of 230 units are compiled. Under LIFO, the ending inventory is composed of the beginning inventory plus the earliest purchases of the current year until the costs of 230 units are compiled. Under weighted average, the ending inventory and cost of goods sold are accumulations based on a unit cost. The latter is the cost of goods available for sale divided by the number of units available for sale: $4,550 ÷ 710 = $6.408.

four cents. The 60¢ − 34¢ = 26¢ difference is a fool's profit because it must be reinvested to maintain the same inventory level as previously. Therefore the twenty-six cents cannot be distributed as a cash dividend without reducing the current level of operations.

□ Problem Three

H. J. Heinz Company has many food products, including Heinz ketchup. Its balance sheets included (in millions):

	MAY 1	
	1985	1984
Inventories	$708	$700

Required:

Suppose clerical errors had been made in tabulating the inventory of May 1, 1984. The correct inventory was $687 million, not $700 million.

1. Would pretax income have been overstated or understated for the year ended May 1, 1984? By how much? For the year ended May 1, 1985? By how much?
2. How would the $708 million inventory have been affected by the errors?

□ Solution to Problem Three

1. The Heinz 1984 pretax income would have been overstated by $700 million minus $687 million, or $13 million. In turn, the 1985 pretax income would have been understated by $13 million. That is, the overstatement of ending inventory would have caused two offsetting errors in 1984 and 1985.
2. The $708 million inventory would have been unaffected by the errors.

□ Problem Four

Fay's Drug Company operates about 120 super drug stores in the Northeast. Some results for fiscal 1985 were (in thousands):

Sales	$366,697
Cost of merchandise sold	$273,135
Net earnings	$ 8,679
Beginning merchandise inventory	$ 43,382
Ending merchandise inventory	$ 56,354

Required:

1. Calculate the 1985 gross profit and gross profit percentage for Fay's Drug Company.
2. Calculate the inventory turnover ratio.
3. What gross profit would have been reported if inventory turnover in 1985 had been 7, the gross profit percentage calculated in requirement 1 had been achieved, and the level of inventory was unchanged?

□ Solution to Problem Four

1. Gross profit = Sales − Cost of merchandise sold
   = $366,697 − $273,135
   = $93,562

$$\text{Gross profit percentage} = \text{Gross profit} \div \text{Sales}$$
$$= \$93{,}562 \div \$366{,}697$$
$$= 25.5\%$$

2. $\text{Inventory turnover} = \text{Cost of merchandise sold} \div \text{Average merchandise inventory}$
$$= \$273{,}135 \div [(\$43{,}382 + \$56{,}354) \div 2]$$
$$= \$273{,}135 \div \$49{,}868$$
$$= 5.5$$

3. $\text{Cost of merchandise sold} = \text{Inventory turnover} \times \text{Average merchandise inventory}$
$$= 7 \times \$49{,}868$$
$$= \$349{,}076$$

$$\text{Gross profit percentage} = (\text{Sales} - \text{Cost of merchandise sold}) \div \text{Sales}$$
$$25.5\% = (S - \$349{,}076) \div S$$
$$.255 \times S = S - \$349{,}076$$
$$S - (.255 \times S) = \$349{,}076$$
$$S \times (1 - .255) = \$349{,}076$$
$$S = \$349{,}076 \div (1 - .255)$$
$$S = \$468{,}558$$

$$\text{Gross profit} = \text{Sales} - \text{Cost of merchandise sold}$$
$$= \$468{,}558 - \$349{,}076$$
$$= \$119{,}482$$

The increase in inventory turnover from 5.5 to 7 raised gross profit from \$93,562 to \$119,482.

HIGHLIGHTS TO REMEMBER

1. Ponder the contents of this chapter and the preceding chapter. Although a sizable part of the preceding chapter was devoted to the mechanics of accounting for the periodic inventory method, most of the space in these two chapters concentrated on decisions faced by accountants and managers. For example, what customer credit policies should be adopted? Should we use bank cards? Should we grant cash discounts? What gross profit percentage and inventory turnover strategies would be most appealing? What inventory method would be best for our company? Note too that investors often raise these same questions.
2. Gross profit percentages and inventory turnover are key financial ratios in many companies.
3. The following table summarizes differences between FIFO and LIFO:

INVENTORY METHOD	INCOME STATEMENT: MEASUREMENT OF COST OF GOODS SOLD	BALANCE SHEET: MEASUREMENT OF INVENTORY ASSET
FIFO	Distant from current replacement cost	Near current replacement cost
LIFO	Near current replacement cost	Distant from current replacement cost

ACCOUNTING VOCABULARY

Conservatism, p. 278   Consistency, 272   First-in, First-out (FIFO), 269   Inventory Turnover, 285   Last-in, First-out (LIFO), 270   LIFO Increment, 276   LIFO Layer, 276   LIFO Pool, 276   LIFO Reserve, 290   Lower-of-Cost-or-Market, 279   Next-in,

APPENDIX 7A: LIFO LIQUIDATION AND RESERVES

☐ LIFO Liquidation

In general, prices have been rising throughout the world for many years. Companies that have been on LIFO for a number of years typically have many LIFO layers, some at unit prices that are relatively old and low. Occasionally, circumstances (such as a prolonged strike or the discontinuance of a segment of the business) call for the liquidation of some or all of the LIFO layers. This decrease in the physical levels of inventories would cause unusually low cost of goods sold, high income, and high income tax expense in comparison with FIFO. For example, the 1985 annual report of CrownAmerica, Inc., a Georgia-based yarn mill and general warehousing company, stated:

☐ During the years ended August 31, 1985 and 1984, inventory quantities were reduced. These reductions resulted in a liquidation of LIFO inventory quantities carried at lower costs prevailing in prior years as compared with the cost of 1985 and 1984 purchases. The effect of these liquidations was to increase net income in 1985 by $304,300, or $.26 per share, and in 1984 by $57,100, or $.05 per share.

The 26 cents per share represented 76% of CrownAmerica's reported net income in 1985.

☐ LIFO Reserve

The business press, financial analysts, and accountants often refer to a company's **LIFO reserve**, which is generally defined as the difference between a company's inventory valued at LIFO and what it would be under FIFO. For example, our cola vendor's LIFO reserve at the end of Thursday would be (see Exhibit 7–2, page 270):

FIFO inventory (not in company accounts)	96¢
LIFO inventory (in company accounts)	70¢
LIFO reserve (not in company accounts)	26¢

Analysts especially desire this information for comparing companies within the same industry that use different inventory methods. Note that companies using FIFO have no LIFO reserve. As Chapter 11 explains, the word *reserve* has a variety of meanings in accounting. In this context, *reserve* was probably adopted because most LIFO companies have inventories far below their FIFO values. Therefore the reserve is the amount of "cushion" or "understatement" of current inventory values that the LIFO method produces in relation to FIFO.

☐ Effects of LIFO Reserve on Income

Some analysts use the *change* in LIFO reserve to compute the difference in income statements under FIFO and LIFO. Because the reserve is the relative "understatement" of current inventory value produced by the LIFO method as compared with FIFO, this may be viewed as a corresponding "understatement" of accumulated reported income before taxes. Therefore any annual increase or decrease in the reserve could be viewed as a corresponding change in the annual "understatement" of reported income before taxes. This can be illustrated by using the chapter's cola vendor example, where there was no reserve at the beginning of the week. The "understatement" of reported income before income taxes for Monday through Thursday would simply be the amount of the reserve at the end of Thursday: 96¢ − 70¢ = 26¢.

On the other hand, if a comparison of FIFO and LIFO values revealed a *decrease* in the LIFO reserve for a certain period, this would measure an "overstatement" of the period's reported income before income taxes as compared with FIFO. Such a situation arises on Friday in our cola vendor example. (See Part II of Exhibit 7-2 on page 270.) Thursday's LIFO reserve of 26¢ *decreased* to zero by the end of Friday. Therefore Friday's LIFO profit of 110¢ is 26¢ *greater* than Friday's FIFO profit of 84¢.

Consider another illustration. M Company has sales of $4,000 and purchases of $3,000 during 19X3. Its results are:

	FIFO		LIFO	
Sales		$4,000		$4,000
Cost of goods sold:				
Beginning inventory	$ 500		$ 300	
Purchases	3,000		3,000	
Available for sale	$3,500		$3,300	
Ending inventory	700	2,800	400	2,900
Gross profit		$1,200		$1,100

Instead of using the comprehensive method as tabulated, many analysts prefer to compare LIFO and FIFO via computing *changes* in LIFO reserves. As can be seen by inspecting the above tabulation, a formula can be developed and used:

Change in LIFO reserve = Difference in cost of goods sold
(and hence pretax income) between FIFO and LIFO

Apply the formula. Compute the LIFO reserve at the beginning and end of 19X3:

	DECEMBER 31	
	19X3	19X2
FIFO inventory	= $700	$500
LIFO inventory	= 400	300
LIFO reserve	= $300	$200
Change in LIFO reserve	= Difference in cost of goods sold	
$300 − $200	= $100	
Therefore:		
Cost of goods sold	= $100 higher under LIFO	
Also:		
Pretax income	= $100 lower under LIFO	
Income tax payable, December 31, 19X3, at assumed 40% rate: .40 × $100	= $40 lower under LIFO	
Retained income, December 31, 19X3, is $100 − $40	= $60 lower under LIFO	

APPENDIX 7B: EFFECTS OF ACCOUNTING METHODS ON PERPETUAL INVENTORY SYSTEMS

Exhibit 7–7 shows a perpetual (continuous) inventory record, using the same data as those employed in the first "Summary Problem" of this chapter. The FIFO method is illustrated, but similar details (applying different cost-flow assumptions) may be kept for average cost and LIFO methods. Such details may be kept on individual cards for each item in stock, on computer tape, or on any record that supports the aggregate dollar amounts assigned to cost of goods sold and inventories.

EXHIBIT 7–7

Perpetual Inventory Card (or similar computer record)

Description   Hand calculator #4326A   Location   Shelf 42B
Cost-Flow Assumption   FIFO   Maximum   250
                                            Minimum   100

	Units*				Dollars†		
Date	Purchased	Sold	Balance	Unit Cost	Purchased	Sold	Balance
19X1							
Dec. 31			200	5			1,000
19X2							
Jan. 25	170			6	1,020		
			{ 200	5			{ 1,000
			170	6			1,020
Jan. 29		150		5		750	
			{ 50	5			{ 250
			170	6			1,020
May 28	190			7	1,330		
			{ 50	5			{ 250
			{ 170	6			{ 1,020
			190	7			1,330
June 7		{ 50		5		{ 250	
		{ 170		6		{ 1,020	
		10		7		70	
			180	7			1,260
Nov. 20	150			8	1,200		
			{ 180	7			{ 1,260
			150	8			1,200
Dec. 15		100		7		700	
			{ 80	7			{ 560
			150	8			1,200

*Entries always the same regardless of cost-flow assumption in use. Many organizations confine their perpetual inventory system to quantities only.
†Entries differ, depending on cost-flow assumptions such as FIFO, specific identification, average cost, or LIFO.

Many perpetual inventory systems are confined to *units* only. Dollar amounts are determined only at year-end through some averaging process or some overall assumptions as to cost flow (such as LIFO) for the year. These systems are best described as combined perpetual-periodic inventory systems. For instance, a full-blown LIFO perpetual inventory system on a day-to-day basis is virtually unknown. Indeed, the LIFO results from using perpetual records would not always coincide exactly with the periodic records.[5]

FUNDAMENTAL ASSIGNMENT MATERIAL

☐ General Coverage

7–1. **COMPARISON OF INVENTORY METHODS.** (Alternates are 7–4, 7–6, and 7–26.) The Strober Co. is a wholesaler of air filters for furnaces and air-conditioning equipment. The company uses a periodic inventory system. The data concerning Filter AG4 for the year 19X2 follow:

	PURCHASES	SOLD	BALANCE
December 31, 19X1			150 @ $4 = $600
January 20, 19X2	90 @ $5 = $ 450		
February 5		80	
May 20	100 @ $6 = $ 600		
June 17		110	
October 24	80 @ $7 = $ 560		
November 29		60	
Total	270 $1,610	250	
December 31, 19X2			170 @ ?

The sales during 19X2 were made at the following selling prices:

80 @	7 = $	560
110 @	9 =	990
60 @	10 =	600
250		$2,150

Required:

1. Prepare a comparative statement of gross profit for the year ended December 31, 19X2, using FIFO, LIFO, and weighted-average inventory methods.
2. By how much would income taxes differ if Strober used LIFO instead of FIFO for Filter AG4? Assume a 40% income tax rate.

7–2. **EFFECTS OF LATE PURCHASES.** (Alternatives are 7–5 and 7–7.) Refer to the preceding problem. Suppose that 100 extra units were acquired on December 30 for $7 each, a total of $700. How would net income and income taxes be affected under FIFO? Under LIFO? Show a tabulated comparison.

---

[5] For instance, in Exhibit 7–7, suppose the January 29 sale were 200 units instead of 150 units. A perpetual LIFO method would show:

	SOLD	BALANCE
Jan. 29	170 @ $6 = $1,020	170 @ $5 = $850
	30 @ $5 = 150	

Note that 30 units from the beginning inventory would be released as Cost of Goods Sold under perpetual LIFO, whereas periodic LIFO would wait until the end of the year and would assign no amounts from the beginning inventory to Cost of Goods Sold unless the physical inventory levels had declined *for the year as a whole*. In other words, interim declines in inventory would be ignored under the periodic LIFO approach.

7–3. INVENTORY ERRORS. (Alternates are 7–8 and 7–9.) The following data are from the 19X1 income statement of the Abbey Carpet Stores (in thousands):

Sales		$1,500
Deduct: Cost of goods sold:		
Beginning inventory	$ 420	
Purchases	690	
Cost of goods available for sale	$1,110	
Deduct: Ending inventory	370	
Cost of goods sold		740
Gross profit		$ 760
Other expenses		610
Income before income taxes		$ 150
Income tax expense at 30%		45
Net income		$ 105

The ending inventory was overstated by $20,000 because of errors in the physical count. The income tax rate was 30% in 19X1 and 19X2.

Required:

1. Which items in the income statement are incorrect? By how much? Use *O* for overstated and *U* for understated. Complete the following tabulation:

	19X1	19X2
Beginning inventory	Unaffected	O $20
Ending inventory	?	?
Cost of goods sold	?	?
Gross margin	?	?
Income before income taxes	?	?
Income tax expense	?	?
Net income	?	?

2. What is the dollar effect of the inventory error on retained income at the end of 19X1? At the end of 19X2?

☐ **Understanding Published Financial Reports**

7–4. COMPARISON OF INVENTORY METHODS. (Alternates are 7–1, 7–6, and 7–26.) Sperry Corporation is a producer of electronic systems for information processing, aerospace, and defense. The following actual data and descriptions are from the company's fiscal 1985 annual report (in millions):

	MARCH 31	
	1985	1984
Inventories	$1,567.1	$1,180.2

A footnote states: "Inventories are valued at the lower of cost or market, cost generally representing average cost."

The income statement for the fiscal year ended March 31, 1985, included (in millions):

Net sales of products	$4,159.3
Cost of sales of products	2,906.6

Assume that Sperry used the periodic inventory system. Suppose its Univac division had the accompanying data regarding the use of its computer parts that it acquires and resells to customers for maintaining equipment:

Data for Problem 7–4
(dollars are *not* in millions)

	UNITS	TOTAL
Inventory (March 31, 1984)	100	$ 400
Purchase (May 20, 1984)	200	1,000
Sales, June 17 (at $9 per unit)	150	
Purchase (September 25, 1984)	140	840
Sales, February 7, 1985 (at $10 per unit)	160	

Required:

1. For these computer parts only, prepare a tabulation of the cost-of-goods-sold section of the income statement for the year ended March 31, 1985. Support your computations. Round totals to the nearest dollar. Show your tabulation for four different inventory methods: (a) FIFO, (b) LIFO, (c) weighted-average, and (d) specific identification.

   For requirement *d*, assume that the purchase of May 20 was identified with the sale of June 17. Also assume that the purchase of September 25 was identified with the sale of February 7; the additional units sold were identified with the beginning inventory.
2. By how much would income taxes differ if Sperry used (a) LIFO instead of FIFO for this inventory item? (b) LIFO instead of weighted-average? Assume a 40% tax rate.

7–5. **EFFECTS OF LATE PURCHASES.** (Alternates are 7–2 and 7–7.) Refer to the preceding problem. Suppose Sperry acquired 60 extra units @ $7 each on March 29, 1985, a total of $420. How would gross margin and income taxes be affected under FIFO? That is, compare FIFO results before and after the purchase of 60 extra units. Under LIFO? That is, compare LIFO results before and after the purchase of 60 extra units. Show computations and explain.

7–6. **COMPARISON OF INVENTORY METHODS.** (Alternates are 7–1, 7–4, and 7–26.) Texas Instruments is a major producer of semiconductors and other electrical and electronic products. Semiconductors are especially vulnerable to price fluctuations. The following actual data and descriptions are from the company's annual report (in millions):

	DECEMBER 31	
	1985	1984
Inventories	$447.1	$489.2

Texas Instruments uses a variety of inventory methods, but for this problem assume that only FIFO is used.

Net sales for the fiscal year ended December 31, 1985, were $4,924.5 million. Cost of sales was $4,071.2 million.

Assume that Texas Instruments had the accompanying data regarding one of its semiconductors. Assume a periodic inventory system.

Data for Problem 7–6

	IN	OUT	BALANCE
December 31, 1984			80 @ $5 = 400
February 25, 1985	50 @ $6 = $ 300		
March 29		60* @ ?	
May 28	80 @ $7 = $ 560		
June 7		90* @ ?	
November 20	90 @ $8 = $ 720		
December 15		50* @ ?	
Total	220 $1,580	200	
December 31, 1985			100 @ ?

* Selling prices were $9, $11, and $13, respectively:

	60 @ $ 9 = $ 540	
	90 @ 11 = 990	
	50 @ 13 = 650	
Total sales	200 $2,180	

Summary of costs to account for:

Beginning inventory	$ 400
Purchases	1,580
Cost of goods available for sale	$1,980
Other expenses for this product	$ 500
Income tax rate, 40%	

Required:

1. Prepare a comparative income statement for the 1985 fiscal year for the product in question. Use the FIFO, LIFO, and weighted-average inventory methods.
2. By how much would income taxes have differed if Texas Instruments had used LIFO instead of FIFO for this product?
3. Suppose Texas Instruments had used the specific identification method. Compute the gross margin if the ending inventory had consisted of (a) 90 units @ $8 and 10 units @ $7, and (b) 60 units @ $5 and 40 units @ $8.

7–7. **EFFECTS OF LATE PURCHASES.** (Alternates are 7–2 and 7–5.) Refer to the preceding problem. Suppose Texas Instruments had acquired 50 extra units @ $8 each on December 30, 1985, a total of $400. How would income before income taxes and income taxes have been affected under FIFO? That is, compare FIFO results before and after the purchase of 50 extra units. Under LIFO? That is, compare LIFO results before and after the purchase of 50 extra units. Show computations and explain.

7–8. **INVENTORY ERRORS.** (Alternates are 7–3 and 7–9.) Claire's Stores, Inc., operates 260 specialty retail stores selling inexpensively priced fashion accessories. The accompanying actual data are from the company's annual report for the 1985 fiscal year:

Net sales	$55,894,795
Cost of sales, occupancy, and buying expenses	26,395,195
Gross profit	$29,499,600
Other expenses (detailed)	16,777,492
Income before income taxes	$12,722,108
Income taxes	6,122,058
Net income	$ 6,600,050

The inventories were $7,737,103 at the end of fiscal 1985 and $5,357,100 a year earlier. The applicable tax rate is 48% for both fiscal years, 1984 and 1985.

Required:

1. Suppose the beginning inventory for fiscal 1985 had been overstated by $100,000 because of errors in physical counts. Which items in the financial statement would be incorrect? By how much? Use O for overstated and U for understated. Complete the following tabulation:

	EFFECT ON FISCAL YEAR	
	1985	1984
Beginning inventory	O by $100,000	Not affected
Ending inventory	?	?
Cost of sales	?	?
Gross profit	?	?
Income before taxes on income	?	?
Taxes on income	?	?
Net income	?	?

2. What is the dollar effect of the inventory error on retained earnings at the end of fiscal 1984? 1985?

7–9. **INVENTORY ERRORS.** (Alternates are 7–3 and 7–8.) Anixter Bros., Inc., is one of the largest independent international specialists in distributing telephone, cable television, and other communications products, and electrical and electronic wire and cable. The accompanying actual data and descriptions are from Anixter's annual report for the year ended July 31, 1985:

(in thousands)	
Net sales	$650,949
Cost of sales	512,053
Gross profit	$138,896

The applicable income tax rate was 42%. Balance sheet items included (in thousands):

	DECEMBER	
	1985	1984
Inventories	$154,262	$153,397

Required:

1. Suppose the inventory on July 31, 1984, had been understated by $2 million because of errors in physical counts. Which items in the financial statements would be incorrect? By how much? Use O for overstated and U for understated. Complete the following tabulation:

	EFFECT ON YEAR	
	1985	1984
Beginning inventory	U by $2 million	Not affected
Ending inventory	?	?
Cost of sales	?	?
Gross margin	?	?
Income taxes	?	?
Net income	?	?

2. What is the dollar effect of the inventory error on retained earnings on July 31, 1984, and July 31, 1985?

ADDITIONAL ASSIGNMENT MATERIAL

☐ General Coverage

7–10. "An inventory profit is a fictitious profit." Do you agree? Explain.

7–11. LIFO produces absurd inventory valuations. Why?

7–12. "There is a single dominant reason why more and more companies have adopted LIFO." What is the reason?

7–13. "Accountants have traditionally favored taking some losses but no gains before an asset is exchanged." What is this tradition or convention called?

7–14. What does *market* mean in inventory accounting?

7–15. "The lower-of-cost-or-market method is inherently inconsistent." Do you agree? Explain.

7–16. "Conservatism now is liberalism later." Do you agree? Explain.

7–17. "Inventory errors are counterbalancing." Explain.

7–18. "Replacement costs of goods sold must appear in income statements in annual reports to stockholders." Do you agree? Explain.

7–19. "There are two major steps in accounting for inventories." What are they?

7–20. "Purchases of inventory at the end of a fiscal period can have a direct effect on income under LIFO." Do you agree? Explain.

7–21. "Conservatism always results in lower reported profits." Do you agree? Explain.

7–22. The term *net* is frequently used in accounting. What does it mean?

7–23. Express the gross profit section of the income statement as an equation.

7–24. Express the cost of goods sold section of the income statement as an equation.

7–25. "Gross profit percentages help the preparation of interim financial statements." Explain.

7–26. **BASIC SUMMARY PROBLEMS.** (Alternates are 7–1, 7–4, and 7–6.) The "Summary Problems for Your Review" section in this chapter provided some facts in Exhibit 7–5 and a solution in Exhibit 7–6 that compared the inventory methods of FIFO, LIFO, and weighted average. Suppose sales had been 430 units instead of 480 units. That is, suppose the final 50 units that were sold @ $13 had not been sold. No other changes occurred. Prepare an altered Exhibit 7–6 that would show the revised net income. Exhibits 7–5 and 7–6 are on pages 286–287.

7–27. **INVENTORY SHORTAGE.** An accounting clerk of the Meecham Company absconded with cash and a truck full of the entire electronic merchandise on March 4, 19X2. The following data have been compiled:

Beginning inventory, January 1	$ 50,000
Sales to March 4, 19X2	120,000
Average gross profit rate	30%
Purchases to March 4, 19X2	100,000

Required: Compute the estimated cost of the missing merchandise.

7–28. **GROSS PROFIT METHOD FOR INTERIM REPORTING.** The average gross profit percentage of Meier Drug Stores is 40%. The following data were accumulated for the month of January (in thousands):

Inventory, December 31, 19X1	$400
Net purchases	700
Net sales	950

Compute the estimated ending inventory, January 31, 19X2.

7–29. **FIRE LOSS.** The Valencia Shoe Store had a fire on March 14, 19X5. Its last physical inventory had been on January 31, 19X5, the close of its fiscal year. For the past three years, Valencia's gross profit percentage had been averaging 35%. The following data were gathered:

Purchases, February 1–March 14, 19X5	$100,000
Inventory, January 31, 19X5	200,000
Sales, February 1–March 14, 19X5	120,000

Required: Estimate the cost of inventory, March 14, 19X5. Show your computations. The insurance company will use this estimate of historical cost as a basis for estimating the replacement cost (which is the usual basis for paying insurance claims).

7–30. **STATEMENT OF GROSS PROFIT.** Serbein Jewelers, Inc., had net purchases of merchandise of $540,000 during 19X3. Ending inventory was $500,000. Beginning inventory was $420,000. Net sales were $900,000.

Required: 1. Prepare a statement of gross profit for 19X3.
2. What was Serbein's inventory turnover?

7–31. **DECISION ABOUT PRICING.** Refer to the preceding problem. Serbein is considering whether to become a "discount" jeweler. For example, given the data in requirement 1, Serbein believed that a cut of 20% in average selling prices would have increased turnover to 1.5 times per year. Suppose Serbein's beliefs were valid. Would the gross profit in 19X3 have improved? Show computations.

7–32. **INCOME TAX AUDIT.** As an auditor for the Internal Revenue Service, you are examining the records of Martin Auto Supply Store, which was purchased at the start of 19X5 by John Martin. For the three preceding years, the store had shown (in thousands):

	19X4	19X3	19X2
Sales	$720	$700	$800
Cost of goods sold	425	427	480

Martin's income tax return for 19X5 had shown:

Sales	$650
Cost of goods sold	442

Required:

As a part of your examination, you conduct a gross profit test. Compute the gross profit percentages for 19X2 through 19X5. List the possible explanations for the gross profit performance in 19X5.

7–33. LIFO, FIFO, PURCHASE DECISIONS, AND EARNINGS PER SHARE. Suppose a company with one million shares of common stock outstanding has had the following transactions during 19X1, its first year in business:

Sales:	1,000,000 units @ $5
Purchases:	800,000 units @ $2
	300,000 units @ $3

The current income tax rate is a flat 50%; the rate next year is expected to be 40%. Prices on inventory are not expected to decline next year.

It is December 20, and as the president, you are trying to decide whether you should buy the 600,000 units you need for inventory now or early next year. The current price is $4 per unit. Prices on inventory are expected to remain stable; in any event, no decline in prices is anticipated.

You have not chosen an inventory method as yet, but you will pick either LIFO or FIFO.

Other expenses for the year will be $1.4 million.

Required:

1. Using LIFO, prepare a comparative income statement assuming the 600,000 units (a) are not purchased, (b) are purchased. The statement should end with reported earnings per share.
2. Repeat requirement 1, using FIFO.
3. Comment on the above results. Which method would you choose? Why? Be specific.
4. Suppose that in Year 2 the tax rate drops to 40%, prices remain stable, 1 million units are sold @ $5, enough units are purchased at $4 so that the ending inventory will be 700,000 units, and other expenses are reduced to $800,000.
   (a) Prepare a comparative income statement for the second year showing the impact of each of the four alternatives on net income and earnings per share for the second year.
   (b) Explain any difference in net income that you encounter among the four alternatives.
   (c) Why is there a difference in ending inventory values under LIFO even though the same amount of physical inventory is in stock?
   (d) What is the total cash outflow for income taxes for the two years together under the four alternatives?
   (e) Would you change your answer in requirement 3 now that you have completed requirement 4? Why?

7–34. GROSS MARGIN AND TURNOVER. Retailers closely watch a number of financial ratios, including the gross margin (gross profit) percentage and inventory turnover. Suppose the annual results for video equipment in a suburban Macy's department store were:

Sales	$2,000,000
Cost of goods sold	1,200,000
Gross margin	$ 800,000
Beginning inventory	$ 500,000
Ending inventory	300,000

Required:

1. Compute the gross margin percentage and the inventory turnover.
2. Suppose the manager of the video section is able to maintain its ending inventory at the same dollar level throughout the succeeding year. What inventory turnover would have to be obtained to achieve the same total gross margin? Assume that the gross margin percentage is unchanged.
3. Suppose the manager maintains the ending inventory at the same dollar level throughout the succeeding year. What gross margin percentage would have to be obtained to achieve the same total gross margin? Assume that the inventory turnover is unchanged.
4. Suppose the average inventory is maintained. Compute the total gross margin in the succeeding year if there is
   (a) A 10% increase of the gross margin *percentage* (that is, 10% of the percentage, not an additional ten percentage points) and a 10% decrease of the inventory turnover; or
   (b) A 10% decrease of the gross margin percentage and a 10% increase of the inventory turnover.
5. Why do retailers find the above types of ratios helpful?

7–35. **REPLACEMENT COST, LIFO, FIFO.** You are a vendor of soft drinks at the fairgrounds. You purchased 100 units on Tuesday, 100 on Wednesday, and 100 on Thursday for forty, fifty, and sixty cents per unit, respectively. You sold 100 units on Friday for ninety cents per can. The replacement cost on Friday was seventy cents per can.

Required:

1. Prepare a comparative tabulation of gross profit for the following three inventory methods: replacement cost, LIFO, and FIFO.
2. What is the total amount required to replenish your inventory? If you paid yourself a dividend equal to your gross profit, how much cash would remain for replenishing your inventory under each of the three inventory methods?

7–36. **REVIEW PERPETUAL AND PERIODIC SYSTEMS.** The Eppler Co. is a wholesaler of hardware for commercial builders. Data concerning Airvent Grill RD8 for the year 19X2 follow:

	PURCHASES		SALES IN UNITS	BALANCE
December 31, 19X1				150 @ $4 = $600
19X2				
February 10	90 @ $5 =	$ 450		
April 14			80	
May 9	100 @ $6 =	600		
July 14			110	
October 21	80 @ $7 =	560		
November 12			60	
Total	270	$1,610	250	

1. Assume FIFO. Using summary journal entries for the year, prepare a compara-tive presentation of the entries for the perpetual and periodic systems. Include the closing entries.

2. Show postings to T-accounts for the entries in requirement 1.

7–37. LIFO AND FIFO. The inventory of the Kiner Gravel Company on June 30 shows 1,000 tons at $6 per ton. A physical inventory on July 31 shows a total of 1,200 tons on hand. Revenue from sales of gravel for July totals $30,000. The following purchases were made during July:

July 5	2,000 tons @ $7 per ton
July 15	500 tons @ $8 per ton
July 25	600 tons @ $9 per ton

1. Compute the inventory value as of July 31, using (a) LIFO and (b) FIFO.

2. Compute the gross profit using each method.

7–38. LOWER OF COST OR MARKET. (Alternate is 7–56.) McGilvray company uses cost or market, whichever is lower. There were no sales or purchases during the periods indicated, although selling prices generally fluctuated in the same directions as replacement costs. At what amount would you value merchandise on the dates listed below?

	INVOICE COST	REPLACEMENT COST
December 31, 19X1	$100,000	$ 80,000
April 30, 19X2	100,000	90,000
August 31, 19X2	100,000	105,000
December 31, 19X2	100,000	65,000

7–39. LIFO OR NIFO. Refer to Problem 7–1. Suppose the Internal Revenue Service allowed a replacement cost method (NIFO) of inventory valuation. The replace-ment cost at December 31, 19X2 is $7 per unit.

1. Compute the gross profit, using FIFO, LIFO, and NIFO.

2. Suppose all transactions are for cash. The cash necessary to replace the 250 units sold in 19X2 would be 250 @ $7, or $1,750. Suppose also that the company had only this product and had no other expenses in 19X2. The company paid cash dividends equal to net income. Tabulate a comparison of cash receipts less disbursements for each inventory method (FIFO, LIFO, and NIFO), as follows:

Gross profit (= pretax income in this case)	xxx
Deduct: Income taxes @ 40%	xxx
Net income	xxx
Sales	xxx
Cash disbursements for:	
Income taxes	xxx
Cash dividends equal to net income	xxx
Subtotal	xxx
Cash remaining for replenishment of inventory	xxx
Cash needed to replace inventory	xxx
Cash remaining (shortage)	xxx

3. Summarize the effects of the three methods on the cash position of the company.

7–40. Lower of Cost or Market.   Refer to Problem 7–1. Suppose the ending FIFO inventory is valued at $1,100 at FIFO cost and $510 at market (based on a sudden decline on December 31, 19X2, to $3 per unit, which leads to 170 units × $3 = $510). The lower market price is indicative of lower ultimate sales prices.

Suppose Strober Co. goes out of business in 19X3. The 170 units are sold in January for $4 each.

Required:

1. Prepare a statement of gross profit for 19X2 and 19X3. Show the results under a strict FIFO cost method in the first two columns and under a lower of FIFO cost or market method in the next two columns.
2. Suppose Strober does not go out of business. Instead the replacement cost price rises in 19X3 to $8 per unit. Would this rise in price affect the inventory valuation of the 170 units? Explain.

7–41. LIFO, FIFO, Cash Effects.   Schreuder Company had sales revenue of $432,000 in 19X2 for a line of hardware supplies. The company uses a periodic inventory system. Pertinent data for 19X2 included:

Inventory, December 31, 19X1	16,000 units @ $6	$ 96,000
January purchases	25,000 units @ $7	175,000
July purchases	28,000 units @ $8	224,000
Sales for the year	36,000 units	

Required:

1. Prepare a statement of gross margin for 19X2. Use columns, one assuming LIFO and one assuming FIFO.
2. Assume a 40% income tax rate. Suppose all transactions are for cash. Which inventory method results in more cash for Schreuder Company? By how much?

7–42. LIFO or NIFO and Cash Effects.   The "Summary Problems for Your Review" section in this chapter (p. 286) provided some facts in Exhibit 7–5 and a solution in Exhibit 7–6 (p. 287). Suppose all transactions were for cash. The company paid cash dividends equal to net income. The replacement cost on December 31 was $8 per unit.

Required:

1. Assume that NIFO is acceptable for income tax purposes. Complete the table at the top of page 304.
2. Summarize the effects of the three methods on the company's cash position.

Table for Problem 7–42
Comparison of Effects of Inventory Methods on Cash

		FIFO	LIFO	NIFO
	Pretax income	$ 1,390*	$ 810*	?
	Income taxes at 40%	556	324	?
	Net income	$ 834	$ 486	?
1.	Sales (assume in cash)	$ 5,180	$5,180	$5,180
	Cash disbursements for:			
2.	Other expenses	$ 1,000	$1,000	$1,000
3.	Income taxes	556	324	?
4.	Dividends equal to net income	834	?	?
5. (2 + 3 + 4)	Subtotal	$ 2,390	?	?
6. (1 − 5)	Cash remaining for replacement of inventory	$ 2,790	?	?
7.	Cash needed for replacement, 480 @ $8	3,840	3,840	3,840
8. (6 − 7)	Cash remaining (shortage)	$(1,050)	?	?

* From Exhibit 7–6.

7–43. LIFO, FIFO, PRICES RISING AND FALLING. The Suarez Company has a periodic inventory system. Inventory on December 31, 19X1, consisted of 10,000 units @ $10 = $100,000. Purchases during 19X2 were 15,000 units. Sales were 14,000 units for sales revenue of $20 per unit.

Required:

Prepare a four-column comparative statement of gross margin for 19X2:

1. Assume purchases were at $12 per unit. Assume FIFO and then LIFO (columns 1 and 2).
2. Assume purchases were at $8 per unit. Assume FIFO and then LIFO (columns 3 and 4).
3. Assume an income tax rate of 40%. Suppose all transactions are for cash. Which inventory method in requirement 1 results in more cash for Suarez Company? By how much?
4. Repeat the preceding requirement. Which inventory method in requirement 2 results in more cash for Suarez Company? By how much?

7–44. INVENTORY ERRORS, THREE YEARS. The Rohm Company had the accompanying data for three successive years (in millions):

	19X3	19X2	19X1
Sales	$200	$160	$175
Deduct: Cost of goods sold:			
Beginning inventory	15	25	40
Purchases	135	100	90
Cost of goods available for sale	150	125	130
Ending inventory	30	15	25
Cost of goods sold	120	110	105
Gross profit	80	50	70
Other expenses	70	30	30
Income before income taxes	10	20	40
Income tax expense	4	8	16
Net income	$ 6	$ 12	$ 24

In early 19X4, a team of internal auditors discovered that the ending inventory for 19X1 had been overstated by $20 million. Furthermore, the ending inventory for 19X3 had been understated by $5 million. The ending inventory for December 31, 19X2, was correct.

Required:

1. Which items in the income statements are incorrect? By how much? Prepare a tabulation covering each of the three years.
2. Is the amount of retained income correct at the end of 19X1, 19X2, and 19X3? If it is erroneous, indicate the amount and whether it is overstated (O) or understated (U).

7–45. MULTIPLE CHOICE: COMPARISON OF INVENTORY METHODS. Information about inventories of Grote-Miller Wholesalers under different valuation methods is shown below. The company began business on January 1, 19X4. Using the information given, you are to choose the phrase that best answers each of the following questions. For each question, give the *letter that identifies the answer* you select.

	INVENTORY			
	LIFO Cost	FIFO Cost	Market	Lower of Specifically Identified Cost or Market
December 31, 19X4	$5,100	$5,000	$4,800	$4,450
December 31, 19X5	4,550	4,500	4,400	4,250
December 31, 19X6	5,150	5,500	6,000	5,450

1. The inventory basis that would show the *highest net income for 19X4* is (a) LIFO cost, (b) FIFO cost, (c) market, (d) lower of cost or market.
2. The inventory basis that would show the *highest net income for 19X5* is (a) LIFO cost, (b) FIFO cost, (c) market, (d) lower of cost or market.
3. The inventory basis that would show the *lowest net income for the three years combined* is (a) LIFO cost, (b) FIFO cost, (c) market, (d) lower of cost or market.
4. For the year 19X5, how much higher or lower would profits be on the *FIFO-cost basis* than on the *lower-of-cost-or-market basis*? (a) $200 higher, (b) $200 lower, (c) $300 higher, (d) $300 lower, (e) $500 higher, (f) $500 lower, (g) $700 higher, (h) $700 lower.
5. On the basis of the information given, it appears that *the movement of prices* for the items in the inventory was (a) up in 19X4 and down in 19X6, (b) up in both 19X4 and 19X6, (c) down in 19X4 and up in 19X6, (d) down in both 19X4 and 19X6.

7–46. FIFO AND LIFO. Two divisions of General Diversified, Inc., are in the scrap metal warehousing business, the Newark Division on the East Coast and the Sacramento Division in the West. The manager of each division receives a bonus based on the division's income before income taxes. The divisions are about the same size and in 19X6 coincidentally encountered seemingly identical operating situations. However, their accounting systems differ; Newark uses FIFO and Sacramento uses LIFO.

Both divisions reported the following data for 19X6:

Beginning inventory, 10,000 tons @ $50 per ton	$ 500,000
Purchase, February 15, 19X6, 20,000 tons @ $70 per ton	$1,400,000
Purchase, October 6, 19X6, 30,000 tons @ $90 per ton	$2,700,000
Sales, 45,000 tons @ $100 per ton	$4,500,000
Other expenses (in addition to cost of goods sold but excluding income taxes)	$ 710,000

The income tax rate is 55%.

Required:

1. Compute net income for the year for both divisions. Show your calculations.
2. Which division had the better performance for the year? Which accounting system would you prefer if you were manager of one of the divisions? Why? Explain fully. Include your estimate of the overall effect of these events on the cash balance of each division, assuming that all transactions during 19X6 were direct receipts or disbursements of cash.

7–47. EFFECTS OF LIFO AND FIFO. (G. Sorter, adapted) The New Delhi Trading Company is starting in business on December 31, 19X0. In each *half year*, from 19X1 through 19X4, it expects to purchase 1,000 units and sell 500 units for the amounts listed below. In 19X5, it expects to purchase no units and sell 4,000 units for the amount indicated below. Monetary amounts are in thousands of rupees (R).

	19X1	19X2	19X3	19X4	19X5
Purchases:					
First 6 months	R 2,000	R 4,000	R 6,000	R 6,000	0
Second 6 months	4,000	9,000	6,000	8,000	0
Total	R 6,000	R13,000	R12,000	R14,000	0
Sales (at selling price)	R10,000	R10,000	R10,000	R10,000	R40,000

Assume that there are no costs or expenses other than those shown above. The income tax rate is 60%, and taxes for each year are payable on December 31 of that year. New Delhi Trading Company is trying to decide whether to use FIFO or LIFO throughout the five-year period.

Required:

1. What was net income under FIFO for each of the five years? Under LIFO? Show calculations. ·
2. Explain briefly which method, LIFO or FIFO, seems more advantageous, and why.

7–48. EFFECTS OF LIFO ON PURCHASE DECISIONS. The Sandmo Corporation is nearing the end of its first year in business. The following purchases of its single product have been made:

	UNITS	UNIT PRICE	TOTAL COST
January	500	$20	$10,000
March	500	20	10,000
May	500	22	11,000
July	500	26	13,000
September	500	28	14,000
November	500	30	15,000
	3,000		$73,000

Sales for the year will be 2,500 units for $120,000. Expenses other than cost of goods sold will be $20,000.

The president is undecided about whether to adopt FIFO or LIFO for income tax purposes. The company has ample storage space for up to 3,500 units of inventory. Inventory prices are expected to stay at $30 per unit for the next few months.

Required:

1. If the president decided to purchase 2,000 units @ $30 in December, what would be the net income before taxes, the income taxes, and the net income after

taxes for the year under (a) FIFO and (b) LIFO? Assume that income tax rates are 30% on the first $25,000 of net taxable income and 50% on the excess.

2. If the company sells its year-end inventory in Year 2 @ $48 per unit and goes out of business, what would be the net income before taxes, the income taxes, and the net income after taxes under (a) FIFO and (b) LIFO? Assume that other expenses in Year 2 are $20,000.

3. Repeat requirements 1 and 2, assuming that 2,000 units, @ $30, were not purchased until January of the second year. Generalize on the effect on net income of the timing of purchases under FIFO and LIFO.

7-49. CHANGING QUANTITIES AND LIFO RESERVE. Study Appendix 7A. Consider the following data for the year 19X2:

	UNITS	UNIT COST
Beginning inventory	2	*
Purchases:	3	24
	3	28
Ending inventory	2	†

* FIFO, $20; LIFO, $16.
† To be computed.

Required:

1. Prepare a comparative table computing the cost of goods sold, using columns for FIFO and LIFO. In a final column, show (a) the LIFO reserve at the beginning of the year and at the end of the year, and (b) how its *change* in amount explains the difference in cost of goods sold.

2. Repeat requirement 1 except assume that the ending inventory consisted of (a) 3 units, (b) 1 unit, (c) zero units.

3. In your own words, explain why, for a given year, the increase in the LIFO reserve measures the amount by which cost of goods sold is higher under LIFO than FIFO.

7-50. PERPETUAL INVENTORY RECORDS. (Alternate is 7-57.) Study Appendix 7B. Eppler Co. is a wholesaler of hardware for commercial builders. The company uses a perpetual inventory system and a FIFO cost-flow assumption. The data concerning Airvent Grill RD8 for the year 19X2 follow:

	PURCHASED	SOLD	BALANCE
December 31, 19X1			150 @ $4 = $600
February 10, 19X2	90 @ $5 = $ 450		
April 14		80	
May 9	100 @ $6 = 600		
July 14		110	
October 21	80 @ $7 = 560		
November 12		60	
Total	270 $1,610	250	

Required:

Prepare a perpetual inventory card. What is the ending balance in units and dollars?

☐ **Understanding Published Financial Reports**

7-51. MEANING OF PERCENTAGES. Here is an excerpt from a letter to the *TWA Ambassador* magazine:

☐ Boy, am I mad! People like Jan Schogel should not be writing columns entitled "Personal Finance." When Hubreth (probably a distant relative) sold his island for twice what he paid, his gross profit was 50 percent, not 100 percent, as stated in the column.

The editor added the following note:

☐ Seethe no more, reader. When the island was sold for twice its cost, the gross profit was equivalent to the purchase price, thus 100 percent. Perhaps you were thinking that 50 percent of the selling price was gross profit—but that's not the way to figure it.

Required: | Do you agree with the editor? Explain.

7–52. **SWITCH FROM LIFO TO FIFO.** Effective January 1, 1970, Chrysler Corporation adopted the FIFO method for inventories previously valued by the LIFO method. The 1970 annual report stated: "This . . . makes the financial statements with respect to inventory valuation comparable with those of the other United States automobile manufacturers."

The *Wall Street Journal* reported:

☐ The change improved Chrysler's 1970 financial results several ways. Besides narrowing the 1970 loss by $20 million it improved Chrysler's working capital. The change also made the comparison with 1969 earnings look somewhat more favorable because, upon restatement, Chrysler's 1969 profit was raised only $10.2 million from the original figures.

☐ Finally, the change helped Chrysler's balance sheet by boosting inventories, and thus current assets, by $150 million at the end of 1970 over what they would have been under LIFO. As Chrysler's profit has collapsed over the last two years and its financial position tightened, auto analysts have eyed warily Chrysler's shrinking ratio of current assets to current liabilities.

☐ To get the improvements in its balance sheet and results, however, Chrysler paid a price. Roger Helder, vice president and comptroller, said Chrysler owed the government $53 million in tax savings it accumulated by using the LIFO method since it switched from FIFO in 1957. The major advantage of LIFO is that it holds down profit and thus tax liabilities. The other three major auto makers stayed on the FIFO method. Mr. Helder said Chrysler now has to pay back that $53 million to the government over 20 years, which will boost Chrysler's tax bills about $3 million a year.

Required: | Given the content of this text chapter, do you think the Chrysler decision to switch from LIFO to FIFO was beneficial to its stockholders? Explain, being as specific and using as many data as you can.

7–53. **YEAR-END PURCHASES AND LIFO.** A company engaged in the manufacture and sale of jewelry maintained an inventory of gold for use in its business. The company used LIFO for the gold content of its products.

On the final day of its fiscal year, the company bought 10,000 ounces of gold at $400 per ounce. Had the purchase not been made, the company would have penetrated its LIFO layers for 8,000 ounces of gold acquired at $260 per ounce.

The applicable income tax rate is 40%.

Required: | 1. Compute the effect of the year-end purchase on the income taxes of the fiscal year.
2. On the second day of the next fiscal year, the company resold the 10,000 ounces of gold to its suppliers. What do you think the Internal Revenue Service should do it if discovers this resale, if anything? Explain.

7-54. ERODING THE LIFO BASE. Many companies on LIFO are occasionally faced with strikes or material shortages that necessitate a reduction in their normal inventory levels in order to satisfy current sales demands. A few years ago several large steel companies requested special legislative relief from the additional taxes that ensued from such events.

A news story stated:

☐ As steelworkers slowly streamed back to the mills this week, most steel companies began adding up the tremendous losses imposed by the longest strike in history. At a significant number of plants across the country, however, the worry wasn't losses but profits—"windfall" bookkeeping profits that for some companies may mean painful increases in corporate income taxes.

☐ These outfits have been caught in the backfire of a special mechanism for figuring up inventory costs on tax returns. It's known to accountants as LIFO, or last in, first out. Ironically, it's designed to slice the corporate tax bill in a time of rising prices.

☐ *Biggest Bite*—Most of the big steel companies—16 out of the top 20—as well as 40 percent of all steel warehousers, use LIFO accounting in figuring their taxes. But the tax squeeze from paper LIFO profits won't affect them all equally. It will put the biggest bite on warehousers that kept going during the strike—and as a result, the American Steel Warehouse Assn. may ask Congress for a special tax exemption on these paper profits. . . .

☐ Companies such as Ryerson and Castle have been caught because they have had to strip their shelves bare in order to satisfy customer demands during the strike. And they probably won't be able to rebuild their stocks by the time they close their books for tax purposes.

To see how this can happen, consider the following example. Suppose a company adopted LIFO in 1980. At December 31, 1985, its LIFO inventory consisted of three "layers":

From 1980:	100,000 units @ $1.00	$100,000
From 1982:	50,000 units @ 1.10	55,000
From 1984:	30,000 units @ 1.20	36,000
		$191,000

In 1986, prices rose enormously. Data follow:

Sales	500,000 units @ $3.00 =	$1,500,000
Purchases	340,000 units @ $2.00 =	$ 680,000
Operating expenses		$ 500,000

A prolonged strike near the end of the year resulted in a severe depletion of the normal inventory stock of 180,000 units. The strike was settled on December 28, 1986. The company intended to replenish the inventory as soon as possible.

The applicable income tax rate is 60%.

Required:

1. Compute the income taxes for 1986.
2. Suppose the company had been able to meet the 500,000-unit demand out of current purchases. Compute the income taxes for 1986 under those circumstances.

7-55. LIFO INVENTORIES AND REPLACEMENT COST. R. J. Reynolds Industries is an international consumer products corporation. Its subsidiaries include R. J. Reynolds Tobacco, Del Monte, and Kentucky Fried Chicken corporations. Footnote 5 to

R. J. Reynolds's 1985 financial statements stated: "At December 31, 1985 and 1984, . . . [part] of the inventory was valued by the LIFO method . . . [and part] by various other methods, principally FIFO. The current cost of inventories at December 31, 1985 and 1984 was greater than the amounts at which these inventories were carried on the balance sheets by $1.4 billion and $1.7 billion, respectively." For this problem, assume that all inventories were valued using LIFO.

The December 1985 balance sheet showed (in millions):

	1985	1984
Inventories	$3,209	$2,493

Assume that R. J. Reynolds was considering measuring year-end inventories at current replacement cost, as advocated by some accountants and managers. Replacement costs would be $4,609 million and $4,193 million at the end of 1985 and 1984.

Required:

1. Indicate the effect on total current assets at December 31, 1985, if inventories were measured at replacement cost.
2. If inventories had consistently been measured at current replacement cost, at what amount would the cost of products sold have been measured in the 1985 income statement? The 1985 income statement, as reported, measured cost of products sold at $10,127 million.
3. Assume that R. J. Reynolds uses the average cost of inventory purchases made during the year to determine the cost of any LIFO layer (the difference between the ending and beginning inventory balances) added. Can you determine from the financial statements if the 1985 average inventory purchase costs were greater than, less than, or equal to the replacement costs on December 31, 1985? Explain.

7–56. **LOWER OF COST OR MARKET.**   (Alternate is 7–38.) Polaroid Corporation's annual report stated: "Inventories are valued on a first-in, first-out basis at the lower of standard cost (which approximates actual cost) or market value." Assume that severe price competition in 1985 necessitated a write-down on December 31 for a class of camera inventories bearing a standard cost of $10 million. The appropriate valuation at market was deemed to be $7 million.

Suppose the product line had been terminated in early 1986 and the remaining inventory had been sold for $7 million.

Required:

1. Assume that sales of this line of camera for 1985 were $20 million and cost of goods sold was $16 million. Prepare a statement of gross margin for 1985 and 1986. Show the results under a strict FIFO cost method in the first two columns and under a lower-of-FIFO-cost-or-market method in the next two columns.
2. Assume that Polaroid did not discontinue the product line. Instead a new marketing campaign spurred market demand. Replacement cost of the cameras in the December 31 inventory was $9 million on January 31, 1986. What inventory valuation would be appropriate if the inventory of December 31, 1985, was still held on January 31, 1986?

7–57. **PERPETUAL INVENTORY RECORDS.**   (Alternate is 7–50.) Study Appendix 7B. Control Data Corporation produces and sells computers, computer systems, and computer services. Its annual report showed inventories of $656.4 million on January 1, 1986. The company uses FIFO for much of its inventory.

Control Data uses a perpetual inventory system for many items, including parts sold in conjunction with servicing. Assume that the data concerning Part 431 for 1986 were:

	PURCHASED	SOLD	BALANCE
December 31, 1985			100 @ $4 = $400
March 4, 1986	90 @ $5 = $ 450		
May 19		60	
July 22	100 @ $6 = 600		
September 9		120	
October 15	80 @ $8 = 640		
December 5		50	
	270	$1,690	230

Required:

Prepare a perpetual inventory card. What is the ending balance in units and dollars?

7–58. FIFO VERSUS LIFO NET INCOME. Thrifty Corporation operates almost 900 retail stores, mostly in the western United States. Pretax income in 1985 was $60,172,000. A footnote to Thrifty's financial statements read: "Merchandise inventories are principally stated on the LIFO cost basis, which is lower than market. If the FIFO method had been used by the Company, inventories would have been greater by $49,554,000 and $47,101,000 at the end of 1985 and 1984, respectively."

Required:

1. Calculate the pretax income that Thrifty would have reported if the FIFO inventory method had been used.
2. Thrifty's income tax rate is 46%. What were Thrifty's income taxes using LIFO? What would they have been if Thrifty had used FIFO?

LIFO LIQUIDATION. Study Appendix 7A. Campbell Soup Company included the following footnote in its 1985 annual report:

☐ Liquidation of LIFO inventory quantities increased net earnings $700 in 1985, $1.9 million in 1984, and $2.6 million in 1983. Inventories for which the LIFO method of determining cost is used represent approximately 80% of inventories in both years.

Required:

1. Suppose the income tax rate was 40% in each of the three years. What was the effect of the LIFO liquidations on the (before tax) operating income in each year? What was the effect on taxes?
2. How could Campbell Soup have avoided the extra taxes?

7–60. EFFECT OF LIFO. Study Appendix 7A. Georgia-Pacific, one of the world's largest forest products companies, reported 1985 operating income of $290 million. Part of Footnote 1 to the financial statements stated:

☐ The last-in, first-out (LIFO) method of inventory valuation is utilized for the majority of inventories at manufacturing facilities and the Corporation's manufactured inventories located at its building products distribution centers. The average cost method is used for all other inventories.

Inventories are valued at the lower of cost or market as follows (in millions):

	DECEMBER 31	
	1985	1984
	(millions)	
Inventories	634	698

If LIFO inventories were valued at the lower of average cost or market, the inventories would have been $105 million and $134 million higher than those reported at December 31, 1985 and 1984, respectively.

Required:

Suppose the weighted-average method had always been used for all inventories. Calculate Georgia-Pacific's operating income for 1985. By how much would the cumulative operating income for all years through 1985 differ from that reported? Would it be more or less than that reported?

7–61. MEANING OF LIFO LIQUIDATION. Study Appendix 7A. A letter to the editor of a business newspaper complained about LIFO:

☐ It is accounting ritual, not accounting reason that causes enterprises to report that a profit—which will never be confirmed by the receipt of cash—has been realized by theoretically dipping into old, low-historic-cost levels of inventory, inventory which in fact was disposed of long ago, but through accounting pretense is still carried on the books.

☐ The sale of an item for $10, that is shown on the books as costing $8, does not result in an increased command over goods, rights, and services of $2, if its replacement cost is $10 or more. The $2 is merely the expression of additional dollar cost of what was sold. The income from the sale of an inventory must discharge its replacement cost, or the firm will run out of cash and out of business.

☐ The tax legislation most needed in the U.S. is to reform the federal and state tax accounting systems. The taxation of spurious "LIFO profits," and various other amounts that do no confer an increase in the ability to consume, is the major cause of the current illiquidity of U.S. industry.

The essence of the complaint is that the dipping into old LIFO layers will produce large profits that will be unjustly taxed.

Required:

Do you agree with the writer of the letter? Explain.

7–62. CHANGE IN INVENTORY METHOD. Study Appendix 7A. This problem is more difficult than most of the others in this chapter. The Raymark Company, a multinational manufacturer and marketer of energy absorption and transmission products, fastening systems, and custom-engineered materials, had the following footnote in an annual report:

☐ The Company changed its cost method for inventories to the first-in, first-out (FIFO) method during the fourth quarter of 1984. The last-in, first-out (LIFO) method had been used in prior years for substantially all inventories. Management believes the FIFO method will result in a better matching of current costs and revenues.

The FIFO inventory on December 31, 1984, was $32,710,000. The annual report stated that financial results for all previous years were adjusted to a FIFO basis. Retained income for December 31, 1981, was increased from $50,561,000 under LIFO to $59,-629,000 under FIFO. The differences in FIFO and LIFO net incomes were:

1984	$5,951,000 lower under FIFO
1983	358,000 higher under FIFO
1982	100,000 lower under FIFO

Assume that the income tax rate for the relevant years was 40%.

1. What was the LIFO reserve on December 31, 1981?
2. If Raymark had continued to use LIFO, what would have been the LIFO reserve on December 31, 1984?

7–63. **LIFO RESERVE.** Study Appendix 7A. This problem is more difficult than most of the others in this chapter. Savin Corporation, a manufacturer in the office copier industry, had the following footnote in an annual report:

Inventories:
Inventories consist of the following (in thousands):

	JANUARY 1, 1985	APRIL 30, 1984	APRIL 30, 1983
At FIFO cost:			
Office machines, principally copiers	$27,483	$15,334	$25,021
Parts, paper, and supplies	40,449	37,699	30,928
Other	6,304	7,454	8,924
Total at FIFO	74,236	60,487	64,873
LIFO reserve	4,171	2,796	2,863
Total at LIFO	$78,407	$63,283	$67,736

At January 1, 1985 and April 30, 1984 and 1983, approximately 82%, 75% and 74%, respectively, of the inventory value was determined by the LIFO method. Inventory at LIFO cost exceeds inventory at FIFO cost, due to the strengthening of the U.S. dollar relative to the Japanese yen, which resulted in lower costs of inventory purchased from the Company's Japanese supplier when compared to earlier periods.

Savin changed fiscal years during 1984, but that has no special bearing on this problem. The income statement for the period ended January 1, 1985, simply covers eight rather than twelve months.

Focus your attention on the LIFO adjustment. Savin uses LIFO for most of its inventories.

Savin's operating *losses* (before taxes) for fiscal periods ending January 1, 1985, and April 30, 1984, were $14,330,000 and $60,982,000, respectively. Cost of sales was $182,983,000 and $260,599,000, respectively.

Required:

1. Compute operating income (or loss) for the fiscal years ending January 1, 1985, and April 30, 1984, if Savin had been using the FIFO inventory method.
2. How does Savin's LIFO reserve differ from the LIFO reserves of most companies?

Chapter 8

INTERNAL CONTROL, CASH, AND SPECIAL JOURNALS

LEARNING OBJECTIVES

After studying this chapter, you should be able to

1. Describe the implications of the Foreign Corrupt Practices Act regarding internal accounting controls
2. Explain the role of the audit committee in a modern corporation
3. Describe and apply the checklist that may be used as a starting point for judging the effectiveness of an internal control system
4. Prepare a bank reconciliation
5. Describe an imprest system for controlling petty cash
6. Describe the retail method of inventory control (Appendix 8A)
7. Describe and apply data-processing techniques using special journals (Appendix 8B)

Internal control was once regarded as a technical subject that belonged in advanced courses in accounting, particularly the course in auditing. But widespread disclosures of secret payments and embezzlements brought internal control to the forefront as a central responsibility of top management. In 1985, a report in the *Wall Street Journal* estimated that so-called white-collar crime cost business $67 billion a year. This chapter explains internal control in general and illustrates its application to cash and inventories.

Chapter Appendix 8A provides more details about inventory control. Appendix 8B explores various ways of data processing, including special journals and subsidiary ledgers.

The problems of internal control extend to nonprofit organizations, which often suffer from defective systems. For example, an auditor's report regarding the U.S. Department of Energy listed many shortcomings of internal control. The auditors commented that the department "does not have an effective system of recording, managing, and disposing of government property."

Another example is a report by California's auditor general. In a 285-page report to the legislature, he reported that twenty-five of the thirty-six major state agencies each "had at least one weakness in the internal controls that apply to financial operations." The weaknesses created an unnecessary $24 million loss.

The problems of internal control are not confined to preventing theft. They are also concerned with adherence to management policies and procedures. Sometimes employees squander an organization's assets, not necessarily for direct personal gain, but to cover up their past mistakes. For example, an employee for Spectra-Physics shocked the top executives of that company, a pioneer manufacturer of lasers. In 1983, the company lost $10 million in a series of unauthorized foreign exchange transactions. The loss occurred when the employee, who was supposed to buy and sell small quantities of foreign currency, suddenly went overboard. The senior vice-president said that the employee with responsibility for trading in foreign exchange ended up with a small loss for the first quarter and did not disclose the facts. Instead he circumvented management controls and expanded his activities in an effort to wipe out the loss.

OVERVIEW OF INTERNAL CONTROL

□ Importance of Accounting Systems

Regardless of an entity's size or type, and regardless of whether it is held privately or publicly, managers and accountants should be alert to the rudiments of accounting systems and controls. Accounting records are kept for a variety of purposes. A major purpose is to help managers operate their entities more efficiently and effectively. Any person who forms a business will soon discover that recordkeeping is absolutely essential. For instance, records of receivables and payables must be created for transactions with customers and creditors, and cash disbursements and receipts must be traced to the individual accounts. Even the simplest of organizations must have some records. The cost-benefit test is easily met. Unless orderly compilation occurs, intolerable chaos results. In short, an accounting system is a wise business investment.

The dictionary defines *system* as "an assemblage of objects united by some form of regular interaction or interdependence." The key word is *regular*. An **accounting system** is a set of records, procedures, and equipment that *routinely* deals with the events affecting the financial performance and position of the entity.

Chapter 5 provides an overview of the heart of the accounting system: source documents, journal entries, postings to ledgers, trial balances, adjustments, and financial reports. The focus of the system is on repetitive, voluminous transactions, which almost always fall into four categories:

1. Cash disbursements
2. Cash receipts
3. Purchases of goods and services, including employee payroll
4. Sales or other rendering of goods and services

The magnitude of the physical handling of records is often staggering. For example, consider the telephone company or the credit-card companies. They must process *millions* of transactions daily. Without computers and photocopying equipment, most modern organizations would be forced to halt operations. Too often, systems are regarded as a necessary evil. But systems deserve a loftier status. Well-designed and well-run accounting systems are positive contributions to organizations and the economy.

Advances in computer technology continue to be awesome. The description of a specific accounting system is likely to be ancient history before it comes off the presses. Consequently, this chapter emphasizes the *general* features of accounting systems that persist regardless of specific computer programs and hardware. The purpose here is not to develop skills as a systems designer; the purpose is to develop an acquaintance with the scope and nature of accounting systems and controls. No manager or would-be manager can afford the risks of not having an awareness of the primary attributes of a suitable internal control system.

☐ Definition of Internal Control

Definitions of internal control vary considerably. In its broadest sense, **internal control** refers to both *administrative* control and *accounting* control:

1. *Administrative controls* include the plan of organization (for example, the formal organization chart concerning who reports to whom) and all methods and proce-

dures that facilitate management planning and control of operations. Examples are departmental budgeting procedures and reports on performance.

2. *Accounting controls* include the methods and procedures for authorizing transactions, safeguarding assets, ensuring the accuracy of the financial records. Good accounting controls help *maximize* efficiency; they help *minimize* waste, unintentional errors, and fraud.

This chapter focuses on **internal accounting controls**, as distinguished from internal administrative controls. The latter subject is covered in books on management accounting.

☐ Management's Responsibility

Chapter 1 explains that outside auditors attest to the financial reports of an entity. However, management bears the *primary responsibility* for a company's financial statements. Today the annual reports of publicly held companies generally contain an explicit statement of management responsibility for its financial statements.

These **management reports** usually state that management is responsible for all audited and unaudited information in the annual report, include a statement on the adequacy of internal control, and include a description of the composition and duties of the audit committee as well as the duties of the independent auditor. These features are highlighted in color in Exhibit 8–1, the statement of H. J. Heinz Company.

EXHIBIT 8–1

H. J. Heinz Company
Responsibility for Financial Statements

Management of H. J. Heinz Company is primarily responsible for the preparation of the financial statements and other information included in this annual report. The financial statements have been prepared in conformity with generally accepted accounting principles, incorporating management's best estimates and judgments where applicable.

Management believes that the company's internal control systems provide reasonable assurance that assets are safeguarded, transactions are recorded and reported appropriately and policies are followed. The concept of reasonable assurance recognizes that the cost of a control procedure should not exceed the expected benefits. Management believes that its systems provide this appropriate balance. An important element of the company's control systems is the ongoing program to promote control consciousness throughout the organization. Management's commitment to this program is emphasized through written policies and procedures (including a code of conduct), an effective internal audit function and a qualified financial staff.

The company engages independent public accountants who are responsible for performing an independent examination of the financial statements. Their report, which appears herein, is based on obtaining an understanding of the company's accounting systems and procedures and testing them as they deem necessary

The company's Audit Committee is composed entirely of outside directors. The Audit Committee meets regularly, and when appropriate separately, with the independent public accountants, the internal auditors and financial management to review the work of each and to satisfy itself that each is discharging its responsibilities properly. Both the independent public accountants and the internal auditors have unrestricted access to the Audit Committee.

U.S. companies must obey the **Foreign Corrupt Practices Act**. The title is misleading because the act's provisions pertain to the internal control systems of all publicly held companies, *even if they do no business outside the United States*. The act contains not only specific prohibitions against bribery and other corrupt practices but also requirements (a) for maintaining accounting records in reasonable detail and accuracy and (b) for maintaining an appropriate system of internal accounting controls. In general, as a part of intelligent management practices, most organizations already abide by these requirements. However, these responsibilities have now been explicitly codified as part of a federal law.

Public reporting on the adequacy of internal control is an explicit responsibility of management under the act. Consequently, management in general, not just accountants, focus on systems of internal control. Boards of directors assure themselves of compliance with the act and with SEC requirements by (a) obtaining documentation of the internal control system and (b) compiling written evidence of management's evaluation and ongoing review of the system. The biggest impact of the act has been the mandatory documentation of evaluation of internal control *by management* rather than only by auditors.[1]

The documentation should systematically refer to (a) management's cost-benefit choices regarding the system and (b) management's evaluation of how well the system is working. Documentation includes memos, minutes of meetings discussing internal control concepts with all affected individuals, written statements of compliance, flow charts, procedures manuals, and the like. Moreover, there should be a written program for ongoing review and evaluation of the system. Finally, there should be letters from independent auditors stating that they found no material weaknesses in internal control during their audit, or that necessary improvements have been made.

The act specifies that internal accounting controls are supposed to provide reasonable assurance concerning

1. *Authorization*. Transactions are executed in accordance with management's general or specific intentions.
2. *Recording*. All authorized transactions are recorded in the correct amounts, periods, and accounts. No fictitious transactions are recorded.
3. *Safeguarding*. Precautions and procedures appropriately restrict access to assets.
4. *Reconciliation*. Records are compared with other independently kept records and physical counts. Such comparisons help ensure that other control objectives are attained.
5. *Valuation*. Recorded amounts are periodically reviewed for impairment of values and necessary write-downs.

---

[1] These requirements were extended to managers in the public sector by the Federal Managers' Financial Integrity Act of 1982. Briefly, the act requires each executive agency to establish a system of internal accounting and administrative control that meets prescribed standards and to report annually, based upon an evaluation conducted in accordance with established guidelines, to the president, Congress, and the public on the extent to which the agency's systems comply with the standards.

The first three general objectives—authorization, recording, and safe-guarding—relate to establishing the system of accountability and are aimed at *prevention* of errors and irregularities. The final two objectives—reconciliation and valuation—are aimed at *detection* of errors and irregularities.

A sixth objective of an internal control system should be added: *promoting operating efficiency*. Although the act is not particularly concerned with efficiency, management should recognize that an internal control system's purpose is as much a positive one (promoting efficiency) as a negative one (preventing errors and fraud).

THE AUDIT COMMITTEE

The first objective of internal accounting control is *authorization*; transactions should be executed in accordance with management's intentions. Moreover, management bears primary responsibility for the entity's financial statements. This authority and responsibility extends upward to the board of directors. Most boards have an *audit committee*. Indeed, such committees are required of companies whose shares are listed on the New York Stock Exchange. The primary responsibility of the audit committee is fiscal vigilance.

Audit committees are typically composed of three or more "outside" board members. Not being everyday employees of the company, they are usually considered to be more independent than the "inside" directors, who, as employees, also serve as part of the corporation's management.[2] The **audit committee** oversees the accounting controls, financial statements, and financial affairs of the corporation. The committee represents the full board and provides personal contact and communication among the board, the external auditors, the internal auditors, the financial executives, and the operating executives. These relationships are depicted in Exhibit 8–2.

Exhibit 8–2 shows only one of many possible arrangements. Above all, note how the audit committee serves as the main pipeline to the board of directors, especially for individuals responsible for the accounting function. In Exhibit 8–2, the internal audit manager is directly responsible (solid line) to the accounting executives, who, in turn, are directly responsible to both the audit committee and the executive vice-president. The dashed lines indicate that the audit committee should communicate with and gather information directly from the external auditors and the internal auditors.

These relationships are evolving. For example, the internal auditing department sometimes is directly responsible to the executive vice-president, or to the president, or to the audit committee itself. Many observers believe that the internal audit department should be totally independent of the financial officers.

The audit committee meets at least twice annually. The first meeting is typically to review the annual external audit plan; the second, to review

---

[2] Goodyear Tire and Rubber Company has a typical board composition. Of eighteen directors, eight are also members of management and ten are "outside" directors. Four of the outside directors form the audit committee.

EXHIBIT 8–2

Typical Corporate Organization Chart

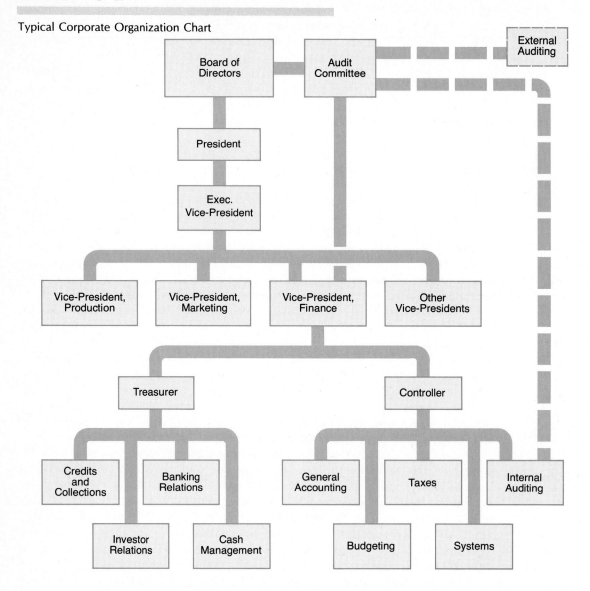

the audited financial statements before their publication. Additional meetings may be held (a) to consider the retention or replacement of the independent external auditors; (b) to review the company's accounting system, particularly the internal controls; and (c) to review any special matters raised by internal audits.

As a minimum, meetings should be attended by the chief financial officer and a representative of the independent auditing firm. At least once a year, the committee should discuss with the independent auditors their evaluation of corporate management (without the presence of the latter). Similarly, the committee should obtain management's evaluation of the independent auditors.

CHECKLIST OF INTERNAL CONTROL

All good systems of internal control have certain features in common. These features can be termed a *checklist of internal control*, which may be used to appraise any specific procedures for cash, purchases, sales, payroll, and the like. This checklist is sometimes called *principles* or *rules* or *concepts* or *characteristics* or *features* or *elements*. The following checklist summarizes the guidance that is found in much of the systems and auditing literature.[3]

1. RELIABLE PERSONNEL WITH CLEAR RESPONSIBILITIES. The most important element of successful control is personnel. Incompetent or dishonest individuals can undermine a system, no matter how well it meets the other items on the checklist. Individuals obviously must be given authority, responsibility, and duties commensurate with their abilities, interests, experience, and reliability. Yet many employers use low-cost talent that may prove exceedingly expensive in the long run, not only because of fraud but because of poor productivity.

Reliability begins at the top of the organization. The entire system deserves surveillance by operating management to see if it is working as prescribed and if changes are warranted. In addition, appropriate overseeing and appraisal of employees are essential. The most streamlined accounting system is deficient if its prescribed procedures are not being conscientiously followed.

Responsibility means tracking actions as far down in the organization as is feasible, so that results can be related to individuals. It means having salesclerks sign sales slips, inspectors initial packing slips, and workers sign time cards and requisitions. The psychological impact of fixing responsibility tends to promote care and efficiency. Employees often perform better when they must explain deviations from required procedures.

2. SEPARATION OF DUTIES. This element not only helps ensure accurate compilation of data but also limits the chances for fraud that would require the collusion of two or more persons. This extremely important and often neglected element can be subdivided into four parts:

a. *Separation of operational responsibility from recordkeeping responsibility.* The entire accounting function should be divorced from operating departments so that objective, independent records may be kept either by other operating people or by clerks. For example, product inspectors, not machine operators, should count units produced; stores record clerks or computers, not storekeepers, should keep perpetual inventory records.

b. *Separation of the custody of assets from accounting.* This practice reduces temptation and fraud. For example, the bookkeeper should not handle cash, and the

---

[3] For an expanded discussion, see Alvin Arens and James Loebbecke, *Auditing*, 3rd ed. (Englewood Cliffs, N.J.: Prentice-Hall, 1984), Chap. 9.

cashier should not have access to ledger accounts such as the individual records of customers.

In a computer system, a person with custody of assets should not have access to programming or any input records. Similarly, an individual who handles programming or input records should not have access to tempting assets.

c. *Separation of the authorization of transactions from the custody of related assets.* To the extent feasible, persons who authorize transactions should not have control over the related asset. For instance, the same individual should not authorize the payment of a supplier's invoice and also sign the check in payment of the bill. Nor should an individual who handles cash receipts have the authority to indicate which accounts receivable should be written off as uncollectible.

The latter separation of powers prevents such embezzlement as the following: A bookkeeper opens the mail, removes a $1,000 check from a customer, and somehow cashes it. To hide the theft, the bookkeeper prepares the following journal entry:

Allowance for bad debts	1,000	
Accounts receivable		1,000
To write off an amount owed		
by a customer.		

d. *Separation of duties within the accounting function.* An employee should not be able to record a transaction from its origin to its ultimate posting in a ledger. Independent performance of various phases will help ensure control over errors.

3. PROPER AUTHORIZATION. The Foreign Corrupt Practices Act has stressed this element. Authorization can be either *general* or *specific*. General authorization is usually found in writing. It often sets definite limits on what price to pay (whether to fly economy or first class), on what price to receive (whether to offer a sales discount), on what credit limits to grant to customers, and so forth. There may also be complete prohibitions (against paying extra fees or bribes or overtime premiums).

Specific authorization usually means that a superior manager must permit (typically in writing) any particular deviations from the limits set by general authorization. For example, the plant manager, rather than the lathe supervisor, may have to approve any overtime. Another example is the need for approval from the board of directors regarding expenditures for capital assets in excess of a specific limit.

4. ADEQUATE DOCUMENTS. Documents and records vary considerably, from source documents such as sales invoices and purchase orders to journals and ledgers. Immediate, complete, and tamper-proof recording is the aim. It is encouraged by having all source documents prenumbered and accounted for, by using devices such as cash registers and locked compartments in invoice-writing machines, and by designing forms for ease of recording.

Immediate recording is especially important for handling cash sales. Devices used to ensure immediate recording include cash registers with loud bells and compiling tapes, private detectives, guaranteeing "rewards" to customers if they are not offered a receipt at the time of sale, and forcing clerks to make change by pricing items at $1.99, $2.99, and $3.99 rather than at $2, $3, and $4.[4]

5. PROPER PROCEDURES. Most organizations have *procedures manuals*, which specify the flow of documents and provide information and instructions to facilitate adequate recordkeeping.

Routine and automatic checks are major ways of attaining proper procedures. In a phrase, this means doing things "by the numbers." Just as manufacturing activities tend to be made more efficient by the division and specialization of repetitive activities, so can recordkeeping activities be made less costly and more accurate. Repetitive procedures may be prescribed for nonmanufacturing activities such as order taking, order filling, collating, and inspecting. The use of general routines permits specialization of effort, division of duties, and automatic checks on previous steps in the routine.

6. PHYSICAL SAFEGUARDS. Obviously, losses of cash, inventories, and records are minimized by safes, locks, guards, and limited access.

7. BONDING, VACATIONS, AND ROTATION OF DUTIES. Key people may be subject to excessive temptation; top executives, branch managers, and individuals who handle cash or inventories should have understudies, be forced to take vacations, and be bonded.

A facet of this idea is also illustrated by the common practice of having receivables and payables clerks periodically rotated in duties. Thus a receivables clerk may handle accounts from A to C for three months and then be rotated to accounts M to P for three months, and so forth.

Incidentally, the act of bonding, that is, buying insurance against embezzlement, is not a substitute for vacations, rotation of duties, and similar precautions. Insurance companies will pay only when a loss is proved; establishing proof is often difficult and costly in itself.

8. INDEPENDENT CHECK. All phases of the system should be subjected to periodic review by outsiders (for example, by independent public accountants) and by internal auditors who do not ordinarily have contact with the operation under review.

The idea of an independent check extends beyond the work performed by professional auditors. For example, bank statements should be reconciled with book balances. The bank provides an independent record of cash. Furthermore, the monthly bank reconciliations should be conducted by some clerk other than the cash, receivables, or payables clerks. Other examples of independent checks include monthly statements sent to credit customers and physical counts of inventory to check against perpetual records.

One of the main jobs of both internal and external auditors is to appraise the effectiveness of internal control; such appraisal affects the extent of the sampling of transactions needed to test the validity of account balances.

9. COST-BENEFIT ANALYSIS. Highly complex systems tend to strangle people in red tape, so that the system impedes rather than promotes efficiency. Besides, there is "a cost of keeping the costs" that sometimes gets out of hand.

---

[4] Historically, such pricing was originally adopted to force clerks to make change as well as for its psychological impact on potential customers.

Investments in more costly systems must be compared with the expected benefits. Unfortunately, such benefits are difficult to measure. It is much easier to relate new lathes or production methods to cost savings in manufacturing than a new computer to cost savings in the form of facilitating new attacks on problems of inventory control, production scheduling, and research. Yet hardheaded efforts, as are used in making other business decisions, must be made to measure alternative costs of various accounting systems. For example, the accounting firm of Peat Marwick completed a study of office automation for a client. After examining the jobs of 2,600 white-collar workers, Peat Marwick quantified a cost-benefit relationship: "A single investment of $10 million would result in a productivity savings equal to $8.4 million every year."

The relationship of costs to benefits sometimes leads to using sampling procedures. Although many companies implement more complex procedures to improve internal control, a few have taken a reverse course. They have decided that the increased costs of additional scrutiny are not worth the expected savings from catching mistakes or crooks. For example, an aerospace manufacturer routinely pays the invoice amounts without checking supporting documentation except on a random-sampling basis. An aluminum company sends out a blank check with its purchase orders, and then the supplier fills out the check and deposits it.

No framework for internal control is perfect in the sense that it can prevent some shrewd individual from "beating the system" either by outright embezzlement or by producing inaccurate records. The task is not total prevention of fraud, nor is it implementation of operating perfection; rather, the task is the designing of a *cost-effective* tool that will help achieve efficient operations and reduce temptation.

EFFECTS OF COMPUTERS ON INTERNAL CONTROL

☐ **Computers Change the Control Environment**

The computer has allowed relatively inexpensive processing of huge volumes of accounting data. Even most small companies use computers for some of their data processing. However, internal control over computerized operations has sometimes been weak. Consider an error that a human might make once a month. Such an error would be repeated thousands of times a day if contained in a computer program for processing vast quantities of data. Further, errors that would be obvious by scanning journal entries could be undetected because data are invisible, stored on tape or disks. Input and output data are transmitted over phone lines. Without appropriate security, anyone with a telephone and computer knowledge could read and possibly change a company's records. Thus the installation of internal control systems must accompany computerization.

Computers are amazingly accurate. The focus of internal control is not *computer* errors. Invariably, the computer has done exactly what it was told (or programmed) to do. Errors usually result because someone entered the wrong data, ran the wrong program, or asked for the wrong output.

The nine items in the checklist on pages 321–324 apply to both computer and manual systems. However, computers change the focus of internal control in two ways:

1. The computer can be used to accomplish some traditional internal control functions more efficiently.
2. Additional controls must be put in place to ensure the accuracy and reliability of computer-processed data.

☐ Types of Controls for Computer Systems

Controls for a computer system are divided into two types: *application controls* and *general controls*. The applications category includes *input, processing,* and *output controls*. The greatest source of errors in computerized systems is the data input. Both the original recording (for example, a sales slip) and the transcription of the data to computer-readable form (for example, key-punching cards or direct entry from a remote terminal) are sources of error. Controls such as using standardized forms and verifying data input are common. Accountants also program the computer to verify that all required data are included on each input document, flag key numbers outside a range of reasonableness, and conduct other such checks. Use of optical scanning equipment can also limit data-recording errors.

Processing controls start with the design and programming of the system, including complete documentation. They also include normal separation and rotation of duties. For example, programmers should not be allowed to operate the computers. A computer consultant commented that he had immense stealing opportunities when he ran computer operations for a large bank: "I alone designed the dividend-payment operation, wrote the program for it, and ran the job on the machine. The operation was so big that it had a mistake tolerance of nearly $100,000. I could have paid at least half that much to myself, in small checks, and the money wouldn't even have been missed."

Processing controls can also be programmed into the computer. For example, files of data can be labeled so that only certain programs can read them or change (or update) the data.

Output controls check output against input, possibly by random manual processing of data. Output controls should also ensure that only authorized persons receive the reports. Computers often generate literally tons of printed output. A paper shredder can be an important control tool to safeguard privileged information.

The general controls focus on the organization and operation of the data-processing activity. Good internal control requires well-defined procedures for developing, testing, and approving new systems and programs or changing old ones. Access to equipment and files should be restricted. But most important, as in any system, manual or computerized, are personnel controls. Hiring reliable personnel and keeping temptation from their doorsteps through commonsense controls are important goals of any internal control system.

INTERNAL CONTROL OF CASH

Cash has the same meaning to organizations that it does to individuals. Cash encompasses all the items that are accepted for deposit by a bank, notably currency, coins, money orders, and checks. Banks do not accept postage stamps (which are really prepaid expenses) or notes receivable as cash. Indeed, although deposits are often credited to the accounts of bank customers on the date received, the checks must be cleared by the banks. Therefore, if a check fails to clear because its writer has insufficient funds, its amount is deducted from the depositor's account.

Sometimes the entire cash balance is not available for unrestricted use. Companies frequently must maintain **compensating balances**, which are required minimum cash balances on deposit with banks from which a company borrows money. The size of the minimum balance often depends on either the amount borrowed or the amount of credit available, or both.

To prevent any misleading information regarding cash, annual reports must disclose the state of any compensating balances. For example, a footnote in the annual report of North Carolina Natural Gas Corporation disclosed a requirement for a compensating balance "of 10% of the annual average loan outstanding."

Cash is almost always the most enticing asset for potential thieves and embezzlers. Therefore internal controls are far more elaborate for cash than for, say, the paper clips and desks on the premises.

☐ Highlights of Checklist

The checklist of internal control has already referred to various aspects of the control of the most tempting asset, cash. The following points are especially noteworthy:

1. As previously mentioned, the function of receiving cash should be separated from the function of disbursing cash. Moreover, individuals who handle cash or checks should not have access to the accounting records.

2. All receipts should be deposited intact each day. That is, none of the currency and checks received each day should be used directly for any other purposes. For example, sales in retail establishments are recorded in a cash register. A supervisor compares the locked cash register tape with the actual cash in the register drawer. Then the cash receipts are deposited, and the tape is forwarded to the accounting department as a basis for acounting entries. If cash from the till is sometimes used to pay suppliers, there is a serious internal control weakness.

3. All major disbursements should be made by serially numbered checks. Gaps should be investigated. The *Wall Street Journal* cited an example of good controls used poorly: "A bookkeeping assistant [was] under strict orders to note every missing number. . . . But no one checked to see how many were missing or why."

4. Bank accounts should be reconciled monthly. (This recommendation also

applies to personal banking accounts.) It is surprising how many businesses (some of substantial size) do not reconcile their bank accounts regularly. This subject is covered later in this chapter.

Many organizations use check protectors that perforate or otherwise establish an unalterable amount on the face of each check. Dual signatures are frequently required.

☐ Skimming of Cash Receipts

Currency is probably the most alluring form of cash. Businesses that handle much currency, such as gambling establishments, restaurants, and bars, are particularly subject to theft and false reporting. For example, many owners of small retail outlets do not record all of their cash receipts, a procedure known as *skimming*. Why? To save income taxes.

A recent news story reported: "Federal undercover agents in New York City opened an attack on the underground economy, which spawns billions of dollars yearly in untaxed income through off-the-books transactions." According to the affidavits, the establishments searched by the agents grossed more than $5.0 million while reporting on their tax returns only $3.6 million.

As explained in Chapter 6, a principal investigative weapon of the taxing authorities is the gross profit test. The agents know what gross profits a restaurant should generate for any specific level of revenues. However, many restaurant owners are aware of this test; they limit their cheating accordingly.

Comparing reported results with averages is not foolproof. An exclusive clothing store in San Francisco paid a percentage of sales for rent. Reported sales for a recent year were $11.2 million; an independent audit later disclosed actual sales of $20.5 million. The lessor always compared sales per square foot of floor space with those of similar stores. No clue to any impropriety arose. In fact, the lessor termed the reported sales per square foot "extraordinary" and the actual results as "unheard of."

BANK RECONCILIATIONS

Exhibit 8–3 demonstrates how an independent check of cash balances works for any bank depositor (individual or entity). First, note how parallel records are kept. The balance on December 31 is an asset (Cash) on the depositor's books and a liability (Deposits) on the bank's books. The terms *debit* and *credit* are used often in banking. They refer to the entries in the bank's books. Banks *credit* the depositor's account for additional deposits and *debit* the account for checks cleared and canceled (paid) by the bank. Thus the $2,000 check drawn by the depositor on January 5 is paid on January 8 when it is presented to the bank for payment. The bank's journal entry would be:

EXHIBIT 8–3

Comparative Cash Balance

Depositor's Records							
Cash in Bank (receivable from bank)				Date	**Depositor's General Journal**	Debit	Credit
		19X2		**19X2**			
12/31/X1 Bal.	11,000	1/5	2,000	1/5	Accounts payable	2,000	
19X2		1/15	3,000		Cash		2,000
1/10	4,000				Check No. 1.		
		1/19	5,000	1/10	Cash	4,000	
1/24	6,000				Accounts receivable		4,000
1/31	7,000	1/29	10,000		Deposit slip No. 1.		
	28,000		20,000				
1/31/X2 Bal.	8,000			1/15	Income taxes payable	3,000	
					Cash		3,000
					Check No. 2.		
Bank's Records				1/19	Accounts payable	5,000	
Deposits (payable)					Cash		5,000
19X2					Check No. 3.		
1/8	2,000	12/31/X1 Bal.	11,000				
1/20	3,000	1/11/X2	4,000	1/24	Cash	6,000	
					Accounts receivable		6,000
1/28	5,000	1/26/X2	6,000		Deposit No. 2.		
1/31	20*						
	10,020		21,000	1/29	Accounts payable	10,000	
					Cash		10,000
		1/31/X2 Bal.	10,980		Check No. 4.		
				1/31	Cash	7,000	
					Accounts receivable		7,000
					Deposit No. 3.		

* Service charge for printing checks.

Jan. 8	Deposits		2,000	
	Cash			2,000
	To debit the depositor's account.			

A credit balance on the bank's books means that the bank owes money to the depositor.

A monthly bank reconciliation is conducted by the depositor to make sure that all cash receipts and disbursements are accounted for. A **bank reconciliation** is an analysis that explains any differences existing between the cash balance shown by the depositor and that shown by the bank. Bank reconciliations can take many formats, but the objective is unchanged: to explain all differences in a cash balance at a given date. Using the data in Exhibit 8–3:

Bank Reconciliation
January 31, 19X2

Balance per books (also called *balance per check register, register balance*)	$ 8,000
Deduct: Bank service charges for January not recorded (also include any other charges by the bank not yet deducted)*	20
Adjusted (corrected) balance per books	$ 7,980
Balance per bank (also called *bank statement balance, statement balance*)	$10,980
Add: Deposits not recorded by bank (also called *unrecorded deposits, deposits in transit*), deposit of 1/31	7,000
Total	$17,980
Deduct: Outstanding checks, check of 1/29	10,000
Adjusted (corrected) balance per bank	$ 7,980

* Note that new entries on the depositor's books are required for all additions and deductions made to achieve the adjusted balance per books.

As the bank reconciliation indicates, an adjustment is necessary on the books of the depositor:

Jan. 31	Bank service charge expense	20	
	Cash		20
	To record bank charges for printing checks.		

This popular format has two major sections. The first section begins with the balance per books (that is, the balance in the Cash T-account). Adjustments are made for items not entered on the *books* but already entered by the *bank*, such as deduction of the $20 service charge. No additions are shown in the illustrated section, but an example would be the bank's collection of a customer receivable on behalf of the company. The second section begins with the balance per bank. Adjustments are made for items not entered by the *bank* but already entered in the books. After adjustments, each section should end with identical adjusted cash balances. This is the amount that should appear as cash in bank on the depositor's balance sheet.

THE BANK STATEMENT

Exhibit 8–4 displays an actual bank statement. The overall format shows that the statement is basically one account among hundreds or thousands of the bank's deposits. Together, these accounts form the subsidiary ledger that supports the bank's general ledger account *Deposits*, a liability. The statement shows checks as debits and deposits as credits, which is consistent with the idea that this is the *bank's* statement of its deposit payable.

The supporting documents for the detailed checks on the statement are canceled checks; for additional deposits, deposit slips. Symbols are often used

EXHIBIT 8–4

An Actual Bank Statement

Bank Statement

648/013	ɔCT 23, 1986	64820-2208	1
STATEMENT OF ACCOUNT	PERIOD ENDING	ACCOUNT NUMBER	PAGE

WITH

UNION BANK

S MID–PENINSULA REG HEAD OFC
400 UNIVERSITY AVENUE
PALO ALTO   94302

Charles Holland
757 Tolman Drive
San Mateo, CA 94301

TOTALS FOR THIS INTERIM STATEMENT				TOTALS FOR THIS STATEMENT PERIOD			
NO. - CHECKS PAID - AMT.		NO. - DEPOSITS MADE - AMT.		NO. - CHECKS PAID - AMT.		NO. - DEPOSITS MADE - AMT.	
3	273000	2	172754	3	273000	2	172754

CHECKS		DATE	DEPOSITS	*	BALANCE	*
CYCLE AVERAGE BALANCE=$	444	09-22	PREVIOUS BALANCE →		134214	S
132500		09-29			1714	*
		10-05	135604		137318	*
136500		10-09			814	*
4000		10-18			31820	OD
		10-19	37150		33968	*
400A		10-23			33568	*

to denote other types of transactions. In Exhibit 8–4, the symbol *S* means subtotal (the previous balance brought forward), *A* means activity charge (the amount frequently depends on whether the average balance is above a specified minimum), and *OD* means overdraft (an overdrawn account, a negative checking account balance arising from the bank's paying a check even though the depositor had insufficient funds available at the instant the check was presented).

Banks do not like overdrafts. Overdrafts are permitted as an occasional courtesy by the bank. However, the depositor is rarely given more than a day or two to eliminate the overdraft by making an additional deposit. Moreover, the bank may levy a fee ($5 or $10) for each overdraft if the depositor is careless and overdraws his or her account more than once every year or two.

Banks often provide (for a fee plus interest) "automatic" loan privileges for valued depositors. This arrangement provides for short-term loans (from ten to thirty days or more) to ensure against overdrafts. That is, when a depositor has an insufficient balance to cover his or her checks, the bank credits the depositor's account with additional money (an "automatic" loan). In this way, overdrafts are avoided. Furthermore, the depositor avoids any embarrassment or risks of a bank's delaying payment of a check to await an additional deposit.

ILLUSTRATION OF VARIOUS BANK TRANSACTIONS

Each passing year brings us closer to so-called paperless banking. For example, many employees never see their payroll checks. Instead the employer deposits the "checks" in the employee's bank accounts. This is an example of an "automatic" deposit. If the employee forgets to add the amount to his or her check register, the bank's books would show a higher balance than the depositor's books.

Suppose an employee, Mary Phelan, has a personal bank account. Her employer deposits her weekly paycheck automatically each Friday. Her check register (checkbook) for March is summarized as follows:

Reconciled cash balance, March 1, 19X7			$1,000
Additions:			
Weekly payroll deposits:	March		
	2		500
	9		500
	16		500
	23		500
Deposit of check received for			
used car sold to brother-in-law	25		800
Deposit of check received as			
birthday gift from parents	31		100
Subtotal			$3,900
Deductions:			
Checks written #291–#303	1–23	$3,000	
Check #304	27	60	
Check #305	30	80	
Check #306	31	430	3,570
Cash in bank, March 31, 19X7			$ 330

Her bank statement is summarized in Exhibit 8–5. Note the code at the bottom of the exhibit, which explains the transactions on the bank's books. The brother-in-law's $800 check "bounced"; that is, when the bank presented the check for payment, his bank refused to honor it. Mary's bank then reversed the $800 deposit of March 25 by charging it back to her on March 28. This led to an overdraft of $60. By prearrangement with Mary, the bank automatically lends sufficient amounts (in multiples of $100) to ensure that her balance is never less than $100. Therefore a loan of $200 was made.

Exhibit 8–6 shows a bank reconciliation of the discrepancies between the bank's books and the depositor's books. Assume that the individual keeps a complete set of personal books on the accrual basis. The bank reconciliation leads to the following compound journal entry by the depositor:

Receivable from brother-in-law	800	
Bank service charge expense	20	
Note payable to bank		200
Salary revenue		500
Cash in bank		120
To update and correct balances in various		
accounts as indicated by monthly		
bank reconciliation.		

EXHIBIT 8–5

Bank Statement of Deposit Account, Mary Phelan

CHECKS AND OTHER CHARGES		DEPOSITS	DATE	BALANCE
			3/1	1,000 BF
#291–#303 various dates		500 AP	3/2	1,500
in March. These would		500 AP	3/9	2,000
be shown by specific		500 AP	3/16	2,500
amounts, but are shown		500 AP	3/23	3,000
here as a total:	3,000		3/1–3/24	0
		800	3/25	800
#304	60		3/27	740
	800 NSF		3/28	60 OD
		200 AL	3/28	140
		500 AP	3/30	640
	20 MA		3/31	620

AL—automatic loan
AP—automatic deposit from employee payroll
BF—balance brought forward

MA—monthly activity charge
NSF—returned check
OD—overdraft

The reconciliation pointed out entries that belonged on the depositor's books but had not yet been entered. After these transactions were recorded with the foregoing journal entry, the depositor's book balance differed from the bank's balance by $620 − $210 = $410. Why? Because two checks ($430

EXHIBIT 8–6

Mary Phelan's Bank Reconciliation
March 31, 19X7

Balance per books		$ 330
Additions:		
Unrecorded automatic deposit of weekly payroll, March 30	$500	
Unrecorded automatic loan by bank to cover overdraft	200	700
Subtotal		$1,030
Deductions:		
Brother-in-law's returned check, often called NSF check (for Not Sufficient Funds)	$800	
Monthly activity fees	20	820
Adjusted (corrected) balance per books		$ 210
Balance per bank		$ 620
Additions:		
Unrecorded deposit of March 31 (deposit in transit)		100
Subtotal		$ 720
Deductions:		
Outstanding checks:		
#305	$ 80	
#306	430	510
Adjusted (corrected) balance per bank		$ 210

and $80) and one deposit ($100) had been recorded by the depositor but were still in transit to the bank.

PETTY CASH

Every organization desires to minimize red tape—for example, avoiding unjustifiably complicated procedures for minor disbursements. Consequently, petty cash funds are usually created and accounted for on an **imprest basis**. An imprest petty cash fund is initiated with a fixed amount of currency and coins. As the currency is used, petty cash receipts or vouchers are prepared to show the purposes of the disbursements. When the balance of currency gets low, the fund is restored to its original level by drawing and cashing a single check for the exact amount of the needed cash replenishment. **The following are typical journal entries:**

Petty cash	100	
Cash in bank		100
To set up a fund for miscellaneous minor office disbursements. (A check is drawn, cashed, and proceeds placed with some responsible person.)		
Postage	10	
Freight in	40	
Miscellaneous office expenses	35	
Cash in bank		85
To replenish the petty cash fund and record expenses paid therefrom.		

Examples of petty cash outlays include special post-office charges for certifying or insuring mail, collections by delivery personnel, and dinner money given to a secretary when working overtime.

Note that after inception the Petty Cash account itself is never directly charged or credited unless the $100 initial amount of the fund is increased or decreased. Further, the cash on hand plus the receipts (or vouchers) should always equal the $100 amount of the petty cash fund.

INTERNAL CONTROL OF INVENTORIES

In many organizations, inventories are more easily accessible than cash. Therefore they become a favorite target for thieves. This section discusses some highlights of controlling inventories.

☐ Inventory Shrinkage

Retail merchants must contend with a major operating problem that is often called inventory shrinkage, a polite term for shoplifting by customers and embezzling by employees. More broadly defined, **inventory shrinkage** is the difference between (a) the value of inventory that would occur if there were no pilferage, misclassifications, breakage, and clerical errors and (b) the value of inventory when it is physically counted. Different types of companies have various levels of inventory shrinkage. Consider the following footnote from the 1985 annual report of Associated Dry Goods, one of the largest operators of department and discount stores in the country: "Physical inventories are taken twice each year. Department store inventory shrinkage at retail, as a percent to retail sales, was 2.4% this year compared with 2.1% last year. Discount store inventory shrinkage as a percent to retail sales was .4% and .3%, respectively." Some department stores have suffered shrinkage losses of 4% to 5% of their sales volume. Compare this with the typical net profit margin of 5% to 6%.

A management consultant firm has demonstrated how widespread shoplifting has become. The firm concentrated on a midtown New York department store. Five hundred shoppers, picked at random, were followed from the moment they entered the store to the time they departed. Forty-two shoppers, or one out of every twelve, took something. They stole $300 worth of merchandise, an average of $7.15 each. Similar experiments were conducted in Boston (1 of 20 shoplifted), Philadelphia (1 of 10), and again in New York (1 of 12).

Experts on controlling inventory shrinkage generally agree that the best deterrent is an alert employee at the point of sale. But other means are also used. Retail stores have gone so far as to use tiny sensitized tags on merchandise; if not detached or neutralized by a salesclerk, these miniature transmitters trip an alarm as the culprit begins to leave the store. Many libraries use a similar system to safeguard their books. Macy's in New York has continuous surveillance with over fifty television cameras. Retailers must also scrutinize their own personnel, because they account for 30% to 40% of inventory shortages.

Some stores have hired actors to pose as shoplifters, who are then subjected to fake, calm arrests. If potential thieves see the arrests, they may be deterred. Such ploys have helped reduce thefts by employees at major retail chains.

The problem of stealing is not confined to profit-seeking entities. According to the student newspaper at Northwestern University, $14,000 worth of silverware, glasses, and china was stolen from the university dining halls annually. That amounts to $4.71 for every regular customer. Signs were posted at the end of each school term requesting the return of "borrowed" goods, but they have had little success. The food service director commented, "Two years ago, we put up really nice signs and set out boxes for returns. Kids saw the boxes and stole them for packing."

The imposing magnitude of retail inventory shrinkage demonstrates how management objectives may differ among industries. For example, consider the grocery business, where the net income percentage on sales hovers around 1%. You can readily see why a prime responsibility of the store manager is to control inventory shrinkage rather than boost gross sales volume. The trade-off is clear: If the operating profit on sales is 2%, to offset a $1,000 increase in shrinkage requires a $50,000 boost in gross sales.

☐ Shrinkage in Perpetual and Periodic Inventory Systems

Measuring inventory shrinkage is straightforward for companies using a perpetual inventory system. Shrinkage is simply the difference between the cost of the inventory identified by a physical count and the clerical inventory balance. Consider the following example:

Sales	$100,000
Cost of goods sold (perpetual inventory system)	$ 80,000
Beginning inventory	$ 15,000
Purchases	$ 85,000
Ending inventory, per clerical records	$ 20,000
Ending inventory, per physical count	$ 18,000

Shrinkage is $20,000 − $18,000 = $2,000. The journal entries under a perpetual inventory system would be:

Inventory shrinkage	2,000	
Inventory		2,000
To adjust ending inventory to its balance per physical count.		

Cost of goods sold	2,000	
Inventory shrinkage		2,000
To close inventory shrinkage to cost of goods sold.		

The total cost of goods sold would be $80,000 + $2,000 = $82,000.

By definition, a periodic inventory system has no clerical balance of the inventory account. Inventory shrinkage is automatically included in cost of goods sold. Why? Because beginning inventory plus purchases less ending inventory measures all inventory that has flowed out, whether it went to customers, shoplifters, or embezzlers or was simply lost or broken. Our example would show:

Beginning inventory	$ 15,000
Plus: Purchases	85,000
Goods available for sale	$100,000
Less: Ending inventory, per physical count	18,000
Cost of goods sold	$ 82,000

To assess shrinkage, we need some way to *estimate* what the ending inventory *should be*. The difference between this *estimate* and the physical count is inventory shrinkage. Appendix 8A describes how these estimates are made. No journal entries are necessary.

Most organizations are managed honestly. Nevertheless, there will always be sinners. A recent news story commented: "The accounting tricks used in recent cases don't appear to be new, but the pattern of scheming is. In the accounting scandals of the early to mid 1970s, employees or executives bled money from operations for their own use. In many of the recent cases, however, employees apparently committed the improprieties under pressure to meet growth goals set by management."

Although many managers may not be directly lured by cash or inventories, they may nevertheless attempt to manipulate financial results. Why? Because bonuses, salary raises, and promotions are frequently affected by reported sales or income. For example, the achieving of a budgeted net income for a specific quarter or year may mean a tidy bonus.

Examples of manipulation of profits appear periodically. For instance, during the 1970s several executives of H. J. Heinz Company felt that they were under pressure to produce smooth earnings growth from quarter to quarter. These executives would prepay for advertising services near the end of a highly profitable quarter, charging the outlay to expense. They would then obtain the actual advertising services in the next quarter. In effect, such manipulation hurts the current quarter's profits by overstating its expenses and helps the subsequent quarter's profits by understating its expenses.

In a highly publicized case in 1985, E. F. Hutton pleaded guilty to two thousand counts of fraud for writing checks for more than it had in its checking accounts. *Business Week* (November 4, 1985) indicated that "Hutton's top management put in place incentives to encourage mid-level employees to boost cash-management income but neglected to set up systems to monitor the overdrafting of checking accounts."

Another common example of manipulation is the unjustifiable recognition of revenue. For example, a news story stated: "Datapoint, a computer maker, recently disclosed that much of its success was based on apparently phantom sales and earnings. Five marketing executives, three of them vice presidents, have resigned."

Undue pressures for profits not only induce the making of phony sales but also tempt marketing executives to sell to marginal customers who never pay.

The best protection against such manipulations is paying attention to these points in the checklist of internal control: (1) reliable personnel, (2) separation of duties, (3) proper authorization, and (8) independent check. Regarding the last, auditors typically conduct sales and purchase "cutoff" tests to see that revenues and expenses are indeed attributed to the correct reporting periods.

Above all, to ensure adequate control, a "control consciousness" must become embedded in the managers throughout the organization. Such consciousness must come from the top down. Unless top managers provide clear messages and examples of proper behavior, subordinates will be unlikely to take their responsibilities for control seriously. A *Business Week* editorial commented: "Middle management in a lot of companies is under excruciating pressure to meet profit goals that are too tough. There may be more indictments unless top management takes a more realistic view of its business."

SUMMARY

The following general characteristics form a checklist that can be used as a starting point for judging the effectiveness of internal control:

1. Reliable personnel with clear responsibilities
2. Separation of duties
3. Proper authorization
4. Adequate documents
5. Proper procedures
6. Physical safeguards
7. Bonding, vacations, and rotation of duties
8. Independent check
9. Cost-benefit analysis

This checklist is equally applicable to both computer and manual systems.

There are many well-established means of obtaining internal control over key assets such as cash and inventories. Independent check is especially popular, as is evidenced by bank reconciliations and surprise counts of inventories.

SUMMARY PROBLEMS FOR YOUR REVIEW

☐ Problem One

Examine Exhibits 8–5 and 8–6, page 332. Consider the following *additional* facts:

1. The bank had erroneously credited a deposit of $120 by Mary Whelan to Mary Phelan's account on March 30.
2. The bank had charged a service fee of $10 for the transaction involving the NSF check.

Required:

1. Indicate specifically what numbers would change in Exhibits 8–5 and 8–6.
2. Prepare the journal entry called for by these additional facts.

☐ Solution to Problem One

1. In Exhibit 8–5, the ending balance would be $620 + $120 − $10 = $730. There would be an additional deposit of $120 on March 30. There would also be a service charge of $10. In Exhibit 8–6, a condensed presentation follows:

Balance per books		$ 330
Additions:		700
Subtotal		$1,030
Deductions	$820	
Additional service charge	10	830
Adjusted (corrected) balance		$ 200
Balance per bank		$ 730
Additions		100
Subtotal		$ 830
Deductions	$510	
Erroneous credit of Whelan's deposit	120	630
Adjusted (corrected) balance		$ 200

2.

Bank service charge expense	10	
Cash in bank		10
To record service charge for NSF check.		

Note that no entry is necessary regarding the Whelan deposit because no error was made on Phelan's books.

☐ Problem Two

A news story reported:

☐ A federal grand jury indicted seven former Cenco Inc. officials, accusing them of an inventory overstatement scheme that led the concern to report about $25 million in false profits. The indictment charged that the overstatement was accomplished by increasing the number of products shown on inventory tabulating cards and making up new cards. The inflation of inventory lessened the reported cost of sales and thereby resulted in a greater reported profit figure.

Given this description, were any assets stolen? What is the major feature in the chapter checklist of internal control that is aimed at preventing such dishonesty? Indicate how such dishonest acts could be accomplished and how the dishonest officials might have expected to benefit from these acts.

☐ Solution to Problem Two

Assets in the form of inventories were probably not stolen. Recall the section "Effects of Inventory Errors" in Chapter 7, page 281; overstatement of ending inventory also causes overstatement of net income in the current period. Major motives were job security (by means of a display of higher net income) and greed (by means of management bonuses and raises in future salaries). Indeed, the manager who began the scheme was hired on a four-year contract with Cenco, giving him a modest annual base salary of $40,000 plus a bonus that added 1% to his salary for every 1% increase in the Cenco Medical Health (CMH) Group's net income. Net profits soared during the life of the manager's contract. The manager reaped total compensation far in excess of his base salary.

Two subordinate managers had no incentive bonus plans, but they played along with the inventory scheme to please their boss. A variety of ways were used to overstate inventories. For example, three boxes of gauze pads would become twenty-three. The auditors were fooled with the help of fake invoices and lies. The scheme was uncovered when a subordinate informed the company treasurer. Three executives were given prison terms ranging from one to three years.

The major feature that should prevent such dishonesty is *separation of duties*. Collusion makes dishonest acts harder to accomplish. Nevertheless, as the Cenco case illustrates, separation of duties is not enough to detect fictitious inventories.

Reliable personnel with clear responsibilities is an additional feature on the checklist that is illustrated by this case. Personnel must not only be competent and honest but also be adequately instructed and supervised. The lack of top-management surveillance undoubtedly contributed to this unfortunate situation. Immediate supervisors should know enough about underlying operations so that they can sense any significant unauthorized conduct.

Independent check is another feature that helps. That is why outside auditors conduct their own physical counts.

HIGHLIGHTS TO REMEMBER

1. Managers at all levels have a major responsibility for the success of a given control system. If managers do not insist on accurate documents, separation of duties, independent checks, and so on, trouble is inevitable.

2. In the United States there is a federal law that explicitly places the ultimate responsibility for the adequacy of internal controls of publicly held companies on top management, including the audit committee of the board of directors.

3. Banks help provide an independent check on the accuracy of an important asset, cash. Monthly reconciliations of the cash balance in the bank versus the balance shown in the organization's books are good illustrations of rudimentary control.

4. Retail merchandise is particularly subject to theft by both customers and employees. Systems help control the level of inventory shrinkage, but managers bear the primary responsibility for safeguarding assets.

5. Pressures for profits sometimes cause managers to manipulate records so that their performance will look better than it really is.

6. How elaborate should internal control systems be? The answer depends on the specific organization's problems. The design ultimately depends on weighing the costs of the system against the potential benefits in the form of more efficiency and less theft.

7. Accountants and managers should recognize that the role of an internal control system is as much a positive one (enhancing efficiency) as a negative one (reducing errors and fraud).

ACCOUNTING VOCABULARY

Accounting System, p. *316*   Audit Committee, *319*   Bank Reconciliation, *328*   Check Register, *350*   Compensating Balances, *326*   Consignment, *342*   Cutoff Error, *342*   Disbursement Voucher, *350*   Foreign Corrupt Practices Act, *318*   Imprest Basis, *333*   Internal Accounting Control, *317*   Internal Control, *316*   Inventory Shrinkage, *333*   Management Reports, *317*   Retail Inventory Method, *339*   Retail Method, *339*   Special Journals, *343*   Voucher, *350*   Voucher Register, *350*   Voucher System, *333*

APPENDIX 8A: INVENTORY CONTROL VIA RETAIL METHOD, COST RATIOS, AND CUTOFFS

RETAIL METHOD OF INVENTORY CONTROL

A popular inventory method, known as the **retail inventory method**, or simply **retail method**, is often used as a control device. Its role in obtaining an inventory valuation (at cost) for financial statement purposes will be discussed in the next section; for now, concentrate on its internal control characteristics. Following is a general version of how food stores use the retail method to control grocery inventories at the store level. All merchandise is accounted for at *retail prices* as follows:

			RETAIL PRICES
	Inventory, January 5 (by surprise count by branch auditors)		$ 15,000
	Purchases (shipments to store from branch warehouse)		101,000
	Additional retail price changes:		
	Markups (from initial retail prices)		2,000
	Markdowns (from initial retail prices)		(5,000)
(1)	Total merchandise to account for		$113,000
	Sales (per cash-register records)		$100,000
	Allowable shrinkage (shoplifting, breakage, etc., usually a predetermined percentage of sales)		1,000
(2)	Total deductions		$101,000
(1) − (2)	Inventory, February 11, should be		$ 12,000
	Inventory, February 11, by physical count		11,100
	Excess shrinkage		$ 900

The total merchandise to account for is $113,000. What happens to it? Most is sold, some disappears as shrinkage, and some remains in ending inventory. Cash-register tabulations indicate sales of $100,000. If there were absolutely no shrinkage, the ending inventory at retail should be $113,000 − $100,000 = $13,000. But suppose an allowable "normal" shrinkage is 1% of sales, or $1,000. Therefore the expected inventory is $13,000 − $1,000 = $12,000.

The actual physical count provides a retail valuation of $11,100. Thus the total shrinkage is $1,900, consisting of $1,000 of allowable shrinkage plus $900 of excess shrinkage ($12,000 − $11,100 = $900).

If the inventory shrinkage is not within predetermined limits, the manager usually bears prime responsibility. There are worrisome behavioral implications here. For utmost accuracy, the retail method requires the prompt application of the directed changes in retail prices that are ordered by the branch managers. For example, to help ensure a good performance regarding control of shrinkage, store managers may be inclined to delay the entering of markdowns on price tags and may be inclined to overstate the retail prices of merchandise if possible. The branch manager usually relies on other means, such as surprise spot checks, to ensure that markup and markdown directives are being followed.

Computerized checkout systems also help to control inventory shrinkage. Such a system records each individual item that is sold, allowing a store to keep an item-by-item perpetual inventory. Such a system pinpoints the items that are disappearing, and additional control measures can be applied to these items.

ROLE OF COST RATIOS AND GROSS MARGIN PERCENTAGES

Inventories carried at retail values provide a satisfactory basis for internal control. However, inventories in financial statements are reported at cost. Therefore the retail values of inventories must be converted to costs. This is accomplished by approximations, using the ratio of cost to retail value based on an average. Consider the data in our illustration:

		RETAIL PRICES	COST
	Inventory, January 5 (by surprise count by branch auditors)	$ 15,000	$12,300
	Purchases (shipments to store from branch warehouse)	101,000	78,100
	Additional retail price changes:		
	Markups (from initial retail prices)	2,000	
	Markdowns (from initial retail prices)	(5,000)	
(1)	Total merchandise to account for	$113,000	$90,400
	Ratio of cost to retail value		80%
	Sales (per cash-register records)	$100,000	$80,000
	Allowable shrinkage (shoplifting, breakage, etc., usually a predetermined percentage of sales)	1,000	800
(2)	Total deductions	$101,000	$80,800
(1) − (2)	Inventory, February 11, should be	$ 12,000	$ 9,600
	Inventory, February 11, by physical count	11,100	8,880
	Excess shrinkage	$ 900	$ 720

The line denoted as (1) provides the basis for a ratio of cost to retail value:

$$\$90,400 \div \$113,000 = .80$$

This critical ratio[5] is then used to develop the key subsequent amounts at cost:

	RETAIL PRICES	AVERAGE RATIO OF COST TO RETAIL VALUE	COST
Allowable shrinkage	$ 1,000 ×	.80	= $ 800
Inventory, by physical count	11,100 ×	.80	= 8,880
Excess shrinkage	900 ×	.80	= 720

These amounts can be used in an income statement for a company with a periodic inventory system:

Sales		$100,000
Cost of sales:		
Beginning inventory per physical count	$12,300	
Purchases	78,100	
Available for sale	$90,400	
Ending inventory per physical count	8,880	
Cost of sales (including $800 allowable shrinkage and $720 excess shrinkage)		81,520
Gross margin (after inventory shrinkage)		$ 18,480

---

[5] Both markdowns and markups are included in this illustrative computation. Many retailers prefer to exclude markdowns because a lower cost ratio is developed:

$$\$90,400 \div (\$113,000 + \$5,000 \text{ Markdowns}) = .7661$$

This ratio would provide a "more conservative" ending inventory. Advocates of this approach say that it yields a better approximation of the lower-of-cost-or-market method.

This approach is used over and over again as periods unfold. The ending inventory of $8,880 becomes the beginning inventory of the next reporting period. Purchases are then added at cost, a new ratio of cost to retail value is developed, and shrinkage and ending inventory values are approximated:

1. Compute the goods available for sale at retail value and cost.
2. Compute the ratio of cost to retail value.
3. Count the ending inventory and value it at retail value.
4. Convert the retail value of the ending inventory to cost by using the ratio of cost to retail value.

The *cost* of shrinkage, which can be divided into allowable and excess components, is approximated by using the ratio of cost to retail value.

Note that the ratio of cost to retail value is the complement of the gross margin ratio. In this illustration, the gross margin percentage is 100% − 80% = 20%. Thus the gross margin percentage or its related ratio of cost to retail value is a key element of internal control.

CUTOFF ERRORS, CONSIGNMENTS, AND INVENTORY VALUATION

The accrual basis of accounting should include the physical counting and careful valuation of inventory at least once yearly. Auditors routinely search for **cutoff errors**, which are failures to record transactions in the correct time period. For example, assume a periodic inventory system. Suppose a physical inventory is conducted on December 31. Inventory purchases of $100,000 arrive in the receiving room during the afternoon of December 31. The acquisition is included in Purchases and Accounts Payable but excluded from the ending inventory valuation. Such an error would overstate cost of goods sold and understate gross profit. On the other hand, if the acquisition were not recorded until January 2, the error would understate the ending inventory and Accounts Payable as of December 31. However, cost of goods sold and gross profit would be correct because Purchases and the ending inventory would be understated by the same amount.

The general approach to recording purchases and sales is keyed to the legal transfer of ownership. Some major points follow:

1. Ownership typically changes hands when the goods are delivered by the seller to the purchaser. These terms are usually F.O.B. destination. If the terms are F.O.B. shipping point, ownership passes to the purchaser when the goods are delivered to the transportation company.

2. Sometimes goods are shipped on **consignment**. These are goods shipped for future sale, title remaining with the shipper (consignor), for which the receiver (consignee), upon his or her acceptance, is accountable. Even though such goods are physically elsewhere, they are part of the consignor's inventory until sold. For example, a manufacturer of bicycles might ship 20 units on consignment to a new retailer. Under such terms, the bicycles are included in the manufacturer's inventory and excluded from the retailer's inventory.

Auditors are especially careful about cutoff tests because the pressure for profits sometimes causes managers to postpone the recording of bona fide purchases of goods and services. Similarly, the same managers may deliberately include sales *orders* near year-end (rather than bona fide completed sales) in revenues. For example, consider the case of Datapoint, a maker of small computers and telecommunications equipment. A news story reported: "Datapoint's hard-pressed sales force was still logging orders that might not hold up after shipment." In the wake of an accounting scandal, Datapoint's president declared a three-week "amnesty period" during which scheduled shipments could be taken off the books, no questions asked.

A similar news story referred to difficulties at McCormick & Co., a firm best known for its spices: "The investigation also found that improprieties included the company's accounting for sales. In a longstanding practice, the company recorded as sales goods that had been selected and prepared for shipment rather than waiting until after they had been shipped as is the customary accounting practice."

APPENDIX 8B: DATA PROCESSING AND SPECIAL JOURNALS

Elsewhere in this textbook, the only book of original entry is a general journal. This appendix describes the use of special journals in addition to a general journal. This material is important to anyone who wants to know the details about how an accounting system processes data.

Chapters 4 and 5 use the general journal as the basic step in data processing. However, in all but the smallest accounting systems, **special journals** (or procedures akin to special journals) are used in addition to the general journal:

IN OTHER CHAPTERS	IN THIS APPENDIX
1. Transaction	1. Transaction
2. Source documents (invoices, receiving reports, checks, etc.)	2. Source documents
3. General journal	3. Sales journal (for credit sales)
	Cash receipts journal
	Purchases journal (for credit purchases of inventory)
	Cash disbursements journal
	General journal (for all other transactions)
4. General ledger	4. General and subsidiary ledgers[6]

Every accounting system has a general journal, whether kept in pen and ink or on computer tape. But a general journal is not an efficient device for recording numerous repetitive transactions. How would you enjoy using a general journal to debit Accounts Receivable and credit Sales for each credit sale made in a department store on a Saturday? Moreover, how would you like to post each journal entry to the general ledger accounts for accounts receivable and sales? Not only would the work be long, tedious, and dull, but it would be outrageously expensive.

More than 90% of most companies' transactions are recorded in one of the four special journals listed. As we will see, all entries in these journals have common features, thereby allowing speed, efficiency, and economy of data processing. The same basic ideas apply to both manual and computerized systems.

SALES JOURNAL

The sales journal in Exhibit 8–7 is probably better called a *credit sales journal* because it includes only credit sales, cash sales being recorded in the cash receipts journal. If a general journal were used for these five credit sales transactions, five separate entries debiting Accounts Receivable and crediting Sales would be required. In addition, five separate postings would be made to these accounts in the general ledger. Obviously, if five thousand sales occurred in June, journalizing and posting each individual transaction would become oppressive.

---

[6] Chapter 6 illustrated a subsidiary ledger for accounts receivable on pages 222–223.

EXHIBIT 8–7

Sales Journal and Postings

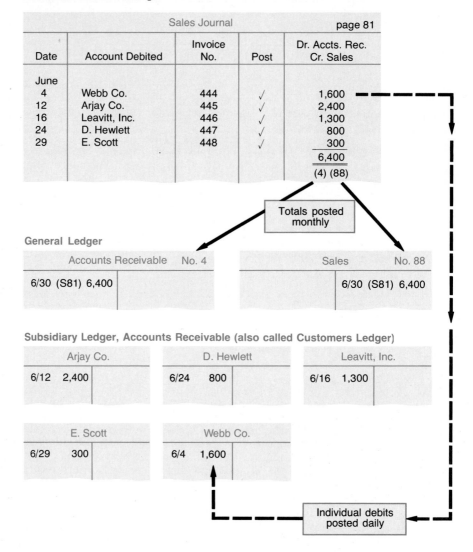

	Sales Journal			page 81
Date	Account Debited	Invoice No.	Post	Dr. Accts. Rec. Cr. Sales
June				
4	Webb Co.	444	✓	1,600
12	Arjay Co.	445	✓	2,400
16	Leavitt, Inc.	446	✓	1,300
24	D. Hewlett	447	✓	800
29	E. Scott	448	✓	300
				6,400
				(4) (88)

Totals posted monthly

General Ledger

Accounts Receivable	No. 4
6/30 (S81) 6,400	

Sales	No. 88
	6/30 (S81) 6,400

Subsidiary Ledger, Accounts Receivable (also called Customers Ledger)

Arjay Co.	
6/12 2,400	

D. Hewlett	
6/24 800	

Leavitt, Inc.	
6/16 1,300	

E. Scott	
6/29 300	

Webb Co.	
6/4 1,600	

Individual debits posted daily

Consider the details in Exhibit 8–7. As each sale is entered, the accountant debits the *subsidiary* ledger account for the particular customer. The invoice reference provides a trail to any underlying details of the sale. A check mark is put in the Post column as each amount is posted to the individual subsidiary accounts.

The general ledger accounts, Accounts Receivable and Sales, are not written out as entries are being made in the sales journal. The dollar amount is entered once, not twice, for each sale. Postings to the general ledger are made only periodically, usually at the end of the month. The $6,400 total is posted to two accounts and has the same effect as if the following general journal entry were made:

	POST	AMOUNTS	
Accounts receivable	4	6,400	
Sales	88		6,400

Of course, the direct posting from the sales journal eliminates having the above general journal entry.

As explained in Chapter 6, the sum of the balances in the subsidiary ledger must agree with the Accounts Receivable account in the general ledger. When there is a subsidiary ledger, its corresponding summary account in the general ledger is often called a controlling account. The existence of a subsidiary ledger for a particular general ledger account is often denoted by adding the word *control* to the latter's title—for example, Accounts Receivable Control.

The sales journal (and other special journals) are being described here to help you visualize various ways of gathering data for posting to ledgers. However, these special journals have been abandoned as being completely unnecessary in many mechanical and computerized systems. For example, copies of all credit sales slips can be accumulated and summarized once a month and posted to ledgers without being journalized at all:

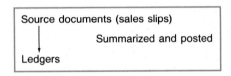

CASH RECEIPTS JOURNAL

Special journals may have a single money column, as in the sales journal just illustrated, or they may have several columns, as Exhibit 8–8 demonstrates. The number of columns depends on the frequency of transactions affecting particular accounts. Moreover, as the cash receipts journal in Exhibit 8–8 shows, the most frequently affected columns might be placed at the far right—regardless of whether the amounts therein are debits or credits. The important point about debits and credits is that they are ultimately entered on the correct sides of the *ledger* accounts, even though the format of some special *journals* seems to put debits on the right.

Cash sales and collections on accounts receivable are generally the two most common types of cash receipts, so special columns are formed for Cash, Sales, and Accounts Receivable. The amounts of the cash sales are entered in the Cash and Sales columns. The amounts of the collections on accounts are entered in the Cash and Accounts Receivable columns. This specialized approach replaces the need for countless repetitions of the following familiar entries that would otherwise have to be made in the general journal:

Cash	xx	
Sales		xx
Cash	xx	
Accounts receivable		xx

Infrequent cash receipts, such as those illustrated for the bank loan and the sale of common stock, are entered in the Cash and the Other Accounts columns.

The columns are totaled at the end of each month to make sure that the total debits equal the total credits: 13,000 + 3,700 + 7,500 = 24,200. Then the totals of

EXHIBIT 8–8

Cash Receipts Journal and Postings

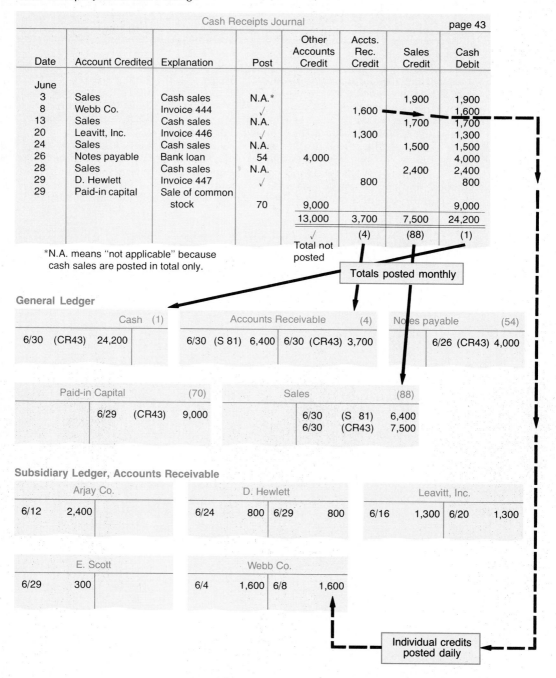

Date	Account Credited	Explanation	Post	Other Accounts Credit	Accts. Rec. Credit	Sales Credit	Cash Debit
June							
3	Sales	Cash sales	N.A.*			1,900	1,900
8	Webb Co.	Invoice 444	√		1,600		1,600
13	Sales	Cash sales	N.A.			1,700	1,700
20	Leavitt, Inc.	Invoice 446	√		1,300		1,300
24	Sales	Cash sales	N.A.			1,500	1,500
26	Notes payable	Bank loan	54	4,000			4,000
28	Sales	Cash sales	N.A.			2,400	2,400
29	D. Hewlett	Invoice 447	√		800		800
29	Paid-in capital	Sale of common stock	70	9,000			9,000
				13,000	3,700	7,500	24,200
				√ Total not posted	(4)	(88)	(1)

Cash Receipts Journal — page 43

*N.A. means "not applicable" because cash sales are posted in total only.

Totals posted monthly

General Ledger

	Cash (1)	
6/30 (CR43) 24,200		

	Accounts Receivable (4)	
6/30 (S 81) 6,400	6/30 (CR43) 3,700	

	Notes payable (54)	
	6/26 (CR43) 4,000	

	Paid-in Capital (70)	
	6/29 (CR43) 9,000	

	Sales (88)	
	6/30 (S 81) 6,400	
	6/30 (CR43) 7,500	

Subsidiary Ledger, Accounts Receivable

	Arjay Co.	
6/12 2,400		

	D. Hewlett	
6/24 800	6/29 800	

	Leavitt, Inc.	
6/16 1,300	6/20 1,300	

	E. Scott	
6/29 300		

	Webb Co.	
6/4 1,600	6/8 1,600	

Individual credits posted daily

each column are posted to the indicated accounts in the general ledger. Of course, the Other Accounts total is not posted. Instead the individual amounts therein are posted to the relevant individual general ledger accounts. The numbers 54 and 70 are placed in the Post column as evidence that the postings have been made. The illustrated general ledger accounts now contain postings from the cash receipts journal and those made previously from the sales journal.

The only subsidiary ledger in this illustration is for Accounts Receivable. The postings from the cash receipts journal are made in the same manner as those from the sales journal. A principal internal control feature is illustrated by the monthly schedule of the individual customer balances. The sum should agree with the general ledger balance, June 30:

Arjay Co.	$2,400
E. Scott	300
Balance, subsidiary ledger	$2,700
Balance, Accounts Receivable in general ledger	$2,700

PURCHASES JOURNAL

The purchases journal in Exhibit 8–9 is the mirror image of the sales journal except that the amounts and individuals differ. The purchases journal is better called a *credit merchandise purchases journal* because cash purchases are recorded in the cash disbursements journal. A perpetual inventory system is assumed, although the subsidiary ledger (composed of stock cards for individual inventory items) is not shown here. If a general journal were used for these five credit purchase transactions, five separate entries debiting Inventory and crediting Accounts Payable would be required. Moreover, five separate postings would be made to these general ledger accounts. (Under a periodic inventory system, the debits would be made to the Purchases account instead of Merchandise Inventory.)

Consider the details in Exhibit 8–9. As each purchase is entered, the name of the account credited is the name of the *subsidiary* account. The invoice date provides a trail to the underlying details. The terms are sometimes listed and used as a guide to scheduling cash disbursements (although more frequently the invoice itself is so used). As in the sales journal, a check mark is placed in the Post column as each amount is put in the individual subsidiary accounts.

As in the sales journal, postings to the general ledger are made only at the end of the month. The $15,000 total is "double posted" and has the same effect as the following general journal entry (which need no longer be made):

	POST	AMOUNTS	
Merchandise inventory	20	15,000	
Accounts payable	51		15,000

CASH DISBURSEMENTS JOURNAL

The cash disbursements journal is often called a *check register* or a *cash payments journal*. Like its counterpart, the cash receipts journal, the cash disbursements journal usually has multiple columns. As Exhibit 8–10 shows, special columns are formed for Cash, Merchandise Inventory, and Accounts Payable. The amounts of the cash

EXHIBIT 8–9

Purchases Journal and Postings

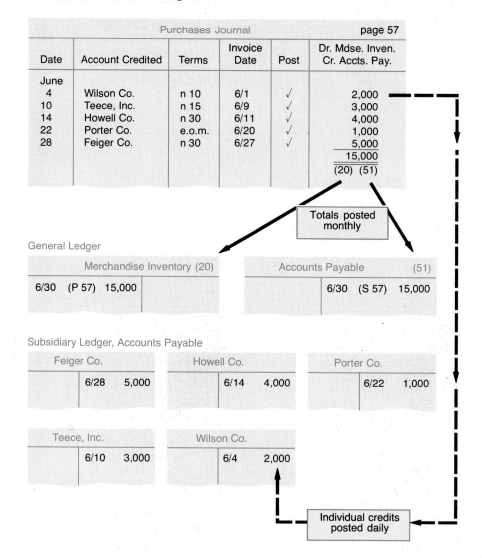

	Purchases Journal				page 57
Date	Account Credited	Terms	Invoice Date	Post	Dr. Mdse. Inven. Cr. Accts. Pay.
June					
4	Wilson Co.	n 10	6/1	✓	2,000
10	Teece, Inc.	n 15	6/9	✓	3,000
14	Howell Co.	n 30	6/11	✓	4,000
22	Porter Co.	e.o.m.	6/20	✓	1,000
28	Feiger Co.	n 30	6/27	✓	5,000
					15,000
					(20) (51)

Totals posted monthly

General Ledger

Merchandise Inventory (20)		Accounts Payable (51)	
6/30 (P 57) 15,000			6/30 (S 57) 15,000

Subsidiary Ledger, Accounts Payable

Feiger Co.		Howell Co.		Porter Co.	
	6/28 5,000		6/14 4,000		6/22 1,000

Teece, Inc.		Wilson Co.	
	6/10 3,000		6/4 2,000

Individual credits posted daily

purchases are entered in the Cash and Merchandise Inventory columns. The amounts of the payments on accounts are entered in the Cash and Accounts Payable columns. Thus countless repetitions of the following familiar general journal entries are avoided:

Merchandise inventory	xx	
Cash		xx
Accounts payable	xx	
Cash		xx

EXHIBIT 8–10

Cash Disbursements Journal and Postings

					Cash Disbursements Journal				page 67

Date	Check No.	Payee	Account Debited	Post	Other Accounts Debit	Accts. Payable Debit	Mdse. Inven. Debit	Cash Credit
June								
6	322	Simpson Co.	Inventory	√*			1,000	1,000
12	323	Wilson Co.	Wilson Co.	√		2,000		2,000
15	324	IRS	Income taxes payable	55	4,000			4,000
19	325	Reese, Inc.	Inventory	√			400	400
23	326	Teece, Inc.	Teece, Inc.	√		3,000		3,000
26	327	Fixit Co.	Repair expense	94	200			200
28	328	Porter Co.	Porter Co.	√		1,000		1,000
					4,200	6,000	1,400	11,600
					√	(51)	(20)	(1)
					Total not posted			

*Posted to subsidiary accounts for Merchandise Inventory, but this subsidiary ledger is not illustrated here.

Totals posted monthly

General Ledger

Cash	(1)
6/30 (CR43) 24,200	6/30 (CD67) 11,600

Merchandise Inventory (20)	
6/30 (P 57) 15,000	
6/30 (CD67) 1,400	

Accounts Payable	(51)
6/30 (CD67) 6,000	6/30 (S57) 15,000

Income Taxes Payable	(55)
6/15 (CD67) 4,000	

Repair Expense	(94)
6/26 (CD67) 200	

Subsidiary Ledger, Accounts Payable

Feiger Co.	
	6/28 5,000

Howell Co.	
	6/14 4,000

Porter Co.	
6/28 1,000	6/22 1,000

Teece, Inc.	
6/23 3,000	6/10 3,000

Wilson Co.	
6/12 2,000	6/4 2,000

Individual debits posted daily

Payments on accounts payable are made so that suppliers receive the checks on the appropriate due dates. For instance, the Porter Co. terms are e.o.m., which means payment is due at the end of the month of the invoice. Therefore a check is sent on June 28 to allow two days for mail delivery.

Infrequent cash disbursements, such as those illustrated for income taxes and repairs, are entered in the columns *Cash* and *Other Accounts*.

Each column is totaled (accountants say *footed*) and the column totals are cross-added (*cross-footed*) to make sure that the total debits equal the total credits:

4,200 + 6,000 + 1,400 = 11,600. Then the totals of each column are posted to the indicated accounts in the general ledger. The total for Other Accounts is not posted. Instead the individual amounts are posted to the relevant individual general ledger accounts, as shown by numbers 55 and 94 in the Post column. The general ledger now has all postings from the pertinent special journals.

The postings from the cash disbursements journal to the subsidiary accounts payable ledger are made in the same way as from the purchases journal. For control purposes, a monthly schedule of the individual accounts payable balances should be compared with the general ledger balance. As of June 30:

Feiger Co.	$5,000
Howell Co.	4,000
Balance, subsidiary ledger	$9,000
Balance, Accounts Payable in general ledger	$9,000

OTHER JOURNALS, INCLUDING VOUCHER REGISTER

As indicated earlier, the general journal exists for all organizations. As a minimum, general journal entries are made for closing entries and for adjusting entries such as depreciation and various accruals.

The four special journals here come in a variety of shapes, sizes, names, and formats and are processed by manual, mechanical, or computerized means. Moreover, additional special journals are frequently justified, particularly in accounting for payroll. Other special journals include those for (a) sales returns and allowances and (b) purchase returns and allowances.

Some companies employ a **voucher system** for controlling cash disbursements. This system is too detailed for thorough coverage here, but a brief description follows.

1. A **voucher** is a form to which purchase orders, receiving reports, and invoices are often attached. The voucher is formal verification of a transaction and authority to prepare journal entries and to write and release a check. Sometimes this formal authority is called a **disbursement voucher**. Indeed, sometimes a copy of the disbursement voucher becomes the formal check itself (called a *voucher check*).

2. These vouchers are listed in a **voucher register**, which is similar to Exhibit 8–10 except that the Check No. column would be replaced by a Voucher No. and the Cash column would be replaced by a Vouchers Payable column.

3. A simple **check register** would be created and would appear as follows:

	Check Register		
Date	Check No.	Payee	Dr. Vouchers Payable Cr. Cash

FUNDAMENTAL ASSIGNMENT MATERIAL

☐ General Coverage

8-1. MANAGEMENT'S RESPONSIBILITY FOR INTERNAL CONTROLS. The Gerberding Company has always tried to prepare informative annual reports. A few years ago, Harold Gerberding, president, heard about the Foreign Corrupt Practices Act, but he assumed that it did not affect his company. After all, not only did Gerberding Company refrain from corrupt foreign practices but the company had no foreign operations or export sales.

Required:

> Explain how the Foreign Corrupt Practices Act affects a company such as Gerberding. How does it affect Gerberding's annual report?

8-2. EMBEZZLEMENT AND CHECKLIST OF INTERNAL CONTROL. (Alternate is 8-28.) Surf Products, Incorporated, manufactures a variety of swimwear, which it sells to hundreds of distributors and retailers.

Surf makes nearly all sales on credit, and payments (less any discounts or allowances) are received through the mail, generally within 30 days of billing. Payment envelopes are opened by Peter Olson. He separates the checks and currency from the accompanying letters and remittance advices. Olson forwards the checks and currency to another employee, who makes daily bank deposits but has no access to the accounting records. He sends the letters and remittance advices, which show the customer and the amount received, to the accounting department where appropriate entries are made in the company's accounts. An employee in the treasurer's office, who has no access to cash or checks, reconciles the monthly bank statements.

Sales returns and allowances must be approved by the sales manager, who determines the appropriate amount. The credit manager decides when an account is uncollectible and should therefore be written off.

The internal auditor for Surf recently discovered that Olson had forged the signatures of the sales manager and the credit manager authorizing sales allowances and bad debt write-offs for several accounts. The accounting department was unaware of the forgeries, so they posted the stated amounts to the customer's accounts.

Required:

> 1. How could Olson have used these forgeries to cover an embezzlement by him? Assume there was no collusion with other employees. Be specific.
> 2. See the chapter checklist of internal control. Identify the items that would be relevant to such an embezzlement, and describe briefly any different procedures that should have been followed by Surf.

8-3. BANK RECONCILIATION. (Alternates are 8-6 and 8-7.) Bellevue Prep, a private high school, has a bank account. Consider the following information:

a. Balances as of July 31: per books, $62,000; per bank statement, $41,880.
b. Cash receipts of July 31 amounting to $10,000 were recorded and then deposited in the bank's night depository. The bank did not include this deposit on its July statement.
c. The bank statement included service charges of $120.
d. Parents had given the school some bad checks amounting to $15,000. The bank marked them NSF and returned them with the bank statement after charging the school for the $15,000. The school had made no entry for the return of these checks.
e. The school's outstanding checks amounted to $5,000.

Required:

> 1. Prepare a bank reconciliation as of July 31.
> 2. Prepare the school's journal entries required by the given information.

8–4. **USE OF CREDIT CARDS.** An executive used her American Express card for a variety of purchases. When checking her monthly bill, she compared her original copy with a duplicate copy for a business luncheon at a local restaurant. The original copy showed a purchase of $24.25; the duplicate had been raised to $26.25.

Who obtained the extra $2? How can the system be improved to prevent such thievery?

8–5. **OVERSTATEMENTS OF RESULTS.** Saxon Industries, Inc., sold office copiers before undergoing bankruptcy proceedings.

Forbes reported that Saxon's inventory had been overstated by at least $100 million out of a reported total inventory of $120 million. A news story reported that possible motives included "inflating earnings or increasing the company's borrowing capacity."

Regarding the manipulations, *Forbes* referred to the Saxon inventory methods as "not LIFO or FIFO but Presto!"

1. How does overstating inventory enhance reported results? Be specific.
2. How are such overstatements accomplished? Prevented? Be specific.

8–6. **BANK RECONCILIATION.** (Alternates are 8–3 and 8–7.) Church's Fried Chicken Incorporated reported an actual cash balance of over $8 million at the end of 1985. During 1986, the company opened many fast-food outlets.

Assume that one of the company's outlets has a checking account with a local bank. The following information is available regarding an April bank statement, which had an April 30 balance of $17,950:

a. The bank had charged $40 against the outlet's account for miscellaneous April services.
b. A customer's check for $50 was stamped NSF, charged against the outlet's account, and returned by the bank.
c. The bank had purchased on credit $60 worth of dinners for employees working overtime. The bank had paid the outlet by crediting the outlet's bank account on April 26. However, the outlet had failed to record the latter transaction.

The above items affecting cash were not shown on the outlet's books, which had an April 30 balance of $20,080. In addition, the outlet manager discovered that the following checks were outstanding at April 30: #430 for $300, #434 for $200, and #435 for $400. Moreover, a $3,000 deposit that was mailed on April 30 did not appear on the April bank statement.

1. Prepare a bank reconciliation as of April 30.
2. Prepare Church's journal entries required by the given information.

8–7. **BANK RECONCILIATION.** (Alternates are 8–3 and 8–6.) American Building Maintenance Industries is the largest janitorial service company in the world. Most of its twenty-five thousand employees clean structures such as the buildings of Bank of America. The company has many branch offices throughout the United States and elsewhere.

A St. Louis branch office has a checking account with a local bank. The branch's cash balance per books was $4,000 on June 30; the bank statement showed a balance of $4,400.

Other information follows:

a. The branch office had two checks outstanding at June 30: #704 for $400 and #706 for $300.

b. The bank had enclosed a branch customer's $2,000 check with the bank statement. It was marked NSF, and the bank had reduced the branch's balance accordingly.

c. The branch office had mailed a $1,200 deposit on June 29, but the June bank statement failed to show it.

d. The branch borrowed $3,000 from the bank on June 30. The bank had credited the branch's deposit account on that date. However, the branch had not recorded the transaction.

e. Miscellaneous bank service charges of $100 were on the bank statement. The branch had not recorded them.

Required:

1. Prepare a bank reconciliation as of June 30. (The correct balance is $9,900.)

2. Prepare the American Building Maintenance Industries journal entries required by the given information.

ADDITIONAL ASSIGNMENT MATERIAL

☐ General Coverage

8–8. Into what four categories can the most repetitive, voluminous transactions in most organizations be divided?

8–9. Distinguish between *internal accounting control* and *internal administrative control*.

8–10. "The primary responsibility for internal controls rests with the outside auditors." Do you agree? Explain.

8–11. "The Foreign Corrupt Practices Act governs the acts of multinational companies." Do you agree? Explain.

8–12. What are the two major ways of ensuring compliance with the Foreign Corrupt Practices Act regarding internal control systems?

8–13. Give three examples of documentation of an internal accounting control system.

8–14. Name five objectives of the Foreign Corrupt Practices Act with respect to internal accounting controls.

8–15. What is the primary responsibility of the audit committee?

8–16. "There are nine check points that I always use as a framework for judging the effectiveness of an internal control system." Name them.

8–17. "The most important element of successful control is personnel." Explain.

8–18. What is the essential idea of separation of duties?

8–19. Authorization can be general or specific. Give an example of each.

8–20. "The words *internal control* are commonly misunderstood. They are thought to refer to those facets of the accounting system that are supposed to help prevent embezzling." Do you agree? Why?

8–21. "Internal control systems have both negative and positive objectives." Do you agree? Explain.

8–22. Internal control of a computerized system consists of applications controls and general controls. What are the three types of applications controls?

8–23. "A compensating balance essentially increases the interest rate on money borrowed." Explain.

8–24. Briefly describe how a bottler of soda water might compile data regarding control of breakage of bottles at the plant, where normal breakage can be expected.

8–25. The branch manager of a national retail grocery chain has stated: "My managers are judged more heavily on the basis of their merchandise-shrinkage control than on their overall sales volume." Why? Explain.

8–26. "Business operations would be a hopeless tangle without the paper work that is often regarded with disdain." Explain.

8–27. Pressure for profits extends beyond managers in profit-seeking companies. A 1986 news story reported: "The profit motive, even in nonprofit hospitals, is steadily eroding the traditional concern to provide care to the medically indigent." Why does the profit motive affect even nonprofit organizations?

8–28. EMBEZZLEMENT OF CASH RECEIPTS. (Alternate is 8–2.) The Kane Company is a small wholesaler of gift and novelty items. It has only a few employees.

The owner of Kane Company, who is also its president and general manager, makes daily deposits of customers' checks in the company bank account and writes all checks issued by the company. The president also reconciles the monthly bank statement with the books when the bank statement is received in the mail.

The assistant to Kane Company's president renders secretarial services, which include taking dictation, typing letters, and processing all mail, both incoming and outgoing. Each day the assistant opens the incoming mail and gives the president the checks received from customers. The vouchers attached to the checks are separated by the assistant and sent to the bookkeeper, along with any other remittance advices that have been enclosed with the checks.

The bookkeeper makes prompt entries to credit customers' accounts for their remittances. From these accounts, the bookkeeper prepares monthly statements for mailing to customers.

Other employees include marketing and warehouse personnel.

Required:

For the thefts described below, explain briefly how each could have been concealed and what precautions you would recommend for forestalling the theft and its concealment:

1. The president's assistant takes some customers' checks, forges the company's endorsements, deposits the checks in a personal bank account, and destroys the check vouchers and any other remittance advices that have accompanied these checks.
2. The same action is taken as above, except that the vouchers and other remittance advices are sent intact to the bookkeeper.

8–29. APPRAISAL OF PAYROLL SYSTEM. (CPA). The Generous Loan Company has one hundred branch loan offices. Each office has a manager and four or five subordinates who are employed by the manager. Branch managers prepare the weekly payroll, including their own salaries, and pay their employees from cash on hand. The employee signs the payroll sheet, signifying receipt of his or her salary. Hours worked by hourly personnel are inserted in the payroll sheet from time cards prepared by the employees and approved by the manager.

The weekly payroll sheets are sent to the home office along with other accounting statements and reports. The home office compiles employee earnings records and prepares all federal and state salary reports from the weekly payroll sheets.

Salaries are established by home-office job-evaluation schedules. Salary adjustments, promotions, and transfers of full-time employees are approved by a home-office salary committee, based on the recommendations of branch managers and area supervisors. Branch managers advise the salary committee of new full-time employees and of terminations. Part-time and temporary employees are hired without referral to the salary committee.

Required:

Based on your review of the payroll system, how might payroll funds be embezzled?

8–30. MULTIPLE CHOICE (CPA, adapted). Choose the best answer for each of the four questions that follow:

1. Which of the following internal control procedures would be *most* likely to prevent the concealment of a cash shortage resulting from the improper write-off of a trade account receivable?
   (*a*) Write-offs must be approved by a responsible officer after review of credit department recommendations and supporting evidence.
   (*b*) Write-offs must be supported by an aging schedule showing that only receivables over-due several months have been written off.
   (*c*) Write-offs must be approved by the cashier who is in a position to know if the receivables have, in fact, been collected.
   (*d*) Write-offs must be authorized by company field sales employees who are in a position to determine the financial standing of the customers.
2. Which of the following is an effective internal accounting control over accounts receivable?
   (*a*) Only persons who handle cash receipts should be responsible for the preparation of documents that reduce accounts receivable balances.
   (*b*) Responsibility for approval of the write-off of uncollectible accounts receivable should be assigned to the cashier.
   (*c*) Balances in the subsidiary accounts ledger should be reconciled to the general ledger control account once a year, preferably at year-end.
   (*d*) The billing function should be assigned to persons other than those responsible for maintaining accounts receivable subsidiary records.
3. Internal control over cash receipts is weakened when an employee who receives customer mail receipts also
   (*a*) Prepares initial cash receipts records
   (*b*) Records credits to individual accounts receivable
   (*c*) Prepares bank deposit slips for all mail receipts
   (*d*) Maintains a petty cash fund
4. Which of the following activities would be *least* likely to strengthen a company's internal control?
   (*a*) Separating accounting from other financial operations
   (*b*) Maintaining insurance for fire and theft
   (*c*) Fixing responsibility for the performance of employee duties
   (*d*) Carefully selecting and training employees

8–31. **INTERNAL CONTROL IN A SMALL COMPANY.** Briefly specify (in one page or less) the possible areas where internal controls should be installed in Ricco's Speedy Messages, described briefly below. Be sure that your suggested controls are feasible for a company of this size and type. Make any reasonable assumptions about management duties and policies not expressly set forth below.

Sophia Ricco owns and operates a fast-growing messenger service in Philadelphia. Currently she has ten messengers riding bicycles or motor scooters. Each messenger makes about 40 stops a day to either pick up or deliver a letter or small parcel. Messengers who pick up a message either deliver it themselves if it is in or near their territory, or they bring it back to "operations central," where another messenger picks it up and delivers it. Delivery within six business hours is guaranteed, and an extra fee will guarantee two-hour delivery.

Customers generally pay the messengers when a message is picked up, although a few regular customers are granted credit. Such customers simply sign an invoice when the message is picked up, and they are billed weekly. Each messenger submits cash and checks to operations central at least twice a day. The company's policy is to avoid having any messenger carry over $200 in cash.

Three dispatchers work at operations central. Part-time help is hired when more messengers or dispatchers are needed. Sophia supervises activities at operations central, and she has one bookkeeper/accountant and a secretary. Messengers are paid weekly based on miles covered and messages delivered. Employees at operations central are paid on a straight hourly basis.

8–32. ASSIGNMENT OF DUTIES. The Cyclometric Corporation is a distributor of several popular lines of drawing and measuring instruments. It purchases merchandise from several suppliers and sells to hundreds of retail stores. Here is a *partial list* of the company's necessary office routines:

1. Daily sorting of incoming mail into items that contain money and items that do not
2. Distributing the above mail: money to cashier, reports of money received to accounting department, and remainder to various appropriate offices
3. Making daily bank deposits
4. Reconciling monthly bank statements
5. Verifying and comparing related purchase documents: purchase orders, purchase invoices, receiving reports, etc.
6. Preparing vouchers for cash disbursements and attaching supporting purchase documents
7. Signing above vouchers to authorize payment (after examining vouchers with attached documents)
8. Preparing checks for above
9. Signing checks (after examining voucher authorization and supporting documents)
10. Mailing checks

The company's chief financial officer has decided that no more than five different people will handle all of these routines, including himself as necessary.

Required: Prepare a chart to show how these operations should be assigned to the five employees, including the chief financial officer. Use a line for each of the numbered routines and a column for each employee: Financial Officer, A, B, C, D. Place a check mark for each line in one or more of the columns. Observe the rules of the textbook checklist for internal control, especially separation of duties.

8–33. MULTIPLE CHOICE; DISCOVERING IRREGULARITIES. In questions 1 through 4, you are given a well-recognized procedure of internal control. You are to identify the irregularity *that will be discovered or prevented by each procedure*. Write the numbers 1 through 4 on your answer sheet. Then place the letter of your chosen answer next to your numbers.

1. The general-ledger control account and the subsidiary ledger of Accounts Receivable are reconciled monthly. The two bookkeepers are independent.
   (*a*) The Accounts Receivable subsidiary-ledger bookkeeper charges a sale to Mr. Smith instead of Mr. Smithe (that is, the wrong customer). The error is due to misreading the sales slip.
   (*b*) The Accounts Receivable subsidiary-ledger bookkeeper charges a customer with $72 instead of $74, the correct amount. The error is due to misreading the sales slip. The credit-sales summary for the day has the correct amount of $74.
   (*c*) The employee opening mail abstracts funds without making a record of their receipt. Customer accounts are not credited with their payments.
   (*d*) The general-ledger bookkeeper takes funds and covers the loss by charging "Miscellaneous General Expenses."
   (*e*) When friends purchase merchandise, the salesclerk allows them an employee discount by using an employee name on the sales slip and deducting the discount on the slip. This is against company policy.
2. Both cash and credit customers are educated to expect a sales ticket. Tickets are serially numbered. All numbers are accounted for daily.
   (*a*) Customers complain that their monthly bills contain items that have already been paid.
   (*b*) Some customers have the correct change for the merchandise purchased. They pay and do not wait for a sales ticket.
   (*c*) Customers complain that they are billed for goods they did not purchase.
   (*d*) Salesclerks destroy duplicate sales tickets for the amount of cash stolen.
   (*e*) Customers complain that goods ordered are not received.

3. The storekeeper should sign a receipt for goods received from the receiving and inspection room, and no payment should be made without the storekeeper's signature.
   (a) Employees send through fictitious invoices and receive payment.
   (b) Invoices are paid twice.
   (c) Materials are withdrawn from the storeroom for personal use rather than for business purposes.
   (d) The storekeeper takes materials and charges them to company use.
   (e) Employees send through purchase requisitions for materials for personal use. After the materials are received and receiving reports have been issued, employees take the merchandise for personal use.

4. At a movie theater box office, all tickets are prenumbered. At the end of each day, the beginning ticket number is subtracted from the ending number to give the number of tickets sold. Cash is counted and compared with the number of tickets sold:
   (a) The ticket taker admits his friends without a ticket.
   (b) The manager gives theater passes for personal expenses. This is against company policy.
   (c) The box office gives too much change.
   (d) A test check of customers entering the theater does not reconcile with ticket sales.
   (e) Tickets from a previous day are discovered in the ticket taker's stub box despite the fact that tickets are stamped "Good on Date of Purchase Only."

8–34. **BANK RECONCILIATION.** The Killebrew Company reconciled its bank statement as of October 31, 19X5. Two checks were outstanding: #411 for $60, and #422 for $44. The bank statement for November follows:

KILLEBREW COMPANY
Statement of Account with Crown National Bank

DATE 19X5	CHECKS	DEPOSITS	BALANCE
Oct. 31	Balance		$1,600.00
Nov. 2	1,300.00		300.00
4	44.00		256.00
15	467.00	1,600.00	1,389.00
17	300.00 NSF		1,089.00
23	64.00		1,025.00
24	512.00		513.00
25	90.00		423.00
28		490.00 CM	913.00
30	20.00 SC		893.00

Code:
EC—error correction
NSF—not sufficient funds

SC—service charge
DM—debit memo
CM—credit memo

Killebrew Company's cash records for November show:

CASH RECEIPTS		CASH DISBURSEMENTS	
DATE	CASH DR.	CHECK #	CASH CR.
Nov. 12	1,600.00	435	1,300.00
Nov. 30	750.00	436	467.00
	2,350.00	437	512.00
		438	89.00
		439	64.00
		440	90.00
			2,522.00

CASH LEDGER ACCOUNT

DATE	DEBIT	CREDIT	BALANCE
Oct. 31			1,496.00
Nov. 17		300.00	1,196.00
Nov. 30	2,350.00		3,546.00
Nov. 30		2,522.00	1,024.00

The $300 NSF check returned by the bank on November 17 has already been recorded by a journal entry on Killebrew Company's books. Included with the bank statement was a credit memorandum indicating that the bank had collected a $500 note receivable for Killebrew Company, charged a $10 collection fee, and credited the remainder to the account.

Required:

1. Prepare a November 30 bank reconciliation that arrives at two equal figures for the adjusted balance.
2. Make journal entries (without explanation) to adjust the book balance of cash to the reconciled balance.

8–35. STRAIGHTFORWARD BANK RECONCILIATION. On February 28, 19X1, the town of Eagle Harbor had a cash balance of $30,000 in its books. Its account at King County Bank also showed $30,000 that day. The following transactions occurred during March:

DATE	CHECK NUMBER	AMOUNT	EXPLANATION
3/1	492	$10,000	Payment of previously billed consulting fee
3/6	493	8,000	Payment of accounts payable
3/10		12,000	Collection of taxes receivable
3/14	494	14,000	Acquisition of equipment for cash
3/17		16,000	Collection of license fees receivable
3/28	495	9,000	Payment of accounts payable
3/30	496	21,000	Payment of interest on municipal bonds
3/31		26,000	Collection of taxes receivable

All cash receipts are deposited via a night depository system after the close of the municipal business day. Therefore the receipts are not recorded by the bank until the succeeding day.

On March 31, the bank charged Eagle Harbor $100 for miscellaneous bank services.

Required:

1. Prepare the journal entries on the bank's books for check 493 and deposit of March 10.
2. Prepare the journal entries for all March transactions on the books of Eagle Harbor.
3. Post all transactions for March to T-accounts for the town's Cash in Bank account and the bank's Deposits account. Assume that only checks 492–494 have been presented to the bank in March, each taking four days to clear the bank's records.
4. Prepare a bank reconciliation for Eagle Harbor, March 31, 19X1. The final three Eagle Harbor transactions of March had not affected the bank's records as of March 31. What adjusting entry in the books of the town of Eagle Harbor is required on March 31?
5. What would be the cash balance shown on the balance sheet of the town of Eagle Harbor on March 31, 19X1?

8–36. SEMICOMPLEX BANK RECONCILIATION. Jenny Garfield has a personal bank account at American Marine Bank. Her employer deposits her weekly paycheck automatically each Friday. Garfield's check register (checkbook) for July is summarized as follows:

Reconciled cash balance, June 30, 19X1			$100
Additions:			
Weekly payroll deposits:	July		
	3		800
	10		800
	17		800
	24		800
Deposit of check received for gambling debt	25		600
Deposit of check received as winner of cereal contest	31		400
Subtotal			$4,300
Deductions:			
Checks written #725–#739	1–23	$3,300	
Check 740	26	70	
Check 741	30	90	
Check 742	31	340	3,800
Cash in bank, July 31, 19X1			$ 500

The bank statement is summarized in Exhibit 8–11. Note the code at the bottom of the exhibit, which explains the transactions on the bank's books. The check deposited on July 25 bounced.

EXHIBIT 8–11

Bank Statement of Deposit Account, Jenny Garfield

CHECKS AND OTHER CHARGES		DEPOSITS	DATE	BALANCE
			6/30	100 BF
#725–739 various dates		800 AP	7/3	900
in July. These would		800 AP	7/10	1,700
be shown by specific		800 AP	7/17	2,500
amounts, but are shown		800 AP	7/24	3,300
here as a total:	3,300		7/24	0
		600	7/25	600
	70		7/27	530
	600 NSF		7/28	80 OD
	10 RC			
		200 AL	7/28	120
		800 AP	7/31	920
	15 MA		7/31	905

AL—automatic loan*
AP—automatic deposit from employee payroll
BF—balance brought forward
MA—monthly activity charge

NSF—returned check
OD—overdraft
RC—returned check charge

* By prearrangement with Garfield, the bank automatically lends sufficient amounts (in multiples of $100) to ensure that her balance is never less than $100.

1. Prepare Garfield's bank reconciliation, July 31, 19X1.
2. Assume that Garfield keeps a personal set of books on the accrual basis. Prepare the compound journal entry called for by the bank reconciliation.

8–37. BANK RECONCILIATION WITH MULTIPLE ERROR CORRECTIONS. An accountant of Hill Building Materials Company has compared its July 19X5 cash-in-bank transactions with the July bank statement of Lester Prairie Bank, a newly formed bank with inexperienced clerical personnel. The bookkeeper's findings are summarized as follows:

Balances, July 31:	
Cash account on Hill's books	$2,545 Dr.
Hill Co. deposit account on bank's books	$5,130 Cr.

a. Bank service charges of $25 for July have not yet been recorded by Hill.
b. Hill's $1,200 deposit of July 31 was not recorded by the bank until August 2.
c. A July 5 bank deposit of $575 by Hillman Co. was erroneously credited by the bank to Hill Company.
d. Hill's $390 bank deposit of July 13 was erroneously credited by the bank to the Hillside Department Store account.
e. On July 25, Hill received a check from Jane Pittsfield, a customer, for $740, but the bookkeeper entered it as $640 in the cash receipts journal. However, when the check was deposited in the bank, it was processed correctly by Hill Company and Lester Prairie Bank.
f. Hilton Company's check to the IRS for $150 was erroneously charged by the bank to the Hill Company account on July 3.
g. Hill's bank deposit of July 19 for $540 was erroneously recorded by the bank as $450.
h. Hill's check #801 to City Utility Co. for $490 was erroneously charged on the bank statement as $940.
i. Hill's check #792 to Ali Oil Co. for $310 was erroneously charged by the bank to the Hiller's Tavern account.
j. A $530 check received on account by Hill on July 26 from Dedman Beet, a customer, was deposited in the Lester Prairie Bank on the same day. However, on July 31 it was returned to Hill by the bank because of insufficient funds on deposit in Beet's bank account. No entry was made by Hill for the return.
k. Hill's monthly payment to S. W. Bell Co. for telephone service was $1,030 (check #793). However, the check was erroneously recorded as $1,300 in Hill's cash disbursements journal.
l. Outstanding Hill Company checks at July 31 total $4,165:

#811	$125	#821	$1,900
#815	$ 80	#822	$ 650
#820	$910	#823	$ 500

Assume that no adjustments or corrections have been made for errors or for transactions not yet recorded on Hill Company books. Prepare

1. Hill Company's bank reconciliation statement that arrives at two equal figures for the corrected balance of cash in bank at July 31, 19X5
2. Hill Company's journal entries to correct and adjust its cash account at July 31

8–38. PETTY CASH FUND. (Alternates are 8–39 and 8–50.) On August 1, 19X7, the treasurer of DeCostella Company established an imprest petty cash fund of $230 by writing a check on the company's regular bank account payable to "Cash." This check was cashed by the office receptionist, who became responsible for the fund. On August 30, there was cash of $123 in the fund along with petty cash "vouchers" (signed receipts for disbursements) as follows: airport limousine fares, $22; postage, $13; office supplies, $35; delivery charges for incoming merchandise, $17; and "supper money" for two secretaries who worked late, $20.

Required:

1. Prepare journal entries for (a) creation of the petty cash fund and (b) reimbursement of the fund on August 31 for the payments made from it.
2. Assume that the petty cash fund had been replenished on August 31. Where would its balance appear in the financial statements?
3. Suppose the cash balance in the fund had been only $118 instead of $123 just before its replenishment. Comment briefly.
4. Suppose that sometime in December 19X7 the treasurer decided to decrease the fund to $180. Prepare the journal entry for the transaction.

8–39. **IMPREST PETTY CASH.** (Alternates are 8–38 and 8–50.) For several years, North Slope Oil Co. has maintained an imprest petty cash fund of $100. When $80 of miscellaneous expense receipts were reimbursed, the company's new bookkeeper made the following entry:

Petty cash fund	80	
Cash in bank		80

The following day was the last day of the company's fiscal year. The books were closed, and the financial statements were prepared.

Required:

1. Explain the effects of the entry on the financial statements. Assume a 40% income tax rate. Be specific.
2. If you had been aware of the entry before the books were closed, what correcting entry, if any, would you have recommended?

8–40. **INVENTORY SHRINKAGE.** José Banaag, owner of Village Auto Parts, was concerned about his control of inventory. In December 19X3, he installed a computerized perpetual inventory system. In April, his accountant brought him the following information for the first three months of 19X4:

Sales	$350,000
Cost of goods sold	285,000
Beginning inventory (per physical count)	50,000
Merchandise purchases	315,000

José had asked his public accounting firm to conduct a physical count of inventory on April 1. The CPAs reported inventory of $45,000.

Required:

1. Compute the ending inventory shown in the books by the new perpetual inventory system.
2. Provide the journal entry to reconcile the book inventory with the physical count. What is the corrected cost of goods sold for the first three months of 19X4?
3. Do your calculations point out areas about which José should be concerned? Why?

8–41. **RETAIL METHOD AND INTERNAL CONTROL.** Study Appendix 8A. The following figures pertain to the Zenith Gift Store for the two-month period November and December, 19X8:

Sales	$170,000	Purchases (at sales price)	$ 80,000
Additional markups	10,000	Inventory at November 1,	
Markdowns	25,000	19X8:	
Purchases (at cost price)	52,000	At cost price	105,000
		At selling price	160,000

Required:

1. What should be the inventory amount at December 31, 19X8, at retail price using the conventional retail inventory method?
2. Suppose the allowable shrinkage is 2% of sales. The physical inventory at retail prices at December 31 amounts to $50,000. What is the excess inventory shrinkage?

8–42. COST TO RETAIL VALUE. Study Appendix 8A. Refer to the preceding problem. Compute Zenith Gift Store's ratio of cost to retail value. Compute the cost value of the ending inventory for inclusion in the financial statements.

8–43. RETAIL METHOD AND INVENTORY SHRINKAGE (suggested by W. Crum). Study Appendix 8A. The following data are for a ladies clothing department in a large department store at retail selling prices:

Net sales	$1,900,000	Transfers in from other	
Discounts granted to		branches	$30,000
employees, churches, etc.	23,500	Transfers out to other	
Beginning inventory	900,000	branches	12,000
Net purchases	2,068,000	Additional markups	14,000
		Markdowns	79,000

Required:

1. What should be the ending inventory at retail prices using the conventional retail inventory method and assuming no allowances for losses (shrinkage)?
2. Suppose the estimated shrinkage is 1% of sales. What should be the ending inventory at retail prices? Suppose the cost ratio is 62%—that is, the *cost* of the ending inventory is approximated at 62% of retail price. What should be the ending inventory at cost? Again, assume 1% shrinkage.
3. The actual ending physical inventory at retail is $950,000. What is the total shrinkage at retail? At cost? Prepare a section of the income statement through gross profit on sales. Assume that beginning inventory at cost was $580,000 and that applicable net purchases (including transfer effects) at cost were $1,-280,000.

8–44. CONTROL OF RETAIL INVENTORY. Study Appendix 8A. Central Sports, Inc., a large retail sporting goods store, reported an ending inventory of merchandise that seemed significantly smaller than usual despite no apparent deviations from the usual amounts of beginning inventory, purchases, and sales. Employee theft was suspected. Reported data included:

Beginning inventory:		Sales	$200,000
At cost prices	$ 55,000	Additional markups	5,000
At retail prices	110,000	Markdowns	25,000
Purchases:		Ending physical	
At cost prices	110,000	inventory, retail	98,700
At retail prices	210,000		

The company's auditing department discovered that the supplementary merchandise records showed an arithmetically incorrect total for purchases at retail prices. The correct total is $220,000.

1. Use the uncorrected data and assume that the allowable inventory shrinkage is 0.4% of sales. Compute the apparent inventory shortage.
2. Compute the apparent inventory shortage by using the corrected figure for purchases at retail prices.
3. Assume that the arithmetical error in determining the total purchases at retail prices had been deliberately committed to conceal a merchandise theft of an equal amount. Using a ratio of cost to retail value of 65%, compute the estimated cost of the inventory that may have been stolen.
4. See the chapter checklist of internal control. Briefly explain what precautions should be used to forestall such a theft and its concealment by employees.

8–45. SPECIAL JOURNALS. (Alternate is 8–46.) Study Appendix 8B. Colonial Products Company uses the periodic inventory system and the following journals with their indicated current page numbers and amount columns:

General journal (page 8): two columns, debit and credit
Sales journal (page 18): single amount column
Purchases journal (page 14): single amount column
Cash receipts journal (page 24): debit columns for Cash and for Sales Discounts: credit columns for Sales, Accounts Receivable, and Other Accounts
Cash payments journal (page 84): credit columns for Cash and for Purchase Discounts; debit columns for Purchases, Accounts Payable, and Other Accounts

The general ledger accounts needed for this problem are shown below with their account numbers and August 1, 19X1, balances, if any:

Cash (11)	$ 2,000	
Accounts receivable (26)	12,000	
Office supplies (30)	1,000	
Office equipment (44)	14,000	
Accounts payable (82)		$ 8,000
Notes payable (83)		
Sales (142)		
Sales returns and allowances (143)		
Sales discounts (144)		
Purchases (162)		
Purchase returns and allowances (163)		
Purchase discounts (164)		
All other accounts	31,000	52,000
Total	$60,000	$60,000

The subsidiary ledger accounts needed and their August 1 balances, if any, are:

Accounts receivable:
  Alberto Co.
  Barry & Thomas
. Davidson, Inc.
  Weldell Bros. $12,000
    debit balance

Accounts payable:
  Austin Corp.
  King & King
  Raleigh Co.
  Sydney, Inc.
  Urban Stores, Inc., $8,000
    credit balance

Note that Colonial Products Company uses the periodic inventory system, not the perpetual inventory system. All merchandise bought is debited to the Purchases account. The cost of goods sold is determined only at the end of the period when the physical inventory is measured (not required in this problem).

1. Set up journals and ledgers, entering beginning account balances, if any.
2. Enter the transactions described below in the appropriate journals.
3. Post amounts from all journals to T-accounts, showing details: dates, account numbers, and posting references.
4. Take a trial balance of the general ledger at August 31.
5. Prepare schedules of the two subsidiary ledgers to prove their agreement with the controlling accounts at August 31.

Transactions:

Aug. 1 Sold merchandise to Alberto Co. for $6,000, terms 2/10, n/30, invoice number 913.

2 Purchased merchandise from Austin Corp., $4,000, terms 1/10, n/30.

3 Purchased office supplies from Wide Co. for cash, $200, check number 209.

4 Sold merchandise to Barry & Thomas, $8,000, terms 2/10, n/30, invoice number 914.

5 Purchased merchandise from Sydney, Inc., $5,000, terms 1/10, n/30.

6 Received cash to settle Alberto Co. invoice 913, less 2% cash discount. (Use only one line for this entry in the cash receipts journal.)

*8 Purchased office equipment from King & King for $3,600, terms n/30.

10 Sold merchandise to Davidson, Inc., $10,000, terms 2/10, n/30, invoice number 915.

12 Issued check number 210 to Austin Corp. to pay for August 2 purchase less 1% cash discount. (Use only one line for this entry in the cash payments journal.)

13 Cash sales of merchandise, $1,200.

15 Issued check number 211 to Rank Co. for cash purchase of merchandise, $1,600.

19 Purchased merchandise from Raleigh Co., $3,600, terms 2/10, n/30.

22 Borrowed $12,000 for ninety days from Capital Bank at 12% interest to be paid at due date of note.

*25 Issued credit memo number 98 for $400 to Barry & Thomas for unsatisfactory merchandise sold August 4.

*27 Received credit memo number 1003 for $600 from Sydney, Inc., for unsatisfactory merchandise purchased August 5.

---

* These transactions are to be entered in the general journal. Be sure to post the debit and credit amounts for receivables and payables to the subsidiary ledger accounts as well as to the related controlling accounts.

8-46. SPECIAL JOURNALS. (Alternate is 8-45.) Study Appendix 8B. The London Trading Company uses a sales journal (journal page 42), a purchases journal (page 74), a cash receipts journal (page 63), a cash disbursements journal (page 81), and a general journal (page 19). It has a general ledger and subsidiary ledgers for accounts receivable and accounts payable. For simplicity, only a few transactions of each kind are illustrated on the following page. Moreover, the beginning balances of the pertinent accounts are not given, nor are they necessary for the purposes of this problem. The currency is British pounds, £.

The numbers of some pertinent accounts are:

Cash	No. 10					
Accounts receivable	30					
Allowance for bad debts	32					
Merchandise inventory	50					
Accounts payable	70					
Notes payable	75					
Property taxes payable	77					
Paid-in capital	80					
Sales	90					
Advertising expense	97					
Bad debts expense	99					

Consider the following list of transactions.

List of Transactions for Problem 8–46

JULY	DESCRIPTION	INVOICE DATE	INVOICE NO.	TERMS	CHECK NO.	AMOUNT
2	Cash sales	—	—	—	—	£2,000
3	Credit sale to Martin	—	319	n30	—	1,400
5	Purchase of merchandise from Riggs	7/3	—	n30	—	2,200
6	Cash purchase of merchandise from Krueger	—	—	—	42	1,100
8	Collection of Invoice 319	—	—	—	—	1,400
10	Credit sale to Ramos	—	320	n30	—	2,800
11	Purchase of merchandise from Ryan	7/10	—	n10	—	2,900
12	Payment of Riggs invoice	—	—	—	43	2,200
13	Cash sales	—	—	—	—	1,900
14	Purchase of merchandise from Gates	7/12	—	n15	—	3,000
15	Payment of City of Hyde property taxes (set up previously as a payable)	—	—	—	44	3,200
16	Credit sale to Haynes	—	321	n30	—	1,800
18	Cash purchase of merchandise from Saucedo	—	—	—	45	500
19	Payment of Ryan invoice	—	—	—	46	2,900
20	Collection of Invoice 321	—	—	—	—	1,800
21	Purchase of merchandise from Goldman	7/19	—	n15	—	1,100
23	Credit sale to Lenz	—	322	n30	—	900
24	Cash sales	—	—	—	—	2,000
25	Advertising for cash to Tribune	—	—	—	47	700
26	Borrowed from bank, 60-day loan	—	—	—	—	5,000
27	Purchase of merchandise from Hunter	7/26	—	n30	—	3,800
28	Cash sales	—	—	—	—	2,500
28	Payment of Gates invoice	—	—	—	48	3,000
29	Credit sale to Holford	—	323	n30	—	600
31	Sale of additional common stock for cash	—	—	—	—	10,000
31	Addition to allowance for uncollectible accounts	—	—	—	—	100

1. Journalize the transactions for July, using the appropriate journals.
2. Post the effects of the transactions to the general and subsidiary ledgers (exclude the subsidiary ledger for merchandise inventory). Show posting details such as dates and account numbers.
3. Prepare a listing of subsidiary ledger balances. Make sure that their totals agree with the related general ledger accounts.
4. Suppose a voucher system were employed by the London Trading Company. Describe in detail how the special journals in requirement 1 would be affected.

☐ Understanding Published Financial Reports

8-47. APPRAISAL OF INTERNAL CONTROL SYSTEM. From the *San Francisco Chronicle*:

☐ The flap over missing ferry fares was peacefully—and openly—resolved at a meeting of the Golden Gate Bridge District finance committee yesterday.

☐ Only a week ago, the subject was a matter of furious dispute in which bridge manager Dale W. Luehring was twice called a liar and there were prospects of a closed meeting on personnel matters.

☐ But yesterday, after a week of investigation, the meeting turned out to be public after all, and attorney Thomas M. Jenkins revealed the full total of stolen ferry tickets equaled $26.20.

☐ The controversy began when auditor Gordon Dahlgren complained that there was an auditing "problem" and that he had not been informed when four children swiped $13.75 worth of tickets February 28. Committee chairman Ben K. Lerer, of San Francisco, ordered a full investigation.

☐ Jenkins said the situation was complicated because children under 5 have been allowed to ride the ferry without a ticket, but after May 1 everyone will have to have a ticket, allowing for a closer audit.

☐ Secondly, Jenkins explained, the "vault" in which tickets are deposited was proved insecure (resulting in two thefts totaling $26.20 worth of tickets) but has been replaced.

☐ In the future, it was decided, all thefts of cash or tickets must be reported immediately to the California Highway Patrol or the local police, the bridge lieutenant on duty, the general manager, the security officer, the auditor-controller, and the transit manager.

☐ In addition, employees must make a full written report within 24 hours to the president of the district board, the chairman of the finance-auditing committee, the auditor controller, the attorney, the bus transit manager, the water transit manager, the toll captain, and the chief of administration and security.

What is your reaction to the new system? Explain, giving particular attention to applicable criteria for appraising an internal control system.

8-48. STATE AND COUNTY FAIRS. Nonprofit entities take various forms. For example, state and county fairs are usually important sources of revenue because the state gets a percentage of the bets made on horse races. In past years, the carnivals would bid for the rights to appear at the fair. The winner would be willing to pay the fairs a higher percentage of some measure of its revenue generated from rides, games, and food booths.

What types of major internal control problems arise from such percentage revenue agreements? Which item or items of the chapter checklist of internal control seem most critical in these cases?

8–49. AUDIT COMMITTEE ROLE. In a recent court decision, an American corporation was required to delegate certain responsibilities to its audit committee, management being required to

1. Consult with its independent auditors before deciding any significant or material accounting question or policy
2. Retain independent auditors to perform quarterly reviews of all financial statements prior to public issuance
3. Conduct internal audits, with personnel reporting directly to the audit committee (internal auditors must report to the audit committee quarterly)
4. Retain or dismiss independent and internal auditors
5. Consult with the independent auditors on their quarterly reviews of financial statements
6. Review all monthly corporate and division financial statements and the auditor's management letter
7. Receive quarterly reports from independent auditors on internal control deficiencies
8. Review and approve all reports to shareholders and the SEC before dissemination

The court also ruled that the audit committee must be composed of at least three outside directors who have no business dealings with the firm other than directors' fees and expense reimbursements.

Required:

a. Prepare a partial corporation organization chart to depict these requirements. Use boxes only for Audit Committee, Independent Auditors, Internal Auditing, Finance Vice-President, and Board of Directors. Connect the appropriate boxes with lines: solid lines for direct responsibility, dashed lines for information and communication. Place numbers on these lines to correspond to the eight items specified by the court decision.
b. Identify the main elements of the chapter checklist of internal control that seem most relevant to this system design.

8–50. IMPREST PETTY CASH. (Alternates are 8–38 and 8–39.) The Stanford Business School created an imprest petty cash fund of $150 on January 2.

During January the following outlays were made from petty cash:

Auto mileage at 20¢ per mile for secretary to deliver documents to alumini office in San Francisco, round trip 80 miles	$16.00
Dinner allowance for mail clerk working overtime	9.00
Postal charges for insuring mail	14.50
Payments to delivery personnel	22.40
Purchase of special posters	12.75
Total	$74.65

Required:

Prepare journal entries for

1. Creation of the fund on January 2
2. Replenishment of the fund on January 31
3. Reduction of the fund from $150 to $100 on February 15

8–51. BANK SERVICE CHARGES. *U.S. News and World Report* contained the following story on the sudden increase in bank fees: "Many banks are experimenting with a new pricing system for checking services. Philadelphia's Girard, for example, gives each depositor a monthly credit based on the average account balance. Each time a check is written, the bank subtracts 30 cents from the credit allowance. If the credit is exhausted, Girard collects as a service fee the difference between the initial credit and the total check charge."

Suppose a Kinney Shoe Store had a checking account at Girard. Its average account balance in March was $1,000. On April 1, Girard credited the Kinney account with 2% of the $1,000 average balance. It then charged Kinney 30 cents for each of the 100 checks written during April.

Required:

1. Prepare the probable journal entries Girard made for these transactions.
2. Prepare the probable journal entries on Kinney's books for these transactions.

8–52. BANK VERSUS BOOK RECORDS. The Mead Corporation, primarily a forest products company, lists the following among its current assets and current liabilities (in millions):

	JANUARY 1	
	1986	1985
As part of current assets:		
Cash and temporary cash investments	$ 17.9	$126.4
As part of current liabilities:		
Accounts payable:		
Trade	122.9	124.2
Affiliated companies	137.3	149.6
Outstanding checks	41.4	24.3

It is unusual to find a liability account labeled "Outstanding Checks."

Required:

1. Most companies have checks outstanding at any balance sheet date. Why is it unusual to have a liability for outstanding checks?
2. Suppose you examined the "Cash and Temporary Cash Investments" account in Mead's general ledger. What balance would you find for January 1, 1986? For January 1, 1985?
3. Why do you suppose Mead reported outstanding checks as a liability?

8–53. CASINO SKIMMING. An article in the *Wall Street Journal* reported that about $7 million in quarters disappeared from the slot machines of four casinos of Argent Corporation in an 18-month period. The coins weighed nearly 150 tons, and the odds against such a payout to players of the slot machines is one in 3,875,000,000,000,000,000,000,000,000,000,000,000,000,000,000,000—an extremely unlikely event, to say the least. The disappearance was part of the biggest known skim operation ever. *Skimming* is taking a portion of gambling revenues before they can be counted for tax purposes.

Internal control is especially important in casinos. Meters in the slot machines record the winnings paid to customers. Coins are taken immediately to the slot counting room when machines are emptied. In the counting rooms coins are weighed, and a portion is returned to the change booths.

Required:

What items in the chapter checklist of internal control seem especially important regarding slot machine operations? How could the money from slot machine operations have been stolen in such large amounts?

8–54. EMPLOYEE DISHONESTY. Consider the following newspaper reports of dishonesty:

a. At a small manufacturer, supervisors had access to time cards and gave out W-2 forms each year. The supervisors pocketed $80,000 a year in paychecks for phantom workers.
b. A manager at a busy branch office of a copying service had a receipt book of his own. Jobs of $200 and $300 were common. The manager stole cash by simply giving customers a receipt from his book instead of one of the company's numbered forms.

c. A purchasing agent received tiny kickbacks on buttons, zippers, and other trims used at a successful dress company. The agent got rich, and the company was overcharged $10 million.

Required: Specify what control or controls would have helped avoid each of the listed situations.

8–55. DISHONESTY AND GAMBLING. A news article reported about Ruth Mishkin, a trusted employee of the Communications Group, a public relations firm in Boca Raton, Florida. She had worked nine years for the company. Her bosses had put her in charge of paying bills, balancing bank accounts, and handling other cash management chores.

When Mishkin took a sick leave, the company discovered that she had been taking company funds for years. In all, the 60-year-old widow allegedly stole about $320,000 to feed a gambling habit. The president of the company was quoted as saying, "We thought she was just playing cards with the girls."

Incidents such as this highlight weaknesses in internal controls, and preventive steps are often taken only after a crime has been committed.

Required: What internal controls would have deterred Mishkin from the thievery? What internal controls would have helped the Communications Group to detect the theft at an earlier date?

8–56. PRESSURE FOR PROFITS. The *Wall Street Journal* stated that "Datapoint Corp. reported its first quarterly loss in nearly a decade, partly reflecting the reversal of about $15 million in revenue generated in previous quarters by questionable sales practices." Datapoint is a maker of small computer systems and telecommunications equipment.

The news report stated that Datapoint was trying to explain the unusually high rate of product returns in recent months, and this led to an investigation of the sales practices of its domestic marketing division. Current and former Datapoint employees asserted that certain marketing officials were determined to continue a string of record profit that had lasted 39 quarters. The officials resorted to increasingly questionable practices of recording revenue. Their methods eventually backfired.

The practices included shipping computer equipment to customers who had not met Datapoint's credit requirements, executives using their own money to pay warehousing fees so that distributors would accept shipments they did not have room for, and, in one instance, shipping to an imaginary customer "just to get a shipment out the door and revenue logged."

Required: On what specific items on the checklist of internal control should Datapoint concentrate to prevent a recurrence of these questionable marketing practices?

8–57. CHEATING ON INVENTORIES. The *Wall Street Journal* reported: "Cheating on inventories is a common way for small business to chisel on their income taxes. . . . A New York garment maker, for example, evades a sizable amount of income tax by undervaluing his firm's inventory by 20 percent on his tax return. He hides about $500,000 out of a $2.5 million inventory."

The news story concluded: "When it's time to borrow, business owners generally want profits and assets to look fat." The garment maker uses a different fiscal period for financial statements to his bank: "After writing down the inventory as of Dec. 31, he writes it up six months later when the fiscal year ends. In this way, he underpays the IRS and impresses his banker. Some describe that kind of inventory accounting as WIFL—Whatever I Feel Like."

Required: **1.** At a 40% income tax rate, what amount of income taxes would the owner evade according to the news story?

INTERNAL CONTROL, CASH, AND SPECIAL JOURNALS

2. Consider the next year. By how much would the ending inventory have to be understated to evade the same amount of income taxes?

Use the following table and fill in the blanks:

| | HONEST REPORTING | | DISHONEST REPORTING | |
	First Year	Second Year	First Year	Second Year
	(in dollars)			
Beginning inventory	3,000,000	?	3,000,000	?
Purchases	10,000,000	10,000,000	10,000,000	10,000,000
Available for sale	13,000,000	?	13,000,000	?
Ending inventory	2,500,000	2,500,000	2,000,000	?
Cost of goods sold	10,500,000	?	11,000,000	?
Income tax savings @ 40%*	4,200,000	?	?	?
Income tax savings for two years together		?		?

* This is the income tax effect of only the cost of goods sold. To shorten and simplify the analysis, sales and operating expenses are assumed to be the same each year.

8–58. RETAIL METHOD AND INVENTORY SHRINKAGE. Study Appendix 8A. Safeway Stores is a large food chain. Its 1986 sales exceeded $20 billion. Safeway uses the retail method of inventory control for many parts of its operations. Suppose the following data pertain to the grocery department of one of its stores for a given period (at retail prices):

Beginning inventory	$200,000	Sales	$1,040,000
Markups	30,000	Purchases	1,020,000
Markdowns	50,000		

Required:

1. Using the retail inventory method, compute the retail value of the ending inventory (in accordance with the given data).
2. Suppose the allowable shrinkage is 1% of sales. The physical inventory at retail prices at December 31 amounts to $142,000. Compute the excess shrinkage.
3. Consider the following additional data (at cost): beginning inventory, $150,000; purchases, $690,000. Compute the ratio of cost to retail value. Compute the cost value of the ending inventory for inclusion in the financial statements.

8–59. MANIPULATION OF PROFITS. Throughout the 1970s, H. J. Heinz Company had a publicly stated objective: to seek an increase in earnings at a steady and consistent rate. For example, the Heinz 1978 annual report said: ". . . the annual compound growth rate has been 11.7% for the past 10 years and 14.0% for the past five years, which is consistent with the company's financial objectives for a compound growth rate in earnings per share of 10% to 12% per year."

In 1979, Heinz disclosed that several managers had engaged in "profit-switching" practices since 1972. These practices resulted in the improper transfer of $16.4 million in pretax income to fiscal 1979 from prior years. A news story reported that "the intent of the practices was to smooth out earnings increases to create the appearance of consistent, orderly growth."

For your information, "profit-switching" and "improper transfer" refer to keeping records so that profits that appropriately belong in one reporting period are actually reported in a different reporting period.

Given this description, were any assets stolen by management? Identify at least one way to falsely defer profit to a future period. What feature in the chapter checklist of internal control is aimed at preventing the practice you describe?

8–60. COOKING THE BOOKS. In *The Accounting Wars* (Macmillan, 1985), author Mark Stevens presents a chapter on "Book Cooking, Number Juggling, and Other Tricks of the Trade." He quotes Glen Perry, a former chief accountant of the SEC's Enforcement Division: "Companies play games with their financial reports for any number of reasons, the most common being the intense pressure on corporate management to produce an unbroken stream of increasing earnings reports." Stevens then lists Perry's "terrible ten of accounting frauds—ploys used to misrepresent corporate financial statements":

1. Recognition of revenues before they are realized
2. Recognition of rentals to customers as sales
3. Inclusion of fictitious amounts in inventories
4. Improper cutoffs at year-end
5. Improper application of LIFO
6. Creation of fraudulent year-end transactions to boost earnings
7. Failure to recognize losses through write-offs and allowances
8. Inconsistent accounting practices without disclosures
9. Capitalization or improper deferral of expenses
10 Inclusion of unusual gains in operating income

Suppose you were a division manager in a major corporation. Briefly explain how you could use each of the ten methods to manipulate income. Be specific.

Chapter 9

LONG-LIVED ASSETS
AND DEPRECIATION

LEARNING OBJECTIVES

After studying this chapter, you should be able to

1. Define and explain depreciation and show how it relates to income measurement, income taxes, and cash balances
2. Define, compute, and compare some typical depreciation methods
3. Explain how gains and losses on sales of fixed assets are computed and presented in financial statements
4. Contrast between accounting for repairs, maintenance, and improvements
5. Define and explain depletion and amortization
6. Define *intangible assets* and explain how they are accounted for regarding both shareholder purposes and income tax purposes

Cost of goods sold and depreciation expense are the two most widely encountered and debated items on an income statement. Chapter 7 emphasized FIFO, LIFO, and other ways of computing cost of goods sold. This chapter emphasizes various ways of computing depreciation as well as similar items like depletion and amortization.

This chapter considers some major assets, such as land, buildings, equipment, natural resources, and patents. These resources are often described as **long-lived assets** because they are held for an extended time. A distinguishing feature of these assets is their underlying purpose: to facilitate the production and sale of goods or services to customers. That is, these assets by themselves are not available for sale in the ordinary course of business. Thus a delivery truck is a long-lived asset for nearly all companies; of course, a truck dealer would regard trucks as merchandise inventory.

During the 1970s and 1980s, much attention has been given to whether depreciation based on acquisition cost is an appropriate measure of expense. Critics have insisted that depreciation should be tied to current values instead. These issues are covered in Chapter 14 rather than here. This chapter discusses depreciation under a historical-cost accounting system.

GENERAL PERSPECTIVE

With the exception of land, the acquisition costs of all long-lived assets are typically charged to expense over a period of years in some systematic way. As Exhibit 9–1 shows, such expenses are called depreciation, depletion, or amortization, depending on the asset in question.

Summary of Accounting for Long-Lived Assets

BALANCE SHEET	INCOME STATEMENT
Land	—
Buildings and equipment ———————————→	Depreciation
Natural resources ———————————→	Depletion
Intangible assets	
(for example, franchises or patents) ————→	Amortization

The word **amortization** is probably the most general in the sense that it means the systematic reduction of a lump-sum amount. Therefore there is nothing inherently wrong with using a single word such as *amortization* to describe the application of the *same fundamental idea* to various types of long-lived assets. However, it is customary to use three words, as shown in Exhibit 9–1.

How do you compute the acquisition cost of long-lived assets? How do you account for useful lives? Residual values? Gains or losses on disposition? Intervening changes in original estimates? This chapter explores these fundamental questions.

The major long-lived assets are often divided into tangible and intangible categories. Examples of tangible assets are land, natural resources, buildings, and equipment. **Tangible assets** are physical items that can be seen and touched. In contrast, **intangible assets** are rights or economic benefits that are not physical in nature. Examples are franchises, patents, trademarks, copyrights, and goodwill.

Tangible assets are often called **fixed assets** for brevity, but *plant assets* is more descriptive. Corporate annual reports generally use the following nomenclature, which is taken from the annual report of the American Telephone and Telegraph Company (AT&T):

AT&T COMPANY

Property, Plant, and Equipment:

(in millions)	AT JANUARY 1, 1986	1985
Land and improvements	$ 480.0	$ 452.6
Buildings and improvements	5,812.5	5,648.8
Machinery and electronic equipment	29,627.0	30,046.7
Transportation equipment, furniture, tools and other	2,742.8	2,359.7
Total property, plant, and equipment	38,662.3	38,507.8
Less: Accumulated depreciation	16,549.4	17,492.8
Property, plant, and equipment—net	$22,112.9	$21,015.0

Shareholders' reports often contain summarized data, as shown by AT&T. However, in the accounting records, accumulated depreciation and amortization are kept in great detail for various categories of plant and equipment.

LAND

The acquisition cost of all long-lived assets is their cash-equivalent purchase price, including incidental costs.

The cost of land includes charges to the purchaser for the cost of land surveys, legal fees, title fees, realtors' commissions, transfer taxes, and even the demolition costs of old structures that might be torn down to get the land ready for its intended use.

Land such as plant sites or building sites is ordinarily accounted for as a separate item. Under historical-cost accounting, land is carried indefinitely at its original cost. As a result, if land is held for many years of persistent inflation, its carrying amount is likely to be far below its current realizable value.

Should land acquired and held since 1932 be placed on a 1987 balance sheet at cost expressed in 1932 dollars? Accountants do exactly that. For example, Weyerhaeuser lists 5.9 million acres of land at $125 million (only $21 per acre). Many critics of accounting point to such extreme examples as illustrations of why the basic historical-cost framework of accounting deserves drastic overhauling. They claim that some type of accounting for inflation should be mandatory. This worrisome problem of inflation is discussed in Chapter 14.

BUILDINGS AND EQUIPMENT

☐ **Acquisition Cost**

The cost of buildings, plant, and equipment should include all costs of acquisition and preparation for use. Consider the following example for some used packaging equipment:

Invoice price, gross	$100,000
Deduct 2% cash discount for payment within 30 days	2,000
Invoice price, net	$ 98,000
State sales tax at 8% of $98,000	7,840
Transportation costs	3,000
Installation costs	8,000
Repair costs prior to use	7,000
Total acquisition cost	$123,840

The $123,840 would be the total "capitalized" cost added to the Equipment account. A cost is described as being "capitalized" when it is added to an asset account, as distinguished from being "expensed" immediately. Note that ordinary repair costs are expensed if incurred *after* the equipment is placed in use.

Generally accepted accounting principles usually regard interest cost as an expense. However, FASB *Statement No. 34* specifies that interest on expenditures during an extended construction period should be added to the acquisition cost of the fixed asset under construction. Suppose a $2 million plant was constructed over two years. If no construction payments were made before the plant was completed, no interest would be capitalized. However, suppose $1 million was paid at the end of the first year, and $1 million at completion. Assume the interest rate on recent borrowing was 12%. Interest of $1,000,000 × .12 = $120,000 would be part of the capitalized cost of the plant.

☐ Basket Purchases

Frequently, more than one type of long-lived asset is acquired for a single overall outlay. For instance, suppose land and a building were acquired for $1 million. The acquisition of two or more types of assets for a lump-sum cost is sometimes called a **basket purchase**. How much of the $1 million should be allocated to each? Invariably, the cost is allocated in proportion to some estimate of their relative sales values as separate items. For example, an appraiser or a tax assessor might indicate that the market value of the land is $480,000 and of the building is $720,000. The cost would be allocated as follows:

	(1) MARKET VALUE	(2) WEIGHTING	(3) TOTAL COST TO ALLOCATE	(2) × (3) ALLOCATED COSTS
Land	$ 480,000	480/1,200 (or 40%)	$1,000,000	$ 400,000
Building	720,000	720/1,200 (or 60%)	$1,000,000	600,000
Total	$1,200,000			$1,000,000

This problem of allocating a basket purchase cost to the individual assets is often extremely important.[1] Why? Because the useful lives of various assets differ. Consequently, the reported income might be affected considerably. The higher the cost allocated to land, the lower the cost of the depreciable assets, the lower the depreciation expense, and the higher the subsequent reported income. In our example, suppose the building bore an $800,000 cost instead of the $600,000 cost above. Then straight-line depreciation based on a twenty-year useful life and zero residual value could be $800,000 ÷ 20, or $40,000, instead of $600,000 ÷ 20, or $30,000.

However, if managers want to reduce their income tax outflows in earlier years, they would tend to take advantage of any doubts (within the bounds of the law) about relative market values by loading as much cost as possible on depreciable assets rather than on land.

☐ Depreciation in General

Fixed assets represent future services that will be used over a prolonged span of time. The major difficulties of measurement center on predicting useful lives, predicting residual values, and choosing whether to use a straight-line pattern of depreciation or some other pattern.

---

[1] The allocation of a lump-sum cost of a sports team, which includes player contracts, has been the subject of litigation between taxpayers and the Internal Revenue Service. Buyers want to allocate as much of the cost to player contracts as possible. Such contracts may be depreciated (amortized) for income tax purposes, but the sports franchise itself may not.

In particular, note that accountants regard depreciation as a process of *allocating the acquisition cost* to the particular periods or products that are related to the use of the assets. Depreciation is frequently misunderstood. It is *not* a process of *valuation*. In everyday use, we might say that an auto depreciates in value, meaning a decrease in its current market value. But to an accountant, depreciation is *not* a technique for approximating current values such as replacement costs or resale values. It is simply *cost allocation*.

The amount of the acquisition cost to be allocated over the total useful life of the asset as depreciation is the difference between the total acquisition cost and the predicted net residual value at the end of the asset's useful life. This difference is sometimes called the **depreciable value**. The ending **residual value** is also called **disposal value**, **salvage value**, **scrap value**, and *terminal value*.

The depreciation allocation to each year may be made on the basis of either time or service. The prediction of useful life, which is a crucial factor in determining the yearly amount of depreciation, is influenced by predictions of physical wear and tear. However, the useful lives are almost always more heavily affected by economic and technological factors than by when equipment may physically wear out.

The following symbols and amounts will be used to compare various depreciation patterns:

	AMOUNTS FOR ILLUSTRATION
Let	
C = total acquisition cost on December 31, 19X7	$41,000
R = residual value	1,000
n = estimated useful life	4 years
D = amount of depreciation (or amortization) per unit of n	

☐ **Straight-Line Depreciation**

Straight-line depreciation is by far the most popular depreciation method for corporate reporting to shareholders. It is used by 95% of major companies for at least part of their fixed assets, and over two-thirds use it exclusively. It was introduced in Chapters 2 and 5, so its rudiments will not be repeated in detail here.

Exhibit 9–2 shows how the asset would be displayed in the balance sheet if a straight-line method of depreciation were used. The annual depreciation expense that would appear on the income statement would be:

$$D = \frac{\text{Acquisition cost} - \text{Residual value}}{\text{Years of useful life}}$$

$$= \frac{C - R}{n}$$

$$= \frac{\$41,000 - \$1,000}{4} = \$10,000 \text{ per year}$$

EXHIBIT 9–2

Straight-Line Depreciation Schedule*

	BALANCES AT END OF YEAR			
	1	2	3	4
Plant and equipment (at original acquisition cost)	41,000	$41,000	$41,000	$41,000
Less: Accumulated depreciation (the portion of original cost that has already been charged to operations as expense)	10,000	20,000	30,000	40,000
Net book value (the portion of original cost that will be charged to future operations as expense)	$31,000	$21,000	$11,000	$ 1,000

* Other patterns of depreciation are discussed later in this chapter.

☐ Depreciation Based on Units

When physical wear and tear is the dominating influence on the useful life of the asset, depreciation may be based on *units of service* or *units of production* rather than on the units of time (years) so commonly used. Depreciation based on units of service is called **unit depreciation**. Suppose the asset in our example were a large truck that would be kept for a useful life of two hundred thousand miles. Depreciation would then be computed on a mileage basis:

$$D = \frac{C - R}{n}$$

$$= \frac{\$41,000 - \$1,000}{200,000 \text{ miles}}$$

$$= \$.20 \text{ per mile}$$

For some assets, such as transportation equipment, this depreciation pattern may have more logical appeal than the straight-line method. However, the unit depreciation method is not widely used, probably for two major reasons:

1. Straight-line depreciation frequently produces approximately the same yearly depreciation amounts.
2. Straight-line depreciation entails less data-collection costs. The entire depreciation schedule can be set at the time of acquisition, and detailed records of units of service are not necessary.

The most commonly encountered example of unit depreciation relates to the use of mining equipment. Instead of writing such costs off on a time basis, the equipment costs are depreciated at a rate per ton of minerals extracted.

☐ Sum-Of-The-Years'-Digits Depreciation

Any pattern of depreciation that writes off depreciable costs more quickly than the ordinary straight-line method based on expected useful life is called **accelerated depreciation.**[2] A form used in the United States is the **sum-of-the-years'-digits (SYD)** method. DuPont and Holly Sugar are among the few companies currently using SYD for reporting to stockholders. Sum of the digits is the total of the numbers representing the years of life; for example, assuming a four-year life, $1 + 2 + 3 + 4 = 10$. This sum becomes the denominator[3] in a key fraction as follows:

$$\text{SYD depreciation} = \text{Fraction} \times \text{Depreciable amount}$$

$$= \frac{\text{Number of remaining years of life}}{\text{Sum of digits}} (C - R)$$

For year 1: $D = \dfrac{4}{1 + 2 + 3 + 4} (\$41,000 - \$1,000)$

$$D = 4/10\ (\$40,000) = \$16,000$$

For year 2: $D = 3/10\ (\$40,000) = \$12,000$
For year 3: $D = 2/10\ (\$40,000) = \$\ 8,000$
For year 4: $D = 1/10\ (\$40,000) = \$\ 4,000$

Companies do not necessarily use the same depreciation policies for all types of depreciable assets. For example, consider the 1985 annual report of the American Telephone and Telegraph Company (AT&T): "Depreciation is calculated principally by using the straight-line method over the useful lives of assets; however, factory facilities placed in service subsequent to December 31, 1979 are depreciated on an accelerated basis."

☐ Double-Declining-Balance Depreciation

Even though companies are permitted to use different depreciation methods for reporting to shareholders and to income tax authorities, some companies use the same depreciation methods for reporting to all interested parties. Until 1954, U.S. companies used straight-line depreciation for their reports to shareholders and to the Internal Revenue Service.

Be careful about the distinctions being made here concerning depreciation methods:

---

[2] About 25% of major U.S. companies use accelerated depreciation for part of their fixed assets in reporting to shareholders.

[3] A general formula for the denominator is $S = \dfrac{n(n+1)}{2}$ where S = sum of the digits and n = useful life: $S = \dfrac{4(4+1)}{2} = 10$

WHEN ASSETS ACQUIRED	REPORTS TO SHAREHOLDERS	REPORTS TO INTERNAL REVENUE SERVICE
Before 1954	Straight-line	Straight-line
1954 to date:		
Most companies	Straight-line	Accelerated
Some companies (such as Dupont and Texas Instruments)	Accelerated	Accelerated

Beginning in 1954, the income tax laws introduced various forms of accelerated depreciation. For assets acquired from 1954 through 1980, the SYD method and the **double-declining-balance (DDB)** method became the most popular forms of *accelerated* depreciation.

DDB is computed as follows:

1. Compute a rate (ignoring the residual value) by dividing 100% by the years of useful life. Then double the rate.[4] In our example, 100% ÷ 4 years = 25%. The DDB rate would be 2 × 25%, or 50%.
2. To compute the depreciation for any year, multiply the beginning book value for the year by the DDB rate.

The DDB method can be illustrated as follows:

$$\text{DDB rate} = 2(100\% \div n)$$
$$\text{DDB rate, 4-year life} = 2(100\% \div 4) = 50\%$$
$$\text{DDB depreciation} = \text{DDB rate} \times \text{Beginning book value}$$

For year 1: $D = .50 \ (\$41{,}000) = \$20{,}500$
For year 2: $D = .50 \ (\$41{,}000 - \$20{,}500)$
           $= .50 \ (\$20{,}500) = \$10{,}250$
For year 3: $D = .50 \ [\$41{,}000 - (\$20{,}500 + \$10{,}250)]$
           $= .50 \ (\$10{,}250) = \$5{,}125$
For year 4: $D = .50 \ [\$41{,}000 - (\$20{,}500 + \$10{,}250 + \$5{,}125)]$
           $= .50 \ (\$5{,}125) = \$2{,}563$

Cumulative total = $35,875

In this example, by coincidence the depreciation amount for each year happens to be half of the preceding year's depreciation. However, this is a special case; it happens only with a four-year life. As the equations show, the basic approach is to apply the depreciation rate to the beginning book value.

Exhibit 9–3 compares the results of these three popular depreciation methods. Note that the DDB method will not write off the full depreciable cost of $40,000. American income tax regulations permit the taxpayer to change to the straight-line method at any time. For example, in Exhibit 9–3 the taxpayer could switch to the straight-line method at the beginning of the fourth year. The total accumulated depreciation for the first three years is $35,875. Because the maximum depreciation allowed for this asset over

---

[4] *Double*-declining-balance requires doubling the rate. Other declining-balance methods use other multiples. For instance, 150% declining-balance requires the straight-line rate to be multiplied by 1.5.

its four-year life is \$40,000, the taxpayer would deduct \$40,000 − \$35,875, or \$4,125, in the fourth year (rather than the \$2,563 shown in Exhibit 9–3). In this way, the taxpayer obtains the complete depreciation deduction allowable.

EXHIBIT 9–3

Depreciation: Three Popular Methods
(Assume equipment costs \$41,000, four-year life, predicted residual value of \$1,000)

			ACCELERATED DEPRECIATION			
	Straight-Line*		Sum-of-Years'-Digits (SYD)†		Declining Balance at Twice the Straight-Line Rate (DDB)‡	
	Annual Depreciation	Book Value	Annual Depreciation	Book Value	Annual Depreciation	Book Value
At acquisition		\$41,000		\$41,000		\$41,000
Year						
1	\$10,000	31,000	\$16,000	25,000	\$20,500	20,500
2	10,000	21,000	12,000	13,000	10,250	10,250
3	10,000	11,000	8,000	5,000	5,125	5,125
4	10,000	1,000	4,000	1,000	2,563	2,562
Total	\$40,000		\$40,000		\$38,438	

* Depreciation is the same each year, 25% of (\$41,000 − \$1,000).
† Sum of digits is $1 + 2 + 3 + 4 = 10$. Then 4/10 × \$40,000; 3/10 × \$40,000; etc.
‡ 100% ÷ 4 = 25%. The double rate is 50%. Then 50% of \$41,000; 50% of (\$41,000 − \$20,500); 50% of [\$41,000 − (\$20,500 + \$10,250)]; etc. Unmodified, this method will never fully depreciate the existing book value. Therefore, in the later years of an asset's life, companies typically switch to a straight-line method. See the text for a fuller explanation.

☐ Accelerated Cost Recovery System (ACRS)

For most fixed assets placed in service after December 31, 1980, the tax regulations require new forms of write-offs for various types of assets. Essentially, these new forms, called the Accelerated Cost Recovery System (ACRS), have assigned shorter useful lives to the assets than previously. In essence, for most assets ACRS approximates (*a*) double-declining balance or 150% declining-balance depreciation (*b*) applied *over shorter lives*. In combination, *a* and *b* provide greater acceleration of depreciation than before ACRS. (Taxpayers always have the option of using straight-line depreciation.) For the most part, these shorter lives are not used for reporting to shareholders. See Chapter 13 for a fuller explanation.

The key word in all variations of depreciation from straight-line based on expected useful service life is *accelerated*. For example, whether declining-balance depreciation is 200%, 175%, or 150% of the straight-line rate, in the early years of an asset's service life there will be higher depreciation than with the straight-line method. Moreover, the use of a straight-line rate over a shorter useful life is also a form of accelerated depreciation. Carried to its extreme, an accelerated depreciation method would call for immediate total write-off in the year of acquisition.

INCOME TAX REPORTING AND SHAREHOLDER REPORTING

☐ Purposes and Income Taxes

Throughout this discussion of long-lived assets, please distinguish between reporting to stockholders and reporting to the income tax authorities. Reports to stockholders must abide by "generally accepted accounting principles (GAAP)." In contrast, reports to income tax authorities must abide by the income tax rules and regulations. These rules comply with GAAP in many respects, but they frequently diverge. Therefore there is nothing immoral or unethical about "keeping two sets of records." In fact, it is necessary.

Keep in mind that the income tax laws are patchworks that are often designed to give taxpayers special incentives for making investments. For example, tax authorities in some countries have permitted taxpayers to write off the full cost of new equipment as expense in the year acquired. Although such a total write-off may be permitted for income tax purposes, it is not permitted for shareholder-reporting purposes.

Major differences between GAAP and the U.S. tax laws are found in accounting for amortization and depreciation. For example, consider how the accounting for perpetual franchises, trademarks, and goodwill differs. Their acquisition costs must be amortized for shareholder reporting. However, the Internal Revenue Service will not allow amortization because such assets are deemed to have indefinite useful lives. Tax reporting and shareholder reporting are *required* to differ.

☐ Straight-Line or Accelerated Depreciation

The vast bulk of companies use straight-line depreciation for reporting to shareholders. Practical reasons for adopting straight-line depreciation are simplicity, convenience, and the reporting of higher earnings in early years than would be reported under accelerated depreciation. Managers tend not to choose accounting methods that hurt reported earnings in the early years of long-lived assets.

An additional reason given in support of straight-line depreciation is the assumption that depreciation is a function of time rather than of use. Therefore the "service potential" of the asset is assumed to decline by an equal amount each period; the total cost of the services consumed in any period is the same regardless of actual use. Further, suppose the benefit from using an asset is the same each period. The matching principle would require that the cost be spread equally to all periods.

For income-tax-reporting purposes, most corporations use *accelerated depreciation*. Why? To postpone payments of income taxes. Most of the same companies simultaneously use straight-line depreciation for shareholder reporting. Chapter 13 discusses the accounting problems that arise from such simultaneous reporting.

A few companies also use some form of accelerated depreciation for reporting to shareholders. For example, Texas Instruments Corporation states that "substantially all depreciation is computed by either the declining balance or the sum-of-the-years'-digits method." Among the reasons for using accelerated depreciation is conservatism. A more persuasive reason is that fixed assets are bundles of services or economic benefits that are used at a faster rate in early years. For example, suppose repair and maintenance expenses increase as an asset ages. If the service obtained is the same each year, the total cost should not increase across time. In essence, the asset is more responsible for the services in early years, and repairs and maintenance are relatively more responsible in later years. Hence depreciation expense should be higher in earlier years and lower in later years.

For simplicity, unless stated otherwise, throughout this chapter we assume that the company uses the same accounting for both income tax reporting and shareholder reporting.

DEPRECIATION AND GENERATION OF CASH

☐ Misunderstood Relationships

Depreciation is widely misunderstood. We have already noted (see page 172) that depreciation expense is an allocation of original cost (the doughnut) and that accumulated depreciation (the enlarging hole in the doughnut) is a compilation of the original cost already written off to expense in prior periods. Thus accumulated depreciation is *not* a pile of cash waiting to be used to replace the asset.

A major objective of this chapter is to pinpoint the relationships between depreciation expense, income tax expense, cash, and accumulated depreciation. Too often, these relationships are confused. For example, the business press frequently contains misleading quotations such as ". . . we're looking for financing $3.75 billion. Of that, about 60% will be recovered in depreciation and amortization." As another example, consider a *Business Week* news report concerning Western Air Lines: "And with a hefty boost from depreciation and the sale of $6 million worth of property, its cash balance rose by $10 million in the year's first quarter." Also consider *Forbes*: "Now, by dragging out their depreciation schedules, firms may run the risk of repeating the errors of the automobile and steel industries, which found themselves hard pressed to replace assets because of years of underdepreciation."

☐ Depreciation Is Not Cash

Suppose a company began business with cash and common stock equity of $100,000. On the same day, equipment was acquired for $41,000 cash. The equipment had an expected four-year life and a predicted residual value of $1,000. The first year's operations generated cash sales of $99,000 and cash operating expenses of $53,000. These relationships are depicted in Exhibit 9–4, using straight-line depreciation and accelerated depreciation, respectively. The form of accelerated depreciation assumed here is sum-of-the-years'-digits. Depreciation for the first year is $4/10 \times \$40,000 = \$16,000$. The ending balance sheets and income statements are shown in Exhibit 9–5 and Exhibit 9–6, respectively.

A comparison of the amounts shown before income taxes stresses the role of depreciation expense most vividly. At the end of the year, the cash balance before taxes is $105,000, regardless of the depreciation method used. Changes in the depreciation method affect only the accumulated depreciation and retained earnings accounts. The ending cash balances are completely unaffected.

Consider the diagram in Exhibit 9–7 (page 387). Each extra dollar of depreciation reduces pretax income by a dollar, leaving the increase in cash unchanged. If depreciation were $40,000, pretax income would be $6,000, and the increase in cash would remain at $46,000.

☐ Effects on Income Taxes

Depreciation is a deductible noncash expense for income tax purposes. Hence the higher the depreciation allowed to be deducted in any given year, the

EXHIBIT 9–4

Analysis of Transactions
(in thousands of dollars)

| | | A | | = L + | SE | |
| | | | Accumulated | | Paid-in | Retained |
	Cash + Equipment −	Depreciation	= Liabilities +	Capital +	Income
I. STRAIGHT-LINE DEPRECIATION						
Initial investment	+100			=	+100	
Acquisition	− 41	+41		=		
Cash sales	+ 99			=		+99 Sales
Cash operating expenses	− 53			=		−53 Expense
Depreciation, year 1			−10	=		−10 Expense
Bal. Dec. 31 before taxes	+105	+41	−10	=	+100	+36
Income taxes (33⅓% of 36)	− 12			=		−12 Expense
Bal. Dec. 31 after taxes	+ 93	+41	−10	=	+100	+24
II. ACCELERATED DEPRECIATION						
Initial investment	+100			=	+100	
Acquisition	− 41	+41		=		
Cash sales	+ 99			=		+99 Sales
Cash operating expenses	− 53			=		−53 Expense
Depreciation, year 1			−16	=		−16 Expense
Bal. Dec. 31 before taxes	+105	+41	−16	=	+100	+30
Income taxes (33⅓% of 30)	− 10			=		−10 Expense
Bal. Dec. 31 after taxes	+ 95	+41	−16	=	+100	+20

EXHIBIT 9–5

ACME SERVICE COMPANY
Balance Sheet
December 31, 19X1
(in thousands)

ASSETS	STRAIGHT LINE DEPRECIATION		ACCELERATED DEPRECIATION		STOCKHOLDERS' EQUITY	STRAIGHT LINE DEPRECIATION	ACCELERATED DEPRECIATION
BEFORE TAXES							
Cash		$105		$105			
Equipment	$41		$41		Paid-in		
Deduct:					capital	$100	$100
Accumulated					Retained		
depreciation	10	31	16	25	income	36	30
Total		$136		$130	Total	$136	$130
AFTER TAXES							
Cash		$ 93		$ 95			
Equipment	$41		$41		Paid-in		
Deduct:					capital	$100	$100
Accumulated					Retained		
depreciation	10	31	16	25	income	24	20
Total		$124		$120	Total	$124	$120

EXHIBIT 9–6

ACME SERVICE COMPANY
Income Statement
For the Year Ended December 31, 19X1
(in thousands)

	Before Taxes		After Taxes	
	STRAIGHT-LINE DEPRECIATION	ACCELERATED DEPRECIATION	STRAIGHT-LINE DEPRECIATION	ACCELERATED DEPRECIATION
Sales	$99	$99	$99	$99
Cash operating expenses	53	53	53	53
Cash provided by operations before income tax	46	46	46	46
Depreciation expense	10	16	10	16
Pretax income	36	30	36	30
Income tax expense (33⅓%)	—	—	12	10
Net income	$36	$30	$24	$20
Supplementary analysis:				
Cash provided by operations before income tax	$46	$46	$46	$46
Income tax expense	—	—	12	10
Cash provided by operations*	$46	$46	$34	$36

* Sometimes called cash flow from operations or just cash flow. But it is usually simply called cash provided by operations, which is typically defined as cash collected on sales (a) less all operating expenses requiring cash and (b) less income taxes.

lower the taxable income and the cash disbursements for income taxes. In short, if depreciation expense is higher, more cash is conserved and kept for use in the business. Therefore, compared with the straight-line method, the accelerated method results in a higher cash balance *after* income tax ($95,000 instead of $93,000). At a 33⅓% income tax rate, a $6,000 higher depreciation expense postpones $2,000 of income taxes.

Some strange results occur here. The reported net income is *lower* under accelerated than under straight-line depreciation, but the cash balance is *higher*. Thus, suppose managers were forced to choose one depreciation method for all purposes. Managers who are concerned about reported net income to shareholders may prefer straight-line to accelerated depreciation. This dilemma is not faced by managers in the United States, where straight-line depreciation is often used for shareholder purposes while accelerated depreciation is used for income tax purposes. See Chapter 13 for additional explanation.

Governments throughout the world have increasingly tolerated a wide variety of depreciation methods "to provide more cash for industrial expansion." The business press and financial analysts' reports are peppered with such phrasing as "cash provided by depreciation" or "funds generated by depreciation." Accountants quarrel with such phrasing because depreciation by itself is *not* a source of cash.

There is only one source of cash from operations: the cash provided through *sales to customers*. As our example shows, the effect of more depreciation on cash is *indirect*; it reduces income taxes by one-third of the extra depreciation of $6,000, or $2,000. Therefore accelerated depreciation keeps more cash in the business for a longer span of time because of the postponement of cash disbursements for income taxes.

Examine the account for accumulated depreciation. *No cash is there.* It is a deduction from an asset, a hole in the doughnut regardless of whether income tax rates are zero, 20%, or 90%.

CHAPTER 15, WHICH MAY BE STUDIED NOW OR LATER WITHOUT BREAKING CONTINUITY, EXPLAINS THE RELATIONSHIP OF DEPRECIATION TO ANOTHER MAJOR FINANCIAL REPORT, THE STATEMENT OF CHANGES IN FINANCIAL POSITION.

GAINS AND LOSSES ON SALES OF FIXED ASSETS

Gains or losses on the disposal of property, plant, and equipment are inevitable. They are usually measured in a cash sale by the difference between the cash received and the net book value (net carrying amount) of the asset given up.[5] Chapter 5, page 173, showed the accounting entries for recording such gains or losses.

---

[5] When an old asset is traded for a similar new asset, the new asset is valued at its cash-equivalent value for purposes of computing gain or loss. For an illustration, see Chapter 6, Appendix 6B, pages 239–240, regarding the trade-in of an old car for a new car. The trading of assets can become complex. It is explained in advanced accounting texts. Also see Accounting Principles Board *Opinion No. 29*, "Accounting for Nonmonetary Transactions."

EXHIBIT 9–7

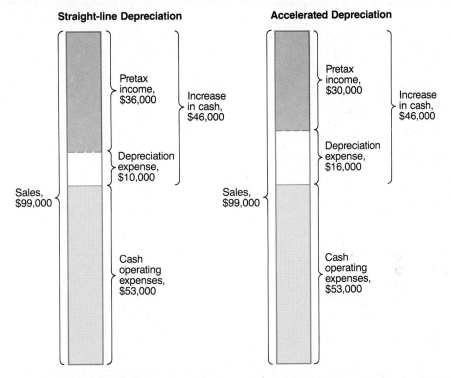

Straight-line Depreciation

Sales, $99,000

Pretax income, $36,000

Depreciation expense, $10,000

Cash operating expenses, $53,000

Increase in cash, $46,000

Accelerated Depreciation

Sales, $99,000

Pretax income, $30,000

Depreciation expense, $16,000

Cash operating expenses, $53,000

Increase in cash, $46,000

Each extra dollar of depreciation reduces pretax income by a dollar, but leaves the increase in cash unchanged. If depreciation were $40,000, pretax income would be only $6,000, but the increase in cash would remain at $46,000.

☐ Income Statement Presentation

Gain on Sale of Equipment is usually shown as a separate item on an income statement as a part of "other income" or some similar category.

In single-step income statements, the gain is shown at the top along with other revenue items. For example:

Revenue:	
Sales of products	$xxx
Interest income (or interest revenue)	x
Other income: Gain on sale of equipment	x
Total sales and other income	$xxx

When a multiple-step income statement is used, the gain (or loss) is usually excluded from the computation of major profit categories such as gross profit or operating profit. Therefore the gain or loss appears in some type of "other income" or nonoperating income section in the lower part of the income statement.

In most instances, gains or losses on disposition of plant assets are not significant, so they are buried as a part of "other income" and are not separately identified. For example, W. R. Grace & Co. includes an item on its income statement immediately after sales labeled "Dividends, interest, and other income." American Telephone and Telegraph (AT&T) shows "Other income, net (Note D)" on a separate line after operating income in its 1985 annual report. Note D lists Gains (loss) on sale of fixed assets, $9.0 million, out of a total of $251.8 million of net other income.

☐ Recording Gains and Losses

Suppose the equipment in Exhibit 9–2 (p. 378) were sold at the end of Year 2 for $27,000. The sale would have the following effects:

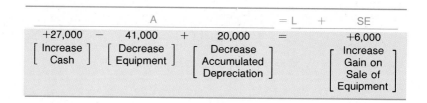

If the selling price were $17,000 rather than $27,000:

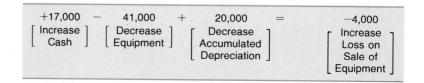

The T-account presentations and journal entries are in Exhibit 9–8. Note especially that the disposal of the equipment necessitates the removal of the doughnut (the original cost of the equipment) *and* the accompanying hole in the doughnut (the accumulated depreciation). Of course, the net effect is to decrease the carrying amount of the equipment by $21,000.

CHANGES IN DEPRECIATION ESTIMATES

Predictions of useful lives and residual values are invariably not accurate. If the inaccuracies are material, how should the affected accounts be adjusted? Consider the example of the $41,000 asset and the straight-line method. Suppose it is the beginning of Year 3. The firm's economists and engineers have

EXHIBIT 9–8

Journal and Ledger Entries
Gain or Loss on Sale of Equipment
(in thousands of dollars)

Sale at $27,000:

		Cash		Equipment		Gain on Sale of Equipment	
Cash	27	27			41		6
Accumulated depreciation	20						
Equipment		41		Accumulated Depreciation, Equipment			
Gain on sale of equipment		6		20			

Sale at $17,000:

		Cash		Equipment		Loss on Sale of Equipment	
Cash	17	17			41	4	
Accumulated depreciation	20						
Loss on sale of equipment	4			Accumulated Depreciation, Equipment			
Equipment		41		20			

altered their expectations; the asset's new expected useful life is five instead of four years. Moreover, the new expected residual value is $3,000 instead of $1,000:

	EXPECTATIONS	
	Original	Revised
Cost	$41,000	$41,000
Useful life	4 years	5 years
Residual value	$ 1,000	$ 3,000
Straight-line depreciation per year:		
Old, $40,000 ÷ 4	$10,000	
New, as computed below		$ 6,000

These modifications to predictions are "changes in accounting estimates." They must be accounted for "prospectively" rather than "retroactively" in the sense that the records through Year 2 would not be adjusted. Instead the *remaining* depreciable amount would be written off over the new *remaining* useful life:

New book value at end of Year 2: $41,000 − 2 ($10,000) =	$21,000
Revised residual value	3,000
Revised depreciable amount	$18,000
Divide by remaining useful life in years, ÷3	
New straight-line depreciation per year	= $ 6,000

Critics of the foregoing "prospective" method assert that it misstates the yearly depreciation throughout the entire life of the asset. That is, depreciation in early years is overstated and in later years is understated. This can be illustrated by comparing the prospective method in our example with the retroactive method (which uses perfect hindsight):

YEAR	PROSPECTIVE METHOD	RETROACTIVE METHOD
1	$10,000	$ 7,600*
2	10,000	7,600
3	6,000	7,600
4	6,000	7,600
5	6,000	7,600
	$38,000	$38,000

* ($41,000 − $3,000) ÷ 5 = $7,600.

Applying the retroactive method would entail restating the accounts of prior periods, a procedure that many accountants oppose mainly on the grounds that the past accounting was as accurate as possible given the knowledge then existing. Although the retroactive way of adjusting the accounts has much logical appeal, Accounting Principles Board *Opinion No. 20* stated: "A change in estimate should not be accounted for by restating amounts reported in financial statements of prior periods."

DEPRECIATION FOR PARTS OF A YEAR

Assets are rarely acquired exactly at the start of a year or a month. To economize on recordkeeping, various simplifying assumptions are made about depreciation within the year. Each assumption must be reasonable and be consistently applied.[6]

For interim reporting, yearly depreciation is usually spread uniformly *within* a given fiscal year (an equal amount for each month), regardless of whether straight-line or accelerated depreciation is used to compute the total amount for the year. Moreover, depreciation for an asset acquired during a month is usually provided for the full month or not at all (depending on specific accounting policies, which vary among companies). For instance, suppose our $41,000 asset had been acquired on October 14, 19X1, and SYD

---

[6] For example, one of two methods might be used to determine when certain specified assets are placed in service:

1. *Half-year convention.* Treat all assets placed in service during the year as if they had been placed in service at the year's midpoint.
2. *Modified half-year convention.* Treat each asset placed in service during the first half of a tax year as if it had been placed in service on the first day of that tax year. Treat each asset placed in service during the last half of the tax year as if it had been placed in service on the first day of the *following* tax year.

depreciation was used. As Exhibit 9–3 shows, the depreciation for Year 1 would be $16,000 and for Year 2 would be $12,000.

Assume that the company's fiscal year and calendar year are the same and that depreciation is to be included for the full month of October. The depreciation schedule could appear as shown below (in thousands of dollars).

The monthly statements in October, November, and December, 19X1, would each have depreciation expense of $4,000 ÷ 3 = $1,333. In turn, the monthly statements of 19X2 would each have depreciation expense of $15,000 ÷ 12 = $1,250. Depreciation is shown as thousands of dollars:

| ASSET YEAR | DEPRECIATION FOR 12-MONTH PERIODS | ALLOCATION TO EACH CALENDAR YEAR | | | | |
		19X1	19X2	19X3	19X4	19X5
1	4/10(40) = 16	4*	12†			
2	3/10(40) = 12		3*	9†		
3	2/10(40) = 8			2*	6†	
4	1/10(40) = 4				1*	3†
10	40	4	15	11	7	3

* 3/12 of column 2 (for example, 19X1: 16 ÷ 12 months = $1.33⅓ per month; 3 months, $1.33⅓ × 3 = $4).

† 9/12 of column 2 (for example, 19X2: 16 ÷ 12 months = $1.33⅓ per month; 9 months, $1.33⅓ × 9 = $12).

EXPENSES VERSUS EXPENDITURES

☐ Types of Expenditures

This section explores the accounting for expenditures. **Expenditures** are defined by accountants as the purchases of goods or services, whether for cash or credit. **Capital expenditures** are those expected to benefit more than the current accounting year. **Revenue expenditures** are those deemed to have a useful life no longer than the current accounting year. Capital expenditures generally add new fixed assets or increase the capacity, efficiency, useful life, or economy of operation of an existing fixed asset.

The terminology here is a good example of entrenched usage that does not provide particularly accurate descriptions of the classification intended. For example, a capital expenditure might better be called an *asset* expenditure. Similarly, a revenue expenditure might better be called an *expense* expenditure.

Every expenditure eventually becomes an expense. Revenue expenditures are matched with current revenues and therefore become expenses in the current period. Capital expenditures benefit *future* revenues. They are charged as expenses over future periods.

Sometimes the distinction between capital and revenue expenditures is subjective. Auditors from both the public accounting firms and the income tax authorities regularly investigate whether a given outlay is a capital expenditure or a revenue expenditure. That is, is a particular outlay for the engine repair or part properly classifed as an asset or an expense? The public accountant (who tends to prefer conservatism) is usually on the alert for any tendencies to understate current expenses through the unjustified charging of a repair to an asset account. In contrast, the income tax auditor is looking for the unjustified charging to an expense account (which provides an immediate income tax deduction).

Wherever doubt exists, there is a general tendency in practice to charge an expense rather than an asset account for repairs, parts, and similar items. First, many of these outlays are minor, so the cost-benefit test of recordkeeping (the concept of materiality) justifies such action. For instance, many companies have a policy of charging all such outlays to expense that are less than a specified minimum such as $100, $500, or $1,000. Second, there is the temptation of an immediate deduction for income tax purposes (if, indeed, the deductions are allowable as reasonable expenses).

☐ Repairs and Maintenance

Repairs and maintenance costs are necessary if a fixed asset is to continue in a specified operating condition. The costs of repairs and maintenance are usually compiled in the same account and are labeled as revenue expenditures because they are regarded as expenses of the current period.

Repairs are sometimes distinguished from *maintenance* as follows. *Repairs* include the occasional costs of restoring a fixed asset to its ordinary operating condition after breakdowns, accidents, or damage. *Maintenance* includes the routine recurring costs of oiling, polishing, painting, and adjusting.

Obviously, distinctions between repairs and maintenance are sometimes hard to draw. For example, is an engine tuneup a repair expense or a maintenance expense? Nobody loses much sleep over such matters, so one account typically contains both repairs and maintenance.

☐ Capital Improvements

An **improvement** (sometimes called a **betterment** or a **capital improvement**) is a capital expenditure that is intended to add to the future benefits from an existing fixed asset. How? By decreasing its operating cost, increasing its rate of output, or prolonging its useful life. An improvement differs from repairs and maintenance because the latter help ensure a specified level of benefits but do not enlarge the expected future benefits.

Examples of capital improvements or betterments include the rehabilitation of an apartment house that will yield above-normal rents and the rebuilding of a packaging machine that increases its speed or extends its useful life.

In Exhibit 9–2 (page 378), suppose that at the start of Year 3 a major overhaul costing $7,000 occurred. If this is judged to extend the useful life from four to five years, the required accounting would be:

1. Increase the book value of the asset (now $41,000 − $20,000 = $21,000) by $7,000. This is usually done by adding the $7,000 to Equipment.[7]
2. Assume straight-line depreciation. Revise the depreciation schedule so that the new unexpired cost is spread over the remaining three years, as follows:

	ORIGINAL DEPRECIATION SCHEDULE		REVISED DEPRECIATION SCHEDULE	
	Year	Amount	Year	Amount
	1	$10,000	1	$10,000
	2	10,000	2	10,000
	3	10,000	3	9,000*
	4	10,000	4	9,000
			5	9,000
Accumulated depreciation		$40,000†		$47,000†

* New depreciable amount is ($41,000 − $20,000 + $7,000) − $1,000 residual value = $27,000. New depreciation expense is $27,000 divided by remaining useful life of 3 years, or $9,000 per year.

† Recapitulation:

	NET BOOK VALUE	
	Original	Revised
Original outlay	$41,000	$41,000
Major overhaul	—	7,000
Total	$41,000	$48,000
Accumulated depreciation	40,000	47,000
Residual value	$ 1,000	$ 1,000

AMORTIZATION OF LEASEHOLDS AND LEASEHOLD IMPROVEMENTS

Leaseholds and *leasehold improvements* are frequently classified with plant assets. A **leasehold** is the right to use a fixed asset (such as a building or some portion thereof) for a specified period of time beyond one year. A **leasehold improvement** incurred by a lessee (tenant) can take various forms. Examples are the installation of new fixtures, panels, walls, and air-conditioning equipment that are not permitted to be removed from the premises when a lease expires.

The costs of leases and leasehold improvements are written off in the same way as depreciation. However, the straight-line method is used almost

---

[7] A few accountants prefer to debit Accumulated Depreciation instead of Equipment. The theory is that a portion of past depreciation is being "reversed" or "made good" by the improvement or betterment. In any event, the effect of the improvement is to increase the net book value of the equipment and increase subsequent depreciation in identical amounts, regardless of whether the debit is made to Equipment or to Accumulated Depreciation. The major justification for debiting Accumulated Depreciation is that old machine parts have been replaced, but their original cost cannot be isolated.

exclusively, probably because accelerated methods have not been permitted for income tax purposes. Furthermore, these systematic write-offs are often described as amortization rather than as depreciation.

Sometimes the useful life of a *leasehold improvement* is expected to exceed the life of the lease. In such cases, amortization must be based on the shorter time span, the life of the lease. For more on leases, see Chapter 10, page 457.

DEPLETION

Natural resources such as minerals, oil, and timber are sometimes called *wasting assets*. **Depletion** is the gradual exhaustion of the original amounts of the resources acquired. Depletion differs from depreciation because the former focuses narrowly on a physical phenomenon and the latter focuses more broadly on any cause of the reduction of the economic value of a fixed asset, including physical wear and tear plus obsolescence.

The costs of natural resources are usually classified as fixed assets. However, the investment in natural resources can be likened to a lump-sum acquisition of massive quantities of inventories under the ground (iron ore) or over the ground (timber). Depletion expense is the measure of that portion of this "long-term inventory" that is used up in a particular period. For example, a coal mine may cost $20 million and originally contain an estimated one million tons. The depletion rate would be $20 per ton. If 100,000 tons were mined during the first year, the depletion would be 100,000 × $20, or $2 million for that year; if 150,000 tons were mined the second year, depletion would be 150,000 × $20, or $3 million; and so forth.

As the above example shows, depletion is measured on a units-of-production basis. The annual depletion may be accounted for as a direct reduction of the mining asset, or it may be accumulated in a separate account similar to accumulated depreciation.

Another example is timber. Boise Cascade Corporation, a large producer of forest products, describes its approach to depletion as follows:

☐ Timber and timberlands are shown at cost, less the cost of company timber harvested. Cost of company timber harvested and amortization of logging roads are determined on the basis of timber removals at rates based on the estimated volume of recoverable timber and are credited to the respective asset accounts.

The "cost of company timber harvested" is Boise Cascade's synonym for "depletion" of timber.

AMORTIZATION OF VARIOUS INTANGIBLE ASSETS

Intangible assets are a class of long-lived assets that are not physical in nature. They are rights to expected benefits deriving from their acquisition and continued possession. Examples of intangible assets are *patents*, *copyrights*, *franchises*, and *goodwill*.

Intangible assets are accounted for like plant and equipment. That is, the acquisition costs are capitalized as assets and are then amortized over estimated useful lives. Because of obsolescence, the *economic lives* of intangible assets tend to be shorter than their *legal lives*.

Patents are grants by the federal government to an inventor, bestowing (in the United States) the exclusive right for 17 years to produce and sell the invention. Suppose a company acquires such a patent from the inventor for $170,000. Suppose further that because of fast-changing technology, the *economic life* (the expected useful life) of the patent is only five years. The amortization would be $170,000 ÷ 5 = $34,000 per year, rather than $170,000 ÷ 17 = $10,000 per year.

The write-offs of intangible assets are usually made via direct reductions of the accounts in question. Thus accounts like Accumulated Amortization of Patents are rarely found. Furthermore, the residual values of intangible assets are nearly always zero.

Copyrights are exclusive rights to reproduce and sell a book, musical composition, film, and similar items. These rights are issued (in the United States) by the federal government and provide protection to a company for 75 years. The original costs of obtaining copyrights from the government are nominal, but a company may pay a large sum to purchase an existing asset from the owner. For example, a publisher of paperback books will pay the author of a popular novel in excess of a million dollars for his or her copyright. The economic lives of such assets are usually no longer than two or three years, so amortization occurs accordingly.

Trademarks are distinctive identifications of a manufactured product or of a service taking the form of a name, a sign, a slogan, or an emblem. An example is an emblem for Coca-Cola. Trademarks, trade names, trade brands, secret formulas, and similar items are property rights with economic lives depending on their length of use. For stockholder-reporting purposes, their costs are amortized over their useful lives, but no longer than 40 years.

Franchises and **licenses** are privileges granted by a government, manufacturer, or distributor to sell a product or service in accordance with specified conditions. An example is the franchise of a baseball team or the franchise of a local owner of a Holiday Inn. The lengths of the franchises vary from one year to perpetuity. Again, the acquisition costs of franchises and licenses are amortized over their economic lives rather than their legal lives.

Goodwill, which is discussed in more detail in Chapter 12, is defined as the excess of the cost of an acquired company over the sum of the fair market values of its identifiable individual assets less the liabilities. For example, General Motors acquired Hughes Aircraft for $5 billion but could assign only $1 billion to various identifiable assets such as receivables, plant, and patents less liabilities assumed by GM; the remainder, $4 billion, is goodwill. Identifiable intangible assets, such as franchises and patents, may be acquired singly, but goodwill cannot be acquired separately from a related business. This excess of the purchase price over the fair market value is called "goodwill" or "purchased goodwill" or, more accurately, "excess of cost over fair value of net identifiable assets of businesses acquired."

The accounting for goodwill illustrates how an *exchange* transaction is a basic concept of accounting. After all, there are many owners who could obtain a premium price for their companies. *But such goodwill is never recorded.* Only the goodwill arising from an *actual acquisition* with arm's-length bargaining is shown as an asset on the purchaser's records.

For shareholder-reporting purposes, goodwill must be amortized, generally in a straight-line manner, over the periods benefited. The maximum amortization period is forty years. The minimum amortization period was not specified by the Accounting Principles Board (*Opinion No. 17*), but a lump-sum write-off on acquisition is forbidden.

HISTORICAL THRUST TOWARD CONSERVATISM

☐ Goodwill

Many managers and accountants insist that some intangible assets have unlimited lives. But the Accounting Principles Board ruled that the values of all intangible assets eventually disappear. The attitudes of the regulatory bodies toward accounting for intangible assets became increasingly conservative during the 1970s. For example, before October 31, 1970, the amortization of goodwill, trademarks, and franchises with indefinite useful lives was not mandatory. The new requirement for amortization was not imposed retroactively. Consequently, many companies *are* currently amortizing goodwill acquired after October 31, 1970, but *are not* amortizing goodwill acquired before that date. For example, American Brands, maker of Titleist golf balls, Master locks, and many other consumer products, states in its annual report: "Intangibles resulting from business acquisitions, comprising brands and trademarks and cost in excess of net assets of businesses acquired, are considered to have a continuing value over an indefinite period and are not being amortized, except for intangibles acquired after 1970, which are being amortized on a straight-line basis over 40 years."

☐ Research and Development

Before 1975, many companies regarded *research and development costs* as assets and amortized them over the years of expected benefit, usually three to six years. Such costs result from planned search or critical investigation aimed at obtaining new products or processes or significant improvements in existing products or processes. For all fiscal years beginning on or after January 1, 1975, the Financial Accounting Standards Board (*Statement No. 2*) has required that all such costs be charged to expense when incurred. The FASB recognized that research and development costs may generate many long-term benefits, but the general high degree of uncertainty about the extent and measurement of future benefits led to conservative accounting in the form of immediate write-off.

An exception to the immediate expensing of all research and development costs is accounting for the costs of developing computer software to be sold or leased. Such costs should be expensed only until *the technological feasibility* of the product is established. Thereafter, software production costs should be capitalized and amortized based on anticipated revenue.

AMORTIZATION OF DEFERRED CHARGES

Sometimes prepaid expenses are lumped with **deferred charges** as a single amount, *prepaid expenses and deferred charges*, that appears on the balance sheet at the bottom of the current asset classification or at the bottom of all the assets as an "other asset." Deferred charges are like prepaid expenses, but they have longer-term benefits. For example, the costs of relocating a mass of employees to a different geographical area, or the costs of rearranging an assembly line, or the costs of developing new markets may be carried forward as deferred charges and written off as expense over a three- to five-year period. This procedure is often described as the amortization of deferred charges.

Another example of deferred charges is *organization costs*, which include certain types of expenditures made in forming a corporation: fees for legal and accounting services, promotional costs for the sale of corporate securities, and the printing costs of stock certificates. These costs theoretically benefit the corporation indefinitely, but they are usually amortized for both shareholder and tax purposes over five years (which happens to be the span specified by the Internal Revenue Service).

INTERNAL COSTS AND EXTERNAL COSTS

As we have seen, accountants tend to be extremely conservative about intangible assets and deferred charges, and most intangibles are swiftly amortized. The contrast between the accounting for tangible and intangible long-lived assets raises some provocative and knotty theoretical issues. Accountants are sometimes overly concerned with physical objects or contractual rights, tending to overlook the underlying reality of future economic benefits.

This preoccupation with physical evidence often results in the expensing of outlays that should be treated as assets. Thus expenditures for research, advertising, employee training, and the like are generally expensed, although it seems clear that in an economic sense such expenditures represent expected future benefits. The difficulty of measuring future benefits is the reason usually advanced for expensing these items. The Financial Accounting Standards Board requires that all *internal* research and development costs be written off to expense as incurred.

In summary, accounting practice for intangible assets is not consistent. An annual report of Omark Industries exemplifies this inconsistency: "Costs of internally developed patents, trademarks and formulas are charged to current operations. Costs of purchased patents, trademarks and formulas are amortized over their legal or economic lives."

CONFLICTS WITH INCOME TAX PURPOSES

As mentioned earlier in this chapter, accounting for shareholder purposes often coincides with but sometimes differs from accounting for income tax purposes. Tax and shareholder accounting for leaseholds, leasehold improvements, patents, and copyrights generally coincide. However, they differ for perpetual franchises, trademarks, and goodwill. The acquisition costs of such assets *must* be amortized for shareholder reporting but *must not* be amortized for income tax purposes; the Internal Revenue Service will not allow amortization because of the indefinite duration of their usefulness.

The following table recapitulates how accounting for two purposes can conflict:

Type of Intangible Asset	MAXIMUM USEFUL LIVES IN YEARS FOR MEASURING ANNUAL AMORTIZATION IN REPORTS*	
	To Shareholders	To Internal Revenue Service
Patents	17	Same as first column
Copyrights	40	Same
Sports player contracts	Length of contract	Same
Franchises and licenses	Length of contract	Same
	or	or
	40 if length is unlimited	No amortization permitted†
Trademarks	40	No amortization permitted†
Goodwill	40	No amortization permitted†
Research and development	Full write-off as incurred	Same
Covenants not to compete‡	Length of contract	Same

* These maximums are frequently far in excess of the economic lives. Thus patents and copyrights are often written off in two or three years because the related products have short lives.
† The Internal Revenue Service does not permit amortization of intangible assets with indefinite useful lives. Examples are franchises of unlimited duration such as a football franchise, goodwill, and trademarks.
‡ For example, the seller of a pest control business promises not to open a competing business within one hundred miles for five years.

SUMMARY

Depreciation, depletion, and amortization are similar concepts, providing for systematic write-offs of the acquisition costs of long-lived assets over their useful lives. By itself, depreciation does not provide cash. Customers provide cash. However, depreciation is deductible for income tax purposes. Therefore the larger the depreciation in any given year, the greater the amount of cash from customers that may be kept by the business instead of being disbursed to the income tax authorities.

Accumulated depreciation is a deduction from an asset, not an increasing pile of cash for replacing assets.

Reporting to shareholders and reporting to income tax authorities sometimes diverge. Keeping two sets of records to satisfy these two purposes is necessary, not illegal or immoral.

Goodwill is never shown as an asset unless it was acquired through the purchase of another business.

SUMMARY PROBLEMS FOR YOUR REVIEW

☐ Problem One

"The net book value of plant assets is the amount that would be spent today for their replacement." Do you agree? Explain.

☐ Solution to Problem One

Net book value of the plant assets is the result of deducting accumulated depreciation from original cost. It is a result of cost allocation, not valuation. This process does not attempt to reflect all the technological and economic events that may affect replacement value. Consequently, there is little assurance that net book value will approximate replacement cost.

☐ Problem Two

"Accumulated depreciation provides cash for the replacement of fixed assets." Do you agree with this quotation from a business magazine? Explain.

☐ Solution to Problem Two

Accumulated depreciation is a contra asset. It is like a "hole in a doughnut" and in no way represents a direct stockpile of cash for replacement.

☐ Problem Three

Refer to Exhibit 9–3 (p. 381). Suppose the predicted residual value had been $5,000 instead of $1,000.

1. Compute depreciation for each of the first two years. Compare straight-line, sum-of-years'-digits, and double-declining-balance.
2. Assume that SYD depreciation is used and that the equipment is sold for $20,000 cash at the end of the second year. Compute the gain or loss on the sale. Show the effects of the sale in T-accounts for the equipment and accumulated depreciation. Where and how would the sale appear in the income statement?

☐ Solution to Problem Three

1.

	STRAIGHT-LINE DEPRECIATION $\dfrac{C - R^{*}}{n}$	SYD DEPRECIATION = FRACTION† × (C − R)	DDB DEPRECIATION = RATE‡ × (BEGINNING BOOK VALUE)
Year 1	$36,000/4 = $9,000	4/10 ($36,000) = $14,400	.50 ($41,000) = $20,500
Year 2	$36,000/4 = $9,000	3/10 ($36,000) = $10,800	.50 ($41,000 − $20,500) = $10,250

* C − R = $41,000 − $5,000 = $36,000.

† $\dfrac{\text{Number of remaining years of life}}{\text{Sum of digits}} = \dfrac{4}{1+2+3+4} = 4/10$ in Year 1 and 3/10 in Year 2.

‡ Rate = 2(100% ÷ n) = 2(100% ÷ 4) = 50%.

Revenue	$20,000
Expense: Net book value of equipment sold is $41,000 − ($14,400 + $10,800), or $41,000 − $25,200 =	15,800
Gain on sale of equipment	$ 4,200

The effect of removing the book value is a $15,800 decrease in assets. Note that the effect of a *decrease* in Accumulated Depreciation (by itself) is an *increase* in assets:

Equipment			
Acquisition cost	41,000	Cost of equipment sold	41,000

Accumulated Depreciation, Equipment			
Accumulated on equipment sold	25,200	Depreciation for: Year 1	14,400
		Year 2	10,800
			25,200

The $4,200 gain is usually shown as a separate item on the income statement as Gain on Sale of Equipment or Gain on Disposal of Equipment.

□ Problem Four

Review the important chapter illustration in the section "Depreciation and Generation of Cash," pages 383–386. Suppose the equipment had been acquired for $82,000 instead of $41,000. Also suppose that the predicted residual value had been $2,000 instead of $1,000.

Required:

1. Prepare a revised Exhibit 9–6, which is on page 386. Assume an income tax rate of $33\frac{1}{3}\%$; round all income tax computations to the nearest thousand.
2. Indicate all items affected by these changes. Also tabulate all differences between the final two columns in your revised exhibit as compared with Exhibit 9–6.

□ Solution to Problem Four

1. The revised income statements are in Exhibit 9–9.

2. The following comparisons of Exhibits 9–9 and 9–6 are noteworthy. *Sales, operating expenses, and cash provided by operations before income taxes are unaffected by the change in depreciation.* Because of higher depreciation, net income would be lower in all four columns of Exhibit 9–9 than in Exhibit 9–6. Comparison of the final two columns of the exhibits follows:

	AS SHOWN IN		
	EXHIBIT 9–9	EXHIBIT 9–6	DIFFERENCE
Straight-line depreciation	20	10	10 higher
Accelerated depreciation	32	16	16 higher
Income tax expense based on:			
Straight-line depreciation	9	12	3 lower
Accelerated depreciation	5	10	5 lower
Net income based on:			
Straight-line depreciation	17	24	7 lower
Accelerated depreciation	9	20	11 lower
Cash provided by operations based on:			
Straight-line depreciation	37	34	3 higher
Accelerated depreciation	41	36	5 higher

Especially noteworthy is the phenomenon that higher depreciation *decreases* net income but also decreases cash outflows for income taxes. As a result, cash provided by operations *increases*.

EXHIBIT 9–9

ACME SERVICE COMPANY
Income Statement
For the Year Ended December 31, 19X1
(in thousands)

	Before Taxes		After Taxes	
	STRAIGHT-LINE DEPRECIATION	ACCELERATED DEPRECIATION	STRAIGHT-LINE DEPRECIATION	ACCELERATED DEPRECIATION
Sales	$99	$99	$99	$99
Cash operating expenses	53	53	53	53
Cash provided by operations before income tax	46	46	46	46
Depreciation expense	20	32	20	32
Pretax income	26	14	26	14
Income tax expense (33⅓%)	—	—	9*	5*
Net income	$26	$14	$17	$ 9
Supplementary analysis:				
Cash provided by operations before income tax	$46	$46	$46	$46
Income tax expense	—	—	9	5
Cash provided by operations	$46	$46	$37	$41

* Income tax expenses rounded to the nearest thousand. Their exact amounts are $8,667 and $4,667, respectively.

HIGHLIGHTS TO REMEMBER

1. This chapter contains an unusually high number of new terms. Check your understanding of the items in the next section, "Accounting Vocabulary."
2. Are you able to distinguish between the terms *expense* and *expenditure*? Consult the

Glossary for definitions. Note that an expenditure may be a *capital expenditure*, whose amount becomes allocated as an expense in each of several years. In contrast, a *revenue expenditure* becomes an expense in the current accounting year.

3. Students of introductory accounting are often confused by the relationships of depreciation to cash. Students are also often confused by the idea that "generally accepted accounting principles" are aimed primarily at reporting to shareholders, not income tax authorities. A careful study of Problem Four of the "Summary Problems for Your Review" should reduce the confusion.

ACCOUNTING VOCABULARY

Accelerated Depreciation, p. *379* Amortization, *373* Basket Purchase, *376* Betterment, *392* Capital Expenditure, *391* Capital Improvement, *392* Copyrights, *395* Deferred Charge, *397* Depletion, *394* Depreciable Value, *377* Disposal Value, *377* Double-Declining Balance Depreciation (DDB), *380* Expenditures, *391* Fixed Assets, *374* Franchise, *395* Goodwill, *395* Improvement, *392* Intangible Assets, *374* Leasehold, *393* Leasehold Improvement, *393* Licenses, *395* Long-Lived Assets, *373* Patents, *395* Residual Value, *377* Revenue Expenditure, *391* Salvage Value, *377* Scrap Value, *377* Straight-Line Depreciation, *377* Sum-of-the-Years'-Digits Depreciation (SYD), *379* Tangible Assets, *374* Trademarks, *395* Unit Depreciation, *378*

FUNDAMENTAL ASSIGNMENT MATERIAL

☐ **General Coverage**

9–1. COMPARISON OF POPULAR DEPRECIATION METHODS. (Alternates are 9–5, 9–6, and 9–32.) Lopez Company acquired equipment for $32,000 with an expected useful life of five years and a $2,000 expected residual value. Prepare a tabular comparison (similar to Exhibit 9–3, p. 381) of the annual depreciation and book value for each year under straight-line, sum-of-the-years'-digits, and double-declining-balance depreciation. (Note that this is a comparison of methods used for reporting to shareholders. Such methods may differ from those used for reporting to the income tax authorities.)

9–2. DEPRECIATION, INCOME TAXES, AND CASH FLOW. (Alternates are 9–7 and 9–8.) Ferragamo Co. had the following balances, among others, at the end of December 19X1: Cash, $200,000; Equipment, $400,000; Accumulated Depreciation, $100,000. Total revenues (all in cash) were $900,000. Cash operating expenses were $600,000. Straight-line depreciation expense was $50,000. If accelerated depreciation had been used, depreciation expense would have been $80,000.

Required:

1. Assume zero income taxes. Fill in the blanks in the accompanying table (on p. 403). Show the amounts in thousands.
2. Repeat requirement 1, but assume an income tax rate of 40%. Assume also that Ferragamo uses the same depreciation method for reporting to shareholders and to income tax authorities.
3. Compare your answers to requirements 1 and 2. Does depreciation provide cash? Explain as precisely as possible.
4. Assume that Ferragamo had used straight-line depreciation for reporting to

shareholders and to income tax authorities. Indicate the change (increase or decrease and amount) in the following balances if Ferragamo had used accelerated depreciation instead of straight-line: Cash, Accumulated Depreciation, Operating Income, Retained Income.

5. Refer to requirement 1. Suppose depreciation were tripled under both straight-line and accelerated methods. How would cash be affected? Be specific.

Table for Problem 9–2
(amounts in thousands)

| | 1. ZERO INCOME TAXES | | 2. 40% INCOME TAXES | |
	Straight-line Depreciation	Accelerated Depreciation	Straight-line Depreciation	Accelerated Depreciation
Revenues	$	$	$	$
Cash operating expenses				
Cash provided by operations before income taxes				
Depreciation expense				
Operating income				
Income tax expense				
Net income				
Supplementary analysis:				
Cash provided by operations before income taxes				
Income tax expense				
Net cash provided by operations	$	$	$	$

9–3. **DISPOSAL OF EQUIPMENT.** (Alternates are 9–9 and 9–10.) Lopez Company acquired equipment for $32,000 with an expected useful life of five years and a $2,000 expected residual value. Straight-line depreciation was used. The equipment was sold at the end of the fourth year for $15,000 cash.

Required:

1. Compute the gain or loss on the sale. Show the effects of the sale on the balance sheet equation, identifying all specific accounts by name. Where and how would the sale appear on the income statement?
2. (a) Show the journal entries and postings to T-accounts for the transaction in requirement 1. (b) Repeat 2a, assuming that the cash sales price was $5,000 instead of $15,000.

9–4. **VARIOUS INTANGIBLE ASSETS.** (Alternates are 9–11 and 9–12.) Consider the following:

1. On December 28, 19X1, Bach Company purchased a patent for a tape recorder for $340,000. The patent has ten years of its legal life remaining. Technology changes fast, so Bach expects the patent to be worthless in four years. What will be the amortization for 19X2?
2. On December 29, 19X1, a publisher acquires the copyright for a book by Ted Kennedy for $2 million. Most sales of this book are expected to take place during 19X2 and 19X3. What will be the amortization for 19X2?
3. On January 4, 19X1, Company X acquires Company Y for $30 million and can assign only $25 million to identifiable individual assets. What is the minimum account of amortization of the goodwill for 19X1? Could the entire amount be written off in 19X1? Why?
4. In 19X1, Company C spent $10 million in its research department, which resulted in new valuable patents. In December 19X1, Company D paid $10 million to an outside inventor for some valuable new patents. How would the income statements for 19X1 for each company be affected? How would the balance sheets as of December 31, 19X1, be affected?

9–5. FUNDAMENTAL DEPRECIATION POLICIES. (Alternates are 9–1, 9–6, and 9–32.) The Seattle office of the United Parcel Service acquired some new package-handling equipment for $2 million. The equipment's predicted useful life is eight years and predicted residual value is $240,000.

Required:

Prepare a depreciation schedule similar to Exhibit 9–3, comparing straight-line, sum-of-the-years'-digits, and declining-balance at twice the straight-line rate. Show all amounts in thousands of dollars (rounded to the nearest thousand). Limit the schedule to each of the first three years of useful life. Show the depreciation for each year and the book value at the end of each year. (Note that this is a comparison of methods used for reporting to shareholders. Such methods may differ from those used for reporting to the income tax authorities.)

9–6. POPULAR DEPRECIATION METHODS. (Alternates are 9–1, 9–5, and 9–32.) The annual report of Alaska Airlines contained the following footnote:

☐ PROPERTY, EQUIPMENT AND DEPRECIATION—Provision is made for depreciation principally by the straight-line method over the estimated useful lives of the related assets, which are as follows:

Buildings	10–30 years
Flight equipment—	
Boeing 727-100	10 years
Boeing 727-200	14 years
Boeing 737-200C	14 years
Other equipment	3–15 years

Required:

Consider a Boeing 727-100 airplane, which was acquired for $24 million on January 1, 19X1. Its expected residual value was $2 million. Prepare a tabular comparison of the annual depreciation and book value for each of the first three years of service life under straight-line, sum-of-the-years'-digits, and double-declining-balance depreciation. Show all amounts in thousands of dollars (rounded to the nearest thousand). (Note that this is a comparison of methods used for reporting to shareholders. Such methods may differ from those used for reporting to the income tax authorities.) *Hint:* See Exhibit 9–3, page 381.

9–7. DEPRECIATION, INCOME TAXES, AND CASH FLOW. (Alternates are 9–2 and 9–8.) The 1985 annual report of NYNEX Corporation, owner of New England Telephone and New York Telephone, listed the following property, plant, and equipment:

Total property, plant, and equipment, gross	$23,561,300,000
Less accumulated depreciation	6,454,600,000
Property, plant, and equipment, net	$17,106,700,000

The cash balance was $170,800,000.

Depreciation expense during 1985 was $1,433,200,000. The condensed income statement follows:

Revenues	$10,313,600,000
Expenses	8,003,500,000
Operating income	$ 2,310,100,000

For purposes of this problem, assume that all revenues and expenses, excluding depreciation, are for cash. Thus cash operating expenses were $8,003,500,000 − $1,433,200,000 = $6,570,300,000.

Required:

1. NYNEX uses straight-line depreciation. Suppose accelerated depreciation for 1985 had been $1,833,200,000 instead of $1,433,200,000. Assume zero income taxes. Fill in the blanks in the accompanying table (in thousands of dollars).
2. Repeat requirement 1, but assume an income tax rate of 40%. Assume also that NYNEX uses the same depreciation method for reporting to shareholders and to income tax authorities.
3. Compare your answers to requirements 1 and 2. Does depreciation provide cash? Explain as precisely as possible.
4. Assume that NYNEX had used straight-line depreciation for reporting to shareholders and to income tax authorities. Indicate the change (increase or decrease and amount) in the following balances if NYNEX had used accelerated depreciation instead of straight-line for 1985 only: Cash, Accumulated Depreciation, Operating Income, Retained Income. What would be the new balances in Cash and Accumulated Depreciation?
5. Refer to requirement 1. Suppose depreciation were increased by an extra $300 million under both straight-line and accelerated methods. How would cash be affected? Be specific.

Table for Problem 9–7
(amounts in thousands)

	1. ZERO INCOME TAXES		2. 40% INCOME TAXES	
	Straight-line Depreciation	Accelerated Depreciation	Straight-line Depreciation	Accelerated Depreciation
Revenues	$	$	$	$
Cash operating expenses				
Cash provided by operations before income taxes				
Depreciation expense				
Operating income				
Income tax expense				
Net income				
Supplementary analysis:				
Cash provided by operations before income taxes				
Income tax expense				
Net cash provided by operations	$	$	$	$

9–8. **DEPRECIATION, INCOME TAXES, AND CASH FLOW.** (Alternates are 9–2 and 9–7.) Federal Express Corporation provides door-to-door overnight delivery of packages and documents throughout the United States. The company's annual report showed the following balances (in thousands):

Revenues	$589,493
Operating expenses	487,396
Operating income	$102,097

Federal Express had "depreciation and amortization" expense of $39,010,000 (included in operating expenses). The company's ending cash balance was $66,108,000.

Federal Express reported the property and equipment in the following way (in thousands):

Flight equipment	$289,700
Package handling and ground support equipment	68,120
Buildings and leasehold improvements	25,632
Other property and equipment	83,742
	467,194
Less accumulated depreciation and amortization	93,944
Net property and equipment	$373,250

For purposes of this problem, assume that all revenues and expenses, excluding depreciation, are for cash.

Required:

1. Federal Express used straight-line depreciation and amortization. Suppose accelerated depreciation had been $49,010,000 instead of $39,010,000. Assume zero income taxes. Fill in the blanks in the accompanying table (in thousands of dollars).
2. Repeat requirement 1, but assume an income tax rate of 45%. Assume also that Federal Express uses the same depreciation method for reporting to shareholders and to income tax authorities.
3. Compare your answers to requirements 1 and 2. Does depreciation provide cash? Explain as precisely as possible.
4. Assume that Federal Express had used straight-line depreciation for reporting to shareholders and to income tax authorities. Indicate the change (increase or decrease and amount) in the following balances if Federal Express had used accelerated depreciation rather than straight-line: Cash, Accumulated Depreciation and Amortization, Operating Income, and Retained Income. What would be the new balances in Cash and Accumulated Depreciation and Amortization?
5. Refer to requirement 1. Suppose depreciation were doubled under both straight-line and accelerated methods. How would cash be affected? Be specific.

Table for Problem 9–8
(amounts in thousands)

	1. ZERO INCOME TAXES		2. 45% INCOME TAXES	
	Straight-line Depreciation	Accelerated Depreciation	Straight-line Depreciation	Accelerated Depreciation
Revenues	$	$	$	$
Cash operating expenses				
Cash provided by operations before income taxes				
Depreciation expense				
Operating income				
Income tax expense				
Net income				
Supplementary analysis:				
Cash provided by operations before income taxes				
Income tax expense				
Net cash provided by operations	$	$	$	$

9–9. **DISPOSAL OF EQUIPMENT.** (Alternates are 9–3 and 9–10.) Alaska Airlines acquired a new Boeing 727-100 airplane for $22 million. Its expected residual value was $2 million. The company's annual report indicated that straight-line depreciation was used based on an estimated service life of ten years. In addition, the company stated: "The cost and related accumulated depreciation of assets sold or retired are removed from the appropriate accounts, and gain or loss, if any, is recognized in Other Income (Expense)."

Show all amounts in millions of dollars.

1. Assume that the equipment is sold at the end of the sixth year for $11 million cash. Compute the gain or loss on the sale. Show the effects of the sale on the balance sheet equation, identifying all specific accounts by name. Where and how would the sale appear on the income statement?
2. (a) Show the journal entries and postings to T-accounts for the transaction in requirement 1. (b) Repeat 2a, assuming that the cash sales price was $8 million instead of $11 million.

9–10. DISPOSAL OF PROPERTY AND EQUIPMENT. (Alternates are 9–3 and 9–9.) Rockwell International is an advanced technology company operating primarily in aerospace and electronics. The company's annual report indicated that both accelerated and straight-line depreciation were used for its property and equipment. In addition, the annual report said: "When assets are sold or retired, accumulated depreciation is charged with the portion thereof applicable to such assets. The resulting gain or loss is recorded in income in the year of sale or retirement."

In 1985 Rockwell received $27.5 million for property and equipment that it sold.

Required:

1. Assume that the total property and equipment in question were originally acquired for $150 million, and the $27.5 million was received in cash. There was a gain of $8.5 million on the sale. Compute the accumulated depreciation on the equipment. Show the effects of the sale on the balance sheet equation, identifying all specific accounts by name.
2. For this requirement, round your entries to the nearest thousand dollars. (a) Show the journal entries and postings to T-accounts for the transaction in requirement 1. (b) Repeat 2a, assuming that the cash sales price was $17,500,000 cash instead of $27,500,000.

9–11. VARIOUS INTANGIBLE ASSETS. (Alternates are 9–4 and 9–12.)

1. The most recent annual report of Associated Hosts, owner and operator of many restaurants and hotels, including the Beverly Hillcrest Hotel, stated: "It is the company's policy to defer preopening costs during periods of construction of new units or remodeling of existing units and to amortize such costs over a period of 12 to 24 months commencing on the opening date."

In 1985, preopening costs of $582,000 were capitalized. The beginning-of-the-year asset balance for preopening costs was $779,000, and the end-of-the-year balance was $617,000. Compute the amortization for 1985.

2. On May 1, 1985, Sanders Associates, Incorporated, maker of advanced technology electronic systems, acquired the Architectural, Engineering, and Construction Division of Personal CAD Systems, Inc., for $7.5 million. Sanders could assign only $4,431,000 to identifiable individual assets. Assume that Sanders Associates has a fiscal year ending on April 30. What is the amount of goodwill created by the acquisition? What is the minimum amount of amortization for the year ended April 30, 1986? Could the entire amount be written off that year?

3. (a) In 1986, DuPont spent over $300 million in its research departments, and this resulted in valuable new patents. (b) Suppose that in December 1986, DuPont had paid $326 million to various outside companies for the same new patents. How would the income statement for 1986 have been affected under a and b? The balance sheet, December 31, 1986?

LONG-LIVED ASSETS AND DEPRECIATION

4. On December 29, 1986, CBS Corporation purchased a patent on some broadcasting equipment for $900,000. The patent has sixteen years of its legal life remaining. Because technology moves rapidly, CBS expects the patent to be worthless in three years. What is the amortization for 1987?

9–12. VARIOUS INTANGIBLE ASSETS. (Alternates are 9–4 and 9–11.) Consider the following:

1. (a) Dow Chemical Company's annual report indicated that research and development expenditures for the year were $507 million. How did this amount affect operating income, which was $848 million? (b) Suppose the entire $507 million arose from outlays for patents acquired from various outside parties on December 30. What would be the operating income for the year? (c) How would Dow's December 31 balance sheet be affected by *b*?

2. On December 30, 1986, American Telephone and Telegraph Company (AT&T) acquired new patents on some communications equipment for $10 million. Technology changes quickly. The equipment's useful life is expected to be five years rather than the seventeen-year life of the patent. What will be the amortization for 1987?

3. Hilton Hotels has an account classified under assets in its balance sheet called preopening costs. A footnote said that these costs "are charged to income over a three-year period after the opening date." Suppose expenditures for preopening costs in 1986 were $2,000,000 and the preopening costs account balance on December 31, 1986, was $1,840,000 and on December 31, 1985, was $2,390,000. What amount was amortized for 1986?

4. The Gannett Co., Inc., publisher of many newspapers, including *USA Today*, purchased radio stations KKBQ–AM and FM in Houston and WDAE–AM in Tampa for a total of $41 million. A footnote in the annual report stated that goodwill is "amortized over a period of 40 years." Assume that both purchases were made on January 2 and that Gannett could assign only $33 million to identifiable individual assets. What is the minimum amount of amortization of goodwill for the first year? Could the entire amount be written off immediately? Explain.

ADDITIONAL ASSIGNMENT MATERIAL

☐ General Coverage

9–13. Distinguish between *tangible* and *intangible* assets.

9–14. "The cash discount on the purchase of equipment is income to the buyer during the year of acquisition." Do you agree? Explain.

9–15. "When an expenditure is capitalized, stockholders' equity is credited." Do you agree? Explain.

9–16. "Accumulated depreciation is like a hole in a doughnut." Explain.

9–17. "Accumulated depreciation is a sum of cash being accumulated for the replacement of fixed assets." Do you agree? Explain.

9–18. "The accounting process of depreciation is allocation, not valuation." Explain.

9–19. "Accelerated depreciation is the reduction of useful life." Do you agree? Explain.

9–20. "Keeping two sets of books is immoral." Do you agree? Explain.

9–21. "Most of the money we'll spend this year for replacing our equipment will be generated by depreciation." Do you agree? Explain.

9–22. Criticize: "Depreciation is the loss in value of a fixed asset over a given span of time."

9–23. What factors influence the estimate of useful life in depreciation accounting?

9–24. "The gain on sale of equipment should be reported fully on the income statement." Explain what the complete reporting would include.

9–25. "Changes in accounting estimates should be reported prospectively rather than retroactively." Explain.

9–26. The manager of a division reported to the president of the company: "Now that our major capital improvements are finished, the division's expenses will be much lower." Is this really what he means to say? Explain.

9–27. Explain how goodwill is computed.

9–28. "Internally acquired patents are accounted for differently than externally acquired patents." Explain the difference.

9–29. "Goodwill may have nothing to do with the personality of the manager or employees." Do you agree? Explain.

9–30. "Accountants sometimes are too concerned with physical objects or contractual rights." Explain.

9–31. Compare the choice between straight-line and accelerated depreciation with the choice between FIFO and LIFO. Give at least one similarity and one difference.

9–32. **FUNDAMENTAL DEPRECIATION APPROACHES.** (Alternates are 9–1, 9–5, and 9–6.) A transportation company acquired some new trucks for $1 million. Their predicted useful life is five years, and predicted residual value is $100,000.

Required:

Prepare a depreciation schedule similar to Exhibit 9–3, comparing straight-line, sum-of-the-years'-digits, and declining-balance at twice the straight-line rate.

9–33. **DEPRECIATION, INCOME TAXES, AND CASH FLOW.** (Alternate is 9–48.) Unitas Company began business with cash and common stock equity of $300,000. The same day, December 31, 19X1, equipment was acquired for $100,000 cash. The equipment had an expected useful life of five years and a predicted residual value of $10,000. The first year's operations generated cash sales of $320,000 and cash operating expenses of $170,000.

Required:

1. Prepare an analysis of transactions for December 31, 19X1, plus the year 19X2, using the balance sheet equation format as illustrated in Exhibit 9–4. Assume (a) straight-line depreciation and (b) sum-of-the-years'-digits depreciation. Assume zero income taxes. Exhibit 9–4 is on page 384.
2. Repeat requirement 1, but assume an income tax rate of 50% (to ease computations). Income taxes are paid in cash. The company uses the same depreciation method for reporting to shareholders and to income tax authorities.
3. Prepare columnar (a) income statements for 19X2 and (b) balance sheets as of December 31, 19X2, that compare the effects of the four alternatives covered in requirements 1 and 2. (*Hint*: See the illustration in the chapter, page 385.)
4. Compare your answers to requirements 1 and 2. Does depreciation provide cash? Explain as precisely as possible.
5. Refer to requirement 1. Suppose depreciation were tripled under straight-line and SYD methods. How would cash be affected? Be specific.

9–34. **COMPUTING ACQUISITION COSTS.** From the following data, calculate the cost to be added to the Land account and the Building account of El Camino Hospital:

On January 1, 19X5, the hospital acquired a thirty-acre parcel of land immediately adjacent to its existing facilities. The land included a warehouse, parking lots, and driveways. The hospital paid $200,000 cash and also gave a note for $1 million, payable at $100,000 per year plus interest of 10% on the outstanding balance.

The warehouse was demolished at a cash cost of $150,000 and replaced with a new hospital building. The building required a cash down payment of $1 million plus a mortgage note of $5 million. The mortgage was payable at $250,000 per year plus interest of 11% on the outstanding balance.

9–35. GOVERNMENT EQUIPMENT. A transportation agency of the state of California acquired some used computer equipment. Installation costs were $9,000. Repair costs prior to use were $7,000. The purchasing manager's salary is $29,000 per annum. The invoice price was $200,000. The seller paid his salesman a commission of 1% and offered the buyer a cash discount of 2% if the invoice was paid within sixty days. Freight costs were $4,200. Repairs during the first year of use were $6,000. Compute the total capitalized cost to be added to the Equipment account. The seller was paid within sixty days.

9–36. BASKET PURCHASE. On January 31, 19X2, McDonald's, a large fast-foods chain, acquired an existing building and land for $900,000 from a local restaurant that had failed. The tax assessor had placed an assessed valuation on May 1, 19X1, as follows:

Land	$ 50,000
Building	200,000
Total	$250,000

Many localities use formulas for assessing property at considerably below its full market value.

Required:

How much of the $900,000 purchase price should be attributed to the building? Why?

9–37. BASKET PURCHASE OF SPORTS FRANCHISE. William Rooney acquired the assets of the San Francisco football team, including the player contracts. The total cost was $12 million. The largest assets were the franchise and the contracts. For reporting to the IRS, the franchise has an indefinite useful life. The contracts had a five-year useful life. Other assets are relatively minor. The seller, Samuel Stefano, showed the following book values of the assets (in millions):

Player contracts	$3
Franchise	5
Total book value	$8

Required:

As Rooney, if you had complete discretion for tax purposes, how much of the $12 million price would you allocate to the contracts? Explain.

9–38. DEPRECIATION FOR PARTS OF YEAR. Fumani Company acquired equipment on April 2, 19X1, for $64,000 cash. Its expected useful life was five years, and its expected residual value was $4,000. The sum-of-the-years'-digits method of depreciation was adopted. Prepare a schedule of depreciation for each calendar year of use. Show the total amount of depreciation for each calendar year affected.

9–39. REPAIRS AND IMPROVEMENTS. Lopez Company acquired equipment for $32,000 with an expected useful life of five years and a $2,000 expected residual value. Straight-line depreciation was used. During its fourth year of service, expenditures related to the equipment were

1. Oiling and greasing, $100.
2. Replacing belts and hoses, $150.
3. Major overhaul during the final week of the year, including the replacement of an engine. The useful life of the equipment was extended from five to seven years. The cost was $8,000. The residual value is now expected to be $4,000 instead of $2,000.

Indicate in words how each of the three items would affect the income statement and the balance sheet. Prepare a tabulation that compares the original depreciation schedule with the revised depreciation schedule.

9–40. CAPITAL AND REVENUE EXPENDITURES. Consider the following transactions:

a. Acquired building for a down payment plus a mortgage payable.
b. Paid interest on building mortgage.
c. Paid principal on building mortgage.
d. Paid cash dividends.
e. Paid janitorial wages.
f. Paid security guard wages.
g. Paid plumbers for repair of leaky faucets.
h. Acquired new air-conditioning system for the building.
i. Replaced smashed front door (not covered by insurance).
j. Paid travel expenses of sales personnel.

Answer by letter:

1. Indicate which transactions are capital expenditures.
2. Indicate which transactions are revenue expenditures.

9–41. UNITS-OF-PRODUCTION METHOD. The Athens Trucking Company has many trucks that are kept for a useful life of 400,000 kilometers. Depreciation is based on kilometers driven. Suppose a new truck is purchased for DR 700,000 cash (*DR* is the Greek drachma). Its expected residual value is DR 20,000. During Year 1 it was driven 80,000 kilometers, and during Year 2, it was driven 110,000 kilometers. What is the depreciation expense for each of the two years?

9–42. DEPRECIATION OF SPECIAL MACHINERY. Large tunnel-boring machines are frequently depreciated on the basis of the number of days the equipment can be operated. Suppose a machine cost $2 million and is expected to be operated for 1,000 days. Its removal cost will just equal its salvage value. The machine was operated 140 days during 19X3. How much depreciation would be recognized for 19X3?

9–43. LEASEHOLD IMPROVEMENTS. Safeway Stores has a twenty-year lease on a store in a shopping center. Near the end of the thirteenth year of its lease, Safeway exercised its rights under the lease, removed the existing shelving and floor coverings, and installed more attractive and serviceable replacements at a cost of $70,000. The useful life of the latter was predicted to be twelve years.

What accounts would be affected by the $70,000 outlay? What would be the annual amortization?

9–44. DEPLETION. A zinc mine contains an estimated 400,000 tons of zinc ore. The mine cost $5 million. The tonnage mined during 19X4, the first year of operations, was 50,000 tons.

1. What was the depletion for 19X4?
2. Suppose that in January 19X5 it was discovered that the mine probably contained 100,000 more tons than originally estimated. What was the estimated depletion for 19X5, assuming that 30,000 tons were mined?

9–45. CHANGES IN DEPRECIATION ESTIMATES. Fleck Company acquired equipment for $32,000 with an expected useful life of five years and a $2,000 expected residual value. Straight-line depreciation was adopted. Suppose it is the end of Year 3. The company's engineers have altered their expectations; the equipment's new expected useful life is eight instead of five years. Furthermore, the expected residual value is $4,000 instead of $2,000.

1. Using the "prospective" method, compute the new annual straight-line depreciation.
2. Critics of the "prospective" method favor using the "retroactive" method instead. Prepare a table comparing annual depreciation throughout the eight-year life using the prospective method and the retroactive method. Which method do you favor? Why?

9–46. NATURE OF RESEARCH COSTS. Three electrical engineers, headed by Janet Hernandez, resigned from the Silicon Valley company for which they worked. Hernandez had supervised a project to develop a powerful, user-friendly personal computer that could be carried in a briefcase. The company had abandoned the project, but Hernandez and her two co-workers believed in its technological and financial feasibility. They knew that at least two or three years of research would be necessary before a marketable product would be produced, but their entrepreneurial spirit drove them to set up their own company. They raised $500,000 and received an additional $3 million through a venture capital firm. Everyone realized the high risk involved in the new company, but the potential returns were very high.

In early 1986 the new company was incorporated, Hernandez was appointed president, and a research staff was hired. By the end of 1986, $1,200,000 had been expended, mostly for researchers' salaries, but also for related research costs.

Hernandez and the other executives were pleased at the end of the first year. As expected, no marketable product had been produced, but considerable progress had been made. Everyone was optimistic that the briefcase computer would be fully developed within one or two years.

Required:

How would you account for the $1,200,000? Would you write it off as an expense in 1986? Carry it indefinitely? Write it off systematically over three years or some longer span? Why? Explain, giving particular attention to the idea of an asset as an unexpired cost.

9–47. MEANING OF BOOK VALUE. Metropolitan Company purchased an office building twenty years ago for $1 million, $200,000 of which was attributable to land. The mortgage has been fully paid. The current balance sheet follows:

Cash		$350,000	Stockholders'	
Land		200,000	equity	$675,000
Building at cost	$800,000			
Accumulated depreciation	675,000			
Net book value		125,000		
Total assets		$675,000		

The company is about to borrow $1.8 million on a first mortgage to modernize and expand the building. This amounts to 60% of the combined appraised value of the land and building before the modernization and expansion.

Required:

Prepare a balance sheet after the loan is made and the building is expanded and modernized. Comment on its significance.

412   CHAPTER 9

9–48. DEPRECIATION, INCOME TAXES, AND CASH FLOW. (Alternate is 9–33.) A newspaper story stated: "The Indiana Steel Company had a cash flow last year of $1,500,000, consisting of $1,000,000 of net income plus $500,000 of depreciation. New plant facilities helped the cash flow, because depreciation was 25% higher than in the preceding year." "Cash flow" is frequently used as a synonym for "cash provided by operations," which, in turn, is cash revenue less cash operating expenses and income taxes.

Grant McCoy was encouraged by the quotation because the McCoy Company had just acquired a vast amount of new computer equipment. These acquisitions had placed a severe financial strain on the company. McCoy was heartened because he thought that the added cash flow from the depreciation of the new equipment should ease the financial pressures on the company.

McCoy Company had income before income taxes last year (19X2) of $200,000. Depreciation was $200,000; it will also be $200,000 on the old equipment in 19X3.

Revenue in 19X2 was $2.9 million (all in cash), and operating expenses other than depreciation were $2.5 million (all in cash).

In 19X3, the new equipment is expected to help increase revenue by $1 million. However, operating expenses other than depreciation will increase by $800,000.

Required:

1. Suppose depreciation on the new equipment for financial-reporting purposes is $100,000. What would be the "cash flow" from operations (cash provided by operations) for 19X3? Show computations. Ignore income taxes.
2. Repeat requirement 1, assuming that the depreciation on the new equipment is $50,000. Ignore income taxes.
3. Assume an income tax rate of 40%. (a) Repeat requirement 1; (b) repeat requirement 2. Assume that the same amount of depreciation is shown for tax purposes and for financial-reporting purposes.
4. In your own words, state as accurately as possible the effects of depreciation on "cash flow." Comment on requirements 1, 2, and 3 above in order to bring out your points. This is a more important requirement than requirements 1, 2, and 3.

□ Understanding Published Financial Reports

9–49. CLASSIC CASE FROM THE BUSINESS PRESS. A news story regarding Chrysler Corporation stated:

□ Yet the $7.5 billion that John J. Riccardo, its money man, estimates the company will need to finance a recovery over the next five years is huge by any standard. But, says Riccardo, "half is charged to the P&L [profit and loss] as incurred, so we're looking for $3.75 billion. Of that, about 60% will be recovered in depreciation and amortization. That leaves a balance of $1.5 billion over the five years, to be financed through earnings, borrowings, and divestitures. Over the period, that overall number is manageable.

Required:

Explain or comment on the following:

1. "Half is charged to the P&L as incurred, so we're looking for $3.75 billion."
2. "Of that, about 60% will be recovered in depreciation and amortization."

9–50. BALANCE SHEET PRESENTATION. Consider the presentation of the Procter & Gamble Company, whose brands include *Tide*, *Jif*, *Charmin*, *Folger's*, and *Crest* (in millions of dollars):

	JUNE 30	
	1985	1984
PROPERTY, PLANT, AND EQUIPMENT, at cost		
Buildings	1,114	1,087
Machinery and equipment	6,082	5,308
Land	118	117
Timberlands, less depletion	152	134
	7,466	6,646
Less accumulated depreciation	2,174	1,978
	5,292	4,668

Required: | Do any features of this presentation seem unusual? Explain.

9-51. DECLINING-BALANCE DEPRECIATION. The annual report of a publishing company, John Wiley & Sons, states: "The Company depreciates buildings on the double-declining balance method over a 50 year life."

Required: | Suppose Wiley acquired a building for $2 million on May 1, 1987, the beginning of its fiscal year. What depreciation expense would be reported on Wiley's income statement for its fiscal years ended April 30, 1988, 1989, and 1990, respectively?

9-52. CAPITAL OR REVENUE EXPENDITURES. Disputes sometimes arise between the taxpayer and the Internal Revenue Service regarding whether legal costs should be deductible as expenses in the year incurred (revenue expenditures) or be considered as capital expenditures because they relate to defending or perfecting title to business property.

Consider three examples from court cases:

EXAMPLE 1: Several years after Rock set up his stone-quarrying business, Smalltown passed an ordinance banning it. Rock spent $1,000 to invalidate the ordinance.

EXAMPLE 2: Now suppose Rock decided to expand his business. So he applied to Smalltown for a permit to build an additional crusher. It was denied because an ordinance prohibited the expansion of nonconforming uses, including quarrying. Rock sued to invalidate the ordinance and won after spending $2,000. He then built the crusher.

EXAMPLE 3: Smalltown's zoning board established a restrictive building (setback) line across Rock's business property. The line lowered the property's value. Rock spent $3,000 trying unsuccessfully to challenge it.

Required: | Indicate whether each example should be deemed (a) a revenue expenditure or (b) a capital expenditure. Briefly explain your answer.

9-53. RENTAL CARS. RCA Corporation's annual report contained the following note:

☐ Depreciable Assets. Plant and equipment, rental automobiles, and other revenue-earning equipment are generally depreciated using the straight-line method over their estimated useful lives or, in the case of leasehold improvements, over the term of the lease, if shorter. Upon disposal of rental automobiles and other revenue-earning equipment, depreciation expense is adjusted for the difference between net proceeds from sale and the remaining book value. Rental automobiles are held for approximately one year and accordingly are classified as current assets.

1. Assume that some new cars are acquired on October 1, 1986, for $120 million. The useful life is one year. Expected residual values are $84 million. Prepare a summary journal entry for depreciation for 1986. The fiscal year ends on December 31.
2. Prepare a summary journal entry for depreciation for the first six months of 1987.
3. Assume that the automobiles are sold for $96 million cash on October 1, 1987. Prepare the journal entry for the sale.
4. What is the total depreciation expense for 1987? If the $96 million proceeds could exactly have been predicted when the cars were originally acquired, what would depreciation expense have been in 1986? In 1987? Explain.

9–54. **ACCOUNTING FOR CASUALTY ITEM.** A fully insured oil tanker owned by the Murphy Oil Company sank in the Gulf of Mexico. It had been fully depreciated and hence its carrying value was zero at the time of the disaster. The insurance company paid Murphy $300,000 in cash, a material amount. How should this transaction be reported in the financial statements? Why? Be specific.

9–55. **AIRPLANE CRASH.** A DC-10 airplane owned by American Airlines crashed. It had been purchased for $18 million but was carried on American's books at $10.8 million. The plane's replacement cost, reflected in the insurance payment, was $37 million.

A news story stated: "American Airlines reported yesterday that second-quarter earnings jumped 117.1 percent over those a year earlier. The quarter's profits included a $24.3 million after-tax gain from the proceeds of insurance . . ."

1. Prepare an analysis of the above facts, including the acquisition of a new airplane. Use the format of the balance sheet equation and also prepare the related journal entries. Because of various complications, the applicable income tax was relatively small.
2. Do you think a casualty should generate a reported gain? Why?

9–56. **DISPOSAL OF EQUIPMENT.** *Airline Executive* reported on an airline as follows:

☐ Lufthansa's highly successful policy of rolling over entire fleets in roughly ten years—before the aircraft have outlived their usefulness—got started in a "spectacular" way when seven first-generation 747s were sold.

☐ The 747s were bought six to nine years earlier for $22–$28 million each and sold for about the same price.

1. Assume an average original cost of $25 million each, an average original expected useful life of ten years, a 10% expected residual value, and an average actual life of eight years before disposal. Use straight-line depreciation. Compute the total gain or loss on the sale of the seven planes.
2. Prepare a summary journal entry for the sale.

9–57. **INTANGIBLE ASSETS.** General Television, a television cable company, acquired three competitors, paying $600,000 for fifty-nine hundred subscriber contracts, nonexclusive municipal franchises, pole rental agreements, right-of-way agreements, and goodwill.

For stockholder-reporting purposes, how would you account for the costs attributable to the subscriber contracts? Be specific. For tax purposes, would the Internal Revenue Service probably accept the accounting you suggest? Explain.

9–58. BASKET PURCHASE AND INTANGIBLES. A tax newsletter stated: "When a business is sold, part of the sales price may be allocated to a 'covenant not to compete' and another part to 'goodwill.' How this allocation is made can have important tax consequences to both the buyer and seller."

A large law firm, organized as a professional services corporation, purchased a successful local firm for $125,000. Only $25,000 was assigned to individual assets. The other $100,000 was for both a covenant not to compete for five years and goodwill. Suppose the buyer has legally supportable latitude concerning how to allocate this amount, as follows:

	ALLOCATION ONE	ALLOCATION TWO
Covenant	$ 65,000	$ 50,000
Goodwill	35,000	50,000
Total for two assets	$100,000	$100,000

Required:

1. For income tax purposes, which allocation would the buyer favor? Why?
2. For shareholder-reporting purposes, which allocation would the buyer favor? Why?

9–59. DEPRECIATION OF PROFESSIONAL SPORTS CONTRACTS. "Accounting Professor Says the Owners Lost $27 Million" read the headline on July 10, 1985. Major league baseball players and owners were engaged in contract negotiations. The owners claimed to have lost $43 million in 1984, and the Players Association maintained that the owners had made a profit of as much as $10 million. George Sorter, professor of accounting at New York University, fixed the loss at $27 million, primarily because he subtracted "initial roster depreciation" from the owners' figure. "That depreciation, an amount that arises when a team is sold and a portion of the purchase price that makes up player contracts is paid off [amortized] over several years, should not be treated as an operating expense," Sorter said. When a team is sold, an amount representing the value of current player contracts is put into an intangible asset account and amortized (or depreciated) over several years.

Required:

Explain why such an intangible asset account is created. Should this asset be amortized (or depreciated), thereby reducing income? Why would Professor Sorter eliminate this expense when assessing the financial operating performance of the major league teams?

9–60. VALUATION OF INTANGIBLE ASSETS OF FOOTBALL TEAM. New owners acquired the Los Angeles Rams football team for $7.2 million. They valued the contracts of their forty players at a total of $3.5 million, the franchise at $3.6 million, and other assets at $100,000. For income tax purposes, the Rams amortized the $3.5 million over five years; therefore they took a tax deduction of $700,000 annually.

The Internal Revenue Service challenged the deductions. It maintained that only $300,000 of the $7.2 million purchase price was attributable to the player contracts, and that the $3.2 million of the $3.5 million in dispute should be attributed to the league franchise rights. Such franchise rights are regarded by the Internal Revenue Service as a valuable asset with an indefinite future life; therefore no amortization is permitted for tax-reporting purposes.

Suppose the operating income for each of the five years (before any amortization) was $1 million.

Required:

1. Consider the reporting to the Internal Revenue Service. Tabulate a comparison of annual operating income (after amortization) according to two approaches,

(a) the Rams's and (b) the IRS's. What is the difference in annual operating income?

2. Consider the reporting to shareholders. Reports to shareholders by American companies do not have to adhere to the same basis used for income tax purposes. The Rams had been using a five-year life for player contracts and a forty-year life for the league franchise rights. Tabulate a comparison of operating income (after amortization) using (a) this initial approach and (b) the approach whereby only $300,000 would have been attributed to player contracts. What is the difference in annual operating income?

3. Comment on the results in requirements 1 and 2. Which alternative do you think provides the more informative report of operating results? Why?

9–61. DEFERRED CHARGES. Simmons Airlines, Inc., is a regional carrier in the Midwest. Consider the following item under "Other assets" in its annual report:

	1984	1985
Deferred development costs, net of amortization (1984, $161,000; 1985, $268,000)	$446,000	$268,000

A footnote to the annual report stated: "Deferred development costs: Significant costs related to obtaining FAA operating certificates, inaugurating service over new routes and introducing new types of aircraft are deferred and amortized over five years."

Required:

1. Suppose no new deferred development costs were recorded during 1985. Calculate the amount of deferred development costs amortized during 1985. *Hint*: Use two T-accounts, one for deferred development costs and one for accumulated amortization of deferred development costs. When a particular deferred development cost is completely amortized, its original amount is deducted from both accounts.

2. Suppose Simmons received delivery of new Boeing 737s halfway through 1986 and incurred $42,000 of training costs associated with the introduction of the new aircraft. Show the journal entries for recording these costs (assume that payment was in cash) and for recognizing amortization at the end of the year.

9–62. ACQUISITION OF INTANGIBLE ASSETS. *Forbes* reported that CGA Computer Associates, a computer software marketer, had acquired another software company, Allen Services Corporation, for $19 million. CGA got only $1.2 million in net tangible assets.

The CGA president insisted that "the premium was justified because Allen had built up a huge inventory of software that was not reflected in the books. The reason: Spending on developing new software systems is treated as research and development and therefore written off immediately. In this case, CGA had to book $11.7 million of the $17.8 million discrepancy as software and the rest as goodwill."

The software would be amortized over its useful life, five years, because of the pace of developments in computers. Goodwill would be amortized over forty years.

Required:

Compute the expenses for (1) amortization of software and (2) amortization of goodwill for the first complete year after the acquisition.

9–63. SOFTWARE DEVELOPMENT COSTS. Microsoft, Incorporated, is one of the largest producers of software for personal computers. In 1985 one of its divisions began working on some special business applications software for Apple MacIntosh computers. Suppose $400,000 had been spent on the project by the end of the year, but it was not yet clear whether the software was technologically feasible.

On about July 1, 1986, after spending another $200,000, management decided that the software was technologically feasible. During the second half of 1986, the division spent another $500,000 on this project. In December 1986 the product was announced, with deliveries to begin in March 1987. No research and development costs for the software were incurred after December 1987. Projected sales were: 1987, $400,000; 1988, $700,000; 1989, $600,000; 1990, $200,000; and 1991, $100,000.

Required:

1. Prepare journal entries to account for the research and development expenses for the software for 1985 and 1986. Assume that all expenditures were paid in cash.
2. Would any research and development expenses affect income in 1987? If so, prepare the appropriate journal entry. Actual 1987 sales were $400,000.

9–64. **DEPRECIATION PRACTICES.** The 1985 annual report of Sperry Corporation contained the following exact descriptions and data (in millions):

	MARCH 31	
	1985	1984
Property, plant and equipment, at cost	$1,270.8	$1,128.2
Less allowance for depreciation and amortization	577.0	501.6
Property, plant and equipment (net)	$ 693.8	$ 626.6

The annual report indicated that no gain or loss arose from the disposition of property, plant, and equipment. The company acquired additional property, plant, and equipment for $191.0 million.

Required:

During 1985, depreciation expense was $104 million and property was sold for $19.8 million cash. Compute (1) the gross amount of assets written off (sold or retired), (2) the amount of accumulated depreciation written off, and (3) the book value of the assets written off. *Hint*: The use of T-accounts may help your analysis.

9–65. **RECONSTRUCTION OF PLANT ASSET TRANSACTIONS** (J. Patell, adapted). The Ford Motor Company's balance sheets included (in millions of dollars):

Ford Motor Company

	DECEMBER 31	
	1985	1984
Property:		
Land, plant and equipment, at cost (Note 9)	21,048	18,500
Less accumulated depreciation	11,885	10,578
Net land, plant and equipment	9,163	7,922
Unamortized special tools	3,258	2,627
Net property	12,421	10,549

The following additional information was available from the income statement for 1985 (in millions):

Depreciation	1,444
Amortization of special tools	948

The account Unamortized Special Tools is increased by new investments in tools, dies, jigs, and fixtures necessary for new models and production processes. These investments are then amortized over various periods of two to four years. Hence the account is called "unamortized" because its amount will become amortized during future periods.

Required: *Hint*: Analyze with the help of T-accounts.

1. There were no disposals of special tools during 1985. Compute the cost of new acquisitions of special tools.
2. Suppose the proceeds from the sales of land, plant, and equipment during 1985 were $92 million, and the loss on sale of land, plant, and equipment was $25 million. Compute the original cost *and* the accumulated depreciation of the land, plant, and equipment that was sold.
3. Compute the cost of the new acquisitions of land, plant, and equipment.

9–66. **CHANGE IN SERVICE LIFE.** An annual report of TWA contained the following footnote:

☐ Note 2. *Change in accounting estimate.* TWA extended the estimated useful lives of Boeing 727-100 aircraft from principally sixteen years to principally twenty years. As a result, depreciation and amortization expense was decreased by $9,000,000.

The TWA annual report also contained the following data: depreciation, $235,-518,000; net income, $42,233,000.

The cost of the 727-100 aircraft subject to depreciation was $800 million. Residual values were predicted as 10% of acquisition cost.

Required: Assume an income tax rate of 46% throughout all parts of these requirements.

1. Was the effect of the change in estimated useful life a material difference? Explain, including computations.
2. The same year's annual report of Delta Airlines contained the following footnote:

   Depreciation—Substantially all of the flight equipment is being depreciated on a straight-line basis to residual values (10% of cost) over a 10-year period from dates placed in service.

   The Delta annual report also contained the following data: depreciation, $220,-979,000; net income, $146,474,000. Suppose Delta had used a twenty-year life instead of a ten-year life. Assume a 46% applicable income tax rate. Compute the new depreciation and net income.
3. Suppose TWA had used a ten-year life instead of a twenty-year life on its 727-100 equipment. Compute the new depreciation and net income. For purposes of this requirement, assume that the equipment cost $800 million and has been in service one year and that reported net income based on a twenty-year life was $42,233,000.

9–67. **ACQUISITION OF INTANGIBLE ASSETS.** In May 1985, American Brands, Inc., maker of Titleist golf balls, Master locks, and many other consumer products, purchased Foot-Joy, Inc., a manufacturer of golf shoes. The cost of $56,897,000 exceeded the fair market value of assets by $21,666,000. A footnote to the 1985 annual report stated: "Intangibles resulting from business acquisitions, comprising brands and trademarks and cost in excess of net assets of businesses acquired, are being amortized on a straight line basis over 40 years. Amortization of intangibles amounted to $6,-743,000 in 1985."

The following was on the balance sheet (in thousands):

	DECEMBER 31	
	1985	1984
Intangibles resulting from business acquisitions	$641,784	$597,727

American Brands acquired no companies other than Foot-Joy in 1985.

Required:

1. Calculate the amount of cost American Brands assigned to the brands and trademarks of Foot-Joy. *Hint*: Use a T-account.
2. Assume that eight months of amortization on the Foot-Joy intangibles was recognized in 1985. How much of the $597,727,000 beginning balance in the intangibles account was amortized in 1985?
3. What is the amount of intangibles recorded before 1970 and therefore not being amortized?

Chapter 10

LIABILITIES AND INTEREST

LEARNING OBJECTIVES

After studying this chapter, you should be able to

1. Explain the nature and presentation of various liabilities, including payroll taxes, product warranties, and contingent liabilities
2. Make the accounting entries for bonds payable and describe their effects on financial statements
3. Explain compound interest and the use of present value tables (Appendix 10A)
4. Compute effective-interest amortization and explain imputed interest (Appendix 10B)
5. Make the computations and accounting entries for leases (Appendix 10C)

This chapter discusses liabilities in more detail than in earlier presentations. The roles of interest and bonds are given particular attention.

To provide maximum flexibility for study, this chapter is organized as follows. The body focuses on an *introductory* coverage of commonly encountered liabilities. *More depth* is provided in the appendixes. Considerations of compound interest are covered in Appendix 10A, and the effective-interest method of amortization is explained in Appendix 10B, along with imputed interest and pensions. Appendix 10C explains leases.

LIABILITIES IN PERSPECTIVE

The accounting literature contains many controversial discussions about when a resource qualifies as an asset, or an obligation as a liability. For introductory purposes, *liability* can be defined as a recognized obligation to pay money or to provide goods or services. Ordinarily, the obligation arises from some transaction with an "outside party" such as a supplier, a lending institution, or an employee. However, obligations also arise from the imposition of taxes or the loss of a lawsuit.

Current liabilities are obligations that fall due within the coming year or within the normal operating cycle if longer than a year. Accounts payable are amounts owed to suppliers who extended credit for purchases on open account. These open account purchases from trade creditors are ordinarily supported by signatures on purchase orders or similar business documents. Notes payable are backed by formal promissory notes held by a bank or business creditors.

As explained in earlier chapters, the accrual basis of accounting recognizes expenses as they pertain to the operations of a given time period regardless of when they are paid for in cash. A report to shareholders may combine liabilities for wages, salaries, commissions, interest, and similar items and show them as a single liability labeled as *accrued expenses payable*. However, each accrued expense liability is listed individually if its magnitude warrants a separate classification. For example, the liability for accrued income taxes payable is usually displayed separately.

Sometimes the adjective "accrued" is deleted, so that these liabilities are labeled simply as taxes payable, wages payable, and so on. Similarly, the term "accrued" may be used and "payable" deleted.

The real-life example of a presentation of liabilities, shown in Exhibit 10–1, is from the 1985 annual report of Gulf & Western Industries, a financial services, publishing, and entertainment company.

Long-term liabilities are obligations that fall due beyond one year from the balance sheet date. As the Gulf & Western presentation illustrates, long-

EXHIBIT 10–1

GULF & WESTERN INDUSTRIES
Liabilities Section of Balance Sheet
(in millions)

	JULY 31	
	1985	1984
Current liabilities:		
Notes payable	$ 5.2	$ 12.5
Current maturities of long-term debt	320.8	106.8
Trade accounts payable	66.3	227.1
Accrued expenses and other liabilities	680.3	745.3
Income taxes payable	5.6	27.8
Total current liabilities	1,078.2	1,119.5
Long-term debt, net of current maturities	1,028.1	858.2
Total liabilities	$2,106.3	$1,977.7

term debt is frequently payable in installments. The current portion is included as a part of current liabilities.

The journal entry for recognizing the current portion of long-term debt reclassifies a noncurrent liability as a current liability. Using the Gulf & Western illustration (in millions):

Long-term debt	320.8	
Current maturities of long-term debt		320.8

Conceptually, a liability is best measured as the amount of cash to be paid in the future discounted to the present time. The discounted amount is the sum that, if invested immediately, would provide enough cash, including interest, to pay off the obligation. This discounting, which is explained in Appendix 10A, is rarely done to measure current liabilities, but it is often done for obligations that are due beyond one year. Exceptions to the preceding sentence will be noted as various liabilities are discussed in more detail.

ACCOUNTING FOR PAYROLL

Most organizations have three major types of routine cash disbursements and corresponding liabilities:

CASH DISBURSEMENTS	CORRESPONDING LIABILITY
1. To suppliers for goods and services	Accounts payable
2. To employees for labor	Accrued wages payable[1]
3. To taxing authorities	Accrued taxes payable

---

[1] Other terms often encountered are *salaries*, *commissions*, *bonuses*, and *payroll*.

Disbursements for accounts payable and for payroll tend to be voluminous and repetitive. Therefore special data-processing and internal control systems are usually designed for these transactions. See Chapter 8, Appendix 8B, for a description of such a system regarding accounts payable.

Payroll accounting is typically an imposing task regardless of the organization's product or service (or regardless of whether the organization is profit seeking).

☐ Payroll Withholdings

Earlier chapters have described the payments to employees in an elementary way. Our implied assumption has been the condition that actually existed years ago when an employee earned, say, $100 per week and, in turn, received $100 in cash on payday. The bookkeeping problems for payroll were relatively straightforward. Only two parties were involved, the employer and the employee.

These days the complexities of payroll accounting are awesome. Many parties are involved, including health insurance companies, labor unions, and, of course, government agencies. The direct involvement of government has at least two noteworthy effects. First, the employer must serve as a collection agent for *employee* income and social security taxes. Second, the *employer* must bear some special payroll taxes.

In the United States, the employer must collect employees' ordinary income taxes and social security taxes. The latter tax provides government

EXHIBIT 10-2

Analysis of Transactions
(in thousands of dollars)

	A =		L		+	SE
	Cash	Accrued Wages Payable	Withheld Income Taxes Payable	Withheld Social Security Taxes Payable		Retained Income
1. Recognize liabilities	=	+79	+15	+6		−100 [Increase wages expense]
2. Pay cash to employees	−79 =	−79				
3. Pay cash to government	−21 =		−15	−6		

pensions and medical benefits to retired workers. It is also called the *Federal Insurance Contributions Act tax* (FICA tax). The series of accounting entries to accomplish this collection service varies, but the basic pattern is shown in Exhibit 10–2. Assume that the wages expense subject to these tax withholdings is $100,000. All amounts earned were paid in cash, except for withholdings.

The journal entries to accompany Exhibit 10–2 would be:

1. Wages expense	100	
Accrued wages payable		79
Withheld income taxes payable		15
Withheld social security taxes payable		6
To recognize liabilities arising from wages earned.		
2. Accrued wages payable	79	
Cash		79
To pay employees.		
3. Withheld income taxes payable	15	
Withheld social security taxes payable	6	
Cash		21
To pay the government.		

The U.S. government is impatient. It wants its taxes quickly. The amount of tax withheld determines the frequency of payment. Large companies must pay eight times each month.

Many other withholdings from employees occur. They are accounted for in the same manner as withheld taxes. Examples are union dues, donations to community charities, hospitalization insurance, group life insurance, auto insurance, pension plans, and employee savings plans.

Above all, note that withholdings by themselves are not employer costs. They are merely those portions of the employees' gross earnings that are being diverted to third parties, primarily for the employees' convenience. Instead of an obligation to an employee, the company lists a liability to a third party.

☐ Additional Employer Payroll Costs

The gross earnings of employees are only part of the payroll costs really borne. In addition to wages expense, the employer incurs other expenses that are based on the gross earnings of employees.

Governments levy special taxes on the *employer*, as distinguished from the *employee*. Examples are social security taxes, federal unemployment taxes, state unemployment taxes, and workmen's accident compensation taxes. Together, these are often called payroll taxes. These tax rates change from year to year, generally in an upward direction. Together they average about 10% of the gross earnings of U.S. employees.

Employers also contribute to programs for employee pensions, health, life, and other insurance. Such programs are called fringe benefits, or simply "fringes." These costs can easily exceed 30% of the gross earnings of U.S. employees.

The journal entries for these additional employer costs have the same basic pattern. The following numbers (in thousands) are typical for gross earnings of $100,000:

Employer payroll tax expenses (could be detailed)	10	
Employer pension expenses	15	
Employer health insurance expenses	5	
Employer payroll taxes payable		10
Employer pensions payable		15
Employer health insurance payable		5
To record various additional expenses related to gross earnings of employees.		
Employer payroll taxes payable	10	
Employer pensions payable	15	
Employer health insurance payable	5	
Cash		30
To record payments of various liabilities. (These individual disbursements occur at different times.)		

The above entries make heavy use of "employer" as part of the names for both expenses and liabilities. These names are often shortened by deleting "employer" therefrom. Furthermore, many of the liabilities that have been shown in detail in these examples are combined if the amounts contributed by the employer plus the employees are to be paid to the same payee.

ACCRUAL OF VACATION PAY

There is often a time lag between incurrence and payment of various payroll fringe costs. A common illustration is payment for vacations. The liability for vacations really accrues from week to week as each employee accumulates a claim to vacation pay. Companies estimate total vacation expenses and spread them over a year. They cannot simply recognize such outlays as expenses when disbursements are made. Such a policy would violate the matching principle.

For example, suppose an employee receives wages of $1,000 per week and is entitled to a two-week vacation after one year. An appropriate journal entry each week would be (ignoring withholdings and other fringe benefits):

```
Wages expense                              1,040
  Accrued payroll                                   1,000
  Accrued vacation pay                                 40
To recognize liabilities for wages earned
including related vacation pay.
Computation is based on liability for
the year, or (2 weeks × $1,000)/(50
weeks × $1,000) = 4%. The accrual
for vacation pay will accumulate to
$40 × 50 = $2,000 at the end of fifty
weeks. The $40 portion of wages
expense might be accounted for in
a separate account, such as Vacation
Pay Expense.


Accrued vacation pay                       2,000
  Cash                                              2,000
The liability account for vacation pay
is decreased as actual vacation
payments occur.
```

Liabilities for vacations and other compensated absences, such as sickness and disabilities, can become significant. Many companies specifically mention such items in their annual reports. For instance, the 1985 annual report of J. C. Penney labeled its liability as "Accrued Salaries, Vacations, Profit-sharing, and Bonuses." Adolph Coors called it "Accrued Salaries and Vacations."

INCOME TAXES PAYABLE

A corporation must pay a tax on its earnings. Like individuals, corporations pay throughout the year rather than paying a lump sum at the end of each year. Corporations make periodic installment payments based on their estimated tax for the year.

To illustrate, suppose a corporation has an estimated taxable income of $100 million for the calendar year 19X4. At a 40% tax rate, the company's estimated taxes for the year would be $40 million. Payments must be made as follows:

	APRIL 15	JUNE 15	SEPTEMBER 15	DECEMBER 15
Estimated taxes (in millions)	$10	$10	$10	$10

The final income tax return and payment date is March 15, 19X5. Suppose the actual taxable income is $110 million instead of the estimated $100 million. On March 15, the corporation must pay the $4 million additional tax on the additional $10 million of taxable income.

As we have seen in earlier chapters, the month-to-month entries for income tax expenses are:

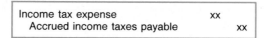

```
Income tax expense                          xx
    Accrued income taxes payable                 xx
```

Quarterly payments reduce the liability:

```
Accrued income taxes payable                xx
    Cash                                         xx
```

For simplicity, the illustration assumed equal quarterly payments. However, the estimated taxable income for a calendar year may change as the year unfolds. The corporation must change its quarterly payments accordingly. Although reasonably accurate estimates are typical, there will nearly always be a relatively small tax payment or refund due on March 15.

Keep in mind that the amounts for monthly entries for income tax expense are generally based on the pretax income of that month. For example, the applicable overall income tax rate for the year as a whole is applied to the January pretax income, or the July pretax income, or the December pretax income. Thus the income tax *expense* for any given year will be quite accurate.

Disbursements for income taxes are determined by laws, not by the pretax income for a specific month. A variety of rules determine the minimum amounts of taxes that must be paid each quarter. For instance, the minimum payment is frequently based on the income taxes paid during the previous year rather than the current year's income. These complications are beyond the scope of this book.

SALES TAXES

When they collect sales taxes, retailers are agents of the state or local government. For example, suppose a 7% sales tax is levied on sales of $10,000. The total collected from the customer must be $10,000 + $700, or $10,700. The impact on the entity is:

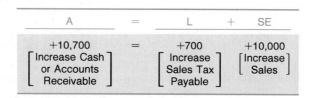

The sales tax payable appears on the balance sheet as a liability until the taxes are paid to the government. The sales shown on the income statement would be $10,000, not $10,700.

When the sales taxes are paid at a later date:

A	=	L	+ SE
−700 [Decrease Cash]		−700 [Decrease Sales Tax Payable]	

The journal entries (without explanations) are:

Cash or accounts receivable	10,700	
Sales		10,000
Sales tax payable		700
Sales tax payable	700	
Cash		700

PRODUCT WARRANTIES

The liabilities discussed so far have borne definite amounts. However, some liabilities have estimated amounts. A noteworthy example is the liability arising from product guarantees and warranties. If warranty obligations are material, they must be accrued when products are sold because the obligation arises then, not when the actual services are performed. General Motors describes its accounting as follows: "Provisions for estimated costs related to product warranty are made at the time the products are sold."

The estimated warranty expenses are typically based on past experience for replacing defective products or remedying the defects of products. Although the estimates should be close, they are bound to be inaccurate. Therefore any differences between the estimated and actual results are usually added to or subtracted from the current warranty expense account as additional information unfolds. The accounting entry at the time of sale is:

Warranty expense	600,000	
Liability for warranties (or some similar title)		600,000
To record the estimated liability for warranties arising from current sales. The provision is 3% of current sales of $20 million, or $600,000.		

When a warranty claim arises, an entry such as the following is made:

Liability for warranties	1,000	
Cash, accounts payable, accrued wages payable, and similar accounts		1,000
To record the acquisition of supplies, outside services, and employee services to satisfy claims for repairs.		

If the estimate for warranty expense is accurate, the entries for all claims will total about $600,000.

RETURNABLE DEPOSITS

Customers occasionally make money deposits that are to be returned in full, sometimes plus interest and sometimes not. The receivers of these deposits view them as a form of payable, although the word "payable" may not be a part of their specific labeling.

The most notable deposits are those with banks and similar financial institutions. Savings deposits bear explicit interest, but many commercial checking deposits do not. Deposits take many forms. For instance, the purchase of traveler's checks from American Express may be shown by the latter as "Traveler's Checks Outstanding," essentially an interest-free deposit.

Other examples of deposits include those for returnable containers such as soft-drink bottles, oil drums, or beer kegs. Moreover, many lessors (landlords) require damage deposits that are to be returned in full if specified conditions are met by their lessees (tenants).

The accounting entries by the recipients of deposits have the following basic pattern (numbers assumed in thousands of dollars):

	INTEREST BEARING			NON-INTEREST BEARING		
1. Deposit	Cash	100		Cash	100	
	Deposits		100	Deposits		100
2. Interest recognized	Interest expense	9		No entry		
	Deposits		9			
3. Deposit returned	Deposits	109		Deposits	100	
	Cash		109	Cash		100

The account "Deposits" is a liability of the company receiving the deposit. Ordinarily the recipient of the cash deposit may use the cash for investment purposes from the date of deposit to the date of its return to the depositor. For example, banks lend the cash to others to earn interest revenue.

UNEARNED REVENUE

Chapter 4 explained that revenue collected in advance was fundamentally a liability (usually a current liability). The seller either must deliver the product or service or is obligated to make a full refund. Examples include lease rentals, magazine subscriptions, insurance premiums, advance airline or theater ticket sales, and advance repair service contracts.

The accounting entries follow (in dollars):

Cash or accounts receivable	100,000	
Unearned sales revenue		100,000
To record advance collections from customers.		
Unearned sales revenue	100,000	
Sales		100,000
To record sales revenue when products are delivered to customers who paid in advance.		

These advance collections are frequently referred to as *deferred credits*. Why? Because, as the second entry shows, the ultimate accounting entry is a "credit" to revenue, but such an entry has been deferred to a later accounting period. Unearned revenues are also called *revenues collected in advance*.

CONTINGENT LIABILITIES

A **contingent liability** is *not* a liability. Instead it is a *potential* (possible) liability that depends on a *future* event arising out of a *past* transaction. Sometimes it has a definite amount. For instance, a company may guarantee the payment on a related company's note payable. This means that the guarantor will pay if, and only if, the primary borrower fails to pay. Such a note is the liability of the primary borrower, and the contingent liability of the guarantor.

More often, a contingent liability has an indefinite amount. A common example is a lawsuit. Many companies have lawsuits pending against them. These are possible obligations of indefinite amounts.

Some companies show contingent liabilities on the balance sheet. Most often they are listed after long-term liabilities but before stockholders' equity. Pioneer Hi-Bred International, the seed corn company, is an example (in thousands):

	1985	1984
Current liabilities	$180,079	$154,947
Other liabilities	49,817	39,946
Contingent liabilities (Note 7)		
Stockholders' equity	461,812	393,570

In contrast, the Toro Company, maker of lawnmowers and other equipment, lists contingent liabilities after stockholders' equity (in thousands):

	1985	1984
Liabilities	$87,290	$89,373
Stockholders' equity	80,560	74,778
Commitments and contingent liabilities (Notes 10 and 11)		

The presentations used by Pioneer and Toro are often called **short presentations**. That is, an item is described as being "short" when it is included in the body of a financial statement, but its amount (if any) is not shown on the face of the balance sheet. Inevitably, a short presentation is accompanied by an explanatory footnote. For example, Pioneer Hi-Bred's footnote included:

☐ Migrant workers in Texas have filed suits against the Company and certain farm labor contractors alleging violations of the Farm Labor Contractor Registration Act (FLCRA). It is unlikely the above-described litigation will result in any recovery that will materially affect the financial position or operating results of the Company.

☐ The Company has guaranteed the repayment of principal and interest on certain obligations of its unconsolidated subsidiaries. At August 31, 1985, such guarantees totaled approximately $10,800,000.

Contingent liabilities do not have to be mentioned in the body of the balance sheet. Many companies merely reveal the contingencies in a footnote. Indeed, the International Business Machines Corporation, one of the world's most heavily sued corporations, reveals its contingent liabilities in a short supplementary note labeled as *litigation*.

The line between a contingent liability and a real liability is sometimes hard to draw. If an obligation is highly probable (likely to occur), it is no longer contingent even if its amount must be estimated. To illustrate, suppose that at the balance sheet date, a hospital has lost a court case for uninsured malpractice, but the amount of damages has not been set. A reasonable estimate is between $1.0 and $2.5 million. The hospital must recognize a loss and a liability for $1.0 million. Moreover, the possibility of an additional loss of $1.5 million must also be disclosed in a footnote.[2]

Although contingent liabilities are "iffy" and hard to measure, they are increasingly important in our litigation-happy society. As a result, fuller disclosure has occurred in corporate reports so investors can make informal judgments. Nevertheless, the investor often has little information that is concrete beyond a fair warning.

To recapitulate, there are definite liabilities of either definite amounts (accounts payable) or of estimated amounts (product warranties). There are also contingent liabilities of either definite amounts (guaranteeing a note) or estimated amounts (income tax dispute with IRS).

---

[2] At one point, the Johns-Manville Corporation's balance sheet showed stockholders' equity of $1.1 billion and *potential* liabilities of $2 billion from fifty-two thousand lawsuits regarding health damage from asbestos.

NATURE OF INTEREST

Interest is the cost of using money. It is the rental charge for cash, just as rental charges are often made for the use of automobiles or boats. Interest cost is often unimportant in the short run. The longer the time span and the higher the rate, the more significant the interest cost. Of course, for financial institutions, interest is a primary revenue and expense.

Contracts that bear interest have many forms, from simple short-term promissory notes to multimillion-dollar issues of long-term notes often called bonds. Commonly encountered terms include

> **Principal**—the amount invested, borrowed, or used on which interest accrues
> **Interest**—the rental charge for the use of principal

Details about interest are presented in Appendix 10A.

NATURE OF BONDS

☐ Mortgage Bonds and Debentures

Bonds are a form of long-term debt. They are described in more detail later in this chapter. A common type of bond is a **mortgage bond**, which is secured by the pledge of specific property. In case of default, the bondholders can sell the property to satisfy their claims. Moreover, the holders of mortgage bonds have a further unsecured claim on the corporation if the proceeds from the pledged property are insufficient.

If no lien exists against specific assets, the bond is called a **debenture**. The holders thereof have no special claims against the assets beyond their general claim against the *total* assets, a claim shared with other general creditors such as trade creditors. **Subordinated debentures** means that such bondholders are junior to the other general creditors in exercising claims against the total assets. If debentures were **unsubordinated**, the holders would have the same priority as holders of accounts payable.

A *mortgage bond*, which has a specific lien on particular assets, is an inherently safer investment than the same company's *debentures*, which have no specific lien on any asset. However, the relative attractiveness of specific bonds depends *primarily* on the credit-worthiness of the issuer. Thus IBM can issue billions of dollars of debentures at relatively low interest rates when compared with the mortgage bonds that might be issued by real estate companies.

☐ Bond Provisions

Corporations issue promissory notes when money is borrowed from a few sources. These issues are known as **private placements** because they are not held or traded among the general public. Instead the creditors are financial institutions such as insurance companies or pension funds. Private placements provide over half the capital borrowed by corporations in the United States.

Corporations have heavy demands for borrowed capital, so they often borrow from the general public by issuing bonds. Fundamentally, bonds are individual promissory notes issued to many lenders.

A **bond** is the most common type of long-term liability. Bonds are formal certificates of indebtedness that are typically accompanied by (1) a promise to pay interest in cash at a specified annual rate (often called the **nominal rate**, **contractual rate, coupon rate**, or **stated rate**) plus (2) a promise to pay the principal (often called the **face amount** or **par amount**) at a specific maturity date. The interest is usually paid every six months.

Bonds typically have a par value of $1,000, but they are quoted in terms of percentages of par. Some bonds are traded on the New York Stock Exchange. A quotation for the Aluminum Company of America (Alcoa) follows:

DESCRIPTION	CURRENT YIELD	VOLUME	HIGH	LOW	CLOSE	NET CHANGE
Alcoa 9s95	8.9	5	101¾ *	101½	101½	−½

* The price of one $1,000 bond is 101¾, or 1.0175 × $1,000 = $1,017.50.

The Aluminum Company of America's bonds carrying a 9% coupon rate and maturing in 1995 traded at a high of $1,017.50 and closed at their low price of $1,015.00 at the end of the day. The **current yield**, based on the closing price, was 9/101.5, or 8.9%. Five bonds were traded, each having a face or par value of $1,000. The closing price was down one-half from that of the previous day. Therefore the preceding closing price must have been 101½ + ½ = 102, or $1,020 per bond.

An issue of bonds is usually accompanied by a **trust indenture** whereby the issuing corporation promises a *trustee* (usually a bank or trust company) that it will abide by stated provisions, often called **protective covenants**. The indenture is designed primarily to protect the safety of the bondholders. The provisions pertain to payments of principal and interest, sales of pledged property, restrictions on dividends, and like matters. The trustee's major function is to represent the collective claims and concerns of the bondholders.

For example, MacMillan Bloedel, the large forest products company, indicated in its 1985 annual report that "*trust indentures* securing the company's debentures contain provisions limiting the amount of indebtedness the company can incur." Gordon Jewelry Corporation, a major jewelry company listed on the New York Stock Exchange, mentioned many constraints in its 1985 annual report: "The note agreement contains restrictive *covenants* regarding the nature of the business, liabilities, financial ratios, indebtedness, lines, investments, leases, company stock, mergers, and acquisitions."

Bonds issued by American industrial corporations are normally **registered**, which means that the interest and maturity payments are made to a specific owner. In contrast, bonds issued before 1983 by American governmental bodies such as municipalities are normally **unregistered** or **bearer** instruments, which means that the interest is paid to the individual who presents the interest *coupons* attached to the bond. Similarly, the principal is paid to the individual who presents the bond at the maturity date. Bearer instruments are like cash; they are more vulnerable to theft than are registered bonds.

Callable, Sinking Fund, and Convertible Bonds

Some bonds are **callable**, which means that they are subject to redemption before maturity at the option of the issuer. The issuer typically provides for a predetermined **call premium** (a redemption price in excess of par). The call premium declines as maturity comes closer. Thus a bond issued in 1974 with a 1994 maturity date may not be callable until 1986. Then it may be subject to call for an initial price in 1986 of 105 (105% of par), in 1987 of 104, in 1988 of 103, and so on. The call premium in 1986 would be $50 per $1,000 bond; $40 in 1987; $30 in 1988; and so on.

Sinking fund bonds are those with indentures that require the issuer to make annual payments into a sinking fund. A **sinking fund** is cash or securities segregated for meeting obligations on bonded debt. It is an asset that is usually classified as part of an asset category called "investments" or "other assets." This helps assure the bondholders that sufficient cash will be accumulated to repay the principal at maturity.

Convertible bonds are those bonds that may, at the holder's option, be exchanged for other securities. The conversion is usually for a predetermined number of common shares of the issuing company. Because of the conversion feature, convertible bondholders are willing to accept a lower interest rate than on a similar bond without the conversion privilege.

Most companies have an assortment of long-term debt, including a variety of bonds payable.[3] The body of the balance sheet usually summarizes such debt on one line. In contrast, the details in the footnotes can occupy an entire page. Payments on debt that are due within a year are classified as current liabilities.

ACCOUNTING FOR BOND TRANSACTIONS

Bonds frequently have *premiums* or *discounts* upon issue. What are these and what roles do they play in bond interest transactions?

Setting the Interest Rate

Bonds are typically sold through a syndicate (special group) of investment bankers called **underwriters**. That is, the syndicate buys the entire issue from the corporation, thus guaranteeing that the company will obtain all of

---

[3] There are many types of bonds, too many to discuss exhaustively here. Textbooks on corporate finance contain detailed descriptions.

its desired funds. In turn, the syndicate sells the bonds to the general investing public.

A company's board of directors sets the stated or nominal interest rate. The investment banker who manages the underwriting syndicate provides advice. The nominal rate is usually set as close to the current market rate as possible. Many factors affect this rate, notably general economic conditions, industry conditions, risks of the use of the proceeds, and specific features of the bonds (examples include callability, sinking fund, convertibility). On the day of issuance, the proceeds to the issuer may be above par or below par, depending on market conditions.[4] If above par, there is a **premium**; if below par, a **discount**. Therefore the **effective interest rate** (**market rate, real rate, yield rate, true rate**) frequently differs from the *nominal interest rate*. The interest paid in cash, usually semiannually, is determined by the nominal rate, not the effective rate.

Note that bonds issued at a discount do not mean that the credit-worthiness of the issuer is especially bad, nor do bonds issued at a premium mean that credit-worthiness is especially good. Discounts and premiums are determined by market forces that fluctuate from day to day and by the choice of the nominal rate of interest, relative to the then-current market rate of interest for bonds of similar risk.

☐ **Accounting for Discount and Premium**

Suppose that on December 31, 1980, a company issued $12 million of ten-year, 10% debentures, at 98. This means that the proceeds were 98% of $12 million, or $11,760,000. There was a discount on bonds at issuance of 2% of $12 million, or $240,000. The discount is the excess of face amount over the proceeds. Therefore the company has the use of only $11,760,000, not $12,000,000. Interest (rental payment for the use of $11,760,000) takes two forms, a semiannual cash outlay plus an extra lump-sum cash payment of $240,000 (total of $12,000,000) at maturity.

The extra $240,000 to be paid at maturity relates to the use of the proceeds over ten years. Therefore the discount is amortized:

Semiannual expense:	
Cash interest payments, .10 × $12,000,000 × ½	$ 600,000
Amortization of discount, ($240,000 ÷ 10 years) × ½	12,000
Semiannual expense	$ 612,000
Annual expense, $612,000 × 2	$1,224,000

---

[4] The interest rate is often established at the last possible minute so that bonds may be issued exactly at par. The highest-quality corporate issues, such as IBM's notes and debentures, are usually priced as close as possible to their U.S. Treasury and corporate equivalents. A spread of one-quarter of one percent above the Treasuries in yield is a customary standard. Thus, if Treasuries of comparable maturities are yielding 10.50%, IBM's new issue would yield 10.75%.

As the above tabulation shows, the discount (or premium) is used as an adjustment of nominal interest to obtain the real interest. The adjustment, which is introduced here using straight-line amortization of a discount, *increases* the interest expense of the issuer. (A premium would have a *decreasing* effect.)

Exhibit 10–3 shows how the issuer would account for the bonds throughout their life, assuming that they are held to maturity. Note that the Discount on Bonds Payable is simply a contra liability, a *negative element* of the Bonds Payable account. (A premium would be a *positive element*.)

EXHIBIT 10–3

Analysis of Bond Transactions: Discount Amortization
(in thousands of dollars)

	A	=	L		+	SE
	Cash	Bonds Payable	Discount on Bonds Payable			Retained Income
Issuer's records 1. Issuance	+11,760 =	+12,000	−240	[Increase Discount]		
2. Semiannual interest (repeated for ten years)	−600 =		+12	[Decrease Discount]	−612	[Increase Interest Expense]
3. Maturity value (final payment)	−12,000 =	−12,000	___			
Bond-related totals		0	0			

The spreading of the $240,000 discount over ten years as expense is usually called **discount amortization**. Since the discount is a *negative* element of the Bonds Payable account, the carrying amount of the bonds gradually *rises* as their maturity date approaches.

When presented on balance sheets, unamortized discounts are deducted from the face value of the related bonds:

	DECEMBER 31		
ISSUER'S BALANCE SHEET	1980	1985	1989
Bonds payable, 10% due December 31, 1990	$12,000,000	$12,000,000	$12,000,000
Deduct: Discount on bonds payable	240,000	120,000	24,000
Net carrying amount	$11,760,000	$11,880,000	$11,976,000

The journal entries for the issuer follow:

```
1. Cash                                    11,760,000
     Discount on bonds payable                240,000
        Bonds payable                                      12,000,000
     To record proceeds upon issuance
     of 10% bonds maturing on
     December 31, 1990.

2. Interest expense                           612,000
      Discount on bonds payable                                12,000
      Cash                                                    600,000
     To record payment of interest and
     amortization of discount on
     straight-line basis of
     $240,000 ÷ 20, or $12,000 per
     six-month period.

3. Bonds payable                           12,000,000
      Cash                                                 12,000,000
     To record payment of maturity
     value of bonds and their
     retirement.
```

The issuer also has "bond issue" costs, such as legal, accounting, and printing costs. FASB Concepts *Statement No. 3* (p. 70) states that debt issue cost

☐   . . . in effect reduces the proceeds of borrowing and increases the effective interest rate and thus may be accounted for the same as debt discount. However, debt issue cost may also be considered to be an expense of the period of borrowing.

A *premium on bonds* at issuance is the excess of the proceeds over the face amount. When an issuance premium exists, its amortization is *deducted* from cash payments to compute the periodic interest expense. Unamortized premiums would be added to the face value of the bonds. See the "Summary Problem for Your Review" for an illustration, page 443.

☐ **Premiums and Discounts in Practice**

Bond premiums and discounts should really be amortized by using the compound interest method explained in Appendix 10B. In this way, the accounting would accord with how bonds are actually valued and how bond yields are actually computed in the bond markets. However, hand calculations of these amortization schedules are cumbersome. Consequently, the simpler straight-line (sometimes called *pro-rata*) method is favored for an introductory presentation in textbooks.

The Accounting Principles Board *Opinion No. 21* prescribed the compound interest method for amortization of discounts and premiums. However, even in practice, the straight-line method may be used "if the results obtained are not materially different from those that would result from the compound interest method."

The major lesson concerning discounts and premiums is that they are essentially part of the Bonds Payable account, and their amortization adjusts the periodic cash (nominal) interest expense. Accountants may debate whether the straight-line and compound interest methods should be used, but the requirement for periodic amortization is beyond question.

☐ Early Extinguishment

Investors often dispose of bonds before maturity by selling them to other investors. Such a sale does not affect the issuer's books. However, the issuer may redeem *its own* bonds by purchases on the open market or by exercising its call option. Gains or losses on these early extinguishments of debt are computed in the usual manner. That is, the difference between the cash paid and the net carrying amount of the bonds (face, less unamortized discount or plus unamortized premium) is the gain or loss.

Suppose that in our example the issuer purchases all of its bonds on the open market for 96 on December 31, 1988 (after all interest payments and amortization were recorded for 1988):

Carrying amount:		
Face or par value	$12,000,000	
Deduct: Unamortized discount on		
bonds*	48,000	$11,952,000
Cash required, 96% of $12,000,000		11,520,000
Difference, gain on early		
extinguishment of debt		$ 432,000

* There are two years until maturity, and the rate of amortization has been $24,000 yearly. Therefore the unamortized amount is 2 × $24,000 = $48,000.

Exhibit 10–4 presents an analysis of the transaction. The $432,000 gain on extinguishment of debt would be shown on an income statement below operating income as a separate classification called an extraordinary item.

EXHIBIT 10–4

Analysis of Early Extinguishment of Debt on Issuer's Records
(in thousands of dollars)

	A =	L	+	SE
	Cash	Bonds Payable	Discount on Bonds Payable	Retained Income
Redemption, December 31, 1988	−11,520 = −12,000		+48 [Decrease Discount]	+432 [Gain on Early Extinguishment]

The journal entry on December 31, 1988, is:

Bonds payable	12,000,000	
Discount on bonds payable		48,000
Gain on early extinguishment of debt		432,000
Cash		11,520,000
To record open-market acquisition of entire issue of 10% bonds at 96.		

□ Bonds Sold Between Interest Dates

Bond interest payments are typically made semiannually. Suppose the company in our example had its bonds printed and ready for issuance, but then market conditions delayed issuance of the bonds. On January 31, 1981, one month after the originally planned issuance date, the bonds were issued at 100. The indenture requires the payment of $600,000 interest every six months, beginning June 30, 1981. Indeed, there may be interest coupons attached to the bonds that require such payment.

When bonds are sold between interest dates, they command the market price *plus accrued interest*. Thus the market quotations you see for bonds *always* mean that the investor must pay an extra amount for any *unearned* interest to be received at the next interest payment date. In our example, the price to be paid is:

Market price of bonds at 100	$12,000,000
Accrued interest, .10 × $12,000,000 × $\frac{1}{12}$,	100,000
Market price plus accrued interest	$12,100,000

Exhibit 10–5 presents an analysis of these transactions. Note that the interest expense for the first half of 1981 is properly measured as $500,000, pertaining

EXHIBIT 10–5

Analysis of Bonds Sold between Interest Dates
(in thousands of dollars)

	A	=	L	+	SE
	Cash	Bonds Payable	Accrued Interest Payable		Retained Income
Issuance, 1/31/81	+12,100 =	+12,000	+100		
Interest payment, 6/30/81	−600 =		−100	−500	[Increase Interest Expense]

to only five months that the money was actually in use. The journal entries follow (in thousands of dollars):

1/31/81	Cash	12,100	
	Bonds payable		12,000
	Accrued interest payable		100
6/30/81	Accrued interest payable	100	
	Interest expense	500	
	Cash		600

Obviously, the analysis of transactions can be made more complicated by combining the acquisitions of bonds between interest dates with discounts and premiums. However, these are mechanical details that do not involve any new accounting concepts.

NON-INTEREST-BEARING INSTRUMENTS

Some notes (and bonds) do not bear explicit interest. Instead they contain a promise to pay a lump sum at a specified date. To call such notes *non-interest-bearing* is misleading. These instruments cannot be marketed at face value. The investor demands interest revenue. Therefore the investor pays less than the face value. The investor discounts the maturity value, using the market rate of interest for notes having similar terms and risks. The discount is amortized as interest over the life of the note.

Banks often discount both long-term and short-term notes when making loans. Consider an example of a six-month note with a face value of $10,000. The bank may provide the borrower with only $9,400, thus discounting the note by the $600 desired implicit interest.

Exhibit 10–6 displays the accounting for such notes on a monthly basis. The discount accounts would be presented in the balance sheets as direct reductions of the notes. Indeed, some accountants would not keep separate accounts for discounts. Instead the notes themselves would initially be carried

EXHIBIT 10–6

Analysis of Transactions of Borrower, Discounted Notes

	A	=	L	+	SE
	Cash	Notes Payable	Discount on Notes Payable		Retained Income
Proceeds of loan	+9,400 =	+10,000	−600		
Monthly amortization (six times, $100 each)			+600	−600	⎡Increase Interest Expense⎤
Payment of note	−10,000 =	−10,000			
Change after six months	−600 =	0	0		−600

at their discounted amounts and then raised by $100 each month (in this case) until maturity.

The appropriate journal entries follow:

Inception:	Cash	9,400	
	Discount on notes payable	600	
	Notes payable		10,000
Monthly entry:	Interest expense	100	
	Discount on notes payable		100
Maturity:	Notes payable	10,000	
	Cash		10,000

DEBT-TO-EQUITY RATIOS

Many ratios are used to measure the relative position of creditors and shareholders. For example, commonly encountered ratios include:

$$\text{Total debt-to-equity ratio} = \frac{\text{Total liabilities}}{\text{Total shareholders' equity}}$$

$$\text{Total long-term debt-to-equity ratio} = \frac{\text{Total long-term debt}}{\text{Total shareholders' equity}}$$

$$\text{Total debt-to-total assets ratio} = \frac{\text{Total liabilities}}{\text{Total assets}}$$

When commenting on the recent increase in the use of debt, *Fortune* (July 22, 1985) cited the last ratio:

☐ In 1960, the total liabilities of Fortune 500 industrial companies averaged 35% of assets; shareholders' equity made up the balance. At the end of 1984 the liabilities figure stood at nearly 55%.

The debt burden varies greatly from firm to firm and industry to industry. For example, retailing companies, utilities, and transportation companies tend to have debt of more than 60% of their assets. Computer companies and textile firms have debt of about 45% of assets. Some computer companies, such as Digital Equipment and Hewlett-Packard, have debt as low as 30% of assets. Companies such as American Motors and Control Data have debt equal to over 80% of their assets.

Standard & Poor's Corporation, a credit-rating company, reviews the ability of corporations to pay their debts. A review of Lear Siegler, an aerospace corporation, commented favorably on the company's "lowering of debt leverage from over 40% to a satisfactory 32%." In other words, the ratio of total debt to total stockholders' equity had fallen from .40 to .32.

SUMMARY

A liability is a recognized obligation to pay money or to provide goods or services. It may have a definite or an estimated amount. A contingent liability is not a liability because it depends on a future event arising out of a past transaction.

Bond premium and bond discount are used as ways of adjusting nominal interest rates to market interest rates at issuance. Amortization is conducted so that interest expense is measured on an accrual basis throughout the life of the bonds.

For balance sheet presentations, discounts are subtractions from and premiums are additions to their related bonds or notes.

Appendix 10A discusses compound interest, and Appendix 10B applies compound interest principles to the accounting for bonds. Appendix 10C discusses leases.

SUMMARY PROBLEM FOR YOUR REVIEW

☐ Problem One

Suppose that on December 31, 1986, Exxon issued $12 million of ten-year, 10% debentures at 103.

Required:

1. Prepare an analysis of transactions for the issuer's records (similar to Exhibit 10–3, page 437). Key your transactions as follows: (1) issuance, (2) semiannual interest using straight-line amortization of bond premium, and (3) payment of maturity value.
2. Prepare sample journal entries keyed as above.

☐ Solution to Problem One

Note that the approach is the same whether a bond premium or a bond discount exists. Of course, the details differ slightly. Exhibit 10–7 provides the solution to requirement 1. The solution to requirement 2 follows:

EXHIBIT 10–7

Analysis of Bond Transactions: Premium Amortization of Issuer
(in thousands of dollars)

	A	=	L	+	SE
	Cash	Bonds Payable	Premium on Bonds Payable		Retained Income
1. Issuance	+12,360 =	+12,000	+360		
2. Semiannual interest (repeated for twenty semiannual periods)	−600 =		−18	−582	⎡Increase⎤ Interest ⎣Expense⎦
3. Maturity value (final payment)	−12,000 =	−12,000			
Bond-related totals	0	0	0		

12/31/86	1. Cash	12,360,000	
	Bonds payable		12,000,000
	Premium on bonds payable		360,000
	To record proceeds upon issuance of 10% bonds maturing on December 31, 1996.		
6/30/87 and every six months thereafter through 12/31/96	2. Interest expense	582,000	
	Premium on bonds payable	18,000	
	Cash		600,000
	To record semiannual amortization of premium and payment of interest.		
12/31/96	3. Bonds payable	12,000,000	
	Cash		12,000,000
	To record payment of maturity value of bonds and their retirement.		

HIGHLIGHTS TO REMEMBER

1. Organizations usually have three large, repetitive drains on cash: (a) to suppliers for goods and services, (b) to employees for labor services, and (c) to tax authorities.

2. *Debenture* is the name for the most popular type of long-term debt. A debenture is a general claim against total assets rather than a specific claim against particular assets.

3. Bonds usually have nominal interest rates that are stated on an annual basis. However, interest is generally paid semiannually, so the nominal rate should be halved when computing the actual cash disbursed for interest. For instance, a 10% debenture of $1,000 would ordinarily require an interest payment of .05 × $1,000, or $50, twice per year.

4. Liabilities can be short-term or long-term. They can also be classified as follows:

DESCRIPTION	EXAMPLE
a. Definite liability of definite amount	Account payable for a repair
b. Definite liability of estimated amount	Liability for warranties

5. Contingent liabilities can have a definite amount (e.g., to pay a $1,000 note payable if a primary borrower fails to pay) or an indefinite amount (e.g., an income tax dispute). These amounts may be substantial, but they are not included in the total liabilities in a balance sheet. They are described in footnotes.

6. Especially in this chapter and its appendixes, solve the "Summary Problems for Your Review" before undertaking any homework assignments.

ACCOUNTING VOCABULARY

Many new terms have been introduced in this chapter. The most important basic terms in the body of the chapter are *contingent liability*, *431 coupon interest rate*, *434 debenture*, *433 discount on bonds*, *436 effective interest rate*, *436 nominal rate*, *434 premium on bonds*, *436* and *subordinated debenture*, *433*. The following list includes terms that are in the chapter or its appendixes:

APPENDIX 10A: ROLE OF COMPOUND INTEREST

Newspapers often contain advertisements of financial institutions citing interest rates that are "compounded." This appendix explains compound interest, including the use of present value tables. Appendix 10B then examines the compound interest method of amortization of bond discounts and premiums.

USE OF PRESENT VALUE TABLES

☐ Nature of Compound Interest

Simple interest is calculated by multiplying an interest rate by an unchanging principal amount. In contrast, **compound interest** is calculated by multiplying an interest rate by a principal amount that is changed each interest period by the previously accumulated (unpaid) interest. The accumulated interest is added to the principal to become the principal for the new period. For example, suppose you deposited $10,000 in a financial institution that promised to pay 10% interest per annum. You let the amount accumulate for three years before withdrawing the full balance of the deposit. The *simple interest* deposit would accumulate to $13,000 at the end of three years:

	PRINCIPAL	SIMPLE INTEREST	BALANCE, END OF YEAR
Year 1	$10,000	$10,000 × .10 = $1,000	$11,000
Year 2	10,000	10,000 × .10 = 1,000	12,000
Year 3	10,000	10,000 × .10 = 1,000	13,000

Compound interest provides interest on interest. That is, the principal changes from period to period. The deposit would accumulate to $10,000 × (1.10)^3 = $10,000 × 1.331 = $13,310:

	PRINCIPAL	COMPOUND INTEREST	BALANCE, END OF YEAR
Year 1	$10,000	$10,000 × .10 = $1,000	$11,000
Year 2	11,000	11,000 × .10 = 1,100	12,100
Year 3	12,100	12,100 × .10 = 1,210	13,310

The accountant would prepare the following initial journal entry for the financial institution:

Cash	10,000	
Deposits (payable)		10,000

Applying compound interest, the financial institution would make the following entries at the end of each of the three years:

	YEAR		
	1	2	3
Interest expense	1,000	1,100	1,210
Deposits (payable)	1,000	1,100	1,210
Deposits (payable)			13,310
Cash			13,310

The "force" of compound interest can be staggering. For example, the same deposit would accumulate as follows:

	AT END OF		
	10 Years	20 Years	40 Years
Simple interest:			
$10,000 + 10 ($1,000) =	$20,000		
$10,000 + 20 ($1,000) =		$30,000	
$10,000 + 40 ($1,000) =			$ 50,000
Compound interest:			
$10,000 \times (1.10)^{10} = $10,000 \times 2.5937 =	$25,937		
$10,000 \times (1.10)^{20} = $10,000 \times 6.7275 =		$67,275	
$10,000 \times (1.10)^{40} = $10,000 \times 45.2593 =			$452,593

Hand calculations of compound interest quickly become burdensome. Therefore compound interest tables have been constructed to ease computations. (Indeed, many hand calculators contain programs that provide speedy answers.) Hundreds of tables are available, but we will use only the two most popular tables for this introduction.[5]

---

[5] For additional tables, see R. Vichas, *Handbook of Financial Mathematics, Formulas and Tables* (Englewood Cliffs, N.J.: Prentice-Hall, 1979).

How should we express a future cash inflow or outflow in terms of its equivalent today (at time zero)? Table 1, page 450, provides factors that give the **present value** of a single, lump-sum cash flow to be received or paid at the *end* of a future period.[6]

Suppose you invest $1.00 today. It will grow to $1.06 in one year at 6% interest; that is, $1 \times 1.06 = $1.06. At the end of the second year its value is ($1 \times 1.06) \times 1.06 = $1 \times (1.06)^2 = $1.124, and at the end of the third year it is $1 \times (1.06)^3 = $1.1910. In general, $1.00 grows to $(1 + i)^n$ in n years at $i\%$ interest.

To determine the *present value*, you reverse this accumulation process. If $1.00 is to be received in one year, it is worth $1 \div 1.06 = $.9434 today. Suppose you invest $.9434 today. In one year you will have $.9434 \times 1.06 = $1.00. Thus $.9434 is the *present value* of $1.00 a year hence at 6%. If the dollar will be received in two years, its present value is $1.00 \div (1.06)^2 = $.8900. The general formula for the present value (PV) of an amount S to be received or paid in n periods at an interest rate of $i\%$ per period is

$$PV = \frac{S}{(1 + i)^n}.$$

Table 1 gives factors for the present value of $1.00 at various interest rates (often called **discount rates**) over several different periods. Present values are also called *discounted* values, and the process of finding the present value is discounting. You can think of this as discounting (decreasing) the value of a future cash inflow or outflow. Why is the value discounted? Because the cash is to be received or paid in the future, not today.

Assume that a prominent city is issuing a three-year non-interest-bearing note payable that promises to pay a lump sum of $1,000 exactly three years from now. You desire a rate of return of exactly 6%, compounded annually. How much would you be willing to pay now for the three-year note? The situation is sketched as follows:

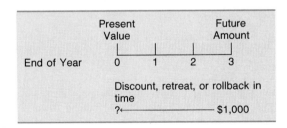

The factor in the Period 3 row and 6% column of Table 1 is .8396. The present value of the $1,000 payment is $1,000 \times .8396 = $839.60. You would be willing to pay $839.60 for the $1,000 to be received in three years.

Suppose interest is compounded semiannually rather than annually. How much

---

[6] The factors are rounded to four decimal places. The examples in this text use these rounded factors. If you use tables with different rounding, or if you use a hand calculator or personal computer, your answers may differ from those given because of a small rounding error.

would you be willing to pay? The three years become six interest payment periods. The rate per period is half the annual rate, or 6% ÷ 2 = 3%. The factor in the Period 6 row and 3% column of Table 1 is .8375. You would be willing to pay $1,000 × .8375, or only $837.50 rather than $839.60.

As a further check on your understanding, review the earlier example of compound interest. Suppose the financial institution promised to pay $13,310 at the end of three years. How much would you be willing to deposit at time zero if you desired a 10% rate of return compounded annually? Using Table 1, the Period 3 row and the 10% column show a factor of .7513. Multiply this factor by the future amount and round to the nearest dollar:

$$PV = .7513 \times \$13,310 = \$10,000$$

A diagram of this computation follows:

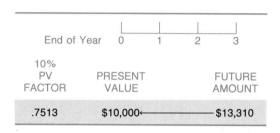

Pause for a moment. Use Table 1 to obtain the present values of

1. $1,600, @ 20%, at the end of 20 years
2. $8,300, @ 10%, at the end of 12 years
3. $8,000, @ 4%, at the end of 4 years

Answers:

1. $1,600 (.0261) = $41.76
2. $8,300 (.3186) = $2,644.38
3. $8,000 (.8548) = $6,838.40

☐ Table 2: Present Value of an Ordinary Annuity of $1

An ordinary annuity is a series of equal cash flows to take place at the *end* of successive periods of equal length. Its present value is denoted PV_A. Assume that you buy a non-interest-bearing serial note from a municipality that promises to pay $1,000 at the end of *each* of three years. How much should you be willing to pay if you desire a rate of return of 6%, compounded annually?

You could solve this problem using Table 1. First, find the present value of each payment, and then add the present values as in Exhibit 10–8. You would be willing to pay $943.40 for the first payment, $890.00 for the second, and $839.60 for the third, a total of $2,673.00.

Since each cash payment is $1,000 with equal one-year periods between them, Table 2 provides a shortcut method. The present value in Exhibit 10–8 can be expressed as

$$PV_A = \$1,000 \times \frac{1}{1.06} + \$1,000 \times \frac{1}{(1.06)^2} + \$1,000 \times \frac{1}{(1.06)^3}$$

$$= \$1,000 \left[\frac{1}{1.06} + \frac{1}{(1.06)^2} + \frac{1}{(1.06)^3} \right]$$

EXHIBIT 10–8

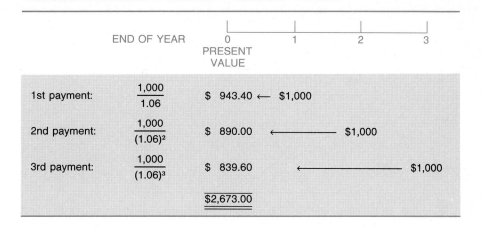

The three terms in brackets are the first three numbers from the 6% column of Table 1, and their sum is in the third row of the 6% column of Table 2: .9434 + .8900 + .8396 = 2.6730. Instead of calculating three present values and adding them, you simply multiply the PV factor from Table 2 by the cash payment: 2.6730 × $1,000 = $2,673.

This shortcut is especially valuable if the cash payments or receipts extend over many periods. Consider an annual cash payment of $1,000 for 20 years at 6%. The present value, calculated from Table 2, is $1,000 × 11.4699 = $11,469.90. To use Table 1 for this calculation, you would perform twenty multiplications and then add the twenty products.

The factors in Table 2 can be calculated using the following general formula:

$$PV_A = \frac{1}{i}\left[1 - \frac{1}{(1+i)^n}\right]$$

Applied to our illustration:

$$PV_A = \frac{1}{.06}(1 - .83962) = \frac{.16038}{.06} = 2.6730$$

Use Table 2 to obtain the present values of the following ordinary annuities:

1. $1,600 at 20% for 20 years
2. $8,300 at 10% for 12 years
3. $8,000 at 4% for 4 years

Answers:

1. $1,600 (4.8696) = $7791.36
2. $8,300 (6.8137) = $56,553.71
3. $8,000 (3.6299) = $29,039.20

In particular, note that the higher the interest rate, the lower the present value.

TABLE 1 (*Put a clip on this page for easy reference.*)

Present Value of $1

$$PV = \frac{1}{(1+i)^n}$$

PERIODS	3%	4%	5%	6%	7%	8%	10%	12%	14%	16%	18%	20%	22%	24%	25%	26%	28%	30%	40%
1	.9709	.9615	.9524	.9434	.9346	.9259	.9091	.8929	.8772	.8621	.8475	.8333	.8197	.8065	.8000	.7937	.7813	.7692	.7143
2	.9426	.9246	.9070	.8900	.8734	.8573	.8264	.7972	.7695	.7432	.7182	.6944	.6719	.6504	.6400	.6299	.6104	.5917	.5102
3	.9151	.8890	.8638	.8396	.8163	.7938	.7513	.7118	.6750	.6407	.6086	.5787	.5507	.5245	.5120	.4999	.4768	.4552	.3644
4	.8885	.8548	.8227	.7921	.7629	.7350	.6830	.6355	.5921	.5523	.5158	.4823	.4514	.4230	.4096	.3968	.3725	.3501	.2603
5	.8626	.8219	.7835	.7473	.7130	.6806	.6209	.5674	.5194	.4761	.4371	.4019	.3700	.3411	.3277	.3149	.2910	.2693	.1859
6	.8375	.7903	.7462	.7050	.6663	.6302	.5645	.5066	.4556	.4104	.3704	.3349	.3033	.2751	.2621	.2499	.2274	.2072	.1328
7	.8131	.7599	.7107	.6651	.6227	.5835	.5132	.4523	.3996	.3538	.3139	.2791	.2486	.2218	.2097	.1983	.1776	.1594	.0949
8	.7894	.7307	.6768	.6274	.5820	.5403	.4665	.4039	.3506	.3050	.2660	.2326	.2038	.1789	.1678	.1574	.1388	.1226	.0678
9	.7664	.7026	.6446	.5919	.5439	.5002	.4241	.3606	.3075	.2630	.2255	.1938	.1670	.1443	.1342	.1249	.1084	.0943	.0484
10	.7441	.6756	.6139	.5584	.5083	.4632	.3855	.3220	.2697	.2267	.1911	.1615	.1369	.1164	.1074	.0992	.0847	.0725	.0346
11	.7224	.6496	.5847	.5268	.4751	.4289	.3505	.2875	.2366	.1954	.1619	.1346	.1122	.0938	.0859	.0787	.0662	.0558	.0247
12	.7014	.6246	.5568	.4970	.4440	.3971	.3186	.2567	.2076	.1685	.1372	.1122	.0920	.0757	.0687	.0625	.0517	.0429	.0176
13	.6810	.6006	.5303	.4688	.4150	.3677	.2897	.2292	.1821	.1452	.1163	.0935	.0754	.0610	.0550	.0496	.0404	.0330	.0126
14	.6611	.5775	.5051	.4423	.3878	.3405	.2633	.2046	.1597	.1252	.0985	.0779	.0618	.0492	.0440	.0393	.0316	.0254	.0090
15	.6419	.5553	.4810	.4173	.3624	.3152	.2394	.1827	.1401	.1079	.0835	.0649	.0507	.0397	.0352	.0312	.0247	.0195	.0064
16	.6232	.5339	.4581	.3936	.3387	.2919	.2176	.1631	.1229	.0930	.0708	.0541	.0415	.0320	.0281	.0248	.0193	.0150	.0046
17	.6050	.5134	.4363	.3714	.3166	.2703	.1978	.1456	.1078	.0802	.0600	.0451	.0340	.0258	.0225	.0197	.0150	.0116	.0033
18	.5874	.4936	.4155	.3503	.2959	.2502	.1799	.1300	.0946	.0691	.0508	.0376	.0279	.0208	.0180	.0156	.0118	.0089	.0023
19	.5703	.4746	.3957	.3305	.2765	.2317	.1635	.1161	.0829	.0596	.0431	.0313	.0229	.0168	.0144	.0124	.0092	.0068	.0017
20	.5537	.4564	.3769	.3118	.2584	.2145	.1486	.1037	.0728	.0514	.0365	.0261	.0187	.0135	.0115	.0098	.0072	.0053	.0012
21	.5375	.4388	.3589	.2942	.2415	.1987	.1351	.0926	.0638	.0443	.0309	.0217	.0154	.0109	.0092	.0078	.0056	.0040	.0009
22	.5219	.4220	.3418	.2775	.2257	.1839	.1228	.0826	.0560	.0382	.0262	.0181	.0126	.0088	.0074	.0062	.0044	.0031	.0006
23	.5067	.4057	.3256	.2618	.2109	.1703	.1117	.0738	.0491	.0329	.0222	.0151	.0103	.0071	.0059	.0049	.0034	.0024	.0004
24	.4919	.3901	.3101	.2470	.1971	.1577	.1015	.0659	.0431	.0284	.0188	.0126	.0085	.0057	.0047	.0039	.0027	.0018	.0003
25	.4776	.3751	.2953	.2330	.1842	.1460	.0923	.0588	.0378	.0245	.0160	.0105	.0069	.0046	.0038	.0031	.0021	.0014	.0002
26	.4637	.3607	.2812	.2198	.1722	.1352	.0839	.0525	.0331	.0211	.0135	.0087	.0057	.0037	.0030	.0025	.0016	.0011	.0002
27	.4502	.3468	.2678	.2074	.1609	.1252	.0763	.0469	.0291	.0182	.0115	.0073	.0047	.0030	.0024	.0019	.0013	.0008	.0001
28	.4371	.3335	.2551	.1956	.1504	.1159	.0693	.0419	.0255	.0157	.0097	.0061	.0038	.0024	.0019	.0015	.0010	.0006	.0001
29	.4243	.3207	.2429	.1846	.1406	.1073	.0630	.0374	.0224	.0135	.0082	.0051	.0031	.0020	.0015	.0012	.0008	.0005	.0001
30	.4120	.3083	.2314	.1741	.1314	.0994	.0573	.0334	.0196	.0116	.0070	.0042	.0026	.0016	.0012	.0010	.0006	.0004	.0000
40	.3066	.2083	.1420	.0972	.0668	.0460	.0221	.0107	.0053	.0026	.0013	.0007	.0004	.0002	.0001	.0001	.0001	.0000	.0000

TABLE 2

Present Value of Ordinary Annuity of $1

$$PV_A = \frac{1}{i}\left[1 - \frac{1}{(1+i)^n}\right]$$

PERIODS	3%	4%	5%	6%	7%	8%	10%	12%	14%	16%	18%	20%	22%	24%	25%	26%	28%	30%	40%
1	.9709	.9615	.9524	.9434	.9346	.9259	.9091	.8929	.8772	.8621	.8475	.8333	.8197	.8065	.8000	.7937	.7813	.7692	.7143
2	1.9135	1.8861	1.8594	1.8334	1.8080	1.7833	1.7355	1.6901	1.6467	1.6052	1.5656	1.5278	1.4915	1.4568	1.4400	1.4235	1.3916	1.3609	1.2245
3	2.8286	2.7751	2.7232	2.6730	2.6243	2.5771	2.4869	2.4018	2.3216	2.2459	2.1743	2.1065	2.0422	1.9813	1.9520	1.9234	1.8684	1.8161	1.5889
4	3.7171	3.6299	3.5460	3.4651	3.3872	3.3121	3.1699	3.0373	2.9137	2.7982	2.6901	2.5887	2.4936	2.4043	2.3616	2.3202	2.2410	2.1662	1.8492
5	4.5797	4.4518	4.3295	4.2124	4.1002	3.9927	3.7908	3.6048	3.4331	3.2743	3.1272	2.9906	2.8636	2.7454	2.6893	2.6351	2.5320	2.4356	2.0352
6	5.4172	5.2421	5.0757	4.9173	4.7665	4.6229	4.3553	4.1114	3.8887	3.6847	3.4976	3.3255	3.1669	3.0205	2.9514	2.8850	2.7594	2.6427	2.1680
7	6.2303	6.0021	5.7864	5.5824	5.3893	5.2064	4.8684	4.5638	4.2883	4.0386	3.8115	3.6046	3.4155	3.2423	3.1611	3.0833	2.9370	2.8021	2.2628
8	7.0197	6.7327	6.4632	6.2098	5.9713	5.7466	5.3349	4.9676	4.6389	4.3436	4.0776	3.8372	3.6193	3.4212	3.3289	3.2407	3.0758	2.9247	2.3306
9	7.7861	7.4353	7.1078	6.8017	6.5152	6.2469	5.7590	5.3282	4.9464	4.6065	4.3030	4.0310	3.7863	3.5655	3.4631	3.3657	3.1842	3.0190	2.3790
10	8.5302	8.1109	7.7217	7.3601	7.0236	6.7101	6.1446	5.6502	5.2161	4.8332	4.4941	4.1925	3.9232	3.6819	3.5705	3.4648	3.2689	3.0915	2.4136
11	9.2526	8.7605	8.3064	7.8869	7.4987	7.1390	6.4951	5.9377	5.4527	5.0286	4.6560	4.3271	4.0354	3.7757	3.6564	3.5435	3.3351	3.1473	2.4383
12	9.9540	9.3851	8.8633	8.3838	7.9427	7.5361	6.8137	6.1944	5.6603	5.1971	4.7932	4.4392	4.1274	3.8514	3.7251	3.6059	3.3868	3.1903	2.4559
13	10.6350	9.9856	9.3936	8.8527	8.3577	7.9038	7.1034	6.4235	5.8424	5.3423	4.9095	4.5327	4.2028	3.9124	3.7801	3.6555	3.4272	3.2233	2.4685
14	11.2961	10.5631	9.8986	9.2950	8.7455	8.2442	7.3667	6.6282	6.0021	5.4675	5.0081	4.6106	4.2646	3.9616	3.8241	3.6949	3.4587	3.2487	2.4775
15	11.9379	11.1184	10.3797	9.7122	9.1079	8.5595	7.6061	6.8109	6.1422	5.5755	5.0916	4.6755	4.3152	4.0013	3.8593	3.7261	3.4834	3.2682	2.4839
16	12.5611	11.6523	10.8378	10.1059	9.4466	8.8514	7.8237	6.9740	6.2651	5.6685	5.1624	4.7296	4.3567	4.0333	3.8874	3.7509	3.5026	3.2832	2.4885
17	13.1661	12.1657	11.2741	10.4773	9.7632	9.1216	8.0216	7.1196	6.3729	5.7487	5.2223	4.7746	4.3908	4.0591	3.9099	3.7705	3.5177	3.2948	2.4918
18	13.7535	12.6593	11.6896	10.8276	10.0591	9.3719	8.2014	7.2497	6.4674	5.8178	5.2732	4.8122	4.4187	4.0799	3.9279	3.7861	3.5294	3.3037	2.4941
19	14.3238	13.1339	12.0853	11.1581	10.3356	9.6036	8.3649	7.3658	6.5504	5.8775	5.3162	4.8435	4.4415	4.0967	3.9424	3.7985	3.5386	3.3105	2.4958
20	14.8775	13.5903	12.4622	11.4699	10.5940	9.8181	8.5136	7.4694	6.6231	5.9288	5.3527	4.8696	4.4603	4.1103	3.9539	3.8083	3.5458	3.3158	2.4970
21	15.4150	14.0292	12.8212	11.7641	10.8355	10.0168	8.6487	7.5620	6.6870	5.9731	5.3837	4.8913	4.4756	4.1212	3.9631	3.8161	3.5514	3.3198	2.4979
22	15.9369	14.4511	13.1630	12.0416	11.0612	10.2007	8.7715	7.6446	6.7429	6.0113	5.4099	4.9094	4.4882	4.1300	3.9705	3.8223	3.5558	3.3230	2.4985
23	16.4436	14.8568	13.4886	12.3034	11.2722	10.3711	8.8832	7.7184	6.7921	6.0442	5.4321	4.9245	4.4985	4.1371	3.9764	3.8273	3.5592	3.3254	2.4989
24	16.9355	15.2470	13.7986	12.5504	11.4693	10.5288	8.9847	7.7843	6.8351	6.0726	5.4509	4.9371	4.5070	4.1428	3.9811	3.8312	3.5619	3.3272	2.4992
25	17.4131	15.6221	14.0939	12.7834	11.6536	10.6748	9.0770	7.8431	6.8729	6.0971	5.4669	4.9476	4.5139	4.1474	3.9849	3.8342	3.5640	3.3286	2.4994
26	17.8768	15.9828	14.3752	13.0032	11.8258	10.8100	9.1609	7.8957	6.9061	6.1182	5.4804	4.9563	4.5196	4.1511	3.9879	3.8367	3.5656	3.3297	2.4996
27	18.3270	16.3296	14.6430	13.2105	11.9867	10.9352	9.2372	7.9426	6.9352	6.1364	5.4919	4.9636	4.5243	4.1542	3.9903	3.8387	3.5669	3.3305	2.4997
28	18.7641	16.6631	14.8981	13.4062	12.1371	11.0511	9.3066	7.9844	6.9607	6.1520	5.5016	4.9697	4.5281	4.1566	3.9923	3.8402	3.5679	3.3312	2.4998
29	19.1885	16.9837	15.1411	13.5907	12.2777	11.1584	9.3696	8.0218	6.9830	6.1656	5.5098	4.9747	4.5312	4.1585	3.9938	3.8414	3.5687	3.3317	2.4999
30	19.6004	17.2920	15.3725	13.7648	12.4090	11.2578	9.4269	8.0552	7.0027	6.1772	5.5168	4.9789	4.5338	4.1601	3.9950	3.8424	3.5693	3.3321	2.4999
40	23.1148	19.7928	17.1591	15.0463	13.3317	11.9246	9.7791	8.2438	7.1050	6.2335	5.5482	4.9966	4.5439	4.1659	3.9995	3.8458	3.5712	3.3332	2.5000

SUMMARY PROBLEMS FOR YOUR REVIEW

Before proceeding to the next section, be sure to solve these review exercises.

☐ Problem Two (Problem One is in the body of the chapter.)

Xerox Corporation plans to enter some new communications business. The company expects to accumulate sufficient cash from its new operations to pay a lump sum of $200 million to Prudential Insurance Company at the end of five years. Prudential will lend money on a promissory note now, will take no payments until the end of five years, and desires 12% interest compounded annually.

Required:

1. How much money will Prudential lend Xerox?
2. Prepare journal entries for Xerox at the inception of the loan and at the end of each of the first two years.

☐ Solution to Problem Two

The initial step in solving present value problems focuses on a basic question, Which table should I use? No computations should be made until you are convinced that you are using the correct table.

1. Use Table 1. The $200 million is a future amount. Its present value is

$$PV = \$200,000,000 \times \frac{1}{(1 + .12)^5}$$

The conversion factor, $1/(1 + .12)^5$, is in row 5 and the 12% column. It is .5674.

$$PV = \$200,000,000 \times .5674 = \$113,480,000$$

2.

Cash	113,480,000	
Long-term note payable		
(or long-term debt)		113,480,000
To record borrowing that is payable in a lump sum at the end of five years at 12% interest compounded annually.		
Interest expense	13,617,600	
Long-term note payable		13,617,600
To record interest expense and corresponding accumulation of principal at the end of the first year: .12 × $113,480,000 = $13,617,600		
Interest expense	15,251,712	
Long-term note payable		15,251,712
To record interest expense and corresponding accumulation of principal at the end of the second year: .12 × ($113,480,000 + $13,617,600).		

Reflect on the entries for interest. Note how the interest expense becomes larger if no interest payments are made from year to year. This mounting interest expense occurs because the unpaid interest is being added to the principal to form a new higher principal each year.

☐ Problem Three

Refer to the preceding problem. Suppose Xerox and Prudential agree on a 12% interest rate compounded annually. However, Xerox will pay a *total* of $200 million in the form of $40 million annual payments at the end of *each* of the next five years. How much money will Prudential lend Xerox?

☐ Solution to Problem Three

Use Table 2. The $40 million is a uniform periodic payment at the end of a series of years. Therefore it is an annuity. Its present value is:

$$PV_A = \text{Annual payment} \times \text{Conversion factor}$$
$$= \$40 \text{ million} \times \text{Conversion factor for 5 years at 12\%}$$
$$= \$40 \text{ million} \times 3.6048$$
$$= \$144,192,000$$

In particular, note that Prudential is willing to lend more than in Problem Two even though the interest rate is the same. Why? Because Prudential will get its money back more quickly.

APPENDIX 10B: AMORTIZATION OF BOND DISCOUNT, IMPUTED INTEREST, AND PENSIONS

This appendix discusses the application of compound interest principles to the accounting for bonds, notes, and pensions.

COMPOUND INTEREST AND AMORTIZATION OF BOND DISCOUNT

☐ Constant Amount or Percentage

As this chapter explained, bond premium or discount emerges when the nominal rate of interest (stated or contractual rate) does not coincide with the effective rate (yield rate or market rate). The premium or discount is the difference between the face value (or maturity value) of a bond and the amount a company receives from issuing the bond. A premium arises when the nominal rate exceeds the effective rate, so that the amount received exceeds the face value. A discount arises when the effective rate exceeds the nominal rate, so that the face value exceeds the amount received.

Accountants amortize the premium or discount to adjust the periodic interest expense so that it approximates the effective rate of interest. A rough approximation is attained by straight-line amortization. The straight-line method allocates a *constant amount* to each period, but it fails to measure interest expense as a *constant percentage* of the net carrying amount of the bond. Thus the interest *rate* gradually increases or decreases from year to year under straight-line amortization.

The compound interest method assigns to each period an amount of interest expense computed at a constant rate. Each interest period bears an interest expense equal to the effective interest rate multiplied by the carrying amount (face amount less unamortized discount or plus unamortized premium). The product is the effective interest amount. **The difference between the effective-interest amount and the nominal-interest amount is the amount of discount or premium amortized for the period.**

☐ Market Valuation of Bonds

A typical bond consists of a promise to pay interest every six months until maturity and a promise to pay a lump sum at maturity. Suppose that on January 1, 19X1, a two-year $1,000 bond is issued that bears a nominal interest rate of 10%. Consider how the investor would value the bond, using the tables on pages 450–451.

Exhibit 10–9 shows how the bond would be valued, using three different interest rates. Note the following about Exhibit 10–9:

EXHIBIT 10–9

Computation of Market Value of Bonds

	PRESENT VALUE FACTOR	TOTAL PRESENT VALUE	SKETCH OF CASH FLOWS				
			0	1	2	3	4
Valuation at 10%, or 5% per period:							
Principal, 4-period line, Table 1							
.8227 × $1,000 = $822.70	.8227	822.70					1,000
Interest, 4-period line, Table 2							
3.5460 × $50 = $177.30	3.5460	177.30	50	50	50		50
Total		1,000.00					
Valuation at 12%, or 6% per period:							
Principal	.7921	792.10					1,000
Interest	3.4651	173.25	50	50	50		50
Total		965.35					
Valuation at 8%, or 4% per period:							
Principal	.8548	854.80					1,000
Interest	3.6299	181.50	50	50	50		50
Total		1,036.30					

1. The quoted bond rates imply a rate per annum, but the bond markets do not mean that rate literally. Thus a 10% bond really pays 5% interest each semiannual period. A two-year bond has four periods, a ten-year bond has twenty periods, and so on.
2. Consider the valuation using 10%. Uninformed investors think that the $1,000 liability represents the face amount and that the interest liability does not have any value when the bonds are issued. They are mistaken because the simple name "bonds payable" is deceptive. A more accurate statement of liability would be:

Present value of $1,000 to be paid at the end of two years, $1,000 × .8227	$ 822.70
Present value of $50 to be paid at the end of each of four semiannual periods, $50 × 3.5460	177.30
Total present value of liability	$1,000.00

3. The *higher* the effective (or market) rate of interest, the *lower* the present value.

☐ Effective-Interest Amortization

Assume the bond is issued at a price of $965.35, which reflects an effective interest rate of 6% per semiannual period, as shown in Exhibit 10–9. The nominal-interest rate of 5% results in cash outlays for interest of $50 per semiannual period. The amortization of discount using the effective-interest method is shown in the following schedule:

For Six Months Ended	(1) .06 × (5) Effective Interest: 6% per Period*	(2) .05 × $1,000 Nominal Interest: 5% per Period	(3) (1) − (2) Discount Amortized	(4) Carrying Amount Unamortized Discount	(5) $1,000 − (4) Carrying Amount Net Liability
1/1/X1				34.65	965.35
7/1/X1	57.92	50.00	7.92	26.73†	973.27
1/1/X2	58.40	50.00	8.40	18.33	981.67
7/1/X2	58.90	50.00	8.90	9.43	990.57
1/1/X3	59.43	50.00	9.43	0	1,000.00

* 6% × the balance of the net liability at the beginning of each period. For example, at 7/1/X1, .06 × $965.35 = $57.92.
† $34.65 − $7.92, $26.73 − $8.40, and so on.

Note that the discount amortized is not the same amount each period, as in the straight-line method. However, the journal entries for amortization affect the same accounts, regardless of whether the straight-line or effective-interest method is used. For example, the journal entry on July 1, 19X1, would be:

Bond interest expense (for effective interest)	57.92	
Discount on bonds payable (for amortization)		7.92
Cash (for nominal interest)		50.00
To record interest payment and discount amortization.		

Compare the amount of amortization over the four interest periods:

	METHOD OF AMORTIZATION	
Period	Effective Interest (see schedule)	Straight-Line ($34.65 ÷ 4)
1	$ 7.92	$ 8.66
2	8.40	8.66
3	8.90	8.66
4	9.43	8.67
Total	$34.65	$34.65

The amount of effective-interest amortization rises each period because the net liability also rises as the maturity date nears. (When bonds are issued at a premium, the reverse will be true.) In contrast, the amount of straight-line amortization is always equal each period.

IMPUTED INTEREST

Transactions often entail the exchange of property for notes. Sometimes these notes bear no interest or a nominal interest rate much below the market rate. When the face amount of a note does not reasonably represent the present value of the consideration in the exchange, the values of the assets and liabilities are erroneous. Moreover, the subsequent interest is also erroneous.

When a noncash exchange occurs, the valuation should be determined by the cash-equivalent value of one of the items exchanged, whichever is more objectively determinable. Suppose a note is exchanged for property such as undeveloped land. The accountant must be assured that the face amount of the note is approximately equal to the current cash sales price of the land (or equivalent land). If comparable sales prices are unobtainable, the accountant must determine the cash-equivalent value of the note. For example, what would a bank be willing to pay for the note?

Suppose Company Y acquires some raw land from a realtor in exchange for a $100,000 non-interest-bearing note payable in ten years. Comparable sales prices for the land are not obtainable. However, a bank offered financing for such land at 12% interest.

Suppose form prevails over substance. Company Y would list a $100,000 asset, land, and a $100,000 liability, note payable, on its balance sheet. No interest expense would ever be recognized.

However, economic substance should prevail over legal form. The nominal rate of zero should be rejected in favor of the market rate. This process is frequently called **imputation**, and the resulting interest rate is called the **imputed rate**. In general, *imputation* is the process that recognizes a pertinent expense or revenue that may not be routinely recognized by ordinary accounting procedures. Table 1 reveals a present value at 12% of $100,000 to be paid in ten years, assuming annual compounding:

Present value of $1.00 from Table 1, 12% column, 10-year row = .3220
Present value of $100,000 note = $100,000 × .3220 = $32,200

Note the heavy importance of interest. The picture changes drastically. This is the accounting if substance prevails over form:

Land	32,200	
Discount on note payable	67,800	
Note payable		100,000
To record the present value of a non-interest-bearing 10-year $100,000 note discounted at the market rate of interest of 12%.		

The entry to record the interest for the first year would be:

Interest expense	3,864	
Discount on note payable		3,864
[Interest expense is recorded even though no cash is paid. The interest is .12 × $32,200 = $3,864. The second year's interest would be .12 × ($32,200 + $3,864); and it would rise each year.]		

The interest expense would rise each year as the discount on the note is amortized in the effective-interest manner that was illustrated earlier in this appendix.

LIABILITIES FOR PENSIONS

In accounting for pensions, companies must recognize a liability to employees when the accumulated benefit obligation exceeds the fair value of the assets in a pension fund. Suppose a company's current pension expense is $100,000, $30,000 of which is paid in cash. The accounting for pensions has the following fundamental framework:

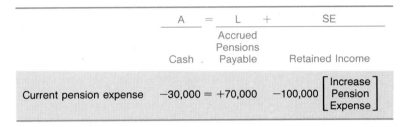

	A	=	L	+	SE	
			Accrued Pensions			
	Cash		Payable		Retained Income	
Current pension expense	−30,000	=	+70,000		−100,000	[Increase Pension Expense]

The journal entry would be:

Pension expense	100,000	
Cash		30,000
Accrued pensions payable		70,000
To record pension expense for the year.		

Accounting for pensions has been controversial. However, the debate is not overly concerned with what accounts should be affected. Rather, it is concerned with how to *measure* current expense and the long-term liability for pensions. This entails compound interest effects and fiery debates about what interest rates are applicable. As the preceding section on imputed interest demonstrated, the choice of an interest rate can have a telling impact on the present value of a liability. Pension liabilities are frequently substantial. FASB *Statements No. 87* and *88* provide detailed rules for many of the controversial measurement issues. For further discussion, see textbooks on intermediate and advanced accounting.

APPENDIX 10C: ACCOUNTING FOR LEASES

Do not proceed with this appendix until you have solved the "Summary Problems for Your Review" in Appendix 10A, page 452.

OPERATING AND CAPITAL LEASES

Leasing is big business. Any asset imaginable, from television sets to jumbo aircraft to buildings, can be acquired via rental. In 1985, *Euromoney* pointed out that "leasing has now blossomed into the biggest single provider of fixed-rate finance for corporate

America." A **lease** is a contract whereby an owner (lessor) grants the use of property to a second party (lessee) for rental payments. This appendix discusses leasing from the lessee's point of view.

In general, the legal form and economic substance of an exchange are straightforward and mutually reinforcing. For example, an ordinary sale of equipment passes title (legal form) of an asset to the purchaser, who subsequently bears the risk and rewards of ownership (economic substance). Generally, accountants do not record the asset and liability on the new owner's records unless legal title has passed.

Statement No. 13 of the Financial Accounting Standards Board (FASB) requires an exception to this rule for certain types of leases. The board asserted that many noncancelable leases are substantially equivalent to purchases. The lessee has full use of the asset and a legal obligation to make payments, the same as if money were borrowed and the asset purchased. Such leases should be recorded by the lessee as a leasehold *asset* and leasehold *liability* even though no legal title has passed. That is, legal passage of title (the form) is secondary; accountants should record the assumption of the risks and rewards of ownership by the lessee (economic substance).

Leases are divided into two major kinds: capital leases and operating leases. **Capital leases** are those that transfer substantially all the risks and benefits of ownership. They are equivalent to installment sale and purchase transactions. The asset must be recorded essentially as having been sold by the lessor and having been purchased by the lessee. All other leases are **operating leases**. Examples of the latter are telephones rented by the month and rooms rented by the day, week, or month. Operating leases are accounted for as ordinary rent expenses; no balance sheet accounts are affected by operating leases.

In its annual report, Roper Corporation, the main supplier to Sears of cooking ranges and rotary lawnmowers, provides an example of how a liability on a capital lease is described:

	JULY 31	
	1985	1984
Capitalized lease obligations with an average interest rate of 7% maturing through 1997	$13,852,000	$16,275,000

Footnote disclosures are required for all significant leases, regardless of whether they are capital leases or operating leases. These footnotes reveal at least the minimum lease payments for the next five years, in the aggregate and year by year. In addition to such footnotes, the parties to lease transactions must, of course, use the accounting and reporting methods that are appropriate for the particular types of leases.

Consider a simple example to see how the accounting differs for operating and capital leases. Suppose B Company can acquire a truck (or a computer or a packaging machine) that has a useful life of four years and no residual value under either of the following conditions:

BUY OUTRIGHT	or	NONCANCELABLE LEASE
Cash outlays, $50,000		Rental of $16,462 per year, payable at the end of each of four years
Borrow $50,000 cash, four-year loan payable at maturity at 12% interest compounded annually		

There is no basic difference between buying outright or irrevocably leasing for four years.[7] B Company uses the asset for its entire useful life and must pay for repairs, property taxes, and other operating costs under either plan.

Most lease rentals are paid at the *start* of each payment period, but to ease our computations we assume that each payment will occur at the end of the year. To earn 12% per year, the lessor would consult Table 2. The 12% column and fourth-period row show a factor of 3.0373:

Let x = rental payment
$50,000 = PV of annuity of x per year for 4 years at 12%
$50,000 = 3.0373x
x = $50,000 ÷ 3.0373
x = $16,462 rental per year, as shown in the comparison above

The present value of the four $16,462 lease payments is

$$\$16{,}462 \times 3.0373 = \$50{,}000$$

From the lessee's perspective, both buying outright and leasing create a $50,000 obligation.

Before the passage of FASB *Statement No. 13* in 1976, the balance sheet of a company electing to lease the asset would have looked very different from that of a company that purchased the asset. Most companies used the operating lease method, with the following straightforward effect:

	A		= L	+	SE
	Cash	Truck Leasehold	Lease Liability		Retained Income
Signing of lease	No entry				
Lease payment:					[Increase Rent Expense]
Year 1	−16,462		=		−16,462
Year 2	−16,462		=		−16,462
Year 3	−16,462		=		−16,462
Year 4	−16,462		=		−16,462
Cumulative totals	−65,848		=		−65,848

Each year the journal entry would be:

Rent expense	16,462	
Cash		16,462
To record lease payment.		

However, under today's accounting rules, such a lease must be accounted for as a *capital lease*. This means that both a leasehold asset and a lease liability must be placed on the balance sheet at the present value of future lease payments, $50,000 in this illustration. The signing of the lease would require the following journal entry:

---

[7] Note the reason why a capital lease is regarded as no different from borrowing the cash and then buying an asset outright. The lessee bears the same risks and rewards as an owner. The difference is only in the form of financing. The management decision in this context is often expressed as, Should we buy or lease? But if you ponder the question more deeply, you will see that the question is better divided into two parts. First, regardless of the form of financing, Should we acquire the asset or not acquire it? If the answer is to acquire it, the second question is, Should we acquire it by leasing or by an outright purchase with borrowed money?

Truck leasehold under capital lease	50,000	
Lease liability		50,000
To record the acquisition of an asset and its accompanying liability.		

At the end of each of the four years, the asset must be amortized. Straight-line amortization, which is used almost without exception, would be $50,000 \div 4 = $12,500 annually. In addition, the annual lease payment must be recorded. Each lease payment consists of interest expense plus an amount that reduces the outstanding liability. The effective-interest method is used, as Exhibit 10–10 demonstrates. Study the exhibit before proceeding.

Exhibit 10–11 uses the balance sheet equation to summarize the accounting for capital leases. The yearly journal entries for the leasehold would be:

| Amortization of leasehold | 12,500 | |
| Truck leasehold | | 12,500 |

The yearly journal entries for lease payments would be:

	YEAR 1		YEAR 2		YEAR 3		YEAR 4	
Interest expense	6,000		4,745		3,339		1,764	
Lease liability	10,462		11,717		13,123		14,698	
Cash		16,462		16,462		16,462		16,462

EXHIBIT 10–10

Analytical Schedule of Lease Payments

	(1)	(2)	(3) (1) + (2)	(4)	(5) (3) − (4)	(6) SAME AS (2)	(7) (4) − (2)
						Supplementary Analysis of Each Payment	
End of Year	Lease Liability at Beginning of Year	Interest at 12% per Year	Accumulated Amount at End of Year	Cash for Lease Payment	Lease Liability at End of Year	Interest Expense	Reduction in Beginning Lease Liability
1	$50,000	$6,000	$56,000	$16,462	$39,538	$ 6,000	$10,462
2	39,538	4,745	44,283	16,462	27,821	4,745	11,717
3	27,821	3,339	31,160	16,462	14,698	3,339	13,123
4	14,698	1,764	16,462	16,462	0	1,764	14,698
						$15,848	$50,000

EXHIBIT 10–11

Accounting for a Capital Lease

	A		= L	+	SE
	Cash	Truck Leasehold	Lease Liability		Retained Income
Signing of lease		+50,000	= +50,000		
Amortization of leasehold:*					
End of Year 1		−12,500* =			−12,500
End of Year 2		−12,500 =			−12,500
End of Year 3		−12,500 =			−12,500
End of Year 4		−12,500 =			−12,500
Lease payments:†					
End of Year 1	−16,462		= −10,462		− 6,000
End of Year 2	−16,462		= −11,717		− 4,745
End of Year 3	−16,462		= −13,123		− 3,339
End of Year 4	−16,462		= −14,698		− 1,764
Cumulative totals	−65,848	0	0		−65,848

(End of Year 1–4 amortization rows bracketed: "Increase Amortization of leasehold")

(End of Year 1–4 lease payment rows bracketed: "Increase Interest Expense")

* Straight-line amortization is followed in practice. A separate account for Accumulated Amortization—Leasehold could be presented, but the Amortization is shown here as a direct reduction of Truck Leasehold.

† Exhibit 10–10 contains the analytical schedule of lease payments.

DIFFERENCES IN INCOME STATEMENTS

Exhibit 10–12 shows the major differences between the accounting for operating leases and the accounting for capital leases. The cumulative expenses are the same, $65,848, but the timing differs. In comparison with the operating-lease approach, the capital-lease approach tends to bunch heavier charges in the early years. The longer the lease, the more pronounced the differences will be in the early years. Therefore immediate reported income is hurt more under the capital-lease approach.

An operating lease affects the income statement as rent expense, which is the amount of the lease payment. A capital lease affects the income statement as amortization (of the asset) plus interest expense (on the liability). For each year of the lease, the difference in pretax income can be expressed as follows:

Difference in pretax income = Operating lease effect − Capital lease effect (1)
= Lease payment − (Amortization + Interest) (2)
= (Lease payment − Amortization) − Interest

Example for Year 1: ($16,462 − $12,500) − $6,000 = $−2,038
Example for Year 4: ($16,462 − $12,500) − $1,764 = $2,198

Neither the lease payment nor the amortization changes from year to year. In early years, when interest is high, the total expense is greater for a capital lease than for an operating lease. In later years the interest falls, and the operating lease expense (that is, the lease payment) is greater. The relationship can be shown as follows:

EXHIBIT 10–12

Year-by-Year Comparison of Accounting for Leases
(amounts are in dollars)

| | OPERATING-LEASE METHOD | CAPITAL-LEASE METHOD | | | | | | DIFFERENCE | |
| | Recognition of asset and liability? No | Yes | | | | | | | |
	(a) Lease Payment*	(b) Asset	(c) Amortization of Asset	(d) Interest Expense	(e) (c) + (d) Total Expense	(f) Lease Liability	(g) (a) − (e) Difference in Pretax Income	(h) Difference in Ending Balance, Retained Income
Balance at inception of lease		50,000				50,000		
Balance at end of year:								
1	16,462	37,500	12,500	6,000	18,500	39,538	(2,038)	(2,038)
2	16,462	25,000	12,500	4,745	17,245	27,821	(783)	(2,821)
3	16,462	12,500	12,500	3,339	15,839	14,698	623	(2,198)
4	16,462	—	12,500	1,764	14,264	—	2,198	—
Cumulative expenses	65,848		50,000	15,848	65,848			

* Rent expense for the year under the operating-lease method.

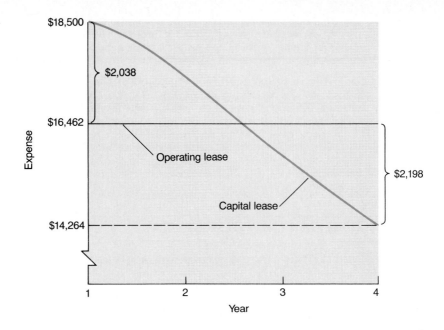

Regardless of the useful life of the asset, the same pattern arises. The expense for an operating lease, which is the lease payment, is constant year to year. The expense for a capital lease is greater than the lease payment in early years and lower in later years.

TESTS FOR CAPITAL LEASES

The capital-lease approach was adopted in 1976 after many years of controversy within the accounting profession regarding which leases deserve capitalization as balance sheet items. Until then, almost no leases were capitalized. Many companies were criticized for "invisible debt" or "off-balance sheet financing" in the sense that noncancelable leases existed but were not included as liabilities on the balance sheet.

A letter to the editor of *Business Week* shows the attitude that still persists among many managers:

☐ The fact is that capital leases do, indeed, have to be carried on a company's balance sheet as assets and liabilities, but operating leases do not. Operating leases are accounted for as expenses.

☐ Consequently operating leases provide considerably greater financial benefits. Companies will show a better return on assets and a lower debt-to-equity ratio. Asset turnover also will be higher. The lease payments are fully deductible.

Whether "considerably greater financial benefits" do in fact occur is a highly debatable, complex point. See Chapter 16, pages 743–745, for additional discussion.

A *capital lease* exists if *one* or more of the following conditions are met:

1. Title is transferred to the lessee by the end of the lease term.
2. A bargain purchase option is available to the lessee.

3. The lease term equals or exceeds 75% of the estimated economic life of the property.
4. At the start of the lease term, the present value of minimum lease payments is at least 90% of the excess of the property's fair value over any related investment tax credit retained by the lessor.

Criteria 3 and 4 are not applicable if the lease term begins during the final 25% of the property's economic life. A lease either meets one of these criteria or does not. Managers cannot choose to treat a given lease as either a capital lease or an operating lease. However, some managers seek to structure leases so that they do not meet any of the criteria and therefore are not shown on the balance sheet.

As you can readily visualize, accounting for leases can rapidly become enormously complicated.[8] For further discussion, see a textbook on intermediate or advanced accounting.

SUMMARY PROBLEM FOR YOUR REVIEW

☐ **Problem Four (Other review problems appear earlier in the chapter.)**

Exxon acquired computer equipment from IBM on a capital lease. There were annual lease payments of $60 million at the end of each of four years. The implicit interest rate was 14% compounded annually.

Required:

1. Compute the present value of the capital lease.
2. Prepare Exxon journal entries at the inception of the lease and for the first two years. Show computations.
3. For simplicity, the earlier presentation of leases ignored short-term and long-term classifications. Recast the initial journal entry in requirement 2 to make this distinction. Also prepare an entry at the end of Year 1 to reclassify the portion of long-term debt that has become current.

☐ **Solution to Problem Four**

1. $PV_A = \$60,000,000 \times$ Annuity factor for 4 years at 14%
$= \$60,000,000 \times 2.9137$
$= \$174,822,000$

2.

Computer equipment leasehold	174,822,000	
Lease liability		174,822,000
To record capital lease.		
Terms are 4 years,		
annual payments of $60 million,		
implicit interest of 14%.		

Entry for amortization of asset for each of first two years:

---

[8] Consider the advertisement in the *Wall Street Journal* with big bold letters in black and white: FAS–13. (That refers to Financial Accounting Standards No. 13, although the ad found it unnecessary to say so.) The ad continues, "We specialize in leases and have developed a complete and easy-to-use system for lessees and lessors. All accounting, tax, disclosure and restatement schedules . . ."

Amortization of computer equipment leasehold	43,705,500	
Computer equipment leasehold		43,705,500
To record straight-line amortization of $174,822,000 ÷ 4 = $43,705,500.		

Entries for reduction of liability:

Interest expense	24,475,080	
Lease liability	35,524,920	
Cash		60,000,000
Interest is .14 × $174,822,000 = $24,475,080. Principal reduction is $60,000,000 − $24,475,080 = $35,524,920		
Interest expense	19,501,591	
Lease liability	40,498,409	
Cash		60,000,000
Interest is .14 ($174,822,000 −$35,524,920) or .14 × $139,297,080 = $19,501,591. Principal reduction is $60,000,000 − $19,501,591 = $40,498,409.		

3.

Computer equipment leasehold	174,822,000	
Lease liability, current		35,524,920
Lease liability, long-term		139,297,080
To record capital lease.		
Lease liability, long-term	40,498,409	
Lease liability, current		40,498,409
To reclassify current installment of long-term debt as short-term debt.		

FUNDAMENTAL ASSIGNMENT MATERIAL

☐ General Coverage

10–1. PAYROLL TAXES. (Alternate is 10–6.) M. J. Greene Company incurred wages expenses of $300,000 for the week ended January 31. Related obligations for withheld income taxes and social security taxes were $29,000 and $18,000, respectively. The employees were paid on February 3, and the government was paid on February 4.

Required:

Show all amounts in thousands of dollars.

1. Show an analysis of the transactions, using the balance sheet equation.
2. Prepare journal entries to accompany the analysis in requirement 1.
3. Assume that the company has additional costs related to the above data, as follows: employer payroll taxes, $21,000; pension obligations, $30,000; and health insurance, $9,000. Prepare journal entries to record (a) the liabilities and (b) the related cash disbursements.

10–2. VARIOUS LIABILITIES. (Alternate is 10–7.)

1. Leverett Company uses a rate of 6% of gross payroll to accrue a liability for vacation pay. As vacations are actually being taken, the liability is extinguished. Prepare journal entries for (a) liabilities relating to a gross payroll of $400,000 and (b) vacation payments of $10,000. Ignore payroll taxes and withholding taxes.
2. A bank received a $24,000 savings deposit on August 1. On September 30, the bank recognized two months' interest thereon at an annual rate of 10%. On October 1, the depositor closed her account with the bank. Interest is payable from the date of deposit through the date before withdrawal. Prepare the bank's journal entries.
3. The New York Mets sold season tickets for $5 million cash in advance of the baseball season, which begins on April 10. These tickets are for eighty game dates.
    (a) What is the effect on the balance sheet, March 31? Prepare the appropriate journal entry for the sale of the tickets.
    (b) Assume that seventy game dates remain after April 30. What is the effect on the balance sheet, April 30? Prepare the related summary journal entry for April.
4. Zellner Corporation sells communications equipment. Experience has shown that warranty costs average 4% of sales. Sales for June were $10 million. Cash disbursements for rendering warranty service during June were $310,000. Prepare the journal entries for these transactions.
5. A 7-Up distributor in Oregon gets cash deposits for its returnable bottles. In July, the distributor received $140,000 cash and disbursed $120,000 for bottles returned. Prepare the journal entries for these transactions.
6. Contingencies are often shown "short" in the balance sheet. What is a "short" presentation?
7. A city zoo has lost a lawsuit. Damages were set at $2 million. The city plans to appeal the decision to a higher court. The city's attorneys are 80% confident of a reversal of the lower court's decision. What liability, if any, should appear on the zoo's balance sheet?

10–3. BOND DISCOUNT TRANSACTIONS. (Alternates are 10–8, 10–31, and 10–55.) On December 31, 1986, a company issued $10 million of ten-year, 12% debentures at 97.

1. Using the balance sheet equation format, prepare an analysis of bond transactions. Assume straight-line amortization. Show entries for both the issuer and the investors regarding (a) issuance, (b) one semiannual interest payment, and (c) payment of maturity value.
2. Show the corresponding journal entries keyed as above.
3. Show how the bond-related accounts would appear on the balance sheets as of December 31, 1986, 1993, and 1995.

10–4. EARLY EXTINGUISHMENT OF DEBT. (Alternate is 10–9.) On December 31, 1980, a company issued $10 million of ten-year, 12% debentures at 97. On December 31, 1986 (after all interest payments and amortization were recorded for 1986), the company purchased all the debentures for $9.5 million. The debentures had been held by a large insurance company throughout their life. Straight-line amortization of discount was used.

Required:

1. Compute the gain or loss on early extinguishment.
2. Using the balance sheet equation, present an analysis of the transaction on both the issuer's and the investor's books. Also show the appropriate journal entries.

10–5. NON-INTEREST-BEARING NOTES. (Alternate is 10–10.) A school borrowed money from a bank on a three-month note due on July 31, 19X1. The face value of the note was $50,000. However, the bank deducted its interest "in advance" at an annual rate of 12% simple interest.

Required:

Using the balance sheet equation, prepare an analysis of transactions. Also prepare journal entries. Show the effects on both the lender's and borrower's records. Show the effects at inception, monthly, and at maturity.

10–6. PAYROLL TAXES. (Alternate is 10–1.) USX Corporation (formerly United States Steel) has 54% of its sales in oil and gas and only 33% in steel. Suppose USX incurred gross wage expenses of $100 million for the week ended March 31. Related obligations for withheld income taxes and social security taxes were $16 million and $7 million, respectively. The employees were paid on April 2, and the government was paid on April 3.

Required:

Show all amounts in millions of dollars.

1. Prepare an analysis of the transactions, using the balance sheet equation format.
2. Prepare journal entries to accompany the analysis in requirement 1.
3. Assume that USX has additional costs related to the above data, as follows (in millions): vacation accruals, $5; pension obligations, $16; health insurance, $6; and employer payroll taxes, $11. Prepare journal entries to record (a) the liabilities and (b) the related cash disbursements.

10–7. VARIOUS LIABILITIES. (Alternate is 10–2.)

1. Whirlpool Corporation sells electric appliances, including automatic washing machines. Experience in recent years has indicated that warranty costs average 3.2% of sales. Sales of washing machines for October were $3 million. Cash disbursements and obligations for warranty service on washing machines during October totaled $81,000. Prepare the journal entries prompted by these facts.
2. Pepsi-Cola Company of New York gets cash deposits for its returnable bottles. In August it received $100,000 cash and disbursed $89,000 for bottles returned. Prepare the journal entries regarding the receipts and returns of deposits.
3. Bank of America received a $2,000 savings deposit on April 1. On June 30, it recognized interest thereon at an annual rate of 5%. On July 1, the depositor closed her account with the bank. Prepare the necessary journal entries.
4. The Schubert Theater sold for $100,000 cash a "season's series" of tickets in advance of December 31 for four plays, each to be held in successive months beginning in January.
   (a) What is the effect on the balance sheet, December 31? What is the appropriate journal entry for the sale of the tickets?
   (b) What is the effect on the balance sheet, January 31? What is the related journal entry for January?
5. In its 1986 annual report, Alcoa shows "contingencies" short in the balance sheet just above the "stockholders' equity" section. What is a "short" presentation?
6. Suppose your local hospital has lost a lawsuit. Damages were set at $600,000. The hospital plans to appeal the decision to a higher court. The hospital's attorneys are 90% confident of a reversal of the lower court's decision. What liability, if any, should be shown on the hospital's balance sheet?

10–8. BOND DISCOUNT TRANSACTIONS. (Alternates are 10–3, 10–31, and 10–55.) On February 1, 1985, New England Telephone issued $200 million of forty-year, 9% debentures at 98.

Required:

Show all amounts in thousands of dollars.

1. Using the balance sheet equation format, prepare an analysis of bond transactions. Assume straight-line amortization. Show entries for the issuer regarding (a) issuance, (b) the first semiannual interest payment, and (c) payment of maturity value.
2. Show all the corresponding journal entries for (a), (b), and (c) in requirement 1.
3. Show how the bond-related accounts would appear on the balance sheets as of February 1, 1985, 2005, and 2024. Assume the February 1 interest payment has been made.

10–9. EARLY EXTINGUISHMENT OF DEBT. (Alternate is 10–4.) On December 31, 1983, Texaco issued $10 million of ten-year, 12% debentures at 97. Suppose that on December 31, 1989 (after all interest payments and amortization had been recorded for 1989), the company purchased all the debentures for $9.5 million. The debentures had been held by a large insurance company throughout their life.

Required:

Show all amounts in thousands of dollars.

1. Compute the gain or loss on early extinguishment.
2. Using the balance sheet equation, present an analysis of the transaction on the issuer's books.
3. Show the appropriate journal entry.

10–10. NON-INTEREST-BEARING NOTES. (Alternate is 10–5.) St. Joseph's Church borrowed money from a bank on a three-month note due on July 31, 1986. The face value of the note was $25,000. However, the bank deducted its interest "in advance" at an annual rate of 12% simple interest.

Required:

Show the effects on the borrower's records. Show the effects at inception, monthly, and at maturity.

1. Using the balance sheet equation, prepare an analysis of transactions.
2. Prepare journal entries.

ADDITIONAL ASSIGNMENT MATERIAL

□ **General Coverage**

10–11. "A liability can be both short-term and long-term simultaneously." Do you agree? Explain.

10–12. Name the three major types of routine cash disbursements and corresponding liabilities.

10–13. Distinguish between *employee* payroll taxes and *employer* payroll taxes.

10–14. "Withholding taxes really add to employer payroll costs." Do you agree? Explain.

10–15. Give three examples of liabilities having estimated amounts.

10–16. "A contingent liability is a liability having an estimated amount." Do you agree? Explain.

10–17. "At the balance sheet date, a private high school has lost a court case for an uninsured football injury. The amount of damages has not been set. A reasonable estimate is between $800,000 and $2 million." How should this information be presented in the financial statements?

10–18. Distinguish between a *mortgage bond* and a *debenture*. Which is safer?

10–19. Distinguish between *subordinated* and *unsubordinated* debentures.

10–20. "The face amount of a bond is what you can sell it for." Do you agree? Explain.

10–21. "Discount *accumulation* is a better descriptive term than discount *amortization*." What would be the justification for making this assertion?

10–22. What is the major lesson concerning discounts and premiums?

10–23. "The quoted bond interest rates imply a rate per annum, but the bond markets do not mean that rate literally." Explain.

10–24. Distinguish between *straight-line* amortization and *effective-interest* amortization.

10–25. "If substance prevails over form, the nominal interest rate will be rejected in favor of the market rate." What is this process called?

10–26. "Because a company never knows how much it will have to pay for pensions, no pension liability is recognized. Pension obligations are simply explained in a footnote to the financial statements." Do you agree? Explain.

10–27. Certain leases are essentially equivalent to purchases. A company must account for such leases as if the asset had been purchased. Explain.

10–28. SALES TAXES. (Alternate is 10–54.) Lynden Market is in a northwestern state where the sales tax is 8%. Total sales for the month of July were $450,000, of which $400,000 was subject to sales tax.

Required:

1. Prepare a journal entry that summarizes sales (all in cash) for the month.
2. Prepare a journal entry regarding the disbursement for the sales tax.

10–29. INCOME TAX ESTIMATES. A corporation has an estimated taxable income of $28 million for the calendar year 19X3. The applicable income tax rate is 40%. Ignore all other possible data regarding income taxes.

Required:

1. Compute the quarterly income tax payment.
2. Suppose pretax income is as follows for the first quarter: January, $4 million; February, $1 million; March, $3 million. Fill in the blanks:

	JANUARY	FEBRUARY	MARCH
Amount of income tax expense	?	?	?

3. Prepare the journal entry for January.
4. Prepare the journal entry for the April 15 payment of first quarter taxes.
5. What is the balance of Accrued Income Taxes Payable after the disbursement on April 15?

10–30. PRIORITIES OF CLAIMS. J. L. Smith Corporation is being liquidated. It has one major asset, an office building, which was converted into $18 million cash. The stockholders' equity has been wiped out by past losses. The following claims exist: accounts payable, $3 million; debentures payable, $5 million; first-mortgage bonds payable, $12 million.

Required:

1. Assume the debentures are unsubordinated. How much will each class of claimants receive?
2. If the debentures are subordinated, how much will each class of claimants receive? How much will each class receive if the cash proceeds from the sale of the building amount to only $13.5 million?

10–31. BOND PREMIUM TRANSACTIONS. (Alternates are 10–3, 10–8, and 10-55.) Suppose that on December 31, 1987, Crowne Company issued $40 million of ten-year, 12% debentures at 102.

Required:

Show all amounts in thousands of dollars.

1. Using the balance sheet equation format, prepare an analysis of transactions for the issuer's records. Key your transactions as follows: (a) issuance, (b) semiannual interest using straight-line amortization of bond premium, and (c) payment of maturity value.
2. Prepare all the corresponding journal entries keyed as above.
3. Show how the bond-related accounts would appear on the balance sheets as of December 31, 1987, 1994, and 1996.

10–32. ANALYSIS OF PRINCIPAL AND INTEREST. (Alternate is 10–56.) Consider a bank loan of $240,000 to Country Day School on August 31, 19X1. The loan bears interest at 10%. Principal and interest are due in one year. Country Day School reports on a calendar-year basis.

Required:

1. Prepare an analysis of transactions, using the balance sheet format. Indicate the entries for Country Day School for August 31, 19X1, December 31, 19X1, and August 31, 19X2. Show all amounts in thousands of dollars.
2. Prepare all the corresponding journal entries for each of the three dates in requirement 1.

10–33. BONDS SOLD BETWEEN INTEREST DATES. On December 31, 19X7, a company had some bonds printed and ready for issuance. But market conditions soured. The bonds were not issued until February 28, 19X8, at 100. The indenture requires payment of semiannual interest on December 31 and June 30. The face value of the bonds is $10 million. The interest rate is 12%.

Required:

1. Compute the total proceeds of the issue on February 28.
2. Prepare an analysis of transactions, using the balance sheet equation. Show amounts in thousands of dollars. Show the effects on the issuer's records on February 28 and June 30, 19X8.
3. Prepare corresponding journal entries.

10–34. NON-INTEREST-BEARING NOTE. A sports club borrowed money from a bank on a six-month note due on September 30, 19X1. The face value of the note was $30,000. However, the bank deducted its interest in advance at an annual rate of 12% simple interest.

Required:

1. Prepare journal entries for the sports club at the inception of the note, for one month's interest, and at maturity.
2. What would be the liability after two months? How would it be presented on the club's balance sheet?

□ **Assignments for Appendixes in Chapter 10**

Special note: These problems are arranged to correspond with the sequence of topics covered in the appendixes.

10–35. EXERCISES IN COMPOUND INTEREST.

1. A savings and loan association offers depositors a lump-sum payment of $10,000 four years hence. If you desire an interest rate of 8% compounded annually, how much will you be willing to deposit? At an interest rate of 12%?
2. Repeat requirement 1, but assume that the interest rates are compounded semiannually.

10–36. EXERCISES IN COMPOUND INTEREST. A reliable friend has asked you for a loan. You are pondering various proposals for repayment.

1. Lump sum of $50,000 four years hence. How much will you lend if your desired rate of return is (a) 10% compounded annually, (b) 20% compounded annually?
2. Repeat requirement 1, but assume that the interest rates are compounded semiannually.
3. Suppose the loan is to be paid in full by equal payments of $12,500 at the end of each of the next four years. How much will you lend if your desired rate of return is (a) 10% compounded annually, (b) 20% compounded annually?

10–37. COMPOUND INTEREST AND JOURNAL ENTRIES. Cheney Company acquired equipment for a $145,000 promissory note, payable five years hence, non-interest-bearing, but having an implicit interest rate of 14% compounded annually. Prepare the journal entry for (1) the acquisition of the equipment and (2) interest expense for the first year.

10–38. **COMPOUND INTEREST AND JOURNAL ENTRIES.** A German company has bought some equipment on a contract entailing a DM 100,000 cash down payment and a DM 400,000 lump sum to be paid at the end of four years. The same equipment can be bought for DM 336,840 cash. DM refers to the German mark, a unit of currency.

Required:

1. Prepare the journal entry for the acquisition of the equipment.
2. Prepare journal entries at the end of each of the first two years. Ignore entries for depreciation.

10–39. **COMPOUND INTEREST AND JOURNAL ENTRIES.** A dry-cleaning company bought new presses for a $100,000 down payment and $100,000 to be paid at the end of each of four years. The applicable imputed interest rate is 10% on the unpaid balance. Prepare journal entries for the acquisition and at the end of the first year.

10–40. **EXERCISES IN COMPOUND INTEREST.**

a. It is your sixty-fifth birthday. You plan to work five more years before retiring. Then you want to take $5,000 for a Mediterranean cruise. What lump sum do you have to invest now in order to accumulate the $5,000? Assume that your minimum desired rate of return is
   (1) 6%, compounded annually
   (2) 10%, compounded annually
   (3) 20%, compounded annually

b. You want to spend $1,000 on a vacation at the end of each of the next five years. What lump sum do you have to invest now in order to take the five vacations? Assume that your minimum desired rate of return is
   (1) 6%, compounded annually
   (2) 10%, compounded annually
   (3) 20%, compounded annually

c. At age sixty, you find that your employer is moving to another location. You receive termination pay of $5,000. You have some savings and wonder whether to retire now.
   (1) If you invest the $5,000 now at 6%, compounded annually, how much money can you withdraw from your account each year so that at the end of five years there will be a zero balance?
   (2) If you invest it at 10%?

d. At 16%, compounded annually, which of the following plans is more desirable in terms of present values? Show computations to support your answer.

	ANNUAL CASH INFLOWS	
Year	Mining	Farming
1	$100,000	$ 20,000
2	80,000	40,000
3	60,000	60,000
4	40,000	80,000
5	20,000	100,000
	$300,000	$300,000

10–41. **BASIC RELATIONSHIPS IN INTEREST TABLES.**

1. Suppose you borrow $15,000 now at 16% interest compounded annually. The borrowed amount plus interest will be repaid in a lump sum at the end of six years. How much must be repaid? Use Table 1 and the basic equation: PV = Future amount × Conversion factor.

2. Assume the same facts as in requirement 1 except that the loan will be repaid in equal installments at the end of each of six years. How much must be repaid each year? Use Table 2 and the basic equation: PV_A = Future annual amounts × Conversion factor.

10–42. DEFERRED ANNUITY EXERCISE. It is your thirty-fifth birthday. On your fortieth birthday, and on three successive birthdays thereafter, you intend to spend exactly $2,000 for a birthday celebration. What lump sum do you have to invest now in order to have the four celebrations? Assume that the money will earn interest, compounded annually, of 8%.

10–43. PRESENT VALUES AND DEFERRED SPORTS SALARIES. Gary Hogeboom, former quarterback for the Dallas Cowboys, signed a 1985 contract that included $6 million in deferred income. The January 13, 1985, issue of the *Dallas Morning News* reported:

☐ The Cowboys will pay Hogeboom $300,000 a year on February 1 from 1994–2013, a total of $6 million. The present value of that money discounted at 12 percent is $600,000–$700,000, a source said.

Required:

Do you agree with the present value that the source reported? If not, what is the appropriate present value? Assume that the calculations are made on February 1, 1985.

10–44. DISCOUNTED PRESENT VALUE. On December 31, 19X1, a company issued a three-year $1,000 bond that bears a nominal interest rate of 12%, payable 6% semiannually. Compute the discounted present value of the principal and the interest as of December 31, 19X1, if the market rate of interest for such securities is 12%, 14%, and 10%, respectively. Show your computations, including a sketch of cash flows. Round to the nearest dollar.

10–45. AMORTIZATION OF DISCOUNT. Baxter Company issued a three-year $1,000 bond with a nominal interest rate of 12%, payable in cash 6% semiannually. Its market rate of interest on December 31, 19X1, the date of issue, was 16%.

Required:

1. Compute the issuance price (discounted present value at December 31, 19X1).
2. Prepare a schedule of amortization of discount for every six months throughout the three-year period. Show dollar amounts for effective interest, nominal interest, discount amortized, unamortized discount, and net liability. Use the effective-interest method.
3. Show the journal entry for the amortization and payment of interest on June 30, 19X2.
4. Prepare a schedule comparing the amounts of amortization each interest period using the effective-interest and straight-line methods.

10–46. IMPUTED INTEREST. Gompers Company purchased some land in a remote area in exchange for a $450,000 non-interest-bearing note payable due in ten years. Comparable sales prices for the land are not obtainable. A bank offered similar financing at 16% interest, compounded annually.

Required:

1. Indicate the journal entries for the acquisition and the first year of holding if form prevails over substance.
2. Repeat requirement 1 if substance prevails over form.

10–47. ACCOUNTING FOR PENSIONS. The current pension expense for Batista Company is $375,000, $140,000 of which is paid in cash. Using the balance sheet equation format, show which accounts are affected by these data. Prepare the corresponding journal entry.

10–48. RETIREMENT OF BONDS. (J. Patell, adapted). This is a more difficult problem than others in this group.

On January 2, 1977, the Wang Financial Corporation sold a large issue of Series A $1,000 denomination bonds. The bonds had a stated coupon rate of 12% (annual), had a term to maturity of twenty years, and made semiannual coupon payments. Market conditions at the time were such that the bonds sold at their face value.

During the ensuing ten years, market interest rates fluctuated widely, and by January 2, 1987, the Wang bonds were trading at a price that provided an annual yield of 10%. Wang's management was considering purchasing the Series A bonds in the open market and retiring them; the necessary capital was to be raised by a new bond issue—the Series B bonds. Series B bonds were to be $1,000 denomination coupon (semiannual) bonds with a stated annual rate of 8% and a twenty-year term. Management felt that these bonds could be sold at a price yielding no more than 10%, especially if the Series A bonds were retired.

Required:

1. On January 2, 1987, at what price could Wang Financial purchase the Series A bonds? *Hint*: The applicable factors are 5% and 20 periods.
2. Show the journal entries necessary to record the following transactions:

   a. Issue of one Series B bond on January 2, 1987.
   b. Purchase and retirement of one Series A bond on January 2, 1987.
   c. The first coupon payment on a Series B bond on July 2, 1987. Wang uses the effective-interest method of accounting for bond premium and discount.
   d. The second coupon payment on a Series B bond on January 2, 1988.

10–49. **CAPITAL OR OPERATING LEASE.** On December 31, 19X1, Koblitz Company acquired a robotic assembly operation. The purchase could be (a) outright for $100,000 cash or (b) on a noncancelable lease whereby rental payments would be made at the end of each year for three years. The robots will become obsolete and worthless at the end of three years. The company can borrow $100,000 cash on a three-year loan payable at maturity at 12% compounded annually.

Required:

1. Compute the annual rental payment, assuming that the lessor desires a 12% rate of return per year.
2. If the lease could be accounted for as an operating lease, what annual journal entry would be made?
3. The lease is a capital lease. Prepare an analytical schedule of each lease payment. Show the lease liability at the beginning of the year, interest, accumulated amount, lease payment, lease liability at end of year, and a supplementary breakdown of each payment into its interest and principal components.
4. Prepare an analysis of transactions, using the balance sheet equation format.
5. Prepare yearly journal entries.

10–50. **CAPITAL LEASE.** A company acquired packaging equipment on a capital lease. There were annual lease payments of $60 million at the end of each of three years. The implicit interest rate was 14% compounded annually.

Required:

1. Compute the present value of the capital lease. Use the appropriate table in this book (not a hand calculator).
2. Prepare journal entries at the inception of the lease and for each of the three years. Distinguish between the short-term and long-term classifications of the lease.

10–51. **COMPARISON OF OPERATING AND CAPITAL LEASES.** Reggie Industries has decided to lease a computer system. Assume that annual lease payments of $40,000 will be made at the end of each of the next three years. The implicit annual interest rate for the lease is 10%. Janice Bolin, the controller of Reggie, must decide whether to structure the lease as an operating lease or a capital lease. To help her, fill in the blanks (and prepare supporting calculations) for the following table:

LEASE EXPENSES	OPERATING LEASE	CAPITAL LEASE	DIFFERENCE
Year 1	?	?	?
Year 2	?	?	?
Year 3	?	?	?
Total	?	?	?

☐ Understanding Published Financial Reports

10–52. TERMINOLOGY. Consult Exhibit 10–1, page 423, the liabilities of Gulf & Western Industries. For each item therein, state at least one other way of describing the liability.

10–53. EMPLOYEE BENEFITS AND LIABILITIES. Many companies provide retirees with medical and life insurance coverage. According to *Forbes* (July 15, 1985), a consulting firm specializing in employee benefits estimates that such benefits amount to "hundreds of billions of dollars." Is a promise to pay such benefits to retirees a liability of the company? Should an estimated amount be listed with liabilities on the company's balance sheet?

10–54. SALES TAXES. (Alternate is 10–28.) Most of the food sold in retail stores in California is not subject to sales taxes (for example, candy), but some items are (for example, soft drinks). Apparently, the candy lobbyists were more effective than soft drinks lobbyists when dealing with the state legislature. Most cash registers are designed to record taxable sales and nontaxable sales and automatically add the appropriate sales tax.

The sales for the past week in the local Safeway store were $110,000, $20,000 of which was taxable at a rate of 7%. Using the $A = L + SE$ equation, show the impact on the entity, both now and when the sales taxes are paid at a later date. Also prepare corresponding journal entries.

10–55. BOND PREMIUM TRANSACTIONS. (Alternates are 10–3, 10–8, and 10–31.) Assume that on December 31, 1986, IBM issued $10 million of ten-year, 12% debentures at 104.

Required:

Show all amounts in thousands of dollars.

1. Using the balance sheet equation format, prepare an analysis of transactions for the issuer's records. Key your transactions as follows: (a) issuance, (b) semiannual interest using straight-line amortization of bond premium, and (c) payment of maturity value.
2. Prepare corresponding journal entries keyed (a), (b), and (c) as above.
3. Show how the bond-related accounts would appear on the balance sheets as of December 31, 1986, 1993, and 1995.

10–56. ANALYSIS OF PRINCIPAL AND INTEREST. (Alternate is 10–32.) A repertory theater borrowed $90,000 from Great Western Savings & Loan on August 31, 19X1. The loan bears interest at 10%. Principal and interest are due in one year. The theater reports on a calendar-year basis.

Required:

Show all amounts in thousands of dollars.

1. Using the balance sheet equation format, prepare an analysis of the transactions for the theater for August 31, 19X1, December 31, 19X1, and August 31, 19X2.
2. Prepare corresponding journal entries.

10–57. BOND QUOTATIONS. Following is a recent bond quotation for American Telephone and Telegraph Company:

DESCRIPTION	CURRENT YIELD	VOLUME	HIGH	LOW	CLOSE	NET CHANGE
AT&T 7s01	7.9	924	90	89	89	+¼

Required:

1. How was the current yield of 7.9% calculated?
2. What price (in total dollars) would you have paid for one bond if you had bought it at a price halfway between its high and low for the day?
3. What was the closing price (in total dollars) for the bond on the preceding day?

10–58. **CONVERTIBLE BONDS.** K Mart has 6% convertible bonds that can each be exchanged for 28.169 shares of common stock. The price of the common stock is $48 per share, and quarterly dividends are $.37 per share.

Required:

1. What is the total market price of the common stock that a holder of one bond could obtain by converting the bond to common stock?
2. What amount of semi-annual dividends would be received on the stock obtained in requirement 1?
3. What amount of semi-annual interest does the holder of the bond receive on the bond?
4. Will the holder of a convertible bond always exchange it for common stock when the market value of the stock exceeds that of the bond? Explain.

10–59. **REVIEW OF CHAPTERS 9 AND 10.** The 1985 annual report of Koppers Company, a $1.4 billion (sales) company in construction materials and chemical products, contained the following:

Koppers Company, Inc.

	DECEMBER	
	1985	1984
	(in millions)	
Gross buildings, machinery, and equipment	$974	$1,141
Less Accumulated Depreciation	610	666
Net buildings, machinery, and equipment	364	475
Long-term debt due within one year	19	13
Long-term debt	215	220

Purchases of buildings, machinery, and equipment during 1985 were $99 million. Depreciation expense for 1985 was $120 million.

The account *Long-term Debt* contained reductions of $20 million during 1985.

Required:

Show all amounts in millions of dollars. (The use of T-accounts should help your analysis.)

1. Compute the dollar amounts of
   (a) Accumulated depreciation relating to properties and plants disposed of during 1985.
   (b) Original acquisition cost of properties and plants disposed of during 1985.

2. Compute the dollar amounts of
   (*a*) Long-term debt additions
   (*b*) The *net increase or decrease* in all long-term debt, including that due within one year
3. What journal entry was probably made to obtain the ending balance in Long-term debt due within one year? Assume that the ending amount arose from a single journal entry.

10–60. **REVIEW OF CHAPTERS 9 AND 10.** (J. Patell, adapted) Here are excerpts from an annual report of Crane Company, a manufacturer of plumbing fixtures and related items.

From income statement (in thousands):

Depreciation	$23,178
Amortization of debt discount	779
Loss on disposal of property, plant and equipment	84

CRANE Crane Company
FROM BALANCE SHEETS (IN THOUSANDS OF DOLLARS)

	DECEMBER 31	
	1984	1983
Investments and Other Assets:		
Unamortized debt discount	1,938	2,717
Property, Plant and Equipment at Cost:		
Land	10,644	10,751
Buildings and improvements	83,320	90,605
Machinery and equipment	303,063	314,732
	397,027	416,088
Less accumulated depreciation	269,078	269,896
	127,949	146,192
Long-Term Debt	138,524	202,232

Additional information (in thousands):

Additions to property, plant, and equipment during 1984 amounted to $14,465. Reductions in long-term debt during 1984 were $64,497.

Required:

(The use of T-accounts should help your analysis.) During 1984, Crane's property, plant, and equipment accounts were affected by both purchases of new assets and disposals (sales) of old assets.

1. Determine the total original cost of the property, plant, and equipment sold by Crane during 1984.
2. Determine the total dollar amount Crane received for the property, plant, and equipment that was sold during 1984.

In 1984, as well as in the several previous years, Crane issued long-term bonds at a discount. Rather than showing the bond discount as a contra account to long-term debt, Crane has shown it on the asset side of the balance sheet under the heading "Investments and Other Assets." All reductions in debt occurred through the normal maturity of outstanding bonds. There were no early retirements.

3. Determine the face (or par) amount of the long-term debt issued during 1984.
4. Determine the actual cash received by Crane for the bonds issued during 1984.

10–61. **ZERO COUPON BONDS.** Study Appendix 10B. Since 1985, the U.S. Treasury has required issuers of "deep-discount" or "zero coupon" debt securities to use an effective-interest approach to amortization of discount rather than straight-line amortization. The Treasury claimed that the old law, which permitted straight-line amortization, resulted in overstatements of deductions in early years.

Required:

1. Assume that General Motors issues a ten-year zero coupon bond having a face amount of $20,000,000 to yield 10%. For simplicity, assume that the 10% yield is compounded annually. Prepare the journal entry for the issuer.
2. Prepare the journal entry for interest expense for the first full year and the second full year using (a) straight-line and (b) effective-interest amortization.
3. Assume an income tax rate of 40%. How much more income tax for the first year would the issuer have to pay because of applying effective-interest instead of straight-line amortization?

10–62. **ZERO COUPON DEBT.** Study Appendix 10B. The 1985 annual report of Caterpillar Tractor Company lists a zero coupon note due in 1992. A footnote states that the "principal at maturity is $300,000 and the original issue discount was $228,000. The effective annual cost [imputed interest rate] is 13.4%." Interest is compounded semiannually.

Required:

1. Prepare the journal entry on the date the bond was issued.
2. Prepare the journal entry to recognize interest expense for the first six months. For the second six months. Omit explanations.
3. The amount listed on the 1985 balance sheet for the note is $122,000. Calculate interest expense for 1986 and for the account balances for the note at the end of 1986.

10–63. **LEASES.** Study Appendix 10C. The following information appeared in a footnote to the annual report of Piedmont Aviation, Incorporated:

☐   The future minimum rental payments, by year and in total, for all noncancelable leases as of January 1, 1985 are as follows (in thousands):

	OPERATING LEASES	CAPITAL LEASES
1985	$ 17,164	$ 35,552
1986	16,446	33,507
1987	16,130	45,511
1988	15,760	30,291
1989	15,518	31,038
Thereafter	168,939	167,737
Total minimum lease payment	$249,957	343,636
Imputed interest, average interest rate of 8%		108,087
Present value of payments		$235,549

1. As of January 1, 1985, what was the present value of the minimum payments on operating leases for the years 1985 through 1987? Use the average interest rate on capital leases, 8% compounded annually. Assume that operating lease payments are made at the end of each fiscal year.
2. Suppose the minimum capital lease payments are made in equal amounts on March 31, June 30, September 30, and December 31 of each year. Compute the interest and principal to be paid on capital leases during the first half of 1985. Assume an interest rate of 8% per annum, compounded quarterly.
3. Prepare the journal entries for the lease payments in requirement 2 on March 31 and June 30, 1985.

10–64. LEASES. Study Appendix 10C. Consider footnote K from the 1985 annual report of American Telephone and Telegraph Company (AT&T):

☐ Footnote K:

The Company leases land, buildings and equipment through contracts that expire in various years. Items leased on a long-term basis or otherwise qualifying under the accounting rules as a capital lease are included in the Company's asset accounts and a corresponding liability is booked for the future minimum lease payments. Items not qualifying as a capital lease are accounted for as an operating lease, i.e., the annual rental is recorded as an operating expense of that year. The Company's future minimum lease payments under capital and noncancelable operating leases at December 31, 1985 are as follows:

(DOLLARS IN MILLIONS)	CAPITAL LEASES	OPERATING LEASES
Minimum lease payments for year ending December 31,		
1986	$195.5	$ 589.1
1987	164.5	494.5
1988	97.9	349.9
1989	52.8	214.6
1990	47.8	175.0
Later years	273.0	814.0
Total minimum lease payments	$831.5	$2,637.1
Less: Estimated executory cost on capital leases	20.2	
Imputed interest on capital leases	286.6	
Present value of net minimum capital lease payments	$524.7	

1. Footnote K contains the minimum future lease payments due under AT&T's capital and operating leases. Compute the net present value of the *operating* lease payments as of December 31, 1985. Use a 10% implicit interest rate. For ease of computation, assume that each payment is made on December 31 of the designated year (i.e., the first $589.1 million payment is made on December 31, 1986) and that the final payment, labeled "Later," is made on December 31, 1991.
2. Suppose AT&T were to capitalize the operating leases examined in requirement 1. Show the journal entries necessary to
   (a) Capitalize the leases on January 1, 1986. Ignore any prior period adjustments and do not break the lease obligation into current and long-term portions.
   (b) Record the first payment on December 31, 1986.

10–65. EFFECT OF CAPITAL LEASES. Study Appendix 10C. Deb Shops, Inc., a chain of specialty women's apparel stores, reported the following information about leases in its annual report (in thousands):

| | JANUARY 31 | |
	1986	1985
Capital lease asset, gross	$1,980	$1,980
Less: Accumulated depreciation	363	264
Capital lease asset, net	$1,617	$1,716
Capital lease obligation	$2,040	$2,040

The only asset under a capital lease is a warehouse and office building. The building has an economic life of 20 years and is being depreciated on a straight-line basis. Deb Shops had operating income of $19,705,000 in fiscal 1986.

Required:

1. Calculate the depreciation on the warehouse and office building for the fiscal year ending January 31, 1986.
2. On what date was the building placed into service? (*Hint*: How long would it take to build up the accumulated depreciation shown?)
3. The implicit interest on the lease obligation is $5,866,000 at January 31, 1986. Compute the total minimum rental commitments under the capital lease.
4. The implicit interest rate is 14.7%. Compute the interest expense (to the nearest thousand dollars) on the capital lease obligation for fiscal 1986.
5. Compute the lease payment on the capital lease during fiscal 1986.
6. Suppose this building had met the requirements for an operating lease rather than a capital lease. Calculate the operating income for Deb Shops in fiscal 1986.

Chapter 11

STOCKHOLDERS' EQUITY AND THE

INCOME STATEMENT

LEARNING OBJECTIVES

After studying this chapter, you should be able to

1. Explain the differences between the major types of bonds, stocks, and dividends

2. Compute and explain some additional financial ratios related to stockholders' equity

3. Account for stock dividends and stock splits and describe their financial effects

4. Explain the accounting for the repurchase of shares, including retirements and treasury stock

5. Explain the accounting for noncash exchanges and the conversion of securities

6. Explain the effects of extraordinary items and discontinued operations on the reporting of income (Appendix 11)

This chapter focuses on the most prominent type of accounting entity, the corporation. In terms of sheer numbers, there may be more sole proprietorships and partnerships than corporations. Nevertheless, there are over a million corporations in the United States. Corporations dominate economic activities in all respects. Look around you. Nearly all the products you use (food, books, gasoline, radios) and services (telephone, electricity) are being supplied by corporations. Moreover, you routinely interact with corporations on various levels, as customers, shareholders, employees, creditors, regulators, or in other capacities.

The highlights of the corporate form of ownership were covered in Chapter 1, pages 14–18. In addition, a separate section of Chapter 1 compared the sole proprietorship, partnership, and corporation. Please review this material before proceeding. Chapter 13, Appendix 13B, describes how income taxes affect the choice of a form of business organization.

Corporations are creatures of the state. They are artificial persons created by law. They exist separately from their owners. As persons, corporations may enter into contracts, may sue, and may even marry (by affiliating with another corporation) and produce offspring (corporate subsidiaries). Corporations are also subject to taxation as separate entities.

This chapter is longer than the other chapters. However, the reading is easier because the concepts presented are not difficult.

SHAREHOLDERS' RIGHTS

Stockholders are entitled to (a) vote, (b) share in corporate profits, (c) share residually in corporate assets upon liquidation, and (d) acquire more shares of subsequent issues of stock. The extent of the stockholders' powers is determined by the number and type of shares held.

Corporations hold annual meetings of shareholders, when votes are taken on important matters. For example, the shareholders elect the board of directors. They may also vote on changing employee bonus plans, choosing outside auditors, and similar matters. Large corporations make heavy use of the proxy system. A **corporate proxy** is a written authority granted by a shareholder to others (usually members of corporate management) to cast the shareholder's votes.

The ultimate power to manage a corporation almost always resides in the common shareholders. But shareholders of publicly owned corporations usually delegate that power via proxies to the top managers. The typical hierarchy is shown in the accompanying diagram.

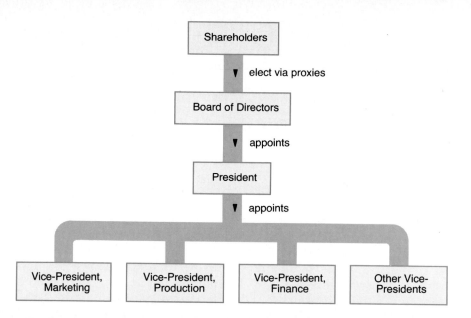

The modern large corporation frequently has a team of professional managers, from the chairman of the board downward. That is, the top managers may have only a token number of shares. The chief executive officer (CEO) is frequently the chairman of the board rather than the president.

Chapter 2 described how stockholders share in corporate profits via dividends. Stockholders also generally have **preemptive rights**, which are the rights to acquire a pro-rata amount of any new issues of capital stock. The preemptive privilege gives the present shareholders the opportunity to purchase additional shares directly from the corporation before the shares can be sold to the general public. In this way, the shareholders are able to maintain their percentage ownership.

AUTHORIZED, ISSUED, AND OUTSTANDING STOCK

A useful illustration of authorized, issued, and outstanding stock is provided by Parker Hannifin Corporation, supplier of fluidpower products to the automotive, space, and marine industries. Consider the presentation in its balance sheet (in thousands of dollars):

	JUNE 30	
STOCKHOLDERS' EQUITY	1985	1984
Serial preferred stock, $.50 par value, authorized 3,000,000 shares, none issued		
Common stock, $.50 par value, authorized 60,000,000 shares; issued:		
27,689,289 shares in 1985 and 26,808,213 shares in 1984 at par value	13,845	13,404
Additional capital	103,659	94,870
Retained earnings	459,663	410,047
Total stockholders' equity	577,167	518,321

The state approves the articles of incorporation, which include authorization of the number and types of capital stock that can be issued. The articles also specify the par value, if any. Parker Hannifin has the two most popular types of stock, preferred and common. Customarily, the articles authorize many more shares of each type than the company plans to issue immediately. In this way, if the corporation grows, it can proceed to issue additional shares without having to get the state's approval. Incidentally, such approval is usually a mere formality.

As Chapter 1 points out, par (or stated) value has no economic significance. Inevitably, as shown by the Parker Hannifin example of $.50 par value, par value per share is extremely small in relation to its market value upon issuance. The Parker Hannifin example has additional paid-in capital of over $103 million as compared with par value of less than $14 million.

Parker Hannifin's stockholders have authorized preferred stock, but no shares have been issued. Thus no dollar amounts appear for preferred stock in the balance sheet. The corporation simply has chosen to reveal the type and number of shares authorized.

Avoid the frequent confusion between the words *authorized*, *issued*, and *outstanding*. Consider the common shares of Parker Hannifin on June 30, 1985:

	NUMBER OF SHARES
Authorized	60,000,000
Unissued	32,310,711
Issued and outstanding	27,689,289

Note that shares may be authorized (an upper limit) but unissued. They become issued when the company receives cash in exchange for the stock certificates. When stock is issued and held by stockholders, it is outstanding.

Many companies subsequently repurchase their own shares but do not retire them. Such shares are called **treasury stock**. They are no longer outstanding in the hands of stockholders. The details of treasury stock are explained later. For the time being, suppose Parker Hannifin had repurchased 500,000 of its own shares on the open market but had not retired them. The following nomenclature and tabulation would be appropriate:

	NUMBER OF SHARES
Authorized	60,000,000
Unissued	32,310,711
Issued	27,689,289
Deduct: Shares held in treasury	500,000
Total shares outstanding	27,189,289

PREFERRED STOCK

☐ Comparison With Bonds

Preferred stocks are essentially a form of stockholders' equity, but they have characteristics of both bonds and common stock. They appeal to an investor who wants a higher rate of return than is offered by long-term debt and a lower risk than is offered by common stock.

As its name implies, **preferred stock** has a claim prior to common stock upon the earnings of a corporation and frequently upon the assets in the event of liquidation. At the same time, the preferred claims come after those of bondholders. The preferred stock usually appears in the top part of the stockholders' equity section of the balance sheet, not in a section with bonds payable, which are liabilities.

☐ Comparison With Common Stock

Preferred shares typically have a specified dividend rate, such as $1 per share or 9% of the par value or stated value printed on the face of the certificates. Many preferred stocks have $100 par values; therefore a 9%, $100-par preferred stock would carry a $9 annual dividend. In contrast, most bonds have a par value of $1,000. A 9% bond usually provides annual interest of $90.

As Chapter 1 points out, par value of common stock has limited importance. Historically, it was used for establishing the maximum legal liability of the stockholder in case the corporation could not pay its debts. Currently, it is set at a nominal amount in relation to the market value of the stock upon issuance (in our Parker Hannifin example, $.50 compared with over $4). It is generally illegal for a corporation to sell an original issue of its common stock below par. Common shareholders typically have limited liability, which means that creditors cannot enforce claims on individuals if the corporation itself cannot pay its debts.

Common stock has no predetermined rate of dividends and has the lowest priority in claims against the assets when the corporation is dissolved. Common shares usually have voting power in the management of the corporation. Common stock is usually the riskiest investment in a corporation, being unattractive in dire times but attractive in prosperous times because, unlike other stocks, there is no limit to the stockholder's potential participation in earnings.

Ordinarily, corporations must declare dividends on preferred stock before any dividends can be declared on common stock.

☐ Cumulative Dividends

Preferred dividends are either *cumulative* or *noncumulative*. **Cumulative** means that unpaid dividends for a particular period (usually quarterly or annually) accumulate as a claim upon future earnings, whereas *noncumulative* dividends do not accumulate. Moreover, in the event of liquidation, cumulative unpaid dividends must be paid before common stockholders receive any cash.

To illustrate these distinctions, consider a corporation with a stockholders' equity on January 1, 19X1, and a series of subsequent net incomes and dividends:

Preferred stock, no par, cumulative, $5 annual dividend per share:	
Issued and outstanding, 1,000,000 shares	$ 50,000,000
Common stock, no par, 5,000,000 shares	100,000,000
Retained income	400,000,000
Total stockholders' equity	$550,000,000

Despite the presence of a huge retained income, the board of directors is not legally obligated to declare dividends at any time. Dividends are paid out of assets, not stockholders' equity. Hence the amount of a dividend declaration depends on the availability of assets (usually cash) for distribution.

Dividends are generally limited by law to the unrestricted balance of retained income. However, the cash to be paid out in dividends is almost always constrained by the amount of available cash, not by the balance in retained income. Pursuing our illustration, consider the following data:

	NET INCOME	PREFERRED DIVIDENDS		COMMON DIVIDENDS DECLARED	ENDING BALANCE, RETAINED INCOME
		Declared	In Arrears		
19X1	$ (4,000,000)	—	$ 5,000,000	—	396,000,000
19X2	(4,000,000)	—	10,000,000	—	392,000,000
19X3	21,000,000	3,000,000	12,000,000	—	410,000,000
19X4	29,000,000	17,000,000	—	2,000,000	420,000,000
19X5	32,000,000	5,000,000	—	17,000,000	430,000,000

The holders of cumulative preferred stock would receive all accumulated unpaid dividends (called **dividend arrearages**) before the holders of common shares receive anything. However, the amount of dividends in arrears is not a liability. Why? Because *no* dividends are liabilities until declared. But dividends in arrears must be disclosed in a footnote to the balance sheet.

A partial payment of arrearages is illustrated in the year 19X3 in the tabulation. In 19X4, the remainder of the arrearages is paid ($12 million) plus the current dividend of $5 million.

Would you rather own cumulative or noncumulative preferred stock? In the above tabulation, a holder of noncumulative preferred stock would not be entitled to receive more than $5 million in any single year. Thus, despite three years of no dividends, the preferred dividend payment in 19X4 would have been only $5 million. Consequently, most buyers of preferred shares insist on cumulative status, and in actual practice such shares far outnumber the noncumulative type.

Preferred shareholders ordinarily do not have voting privileges regarding the management of the corporation. Sometimes voting privileges arise when dividends in arrears reach a predetermined level.

□ Preferences as to Assets

In addition to the cumulative dividend feature, preferred stock usually has a **liquidating value**, which is a preference to receive assets in the event of corporate liquidation. The exact liquidating value is stated on the stock certificate; it is often the same as par value. As already mentioned, any dividends in arrears would also have preference ahead of common shareholders.

The liquidating value is typically indicated either in the body of the financial statement or in footnotes. For example, the 1985 annual report of Instrument Systems Corporation, a maker of home furnishings, specialty hardware, and electronic communications equipment, describes the company's $.25 par value preferred stock as follows:

Preferred stock—authorized 2,950,000 shares, issued 1,707,283 shares (liquidation value $17,072,830)	$427,000

The liquidation value is $10 per share, although the par value is only $.25 per share.

Consider an illustration of the liquidation of assets when short- and long-term debt, preferred stock, and common stock are all present. Recall the discussion of subordinated debentures in Chapter 10, page 433. Study Exhibit 11–1, which shows the distribution of cash for various levels of cash proceeds.

The cash available upon liquidation almost never coincides with the account balances for liabilities and stockholders' equity. The order of priorities is clearly displayed in Exhibit 11–1.

The common shareholders are frequently called the residual owners because they are last in line for cash distributions. Suppose there is bountiful cash because the proceeds exceeded the book values of the assets sold. For instance, assets listed at $1.0 million may have been sold for $1.5 million, as illustrated by the first distribution. Then the common shareholders benefit handsomely. However, if the cash proceeds are lower than the book value, the common shareholders may get as little as zero.

Because of their *limited liability*, stockholders are not subject to having their personal assets seized to satisfy corporate debts. In contrast, proprietors and partners have **unlimited liability** for the debts of their businesses.

Preferred shareholders in this example have a claim in liquidation of up to $120 per share plus dividends in arrears (if any), even though the corporation may originally have issued its stock for less ($100 per share in this example). Note how preferred shareholders rank lower in priority of claim than the holders of subordinated debentures. As Chapter 10 explained, holders of

EXHIBIT 11–1

Liquidation of Claims under Various Alternatives
(in thousands)

	Account Balances	ASSUMED TOTAL CASH PROCEEDS TO BE DISTRIBUTED						
		$1,500	$1,000	$500	$450	$350	$200	$100
Accounts payable	$ 100	$ 100	$ 100	$100	$100	$100	$100	$ 50*
Unsubordinated debentures	100	100	100	100	100	100	100	50*
Subordinated debentures	200	200	200	200	200	150		
Preferred stock ($100 par value and $120 liquidating value per share)	100	120	120	100	50			
Common stock and retained income	500	980	480					
Total liabilities and shareholders' equity	$1,000							
Total cash proceeds distributed		$1,500	$1,000	$500	$450	$350	$200	$100

* Ratio of 50:50 because each has a $100,000 claim.

unsubordinated debt have a general claim against assets just like ordinary trade creditors. In contrast, the claims of holders of subordinated debt rank below those of all other creditors.

Like long-term debt, preferred stocks are frequently callable at the option of the corporation. The call price, which is often described as the **redemption price**, is typically 5% to 10% above the par value of the stock. It is frequently the same as the liquidating value.[1]

FINANCIAL RATIOS AND MEANING OF STOCKHOLDERS' EQUITY

Previous chapters described assorted financial ratios applicable to the subjects being discussed. For example, Chapter 2 introduced earnings-per-share and price-earnings ratios. This section introduces two additional important ratios that relate to stockholders' equity.

Consider the following data for Company Y:

---

[1] Two other features of preferred stock are sometimes encountered. First, a few preferred stocks have a *participation* feature, which means that preferred will share with common in dividends after both preferred and common have received dividends at the stated preferred rate. This specialized topic is discussed in intermediate accounting texts. Second, many preferred stocks have a *convertible* feature, which means that holders have the option of exchanging their shares for common shares at predetermined rates of exchange. Convertibles are discussed later in this chapter.

| | DECEMBER 31 | |
	19X2	19X1
Stockholders' equity:		
$10 preferred stock, 100,000 shares,		
$100 par	$ 10,000,000	$ 10,000,000
Common stock, 5,000,000 shares,		
$1 par	5,000,000	5,000,000
Additional paid-in capital	35,000,000	35,000,000
Retained income	87,400,000	83,000,000
Total stockholders' equity	$137,400,000	$133,000,000
Net income		$11,000,000
Preferred dividends @ $10 per share		1,000,000
Net income available for common stock		$10,000,000

The common stockholders received dividends of $1.12 per share during 19X2, or 5 million × $1.12 = $5,600,000.

The rate of return on common equity is naturally of great interest to common stockholders. The rate focuses on the ultimate profitability based on the book value of the common equity. To determine the numerator of the ratio, preferred dividends are subtracted from net income to obtain net income available for common stock. The denominator is the average of the beginning and ending *common* equity balances. Note that the *common* equity balance is the total stockholders' equity less the preferred stock at book value:[2]

$$\text{Rate of return on common equity} = \frac{\text{Net income} - \text{Preferred dividends}}{\text{Average common equity}}$$

$$= \frac{\$11,000,000 - \$1,000,000}{\frac{1}{2}[(\$133,000,000 - \$10,000,000) + (\$137,400,000 - \$10,000,000)]}$$

$$= \frac{\$10,000,000}{\frac{1}{2}(\$123,000,000 + \$127,400,000)}$$

$$= \frac{\$10,000,000}{\$125,200,000} = 8.0\%$$

Return on stockholders' equity varies considerably among companies and industries. For example, Coors's return on equity in 1985 was a paltry 5.8% compared with the beverage industry average of 16.3% and an average for all manufacturing industries of 11.4%. In contrast, Coca-Cola's return was 22.7%.

Another often-quoted statistic is

$$\begin{aligned}\text{Book value per share} \\ \text{of common stock}\end{aligned} = \frac{\begin{aligned}\text{Total stockholders' equity} \\ - \text{ Book value of preferred stock}\end{aligned}}{\text{Number of common shares outstanding}}$$

$$= \frac{\$137,400,000 - \$10,000,000}{5,000,000} = \$25.48$$

---

[2] If the liquidating value of a company's preferred stock exceeds the book value, the liquidating value is deducted from the total stockholders' equity to determine the common equity balance.

Suppose the market value is $31. Note the low book value as compared with market value. The shareholders are paying for earning power rather than for assets per se. The usefulness of this computation is highly questionable for most companies. Supposedly, if a stock's market price is below its book value, the stock is attractively priced. The trouble is that book values are based on balance sheet values, which show the historical cost of assets. The current value of those assets may differ greatly from their historical cost. Consequently, some companies may consistently have market prices in excess of book values, and vice versa. Book value may, however, be pertinent when companies have heavy investments in liquid assets and are contemplating liquidation. In these cases, book values probably approximate the market values of the assets.

The market value of common stock is sometimes less than its book value. This encourages takeovers of the corporation by other companies, particularly if the assets are relatively liquid. Sometimes the new owners sell assets that are valuable individually, even though the earning power of the entire firm has been weak.

ISSUANCE OF SHARES

Other than revenue and expense transactions, the typical transactions affecting stockholders' equity entail issuance of shares, distribution of dividends, and repurchase of shares. These items will now be discussed.

☐ Original Issue

Recall that Chapter 1 explains the accounting for the issuance of capital stock. The amount initially paid in by the shareholder is often referred to as *contributed capital*. The word "contributed" has a narrow meaning here and should not be confused with the contributions or donations made by individuals to churches or other charitable organizations. That is why we will use *paid-in capital* instead.

A summary journal entry portrays the Parker Hannifin issuance of common shares for cash:

Cash	117,503,651	
Common stock at par		13,844,644
Additional paid-in capital		
on common stock		103,659,007
To record the issuance of 27,689,289		
shares of $.50 par value for an		
average price of $4.24365 per share.		

As already explained, for antiquated legal reasons the corporation may have two accounts for its common stock, one for par and one for additional paid-in capital. However, the economic substance of the issuance could be portrayed with one account, as indicated by the following journal entry:

Cash	117,503,644	
Paid-in capital, common stock		117,503,644

Indeed, as you pursue your study of this chapter, keep in mind that distinguishing between the par or stated value, the additional paid-in capital, and retained income has little practical importance for ongoing corporations. To keep perspective, whenever feasible, think of stockholders' equity as a single amount.

The amounts in excess of par value are described in various ways in corporate balance sheets, but they all have substantially the same meaning. For instance, the term *premium on stock* is used occasionally. Examples of similar terms follow:

> Paid-in capital (R. J. Reynolds Industries)
> Additional paid-in capital (Cluett, Peabody & Co.)
> Capital in excess of par value (Ralston-Purina)
> Capital surplus (Coca-Cola Company)
> Other paid-in capital (PanAm Corporation)

When more than one type of shares are outstanding, the additional paid-in capital is identified accordingly. For example:

> Additional paid-in capital, preferred stock
> Additional paid-in capital, common stock

Such labels merely designate the *sources* of capital, not the *liquidation claims* of the particular classes of stockholders. Their importance relates to state laws and loan agreements that may restrict the power of corporations to declare dividends or repurchase shares.

☐ Stock Splits

Many companies occasionally split their stock. A **stock split**, or split-up, refers to the issuance of additional shares for no payments by stockholders and under conditions indicating that the objective is to increase the number of outstanding shares for the purpose of *reducing their unit market price*, in order to bring the stock price down into a more popular range. This supposedly encourages wider distribution and a *higher total market value* for the same ownership interest. Corporate management naturally wants the stock to be as attractive as possible, easing the task of raising additional investment capital when needed. For a given ownership interest, the higher the total market value, the more capital can be raised by issuance of a specified number of additional shares.

Stock splits can be achieved by issuing new shares for old shares. Suppose Company A has the following stockholders' equity section:

	BEFORE 2-FOR-1 SPLIT	CHANGES	AFTER 2-FOR-1 SPLIT
Common stock, 100,000 shares @ $10 par	$ 1,000,000	[−100,000 shares @ $10 par + 200,000 shares @ $5 par]	$ 1,000,000
Additional paid-in capital	4,000,000		4,000,000
Total paid-in capital	$ 5,000,000		$ 5,000,000
Retained income	6,000,000		6,000,000
Stockholders' equity	$11,000,000		$11,000,000
Overall market value of stock @ assumed $150 per share	$15,000,000	@ assumed $80 per share	$16,000,000

There is no effect on the reported amount of the total stockholders' equity. A person who previously owned 1,000 shares (a 1% interest) now owns 2,000 shares (still a 1% interest). Professor Willard Graham explained a stock split as being akin to taking a gallon of whiskey and pouring it into five individual bottles. The resulting packaging might attract a price for each fifth that would produce a higher total value than if the gallon were not split (less the amount spilled when pouring into the five bottles—that's the legal, printing, and clerical costs). Therefore Company A splits its stock with the hope[3] that the market value of the total ownership interest will increase from $15 million to $16 million because one share that previously sold for $150 will now be in the form of two shares that might sell for $80 each, or a total of $160.

The accounting for the stock split illustrated here would entail no journal entry or change in the amounts of any accounts, as the above tabulation shows. However, there would be plenty of paper work. Each shareholder would have to exchange the $10 par certificates for the $5 par certificates, receiving two shares of the latter for one of the former. In sum, a stock split changes the evidence of ownership in form but not in substance.

DIVIDENDS

☐ Asset Dividends

Dividends are generally distributions of assets (almost always cash) to reduce stockholders' claims arising from the generation of net income. The meaning of dividends is explained in Chapter 2, pages 48–49, so the details are not repeated here. Please reread that section now.

Recall that dividends must be *declared* by the board of directors. When dividends are declared, the shareholders simultaneously become creditors (with the same priorities as to assets as accounts payable) for the amount of the dividends. If a balance sheet is prepared between the date of declaration

---

[3] This hope is not justified by the evidence. The myth is that a lower price will enhance total demand and total market value. But investors are not easily fooled by new wrappers placed on unchanged merchandise.

and the date of payment, the corporation must show a liability for dividends payable arising from the following journal entry (suppose the amount is $20,000):

Sept. 26	Retained income	20,000	
	Dividends payable		20,000
	To record the declaration of dividends to be paid on November 15 to shareholders of record as of October 25.		

No journal entry is necessary on October 25. An entry is made when the dividend is paid:

Nov. 15	Dividends payable	20,000	
	Cash		20,000
	To pay dividends declared on September 26 to shareholders of record as of October 25.		

☐ Amount Declared

The amount of cash dividends declared by a board of directors depends on many factors. The least important factor is the amount of retained income, except in cases where the company is on the brink of bankruptcy or where the company has just been incorporated. In either case, the wisdom of declaring dividends is highly questionable.

The more important factors that affect dividends include the stock market's expectations that have crystallized over a series of years, current and predicted earnings, and the corporation's current cash position and financial plans regarding spending on plant assets and repayments of debts.

Some corporations try to increase the attractiveness of their shares by maintaining a stable quarterly dividend payment on common shares (say, $1 per share). Others pay a predictable fraction of current earnings per share (say, 60% of whatever is earned in the current year). Some corporations also try to show steady growth in dividends by increasing the dividend per share each year. Sometimes an "extra" payment occurs at the end of an especially profitable year. General Motors has followed the latter practice.

If a company has maintained a series of uninterrupted dividends over a span of years, it will make every effort to continue such payments even in the face of net losses. Indeed, companies occasionally borrow money for the sole purpose of maintaining dividend payments.

☐ Small-Percentage Stock Dividends

Cash dividends are a straightforward means of rewarding the shareholder for investing in the corporation. In contrast, so-called stock dividends are often misunderstood. The term *stock dividends* is a misnomer because such dividends are totally different from cash dividends. A **stock dividend** is a distribution to stockholders of additional shares of the distributing company's stock; the stockholders make no additional investment in the corporation. The most frequently encountered type of stock dividend is the distribution of additional common stock to existing holders of outstanding common stock; usually anywhere from 1% to 10% of the number of common shares already outstanding are distributed.

In substance, stock dividends are not dividends at all, as the term is usually understood. Each shareholder's proportionate interest in the corporation is unchanged; the unit market price of each share tends to decline just enough to leave the total market value of the company unchanged. Reconsider our example of Company A (before the split). Suppose the market value of common shares is $150 at the time of issuance of the stock dividend. A common stock dividend of 2% would affect the stockholders' equity section as shown in the following table.

	BEFORE 2% STOCK DIVIDEND	CHANGES	AFTER 2% STOCK DIVIDEND
Common stock, 100,000 shares @ $10 par	$ 1,000,000	+(2,000 shares @ $10 par) = +20,000	$ 1,020,000
Additional paid-in capital	4,000,000	+[2,000 shares @ ($150 − $10)] = +280,000	4,280,000
Retained income	6,000,000	−(2,000 @ $150) = −300,000	5,700,000
Stockholders' equity	$11,000,000		$11,000,000
Overall market value of stock @ assumed $150 per share	$15,000,000	@ assumed $147.06 per share*	$15,000,000*
Total shares outstanding	100,000		102,000
Individual shareholder: Assumed ownership of shares	1,000		1,020
Percentage ownership interest	1%		Still 1%

* Many simultaneous events affect the level of stock prices, including expectations regarding the general economy, the industry, and the specific company. Thus the market price of the stock may move in either direction when the stock dividend is declared. Theory and complicated case studies indicate that a stock dividend should have zero effect on the total market value of the firm. Accordingly, the new market price per share should be $15,000,000 ÷ 102,000 shares = $147.06.

First, note that the individual shareholder receives no assets from the corporation. Moreover, the shareholder's fractional interest is unchanged; if the shareholders sell the dividend shares, their proportionate ownership interest in the company will decrease.

Second, the company records the transaction by transferring the *market value* of the additional shares from retained income to common stock and additional "paid-in capital." This entry is often referred to as being a "capitalization of retained income." It is basically a signal to the shareholders that $300,000 of retained income is no longer available as part of their claim to future cash dividends.

Stock dividends are prime examples of have-your-cake-and-eat-it-too manipulations that in substance are meaningless but seemingly leave all interested parties happy. The company pays a "dividend" but gives up no assets. Some stockholders may think they are getting a dividend even though to realize it in cash they must sell a proportion of their predividend fractional interest in the company.

The stock dividend device is particularly effective where such a low percentage, such as 1% or 2%, of additional shares are issued that the effect on the market price is almost imperceptible. The recipient, who is not particularly concerned about the fractional ownership interest anyway, may hold 1,000 shares at a $150 market price before the dividend and 1,020 shares at close to the same $150 market price after the dividend. A favorable reaction may occur because it appears that the dividend increased the recipient's wealth by 20 × $150 = $3,000. But the recipient still owns the same percentage of the same company.

The major possible economic effect of a stock dividend is to signal increased cash dividends. Suppose the company in our example consistently paid cash dividends of $1 per share. Often this cash dividend level per share is maintained after a stock dividend. The recipient of the stock dividend can now expect a future annual cash dividend of $1 × 1,020 = $1,020 rather than $1 × 1,000 = $1,000.

Accounting for a stock dividend entails transferring an amount from retained income to common stock and additional paid-in capital. Some accountants think that the appropriate entry for a stock dividend is to transfer merely the par value of the additional shares, not the market value, from retained income to paid-in capital. Why? Because using market values compounds the false notion that the recipients are getting a dividend akin to a cash dividend. Nevertheless, the U.S. authoritative bodies require that market values be transferred. One major reason is that larger amounts of retained income are thus transferred to become a part of "permanent" stockholders' equity. This requirement helps put a brake on the practice of declaring a long series of stock dividends that may give a misleading appearance of greater profitability. In our example, the required journal entry would be:

Retained income	300,000	
Common stock		20,000
Additional paid-in capital		280,000
To record a 2% common stock dividend, resulting in the issuance of 2,000 shares. Retained income is reduced at the rate of the market value of $150 per share at date of issuance.		

☐ Large-Percentage Stock Dividends

The U.S. accounting authorities differentiate between the sizes of stock dividends. That is, the small-percentage dividends just described are really "stock dividends" and must be accounted for on the basis of the market prices of the shares. However, large-percentage dividends (typically those 20% or higher) must be accounted for differently.

The principal reason why large-percentage dividends require different accounting treatment is their effect on the market price of the shares. That is, a large percentage of additional shares issued as a stock dividend will materially reduce the market value per share. In large-percentage cases, the accounting authorities generally require capitalization of the par value of the shares issued. Such capitalization is usually achieved by transferring the par amount from Retained Income to the Common Stock (at par) account. However, the regulations are not ironclad. The amounts of large-percentage dividends are often shifted from additional paid-in capital instead of retained income.

Review the typical accounting for stock splits and stock dividends:

Stock splits—no rearrangement of the amounts in paid-in capital and retained income.

Stock dividends—shift from retained income to paid-in capital:

1. Small-percentage dividends—reduce retained income by market value of the additional shares issued.
2. Large-percentage dividends—reduce retained income or additional paid-in capital by only the par value of the additional shares issued.

RELATION OF DIVIDENDS AND SPLITS

Companies typically use large-percentage stock dividends to accomplish exactly the same purpose as a stock split. That is, the companies want a material reduction in the market price of their shares. *Therefore the use of large-percentage stock dividends is merely another way of obtaining the purpose of a stock split.* For example, if the two-for-one split described earlier (see the section entitled "Stock Splits") were achieved through an equivalent 100% stock dividend, the total amount of stockholders' equity would be unaffected. However, its composition would change:

	BEFORE 100% STOCK DIVIDEND	CHANGES	AFTER 100% STOCK DIVIDEND
Common stock, 100,000 shares @ $10 par	$ 1,000,000	+(100,000 shares @ $10 par = $1,000,000)	$ 2,000,000
Additional paid-in capital	4,000,000		4,000,000
Total paid-in capital	$ 5,000,000		$ 6,000,000
Retained income	6,000,000	−$1,000,000 par value of "dividend"	5,000,000
Stockholders' equity	$11,000,000		$11,000,000

In substance, there is absolutely no difference between the 100% stock dividend and the 2-for-1 stock split. *In form*, the shareholder in this example has $10 par shares rather than $5 par shares. The 2-for-1 split requires no journal entry, but the stock dividend requires the following entry:

| Retained income (or Additional paid-in capital) | 1,000,000 | |
| Common stock, at par | | 1,000,000 |

Be on the alert for the most apt description of this large-percentage dividend: "a stock split effected in the form of a stock dividend." This requires a decrease in Retained Income or Additional Paid-in Capital and an increase in Common Stock in the amount of only the *par value* (rather than the market value) of the additional shares.

Stock splits frequently occur in the form of a stock "dividend" instead of in the classical form described earlier. Why? The major reason is to save clerical costs and the bothering of shareholders. After all, the swapping of old $10-par certificates for new $5-par certificates is more expensive than the mere printing and mailing of additional $10-par certificates.

FRACTIONAL SHARES

Corporations ordinarily issue shares in whole units. However, some shareholders are entitled to stock dividends in amounts equal to fractional units. Consequently, corporations issue additional shares for whole units plus cash equal to the market value of the fractional amount.

An example will clarify the problem. Suppose a corporation issues a 3% stock dividend. A shareholder has 160 shares. The market value per share on the date of issuance is $40. Par value is $2. The shareholder would be entitled to .03 × 160 = 4.8 shares. The company would issue 4 shares plus .8($40) = $32 cash. The journal entry would be:

Retained income (4.8 × $40)	192	
Common stock, at par (4 × $2)		8
Additional paid-in capital (4 × $38)		152
Cash (.8 × $40)		32
To issue a stock dividend of 3%		
to a holder of 160 shares.		

INVESTOR'S ACCOUNTING

To crystallize understanding, consider the *investor's* entries for the transactions described so far. Suppose the investor is passive and takes no active voice in management. The investor buys 1,000 shares of the original issue of Company A (described earlier) for $50 per share:

Investment in common stock of Company A	50,000	
Cash		50,000
To record investment in 1,000 shares		
of an original issue of Company A		
common stock at $50 per share.		
The par value is $10 per share.		

The investor holds the shares indefinitely. Note that if Investor J sold the shares to Investor K at a subsequent price other than $50, a gain or loss would be recorded by J. K would carry the shares at whatever amount was paid to J. Meanwhile the stockholders' equity of Company A would be completely unaffected by this sale by one investor to another. The company's underlying shareholder records simply would be changed to delete J and add K as a shareholder.

The *investor* would proceed to record the transactions described earlier as follows:

a.	Stock split at 2 for 1:	No journal entry, but a memorandum would be made in the investment account to show that 2,000 shares are now held at a cost of $25 each instead of 1,000 shares at a cost of $50 each.		

b.	Cash dividends of $2 per share:	Cash	2,000	
		Dividend income		2,000
		To record cash dividends on Company A stock. If financial statements must be prepared between the declaration date and the payment date instead of this one entry, the two following entries would be made:		
	Date of declaration:	Dividends receivable	2,000	
		Dividend income		2,000
		To record dividends declared by Company A, and		
	Date of receipt:	Cash	2,000	
		Dividends receivable		2,000

c.	Stock dividends of 2%:	No journal entry, but a memorandum would be made in the investment account to show that (assuming the stock split in **a** had not occurred) 1,020 shares are now owned at an average cost of $50,000 ÷ 1,020, or $49.02 per share.

d.	Stock split in form of a 100% dividend	No journal entry, but a memorandum would be made in the investment account to show that (assuming the stock splits and stock dividends in **a** and **c** had not occurred) 2,000 shares are now owned at an average cost of $25 instead of 1,000 shares @ $50. Note that this memorandum has the same effect as the memorandum in **a** above.

REPURCHASE OF SHARES

☐ Contraction of Equity

Companies repurchase their own shares for two main purposes: (1) to permanently reduce shareholder claims, called retiring stock, and (2) to temporarily hold shares for later use, most often to be granted as part of employee bonus or stock purchase plans. Temporarily held shares are called *treasury stock* or *treasury shares*. By repurchasing shares, for whatever reason, a company liquidates some shareholders' claims:

```
Stockholders' equity                          xxx
   Cash                                               xxx
Repurchase of outstanding shares.
```

The purpose of the repurchase determines *which stockholders' equity accounts* are affected. Consider an illustration of Company B, whose stock has a market value of $15 per share:

Common stock, 1,000,000 shares at $1 par	$ 1,000,000
Additional paid-in capital	4,000,000
Total paid-in capital	$ 5,000,000
Retained income	6,000,000
Stockholders' equity	$11,000,000
Overall market value of stock @ assumed $15 per share	$15,000,000
Book value per share = $11,000,000 ÷ 1,000,000 = $11.	

☐ **Retirement of Shares**

Suppose the board of directors has decided that the $15 market value of its shares is "too low." Of course, the **book value per share of common stock**, which is defined as the stockholders' equity attributable to common stock divided by the number of shares outstanding, is only $11. Nevertheless, even though the market value exceeds the book value by $4 per share ($15 − $11), the board may think the market is too pessimistic regarding the company's shares. Because of inflation and other factors, it is not unusual to have the market value vastly exceed the book value.

The board might believe that the best use of corporate cash would be to purchase and retire a portion of the outstanding shares. In this way, the remaining shareholders would have the sole benefit of the predicted eventual increase in market value per share. (Of course, the board is usually more eager to retire its shares if the market value is less than the book value, rather than the vice versa situation illustrated here.) It is not unusual for a firm to buy back its own shares. In late 1985, the *Economist* reported that "about 150 public companies in America have spent $50 billion on their own shares in the past 18 months." For example, Exxon bought $5 billion of its own stock between 1983 and 1985, and Ralston-Purina repurchased 5 million shares.

Suppose the board of Company B purchases and retires 5% of its outstanding shares @ $15 for a total of 50,000 × $15, or $750,000 cash. The total stockholders' equity is reduced or contracted. The stock certificates would be canceled, and the shares would no longer be issued and outstanding:

	BEFORE REPURCHASE OF 5% OF OUTSTANDING SHARES	CHANGES BECAUSE OF RETIREMENT	AFTER REPURCHASE OF 5% OF OUTSTANDING SHARES
Common stock, 1,000,000 shares @ $1 par	$ 1,000,000	{ −(50,000 shares @ $1 par) = −$50,000	$ 950,000
Additional paid-in capital	4,000,000	{ −(50,000 shares @ $4) = −$200,000	3,800,000
Total paid-in capital	$ 5,000,000	{ −(50,000 @ $10*) = −$500,000	$ 4,750,000
Retained income	6,000,000		5,500,000
Stockholders' equity	$11,000,000		$10,250,000
Book value per common share:			
$11,000,000 ÷ 1,000,000	$11.00		
$10,250,000 ÷ 950,000			$10.79

* $15 − the $5 (or $1 + $4) originally paid in.

The journal entry would reverse the original average paid-in capital per share and would charge any additional amount to retained income. The additional $10 is sometimes described as being tantamount to a special cash dividend paid to the owners of the 50,000 retired shares:

```
Common stock                          50,000
Additional paid-in capital           200,000
Retained income                      500,000
    Cash                                        750,000
To record retirement of 50,000 shares
of stock for $15 cash per share. The
original paid-in capital was $5 per
share, so the additional $10 per share
is debited to Retained Income.
```

Note how the book value per share of the outstanding shares has declined from $11.00 to $10.79. This phenomenon is called *dilution* of the common shareholders' equity. **Dilution** is usually defined as a reduction in shareholders' equity per share or earnings per share that arises from some changes among shareholders' proportionate interests. As a rule, boards of directors avoid dilution. However, the board sometimes favors deliberate dilution if expected future profits will more than compensate for a temporary undesirable reduction in book value per share.

☐ **Treasury Stock**

Suppose the board of directors in the foregoing example decided that the 50,000 repurchased shares would be held only temporarily and then resold. Therefore the shares are treasury stock. As in the retirement of shares, the repurchase is a *decrease in stockholders' equity*. Treasury stock is NOT an asset. It indicates a liquidation of the ownership claim of one or more stockholders. The shares had been issued previously but would no longer be outstanding:

Shares issued	1,000,000
Less: Treasury stock	50,000
Total shares outstanding	950,000

Cash dividends are not paid on shares held in the treasury; cash dividends are distributed only to the shares outstanding (in the hands of stockholders), and treasury stock is not outstanding.

In the foregoing example, the stockholders' equity section would be affected as follows:

	BEFORE REPURCHASE OF 5% OF OUTSTANDING SHARES	CHANGES BECAUSE OF TREASURY STOCK	AFTER REPURCHASE OF 5% OF OUTSTANDING SHARES
Common stock, 1,000,000 shares @ $1 par	$ 1,000,000		$ 1,000,000
Additional paid-in capital	4,000,000		4,000,000
Total paid-in capital	$ 5,000,000		$ 5,000,000
Retained income	6,000,000		6,000,000
Total	$11,000,000		$11,000,000
Deduct:			
Cost of treasury stock	—	−$750,000*	750,000
Stockholders' equity	$11,000,000		$10,250,000

The journal entry would be:

Treasury stock	750,000	
Cash		750,000
To record acquisition of 50,000 shares of common stock @ $15 (to be held as treasury stock).		

Like the retirement of shares, the purchase of treasury stock decreases stockholders' equity by $750,000. Unlike retirements, common stock at par value, additional paid-in capital, and retained income remain untouched by treasury stock purchases. A separate treasury stock account is a deduction from total stockholders' equity on the balance sheet.

Remember that treasury stock is not an asset. A company's holding of shares in *another company* is an asset; its holding of *its own shares* is a negative element of stockholders' equity.

☐ Disposition of Treasury Stock

Treasury shares are usually resold at a later date, often in conjunction with an employee stock purchase plan. The sales price usually differs from the acquisition cost. Suppose the sales price is $18. The journal entry would be:

Cash	900,000	
Treasury stock		750,000
Additional paid-in capital		150,000
To record sale of treasury stock, 50,000 shares @ $18. Cost was $15 per share.		

Suppose the price is $13:

Cash	650,000	
Additional paid-in capital	100,000	
Treasury stock		750,000
To record sale of treasury stock, 50,000 shares @ $13. Cost was $15 per share.		

If the treasury shares are resold below their cost, accountants tend to debit Additional Paid-in Capital for the difference, $2 per share in this case Additional Paid-in Capital is sometimes divided into several separate accounts that identify different sources of capital. For example:

    Additional paid-in capital—preferred stock
    Additional paid-in capital—common stock
    Additional paid-in capital—treasury stock transactions

If such accounts are used, a consistent accounting treatment would call for debiting only Additional Paid-in Capital—Treasury Stock Transactions (and no other paid-in capital account) for the excess of the cost over the resale price of treasury shares. If there is no balance in such a paid-in capital account, the debit should be made to Retained Income.

Suppose 25,000 of the treasury shares in the foregoing example were sold for $17 and later the other 25,000 shares were sold for $12. The company had no previous sales of treasury stock. The journal entries would be:

Cash	425,000	
Treasury stock		375,000
Additional paid-in capital—treasury stock transactions		50,000
To record sale of treasury stock, 25,000 shares @ $17. Cost was $15 per share.		

Cash	300,000
Additional paid-in capital—treasury stock transactions	50,000
Retained income	25,000
Treasury stock	375,000
To record sale of treasury stock, 25,000 shares @ $12. Cost was $15 per share.	

Although the specific accounting for transactions in the company's own stock may vary from company to company, one rule is paramount. Any differences between the acquisition costs and the resale proceeds of treasury stock must never be reported as losses, expenses, revenues, or gains in the income statement. Why? A corporation's own capital stock is part of its capital structure. It is *not* an asset of the corporation. Nor is stock intended to be treated like merchandise for sale to customers at a profit. Therefore changes in a corporation's capitalization should produce no gain or loss but should merely require direct adjustments to the owners' equity.

There is essentially no difference between unissued shares and treasury shares. In our example, a corporation can accomplish the same objective by acquiring 50,000 shares, retiring them, and issuing 50,000 new shares (which would be accounted for as an original issue giving rise to no gain or loss upon issuance).

RETAINED INCOME RESTRICTIONS

Directors can make decisions that benefit shareholders but hurt creditors. For example, directors might pay such large dividends that payments of creditors' claims would be threatened. To protect creditors, dividend-declaring power is restricted by either state laws or contractual obligations or both. Moreover, boards of directors can voluntarily restrict their declarations of dividends.

States typically do not permit dividends if stockholders' equity is less than total paid-in capital. Therefore retained income must exceed the cost of treasury stock. If there is no treasury stock, retained income must be positive. A lack of this restriction could jeopardize the position of the creditors. For example, consider the following for a company (in millions):

	BEFORE DIVIDENDS	AFTER DIVIDEND PAYMENTS OF	
		10	4
Paid-in capital	$25	$25	$25
Retained income	10	—	6
Total	$35	$25	$31
Deduct:			
Cost of treasury stock	6	6	6
Stockholders' equity	$29	$19	$25

Without a restriction of retained income of $6 million, the cost of the treasury stock, the corporation could pay a dividend of $10 million and thus reduce the stockholders' equity below the paid-in capital of $25 million. With the restriction, unrestricted retained income (and maximum legal payment of dividends) would be $10 − $6, or $4 million. The **restricted retained income** cannot be reduced by dividend declarations.

Most of the time, restrictions of retained income are disclosed by footnotes. Some companies show the restrictions in the stockholders' equity section. For example, consider the recent annual reports of two companies:[4]

Alatenn Resources:	
Retained earnings ($1,353,494 restricted as	
to cash dividends)	$18,233,000

H. F. Ahmanson & Company:	
Retained earnings:	
Restricted	$750,855
Unrestricted	48,962
Total retained earnings	$799,817

EXCHANGES AND CONVERSIONS

☐ Noncash Exchanges

Securities are sometimes issued for assets other than cash. For example, many assets or entire companies are acquired in exchange for the buyer's common stock. Such exchanges raise the question of the proper dollar value of the transaction to be recorded in both the buyer's and the seller's books. The proper amount is the "fair value" of either the securities or the exchanged assets, whichever is more objectively determinable. That amount should be used by both companies.

For example, suppose Company A acquires some equipment from Company B in exchange for 10,000 newly issued shares of A's common stock. The equipment was carried on B's books at the $200,000 original cost less accumulated depreciation of $50,000. Company A's stock is listed on the New York Stock Exchange; its current market price is $18 per share. Its par value is $1 per share. In this case, the market price of A's common stock would be regarded as a more objectively determinable fair value than the book value or the undepreciated cost of B's equipment. The amounts would be affected as follows:

---

[4] Restrictions of retained income are sometimes called **appropriated retained income** and sometimes *reserves*. The term *reserve* can be misleading. Accountants *never* use the word reserve to indicate cash set aside for a particular purpose; instead they call such assets a *fund*. The word **reserve** has one of three broad meanings in accounting: (a) restrictions of dividend declarations, (b) offset to an asset, and (c) estimate of a definite liability of indefinite or uncertain amount.

	ASSETS		= LIABILITIES +	STOCKHOLDERS' EQUITY	
	Equipment			Common Stock	Additional Paid-in Capital
Issuance of stock by A	+180,000		=	+10,000	+170,000

	Investment in A Common Stock	Equipment	Accumulated Depreciation		Retained Income
Disposal of equipment by B	+180,000	−200,000	+50,000 =	+30,000	[gain on disposal of equipment]

The journal entries would be:

```
On issuer's      Equipment                              180,000
books (A):          Common stock                                  10,000
                    Additional paid-in capital                   170,000

On investor's    Investment in A common stock           180,000
books (B):       Accumulated depreciation, equipment     50,000
                    Equipment                                    200,000
                    Gain on disposal of equipment                 30,000
```

☐ Convertible Securities

To make bonds and preferred stock more attractive, many companies add a conversion feature. Convertible bonds and convertible preferred stocks can be transformed into common shares at the option of the holder. They have widespread popularity.

When securities are exchanged pursuant to a conversion privilege, no gain or loss is recognized for tax purposes. Opinion is unsettled regarding whether gain or loss should be recognized for financial-accounting purposes. Market quotations, when available, are an objective basis for computing gain or loss on a conversion; however, most accountants maintain that there is no actual realization of gain or loss—that a mere cost transfer has taken place. The form of the investment has been changed in accordance with a "deferred common stock" privilege that was obtained upon the purchase of the old asset. In this sense, all investments in convertible securities are made with the intention and expectation of their eventually being transformed into common stock. Therefore the conversion itself is a transaction of form rather than substance; no realization test has been met. The accounts are simply adjusted to reflect what would have been recorded if the common stock had been initially issued instead of the convertible preferred stock.

For example, suppose Company B had paid $160,000 for an investment in 5,000 shares of the $1 par value convertible preferred stock of Company

A in 19X1. The preferred stock was converted into 10,000 shares of Company A common stock ($1 par value) in 19X8. The accounts would be affected as shown in Exhibit 11–2.

The journal entries would be as follows:

On issuer's books (A):

Cash	160,000	
Preferred stock, convertible		5,000
Additional paid-in capital, preferred		155,000
To record issuance of 5,000 shares of $1 par preferred stock convertible into two common shares for one preferred share.		
Preferred stock, convertible	5,000	
Additional paid-in capital, preferred	155,000	
Common stock		10,000
Additional paid-in capital, common		150,000
To record the conversion of 5,000 preferred shares to 10,000 common shares.		

On investor's books (B):

Investment in Company A convertible preferred stock	160,000	
Cash		160,000
To record acquisition of 5,000 shares convertible into common at the rate of two common shares for one preferred.		
Investment in Company A common stock	160,000	
Investment in Company A preferred stock		160,000
To record conversion of 5,000 preferred shares for 10,000 common shares.		

The relation of convertible securities to earnings per share is discussed later in this chapter.

STOCK OPTIONS

Stock options are rights to purchase a corporation's capital stock. Various conditions are specified for the options, including times, prices, and amounts. Options are frequently given to corporate officers as a form of incentive compensation. Although options have assorted conditions, a typical form consists of granting executives the right to purchase shares (exercise the option) during some specified time in the *future* at *today's* market price (the exercise price, which is set at the date of grant).

Suppose Company A granted its top executives options to purchase 60,000 shares of $1 par value common stock at $15 per share, the market price today (date of grant). The options can be exercised over a five-year span, beginning three years hence. Such options clearly are valuable rights. The executives can gain the benefits of price increases without bearing the risks of price declines. However, measurement of the value of options at the time of grant is difficult because executive options may not be sold to others. There-

EXHIBIT 11–2

Analysis of Convertible Preferred Stock

Company A's Books

	ASSETS	= LIABILITIES +	STOCKHOLDERS' EQUITY			
	Cash		Preferred Stock	Additional Paid-In Capital, Preferred	Common Stock	Additional Paid-In Capital, Common
Issuance of preferred (19X1)	+160,000	=	+5,000	+155,000		
Conversion of preferred (19X8)		=	−5,000	−155,000	+10,000	+150,000

Company B's Books

	ASSETS			= LIABILITIES +
	Cash	Investment in A Preferred	Investment in A Common	
Acquisition of preferred (19X1)	−160,000	+160,000		=
Conversion of preferred (19X8)		−160,000	+160,000	=

fore currently accepted accounting attributes zero value to most of them[5] as long as the exercise price is the same as the market price at date of grant. Thus the accounting approach is to make no entry at the time of grant. Subsequent financial statements must reveal (usually by a footnote) the number and type of options outstanding.[6]

Suppose all options are exercised three years hence. The journal entry would be as shown below.

Cash	900,000	
Common stock		60,000
Additional paid-in capital		840,000
To record issue of 60,000 shares upon exercise of options to acquire them @ $15 per share.		

Executives sometimes let their options lapse. For example, here the options will become worthless if the price of the common stock is no higher than $15 per share during the time they may be exercised. In such a case, no journal entry is made.

Many observers have severely criticized the above practice because no compensation (the value of the options) is ever recorded as salary expense. For example, if the options were required to be valued at date of grant at, say, $2 each, or $120,000, the following entry would be logical but is not generally accepted:

Salary or bonus expense	120,000	
Additional paid-in capital		120,000
To record the value of 60,000 options issued to buy 60,000 shares of common stock at $15 per share. The value of each option is $2.		

The $120,000 entry would be made regardless of whether the options are later exercised. The basic idea underlying the granting of options is to give key employees incentive to work harder on behalf of the corporation. Hence the $120,000 credit to Additional Paid-in Capital represents an additional stake in the corporation by these employees.

PROMINENCE OF EARNINGS PER SHARE

The importance of earnings per share (EPS) was illustrated in Chapter 2. When the capital structure is relatively simple, computations of EPS are straightforward. For example, consider the following calculation (figures assumed):

---

[5] There are many exceptions. See Accounting Principles Board *Opinion No. 25*.

[6] An example is provided by the 1985 annual report of Procter & Gamble: ". . . options have been granted to key employees to purchase common shares of the company at the market value on the dates of the grants. Options for 3,347,680 shares were exercisable at June 30, 1985." Procter & Gamble has approximately 167 million common shares outstanding.

$$\frac{\text{Earnings per share}}{\text{of common stock}} = \frac{\text{Net income}}{\text{Weighted-average number of shares}}\\\text{outstanding during the period}$$

$$= \frac{\$1,000,000}{800,000} = \$1.25$$

Computations of EPS are based on the weighted-average number of shares outstanding during a period. For example, suppose 750,000 shares were outstanding at the beginning of a calendar year, and 200,000 of additional shares were issued on October 1 (three months before the end of the year). The weighted average is based on the number of months that the shares were outstanding during the year. The basic computation is:

```
750,000 × weighting of 12/12 = 750,000
200,000 × weighting of 3/12  =  50,000
Weighted average             = 800,000    shares
```

However, if the capital structure includes preferred stock that is nonconvertible, the dividends on preferred stock applicable to the current period, whether or not paid, should be deducted in calculating earnings applicable to common stock (figures assumed):

$$\frac{\text{Earnings per share}}{\text{of common stock}^7} = \frac{\text{Net income} - \text{Preferred dividends}}{\text{Weighted-average number of shares}}\\\text{outstanding during the period}$$

$$= \frac{\$1,000,000 - \$200,000}{800,000} = \$1.00$$

Historical summaries of EPS must be made comparable by adjusting for changes in capitalization structure (for example, stock splits and stock dividends).

PRIMARY AND FULLY DILUTED EPS

Accounting Principles Board *Opinion No. 15*, "Earnings per Share," stresses that the foregoing simple computations are inadequate when companies have convertible securities, stock options, or other financial instruments that can be exchanged for or converted to common shares. For example, suppose a firm has some convertible preferred stock in its capital structure:

---

[7] When preferred stock exists, the number of times that *preferred* dividends have been earned (net income ÷ preferred dividends, sometimes called earnings coverage) may be revealed in footnotes. Net income ÷ weighted-average preferred shares outstanding should *not* be called earnings per share of preferred stock.

5% convertible preferred stock, $100 par, each share convertible into 2 common shares	100,000 shares
Common stock	1,000,000 shares

The simple EPS computation follows:

Computation of earnings per share:	
Net income	$10,500,000
Preferred dividends	500,000
Net income to common stock	$10,000,000
Earnings per share of common stock:	
$10,000,000 ÷ 1,000,000 shares	$ 10.00

However, note how EPS would be affected if the preferred stock were converted, that is, exchanged into common stock. Dilution, a reduction in EPS, will occur. EPS can be calculated *as if* conversion had occurred at the beginning of the fiscal year:

Net income	$10,500,000
Preferred dividends	0
Net income to common stock	$10,500,000
Earnings per share of common stock—assuming conversion:	
$10,500,000 ÷ 1,200,000 shares	$ 8.75

The potential earnings dilution of common stock is $10.00 − $8.75 = $1.25 per share.

APB *Opinion No. 15* requires companies to divide securities that could cause dilution into two categories: (1) common stock equivalents[8] and (2) other sources of dilution. Common stock equivalents are securities whose major value is attributable to their being exchangeable for or convertible to common stock. There are complex rules, beyond the scope of this text, for identifying common stock equivalents. **Primary EPS** is the EPS calculated as if *common stock equivalents* that dilute EPS were converted. **Fully diluted EPS** is an EPS that includes assumed conversion of *all* potentially dilutive securities. Primary EPS is reported on the income statement. If primary and fully diluted EPS differ by more than 3%, both must be reported.

Assume that the convertible preferred stock in our example is not a common stock equivalent. EPS would be presented as follows:

---

[8] All stock options and warrants and a few convertible securities have characteristics that qualify them as common stock equivalents. Complicated tests and assumptions are applied to determine the existence of common stock equivalents and how to measure their impact on EPS. These matters are described in APB *Opinion No. 15*.

| Primary earnings per common share (Note A) | $10.00 |
| Fully diluted earnings per common share (Note B) | $ 8.75 |

Note A: Per share data are based on the average number of common shares outstanding during each year, after recognition of the dividend requirements on the 5% preferred stock.

Note B: Per share data based on the assumption that the outstanding preferred stock is converted into common shares at the beginning of the year, reflecting the 200,000 shares issuable on conversion and eliminating the preferred dividend requirements.

SUMMARY

Stockholders' equity is essentially a residual claim against (or interest in) the total assets of the entity. It can be very simple or enormously complex.

The composition of stockholders' equity is affected by a wide variety of transactions, including issuance of shares of various types, cash dividends, stock dividends, stock splits, retirement of shares, purchase and sale of treasury stock, exercise of stock options, and restrictions of retained income.

Earnings per share is the single number that gets the widest attention as a measure of the performance of publicly traded stocks. Its surface appeal is probably attributable to its deceptive simplicity. However, the difficulties of measuring net income plus the complexities of modern capitalization structures mean that both the numerator and the denominator are far from being simple computations.

Should an organization be formed as a corporation (the focus of this chapter), a partnership, or a sole proprietorship? The form of organization is heavily influenced by income taxes. See Appendix 13B for the discussion of this important topic.

SUMMARY PROBLEMS FOR YOUR REVIEW

☐ Problem One

From the following data, prepare a detailed statement of stockholders' equity for the Sample Corporation, December 31, 19X1:

Additional paid-in capital, preferred stock	$ 50,000
Additional paid-in capital, common stock	1,000,000
Retained income restricted as to dividends because of loan agreement	500,000
9% preferred stock, $50 par value, callable at $55, authorized 20,000 shares, issued and outstanding 12,000 shares	
Common stock, no par, stated value $2 per share, authorized 500,000 shares, issued 400,000 shares of which 25,000 shares are held in the treasury	
Dividends payable	90,000
Unrestricted retained income	1,500,000

The 25,000 shares of treasury stock cost $250,000.

☐ Solution to Problem One

Dividends payable is a *liability*. It must therefore be excluded from a statement of stockholders' equity:

SAMPLE CORPORATION
Statement of Stockholders' Equity
December 31, 19X1

9% preferred stock, $50 par value, callable at $55, authorized 20,000 shares, issued and outstanding 12,000 shares		$ 600,000
Common stock, no par, stated value $2 per share, authorized 500,000 shares, issued 400,000 shares of which 25,000 shares are held in the treasury		800,000
Additional paid-in capital:		
Preferred	$ 50,000	
Common	1,000,000	1,050,000*
Retained income:		
Restricted	$ 500,000	
Unrestricted	1,500,000	2,000,000†
Subtotal		$4,450,000
Less: Cost of 25,000 shares of common stock reacquired and held in treasury		250,000
Total stockholders' equity		$4,200,000

* Many presentations would not show the detailed breakdown of additional paid-in capital into preferred and common portions.

† Many presentations would show the restrictions parenthetically, as follows:

Retained income ($500,000 restricted as to dividends because of loan agreement) $2,000,000

Although not shown here, an additional $250,000 restriction in the amount of the cost of the treasury stock would be required by many state laws. This would reduce the unrestricted retained income from $1,500,000 to $1,250,000.

☐ Problem Two

B Company splits its $10 par common stock 5 for 1. How will its balance sheet be affected? Its earnings per share?

☐ Solution to Problem Two

The total amount of stockholders' equity would be unaffected, but there would be five times more outstanding shares than previously at $2 par rather than $10 par. Earnings per share would be one-fifth of that previously reported, assuming no change in total net income applicable to the common stock.

☐ Problem Three

C Company distributes a 2% stock dividend on its 1 million outstanding $5 par common shares. Its stockholders' equity section before the dividend was:

Common stock, 1,000,000 shares @ $5 par	$	5,000,000
Paid-in capital in excess of par		20,000,000
Retained income		75,000,000
Total stockholders' equity		$100,000,000

The common was selling on the open market for $150 per share when the dividend was distributed.

How will the stockholders' equity section be affected? If net income were $10.2 million next year, what would earnings per share be before considering the effects of the stock dividend? After considering the effects of the stock dividend?

☐ Solution to Problem Three

Stockholders' equity:

	BEFORE 2% STOCK DIVIDEND	CHANGES	AFTER 2% STOCK DIVIDEND
Common stock, 1,000,000 shares @ $5 par	$ 5,000,000	+ (20,000 @ $5)	$ 5,100,000
Paid-in capital	20,000,000	+ [20,000 @ ($150 − $5)]	22,900,000
Retained income	75,000,000	− (20,000 @ $150)	72,000,000
Total	$100,000,000		$100,000,000

Earnings per share before considering the effects of the stock dividend would be $10,200,000 ÷ 1,000,000, or $10.20. After the dividend: $10,200,000 ÷ 1,020,000, or $10.

Note that the dividend has no effect on net income, the numerator of the earnings-per-share computation. But it does affect the denominator and causes a mild dilution which, in theory, should be reflected by a slight decline in the market price of the stock.

☐ Problem Four

Metro-Goldwyn-Mayer Film Co. declared and distributed a 3% stock dividend. The applicable market value per share was $7.75. The par value of the 966,000 additional shares issued was $1.00 each. The total cash paid to shareholders in lieu of issuing fractional shares was $70,000. Prepare the appropriate journal entry.

☐ Solution to Problem Four

Retained income	7,556,500	
Common stock, $1.00 par value		966,000
Capital in excess of par value		6,520,500
Cash		70,000

To record 3% stock dividend. Total shares issued were 966,000 at $7.75, a total market value of $7,486,500. In addition, cash of $70,000 was paid in lieu of issuing fractional shares. Total charge to retained earnings was $70,000 + (966,000 × $7.75) = $7,556,500. The account Capital in Excess of Par Value was the description actually used by MGM.

HIGHLIGHTS TO REMEMBER

1. A company may have plenty of retained income but almost no cash. The *practical ability* to pay dividends depends on the cash position and other requirements for cash, not the *legal ability* as often measured by balances in retained income.

2. At first glance, accounting for stockholders' equity may seem complex. However, do not be frightened by the many new labels and accounts. As you analyze each transaction, first ask yourself how the fundamental balance sheet equation is affected. For example, stock splits and stock dividends do not affect assets or liabilities (except for minor cash outlays in lieu of issuing fractional shares).

3. Treasury stock is usually carried at cost and is deducted from the total stockholders' equity. It is *issued* stock, but it has been repurchased by the company, so it is no longer *outstanding*.

4. Convertible preferred shares and convertible debentures are frequently used. When conversion occurs, additional common shares are issued in their place, using some predetermined ratio of exchange.

5. Become familiar with the basic computation of earnings per share of common stock. It is the only "financial ratio" that is in the body of publicly issued financial statements.

ACCOUNTING VOCABULARY

Appropriated Retained Income, p. *503*   Book Value per Share of Common Stock, *498*   Corporate Proxy, *481*   Cumulative Dividends, *484*   Dilution, *499*   Dividend Arrearages, *485*   Extraordinary Item, *514*   Fully Diluted Earnings per Share, *509*   Liquidating Value, *486*   Preemptive Rights, *482*   Preferred Stock, *484*   Primary Earnings per Share, *509*   Rate of Return on Common Equity, *488*   Redemption Price, *487*   Reserve, *503*   Restricted Retained Income, *503*   Stock Dividend, *493*   Stock Option, *505*   Stock Split, *490*   Treasury Stock, *483*   Unlimited Liability, *486*

APPENDIX 11: A CLOSER LOOK AT THE INCOME STATEMENT

This appendix describes the characteristics of some special items that sometimes appear on income statements: gains or losses from (a) extraordinary items and (b) discontinued operations. Above all, note that the income tax effects of these items, as shown in Exhibit 11–3, are computed and shown separately, item by item.

The income statement that you are used to seeing ends as follows:

Income before income taxes	$50
Income taxes	20
Net income	$30

In contrast the income statement in Exhibit 11–3 has a more elaborate ending. The $30 net income is relabeled as *income from continuing operations*, which is followed by the effects of *discontinued operations* and *extraordinary items* (net of their impact on income taxes).

EXHIBIT 11–3

Illustrated Partial Income Statement
(in millions, data assumed)

Income from continuing operations before income taxes		$ 50
Deduct applicable income taxes		20
Income from continuing operations		$ 30
Discontinued operations (Note _____):		
Income from operations of discontinued Division X (less applicable income taxes of $4)	$ 6	
Loss on disposal of Division X, including provision of $3 for operating losses during phase-out period (less applicable income taxes of $6)	(9)	3
Income before extraordinary items		$ 27
Add extraordinary items:		
Loss from earthquake (less applicable income taxes of $2)	(3)	
Gain from early extinguishment of debt (less applicable income taxes of $8)	12	9
Net income		$ 36
Per share amounts (in dollars), assuming 4 million shares of common stock outstanding:		
Income from continuing operations		$7.50
Loss on discontinued operations		.75
Income before extraordinary items		$6.75
Extraordinary items		2.25
Net income		$9.00

EXTRAORDINARY ITEMS

The FASB and SEC insist that nearly all items of revenue, expense, gain, and loss recognized during the period be shown in the current income statement.[9] In contrast, in earlier years, some special or **extraordinary items** were shown in the Statement of Retained Income and never appeared as a part of the computation of net income or EPS for any year. Today they are listed in a special section of the income statement and are included in net income.

The regulators also insist that the following items should be *excluded* from the determination of net income under all circumstances:

a. Charges or credits resulting from transactions in the company's own capital stock

b. Transfers to and from accounts properly designated as appropriated retained earnings (such as general purpose contingency reserves or provisions for replacement costs of fixed assets)

Extraordinary items would affect net income but would be segregated as follows:

a. Income before extraordinary items

b. Extraordinary items (less applicable income tax)

c. Net income

In addition, EPS amounts *must* be reported for both *a* and *c* above, but most companies report EPS in a format that shows per share amounts for *a*, *b*, and *c*.

Many users of income statements have tried to distinguish between "normal" and "unusual" items affecting earnings. This distinction is supposed to assist in predict-

---

[9] There are three exceptions: (1) correction of errors, such as the failure to recognize depreciation in a previous period, (2) tax effects of preacquisition loss carryforwards of purchased subsidiaries, and (3) specified foreign currency translation adjustments.

ing future earnings; presumably, the unusual items will not be considered as heavily in any projections.

Through the years, the definition of extraordinary items has been narrowed considerably. Accounting Principles Board *Opinion No. 30* concluded that an event or transaction should be presumed to be an ordinary and usual activity of the reporting entity, and hence includable in income before extraordinary items, unless the evidence clearly supports its classification as an extraordinary item as defined in *Opinion No. 30*. Extraordinary items result from events that must have both an *unusual nature* and an *infrequency of occurrence*.

The environment in which an entity operates is a primary consideration in determining whether some specific event is abnormal and significantly different from the ordinary activities of the entity. Moreover, extraordinary events cannot reasonably be expected to recur in the foreseeable future. Therefore write-downs of receivables and inventories are ordinary items, as are gains or losses on the sale or abandonment of fixed assets. The effects of a strike and many foreign currency revaluations are also ordinary items. In short, the burden of proof is on the reporting company to demonstrate that a special item is extraordinary. *Opinion No. 30* specifically states that casualties such as an earthquake or government expropriation or prohibition are examples of events that are likely to qualify as extraordinary items. Other examples of extraordinary items include gains or losses arising from governmental condemnation or early extinguishment of debt (except for purchases of debt to satisfy sinking fund requirements).

In an average year, fewer than 15% of major U.S. companies report an extraordinary item; fewer than 5% have an extraordinary item greater than 10% of their net income. About three-fourths of the extraordinary items arise either from extinguishment of debt or from items related to income taxes.

A tragic illustration of an extraordinary charge was caused by criminal tampering with Tylenol capsules. The manufacturer, Johnson & Johnson, reported the following on its income statement (in millions):

Earnings before extraordinary charge	$146.5
Extraordinary charge—costs associated with the withdrawal of TYLENOL capsules (less applicable tax relief of $50.0)	50.0
Net earnings	$ 96.5

Another example of an extraordinary item is described in a footnote to the 1985 annual report of the Toro Company:

☐ The company partially retired $3,725,000 of industrial bonds originally used to finance the Mason City, Iowa, facility. This retirement resulted in an after tax gain of $466,000 or $.08 per share and is reflected as an extraordinary item.

DISCONTINUED OPERATIONS

Opinion No. 30 states that the results of continuing operations should be reported separately from discontinued operations, although both must be reported on the income statement. Moreover, any gain or loss from the disposal of a segment of a business should be reported in conjunction with the related results of discontinued operations and not as an extraordinary item.

The net income of a company that regularly acquires and disposes of parts of its operations can be greatly affected by the results of discontinued operations. Consider Gulf + Western Industries. In 1985 G+W disposed of operations generating nearly $3 billion of sales. The 1985 annual report separates the results of the discontinued operations from the results of continuing operations as follows (in millions):

	1985	1984	1983
Earnings from continuing operations	$129.6	$155.8	$ 161.4
Earnings (loss) from discontinued operations	104.7	104.1	(373.5)
Net earnings (loss)	$234.3	$259.9	$(212.1)

Exhibit 11–3 shows how discontinued operations should be reported. Amounts of income taxes applicable to the results of discontinued operations and the gain or loss from disposal of the segment should be disclosed on the face of the income statement or in related notes. Revenues applicable to the discontinued operations should be disclosed separately in the related notes.

In a two-year comparative income statement, the income or loss of the discontinued segment's operations during the first of the two years should be condensed and reclassified from continuing operations to discontinued operations. In this way, the income from continuing operations is placed on a comparable basis.

As a general rule, each item below income from continuing operations should be shown net of applicable income taxes. Moreover, separate and detailed disclosures are highly recommended.

Exhibit 11–3 shows how discontinued operations and extraordinary items should be presented separately on the income statement. The exhibit also shows how separate EPS figures must be displayed. You can readily visualize even more complicated presentations involving primary and fully diluted earnings per share.

Financial presentations such as those in Exhibit 11–3 are often criticized as being unnecessarily complex. However, the financial results of an entity are often produced by a variety of complicated forces. Consequently, the simplifying of innately complex data is not easy. Indeed, too much condensation and summarization may be undesirable.

FUNDAMENTAL ASSIGNMENT MATERIAL

☐ General Coverage

11–1. STOCKHOLDERS' EQUITY SECTION.   (Alternate is 11–5.) From the following data, prepare for the Ramirez Corporation a detailed stockholders' equity section as it would appear in the balance sheet at December 31, 19X3:

Dividends payable	$ 64,000
Unrestricted retained income	7,000,000
Additional paid-in capital, preferred stock	1,000,000
Common stock, $5 par value per share, authorized 900,000 shares, issued 600,000 shares of which 30,000 are held in the treasury	3,000,000
8% preferred stock, $40 par value, callable at $42, authorized 100,000 shares, issued and outstanding 80,000 shares	3,200,000
Treasury stock, common (at cost)	6,000,000
Additional paid-in capital, common stock	9,000,000
Restricted retained earnings because of loan agreement	5,000,000

11–2. ISSUANCE, SPLITS, DIVIDENDS.   (Alternate is 11–6.)

1. G Company issued 100,000 shares of common stock, $2 par, for $25 cash per share on December 31, 19X1. Prepare the journal entry.
2. G Company had accumulated earnings of $5 million by December 31, 19X5. The board

of directors declared a two-for-one stock split and immediately exchanged two $1 par shares for each share outstanding. Prepare the journal entry, if any. Present the stockholders' equity section of the balance sheet before and after the split.

3. Repeat requirement 2, but assume that instead of exchanging two shares for each share outstanding, one *additional* $3 par share was issued for each share outstanding.

4. What journal entries would be made by the investor who bought 1,000 shares of G Company common stock and held this investment throughout the time covered in requirements 1, 2, and 3?

11–3. **DIVIDENDS.** (Alternate is 11–7.)

1. H Company issued 300,000 shares of common stock, $4 par, for $20 cash per share on December 31, 19X1. Prepare the journal entry.

2. H Company declared and paid a cash dividend of $1 per share on December 31, 19X2. Prepare the journal entry. Assume that only the 300,000 shares from part 1 are outstanding.

3. H Company had accumulated earnings of $7 million by December 31, 19X5. The market value of the common shares was $60 each. A common stock dividend of 3% was declared; the shares were issued on December 31, 19X5. Prepare the journal entry. Also present a tabulation that compares the stockholders' equity section before and after the declaration and issuance of the stock dividend. Also include at the bottom of the tabulation the effects on the overall market value of the stock, the total shares outstanding, and the number of shares and percentage ownership of an individual owner who originally bought 6,000 shares.

4. What journal entries would be made by the investor who bought 6,000 shares of H Company common stock and held this investment throughout the time covered in requirements 1, 2, and 3?

5. Refer to requirement 4. Suppose the investor sold 180 shares for $58 each the day after he or she received the stock dividend. Prepare the investor's journal entry for the sale of the shares.

11–4. **TREASURY STOCK.** (Alternate is 11–8.) Company Y has the following:

Common stock, 2,000,000 shares @ $2 par	$ 4,000,000
Paid-in capital in excess of par	36,000,000
Total paid-in capital	$40,000,000
Retained income	18,000,000
Stockholders' equity	$58,000,000
Overall market value of stock @ assumed $40	$80,000,000
Book value per share = $58,000,000 ÷ 2,000,000 = $29.	

Required:

1. The company used cash to reacquire 75,000 shares for $40 each and held them in the treasury. Prepare the stockholders' equity section before and after the acquisition of treasury stock. Also prepare the journal entry.

2. All the treasury stock is sold for $50 per share. Prepare the journal entry.

3. All the treasury stock is sold for $30 per share. Prepare the journal entry.

☐ **Understanding Published Financial Reports**

11–5. **SHAREHOLDERS' EQUITY SECTION.** (Alternate is 11–1.) Consider the following data, which are from the body of the balance sheet in the 1985 annual report of Johnstown American Companies, a real estate services company that manages income producing properties:

Retained earnings	$16,084,000
Convertible preferred shares: $10 par value, unlimited authorization, 500,000 shares issued and outstanding	27,500,000
Common Shares held in treasury, 58,200 shares at cost	(444,000)
Capital in excess of par value	5,916,000
Common Shares: $1 par value, unlimited authorization, 8,492,673 shares issued and outstanding	8,493,000

Required:

1. Johnstown American classified the above amounts as shareholders' equity. Prepare that section of the balance sheet.
2. Assume that $5 million of retained income was restricted as to payment of dividends because of loan agreements. Suppose the company wanted to indicate these restrictions in the body of the balance sheet rather than a footnote. Indicate specifically how your answer to requirement 1 would be changed.

11–6. **ISSUANCE, SPLITS, DIVIDENDS.**   (Alternate is 11–2.) The Gillette Company has many popular products, including razors, blades, and grooming aids. The company's annual report contained the following:

Common stock, par value $1.00 per share	$30,800,000

Required:

1. Suppose Gillette had originally issued 200,000 shares of common stock, $3 par, for $15 cash per share many years ago, say, on December 31, 19X1. Prepare the journal entry.
2. Gillette had accumulated earnings of $5 million by December 31, 19X5. The board of directors declared a three-for-one stock split and immediately exchanged three $1 par shares for each share outstanding. Prepare the journal entry, if any. Present the stockholders' equity section of the balance sheet before and after the split.
3. Repeat requirement 2, but assume that two additional $3-par shares are issued by Gillette for each share outstanding (instead of exchanging shares).
4. What journal entries would be made by the investor who bought 1,000 shares of Gillette common stock and held this investment throughout the time covered in requirements 1, 2, and 3?

11–7. **DIVIDENDS.**   (Alternate is 11–3.) John Fluke Manufacturing Company is a fast-growing, Seattle-based electronics company. Fluke pays both cash dividends and stock dividends. Consider the following assumed data:

1. The company issued 400,000 shares of common stock, $4 par, for $20 cash per share on March 31, 19X1. Prepare the journal entry.
2. The company declared and paid a cash dividend of $2 per share on March 31, 19X2. Prepare the journal entry.
3. The company had accumulated earnings of $9 million by March 31, 19X5. The market value of the common shares was $60 each. A common stock dividend of 5% was declared; the shares were issued on March 31, 19X5. Prepare the journal entry. Also present a tabulation that compares the stockholders' equity section before and after the declaration and issuance of the stock dividend. Also include at the bottom of the tabulation the effects on the overall market value of the stock, the total shares outstanding, and the number of shares and percentage ownership of an individual owner who originally bought 6,000 shares.
4. What journal entries would be made by the investor who bought 6,000 shares of the company common stock and held this investment throughout the time covered in requirements 1, 2, and 3?

5. Refer to requirement 4. Suppose the investor sold 180 shares for $58 each the day after he or she received the stock dividend. Prepare the investor's journal entry for the sale of the shares.

11–8. **TREASURY STOCK.**   (Alternate is 11–4.) Dow Chemical Company presented the following data in a recent annual report:

	JANUARY 1	
	1985	1984
	(In millions)	
Stockholders' Equity:		
Common stock (authorized 500,000,000 shares of $2.50 par value each; issued 1985, 208,613,652; 1984, 206,549,098)	$ 522	$ 516
Additional paid-in capital	597	552
Retained earnings	4,326	4,131
Total	5,445	5,199
Less—Treasury stock, at cost (1985, 18,521,367; 1984, 10,703,413 shares)	383	153
Net Stockholders' Equity	5,062	5,046

Required:

1. Suppose that on January 2, 1985, Dow used cash to reacquire 175,000 shares for $40 each and held them in the treasury. Prepare the stockholders' equity section after the acquisition of treasury stock. Also prepare the journal entry.
2. The 175,000 shares of treasury stock are sold for $50 per share. Prepare the journal entry.
3. The 175,000 shares of treasury stock are sold for $30 per share. Prepare the journal entry.

ADDITIONAL ASSIGNMENT MATERIAL

☐ General Coverage

11–9.   In what way are corporations "artificial persons"?

11–10.   What is the purpose of preemptive rights?

11–11.   Can a share of common stock be outstanding but not authorized or issued? Why?

11–12.   "Treasury stock is unissued stock." Do you agree? Explain.

11–13.   "Cumulative dividends are liabilities that must be paid to preferred shareholders before any dividends are paid to common shareholders." Do you agree? Explain?

11–14.   "The liquidating value of preferred stock is the amount of cash for which it can currently be exchanged." Do you agree? Explain.

11–15.   "Common shareholders have limited liability." Explain.

11–16.   "The only real dividends are cash dividends." Do you agree? Explain.

11–17.   "The term *stock dividends* is a misnomer." Why?

11–18.   "A stock split can be achieved by means of a stock dividend." Do you agree? Explain.

11–19.   "A 2% stock dividend increases every shareholder's fractional portion of the company by 2%." Do you agree? Explain.

11–20.   "When a company retires shares, it must pay the stockholders an amount equal to the original par value and additional capital contributed for those shares plus the stockholders' fractional portion of retained earnings." Do you agree? Explain.

11-21. "A common stock selling on the market far below its book value is an attractive buy." Do you agree? Explain.

11-22. "Treasury stock is not an asset." Explain.

11-23. "Gains and losses are not possible from a corporation's acquiring or selling its own stock." Do you agree? Explain.

11-24. Restrictions on dividend-declaring power may be voluntary or involuntary. Give an example of each.

11-25. Why might a board of directors voluntarily restrict its dividend-declaring power?

11-26. What is the proper measure for an asset newly acquired through an exchange (e.g., an exchange of land for securities)? Explain.

11-27. What are convertible securities?

11-28. "Earnings per share is net income divided by the number of common shares outstanding." Do you agree? Explain.

11-29. Explain the difference between *primary* and *fully diluted* earnings per share.

11-30. How may the distinction between contributed and accumulated capital be blurred by traditional accounting?

11-31. **DISTINCTIONS BETWEEN TERMS.** First Federal Savings Bank had 4 million shares of common stock authorized on August 31, 19X8. Shares issued were 3,073,178. There were 22,000 shares held in the treasury. How many shares were issued and outstanding? How many shares were unissued? Label your computations.

11-32. **CUMULATIVE DIVIDENDS.** In recent years, the Pulanski Company had severe problems. In 19X4, the company suspended payment of common stock dividends. In 19X5, it ceased payment on its $2 million of outstanding 8% cumulative preferred stock. No common or preferred dividends were paid in 19X5 or 19X6. In 19X7, Pulanski's board of directors decided that $500,000 was available for cash dividends. Compute the preferred stock dividend and the common stock dividend for 19X7.

11-33. **CUMULATIVE DIVIDENDS.** E Corporation was founded on January 1, 19X1:

Preferred stock, no par, cumulative, $8 annual dividend per share:	
Issued and outstanding, 1,000,000 shares	$ 40,000,000
Capital stock, no par, 6,000,000 shares	90,000,000
Total stockholders' equity	$130,000,000

The corporation's subsequent net incomes (losses) were:

19X1	$ (5,000,000)
19X2	(4,000,000)
19X3	14,000,000
19X4	30,000,000
19X5	15,000,000

Required:

Assume that the board of directors declared dividends to the maximum extent permissible by law throughout the five years. Tabulate the annual dividend declarations on preferred and common shares. There is no treasury stock.

11-34. **PREFERENCES AS TO ASSETS.** The following are account balances of Food Good Corporation (in thousands): common stock and retained income, $200; accounts payable, $300; preferred stock ($20 par and $22 liquidating value per share), $100; subordinated debentures, $300; and unsubordinated debentures, $100. Prepare a table showing the distribution of the cash proceeds upon liquidation and dissolution of the corporation. Assume cash proceeds of (in thousands): $1,400; $1,000; $790; $500; $400; $200; and $100, respectively.

11–35. **FINANCIAL RATIOS AND STOCKHOLDERS' EQUITY.** Consider the following data for Company H:

	DECEMBER 31	
	19X2	19X1
Stockholders' equity:		
Preferred stock, 100,000 shares, $40 par	$ 4,000,000	$ 4,000,000
Common stock, 2,000,000 shares, $3 par	6,000,000	6,000,000
Additional paid-in capital	7,000,000	7,000,000
Retained income	2,000,000	1,400,000
Total stockholders' equity	$19,000,000	$18,400,000

Net income was $2 million for 19X2. The preferred stock is 10% cumulative. The regular annual dividend was declared on the preferred stock, and the common shareholders received dividends of $.50 per share. The market price of the common stock on December 31, 19X2, was $6 per share.

Required:

Compute the following statistics for 19X2: rate of return on common equity, earnings per share of common stock, price-earnings ratio, dividend-payout ratio, dividend-yield ratio, and book value per share of common stock. (You may want to review pages 58–61.)

11–36. **BOOK VALUE AND RETURN ON EQUITY.** Gonzalez Company had net income of $9 million in 19X8. The stockholders' equity section of its 19X8 annual report follows:

	19X8	19X7
Stockholders' Equity:		
9% Preferred stock, $100 par value, 200,000 shares authorized, 150,000 shares issued	$ 15,000,000	$ 15,000,000
Common stock, $1 par, 5,000,000 authorized, 2,000,000 and 1,800,000 issued	2,000,000	1,800,000
Additional paid-in capital	32,000,000	30,000,000
Retained earnings	69,000,000	65,000,000
Total stockholders' equity	$118,000,000	$111,800,000

Required:

1. Compute the book value per share of common stock at the end of 19X8.
2. Compute the rate of return on common equity for 19X8.
3. Compute the amount of cash dividends on common stock declared during 19X8. (*Hint*: Examine the retained earnings T-account.)

11–37. **EFFECTS OF TREASURY STOCK ON RETAINED INCOME.** Assume that a company has retained income of $7 million, paid-in capital of $40 million, and cost of treasury stock of $4 million.

Required:

1. Tabulate the effects of dividend payments of (a) $7 million and (b) $3 million on retained income and total stockholders' equity.
2. Why do states forbid the payment of dividends if retained income does not exceed the cost of any treasury stock on hand? Explain, using the numbers from your answer to requirement 1.

11–38. STOCK SPLIT AND 100% STOCK DIVIDEND. The Walcott Company wishes to double its number of shares outstanding. The company president asks the controller how a two-for-one stock split differs from a 100% stock dividend. Walcott has 100,000 shares ($1 par) outstanding at a market price of $50 per share.

The current stockholders' equity section is:

Common shares, 100,000 issued	
and outstanding	$ 100,000
Additional paid-in capital	2,400,000
Retained income	4,500,000

Required:

1. Prepare the journal entry for a two-for-one stock split.
2. Prepare the journal entry for a 100% stock dividend.
3. Explain the difference between a two-for-one stock split and a 100% stock dividend.

11–39. RETIREMENT OF SHARES. Solimon Company has the following:

Common stock, 5,000,000 shares @ $1 par	$ 5,000,000
Paid-in capital in excess of par	40,000,000
Total paid-in capital	$ 45,000,000
Retained income	15,000,000
Stockholders' equity	$ 60,000,000
Overall market value of stock @ assumed $20	$100,000,000
Book value per share = $60,000,000 ÷ 5,000,000 = $12.	

Required:

The company used cash to reacquire and retire 150,000 shares for $20 each. Prepare the stockholders' equity section before and after this retirement of shares. Also prepare the journal entry.

11–40. RESTRICTIONS OF DIVIDENDS. Lawrence Company has total retained income of $50 million. It also has treasury stock that cost $10 million. The company also has loan agreements that restrict dividends in the amount of $28 million. State laws do not permit dividends if retained income does not exceed the cost of treasury stock on hand. Present at least two different ways of disclosing these facts on the balance sheet.

11–41. NONCASH EXCHANGES. Suppose Company S acquires some equipment from Company T in exchange for issuance of 30,000 shares of S's common stock. The equipment was carried on T's books at the $300,000 original cost less accumulated depreciation of $120,000. Company S's stock is listed on the New York Stock Exchange; its current market value is $12 per share. Its par value is $1 per share.

Required:

1. Using the balance sheet equation, show the effects of the transaction on the accounts of Company S and Company T.
2. Show the journal entry on the books of Company S. On the books of Company T.

11–42. CONVERTIBLE SECURITIES. Suppose Chan Company had paid $350,000 to Schwartz Company for an investment in 10,000 shares of the $5 par value preferred stock of Schwartz Company. The preferred stock was later converted into 30,000 shares of Schwartz Company common stock ($.50 par value).

1. Using the balance sheet equation, prepare an analysis of transactions of Chan Company and Schwartz Company.

2. Prepare the journal entries to accompany your analysis in requirement 1.

11–43. STOCK OPTIONS. Company Z granted its top executives options to purchase 5,000 shares of common stock (par $1) at $40 per share, the market price today. The options may be exercised over a four-year span, starting three years hence. Suppose all options are exercised three years hence when the market value of the stock is $40 per share. Prepare the appropriate journal entry on the books of Company Z.

11–44. EARNINGS PER SHARE. B Company had 500,000 shares of common stock outstanding at the start of 19X1. There were 450,000 additional shares issued on April 30. Net income for 19X1 was $5.4 million. Throughout 19X1 there were 200,000 shares of 7% preferred stock, $100 par, outstanding. Compute the earnings per share of common stock.

11–45. EARNINGS DILUTION. C Company had 600,000 shares of common stock outstanding at the start of 19X1. On September 1, 300,000 additional shares were issued. Net income for 19X1 was $7.3 million. Throughout 19X1 there were 300,000 shares of 8% preferred stock, $100 par, outstanding. Each share was convertible into two shares of common stock. It is not a common stock equivalent.

Required:

1. Compute the primary earnings per share of common stock.

2. Compute the earnings per share of common stock assuming full dilution.

11–46. PRIMARY AND FULLY DILUTED EPS. Goldberg Jewelry Exchange has 100,000 shares of common stock. It also has two types of convertible preferred stock. Series A preferred stock is convertible into 10,000 shares of common stock, and it is a common stock equivalent. Series A preferred dividends are $80,000 per year. Series B preferred stock is convertible into 20,000 shares of common stock, and it is not a common stock equivalent. Series B preferred dividends are $120,000 per year. Net income in 19X9 was $1,500,000.

Required:

1. Calculate primary earnings per share.

2. Calculate fully diluted earnings per share.

11–47. UNUSUAL ITEMS AND EPS. Study Appendix 11. The Mercker Company has the following data pertaining to the year 19X2 (in millions): gain from early extinguishment of debt, $30; income from continuing operations before income taxes, $120; income from operations of discontinued Division B, $20; loss from government prohibition of saccharin, $10; and loss on disposal of Division B (including provision of $4 for operating losses during phase-out period), $25.

The applicable income tax rate for all items is 40%.

Required:

Prepare a partial income statement that begins with income from continuing operations before income taxes. At the bottom, show all relevant earnings-per-share amounts. Assume that 10 million shares of common stock are outstanding.

□ Understanding Published Financial Reports

11–48. DISTINCTIONS BETWEEN TERMS. The 1985 annual report of Procter & Gamble Company indicated that 250 million shares of common stock were authorized on June 30, 1985. There were 165,921,215 shares issued, and 1,507,705 shares held as treasury stock. How many shares were issued and outstanding? How many shares were unissued? Label your computations.

11–49. DIVIDENDS AND CUMULATIVE PREFERRED STOCK. Commercial Decal, Inc., maker of ceramic decals and plastic foils, started fiscal 1986 with retained income of $2,210,000. Commercial Decal's balance sheet showed:

6% Cumulative Convertible Preferred Stock, par value $10 a share, authorized 200,000 shares; issued 53,246 shares	532,000
Common stock, par value $.20 a share, authorized 2,000,000 shares, issued 1,321,740 shares	264,000
Additional paid-in capital	2,052,000
Retained income	2,210,000
Less: Treasury stock, at cost:	
Preferred stock, 11,344 shares	(79,000)
Common stock, 92,941 shares	(166,000)
Total stockholders' equity	$4,813,000

Required:

1. Suppose Commercial Decal had paid no dividends, preferred or common, in 1985. All preferred dividends had been paid through 1984. Management decided at the end of 1986 to pay $.05 per share common dividends. Calculate the preferred dividends that would be paid during 1986. Prepare journal entries for recording both preferred and common dividends. Assume that no preferred or common shares were issued or purchased during 1986.
2. Suppose 1986 net income was $200,000. Compute the ending balance in the Retained Income account.

11–50. ISSUE OF COMMON SHARES. Intermec Corporation, a leader in the field of bar code data collection, issued the following common shares during fiscal 1985:

a. 780,000 shares through a public offering for net cash of $10,765,977, an average price of $13.80 per share.
b. 16,900 shares as part of an employee stock purchase plan; $218,093, or $12.90 per share, was received.
c. 88,283 shares for the exercise of stock options; $355,275, or $4.02 per share, was received.

The stockholders' equity section of Intermec's balance sheet at the beginning of the year was the following:

Common stock: authorized 10,000,000 shares with $.60 par value, issued and outstanding 4,510,908 shares	$ 2,706,545
Additional paid-in capital	4,603,092
Retained earnings	8,128,230
Total stockholders' equity	$15,437,867

Net income for fiscal 1985 was $4,008,991. No dividends were paid.

Required:

1. Prepare journal entries for the common stock issues in a, b, and c. Omit explanations.
2. Present the stockholders' equity section of the balance sheet at the end of fiscal 1985.

11–51. REVERSE STOCK SPLIT. According to a news story, on November 14, 1985, "The shareholders of QED approved a one-for-ten reverse split of QED's common stock." Accounting for a reverse stock split applies the same principles as accounting for a regular stock split. QED Exploration, Inc., is an oil development company operating in Texas and Louisiana. On July 31, 1985, QED's stockholders' equity section included:

Common stock, authorized 30,000,000 shares, issued 23,530,000 shares	$ 287,637
Additional paid-in capital	3,437,547
Retained income	2,220,895
Less treasury stock, at cost, 1,017,500 shares	(305,250)
Total stockholders' equity	$5,640,829

Required: | Prepare QED's stockholders' equity section after the reverse stock split.

11–52. MEANING OF STOCK SPLITS. A letter of January 31 to shareholders of United Financial, a California savings and loan company, said:

☐ Once again, I want to take the opportunity of sending you some good news about recent developments at United Financial. Last week the board raised United's quarterly cash dividend 12½ percent and then declared a 5-for-4 stock split in the form of a 25 percent stock dividend. The additional shares will be distributed on March 15 to shareholders of record February 15.

On March 16, the board approved a merger between National Steel Corporation and United Financial. The agreement called for a cash payment of $33.60 on each outstanding United Financial share. The original National Steel offer (in early February) was $42 per share for the 5.8 million shares outstanding.

Required: | 1. As a recipient of the letter of January 31, you were annoyed by the five-for-four stock split. Prepare a letter to the chairman indicating the reasons for your displeasure.
2. A shareholder wrote to the chairman in early March: "I'm confused about the price per share, because of the recent stock split. I owned 100 shares and thought I'd receive $4,200. Now the price has dropped from $42.00 to $33.60." Prepare a response to the shareholder.

11–53. STOCK DIVIDENDS. The St. Regis Paper Company had 13.7 million shares of $5 par value common stock issued and outstanding when a 2% stock dividend was issued. The market value of the stock at the time was $36 per share.

Required: | Indicate what accounts would be affected by the issuance of the dividend and by how much.

11–54. STOCK SPLIT. The annual report of Dean Foods Company included the following in the statement of consolidated retained earnings:

Charge for stock split	$4,401,000

The balance sheets before and after the split showed:

	AFTER	BEFORE
Common stock $1 par value	$13,203,000	$8,802.000

Required: | Define *stock split*. What did Dean Foods do to achieve its stock split? Does this conflict with your definition? Explain fully.

11–55. REPURCHASE OF SHARES AND BOOK VALUE PER SHARE. In October 1985, Exxon announced that in the past year it had repurchased 46,553,000 of its own common shares for $2.34 billion. Suppose 800 million shares were outstanding before the purchase, and the shareholders' equity section of the balance sheet showed (in millions):

Common stock, $1 par, 800 million shares outstanding	$ 800
Additional paid-in capital	2,000
Retained earnings	32,300

Required:

1. Prepare the journal entry for the retirement of the 46,553,000 shares.
2. Compute the book value per share before the retirement.
3. Compute the book value per share after the retirement.

11–56. TREASURY STOCK. Ford Motor Company included the following in a footnote to a recent annual report:

☐ There were 850,666 shares of common stock of the company, with a cost of $37 million, included in Other Assets in the company's balance sheet. Such shares were acquired for various purposes.

Required: Comment on Ford's accounting for ownership of its own stock.

11–57. SMALL STOCK DIVIDEND. A news story stated:

☐ The Board of Directors of Wickes Companies Inc. today declared a 2½% stock dividend. . . . This is in lieu of the quarterly cash dividend, which had been 26¢ per share . . .

☐ The chairman said, "This dividend continues Wickes' 88-year record of uninterrupted dividend payments."

Required: Do you agree with the chairman? Explain.

11–58. DIVIDEND REINVESTMENT PLANS. Many corporations have automatic dividend reinvestment plans. The shareholder may elect not to receive his or her cash dividends. Instead an equivalent amount of cash is invested in additional stock (at the current market value) that is issued to the shareholder.

Holiday Inns, Inc., had the following data during a recent year:

Holiday Inns, Inc.

Common stock: authorized 120,000,000 shares; $1.50 par value; issued 34,786,931 shares	$ 52,180,396
Capital surplus	271,004,000
Retained earnings	710,909,000

Required:

1. Suppose Holiday Inns declared a cash dividend of $.14 per share. Holders of 10% of the company's shares decided to reinvest in the company under an automatic dividend reinvestment plan rather than accepting the cash. The market price of the shares upon issuance was $30 per share. Prepare the journal entry (or entries) for these transactions. There was no treasury stock.
2. A letter to the editor of *Business Week* commented:

☐ Stockholders participating in dividend reinvestment programs pay taxes on dividends not really received.

☐ If a company would refrain from paying dividends only to take them back as reinvestments, it would save paper-work, and the stockholder would save income tax.

Do you agree with the writer's remarks? Explain in detail.

11–59. EFFECTS ON STOCKHOLDERS' EQUITY. Indicate the effect (+, −, or 0) on *total* stockholders' equity of IBM of each of the following:

1. Sale of 100 shares of IBM by Jay Rockefeller to Tom Jones
2. Operating loss for the period
3. Declaration of a stock dividend on common stock
4. Issuance of a stock dividend on common stock
5. Failing to declare a regular dividend on cumulative preferred stock
6. Declaration of a cash dividend
7. Payment of item 6
8. Purchase of ten shares of treasury stock for $1,000 cash
9. Sale of treasury stock, purchased in item 8, for $1,200
10. Sale of treasury stock, purchased in item 8, for $900

11–60. STOCK OPTIONS. Barris Industries is a producer of television shows including "The Newlywed Game" and "The Dating Game." During 1985, Barris issued 690,000 new shares at a net price of $13.1145 per share. (Shares were sold for $14.25 and selling expenses were $783,495.) Executives exercised stock options for 150,723 shares at an average price of $4.8703 per share. Shares have a $.50 par value.

Required:

1. Prepare journal entries for (a) the newly issued shares and (b) the stock options that were exercised. Omit explanations. Round calculations to the nearest thousand dollars.
2. Suppose that all the stock options were exercised when the stock price for Barris was $14.25. How much did the executives gain from exercising the stock options?
3. How much compensation expense did Barris record when the options were granted? When they were exercised?

11–61. DILUTION. Allied Stores Corporation is a large retail organization that operates department stores such as Jordan Marsh and specialty stores such as Bonwit Teller. In fiscal 1985 Allied reported primary earnings per share (EPS) of $6.71, fully diluted EPS of $5.98, and net income of $140,733,000. Suppose Allied's only convertible security is preferred stock that is not a common stock equivalent. Suppose Allied had 20,482,014 common shares outstanding at the beginning of the fiscal year and issued 972,084 common shares halfway through the year.

Required:

1. Compute Allied's average common shares outstanding during the year.
2. Compute Allied's preferred stock dividends for fiscal 1985. *Hint*: How was primary EPS of $6.71 computed?
3. Compute the number of common shares into which the preferred stock can be converted. *Hint*: How was fully diluted EPS of $5.98 computed?

11–62. CASH DIVIDENDS, STOCK DIVIDENDS, STOCK SPLITS, AND STOCK OPTIONS. In a recent annual report, SL Industries, a manufacturer of specialty industrial products in the electrical, metalworking, and plastics industries, disclosed the following facts affecting stockholders' equity:

a. Cash dividends of $631,000 were declared and paid.
b. A 6% stock dividend was declared and distributed to owners of 2,400,000 shares when the market price was $11.20 per share. Cash of $10,000 was issued in lieu of issuing fractional shares.

c. A three-for-two stock split occurred after the stock dividend was distributed.

d. Stock options for 2,000 common shares were exercised at an average exercise price of $11 per share. This occurred after the stock dividend and stock split.

e. Net income for the year was $3,493,000.

The stockholders' equity at the beginning of the year was:

Common stock, $.20 par, 2,400,000 shares	$ 480,000
Capital in excess of par value	11,149,000
Retained earnings	11,192,000
Less: Treasury stock (160,000 shares) at cost	(3,817,000)
Total stockholders' equity	$19,004,000

Required:

1. Prepare journal entries for all five items listed. Round all calculations (both dollars and number of shares) to the nearest thousand. Include any journal entries needed to close the books at the end of the year.
2. Present the stockholders' equity section at the end of the year.

11–63. EXTRAORDINARY ITEM. Study Appendix 11. United Cable Television Corporation owns and manages forty-one cable television systems. A footnote to the company's 1985 annual report contained the following:

☐ In May 1985 the company repaid $2,297,000 of 9½% Senior Notes, and in June 1985 the company extinguished the remaining 28,007,000 of 9⅞% Senior Notes. The prepayment penalties, deferred debt expense and the debt discount expensed in fiscal 1985 for both the 9½% and 9⅞% Senior Notes totaled $2,149,000. These amounts, net of the applicable income tax benefit of $224,000, were classified as an extraordinary item.

United Cable Television paid $1,550,000 in preferred dividends in 1985, and an average of 18,039,000 common shares were outstanding during the year. Assume the company has no potentially dilutive securities. Using the following condensed data for the 1985 fiscal year, prepare an income statement including amounts for earnings per share. The descriptions are those used by United Cable Television:

General administrative expenses	$ 39,154,000
Extraordinary loss, net of applicable tax benefit of $224,000	(1,925,000)
Other expenses	54,156,000
Revenues	168,996,000
Net earnings	?
Operating expenses	61,339,000
Income tax provision	1,880,000
Income before income taxes	?

Chapter 12

INTERCORPORATE INVESTMENTS, INCLUDING CONSOLIDATIONS

LEARNING OBJECTIVES

After studying this chapter, you should be able to

1. Distinguish between accounting for short-term investments in debt securities and equity securities
2. Explain the basic approach to accounting for long-term investments in bonds
3. Contrast accounting for investments using the equity method and the cost method
4. Explain the basic ideas and methods used in the preparation of consolidated financial statements
5. Describe how goodwill arises and is accounted for
6. Explain the major features of segment reporting
7. Contrast the purchase method and the pooling-of-interests method of accounting for business combinations (Appendixes 12A and 12B)

This chapter begins with a discussion of short-term investments. It then examines accounting for intercorporate long-term investments in bonds and in equity securities. Consolidated statements, goodwill, and segment reporting are also covered. Pooling of interests is introduced in the first appendix and pursued in greater depth in the second appendix.

Although this chapter covers much territory, it concentrates on underlying concepts rather than tedious details. Moreover, the topics can be studied separately. Consider the following convenient chunks: short-term investments, long-term investments in bonds, equity method for intercorporate investments, consolidated financial statements, and accounting for goodwill.

SHORT-TERM INVESTMENTS

Investments are classified on a balance sheet according to *purpose* or *intention*. An investment should be carried as a current asset if it is a short-term investment. All other investments are classified as noncurrent assets. The latter usually appear as either (1) a separate *investments* category between current assets and property, plant, and equipment or (2) a part of *other assets* below the plant assets category.

☐ Types of Securities

As its name implies, a **short-term investment** is a temporary investment of otherwise idle cash; the investment portfolio (total of securities owned) usually consists largely of notes and bonds with maturities of one year or less. Favorite investments are **certificates of deposit**, which are short-term obligations of banks, and **commercial paper**, which consists of short-term notes payable issued by large corporations with top credit ratings. The aim is usually the highest safety, so investments in stocks tend to be minor. The investments frequently are highly liquid (easily convertible into cash) and have stable prices.

Ordinarily, short-term investments are expected to be completely converted into cash within a year after the balance sheet date. But some companies hold part of their portfolio of investments beyond a twelve-month period. Nevertheless, these investments are still classified as current assets if management intends to convert them into cash *when needed*. The key point is that cash from the sale of the securities is immediately available at the option of management.

Some companies use the ill-chosen term *marketable securities* to describe their short-term investments. **Marketable securities** are any notes, bonds, or stocks that can readily be sold via public markets. Strictly speaking, marketable securities may be held as *either* short-term investments or long-term investments. Thus 100 shares of General Electric (GE) common stock may be held as a short-term investment by one company and another 100 shares of GE may be held as a long-term investment by a second company. Consequently, this book will not use the term *marketable securities* as a synonym for the more descriptive term *short-term investments*.

☐ Short-Term Debt Securities

Balance sheets show short-term investments immediately after cash. Because short-term investments tend to be in *debt* securities such as highly stable notes and bonds with early maturities, most companies follow the reporting practice illustrated by Pacific Gas and Electric Company:

Short-term investments (at cost which approximates market)	$374,035,000

Some companies combine cash and short-term investments, as exemplified by the current asset section of Koppers Company, Inc.:

Cash, including short-term investments of $44,225,000	$57,777,000

Short-term investments in *debt securities* are usually carried at cost. What if their market values fall below cost? There is no requirement to write them down unless the decline is a substantial amount and is deemed to be "permanent."

☐ Short-Term Equity Securities

When marketable *equity* securities (common and preferred stocks) are held as short-term investments, their balance sheet value must be the lower of the *aggregate* cost or current market value of the portfolio. The changes in the market value of the portfolio would affect the financial reporting. Suppose a portfolio cost $50 million, as follows (in millions of dollars):

	END OF PERIOD			
	1	2	3	4
Assumed market values	50	45	47	54
Balance Sheet Presentation:				
Short-term investments in equity securities, at cost	50	50	50	50
Contra asset account to reduce to lower of cost or market	0	5	3	0
Net short-term investments, lower of cost or market (balance sheet value)	50	45	47	50

	FOR PERIOD			
	1	2	3	4
Income Statement Presentation: Unrealized gain (loss) on portfolio of short-term investments in equity securities	0	(5)	2	3

The tabulation shows the results for four periods. Assume these are four quarters rather than four years. (The investments hardly qualify as short-term if they are held untouched for four years.) Current accounting rules require the write-down of the short-term investment to affect income in the period when the market falls below cost. If the market subsequently recovers, the net investment may be written up—but never above cost. Thus, even though the market value rises by $7 million in period 4, only $3 million will be shown as income for that period. Journal entries for periods 2, 3, and 4 follow:

Unrealized loss on short-term investment portfolio	5	
Allowance to reduce short-term investment		5
To record unrealized loss on portfolio. (A more descriptive valuation account such as the one illustrated in the table could be used, but Allowance to Reduce Short-Term Investment is used here.)		
Allowance to reduce short-term investment	2	
Unrealized gain on short-term investment portfolio		2
To record recovery of market value and restore previously recorded unrealized loss.		
Allowance to reduce short-term investment	3	
Unrealized gain on short-term investment portfolio		3
To record recovery of market value and restore previously recorded unrealized loss. (The total unrealized gain was $7 million, but no write-ups above original cost are permissible.)		

The accounting for short-term debt securities and short-term equity securities is obviously inconsistent. Why? Because the lower-of-cost-or-market method must be routinely applied to equity securities but not to debt securities. This inconsistency is an excellent illustration of how accounting principles have developed in piecemeal fashion. Regulatory bodies seldom have the time to make pronouncements that envelop many similar items. For various reasons, including severe time pressures, the FASB chose to confine its pronouncement to certain marketable securities, excluding debt securities.

LONG-TERM INVESTMENTS IN BONDS

☐ Acquisition and Holding

Chapter 10 explained the fundamental approach to accounting for bonds payable. Recall that the issuer amortizes bond discounts and premiums as periodic adjustments of interest expense. Investors analyze bonds in a parallel fashion.

However, while the issuer typically keeps a separate account for unamortized discounts and premiums, investors do not (although they could if desired). Consider the same illustration that was used in Chapter 10, pages 436–438: Suppose that on December 31, 1980, a company issued $12 million of ten-year, 10% debentures, at 98. This means that the proceeds were 98% of $12 million, or $11,760,000. There was a discount on bonds at issuance of 2% of $12 million, or $240,000. The discount is the excess of face amount over the proceeds. Therefore the company has the use of $11,760,000, not $12,000,000. Interest (rental payment for $11,760,000) will take two forms, a semiannual cash outlay plus an extra lump-sum cash payment of $240,000 (total of $12,000,000) at maturity.

The extra $240,000 to be paid at maturity relates to the use of the proceeds over ten years. Therefore the discount is amortized:

Semiannual expense:	
Cash interest payments, $.10 \times \$12,000,000 \times \frac{1}{2}$	$ 600,000
Amortization of discount, $(\$240,000 \div 10 \text{ years}) \times \frac{1}{2}$	12,000
Semiannual expense (or revenue)	$ 612,000
Annual expense (or revenue) $\$612,000 \times 2$	$1,224,000

As the above tabulation shows, the discount (or premium) is used as an adjustment of nominal interest to obtain the real interest. The adjustment, which for simplicity uses straight-line amortization of a discount, *increases* the interest revenue of the investors. (A premium would have a *decreasing* effect.)

Exhibit 12–1 shows how the investors would account for the bonds throughout their life, assuming that they are held to maturity. The top of the exhibit analyzes the balance sheet equation; the bottom shows the journal entries.

☐ Early Extinguishment of Investment

Consider another illustration of parallel recording. Suppose in our example that the issuer purchases all of its bonds on the open market for 96 on December 31, 1988 (after all interest payments and amortization were recorded for 1988):

Carrying amount:		
Face or par value	$12,000,000	
Deduct: Unamortized discount on bonds*	48,000	$11,952,000
Cash received, 96% of $12,000,000		11,520,000
Difference, loss on sale		$ 432,000

* There are two years until maturity, and the rate of amortization has been $24,000 yearly. Therefore the unamortized amount is $2 \times \$24,000 = \$48,000$.

EXHIBIT 12–1

Investor's Records
(in thousands of dollars)

BALANCE SHEET EQUATION	A		= L +	SE
	Cash	Investment in Bonds		Retained Income
a. Acquisition	−11,760	+11,760 =		
b. Semiannual interest (repeated for ten years)	+600	+12 =	+612	Increase Interest Revenue
c. Maturity value (final receipt)	+12,000	−12,000 =		
Bond-related total		0		

JOURNAL ENTRIES:

a.	Investment in bonds	11,760,000	
	Cash		11,760,000
	To record the acquisition of 10% bonds maturing on December 31, 1990. Price paid was 98.		
b.	Cash	600,000	
	Investment in bonds	12,000	
	Interest revenue (or interest income)		612,000
	To record receipt of interest and straight-line amortization of discount.		
c.	Cash	12,000,000	
	Investment in bonds		12,000,000
	To record collection of bonds at maturity date.		

The appropriate journal entry for the investor, December 31, 1988, would be:

Cash	11,520,000	
Loss on disposal of bonds	432,000	
Investment in bonds		11,952,000
To record the sale of bonds on the open market.		

EQUITY METHOD FOR INTERCORPORATE INVESTMENTS

Equity securities were discussed from the issuer's point of view in Chapter 11. In this chapter we are concerned with the investor's records. Investments in the equity securities of one company by another company are accounted for in different ways, depending on the type of relationship between the "investor" and the "investee." For example, the ordinary stockholder who is a passive investor follows the **cost method** whereby the initial investment is recorded at cost and dividends are recorded as income when received.

United States companies must use the equity method instead of the cost method if the investor exerts a "significant influence" over the operating and financial policies of an investee. Such influence can exist even when the investor holds 50% or less of the outstanding voting stock. The **equity method** accounts for the investment at acquisition cost adjusted for the investor's share of dividends and earnings or losses of the investee subsequent to the date of investment. Accordingly, the carrying amount of the investment is increased by the investor's share of investee's earnings. The carrying amount is reduced by dividends received from the investee and by the investor's share of investee's losses. The equity method is generally used for a 20% through 50% interest, because such a level of ownership is regarded as a presumption that the investor has the ability to exert significant influence, whereas the cost method is generally used to account for interests of less than 20%. The treatment of an interest in excess of 50% is explained in the following section, "Consolidated Financial Statements."

Compare the cost and equity methods. Suppose Company A acquires 40% of the voting stock of Company B for $80 million. In Year 1, B has a net income of $30 million and pays cash dividends of $10 million. A's 40% shares would be $12 million and $4 million, respectively. The balance sheet equation of A would be affected as follows:

| | EQUITY METHOD | | | | COST METHOD | | | |
| | Assets | | = Liab. and Stk. Eq. | | Assets | | = Liab. and Stk. Eq. | |
	Cash	Investments	Liab.	Stk. Eq.	Cash	Investments	Liab.	Stk. Eq.
1. Acquisition	−80	+80	=		−80	+80	=	
2. Net income of B		+12	=	+12	No entry and no effect			
3. Dividends from B	+4	−4	=	____	+4	____	=	+4
Effects for year	−76	+88	=	+12	−76	+80	=	+4

The investment account will have a net increase of $8 million for the year. The dividend will increase the cash account by $4 million.

The investment account will be unaffected. The dividend will increase the cash amount by $4 million.

The following journal entries would accompany the above table:

EQUITY METHOD			COST METHOD		
1. Investment in B	80		1. Investment in B	80	
Cash		80	Cash		80
2. Investment in B	12		2. No entry		
Investment revenue*		12			
3. Cash	4		3. Cash	4	
Investment in B		4	Dividend revenue†		4

* Frequently called "equity in earnings of affiliated companies."
† Frequently called "dividend income."

Under the equity method, income is recognized by A as it is earned by B rather than when dividends are received. Cash dividends do not affect net income; they increase Cash and decrease the Investment balance. In a sense, A's claim on B grows by its share of B's net income. The dividend is a partial liquidation of A's "claim." The receipt of a dividend is similar to the collection of an account receivable. The revenue from a sale of merchandise on account is recognized when the receivable is created; to include the collection also as revenue would be double-counting. Similarly, it would be double-counting to include the $4 million of dividends as income after the $12 million of income is already recognized as it is earned.

The major justification for using the equity method instead of the cost method is that it more appropriately recognizes increases or decreases in the economic resources underlying the investments. Further, the cost method may allow management of the investor company to unduly influence its own reported net income. How? Under the cost method, the reported net income of the investor is directly affected by the dividend policies of the investee, over which the investor might have significant influence. Under the equity method, the investor's reported net income could not be influenced by the manipulation of the investee's dividend policies.

Sears, the world's largest retailer of general merchandise, holds ownership in several companies. An example is Sears's 23% interest in Roper Corporation, a manufacturer of household appliances. Sears must use the equity method in accounting for such investments because an ownership interest in excess of 20% is presumed to be evidence of ability to exert significant influence.[1]

CONSOLIDATED FINANCIAL STATEMENTS

United States companies having substantial ownership of other companies must issue consolidated financial statements, which are explained in this section. A reader cannot hope to understand a corporate annual report without understanding the assumptions underlying consolidations. Consolidated financial statements have been required for many years in the United States. Moreover, many other countries have adopted such requirements in recent years.

A publicly held business is typically composed of two or more separate legal entities that constitute a single overall economic unit. This is almost always a parent-subsidiary relationship where one corporation (the **parent**) owns more than 50% of the outstanding voting shares of another corporation (the **subsidiary**).

---

[1] The equity method is generally attractive to investors because it requires the recognition of a pro-rata share of income as earned regardless of whether dividends are paid by the investee. Although the 20% ownership interest is the usual rule, significant influence must indeed exist before the equity method can be justified. For example, the Securities and Exchange Commission accused McLouth Steel of abusing the equity method with its 19.87% interest in Jewell Coal & Coke Co. McLouth had so little practical control it was unable to get a director on Jewell's board, as the remainder of the company was closely held by the Thompson family.

Why have subsidiaries? Why not have the corporation take the form of a single legal entity? The reasons include limiting the liabilities in a risky venture, saving income taxes, conforming with government regulations with respect to a part of the business, doing business in a foreign country, and expanding in an orderly way. For example, there are often tax advantages in acquiring the capital stock of a going concern rather than its individual assets.

Consolidated statements combine the financial positions and earnings reports of the parent company with those of various subsidiaries into an overall report as if they were a single entity. The aim is to give the readers better perspective than could be obtained by their examining a large number of separate reports of individual companies.

☐ The Acquisition

When parent and subsidiary financial statements are consolidated, double-counting of assets and equities must be avoided via "intercompany elimina-tions." Suppose Company P (Parent) acquired a 100% voting interest in S (Subsidiary) for $213 million cash at the beginning of the year.[2] Their balance sheet accounts are analyzed in the equation form below. Investment in S is presented in the first column because it is a focal point in this chapter, not because it appears first in actual balance sheets. Figures in this and subsequent tables are in millions of dollars:

	ASSETS		= LIABILITIES +		STOCKHOLDERS' EQUITY
	Investment + in S	Cash and Other = Assets	Accounts Payable, + etc.		Stockholders' Equity
P's accounts, Jan. 1:					
Before acquisition		650 =	200	+	450
Acquisition of S	+213	−213 =			
S's accounts, Jan. 1		400 =	187	+	213
Intercompany					
eliminations	−213	=			−213
Consolidated, Jan. 1	0	+ 837 =	387	+	450

Note that the $213 million is paid to the *former owners* of S as private investors. The $213 million is *not* an addition to the existing assets and stockholders' equity of S. *That is, the books of S are completely unaffected by P's initial investment and P's subsequent accounting thereof.* S is not dissolved; it lives on as a separate legal entity.

The following journal entry would occur:

---

[2] In this example, the purchase price equals the stockholders' equity of the acquired com-pany. The preparation of consolidated statements in situations where these two amounts differ is discussed later in the section entitled "Accounting for Goodwill," pages 548–551.

P BOOKS			S BOOKS
Investment in S	213		No entry
Cash		213	

Each legal entity has its individual set of books; the consolidated entity does not keep a separate set of books. Instead working papers are used to prepare the consolidated statements.

A *consolidated* balance sheet reports all assets and liabilities of both the parent and the subsidiary. Suppose a consolidated balance sheet were prepared immediately after the acquisition. The consolidated statement shows the details of all assets and liabilities of both the parent and the subsidiary. The *Investment in S* account on P's books is the evidence of an ownership interest, which is held by P but is really composed of all the assets and liabilities of S. The consolidated statements cannot show both the evidence of interest *plus* the detailed underlying assets and liabilities. So this double-counting is avoided by eliminating the reciprocal evidence of ownership present in two places: (a) the Investment in S on P's books, and (b) the Stockholders' Equity on S's books.

In summary, if the $213 million elimination of the reciprocal accounts did not occur, there would be a double-counting in the consolidated statement:

ENTITY	TYPES OF RECORDS
P	Parent books
+ S	Subsidiary books
= Preliminary consolidated report	No separate books, but periodically P and S assets and liabilities are added together via work sheets
− E	"Eliminating entries" remove double-counting
= Consolidated report to investors	

On the work sheet for consolidating the balance sheet, the eliminating entry in journal format would be:

Stockholders' equity (on S books)	213	
Investment in S (on P books)		213

☐ **After Acquisition**

Long-term investments in equity securities, such as this investment in S, are carried in the *investor's* balance sheet by the equity method, the same method of accounting for an unconsolidated ownership interest of 20% through 50%, as previously described. Suppose S has a net income of $50 million for the year. If the parent company were reporting alone, it would have to account for the net income of its subsidiary by increasing its Investment in S account and its Stockholders' Equity account (in the form of Retained Income) by 100% of $50 million.

The income statements for the year would contain (numbers in millions assumed):

	P	S	CONSOLIDATED
Sales	$900	$300	$1,200
Expenses	800	250	1,050
Operating income	$100	$ 50	$ 150
Pro-rata share (100%) of subsidiary net income	50	—	
Net income	$150	$ 50	

P's parent-company-only income statement would show its own sales and expenses plus its pro-rata share of S's net income (as the equity method requires). The journal entry on P's books would be:

Investment in S	50	
Investment revenue*		50
* Or "equity in net income of subsidiary."		

The eliminating entry on the work sheet used for consolidating the balance sheets would be for $213 + $50 = $263.

Reflect on the changes in P's accounts, S's accounts, and the consolidated accounts (in millions of dollars):

		ASSETS		= LIABILITIES +		STOCKHOLDERS' EQUITY
	Investment + in S		Cash and Other = Assets	Accounts Payable, + etc.		Stockholders' Equity
P's accounts:						
Beginning of year	213	+	437 =	200	+	450
Operating income			+100 =			+100*
Share of S income	+50		=			+50*
End of year	263	+	537 =	200	+	600
S's accounts:						
Beginning of year			400 =	187	+	213
Net income			+50 =			+50*
End of year			450 =	187	+	263
Intercompany eliminations	−263		=			−263
Consolidated, end of year	0	+	987 =	387	+	600

* Changes in the retained income portion of stockholders' equity.

Review at this point to see that consolidated statements are the summation of the individual accounts of two or more separate legal entities. They are prepared periodically via work sheets. The consolidated entity does not have a separate continuous set of books like the legal entities. Moreover, a consolidated income statement is merely the summation of the revenue and expenses of the separate legal entities being consolidated after eliminating double-counting.[3] The income statement for P shows a $150 million net income; for S, a $50 million net income; for consolidated, a $150 million net income.

☐ Minority Interests

A consolidated balance sheet often includes an account on the equities side called *Minority Interests in Subsidiaries*, or simply **Minority Interests**. The account shows the outside stockholders' interest, as opposed to the parent's interest, in a subsidiary corporation. It arises because the consolidated balance sheet is a combination of all the assets and liabilities of a subsidiary. If the parent owns, for example, 90% of the subsidiary stock, then outsiders to the consolidated group own the other 10%. The Minority Interest in Subsidiaries account is a measure of the outside stockholders' interest. The diagram that follows shows the area encompassed by the consolidated statements; it includes all the subsidiary assets, item by item. The creation of an account for minority interests, in effect, corrects this overstatement. The remainder after deducting minority interests is P's total ownership interest:

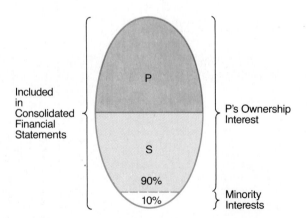

---

[3] An example of double-counting is sales by P to S (or by S to P). A consolidated income statement should not include the sale when P sells the item to S and again when S sells it to an outsider. Suppose P bought an item for $1,000 and sold it to S for $1,200. P recognized revenue of $1,200, cost of goods sold of $1,000, and income of $200. S recorded an inventory item of $1,200. In consolidation, this transaction must be eliminated. After adding together the individual accounts of P and S, you must deduct $1,200 from revenue, $1,000 from cost of goods sold, and $200 from inventory. This eliminates the $200 of income that P recognized and reduces inventory to the original $1,000 that P paid for the item.

The next table, using the basic figures of the previous example, shows the overall approach to a consolidated balance sheet immediately after the acquisition. P owns 90% of the stock of S for a cost of .90 × $213, or $192 million. The minority interest is 10%, or $21 million. (All dollar amounts are rounded to the nearest million.)

	ASSETS		= LIABILITIES +	STOCKHOLDERS' EQUITY	
	Investment + in S	Cash and Other = Assets	Accounts Payable, etc.	+ Minority + Interest	Stockholders' Equity
P's accounts, Jan. 1: Before acquisition		650 =	200	+	450
Acquisition of 90% of S	+192	−192 =			
S's accounts, Jan. 1:		400 =	187	+	213
Intercompany eliminations	−192	=		+21	−213
Consolidated, Jan. 1	0 +	858 =	387	+ 21 +	450

Again, suppose S has a net income of $50 million for the year. The same basic procedures are followed by P and by S regardless of whether S is 100% owned or 90% owned. However, the presence of a minority interest changes the *consolidated* income statement slightly, as follows:

	P	S	CONSOLIDATED
Sales	$900	$300	$1,200
Expenses	800	250	1,050
Operating income	$100	$ 50	$ 150
Pro-rata share (90%) of subsidiary net income	45	—	
Net income	$145	$ 50	
Outside interest (10%) in subsidiary's net income (minority interest in income)			5
Net income to consolidated entity			$ 145

Consolidated balance sheets at the end of the year would also be affected, as follows:

	ASSETS		= LIABILITIES +		STOCKHOLDERS' EQUITY
	Investment + in S	Cash and Other = Assets	Accounts Payable, etc.	+ Minority + Interest	Stockholders' Equity
P's accounts:					
Beginning of year, before acquisition		650 =	200	+	450
Acquisition	192	−192 =			
Operating income		+100 =			+100
Share of S income	+45	=			+45
End of year	237 +	558 =	200	+	595
S's accounts:					
Beginning of year		400 =	187	+	213
Net income		+50 =			+50
End of year	+	450 =	187	+	263
Intercompany eliminations	−237	=		+26*	−263
Consolidated, end of year	0 +	1,008 =	387	+ 26 +	595

* Beginning minority interest plus minority interest in net income: 21 + .10(50) = 21 + 5 = 26.

As indicated in the table, the eliminating entry on the work sheet used for consolidating the balance sheet would be:

Stockholders' equity (on S books)	263	
Investment in S (on P books)		237
Minority interest (on consolidated statements)		26

Thus the minority interest can be regarded as identifying the interests of those shareholders who own the 10% of the *subsidiary* stockholders' equity that is not eliminated by consolidation.

PERSPECTIVE ON CONSOLIDATED STATEMENTS

☐ Consolidated Subsidiaries

Exhibits 12–2 and 12–3 provide an overall look at how the balance sheet and income statement appear in corporate annual reports. The circled items ① and ② in the exhibits deserve special mention:

① The headings indicate that these are *consolidated* financial statements.

② On balance sheets the minority interest typically appears just above the stockholders' equity section, as Exhibit 12–2 shows. On income statements, the minority interest in net income is deducted as if it were an expense of the consolidated entity, as Exhibit 12–3 demonstrates. It generally follows all other expenses. Note that minority interest is a claim of outside stockholders' interest in a *consolidated subsidiary* company. Note also that minority interests arise only in conjunction with *consolidated* financial statements.

EXHIBIT 12-2 *(Place a clip on this page for easy reference.)*

GOLIATH CORPORATION
Consolidated Balance Sheets
As of December 31
(in millions of dollars)

①

ASSETS	19X3	19X2	CHANGE
Current assets:			
Cash	$ 90	$ 56	
Short-term investments in debt securities at cost (which approximates market value)	—	28	
Accounts receivable (less allowance for doubtful accounts of $2,000,000 and $2,100,000 at their respective dates)	91	95	
Inventories at average cost	120	130	
Total current assets	301	309	(8)
Investments in unconsolidated subsidiaries	63	55	8
Investments in affiliated companies	10	9	1
Property, plant, and equipment:			
Land at original cost	50	39	11

	19X3	19X2	
Plant and equipment			
Original cost	$192	$135	57
Accumulated depreciation	126	112	(14)

	19X3	19X2	CHANGE
Net plant and equipment	66	23	
Total property, plant, and equipment	116	62	57
Other assets:			
Franchises and trademarks	15	16	
Deferred charges and prepayments	3	4	
Total other assets	18	20	(2)
Total assets	$508	$455	53

③④

LIAB. AND STK. EQUITY	19X3	19X2	CHANGE
Current liabilities			
Accounts payable	$100	$ 84	
Notes payable	10	—	
Accrued expenses payable	32	22	
Accrued income taxes payable	34	38	
Total current liabilities	176	144	32
Long-term liabilities:			
First mortgage bonds, 5% interest, due Dec. 31, 19X6	25	25	
Subordinated debentures, 6% interest, due Dec. 31, 19X9	30	20	10
Total long-term liabilities	55	45	
Unearned income*	12	9.3	2.7
② Outside stockholders' interest in consolidated subsidiaries (minority interests)	6	5.7	0.3
Total liabilities	249	204	
Stockholders' equity:			
Preferred stock, 100,000 shares, $30 par†	3	3	
Common stock, 1,000,000 shares, $1 par	1	1	
Paid-in capital in excess of par	55	55	
Retained income	200	192	8
Total stockholders' equity	259	251	
Total liab. and stk. equity	$508	$455	53

* Advances from customers on long-term contracts. Other examples are collections for rent and subscriptions, which often are classified as current liabilities.

† Dividend rate is $5 per share; each share is convertible into two shares of common stock. The shares were originally issued for $100. The excess over par is included in "paid-in capital in excess of par." Liquidating value is $100 per share.

To help understand, consider the following hypothetical relationships that exist for Goliath Corporation, which for more realism could be viewed as a simplified version of General Motors.

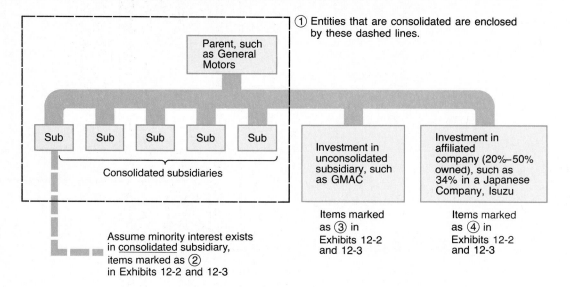

① Entities that are consolidated are enclosed by these dashed lines.

Parent, such as General Motors

Sub Sub Sub Sub Sub

Consolidated subsidiaries

Assume minority interest exists in <u>consolidated</u> subsidiary, items marked as ② in Exhibits 12-2 and 12-3

Investment in unconsolidated subsidiary, such as GMAC

Items marked as ③ in Exhibits 12-2 and 12-3

Investment in affiliated company (20%–50% owned), such as 34% in a Japanese Company, Isuzu

Items marked as ④ in Exhibits 12-2 and 12-3

☐ Unconsolidated Subsidiaries

We have already seen how the equity method is used on a parent company's books to account for its investment in subsidiaries. Most often, such investment accounts are eliminated when consolidated statements are prepared, as was just illustrated. Sometimes there is justification for not consolidating one or two subsidiaries with businesses totally different from the parent and other subsidiaries. Examples are a manufacturer's subsidiary finance companies and insurance companies. For instance, many accountants believe that a consolidated statement of General Motors (GM) and its finance company subsidiary, General Motors Acceptance Corporation (GMAC), would produce a meaningless hodgepodge. Therefore the interest in GMAC is shown as an Investment on the GM consolidated balance sheet, even though the GM interest is 100%. A separate set of GMAC statements is included in the GM annual report.

Investments in domestic unconsolidated subsidiaries are carried via the equity method. The parent's income statement includes its share of unconsolidated subsidiary net income. This income usually appears as a separate item in the consolidated income statement (see ③ in Exhibit 12–3). Note also that the beginning balance of the Investment account in Exhibit 12–2 (see ③) was $55 million. It has risen $8 million for the year because of the consolidated enterprise's share in the unconsolidated subsidiary net income.

Exhibits 12–2 and 12–3 indicate that the unconsolidated subsidiary did not declare dividends during 19X3. But suppose the parent received $6 million in dividends. The equity method would have the following effects:

Original investment	$55	
Share of subsidiary net income	8 →	Same as now appears in the
Balance	$63	income statement in
Dividends received	6	Exhibit 12–3
Balance, December 31, 19X3	$57	

The $6 million dividend would not appear in the income statement because it would represent a double-counting. Instead it is regarded as a partial liquidation of the $63 million ownership "claim" as measured in the Investment account. Thus net income of the subsidiary increases this claim, and dividends reduce this claim.

Investments in foreign subsidiaries are sometimes carried at cost because of a longstanding reluctance to recognize gains prior to the receipt of a corresponding amount of funds from the foreign subsidiaries. The conservative approach is an outgrowth of many unhappy experiences with wars, expropriations of assets, devaluations of currencies, and currency restrictions.

EXHIBIT 12–3

GOLIATH CORPORATION
① Consolidated Income Statements
for the Year Ended December 31
(000's omitted)

	19X3	19X2
Net sales and other operating revenue	$499,000	$599,100
Cost of goods sold and operating expenses, exclusive of depreciation	468,750	554,550
Depreciation	14,000	11,000
Total operating expenses	482,750	565,550
Operating income	16,250	33,550
④ Equity in earnings of affiliates	1,000	900
③ Equity in earnings of unconsolidated subsidiary	8,000	10,000
Total income before interest expense and income taxes	25,250	44,450
Interest expense	2,450	2,450
Income before income taxes	22,800	42,000
Income taxes	12,000	21,900
Income before minority interests	10,800	20,100
② Outside stockholders' interest (minority interests) in consolidated subsidiaries' net income	300	600
Net consolidated income to Goliath Corporation*	10,500	19,500
Preferred dividends	500	500
Net income to Goliath Corporation common stock	$ 10,000	$ 19,000
Earnings per share of common stock:		
On shares outstanding (1,000,000 shares)	$10.00†	$19.00
Assuming full dilution, reflecting conversion of all convertible securities (1,200,000 shares)	$ 8.75‡	$16.25

* This is the total figure in dollars that the accountant traditionally labels net income. It is reported accordingly in the financial press.

† This is the figure most widely quoted by the investment community: $10,000,000 ÷ 1,000,000 = $10.00, $19,000,000 ÷ 1,000,000 = $19.00.

‡ Computed, respectively: $10,500,000 ÷ 1,200,000 = $8.75; $19,500,000 ÷ 1,200,000 = $16.25.

As described earlier in the chapter, investments in equity securities that represent 20% to 50% ownership are usually accounted for under the equity method. These investments are frequently called Investments in **Affiliated Companies** or Investments in Associates. For example, see the items marked as ④ in Exhibits 12–2 and 12–3. General Motors would account for its 34% investment in Isuzu in this manner. Exhibit 12–2 shows how the Investment account in the balance sheet has risen by the pro-rata share of the current earnings of affiliates, the $1 million shown in the income statement in Exhibit 12–3.[4]

RECAPITULATION OF INVESTMENTS IN EQUITY SECURITIES

Exhibit 12–4 summarizes all the relationships depicted in the preceding exhibits. Take a few moments to review Exhibits 12–2 and 12–3 in conjunction with Exhibit 12–4. In particular, note that minority interests arise only in conjunction with *consolidated* subsidiaries. Why? Because consolidated balance sheets and income statements aggregate 100% of the detailed assets, liabilities, sales, and expenses of the subsidiary companies. Thus, if a minority interest were not recognized, the stockholders' equity and net income of the consolidated enterprise would be overstated.

In contrast, minority interests do not arise in connection with the accounting for investments in *unconsolidated* subsidiaries or investments in affiliated companies. Why? Because no detailed assets, liabilities, revenues, and expenses of the unconsolidated subsidiaries or affiliated companies are included in the consolidated statements. The investor's interests in these companies have been recognized on a pro-rata basis only.

As we have seen, the accounting for investments *in voting stock* depends on the nature of the investment:

1. Except for those subsidiaries in insurance and finance activities, investments that represent more than a 50% ownership interest are usually consolidated. A *subsidiary* is a corporation controlled by another corporation. The usual condition for control is ownership of a majority (more than 50%) of the outstanding voting stock.

2. **a.** If the subsidiary is not consolidated, it is carried by the parent under the equity method, which is cost at date of acquisition adjusted for the investor's share of the earnings or losses of the investee subsequent to the date of investment. Dividends received from the investee reduce the carrying amount of the investment.

   b. The equity method is also generally used for a 20% through 50% interest because such a level of ownership is regarded as a presumption that the owner has the ability to exert significant influence.

   c. Investments in corporate joint ventures should also be accounted for under the equity method. "Corporate joint ventures" are corporations owned and

---

[4] Appendix 15A and Problems 15–36 and 15–50 explore how investments carried by the equity method relate to the statement of changes in financial position.

EXHIBIT 12-4

Summary of Equity Method and Consolidations

ITEM IN EXHIBITS 12-2 AND 12-3	PERCENTAGE OF OWNERSHIP	TYPE OF ACCOUNTING	BALANCE SHEET EFFECTS	INCOME STATEMENT EFFECTS	MAJOR JOURNAL ENTRIES
①	100%	Consolidation	Individual assets, individual liabilities added together	Individual revenues, individual expenses added together	None, except in work sheets for preparing consolidated statements; to eliminate reciprocal accounts, to avoid double-counting, and to recognize any goodwill or minority interests
②	Greater than 50% and less than 100%	Consolidation	Same as 1, but recognition given to minority interest in liability section	Same as 1, but recognition given to minority interest near bottom of statement when consolidated net income is computed	

③	Greater than 50% up to 100%, but subsidiary in totally different business, so not consolidated	Equity method	Investment carried at cost plus pro-rata share of subsidiary earnings less dividends received	Equity in earnings of *unconsolidated subsidiary* shown on one line as addition to income	Investment xx
					  Equity in earnings xx
					To record earnings.
					
					Cash xx
					  Investment xx
					To record dividends received.

④	20% to and including 50%	Equity method	Same as 3	Same as 3, often called equity in earnings of *affiliated* or *associated* companies	Same as 3

operated by a small group of businesses (the "joint venturers") as a separate business or project for the mutual benefit of the members of the group. Joint ventures are common in the petroleum and construction industries.

3. Marketable *equity* securities held as short-term investments are generally carried at the lower-of-cost-or-market value.[5] These investments are typically passive in the sense that the investor exerts no significant influence on the investee.

ACCOUNTING FOR GOODWILL

☐ Purchased Goodwill

The major example on consolidated financial statements assumed that the acquisition cost of Company S by Company P was equal to the *book value* of Company S. However, the total purchase price paid by P often exceeds the book values of the assets acquired. In fact, the purchase price also often exceeds the sum of the fair market values (current values) of the identifiable individual assets less the liabilities. Such excess of purchase price over fair market value is called *goodwill* or *purchased goodwill* or, more accurately, *excess of cost over fair value of net identifiable assets of businesses acquired*. Recall that Chapter 9 discusses goodwill on pages 395–396.

To see the impact of goodwill on the consolidated statements, refer to our initial example on consolidations, where there was an acquisition of a 100% interest in S by P for $213 million. Suppose the price were $40 million higher, or a total of $253 million cash. For simplicity, assume that the fair values of the individual assets of S are equal to their book values. The balance sheets immediately after the acquisition are:

	ASSETS		= LIABILITIES +		STOCKHOLDERS' EQUITY
	Investment + in S	Cash and Other Assets	Accounts Payable, etc.	+	Stockholders' Equity
P's accounts:					
Before acquisition		650 =	200	+	450
Acquisition	+253	−253 =			
S's accounts		400 =	187	+	213
Intercompany eliminations	−213	=			−213
Consolidated	40* +	797 =	387	+	450

* The $40 million "goodwill" would appear in the consolidated balance sheet as a separate intangible asset account. It is often shown as the final item in a listing of assets. It is usually amortized in a straight-line manner as an expense in the consolidated income statement over a span of no greater than forty years.

---

[5] FASB *Statement No. 12*, "Accounting for Certain Marketable Securities," requires that a portfolio of securities (rather than each security as an individual investment) should be stated at the lower of cost or market. If the investment is classified as a current asset, any write-down to market should affect current net income. If the investment is a noncurrent asset, the write-down should be recorded directly in the stockholders' equity section of the balance sheet as a separate valuation account and not as a component of the determination of net income.

As indicated in the table, the eliminating entry on the work sheet for consolidating the balance sheet would be:

Stockholders' equity (on S books)	213	
Goodwill (on consolidated balance sheet)	40	
Investment in S (on P books)		253

Fair Values of Individual Assets

If the book values of the individual assets of S are not equal to their fair values, the usual procedures are:

1. S continues as a going concern and keeps its accounts on the same basis as before.
2. P records its investment at its acquisition cost (the agreed purchase price).
3. For consolidated reporting purposes, the excess of the acquisition cost over the book values of S is identified with the individual assets, item by item. (In effect, they are revalued at the current market prices prevailing when P acquired S.) Any *remaining excess* that cannot be identified is labeled as purchased goodwill.

Suppose that the fair value of the other assets of S (e.g., machinery and equipment) exceeded their book value by $30 million in our example. The balance sheets immediately after acquisition would be the same as above, with a single exception. The $40 million goodwill would now be only $10 million. The remaining $30 million would appear in the consolidated balance sheet as an integral part of the other assets. That is, the S equipment would be shown at $30 million higher in the consolidated balance sheet than the carrying amount on S's books. Similarly, the depreciation expense on the consolidated income statement would be higher. For instance, if the equipment had five years of useful life remaining, the straight-line depreciation would be $30 ÷ 5, or $6 million higher per year.

As in the preceding tabulation, the $10 million goodwill would appear in the consolidated balance sheet as a separate intangible asset acccount. The eliminating entry on the working papers for consolidating the balance sheet would be:

Stockholders' equity (on S books)	213	
Equipment (on consolidated balance sheet)	30	
Goodwill (on consolidated balance sheet)	10	
Investment in S (on P books)		253

Goodwill and Abnormal Earnings

Goodwill is frequently misunderstood. The layperson often thinks of goodwill as being the friendly attitude of the neighborhood store manager. But goodwill has many aspects that some observers have divided into causes (sources) and effects (fruits). A purchaser may be willing to pay more than the current values of the individual assets received because the acquired company is able to generate abnormally high earnings (the effects, or fruits). The causes of this excess earning power may be traceable to personalities, skills, locations, operating methods, and so forth. For example a purchaser may be willing to pay extra (the fruits) because excess earnings can be forthcoming from

1. Saving in time and costs by purchasing a corporation having a share of the market in a type of business or in a geographical area where the acquiring corporation planned expansion
2. Excellent general management skills or a unique product line
3. Potential efficiency by combination, rearrangement, or elimination of duplicate facilities and administration

Of course, goodwill is originally generated internally. For example, a happy combination of advertising, research, management talent, and timing may give a particular company a dominant market position (the cause) for which another company is willing to pay dearly (the fruit). This ability to command a premium price for the total business is goodwill. Nevertheless, such goodwill should never be recorded by the selling company. Therefore the *only* goodwill generally recognized as an asset is that identified when one company is purchased by another. The consolidated company must then show in its financial statements the purchased goodwill.

As you might suspect, the final price paid by the purchaser of an ongoing business is the culmination of a bargaining process. Therefore the exact amount paid for goodwill is subject to the negotiations regarding the total purchase price. A popular logic for determining the maximum price follows.

Goodwill is fundamentally the price paid for "excess" or "abnormal" earning power. The following steps might be taken regarding the possible acquisition of Company M or Company N:

	ORDINARY COMPANY M	EXTRAORDINARY COMPANY N
1. Fair market value of identifiable assets, less liabilities	$800,000	$800,000
2. Normal annual earnings on net assets at 10%	80,000	80,000
3. Actual average annual earnings for past five years (including for Co. N an excess or abnormal return of $20,000)	80,000	100,000
4. Maximum price paid for normal annual earnings is ten times line 2	800,000	800,000
5. Maximum price paid for abnormal annual earnings (which are riskier and thus less valuable per dollar of expected earnings) is six times $20,000	—	120,000*
6. Maximum price a purchaser is willing to pay for the company (line 1 plus line 5)	800,000	920,000

* This is the most the purchaser is willing to pay for goodwill.

The above table uses a "capitalization rate" of 10% (earnings divided by .10 or earnings multiplied by 10) to arrive at a purchase price for a normal company. This normal rate varies by risk and by industry. For example, the normal rate for an oil exploration company will be higher (and the earnings multiplier lower) than for a retail food chain. Goodwill is attributed to the exceptional company, and the earnings multiplier paid for extra earnings (the abnormal layer) is less than the multiplier used for the basic earnings (the normal layer). The capitalization rate for the abnormal layer is $16\frac{2}{3}\%$ (earnings divided by .1667 or earnings multiplied by 6):

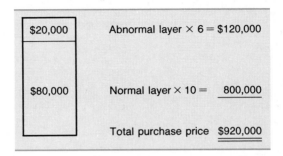

For shareholder-reporting purposes, goodwill must be amortized by systematic charges in the income statement over the period estimated to be benefited. The maximum amortization period should not exceed forty years.[6] In our Company N example, a strong case could be made for amortization over six years or less.

Managers, investors, and accountants tend to be uncomfortable about the presence of goodwill on the balance sheet. Somehow it is regarded as an inferior asset even though management decided that it was valuable enough to warrant a total outlay in excess of the total current value of the individual assets. As a practical matter, many accountants feel that the income-producing factors of goodwill are unlikely to have a value in perpetuity even though expenditures may be aimed at maintaining their value. Nevertheless, the Accounting Principles Board did not permit the lump-sum write-off of goodwill upon acquisition.

SEGMENT REPORTING

The 1970s and 1980s can accurately be described as the years of fuller disclosure. The financial statements became thicker and more complex and were impressively adorned with detailed footnotes and supplementary information. Among the more controversial requirements was the issuance by the FASB in 1976 of *Statement No. 14*, "Financial Reporting for Segments of a Business Enterprise." Corporations must now disclose data about their operations in different industries and in foreign countries, their export sales, and their major customers.

---

[6] Before October 31, 1970, amortization was not required. Some companies still have large amounts of such goodwill purchased before 1970 that is not being amortized. For example, about half of the $640 million of intangible assets of American Brands, Inc., is not being amortized.

EXHIBIT 12-5

Main Provisions of FASB Statement No. 14

TYPE OF DISCLOSURE	CRITERIA FOR DISCLOSURE	ITEMS TO BE DISCLOSED
1. Industry segment	a. Revenue at least 10% of company revenue, b. Profit at least 10% of company profit, or c. Assets at least 10% of company assets.	a. Segment revenue b. Segment profit c. Segment assets d. Other (e.g., segment depreciation and capital expenditures)
2. Geographic segment	a. Foreign operations contribute at least 10% of company's revenue, or b. Foreign operations use more than 10% of the company's assets	a. Segment revenue b. Segment profit c. Segment assets
3. Export disclosures	At least 10% of revenues from export sales	Export sales by geographic area
4. Major customers	Any customer providing more than 10% of company's revenue	Customer identity and amount of revenue

The purpose of consolidated financial statements is to provide an overall view of an economic entity. However, consolidated data can hide some of the details that might be useful in predicting profitability, risk, and growth. The purpose of segment disclosures is to facilitate such prediction.

Exhibit 12-5 lists the four types of disclosures required by *Statement No. 14*. An *industry segment* is a product or service or a group of related products or services. Management has much discretion in defining industry segments. The nature of the product, the nature of the production process, and the markets or marketing methods should be considered in identifying a company's segments. Examples of industry segments include the following:

American Express Company: travel-related services; international banking services; investment services; IDS financial services; insurance services

Alcoa: aluminum processing; finished products

If an industry segment meets any one of the three criteria for disclosure in Exhibit 12-5, the segment's revenue, profit, assets, depreciation, and capital expenditures must be reported.

Companies with significant operations in foreign countries must separately disclose the results of operations by geographic area. For example, American Express Company reports revenue, profits, and assets for the United States, Europe, and Asia/Pacific. Even companies without foreign operations must disclose foreign *sales* by geographic area if such export sales are 10% or more of total revenues.

Finally, companies must report aggregate sales to any customer accounting for more than 10% of revenues. For example, Sanders Associates, Inc., reports sales to IBM of $142 million, 16% of total revenues.

EXHIBIT 12–6

AMERICAN BRANDS, INC. AND SUBSIDIARIES
Information on Business Segments
(in millions)

BUSINESS BY INDUSTRY SEGMENTS	1985	1984		1985	1984
Net sales			**Depreciation and amortization**		
Tobacco products	$4,390.0	$4,229.0	Tobacco products	$ 36.9	$ 35.4
Hardware and security	569.3	519.3	Hardware and security	13.2	11.8
Distilled beverages	249.8	246.4	Distilled beverages	13.7	14.4
Food products	507.0	493.8	Food products	10.7	9.7
Office products	336.7	335.5	Office products	9.1	8.6
Other	1,255.5	1,171.2	Other	26.6	22.9
	$7,308.3	$6,995.2	Total	$110.2	$102.8
Operating income			**Capital expenditures**		
Tobacco products	$519.6	$496.7	Tobacco products	$ 62.5	$ 63.5
Hardware and security	43.4	48.4	Hardware and security	16.8	9.2
Distilled beverages	40.2	39.3	Distilled beverages	14.6	16.4
Food products	27.4	28.6	Food products	18.2	18.4
Office products	17.1	33.8	Office products	13.6	14.3
Other	76.5	72.5	Other	43.8	42.1
	724.2	719.3	Total	$169.5	$163.9
Financial services	174.1	172.9			
	$898.3	$892.2	**BUSINESS BY GEOGRAPHIC AREAS**	1985	1984
			Net sales		
Identifiable assets			United States	$3,150.0	$3,064.9
Tobacco products	$1,647.5	$1,439.6	Europe	3,930.4	3,704.8
Hardware and security	458.2	422.9	Other	227.9	225.5
Distilled beverages	259.5	259.3		$7,308.3	$6,995.2
Food products	178.7	174.8			
Office products	427.5	420.3	**Operating income**		
Other	760.8	591.4	United States	$551.4	$550.5
	$3,732.2	$3,308.3	Europe	163.3	156.1
			Other	9.5	12.7
				724.2	719.3
			Financial services (U.S.)	174.1	172.9
				$898.3	$892.2
			Identifiable assets		
			United States	$2,059.8	$1,995.1
			Europe	1,565.7	1,201.0
			Other	106.7	112.2
				$3,732.2	$3,308.3

Exhibit 12–6 displays the segment information of American Brands, Inc., for two years (six years were included in the annual report). Examples of American Brands products include Carlton and Pall Mall cigarettes, Master locks, Sunshine biscuits, Wilson Jones office supplies, Jim Beam whiskey, Titleist golf balls, and Franklin life insurance.

SUMMARY

Nearly all corporate annual reports contain consolidated financial statements, as well as "investment" accounts of various sorts. Acquiring a fundamental understanding of accounting for intercorporate investments is therefore essential for intelligent use of financial reports.

Exhibits 12–2 and 12–3 summarize how to account for intercorporate investments. Note how the equity method is applied. The $8 million increase in the Investments account is attributable to the pro-rata share of the *unconsolidated* subsidiary net income shown in Exhibit 12–3. See pages 543 and 545.

Minority interests are also displayed in Exhibits 12–2 and 12–3. Consider the $300,000 increase (Exhibit 12–2) in Outside Stockholders' Interest in Consolidated Subsidiaries. It is attributable to the minority interests' share of the income of *consolidated* subsidiaries, as indicated in the income statement in Exhibit 12–3.

Even though consolidated statements are regarded as the heart of the financial report, companies must also disclose as supplementary data information regarding significant business segments.

SUMMARY PROBLEMS FOR YOUR REVIEW

☐ Problem One

Dow Chemical's annual report used the following asset nomenclature and classifications as of December 31 (in millions):

	$:
Marketable securities and interest-bearing deposits (at cost, approximately market)	102
	:
Total Current Assets	3,931
Investments:	
Capital stock of related companies—at cost plus equity in accumulated earnings:	
Banking and insurance subsidiaries	214
Associated companies (50% owned)	833
20%–49% owned companies	105
Other investments (at cost)	413
Noncurrent receivables	384
Total Investments	1,949
Plant Properties	11,256
Less–Accumulated depreciation	6,083
Net Plant Properties	5,173
Goodwill	202
Deferred Charges and Other Assets	164
TOTAL	$11,419

Dow also shows "Minority Interests in Subsidiary Companies" of $21 million among its "other liabilties."

1. Suppose "Marketable Securities" included a $24 million portfolio of equity securities. Their market values on March 31, June 30, and September 30 were $20, $23, and $28, respectively. Compute
   (a) Carrying amount of the portfolio on each of the three dates
   (b) Unrealized gain (loss) on the portfolio for each of the three quarters
2. Suppose the $413 million of "Other Investments" included a $9 million investment in the debentures of an affiliate. The debentures had a par value of $10 million and a 10% nominal rate of interest, payable June 30 and December 31. Their market rate of interest when the investment was made was 12%. Prepare the Dow journal entry for the semiannual receipt of interest.
3. Suppose Dow's "Associated Companies" had net income of $200 million. Dow received cash dividends of $70 million from these companies. No other transactions occurred. Prepare the pertinent journal entries.

☐ Solution to Problem One

1. **a.** Lower of cost or market: $20, $23, and $24.
   b. $24 − $20 = $4 loss; $23 − $20 = $3 gain; $28 − $23 = $5 gain, but only $1 gain would appear on the income statement because the portfolio should not be written up above cost.

2.

Cash	500,000	
Other investments (in bonds)	40,000	
Interest revenue		540,000
Six months' interest earned is		
.5 × .12 × $9,000,000 = $540,000.		
Amortization is $540,000 − cash received		
of .5 × .10 × $10,000,000 = $540,000 − $500,000.		

3.

Investments in associated companies	100,000,000	
Investment revenue		100,000,000
To record 50% share of $200 million income.		
Cash	70,000,000	
Investments in associated companies		70,000,000
To record dividends received from associated companies.		

☐ Problem Two

1. Review the section on minority interests, pages 540–542. Suppose P owns 60% of the stock of S for a cost of .60 × $213, or $128 million. The total assets of P consist of this $128 million plus $522 million of other assets, a total of $650 million. The S assets and equities are unchanged from the amount given in the example on page 541. Prepare an analysis showing what amounts would appear in a consolidated balance sheet immediately after the acquisition.
2. Suppose S has a net income of $50 million for the year, and P has an operating income of $100 million. Other details are described in the example on page 541. Prepare an analysis showing what amounts would appear in a consolidated income statement and year-end balance sheet.

☐ Solution to Problem Two

1.

	ASSETS		= LIABILITIES +	STOCKHOLDERS' EQUITY	
	Investment in S	+ Cash and Other Assets =	Accounts Payable, etc.	Minority + Interest +	Stockholders' Equity
P's accounts, Jan. 1: Before acquisition		650 =	200	+	450
Acquisition of 60% of S	+128	−128 =			
S's accounts, Jan. 1		400 =	187	+	213
Intercompany eliminations	−128	=		+85	−213
Consolidated, Jan. 1	0	+ 922 =	387	+ 85 +	450

2.

	P	S	CONSOLIDATED
Sales	$900	$300	$1,200
Expenses	800	250	1,050
Operating income	$100	$ 50	$ 150
Pro-rata share (60%) of unconsolidated subsidiary net income	30	—	
Net income	$130	$ 50	
Outside interest (40%) in consolidated subsidiary net income (minority interest in income)			20
Net income to consolidated entity			$ 130

	ASSETS		= LIABILITIES +	STOCKHOLDERS' EQUITY	
	Investment in S	+ Cash and Other Assets =	Accounts Payable, etc.	Minority + Interest +	Stockholders' Equity
P's accounts:					
Beginning of year	128	+ 522* =	200	+	450
Operating income		+100 =		+	+100
Share of S income	+ 30	=			+ 30
End of year	158	+ 622 =	200	+	580
S's accounts:					
Beginning of year		400 =	187	+	213
Net income		+ 50 =			+ 50
End of year		450 =	187	+	263
Intercompany eliminations	−158	=		+105†	−263
Consolidated, end of year	0	+ 1,072 =	387	+ 105 +	580

* 650 beginning of year − 128 for acquisition = 522.

† 85 beginning of year + .40 (50) = 85 + 20 = 105.

HIGHLIGHTS TO REMEMBER

1. Generally accepted accounting principles evolve in a patchwork way. Ponder the assortment of approaches to current assets:

TYPE OF CURRENT ASSET	APPLICATION OF LOWER OF COST OR MARKET
Investments in debt securities	Write down if "permanent" decline
Investments in equity securities	Write down and then write up recoveries, but not above original cost
Inventories	Write down, but do not write up any subsequent recoveries

2. The accounting for long-term investments in bonds is usually similar to the accounting on the issuer's books. That is, the investor's acquisition premium or discount is amortized over the remaining life of the bond.

3. Exhibit 12–4 (p. 547) summarizes the accounting for long-term investments in equity securities. Please review it before you try to solve any problems in these categories.

ACCOUNTING VOCABULARY

Affiliated Companies, *546* Certificates of Deposit, *530* Commercial Paper, *530* Consolidated Statements, *537* Cost Method for Investments, *534* Equity Method, *535* Marketable Securities, *530* Minority Interests, *540* Parent Company, *536* Pooling-of-Interests Method, *557* Purchase Method, *557* Short-Term Investment, *530* Subsidiary, *536*

APPENDIX 12A: POOLING OF INTERESTS

☐ Nature of Pooling

The business combinations described in the body of the chapter were accounted for by using the *purchase method*, as contrasted with the *pooling-of-interests method*. The focus is on the acquired company. The **purchase method** accounts for a business combination on the basis of the *market prices* actually paid for the acquired company's assets. In contrast, the **pooling-of-interests method** is based on the *book values* of the acquired company's assets.

Both the purchase and the pooling methods are acceptable under the appropriate circumstances, but not as alternatives for the same business combination. Pooling is a uniting of ownership interests of two or more companies by the exchange of common stock. In theory, neither company *purchases* the other. The recorded assets and liabilities of the fused companies are carried forward at their book values by the combined corporation. The market values of both corporations are ignored on the grounds that no purchase has occurred; instead two going concerns have merely combined existing resources that are already being accounted for. To use pooling-of-interests accounting, the combination must completely adhere to a long list of restrictive conditions, including most importantly:

1. The acquirer must issue voting common shares (not cash) in exchange for substantially all (at least 90%) of the voting common shares of the acquired company.
2. The acquisition must occur in a single transaction.

Consider the way actual business combinations commonly occur:

1. The management of P and the management of S discuss the feasibility of P's acquiring S.
2. The *market value* of S as a going concern is established in a variety of ways, including the market values of securities, the appraisal values of individual assets, and negotiations between P and S. A final price is agreed upon.
3. S is acquired by P. The cash or stock issued by P is ultimately distributed to the individual shareholders of S, not to S itself. Thus, after the acquisition has been completed, S's assets, liabilities, and stockholders' equity are unchanged.
   (*a*) P may issue shares for cash and then use the cash to buy S. The acquisition would be accounted for as a *purchase*.
   (*b*) P may issue *the same number* of shares directly to S. If various conditions are met, the acquisition would be accounted for as a *pooling*.
   (*c*) Note especially that the owners of S would expect the *same total market value* for their shares sold to P, regardless of whether the transaction is accounted for as a purchase or a pooling. Also note that not all acquisitions by P's issuance of stock would necessarily be accounted for as a pooling. For example, P may fail to acquire at least 90% of the common shares of S. Or P may pay for S with half cash and half P shares. In either case, the transaction should be accounted for as a purchase.

☐ Illustration of Pooling

The basic data in the section "Purchased Goodwill," page 548, are reproduced at the top of Exhibit 12–7 for your reconsideration. Suppose P had issued stock for $253 million cash at the beginning of the year and then used the cash to acquire all the shares of S. This combination should be accounted for by using the purchase method.

EXHIBIT 12–7

Comparison of Purchase and Pooling for Business Combinations
(in millions of dollars)

	Investment in S	+	Cash and Other Assets =	Accounts Payable, etc.	+	Stockholders' Equity
	ASSETS			= LIABILITIES +		STOCKHOLDERS' EQUITY
PURCHASE METHOD						
P's accounts:						
Before issuance of stock			397 =	200	+	197
Issuance of stock			+253 =			+253
Acquisition of S	+253		−253 =			
S's accounts			400	187	+	213
Intercompany eliminations	−213					−213
Consolidated	40*	+	797 =	387	+	450
POOLING METHOD						
P's accounts:						
Before issuance of stock			397 =	200	+	197
Issuance of stock in acquisition of S	+213		=			+213
S's accounts			400 =	187	+	213
Intercompany eliminations	−213		=			−213
Consolidated	0	+	797 =	387	+	410

* Goodwill, as explained in the body of the chapter. See the section "Purchased Goodwill," page 548.

Instead of issuing its shares for $253 million cash, suppose P exchanges *the same number* of its shares for the shares of S. Assuming that all the conditions of pooling are met, the accounting would appear as shown in the bottom half of Exhibit 12–7.

The current value of Company S exceeds the recorded values by $40 million. Purchase accounting recognizes the fair values (current values) of the assets acquired, but pooling does not. Moreover, the future consolidated income statements will show higher income under pooling. Why? Because pooling has no $40 million goodwill to amortize as expense.

The magnitude of the difference between purchasing and pooling would become even more pronounced if S had several individual assets whose fair market values far exceeded book values. Examples are companies with large holdings of internally developed patents, copyrights, and trademarks. Under pooling, the combined company does not have to account for these market values either on its consolidated balance sheet or as a part of its expenses on future consolidated income statements.

□ Criticisms of Pooling

Many critics maintain that pooling-of-interests accounting should be completely banned. Pooling is defective because it ignores the asset values on which the parties have traded and substitutes a wholly irrelevant figure—the amount on the seller's books. Such accounting also permits the reporting of erroneous profits upon subsequent disposition of such assets. If the assets had been acquired for cash, the buyer's cost would be the amount of the cash. Acquisition for stock should make no difference.

The accounting essence is the amount of consideration, not its nature. Payment in cash or stock can be a matter of form, not substance. Suppose the seller wants cash. The buyer can first sell stock and turn over the proceeds to the seller, or the seller can take stock and promptly sell the stock for cash.

Some say that the elimination of pooling would impede mergers and thus is not in the national interest. Others say that accounting does not exist to aid or discourage mergers, but to account for them fairly. Elimination of pooling would remove the confusion that comes from the coexistence of pooling and purchase accounting. Above all, the elimination of pooling would remove an aberration in historical-cost accounting that permits an acquisition to be accounted for on the basis of the seller's cost rather than the buyer's cost of the assets obtained in a bargained exchange.

APPENDIX 12B: MORE ON POOLING OF INTERESTS

Exhibit 12–7 does not provide a detailed illustration of the consolidation process for pooling. A detailed approach follows:

1. Sum the individual assets and liabilities of P and S, line by line.
2. Sum the individual retained incomes. By definition of pooling, the retained incomes are combined in this way.
3. Adjust the accounts for changes in par and additional paid-in capital. This adjustment is usually small; it involves increasing or decreasing two accounts.

To illustrate, reconsider Exhibit 12–7. Suppose the following detailed stockholders' equity accounts had existed before the pooling of interests (in millions of dollars):

	P		S	
Common stock, at par	8,000,000 shares @ $5 =	40	5,000,000 shares @ $4 =	20
Additional paid-in capital		87		140
Retained income		70		53
Total stockholders' equity		197		213

Assume that the market value of the additional P shares is $55 each. If the acquisition of S is based on a total market value of $253 million, then $253,000,000 ÷ $55 = 4,600,000 additional P shares that would be issued. In accounting for a pooling, the *number* of shares is pertinent, but their *value* is ignored.

In concept, a straightforward pooling would call for the following simple addition of all accounts:

	P	+	S	= CONSOLIDATED
Cash and other assets	397	+	400 =	797
Accounts payable	200	+	187 =	387
Common stock, par	40	+	20 =	60*
Additional paid-in capital	87	+	140 =	227*
Retained income	70	+	53 =	123
	397		400	797

* Total paid-in capital = 60 + 227 = 287.

Indeed, *in practice* the above addition does occur, including the noteworthy summing of retained incomes. However, a modest change in the Common Stock and Additional Paid-in Capital accounts is necessary to show the consolidated picture to the outside investor:

	CONSOLIDATED	
Common stock at par	Old P, 8,000,000 shares @ $5 =	40
	New P, 4,600,000 shares @ $5 =	23
	New total	63*
Additional paid-in capital	Old P	87
	Old S	140
	Adjustment	(3)
	New total	224*

* Total paid-in capital = 63 + 224 = 287.

Compare the $63 with the $60 in the preceding tabulation; also compare the $224 with the $227. The numbers differ only because the $23 million par value of the new P shares differs from the $20 million par value of the S shares. To bring the par value account up to the required $63 million, $3 must be transferred from additional paid-in capital to common stock, at par.

A consolidating journal entry (for the work sheet) may clarify the pooling transaction. The book values of S are added to P:

Cash and other assets	400	
Accounts payable		187
Common stock		23
Additional paid-in capital		137
Retained income		53

To issue 4,600,000 shares of P @ $5 par in a pooling of interests with S. S's retained income is added intact. The book value ($20 + $140) of S common stock and additional paid-in capital is also added, after recognizing that P's par value is different from S's. So instead of adding $20 + $140, the addition takes the form of $23 + $137.

Ponder the accounting for pooling. A "parent" is identified. The par value of P stock governs the new totals for common stock and for additional paid-in capital. The latter plays a residual role. That is, the new total for the par value of the consolidated company is the old P total of $40 plus the par value of the additional P shares issued of $23 = $63. But the total of $287 for both par and additional paid-in capital still holds. Consequently, the additional paid-in capital is a residual of $287 − $63 = $224. The consolidated balance sheet on the pooling basis would include the following:

ASSETS		LIABILITIES AND STOCKHOLDERS' EQUITY	
Cash and other assets	$797	Accounts payable	$387
		Common stock, 12,600,000 shares @ $5 par	63
		Additional paid-in capital	224
		Retained income	123
			$797

In contrast, the consolidated balance sheet on the purchase basis follows:

ASSETS		LIABILITIES AND STOCKHOLDERS' EQUITY	
Cash and other assets	$797	Accounts payable	$387
Goodwill	40	Common stock, 12,600,000 shares @ $5 par	63
	$837	Additional paid-in capital	317*
		Retained income	70
			$837

* Identified with the first 8,000,000 shares	$ 87
Identified with new 4,600,000 shares @ ($55 − $5)	230
	$317

Compare the two consolidated balance sheets immediately after P acquires S:

	POOLING	PURCHASE COMPARED WITH POOLING
1. Assets	No goodwill No fair value of other assets	Higher because of goodwill and fair values of other assets such as property, plant, and equipment
2. Retained income	P and S added together	Lower because S retained income not added; the consolidated retained income equals P retained income
3. Common stock at par	Sum of all P shares	Same as pooling
4. Additional paid-in capital	Adjusted to accommodate changes in par values	Higher because new shares affect equity at market values at time of acquisition of S

How do income statements differ between purchasing and pooling? Consider the year of the acquisition. Pooling merely sums revenues and expenses as though both P and S were together throughout the year:

	POOLING	PURCHASE COMPARED WITH POOLING
Revenue and expenses	Added together for entire year regardless of when acquisition occurred during the year	Added together only for time span subsequent to date of acquisition
Goodwill amortization	No goodwill	Amortized for time span subsequent to acquisition
Depreciation expense	Based on old book values	Based on fair values at date of acquisition

A widespread criticism of pooling has been that a P company can "artificially" boost its net income by acquiring an S company late in a year. Under pooling, P can include the S income for the entire year in consolidated results. Under purchasing, P can include only the S income earned subsequent to the acquisition.

FUNDAMENTAL ASSIGNMENT MATERIAL

☐ **General Coverage**

12–1. COST OR EQUITY METHOD. (Alternates are 12–7 and 12–33.) Company D acquired 30% of the voting stock of Company E for $30 million cash. In Year 1, E had a net income of $20 million and paid a cash dividend of $13,333,333.

Required:

Using the equity and the cost methods, show the effects of the three transactions on the accounts of D. Use the balance sheet equation format. Also show the accompanying journal entries.

12–2. CONSOLIDATED FINANCIAL STATEMENTS. (Alternate is 12–8.) Company P acquired a 100% voting interest in Company S for $110 million cash at the start of the year. Immediately before the business combination, each company had the following condensed balance sheet accounts (in millions):

	P	S
Cash and other assets	$600	$200
Accounts payable, etc.	$250	$ 90
Stockholders' equity	350	110
Total liab. and stk. eq.	$600	$200

1. Prepare a tabulation of the consolidated balance sheet accounts immediately after the acquisition. Use the balance sheet equation format.
2. Suppose P and S have the following results for the year:

	P	S
Sales	$700	$400
Expenses	550	360

Prepare income statements for the year for P, S, and the consolidated entity.
3. Present the effects of the operations for the year on P's accounts and on S's accounts, using the balance sheet equation. Also tabulate the consolidated balance sheet accounts at the end of the year. Assume that liabilities are unchanged.
4. Suppose S paid a cash dividend of $30 million. What accounts in requirement 3 would be affected and by how much?

12–3. **MINORITY INTERESTS.** This extends the preceding problem. However, this problem is self-contained because all the facts are reproduced below. Company P acquired a 70% voting interest in Company S for $77 million cash at the start of the year. Immediately before the business combination, each company had the following condensed balance sheet accounts (in millions):

	P	S
Cash and other assets	$600	$200
Accounts payable, etc.	$250	$ 90
Stockholders' equity	350	110
Total liab. and stk. eq.	$600	$200

1. Prepare a tabulation of the consolidated balance sheet accounts immediately after the acquisition. Use the balance sheet equation format.
2. Suppose P and S have the following results for the year:

	P	S
Sales	$700	$400
Expenses	550	360

Prepare income statements for the year for P, S, and the consolidated entity.
3. Using the balance sheet equation format, present the effects of the operations for the year on P's accounts and S's accounts. Also tabulate consolidated balance sheet accounts at the end of the year. Assume that liabilities are unchanged.
4. Suppose S paid a cash dividend of $30 million. What accounts in requirement 3 would be affected and by how much?

12–4. **GOODWILL AND CONSOLIDATIONS.** This extends Problem 12–2. However, this problem is self-contained because all the facts are reproduced below. Company P acquired a 100% voting interest in Company S for $170 million cash at the start of the year. Immediately before the business combination, each company had the following condensed balance sheet accounts (in millions):

	P	S
Cash and other assets	$600	$200
Accounts payable, etc.	$250	$ 90
Stockholders' equity	350	110
Total liab. and stk. eq.	$600	$200

Assume that the fair values of the individual assets of S were equal to their book values.

Required:

1. Prepare a tabulation of the consolidated balance sheet accounts immediately after the acquisition. Use the balance sheet equation format.
2. If goodwill is going to be amortized over forty years, how much was amortized for the first year? If over five years, how much was amortized for the first year?
3. Suppose the book values of the S individual assets are equal to their fair market values except for equipment. The net book value of equipment is $30 million and its fair market value is $70 million. The equipment has a remaining useful life of four years. Straight-line depreciation is used.
   (*a*) Describe how the consolidated balance sheet accounts immediately after the acquisition would differ from those in requirement 1. Be specific as to accounts and amounts.
   (*b*) By how much will consolidated income differ in comparison with the consolidated income that would be reported in requirement 2? Assume amortization of goodwill over a forty-year period.

12–5. **SHORT-TERM INVESTMENT PORTFOLIO.** The Turner Company has a portfolio of short-term investments consisting of common and preferred stocks. The portfolio cost $100 million on January 1. The market values of the portfolio were (in millions): March 31, $100; June 30, $92; September 30, $95; and December 31, $109.

Required:

1. Prepare a tabulation showing the balance sheet presentations and income statement presentations for quarterly reporting purposes.
2. Show the journal entries for quarters 2, 3, and 4.

12–6. **PREPARE CONSOLIDATED FINANCIAL STATEMENTS.** From the following data, prepare a consolidated balance sheet and income statement of the Lumsden Corporation. All data are in millions and pertain to operations for 19X2 or to December 31, 19X2:

Retained income	$198
Accrued income taxes payable	30
Investments in unconsolidated subsidiaries (which are two insurance companies)	60
Cost of goods sold and operating expenses, exclusive of depreciation and amortization	700
Paid-in capital in excess of par	82
Interest expense	25
Subordinated debentures, 11% interest, due December 31, 19X9	100
Outside stockholders' interest in consolidated subsidiaries' net income	15
Goodwill	120
Net sales and other operating revenue	900
Investments in affiliated companies	20
Common stock, 10,000,000 shares, $1 par	10
Depreciation and amortization	20
Accounts payable	200
Equity in earnings of unconsolidated subsidiary	18
Cash	50
First-mortgage bonds, 10% interest, due December 31, 19X8	80
Property, plant, and equipment, net	120
Preferred stock, 2,000,000 shares, $50 par, dividend rate is $5 per share, each share is convertible into five shares of common stock	100
Short-term investments at cost, which approximates current market	40
Income tax expense	70
Accounts receivable, net	100
Outside stockholders' interest in subsidiaries (minority interests)	90
Inventories at average cost	400
Dividends declared and paid on preferred stock	10
Equity in earnings of affiliated companies	2

☐ Understanding Published Financial Reports

12–7. **EQUITY METHOD.** (Alternates are 12–1 and 12–33.) Sears acquired one-third of the voting stock of Whirlpool Company for $25 million cash. In Year 1, Whirlpool had a net income of $21 million and paid cash dividends of $12 million.

Required:

Prepare a tabulation that compares the equity method and the cost method of accounting for Sears's investment in Whirlpool. Show the effects on the balance sheet equation under each method. What is the year-end balance in the Investment in Whirlpool account under the equity method? Under the cost method? Also show the accompanying journal entries.

12–8. **CONSOLIDATED FINANCIAL STATEMENTS.** (Alternate is 12–2.) Consider the purchase of Heublein (maker of Smirnoff vodka and Inglenook wines) by R. J. Reynolds, a major food, beverage, and tobacco company (Del Monte, Canada Dry, Sunkist, and Winston). The purchase price was $1.4 billion. Assume that a 100% interest was acquired.

The balance sheet accounts immediately after the transaction were approximately (in millions):

	R. J. REYNOLDS	HEUBLEIN
Investment in Heublein	$1,400	—
Cash and other assets	6,900	$1,800
Total assets	$8,300	$1,800
Liabilities	$4,400	$ 400
Shareholders' equity	3,900	1,400
Total liab. and stk. eq.	$8,300	$1,800

Required:

1. Using the balance sheet equation format, prepare a tabulation of the consolidated balance sheet accounts immediately after the acquisition.
2. Suppose Heublein had sales of $2,000 million and expenses of $1,900 million for the year. R. J. Reynolds had sales of $9,400 million and expenses of $8,600 million. Prepare income statements for R. J. Reynolds, for Heublein, and for the consolidated company. Assume that neither R. J. Reynolds nor Heublein sold items to the other.
3. Using the balance sheet equation, present the effects of the operations for the year on the accounts of Heublein and R. J. Reynolds. Also tabulate the consolidated balance sheet accounts at the end of the year. Assume that liabilities are unchanged.
4. Suppose Heublein paid a cash dividend of $50 million. What accounts in requirement 3 would be affected and by how much?

12–9. INVESTMENTS IN EQUITY SECURITIES. Barris Industries, a producer of television shows, including "The Gong Show," "The Dating Game," and "The Newlywed Game," holds a 32% interest in Ply*Gem. This investment is recorded on the 1984 balance sheet at $6,542,000, comprising a significant part of the $18,353,000 total assets of Barris.

Ply*Gem's net income for fiscal 1984 was $3,117,000, and Barris's "accumulated equity in undistributed earnings, after consideration of dividends received of $253,000, amounted to $769,000."

Required:

1. How much did Barris Industries pay for its shares of Ply*Gem?
2. Suppose Ply*Gem paid 25% of its 1984 net income in cash dividends:
   (a) By how much did Barris's Investment in Subsidiaries account change during 1984 as a result of its interest in Ply*Gem?
   (b) How much income did Barris recognize from its investment in Ply*Gem in 1984?
3. How should Barris Industries report the investments in which it owned more than 50% interest? Indicate briefly how the following three classes of investments should be accounted for: (a) greater than 50% interest; (b) 20% through 50% interest; and (c) less than 20% interest.

12–10. EQUITY METHOD OF ACCOUNTING FOR UNCONSOLIDATED SUBSIDIARIES. TransWorld Airlines once owned 100% of Hilton International Company. The hotel operations were not consolidated with the airline operations for financial-reporting purposes. The following data have been extracted from an old TWA annual report (in millions):

From statement of income:	
Income from airline operations (detailed)	(5.3)
Income from hotel operations (on one line)	8.8
Net income for the year	$ 3.5
From balance sheet:	
Investments: Beginning equity in Hilton International	$38.2
Ending equity in Hilton International	47.0

Required:

Assume that Hilton paid no dividends. If Hilton had paid cash dividends of $4.1 million, how would the payment have affected TWA net income for the year? How would it have affected the investment balance at the end of the year?

ADDITIONAL ASSIGNMENT MATERIAL

☐ General Coverage

12–11. "The lower-of-cost-or-market rule is applied to investments in short-term securities." Do you agree? Explain.

12–12. Why is *marketable securities* an ill-chosen term to describe short-term investments?

12–13. What is the equity method?

12–14. "The equity method is usually used for long-term investments." Do you think this is appropriate? Explain.

12–15. Contrast the *cost* method with the *equity* method.

12–16. What criterion is used to determine whether a parent-subsidiary relationship exists?

12–17. Why have subsidiaries? Why not have the corporation take the form of a single legal entity?

12–18. What is a minority interest?

12–19. When is there justification for not consolidating subsidiaries in accounting reports?

12–20. "A consolidated balance sheet can contain an asset, Investment in Unconsolidated Subsidiary." Do you agree that this is appropriate? Explain.

12–21. "A company can carry some investments in unconsolidated subsidiaries at cost." Under what circumstances is this a correct statement?

12–22. Distinguish between *control of* a company and *significant influence over* a company.

12–23. "Goodwill is the excess of purchase price over the book values of the individual assets acquired." Do you agree? Explain.

12–24. Why are segment disclosures required?

12–25. What four types of disclosures are required by FASB *Statement No. 14*, "Financial Reporting for Segments of a Business Enterprise"?

12–26. "If a company is acquired by an exchange of stock, pooling-of-interests accounting must be used." Do you agree? Explain.

12–27. "Pooling is an inferior accounting method." What major reason is usually offered for making such a comment?

12–28. "Pooling should be allowed because its elimination would impede business combinations and thus would not be in the national interest." What is the counterargument to this assertion?

12–29. LONG-TERM INVESTMENTS IN BONDS. On December 31, 1986, a company issued $10 million of ten-year, 10% debentures at 104.

Required:

1. Prepare an analysis of transactions for the investors' records (similar to Exhibit 12–1). Key your transactions as follows: (a) issuance, (b) semiannual interest using straight-line amortization of bond premium, and (c) payment of maturity value.
2. Prepare sample journal entries keyed as above.

12–30. BOND DISCOUNT TRANSACTIONS. (Alternate is 12–32.) On December 31, 1986, a company issued $12 million of ten-year, 10% debentures at 97.

Required:

1. Using the balance sheet equation format, prepare an analysis of bond transactions. Assume straight-line amortization. Show entries for the long-term investors regarding (a) issuance, (b) one semiannual interest payment, and (c) payment of maturity value.
2. Show the corresponding journal entries for (a), (b), and (c) above.
3. Show how the bond investment would appear on the balance sheets as of December 31, 1986, 1993, and 1995.

12–31. EARLY EXTINGUISHMENT OF INVESTMENT. On December 31, 1986, a company issued $20 million of ten-year, 12% debentures at 97. On December 31, 1992 (after all interest payments and amortization had been recorded for 1992), the company purchased all the debentures for $19 million. The debentures had been held by a large insurance company throughout their life.

Required:

1. Compute the gain or loss on the sale for the investor.
2. Prepare the appropriate journal entries for the investor.

12–32. BOND PREMIUM TRANSACTIONS. (Alternate is 12–30.) On December 31, 1986, a company issued $12 million of ten-year, 10% debentures at 104.

Required:

1. Using the balance sheet equation format, prepare an analysis of transactions for the long-term investors' records. Key your transactions as follows: (a) issuance, (b) semiannual interest using straight-line amortization of bond premium, and (c) payment of maturity value.
2. Prepare sample journal entries keyed as above.
3. Show how the bond-related accounts would appear on the balance sheets as of December 31, 1986, 1993, and 1995.

12–33. EQUITY METHOD. (Alternates are 12–1 and 12–7.) Company A acquired 30% of the voting stock of Company B for $90 million cash. In Year 1, B had a net income of $50 million and paid cash dividends of $30 million.

Required:

Prepare a tabulation that compares the equity method and the cost method of accounting for A's investment in B. Show the effects on the balance sheet equation under each method. What is the year-end balance in the Investment in B account under the equity method? Under the cost method?

12–34. CONSOLIDATED STATEMENTS. Consider the following for D company as of December 31, 19X4:

	PARENT	SUBSIDIARY*
Assets	$700,000	$200,000
Liabilities to creditors	$200,000	$ 80,000
Stockholders' equity	500,000	120,000
Total liab. and stk. eq.	$700,000	$200,000

* 80% owned by parent.

The $700,000 of assets of the parent includes a $96,000 investment in the subsidiary. The $96,000 includes the parent's pro-rata share of the subsidiary's net income for 19X4. The parent's sales were $990,000 and operating expenses were $922,000. These figures exclude any pro-rata share of the subsidiary's net income. The subsidiary's sales were $700,000 and operating expenses were $660,000. Prepare a consolidated income statement and a consolidated balance sheet. Assume no intercompany sales.

12–35. **CONSOLIDATED FINANCIAL STATEMENTS.** Fresno Company (the parent) owns 100% of the common stock of Grand Company (the subsidiary), which was acquired at the start of 19X3. Their financial statements follow:

	FRESNO (PARENT)	GRAND (SUBSIDIARY)
INCOME STATEMENTS FOR 19X3		
Revenue and "other income"	$40,000,000	$10,000,000
Expenses	38,000,000	9,000,000
Net income	$ 2,000,000	$ 1,000,000
BALANCE SHEETS, DECEMBER 31, 19X3		
Assets	$10,000,000	$ 4,000,000
Liabilities to creditors	$ 4,500,000	$ 1,000,000
Stockholders' equity	5,500,000	3,000,000
Total liabilities and stk. equity	$10,000,000	$ 4,000,000

Required:

1. The subsidiary had enjoyed a fantastically profitable year in 19X3. The parent's income statement had been prepared by showing the parent's claim to the subsidiary's income as a part of the parent's "other income." On the other hand, the parent's balance sheet is really not completed. The $10 million of assets of the parent company includes a $2 million investment in the subsidiary and does *not* include the parent's claim to subsidiary's 19X3 net income.

   Prepare a consolidated income statement and a consolidated balance sheet. Use the balance sheet equation format for the latter.

2. Suppose Fresno Company owned 60% of the Grand Company. Liabilities to creditors are unchanged. The assets of the parent company include a $1.2 million investment in the subsidiary instead of $2.0 million. However, assume the total assets are $10.0 million. The balance sheet is really not completed because the investment account does not reflect the claim to the subsidiary's 19X3 net income. Similarly, the parent's revenue and other income is $39.6 million, not $40.0 million, but expenses remain at $38 million as in requirement (1).

   Prepare a consolidated income statement and a consolidated balance sheet. Use the balance sheet equation format for the latter.

12–36. **DETERMINATION OF GOODWILL.** Refer to the preceding problem, requirement 1. Suppose the investment in the subsidiary in requirement 1 was $2.8 million instead of the $2.0 million as stated. This would mean that the "other assets" would be $7.2 million instead of $8.0 million. Would the consolidated income differ? How? Be as specific as possible. Would the consolidated balance sheet differ? How? Be as specific as possible.

12–37. GOODWILL AND ABNORMAL EARNINGS. As the chief executive of a large drug corporation, you are attempting to determine the maximum price that your company would be willing to pay for a medical instruments company. The latter's net income, which has been $416,000 per year for each of the previous five years, is expected to continue at this steady level.

"Average" companies in the industry have been selling for eight times annual earnings. This medical instruments company, however, has been exceptionally profitable. Its earnings are probably 30% higher than normal.

Required:

1. You have decided on a maximum price of eight times normal earnings plus five times earnings above normal. What is the maximum price?
2. Describe why the maximum price might be adjusted.
3. Describe how the total price is allocated among the individual assets of the consolidated company.

12–38. PURCHASED GOODWILL. Consider the following balance sheets (in millions of dollars):

	COMPANY A	COMPANY B
Cash	750	80
Inventories	360	70
Plant assets, net	360	60
Total assets	1,470	210
Common stock and paid-in surplus	470	120
Retained income	1,000	90
Total liab. and stk. eq.	1,470	210

A paid $300 million to B stockholders for all their stock. The "fair value" of the plant assets of B is $150 million. The fair value of cash and inventories is equal to their carrying amounts. A and B continued to keep separate books.

Required:

1. Prepare a tabulation showing the balance sheets of A, of B, Intercompany Eliminations, and Consolidated immediately after the acquisition.
2. Suppose that only $90 million rather than $150 million of the total purchase price of $300 million could be logically assigned to the plant assets. How would the consolidated accounts be affected?
3. Refer to the facts in requirement 1. Suppose A had paid $324 million rather than $300 million. State how your tabulation in requirement 1 would change.

12–39. AMORTIZATION AND DEPRECIATION. Refer to the preceding problem, requirement 3. Suppose a year passes, and A and B generate individual net incomes of $90 million and $40 million, respectively. The latter is after a deduction by B of $12 million of straight-line depreciation. Compute the consolidated net income if goodwill is amortized (1) over forty years and (2) over ten years. Ignore income taxes.

12–40. ALLOCATING TOTAL PURCHASE PRICE TO ASSETS. Two entities had the following balance sheet accounts as of December 31, 19X1 (in millions):

	GREYMONT	PARADELT		GREYMONT	PARADELT
Cash and receivables	$ 30	$ 22	Current liabilities	$ 50	$ 20
			Common stock	100	10
Inventories	120	3	Retained income	150	90
Plant assets, net	150	95			
Total assets	$300	$120	Total liab. and stk. eq.	$300	$120
Net income for 19X1	$ 19	$ 4			

On January 4, 19X2, these entities combined. Greymont issued $180 million of its shares (at market value) in exchange for all the shares of Paradelt, a motion picture division of a large company. The inventory of films acquired through the combination had been fully amortized on Paradelt's books.

During 19X2, Paradelt received revenue of $21 million from the rental of films from its inventory. Greymont earned $20 million on its other operations (that is, excluding Paradelt) during 19X2. Paradelt broke even on its other operations (that is, excluding the film rental contracts) during 19X2.

Required:

1. Prepare a consolidated balance sheet for the combined company immediately after the combination on a purchase basis. Assume that $80 million of the purchase price was assigned to the inventory of films.
2. Prepare a comparison of Greymont's net income between 19X1 and 19X2 where the cost of the film inventories would be amortized on a straight-line basis over four years. What would be the net income for 19X2 if the $80 million were assigned to goodwill rather than to the inventory of films, and goodwill were amortized over forty years?

12–41. **CONSOLIDATED FINANCIAL STATEMENTS.** The Parent Company owns 80% of the common stock of Company S-1 and 60% of the common stock of Company S-2. The balances as of December 31, 19X8, in the condensed accounts follow (in thousands):

	PARENT	S-1	S-2
Sales	$510,000	$80,000	$210,000
Investment in subsidiaries*	71,000	—	—
Other assets	129,000	90,000	30,000
Liabilities to creditors	100,000	20,000	5,000
Expenses	490,000	90,000	195,000
Stockholders' equity, including current net income	100,000	70,000	25,000

* Carried at equity in subsidiaries.

Required:

Prepare a consolidated balance sheet as of December 31, 19X8, and a consolidated income statement for 19X8.

12–42. **PREPARING INDIVIDUAL STATEMENTS FROM CONSOLIDATED STATEMENTS AND OTHER INFORMATION.** Using the following, prepare *individual* balance sheets (in a balance sheet equation format) and income statements for P and S. P owns 60% of the stock of S and carries its investment at its underlying equity in Company S. All figures are expressed in millions of dollars:

Total minority interest	10
Consolidated assets	141
Outside interest in consolidated	
subsidiaries' net income	2
Consolidated liabilities	55
Consolidated sales	371
Consolidated expenses	360
Company P sales	301
Company P total assets	125

12–43. **EQUITY METHOD, CONSOLIDATION, AND MINORITY INTEREST.** On January 2, 19X6, Gretzky Oil Company purchased 40% of Great Slave Lake Mining Company (GSLM) for $2 million cash. Before the acquisition, Gretzky had assets of $10 million and stockholders' equity of $8 million. GSLM had stockholders' equity of $5 million and liabilities of $1 million, and the fair values of its assets were equal to their book values.

GSLM reported 19X6 net income of $400,000 and declared and paid dividends of $200,000. Assume that Gretzky and GSLM had no sales to one another. Separate income statements for Gretzkv and GSLM were as follows:

	GRETZKY	GSLM
Sales	$12,500,000	$4,400,000
Expenses	11,100,000	4,000,000
Operating income	$ 1,400,000	$ 400,000

Required:

1. Prepare the journal entries for Gretzky Oil to record the acquisition of GSLM. To record its share of GSLM net income and dividends for 19X6.
2. Prepare Gretzky Oil's income statement for 19X6 and balance sheet as of December 31, 19X6.
3. Suppose Gretzky had purchased 60% of GSLM for $3 million. Using the balance sheet equation format, prepare a tabulation of the consolidated balance sheet immediately after acquisition. Prepare the journal entries for both Gretzky and GSLM to record the acquisition. Omit explanations.
4. Prepare a consolidated income statement for 19X6, using the facts of requirement 3.

12–44. **PURCHASE OR POOLING.** Study Appendix 12A. Two companies had the following condensed balance sheet accounts at December 31, 19X1 (in millions):

	P	S
Cash and other assets	$700	$220
Accounts payable, etc.	$300	$100
Stockholders' equity	400	120
Total liab. and stk. eq.	$700	$220

The fair values of the individual S assets are the same as their book values.

Required:

1. Company P issued stock for $210 million cash at the beginning of 19X2 and then immediately used the cash to acquire all the shares of Company S. Prepare a consolidated balance sheet after the acquisition of S by P.

2. Instead of issuing its shares for $210 million cash, suppose P exchanges the same number of its shares for the shares of S. Assume that all conditions of pooling are met. Prepare a consolidated balance sheet.
3. Which set of future consolidated income statements will show higher income, the ones resulting from purchasing or from pooling? Explain.

12–45. **PURCHASE AND POOLING.** Study Appendix 12A. The B Company and the Y Company have the following accounts at December 31, 19X1:

	B	Y
Net assets	$99,000,000	$27,000,000
Stockholders' equity	$99,000,000	$27,000,000
Net income	$10,000,000	$10,000,000

On December 31, 19X1, B combined with Y by issuing stock with a market value of $67 million in exchange for the shares of Y. Assume that the book value and the current value of the individual assets of Y were equal.

Required:

1. Show the balance sheet accounts and net income for 19X1 for the combined companies as they would appear if the combination were accounted for as (a) a $67 million purchase with recognition of purchased goodwill and (b) a pooling.
2. Assume that the same net incomes of $10 million each are generated by the subparts of the combined entity in 19X2 (before considering amortization of goodwill). Show the net income for 19X2 for the combined companies if the business combination had been accounted for as (a) a purchase and (b) a pooling. Any goodwill amortized is to be written off on a straight-line basis over five years.
3. Comment on the possible net incomes reported in 19X1 and 19X2.

12–46. **MORE ON POOLING OF INTERESTS.** Study Appendix 12B. Two companies had the following condensed balance sheet accounts at December 31, 19X1 (in millions of dollars):

	P	S
Cash and other assets	$700	$220
Accounts payable, etc.	$300	$100
Stockholders' equity:		
Common stock:		
4 million shares @ $4 par	16	
12 million shares @ $1 par		12
Additional paid-in capital	84	40
Retained income	300	68
Total stockholders' equity	$400	$120
Total liab. and stk. eq.	$700	$220

The fair values of the individual assets are the same as their book values.

Required:

1. Company P issued 5 million shares of stock @ $40 for $200 million cash at the beginning of 19X2 and then immediately used the cash to acquire all the shares of Company S. Prepare a consolidated balance sheet after the acquisition of S by P.

2. Instead of issuing its shares for $200 million cash, suppose P exchanges the same number of its shares for the shares of S. Assume that all conditions of pooling are met. Prepare a consolidated balance sheet.

3. List the major differences between the two consolidated balance sheets immediately after the acquisition.

4. Suppose the acquisition occurred on December 1, 19X2. All other information is unchanged. How will the income statements differ for 19X2? Respond by listing the major differences. No numerical differences are required.

□ Understanding Published Financial Reports

12–47. CLASSIFICATION ON BALANCE SHEET. The following accounts appeared in an annual report of the Jewel Companies, Inc.:

1. Accumulated earnings—reserved for self-insured losses and general contingencies
2. Long-term indebtedness, due within one year
3. Investments: minority interest in foreign affiliates (at cost)
4. Prepaid expenses and supplies
5. Dividends payable
6. Treasury stock at cost

Required: Indicate in detail in what section of the balance sheet each account should appear.

12–48. MEANING OF ACCOUNT DESCRIPTIONS. The following account descriptions were found in two annual reports:

DuPont: Minority interests in earnings of consolidated subsidiaries, Minority interests in consolidated subsidiaries

Philip Morris: Investments in unconsolidated subsidiaries and affiliates, Equity in net earnings of unconsolidated subsidiaries and affiliates

In your own words, explain what each type of account represents. Indicate whether the item appears on the balance sheet or the income statement.

12–49. MEANING OF ACCOUNT DESCRIPTIONS. The following account descriptions were found in various annual reports:

Montgomery Ward: Net earnings of subsidiaries not consolidated

Tenneco: Equity in undistributed earnings of 50%-owned companies

St. Regis Paper: Equity in net earnings of subsidiaries not consolidated and associated companies

In your own words, explain what each type of account represents. Also indicate whether the item appears on the balance sheet or the income statement.

12–50. CONSOLIDATIONS IN JAPAN. A few years ago, Japan's finance ministry issued a directive requiring the six hundred largest Japanese companies to produce consolidated financial statements. The previous practice had been to use parent-company-only statements. A story in *Business Week* said: "Financial observers hope that the move will help end the tradition-honored Japanese practice of 'window dressing' the parent company financial results by shoving losses onto hapless subsidiaries, whose red ink was seldom revealed. . . . When companies needed to show a bigger profit, they would sell their product to subsidiaries at an inflated price. . . . Or the parent company charged a higher rent to a subsidiary company using its building."

Required: Could a parent company follow the quoted practices and achieve window dressing in its parent-only financial statements if it used the equity method of accounting for its intercorporate investments? The cost method? Explain.

12–51. MARKETABLE SECURITIES. Entertainment Publications, Inc., a leading publisher of discount coupon books, included the following footnote in its annual report:

☐ Marketable securities: Marketable securities are carried at the lower of aggregate cost or market. The cost of marketable securities exceeded their market value by $49,454 and $236,179 at June 30, 1985 and 1984, respectively.

The market value of marketable securities exceeded their cost at June 30, 1983. They are shown as current assets.

Required:

1. Compute the unrealized gain (loss) on marketable securities for the fiscal years ending June 30, 1985 and 1984. Label each as a gain or loss.
2. Suppose that on June 30, 1986, the market value of marketable securities exceeded their cost by $45,000. Compute the loss or gain to be recognized in fiscal 1986.
3. Comment on the differences in accounting for gains versus losses.

12–52. **EFFECT OF TRANSACTIONS UNDER THE EQUITY METHOD.** (J. Patell adapted and updated). Koppers Company Inc. is a diversified manufacturer. Its balance sheet shows (in thousands):

	DECEMBER 31	
	1985	1984
Investments, affiliated companies, at equity	$23,107	$27,842

These affiliated companies were owned by Koppers in various proportions from 20% to 50%. Dividends received from these companies during 1985 totaled $4,590,000.

The income statement for 1985 showed (in thousands):

Equity in earnings (losses) of affiliates	$(438)

Required:

1. Did Koppers purchase more shares in affiliated companies during 1985 or sell off part of its holdings (in aggregate)? Give the dollar amount of the transaction, and label it as a purchase or sale. *Hint*: Use a balance sheet equation or a T-account to aid your analysis.
2. Pretax loss in 1985 was $47,696,000. What would Koppers's 1985 pretax loss have been if it had accounted for its Investment in Affiliated Companies by the cost method?

12–53. **EFFECT OF TRANSACTIONS UNDER THE EQUITY METHOD.** Pioneer Hi-Bred International, producer of seed corn and other farm products, has nineteen foreign subsidiaries that are not consolidated. They are accounted for by the equity method. Pioneer's balance sheet showed:

	AUGUST 31	
	1985	1984
Equity in unconsolidated subsidiaries	$49,809,000	$31,667,000

The last three lines of Pioneer's income statement were:

	1985
Equity in net income of unconsolidated subsidiaries	$ 7,748,000
Net income	$102,592,000
Earnings per share	$3.21

During fiscal 1985 Pioneer invested an additional $10,394,000 in the subsidiaries.

Required:

1. What was the total amount of dividends paid by the subsidiaries to Pioneer in 1985?
2. Some foreign subsidiaries can be accounted for using the cost method instead of the equity method. What would Pioneer's 1985 net income have been if it had accounted for its unconsolidated subsidiaries using the cost method?

12–54. EQUITY METHOD OF ACCOUNTING FOR UNCONSOLIDATED SUBSIDIARIES. Gulf + Western Industries owns 100% of Associates First Capital Corporation (First Capital). The financial statements of First Capital are not consolidated with those of Gulf + Western. The following data are from Gulf + Western's annual report (in millions):

First Capital, Net income, 1985	$144
Gulf + Western, Investment in First Capital, 1984	$743
Gulf + Western, Investment in First Capital, 1985	$826
Gulf + Western, Net income, 1985	$234

Required:

1. Suppose Gulf + Western had not owned First Capital. Compute Gulf + Western's net income for 1985.
2. Compute the amount of dividends paid by First Capital to Gulf + Western in 1985. *Hint*: Examine the T-account for Gulf + Western's investment in First Capital.
3. Suppose Gulf + Western had used the cost method to account for its investment in First Capital. Compute Gulf + Western's net income for 1985. How could Gulf + Western influence its own income if the cost method is used?

12–55. MINORITY INTEREST. The first footnote to the 1985 annual report of Caesars World, Inc., stated:

☐ Principles of Consolidation:
The consolidated financial statements include the accounts of the Company and its subsidiaries, including Caesars New Jersey, Inc., an 86.6%-owned subsidiary.

Assume that Caesars New Jersey is Caesars World's only consolidated subsidiary. Caesars World's 1985 income statement contained the following (in thousands):

Income before minority interest	$33,110
Minority interest in earnings of consolidated subsidiary	1,298
Net income	$31,812

Caesars World's account "Minority interest in consolidated subsidiary" listed $10,-827,000 at the beginning of 1985. Caesars New Jersey paid no dividends in 1985. Assume that Caesars World did not buy or sell any of its interest in Caesars New Jersey during 1985.

Required:

1. Compute the 1985 net income of Caesars New Jersey.
2. What proportion of Caesars World's $31,812,000 net income was contributed by Caesars New Jersey?
3. Compute Caesars World's balance in "Minority interest in consolidated subsidiary" at the end of 1985.
4. Comment on the reason for including a line for minority interest in the income statement and balance sheet of Caesars World.

12–56. PURCHASE AND POOLING. Study Appendix 12B. Suppose LTV Corporation acquired the common stock of Grumman in exchange for its own common stock. For purposes of this question, you are to assume the following:

The acquisition occurred on the last day of the year.
The market price of LTV stock at the time of acquisition was $22.50 per share.
The market price of Grumman stock at the time of acquisition was $45.00 per share.
The market value of Grumman's assets equals the book value of Grumman's assets.
Any purchased goodwill is amortized over forty years on a straight-line basis.

The following data are from the financial reports of LTV and Grumman (in thousands):

	LTV	GRUMMAN
Net income for the year just ending	$127,893	$30,668

LTV shareholders' equity, end of the year:

Common stock (50¢ par value per share)	$ 17,896
Additional capital	501,038
Retained earnings	318,398
	$837,332

Grumman shareholders' equity, end of the year:

Preferred Stock—$1.00 par value, authorized 10,000,000 shares	
Redeemable preferred stock—$2.80 cumulative preferred:	
redemption value $25 per share;	
outstanding 2,000,000 shares	$ 50,000
Non-redeemable preferred stock—$.80 convertible preferred:	
outstanding 14,216 shares	180
Common Stock—$1.00 par value, authorized 20,000,000 shares:	
outstanding 10,030,773 shares	
(net of 8,100 shares held in treasury)	82,607
Retained Earnings	183,594
	$316,381

Required:

Assume that the business combination occurred under each of the following scenarios:

1. LTV issued additional common stock for 100% of Grumman's outstanding common stock. Assume a pooling of interests.
2. LTV issued additional common stock for 80% of Grumman's outstanding common stock. Because at least 90% of the outstanding voting common shares was not acquired, the transaction would have been a purchase.

Compute for each of these two assumptions for a consolidated LTV–Grumman:

a. Retained earnings at the end of the year
b. Additional capital at the end of the year
c. Purchased goodwill at the end of the year
d. Net income for the year just ended

12–57. ACQUISITION OF RCA. On February 13, 1986, the stockholders of RCA approved the sale of 100% of RCA's common stock to General Electric for $66.50 per share. Of the votes cast, over 90% were in favor of the $6.28 billion cash sale, the largest non-oil acquisition to date. Assume that the $6.28 billion price was twice RCA's book value.

Required:

1. Suppose the fair market values of RCA's net assets were $6.28 billion. Prepare the journal entry or entries to record the acquisition on General Electric's books.
2. Suppose the fair market values of RCA's tangible assets were equal to their book values. Fair market value of identifiable intangible assets was $800 million; their useful life was eight years. None of the intangible assets appeared on RCA's balance sheet. Prepare the journal entry or entries to record the acquisition on General Electric's books.
3. Refer to requirement 2. Assume that the acquisition took place on January 2, 1986. Prepare the December 31, 1986, journal entry or entries to amortize the goodwill and other intangible assets. Assume that goodwill is amortized as slowly as possible.
4. Assume that the acquisition occurred on July 1, 1986, and that 1986 net income for RCA was $500 million. RCA's net income was earned at a constant rate per unit of time during 1986. How much of that net income would appear in General Electric's consolidated net income for the year ended December 31, 1986?

12–58. **SEGMENT DISCLOSURES.** Rockwell International, a multi-industry advanced technology company, disclosed the business segment data in Exhibit 12–8. The only customer of the company that accounted for 10% or more of consolidated sales is the United States Government and its agencies. Such sales by business segment are as follows:

Sales to United States Government

	1985	1984
Aerospace	$5,281	$4,280
Electronics	1,565	1,361
Other business segments	143	202
Total	$6,989	$5,843

Required:

1. Compute the percentage of Rockwell's 1984 and 1985 sales in each industry segment. Point out any significant changes from 1984 to 1985.
2. Compute the percentage of capital expenditures in each industry segment for 1985. In what industry segment did most investment take place?
3. Assume that none of Rockwell's foreign operations had any sales in the United States. What percentage of Rockwell's total 1985 sales were to customers outside the United States? Did foreign sales increase or decrease from 1984 to 1985 in total dollars? In percentage of total sales?
4. Does Rockwell rely heavily on sales to a single customer? What percentage of sales are to the largest customer? What industry segment depends most heavily on sales to a single customer?

EXHIBIT 12-8

ROCKWELL INTERNATIONAL
Business Segment Data
(in millions)

	SALES		EARNINGS		IDENTIFIABLE ASSETS		CAPITAL EXPENDITURES		PROVISION FOR DEPRECIATION AND AMORTIZATION	
	1985	1984	1985	1984	1985	1984	1985	1984	1985	1984
Aerospace	$ 5,309	$4,332	$ 493.8	$397.7	$1,499	$1,331	$163.6	$198.9	$101.9	$ 84.0
Electronics	3,412	2,387	354.2	220.2	3,457	1,419	268.2	199.2	212.8	99.8
Automotive	1,722	1,758	225.9	214.8	963	1,006	67.0	69.9	67.2	64.9
General Industries	895	845	104.3	86.6	572	515	46.8	35.5	29.2	28.8
Total	$11,338	$9,322	$1,178.2	$919.3	$6,491	$4,271	$545.6	$503.5	$411.1	$277.5

Sales, Operating Earnings, and Assets, by Geographic Area

Geographic Area	SALES		OPERATING EARNINGS		IDENTIFIABLE ASSETS	
	1985	1984	1985	1984	1985	1984
United States	$10,381	$8,521	$1,055.9	$845.1	$5,722	$3,710
Europe	525	423	47.8	22.4	482	354
Canada	330	257	61.4	41.9	187	110
Other	102	121	13.1	9.9	100	97
Total	$11,338	$9,322	$1,178.2	$919.3	$6,491	$4,271

Note: United States sales include export sales of $445 million in 1985 and $412 million in 1984.

Chapter 13

INCOME TAXES, INCLUDING INTERPERIOD ALLOCATION

LEARNING OBJECTIVES

After studying this chapter, you should be able to

1. Distinguish tax credits from tax deductions and contrast the financial statement effects of the two methods of accounting for tax credits associated with investments in business property: flow-through and deferral

2. Demonstrate how the accounting for deferred income taxes affects the balance sheet and the measurement of net income

3. Explain why interperiod tax allocation has become generally accepted accounting

4. Distinguish between timing differences and permanent differences in reporting revenues and expenses to stockholders and tax authorities (Appendix 13A)

5. Explain how operating losses are carried back and forward (Appendix 13A)

6. Compare and explain the major accounting and income tax distinctions between corporations, proprietorships, and partnerships (Appendix 13B)

The income tax is pervasive. Hence it has been discussed frequently in conjunction with various topics in preceding chapters. Obviously, an introductory book on financial accounting can only touch on some aspects of this huge, complex subject. Still, the subject of income taxes provides an excellent opportunity for reviewing financial statements as a whole.

Income tax returns filed with the Internal Revenue Service frequently differ from financial reports to shareholders and others. This chapter focuses on why these differences arise and how they are reconciled. The study of these differences accomplishes at least two important purposes. First, knowledge is gained about how to account for a prominent expense, income taxes. Second, understanding is enriched about fundamental ideas underlying the accrual accounting method in its entirety.

There are also two chapter appendixes. Appendix 13A explores some income tax topics in more depth, including timing differences, permanent differences, and operating losses. Appendix 13B describes differences between forms of business organization, emphasizing income tax aspects.

AN OVERVIEW OF INCOME TAXES

Throughout your study, remember that the income tax laws are designed as an arm of the fiscal policies of a government. For example, special tax incentives are created or changed to spur or discourage business investments and employment. Thus the taxable income reported on the income tax form may not necessarily coincide with the pretax income reported to shareholders and others.

Also remember that intelligent managers try to pay the least amount of income taxes at the latest possible time permitted within the law. This "least-latest" strategy often leads to situations where the accounting allowed in the income tax returns may not be acceptable in reports to others. For example, tax laws in some countries permit the entire cost of equipment to be deducted as an expense during the year of acquisition. However, for shareholder reporting, the accrual accounting method is required, which means that the equipment cost must be matched with the revenues generated by its use. This requires the equipment to be depreciated over its useful life.

The bulk of federal government revenue comes from income taxes collected from two types of taxpayers: individuals and corporations. In addition, all taxpayers are subject to a variety of other taxes, including state income taxes, social security taxes (which are based on income), and local property taxes. We concentrate here on the federal income taxes of corporations, which pay graduated rates up to 34% of their pretax income. However, to simplify our illustrations, we assume that a flat (nongraduated) tax rate applies.

Income tax rates obviously affect a corporation's total tax bill. Moreover, laws affect a company's taxes by (a) permitting *deductions* of expenses and (b) granting *tax credits*.

Deductible items (or *tax deductions*) are expenses that can be subtracted from revenues to determine taxable income. Income taxes are determined by multiplying taxable income by the applicable tax rate. Most company expenses are *deductible*, although a few, such as amortization of goodwill, are not. Some expenses, such as business meals, are only partially deductible.

Tax laws also specify *when* an item should be deducted. For example, everyone agrees that the cost of equipment is deductible. However, there is considerable controversy over *when* the cost should be deducted. Companies prefer to have the deduction (and the related tax saving) sooner; the Internal Revenue Service (IRS) prefers to delay the deduction to speed up the collection of taxes.

Tax credits differ from deductible items; **tax credits** are direct reductions of the income tax itself. For instance, at a 40% tax rate, the tax effect of a $15,000 deductible expense would be a tax savings of only .40 × $15,000 = $6,000. In contrast, the tax effect of a $15,000 tax credit would be a tax savings of the full $15,000. The tax reduction is called a credit because in this illustration the U.S. government has the following financial position:

Determination of a tax before a tax credit:			
	Accounts receivable	40,000	
	Revenue from income taxes		40,000
If there is also a tax credit, it is "credited" to the taxpayer's account:			
	Revenue from income taxes	15,000	
	Accounts receivable		15,000

Thus the credit is issued by the federal government to reduce the accounts receivable from the taxpayer.

Tax credits have many forms, amounts, and labels. The government institutes new credits and removes old ones as fiscal and social policy objectives change. Tax credits are permanent reductions in taxes. They are not offset by higher taxes at a later date.

The most significant tax credit for many years was the *investment tax credit* (ITC). Since 1962, the ITC has been enacted, repealed, enacted, and repealed. The Internal Revenue Code of 1986 eliminated the ITC. However, when investment needs to be stimulated, the ITC may again be enacted.

The ITC allowed a tax credit equal to a percentage of the cost of business property (notably machinery and equipment) when it was placed in service. The percentage and other details were changed periodically. For many years, investments generated a tax credit equal to 10% of the cost of the depreciable assets. In addition, the total cost of the assets was *deductible* as depreciation expense. For example, when AT&T invested $1 million in switching equipment in a year with a 10% ITC, its taxes were decreased immediately by a tax credit of $100,000. Moreover, the full $1 million was deductible across the years as depreciation expense. (In some years, the tax law required the depreciable amount to be slightly reduced if the full investment tax credit was taken.)

Illustration of Financial Reporting Methods

The cost of equipment that generated an ITC must be spread over future years as depreciation expense. The tax saving from the associated ITC is received in the year the investment is made. Should the financial statements for investors recognize the entire tax savings from such a tax credit as an increase in net income for the year of purchase (the **flow-through method**)? Or should the tax savings be spread over the useful life of the asset (**deferral method**)? What do you think? Both methods have been permitted, but controversy has raged on this issue for many years. In many industries (such as airlines and others that have heavy capital expenditures), the method chosen for the investment tax credit has had a material effect on reported net income. Keep in mind that the controversy concerns reports to stockholders, not reports to the income tax authorities.

To see the essence of the controversy regarding tax credits associated with investments in business property, consider the following problem:

☐ A company begins business on January 1, 19X1, with $500,000 cash raised by an issue of common stock. All of its transactions throughout 19X1 were for cash. On December 31, it had pretax income of $100,000. The income tax rate is 40%. No income taxes will be due before early 19X2. An investment in equipment of $150,000 cash was made on December 31, 19X1. The equipment has a ten-year life and an expected residual value of zero.

Required:

1. Prepare an analysis of transactions using the A = L + SE format. Show the (a) effects of formation of the company, (b) effects of operating income on cash and retained income, (c) effects of acquisition of equipment, and (d) computation and effects of income taxes. Show the ending balances in all accounts, December 31, 19X1.
2. Suppose the company is eligible for a $15,000 tax credit because of its acquisition of equipment. Prepare an analysis of the flow-through effects. Label as *e1*. Also prepare an analysis of the deferral effects. Label as *e2*.

Try to prepare your own solution before proceeding.

Exhibit 13–1 contains the complete analysis of transactions. Concentrate on items *a* through *d*. Note that the reporting to stockholders would show an income tax liability of $40,000 and an income tax expense of $40,000. If there is no tax credit available, the matter ends here. That is, there is basically nothing new in the analysis of transactions *a* through *d*.

EXHIBIT 13–1

Analysis of Transactions
(in thousands of dollars)

	A		=	L	+	SE	
				Income Tax	Deferred Tax	Paid-in	Retained
	Cash	Equipment		Payable	Credit	Capital	Income
a. Formation	+500		=			+500	
b. Operations	+100		=				+100
c. Acquisition of equipment	−150	+150	=				
d. Income taxes			=	+40			− 40
Bal. Dec. 31, 19X1	+450	+150	=	+40		+500	+ 60
e1. Flow-through			=	−15			+ 15
Bal. Dec. 31, 19X1, after e1	+450	+150	=	+25		+500	+ 75
e2. Deferral			=	−15	+15		
Bal. Dec. 31, 19X1, after e2 rather than e1	+450	+150	=	+25	+15	+500	+ 60

☐ **Flow-Through**

The flow-through method is shown as *e1* in Exhibit 13–1. The journal entries would be:

d. Income tax expense	40,000	
Income tax payable		40,000
e1. Income tax payable	15,000	
Income tax expense		15,000

The proponents of the flow-through method claim that the entire amount of the tax credit is a selective reduction of income tax expense in the year in which taxes otherwise payable are reduced by the credit. It is not a determinant of cost of acquisition or use of the related assets. The majority of companies use this method.

☐ **Deferral**

The deferral method is shown as *e2* in Exhibit 13–1. The journal entries would be:

d. Income tax expense	40,000	
Income tax payable		40,000
e2. Income tax payable	15,000	
Deferred tax credits		15,000

The deferral account would appear in the noncurrent liability section of the balance sheet, even though the label "liability" may not be associated therewith. That is, the subtotal may be labeled as "total liabilities and deferred credits" instead of merely "total liabilities."

Supporters of the deferral method are particularly critical of the idea that the amount spent for depreciable assets in a given year can directly affect net income; within constraints, the more the company *buys*, the more it earns. Such an implication conflicts with the generally accepted concept that net income is earned only by *using* assets to produce revenue from customers. The deferral method prevents current net income from being so significantly affected by unrelated management actions in buying depreciable assets.

Suppose 19X2 was a repetition of 19X1 in the sense that pretax income was again $100,000. However, no additional equipment is acquired. The journal entries for the deferral method would be:

d. Income tax expense	40,000	
Income tax payable		40,000
To recognize income tax owed to government.		
e2. Deferred tax credits	1,500	
Income tax expense		1,500
Amortization for 19X2 of tax credits, $15,000 ÷ 10 years.		

The amortization of the deferral spreads the $15,000 tax credit over the ten years of useful life of the related equipment. (Remember that the equipment was acquired at the *end* of 19X1.) The effect will be to reduce income tax expense (by crediting the Income Tax Expense account) and hence increase reported net income by $1,500 for each of ten years. Note that flow-through companies report considerably higher net income than deferral companies in the year a tax credit is granted. In contrast, deferral companies report slightly higher net income each year of the deferral period.

The advocates of deferral maintain that the amount of the tax credit is associated primarily with the use of the property qualifying for the credit. Deferral of the credit and its subsequent amortization associates the credit with the useful life of the related property. This matching is consistent with the objectives of income measurement on the accrual basis because it spreads a purchase discount over the useful life of the asset purchased.

ACCELERATED COST RECOVERY SYSTEM (ACRS)

Depreciation for tax purposes is generally based on the **Accelerated Cost Recovery System (ACRS)**. Depreciation deductions depend on arbitrary "recovery" periods instead of useful lives. As Exhibit 13–2 shows, property is

EXHIBIT 13-2

Examples of Classifications in Accelerated Cost Recovery System (ACRS)

CLASS	EXAMPLES OF TYPES OF ASSETS
3-year	Special tools for several specific industries; tractor units for over-the-road.
5-year	Automobiles; trucks; research equipment; computers; airplanes; machinery and equipment in selected industries.
7-year	Office furniture; railroad cars; railroad track; machinery and equipment in a majority of industries.
10-year	Water transportation equipment (vessels, tugs, barges); machinery and equipment in selected industries.
15-year	Most land improvements; machinery and equipment in selected industries.
20-year	Farm buildings, railroad structures, telephone and electricity distribution (poles, cables, etc.); most electricity generation equipment.
27.5-year	Residential rental property.
31.5-year	Most nonresidential real property.

classified by the number of years over which the acquisition cost is to be recovered through deductions. Estimates of future residual values are not required under ACRS. The entire acquisition cost is expensed over the recovery period.

The 1986 Internal Revenue Code specifies that three-, five-, seven-, and ten-year assets be depreciated using a double-declining-balance method (which is described on pages 379–381), switching to straight-line at a time that maximizes the depreciation allowance. A 150%-declining-balance method applies to fifteen- and twenty-year assets, and the straight-line method to 27.5- and 31.5-year assets. (A company can choose to use straight-line depreciation rather than the appropriate declining-balance method for any asset.)

The *half-year convention* should be used with the declining-balance methods. This calls for a half year of depreciation in the year an asset is acquired, regardless of the month of purchase. There is also a half year of depreciation in the year an asset is sold or retired from service.

The ACRS depreciation schedules for three-, five-, and seven-year assets are shown in Exhibit 13–3. For example, if an asset in the five-year property class is acquired any time in 1987 at a cost of $1,000, the 1987 depreciation deduction would be $200 (or 20% × $1,000). In 1988 the deduction would be 32% × $1,000, or $320. Notice that the schedule for a five-year asset extends into a sixth year because of the half-year convention.

The ACRS method provides *accelerated* depreciation by (a) using depreciation periods shorter than useful lives, and (b) assigning higher depreciation percentages in the earlier years. Compare ACRS to straight-line and sum-of-the-year's-digits schedules. Suppose General Motors bought a special tool for the manufacture of Buicks. The acquisition cost was $14,000, and the

EXHIBIT 13–3

Examples of ACRS Depreciation Percentages*

YEAR	3-YEAR PROPERTY	5-YEAR PROPERTY	7-YEAR PROPERTY
1	33%	20%	14%
2	45	32	24
3	15	19	18
4	7	12	13
5		12	9
6		5	9
7			9
8			4

* Rounded. For simplicity, these rounded percentages will be used in the examples in this chapter. Underlying rates are from *Highlights of the Tax Reform Act of 1986,* published by Prentice-Hall, Inc.

useful life was seven years. This is a three-year asset for ACRS purposes. Depreciation under the three methods is the following:

YEAR	STRAIGHT-LINE	SUM-OF-THE-YEARS'-DIGITS	ACRS*
1	$ 2,000	$ 3,500	$ 4,620
2	2,000	3,000	6,300
3	2,000	2,500	2,100
4	2,000	2,000	980
5	2,000	1,500	
6	2,000	1,000	
7	2,000	500	
Total	$14,000	$14,000	$14,000

* Uses the rounded percentages as listed in Exhibit 13–3; 33% × $14,000 = $4,620, 45% × 14,000 = $6,300, etc.

In sum, for many assets, ACRS accelerates depreciation even faster than the sum-of-the-years'-digits method. Why? Because the recovery periods are shorter than useful lives.

DEFERRED FEDERAL INCOME TAXES

Most corporations try to take advantage of all the ways offered by governments to minimize immediate income tax disbursements. Hence ACRS depreciation methods are employed for reporting to the income tax authorities and straight-line depreciation for reporting to others. This section explores the meaning of the "deferred" income taxes that are engendered by using different measures of depreciation (and several other items) for tax purposes and other purposes.

□ A Matter of Timing

Accelerated methods of depreciation allow companies an opportunity to postpone disbursements for income taxes. Income tax payments are lower in the early years of the useful life of the asset and higher in the later years than they would be if straight-line depreciation were used for both tax and stock holder-reporting purposes.

Timing differences can be defined as measures of the income tax effects of transactions that affect the computation of pretax income reported to shareholders either earlier or later than they affect taxable income reported to the income tax authorities. These timing differences have spurred great controversy regarding how income should be measured for stockholder-reporting purposes. An example should clarify the issues. Suppose B Company is begun on January 1, 19X1, with initial paid-in capital of $200 million cash. On January 2, 19X1, the company purchases a three-year ACRS asset for $100 million cash. The estimated useful life is five years, and the estimated residual value is zero. Although ACRS depreciation is used for tax reporting, the straight-line method is used for shareholder-reporting purposes. Prospective annual income before depreciation and income taxes is $45 million. The income tax rate is 60%. Assume that all taxes are paid early in the next year after the income is earned.

Exhibit 13–4 analyzes these transactions as they would be prepared *for shareholder reporting*. Study the exhibit, but stop momentarily after transaction *c*. Consider the presentation on the *income tax return*:[1]

Income before depreciation	$45,000,000
ACRS depreciation, 33% × $100,000,000	33,000,000
Taxable income	$12,000,000
Income tax to be paid:	
.60 × $12,000,000, or	$ 7,200,000

If straight-line depreciation is used for shareholder-reporting purposes, should *income tax expense* be based on ACRS cost recovery or straight-line depreciation? Entry *e1* in Exhibit 13–4 shows what would happen if no deferral occurred. Many accountants believe that the income tax expense on the income statement to shareholders should be the actual amount paid or payable to

---

[1] Exhibits 13–4, 13–5, and 13–6 use ACRS percentages in effect for 1987. If the percentages change for later years, the specific numbers will be different but the general relationships will not.

EXHIBIT 13–4

Analysis of Transactions
for Shareholder Reporting
(in millions of dollars)

	Cash	Equipment	Income Tax Payable	Deferred Income Taxes	Paid-in Capital	Retained Income
	A	=	L	+	SE	
a. Formation	+200		=		+200	
b. Acquisition of equipment	−100	+100	=			
c. Income before depreciation and taxes	+ 45		=			+45
d. Straight-line depreciation		− 20	=			−20
e1. Income tax expense—no deferral			= +7.2			− 7.2
Bal. Dec. 31, 19X1, after e1	+145	+ 80	= +7.2		+200	+17.8
e2. Income tax expense—deferral			= +7.2	+7.8		−15
Bal. Dec. 31, 19X1, after e2						
rather than e1	+145	+ 80	= +7.2	+7.8	+200	+10

Notes:

e1. The 7.2 represents income taxes payable as calculated when using ACRS on the income tax return: .60 × 12 taxable income = 7.2.

e2. The 15 represents the income tax that would be payable if straight-line depreciation had been used on the income tax return. Taxable income would be 45 − 20 = 25; income tax expense would be .60 × 25 = 15. The deferred income tax is 15 − 7.2 = 7.8.

the government for the year in question—no more, no less. Of course, this approach would show reported net income of $17.8 million, a happy combination based on *straight-line* depreciation and on tax payments geared to ACRS cost recovery. On the other hand, entry e2 in Exhibit 13–4 shows the effects if deferral is recognized. Note that the income tax expense is now $15 million and net income is only $10 million. The $7.8 million balance in Deferred Income Taxes at the end of the first year represents extra taxes that would have to be paid if straight-line depreciation were used in the tax returns as opposed to ACRS cost recovery.

Another summary of this illustration appears in Exhibit 13–5. The first column of the exhibit shows reporting.of income to the government, which has already been discussed. The second column shows how reporting to shareholders would appear if no deferral were recognized. However, accountants have banned the no-deferral method in favor of the deferral method shown in entry e2 in Exhibit 13–4 and in the third column of Exhibit 13–5.

☐ **Interperiod Tax Allocation**

Before considering the relative merits of deferral and no deferral, study all parts of Exhibit 13–6. This exhibit provides a comparison for five years. The first part is a tabulation of the reports made to the IRS on income tax returns. The second part shows reports made to shareholders. It displays, in turn,

EXHIBIT 13–5

Comparison of Reporting of Income

	YEAR 1* REPORTING		
	To Income Tax Authorities	No Deferral (Banned)	Deferral (Required)
Income before depreciation and income taxes	$45,000,000	$45,000,000	$45,000,000
Depreciation:			
ACRS cost recovery	33,000,000		
Straight-line		20,000,000	20,000,000
Pretax income	$12,000,000	$25,000,000	$25,000,000
Income tax expense:			
Paid or payable almost immediately	$ 7,200,000	$ 7,200,000	$ 7,200,000
Deferred	—	—	7,800,000†
Total income tax expense	$ 7,200,000	$ 7,200,000	$15,000,000‡
Net income	$ 4,800,000	$17,800,000	$10,000,000

* These comparisons are also displayed as part of Exhibit 13–6.

† The $7,800,000 deferred tax is the difference between the $15,000,000 total income tax expense and the $7,200,000 tax paid or payable almost immediately.

‡ Total income tax expense is 60% of the $25,000,000 income before income taxes, or $15,000,000.

for five years (a) the banned no-deferral method and (b) the required deferral method.

Note in all the tabulations how the cumulative income tax paid is $75 million and the cumulative net income is $50 million. Furthermore, tabulations 1 and 2a clearly demonstrate how the favorable effect of lower taxes and higher net income in earlier years is offset by higher taxes and lower net income in later years. The Accounting Principles Board emphasized that timing differences originate in one period and reverse, or "turn around," in one or more subsequent periods, as Exhibit 13–6 demonstrates.

As tabulation 2b in Exhibit 13–6 shows, the Accounting Principles Board favored *deferral*, which in this context is more frequently called **interperiod tax allocation**, or simply **tax allocation**. After heated debate, the board concluded in favor of this interperiod allocation of income taxes, "both in the manner in which tax effects are initially recognized and in the manner in which deferred taxes are amortized in future periods." Method 2b demonstrates that the effect for a particular asset would be to regard any reported income as if it were subject to the full current tax rate even though a more advantageous depreciation method were used for tax purposes. As Exhibit 13–6 shows, this results in a *smoothing effect* on income in these particular circumstances when the year-by-year effects are viewed over the five-year span.

The deferred income tax is a deferred credit in the sense that it is intended to offset the income tax expense in future years. Years 4 and 5 show how the credit is used to bring the reported tax expense down to a lower amount. More fundamentally, the deferred tax is a *liability* (rather than a part of stockholders' equity) that should be recognized under the accrual basis of

EXHIBIT 13–6

Comparison of Alternative Reporting Practices for Depreciation and Income Taxes
Facts: Purchase asset for $100 million; five-year life; 60% tax rate. Company uses ACRS for tax purposes but straight-line depreciation for financial reporting purposes.

1. REPORTING ON INCOME TAX RETURNS

YEAR	INCOME BEFORE DEPRECIATION AND TAXES	ACRS COST RECOVERY	PRETAX INCOME	INCOME TAX PAID*	NET INCOME
1	$ 45	.33 × $100 = $ 33	$ 12	$ 7.2	$ 4.8
2	45	.45 × $100 = 45	0	0.0	0.0
3	45	.15 × $100 = 15	30	18.0	12.0
4	45	.07 × $100 = 7	38	22.8	15.2
5	45		45	27.0	18.0
Cumulative	$225	$100	$125	$75.0	$50.0

2. REPORTING TO STOCKHOLDERS

a. Straight-Line Depreciation and No Tax Deferral (Banned)

YEAR	INCOME BEFORE DEPRECIATION AND TAXES	STRAIGHT-LINE DEPRE-CIATION	PRETAX INCOME	INCOME TAX EXPENSE	NET INCOME	BALANCE SHEET EFFECT: DEFERRED INCOME TAXES
1	$ 45	$ 20	$ 25	$ 7.2	$17.8	—
2	45	20	25	0.0	25.0	—
3	45	20	25	18.0	7.0	—
4	45	20	25	22.8	2.2	—
5	45	20	25	27.0	−2.0	—
Cumulative	$225	$100	$125	$75.0	$50.0	

b. Straight-Line Depreciation and Tax Deferral (Required)

YEAR	INCOME BEFORE DEPRECIATION AND TAXES	STRAIGHT-LINE DEPRE-CIATION	PRETAX INCOME	INCOME TAX EXPENSE Tax Paid	INCOME TAX EXPENSE Tax Deferred	INCOME TAX EXPENSE Total Tax Expense	NET INCOME	BALANCE SHEET EFFECT: DEFERRED INCOME TAXES†
1	$ 45	$ 20	$ 25	$ 7.2	$ 7.8	$15	$10	$ 7.8
2	45	20	25	0.0	15.0	15	10	22.8
3	45	20	25	18.0	−3.0	15	10	19.8
4	45	20	25	22.8	−7.8	15	10	12.0
5	45	20	25	27.0	−12.0	15	10	0
Cumulative	$225	$100	$125	$75.0	$ 0	$75	$50	—

* Or payable on that year's income.

† This would ordinarily appear in the liability section of the balance sheet as a separate item just above the stockholders' equity section. Although it clarifies thinking to consider this item as a liability, in practice the word *payable* usually is not added to the term *deferred income taxes*.

INCOME TAXES, INCLUDING INTERPERIOD ALLOCATION

accounting.[2] Proponents of allocation maintain that failure to allocate is tantamount to retrogressing to a cash basis of accounting. Therefore deferred income taxes should be recognized as a legitimate claim on the assets of the enterprise; the deferral is an obligation to the government that arises because the firm elects to postpone some income tax payments from the present to some future date.

Sample journal entries follow:

Year 1	Income tax expense	15,000,000	
	Deferred income taxes (liability)		7,800,000
	Income taxes payable (or cash)		7,200,000
Year 5	Income tax expense	15,000,000	
	Deferred income taxes	12,000,000	
	Income taxes payable (or cash)		27,000,000

☐ Growth of Deferred Taxes

For growing companies, deferred income tax accounts are likely to accumulate to enormous amounts that will never diminish unless the company discontinues the replacement of old facilities used in its operations. For example, in Exhibit 13–6, if the company spent $100 million each year for more plant assets, the additional deferrals in each of these years would more than offset the decline in deferrals in Years 4 and 5 associated with the original $100 million outlay. Exhibit 13–7 summarizes this point.

The objectors to the deferral method point out that tax-allocation procedures should not apply to the recurring differences between taxable income and pretax accounting income in Exhibit 13–7 if there is a relatively stable or growing investment in depreciable assets. This results in an indefinite postponement of the additional tax, a mounting deferred taxes account that may never be reduced, and a consequent understatement of net income. Note from Year 6 in Exhibit 13–7 that the deferred income taxes will never decline unless the company fails to maintain its $100 million annual expenditure each year.

The proponents of deferral reject the growing-firm argument as fallacious. The ever-increasing aggregate amount of deferred income taxes is an example of a typical characteristic of growing companies that is also reflected in many other accounts. For example, accounts payable and liabilities for product warranties may also grow, but that is not justification for assuming that liabilities for these obligations are unnecessary.

Whatever your reactions to these conflicting arguments, the board's accounting *requirements* are clear. Income tax expense on the income statement for shareholders is based on the revenue and expenses on that statement, not those on the tax statement. Therefore income tax expense seldom equals

---

[2] Many observers who maintain that deferred taxes are liabilities rightly state that the deferral should be measured by estimating the discounted present value of future payments. See Chapter 10, pages 447–449, for an explanation of discounted present value.

EXHIBIT 13-7

Analysis of Growing Firm and Deferred Income Taxes

Facts: Same as in Exhibit 13–6 except that $100 million is spent each year for additional assets and income increases $45 million each year until leveling off in Year 6. In Year 6, the $100 million represents a replacement of the asset originally purchased in Year 1.

REPORTING FOR TAX PURPOSES

YEAR	INCOME BEFORE DEPRECIATION AND TAXES	ACRS COST RECOVERY	PRETAX INCOME	INCOME TAX PAID	NET INCOME
1	$ 45	$33	$ 12	$ 7.2	$ 4.8
2	90	45 + 33 = 78	12	7.2	4.8
3	135	15 + 45 + 33 = 93	42	25.2	16.8
4	180	7 + 15 + 45 + 33 = 100	80	48.0	32.0
5	225	7 + 15 + 45 + 33 = 100	125	75.0	50.0
6	225	7 + 15 + 45 + 33 = 100	125	75.0	50.0

REPORTING TO STOCKHOLDERS
Straight-Line Depreciation and Tax Allocation

YEAR	INCOME BEFORE DEPRECIATION AND TAXES	STRAIGHT-LINE DEPRECIATION	PRETAX INCOME	INCOME TAX EXPENSE Tax Paid	INCOME TAX EXPENSE Tax Deferred	INCOME TAX EXPENSE Total Tax Expense	NET INCOME	BALANCE SHEET EFFECT: DEFERRED INCOME TAXES
1	$ 45	$ 20	$ 25	$ 7.2	$ 7.8	$15	$10	$ 7.8
2	90	40	50	7.2	22.8	30	20	30.6
3	135	60	75	25.2	19.8	45	30	50.4
4	180	80	100	48.0	12.0	60	40	62.4
5	225	100	125	75.0	—	75	50	62.4
6	225	100	125	75.0	—	75	50	62.4

the taxes payable to the government for any given period. Deferred taxes are found on the balance sheets of nearly every company.

WHY BOTHER WITH INTERPERIOD TAX ALLOCATION?

☐ Effects on Assets

Many students, managers, and accountants are bewildered by the subject of deferred income taxes. Their general attitude can be described as a "cash-basis" attitude: "Why get complicated? Why don't we simply show as income tax expense and as income tax liability the actual amount payable in cash as computed on the company's income tax return?" The accounting regulators have rejected the cash-basis approach in favor of an "accrual-basis" approach. An extreme illustration may clarify why the concept of deferred income taxes is generally accepted. Until recently, in England companies were permitted to buy specified equipment and deduct its entire cost on their current income tax returns. Suppose an English company paid £10 million for equipment in early 19X7. (The British unit of currency is the pound, £.) The equipment has an expected useful life of ten years and no residual value. Compare the approaches if pretax income were £30 million before considering depreciation effects. Assume that the income tax rate is 60%:

| | STOCKHOLDER REPORTING | |
	"Cash Basis"	"Accrual Basis"
(In millions of British pounds)		
Income accounts for 19X7		
Pretax income before depreciation	30.0	30.0
Depreciation	10.0	1.0*
Pretax income	20.0	29.0
Income tax expense:		
Current portion	12.0	12.0
Deferred portion	—	5.4
Total income tax expense	12.0	17.4†
Net income	8.0	11.6
Balance sheet accounts at end of 19X7		
Assets:		
Equipment, net	0	9.0
Liabilities:		
Income tax payable	12.0	12.0
Deferred income taxes	—	5.4
Retained income (increase due to		
net income)	8.0	11.6

* Straight-line depreciation = £10 million ÷ 10 years = £1 million per year.
† .60 × 29 million = 17.4 million; 17.4 million less 12 million currently payable is the 5.4 million deferred portion.

Those who favor deferral essentially maintain that the underlying economic impact of taxes is measured more accurately via interperiod tax allocation. Unless tax allocation occurs, income, assets, and liabilities will be misstated. The most obvious faulty measurement is to show zero value for a one-year-old asset with a remaining useful life of nine years.

☐ Installment Method

Timing differences are not confined to depreciation. For example, the Internal Revenue Service permits retailers, such as J. C. Penney, to use the *installment method* rather than the ordinary accrual basis for some installment sales.[3] The **installment method** records the revenue and associated costs for an installment sale in the years during which the selling price is collected in cash, not necessarily during the year of sale. In contrast, reports to shareholders must be on the accrual basis. To illustrate, suppose a refrigerator is sold for $1,200 on January 2, 19X1. There is no cash down payment. Instead the buyer must pay $50 at the end of January and at the end of each month until twenty-four payments have been made. For our purposes, ignore interest

[3] The Internal Revenue Code of 1986 placed limits on the use of the installment method. However, many companies will be able to continue using the method for tax reporting for at least some of their installment sales.

and carrying charges. Assume that the gross margin rate is 40% and the income tax rate is 50%.

Compare the effects on income of the two bases:

	19X1	19X2
For shareholder reporting (accrual basis):		
Sales revenue	$1,200	—
Cost of goods sold	720	—
Gross margin @ 40% of revenue	$ 480	—
Effect on income tax expense @ 50%	$ 240	—
For income tax reporting (installment method):		
Revenue collected	$ 600	$600
Gross margin subject to income tax		
@ 40% of revenue	$ 240	$240
Effect on income tax outlay @ 50%	$ 120	$120

The pertinent journal entries for 19X1 and 19X2 (without explanations) would be:

19X1	Installment accounts receivable	1,200	
	Sales revenue		1,200
	Cash	600	
	Installment accounts receivable		600
	Income tax expense	240	
	Deferred income taxes		120
	Cash		120
19X2	Cash	600	
	Installment accounts receivable		600
	Deferred income taxes	120	
	Cash		120

Retailers ordinarily classify their installment accounts receivable as current assets, even though their ultimate collection may extend beyond one year. Accordingly, the related deferred income taxes are classified as current liabilities.

☐ Percentage-of-Completion and Completed-Contract Methods

Another timing difference between shareholder and tax reporting arises for companies with long-term construction contracts. Suppose a company signs a contract with the state transportation department on January 2, 19X1, to build a new highway. The completion date is December 31, 19X4. The company expects revenue of $40 million and costs of $32 million on the project. When are the revenues and the associated costs recorded on the income statement? There are two alternatives: (1) all revenues and costs are recognized at the completion of the contract, called the **completed-contract method**; and (2) revenues and costs are allocated to each year based on the percentage of the project's projected total costs that have been expended by the end of the year, called the **percentage-of-completion method**.

For example, suppose $8 million of the projected $32 million cost had been incurred by December 31, 19X1. Then 8 ÷ 32 = 25% of the projected

EXHIBIT 13–8

Analysis of Tax Deferral Under Completed-Contract and Percentage-of-Completion Methods:
4-Year, $40 Million Contract
(numbers in millions of dollars)

1. REPORTING ON INCOME TAX RETURNS

YEAR	REVENUE	EXPENSES	PRETAX INCOME	INCOME TAX PAID	NET INCOME
19X1	0	0	0	0	0
19X2	0	0	0	0	0
19X3	0	0	0	0	0
19X4	40	32	8	4	4
Total	40	32	8	4	4

2. REPORTING TO STOCKHOLDERS
a. No Tax Deferral (Banned)

YEAR	REVENUE	EXPENSES	PRETAX INCOME	INCOME TAX PAID	NET INCOME	BALANCE SHEET EFFECT: DEFERRED INCOME TAXES
19X1	10	8	2	0	2	—
19X2	10	8	2	0	2	—
19X3	10	8	2	0	2	—
19X4	10	8	2	4	−2	—
Total	40	32	8	4	4	

b. With Tax Deferral (Required)

YEAR	REVENUE	EXPENSES	PRETAX INCOME	INCOME TAX EXPENSE: Tax Paid	Tax Deferred	Tax Expense	NET INCOME	BALANCE SHEET EFFECT: DEFERRED INCOME TAXES
19X1	10	8	2	0	1	1	1	1
19X2	10	8	2	0	1	1	1	2
19X3	10	8	2	0	1	1	1	3
19X4	10	8	2	4	−3	1	1	0
Total	40	32	8	4	0	4	4	

revenues and the $8 million incurred cost would appear on the 19X1 income statement under the percentage-of-completion method. No revenues or costs for the project would be on the 19X1 income statement under the completed-contract method.

Both the completed-contract method and the percentage-of-completion method have been allowed for either shareholder or tax reporting. Many companies use the percentage-of-completion method for shareholder reporting and the completed-contract method for tax reporting.[4] Exhibit 13–8 shows tax and shareholder reports for our example, assuming that $8 million of cost

---

[4] Until February 28, 1986, an entire contract could be accounted for by the completed-contract method for tax reporting. For contracts entered into after that date, the percentage-of-completion method must be used for at least 40% of the costs and revenues. The completed-contract method can be used for only the other 60%. For simplicity, assume that the entire $40 million of revenue and $32 million of costs in our example relate to the part of a contract for which the completed-contract method is permitted for tax purposes.

was incurred during each of the four years of the contract. Note that tax deferral spreads the $4 million net income evenly to each of the four years. Without deferral, the large tax payment in 19X4 makes it appear that 19X1, 19X2, and 19X3 were highly profitable, but 19X4 was not.[5]

Deferral of income taxes for revenue recognition on long-term contracts can make a large difference in the net income of construction companies. For example, Morrison-Knudsen Company, a construction company with projects throughout the world, reported net income of approximately $40 million for each of the last three years. Morrison-Knudsen used the percentage-of-completion method for shareholder reporting and the completed-contract method for tax purposes. Because of this difference in methods, the company deferred taxes. Without the required tax deferral, the company's net income would have been $7 million, $53 million, and $60 million. Revenue recognition provided the largest tax deferrals for Morrison-Knudsen; depreciation timing differences created deferrals only one-quarter as large.

CLASSIFICATION ON FINANCIAL STATEMENTS

Most companies list only one line labeled "income taxes," or "provision for income taxes," on their income statements. They provide details about deferred taxes in a footnote. Pacific Gas and Electric (PG&E) is such a company. Its footnotes include the data shown in Exhibit 13–9. Deferred taxes are listed by the source of the deferrals.

EXHIBIT 13–9

PG&E   Pacific Gas and Electric Company

The detail of income tax expense (credit) is:

	1985	1984
	In Thousands	
Current:		
Federal	$113,867	$ (12,644)
State and other	84,909	52,277
Deferred:		
ACRS	227,756	114,469
Investment tax credits:		
Current deferrals	139,699	108,798
Amortization of previously		
deferred ITC	(34,376)	(20,104)
Other deferred taxes—net	81,254	301,985
Total	$613,109	$544,781

---

[5] We assume that all costs and revenues are incurred as predicted. Complications beyond the scope of this text arise when actual results differ from the predictions.

Note that PG&E uses the deferral method for its investment tax credits. Although the 1986 tax law repealed the investment tax credit, amortization of previously deferred credits will continue.

A few companies, such as La-Z-Boy Chair Company, list details on the face of the income statement:

Income before income taxes		$38,687,000
Provision for income taxes:		
Federal—current	$9,201,000	
—deferred	6,508,000	
State	1,619,000	
Total		17,328,000
Net income for the year		$21,359,000

A company's balance sheet should list the current portion of deferred taxes separately from the long-term portion. The balance sheet for PG&E includes the following lines:

[listed with current liabilities]	
Deferred income taxes—current portion	$157,490,000
[listed before stockholders' equity]	
Deferred credits:	
Deferred investment tax credits	$504,710,000
Deferred taxes	$783,316,000

SUMMARY

Tax credits are granted by the federal government for various purposes. Such credits are direct reductions of the income tax itself. For financial reporting to shareholders, tax credits linked to the purchase of business property may be accounted for under either the flow-through method or the deferral method.

Deferred federal income taxes arise when the straight-line method of depreciation is used for shareholder-reporting purposes and accelerated depreciation is used for income-tax-reporting purposes. Deferral of income taxes is also often called interperiod tax allocation. Deferral is caused by other items besides depreciation. See Appendix 13A for additional discussion.

SUMMARY PROBLEMS FOR YOUR REVIEW

☐ **Problem One**

Company F was granted a tax credit of $15,000 for purchasing a machine with a 10-year useful life. Pretax income was $100,000, and the income tax rate was 40%. The deferral method would reduce income taxes by $1,500 in Year 1. How would the relevant balance sheet and income statement accounts be affected by the deferral method? Show accounts and amounts for each of the first three years.

☐ Solution to Problem One

The deferral method would appear as follows in each of the three years:

Pretax income		$100,000
Income tax expense:		
Taxes before tax credit	$40,000	
Less amortization of credit (10% × $15,000)	1,500	38,500
Net income		$ 61,500

The balance sheet at the end of the first year would show a deferred credit of $15,000 − $1,500, or $13,500. This balance would decline by $1,500 annually as the beneficial effects of the tax credit were spread out over the useful life of the asset in the form of an annual reduction of income taxes. At the end of Year 3, the balance in deferred tax credits would be $15,000 − 3($1,500), or $10,500.

☐ Problem Two

Examine Exhibit 13–7 on page 593. Suppose that $200 million was spent in Year 7 on additional three-year ACRS class assets with five-year useful lives and that income before depreciation and taxes reached $270 million. For Year 7, fill in all the columns in Exhibit 13–7.

☐ Solution to Problem Two

For income tax authorities (in millions):

INCOME BEFORE DEPRECIATION AND TAXES	ACRS COST RECOVERY	PRETAX INCOME	INCOME TAX PAID	NET INCOME
$270	$7 + 15 + 45 + 66* = $133	$137	$82.2	$54.8

* .33 × 200 million = $66 million.

For stockholders (in millions):

INCOME BEFORE DEPRECIATION AND TAXES	STRAIGHT-LINE DEPRECIATION	PRETAX INCOME	INCOME TAX EXPENSE			NET INCOME	BALANCE SHEET EFFECT: DEFERRED INCOME TAXES
			Paid	Deferred	Total		
$270	$120	$150	$82.2	$7.8	$90	$60	$70.2

Computations: 25 + 25 + 25 + 25 + 50 = 150; .60 × 150 = 90; 90 − 82.2 = 7.8; 62.4 + 7.8 = 70.2

Problem Three

Examine Exhibit 13–9 (page 597) regarding Pacific Gas and Electric Company (PG&E). Suppose the investment tax credit had been eliminated as of January 1, 1985. Therefore PG&E would have received and deferred zero investment tax credit during 1985 instead of the $139,699,000 shown in the exhibit. By how much would net income be affected?

Solution to Problem Three

PG&E uses the deferral method rather than the flow-through method. Assume that the $34,376,000 amortized tax credits are solely the aftermath of capital expenditures made before 1985. Then current taxes would have been higher by $139,699,000, but the $139,699,000 of deferred income tax expense would not be shown. Therefore, net income would not change. If some of the $34,376,000 includes amortization of 1985 expenditures, net income would be lower by the amount of such amortization.

HIGHLIGHTS TO REMEMBER

1. Income tax laws change frequently. Therefore beginners in accounting should not be overly concerned with the specific tax rates or deductions applicable to a particular year. Instead they should concentrate on how the general provisions of income tax laws affect reporting (a) to the government and (b) to the shareholders. Frequently, there are conflicts in reporting requirements between *a* and *b*.

2. Taxation is not a simple subject, nor is the reporting to shareholders by most corporations. In combination, the complexities multiply rapidly. In such circumstances, students should be especially concerned with the forest rather than the trees. For example, deferred tax accounts are creatures of reporting to shareholders; there are no deferred tax accounts when reporting to income tax authorities.

3. *Accelerated depreciation* is any depreciation method that writes off depreciable costs more quickly than the typical straight-line method. Acceleration takes various forms. The Accelerated Cost Recovery System (ACRS) achieves acceleration primarily by shortening the lives of the write-off for depreciation and secondarily by writing off more cost in the early years of the recovery period than in the later years.

ACCOUNTING VOCABULARY

Accelerated Cost Recovery System (ACRS), p. *585* Completed-Contract Method, *595* Deductible Items, *582* Deferral Method, *583* Flow-Through Method, *583* Installment Method, *594* Interperiod Tax Allocation, *590* Percentage-of-Completion Method, *596* Permanent Differences, *602* Tax Allocation, *590* Tax Credit, *582* Timing Differences, *588*

APPENDIX 13A: TIMING DIFFERENCES AND PERMANENT DIFFERENCES

This appendix covers timing differences in more depth than in the body of the chapter. It also covers permanent differences and operating losses.

□ Timing Differences

The body of this chapter describes how interperiod tax allocation accounts for timing differences. There are four major categories of timing differences:

1. *Expenses* are deducted in determining taxable income *earlier* than they are deducted in determining pretax income for stockholder-reporting purposes. The major example is accelerated depreciation. A similar example is the promotion cost that accompanies the opening of a new retail store. The cost may be deducted on the tax return, but it is deferred and amortized for financial reporting.

2. *Revenues* are included in taxable income *later* than they are included in pretax income for stockholder reporting. For instance, as discussed earlier in this chapter, income tax laws permit retailers and others who sell on installment plans to postpone some related income tax payments until the cash installments have actually been collected. Another example covered in the chapter is the use of the percentage-of-completion method on long-term contracts for stockholder reporting together with the use of the completed contracts method on some part of these contracts for income tax returns. Revenue and profits are recognized earlier under the percentage-of-completion method but are permitted to be shown later on income tax returns.

3. *Expenses* are deducted for income tax purposes *later* than they are deducted for stockholder-reporting purposes. For instance, the estimated costs of product warranty contracts are not permitted to be deducted for tax purposes until the period paid or in which the liability becomes fixed. In contrast to the deferred income tax arising from accelerated depreciation, the deferred income tax arising from product warranty contracts is an *asset* (a deferred charge) rather than a liability. Automobile companies recognize estimated costs of product warranties as expenses when the related products are sold. However, no deductions are allowed on income tax returns until cash is disbursed to dealers as warranty service is rendered. Consider a concrete example. For simplicity, assume that a company stops offering warranty service on new sales at the start of Year 2 and that the first-year warranties are not paid in cash until the second year. The effects are (numbers assumed and in dollars):

	YEAR 1 REPORTING		YEAR 2 REPORTING	
	To Shareholders	On Income Tax Return	To Shareholders	On Income Tax Return
Income before warranty expenses	600,000	600,000	600,000	600,000
Warranty expenses estimated based on sales	100,000	—	—	100,000
Pretax income	500,000	600,000	600,000	500,000
Income tax expense @ 40%	200,000	240,000	240,000	200,000

The $40,000 timing difference in income taxes would be reported as an asset, deferred income taxes. Some accountants prefer to call the $40,000 a prepaid income tax.

The journal entries follow:

Year 1	Warranty expense	100,000	
	Estimated liability for warranties		100,000
	Income tax expense	200,000	
	Deferred income taxes	40,000	
	Income tax payable (or cash)		240,000
Year 2	Estimated liability for warranties	100,000	
	Cash		100,000
	Income tax expense	240,000	
	Deferred income taxes		40,000
	Income tax payable (or cash)		200,000

4. *Revenues* are included in income for tax purposes *earlier* than they are included in pretax income for stockholder purposes. For instance, some fees, dues, and service contracts are taxed when collected but are usually deferred as unearned revenue for financial-reporting purposes. As in point 3 above, the deferred tax would be an *asset*.

□ Permanent Differences

A **permanent difference** affects the computation of either pretax income as reported to shareholders or taxable income as reported to the government, but not both. Permanent differences will not "reverse," or "turn around," in subsequent periods. An example is nontaxable income: Interest received on municipal obligations is "permanently" exempt from tax. Other examples are nondeductible expenses: The costs of purchased goodwill and perpetual franchise rights are *not* deductible as expenses for income tax purposes but *must* be amortized for shareholder-reporting purposes.

No interperiod income tax allocation (and therefore no deferred income tax) is appropriate in relation to these permanent differences. Consider an example (in dollars):

	REPORTING	
	To Shareholders	On Income Tax Return
No permanent difference		
Pretax income	120,000	120,000
Income taxes @ 40%	48,000	48,000
Permanent difference		
Income before amortization	120,000	120,000
Permanent difference is amortization of goodwill of $30,000	30,000	—
Pretax income	90,000	120,000
Income taxes	48,000	48,000

The income tax rate in reports to shareholders would be higher than the statutory rate of 40%; it would be $48,000 \div \$90,000 = 53.3\%$. Because this condition is deemed a "permanent difference," no interperiod tax allocation would occur. The report to shareholders would indeed show a 53.3% rate, which would be explained by the fact that the amortization of goodwill is mandatory for shareholder reporting but forbidden for reporting to the income tax authorities.

In contrast, suppose the above company has a large portfolio of investments in tax-exempt municipal bonds and no purchased goodwill:

| | REPORTING | |
	To Shareholders	On Income Tax Return
Permanent difference		
Income from all sources	120,000	120,000
Permanent difference is interest revenue on municipal obligations	—	30,000
Pretax income	120,000	90,000
Income taxes	36,000	36,000

The income tax rate in reports to shareholders would be lower than the statutory rate of 40%; it would be $36,000 ÷ $120,000 = 30%. No interperiod income tax allocation would be applicable.

☐ Operating Losses

Suppose a company reported a net operating loss (NOL) of $100,000 on its 19X4 income statement prepared for tax purposes. In other words, its tax deductions exceeded its taxable revenues by $100,000. The tax effects are as follows:

	NET OPERATING INCOME (LOSS)	19X4 CARRYBACK OR CARRYFORWARD	TAXABLE INCOME
19X1	$ 5,000	$ (5,000)	—
19X2	15,000	(15,000)	—
19X3	35,000	(35,000)	—
19X4	(100,000)	—	—
19X5	5,000	(5,000)	—
19X6	8,000	(8,000)	—
19X7	10,000	(10,000)	—
19X8	10,000	(10,000)	—
19X9	5,000	(5,000)	—
19X0	1,000	(1,000)	—
Next nine years combined	2,000	(2,000)	—
Used		(96,000)	
Unused and nondeductible		(4,000)	
Accounted for		(100,000)	

The NOL can be used to reduce the taxable income of the three preceding or fifteen following years. The company receives a refund of taxes paid in 19X1, 19X2, and 19X3. In addition, the NOL reduces tax disbursements in future years. Any loss carryforward unused after fifteen years becomes nondeductible.

NOL carrybacks result in tax refunds and are recognized on the financial reports for shareholders in the period of the loss. The tax benefits of NOL carryforwards depend on future profitability, and they generally are not recognized until the tax benefits are actually received. Suppose a $100,000 NOL created a $40,000 tax benefit, consisting of a $25,000 tax refund for the preceding three years and a $15,000 potential reduction in future tax disbursements. The usual journal entry would be the following:

Income tax refund receivable	25,000	
Income tax benefit (a reduction of a loss)		25,000
Carryback of the tax effect of a net		
operation loss.		

The bottom of the income statement would show:

Pretax loss	$(100,000)
Add: Income tax benefit of operating	
loss carryback	25,000
Net loss	$ (75,000)

Suppose the benefit of a reduction in future taxes is assured beyond any reasonable doubt.[6] Then its effect is also recognized in the year of the operating loss:

Income tax refund receivable	25,000	
Future tax reduction from		
NOL carryforward (an asset)	15,000	
Income tax benefit		40,000
Carryback and carryforward of the tax		
effect of a net operating loss.		

The bottom of the income statement would show:

Pretax loss	$(100,000)
Add: Income tax benefit of operating loss	
carryback and carryforward	40,000
Net loss	$ (60,000)

APPENDIX 13B: PROPRIETORSHIPS AND PARTNERSHIPS

This appendix examines the fundamental distinctions between proprietorships, partnerships, and corporations. Particular attention is given to the role of income taxes in choosing the form of organization.

☐ Comparison of Transactions

Chapter 1 compares the three major types of ownership, so the details of such comparisons will not be repeated here. The fundamental accounting concepts that underlie the owner's equity are unchanged regardless of whether the organization is a corporation, a proprietorship, or a partnership. Furthermore, the typical business transactions such as sales, cost of goods sold, and operating expenses are accounted for exactly alike for all organizations.

---

[6] In a recent sample of four thousand companies, only one company recognized future tax benefits.

Consider the following facts as a basis for illustrating the accounting for proprietorships and partnerships. On January 1, 19X1, Jane Smith invests $100,000 in a public accounting firm, Azure Accounting Services, as a sole proprietorship. Revenue of $460,000 and expenses of $270,000 apply to the year 19X1 (before considering any withdrawals or salaries for herself). Her withdrawals (called *drawings*) of cash were $10,000 monthly.

Similarly, Smith and Jones form a partnership that has identical operations during 19X1. Smith invests $60,000 and Jones invests $40,000. Although they can split the profits in any way they choose, their partnership agreement specifies 60% for Smith and 40% for Jones. Smith withdrew $6,000 monthly and Jones $4,000 monthly.

Exhibit 13–10 shows how these transactions would affect the accounts. Transactions *a*, *b*, and *c* are the familiar investment, revenue, and expense transactions that are the same regardless of the form of organization. The net income for the year is $460,000 − $270,000 = $190,000.

The journal entries follow (in thousands of dollars). The Income Summary account obviously would not be used on a day-to-day basis. It is used here for convenience. Notice that the sum of Smith's drawings and her addition to capital ($72,000 + $42,000) are 60% of net income; Jones's are 40%.

a. Initial investment	Cash	100		Cash	100	
	Smith, capital		100	Smith, capital		60
				Jones, capital		40
b. Revenues	Cash	460		Cash	460	
	Income summary		460	Income summary		460
c. Expenses	Income summary	270		Income summary	270	
	Cash		270	Cash		270
d. Withdrawals	Smith, drawings	120		Smith, drawings	72	
	Cash		120	Jones, drawings	48	
				Cash		120
e. Transfers to capital	Income summary	190		Income summary	190	
	Smith, drawings		120	Smith, drawings		72
	Smith, capital		70	Jones, drawings		48
				Smith, capital		42
				Jones, capital		28

☐ Comparison With Corporations

From a legal and income tax standpoint, proprietorships and partnerships are not separate entities with limited liability and separate taxability. The owners have unlimited personal liability for all the debts of their businesses. Unlike the corporate entity, proprietorships and partnerships are not subject to income taxes as entities. Instead the entire net income (*before* withdrawals, which are regarded as similar to corporate dividends, *not* as expenses) is taxable as personal income of the owners. In particular, note that the income is fully taxable regardless of whether withdrawals are zero or any percentage of the entity's net income.

Exhibit 13–11 compares the financial statements of the accounting firm under three forms of organization. Please read the footnote therein. The withdrawals in transaction *d* for proprietorships and partnerships are in lieu of the combination salaries-dividends paid by small corporations to their owner-managers. From a legal and income tax standpoint, an owner may be *both* an employee manager (one role) and a stockholder (a separate role). As an employee *manager*, the owner receives a salary; as an *owner*, he or she receives dividends.

EXHIBIT 13–10

Analysis of Transactions for Proprietorship and Partnership
(in thousands of dollars)

	CASH AND OTHER ASSETS =	LIABILITIES +	OWNERS' EQUITY		
			Smith, Capital	Smith, Drawings	Income Summary
Proprietorship					
a. Initial investment	+100	=	+100		
b. Revenues	+460	=			+460
c. Expenses	−270	=			−270
d. Withdrawals	−120	=		−120	
e. Transfer of net income to capital		=	+70	+120	−190
Ending balances	+170	=	+170	0	0

			Smith, Capital	Jones, Capital	Smith, Drawings	Jones, Drawings	Income Summary
Partnership							
a. Initial investment	+100	=	+60	+40			
b. Revenues	+460	=					+460
d. Expenses	−270	=					−270
d. Withdrawals	−120	=			−72	−48	
e. Transfer of net income to capital		=	+42	+28	+72	+48	−190
Ending balances	+170	=	+102	+68	0	0	0

How reasonable are the salaries of $72,000 and $48,000 shown in the corporate income statement? The Internal Revenue Service sometimes challenges such salary levels of closely held corporations. Why? Suppose one-third of the $120,000 could be established as being an unreasonable overpayment of salaries (given what these managers could command as salaried employees of other accounting firms). The $40,000 would be regarded as dividends. The salaries allowed by the IRS would therefore be only $48,000 and $32,000, respectively. Then the corporation would have to pay $8,000 more income taxes, $22,000 instead of $14,000. The entity would have $8,000 less cash, $156,000 (see Exhibit 13–11) minus $8,000, or $148,000. The corporate statements would be revised:

INCOME STATEMENT			STATEMENT OF RETAINED INCOME		BALANCE SHEET	
Revenues		$460	Retained income,		Cash and other	
Expenses	$270		January 1, 19X1	$ 0	assets	$148
Salary expenses,			Net income	88	Capital stock	$100
$48 + $32	80	350	Total	$88	Retained income	48
Income before			Deduct dividends*	40	Total	$148
taxes		$110	Retained income,			
Income tax @ 20%		22	December 31, 19X1	$48		
Net income		$ 88				

* $120,000 total paid as "salaries," but one-third (or $40,000) disallowed by IRS and deemed to be dividends.

EXHIBIT 13–11

AZURE ACCOUNTING SERVICES
Financial Statements
(in thousands of dollars)

SOLE PROPRIETORSHIP	PARTNERSHIP	CORPORATION

INCOME STATEMENTS
FOR THE YEAR ENDED DECEMBER 31, 19X1

Revenues	$460	Revenues		$460	Revenues		$460
Expenses	270	Expenses		270	Expenses	$270	
Net income	$190	Net income		$190	Salary expenses,*		
		Allocation of net			$72 + $48	120	390
		income:			Income before tax		70
		To Smith (60%)	$114		Income tax @ 20%		14
		To Jones (40%)	76	$190	Net income		$ 56*

STATEMENTS OF CAPITAL OR RETAINED INCOME
FOR THE YEAR ENDED DECEMBER 31, 19X1

			Smith	Jones		
Capital, January 1, 19X1	$100	Capital, January 1, 19X1	$ 60	$ 40	Retained income,	
Net income	190	Net income	114	76	January 1, 19X1	$ 0
Total	$290	Total	$174	$116	Net income	56
Drawings	120	Drawings	72	48	Retained income,	
Capital, December 31,		Capital, December 31,			December 31, 19X1	$ 56
19X1	$170	19X1	$102	$ 68		

BALANCE SHEETS
DECEMBER 31, 19X1

Assets
(same for each entity)

Cash and other assets	$170	Cash and other assets		$170	Cash and other assets	$156*

Liabilities and Stockholders' Equity

Smith, capital	$170	Smith capital		$102	Capital stock	$100
		Jones, capital		68	Retained income	56*
		Total capital		$170	Stockholders' equity	$156

* The corporate entity is subject to an income tax, assumed here to be 20% paid in cash. Furthermore, the withdrawals are assumed to be paid as executive salary expenses, which are deductible in computing the net income of the corporate entity.

☐ Comparison of Results of Operations

Consider the statements of income and partners' capital of Deloitte Haskins & Sells, a public accounting firm with hundreds of partners.

Deloitte Haskins & Sells (USA)
Statement of Earnings
(in millions of dollars)

	1985	1984
Fees for professional services	$500	$463
Operating expenses:		
Employee compensation and related benefits	228	208
Occupancy, including depreciation and amortization	41	34
Other	120	107
Total operating expenses	389	349
Earnings attributable to active partners	$111	$114

Statement of Changes in Partners' Capital

	1985	1984
Balance at beginning of year	$118	$105
Additions:		
Earnings attributable to active partners	111	114
Capital contributed by partners	4	8
Reductions:		
Distributions to active partners	104	98
Capital returned to partners who retired or resigned	13	11
Balance at end of year	$116	$118

Note how the compensation of the partners is regarded as an allocation (or apportionment or distribution) of the income of the partnership, not as an operating expense. Under the corporate form, however, as the previous illustrations show, a "salary and bonus" expense would be deducted in the computation of the net income of a corporation.

Be on guard when you compare the income statements of incorporated and unincorporated businesses. To be strictly comparable, some "salaries" of the owner-managers of proprietorships and partnerships should be estimated as being equivalent to expenses.

For instance, suppose the drawings of Smith and Jones in our example were indeed reasonable approximations of the salaries they could earn in a comparable accounting firm. For comparison of their results with those of similar professional service *corporations*, their income statement would have to be revised as follows:

Revenues		$460
Expenses	$270	
Partner "salaries"	120	390
Operating income to be compared with the income before taxes of professional service corporations		$ 70

This approximation of partner "salaries" as an expense is highly desirable for routine internal reports to owner-managers. In this way, the partners can get a better measure of their overall compensation for their efforts. As managers, they wish to be compensated in an amount that they could earn for comparable work elsewhere. As owners, they wish a reasonable return on their ownership capital. If they fail to run an entity that can generate sufficient amounts of both types of rewards, the partners may take a variety of actions, including bringing in new partners or ceasing operations. In short, corporate and noncorporate income statements are not comparable unless approximations are made of partner or proprietor "salaries."

FUNDAMENTAL ASSIGNMENT MATERIAL

☐ General Coverage

13–1. **COMPARISON OF FLOW-THROUGH AND DEFERRAL.** (Alternate is 13–4.) Bayside Metals Corporation had $10 million of investment tax credits from acquisitions in late December 19X5.

Required

1. Compare the effects of two accounting methods by filling in the blanks (in millions of dollars):

	FLOW-THROUGH			DEFERRAL			
	A =	L +	SE	A =	L	+	SE
		Income Tax Payable	Retained Income		Income Tax Payable	Deferred Investment Tax Credits	Retained Income
Effect on balances, 12/31/X5	0 =	−10	+10	0 =	−10	+10	
Four years later @ $1 per year		___	___	=	?	−4	?
Cumulative effect on balances, 12/31/X9	0 =	−10	+10	0 =	?	+6	?

2. Prepare the journal entries for all data in the table.

13–2. **DEFERRED INCOME TAXES.** (Alternates are 13–5 and 13–7.) Palomo Company is begun on January 1, 19X7, with initial paid-in capital of $50 million cash. On January 2, 19X7, the company purchases an asset for $30 million cash with an estimated useful life of five years and an estimated scrap value of zero. ACRS depreciation is used for tax purposes. The asset has an ACRS recovery period of three years. However, *the straight-line method is used for shareholder-reporting purposes*. Prospective annual income before depreciation and income taxes is $14 million. The income tax rate is 40%. Assume that all taxes are paid early in the next year after the income is earned.

Required:

1. Prepare an analysis of transactions for external reporting, using the balance sheet format. Show the effects of (a) formation, (b) acquisition, (c) income before depreciation and taxes, and (d) straight-line depreciation. Show the effects of (e1) no deferral and (e2) deferral of income taxes.
2. Prepare a three-column comparison of reporting of income for 19X7 (a) to income tax authorities, (b) to shareholders if no deferral is used, and (c) to shareholders if deferral is used.

13–3. **TABULATION OF EFFECTS OF DEFERRAL.** (Alternates are 13–6 and 13–8.) Refer to the data in the preceding problem. Prepare a five-year schedule like Exhibit 13–6 (p. 591) for each of the three reporting methods of the problem requirement 2. Show all amounts in millions of dollars.

13–4. COMPARISON OF FLOW-THROUGH AND DEFERRAL. (Alternate is 13–1.) Eastman Kodak had $5 million of investment tax credits from acquisitions in late December 1985.

Required:

1. Compare the effects of two accounting methods by filling in the blanks (in millions of dollars):

	FLOW-THROUGH			DEFERRAL		
	A =	L +	SE	A =	L	+ SE
		Income Tax Payable	Retained Income		Income Tax Payable	Deferred Investment Tax Credits	Retained Income
Effect on balances, 12/31/85	0 =	?	?	0 =	−5	+5	
Three years later @ $1 per year				=	?	−3	?
Cumulative effect on balances, 12/31/88	0 =	−5	+5	0 =	?	+2	?

2. Prepare the journal entries for all data in the table.

13–5. DEFERRED INCOME TAXES. (Alternates are 13–2 and 13–7.) Monsanto Company produces chemicals and pharmaceuticals. The company's capital expenditures exceed $500 million annually. Suppose that on January 4, 1987, Monsanto purchased some special tools for the production of plastics. The acquisition cost was $10 million. The equipment's expected useful life is five years; expected residual value is zero. The ACRS class is three-year.

Assume that the income tax rate is 40%. No income tax payments will be due before early 1988. Assume that in 1987 Monsanto had pretax income of $550 million before considering depreciation related to this acquisition. For simplicity, assume also that this $550 million was the same for reporting to income tax authorities and to stockholders.

Regarding the $10 million acquisition, Monsanto uses straight-line depreciation for reporting to stockholders. However, the company uses the prescribed ACRS schedule for income tax purposes. There is no investment tax credit.

Required:

1. Fill in the blanks in millions (based solely on the given data):

	1987 REPORTING	
	To Income Tax Authorities	To Stockholders
Pretax income as given	$550.0	$550.0
Depreciation:		
ACRS (3-year recovery basis)	?	?
Straight-line (5-year useful life)	?	?
Pretax income	?	?
Income tax expense:		
To be paid in early 1988	?	?
Deferred	?	?
Total income tax expense	?	?
Net income	$?	$?

2. Prepare the summary journal entry, December 31, 1987, for Monsanto's 1987 income taxes.

13–6. LONG-RUN EFFECTS OF DEFERRAL. (Alternates are 13–3 and 13–8.)

1. Refer to the data in the preceding problem. Prepare a five-year schedule like Exhibit 13–6 (p. 591) for the two reporting methods of requirement 1. For each year, assume that income before the depreciation in question is $550 million and the income tax rate is 40%. Show all amounts in millions of dollars. Prepare only two schedules; omit the presentation similar to schedule 2(a) in Exhibit 13–6.
2. Prepare the journal entry for income tax expense for Year 5.

13–7. DEFERRED INCOME TAXES. (Alternates are 13–2 and 13–5.) Suppose that on January 5, 1987, Northwest Orient Airlines purchased some DC-10 aircraft for $400 million. The aircraft's expected useful life is ten years; expected residual value, zero.

Assume that the income tax rate is 40%. No income tax payments will be due before early 1988. Assume that in 1987 Northwest had pretax income of $160 million before considering depreciation related to this acquisition. For simplicity, assume also that this $160 million was the same for reporting to income tax authorities and to stockholders.

Regarding the $400 million acquisition, Northwest uses straight-line depreciation for reporting to stockholders. However, Northwest uses the prescribed ACRS schedule for income tax purposes. Aircraft have a 5-year recovery period. There is no investment tax credit.

Required:

1. Fill in the blanks in millions (based solely on the given data):

	1987 REPORTING	
	To Income Tax Authorities	To Stockholders
Pretax income as given	$160	$160
Depreciation:		
ACRS (5-year recovery basis)	?	?
Straight-line (10-year useful life)	?	?
Pretax income	?	?
Income tax expense:		
To be paid in early 1988	?	?
Deferred	?	?
Total income tax expense	?	?
Net income	$?	$?

2. Prepare the summary journal entry, December 31, 1987, for Northwest's 1987 income taxes.

13–8. LONG-RUN EFFECTS OF DEFERRAL. (Alternates are 13–3 and 13–6.)

1. Refer to the data in the preceding problem. Prepare a seven-year schedule like Exhibit 13–6 (p. 591) for the two reporting methods in requirement 1. For each year, assume that the income before the depreciation in question is $160 million and the income tax rate is 40%. Show all amounts in millions of dollars. Do not continue the schedule beyond the seventh year; instead explain how the final three years would appear in a ten-year schedule. Prepare only two schedules; omit the presentation similar to schedule 2(a) in Exhibit 13–6.
2. Prepare the journal entry for income tax expense for Year 7.

ADDITIONAL ASSIGNMENT MATERIAL

☐ **General Coverage**

13–9. "Taxes are a fact of life, and they have little effect on business decisions." Do you agree? Explain.

13–10. "Tax credits are better than deductible items because they directly reduce taxes." Critically discuss this statement.

13–11. "Tax credits are deductible as expenses for income tax purposes." Do you agree? Explain.

13–12. What are the two most widely used methods of accounting for the investment tax credit?

13–13. Which of the two methods of accounting for the investment tax credit will benefit reported current income the most?

13–14. "ACRS results in an acceleration of income tax disbursements." Do you agree? Explain.

13–15. Why do deferred federal income taxes arise?

13–16. "Deferred income taxes are also known as allocated income taxes." Do you agree? Explain.

13–17. In brief, why did the Accounting Principles Board favor deferral of income taxes?

13–18. "Interperiod income tax allocation is the spreading of the year's income tax expense among the months within the year." Do you agree? Explain.

13–19. Companies that use deferral of tax credits rather than flow-through show lower retained income. Why?

13–20. Give an example of a timing difference where revenues are included in taxable income later than they are included in pretax income for stockholder reporting.

13–21. Give an example of a timing difference where expenses are deducted from taxable income later than they are deducted for financial-reporting purposes.

13–22. Give an example of a timing difference where revenues are included in income for tax purposes earlier than they are for stockholder-reporting purposes.

13–23. "Permanent differences are those timing differences that persist beyond five years." Do you agree? Explain.

13–24. Give two examples of permanent differences.

13–25. "Operating losses are beneficial." Explain.

13–26. Suppose a company's income tax rate is 40%. The company has a $100,000 expenditure that can either be a deductible item or receive a 25% tax credit. Which does the company prefer? Why?

13–27. "Corporations are so different from proprietorships that completely different concepts of accounting apply to each." Do you agree? Explain.

13–28. TAX CREDITS.

1. Felix Company has sales of $900,000, tax-deductible expenses of $790,000, and an income tax rate of 40%. The company is also entitled to a tax credit of $9,000. Compute the company's taxable income and income tax to be paid.
2. By using journal entries, and assuming the accrual basis of accounting, indicate how the government would record the above information (a) after considering the taxes but before considering the tax credit and (b) after considering the tax credit.

13–29. EFFECTS OF DEFERRAL AND FLOW-THROUGH. (Alternate is 13–43.) Hiramatzu Company began business on January 1, 19X5, with $2 million cash raised by an issue of common stock. All of its transactions throughout 19X5 were for cash. On

December 31, it had income before income taxes of $600,000. The income tax rate is 35%. No income tax payments will be due before early 19X6. An investment in equipment of $480,000 cash was made on December 31, 19X5. The equipment has a ten-year life and an expected residual value of zero.

Required:

1. Prepare an analysis of transactions in thousands of dollars, using the A = L + SE format. Show the (a) effects of formation of the company, (b) effects on cash and retained income of income before income taxes, (c) effects of acquisition of equipment, and (d) computation and effects of income taxes. Show the ending balances in all accounts, December 31, 19X5.
2. Suppose the company were eligible for a $20,000 tax credit because of its acquisition of equipment. Prepare an analysis of the flow-through effects in thousands of dollars. Label as *e1*. Also prepare an analysis of the deferral effects. Label as *e2*.
3. Prepare journal entries, December 31, 19X5, for the income tax expense before considering the investment tax credit. Also prepare entries for the investment tax credit using (a) flow-through and (b) deferral.
4. Suppose 19X6 were a repetition of 19X5 in the sense that taxable income was again $600,000. However, no tax credit was permitted on the equipment acquired. Prepare journal entries for the investment tax credit of 19X5 as it affects 19X6 using (a) flow-through and (b) deferral.

13–30. **AMORTIZATION SCHEDULE FOR INVESTMENT TAX CREDIT.** AAX Auto Parts's taxable income is $250,000. Income taxes, before considering any investment tax credit, are $100,000. On December 31, 19X1, the company spent $200,000 cash for equipment with an applicable investment tax credit of $20,000. The equipment will be used for eight years and will have no residual value. Prepare a schedule comparing flow-through and deferral effects on net income for external reports during the life of the asset. Assume that the annual taxable income of $250,000 will persist during the life of the asset.

13–31. **INVESTMENT TAX CREDIT.** The Gulf Steel Company purchased machinery for $300,000. Its estimated useful life is eight years; its expected scrap value is zero. An investment tax credit equal to 10% of the purchase price is allowed. Net income (after taxes but before considering the investment tax credit) is $160,000 annually. Income taxes before considering the investment credit were $100,000.

Required:

1. Net income for Year 1 under the flow-through method.
2. Net income for Years 1, 2, and 3 under the deferral method. Show how the income statement and balance sheet accounts will be affected by the deferral method for each of the first three years.

13–32. **RESEARCH TAX CREDIT.** An income tax credit is allowed for a company's research expenditures that exceed a base amount. The base amount is generally the average research expenditures for the past three years. Suppose the current rate for the credit is 25% of expenditures exceeding the base amount, and the income tax rate is 40%.

The Reynaldo Company had the following 19X6 income statement for tax purposes before considering research expenses:

Revenues	$250,000
Cost of goods sold	150,000
Gross margin	$100,000
General and administrative expenses (except for research expenses)	35,000
Pretax income (before research expenses)	$ 65,000

The Reynaldo Company incurred research expenses of $42,000 in 19X6, and research expenses for each of the past three years were $24,000. Assume that all expenses were paid in cash. The research tax credit was Reynaldo's only tax credit in 19X6.

Required:

1. Compute Reynaldo Company's taxable income for 19X6.
2. Compute the 19X6 income tax expense.
3. How much benefit did the Reynaldo Company receive from the 19X6 tax credit?
4. Suppose annual research expenses continue at $42,000 for 19X7, 19X8, and 19X9. Compute the research tax credit for each of the three years.

13–33. **ACRS RECOVERY PERIODS.** Consider the following business assets: (1) heavy-duty truck, (2) underground power transmission lines, (3) commercial building, and (4) electron microscope used in industrial research. What is the recovery period for each of these assets under the prescribed ACRS method?

13–34. **ACRS DEPRECIATION.** Consider the following acquisitions of business assets on October 1, 1987: (1) office furniture, $4,000; (2) light truck, $16,000; and (3) tractor units for over-the-road, $50,000. For each asset, compute the depreciation for tax purposes for 1987 and 1988, as prescribed by ACRS.

13–35. **ACRS DEPRECIATION.** In 1987, the Kowalski Manufacturing Company acquired the following assets and immediately placed them into service:

1. Machinery with a 7-year ACRS life, a useful life of twenty-seven years, and a cost of $30 million
2. A desk-top computer that cost $16,000
3. An office desk that cost $2,000 but was sold sixteen months later

Required:

Compute the depreciation for tax purposes, under the prescribed ACRS method, in 1987 and 1988. Assume that all assets were acquired on March 1, 1987. There is no investment tax credit.

13–36. **DEFERRED INCOME TAXES.** Examine Exhibit 13–7. Suppose that in Year 7, $160 million was spent on three-year ACRS assets with five-year useful lives and that income before depreciation and taxes reached $270 million. For Year 7, fill in all the columns as shown in Exhibit 13–7, page 593.

13–37. **GROWTH OF DEFERRED TAXES.** The facts are the same as in Problem 13–2. However, $30 million is spent *each year* for additional assets, and income increases $14 million each year until leveling off in Year 6. The $30 million spent in Year 6 represents a replacement of the asset originally acquired in Year 1.

Required:

Prepare two tabulations in millions of dollars. The first tabulation should display the effects of reporting for income tax purposes, assuming ACRS depreciation, including pretax income, income tax paid, and net income. The second tabulation should display the effects of reporting to stockholders, assuming straight-line depreciation and deferred income taxes. The second tabulation should include columns for pretax income, tax paid, tax deferred, total tax expense, net income, and the ending balance sheet effect on Deferred Income Taxes.

13–38. **INVESTMENT CREDIT AND DEFERRED TAXES.** Gulf Coast Electronics had used SYD depreciation for financial-reporting and ACRS for tax purposes. It had also used the deferral method for the investment tax credit for financial-reporting purposes. After enjoying steady growth in earnings for several years, the company encountered severe competition from foreign sources. This had a leveling effect on reported earnings per share.

In 19X8, the company invested over $60 million to update the equipment in one of its plants. The investment generated an investment tax credit of $3 million for 19X8. Management is seriously considering changing its method of reporting from that in requirement 2*a* to that in 2*d* below. Other data:

Useful life of the equipment, 15 years with no scrap value

Net income before depreciation on new assets and income taxes and investment tax credit effects, $19 million

If the investment credit is deferred, a full year of amortization is taken in 19X8.

Depreciation on new assets for 19X8:

Straight-line	$4,000,000
SYD	7,500,000
ACRS	9,000,000

Required:

Show all total amounts in thousands of dollars.

1. Compute taxable income and the total income taxes for 19X8. The tax rate is 40%.
2. Suppose Gulf Coast Electronics has a simple capital structure with 10 million common shares outstanding and no preferred shares outstanding. For financial-reporting purposes, compute net income and earnings per share where
   a. The company uses SYD depreciation and defers the investment credit
   b. The company uses SYD depreciation and "flows through" the investment credit
   c. The company uses straight-line depreciation and defers the investment credit
   d. The company uses straight-line depreciation and "flows through" the investment credit

13–39. PERCENTAGE-OF-COMPLETION AND COMPLETED-CONTRACT METHODS. On January 2, 19X6, the Jefferson Company signed a $500 million contract to design and build an automated assembly facility for Gray Motor Company. Completion is scheduled for December 31, 19X9. Engineers estimated Jefferson's total cost for the project to be $420 million. During 19X6 Jefferson spent $105 million on the project, and it expected to spend another $315 million to complete the project.

Jefferson uses the completed-contract method for tax reporting and percentage-of-completion for reporting to stockholders. Assume that tax authorities allow the entire contract to be accounted for using the completed-contract method and that Jefferson Company worked on no other projects during 19X6. The income tax rate is 33%.

Required:

1. Compute the income taxes that Jefferson Company will pay for 19X6.
2. Prepare a 19X6 income statement for reporting to shareholders assuming no tax allocation.
3. Repeat requirement 2 assuming that Jefferson Company uses tax allocation.
4. Assume that Jefferson completed the project in 19X9 after spending exactly the predicted $420 million on it, $105 million each year for 19X6, 19X7, 19X8, and 19X9. Prepare 19X9 income statements for reporting to stockholders assuming (a) no tax allocation and (b) with tax allocation.
5. Which of the methods, the one in requirement 2 or the one in requirement 3, is the generally accepted method for reporting to shareholders?

13–40. OWNERS' EQUITY OF PROPRIETORS AND PARTNERS. Study Appendix 13B. On December 31, 19X1, Jennifer Bevis invested $500,000 in a restaurant, Downtown Grill and Oyster House, as a sole proprietorship. Revenues of $650,000 and expenses of $404,000 apply to the year 19X2 (before considering withdrawals or salaries for herself). Her withdrawals (called drawings) of cash were $8,000 monthly.

Similarly, Bevis and Leonard Miller formed a partnership that had identical operations during 19X1. Bevis invested $300,000 and Miller invested $200,000. They decided to split the profits fifty-fifty even though their capital investments differed. Each withdrew $4,000 monthly.

1. Prepare an analysis of transactions for the proprietorship and partnership, using the balance sheet equation format. Use amounts in thousands.
2. Prepare summary journal entries for the proprietorship and the partnership.

13–41. COMPARISON OF CORPORATIONS, PARTNERSHIPS, AND PROPRIETORSHIPS. Study Appendix 13B. Refer to the facts in the preceding problem. Also assume that a corporation existed that had exactly the same transactions as the partnership except (a) the drawings were salaries, and (b) the corporation paid an income tax in cash of 40%.

1. Prepare balance sheets, income statements, and statements of capital (or retained income) for each of the three entities.
2. Suppose the Internal Revenue Service established that the reasonable salary levels should be $43,000 each instead of $48,000. Prepare the revised corporate financial statements.

13–42. CHOOSING FORM OF ENTITY. Study Appendix 13B. Irene Herbison is subject to a marginal 40% income tax rate (because of other income). She is considering how to organize her wholly owned business. She anticipates the following average performance over the next few years: sales, $1,150,000; owner's salary, $70,000; other expenses, $980,000. Assume that the corporate income tax rate is 20%. Assume also that Herbison plans to withdraw an amount equal to all net income generated by the entity.

1. Prepare a comparative income statement for the corporation and sole proprietorship.
2. Prepare an analysis of the cash available to the owner under each form of organization. Which form is more desirable (a) if the purpose is to maximize the cash available to the owner after personal income taxes and (b) if the purpose is to maximize the cash retention in the business? Explain.

☐ Understanding Published Financial Reports

13–43. EFFECTS OF DEFERRAL AND FLOW-THROUGH. (Alternate is 13–29.) Emery Air Freight used the flow-through method in accounting for its investment tax credits. Suppose Emery acquired new DC-9 airplanes for $25 million cash on December 31, 1986, and had 1986 pretax income of $30 million.

Assume that the income tax rate is 40%; no income tax payments will be due before early 1987; the airplanes have a ten-year life and an expected residual value of zero; and Emery is eligible for a $2.5 million tax credit because of its acquisition of this equipment.

1. Fill in the blanks in millions of dollars (based solely on the given data):

	SHAREHOLDER REPORTING	
	Deferral Method	Flow-through Method
Balances, December 31, 1986:		
Income before income taxes	?	?
Income tax expense	?	?
Net income	?	?
Income tax payable	?	?
Deferred investment tax credits	?	?

2. Prepare journal entries, December 31, 1986, (a) for the income tax expense before considering the investment tax credit. Also prepare entries for the investment tax credit using (b) deferral and (c) flow-through.
3. Suppose 1987 were a repetition of 1986 in the sense that pretax income was again $30 million. However, no tax credit was allowed on equipment acquired. Journal entry 3a would be the same as 2a. Prepare journal entries for the tax credit of 1986 as it affects 1987 using (b) deferral and (c) flow-through.

13–44. **INVESTMENT TAX CREDIT.** Consolidated Edison Company of New York, the electric utility serving New York City and Westchester County, received investment tax credits totaling $37 million in 1985. The company's capital expenditures were $459 million. Net income after considering all expenses, including taxes, but before considering the investment tax credit, was $553 million. A footnote in Con Edison's annual report showed:

Investment tax credits deferred:	
Credits generated and utilized	$37,000,000
Less: Amortization	11,000,000
Total	$26,000,000

Required:

1. What method does Con Edison use to account for the investment tax credit?
2. Compute Con Edison's 1985 net income using the deferral method.
3. Compute Con Edison's 1985 net income using the flow-through method.
4. Suppose Congress had increased the investment tax credit to 40% of capital expenditures for 1985 only. Compute 1985 net income (a) under the deferral method and (b) under the flow-through method. Assume under the deferral method that none of the investment tax credit on 1985's investments is amortized in 1985. Which of the two methods do you prefer? Explain.

13–45. **FUNDAMENTALS OF INCOME TAX ALLOCATION.** Suppose the railroad division of Burlington Northern purchases a group of highly specialized freight cars for $2.1 million. The cars have a ten-year life and no residual value. The company uses ACRS depreciation for tax purposes and straight-line depreciation for financial-reporting purposes. The freight cars are seven-year ACRS property.

Assume that the income of this division before depreciation and taxes is $800,000. The applicable income tax rate is 30%.

Required:

Show all amounts in thousands of dollars.

1. For the ten years, tabulate the details of how these facts would influence the Burlington Northern reporting for tax purposes and for reporting to stockholders. There is no investment tax credit. *Hint*: See Exhibit 13–6 (p. 591).
2. How will the Deferred Income Taxes account be affected if capital expenditures are the same each year? If they grow each year?

13–46. **ACRS DEPRECIATION.** United Parcel Service (UPS) provides delivery of packages throughout the United States. Consider a light-duty van acquired for $22,000. Using the prescribed ACRS method, compute the depreciation deduction for tax purposes for each of six years.

13–47. **ACRS AND DEFERRED TAXES.** Emery Air Freight Corporation provides overnight delivery of packages throughout the United States. The company acquired new equipment to expand its "Dayton Superhub" as part of its goal to reach $1 billion of sales. Suppose the equipment was acquired for $10 million cash and installed on January 2, 1987. For shareholder-reporting purposes, the equipment's useful life is ten years. There is zero expected residual value. However, for income tax purposes, assume that ACRS prescribes a five-year recovery period.

Show all dollar amounts in millions. There is no investment tax credit.

1. For simplicity, assume that this equipment is the only fixed asset subject to depreciation. Prepare a tabulation (similar to Exhibit 13–6, page 591) summarizing reporting to the Internal Revenue Service for the first six years. Assume that income before depreciation is $20 million and that the income tax rate is 40%.
2. Prepare a similar table summarizing reporting to shareholders. However, prepare a table for seven years. In the final column, show the balance sheet account Deferred Income Taxes at the end of each year. Assume straight-line depreciation.
3. Prepare the journal entry for Years 1 and 7 for income tax expense.

13–48. INSTALLMENT METHOD, DEFERRED TAXES. Suppose J. C. Penney sells kitchen appliances to a customer for $2,000 on January 2, 1987. There is no cash down payment. Instead the buyer must pay $100 per month for twenty successive months, beginning on January 31. Ignore interest and carrying charges. Assume that the gross margin rate is 50% and the income tax rate is 40%.

1. Compare the effects on income by filling in the blanks:
   a. Reporting to stockholders (accrual basis)

	1987	1988
Sales revenue	?	?
Cost of goods sold	?	?
Gross margin	?	?
Effect on income tax expense	?	?

   b. Reporting to income tax authorities on installment method

	1987	1988
Revenue collected	?	?
Gross margin subject to income tax	?	?
Effect on income tax outlay	?	?

2. Prepare the pertinent journal entries for 1987 and 1988. Explanations are not required. Use the accrual basis.

13–49. INSTALLMENT SALES AND TAXES. Sears uses the accrual method for reporting to shareholders, whereby all sales, including installment sales, are recognized as realized revenue as sales occur. In contrast, Sears used the installment method for reporting to income tax authorities. On January 2, 19X1, Sears sold a refrigerator for $540 on an installment sale basis. The sales contract required no down payment and thirty-six payments of $15 per month plus interest on the unpaid balance. The gross margin was 20% of the sales price. For purposes of this problem, ignore interest and any carrying charges.

1. For financial-reporting purposes, what is the pretax gross profit on the sale? The Internal Revenue Code gives the retailer the option of using either the accrual or the installment method (within limits), whereby 20% of each installment payment would be taxable in the period received. Under the installment method, what would be the pretax gross profit for each of the three years?
2. Assume a 50% tax rate. Prepare a table for three years showing the effects of income tax deferral. Use the following columns: pretax gross profit, tax paid,

tax deferred, total tax expense, net income, and balance sheet effect: balance of deferred income taxes.

3. Repeat requirement 2, assuming that a refrigerator is sold for the same price and terms on January 2, 19X2, and also on January 2 of 19X3, 19X4, and 19X5. Extend the analysis through Year 5.
4. Repeat requirement 3, assuming that two units are sold on January 2, 19X2, three in 19X3, four in 19X4, and five in 19X5.
5. Study the results in the above parts. What conclusions can you draw about the long-run effects of interperiod income tax allocation on financial statements?

13–50. **MEANING OF INCOME OF PARTNERSHIPS AND CORPORATIONS.** Study Appendix 13B. Peat Marwick International, a large public accounting partnership, had the following income statement (in millions):

Fees earned for professional services		$586
Operating expenses:		
Employee compensation and fringe benefits	$282	
Occupancy and equipment rentals including		
depreciation and amortization	40	
Other expenses	97	419
Available for allocation		$167
Allocated to:		
Partners formal retirement plans	$ 5	
Retired partners	6	
Active partners for compensation, insurance and		
other fringe benefit costs, and return on capital	156	$167

Required:

1. Suppose Peat Marwick International were a corporation rather than a partnership. Recast its income statement as a corporation.
2. Note how the $156 million is described in the above statement. State some major differences regarding compensation between being a partner in a public accounting firm and being a top executive in a corporation.

13–51. **COMPENSATION OF PARTNERS.** Study Appendix 13B. The business press frequently cites the high compensation of partners of public accounting firms. Arthur Andersen & Co., a large public accounting firm, included the following analysis in an annual report:

Average earnings per partner		$101,656
Deduct:		
Return on capital at risk	$16,147	
Retirement, insurance, etc.	10,500	26,647
Average executive compensation		
equivalent per partner		$ 75,009

Required:

What amount is subject to personal income tax currently for an average partner? For a comparable corporate executive? What reasoning would be used in formulating the above analysis?

13–52. **AMORTIZATION OF INVESTMENT TAX CREDIT.** On December 31, 1985, General Telephone and Electronics (GTE) had deferred investment tax credits of $1,074 million and retained earnings of $2,941 million. No investment tax credits were available to GTE in 1986 or later years. Assume that GTE's income after tax but before considering amortization of the investment tax credit is $1 billion for each of 1986,

1987, and 1988. Also assume that 15% of the December 31, 1985, amount of deferred investment tax credits will be amortized in each of the next three years and that no dividends will be paid.

Required:

| 1. Fill in the blanks in the following table (in millions, round to the nearest million):

	YEAR ENDED DECEMBER 31		
	1986	1987	1988
Income statement items:			
Income after tax but before			
amortization of ITC	$1,000	$1,000	$1,000
Amortization of ITC	?	?	?
Net income	?	?	?
Balance sheet items:			
Deferred investment tax			
credit	?	?	?
Retained earnings	?	?	?

2. Repeat requirement 1 except assume that GTE uses and has always used the flow-through method for the investment tax credit. (*Hint*: First compute the December 31, 1985, *retained earnings* balance *as if* GTE had been using the flow-through method.)
3. Assume that the entire $1,074 million of deferred investment tax credits is amortized in 1986, 1987, and 1988. Compute GTE's December 31, 1988, retained income under the conditions of requirement 1.
4. Assume that Congress does not reenact the investment tax credit. How long will GTE's financial statements be influenced by its accounting for the investment tax credit?

13–53. **RECONSTRUCTION OF INCOME TAX TRANSACTIONS.** The Sherwin-Williams Company makes paints such as Dutch Boy and Kem-Tone and operates 1,627 paint and wallcovering stores in forty-eight states. The company showed various balances in its 1985 annual report. Actual descriptions and amounts follow (dollar amounts in thousands):

	1985	1984
As part of Current Liabilities:		
Accrued income taxes	$30,262	$23,737
As part of Noncurrent Liabilities:		
Deferred income taxes	36,037	29,489

The income statement showed "income taxes" of $54,000,000. No other data regarding income taxes were in the income statement. A footnote stated: "Investment tax credits (accounted for by the flow-through method) aggregated $3,354,000 for 1985."

Required:

Prepare summary 1985 journal entries for (a) the investment tax credit, (b) income taxes as an expense for the fiscal year, and (c) disbursements for income taxes. *Hint*: T-accounts may help.

13–54. **DECLINE IN BALANCE OF DEFERRED INCOME TAXES.** The following are excerpts from the 19X3 annual report of American Machine and Foundry Company (AMF).

	DECEMBER 31	
	19X3	19X2
Included in current liabilities: Federal income taxes (including deferred taxes applicable to installment obligations: 19X3—$5,223,000, 19X2—$9,636,000)	$12,769,618	$28,405,310
As a separate item above stockholders' equity: Deferred federal income taxes (due principally to accelerated depreciation)	16,533,000	20,413,000
In the income statement for the year ending December 31: Federal taxes on income	19,467,000	19,052,000

Required:

1. Explain the accounting options in the areas of installment sales and depreciation accounting that would give rise to the deferred tax liabilities.
2. The deferred tax liabilities declined between 19X2 and 19X3. What specific underlying relationship(s) would yield this result?
3. Estimate the taxable income reported by AMF on its federal tax return in 19X3. (For purposes of this estimate, assume a 50% tax rate.) Show all your calculations. Assume that there were no acquisitions of assets that qualified for the investment tax credit during 19X3. (You may wish to do requirements 3 and 4 together.)
4. Prepare a T-account analysis of the income tax accounts for the year. Show three accounts: Deferred Taxes—Current; Deferred Taxes—Noncurrent; and Accrued Income Taxes Payable. Prepare two summary journal entries, one for the income tax expense for the year and another for the cash paid to the income tax authorities.

13–55. RECONSTRUCTION OF INCOME TAX TRANSACTION. Adolph Coors Company produces beers. Its 1985 annual report contained the following actual descriptions and amounts (in thousands):

Income Statement

Income taxes:	
Current	
Federal	$ 7,773
State	3,090
	$10,863
Deferred—net	32,137
	$43,000

Balance Sheet

	DECEMBER 29	
	1985	1984
Current assets: Refundable income taxes	—	14,400
Current liabilities: Federal and state income taxes	5,127	4,846
Noncurrent liabilities: Accumulated deferred income taxes	165,462	136,409

Footnotes disclosed that the investment tax credit was $3,953,000 in 1985. It was applied as a reduction of income tax expense.

Required:

Prepare summary journal entries for income tax transactions for 1985. Include entries for (a) the investment tax credit, (b) income taxes as an expense for the year, and (c) cash disbursements for income taxes. *Hint*: T-accounts may help.

13–56. COMPLETED-CONTRACT AND PERCENTAGE-OF-COMPLETION METHODS. (This is a more difficult problem.) Sanders Associates produces advanced technology electronic systems and products. Much of the company's work is on a long-term contract basis. Sanders used the completed-contract method for tax purposes and the percentage-of-completion method for reporting to stockholders. The company's $32,651,000 addition to the Deferred Federal Taxes account for 1985 was explained in a footnote:

Completed contract method for long-term contracts	$23,699,000
Other timing differences on contract income	4,600,000
Depreciation	3,711,000
Other timing differences, net	641,000
Total	$32,651,000

The 1985 net income for Sanders Associates was $37,116,000 on sales of $885,-790,000. The average pretax margin on long-term contracts was 20% of the revenue. The tax rate was 38%, and a refund of $14,156,000 was received from the federal government for 1985 income taxes. Foreign income taxes were $4,254,000. Sanders paid no state income taxes.

Required:

1. Compute the provision for income taxes as shown on Sanders's 1985 income statement for stockholders.
2. Compute the pretax income on the report to stockholders.
3. Suppose Sanders had used the percentage-of-completion method for both tax purposes and for reporting to stockholders. Compute the taxes paid (or immediately payable) in 1985.
4. Suppose Sanders had used the completed-contract method for both tax purposes and for reporting to stockholders. Compute the revenue, pretax income, and net income that would have been reported to stockholders.

13–57. RECONSTRUCTION OF INCOME TAX TRANSACTIONS. (This is a more difficult problem.) American Greetings Corporation produces greeting cards, including cards based on the characters Ziggy, Strawberry Shortcake, and the Care Bears. An annual report showed the following (in thousands except per share amounts):

American Greetings

	BALANCE SHEET ITEMS AS OF FEBRUARY 28	
	1986	1985
Under current liabilities:		
Income taxes	$ 18,988	$ 27,465
Immediately after long-term debt:		
Deferred income taxes	27,356	14,406

	INCOME STATEMENT ITEMS FOR THE YEAR ENDED FEBRUARY 28	
	1986	1985
Income before income taxes	$136,060	$135,703
Income taxes:		
Current, net of investment tax credits of $2,449 in 1986 and $2,578 in 1985	48,685	49,387
Deferred	12,950	11,951
Total	$ 61,635	$ 61,338
Net income	$ 74,425	$ 74,365
Net income per common share	$ 2.32	$ 2.35

A footnote stated:

☐   Investment tax credits are accounted for by the "flow-through" method.

Required:

1. What was the dollar amount of the income tax payment that American Greetings made during the fiscal year 1986?
2. (a) Provide the journal entries to record the gross tax expense and gross tax liability (before recording the investment tax credit) for American Greetings in fiscal years 1985 and 1986.
   (b) Record in journal entry form the effects of investment tax credits taken in fiscal years 1985 and 1986.
3. If American Greetings had elected to use the deferral method over ten years to account for the investment tax credit in reporting to shareholders, by how much would the income tax cash payments have been reduced in 1985 and 1986?
4. Suppose fiscal year 1985 was the first year in which American Greetings purchased assets that qualified for the investment tax credit. If the deferral method had been used as described in requirement 3, determine the unamortized investment tax credits as of February 28, 1986. Assume a full year's amortization in the year of purchase.

Chapter 14

FINANCIAL REPORTING AND CHANGING PRICES

LEARNING OBJECTIVES

After studying this chapter, you should be able to

1. Describe the major differences between financial capital and physical capital
2. Explain and illustrate four different ways of measuring income: (a) historical cost/nominal dollars, (b) current cost/nominal dollars, (c) historical cost/constant dollars, and (d) current cost/constant dollars
3. Explain the difference between monetary and nonmonetary items (Appendix 14A)
4. Compute general purchasing-power gains and losses (Appendix 14A)
5. Describe the major provisions of FASB Statement No. 33, "Financial Reporting and Changing Prices" (Appendixes 14A and 14B)

The measurement of income is easily the most controversial subject in accounting. This chapter focuses on how inflation affects the income statement. The chapter appendixes explore the problems of accounting for inflation in more depth, although still at an introductory level. This chapter illustrates the imprecision of a reported net income figure, the assumptions on which traditional accounting is based, and the limitations of the typical financial statements.

INFLATION AND INCOME MEASUREMENT

For the past two decades, inflation has been a major source of price changes. During this period, a pet theme of politicians and others has been the "unconscionable" or "obscene" profits reported by American companies. In turn, business executives maintain that our well-known historical-cost basis for measuring income produces misleading results, especially during a time of rising prices. Some managers have complained that inflation causes reported profits to be so badly overstated that income taxes have been unfairly levied. In many cases, invested capital, rather than earned income, has been taxed. This chapter concentrates on these issues. Its purpose is to deepen your understanding of the various concepts of income and capital.

The industries with huge investments in plant and equipment claim that their profits are badly misstated by generally accepted accounting principles. For instance, consider NYNEX, a company that emerged from the breakup of the Bell System. NYNEX reported 1985 net income of $1,095 million, which would have been a net loss of $82 million if depreciation had been computed on a replacement-cost basis.

Inflation led many critics to attack the traditional financial statements as being "unrealistic," "misleading," "useless," and so on. Suggestions for change led to regulatory actions that departed from the historical-cost measures that had almost exclusively dominated financial reporting throughout the century. These departures will now be described. In essence, the controversies center on how income and capital should be defined. Different sets of concepts of income and capital will lead to different measurement methods.

INCOME OR CAPITAL

At first glance, the concept of income seems straightforward. Income is increase in wealth. But what is wealth? It is capital. But what is capital? An endless chain of similar questions can be constructed. The heart of the issue is the distinction between invested capital and income. The time-honored interpretation is that invested capital is a *financial* concept (rather than a *physical* concept). The focus is on the potential profitability of the money invested, no matter what types of inventory, equipment, or other resources have been acquired.

Financial resources (capital) are invested with the expectation of an eventual return *of* that capital together with additional amounts representing the return *on* that capital. Controversies have arisen regarding whether the financial resources generated by the invested capital qualify as returns *of* or *on* capital.

The Financial Accounting Standards Board distinguishes between financial and physical capital maintenance concepts:

☐ Capital is maintained when Revenues are at least equal to all costs and expenses. The appropriate measurement of costs and expenses depends on the concept of capital maintenance adopted.[1]

Consider an example where a company begins with owners' investment (capital) of $1,000, which is immediately used to purchase inventory. The inventory is sold a year later for $1,500. Meanwhile an increase in the supplier's selling prices has caused the cost of replacing the inventory to rise to $1,200.

	Financial Capital Maintenance	Physical Capital Maintenance
Sales	$1,500	$1,500
Cost of goods sold	1,000	1,200
Income	$ 500	$ 300

Most accountants and managers believe that income emerges after *financial* resources are recovered, a concept called **financial capital maintenance**. Income is $500 after recovering the $1,000 financial investment in inventory.

On the other hand, some accountants and managers believe that income emerges only after recovering an amount that allows *physical operating capability* to be maintained, called **physical capital maintenance**. Because $1,200 is the current cost of inventory (cost of maintaining physical capability) at the date of sale, $300 is the measure of income.

MEASUREMENT ALTERNATIVES

Study the four definitions in this paragraph; they are critical for understanding inflation accounting. **Nominal dollars** are dollar measurements that are not restated for fluctuations in the general purchasing power of the monetary

---

[1] Financial Accounting Standards Board, *Statement No. 33*, "Financial Reporting and Changing Prices."

unit, whereas **constant dollars** are nominal dollars restated in terms of current purchasing power. The **historical cost** of an asset is the amount originally paid to acquire it; the **current cost** of an asset is generally the cost to replace it. Traditional accounting uses *nominal* (rather than constant) dollars and *historical* (rather than current) costs. Such accounting has almost exclusively dominated financial reporting throughout this century. Using historical costs implies maintenance of *financial* capital; current costs imply *physical* capital maintenance.

Two approaches, which can be applied separately or in combination, address problems caused by inflation: (1) constant-dollar disclosures account for *general* changes in the purchasing power of the dollar, and (2) current-cost disclosures account for changes in *specific* prices. The two approaches create the following four alternatives for measuring income:

	Historical Cost	Current Cost
Nominal Dollars	Historical cost/ Nominal dollars	Current cost/ Nominal dollars
Constant Dollars	Historical cost/ Constant dollars	Current cost/ Constant dollars

The G Company situation described below is used to compare various concepts of income and capital. The four basic methods of income measurement are presented.

G Company has the following comparative balance sheets at December 31 (based on historical costs in nominal dollars):

	19X1	19X2
Cash	$ 0	$10,500
Inventory, 400 and 100 units, respectively	8,000	2,000
Total assets	$8,000	$12,500
Original paid-in capital	$8,000	$ 8,000
Retained income	—	4,500
Stockholders' equity	$8,000	$12,500

The company had acquired all of its four hundred units of inventory at $20 per unit (total of $8,000) on December 31, 19X1, and had held the units until December 31, 19X2. Three hundred units were sold for $35 per unit (total of $10,500 cash) on December 31, 19X2. The replacement cost of the inventory at that date was $30 per unit. The general-price-level index was 100 on December 31, 19X1, and 110 on December 31, 19X2. Assume that these are the only transactions. There are no liabilities. Ignore income taxes.

☐ Historical Cost/Nominal Dollars

Exhibit 14–1 is the basis for the explanations that follow in the next several pages. The first set of financial statements in Exhibit 14–1 shows the time-honored method that uses historical cost/nominal dollars (Method 1). Basically, this method measures invested capital in nominal dollars. It is the most popular approach to income measurement and is commonly called the historical-cost method. Operating income (equals net income in this case) is the excess of realized revenue ($10,500 in 19X2) over the "not restated" historical costs of assets used in obtaining that revenue. As we have already seen,

EXHIBIT 14–1 *(Put a clip on this page for easy reference)*

Four Major Methods to Measure Income and Capital

	NOMINAL DOLLARS*				CONSTANT DOLLARS*			
	(METHOD 1)		(METHOD 2)		(METHOD 3)		(METHOD 4)	
	Historical Cost		Current Cost		Historical Cost		Current Cost	
(in dollars)	19X1	19X2	19X1	19X2	19X1	19X2	19X1	19X2
Balance sheets as of December 31								
Cash	—	10,500	—	10,500	—	10,500	—	10,500
Inventory, 400 and 100 units, respectively	8,000	2,000[b]	8,000	3,000[c]	8,800[e]	2,200[e]	8,800[e]	3,000[c]
Total assets	8,000	12,500	8,000	13,500	8,800	12,700	8,800	13,500
Original paid-in capital	8,000	8,000	8,000	8,000	8,800[f]	8,800[f]	8,800[f]	8,800[f]
Retained income (confined to income from continuing operations)		4,500		1,500		3,900		1,500
Revaluation equity (accumulated holding gains)				4,000				3,200
Total stockholders' equity	8,000	12,500	8,000	13,500	8,800	12,700	8,800	13,500
Income statements for 19X2								
Sales, 300 units @ $35		10,500		10,500		10,500		10,500
Cost of goods sold, 300 units		6,000[b]		9,000[c]		6,600[e]		9,000[c]
Income from continuing operations (to retained income)		4,500		1,500		3,900		1,500
Holding gains:[a]								
on 300 units sold				3,000[d]				2,400[g]
on 100 units unsold				1,000[d]				800[g]
Total holding gains[a] (to revaluation equity)				4,000				3,200

* Nominal dollars are not restated for a general price index, whereas constant dollars are restated.

[a] Many advocates of this current-cost method favor showing these gains in a completely separate statement of holding gains rather than as a part of the income statement. Others favor including some or all of these gains as a part of income for the year; see Appendix 14B for further discussion.

[b] $100 \times \$20$ [c] $100 \times \$30$ [d] $300 \times (\$30 - \$20)$ [e] $110/100 \times \$8,000$ [f] $110/100 \times \$8,000$
  $300 \times \$20$ $300 \times \$30$ $100 \times (\$30 - \$20)$ $110/100 \times \$2,000$
                                                      $110/100 \times \$6,000$

[g] $\$9,000 -$ Restated cost of $\$6,600 = \$2,400$ $\$3,000 -$ Restated cost of $\$2,200 = \$800$
  or   or
  $300 \times (\$30 - 110\%$ of $\$20) = \$2,400$ $100 \times (\$30 - 110\%$ of $\$20) = \$800$

when the conventional accrual basis of accounting is used, an exchange transaction is ordinarily necessary before revenues (and resulting incomes) are deemed to be realized. Thus no income generally appears until the asset is sold; intervening price fluctuations are ignored.

□ Current Cost/Nominal Dollars

The second set of financial statements in Exhibit 14–1 illustrates a *current-cost* method that has especially strong advocates in the United Kingdom and Australia (Method 2). This method uses current cost/nominal dollars. In general, the current cost of an asset is the cost to replace it. The focus is on income from continuing operations. This model emphasizes that operating income should be "distributable" income. That is, G Company could pay dividends in an amount of only $1,500, leaving enough assets to allow for replacement of the inventory that has just been sold.

Critics of the historical-cost approach claim that the $4,500 measure of income from continuing operations is misleading because it inaccurately reflects (it overstates) the net increment in distributable assets. If a $4,500 dividend were paid, the company would be less able to continue operations at the same level as before. The $3,000 difference between the two operating incomes ($4,500 − $1,500 = $3,000) is frequently referred to as an "inventory profit" or an "inflated profit." Why? Because $9,000 instead of $6,000 is now necessary to replace the 300 units sold (300 × the increase in price from $20 to $30 equals the $3,000 difference).

□ Holding Gains and Physical Capital

The current-cost method stresses a separation between *income from continuing operations*, which is defined as the excess of revenue over the current costs of the assets consumed in obtaining that revenue, and **holding gains** (or **losses**), which are increases (or decreases) in the replacement costs of the assets held during the current period. Accountants differ sharply on how to account for holding gains. The "correct" accounting depends on distinctions between capital and income. That is, income cannot occur until invested capital is "recovered" or "maintained." The issue of capital versus income is concretely illustrated in Exhibit 14–1. The advocates of a physical concept of capital maintenance claim that *all* holding gains (both those gains related to the units sold and the gains related to the units unsold) should be excluded from income and become a part of revalued capital, called **revaluation equity**. That is, for a going concern no income can result unless the physical capital devoted to operations during the current period can be replaced.

For simplicity, income taxes are ignored in Exhibit 14–1. The historical cost/nominal dollar method (*Method 1*) is the only acceptable method for reporting on income tax returns in English-speaking countries. As Appendix 14A discusses in more detail, many managers of heavy industries such as steel and aluminum claim that their capital is being taxed under the historical cost/nominal dollar method. These managers maintain that taxes should be levied only on *income from continuing operations*, as computed under the current cost/nominal dollar method (Method 2).

☐ Historical Cost/Constant Dollars

Method 3 of Exhibit 14–1 shows the results of applying general index numbers to historical costs. Essentially, the income measurements in each year are restated in terms of *constant dollars* (possessing the same general purchasing power of the current year) instead of the *nominal dollars* (possessing different general purchasing power of various years).

The fundamental reasoning underlying the Method 3 approach goes to the heart of the measurement theory itself. Additions or subtractions must use a *common measuring unit*, be it dollars, francs, meters, ounces, or any chosen measure.

Consider the objections to Method 1. Deducting 6,000 19X1 dollars from 10,500 19X2 dollars to obtain $4,500 is akin to deducting 60 *centimeters* from 105 *meters* and calling the result 45. Grade-school tests are marked wrong when such nonsensical arithmetic is discovered, but accountants have been paid well for years for performing similar arithmetic.

Method 3, historical cost/constant dollars, shows how to remedy the foregoing objections. General indexes can be used to restate the amounts in a historical cost/nominal dollar statement. Examples of such indexes are the Gross National Product Implicit Price Deflator and the Consumer Price Index for All Urban Consumers (CPI). Anyone who has lived long enough to be able to read this book is aware that the purchasing power of the dollar is unstable. Index numbers are used to gauge the relationship between current conditions and some norm or base condition (which is assigned the index number of 100). For our purpose, a general price index compares the average price of a group of goods and services at one date with the average price of a similar group at another date. A price index is an average. It does not measure the behavior of the individual component prices. Some individual prices may move in one direction and some in another. The general consumer price level may soar while the prices of eggs and chickens decline.

Do not confuse *general* indexes, which are used in constant-dollar accounting, with *specific* indexes. The two have entirely different purposes. Sometimes specific price indexes are used as a means of approximating the *current costs* of particular assets or types of assets. That is, companies have found specialized indexes to be good enough to get approximations of current costs. This avoids the hiring of professional appraisers or the employing of other expensive means of valuation. For example, Inland Steel uses the Engineering News Record Construction Cost Index to value most of its property, plant, and equipment for purposes of using the current-cost method.

☐ Maintaining Invested Capital

The historical cost/constant dollar approach (Method 3) is *not* a fundamental departure from historical costs. Instead it maintains that all historical costs to be matched against revenue should be restated on some constant-dollar basis so that all revenue and all expenses can be expressed in dollars of the same (usually current) purchasing power. The restated figures *are historical costs* expressed in constant dollars via the use of a general price index.

The *current* dollar is typically employed because users of financial statements tend to think in such terms instead of in terms of old dollars with significantly different purchasing power. The original units in inventory would be updated on each year's balance sheet along with their effect on stockholders' equity. For example, the December 31, 19X1, balance sheet would be restated for comparative purposes on December 31, 19X2:

	NOT RESTATED COST	MULTIPLIER	RESTATED COST
Inventory	$8,000	110/100	$8,800
Original paid-in capital	8,000	110/100	8,800

To extend the illustration, suppose all the inventory was held for two full years. The general price index rose from 110 to 132 during 19X3. The December 31, 19X2, balance sheet items would be restated for comparative purposes on December 31, 19X3:

	RESTATED COST 12/31/X2	MULTIPLIER	RESTATED COST 12/31/X3
Inventory	$8,800	132/110	$10,560*
Original paid-in capital	8,800	132/110	10,560*

* The same result could be tied to the year of acquisition:
Inventory $8,000 × 132/100 = $10,560
Original paid-in capital $8,000 × 132/100 = $10,560

The restated amount is just that—a restatement of original *cost* in terms of current dollars—not a gain in any sense. Therefore this approach should *not* be labeled as an adoption of "current-cost" accounting. Under this approach, if the specific current cost of the inventory goes up or down, the restated cost is unaffected.

The restated historical-cost approach harmonizes with the concept of *maintaining the general purchasing power* of the invested capital (a *financial* concept of capital maintenance) in total rather than maintaining "specific invested capital," item by item. More will be said about this distinction after we examine Method 4.

☐ Current Cost/Constant Dollars

Method 4 of Exhibit 14–1 shows the results of applying general index numbers to current costs. As the footnotes of the exhibit explain in more detail, the nominal gains reported under Method 2 are adjusted so that only gains in constant dollars are reported. For example, suppose you buy 100 units on December 31, 19X1, for $2,000 cash. If the current replacement cost of your inventory at December 31, 19X2, is $3,000 but the general price index has risen from 100 to 110, your nominal gain is $1,000 but your "real" gain in constant dollars in 19X2 is only $800: the $3,000 current cost minus the restated historical cost of $2,000 × 1.10 = $2,200.

Suppose the 100 units are held throughout 19X3. The general price index rises from 110 to 132. The replacement cost rises from $30 to $34, a nominal holding gain for 19X3 of $4 × 100 = $400. However, the current cost/constant dollar approach (Method 4) would report a real holding loss:

Current cost, restated, December 31, 19X2:	
$3,000 × 132/110	$3,600
Current cost, December 31, 19X3, 100 × $34	3,400
Holding loss	$ 200

Many theorists disagree on the relative merits of historical-cost approaches versus miscellaneous versions of current-cost approaches to income measurement. But there is general agreement among the theorists that restatements in constant dollars would be an improvement (ignoring practical barriers), because otherwise income includes illusory gains caused by using an unstable measuring unit.

FASB PRESENTATION

During the late 1970s, soaring inflation raised questions about the usefulness of historical cost/nominal dollar statements. Accountants in many countries struggled with the problem of measuring the current cost of assets.

After extensive public hearings, the Financial Accounting Standards Board issued *Statement No. 33*, "Financial Reporting and Changing Prices," in 1979. The statement applies to public companies that have either (1) inventories and property, plant, and equipment (before deducting accumulated depreciation) amounting to more than $125 million or (2) total assets amounting to more than $1 billion (after deducting accumulated depreciation). No changes must be made in the primary financial statements. All the information required by *Statement No. 33* is to be presented as supplementary schedules in published annual reports.

Statement No. 33 is experimental, but in 1985 the FASB committed to requiring the supplementary reports for at least several more years. Appendix 14A has a fuller description of the FASB requirements.

Exhibit 14–2 recasts the income statement in Exhibit 14–1 (p. 628) in accordance with the FASB preferences. Compare the two exhibits:

1. The FASB avoids using the term *holding gain*. Instead it uses verbose descriptions of the final three numbers in Exhibit 14–2. Why? Probably because accountants and managers continue to disagree about whether all, some, or none of the holding

EXHIBIT 14–2

Recasting of Preceding Exhibit
(To reflect FASB preferences per FAS 33)
Statement of Income from Continuing Operations Adjusted for Changing Prices
For the Year Ended December 31, 19X2

	AS REPORTED IN THE PRIMARY STATEMENTS	ADJUSTED FOR CHANGES IN SPECIFIC PRICES (CURRENT COSTS)
Sales, 300 units @ $35	$10,500	$10,500
Cost of goods sold, 300 units	6,000	9,000
Income from continuing operations	$ 4,500	$ 1,500
Increase in specific prices (current cost) of inventories held during the year: 400 units × ($30 − $20)		$ 4,000
Less effect of increase in general price level: 10% × 400 × $20		800
Excess of increase in specific prices over increase in the general price level		$ 3,200

gains are really "net income." Note too that in both exhibits these numbers are reported but are not added to income from continuing operations.

2. Exhibit 14–2 is similar to the Method 4 format used in Exhibit 14–1. The income from continuing operations is identical. The only difference is that the total holding gain, $3,200, is divided into different components. Exhibit 14–2 lists the holding gain from Method 2, $4,000, and then deducts the holding gain caused by general inflation, $800. In essence, the specific prices of the company's assets increased by $4,000, although the general-price-level increase would have caused only an $800 increase. Therefore the firm's assets increased in value by $3,200 *more than* the increase caused by general inflation.

The impact of adjustments for current costs differs across companies. The following list shows the fiscal 1985 income (loss) for six companies on both historical cost/nominal dollars and current cost/constant dollars bases (in millions):

COMPANY	HISTORICAL COST/ NOMINAL DOLLARS	CURRENT COST/ CONSTANT DOLLARS
Alcoa	$ (17)	$ (54)
American Telephone & Telegraph	1,557	392
General Motors	3,399	3,220
Safeway	231	164
Sears	1,303	1,027
U.S. Steel	313	(351)

As recently as 1983, current-cost earnings averaged only 28% of the familiar historical-cost numbers. However, because of the decline in the rate of inflation, average current-cost earnings are now over half of historical-cost earnings. But note that current-cost earnings are 95% of historical-cost earnings for General Motors and only 25% for AT&T. Furthermore, a historical-cost income becomes a current-cost loss for U.S. Steel.

SUMMARY

The matching of historical costs with revenue is the generally accepted means of measuring net income. But basing such computations on some version of current costs has been proposed as a better gauge of the distinctions between income (the return *on* capital) and capital maintenance (the return *of* capital).

General price indexes are used to adjust historical costs so that all expenses are measured in current dollars of the same purchasing power. Such adjustments do not represent a departure from historical cost. In contrast, specific price indexes are often used to implement the current-cost approach to measuring income and capital.

SUMMARY PROBLEMS FOR YOUR REVIEW

☐ Problem One

In 1967, a parcel of land, call it parcel #1, was purchased for $1,200. An identical parcel, #2, was purchased today for $3,600. The general-price-level index has risen from 100 in 1967 to 300 now. Fill in the blanks.

PARCEL	(1) HISTORICAL COST MEASURED IN 1967 PURCHASING POWER	(2) HISTORICAL COST MEASURED IN CURRENT PURCHASING POWER	(3) HISTORICAL COST AS ORIGINALLY MEASURED
1			
2	___	___	___
Total	___	___	___

1. Compare the figures in the three columns. Which total presents a nonsense result. Why?
2. Does the write-up of parcel #1 in Column 2 result in a gain? Why? Assume that these parcels are the only assets of the business. There are no liabilities. Prepare a balance sheet for each of the three columns.

☐ Solution to Problem One

PARCEL	(1) HISTORICAL COST MEASURED IN 1967 PURCHASING POWER	(2) HISTORICAL COST MEASURED IN CURRENT PURCHASING POWER	(3) HISTORICAL COST AS ORIGINALLY MEASURED
1	$1,200	$3,600	$1,200
2	1,200	3,600	3,600
Total	$2,400	$7,200	$4,800

1. The addition in column 3 produces a nonsense result. In contrast, the other sums are the results of applying a standard unit of measure. The computations in columns 1 and 2 are illustrations of a restatement of historical cost in terms of a common dollar, a standard unit of measure. Such computations have frequently been termed as adjustments for changes in the general price level. Whether the restatement is made using the 1967 dollar or the current dollar is a matter of personal preference; columns 1 and 2 yield equivalent results. Restatement in terms of the current dollar (column 2) is more popular because the current dollar has more meaning than the old dollar to the reader of the financial statements.

2. The mere restatement of identical assets in terms of different but equivalent measuring units cannot be regarded as a gain. Expressing parcel #1 as $1,200 in column 1 and $3,600 in column 2 is like expressing parcel #1 in terms of, say, either 1,200 square yards or 9 × 1,200 = 10,800 square feet. Surely, the "write-up" from 1,200 square yards to 10,800 square feet is not a gain; it is merely another way of measuring the same asset. The 1,200 square yards and the 10,800 square feet are equivalent; they are different ways of describing the same asset. That is basically what general-price-level accounting is all about. It says you cannot measure one plot of land in square yards and another in square feet and add them together before converting to some common measure. Unfortunately, column 3 fails to perform such a conversion before adding the two parcels together; hence the total is internally inconsistent.

The balance sheets would be:

	(1)	(2)	(3)
Land	$2,400	$7,200	$4,800
Paid-in capital	$2,400	$7,200	$4,800

Note that (1) is expressed in 1967 dollars, (2) is in current dollars, and (3) is a mixture of 1967 and current dollars.

☐ Problem Two

Reexamine Exhibit 14–1, page 628. Suppose the replacement cost at December 31, 19X2, had been $25 instead of $30. Suppose also that the general price index had been 120 instead of 110. All other facts are unchanged. Use four columns to prepare balance sheets as of December 31, 19X2 (only) and income statements for 19X2 under the four concepts shown in Exhibit 14–1.

☐ Solution to Problem Two

The solution is in Exhibit 14–3. In particular, compare Methods 2 and 4. The current cost of inventory items has risen 25% during a period when the general level has risen 20%.

Note too that the historical cost/constant dollar concept restates the old historical-cost amounts in 19X2 dollars rather than 19X1 dollars by multiplying the old dollars by 120/100.

EXHIBIT 14–3

Solution Exhibit for Summary Problem Two for Your Review

	NOMINAL DOLLARS		CONSTANT DOLLARS	
	(METHOD 1) Historical Cost[a]	(METHOD 2) Current Cost	(METHOD 3) Historical Cost	(METHOD 4) Current Cost
Balance sheets, December 31, 19X2				
Cash	10,500	10,500	10,500	10,500
Inventory, 100 units	2,000	2,500[b]	2,400[d]	2,500[b]
Total assets	12,500	13,000	12,900	13,000
Original paid-in capital	8,000	8,000	9,600[e]	9,600[e]
Retained income (confined to income from continuing operations)	4,500	3,000	3,300	3,000
Revaluation equity (accumulated holding gains)	—	2,000	—	400
Total stockholders' equity	12,500	13,000	12,900	13,000
Income statements for 19X2				
Sales, 300 units @ $35	10,500	10,500	10,500	10,500
Cost of goods sold, 300 units	6,000	7,500[b]	7,200[d]	7,500
Income from continuing operations	4,500	3,000	3,300	3,000
Holding gains (losses):				
On 300 units sold		1,500[c]		300[f]
On 100 units unsold		500[c]		100[f]
Total holding gains		2,000		400

[a] All numbers are the same as in Exhibit 14–1, p. 628.
[b] $100 \times \$25$ [c] $300 \times (\$25 - \$20)$ [d] $120/100 \times \$2,000$ [e] $120/100 \times \$8,000$
    $300 \times \$25$ $100 \times (\$25 - \$20)$ $120/100 \times \$6,000$
[f] $\$7,500$ − restated cost of $\$7,200 = \$300$
   $\$2,500$ − restated cost of $\$2,400 = \$100$

HIGHLIGHTS TO REMEMBER

Restatements in constant dollars can be applied to both the historical-cost and the current-cost basis of income measurement, as Methods 3 and 4 illustrate. Avoid the misconception that the choices are among the first three methods only. In fact, many advocates of the current cost/constant dollar method insist that it provides the most useful approximation of net income. In any event, any measurement of income should be based on constant dollars.

When inflation accounting is discussed, accountants and managers frequently confuse and blur the various concepts of income just covered. Highlights of Exhibit 14–1 (p. 628) include:

1. The choice among accounting measures is often expressed as either historical-cost accounting or general-price-level accounting or current-cost (specific-price-level) accounting. But this is an inaccurate statement of choices.

2. A correct statement would be that there are four major concepts. Nominal dollars can be combined with either historical cost (Method 1) or current cost (Method 2). In addition,

general-price-level (constant-dollar) accounting can be combined with either historical cost (Method 3) or current cost (Method 4).

3. Method 3, the historical cost/constant dollar method, is *not* concerned with current-cost concepts of income, whatever their strengths and weaknesses.

4. The current-cost Methods 2 and 4 for measuring income from operations are based on *physical* rather than *financial* concepts of maintenance of invested capital.

5. Write-ups of nonmonetary assets (inventory in this example) under Method 3 do *not* result in the recognition of gains. They are restatements of *costs* in dollars of equivalent purchasing power. See Appendix 14A for a discussion of the distinction between monetary and nonmonetary assets, as well as other aspects of inflation accounting.

ACCOUNTING VOCABULARY

Capital Maintenance, p. *626* Constant Dollars, *627* Current Cost, *627* Current-Cost/Constant Dollar Method, *631* Current-Cost/Nominal Dollar Method, *629* Financial Capital Maintenance, *626* Historical Cost, *627* Historical Cost/Constant Dollar Method, *630* Historical Cost/Nominal Dollar Method, *628* Holding Gains or Losses, *629* Monetary Items, *640* Net Monetary Position, *641* Nominal Dollars, *626* Physical Capital Maintenance, *626* Revaluation Equity, *629*

APPENDIX 14A: MORE ON INFLATION ACCOUNTING

This appendix extends the discussion in the body of the chapter, emphasizing current-cost depreciation and monetary items. Special attention is given to the FASB requirements regarding these topics.

MEANING OF CURRENT COST

Current cost is the most popular term for describing the fundamental basis for valuing the inventory as shown for Method 2 in Exhibit 14–1. However, it is a general term having several variations. Be on guard as to its meaning in a particular situation. As illustrated in Exhibit 14–1, the current-cost method stresses that income cannot emerge until deducting the current (or reproduction) cost of replenishing the item at today's prices. The regulatory authorities in most of the English-speaking countries have proposed that the current-cost approach be based on replacement costs. In most instances, *replacement cost* means today's cost of obtaining a similar asset that would produce the same expected cash flows as the existing asset. For a particular company, these replacement costs would be obtained via price quotations, specific appraisals, or specific indexes for materials or construction.

The FASB uses current replacement cost as its dominant requirement for measuring current cost. However, sometimes the replacement cost of a particular asset exceeds its *recoverable amount*. For example, some equipment or inventory may be obsolete. *Recoverable amount* is defined as (1) the net realizable value of an asset that is about to be sold or (2) the net present value of expected cash flows (called *value in use*) of an asset that is not about to be sold. *Net realizable value* is the amount of cash (or its equivalent) expected to be derived from sale of an asset, net of costs required to be incurred as a result of the sale. In sum, the FASB rule is current cost or lower recoverable amount.

The general idea of current cost is the same for equipment as for inventories. Nevertheless, the application of the idea is more difficult. An illustration will help to clarify the issues. Extending the example in Exhibit 14–1, suppose that on January 2, 19X3, $5,000 of the $10,500 cash was used to buy sales equipment. The equipment was being fully depreciated over a five-year life on a straight-line basis. The replacement cost of the equipment (new) at the end of 19X3 was $8,000. The general price index was 110 at the end of 19X2 and 132 at the end of 19X3. Exhibit 14–4 shows the effects and why manufacturers of heavy goods would like the IRS to adopt the current-cost approach. That is, the manufacturers would want depreciation expense of $1,600 to be deductible for income tax purposes. At the same time, the "holding gain" of $3,000 should not be subject to tax because it represents capital maintenance rather than income.

Current-cost depreciation is computed by multiplying the depreciation percentage based on useful life ($1 \div 5$ years = 20%) by the new *gross* carrying amount at current cost: $.20 \times \$8,000 = \$1,600$.

The holding gain in Method 2 (current cost/nominal dollars) is computed by multiplying the percentage increase in gross carrying amount for the year (from $5,000 to $8,000 is a 60% increase) by the beginning *net* carrying amount at current cost: $.60 \times \$5,000 = \$3,000$.

Pursuing the example for one more year, suppose the replacement cost of the equipment (new) at the end of 19X4 was $12,000. The percentage increase in gross carrying amount would be 50% (from $8,000 to $12,000). Method 2 (current cost/ nominal dollars) would show the following effects on the 19X4 income statement:

1. Restate the beginning asset value into end-of-the-year dollars, recognizing a holding gain:[2]
   Holding gain, equipment: percentage price increase × the beginning net carrying amount at beginning-of-year current cost = $.50 \times \$6,400 = \$3,200$.
2. Calculate depreciation based on the restated (end-of-the-year) value of the asset:
   Depreciation expense: depreciation percentage × gross carrying amount at end-of-year current cost = $.20 \times \$12,000 = \$2,400$.

A complete schedule of depreciation and holding gains for all five years of the equipment's life is provided in Exhibit 14–5. Replacement costs (new) for years 3 through 5 are assumed. Note that total depreciation ($16,000) equals the original cost plus total holding gains ($5,000 + $11,000).

Income tax laws in the English-speaking countries have been changed to permit accelerated write-offs of the historical costs of depreciable assets. However, no departures from historical-cost methods have been permitted. Managers of companies having large investments in inventories and property, plant, and equipment generally favor the adoption of a current-cost approach to measuring taxable income. Why? Because in times of rising prices, cost of goods sold and depreciation are higher based on current costs than on historical costs. Therefore taxable income would be less and income tax outflows would be less—as long as no holding gains are subject to taxes.[3]

---

[2] Computations of holding gains can rapidly become complex. For instance, this introductory explanation has avoided such intricacies as (1) using average current cost for the year, rather than end-of-the-year current cost, as a basis for depreciation and (2) restating current costs through a series of years in constant dollars. The basic concepts are unchanged, but the arithmetic is tedious.

[3] If taxes were levied as indicated, the capital-goods industries would have relatively lower incomes subject to tax than other industries. However, keep in mind that a country usually has the same target *total* income taxes to be generated by the corporate sector. If the taxable income of all corporations declined, all income tax *rates* would undoubtedly be raised so as to produce the same *total* tax collections as before. Thus a replacement-cost basis may redistribute the tax burden among companies so that capital-goods industries pay less total tax. But the chances are high that the overall percentage rate would increase, so that the tax savings in capital-goods industries would be offset by tax increases in other industries.

EXHIBIT 14–4

Relation of Depreciation to Four Methods of Measuring Income

19X3 (in dollars)	NOMINAL DOLLARS (METHOD 1) Historical Cost Jan. 2	Dec. 31	(METHOD 2) Current Cost Jan. 2	Dec. 31	CONSTANT DOLLARS (METHOD 3) Historical Cost Jan. 2	Dec. 31	(METHOD 4) Current Cost Jan. 2	Dec. 31
Balance Sheet Accounts								
Equipment	5,000	5,000	5,000	8,000	6,000^d	6,000	6,000	8,000
Accumulated depreciation	—	1,000	—	1,600	—	1,200	—	1,600
Net carrying amount	5,000	4,000	5,000	6,400	6,000	4,800	6,000	6,400
Income Statement Effects for 19X3								
Depreciation expense		1,000^a		1,600^b		1,200^e		1,600
Holding gain, equipment		—		3,000^c		—		2,000^f

^{a} $.20 \times 5,000$ ^{c} $.60 \times 5,000$ ^{e} $.20 \times 6,000$
^{b} $.20 \times 8,000$ ^{d} $^{132}/_{110} \times 5,000$ ^{f} $8,000 - 6,000$

EXHIBIT 14–5

Current-Cost Depreciation and Holding Gains

YEAR	(1) NET REPLACEMENT COST, BEGINNING OF YEAR	(2) DEPRECIATION	(3) HOLDING GAIN	(4) NET REPLACEMENT COST, END OF YEAR	(5) REPLACEMENT COST (NEW), END OF YEAR
Purchase				$5,000	$ 5,000
1	$5,000	$ 1,600	$ 3,000	6,400	8,000
2	6,400	2,400	3,200	7,200	12,000
3	7,200	3,000	1,800	6,000	15,000
4	6,000	4,000	2,000	4,000	20,000
5	4,000	5,000	1,000	0	25,000
Total		$16,000	$11,000		

Notes:
Col. (1) = col. (4) from preceding row.
Col. (2) = .20 × col. (5).
Col. (3) = {[col. (5) ÷ col. (5) of preceding row] × col. (1)} − col. (1).
Col. (4) = col. (1) + col. (3) − col. (2).
Col. (5) is assumed.

Annual reports frequently contain complaints about high income tax rates. Comparative effective income tax rates are often tabulated to demonstrate striking differences. For example, NYNEX showed 1985 effective income tax rates of 42.1% of pretax earnings based on historical cost/nominal dollars (as reported to the IRS) and 111.6% based on current cost.

GENERAL PURCHASING-POWER GAINS AND LOSSES

We now turn to constant-dollar accounting. First we compare Methods 1 (historical cost/nominal dollar) and 2 (historical cost/constant dollar) from Exhibit 14–1, page 628. Then we briefly discuss the addition of constant-dollar effects to current-cost statements.

☐ **Monetary Items**

A **monetary item** is a claim receivable or payable in a specified number of dollars; the claim remains fixed regardless of changes in either specific or general price levels. Examples are cash, accounts receivable, accounts payable, and bonds payable. In contrast, nonmonetary items have prices that can vary. Examples are inventory, land, equipment, and liabilities for product warranties.

The distinction between monetary and nonmonetary assets is the key to understanding the impact of constant-dollar accounting on income measurement and stockholders' equity. Reconsider the facts depicted in Exhibit 14–1 except that we extend matters throughout 19X3. Suppose the inventory was not replaced. Instead, the $10,500 cash received on December 31, 19X2, was held throughout 19X3 in a non-interest-bearing checking account. Furthermore, assume that the 100 units of inventory on December 31, 19X2, were held throughout 19X3 and remained unsold on December 31, 19X3. The general-price-level index rose from 110 to 132 during 19X3. The familiar historical cost/nominal dollar (Method 1) statement would be:

	19X2	19X3
Balance Sheets as of December 31		
Cash	$10,500	$10,500
Inventory	2,000	2,000
Total assets	$12,500	$12,500
Original paid-in capital	$ 8,000	$ 8,000
Retained income	4,500	4,500
Total stockholders' equity	$12,500	$12,500
Income Statement for 19X3		
None (no revenue or expenses)		

Before reading on, reflect on the intuitive meaning of holding cash during a time of inflation. The holder of cash or claims to cash gets burned by inflation. In contrast, the debtor benefits from inflation because the debtor can pay creditors with a fixed amount of dollars that have less current purchasing power than when the debt was originally contracted.

How do we measure the economic effects of holding cash during inflation? Using the basic historical cost/constant dollar method in Exhibit 14–1, let us restate in constant dollars, using 19X3 dollars. Because the general-price-level index rose from 110 to 132, the restatements would be as follows:

	19X2	19X3
Balance Sheets as of December 31		
Cash: 132/110 × 10,500 19X2 dollars	$12,600	$10,500
Inventory: 132/100 × 2,000 19X1 dollars	2,640	2,640
Total assets	$15,240	$13,140
Original paid-in capital:		
132/100 × 8,000 19X1 dollars	$10,560	$10,560
Retained income	4,680[a]	4,680
Revaluation equity	—	(2,100)[b]
Total stockholders' equity	$15,240	$13,140
Income Statement for 19X3		
Holding gain (loss) on monetary item		$ (2,100)

[a] $15,240 − $10,560   [b] $12,600 − $10,500

The cash balance is not restated in 19X3 because it is already measured in 19X3 dollars. The formal constant-dollar income statement, assuming no operating activities, would consist of the lone item as in the above table: holding loss on monetary item, $2,100. The monetary item in this case is cash; its loss of purchasing power is $12,600 − $10,500 = $2,100. In turn, stockholders' equity would be reduced by $2,100, as shown by the amount of the revaluation equity.

In times of inflation, owning monetary assets creates holding losses, and having monetary liabilities creates holding gains. A company's **net monetary position**, monetary assets less monetary liabilities, determines whether the total effect is a gain or a loss.

The label "holding loss" on the monetary item is not used by FASB *No. 33*. Instead, the following nomenclature is favored: gain (loss) from decline in purchasing power of net monetary items. By using such labels, the FASB tries to dampen the controversy regarding whether holding gains are really a part of net income. For this reason, the accompanying tables here include holding gains and losses in revaluation equity rather than in retained income.

☐ Nonmonetary Items

Before reading on, reflect on the intuitive meaning of holding a nonmonetary asset during a time of inflation. Assets in the form of physical things have prices that can fluctuate and thus, unlike cash, offer more protection against the risks of inflation.

The purchasing power of cash fluctuates. A 19X2 cash balance of $10,500 needs to grow to $12,600 during 19X3 to maintain purchasing power. If it stays at $10,500, $2,100 of purchasing power in 19X3 dollars is lost. In contrast, the purchasing power of the amount paid for an asset does not change. The $2,000 19X1 dollars paid for inventory can be measured with different yardsticks, for example 19X3 dollars, but the purchasing power always remains the same. In 19X3, this purchasing power is expressed as (132 ÷ 100) × $2,000 = $2,640. The $640 increase in inventory is not a gain; it simply arises because a new yardstick is being used.

In summary, the purchasing power paid for a nonmonetary asset is fixed, but measurements of this amount depend on which year's dollar is used to measure it. The purchasing power of monetary assets, on the other hand, can vary. Therefore holding monetary assets and liabilities can create gains or losses in purchasing power.

As of the end of 19X2, the $10,500 cash balance represented the equivalent of

$12,600 in terms of 19X3 purchasing power, but at the end of 19X3 it is worth only $10,500. In contrast, the $2,000 historical investment in inventory, which does not represent a fixed monetary claim, represented $2,640 in terms of *19X3 purchasing power*; its purchasing power has not been eroded. The inventory is *restated* to an amount of $2,640. But the $2,640 investment in inventory is unaffected by changes in the general-price-level index during 19X3.

Two difficulties and subtleties of constant-dollar accounting deserve emphasis here. First, all past balance sheets are restated in today's dollars. Second, the balance sheet changes are computed among the *monetary* items to produce purchasing-power gains or losses. No such gains or losses will ever appear for nonmonetary items. For example, suppose the $10,500 cash had been immediately reinvested in 300 more units of inventory. How would the constant-dollar statements be affected? No purchasing-power loss or gain would have occurred in 19X3:

	DECEMBER 31, 19X2	DECEMBER 31, 19X3
Inventory (instead of cash)		
132/110 × $10,500	$12,600	$12,600
Inventory (as before)	2,640	2,640
Total assets	$15,240	$15,240
Original capital	$10,560	$10,560
Retained income	4,680	4,680
Total stockholders' equity	$15,240	$15,240

Many accountants and managers confuse these restatements of *historical-cost* statements with current-cost notions of income. However, these constant-dollar statements (Method 3 in Exhibit 14–1) adhere to historical cost. The aim is to see whether the *general* purchasing power of the original invested capital has been maintained. Hence, whether *specific* inventory prices have gone up, down, or sideways is of no concern.

In sum, constant-dollar accounting will modify historical-cost statements in two major ways. First, historical costs are restated in constant dollars. Second, purchasing-power gains and losses arising from holding monetary assets and monetary liabilities will be recognized.

Note that holding gains on monetary items are linked with constant-dollar accounting. They do not exist under nominal-dollar accounting. Holding gains on non-monetary items are associated exclusively with "current-cost" accounting and are not an integral part of "historical-cost" accounting.

Finally, constant-dollar accounting may be linked with *either* historical-cost statements or current-cost statements. Thus the $2,100 holding loss on the monetary item computed above would also appear under the current cost/constant dollar method as well as the historical cost/constant dollar method of Exhibit 14–1.

Constant-dollar adjustments also divide current-cost holding gains into two categories: (1) changes in asset values that result from using a new yardstick for measuring the values, and (2) increases (or decreases) in asset values caused by changes in the specific asset values that differ from general changes in purchasing power. For example, the holding gain of $4,000 in column 2 of Exhibit 14–1, p. 628, represents an increase of inventory value from $20 × 400 = $8,000 in 19X1 dollars to $30 × 400 = $12,000 in 19X2 dollars. The general price index increased 10% in 19X2, making the $8,000 in 19X1 dollars equal to 1.1 × $8,000 = $8,800 in 19X2 dollars. Therefore, of the apparent $4,000 holding gain in column 2, $800 is because of a change in yardstick; only $3,200 is a true increase in value.

SUMMARY PROBLEMS FOR YOUR REVIEW

The first two problems appeared earlier in the chapter.

☐ PROBLEM THREE

You purchased a parcel of land ten years ago for $40,000 when the general-price-level index was 90. You also placed $40,000 cash in a safety deposit box. The general-price-level index is now 135. A local real estate appraiser maintains that you could obtain $220,000 for the land today.

Required:

1. Prepare a four-column tabulation of the holding gain (loss) on the monetary item and holding gain (loss) on the nonmonetary item for the ten-year period. The four methods of measurement to be shown are historical cost/nominal dollar, current cost/nominal dollar, historical cost/constant dollar, and current cost/constant dollar.
2. Prepare a summary of the four methods. For each method:
   a. Specify whether a financial or a physical concept of capital maintenance is used for determining income from continuing operations.
   b. Does the method explicitly identify holding gains (losses) on monetary items, frequently called gains (losses) in general purchasing power? Answer *yes* or *no* here and in requirements c, d, and e.
   c. Does the method explicitly identify holding gains (losses) on nonmonetary items?
   d. Does the method use general price indexes such as the Consumer Price Index?
   e. Does the method use specific price indexes such as a construction index?
3. Of the four methods, which do you prefer as the most accurate measure of income? Why?

☐ Solution to Problem Three

1. All amounts are in thousands of dollars.

	MEASUREMENT METHOD			
	(1) Historical Cost/ Nominal Dollar	(2) Current Cost/ Nominal Dollar	(3) Historical Cost/ Constant Dollar	(4) Current Cost/ Constant Dollar
Holding loss on monetary item, commonly called loss in general purchasing power	—	—	(20)[a]	(20)[a]
Holding gain on nonmonetary item	—	180[b]	—	160[c]
Total	—	180	(20)	140

[a] Cash held today, expressed in current purchasing power $= 40$

Cash held ten years ago, expressed in current purchasing power, $40 \times \dfrac{135}{90} = 60$

Holding loss $\underline{\underline{(20)}}$

[b] Current value of $220 -$ Historical cost of $40 = 180$.

[c] Current value of $220 - \left(\text{Restated historical cost of } 40 \times \dfrac{135}{90}, \text{ or } 60\right) = 160$.

2. The relationships among the four methods are shown in the following table:

	MEASUREMENT METHOD			
	(1) Historical Cost/ Nominal Dollar	(2) Current Cost/ Nominal Dollar	(3) Historical Cost/ Constant Dollar	(4) Current Cost/ Constant Dollar
a. Concept of capital maintenance for determining income from continuing operations	Financial	Physical	Financial	Physical
Explicit identification of holding gains:				
b. On monetary items	No	No	Yes	Yes
c. On nonmonetary items	No*	Yes	No	Yes
d. Use of general price indexes	No	No	Yes	Yes
e. Use of specific price indexes	No	Yes	No	Yes

* Recognizes losses, not gains, under lower-of-cost-or-market valuations, which are most often applicable in accounting for inventories and marketable equity securities.

3. Accountants and others have been unable to agree on which method (or model) provides the "most accurate" measure of income. Those who favor Method 1 maintain that no income emerges until an actual sale occurs. Those who favor Method 2 assert that there has been an overall increase in wealth of $180,000 and that the actual sale of land is an incidental factor. Those who favor Method 3 essentially favor the historical-cost approach to measuring income but believe that gains or losses on monetary items are actually realized by mere holding.

Economists tend to favor Method 4 as the most comprehensive way of calibrating an entity's income because it aims at measuring changes in overall command over goods and services, measured in constant purchasing power.

Economists have frequently distinguished between "real" and "nominal" income and capital. The historical-cost method has been severely criticized because it uses a "nominal" measure in the form of unrestated dollars rather than a "real" measure in the form of restated dollars with constant purchasing power. Adherents of the current cost/constant dollar model insist that no income can emerge without the maintenance of real capital, that is, nominal capital restated in terms of constant purchasing power.

Essentially, the FASB has avoided answering the tough question that professors and others have debated for years: If you must pick a single number as a measure of net income, which would you choose? As mentioned earlier, the FASB requires disclosures in accordance with Method 1 for primary financial statements and Method 4 for supplementary information. However, the holding gains under Method 4 are merely reported; they are not added to income from continuing operations. In short, the FASB has decided to provide an array of income measurements that may be useful. The user of financial statements can then select the numbers that seem best.

As an example of different views as to what really constitutes income, some accountants maintain that a holding gain on a monetary liability is really an adjustment to interest expense. Why? Because lenders raise interest rates to compensate for expected inflation. Therefore the interest expense component of income from continuing operations should be reduced by the holding gain. Following this theory often boosts income considerably. For instance, Puget Sound Power and Light's supplementary disclosures included the following current cost/constant dollar information (in millions):

Income from continuing operations	$44.5
Gain attributable to holding net monetary liabilities	36.0
Income including gain attributable to holding net monetary liabilities	$80.5

The $80.5 million is 80% higher than the $44.5 million income from continuing operations. Over the first half of the 1980s, Puget Power's holding gain on net monetary liabilities *exceeded* its operating income by an average of over $12 million per year.

☐ Problem Four

H Company began business on December 31, 19X1. Its opening balance sheet contained Cash, $3,000; Inventory, $8,000; Equipment, $5,000; and Note Payable, $5,000.

The company had acquired all of its four hundred units of inventory at $20 per unit and had held them throughout 19X2. Three hundred units were sold for $35 each (total of $10,500 cash) on December 31, 19X2. The replacement cost of the inventory at that date was $30 per unit.

The equipment was new and was to be fully depreciated over five years, using the straight-line basis. The replacement cost (new) of the equipment on December 31, 19X2, was $8,000.

The note payable is due on December 31, 19X5.

The general price index was 160 on December 31, 19X1, and 192 on December 31, 19X2.

Required:

Prepare comparative financial statements for 19X2, using Exhibit 14–1 as a general model. Thus four methods of measuring income and capital will be presented. For simplicity, ignore interest and income taxes.

☐ Solution to Problem Four

The complete solution is in Exhibit 14–6. In particular, note how the gain on the *net monetary position* (total monetary assets minus total monetary liabilities) is computed. The computation ignores the $10,500 received on December 31, 19X2, because that cash was not held for more than one day.

REQUIREMENTS OF FASB

As briefly described in the body of this chapter, FASB *Statement No. 33*, "Financial Reporting and Changing Prices," requires large companies to report the effects of inflation as supplementary information. The chairman of the FASB said that *Statement No. 33* "meets an urgent need for information about the effects of changing prices." If that information is not provided, he said:

☐ Investors' and creditors' understanding of the past performance of an enterprise and their ability to assess future cash flows may be severely limited; and people in government who participate in decisions on economic policy may lack important information about the implications of their decisions. The requirements of the Statement are expected to promote a better understanding by the general public of the problems caused by inflation. Statements by business managers about those problems are unlikely to have sufficient credibility until financial reports provide quantitative information about the effects of inflation.

EXHIBIT 14-6

Solution Exhibit for Summary Problem Four for Your Review (in dollars)

| | NOMINAL DOLLARS | | | | CONSTANT DOLLARS | | | |
| | (METHOD 1) Historical Cost | | (METHOD 2) Current Cost | | (METHOD 3) Historical Cost | | (METHOD 4) Current Cost | |
	19X1	19X2	19X1	19X2	19X1	19X2	19X1	19X2
Balance sheets as of December 31								
Cash	3,000	13,500	3,000	13,500	3,600d	13,500	3,600d	13,500
Inventory, 400 and 100 units, respectively	8,000	2,000a	8,000	3,000b	9,600d	2,400d	9,600d	3,000
Equipment, end of 19X2	5,000	8,000			6,000	8,000		
Accumulated depreciation	1,000	1,600			1,200	1,600		
Net carrying amount	5,000	4,000	5,000	6,400	6,000d	4,800d	6,000d	6,400
Total assets	16,000	19,500	16,000	22,900	19,200	20,700	19,200	22,900
Note payable	5,000	5,000	5,000	5,000	6,000d	5,000e	6,000d	5,000
Original paid-in capital	11,000	11,000	11,000	11,000	13,200d	13,200d	13,200	13,200
Retained income (confined to income from continuing operations)	—	3,500	—	(100)	—	2,100	—	(100)
Revaluation equity (accumulated holding gains)	—	—	—	7,000c	—	400e	—	4,800g
Total liabilities and stockholders' equity	16,000	19,500	16,000	22,900	19,200	20,700	19,200	22,900
Income statement for 19X2								
Sales, 300 units @ $35		10,500		10,500		10,500		10,500
Cost of goods sold		6,000a		9,000b		7,200		9,000b
Depreciation expense		1,000		1,600c		1,200		1,600
Total operating expenses		7,000		10,600		8,400		10,600
Income from continuing operations (to retained income)		3,500		(100)		2,100		(100)
Holding gains, net monetary items						400e		400
Holding gains on inventory and equipment				7,000c				4,400f

Schedule of Key Computations (Also see comments in text about this exhibit)

a 100 × $20 and 300 × $20

b 100 × $30 and 300 × $30

c Current-cost depreciation, .20 × new gross carrying amount at current cost .20 × $8,000 = $1,600

Holding gain, equipment: ($8,000 − $5,000 = $3,000, which is a 60% increase), or .60 × beginning net carrying amount at current cost = .60 × $5,000 = $3,000

Holding gain, inventory: ($30 − $20) × 400 units held throughout the year   4,000

Total holding gain, inventory and equipment = $7,000

d Multiply by 192/160 to restate in dollars of 12/31/X2 purchasing power

e Beginning net monetary position, a net liability of $5,000 − $3,000 = $2,000, restated in 12/31/X2 dollars, $2,000 × 192/160 = $(2,400)

Nominal amount held throughout the year, resulting in ending net liability of $5,000 − $3,000 =   (2,000)

Difference: holding gain $ 400

f To obtain gains in terms of 12/31/X2 purchasing power, the nominal amounts must be reduced by those portions representing rises due to general inflation:

inventories, nominal holding gain $4,000

Less portion attributable to restatement of 12/31/X1 inventory, a 20% general-price-level rise (or $4 per unit) applicable to $8,000, or .20 × $8,000 =   1,600

Holding gain in 12/31/X2 dollars $2,400

Equipment, nominal holding gain $3,000

Less 20% general-price-level rise applicable to $5,000 =   1,000

Holding gain in 12/31/X2 dollars   2,000

Total holding gain $4,400

g $4,400 + $400 = $4,800

Exhibit 14–7 contains the format and wording suggested by the FASB to display the same data shown in the income statement in Exhibit 14–6. For simplicity, data have been ignored for other operating expense, interest expense, and provision for income taxes. If such numbers were included, they would be identical in all three columns. Why? Because the FASB has not required a complete new model of income, nor has it required revamped balance sheets. Instead the board has taken a piecemeal approach. To comply with *Statement No. 33*, an enterprise must measure the effects of changing prices on inventory, property, plant and equipment, cost of goods sold, and depreciation, depletion, and amortization expense. No adjustments are required to other revenues, expenses, gains, and losses.

Why did the FASB settle for half a loaf? Why did the board fail to require a complete set of financial statements based on at least one model beyond the primary model of historical cost/nominal dollars? The board believes that its approach is simpler and thus easier to understand than a full-fledged set of supplementary financial statements. Furthermore, the board and affected parties were unable to agree on a single answer regarding whether the supplementary information should focus on general or specific price effects. Many preparers and public accounting firms stressed the need to deal with the effects of general inflation; in contrast, users preferred information dealing with the effects of specific price changes.

Despite the piecemeal approach, the information required by *Statement No. 33* is the biggest experiment to date in published financial reports with respect to changing prices.

EXHIBIT 14–7

Statement of Income from Continuing Operations
Adjusted for Changing Prices
For the Year Ended December 31, 19X2
(in 12/31/X2 dollars)

	AS REPORTED IN THE PRIMARY STATEMENTS	ADJUSTED FOR CHANGES IN SPECIFIC PRICES (CURRENT COSTS)
Net sales and other operating revenues	$10,500	$10,500
Cost of goods sold	6,000	9,000
Depreciation and amortization expense	1,000	1,600
Other operating expense	—	—
Interest expense	—	—
Provision for income taxes	—	—
	7,000	10,600
Income (loss) from continuing operations	$ 3,500	$ (100)
Gain from decline in purchasing power of net amounts owed*		$ 400
Increase in specific prices (current cost) of inventories and property, plant, and equipment held during the year*		$ 7,000
Effect of increase in general price level		2,600†
Excess of increase in specific prices over increase in the general price level		$ 4,400

* FASB description of holding gain.

† See footnote *f* in Exhibit 14–6: 20% price-level rise attributable to 12/31/X1 balances of inventory and equipment, (.20 × $8,000) + (.20 × $5,000) = $1,600 + $1,000 = $2,600.

APPENDIX 14B: EVEN MORE ON INFLATION

This appendix explores some technical aspects of accounting for changing prices: schedules of holding gains and losses, use of average price indexes, and five-year comparative statistics.

SCHEDULE OF HOLDING GAINS AND LOSSES: MONETARY ITEMS

A shortcut approach to computing holding gains or losses on monetary items is shown in Exhibit 14–6. A more elaborate schedule, which can be applied generally, is suggested by FASB *No. 33* (paragraph 232). Under this approach, the amount of net monetary items at the beginning of the year, changes in the net monetary items, and the amount at the end of the year are restated into the desired constant dollars (12/31/X2 in the example given below). The holding gain (that is, the purchasing-power gain or loss on net monetary items) is the difference between the amounts to account for (expressed in constant dollars) and the year-end balance. In these schedules, a capital C is placed next to the items in the final column to emphasize their focus on constant dollars.

Monetary items:

	DECEMBER 31	
	19X1	19X2
Cash	3,000	13,500
Note payable	5,000	5,000
Net monetary items	(2,000)	8,500

Holding gain or loss on net monetary items:

	NOMINAL DOLLARS	CONVERSION FACTOR TO RESTATE IN 12/31/X2 DOLLARS	12/31/X2 DOLLARS
Balance, December, 31, 19X1	(2,000)	192/160	C(2,400)
Increase in net monetary items during the year	10,500	192/192	10,500
Purchasing power to account for			8,100
Balance, December 31, 19X2	8,500	192/192	8,500
Difference: purchasing-power gain on net monetary items			C 400*

* Always check this final holding gain or loss against your intuitive knowledge about whether a gain or loss would be expected. In this example, a gain would be expected because the company held a net monetary liability position throughout the year.

SCHEDULE OF HOLDING GAINS AND LOSSES: NONMONETARY ITEMS

Holding gains or losses on nonmonetary items (increases or decreases in current costs of nonmonetary items held) are expressed in nominal dollars and in constant dollars. The FASB refers to the difference between the two as the "inflation component." Footnote *f* in Exhibit 14–6 showed the shortcut approach to computing holding gains in constant dollars. The following schedules begin with the computations in nominal dollars and then convert to constant dollars:

INVENTORIES	CURRENT COST/ NOMINAL DOLLARS	CONVERSION FACTOR TO RESTATE IN 12/31/X2 DOLLARS	CURRENT COST/ 12/31/X2 DOLLARS
Balance, December 31, 19X1	8,000*	192/160	C 9,600
Purchases or production during the year	—	—	—
Available for sale	8,000		9,600
Cost of goods sold	9,000	192/192	9,000
Balance, December 31, 19X2, to account for	(1,000)		600
Balance, December 31, 19X2, at current cost	3,000	192/192	3,000
Difference: increase in current cost of inventories	4,000		C 2,400

* Historical cost and current cost coincide at the inception of the firm, but thereafter the relevant carrying amount for computing holding gains is current cost, not historical cost.

The total cost of inventories held during the year increased by $4,000 because of price changes. Of the $4,000 increase, $1,600 was caused by a general increase in prices (inflation) and $2,400 by additional increases in the specific costs of the inventory beyond the general price effect.

EQUIPMENT	CURRENT COST/ NOMINAL DOLLARS	CONVERSION FACTOR TO RESTATE IN 12/31/X2 DOLLARS	CURRENT COST/ 12/31/X2 DOLLARS
Balance, December 31, 19X1	5,000	192/160	C 6,000
Additions	—	—	—
Depreciation expense	(1,600)	192/192	(1,600)
Balance, December 31, 19X2, to account for	3,400		4,400
Balance, December 31, 19X2, at current cost	6,400	192/192	6,400
Difference: increase in current cost of equipment	3,000		C 2,000

Summary of the holding gains:

	INVENTORY	EQUIPMENT	TOTAL*
Increase in current cost (nominal dollars)	4,000	3,000	7,000
Increase in current cost (constant dollars)	C 2,400	C 2,000	C 4,400
Inflation component	1,600	1,000	2,600

* Exhibit 14–7 shows how these totals would be presented using the FASB format and elaborate wording. The $7,000 is shown and then the $2,600 is deducted to obtain the $4,400 holding gain net of inflation.

CHOICE OF INDEX NUMBERS

FASB *No. 33* requires the use of the Consumer Price Index for All Urban Consumers (CPI). Published monthly, the CPI measures inflation by comparing costs for a chosen group of goods and services that represent a typical manner of personal spending. The average index for the base year, 1967, has a value of 100; by 1987 the index had risen to more than 330.

Some observers favor using some other general index, such as the gross national product deflator. However, the FASB decided that the CPI was a reasonable choice. Moreover, unlike the gross national product index, the CPI is issued monthly without prolonged delay and is seldom revised.

All constant-dollar information must be based on the average level of the CPI over the fiscal year. However, an enterprise may use end-of-year constant dollars if it chooses to present comprehensive financial statements, such as the complete balance sheets and income statements in Exhibits 14–1 and 14–6. Most published financial reports use the average CPI because they confine their supplementary disclosures to the minimum required information.

ROLLING FORWARD FOR SERIES OF YEARS

Exhibit 14–8 contains a five-year comparison of selected financial data for Gulf + Western, which has operations in financial services, publishing, and entertainment. These disclosures are the minimum required by the FASB.

Constant-dollar measurements may be based on any year or any specific date desired. Nearly all companies use the latest year, primarily because most individuals tend to think of the dollar in terms of what it can buy today rather than in former times. Consequently, a set of financial statistics for a series of years must be updated when a new year is added. This updating requires a "roll forward" process that restates all previous statistics in terms of the purchasing power of the current year.

Rolling forward can be clarified by using the statistics in Exhibit 14–8. The 1983 net sales of $1,276.2 million nominal dollars are converted to average 1985 dollars. (The more accurate $1,276.2 is used rather than $1,276 to reduce the rounding error.) The conversion factor is a fraction that has a numerator index representing the time into which the item is to be restated and a denominator index of the actual time when sales occurred.

Net sales in historical cost/constant 1985 dollars

$$= \text{net sales in historical cost/nominal dollars} \times \frac{\text{Average CPI, 1985}}{\text{Average CPI, 1983}}$$

$$= \$1,276.2 \times \frac{318}{295}$$

$$= \$1,376$$

These restatements essentially say that the $1,276 million of 1983 sales had the same general purchasing power as $1,376 million of 1985 sales. What does this adjustment tell the reader? In nominal dollars, sales increased from 1983 to 1985, from $1,276 million to $1,677 million, a rise of 31%. In constant 1985 dollars, sales increased from $1,376 million to $1,677 million, an increase of only 22%.

Gulf + Western's annual report commented on the computations in Exhibit 14–8 as follows:

☐ In a limited attempt to portray the effects of inflation, the Statement of Financial Accounting Standards No. 33, as amended, requires disclosure of the estimated impact on operations and financial position of the change in current cost of

EXHIBIT 14-8

GULF + WESTERN INDUSTRIES, INC.
Five-Year Comparison of Selected Supplementary Financial Data Adjusted for Effects of
Changing Prices (dollars in millions, except per share):

	IN AVERAGE 1985 DOLLARS (EXCEPT "AS REPORTED" AMOUNTS)				
YEAR ENDED OR AT JULY 31	1985	1984	1983	1982	1981
As Reported					
Net sales	$1,677	$1,492	$1,276	$1,190	$1,035
Earnings from continuing operations	130	156	161	22	48
Earnings from continuing operations per share—fully diluted	1.83	2.13	2.01	.20	.54
Net assets (stockholders' equity)	2,052	1,837	1,894	2,177	2,179
Current Cost Information					
Net sales	1,677	1,549	1,376	1,334	1,256
Earnings from continuing operations	99	136	142	8	30
Earnings from continuing operations per share—fully diluted	1.40	1.86	1.78	.10	.36
Net assets (stockholders' equity)	2,427	2,246	2,869	3,985	4,638
Increase in general price level over (under) increase in the specific cost changes (current cost) of inventories and property, plant and equipment held during the year	(188)	(70)	28	173	47
Other Information Adjusted for General Inflation					
Gain from decline in purchasing power of net monetary items	45	48	41	172	306
Cash dividends paid per common share					
As reported	.90	.90	.75	.75	.75
In average 1985 constant dollars	.90	.93	.81	.84	.91
Market price per common share at year-end					
As reported	38.38	27.25	26.88	11.50	18.75
In average 1985 constant dollars	37.77	27.77	28.53	12.50	21.71
Average consumer price index	318	306	295	283	262

inventories and property, plant and equipment from their historical costs. Under
this approach inventories, property, plant and equipment and their related expenses, cost of goods sold and depreciation, are adjusted upward based on the
estimated cost of the assets at the latest balance sheet date.

These estimated costs are determined through use of current vendor quotations,
production costs, appraisals and/or price indexes applicable to the Company's
specific industries. . . . All adjusted current cost amounts are then stated in
average dollars of purchasing power for the most recent year.

Adjusted "Current Cost" earnings from continuing operations of $99 million
[in 1985] compare with reported earnings from continuing operations of $130
million, reflecting the increased cost of replacing assets during inflationary periods. This hypothetical decrease in earnings from continuing operations is due
to higher depreciation expense on property, plant and equipment and higher
costs of inventories sold. Depreciation expense under both methods was based
on the same methods and depreciable lives as used in the "As Reported" financial
statements. Although these computations result in lower earnings from continuing operations before income taxes, the provision for income taxes was not ad-

justed since income taxes are based on historical costs. As a result, income tax expense increases as a percent of earnings before income taxes, pointing out the higher real tax burden during times of inflation.

Inflation generally causes an understatement of net asset values in the balance sheet based on historical costs. When prices are increasing, monetary assets lose purchasing power since a given number of dollars buys less at the end of a period, whereas, monetary liabilities gain purchasing power since dollars of a lesser value are used to pay them, and inventories and property, plant and equipment cost more to replace. Thus the net assets (stockholders' equity), in inflationary times, is understated in terms of current dollars.

INDEXES WITHIN A YEAR

The use of an average index rather than a year-end index ordinarily reduces the calculations for the restating of *income statement items*. For instance, sales for a given year would not have to be "rolled forward" and adjusted to year-end dollars. Consider the data in Exhibit 14–6 (p. 646). Suppose the sales had been made throughout 19X1 instead of on the final day of the year. Suppose also that an average 19X2 index of 176 had been used instead of the year-end index of 192. Then no adjustment of sales would be required for the 19X2 income statement in constant dollars. But if a year-end index had been used, the sales would have to be restated as follows:

	CURRENT COST/ NOMINAL DOLLARS	CONVERSION FACTOR TO RESTATE IN 12/31/X2 DOLLARS	CURRENT COST/ 12/31/X2 DOLLARS
Sales	$10,500	192/176	$11,455

FUNDAMENTAL ASSIGNMENT MATERIAL

Special note: For coverage of the basic ideas of inflation accounting, Problem 14–1 is especially recommended; for a fundamental look at Appendix 14A, Problem 14–29 is recommended.

☐ **General Coverage**

14–1. **FOUR VERSIONS OF INCOME AND CAPITAL.** (Alternate is 14–27.) Zenith Supplies, Inc., has the following comparative balance sheets as of December 31 (based on historical costs in nominal dollars):

	19X4	19X5
Cash	$ —	$6,000
Inventory, 50 and 20 units, respectively	5,000	1,000
Total assets	$5,000	$7,000
Paid-in capital	$5,000	$5,000
Retained income	—	2,000
Stockholders' equity	$5,000	$7,000

The Consumer Price Index was 320 on December 31, 19X4, and 368 on December 31, 19X5. The company had acquired fifty units of inventory on December 31, 19X4, for $100 each and had held them throughout 19X5. Forty units were sold on December 31, 19X5, for $150 cash each. The replacement cost of the inventory at that date was $120 per unit. Assume that these are the only transactions. Ignore income taxes.

Required:

Use four sets of columns to prepare comparative balance sheets as of December 31, 19X4 and 19X5, and income statements for 19X5 under (1) historical cost/nominal dollars, (2) current cost/nominal dollars, (3) historical cost/constant dollars, and (4) current cost/constant dollars.

□ Understanding Published Financial Reports

14–2. **FASB FORMAT FOR REPORTING ON CHANGING PRICES.** Transamerica Corporation, a large diversified company, reported operating income of $151 million on sales of $5,399 million. After adjusting for changes in specific prices (current costs), operating income was $107 million. Three other accounts reported were (in millions):

Excess of increase in specific prices over increase in general price level	$23
Effect of increase in general price level	64
Increase in specific prices of inventories and property and equipment held during the year	87

Required:

Prepare a current-cost income statement using the FASB format as illustrated by Exhibit 14–2, page 633. Place all expenses in a single category so that Sales — Expenses = Operating income.

ADDITIONAL ASSIGNMENT MATERIAL

□ General Coverage

14–3. What are the two major approaches to recognizing changing prices in measuring income?

14–4. Distinguish between the *physical* and the *financial* concepts of maintenance of invested capital.

14–5. Enumerate four ways to measure income.

14–6. "The choice among accounting measures of income is often expressed as either historical-cost accounting or general-price-level accounting or current-cost accounting." Do you agree? Explain.

14–7. Explain how net income is measured under the current-cost approach.

14–8. What is *distributable income*?

14–9. What is the common meaning of *current cost*?

14–10. "Net realizable value and replacement cost are generally equal." Do you agree? Explain.

14–11. Why do managers in heavy industries such as steel favor the current-cost concept for income tax purposes?

14–12. "General-price-level accounting is a loose way of achieving replacement-cost accounting." Do you agree? Explain.

14–13. Explain what a general price index represents.

14–14. Distinguish between *general* indexes and *specific* indexes.

14–15. "Specific indexes are used in nominal-dollar accounting but not in constant-dollar accounting." Do you agree? Explain.

14–16. "All holding gains should be excluded from income." What is the major logic behind this statement?

14–17. What are three basic positions regarding whether holding gains are income?

14–18. "A holding gain can be recognized but unrealized." Do you agree? Explain.

14–19. "A holding gain may simultaneously be a holding loss." Do you agree? Explain.

14–20. "Because of pressure from the SEC, the FASB issued a revolutionary statement in 1979 abandoning the historical-cost method of income measurement and replacing it with a current-cost method." Do you agree? Explain.

14–21. "Holding gains on nonmonetary items are not recognized in historical cost/constant dollar accounting." Do you agree? Explain.

14–22. "The debtor benefits from inflation." Why?

14–23. "Constant-dollar accounting modifies historical-cost accounting in two major ways." Describe the two ways.

14–24. Net monetary position is the relationship of current assets to current liabilities." Do you agree? Explain.

14–25. What is the argument for departing from the use of historical cost as a basis of recording depreciation of fixed assets?

14–26. MEANING OF GENERAL INDEX APPLICATIONS AND CHOICE OF BASE YEAR. Van Dyke Company acquired land in mid-1967 for $3 million. In mid-1987 it acquired a substantially identical parcel of land for $7 million. The general-price-level index annual averages were:

1987—300.0	1977—150.0	1967—90.0

Required:

1. In four columns, show the computations of the total cost of the two parcels of land expressed in (a) costs as traditionally recorded, (b) dollars of 1987 purchasing power, (c) 1977 purchasing power, and (d) 1967 purchasing power.
2. Explain the meaning of the figures that you computed in requirement 1.

14–27. CONCEPTS OF INCOME. (Alternate is 14–1.) Suppose you are in the business of investing in land and holding it for resale. On December 31, 19X2, a parcel of land has a historical cost of $100,000 and a current value (measured via use of a specific price index) of $400,000; the general price level had tripled since the land was acquired. Suppose also that the land is sold on December 31, 19X3, for $460,000. The general price level rose by 5% during 19X3.

Required:

1. Prepare a tabulation of income from continuing operations and holding gains for 19X3, using the four methods illustrated in Exhibit 14–1.
2. In your own words, explain the meaning of the results, giving special attention to what income represents.

14–28. DEPRECIATION AND PRICE-LEVEL ADJUSTMENTS. The Wentworth Company purchased a conveyor system for $600,000. This system has an expected life of four years and an expected residual value of zero. Straight-line depreciation is used. The general price index is 300 at the date of acquisition; it increases 60 points annually during each of the next three years. The results follow:

YEAR	PRICE-LEVEL INDEX	HISTORICAL COST/ NOMINAL DOLLAR DEPRECIATION	MULTIPLIER	HISTORICAL COST/ CONSTANT DOLLAR DEPRECIATION AS RECORDED
1	300	$150,000	$\dfrac{300}{300}$	$150,000
2	360	$150,000	$\dfrac{360}{300}$	180,000
3	420	$150,000	$\dfrac{420}{300}$	210,000
4	480	$150,000	$\dfrac{480}{300}$	240,000
		$600,000		

Required:

1. Convert the figures in the last column so that they are expressed in terms of fourth-year dollars. For example, the $180,000 second-year dollars would have to be restated by multiplying by 480/360.
2. Suppose in requirement 1 that revenue easily exceeds expenses for each year and that cash equal to the annual depreciation charge was invested in a non-interest-bearing cash account. If amounts equal to the unadjusted depreciation charge were invested each year, would sufficient cash have accumulated to equal the general purchasing power of $600,000 invested in the asset four years ago? If not, what is the extent of the total financial deficiency measured in terms of fourth-year dollars?
3. Suppose in requirement 2 that amounts equal to the constant-dollar depreciation for each year were used. What is the extent of the total financial deficiency?
4. Suppose in requirement 3 that the amounts were invested each year in assets that increased in value at the same rate as the increase in the general price level. What is the extent of the total financial deficiency?

☐ **Assignment Material For Appendixes To Chapter 14**

14–29. **MONETARY AND NONMONETARY ITEMS.** Westwood Company began business on December 31, 19X1, with the balance sheet shown below. The assets were held throughout 19X2, when the general-price-level index rose from 120 to 144. The familiar historical cost/nominal dollar statements would be:

	19X1	19X2
Balance sheets as of December 31:		
Cash	$100,000	$100,000
Land	60,000	60,000
Total assets	$160,000	$160,000
Paid-in capital	$160,000	$160,000

Required:

1. Using the historical cost/constant dollar approach, prepare comparative balance sheets and an income statement. Ignore interest and income taxes.
2. Repeat requirement 1. However, assume that a long-term note payable was issued for $50,000 on December 31, 19X1, and that paid-in capital was therefore $160,000 − $50,000 = $110,000.

14–30. MONETARY ITEMS. Suppose Rio Company has Cr$1.5 million cash, which it had acquired at the end of 19X3. *Cr$* is the abbreviation for Brazilian Cruzeiro. Rio held the cash in a safety deposit box through the end of 19X4. The general-price-level index was 200 on December 31, 19X3, and 500 on December 31, 19X4.

Required:

1. Fill in the blanks for the cash held in the safety deposit box:

	(1) MEASURED IN 12/31/X3 PURCHASING POWER	(2) MEASURED IN 12/31/X4 PURCHASING POWER	(3) AS CONVENTIONALLY MEASURED
Cash balance, December 31, 19X3			
Cash balance, December 31, 19X4			
Purchasing-power loss from holding monetary item			

2. Suppose the company had purchased land for Cr$1.5 million cash on December 31, 19X3, and held the land throughout 19X4. Prepare a similar tabulation for the land balance except that the final line would refer to a "nonmonetary" rather than a "monetary" item.

14–31. MONETARY VERSUS NONMONETARY ASSETS. Kowalski Company owns land acquired for $150,000 one year ago when the general price index was 100. It also owns $150,000 of government bonds acquired at the same time. The index today is 110. Operating expenses and operating revenue, including interest income, resulted in net income (and an increase of cash) of $6,000 measured in historical-dollar terms. Assume that all income and expense transactions occurred yesterday. The Kowalski Company has no other assets and no liabilities. Its cash balance one year ago was zero.

Required:

1. Prepare comparative balance sheets for the two instants of time plus an income statement summary based on the historical cost/nominal dollar method. Then prepare such statements using the historical cost/constant dollar method.
2. This is a more important requirement. In your own words, explain the meaning of the historical cost/constant dollar statements. Why should the holding of a monetary asset generate a monetary loss while the holding of land causes neither a loss nor a gain?

14–32. HISTORICAL COST/CONSTANT DOLLAR QUESTIONNAIRE (J. Shank).

1. In historical cost/constant dollar financial statements, "monetary" items consist of
   (a) Only cash
   (b) Cash, other assets expected to be converted into cash, and current liabilities
   (c) Assets and liabilities with amounts fixed by contract or otherwise in terms of dollars, regardless of price-level changes
   (d) Assets and liabilities that are classified as current on the balance sheet
   (e) None of the above
2. An unacceptable practice in presenting historical cost/constant dollar financial statements is
   (a) The inclusion of general-price-level gains and losses on monetary items in the general-price-level adjusted income statement

(**b**) The inclusion of extraordinary gains and losses in the general-price-level adjusted income statement

(**c**) The use of charts, ratios, and narrative information

(**d**) The use of specific price indexes to restate inventories, plant, and equipment

(**e**) None of the above

3. Historical cost/constant dollar financial statements do not incorporate

(**a**) The "lower-of-cost-or-market" rule in the valuation of inventories

(**b**) Replacement cost in the valuation of plant assets

(**c**) The historical-cost basis in reporting income tax expense

(**d**) The actual amounts payable in reporting liabilities on the balance sheet

(**e**) Any of the above

4. During a period of rising price levels, if a firm's combined holdings of cash, short-term marketable securities, and accounts receivable exceed its total liabilities, the historical cost/constant dollar financial statements will exhibit

(**a**) Purchasing-power gains increasing net income

(**b**) Purchasing-power losses decreasing net income

(**c**) Purchasing-power gains with no effect on net income

(**d**) Purchasing-power losses with no effect on net income

(**e**) None of the above

5. With regard to a firm's holdings of plant and equipment, when general price levels are rising, its historical cost/constant dollar financial statements will show

(**a**) Holding gains that increase net income

(**b**) Holding gains credited directly to capital with no effect on net income

(**c**) Holding losses that reduce net income

(**d**) Holding losses charged directly against capital with no effect on net income

(**e**) None of the above

The following information is applicable to items 6 and 7: Equipment was purchased for $120,000 on January 1, Year 1, when the general price index was 100. It was sold on December 31, Year 3, at a price of $85,000. The equipment originally was expected to last six years with no salvage value and was depreciated on a straight-line basis. The general price index at the end of Year 1 was 125, at the end of Year 2 was 150, and at the end of Year 3 was 175.

6. In comparative historical cost/constant dollar balance sheets prepared at the end of Year 2, the end-of-Year 1 balance sheet would show equipment (net of accumulated depreciation) at

(**a**) $150,000

(**b**) $125,000

(**c**) $100,000

(**d**) $80,000

(**e**) None of the above

7. The historical cost/constant dollar income statement prepared at the end of Year 2 should include depreciation expense of

(**a**) $35,000

(**b**) $30,000

(**c**) $24,000

(**d**) $20,000

(**e**) None of the above

14–33. **EQUIPMENT AND CURRENT COSTS.** Calderon Company purchased equipment for $2,500 on January 2, 19X1. The $2,500 purchase was financed by paid-in capital. Assume an expected useful life of four years, straight-line depreciation, and no residual value. Assume also that the current cost of applicable new equipment increases to $5,000 on December 31, 19X1, and sequentially to $10,000, $15,000, and $20,000 on December 31 of the next three years. Fill in the accompanying blanks. (*Hint*: See Method 2 in Exhibit 14–4, p. 639.)

	NOMINAL DOLLAR/ CURRENT COST			
	19X1	19X2	19X3	19X4
Balance Sheet Effects as of December 31				
Equipment				
Accumulated depreciation				
Net carrying amount				
Original paid-in capital	1,000			
Revaluation equity (accumulated holding gains)				
Retained income (from continuing operations)	(1,250)*			
Total effects on stockholders' equity				
Income Statement Effects for Each Year				
Depreciation (based on current costs)	(1,250)*			
Holding gain, equipment				

* Negative effects are in parentheses.

14–34. **COMPREHENSIVE REVIEW OF APPENDIX 14A.** A company has the following comparative balance sheets at December 31 (based on historical cost in nominal dollars):

	19X1	19X2
Cash	$2,000	$3,400
Inventory, 20 units and 10 units, respectively	2,000	1,000
Total assets	$4,000	$4,400
Original capital	$4,000	$4,000
Retained income	—	400
Stockholders' equity	$4,000	$4,400
General-price-level index	160	176

The company had acquired all the inventory at $100 per unit on December 31, 19X1, and had held the inventory throughout 19X2; ten units were sold for $140 cash each on December 31, 19X2. The replacement cost of the inventory at that date was $125.

Note: If you are going to solve the next problem too, ignore the requirements of this problem and proceed directly to the more comprehensive problem that follows.

Required:

Prepare a four-column tabulation of income statements: (1) historical cost/nominal dollars; (2) current cost/nominal dollars; (3) historical cost/constant dollars, and (4) current cost/constant dollars. Also show beginning and ending balance sheet accounts for each of the four columns. For example, the above accounts accompany column 1.

14–35. **EXTENSION OF APPENDIX 14A PROBLEM.** Suppose in the preceding problem that sales equipment had been purchased on December 31, 19X1, for $2,000 cash provided by an extra $2,000 of capital. The equipment was being fully depreciated over a ten-year life on a straight-line basis. The replacement cost of the equipment (new) at the end of 19X2 was $3,000.

Prepare a four-column tabulation in the same manner described in the requirement to the preceding problem.

14–36. **REVIEW OF FOUR MAJOR METHODS.** Study Appendix 14A. Review the basic facts concerning G Company and its results for 19X2, as depicted in Exhibit 14–1 (p. 628).

Balance sheet accounts at December 31, 19X2, using the familiar historical cost/nominal dollar concept were:

Cash	$10,500	Original paid-in capital	$ 8,000
Inventory (100 units)	2,000	Retained income	4,500
Total assets	$12,500	Total equities	$12,500

The general-price-level index rose from 110 on December 31, 19X2, to 132 on December 31, 19X3. The following transactions occurred during 19X3:

1. On January 2, 19X3, 300 units of inventory were acquired for $30 each, a total of $9,000. This disbursement plus a cash dividend of $1,500 on the same day reduced the cash balance to zero.
2. Sales equipment was acquired on January 2, 19X3, in exchange for a $5,000 note payable due on January 2, 19X5. The replacement cost (new) of the equipment on December 31, 19X3, was $8,000.
3. The company had held all of its inventory throughout 19X3, selling 250 units on December 31, 19X3, for $47 each, a total of $11,750 cash. The replacement cost of the 150 units in inventory at that date was $40 each. The company uses a FIFO historical-cost inventory method.

The income statement items for 19X3 were:

Sales, 250 units @ $47		$11,750
Cost of goods sold (100 @ $20) + (150 @ $30)	$6,500	
Depreciation, ⅕ × $5,000	1,000	7,500
Income from continuing operations		$ 4,250

The balance sheet items at December 31, 19X3, were:

Cash ($10,500 − $9,000 − $1,500 + $11,750)		$11,750
Inventory ($2,000 + $9,000 − $6,500)		4,500
Equipment, original cost	$5,000	
Accumulated depreciation	1,000	4,000
Total assets		$20,250
Note payable		$ 5,000
Original paid-in capital		8,000
Retained income ($4,500 − $1,500 dividend		
+ net income for 19X3, $4,250)		7,250
Total equities		$20,250

Required: Prepare a comparative tabulation using four major methods of the balance sheet and income statements, using Exhibit 14–6 (page 646) as a general model. For simplicity, ignore interest and income taxes. Prepare complete footnotes.

Except for Problem 14–41, these problems require a knowledge of Appendix 14A.

14–37. **REVENUES IN CONSTANT DOLLARS.** Alcoa, the aluminum company, reported the following total revenues (in millions):

	1985	1984	1983	1982	1981
Historical basis	$5,163	$5,799	$5,285	$4,676	$5,032
In average 1985 dollars	5,163	6,006	5,706	5,212	?

The average Consumer Price Index was 322.2 in 1985 and 272.4 in 1981.

Required:

Compute the following:

1. Total revenues for 1981 in average 1985 dollars. Round to the nearest million.
2. Percentage increase (decrease) in revenues between 1981 and 1985 on a historical-cost basis.
3. Percentage increase (decrease) in revenues between 1981 and 1985 in average 1985 dollars.
4. Average Consumer Price Index for 1983.

14–38. **HOLDING GAINS ON EQUIPMENT.** On January 2, 1987, Burlington Northern Corporation acquired new equipment for $800,000. The equipment has an estimated useful life of ten years and no expected terminal value. Assume that on January 2, 1987, the CPI is 340; on December 31, 1987, the CPI is 374. On December 31, 1987, the replacement cost of similar new equipment is $900,000.

Required:

Prepare a tabular comparison for a December 31, 1987, balance sheet and a 1987 income statement of the four methods of accounting for changing prices discussed in the chapter. Show the amounts for the following: gross valuation of the equipment, accumulated depreciation, net carrying amount, depreciation expense, and holding gain. For constant-dollar measures, use the December 31, 1987, dollar.

14–39. **EXTENSION OF PRECEDING PROBLEM.** Refer to the preceding problem. The equipment continues to be used in 1988. On December 31, 1988, the CPI is 392.7. On December 31, 1988, the replacement cost of similar new equipment is $1 million; of similar two-year-old equipment, $800,000.

Required:

For 1988, repeat the requirements in the preceding problem. For constant-dollar measures, use the December 31, 1988, dollar.

14–40. **EFFECTS OF GENERAL VERSUS SPECIFIC PRICE CHANGES.** The following data are from the annual reports of Gannett Co., owner of 120 newspapers; Zayre Corporation, operator of 290 discount stores; and Goodyear Tire and Rubber Company:

(in millions)	GANNETT	ZAYRE	GOODYEAR
Increase in specific prices of assets held during the year	$45.8	$ 24.9	$ (4.7)
Less effect of increase in general price level	37.5	55.5	252.0
Excess of increase in specific prices over increase in the general price level	$ 8.3	$(30.6)	$(256.7)

Compare and contrast the relationship between changes in the general price level and changes in the prices of the specific assets of each of the three companies.

14–41. REPLACEMENT COSTS (P. Griffin).   This problem does not require knowledge of Appendix 14A. Accompanying this problem are excerpts from an annual report of Barber-Ellis Limited of Canada. Note 1 to the financial report includes the following passage:

☐   The current replacement costs of inventories and of property, plant and equipment are shown on the balance sheet, and earnings are determined by matching current costs with current revenues. Adjustments of the historical cost of physical assets to their current replacement cost are considered as restatements of shareholders' equity and are shown on the balance sheet under "Revaluation Surplus."

BARBER-ELLIS OF CANADA, LIMITED
Current Replacement Cost Balance Sheet
As of December 31

	CURRENT REPLACEMENT COST	HISTORICAL COST		CURRENT REPLACEMENT COST	HISTORICAL COST
assets			**liabilities**		
Current:			Current:		
Cash	$ 29,783	$ 29,783	Bank indebtedness	$ 7,573,983	$ 7,573,983
Accounts receivable	12,074,945	12,074,945	Accounts payable and accrued liabilities	4,109,189	4,109,189
Inventories	(1)	10,117,804	Income taxes	1,296,693	1,296,693
Prepaid expenses	249,545	249,545	Dividends—preference shares	700	700
Current assets	$22,721,077	$22,472,077	Current portion of long-term debt	486,650	486,650
			Current liabilities	$13,467,215	$13,467,215
Property, plant and equipment	(2)	11,261,927	Deferred income taxes	278,362	278,362
Accumulated depreciation	(3)	(5,817,772)	Long-term debt (Note 1)	4,133,650	4,133,650
Unamortized excess of purchase price of subsidiaries over fair value of net assets acquired	—	816,067	Total liabilities	$17,879,227	$17,879,227
			shareholders' equity		
			Capital Stock	$ 565,705	$ 565,705
			Contributed surplus	45,000	45,000
			Retained earnings	(5)	10,242,367
			Revaluation surplus	4,319,204	—
Total	$ (4)	$28,732,299	Total	$ (4)	$28,732,299

(cont. on next page)

(cont. from previous page)

Current Replacement Cost Statement of
Earnings and Retained Earnings for the
Year Ended December 31

	CURRENT REPLACEMENT COST	HISTORICAL COST
Net sales	$69,058,300	$69,058,300
Cost of products sold	$ (6)	$50,389,580
Selling, general and administration	10,705,281	10,705,281
Depreciation and amortization	1,095,567	786,969
Interest—long-term debt	381,884	381,884
Interest—current	590,284	590,284
Cost and expenses	$	$62,853,998
Earnings before income taxes	$	$ 6,204,302
Provision for income taxes	2,927,442	2,927,442
Net Earnings	$ (7)	$ 3,276,860
Retained earnings, beginning of year	7,939,344	7,939,344
Sub-total	$	$11,216,204
Adjustment of prior years' depreciation on current replacement cost of plant and equipment	$ 1,948,116	—
Dividends	973,837	$ 973,837
Retained Earnings, End of Year	$	$10,242,367
Earnings Per Share		
Basic	$ 4.30	$ 7.09
Fully diluted	4.22	6.96

Statement of Revaluation Surplus for the
Year Ended December 31

Revaluation of physical assets to reflect current replacement cost as at December 31

Inventories	$ 249,000
Property, plant and equipment	3,902,271
Excess of purchase price over fair value of assets acquired	(816,067)

Revaluation of cost of products sold during the year ended December 31

Portion of earnings determined on historical cost basis which are required to replace inventory sold at the current cost in effect at the date of sale	984,000
Revaluation surplus December 31	$4,319,204

Report on Supplementary Financial Statements

To the Shareholders,
Barber-Ellis of Canada, Limited
In conjunction with our examination of and report on the financial statements of Barber-Ellis of Canada, Limited we have also examined the accompanying supplementary financial statements which have been prepared on a current replacement cost basis.

Uniform criteria for the preparation and presentation of such supplementary financial information have not yet been established and accordingly, acceptable alternatives are available as to their nature and content. In our opinion, however, the accounting basis described in the notes to the supplementary financial statements has been applied as stated and is appropriate in these circumstances.

Touche Ross & Co.   Toronto, Ontario
Chartered Accountants

Since this is the first year that the company has prepared current replacement cost financial statements, comparative figures are not available.

From information in the balance sheet, statement of earnings and retained earnings, and statement of revaluation surplus, determine, as of December 31:

1. Current replacement cost "Inventories"
2. Current replacement cost "Property, Plant and Equipment"
3. Current replacement cost "Accumulated Depreciation"
4. Current replacement cost "Total Assets"
5. Current replacement cost "Retained Earnings"

Also, for the year ended December 31, determine the following income statement items:

6. Current replacement cost "Cost of Products Sold"

7. Current replacement cost "Net Earnings"

Finally, explain in words the nature of

8. The difference between the current replacement-cost "Net Earnings" and the historical-cost "Net Earnings"

14–42. HOLDING GAINS ON MONETARY AND NONMONETARY ITEMS. Study Appendix 14B. Refer to the data in the preceding problem. The following information is available:

Items from the January 2 (beginning of the year) historical-cost balance sheet of Barber-Ellis:

Cash: $25,200
Long-term debt: $4,133,650

General-price-level index:

January 2: 140
December 31: 154
Average for the year: 147

For all constant-dollar calculations, use the December 31 dollar.

1. Assume that long-term debt did not change during the year. Calculate the purchasing-power gain or loss associated with Long-term debt (a monetary item). Label it as a gain or loss.

2. Calculate the purchasing-power gain or loss associated with cash and label it as a gain or loss. You may assume that a $4,583 increase in cash occurred uniformly throughout the year.

3. Assume that Barber-Ellis purchased *all* of its inventory on January 2 (no other purchases prior to or subsequent to that date). Also assume that goods were sold continuously throughout the year. What are the following numbers?
   a. Holding gain on inventory, using the current cost/nominal dollar method?
   b. Holding gain on inventory *net* of inflation (that is, based on the current cost/constant dollar method)?

14–43. AVERAGE DOLLAR INSTEAD OF YEAR-END DOLLAR. Repeat the preceding problem; however, for all constant-dollar calculations use the average-for-the-year dollar.

14–44. FASB FORMAT AND CONSTANT-DOLLAR DISCLOSURES. B. F. Saul Real Estate Investment Trust is a company with investments in income-producing properties, primarily shopping centers. The company's 1985 financial statement included some constant-dollar data that were required by the FASB before 1985 but are no longer required.

Examine the comparative income statements for B. F. Saul in Exhibit 14–9.

1. Recast the bottom of the income statements (beginning with loss from continuing operations) in the four-method format of Exhibit 14–6 (p. 646). Use the descriptive terms as shown in Exhibit 14–6.

2. The FASB no longer requires reporting of the middle column, labeled "Adjusted for General Inflation." What information would not be available if that column were eliminated?

EXHIBIT 14–9

B. F. SAUL REAL ESTATE INVESTMENT TRUST

Condensed Consolidated Statement of Operations Adjusted for Changing Prices (in thousands)
Year Ended September 30, 1985

	FINANCIAL STATEMENTS (HISTORICAL COST)	ADJUSTED FOR GENERAL INFLATION (CONSTANT DOLLAR)	ADJUSTED FOR CHANGES IN SPECIFIC PRICES (CURRENT COST)
Total income	$ 65,337	$ 65,337	$ 65,337
Expenses:			
Direct operating expenses	39,437	39,437	39,437
Interest and debt expense	39,717	39,717	39,717
Interest capitalized	(9,147)	(9,147)	(9,147)
Depreciation	7,180	8,154	8,784
Advisory fee	2,480	2,480	2,480
General and administrative	792	792	792
Total expenses	80,459	81,433	82,063
Operating loss	(15,122)	(16,096)	(16,726)
Reduction of property inflation values to lower recoverable amounts		(2,478)	
Equity in earnings of savings and loan	932	932	932
Provision for income taxes	(75)	(75)	(75)
Loss from continuing operations	$(14,265)	$(17,717)	$(15,869)
Increase in specific prices of income-producing properties held during the year*			$ 9,181
Less effect of increase in the general price level			1,661
Excess of increase in specific prices over increase in the general price level			$ 7,520
Gain from decline in purchasing power of net monetary liabilities		$ 9,502	$ 9,502

* At September 30, 1985, current cost of income-producing properties, net of accumulated depreciation, was $241,197,000.

14–45. CONSTANT DOLLAR AND LOWER-OF-COST-OR-MARKET. Refer to the preceding problem. You may want to review the section on "Lower of Cost or Market" in Chapter 7, pages 278–281.

1. Interpret the item "Reduction of property inflation values to lower recoverable amounts." Why does the $2,478,000 appear only in the middle column?
2. On average, did the current cost of B. F. Saul's specific assets increase faster or slower than the general inflation rate in fiscal 1985? Explain how you determined this.

14–46. CONSTANT DOLLARS IN DIFFERENT YEARS. Study Appendix 14B. Aetna Life and Casualty Company, one of the largest insurance companies in the United States, uses a constant 1967 dollar when it presents a ten-year comparison of selected data adjusted for the effects of general inflation. However, Aetna uses the current constant dollar in its schedule of income adjusted for changing prices.

The average CPIs were as follows: 1985, 322.2; 1984, 311.1; 1967, 100.0.

1. In 1985, Aetna showed a $109.2 million "loss from decline in purchasing power of net monetary assets owned" in its schedule of income adjusted for changing prices. Using a constant 1967 dollar, what was the amount for this same item that appeared in the company's ten-year comparison in its 1985 annual report? In its 1986 annual report?
2. The cash dividends per share in 1985 were $2.64. Compute the dividends per share in 1967 dollars.

14–47. SERIES OF YEARS. Study Appendix 14B. Examine the accompanying excerpts from the annual report of PPG Industries, Inc. (formerly Pittsburgh Plate Glass), a major producer of glass, coatings and resins, and chemicals.

As measured by historical cost/nominal dollars, sales in 1984 were $4,242.2 million and income tax expense was $223.9 million. The December 31, 1985, balance sheet listed inventories of $527.6 million and property (net of depreciation) of $2,478.5 million.

Compute the following:

1. As of December 31, 1985: cumulative holding gains (on a current-cost nominal dollar basis) on (a) inventories and (b) net property.
2. For the year *1984*: the current "cost of sales, depreciation, and other expenses" (in average 1985 dollars).
3. Assume that the Consumer Price Index as of December 31, 1985, was 330 and as of December 31, 1984, was 315. Assume further that the tabular five-year comparison is to be restated to reflect constant dollars of December 31, 1985 (rather than average 1985 dollars as actually reported by PPG). What amount would be placed in the table for 1985 net sales?
4. Use the same assumptions as in requirement 3. What amount would be placed in the table for 1984 net sales?

Supplemental Financial Data for the Year Ended December 31, 1985
(in millions except per share data)

	HISTORICAL FINANCIAL DATA	ADJUSTED FOR CURRENT COST
Net sales	$4,345.5	$4,345.5
Cost of sales	2,644.2	2,649.6
Depreciation	213.5	285.8
Other expenses	950.7	950.7
Income taxes	234.4	234.4
Net earnings	$ 302.7	$ 225.0
Earnings per share	$ 4.54	$ 3.37
Gain on net monetary items held during year		$ 33.8
Effect of inflation on inventories and property held during the year		$ 125.6
Increase in current cost		41.6
Excess of increase in inflation over increase in current cost		$ 84.0
December 31, 1985 balances Inventories		$ 757.9
Property (net of depreciation)		$3,018.1

Five-Year Comparison of Selected Data (Stated in Average 1985 Dollars)
(in millions except per share data)

	1985	1984	1983	1982	1981
Net sales	$4,346	$4,392	$3,980	$3,674	$3,974
Dividends per share	1.64	1.45	1.33	1.31	1.38
Market price per share at year-end	50¼	33⅜	36⅞	28½	21⅝
Net earnings—current cost basis	225	223	164	46	141
Earnings per share— current cost basis	3.37	3.18	2.34	.65	2.08
Assets less liabilities— current cost basis	2,449	2,880	2,800	2,845	3,080
Excess of increase in general inflation over increase in current cost	84	66	42	62	(28)
Gain on monetary items held during year	34	27	34	22	48
Average Consumer Price Index	322	311	298	289	272

14–48. **COMPREHENSIVE CASE ON CHANGING PRICES.** Study Appendix 14B. Koppers Company is a diversified manufacturer, featuring many products for the construction and chemical industries. Examine the accompanying tables, A and B, pertaining to the effects of changing prices on Koppers.

Required:

1. What was the 1985 holding gain on inventory and property, plant, and equipment on a current cost/nominal dollar basis?

Table A. Consolidated Statement of Income From Continuing Operations Adjusted for Changing Prices (unaudited)

FOR THE YEAR ENDED DECEMBER 31, 1985 ($ THOUSANDS, EXCEPT PER SHARE FIGURES)	DOLLARS OF CURRENT PURCHASING POWER*	
	As Reported in 1985 Financial Statements (Historical Cost)	Adjusted for Changes in Specific Prices (Current Cost)
Net sales	$1,400,166	$1,400,797
Operating expenses:		
Cost of sales	1,108,382	1,103,673
Depreciation, depletion and amortization	66,373	148,274
Taxes, other than income taxes	39,630	39,630
Selling, research, general and administrative expenses	149,879	149,879
	1,364,264	1,441,456
Operating profit (loss)	35,902	(40,659)
Other income (expense)	(59,925)	(86,831)
Interest expense	23,673	23,673
Loss before income taxes	(47,696)	(151,163)
Income tax benefit	(17,693)	(17,693)
Loss from continuing operations	$ (30,003)	$ (133,470)
Dividends on:		
Redeemable convertible preference stock	$ 4,577	$ 4,577
Cumulative preferred stock	600	600
Loss applicable to common stock	$ (35,180)	$ (138,647)
Average number of shares of common stock outstanding during year (thousands)	28,574	28,574
Loss per share of common stock	$ (1.23)	$ (4.85)
Loss from decrease in purchasing power of net amounts owed		$ (217)
Increase in current cost of inventory and property, plant and equipment held during the year†		$ 243,478
Effect of increase in general price level		38,274
Increase in specific prices net of increase in general price level		$ 205,204

* Current-cost amounts are expressed in average 1985 dollars. Changes are measured by the Consumer Price Index.

† At December 31, 1985, the current cost of inventories was $175,110, and the current cost of property, plant and equipment, net of accumulated depreciation, was $528,119.

Table B. Comparison of Selected Supplementary Financial Data Adjusted for Effects of Changing Prices (unaudited)

($ THOUSANDS; EXCEPT PER SHARE FIGURES)	AS REPORTED IN 1985 FINANCIAL STATEMENTS (HISTORICAL COST)	YEARS ENDED DECEMBER 31, (IN AVERAGE 1985 DOLLARS)				
		1985	1984*	1983*	1982*	1981*
Net sales	$1,400,166	$1,400,797	$1,499,639	$1,277,931	$1,268,117	$1,523,940
Loss from continuing operations	$ (30,003)	$ (133,470)	$ (50,714)	$ (63,608)	$ (117,257)	$ (27,381)
Net assets at year end	$ 478,946	$ 634,888	$ 929,326	$ 970,026	$ 994,262	$1,163,036
Gain (loss) from increase/decrease in purchasing power of net amounts owed	—	$ (217)	$ 179	$ (1,277)	$ 3,550	$ 25,271
Excess (deficit) of increase/decrease in specific prices net of increase in general price level	—	$ 243.478	$ (53,171)	$ (66,878)	$ (150,861)	$ 22,862
Per share information:						
Loss from continuing operations	$ (1.23)	$ (4.85)	$ (2.00)	$ (2.56)	$ (4.53)	$ (1.33)
Cash dividends declared	$ 0.80	$ 0.80	$ 0.83	$ 0.87	$ 1.56	$ 1.67
Market price at year end	$ 21.00	$ 20.67	$ 18.13	$ 23.27	$ 19.11	$ 22.79
Average Consumer Price Index		322.2	311.1	298.4	289.1	272.4

* Restated to conform with 1985 classifications (Note 7).

2. Suppose in Table B that Koppers chose to report 1985 sales in average 1983 dollars rather than average 1985 dollars. What number would replace the $1,400,797?

3. Assume that the CPI increased the same number of points each month throughout 1985. Were the company's actual dollar sales higher in the first half or in the second half of 1985? Explain.

4. Assume that the CPI increased the same number of points each month from June 30 to June 30 in fiscal 1983, 1984, and 1985. What were the values of the CPI on December 31, 1983 and 1984? Assume also that the CPI increased the same number of points each month throughout the calendar year 1985. What was the value of the CPI on December 31, 1985?

5. The company's long-term debt was $220 million on December 31, 1984, and $215 million on December 31, 1985. How much of the 1985 "gain (loss) from increase/decrease in purchasing power of net amounts owed" was attributable to long-term debt? Round your answer to the nearest million. (Keep in mind that this answer is not the amount shown in the table. Why? Because the latter is affected by both monetary assets and monetary liabilities.)

6. Koppers prepared a similar five-year statistical comparison a year earlier for years through December 31, 1984. (a) Compute the number that was shown for the gain from decline in purchasing power of net amounts owed for 1984. (b) Suppose long-term debt of $220 million had been held throughout 1984. If a comparative balance sheet were shown in average 1984 dollars, what amount of long-term debt would have been shown for December 31, 1983?

Chapter 15

STATEMENT OF CHANGES
IN FINANCIAL POSITION

LEARNING OBJECTIVES

After studying this chapter, you should be able to

1. Explain the concept of a statement of changes in financial position and how it relates to the income statement, retained income statement, and balance sheet

2. Prepare a statement of changes in financial position, including two different ways of presenting the working capital provided by operations

3. Explain the role of depreciation in the changes statement

4. Summarize the major criticisms of the focus on working capital in the changes statement

5. Prepare a statement of changes in financial position that focuses on cash instead of working capital

6. Show how some typical transactions affect income and working capital differently and how such effects are presented on the changes statement (Appendix 15A)

7. Use the T-account method to prepare a statement of changes in financial position (Appendix 15B)

The accrual basis of accounting is widely used as the primary means of presenting financial position (balance sheet) and performance (income statement). But investors and managers are also concerned about cash and other current accounts. This chapter shows how external reports focus on such questions as "If we have impressive earnings, why are we always scrambling for more cash?"

This chapter is presented near the end of this book, but it is by no means the least important. Indeed, the body of the chapter is designed for serious study at any time beyond Chapter 5. The chapter appendixes are highly recommended for anybody who wants a comprehensive review of *all* financial statements, particularly on how they are interlocked. (Few homework assignments are more enlightening than using balance sheets and income statements as a basis for preparing a statement of changes in financial position.)

The body of the chapter concentrates first on a statement of changes in financial position that focuses on changes in working capital. This was the most popular focus for many years. Later in the chapter such a statement is expanded to provide a focus on cash, which is currently most popular. The FASB is expected to issue a pronouncement shortly that requires companies to use a focus on cash.

Appendix 15A considers items on the statement in more detail, particularly with reference to material covered in specific chapters beyond Chapter 8. Appendix 15B presents a T-account approach to the construction of the statement.

OPERATING AND FINANCIAL MANAGEMENT

Chapter 2 introduced the distinction between operating management and financial management. **Operating management** is largely concerned with the major day-to-day activities that generate revenues and expenses (that is, using a given set of resources). The major purpose of the income statement is to provide a detailed presentation of the results of operating management.

Financial management is largely concerned with where to get cash (*financing activities*) and how to use cash (*investing activities*) for the benefit of the entity. Examples of financial management include decisions regarding the issuance or retirement of long-term debt or additional capital stock, and deciding how to invest the capital raised. The major purpose of the statement of changes in financial position is to provide a detailed presentation of the results of financial management.

A **statement of changes in financial position** must be presented as a basic financial statement in corporate annual reports. Historically, the statement has been most widely known as **statement of sources and applications of funds**. For brevity in the ensuing discussion, the statement will frequently be called a **changes statement**. Many accountants call it a **funds statement**; the term is convenient, but not descriptive. The FASB is considering a proposal to rename it **Statement of Cash Flows.**[1]

The changes statement summarizes the financing and investing activities of the enterprise. The statement shows directly information that readers of financial reports could otherwise obtain only by makeshift analysis and interpretation of published balance sheets and statements of income and retained income.

Balance sheets are statements of financial position, whereas changes statements are obviously statements of *changes* in financial position. Balance sheets show the status at a day in time. In contrast, changes statements, income statements, and statements of retained income cover periods of time; they provide the explanations of why the balance sheet items have changed. This linkage can be depicted as shown in the accompanying diagram:

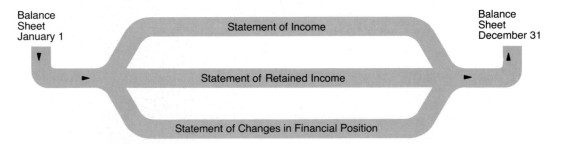

The statement of changes in financial position was devised to provide the reader with a glimpse of where the resources came from during the year and where they went.

STATEMENT OF CHANGES IN WORKING CAPITAL

☐ Focus on Working Capital

The fundamental approach to the changes statement is simple: (1) list the activities that increased resources (*sources*) and those that decreased resources (*uses*), and (2) separate the changes caused by operations from those caused by *financing* and *investment* activities. Two definitions of *resources* have been commonly used: working capital and cash.

A popular approach has been to view the changes statement as an expla-

---

[1] A statement of changes in financial position can have a focus on either cash or working capital, as we will explain. If the FASB requires a focus on cash, which has been proposed, the more descriptive *statement of cash flows* will be appropriate.

nation of working capital changes. A focus on working capital provides a perspective on the entire natural operating cycle rather than just one part thereof (such as cash). A focus on cash differs primarily in form, not substance. A cash focus will be discussed beginning on page 685.

Chapter 2 describes the *operating cycle* of a business as the total time necessary for cash to be transformed into inventories, which are transformed into receivables, which are transformed back into cash:

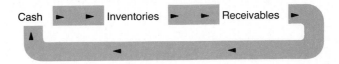

A company often receives short-term credit from suppliers and offers short-term credit to customers. In such cases, the *purchase* of inventory, which creates a short-term liability, is often more important than the actual disbursement of cash. Likewise, the *sale* creating a receivable can be more significant than the subsequent receipt of cash. To provide a broader perspective than cash receipt and disbursement, accountants often focus on a working capital cycle. Accountants define *working capital* as the excess of current assets over current liabilities. A **working capital cycle** is the continuous, rhythmic process of using working capital to generate additional working capital. It begins with the purchase of inventory, whether for cash or on open account; it ends with a sale, regardless of whether cash is received or a receivable is created.

As used in a statement of changes in financial position, working capital is a residual concept, a relatively abstract idea. You cannot borrow it or spend it. Working capital is akin to stockholders' equity. The only difference is that working capital is confined to current assets minus current liabilities, whereas stockholders' equity encompasses all assets minus all liabilities.

☐ Typical Sources and Uses

Most changes statements have displayed the sources and uses of working capital as follows:

SOURCES OF WORKING CAPITAL
(OR WORKING CAPITAL PROVIDED):

Operations (excess of revenue over charges against revenue requiring working capital)
Sale of noncurrent assets (plant, equipment, long-term investments in securities)
Issuance of long-term debt
Issuance of capital stock

USES OF WORKING CAPITAL
(OR WORKING CAPITAL APPLIED):

Declaration of cash dividends
Purchase of noncurrent assets (plant, equipment, long-term investments in securities)
Reduction of long-term debt
Repurchase of outstanding capital stock

Financial analysts have cited the following useful information as being revealed by a changes statement: the major sources from which working capital has been obtained (that is, profitable operations, borrowing, sale of capital stock); clues as to the financial management habits of the executives (that is, management attitudes toward spending and financing); the proportion of working capital applied to plant, dividends, debt retirement, and so forth; indications of the impact of working capital flows upon future dividend-paying probabilities; and an indication of the company's trend toward general financial strength or weakness.

☐ Example of Changes Statement

The preparation of a changes statement can appear complex at first glance because so many different formats are used. However, the basic ideas are straightforward. Generally, as an example will show, accountants build the changes statement from the changes in balance sheet items, the use of a few additional facts, and a familiarity with the typical sources and uses of working capital listed on the preceding page.

Consider the example of the B Company, which had the following condensed income statement for 19X2:

B COMPANY
Statement of Income
For the Year Ended December 31, 19X2
(in thousands)

Sales		$200
Deduct expenses:		
Expenses requiring working capital	$140	
Depreciation	17	157
Net income		$ 43

The B Company had the following condensed balance sheets (in thousands of dollars):

	DECEMBER 31				DECEMBER 31		
	19X2	19X1	Change		19X2	19X1	Change
Current assets:				Current			
Cash	$ 5	$ 25	$ (20)	liabilities	$100	$ 10	$ 90
Net receivables	45	25	20	Long-term debt	105	5	100
Inventories	100	60	40	Total liabilities	$205	$ 15	$190
Total current				Stockholders'			
assets	$150	$110	$ 40	equity	425	315	110
Plant assets, net							
of accumulated							
depreciation	480	220	260				
				Total liab. and			
Total assets	$630	$330	$300	stk. eq.	$630	$330	$300

Additional information: In 19X2, the company issued long-term debt and capital stock for cash of $100,000 and $87,000, respectively. Cash dividends were $20,000. New equipment was acquired for $277,000 cash.

Because the changes statement explains the *causes* for the change in working capital, the first step is to compute the amount of the change (which represents the *net effect*):

	DECEMBER 31	
	19X2	19X1
Current assets	$150	$110
Current liabilities	100	10
Working capital	$ 50	$100
Net decrease in working capital		$50

(Exhibit 15–1 illustrates how this computation is usually shown in detail in the second part of the changes statement in the section called *changes in components of working capital*.)

When business expansion occurs, as in this case, and where there is a strong working capital position at the outset, working capital often declines. Why? Because the managers tend to postpone paying short-term payables as long as seems prudent. Cash balances will also tend to fall to a bare minimum because the cash is usually needed for investment in various business assets required for expansion.

The statement in Exhibit 15–1 gives a direct picture of where the working capital came from and where it went. In this instance, the excess of uses over sources reduced working capital by $50,000. Without the statement of changes, the readers of the annual report would have to conduct their own analysis of the balance sheets, income statement, and statement of retained income to get a grasp of the impact of financial management decisions.

☐ Changes in Balance Sheet Equation

The balance sheet equation is again useful because it can provide the conceptual framework underlying the statement of changes in financial position. Consider the following:

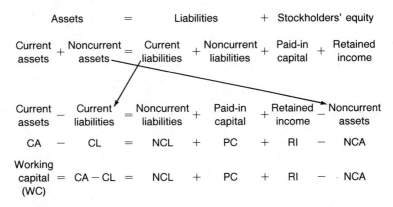

$$\text{Assets} = \text{Liabilities} + \text{Stockholders' equity}$$

$$\underset{\substack{\text{Current} \\ \text{assets}}}{} + \underset{\substack{\text{Noncurrent} \\ \text{assets}}}{} = \underset{\substack{\text{Current} \\ \text{liabilities}}}{} + \underset{\substack{\text{Noncurrent} \\ \text{liabilities}}}{} + \underset{\substack{\text{Paid-in} \\ \text{capital}}}{} + \underset{\substack{\text{Retained} \\ \text{income}}}{}$$

$$\underset{\substack{\text{Current} \\ \text{assets}}}{} - \underset{\substack{\text{Current} \\ \text{liabilities}}}{} = \underset{\substack{\text{Noncurrent} \\ \text{liabilities}}}{} + \underset{\substack{\text{Paid-in} \\ \text{capital}}}{} + \underset{\substack{\text{Retained} \\ \text{income}}}{} - \underset{\substack{\text{Noncurrent} \\ \text{assets}}}{}$$

$$\text{CA} - \text{CL} = \text{NCL} + \text{PC} + \text{RI} - \text{NCA}$$

$$\underset{\text{(WC)}}{\substack{\text{Working} \\ \text{capital}}} = \text{CA} - \text{CL} = \text{NCL} + \text{PC} + \text{RI} - \text{NCA}$$

EXHIBIT 15–1

B COMPANY
Statement of Changes in Financial Position
For the Year Ended December 31, 19X2
(in thousands of dollars)

SOURCES AND USES OF WORKING CAPITAL

Sources:		
Working capital provided by operations		
(Schedule A)		$ 60
Issuance of long-term debt		100
Issuance of additional capital stock		87
Total sources		$247
Uses:		
Payment of cash dividends	$ 20	
Acquisition of plant and equipment	277	
Total uses		297
Decrease in working capital		$ (50)

CHANGES IN COMPONENTS OF WORKING CAPITAL

	DECEMBER 31		INCREASE (DECREASE) IN WORKING CAPITAL
	19X2	19X1	
Current assets:			
Cash	$ 5	$ 25	$(20)
Net receivables	45	25	20
Inventories	100	60	40
Total current assets	$150	$110	$ 40
Current liabilities (detailed)	100	10	(90)
Working capital	$ 50	$100	
Decrease in working capital			$(50)

SCHEDULE A

Working Capital Provided by Operations

First Alternative Presentation (using the Addback Method):	
Net income (from income statement)	$ 43
Add: Charges against income not requiring	
working capital: Depreciation	17
Working capital provided by operations	$ 60
Second Alternative Presentation* (Using the Straightforward Method):	
Sales	$200
Deduct: All expenses requiring working capital	
(detailed)	140
Working capital provided by operations	$ 60

* Although the straightforward method is frequently easier to understand, the addback method is used almost exclusively in annual reports. Be sure you see why each method produces the same figure, $60.

Any change (Δ) in WC must be accompanied by a change in one or more items on the right side to keep the equation in balance:

$$\Delta WC = \Delta NCL + \Delta PC + \Delta RI - \Delta NCA$$

Therefore:

Change in working capital = Change in all nonworking capital accounts

or

What happened to working capital = Why it happened

The statement of changes in financial position focuses on the changes in the nonworking capital accounts (that is, the noncurrent accounts) as a way of explaining how and *why* the level of working capital has gone up or down during a given period. Thus the major changes in the accounts *on the right side* of the above equation appear in the statement of changes in financial position as *causes* of the change in working capital. The left side of the equation measures the *net effect* of the change in working capital.

Applying the equation to our data, we can see, step by step, how the changes statement in Exhibit 15–1 is based on the same theoretical foundation that underlies the other financial statements (in thousands of dollars):

	$\Delta WC = \Delta NCL + \Delta PC + \Delta RI - \Delta NCA$				
Sales	+200 =			+200	
Expenses requiring working capital	−140 =			−140	
Working capital provided by operations	+ 60 =			+ 60	
Expense not requiring working capital:					
depreciation	0 =			− 17	− (−17)
Net income, a subtotal				+ 43	
Issuance of long-term debt	+100 = +100				
Issuance of capital stock	+ 87 =		+87		
Cash dividends	− 20 =			− 20	
Acquisition of new equipment	−277 =				− (+277)
Net changes	− 50 = +100		+87	+ 23	− (+260)
	−50				

When statements become complicated, accountants prefer to use work sheets or T-accounts to help their analysis. (See Appendix 15B for a description of the latter.) In any event, the totals in the above tabulation show that all transactions affecting working capital have been accounted for. The $50,000 *change* in working capital is explained by the *changes* in the non-working-capital accounts. Each noncurrent account can be analyzed in detail if desired.

The relationships among the balance sheet accounts can also be depicted in diagrams:

Conventional Balance
Sheet Format

CA	CL
	NCL
NCA	PC
	RI

WC = CA−CL

WC	NCL
NCA	PC
	RI

Therefore:
ΔWC = ΔNoncurrent Accounts

ΔWC	ΔNCL
WC	NCL
NCA	PC
	RI

Example: Assume additional
long-term debt issued
for cash (shaded panels).

☐ **Preparing a Changes Statement**

Most companies prepare a changes statement by using the format of Exhibit 15–1, with two major categories: *sources* (increases in working capital) and *uses* (decreases in working capital).

You can prepare a changes statement in six steps:

Step 1. Prepare a schedule of changes in the components of working capital. (See the second section of Exhibit 15–1.) The total change is the amount to be explained by the sources and uses of working capital listed on the changes statement.

Step 2. Calculate working capital provided by operations. (See Schedule A in Exhibit 15–1.) This is the first item listed under sources of working capital, $60,000 for B Company. The next section of the chapter gives further details.

Step 3. Determine other sources and uses of working capital by gathering additional information (given in this case). In an actual case, the keys are (a) to know the typical sources and uses and (b) to search systematically for them through the annual report. Nonoperating sources and uses generally arise from activities such as *financing* and *investment* transactions.

Step 4. If all the necessary information is not directly available, analyze changes in all balance sheet items *except* current assets and current liabilities. The following rule will help determine whether such changes are sources or uses:

> *Sources of working capital*
> Increases in long-term liabilities or stockholders' equity
> Decreases in noncurrent assets
> *Uses of working capital*
> Decreases in long-term liabilities or stockholders' equity
> Increases in noncurrent assets

Consider B Company's balance sheet on page 674. Three noncurrent accounts must be analyzed: plant assets, long-term debt, and stockholders' equity.

a. Plant assets increased by $260,000 in 19X2. Three items in the changes statement usually explain changes in net plant assets: assets acquired, asset dispositions, and depreciation expense for the period:

Increase in net plant assets = Acquisitions − Disposals − Depreciation expense

No information is provided about B Company's asset disposals. However, the amount of disposals can be computed from the above equation:

$$\text{\$260,000} = \text{\$277,000} - \text{Disposals} - \text{\$17,000}$$
$$\text{Disposals} = \text{\$277,000} - \text{\$17,000} - \text{\$260,000}$$
$$\text{Disposals} = \text{\$0}$$

If the amount of disposals were known but either acquisitions or depreciation expense were unknown, the missing item could be determined by applying this same equation.

b. Long-term debt increased by $105,000 − $5,000 = $100,000. Long-term debt was issued, a source of working capital.

c. The $110,000 increase in stockholders' equity can be explained by three factors in the changes statement: issuance of capital stock, net income (or loss), and dividends:

Increase in stockholders' equity = New issuance + Net income − Dividends

Suppose data about the issuance of new capital stock had not been provided:

$$\text{\$110,000} = \text{New issuance} + \text{\$43,000} - \text{\$20,000}$$
$$\text{New issuance} = \text{\$110,000} - \text{\$43,000} + \text{\$20,000}$$
$$\text{New issuance} = \text{\$ 87,000, a source of working capital}$$

Step 5. The difference between the total sources and uses is the net change in working capital. This change must agree with the amount in Step 1, a $50,000 decrease for B Company.

Step 6. Major investment and financing activities must be included in the changes statement even though working capital is unaffected. For example, consider the acquisition of a building in exchange for the issuance of capital stock. The changes statement would show the issuance of capital stock as a source of working capital, *as if* cash had been received. The acquisition of the building would be a use of working capital, *as if* the cash had immediately been spent for the building. B Company did not have such transactions in 19X2.

☐ Working Capital Provided by Operations

The first major item in the sources section is working capital provided by operations. Sales to customers are almost always *the* major source of working capital. Correspondingly, outlays for cost of goods sold and operating expenses are almost always *the* major uses of working capital. The excess of sales over all the expenses requiring working capital is, by definition, the working capital provided by operations. There are two ways to compute the amount of this item: the *addback method* and the *straightforward method,* shown in Schedule A of Exhibit 15–1. Because it is easier to understand, please initially consider the **straightforward method** (also called the *direct method*). It is shown as the second alternative presentation in Schedule A: sales of $200,000 minus the $140,000 of expenses requiring working capital equals working capital provided by operations, $60,000.

An alternative, often convenient, way to compute working capital provided by operations is to begin with net income. Then adjust for those items that entered the computation of net income but did not affect working capital. This is called the **addback method** (or the *indirect method*). The two methods can be compared as follows:

Sales	$200,000 (A)	⎫
Deduct expense requiring working capital	−140,000 (B)	⎬ Straightforward
Working capital provided by operations (A − B)	$60,000 (C)	⎭ Method
Deduct expenses not requiring working capital:		
Depreciation	−17,000 (D)	
Net income (C − D)	$43,000 (E)	⎫
Add expenses not requiring working capital:		⎬ Addback
Depreciation	+17,000 (D)	Method
Working capital provided by operations (E + D = A − B)	$60,000 (C)	⎭

Note that depreciation of $17,000 was subtracted from working capital provided by operations to calculate net income. Therefore $17,000 must be added back to net income to measure working capital provided by operations.

As the footnote to Schedule A of Exhibit 15–1 indicates, the first alternative presentation, here called the *addback method*, is used almost exclusively in annual reports even though it may require a bit more effort to understand. The usual presentation would omit Schedule A and include its content in the body of the changes statement as follows:

Sources:	
Net income	$ 43,000
Add charges not requiring working capital:	
Depreciation	17,000
Working capital provided by operations	$ 60,000
Other sources:	
Issuance of long-term debt	100,000
Issuance of additional capital stock	87,000
Total sources	$247,000

If the addback method is somewhat more difficult to fathom, why is it used so heavily? There are two main reasons besides the unsatisfying reason: "Because we've always done it that way." First, beginning with net income shows the important link with the income statement. Second, the straightforward method (which begins with sales) can require a detailed listing of expenses that is cumbersome and duplicates much of what is already contained in the income statement. The addback method is really a shortcut computation of the target number, working capital provided by operations.

☐ Role of Depreciation

The most crucial aspect of a changes statement is how depreciation and other expenses that do not require working capital relate to the flow of working capital. There is widespread misunderstanding of the role of depreciation in financial reporting, so let us examine this point in detail.

Accountants view depreciation as an allocation of historical cost to expense. Therefore depreciation expense does not entail a current outflow of cash, which is the prime form of working capital. Consider again the comparison of the straightforward and addback methods on page 680. Net income is a residual; by itself, it provides no working capital. Instead of beginning with the Sales total and working down (A − B = C on page 680), accountants usually start with Net Income and add back all charges not requiring working capital (E + D = C, or $43,000 + $17,000 = $60,000).

Unfortunately, the use of this shortcut method may at first glance create an erroneous impression that depreciation is, by itself, a source of working capital. If that were really true, a corporation could merely double or triple its bookkeeping entry for depreciation expense when working capital was badly needed! What would happen? Working capital provided by operations would be unaffected. Suppose depreciation for B Company is doubled:

Sales	$200,000
Less: All expenses requiring working capital (detailed)	140,000
Working capital provided by operations	$ 60,000
Less: Depreciation, 2 × $17,000	34,000
Net income	$ 26,000

The doubling affects depreciation *and* net income, but it has no direct influence on working capital provided by operations, which, of course, still amounts to $60,000, the sum of net income and depreciation. (For additional discussion, see Chapter 9, page 383, the section called "Depreciation and Generation of Cash." The effects of depreciation on income tax outflows are explained there.)

☐ Adjustments to Net Income

We have seen that net income rarely coincides with working capital provided by operations. Consequently, the necessary adjustments are commonly shown using the addback method to convert net income to working capital provided by operations, as explained above for depreciation.

A list of some additional possible adjustments is shown below. However, for our purposes in the body of this chapter, we need only be concerned with depreciation. Chapter references are shown in parentheses for readers who want to study the nature of the items in more depth:

ADD CHARGES AGAINST INCOME (EXPENSES) NOT REQUIRING WORKING CAPITAL FOR OPERATIONS	SUBTRACT CREDITS TO INCOME (REVENUES) NOT PROVIDING WORKING CAPITAL FOR OPERATIONS
Depreciation (Chapter 9)	Amortization of premium on bonds payable (Chapter 10)
Depletion (Chapter 9)	Extraordinary and nonoperating gains (Chapter 11)
Amortization of long-lived assets such as patents, copyrights, and goodwill (Chapter 9)	Equity in earnings of unconsolidated subsidiaries and affiliates (Chapter 12)
Amortization of discount on bonds payable (Chapter 10)	
Income tax expense arising from deferred income taxes (Chapter 13)	
Extraordinary and nonoperating losses (Chapter 11)	

Exhibit 15–2 contains the changes statement of G. Heileman Brewing Company, maker of Heidelberg, Special Export, Rainier, Schmidt, Lone Star, and many other brands of beer. Other publicly held corporations may show more details, but the general format of the changes statements is similar to that of Heileman. Every item in Exhibit 15–2 has been discussed earlier in this chapter, with the exception of income tax deferrals and amortization of bond discounts. Both are "added back" to net income because, although they were deducted in computing net income, they did not require working capital. Deferred income taxes are those taxes not currently payable. Amortization of bond discount is interest expense that increases the amount of the bond payable rather than being paid in cash. Also, stock options exercised measures proceeds from the sale of shares of common stock under a stock option plan. Appendix 15A contains a fuller discussion of the contents of the changes statement.

☐ Transactions Not Affecting Working Capital

Exhibit 15–3 analyzes the effects of most major transactions on working capital. It is worth studying to solidify understanding of the conceptual underpinnings of the changes statement. Note especially the final set of transactions, those that do *not* affect working capital. By themselves, the purchases of current assets, short-term borrowing of cash, collections of receivables, and payments that reduce short-term liabilities have no effect (numbers assumed to be $1,000 for each type):

	ΔCA	$- \Delta CL$	$= \Delta WC$
Purchases of current assets for cash	(+1)	(−1) − 0	= 0
Purchases of current assets on open account	(+1)	− (+1)	= 0
Collections of accounts receivable	(+1)	(−1) − 0	= 0
Borrowing cash on short-term note	(+1)	− (+1)	= 0
Payments that reduce short-term liabilities	(−1)	− (−1)	= 0

EXHIBIT 15–2

G. HEILEMAN BREWING COMPANY, INC.
Consolidated Statements of Changes in Financial Position
For the Years Ended December 31

	1985	1984
WORKING CAPITAL PROVIDED BY:		
Operations:		
Net income	$ 43,303,000	$ 45,798,000
Depreciation and amortization	27,840,000	24,943,000
Income tax deferrals	26,586,000	21,832,000
Amortization of bond discount	2,875,000	—
Working capital provided from operations	$100,604,000	$ 92,573,000
Issuance of long-term debt	97,295,000	721,000
Stock options exercised	120,000	119,000
Sale of non-operating properties	—	10,771,000
Total working capital provided	$198,019,000	$104,184,000
WORKING CAPITAL USED FOR:		
Reduction of long-term debt	$ 15,082,000	$ 37,346,000
Plant and equipment additions, net	23,158,000	40,029,000
Payment of cash dividends	13,145,000	12,725,000
Acquisitions	12,986,000	449,000
Other	5,149,000	4,949,000
Total working capital used	$ 69,520,000	$ 95,498,000
Increase in working capital	$128,499,000	$ 8,686,000
CHANGES IN WORKING CAPITAL:		
Increase (decrease) in current assets:		
Cash and temporary investments	$114,446,000	$ 2,914,000
Receivables	2,625,000	(2,010,000)
Inventories	687,000	(15,248,000)
Prepaid expenses	406,000	693,000
	$118,164,000	$ (13,651,000)
Decrease (increase) in current liabilities:		
Current maturities of long-term debt	$ (1,870,000)	$ 168,000
Accounts payable	18,691,000	12,070,000
Accrued expenses	(2,634,000)	3,542,000
Income taxes	(3,852,000)	6,557,000
	$ 10,335,000	$ 22,337,000
Increase in working capital	$128,499,000	$ 8,686,000

Opinion No. 19 points out that related items should be shown in proximity when the result contributes to the clarity of the changes statement. For instance, a building might be acquired for a total price of $900,000 in exchange for $200,000 cash plus a mortgage of $700,000. One way to report this transaction would be to show the $700,000 as a source and the $900,000 as a use. A second way would be to report the entire transaction in the section on uses:

Acquisition of building:		
Total cost	$900,000	
Deduct: Mortgage	700,000	
Working capital used		$200,000

EXHIBIT 15–3

Analysis of Effects of Transactions on Working Capital

TYPE OF TRANSACTION	ΔWC	=	ΔNCL	+	ΔPC	+	ΔRI	−	ΔNCA
Sources of working capital:									
Increase long-term debt	+	=	+						
Increase paid-in capital	+	=			+				
Sell plant, equipment, long-term investments*	+	=						−	(−)
Uses of working capital:									
Reduction of long-term debt	−	=	−						
Repurchase of outstanding capital stock	−	=			−				
Purchase of noncurrent assets (plant, long-term investments in securities)	−	=						−	(+)
Declaration of cash dividends	−	=					−		
Reclassification of long-term debt as short-term debt	+	=	−						
Effects of operations, which have the net effect of being a source:									
Sales of goods and services	+	=					+		
Acquisition of goods and services	−	=					−		
Difference, called working capital provided by operations	+	=					+		
Typical transactions not affecting working capital:									
Purchases of current assets, such as inventories or prepaid expenses for cash	0†								
Purchases of current assets, such as inventories or prepaid expenses on open account	0†								
Collections of accounts receivable	0†								
Borrowing cash on short-term note	0†								
Payments that reduce short-term liabilities	0†								
Depreciation and write-offs of noncurrent assets:									
Example: Depreciation of $17,000 results in reduction of net income and of fixed assets	0†						−17,000	−	(−17,000)

* Assumed sold at book value.
† There is no net effect on working capital, as explained more fully in the text.

In sum, although *Opinion No. 19* has required a statement of changes in financial position, it permits flexibility (some commentators might say fuzziness) in form, content, and terminology. Thus "net change in financial position" may be expressed in terms of any of the alternative concepts enumerated above (cash, working capital, and so on).

FOCUS ON CASH

☐ Computing Cash Provided by Operations

During the 1980s, users of financial statements became increasingly concerned with companies' ability to pay debts. To focus on debt-paying ability, a changes statement that emphasizes changes in *cash* became popular. Differences between a focus on cash and a focus on working capital for the changes statement are more of form than substance.

Since 1984, a majority of the largest companies in the United States have presented a changes statement that focuses on cash. The FASB may soon require a cash focus. There are many possible ways for the changes statement to focus on cash rather than working capital. Probably the easiest format is shown in Exhibit 15–4. The steps are identical to the working capital

EXHIBIT 15–4

B COMPANY
Statement of Changes in Financial Position (Cash)
For the Year Ended December 31, 19X2
(in thousands of dollars)

SOURCES AND USES OF CASH

Sources:		
Net income	$ 43	
Add charges not requiring working capital:		
Depreciation	17	
Working capital provided by operations	$ 60	
Add decreases in noncash working capital:		
Current liabilities (detailed)	90	
Deduct increases in noncash working capital:		
Net receivables	(20)	
Inventories	(40)	
Cash provided by operations*		$ 90
Issuance of long-term debt		100
Issuance of additional capital stock		87
Total sources		$277
Uses:		
Payment of cash dividends	$ 20	
Acquisition of plant and equipment	277	
Total uses		297
Decrease in cash		$ (20)
Cash, December 31, 19X1		25
Cash, December 31, 19X2		$ 5

* Frequently called *cash flow from operations* or just plain *cash flow*.

focus, except that the increases in noncash working capital items are deducted from (or decreases added to) the working capital from operations to obtain **cash provided by operations**. In Exhibit 15–4, $90 is added to and $40 and $20 are subtracted from $60 to obtain the $90 cash provided by operations.

Compare Exhibits 15–4 and 15–1 (p. 676). The only substantive difference is the addition of the sections, "Add decreases in noncash working capital" and "Deduct increases in noncash working capital" in the changes statement in Exhibit 15–4. These sections convert working capital provided by operations to *cash provided by operations*. Increases in receivables and inventories mean that operating cash has been invested therein, so the resulting cash provided by operations would decline. For example, cash provided by operations is diminished by the immediate reinvestment of cash collections in the expansion of inventory.

On the other hand, increases in current liabilities such as trade accounts payable, short-term bank loans, and various accruals have favorable effects on operating cash. For example, cash provided by operations is increased by a ninety-day bank loan, and drains on cash are postponed when suppliers give credit instead of demanding immediate payment.

In a nutshell, when cash is tied up in inventories, it cannot be used to pay creditors. Therefore, when inventories go up, cash provided by operations goes down. In contrast, when a company has less receivables and more payables, it has more cash.

Some typical adjustments to convert from working capital provided by operations to cash provided by operations are:

Add
  Increases in current liabilities
  Decreases in noncash current assets
Deduct
  Decreases in current liabilities
  Increases in noncash current assets

When resources are defined as cash rather than working capital, changes in noncash working capital become part of what *explains* the changes in resources, and only cash is left *to be explained*. In essence, the last two lines of the sources and uses of cash statement in Exhibit 15–4 (beginning and ending cash balance) serve the same function as the schedule of changes in components of working capital did in the working capital-basis statement. They confirm that the activities in the body of the statement did indeed explain the change in resources.

□ Operating, Investing, and Financing Activities

An alternative format for the cash-focused changes statement, shown in Exhibit 15–5, has three major sections: (1) operating activities, (2) investing activities, and (3) financing activities. A statement with this format will be called

EXHIBIT 15–5

B COMPANY
Statement of Cash Flows
For the Year Ended December 31, 19X2
(in thousands of dollars)

Cash flows from operating activities:		
Net income	$ 43	
Add charges not requiring working capital:		
Depreciation	17	
Working capital provided by operations	60	
Add decreases in noncash working capital:		
Current liabilities (detailed)	90	
Deduct increases in noncash working capital:		
Net receivables	(20)	
Inventory	(40)	
Net cash flow from operating activities		$ 90
Cash flows from investing activities:		
Acquisition of plant and equipment	$(277)	
Net cash used by investing activites		$(277)
Cash flows from financing activities:		
Issuance of long-term debt	$ 100	
Issuance of additional capital stock	87	
Payment of cash dividends	(20)	
Net cash provided by financing activities		$ 167
Net decrease in cash		$ 20
Cash, December 31, 19X1		25
Cash, December 31, 19X2		$ 5

a Statement of Cash Flows. Such a format highlights the results of financial management as compared to operating management. Notice that the terms *sources* and *uses* are not used. Instead, the accountant places each item affecting cash into one of the three activities categories, depending on the type of management activity that caused the change. For example, all items that arise from investing activities are listed together, those increasing cash as positive numbers and those decreasing cash as negative.

The section "Cash flows from operating activities" in Exhibit 15–5 is identical to the subsection that shows "Cash provided by operations" in the *sources* section of Exhibit 15–4. The four nonoperating sources and uses of cash in Exhibit 15–4 are shown under *investing activities* or *financing activities* in Exhibit 15–5.

☐ Cash Flow

Rampant inflation in the late 1970s and early 1980s engendered many criticisms of the historical cost/nominal dollar accrual measures of income and financial position. One response, as Chapter 14 described, has been supplementary disclosures using constant dollars and current costs. Another response has been a more intense focus on cash provided by operations and a trend toward focusing on cash rather than working capital in the statement of changes in financial position. Synonyms have arisen for *cash provided by operations*, most notably **cash flow**, which is shortened nomenclature for **cash flow from operations**. These terms are used interchangeably, but *cash flow* is used more frequently. The importance of cash flow has been stressed by Harold Williams, the former chairman of the Securities and Exchange Commission, quoted in *Forbes*: "If I had to make a forced choice between having earnings information and having cash flow information, today I would take cash flow information." The FASB's response has been a proposal to require the format of Exhibit 15–5 for the changes statement. The name of the statement would be changed from statement of changes in financial position to statement of cash flows.

Some companies like to stress a *cash-flow-per-share* figure (or a working-capital-generated-per-share figure) and provide it in addition to the required earnings-per-share figure. Net income is an attempt to summarize management performance. Cash flow or working capital provided by operations gives an incomplete picture of that performance because it ignores noncash expenses that are just as important as cash expenses for judging overall company performance. Moreover, such reported cash flows per share say nothing about the funds needed for replacement and expansion of facilities, thus seeming to imply that the entire per-share cash flows from operations may be available for cash dividends. Because they give an incomplete picture, cash-flow-per-share figures can be quite misleading. They should be interpreted very cautiously.

Both cash flow and accrual earnings data are useful. Bryan Carsberg, as a representative of the FASB, said that "asking which one is better, cash flow or earnings, is like asking which you should cut out, your heart or your lungs."

SUMMARY

Statements of changes in financial position attempt to answer two basic questions: Where did the resources (most often defined as either cash or working capital) come from? and Where did the resources go? The usual sources are operations and issuances of long-term debt and capital stock. The usual uses are dividends, various investments, and extinguishment of debt.

The changes statement also directly explains why a company with high net income may nevertheless be unable to pay dividends because of the weight of other financial commitments to plant expansion or retirement of debt.

SUMMARY PROBLEM FOR YOUR REVIEW

☐ **Problem**

The Buretta Company has prepared the data below and on page 690.

Debits	TRIAL BALANCES DECEMBER 31 (IN MILLIONS) 19X2	19X1	INCREASE (DECREASE)
Cash	$ 1	$20	$(19)
Accounts receivable	20	5	15
Inventory	46	15	31
Prepaid general expenses	4	2	2
Fixed assets, net	91	50	41
	$162	$92	$ 70
Credits			
Accounts payable for merchandise	$ 39	$14	$ 25
Accrued property tax payable	3	1	2
Mortgage payable in 19X9	40	—	40
Capital stock	70	70	—
Retained earnings	10	7	3
	$162	$92	$ 70

On December 28, 19X2, Buretta paid $9 million in cash and signed a $40 million mortgage on a new building acquired to accommodate an expansion of operations.

Because the net income of $4 million was the highest in the company's history, Mr. Buretta, the chairman of the board, was perplexed by the company's extremely low cash balance.

Required:

1. Prepare a statement of changes in financial position that focuses on working capital. Ignore income taxes. You may wish to use Exhibit 15–1 as a guide. However, incorporate the First Alternative Presentation (as illustrated there in Schedule A) in the body of your changes statement. That is, the sources section will begin with net income (like the one on page 680).
2. Redo the sources section (only) in requirement 1 by incorporating the Second Alternative Presentation (as illustrated in Schedule A of Exhibit 15–1) in the body of your changes statement. That is, the body of the sources section will begin with sales.
3. What is revealed by the statement of changes in financial position? Does it help you reduce Mr. Buretta's puzzlement? Why? Prepare a statement of changes in financial position that focuses on cash rather than working capital.
4. Briefly explain to Mr. Buretta why cash has decreased even though working capital has increased and net income was $4 million.
5. Refer to requirement 1. Support your financial statement by using a form of the balance sheet equation. Step by step, show in equation form how each item in the changes statement affects working capital.

BURETTA CO.
Income Statement and Statement of
Retained Earnings
For the Year Ended December 31, 19X2
(in millions)

Sales		$100
Less cost of goods sold:		
Inventory, December 31, 19X1	$ 15	
Purchases	104	
Cost of goods available for sale	$119	
Inventory, December 31, 19X2	46	73
Gross profit		$ 27
Less other expenses:		
General expenses	$ 11	
Depreciation	8	
Property taxes	4	23
Net income		$ 4
Retained earnings, December 31, 19X1		7
Total		$ 11
Dividends		1
Retained earnings, December 31, 19X2		$ 10

☐ **Solution**

1. See Exhibit 15–6. APB *Opinion No. 19* suggests the presentation of the mortgage as a source and the purchase of the building as a use. However, the following presentation under "uses" would probably be at least as informative:

Purchase of fixed assets (building)	$49	
Less: Mortgage thereon	40	
Working capital used		$9

2. See Exhibit 15–7. This is clearer for many readers, but longer.
3. Exhibit 15–6 focuses on working capital. It shows where new working capital has come from and where it has gone. Operations have added $12 million to working capital. But the $10 million uses of working capital ($1 million in dividends plus the $9 million required for fixed assets) reduced the net increase in working capital to only $2 million for the year.

Mr. Buretta's puzzlement can be reduced but not eliminated. A careful reading of the changes statement in Exhibit 15–6 should include the section showing the changes in components, where the drain on cash is revealed. Working capital is increased, but additional cash was needed to finance increases in receivables, inventories, and prepaid general expenses.

Exhibit 15–8 is a changes statement that focuses on cash rather than working capital. This statement shows a format that presents the details of increases and decreases in noncash working capital in a separate schedule rather than in the body of the statement. The statement is less puzzling than Exhibit 15–6. More cash was needed:

For operations	$ 9
For dividends	1
For purchase of the building, $49 − $40	9
Total cash needed	$19

EXHIBIT 15–6

BURETTA CO.
Statement of Changes in Financial Position
For the Year Ended December 31, 19X2
(in millions)

SOURCES AND USES OF WORKING CAPITAL

Sources:		
Net income (from income statement)	$ 4	
Add: Depreciation, which was deducted in the computation of net income but does not decrease working capital	8	
Working capital provided by operations		$12
Mortgage on building acquired		40
Total sources		$52
Uses:		
Dividends	$ 1	
Purchase of fixed assets (building)	49	
Total uses		50
Increase in working capital		$ 2

CHANGES IN COMPONENTS OF WORKING CAPITAL

	DECEMBER 31 19X2	DECEMBER 31 19X1	INCREASE (DECREASE) IN WORKING CAPITAL
Current assets:			
Cash	$ 1	$20	$(19)
Accounts receivable	20	5	15
Inventory	46	15	31
Prepaid general expenses	4	2	2
Total current assets	$71	$42	$ 29
Current liabilities:			
Accounts payable	$39	$14	$(25)
Accrued property tax payable	3	1	(2)
Total current liabilities	$42	$15	$(27)
Working capital	$29	$27	
Increase in working capital			$ 2

EXHIBIT 15–7

BURETTA CO.
Statement of Sources of Working Capital
For the Year Ended December 31, 19X2
(in millions)

Sales		$100
Deduct: All expenses requiring working capital:		
Cost of goods sold	$73	
General expenses	11	
Property taxes	4	88
Working capital provided by operations		$ 12
Mortgage on building acquired		40
Total sources		$ 52

EXHIBIT 15-8

BURETTA CO.
Statement of Changes in Financial Position (Cash)
For the Year Ended December 31, 19X2
(in millions)

SOURCES AND USES OF CASH

Sources:		
Net income (from income statement)	$ 4	
Add: Depreciation, which was deducted in the computation of net income but does not decrease working capital	8	
Working capital provided by operations	$12	
Deduct net increase in noncash working capital (see components)	21	
Cash provided by operations (negative)		$ (9)
Mortgage on building acquired		40
Total sources		$ 31
Uses:		
Dividends	$ 1	
Purchase of fixed assets (building)	49	
Total uses		50
Decrease in cash		$(19)
Cash, December 31, 19X1		20
Cash, December 31, 19X2		$ 1

CHANGES IN COMPONENTS OF NONCASH WORKING CAPITAL

	DECEMBER 31		INCREASE (DECREASE) IN NONCASH WORKING CAPITAL
	19X2	19X1	
Accounts receivable	$20	$ 5	$ 15
Inventory	46	15	31
Prepaid general expenses	4	2	2
Accounts payable	39	14	(25)
Accrued property tax payable	3	1	(2)
Increase in noncash working capital			$ 21

Thus the cash balance declined from $20 million to $1 million, a decrease of $19 million; as Exhibit 15-8 shows, cash provided by operations was negative.

4. Severe squeezes on cash commonly accompany quick corporate growth. There may be ample net income and working capital provided by operations, but the heavy demand for cash to expand fixed assets, inventories, and receivables may diminish the cash on hand despite profitable operations. That is why so many so-called growth companies usually pay little or no dividends.

5. Each item in the changes statement affects working capital as follows:

$$\Delta WC = \Delta NCL + \Delta PC + \Delta RI - \Delta NCA$$

	ΔWC	ΔNCL	$\Delta PC + \Delta RI$	$-\Delta NCA$
Sources:				
Effects of operations:				
Net income	+ 4 =		+4	
Depreciation addback	+ 8 =			− (−8)
Mortgage on building				
acquired	+40 =	+40		
Uses:				
Dividends	− 1 =		−1	
Purchase of fixed assets	−49 =			− (+49)
Net changes	+ 2 =	+40	+3	− (+41)

HIGHLIGHTS TO REMEMBER

1. When it focuses on working capital, the changes statement shows the reasons for changes in current assets and current liabilities in terms of changes in *non-working-capital* accounts.
2. When it focuses on cash, the changes statement shows the reasons for changes in cash in terms of changes in the non-working-capital accounts and all noncash working-capital accounts.
3. Sales to customers are almost always the major source of working capital or cash.
4. *Cash flow*, *cash provided by operations*, and *cash flow from operations* are synonyms.

ACCOUNTING VOCABULARY

Addback Method, p. *680* Cash Flow, *688* Cash Flow from Operations, *688* Cash Provided by Operations, *686* Changes Statement, *672* Financial Management, *671* Funds Statement, *672* Operating Management, *671* Statement of Cash Flows, *672* Statement of Changes in Financial Position, *672* Statement of Sources and Application of Funds, *672* Straightforward Method, *680* Working Capital Cycle, *673*

APPENDIX 15A: MORE ON THE CHANGES STATEMENT

This appendix describes how some common items affect the statement of changes in financial position and distinguishes such effects from the income statement effects of these items. The appendix also presents details on some adjustments to net income encountered when using the addback method.

Exhibit 15–9 shows the effects of the selected transactions on the statement of changes in financial position. The transactions are generally organized in chapter sequence and can be referred to in conjunction with your study of the indicated chapters.

Although all changes statements contain basically the same information, a company can elect to present that information in many different ways. We have already

EXHIBIT 15–9

Effects of Selected Transactions on Statement of Changes in Financial Position

DISCUSSED MAINLY IN CHAPTER	TYPE OF TRANSACTION	DESCRIPTIONS USED IN PUBLISHED FINANCIAL REPORTS	SECTION OF CHANGES STATEMENT	EFFECTS ON BALANCE SHEET EQUATION				
				ΔWC =	ΔNCL +	ΔPC +	ΔRI −	ΔNCA
9	Amortization (like depreciation) is "added back" to net income to obtain working capital provided by operations	Amortization Depreciation and amortization	Sources (operations) as addback	+1 =				−(−1)
10	Amortization of discounts on bonds payable	Same as above	Sources (operations) as addback	+1 =	+1			
	Amortization of premium on bonds payable	Same as above	Sources (operations) as subtraction	−1 =	−1			
11	Treasury stock acquisitions	Treasury stock acquired	Uses	−1 =		−1		
	Retirement of stock	Stock retired	Uses	−1 =		−1		
12	Recognition of income and dividends received under the equity method of accounting for investments in unconsolidated subsidiaries and affiliates. For illustration, assume income is 3 and dividends are 1	Several alternatives are found in practice. Note that the recognition of income increases net income but does **not** increase working capital. In contrast, the receipt of dividends increases working capital but does **not** increase net income	Income shown as a source (operations) as subtraction	−3 =				−(+3)
			Dividends shown as "other source"	+1 =				−(−1)
			The two are netted and shown as a source (operations) as subtraction	−2 =				−(+2)
13	Deferred taxes increased. This means that income tax expense on the income statement is higher than on the tax return	Deferred taxes	Sources (operations) as addback	+1 =	+1			
13	Deferred tax credits increased. This means that income tax expense on the income statement is higher than on the tax return	Same as above	Sources (operations) as addback	+1 =	+1			

discussed the difference between a focus on working capital and a focus on cash. In addition, companies can choose among alternative ways of presenting the same detailed data.

☐ Gain on Disposal of Property

Consider the disposal of a piece of property or equipment. In 1985, the United States Steel Corporation disposed of assets with a book value of $181 million and received proceeds of $236 million, recognizing a gain of $236 million − $181 million = $55 million. How should these data be shown in the changes statement?

Consider first the disposal's net effect on working capital (which is the same as its effect on cash):

$$
\begin{array}{lllll}
\Delta WC & = \Delta NCL + \Delta PC + & \Delta RI & - & \Delta NCA \\
\text{Proceeds} = & & \text{Gain} & -(-\text{Book value}) \\
\$236\ \text{million} = & & \$55\ \text{million} + & \$181\ \text{million}
\end{array}
$$

Whatever method is used to present these data, the net increase in working capital from the disposal of property and equipment must be $236 million.

U.S. Steel includes the $236 million proceeds as a nonoperating source of working capital, essentially an increase in cash. However, net income, which is the starting point for computing working capital from operations, already includes the $55 million gain. To avoid double counting in computing sources of working capital, U.S. Steel deducts from net income the $55 million gain on disposal of assets (in millions):

Total income	$ 313
Adjustments for items not affecting working capital from operations:	
Depreciation, depletion, and amortization	1,294
Deferred taxes on income	121
Gain on disposal of assets	(55)
Other	(50)
Working capital from operations	$1,623

Many companies (for example, Alcoa) would not show the $236 million proceeds in one place. Instead no adjustment would be made to net income, and the *book value* of the assets would replace the proceeds as a nonoperating source of working capital. If U.S. Steel used this method, working capital from operations would be $55 million higher, nonoperating sources of working capital would be $55 million lower, and total sources would be unaffected.

☐ Equity Method Investments

Brunswick Corporation uses the equity method to account for its investments in unconsolidated subsidiaries. Therefore Brunswick's share of the subsidiaries' net income is included in Brunswick's income. In 1985, Brunswick's share of the subsidiaries' net income was $7,015,000, and it received dividends of $5,067,000. How should these items be shown on the changes statement?

Consider again the balance sheet equation:

$$
\begin{array}{lllll}
\Delta WC & = \Delta NCL + \Delta PC + & \Delta RI & - & \Delta NCA \\
(1) & = & + \$7,015,000 & - (+\$7,015,000) \\
(2) \quad +\$5,067,000 = & & & - (-\$5,067,000)
\end{array}
$$

Line (1) records Brunswick's share of the subsidiaries' net income, adding it to Brunswick's income (and hence to retained income) and to the investment account. Line (2) records Brunswick's receipt of dividends from the subsidiaries.

The net source of working capital is $5,067,000, but Brunswick's net income includes the amount $7,015,000. Brunswick makes the needed adjustment in two steps. First, its share of net income of the subsidiaries is deducted from net income. Second, the dividends received are shown as a source:

Provided by operations:	
Net earnings	$100,314,000
Items not requiring (providing) working capital	
Depreciation and amortization	49,569,000
Deferred items	17,633,000
Equity in earnings of unconsolidated subsidiaries	(7,015,000)
Dividends received from unconsolidated subsidiaries	5,067,000
Other (summarized here)	612,000
Working capital provided by operations	$166,180,000

The same adjustment would be made on a changes statement focused on cash. Many companies make this adjustment in one step, showing only the net amount, $7,015,000 − $5,067,000 = $1,948,000. If Brunswick used the terminology of American Can Company, it would show:

Unremitted earnings of unconsolidated subsidiaries (net of $5,067,000 dividend)	$1,948,000

Alcoa labels this net amount "Equity earnings (greater) or less than dividends received."

APPENDIX 15B: T-ACCOUNT APPROACH TO STATEMENT OF CHANGES

Many statements of changes in financial position can be prepared by using the steps described in the body of the chapter. Work sheets or T-accounts are frequently a hindrance instead of a help. However, if the facts become complicated, a T-account approach deserves serious consideration. This appendix presents an overview of the T-account approach.

The procedure begins by preparing a T-account that combines all the current assets and current liabilities in a single account, Working Capital. The data from the B Company illustration used in the body of the chapter will also be used here. For convenient reference, Exhibit 15–1 has been reproduced, using the addback format, as Exhibit 15–10. The $50,000 decrease in working capital is entered on the credit side at the top of the account, and a single line is drawn beneath the entry.

Exhibit 15–11 displays the entire T-account approach to the statement of changes in financial position (working capital). Compare the first account, Working Capital, with the current assets and current liabilities shown in Exhibit 15–10. The $50,000 decrease is the sum of the $20,000 and $90,000 changes in Cash and Current Liabilities minus the $20,000 and $40,000 changes in Receivables and Inventories:

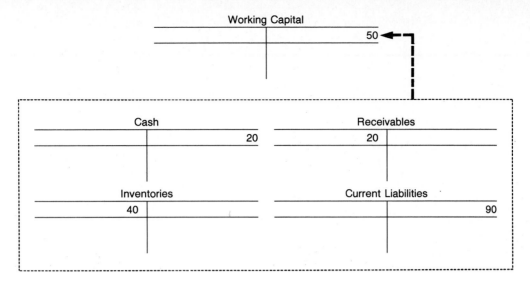

Working Capital

	50

Cash		Receivables	
	20	20	

Inventories		Current Liabilities	
40			90

EXHIBIT 15–10

B COMPANY
Statement of Changes in Financial Position
For the Year Ended December 31, 19X2
(in thousands of dollars)

SOURCES AND USES OF WORKING CAPITAL

Sources:		
Net income		$ 43
Add charges not requiring working capital:		
Depreciation		17
Working capital provided by operations		$ 60
Issuance of long-term debt		100
Issuance of additional capital stock		87
Total sources		$247
Uses:		
Acquisition of plant and equipment	$277	
Payment of cash dividends	20	
Total uses		297
Decrease in working capital		$ 50

CHANGES IN COMPONENTS OF WORKING CAPITAL

	DECEMBER 31		INCREASE (DECREASE) IN WORKING CAPITAL
	19X2	19X1	
Current assets:			
Cash	$ 5	$ 25	$(20)
Net receivables	45	25	20
Inventories	100	60	40
Total current assets	$150	$110	$ 40
Current liabilities (detailed)	100	10	(90)
Working capital	$ 50	$100	
Decrease in working capital			$(50)

EXHIBIT 15–11

B COMPANY
T-Account Approach Using Addback Method
Statement of Changes in Financial Position (Working Capital)
For the Year Ended December 31, 19X2
(in thousands of dollars)

Working Capital

		Change		50
Sources			**Uses**	
1. Net income	43			
2. Depreciation	17			
Working capital from operations	60			
3. Issuance of long-term debt	100		5. Dividends declared	20
4. Issuance of stock	87		6. Equipment acquired	277
Total debits	247		Total credits	297

Plant Assets, Net

260			
6. Acquisition	277	2. Depreciation	17

Long-Term Debt

	100
3. New debt	100

Stockholders' Equity

			110
5. Dividends	20	1. Net income	43
		4. Stock issuance	87
Total debits	20	Total credits	130

The T-account approach displayed in Exhibit 15–11 is merely another way of applying the balance sheet equation described in the body of the chapter:

$$\Delta \text{Working capital} = \Delta \text{Noncurrent liabilities} + \Delta \text{Stockholders' equity} - \Delta \text{Noncurrent assets}$$

Working capital	=	Long-term debt	+	Stockholders' equity	−	Plant assets, net
	50		100		110	260

$$-50 = 100 + 110 - 260$$
$$-50 = -50$$

Again, the focus is on the changes in the *noncurrent* accounts in order to explain why the *current* accounts changed.

The summarized transactions for 19X2 entered in the Working Capital account are the basis for the preparation of the formal statement of changes in financial position (Exhibit 15–10).

If the accountant prefers to use the addback method, the starting point in the Working Capital account is typically net income. A summary of the net income effect is entered as entry 1 in Exhibit 15–11 and can also be shown in journal entry form:

1. Working capital	43	
Stockholders' equity		43

As explained in the body of the chapter, net income does not directly reflect the impact of operations on Working Capital. Net income is a residual figure, the difference between revenue and all expenses—including some expenses (such as depreciation) that do not affect Working Capital. To obtain the desired figure of working capital provided by operations, the accountant adds back all charges not requiring working capital. Thus entry 2 would be:

2. Working capital (addback to net income)	17	
Plant assets, net		17

Sufficient space should be allowed in the Working Capital T-account for the grouping of shortcut addbacks to, or subtractions from, net income to calculate the working capital from operations. The subtotal ($60,000 in Exhibit 15–11) stresses this phase of the analysis.

The remaining entries are shown in journal entry form as follows:

3. Borrowing for long term:		
Working capital	100	
Long-term debt		100
4. Issuance of stock:		
Working capital	87	
Stockholders' equity		87
5. Dividends paid:		
Stockholders' equity	20	
Working capital		20
6. Acquisition of equipment:		
Plant assets, net	277	
Working capital		277

Note that many everyday transactions do not influence working capital. Collections of accounts receivable do not affect working capital because one current asset is merely transformed into a different current asset. Similarly, the payments of current liabilities do not affect working capital because current assets and current liabilities are reduced by the same amount. Furthermore, the acquisition of inventories on open account does not affect working capital because current assets and current liabilities are increased by the same amount.

FUNDAMENTAL ASSIGNMENT MATERIAL

☐ **General Coverage**

Note: Instructors who prefer to focus on cash rather than working capital may wish to assign one or more of the following problems: 15–2, 15–32, 15–37 to 15–41, 15–47, and 15–48.

15–1. **CHANGES STATEMENT.** (Alternate is 15–30). The Redondo Company has the following balance sheets (in millions of dollars):

	AS OF DECEMBER 31			AS OF DECEMBER 31	
	19X7	19X6		19X7	19X6
Current assets (detailed)	$ 90	$ 80	Current liabilities (detailed)	$ 50	$ 45
Fixed assets (net of depreciation)	65	40	Long-term debt	5	—
Goodwill	5	10	Stockholders' equity	105	85
	$160	$130		$160	$130

Net income in 19X7 was $26 million. Cash dividends paid were $6 million. Depreciation was $7 million. Half the goodwill was amortized. Fixed assets of $32 million were purchased.

Required: Prepare a statement of changes in financial position using a focus on working capital.

15–2. PREPARE A CASH-BASIS CHANGES STATEMENT. (Problem 15–32 is an extension of this problem.) Galvez Company had net income of $80,000 on sales of $990,000 in 19X3. The statement of changes of financial position for 19X3 was (in thousands):

Sources and Uses of Working Capital

Sources:		
Working capital provided by operations		$ 200
Issuance of additional capital stock		400
Total sources		$ 600
Uses:		
Redemption of long-term debt	$400	
Acquisition of plant and equipment	300	
Payment of cash dividends	100	
Total uses		800
Decrease in working capital		$(200)

Changes in Components of Working Capital

	DECEMBER 31		INCREASE (DECREASE) IN WORKING CAPITAL
	19X3	19X2	
Current assets:			
Cash	$ 20	$ 60	$ (40)
Accounts receivable	240	150	90
Inventories	450	350	100
Total current assets	$710	560	$ 150
Current liabilities:			
Accounts payable	$560	300	$(260)
Accrued payables	100	10	(90)
Total current liabilities	$660	$310	$(350)
Working capital	$ 50	$250	
Decrease in working capital			$(200)

Required:
1. Prepare a statement of changes in financial position that focuses on cash.
2. Point out the differences between your cash-basis statement and the given working capital-basis statement.

15–3. Depreciation and Working Capital. Delahanty Company has the following data for 19X5: All expenses requiring working capital, $630,000; depreciation, $80,000; sales, $910,000. Ignore income taxes.

Required:

1. Compute working capital provided by operations and net income.
2. Assume that depreciation is tripled. Compute working capital provided by operations and net income.

Understanding Published Financial Reports

15–4. Cash and Working Capital Provided by Operations. Sherwin-Williams Company produces Dutch Boy paints and operates drug and paint stores. Its 1985 annual report included the following items in its statement of changes in consolidated financial position (in thousands):

Net increase in noncash current items	$23,549
Increase in cash and short-term investments	3,792
Net cash flow provided by operations	20,585
Cash dividends	21,064

Required:

Compute the working capital provided by operations.

15–5. Items in a Changes Statement. Knight-Ridder Newspapers, Inc., operates twenty-seven daily newspapers, eight television stations, and various other communications businesses. The company's 1985 changes statement contained the following items:

1) Depreciation	$ 61,005,000
2) Sale of common stock to employees	$ 22,399,000
3) Proceeds from bank borrowings	$356,996,000
4) Payment of cash dividends	$ 46,077,000
5) Amortization of goodwill, publication and broadcast rights	$ 7,827,000
6) Additions to property, plant and equipment	$106,279,000

Required:

Indicate which of the following three sections of the changes statement would contain each of the above items: (a) charges to income not affecting working capital, (b) additional sources of working capital, and (c) additional uses of working capital.

ADDITIONAL ASSIGNMENT MATERIAL

General Coverage

15–6. "The statement of changes in financial position, more recently called the statement of sources and uses of funds, is an optional statement included by most companies in their annual reports." Do you agree? Explain.

15–7. What types of insights are provided by a changes statement?

15–8. Define *funds statement*.

15–9. What is working capital?

15–10. What types of activities are summarized in the changes statement?

15–11. What are the major sources of working capital? Applications?

15–12. "The schedule of changes in components of working capital is an integral part of the statement of changes in financial position." Do you agree? Explain.

15–13. "Net losses mean drains on working capital." Do you agree? Explain.

15–14. Demonstrate how the fundamental balance sheet equation can be recast to focus on working capital.

15–15. What are the two major ways of computing working capital provided by operations?

15–16. Evaluate the following presentation of part of a changes statement:

Sources:	
Sales	$100,000
Less expenses requiring working capital	70,000
Funds provided by operations	$ 30,000

15–17. "Depreciation is usually a big source of working capital." Do you agree? Explain.

15–18. "The ordinary purchase of inventory has no effect on working capital." Why?

15–19. What are some examples of expenses and losses not affecting working capital?

15–20. What are some weaknesses of the idea that funds are working capital?

15–21. Give definitions of *funds* other than working capital.

15–22. What is the major difference between a statement of changes in financial position that focuses on cash and one focused on working capital?

15–23. "Cash flow per share can be downright misleading." Why?

15–24. The changes statement that focuses on cash is becoming more popular. Why?

15–25. The gain on the sale of a fixed asset represents part of the working capital received by the X Company. How should this item be presented on a changes statement? Why?

15–26. What are the effects on working capital of the following transaction: The purchase of fixed assets at a cost of $100,000, of inventories at a cost of $200,000, and of receivables at a cost of $50,000, paid for by the assumption of a $70,000 mortgage on the fixed assets and the giving of a ninety-day promissory note for $280,000.

15–27. The net income of the Lear Company was $1 million. Included on the income statement are the following:

Uninsured loss of inventory, by flood (classified as a part of operating expenses)	$100,000
Gain on the sale of equipment	200,000
Dividend income	10,000
Interest income, including $5,000 not yet received	20,000
Amortization of patents	50,000
Depreciation	400,000

Compute the working capital provided by operations, assuming that interest and dividend income are a part of operating income.

15–28. An asset with a book value of $80,000 was sold for $100,000. The gain of $20,000 was included in income. Correct the following sources section of the changes statement:

Sources:	
Net income	$250,000
Plus depreciation	70,000
Working capital provided by operations	$320,000
Proceeds from sale of equipment	100,000
Total Sources	$420,000

15–29. ITEMS NOT AFFECTING WORKING CAPITAL. Suppose some plant and equipment was acquired for a total price of $950,000, consisting of a cash down payment of $350,000 and a mortgage payable of $600,000. Show at least two ways of presenting the effects of this transaction on the statement of changes in financial position.

15–30. CHANGES STATEMENT AND ANALYSIS OF GROWTH.   (Alternate is 15–1.) The Aztec Company has the following balance sheets (in millions):

	DECEMBER 31			DECEMBER 31	
	19X7	19X6		19X7	19X6
Current assets:			Current liabilities		
Cash	$ 3	$ 10	(detailed)	$105	$ 30
Receivables, net	60	30	Long-term debt	150	—
Inventories	100	50	Stockholders' equity	208	160
Total current assets	$163	$ 90			
Plant assets (net of accumulated depreciation)	300	100			
Total assets	$463	$190	Total liab. and stk. eq.	$463	$190

Net income was $54 million. Cash dividends paid were $6 million. Depreciation was $20 million. Fixed assets were purchased for $220 million, $150 million of which was financed via the issuance of long-term debt outright for cash.

Renee Alvarez, the president and majority stockholder of Aztec, was a superb operating executive. She was imaginative and aggressive in marketing and ingenious and creative in production. But she had little patience with financial matters. After examining the most recent balance sheet and income statement she muttered, "We've enjoyed ten years of steady growth; 19X7 was our most profitable ever. Despite such profitability, we're in the worst cash position in our history. Just look at those current liabilities in relation to our available cash! This whole picture of the more you make, the poorer you get, just does not make sense. These statements must be cockeyed."

Required:

1. Prepare a statement of changes in financial position (sources and applications of working capital).
2. Using the changes statement and other information, write a short memorandum to Alvarez, explaining why there is such a squeeze on cash.

15–31. PREPARE CHANGES STATEMENT.   The Friedlander Company has assembled the accompanying (a) balance sheet and (b) income statement and reconciliation of retained earnings for 19X9.

Balance Sheet
December 31
(in millions)

	19X9	19X8	CHANGE
Assets:			
Cash	$ 10	$ 25	$(15)
Accounts receivable	40	28	12
Inventory	70	50	20
Prepaid general expenses	4	3	1
Plant assets, net	202	150	52
	$326	$256	$ 70
Liabilities and Shareholders' Equity:			
Accounts payable for merchandise	$ 74	$ 60	$ 14
Accrued property tax payable	3	2	1
Mortgage payable	50	—	50
Capital stock	100	100	—
Retained earnings	99	94	5
	$326	$256	$ 70

FRIEDLANDER CO.
Income Statement and Reconciliation of Retained
Earnings For the Year Ended December 31, 19X9
(in millions)

Sales		$250
Less cost of goods sold:		
Inventory, Dec. 31, 19X8	$ 50	
Purchases	160	
Cost of goods available for sale	$210	
Inventory, Dec. 31, 19X9	70	140
Gross profit		$110
Less other expenses:		
General expense	$ 51	
Depreciation	40	
Property taxes	10	101
Net income		$ 9
Dividends		4
Net income of the period retained		$ 5
Retained earnings, Dec. 31, 19X8		94
Retained earnings, Dec. 31, 19X9		$ 99

On December 30, 19X9, Friedlander paid $42 million in cash and signed a $50 million mortgage on a new plant acquired to expand operations. Because net income was $9 million, the highest in the company's history, Sidney Friedlander, the chief executive officer, was distressed by the company's extremely low cash balance.

Required:

1. Prepare a statement of changes in financial position that focuses on working capital. You may wish to use Exhibit 15–1, page 676, as a guide. However, incorporate the First Alternative Presentation (as illustrated there in Schedule A) in the body of your changes statement. That is, the sources section will begin with net income.
2. Redo the sources section (only) in requirement 1 by incorporating the Second Alternative Presentation (as illustrated in Schedule A of Exhibit 15–1, page

676) in the body of your changes statement. That is, the body of the sources section will begin with sales.

3. What is revealed by the statement of changes in financial position? Does it help you reduce Mr. Friedlander's distress? Why?

4. Briefly explain to Mr. Friedlander why cash has decreased even though working capital has increased and net income was $9 million.

5. Refer to requirement 1. Support your financial statement by using a form of the balance sheet equation. Step by step, show in equation form how each item in the changes statement affects working capital.

15–32. **INTERPRET A CHANGES STATEMENT.** Refer to the facts in Problem 15–2, page 700.

Required:

1. Prepare two alternative presentations of a supporting schedule of working capital provided by operations.

2. Prepare a short memorandum summarizing the information contained in the changes statement. Include a discussion of operations, financing activities, and investment activities.

15–33. **CHANGES STATEMENT.** The following comparative trial balances and additional information pertain to the Quick Manufacturing Co. Prepare a statement of changes in financial position (working capital focus) for the year 19X2.

QUICK MANUFACTURING CO.
Comparative Trial Balances

	DEC. 31 19X2	DEC. 31 19X1	INCREASE (DECREASE)
Debits:			
Cash	$ 43,000	$ 50,000	$ (7,000)
Receivables	76,000	65,000	11,000
Inventories	118,000	98,000	20,000
Prepaid rent	5,000	7,000	(2,000)
Patents	50,000	48,000	2,000
Fixed assets	205,000	182,000	23,000
	$497,000	$450,000	$47,000
Credits:			
Accounts payable	$ 71,000	$ 63,000	$ 8,000
Taxes payable	20,000	18,000	2,000
Bank loan	25,000	16,000	9,000
4% serial bonds (current)	20,000	20,000	0
Accumulated depreciation	82,000	76,000	6,000
4% serial bonds (noncurrent)	—	20,000	(20,000)
Capital stock ($10 par value)	110,000	100,000	10,000
Additional paid-in capital	55,000	50,000	5,000
Retained earnings	114,000	87,000	27,000
	$497,000	$450,000	$47,000

Additional information pertaining to 19X2:

1. Old machinery, having an original cost of $22,000 and accumulated depreciation of $18,000, was sold for $5,000.

2. In late December, another patent was acquired at a cost of $5,000.

3. Net income amounted to $27,000, after deductions amounting to $24,000 for depreciation and $3,000 for amortization of patents. No dividends were declared or paid during 19X2.

4. During the year the company received $15,000 for a new issue of 1,000 shares of capital stock.

15–34. WORKING CAPITAL FROM OPERATIONS. Study Appendix 15A. Suppose you use the addback conversion of net income to working capital provided by operations. Indicate whether each of the following items should be added to or subtracted from net income:

a. Amortization of patents
b. Amortization of goodwill
c. Extraordinary loss from earthquake
d. Extraordinary gain on extinguishment of debt
e. Amortization of discount on bonds payable
f. Depletion
g. Amortization of premium on bonds payable
h. Nonoperating gain on sale of investments in equity securities
i. Income tax expense arising from deferred income taxes

15–35. IDENTIFYING CHANGES. Study Appendix 15A. For each of the following items, state whether working capital has increased (I), decreased (D), or been unaffected (U):

1. Net income for year
2. Sales on credit
3. Sales for cash
4. Depreciation
5. Amortization of discount on bond payable
6. Amortization of premium on bond payable
7. Dividend received on investment in unconsolidated subsidiary
8. Recognition of income of unconsolidated subsidiary
9. Recognition of tax expense that increases deferred taxes, noncurrent
10. Acquired treasury stock
11. Acquired inventory for cash
12. Acquired inventory on trade credit
13. Acquired equipment for cash
14. Acquired equipment on short-term credit

15–36. CHANGES STATEMENT AND REVIEW OF CONSOLIDATIONS. Study Appendix 15A. (This problem is harder than the other problems in this chapter. It requires knowledge through Chapter 12.) Using Exhibits 12–2 and 12–3, prepare a 19X3 consolidated statement of changes in financial position using the working capital concept of "funds" for the Goliath Corporation. Goliath paid cash dividends on common shares of $2,000,000. (See pp. 542–545.)

15–37. CASH AND WORKING CAPITAL PROVIDED BY OPERATIONS. Consider the following (in millions):

Net income	$50
Reduction of long-term debt	30
Decrease in accounts payable	12
Amortization of goodwill	4
Decrease in accounts receivable	7
Increase in inventories	29
Depreciation expense	19
Purchase of treasury stock	5

Required:

| Compute working capital provided by operations and cash provided by operations.

15–38. **FOCUS ON CASH.** Refer to the facts in Problem 15–30. Prepare a statement of changes in financial position (cash). Then briefly explain to Alvarez why cash has decreased even though net income was $54 million.

15–39. **FOCUS ON CASH.** Refer to the facts in Problem 15–31. Prepare a statement of changes in financial position (cash). Then briefly explain to Friedlander why cash has decreased even though working capital has risen by $3 million and net income was $9 million.

15–40. **FOCUS ON CASH.** Refer to the facts in Problem 15–33. Compute the cash provided by operations. Explain why a change in cash may differ in direction from a change in working capital.

15–41. **COMPARE CASH WITH WORKING CAPITAL APPROACH.** Williams Company had a net income of $50,000 in 19X3. Sales were $870,000; expenses requiring working capital, $700,000; and depreciation, $120,000. Williams Company had the following balance sheets (in thousands):

| | DECEMBER 31 | | | DECEMBER 31 | |
	19X3	19X2		19X3	19X2
Current assets:			Current liabilities:		
Cash	$ 20	$ 60	Accounts payable	$ 570	$ 300
Net receivables	230	150	Accrued payables	90	10
Inventories	450	350	Total current liabilities	$ 660	$ 310
Total current assets	$ 700	$ 560	Long-term debt	—	400
Plant assets, net			Stockholders' equity	890	520
of accumulated					
depreciation	850	670			
Total assets	$1,550	$1,230	Total equities	$1,550	$1,230

In 19X3, the company issued additional capital stock for $420,000 cash. The long-term debt was retired for cash. Cash dividends declared and paid were $100,000. New equipment was acquired for $300,000 cash.

Required:

1. Prepare a statement of changes in financial position (working capital focus) including two alternative presentations of a supporting schedule of working capital provided by operations.
2. Write a short memorandum summarizing the information contained in the statement.
3. Refer to requirement 1. Support your financial statement by using a form of the balance sheet equation. Step by step, show in equation form how each item in the changes statement affects working capital.

4. Prepare a statement of changes in financial position that focuses on cash. How does this statement differ from the statement prepared in requirement 1?

15–42. **T-ACCOUNT APPROACH.** Study Appendix 15B. Refer to the facts concerning the Buretta Company, the "Summary Problem for Your Review" in the chapter (page 689). Prepare a set of T-accounts that supports the statement of changes in financial position shown in Exhibit 15–5. Assume that the sources section begins with net income. Key your postings by number.

15–43. **T-ACCOUNT APPROACH.** Study Appendix 15B. Refer to the facts concerning the Friedlander Company, Problem 15–31. Prepare a set of T-accounts that supports the statement of changes in financial position. Assume that the sources section begins with net income. Key your postings by number.

15–44. **T-ACCOUNT APPROACH.** Study Appendix 15B. Refer to the facts concerning the Quick Company, Problem 15–33. Prepare a set of T-accounts that supports the statement of changes in financial position. Assume that the sources section begins with net income. Key your postings by number.

15–45. **T-ACCOUNT APPROACH.** Study Appendix 15B. Salgo Company's net income for 19X5 was $36,000. The company's 19X5 annual report included the accompanying comparative balance sheets.

SALGO COMPANY
Comparative Balance Sheets

		DECEMBER 31		
ASSETS		19X5		19X4
Cash		$ 70,000		$ 59,000
Marketable securities (short-term)		—		31,000
Accounts receivable		91,500		95,000
Inventories		124,000		126,000
Prepaid insurance		6,000		4,000
Total current assets		$291,500		$315,000
Long-term notes receivable		50,000		55,000
Plant, property, and equipment	$365,000		$285,000	
Less: Accumulated depreciation	126,000	239,000	112,000	173,000
		$580,500		$543,000

LIABILITIES AND STOCKHOLDERS' EQUITY				
Accounts and notes payable		$110,000		$106,000
Taxes payable		35,000		38,000
Dividends payable		32,000		—
Total current liabilities		$177,000		$144,000
Debentures	$ 50,000		$ 50,000	
Less: Unamortized discount	4,500	45,500	5,000	45,000
Capital stock ($5 par value)		80,000		80,000
Paid-in surplus		112,000		112,000
Retained earnings		166,000		162,000
		$580,500		$543,000

On July 1, 19X5, a fire completely destroyed a small Houston warehouse that Salgo had used only during peak periods to supply customers in the Southwest. Fortunately, the warehouse was empty at the time of the fire. Salgo paid $80,000 for the warehouse on December 31, 19X0, of which $60,000 was for the building and $20,000 for the land. The building was being depreciated on a straight-line basis with a useful life of ten years and no estimated residual value. Salgo received $30,000 from an insurance policy on the warehouse.

Required:

Prepare a statement of changes in financial position (working capital). Use the T-account approach and include the final statement in good form in your answer.

☐ Understanding Published Financial Reports

15–46. **FORMAT OF FUNDS STATEMENT.** Criticize the following excerpts from actual annual reports.

FMC Corporation:

Source of funds:	
Net income	$ 60,822,770
Provision for depreciation and amortization	49,296,594
Cash flow from operations	$110,119,364

Trans World Airlines:

Source of funds:	
Operations:	
Net income for the year	$ 21,500,000
Add noncash expense:	
Depreciation and amortization	83,300,000
Total from operations	$104,800,000

Tenneco, Inc:

Source of funds:	
Net income	$166,931,748
Depreciation, depletion and amortization	156,901,757
Preferred stock sold	30,000,000
Disposal of properties	50,506,439
Etc.	Etc.

St. Regis Paper Company:

Source:	
Operations:	
Net earnings	$ 34,022,000
Expenses that did not require outlay of cash:	
Depreciation	36,365,000
Deferred items	6,101,000
Other	1,569,000
Total	$ 78,057,000

15–47. **CASH AND WORKING CAPITAL PROVIDED BY OPERATIONS.** Examine the accompanying statement of changes in financial position of NYNEX Corporation, provider of telephone services in the Northeast section of the United States.

1. Compute 1985 net income (loss).
2. Some companies place the focus of a changes statement on cash and temporary (short-term) investments. Suppose NYNEX had prepared such a changes statement. Compute the cash (and temporary cash investments) provided by operations.

NYNEX CORPORATION
Statements of Changes in Financial Position

(In millions)	YEAR ENDED DECEMBER 31, 1985
Sources of Working Capital	
From operations:	
Net income	$?
Add expenses not requiring working capital:	
Depreciation	1,433.2
Deferred income taxes—net	302.9
Deferred tax credits—net	75.0
Deduct income not providing working capital:	
Interest charged construction	(61.1)
Income from equity investments	(12.8)
Total working capital from operations	?
Issuance of long-term debt	197.3
Issuance of common stock	45.4
Total Sources of Working Capital	?
Applications of Working Capital	
Additions to property, plant and equipment	2,087.6
Dividends	647.0
Increase in other assets	74.2
Reduction in long-term debt	231.2
Other—net	55.1
Total Applications of Working Capital	3,095.1
Decrease in Working Capital	$ 19.9
Analysis of Changes in Components of Working Capital	
Cash and temporary cash investments	$ (281.3)
Receivables	118.4
Inventories	37.6
Prepaid expenses	18.4
Deferred charges	36.4
Accounts payable	(142.9)
Short-term debt	212.9
Other current liabilities	(19.4)
Increase (Decrease) in Working Capital	$ (19.9)

15–48. FORMAT FOR A CHANGES STATEMENT. Each of the following items was a line in the 1985 changes statement of Rockwell International Corporation, a major defense contractor (in millions):

Deferred income taxes	$ 13.8
Other sources of cash	16.6
Net income	595.3
Other uses of cash	38.8
Property additions	614.4
Acquisition of Allen-Bradley	1,605.8
Long-term borrowings	538.0
Purchase of treasury stock	30.6
Issuance of common stock	10.8
Depreciation and amortization	448.2
Proceeds from dispositions of property and businesses	27.5
Total cash used	2,488.0
Decrease in cash	696.9
Cash provided by changes in noncash working capital	118.1
Other cash provided by operations	22.8
Reduction in long-term debt	39.7
Cash provided by operations	1,198.2
Dividends	158.7
Total cash provided	?

Required:

1. Prepare Rockwell's statement of changes in financial position with a focus on cash. Include the appropriate number where the question mark is shown.
2. Prepare Rockwell's statement of changes in financial position with a focus on working capital. Be sure to relabel and recompute totals where appropriate.

15–49. **FORMATS AND APPROACHES TO DISPOSITIONS OF PROPERTY.** Study Appendix 15A. The Stanford University Bookstore used the following approach in its statement of changes in financial position.

Financial resources were provided by:	
Operations:	
Net income	$ 406,751
Items not requiring working capital:	
Depreciation and amortization	26,831
Gain on disposition of fixed assets	(142)
Working capital provided by operations	433,440
Decrease in investments held for expansion	329,968
Proceeds from disposition of fixed assets	5,303
	768,711
Financial resources were used for:	
Construction advances	1,552,602
Acquisitions of fixed assets	212,071
	1,764,673
Increase (decrease) in working capital	$ (995,962)

Required:

1. What was the book value of the fixed assets disposed of by the bookstore?
2. Koppers Company included the following two items in its changes statement:

Book value of fixed assets and other noncurrent assets disposed of or sold	$ 15,471,000
Capital investments	$110,569,000

The first was under "Sources of Funds," following sources from operations. The second was under "Disposition of funds." The company made no other mention of property acquisitions or disposals in its changes statement. Suppose the Stanford Bookstore used the Koppers approach. Compute the amounts that would be listed under "Total sources from operations," "Total sources," "Capital investments," and "Book value of fixed assets and other noncurrent assets disposed of or sold."

3. American Telephone and Telegraph Company (AT&T) has only one line relating to fixed asset acquisitions and disposals in its changes statement, appearing under "Uses" (in millions):

| Additions to property, plant and equipment, net | $4,177.5 |

Suppose the Stanford Bookstore used the AT&T approach. Compute the amount that would be listed under "Additions to fixed assets, net." Compute total sources and total uses.

4. What might be a major reason for adopting the AT&T approach?

15–50. EQUITY METHOD AND THE CHANGES STATEMENT. (Requirement 3 is more difficult.) Study Appendix 15A.

1. American Brands, maker of Titleist golf equipment, Master locks, and Jergens lotion, also owns 100% of the Franklin Life Insurance Company. Franklin is accounted for as an unconsolidated subsidiary. American Brands's 1985 changes statement included "Equity in undistributed earnings of The Franklin Life Insurance Company" of $47,177,000. The income statement included "Equity in the pretax earnings of The Franklin Life Insurance Company" of $174,080,000. Compute the amount of dividends American Brands received from Franklin in 1985.

2. General Electric Company owns 100% of General Electric Financial Services, Inc., an unconsolidated subsidiary. In 1985, GE Financial Services had net income of $413 million and paid no dividends. How should this affect General Electric's 1985 changes statement?

3. Koppers Company listed $4,475,000 on its 1985 changes statement under the title "Equity in losses of affiliated companies, less dividends received." This is the only changes statement account relating to affiliated companies. The $4,475,000 was added to net income in calculating working capital from operations. Suppose Koppers received $2,000,000 in dividends from its affiliated companies. Compute the amount of equity in losses of affiliated companies.

15–51. RECONSTRUCTION OF A CHANGES STATEMENT. Study Appendix 15A. Claire's Stores operates a chain of 260 specialty stores. Study the accompanying statement of changes in financial position, part of which has been omitted. Also study the other excerpts from the company's 1985 annual report. Claire's Stores acquired no companies during fiscal 1985.

Required: Fill in the items labeled (a) through (l) in the changes statement. Note that (a) and (b) are account titles and (c) through (l) are dollar amounts.

2. Compute the cash provided by operations during 1985.

CLAIRE'S STORES, INC.
Consolidated Statement of Changes in Financial Position

	1985
Working capital provided from:	
Continuing operations:	
(a)	$ (c)
Add charges not affecting working capital:	
Depreciation and amortization	1,223,017
Amortization of goodwill	(d)
Deferred income taxes	(e)
Loss on retirement of property and equipment	(f)
Working capital provided from operations	8,372,372
Cash proceeds from common stock and warrants	755,313
Other	593,872
Total working capital provided	(g)
Working capital used for:	
Decrease in long-term debt	170,866
Acquisition of property and equipment in excess of proceeds from retirements	5,929,982
Increase in other assets	463,814
Cash dividends	(h)
Total working capital used	(i)
Increase in working capital	$ (j)
Changes in working capital:	
Increase (decrease) in current assets:	
(b)	$ 693,887
Inventories	2,380,003
Prepaid expenses and other current assets	(k)
	2,900,241
Increase (decrease) in current liabilities:	
Current maturities of long-term debt	(1,829,134)
Trade accounts payable	920,669
Income taxes payable	324,791
Accrued expenses	674,935
Dividends payable	(l)
	357,639
Increase in working capital	$2,542,602

CLAIRE'S STORES (excerpts from annual report)

Net sales	$55,894,795
Income before income taxes	12,722,108
Income taxes	6,122,058
Net income	$ 6,600,050

Provision for income taxes has been made as follows:

	1985
Federal:	
Current	$4,985,089
Deferred	442,000
	5,427,089
State	694,969
Total	$6,122,058

	FEBRUARY 1	
	1985	1984
Property, plant and equipment	$15,991,897	$10,700,858
Less accumulated depreciation and amortization	(5,870,355)	(5,191,024)
	$10,121,542	$ 5,509,834
Goodwill, less accumulated amortization of $132,204 and $120,156	$ 351,014	$ 363,062
Other assets	$ 668,460	$ 204,646

15–52. INTERPRETING A CHANGES STATEMENT. Study Appendix 15A. Marantz Company, Inc., maker of recording and playback equipment, had a net loss of $2,584,000 for the nine months ended September 30, 1985. The following statement of changes in financial position was included in the quarterly report (in thousands):

	NINE MONTHS ENDED SEPTEMBER 30, 1985
Applications of working capital:	
Absorbed by operations	$2,325
Reduction of long-term debt	96
Additions to property and equipment	77
Total applications	$2,498
Sources of working capital:	
Sales of property and equipment	0
Decrease in other assets	42
Total sources	$ 42
Decrease in working capital	$2,456

During the first nine months of 1985, cash increased from $1,185,000 to $1,451,000 and property and equipment decreased from $1,740,000 to $1,558,000.

Required:

1. Calculate the charges against income in the first nine months of 1985 that did not require working capital.
2. Explain the $182,000 decrease in property and equipment.
3. Explain how cash could increase by $266,000 while working capital decreased by $2,456,000.

Chapter 16

FINANCIAL STATEMENTS: CONCEPTUAL FRAMEWORK AND INTERPRETATION

LEARNING OBJECTIVES

After studying this chapter, you should be able to

1. Explain the objectives of financial reporting as determined by the FASB
2. Identify the elements of financial statements as suggested by the FASB
3. Explain the role of general acceptance in the setting of financial-accounting standards
4. Compute and interpret a variety of popular financial ratios
5. Identify the major implications that "efficient" stock markets have for accounting
6. Review and integrate the concepts, conventions, and subject matter of the preceding chapters
7. Explain the meaning and implications of trading on the equity (Appendix 16)

This chapter provides an overview, pulling together many ideas scattered throughout previous chapters. There are two major parts, which may be studied independently. Part One explores some variations in income measurement, describes the FASB's project on the conceptual framework of accounting, and discusses the problems of policy making and gaining general acceptance for financial-reporting standards. Part Two examines some popular financial ratios and summarizes the implications of efficient markets for accounting.

Note particularly that some of the assignment material serves as a comprehensive review of the entire book.

□ PART ONE: Income, Conceptual Framework, and Acceptance

Part One shows the relationships of some key topics and concepts that have necessarily been taught individually as the book has unfolded.

VARIATIONS IN INCOME MEASUREMENT

The most popular approach to income measurement is commonly labeled the historical-cost method. It has been described at length in this book.

□ Historical Costs and Accrual Basis

Some disputes in accounting focus on alternative methods of measuring income (as described in Chapter 14). In addition, disputes often occur in applying the historical-cost method. The majority of these disputes center on timing. For example, when are revenues realized? When do the costs of assets become expenses?

Nearly every way of applying the historical-cost approach to income measurement has supporters and critics. However, the crudest approach, that of matching cash disbursements against cash receipts in a given period, has generally been rejected in favor of the accrual basis that was discussed in Chapter 2. To illustrate, nearly all "cash-basis" income measurement systems have at least been modified to provide for depreciation. After all, depreciation is central to an accrual basis. All variations in the concepts of income discussed below have the accrual basis as an anchor.

□ Realization

This book introduced the measurement convention (principle) of realization in Chapter 2. It is a major feature of accrual accounting because it determines when revenues and the associated (matched) costs will be recorded. Thus it specifies when income will be reported.

To be realized, revenue must ordinarily meet the following three tests: First, the earning process must be virtually complete in the sense that the goods or services must be fully delivered. Second, an exchange of resources evidenced by a market transaction must occur. Third, the collectibility of the asset (for example, an account receivable) must be reasonably assured. Reflect on the reasoning underlying these three tests:

1. The realization concept focuses on the recording of revenue from sales of products and services to customers. When is revenue realized by a seller? Generally, revenue is realized when the goods or services are *delivered* to customers, even though delivery is only one of a series of events related to the sale. For most businesses, delivery is the occasion that validates a legal claim against the customer for goods or services rendered. Accountants maintain that although the importance of purchasing, production, and distribution may differ from business to business, revenue is generally regarded as an indivisible totality. In this sense, revenue cannot be allocated in bits and pieces to individual business functions such as purchasing inventory, obtaining orders, manufacturing products, delivering goods, and collecting cash.

2. There are two major exceptions to the notion that an exchange (delivery, in most cases) is needed to justify the realization of revenue. First, long-run construction contracts often necessitate a *percentage-of-completion method*. For example, the builder of an ocean liner may portray performance better by spreading prospective revenues, related costs, and resulting net income over the life of the contract in proportion to the work accomplished. Otherwise all the net income would appear in one chunk upon completion of the project, as if it had been earned on a single day. See pages 595–597 for details about the percentage-of-completion method.

   Second, in exceptionally rare cases, revenue is regarded as realized in proportion to cash collections under long-run installment contracts. An illustration is the retail sales of undeveloped lots. These receivables are collectible over an extended period of time, and there is no reliable basis for estimating the degree of collectibility.

   Under the percentage-of-completion method, revenue is realized before delivery takes place; under the installment method, revenue is realized well after the delivery.

3. Uncertainty about the collectibility of receivables does not always delay the recording of revenue. Many accountants regard the revenue as realized but provide an ample allowance for uncollectible accounts. For example, a hospital can recognize revenue on the accrual basis as its services are delivered. However, its bad debts expense (which is conceptually an offset of gross revenue because it represents revenue never to be received) is a much higher percentage of revenue than in, for example, retail food stores.

CONCEPTUAL FRAMEWORK AND THE PROCESS OF SETTING STANDARDS

For years, accountants have sought a conceptual framework. But they still have a patchwork of generally accepted accounting principles (GAAP) that has slowly evolved over many years of accounting practice and regulatory effort. As a result, various accounting rules seem inconsistent within any single framework. For example, the lower-of-cost-or-market basis is applied differently to inventories, to short-term investments, and to long-term investments.

☐ Objectives of Financial Reporting

In late 1984, the Financial Accounting Standards Board completed the primary development of a conceptual framework for financial reporting by business enterprises. The board issued a series of Statements on Financial Accounting Concepts. *Concepts Statement No. 1*, issued in November 1978, is entitled "Objectives of Financial Reporting by Business Enterprises." It establishes that financial reporting should provide useful information to investors and creditors; that objectives change with the economic, legal, political, and social environment; and that the main focus of financial reporting is on earnings. The FASB chairman said, "Objectives and concepts are to be tools for solving problems and for serving the public interest in providing evenhanded information that facilitates efficient functioning of capital and other markets."

Concepts Statement No. 1 emphasizes that

1. Information about enterprise earnings and its components measured by *accrual accounting* provides a better indication of enterprise performance than information about *current cash receipts and payments* (paragraphs 44–48 of *Concepts Statement No. 1*).
2. Financial reporting should also provide information about an enterprise's economic resources, obligations, and owners' equity (paragraph 41), liquidity or solvency (paragraph 49), and management's stewardship (paragraphs 50–53), as well as management's explanations and interpretations of information provided (paragraph 54).

The dominance of net earnings, the "bottom line" in the minds of managers, accountants, and others, is gradually diminishing. FASB *Concepts Statement No. 1* cited earnings as being an important measure of performance, but the board has become increasingly reluctant to bless a *single* number as being sufficient to tell a complete financial story. Instead, reporting several earnings numbers (such as those based on current costs and historical costs) and making ample narrative disclosure seem to be the wave of the future. Economic activities are too diverse and complex to be portrayed by a lone earnings figure.

☐ Qualitative Characteristics

In 1980, the FASB published *Concepts Statement No. 2*, "Qualitative Characteristics of Accounting Information." Accounting policy making is the principal task of the FASB. Some persons may prefer to describe the board's function with some other term, such as standard setting or rule making. **Accounting policy making** is choosing the accounting measurement and disclosure methods to be followed in financial reporting. As a policy-making body, the board must select among alternatives by exercising value judgments instead of being able to rely on more objective criteria.

The "Qualitative Characteristics" statement is designed to aid the board in its choosing among alternative accounting and reporting methods or disclosures. The qualitative criteria are aimed at helping produce the "best" or most useful information. The statement contains a hierarchy of accounting qualities, as depicted in Exhibit 16–1. The hierarchy's major features will

EXHIBIT 16–1

A Hierarchy of Accounting Qualities

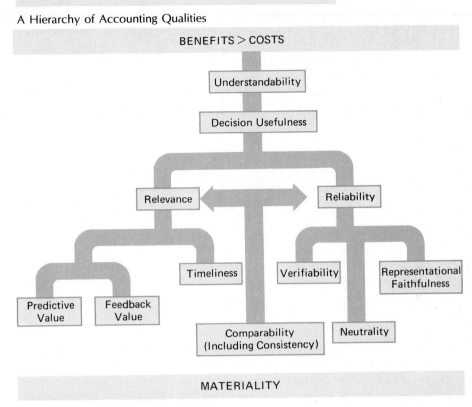

BENEFITS > COSTS

Understandability

Decision Usefulness

Relevance ← → Reliability

Predictive Value   Feedback Value   Timeliness   Verifiability   Representational Faithfulness

Comparability (Including Consistency)   Neutrality

MATERIALITY

Source: *Qualitative Characteristics of Accounting Information* (Stamford, Conn.: FASB, 1980), p. 15.

now be summarized. Choices will inevitably require trade-offs among the various desirable characteristics in Exhibit 16–1.

☐ Decision Usefulness at a Cost

As the top three items in Exhibit 16–1 indicate, accounting should help decision making. This is a benefit. But accounting information is a commodity, an economic good. It will not be sought unless its benefits exceed its costs. A policy-making body such as the FASB must do its best to issue its pronouncements so that their perceived benefits exceed their perceived costs for the whole of society. The costs and benefits are widely diffused and fall unevenly throughout the economy. Therefore the FASB's task of assessment is complex and subjective. Nevertheless, the board should never lose sight of the fundamental cost-benefit test. That is why Exhibit 16–1 shows a benefits > costs band at its top. Indeed, the top three boxes could be recast as:

Decision Usefulness so that Benefits > Costs

The costs to provide information include the costs of collecting and processing, costs of auditing, costs of educating, and disclosure costs in terms of a loss of competitive advantages or in terms of increased labor union pressures. The costs to users of information include those passed on by the providers plus the costs of education, analysis, and interpretation.

The benefits of accounting information surely exist, but they are harder to pinpoint than the costs. Better individual decisions lead to greater personal welfare. Furthermore, a highly developed economy depends on accounting to help obtain the efficient and equitable allocation of resources.

☐ Relevance and Reliability

Relevance and *reliability* are the two major qualities that make accounting useful for decision making. **Relevance** is defined as the capability of information to make a difference to the decision maker. To be relevant, information must be timely and understandable. **Reliability** is defined as the quality of information that allows users to depend on it to represent the conditions or events that it purports to represent. Reliability depends on the degree to which the accounting description or measurement is *representationally faithful, verifiable,* and *neutral*. Comparable information prepared consistently over time enhances both reliability and relevance.

Representational faithfulness is a mouthful (try saying the words) that essentially means correspondence between the accounting numbers and the resources or events that those numbers purport to represent. A synonym is *validity*. However, a high level of correspondence does not ensure that an accounting measurement will be relevant; the resources or events represented may be inappropriate to the purpose at hand. For example, when depreciable assets are restated in constant dollars in a balance sheet, the figures do not purport to represent current values. Yet because of misunderstandings, the constant-dollar amounts are criticized as being unreliable indicators of what the assets are worth.

Verifiability, which is also called *objectivity* by many accountants, is the quality that may be established by getting a high extent of consensus among independent measurers (for example, outside auditors) using the same measurement methods. It was discussed in Chapter 3 on page 95.

The accounting literature is filled with arguments about the trade-offs between relevance and verifiability. Ideally, information should have both traits to the highest degree. But many accountants and managers are reluctant to depart very far from producing or using information that is not easily verifiable. They maintain that verifiability is the main characteristic that gives accounting information an advantage over information from other sources. Thus many oppose departures from the historical cost/nominal dollar method for other, less verifiable, methods (described in Chapter 14). On the other hand, critics maintain that the use of some type of current-cost method is preferable because it is more relevant. They claim that "it is better to be roughly right than precisely wrong."

☐ Neutrality

Neutrality, or *freedom from bias*, means choosing accounting policies without attempting to achieve purposes other than measuring economic impact. An example may clarify the meaning of neutrality.

From time to time, controversies about impending regulatory pronouncements have focused on the impact of financial reporting on achieving national policy goals. The arguments maintain that financial-reporting rules should be used to achieve national goals. For instance, some say that the flow-through method of accounting for the investment tax credit should be permitted because (it is asserted) more capital investment will result. The FASB disagrees. Accounting measurements should be as neutral as possible and not be used to manipulate economic behavior. That is, if the flow-through method is justified, its logic must be anchored to the production of "better" economic measures of performance, not to national goals.

Tampering with accounting policies (standards or principles) to promote national goals is a dangerous path. First, research has demonstrated that accounting measurements per se are unlikely to affect investors' decisions if the timing and amounts of the underlying cash flows are unaffected. Therefore such tampering is not likely to achieve its objectives. Second, the credibility of financial reporting would quickly erode to the detriment of the public interest.

The quality of neutrality underscores a fundamental approach taken by the FASB. Arguments about accounting issues should concentrate on how measurements and disclosure can improve the communication of economic phenomena. These issues should be resolved, however imperfectly, by determining how economic information is best disseminated in light of the costs and benefits for society as a whole.

☐ Materiality

Information is *material* when its inclusion or correct presentation would probably change the judgment of a reasonable person. Determining whether an item is material is a pervasive problem that is usually resolved by professional judgment on a case-by-case basis. Exhibit 16–2 displays three of the very few areas where quantitative guidelines of materiality have been mandated.

☐ Elements of Financial Statements

In a major effort to obtain consensus on the definitions of key components of financial statements, the FASB released *Concepts Statement No. 3*, "Elements of Financial Statements of Business Enterprises." The document defines the key elements shown in Exhibit 16–3. Collectively, these elements are "the building blocks with which financial statements are constructed—the classes of items that financial statements comprise," and their definitions are "a significant step in determining the content of financial statements."

The FASB distinguishes between definition and recognition, measure-

EXHIBIT 16–2

Examples of Quantitative Materiality Guidelines

SUBJECT	AUTHORITY	MATERIALITY GUIDELINE
Dilution of earnings per share (EPS)	APB Opinion No. 15	Reduction in EPS of less than 3% in the aggregate not material.
Segmental reporting—recognition of reportable segment	Statement of Financial Accounting standards No. 14	Revenue equals or exceeds 10% of combined revenues, etc.
Gross rental expense under leases	SEC Accounting Series Release No. 147	Disclose total rental expense, etc., if gross rents exceed 1% of consolidated revenue.

Source: *Qualitative Characteristics of Accounting Information* (Stamford, Conn.: FASB, 1980), p. 70.

ment, and display. To be displayed in a particular set of financial statements, an item not only must qualify as one of the elements but must also meet recognition and measurement tests. Thus some items that qualify under the definitions may have to be excluded from financial statements because of recognition or measurement considerations stemming primarily from the uncertainty that pervades business and economic activities.

Present accounting for research and development costs is an illustration of the latter distinctions. A major reason for recording expenditures for research and development activities as expenses when incurred instead of as assets is not because these activities never generate future economic benefits. They frequently do, but the existence, amounts, and duration of those benefits are highly uncertain.

Most assets and liabilities in present practice will continue to qualify as such under the proposed definitions. The board emphasized that the definitions in the Elements Statement do not require changes in present practice, although they may eventually lead to changes. The FASB itself is likely to be the most direct beneficiary of the guidance provided by the definitions as the board considers the promulgation of individual accounting standards.

☐ **Recognition and Measurement**

The capstone of the conceptual framework project for business enterprises is *Concepts Statement No. 5*, "Recognition and Measurement in Financial Statements of Business Enterprises."[1] This statement is the most specific of

---

[1] The FASB has also issued two statements on a conceptual framework for nonbusiness organizations. The statements apply to "most human service organizations, churches, foundations, and some other organizations, such as those private nonprofit hospitals and nonprofit schools that receive a significant portion of their financial resources from sources other than the sale of goods and services." See *Concepts Statement No. 4*, "Objectives of Financial Reporting by Nonbusiness Organizations" (Stamford, Conn.: FASB, 1980); and *Concepts Statement No. 6*, "Elements of Financial Statements" (Stamford, Conn.: FASB, 1985).

EXHIBIT 16–3

Definitions of Elements of Financial Statements

— **Assets** are probable future economic benefits obtained or controlled by a particular entity as a result of past transactions or events.
— **Liabilities** are probable future sacrifices of economic benefits arising from present obligations of a particular entity to transfer assets or provide services to other entities in the future as a result of past transactions or events.
— **Equity** is the residual interest in the assets of an entity that remains after deducting its liabilities. In a business enterprise, the equity is the ownership interest. [Notice how this definition basically means *owners' equity*.]
— **Comprehensive income** is the change in equity (net assets) of an entity during a period from transactions and other events and circumstances from nonowner sources. It includes all changes in equity during a period except those resulting from investments by owners and distributions to owners.*
— **Revenues** are inflows or other enhancements of assets of an entity or settlements of its liabilities (or a combination of both) during a period from delivering or producing goods, rendering services, or other activities that constitute the entity's ongoing major or central operations.
— **Expenses** are outflows or other using up of assets or incurrences of liabilities (or a combination of both) during a period from delivering or producing goods, rendering services, or carrying out other activities that constitute the entity's ongoing major or central operations.
— **Gains** are increases in equity (net assets) from peripheral or incidental transactions of an entity and from all other transactions and other events and circumstances affecting the entity during a period except those that result from revenues or investments by owners.
— **Losses** are decreases in equity (net assets) from peripheral or incidental transactions of an entity and from all other transactions and other events and circumstances affecting the entity during a period except those that result from expenses or distributions to owners.

Source: *Elements of Financial Statements of Business Enterprises* (Stamford, Conn.: FASB, 1980), pp. xi–xii.

* The Statement does not define the term "earnings," which is reserved for possible use to designate a component part of comprehensive income.

the concepts statements. It "sets forth recognition criteria and guidance on what information should be incorporated into financial statements and when." The statement generally supports current GAAP, although it allows for gradual change.

Concepts Statement No. 5 refers only to the financial statements themselves. As Exhibit 16–4 shows, the FASB standards affect items beyond the body of the financial statements. Furthermore, much of the information useful for investment, credit, and similar decisions is outside the purview of the FASB.

The distinction between earnings and comprehensive income is made explicit in *Concepts Statement No. 5*. *Earnings* is similar to the current net income, with only some technical differences. It measures performance for a particular period. **Comprehensive income** is a broad measure of the change in owners' equity (net assets) of an enterprise during a period from transactions and other events and circumstances from nonowner sources. It includes all

EXHIBIT 16–4

Scope of FASB Activities

All information useful for investment, credit, and similar decisions
(Concepts Statement 1, paragraph 22; partly quoted in footnote 6)

Financial reporting
(Concepts Statement 1, paragraphs 5-8)

Area directly affected by existing FASB standards

Basic financial statements
(in AICPA auditing standards literature)

Scope of recognition
and measurement
Concepts Statement

Financial statements	Notes to financial statements (& parenthetical disclosures)	Supplementary information	Other means of financial reporting	Other information
☐ Statement of financial position ☐ Statements of earnings and comprehensive income ☐ Statement of cash flows ☐ Statement of investments by and distributions to owners	Examples: ☐ Accounting policies ☐ Contingencies ☐ Inventory methods ☐ Number of shares of stock outstanding ☐ Alternative measures (market values of items carried at historical cost)	Examples: ☐ Changing prices disclosures (FASB Statement 33 as amended) ☐ Oil and gas reserves information (FASB Statement 69)	Examples: ☐ Management discussion and analysis ☐ Letters to stockholders	Examples: ☐ Discussion of competition and order Backlog in SEC form 10-K (under SEC Reg. S-K) ☐ Analysts' reports ☐ Economic statistics ☐ News articles about company

Source: *Recognition and Measurement in Financial Statements of Business Enterprises* (Stamford, Conn.: FASB, 1984).

changes in owners' equity during a period except those resulting from investments in the enterprise by owners and distributions by the enterprise to owners.

Both earnings and comprehensive income contain revenues, expenses, gains, and losses. The two differ because certain gains and losses are included in comprehensive income but not in earnings. For example, both the cumulative effects of changes in accounting methods and the changes in the market value of certain marketable equity securities held as long-term investments would be included in comprehensive income but not in earnings.

☐ Time for Review

Exhibit 16–5 recaps the qualitative characteristics discussed earlier in this chapter. A concrete example of each is provided, as is a listing of other chapters in this text that contain additional discussion or examples of the individual characteristics.

In addition to the qualitative characteristics, other key concepts are listed, described, and illustrated in Exhibit 16–5. This entire tabulation should be a convenient guide for recalling and comparing some major ingredients of accounting theory.

Accounting theory (as expressed by a conceptual framework) and practice are intertwined and indivisible. There is some inclination, especially among students and young practitioners, to view accounting theory as chiefly an ivory tower endeavor that should be given only secondary recognition in everyday practice. This inclination probably arises from confusion of the word *practice* and the word *practical*, as if practice means something practical and theory means something merely abstract. This false distinction confuses the basic function of accounting theory, which is to establish the broad guidelines and methods that should govern the use of the discipline of accounting in a given situation. In other words, without underlying theory, practice becomes more chaotic, less satisfying, and harder to understand.

☐ Lessons From History

Until the early 1930s, when the Securities and Exchange Commission was created by Congress, accounting practices evolved in accordance with the best professional judgment of CPAs and managers. The leadership of thoughtful practitioners dominated. Then private and public regulators entered the picture. To refresh your memory, see pages 54–56 for a description of the relationships among the Securities and Exchange Commission, the private regulatory bodies, and other interested groups such as managers, auditors, and investors. The Accounting Principles Board was the senior private regulatory body from 1959 to 1973, when it was succeeded by the FASB.

All regulatory bodies have been criticized for using piecemeal approaches, solving one accounting issue at a time. Observers have alleged that not enough tidy rationality has been used in the process of accounting policy making. Again and again, critics have cited a need for a conceptual framework.

As we saw earlier, the FASB worked on constructing a conceptual framework for over ten years. Meanwhile the board also had to contend with an unending stream of specific accounting controversies that demanded immediate attention. Is there a lesson here? Why has the piecemeal approach persisted? The answer lies in a careful look at the policy-making process.

The term *generally accepted* is a key part of the familiar term *generally accepted accounting principles*. The policy-making process is much more complicated than having some intelligent, experienced regulators apply logic and evidence to an issue and then promulgate rules that are subsequently followed by the affected parties. The use of logic and evidence is absolutely necessary, but it is insufficient. When the FASB considers a financial-accounting standard, assorted interested parties present arguments to support their favored choices. The standards issued are often compromises among the contending interests; therefore the standards are not necessarily products of airtight logic.

The FASB's task has been described as being not only technical but also political or educational. When the term *political* is used in this context, it means the ways of convincing interested persons about the wisdom of the board's decisions. As stated in *Forbes* (June 16, 1986, p. 70): "Good accounting

EXHIBIT 16-5

Frequently Encountered Terminology in Conceptual Frameworks of Accounting

TERM	SHORT DESCRIPTION	EXAMPLE	CHAPTERS IN THIS TEXT*
Cost and benefits	Accounting information is an economic good. It should be gathered as long as its benefits exceed its costs.	Decisions must be improved sufficiently to justify recording current values in addition to historical costs.	Mainly in 3, 8, 14
Relevance	Capability of information to make a difference to the decision maker	Report of cash in bank is essential to determine how much money to borrow.	4, 14
Reliability	Dependability of information as representing what it purports to represent.	The cost of the land was $1 million 1983 dollars.	4, 14
Verifiability (objectivity)	Characteristic of information that results in its reproducibility by a consensus of independent measurers.	Cash has high verifiability, accounts receivable less, inventories less, depreciable assets less, and so on.	3, 1, 14
Representational faithfulness	Correspondence between numbers and effects portrayed.	The historical cost/constant dollar cost of the land described above may be $1.2 million 1988 dollars, but the $1.2 million does not represent the current cost or market value of the land.	14
Consistency	Applying the same accounting methods over a series of reporting periods.	Use of FIFO inventory over a series of years, not FIFO for two years, LIFO for three, and so on.	6
Neutrality (evenhandedness)	Choosing accounting policies on the basis of quantifying without bias, that is, without purposes other than measuring economic impact.	An example of lack of neutrality may clarify: choosing the flow-through method in accounting for the investment tax credit for purposes of achieving national goals of encouraging capital expenditures.†	13
Materiality	An item is material if the judgment of a reasonable person would have been changed or influenced by its omission or misstatement.	Accounting policy to charge all capital expenditures of under $1,000 to expense regardless of useful life of the asset.	3
Conservatism	Way of dealing with uncertainties and is intended to avoid recognition of income on the basis of inadequate evidence but to require recognition of losses when assets have been impaired or liabilities incurred. In short, when in doubt, write it off.	Charging all research and development costs to expense as incurred. Applying lower-of-cost-or-market methods to asset valuation.	6, 9, 12
Continuity (going concern)	Assumption that entity will continue indefinitely or at least will not be liquidated in the near future.	Letterhead stationery: supplies or rubbish, depending on going concern assumption. This assumption is frequently cited as a major justification for adhering to historical cost (less depreciation, if any) for valuing inventories, land, buildings, equipment, and similar assets.	3
Entity	The unit of accountability.	A parent corporation, a subsidiary, a retail store.	1, 12

EXHIBIT 16-5 (*continued*)

TERM	SHORT DESCRIPTION	EXAMPLE	CHAPTERS IN THIS TEXT*
Accrual accounting	Record financial effects in the periods affected regardless of when cash is received or paid.	Recognition of receivables and payables.	2, 3, 4
Realization	Delivery of goods or services in exchange for a liquid asset. Evidenced by completed transaction.	Sale of goods for cash or claims to cash.	2, 4, 14
Recognition	Formally recording or incorporating an item in accounts and financial statements. An element may be recognized (recorded) or unrecognized (unrecorded).	Realization and recognition are not synonyms. A sale of goods for cash may be both recognized and realized. However, a gain or loss on changes in values of securities or land may be recognized but unrealized; moreover, under historical-cost accounting such gains are generally unrecognized until realized.	1, 2, 4, 14
Matching and cost recovery	Matching is relating revenues and expenses to a particular period. Combined or simultaneous recognition of revenues and expenses is the direct criterion for establishing a matching. However, other expenses are indirectly matched with revenues if their recovery from future revenues is not easily demonstrable.	Sales commission expenses are "matched" directly against related sales. Sales salaries, costs of heating, and depreciation on equipment are "matched" indirectly against current revenues because their benefits are considered to be exhausted in the current period.	2, 4, 6, 14

* Many of these criteria or basic ideas underlie this entire textbook.

† However, neutrality exists if flow-through is chosen because it is deemed to be the best possible measure of the economic impact on the enterprise.

standards are like Caesar's wife. They must not only be fair, they must be perceived to be fair." In short, the FASB must tackle the task of obtaining general acceptance, particularly general acceptance by the SEC and Congress.

☐ Future Role of Government

Chapter 2 described the basic relationships between the private and public sectors concerning accounting policy making. As private sector institutions, the FASB and APB have had the general backing of the SEC. The SEC is an agency of the federal government created by the Securities Acts of 1933 and 1934. It is empowered to ensure "full and fair" disclosures by corporations. The SEC has the ultimate legal authority over most financial reporting to investors. Through its Accounting Series Releases (ASR), the SEC issues its own pronouncements on accounting.

On several occasions, the SEC has taken an active role in the setting of accounting standards. For instance, it put pressure on the FASB toward wider use of "current-cost" accounting.

The SEC also favors the publication of earnings forecasts and management objectives by companies. The commission does not require such forecasts, but it has taken steps to give "safe harbor" to companies. That is, companies that make such predictions will be given protection if the forecasts turn out wrong. The companies will have no liability as long as the projection is made with a "reasonable basis" and in good faith.

The FASB is very conscious that its pronouncements need the support of the SEC. So the board and the SEC are in constant touch. In turn, Congress maintains oversight of the SEC. If Congress becomes sufficiently unhappy with progress in the setting of financial-accounting standards, it could specifically require that the role of the FASB be dampened or eliminated.

What looms ahead? Probably more government exercise of authority through the SEC. Although both the SEC and the FASB have been exceedingly active in recent years, congressional committees and others have stated that more activity is warranted. Despite the increasing activist role of the public sector, it is nevertheless highly likely that during the next ten years the FASB will continue to be the major single influence on changes in financial-accounting standards.

☐ Future of Conceptual Framework

In terms of long-run influence, the FASB conceptual framework and FASB *Statement No. 33*, "Financial Reporting and Changing Prices," deserve close watching as we proceed into the 1990s. The reactions of diverse interested parties, including the SEC, to the effects of these pronouncements will be crucial to their long-run acceptability.

The final contents of the FASB Statements of Financial Accounting Concepts have been both praised and condemned. Critics claim that they are bland and overly general.[2] The conceptual framework has fallen short of the expectations of those who expected it to resolve all accounting disputes. On the other hand, its usefulness as a guide to the FASB is still being tested. If the board is able to use the framework for guidance in creating more consistency in accounting standards, a new era of policy making will occur.

The generality of the conceptual framework was probably inevitable. The more specific the document, the more heated the debate and the less the probability of achieving general acceptance. The enormity of getting acceptance on a conceptual framework was expressed by a chairman of the FASB:

☐ In our first discussion memorandum on the Conceptual Framework of Accounting we sought an expression of opinion from respondents on the following as a basic objective of financial statements:

☐ *The basic objective of financial statements is to provide information useful for making economic decisions.*

☐ Could there be disagreement with a statement such as this? I am sure you will be astounded when I tell you that only thirty-seven percent of our respondents were able to recommend the adoption of this objective. Thirty-seven percent! Twenty-two percent recommended that it be rejected out-of-hand; and ten percent insisted that it needed further study. . . . I think this suggests the problem quite clearly.[3]

Almost everybody says that there is a need for a conceptual framework, but *his* or *her* conceptual framework may not be *yours*. For example, four general methods of measuring income and capital were compared in Chapter 14, "Financial Reporting and Changing Prices." Each method has strong advocates, and each method has its variations. Given the historical setting and the diverse interest groups, agreement on an operational conceptual framework that favors one of the four methods would have been hard to achieve. Thus even the issuance of a statement on a conceptual framework cannot escape some political dimensions.

In sum, accounting policy making is obviously complex. Progress will continue to come in fits and starts. It will always be considered as too fast by some critics and too slow by other critics. Most people favor "improvements" in accounting—the quicker the better. But one person's improvement is often another person's impairment. These trade-offs are the nucleus of policy making.

Above all, students, accountants, managers, and others should recognize that the process of setting accounting standards is not confined to the development of a conceptual framework and its application to specific issues via exercises in impeccable logic and fact gathering. The process also includes the gaining of general acceptance and support. A major role of the conceptual framework is ultimately to enhance the likelihood that proposed statements

---

[2] David Solomons, "The FASB's Conceptual Framework: An Evaluation," *Journal of Accountancy*, June 1986, pp. 114–24.

[3] Marshall S. Armstrong, "The Politics of Establishing Accounting Standards" (Address before the Third Annual Securities Regulation Institute, San Diego, Calif., January 16, 1976).

will be generally accepted. The more plausible the logic and the more compelling the facts, the greater the chance of winning the support of diverse interests.

VARIETY OF ACCOUNTING PRACTICES

☐ **Impact on Reported Earnings**

Previous chapters have described a wide variety of generally accepted accounting practices. To be more easily comparable, the financial statements of companies within an industry must be placed on a uniform basis. Suppose two companies, M and N, began business in the same industry in 19X1. Each company had the following for 19X1 (in millions):

		DIFFERENCE
Beginning inventory	$ 0	
Purchases	270	
Ending inventory, FIFO	110 ⎫	
Ending inventory, LIFO	70 ⎭	40
Depreciation, accelerated	20 ⎫	
Depreciation, straight-line	10 ⎭	10
Product introduction costs, original total amount	30 ⎫	
Product introduction costs, amortized amount	10 ⎭	20
Investment tax credit, total received on tax returns for 19X1	5 ⎫	
Investment tax credit, amortized amount per year	1 ⎭	4
Revenue	400	
Other expenses	100	
Common shares outstanding	10,000,000	
Income tax rate	40%	

For income-tax-reporting purposes, the top managements of M and N have both used accelerated (ACRS) depreciation, the flow-through of the investment tax credit, and the immediate write-off of all product introduction costs. For all other items, assume that the same method would be used for tax purposes and stockholder-reporting purposes.

For stockholder-reporting purposes, the choice of accounting policies can have a dramatic effect on net income and earnings per share. Assume that M takes one extreme stance; N, the other extreme. As Exhibit 16–6 shows, the choices of LIFO, accelerated depreciation (assumed equal to ACRS depreciation), and immediate write-off of product introduction costs will result in M's earnings per share of $3.10. In contrast, N's earnings per share would be $7.70.

EXHIBIT 16–6

Stockholder Reporting
Possible Income Statements
For the Year Ended December 31, 19X1
(in millions of dollars)

	INDIVIDUAL EFFECTS					
	(1) M Company	(2) FIFO	(3) Straight Line	(4) Amortization	(5) Flow Through	(6) N Company
Revenue	400					400
Expenses:						
Cost of goods sold	200	40				160
Depreciation	20		10			10
Product introduction costs	30			20		10
Other expenses	100					100
Total expenses	350					280
Income before income taxes	50					120
Income taxes:						
Total before adjustments	20*	16				36†
Income tax deferred	—		4	8		12‡
Investment credit	(1)				(4)	(5)
Income tax expense after adjustments	19					43
Net income reported	31	24	6	12	4	77
Earnings per share on 10,000,000 shares	3.10	2.40	.60	1.20	.40	7.70

* Income tax per the tax return (before considering the investment credit) would be .40 × $50 = $20. However, income taxes actually paid would be $20 less the full investment tax credit of $5 = $15.

† Same as for M Company except that FIFO would boost the current income tax per the tax return by .4 × $40 = $16. Therefore the total would be $20 + $16 = $36. Income taxes actually paid would be $36 less the tax credit of $5 = $31.

‡ Additional income tax expense equal to the income tax deferred liability must be reported as the result of showing $10 less depreciation expense and $20 less amortization expense, a total of $30 multiplied by the tax rate of 40% = $12.

Many managers regard the maximizing of immediate reported earnings per share as a worthy objective. They tend to choose the accounting policies like those favored by N Company. Others tend to be more conservative and tend to choose the M Company policies. The point here is that similar operations may be portrayed differently in income statements. Note that all the data are the same as far as the underlying cash flows are concerned, with one exception: A company that uses FIFO for stockholder reporting cannot use LIFO for tax purposes. Therefore N Company's current payments for income taxes are $16 million larger than M Company's.

Perhaps accounting measurements will eventually become better standardized and identical operations will be reported in more nearly identical figures. In the meantime, accountants and corporate executives should view increased disclosure and amplified description as the most pressing requirements in financial reporting. These requirements must be met if investors are to have sufficient data for making their own comparisons between companies.

☐ Statement of Accounting Policies

As Exhibit 16–6 shows, there are a variety of generally accepted accounting practices. Information about the accounting principles, practices, procedures, or policies (words like these are used loosely) is essential for the intelligent analysis of financial statements. APB *Opinion No. 22* requires reporting companies to include a description of all significant accounting policies as an integral part of the financial report. The disclosure usually appears as a separate Summary of Significant Accounting Policies preceding the footnotes of financial statements.

Exhibit 16–7 displays a typical summary, that of Procter & Gamble Company. A reader can quickly obtain a general understanding of the financial statements by reading Exhibit 16–7. The Procter & Gamble summary of accounting policies mentions many items covered in earlier chapters: consolidated statements, LIFO, goodwill, depreciation methods, and income taxes.

EXHIBIT 16–7

THE PROCTER & GAMBLE COMPANY
Summary of Significant Accounting Policies

PRINCIPLES OF CONSOLIDATION: The financial statements include the accounts of The Procter & Gamble Company and its majority-owned subsidiaries. Investments in 20% to 50% owned affiliates in which significant management control is exercised are included at original cost adjusted for the change in equity since acquisition. Other investments in affiliates are carried at cost.

MARKETABLE SECURITIES: Substantially all of the marketable securities are government and corporate debt instruments which are carried at cost which approximates market.

INVENTORY VALUATION: Inventories are valued at the lower of cost or market. Cost for most inventories is determined by the last-in, first-out method. For the remaining inventories, cost is determined primarily by the average cost method.

GOODWILL: The excess of the purchase price over the value ascribed to net tangible assets of businesses acquired after October 31, 1970 is amortized on a straight-line basis over forty years. Goodwill arising prior to that date is not amortized.

DEPRECIATION: Depreciation is calculated on a straight-line basis over the estimated useful lives of the properties for financial accounting purposes.

INCOME TAXES: Provision is made for the income tax effects of all transactions in the consolidated statement of earnings, including those for which actual tax payment or tax relief is deferred to future years. These deferrals result primarily from the use of shorter equipment lives and accelerated methods of depreciation for tax purposes.

Investment tax credits are recognized as a reduction of the tax expense in the year in which the related assets are placed in service or earlier where permitted by tax regulations.

OTHER EXPENSES: Advertising and research and development costs are charged against earnings in the year incurred.

□ PART TWO: Analysis of Financial Statements

Part Two, which can be studied in whole or in part any time after Chapter 5, examines how the typical financial statements have aided users. A major use of financial statements is to *evaluate past* performance and current position in order to *predict future* performance and position.

USE OF RATIOS IN INTERPRETATION

□ Coverage in Other Chapters

Although the typical financial statements based on historical costs have notable limitations, they have stood the test of time as being *one* major source of information about an entity. Earlier chapters have illustrated how financial ratios have aided managers and investors in evaluating the performance and position of an entity.

A primary reason for integrating the financial ratios into the appropriate earlier chapters is to link the particular uses with the introduction of the particular item on a financial statement. Examples include the following:

Chapter 2 introduced earnings-per-share, price-earnings, and dividend ratios.

Chapter 4 introduced the current ratio, gross profit percentages, return on sales, and return on stockholders' equity.

Chapter 6 showed how various percentages in the income statement are used to judge performance (for example, the percentages of sales discounts and sales returns). Chapter 6 also demonstrated how the collection period is used to appraise management's control of accounts receivable.

Chapters 7 and 8 demonstrated the uses of cost-of-goods-sold ratios, gross margin percentages, and inventory turnover.

Chapter 10 presented debt-to-equity ratios as examples of how risk of repayment is sometimes measured. (Also see Appendix 16.)

Chapter 11 introduced financial ratios and related statistics concerning stockholders' equity, including book value of common stock.

Because many financial ratios have already been introduced, this chapter includes a review and illustration of all the ratios in one place. For additional discussion of particular ratios, please consult the earlier chapters as indicated above.

□ Focus on Interest and Sources of Information

Published financial statements are properly oriented toward the long-term investor, who is mainly interested in long-term earning power. Short-term creditors, such as major suppliers or banks, are usually more interested in the short-run ability of the corporation to satisfy its obligations as they mature. The amount of time allotted by analysts and the quantity of information they seek depend directly on the size of the investment they are considering and on their general familiarity with the company. Financial analysts usually use a company's annual report as the springboard for their review.

Heavy financial commitments, either by investors purchasing many shares of the common stock of a company or by banks making large loans to a new customer, are preceded by thorough investigations. These investigations use many sources of information: personal interviews with management,

EXHIBIT 16–8 *(Place a clip on this page for easy reference)*

OXLEY COMPANY
Balance Sheet (in thousands)

	DECEMBER 31	
Assets	19X2	19X1
Current assets:		
Cash	$150	$ 57
Accounts receivable	95	70
Accrued interest receivable	15	15
Inventory of merchandise	20	60
Prepaid rent	10	—
Total current assets	$290	$202
Long-term assets:*		
Long-term note receivable	288	288

	DECEMBER 31			
	19X2	19X1		
Equipment, at original cost	$200	$200		
Deduct: Accum. depreciation	120	80		
Equipment, net			80	120
Total assets			$658	$610

Liabilities and Stockholders' Equity		
Current liabilities:		
Accounts payable	$ 90	$ 65
Accrued wages payable	24	10
Accrued income taxes payable	16	12
Accrued interest payable	9	9
Unearned sales revenue	—	5
Note payable—current portion	80	—
Total current liabilities	$219	$101
Long-term note payable	40	120
Total liabilities	$259	$221
Stockholders' equity:		
Paid-in capital†	$102	$102
Retained income	297	287
Total stockholders' equity	$399	$389
Total liabilities and stockholders' equity	$658	$610

* This caption is frequently omitted. Instead, the long-term note receivable, the equipment, and other categories are merely listed as separate items following the current assets.

† Details are often shown in a supplementary statement or in footnotes. In this case, there are 200,000 common shares outstanding, $.25 par per share, or 200,000 × $.25 = $50,000. Additional paid-in capital is $52,000.

prospectuses (i.e., detailed financial descriptions), statistical services, annual detailed (Form 10-K) reports to the Securities and Exchange Commission, and subscriptions to the services of investment research organizations that have the contacts necessary for obtaining the desired information. However, the typical trade creditor, unlike large investors and lenders, cannot afford the time or resources for a thorough investigation of every customer. This creditor relies mostly on personal experience with customers and reports from credit agencies such as Dun & Bradstreet.

☐ Objective of Analysis

The primary uses of financial statements consist of evaluating past performance and predicting future performance. Both of these uses can be facilitated by *comparisons*. The ultimate effect of analyzing statements is usually some financial decision. After comparing financial statements with past statements, with those of similar companies, or with industry averages, the analyst will *predict* how the organization will fare. The analyst will then *decide* to buy, sell, or hold the common stock (or lend or not lend).

The financial statements in Exhibits 16–8, 16–9, and 16–10 will be the focus of our extended illustration of the computation of financial ratios. They

EXHIBIT 16–9

OXLEY COMPANY
Statement of Income
(in thousands except earnings per share)

	FOR THE YEAR ENDED DECEMBER 31, 19X2		FOR THE YEAR ENDED DECEMBER 31, 19X1	
Sales		$999		$800
Cost of goods sold		399		336
Gross profit (or gross margin)		$600		$464
Operating expenses:				
Wages	$214		$150	
Rent	120		120	
Miscellaneous	100		50	
Depreciation	40	474	40	360
Operating income (or operating profit)		$126		$104
Other revenue and expense:				
Interest revenue	$ 36		$ 36	
Deduct: Interest expense	12	24	12	24
Income before income taxes		$150		$128
Income tax expense		60		48
Net income		$ 90		$ 80
Earnings per common share*		$ .45		$ .40

* Dividends per share, $.40 and $.20, respectively. For publicly held companies, there is a requirement to show earnings per share on the face of the income statement, but it is not necessary to show dividends per share. Calculation of earnings per share: $90,000 ÷ 200,000 = $.45, and $80,000 ÷ 200,000 = $.40.

EXHIBIT 16–10

OXLEY COMPANY
Statement of Retained Income
(in thousands)

	FOR THE YEAR ENDED DECEMBER 31	
	19X2	19X1
Retained income, beginning of year	$287	$247
Add: Net income	90	80
Total	$377	$327
Deduct: Dividends declared	80	40
Retained income, end of year	$297	$287

are identical to those introduced in Chapter 5 in the Oxley Company illustration. (Recall that Oxley is a retailer of lawn and garden products.) Both managers and investors find ratios helpful for comparing and predicting.

The managers and the financial community (for example, bank officers and stockholders) want clues to help evaluate the operating and financial outlook for an entity. For example, creditors want assurance of being paid in full and on time. Where the amounts are significant, the creditor will often ask the debtor for a set of budgeted financial statements. A *budget*, or **pro forma statement**, is a carefully formulated expression of predicted results, including a schedule of the amounts and timings of cash repayments. For example, the holder of the Oxley note payable may have insisted on getting a budget from Oxley before granting the loan. As a result, the creditor can be confident that the $80,000 short-term portion (see Exhibit 16–8, December 31, 19X2) will be paid in 19X3.

☐ Ratios and Comparisons

In addition to obtaining a budget, the supplier of large amounts of credit will inevitably conduct further analysis. Moreover, many lenders do not extend large amounts of credit to a single entity, so they do not probe deeply enough to obtain budgets. In addition to or instead of budgets, investors and creditors often use ratios computed from published financial statements. Exhibit 16–11 shows how some typical ratios are computed. As you can readily imagine, various combinations of financial ratios are possible. Exhibit 16–11 contains only the most popular.[4]

Evaluation of a financial ratio requires a comparison. There are three main types of comparisons: (1) with a company's own historical ratios (called **time-series comparisons**), (2) with general rules of thumb or **bench marks**, and (3) with ratios of other companies or with industry averages (called **cross-sectional comparisons**).

---

[4] For more details, see George Foster, *Financial Statement Analysis*, 2nd ed. (Englewood Cliffs, N.J.: Prentice-Hall, 1986).

EXHIBIT 16–11

Some Typical Financial Ratios

TYPICAL NAME OF RATIO	NUMERATOR	DENOMINATOR	USING APPROPRIATE OXLEY NUMBERS APPLIED TO DECEMBER 31 OF YEAR 19X2	19X1
Short-term ratios:				
Current ratio	Current assets	Current liabilities	$290 \div 219 = 1.3$	$202 \div 101 = 2.0$
Inventory turnover	Cost of goods sold	Average inventory at cost	$399 \div \frac{1}{2}(20 + 60) = 10$	Unknown*
Average collection period in days	Average accounts receivable × 365	Sales on account	$[\frac{1}{2}(95 + 70) \times 365] \div 999 = 30$†	Unknown*
Debt-to-equity ratios:				
Current debt to equity	Current liabilities	Stockholders' equity	$219 \div 399 = 54.9\%$	$101 \div 389 = 26.0\%$
Total debt to equity	Total liabilities	Stockholders' equity	$259 \div 399 = 64.9\%$	$221 \div 389 = 56.8\%$
Profitability ratios:				
Gross profit rate or percentage	Gross profit or gross margin	Sales	$600 \div 999 = 60\%$	$464 \div 800 = 58\%$
Return on sales	Net income	Sales	$90 \div 999 = 9\%$	$80 \div 800 = 10\%$
Return on stock-holders' equity	Net income	Average stock-holders' equity	$90 \div \frac{1}{2}(399 + 389) = 22.8\%$	Unknown*
Earnings per share	Net income less dividends on preferred stock, if any	Average common shares outstanding	$90 \div 200 = \$.45$	$80 \div 200 = \$.40$
Price-earnings	Market price of common share (assume $3 and $2)	Earnings per share	$3 \div .45 = 6.667$	$2 \div .40 = 5$
Dividend ratios:				
Dividend-yield	Dividends per common share	Market price of common share (assume $3 and $2)	$.40 \div 3 = 13.3\%$	$.20 \div 2 = 10\%$
Dividend-payout	Dividends per common share	Earnings per share	$.40 \div .45 = 89\%$	$.20 \div .40 = 50\%$

* Insufficient data available because the *beginning* balance sheet balances for 19X1 are not provided. Without them the *average* investment during 19X1 cannot be computed.

† This may be easier to see as follows: Average receivables = $\frac{1}{2}(95 + 70) = 82.5$. Average receivables as a percentage of annual sales = $82.5 \div 999 = 8.25\%$. Average collection period = $8.25\% \times 365$ days = 30 days.

Much can be learned by examining the trend of a company's ratios. That is why annual reports typically contain a table of comparative statistics for five or ten years. For example, some of the items listed in the 1986 annual report of Albertson's (the 444-store grocery chain) are:

	1986	1985	1984	1983	1982
Earnings as a percent of sales	1.68%	1.68%	1.64%	1.48%	1.39%
Earnings per share	$ 2.57	$ 2.42	$ 2.15	$ 1.91	$1.57
Book value per share	$15.60	$13.75	$11.93	$10.44	$8.03

Broad rules of thumb often serve as bench marks for comparison. For instance, the most quoted bench mark is a current ratio of 2 to 1. Others are described in *Key Business Ratios* by Dun & Bradstreet, a financial services firm. For example:

Fixed assets to tangible net worth. Ordinarily this relationship should not exceed 100% for a manufacturer and 75% for a wholesaler or retailer.

Current debt to tangible net worth. Ordinarily a business begins to pile up trouble when this relationship exceeds 80%.

Obviously, such bench marks are only general guides. More specific comparisons come from examining ratios of similar companies or from industry averages. Dun & Bradstreet also informs its subscribers of the credit-worthiness of thousands of individual companies. In addition, the firm regularly compiles many ratios of the companies it monitors. Consider each ratio in Exhibit 16–11 in relation to the industry statistics. For example, some of the 1985 Dun-Bradstreet ratios for 1,585 retail nurseries, lawn, and garden and farm supplies companies showed:

	CURRENT RATIO	CURRENT DEBT TO STOCK-HOLDERS' EQUITY	TOTAL DEBT TO STOCK-HOLDERS' EQUITY	NET INCOME ON SALES	NET INCOME ON STOCK-HOLDERS' EQUITY
	(Times)	(Percent)	(Percent)	(Percent)	(Percent
1,585 companies:					
Upper quartile*	4.3	16.9	25.0	8.5	34.3
Median	2.0	51.4	81.8	3.6	15.4
Lower quartile	1.3	149.5	205.3	1.3	4.4
Oxley†	1.3	54.9	64.9	9.0	22.8

* The individual ratios are ranked from best to worst. The middle figure is the median. The figure halfway between the median and the best is the upper quartile. Similarly, the figure halfway between the median and the worst is the lower quartile.

† Ratios are from Exhibit 16–11. Please consult that exhibit for an explanation of the components of each ratio.

Our illustrative analysis focuses on one company and one or two years. This is sufficient as a start, but other firms in the industry, industry averages, and a series of years should be examined to get a better perspective. Above all, recognize that a ratio by itself is of limited use. There must be a standard for comparison—a history, a similar entity, an industry average, a bench mark, or a budget (or similar target).

☐ **Component Percentages**

To aid the general comparison of companies that differ in size, the income statement and the balance sheet are often analyzed by percentage relationships, called **component percentages** (see Exhibit 16–12). The resulting state-

EXHIBIT 16–12

OXLEY COMPANY
Component Percentages
(in thousands except percentages)

	FOR THE YEAR ENDED DECEMBER 31			
	19X2		19X1	
Statement of Income				
Sales	$999*	100%	$800	100%
Cost of goods sold	399	40	336	42
Gross profit (or gross margin)	$600	60%	$464	58%
Wages	$214	21%	$150	19%
Rent	120	12	120	15
Miscellaneous	100	10	50	6
Depreciation	40	4	40	5
Operating expenses	$474	47%	$360	45%
Operating income	$126	13%	$104	13%
Other revenue and expense	24	2	24	3
Pretax income	$150	15%	$128	16%
Income tax expense	60	6	48	6
Net income	$ 90	9%	$ 80	10%

	DECEMBER 31			
	19X2		19X1	
Balance Sheet				
Current assets	$290	44%	$202	33%
Long-term note receivable	288	44	288	47
Equipment, net	80	12	120	20
Total assets	$658	100%	$610	100%
Current liabilities	$219	33%	$101	16%
Long-term note	40	6	120	20
Total liabilities	$259	39%	$221	36%
Stockholders' equity	399	61	389	64
Total liab. and stk. eq.	$658	100%	$610	100%
Working capital	$ 71		$101	

* Note the use of dollar signs in columns of numbers. Frequently, they are used at the top and bottom only and not for every subtotal. Their use by companies depends on the preference of management.

ments are called **common-size statements**. For example, it is difficult to compare Oxley's $290,000 of current assets with another company's $480,000 if the other company is larger. But suppose the other company has total assets of $1 million. Oxley's 44% current asset *percentage* (shown in Exhibit 16–12) can be directly compared with the other company's $480,000 ÷ $1,000,000 = 48%.

The income statement percentages are usually based on sales = 100%. Oxley seems very profitable, but such percentages have more meaning when compared with the budgeted performance for the current year, 19X2 (not shown here). The gross margin rate seems high; Oxley may be vulnerable to price competition. The behavior of each expense in relation to changes in total revenue is often revealing. That is, which expenses go up or down as sales fluctuate? For example, during these two years rent, depreciation, and interest have been fixed in total but have decreased in relation to sales. In contrast, the wages have increased in total and as a percentage of sales. The latter is not a welcome sign. Exhibit 16–12 indicates that wages in 19X1 were $150 ÷ $800 = 19% of sales, whereas wages in 19X2 were $214 ÷ $999 = 21% of sales.

Corporate annual reports to the public must contain a section that is usually labeled *management's discussion and analysis*. This section concentrates on explaining the major changes in the income statement and the major changes in liquidity and capital resources. The focus is on a comparison of one year with the next. For example, consider the 1986 annual report of American Greetings Corporation, the largest publicly held producer of greeting cards in the United States. It contained five pages of detailed comparisons such as the following: "As a percent of total revenue, administrative and general expenses continued to decline, as the 1986 level of 12.7% was lower than both 1985 (13.1%) and 1984 (13.4%)."

The balance sheet percentages are usually based on total assets = 100%. See Exhibit 16–12. The most notable feature of the balance sheet percentages is that both current assets and current liabilities are more prominent at the end of 19X2. Moreover, the working capital has declined largely because $80,000 of the long-term debt has become a current liability (because it is now less than one year from maturity). Some careful planning for 19X3 should provide for the orderly payment of this $80,000 and the probable increase of inventory levels.

☐ Discussion of Individual Ratios

The current ratio is a widely used statistic. Other things being equal, the higher the current ratio, the more assurance the creditor has about being paid in full and on time. As Exhibit 16–11 shows, Oxley's current ratio of 1.3 has declined from 2.0 and is unimpressive in relation to the industry median of 2.0.

The next two ratios in Exhibit 16–11 are not available from Dun & Bradstreet on an industry-comparable basis. Still, the inventory turnover and the average collection period are closely watched signals. Deteriorations through time in these ratios help alert managers to problem areas. For example, a decrease in inventory turnover may suggest slower-moving (or even unsalable) merchandise or a worsening coordination of the buying and selling functions. An increase in the average collection period of receivables may indicate increasing acceptance of poor credit risks or less-energetic collection efforts. Whether the inventory turnover of 10 and the average collection period of thirty days are "fast" or "slow" depends on past performance and the performance of similar companies.

Note how the average collection period is affected by sales *on account*. The computation in Exhibit 16–11 assumes that all sales are credit sales. However, if we relax our assumption, the thirty-day period would rise markedly. For example, if half the sales were for cash, the average collection period for accounts receivable would change from thirty to sixty days:

$$\frac{\frac{1}{2}\,(95 + 70) \times 365}{\frac{1}{2}\,(999)} = 60 \text{ days}$$

Ratios of debt to equity are shown in the second and third columns of the Dun & Bradstreet tabulation. Both creditors and shareholders watch these ratios to judge the degree of risk of insolvency and of stability of profits. Typically, companies with heavy debt in relation to ownership capital are in greater danger of suffering net losses or even insolvency when business conditions sour. Why? Because revenue and many expenses decline, but interest expenses and maturity dates do not change. Oxley's ratios of 54.9% and 64.9% are close to their medians for the industry, reflecting average stability of profits and risk or uncertainty concerning the company's ability to pay its debts on time.

The final two columns in the Dun & Bradstreet tabulation are examples of profitability ratios. Chapter 4 (p. 131) discussed how managers and investors study the ratios of net profit to sales and gross profit to sales as indicators of *operating success*. To owners, however, the ultimate measure of *overall accomplishment* is the rate of return on their invested capital. Hence the final column displays the ratio of net profit to stockholders' equity. Oxley's rate of return is splendid. The opportunities to make more handsome returns than 22% after income taxes are rare.

To summarize, in comparison with the Dun & Bradstreet ratios, Oxley's current ratio is unimpressive, but its profit ratios are outstanding. Its debt management ratios are average. All in all, Oxley's operating and financial performance seem excellent. The main question raised by the ratio analysis is whether Oxley can meet the current portion of its long-term debt without disrupting its normal operations. Oxley's large cash balance will help in the meeting of its short-term commitments.

The meaning of earnings per share was discussed in the appendix to Chapter 2, page 59.

☐ Operating Performance

An important measure of overall accomplishment is the rate of return on invested capital:

$$\text{Rate of return on investment} = \frac{\text{Income}}{\text{Invested capital}} \qquad (1)$$

On the surface, this measure is straightforward, but its ingredients may differ according to the purpose it is to serve. What is *invested capital*, the denominator of the ratio? What income figure is appropriate?

The measurement of *operating* performance (i.e., how profitably assets are employed) should not be influenced by the management's *financial* decisions (i.e., how assets are obtained). Operating performance is best measured by **pretax operating rate of return on total assets**:

$$\frac{\text{Pretax operating rate}}{\text{of return on total assets}} = \frac{\text{Operating income}}{\text{Average total assets available}} \qquad (2)$$

The right side of Equation 2 consists, in turn, of two important ratios:

$$\frac{\text{Operating income}}{\text{Average total assets available}} = \frac{\text{Operating income}}{\text{Sales}} \times \frac{\text{Sales}}{\text{Average total assets available}} \qquad (3)$$

Using Exhibits 16–8 and 16–9, pages 734–735, we can compute the following 19X2 results for Oxley Company:

$$\frac{\$126}{\frac{1}{2}\,(\$658 + \$610)} = \frac{\$126}{\$999} \times \frac{\$999}{\$634}$$

These relationships are displayed in a boxed format in Exhibit 16–13.

The right-side terms in Equation 3 are often called the **operating income percentage on sales** and the **total asset turnover**, respectively. Equation 3 may be reexpressed:

$$\text{Pretax operating rate of return on total assets} = \text{Operating income percentage on sales} \times \text{Total asset turnover} \qquad (4)$$

$$19.9\% = 12.6\% \times 1.576 \text{ times}$$

EXHIBIT 16–13

Major Ingredients of Return on Total Assets

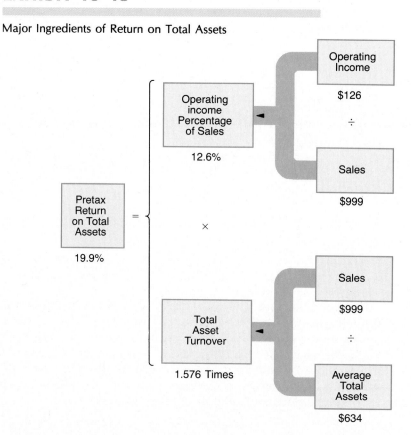

If ratios are used to evaluate operating performance, they should exclude extraordinary items which are regarded as nonrecurring items that do not reflect normal performance.

A scrutiny of Equation 4 shows that there are two basic factors in profit making: operating margin percentage and turnover. An improvement in either will, by itself, increase the rate of return on total assets.

The ratios used can also be computed on the basis of figures after taxes. However, the peculiarities of the income tax laws may sometimes distort results—for example, the tax rate may change, or losses carried back or forward might eliminate the tax in certain years.

Many more ratios could be computed. For example, Standard and Poor's Corporation sells a COMPUSTAT service, which via computer can provide financial and statistical information for thousands of companies. The information includes twenty-two income statement items, nineteen balance sheet items, and a variety of financial ratios for up to twenty past years.

□ Operating Management and Financial Management

Operating income is a popular subtotal because of the oft-made distinction between *operating management* and *financial management*. Operating management is mainly concerned with the major day-to-day activities that generate sales revenue (that is, efficiently using a given set of resources). In contrast, financial management is mainly concerned with where to get cash and how to use cash for the benefit of the entity (that is, obtaining and investing the needed capital). Examples of questions of financial management include: How much cash should be held in checking accounts? Should we pay a dividend? and Should we borrow or issue common stock? The best managements perform both operating management and financial management superbly. However, many managers are superior operating managers and inferior financial managers, or vice versa.

EFFICIENT MARKETS AND INVESTOR DECISIONS

Much recent research in accounting and finance has concentrated on whether the stock markets are "efficient." An **efficient capital market** is one in which market prices "fully reflect" all information available to the public. Therefore searching for "underpriced" securities in such a market would be fruitless unless an investor has information that is not generally available. If the real-world markets are indeed efficient, a relatively inactive portfolio approach would be an appropriate investment strategy for most investors. The hallmarks of the approach are risk control, high diversification, and low turnover of securities. The role of accounting information would mainly be in identifying the different degrees of risk among various stocks so that investors can maintain desired levels of risk and diversification.

Research in finance and accounting during the past twenty years has reinforced the idea that financial ratios and other data such as reported earnings provide inputs to predictions of such economic phenomena as financial failure or earnings growth. Furthermore, many ratios are used simultaneously rather than one at a time for such predictions. Above all, the research showed that accounting reports are only one source of information and that in the aggregate the market is not fooled by companies that choose the least-conservative accounting policies. In sum, the market as a whole sees through any attempts by companies to gain favor through the choice of accounting policies that tend to boost immediate income. Thus there is evidence that the stock markets may indeed be "efficient," at least in their reflection of most accounting data.

Suppose you are the chief executive officer of Company A. Reported earnings are $4 per share and the stock price is $40. You are contemplating changing your method of depreciation for investor-reporting purposes from accelerated to straight-line. Your competitors use straight-line. You think the Company A stock price unjustifiably suffers in comparison with other companies in the same industry.

If straight-line depreciation is adopted by Company A, reported earnings will be $5 instead of $4 per share. Would the stock price rise accordingly from $40 to $50? No, the empirical research on these issues indicates that the stock price would remain at $40 (all other things equal).

The chief executive's beliefs as shown in the above example are shared by many managers, who essentially adhere to an extremely narrow view of the role of an income statement. Such a "bottom-line" mentality is slowly, surely, and sensibly falling into disrepute. At the risk of unfair exaggeration, the view is summarized as:

1. The income statement is the sole (or at least the primary) source of information about a company.
2. Lenders and shareholders invest in a company because of its reported earnings. For instance, the higher the reported earnings per share, the higher the stock price, and the easier it is to raise capital.

Basically, these arguments assume that investors can be misled by how reported earnings are measured. But there is considerable evidence that securities markets are not fooled with respect to accounting changes that are devoid of economic substance (that have no effect on cash flows). Why? Because the change generally reveals no new information, so no significant change in stock price is likely.

Remember that the market is efficient only with respect to *publicly available* information. Therefore significant accounting issues deal with the disclosure of new information, not the format for reporting already available data. William Beaver has commented on the implications of market efficiency for accounting regulators:

☐ Many reporting issues are trivial and do not warrant an expenditure of FASB resources. The properties of such issues are twofold: (1) There is essentially no difference in cost to the firm of reporting either method. (2) There is essentially no cost to statement users in adjusting from one method to the other. In such cases, there is a simple solution. Report one method, with sufficient footnote disclosure to permit adjustment to the other, and let the market interpret implications of the data for security prices.

☐ Unfortunately, too many resources have been devoted to issues that warrant this straightforward resolution. For example, the investment credit controversy belongs in this category, as do the issues regarding the definition of extraordinary items, interperiod tax allocation, earnings per share computations involving convertible securities, and accounting for marketable equity securities. By contrast, the FASB should shift its resources to those controversies where there is non-trivial additional cost to the firms or to investors in order to obtain certain types of information (for example, replacement cost accounting for depreciable assets). Whether such information should be a required part of reporting standards is a substantive issue.[5]

Be aware also that accounting statements are not the only source of financial information about companies. Some alternative sources are the following: company press releases (e.g., capital expenditure announcements); trade association publications (e.g., reports with industry statistics); brokerage house analyses (e.g., company or industry studies); and government economic reports (e.g., GNP and unemployment figures). If accounting reports are to be useful, they must have some advantage over alternative sources in disclosing new information. Financial statement information may be more directly related to the item of interest, and it may be more reliable, lower-cost, or more timely than information from alternative sources.

The research described above concentrates on the effects of accounting on investors in the aggregate. Individual investors vary in how they analyze financial statements. One by one, individual users must either incur the costs of conducting careful analyses or delegate that chore to professional analysts. In any event, intelligent analysis cannot be accomplished without an understanding of the assumptions and limitations of financial statements, including the presence of various alternative accounting methods.

SUMMARY

There are many variations in how income is measured. For example, earnings are sometimes realized earlier than when the product is delivered and sometimes later. An example of the former is the percentage-of-completion method; an example of the latter, the installment method. The majority of disputes in accounting center on when revenues are realized and when the costs of assets become expenses.

Accountants have sought a conceptual framework for years, but financial accounting standards are still largely set on a piecemeal basis. The entire standard-setting process is complex. It involves far more than technical aspects because the gaining of general acceptance is a political task.

The assortment of alternatives among generally accepted accounting principles means that managers and accountants have some latitude in selecting the accounting policies of a specific entity. Publicly held companies must publish a statement of their accounting policies as a part of their annual financial reports.

Financial ratios aid the intelligent analysis of statements. They are used as a

---

[5] William H. Beaver, "What Should Be the FASB's Objectives?" *Journal of Accountancy*, August 1973, p. 52.

basis of evaluation, comparison, and prediction. The rate of return on invested capital is a very popular means of comparing performance.

Financial statements are only one of many sources of information about a company. Market efficiency implies that accounting regulators should focus on issues of disclosure, not format.

SUMMARY PROBLEM FOR YOUR REVIEW

☐ Problem

Examine Exhibits 16–8 and 16–9, pages 734–735. Assume some new data in place of certain old data for the December 31, 19X2, balance sheet (in thousands):

	OLD DATA	NEW DATA
Accounts receivable	$ 95	$130
Inventory	20	40
Total current assets	290	345
Paid-in capital	102	157
Total stockholders' equity	399	454

Required:

Compute the following ratios applicable to December 31, 19X2, or to the year 19X2, as appropriate: current ratio, inventory turnover, average collection period, working capital, and return on stockholders' equity. Compare this new set of ratios with the old set of ratios. Are the new ratios more desirable? Explain.

☐ Solution

$$\text{Current ratio} = \frac{\text{Current assets}}{\text{Current liabilities}}$$

$$= \frac{345}{219} = 1.6 \text{ to 1 instead of 1.3 to 1.}$$

$$\text{Inventory turnover} = \frac{\text{Cost of goods sold}}{\text{Average inventory}}$$

$$= \frac{399}{\frac{1}{2}(40 + 60)}$$

$$= \frac{399}{50} = 8 \text{ times instead of 10 times.}$$

$$\text{Average collection period} = \frac{\text{Average accounts receivable}}{\text{Sales on account}} \times 365$$

$$= \frac{\frac{1}{2}(130 + 70)}{999} \times 365$$

$$= \frac{100 \times 365}{999} = 37 \text{ days instead of 30 days.}$$

Working capital is current assets minus current liabilities, which is 345 − 219 = 126 instead of 71.

$$\text{Return on stockholders' equity} = \frac{\text{Net income}}{\text{Average stockholders' equity}}$$

$$= \frac{90}{\frac{1}{2}(389 + 454)}$$

$$= 21.4\% \text{ instead of } 22.8\%.$$

The new ratios contain good news and bad news. The good news is that the company would appear to be slightly more liquid (a current ratio of 1.6 instead of 1.3) and to have more working capital ($126 instead of $71). The bad news is that the inventory turnover, the average collection period, and the rate of return on stockholders' equity are less attractive.

HIGHLIGHTS TO REMEMBER

1. Avoid the temptation to dismiss a conceptual framework as being mere theory having no practical importance. A conceptual framework aids communication among all interested parties. Practice becomes less chaotic and easier to understand.
2. Exhibit 16–5, pages 726–727, deserves your review. It provides a convenient summary of key concepts used throughout this book.
3. Recent research has indicated that capital markets are "efficient" in the sense that investors in the aggregate are not fooled by companies that try to look good by choosing less-conservative accounting policies. Accounting is a major source of information, but it is not the sole source.

ACCOUNTING VOCABULARY

Accounting Policy Making, p. 718 Asset Turnover, 742 Bench Mark, 736 Capital Structure, 748 Capitalization, 748 Capitalization Structure, 748 Common-Size Statements, 739 Component Percentages, 738 Comprehensive Income, 723 Cross-Sectional Comparisons, 736 Debt Leverage, 748 Efficient Capital Markets, 743 Financial Leverage, 748 Gearing, 749 Leveraging, 749 Neutrality, 721 Operating Income Percentage on Sales, 742 Pretax Operating Rate of Return on Total Assets, 741 Pro Forma Statement, 736 Rate of Return on Stockholders' Equity, 748 Relevance, 720 Reliability, 720 Representational Faithfulness, 720 Return on Total Assets, 748 Time-Series Comparisons, 736 Times Interest Earned, 751 Total Asset Turnover, 742 Trading on the Equity, 748.

APPENDIX 16: DEBT, TRADING ON THE EQUITY, AND FINANCIAL RATIOS

REASONS FOR DEBT

Debt surrounds us. Governments issue debt securities of all kinds for many purposes. Businesses do likewise. Individuals have small loans (on refrigerators) and big loans (on homes).

Business borrowing takes many forms. Short-term debt is usually created through trade credit (accounts payable) and bank credit (notes payable due within one year). This financing should ordinarily be for investments in current assets. The working capital cycle moves from cash to inventories to receivables to the cash that should be used to repay the short-term debts. Many entities have edged into deep financial water by using short-term debt for long-term investments (for example, plant and equipment) and then not having the cash when due. A notable example is the city of New York, which was unable to pay its debts during the 1970s.

Long-term investments should be financed by long-term capital: debt or stock. Debt is often a more attractive vehicle than common stock because (1) interest payments are deductible for income tax purposes but dividends are not, and (2) the ownership rights to voting and profits are kept by the present shareholders.

Creditors are willing to lend for many reasons. For example, suppliers grant trade credit as a way of increasing sales (and net income). Financial institutions and other investors lend money because they are willing to accept a limited interest income as long as they are assured that the borrower will meet its obligations. In other words, lenders want to limit their risks of loss, so they accept a limited rate of return.

TRADING ON THE EQUITY

Most companies have two basic types of long-term financing: long-term debt and stockholders' equity. The total of long-term financing is often called the **capitalization**, **capitalization structure**, or simply **capital structure** of a corporation. Suppose a company has long-term debt (in the form of bonds payable) and common stock as its capital structure. This means that common shareholders enjoy the benefits of all income in excess of interest on the bonds.

Trading on the equity, which is also referred to as using **financial leverage**, or **debt leverage**, generally means using borrowed money at fixed interest rates with the objective of enhancing the rate of return on common shareholders' equity. There are costs and benefits to shareholders from trading on the equity. The costs are interest payments and increased risk, and the benefits are the larger returns to the common shareholders—as long as overall income is sufficiently large.

Examine Exhibit 16–14. The computation in column 7 is based on the following formula for **return on total assets**:

$$\text{Rate of return on total assets} = \frac{\text{Income before interest expense}}{\text{Average total assets}}$$

$$= \frac{\$16,000}{\$80,000} = 20\%$$

The computation in column 8 is based on the following formula for **rate of return on stockholders' equity**:

$$\text{Rate of return on stockholders' equity} = \frac{\text{Net income}}{\text{Average stockholders' equity}}$$

$$= \frac{\$13,000}{\$50,000} = 26\%$$

The numerator in the latter formula is the net income that results after the deduction of all expenses, including interest expense. Interest expense is the return to the lenders, whereas net income is the return to the owners who provided the stockholders' equity.

Exhibit 16–14 shows how borrowing can be a two-edged sword. In Year 1, Company A paid 10% for the use of $30 million, which in turn earned 20%. This method of financing benefited the shareholders handsomely, resulting in an ultimate return on equity of 26%, compared with the 20% earned by debt-free Company B.

EXHIBIT 16–14

Trading on the Equity
Effects of Debt on Rates of Return
(in thousands of dollars)

	(1)	(2)	(3)	(4)	(5) 10% of (2)	(6) (4) − (5)	(7) (4) ÷ (1)	(8) (6) ÷ (3)
							Return on	
	Average Assets	Average Bonds Payable	Average Stockholders' Equity	Income before Interest	10% Interest	Net Income*	Assets	Stockholders' Equity
Year 1								
Co. A	$80,000	$30,000	$50,000	$16,000	$3,000	$13,000	20%	26%
Co. B	80,000	—	80,000	16,000	—	16,000	20	20
Year 2								
Co. A	80,000	30,000	50,000	8,000	3,000	5,000	10	10
Co. B	80,000	—	80,000	8,000	—	8,000	10	10
Year 3								
Co. A	80,000	30,000	50,000	4,000	3,000	1,000	5	2
Co. B	80,000	—	80,000	4,000	—	4,000	5	5

* Income taxes are ignored in this illustration (to highlight the major point).

In Year 3, the picture is reversed. When a company is unable to earn at least the interest rate on the money borrowed, the return on equity will be lower than for the debt-free company. If earnings are low enough that the interest and principal payments on debt cannot be made, a company may be forced into bankruptcy. The possibility of bankruptcy increases the risk to the common stockholders as well as to debtholders.

Real estate promoters are examples of heavy traders on the equity. They use layers of mortgage debt and a minimum amount of owners' equity, and they enjoy extremely high returns on equity as long as revenues are ample. They are also prime candidates for bankruptcy when revenues decrease.

Obviously, the more stable the income, the less dangerous it is to trade on the equity (or, as it is often called, to use **leveraging** or **gearing**). Therefore regulated utilities such as electric, gas, and telephone companies tend to have a much heavier proportion of debt than manufacturers of computers or steel. The *prudent* use of debt is part of intelligent financial management. Managers who brag about having no long-term debt may not be obtaining the maximum returns on equity through the years. On the other hand, too much debt can cause financial disaster when operations become unprofitable (as the owners of Braniff common stock will attest).

USE DEBT OR EQUITY?

☐ Income Tax Effects

Corporations can raise additional invested capital through debt or equity. Debt has at least two major characteristics that differ from equity. First, principal and interest payments are obligatory. Second, the interest payments are deductible as an expense for income tax purposes, but dividends are not. Therefore, if all other things are equal, the use of debt is less costly to the corporation than equity.

Suppose additional capital of $10 million is going to be raised by a company either through long-term debt or through preferred stock. The latter is discussed in Chapter 11, pages 484–487. The typical preferred stock is a part of shareholders' equity, and the dividend thereon is not deductible for income tax purposes. Moreover, the rate of preferred dividends is usually higher than the rate of interest because the preferred stockholders have a greater risk due to their lower-priority claim on the total assets of a company. Assume that an interest rate of 10% for debt and a preferred dividend rate of 11% are applicable. The income tax rate is 40%. Compare the effects of obtaining additional capital by these two methods shown in the accompanying table.

	$10 MILLION LONG-TERM DEBT	$10 MILLION PREFERRED STOCK
Income before interest expense (assumed)	$5,000,000	$5,000,000
Interest expense at 10% of long-term debt	1,000,000	—
Income before income taxes	$4,000,000	$5,000,000
Income tax expense at 40%	1,600,000	2,000,000
Net income	$2,400,000	$3,000,000
Dividends to preferred shareholders at 11%	—	1,100,000
Net income less dividends	$2,400,000	$1,900,000
Pretax cost of capital raised	10%	11%
After-tax cost of capital raised:		
$600,000* ÷ $10,000,000	6%	
$1,100,000 ÷ $10,000,000		11%

* Interest expense	$1,000,000
Income tax savings because of interest deduction:	
.40 × $1,000,000	400,000
Interest expense after tax savings	$ 600,000

Two points deserve emphasis:

1. Interest is tax deductible, so its after-tax cost can be considerably less than dividends on preferred stock. In other words, *net income attributable to common shareholders* can be substantially higher if debt is used.
2. Interest is an expense, whereas preferred dividends are not. Therefore *net income* is higher if preferred shares are used. Note that trading on the equity can benefit the common stockholders by the issuance of either long-term debt securities or preferred stock, provided that the after-tax earnings on the additional assets acquired exceed the after-tax costs of obtaining the funds: in this case, 11% for the preferred stock but only 6% for the long-term debt.

□ **Measuring Safety**

Investors in debt securities want assurance that future operations will easily provide cash sufficient to make the scheduled payments of interest and principal. Corporate borrowers have a natural concern for the degree of risk they assume by trading on the equity through borrowing. Thus both lenders and borrowers may have a somewhat mutual aversion to excessive risks from debt, although lenders understandably tend to have the stronger aversion to risk.

Debt securities often have protective provisions, such as mortgage liens on real estate or restrictions on dividend payments to holders of common stock. However, these provisions are of minor importance compared with prospective earnings. Bond-holders would like to avoid the trouble, costs, and inconvenience of foreclosure or bankruptcy litigation; they would rather receive a steady stream of interest and repayments of principal.

Debt-to-equity ratios are popular measures of risks. But they do not focus on the major concern of the holders of long-term debt: the ability to meet debt obligations on schedule. A ratio that focuses on interest-paying ability is interest coverage (sometimes called earnings coverage). For example, in the above table, interest coverage is shown by the **times interest earned** ratio:

$$\text{Times interest earned} = \frac{\text{Income before interest expense and income taxes}}{\text{Interest expense}}$$

$$= \frac{\$5,000,000}{\$1,000,000} = 5.0 \text{ times}$$

The equation is self-explanatory. A rule of thumb for adequate safety of an industrial bond is that all interest charges should be earned at least five times in the poorest year in a span of seven to ten years that might be under review. The numerator does not deduct income taxes because interest expense is deductible for income tax purposes. In effect, income taxes, as a periodic "claim" on earnings, have a lower priority than interest. For instance, if the numerator were only $1 million, interest would be paid, leaving a net taxable income of zero. This tax-deductibility feature is a major reason why bonds are used so much more widely than preferred stock.

Regarding interest coverage, a recent news story stated:

☐ The implications of the nuclear plant accident in Pennsylvania won't easily be sorted out by investors and promise to be an uncertainty of long duration. Even without this development, however, the operating climate for the utility industry doesn't provide much comfort for electric utility investors.

☐ Among other things, such investors will have to renew their vigilance about the investment quality of stocks in the group. There's some evidence of erosion recently in one key financial measure—*the ratio of income before interest expense to interest expense*.

FUNDAMENTAL ASSIGNMENT MATERIAL

Special note. Problems 16–44 and 16–45 provide a general review of the whole book. They can be solved without necessarily studying the material in this chapter. Those problems focus on material from actual companies and on coverage of more than one accounting topic simultaneously.

☐ General Coverage

16–1. **EFFECTS OF VARIOUS ACCOUNTING METHODS ON NET INCOME.** (Alternate is 16–2). Nimitz Company is a profitable new company that has high potential growth. It is nearing the end of its first year in business and the company's president must make some decisions regarding accounting policies for financial reporting to stockholders. Her controller and certified public accountant have gathered the following information (all figures in thousands except tax rate):

Revenue	$30,000
Beginning inventory	–0–
Purchases	14,000
Ending inventory—if LIFO is used	4,000
Ending inventory—if FIFO is used	5,000
Depreciation—if straight-line is used	1,000
Depreciation—if accelerated depreciation is used	2,000
Store-opening costs	2,000
Store-opening costs (amortized amount)	400
Other expenses	4,000
Common shares outstanding (in thousands)	1,000
Income tax rate	50%
Investment credit—total received on tax returns this year	500
Investment credit—amortized amount per year	50

ACRS accelerated depreciation and flow-through of the investment credit will be used for tax purposes regardless of the method chosen for reporting to stockholders. For all other items, assume that the same method is used for tax purposes and for financial-reporting purposes.

Required:

1. Prepare a columnar income statement. In column 1 show the results using LIFO, accelerated depreciation (assumed equal to ACRS depreciation), direct write-off of store-opening costs, and amortization of the investment credit. Show earnings per share as well as net income. In successive columns, show the separate effects on net income and earnings per share of substituting the alternative methods: column 2, FIFO inventory; column 3, straight-line depreciation; column 4, amortization of store-opening costs; column 5, flow-through of investment credit. In column 6, show the total results of choosing all the alternative methods (columns 2 through 5). Note that in columns 2 through 5 only single changes in column 1 should be shown; that is, column 3 does not show the effects of columns 2 and 3 together, nor does column 4 show the effects of columns 2, 3, and 4 together.
2. Which accounting policies would you advise the company's president to adopt? Why?

☐ Understanding Published Financial Reports

16–2. **EFFECTS OF VARIOUS ACCOUNTING METHODS ON INCOME.** (Alternate is 16–1.) General Electric had the following account descriptions and data in its 1985 annual report (in millions of dollars except for earnings per share):

Sales of products and services to customers	$28,285
Cost of goods sold	19,775
Depreciation, depletion and amortization	1,226
Other expenses (summarized here)	3,744
Total expenses	24,745
Earnings before income taxes	3,540
Provision for income taxes	1,192
Net earnings	$ 2,348
Net earnings per share (in dollars)	$ 5.13

Inventories on December 31, 1985, were $3,949 million and on December 31, 1984, were $3,670 million. If FIFO had been used instead of LIFO, the FIFO inventories would have been higher by $1,856 million at December 31, 1985, and $2,027 million at December 31, 1984.

The company stated that most depreciation is computed by accelerated methods, primarily sum-of-the-years'-digits. The company also stated that the investment tax credit "is deferred and then amortized as a reduction of the provision for income taxes over the lives of the facilities to which the credit applies."

General Electric's effective 1985 income tax rate was $1,192 ÷ $3,540 = 33.67%. Investment tax credit amortization reduced the provision for income taxes by $76 million in 1985. General Electric actually reported $111 million of investment tax credits on its 1985 income tax return.

Required:

Suppose General Electric had used straight-line depreciation for reporting to shareholders, resulting in depreciation, depletion, and amortization expense of $926 million rather than $1,226 million in 1985. Also suppose the company had used FIFO instead of LIFO. Recast all the above data for 1985, including the amount earned per common share. Show supporting computations. (*Hint*: Compute the effective tax rate that would have applied if there were no investment tax credit.)

16–3. **FINANCIAL RATIOS.** Albertson's has 444 stores and is the eighth largest retail food and drug chain in the United States. Excerpts from the company's 1986 annual report are in Exhibit 16–15. Albertson's paid cash dividends of $.76 per common share in fiscal 1986, and an average of 33,170,000 shares were outstanding during the year. Assume that Albertson's has no stock options or convertible securities. The company's current market price is $32 per share.

EXHIBIT 16–15

ALBERTSON'S INC.
For the Year Ended January 31, 1986
(In thousands)

Income Statement

Sales	$5,060,265
Cost of sales	3,948,698
Gross profit	$1,111,567
Other expenses (summarized)	956,793
Earnings before income taxes	$ 154,774
Income taxes	69,664
Net earnings	$ 85,110

	JANUARY 31	
	1986	1985
Balance Sheet		
Assets:		
Inventories	$ 301,985	$ 266,906
Other current assets (summarized)	259,835	262,873
Total current assets	$ 561,820	$ 529,779
Land, buildings and equipment (net)	539,744	482,789
Other assets	23,053	20,308
Total assets	$1,124,617	$1,032,876
Liabilities and stockholders' equity:		
Current liabilities (summarized)	$ 350,562	$ 335,180
Long-term liabilities (summarized)	255,346	243,277
Total liabilities	$ 605,908	$ 578,457
Stockholders' equity (summarized)	518,709	454,419
Total liabilities and stockholders' equity	$1,124,617	$1,032,876

Compute the following financial ratios for fiscal 1986:

1. Current ratio
2. Inventory turnover
3. Current debt to equity
4. Total debt to equity
5. Gross profit rate
6. Return on sales
7. Return on stockholders' equity
8. Earnings per share
9. Price-earnings
10. Dividend-yield
11. Dividend-payout

ADDITIONAL ASSIGNMENT MATERIAL

☐ General Coverage

16–4. What three tests must be met before revenue can be realized?

16–5. "Realization of revenue occurs at the time of delivery of a good or service." Do you agree? Explain.

16–6. What are the major objectives of financial reporting as chosen by the FASB?

16–7. According to FASB *Concepts Statement No. 1*, what types of information should be supplied by financial reporting?

16–8. Why is a lone earnings figure regarded as misleading?

16–9. What is the fundamental cost-benefit test in accounting policy making?

16–10. Name three types of costs of producing accounting information.

16–11. "It is better to be roughly right than precisely wrong." Interpret this statement in light of the qualitative characteristics of accounting.

16–12. "The ability of a dozen independent accountants to apply the same measurement methods and obtain the same result is an example of representational faithfulness." Do you agree? Explain.

16–13. What is accounting policy making?

16–14. What is the role of the *Qualitative Characteristics Statement* of the FASB?

16–15. "Neutrality underscores a fundamental approach that should be taken by the FASB." Describe the approach.

16–16. "Accounting theory is unimportant because it is impractical." Do you agree? Explain.

"Accounting policy making is a political endeavor." Do you agree? Explain.

16–18. What does *uniformity* mean in accounting?

16–19. What is a statement of accounting policies?

16–20. "Ratios are mechanical and incomplete." Explain.

16–21. "An efficient capital market is one where securities are traded through stockbrokers." Do you agree? Explain.

16–22. Give three sources of information for investors besides accounting information.

16–23. Suppose the president of your company wanted to switch depreciation methods to increase reported net income: "Our stock price is 10% below what I think it should be; changing the depreciation method will increase income by 10%, thus getting our share price up to its proper level." How would you respond?

16–24. Evaluate the following quotation from *Forbes*: "If IBM had been forced to expense [the software development cost of] $785 million, its earnings would have been cut by 72 cents a share. With IBM selling at 14 times earnings, expensing the costs might have knocked over $10 off IBM's share price."

16–25. "Trading on the equity means exchanging bonds for stock." Do you agree? Explain.

16–26. "Borrowing is a two-edged sword." Do you agree? Explain.

16–27. Why are companies with heavy debt in relation to ownership capital in greater danger when business conditions sour?

16–28. **TIMING OF RECOGNITION OF REVENUE.** Massive Enterprises, a huge conglomerate company, has recently acquired the Galaxy Publishing Company.

The president of Massive, Martin Mass, is surprised that the Galaxy income statement assumes that an equal proportion of the revenue is earned with the publication of every issue of the company's magazines: "The critical event in the process of earning revenue in the magazine business is the cash sale of the subscription. Therefore, why can't most of the revenue be realized in the period of sale?"

Required:

Discuss the propriety of timing the recognition of revenue in relation to (1) the cash sale of the subscription, (2) the publication of magazines every month, (3) both events—by recognizing a portion of the revenue with the cash sale of the magazine subscription and a portion of the revenue with the publication of the magazine every month.

16–29. **CONTRACTOR ACCOUNTING.** Sikma Construction Company contracted to build a large river bridge for New York City. The board of directors is about to meet to decide whether to adopt the completed-contract or the percentage-of-completion method of accounting. Sikma began business on January 1, 19X4. Construction activity for the year ended December 31, 19X4, revealed (in millions):

Total contract price	$36
Billings through December 31, 19X4	15
Cash collections	12
Contract costs incurred	18
Estimated additional costs to complete the contract	6

Any work remaining to be done is expected to be completed in 19X5.

Required:

Prepare a schedule computing the amount of revenue and income that would be reported for 19X4 under

a. The completed-contract method
b. The percentage-of-completion method (based on estimated costs)

Ignore selling and other expenses as well as income taxes.

The percentage-of-completion method recognizes income based on a percentage:

$$\frac{\text{Percentage}}{\text{of completion}} = \frac{\text{Costs incurred to date}}{\left(\begin{array}{c}\text{Costs incurred}\\\text{to date}\end{array}\right) + \left(\begin{array}{c}\text{Estimated additional}\\\text{costs to complete}\end{array}\right)}$$

The percentage is applied to the total contract price to determine the realized revenue for the period.

16–30. **EFFECTS OF TRANSACTIONS ON FINANCIAL STATEMENTS.** For each of the following numbered items, select the lettered transaction that indicates its effect on the corporation's financial statements. If a transaction has more than one effect, list all applicable letters. Assume that the total current assets exceed the total current liabilities both before and after every transaction described.

NUMBERED TRANSACTIONS

1. Issuance of additional common shares as a stock dividend.
2. Sale for cash of factory building at a selling price that substantially exceeds the book value.
3. The destruction of a building by fire. Insurance proceeds, collected immediately, slightly exceed book value.
4. The appropriation of retained earnings as a reserve for contingencies.
5. Issue of new shares in a three-for-one split of common stock.
6. Collection of account receivable.
7. Sale on account at a gross profit.
8. Payment of trade account payable.
9. Purchase of inventory on open account.

LETTERED EFFECTS

a. Increases the book value per share of common stock.
b. Decreases the book value per share of common stock.
c. Increases total retained earnings.
d. Decreases total retained earnings.
e. Increases current ratio.
f. Decreases current ratio.
g. Increases working capital.
h. Decreases working capital.
i. Increases total stockholders' equity.
j. Decreases total stockholders' equity.
k. None of the above.

16–31. **RATE-OF-RETURN COMPUTATIONS.**

1. Presley Company reported a 4% operating margin on sales, an 8% pretax operating return on total assets, and $200 million of total assets. Compute (a) operating income, (b) total sales, and (c) total asset turnover.
2. McGillivray Corporation reported $600 million of sales, $32 million of operating income, and a total asset turnover of 4 times. Compute (a) total assets, (b) operating margin percentage on sales, and (c) pretax operating return on total assets.

16–32. **EPS AND TIMES-INTEREST-EARNED COMPUTATIONS.** Study Appendix 16. Far East Shipping Co. has outstanding 400,000 shares of common stock, $4 million of 8% preferred stock, and $8 million of 10% bonds payable. Its income tax rate is 40%.

1. Assume the company has $6 million of income before interest and taxes. Compute (a) EPS and (b) number of times bond interest has been earned.
2. Assume $4 million of income before interest and taxes, and make the same computations.

16–33. **COMMON STOCK RATIOS AND BOOK VALUE.** You may wish to review Chapter 11. The Ramos Corporation has outstanding 500,000 shares of 8% preferred stock with a $100 par value and 10.5 million shares of common stock of $1 par value. The current market price of the common is $24, and the latest annual dividend rate is $2 per share. Common treasury stock consists of 500,000 shares costing $7.5 million. The company has $150 million of additional paid-in capital, $15 million of retained income, and a $12 million bond sinking fund. Net income for the current year is $20 million.

Required:

1. Total stockholders' equity
2. Common price-earnings ratio
3. Common dividend-yield percentage
4. Common dividend-payout percentage
5. Book value per share of common

16–34. **FINANCIAL RATIOS.** Comparable Products Company furnished the following condensed data (in thousands):

	DECEMBER 31		
	19X3	19X2	19X1
Cash	$ 25	$ 20	$ 15
Accounts receivable	90	70	50
Merchandise inventory	85	75	65
Prepaid expenses	10	10	10
Land	30	30	30
Building	70	75	80
Equipment	60	50	40
Total assets	$370	$330	$290
Accounts payable	$ 50	$ 40	$ 30
Taxes payable	20	15	10
Accrued expenses payable	15	10	5
Long-term debt	45	45	45
Paid-in capital	150	150	150
Retained income	90	70	50
Total liab. and stk. eq.	$370	$330	$290

	YEAR ENDED DECEMBER 31	
	19X3	19X2
Sales (all on credit)	$800	$750
Cost of goods sold	440	420
Net income	40	30

Required:

1. Compute the following ratios for each of the last two years, 19X2 and 19X3:
   a. Current ratio
   b. Gross profit rate
   c. Percentage of net income to sales
   d. Ratio of current debt to stockholders' equity
   e. Inventory turnover
   f. Percentage of net income to stockholders' equity
   g. Average collection period for accounts receivable
   h. Ratio of total debt to stockholders' equity
2. For each of the following items, indicate whether the change from 19X2 to 19X3 for Comparable Products seems to be favorable or unfavorable, and identify

the ratios you computed above that most directly support your answer. The first item below is given as an example.

a. Gross margin: favorable, b
b. Return to owners
c. Ability to pay current debts on time
d. Collectibility of receivables
e. Risks of insolvency
f. Salability of merchandise
g. Return on sales

h. Operating success
i. Overall accomplishment
j. Future stability of profits
k. Coordination of buying and selling functions
l. Screening of risks in granting credit to customers

16–35. **FINANCIAL RATIOS.** Examine the accompanying financial statements of Diaz Lumber.

Dun & Bradstreet compiles many ratios of the companies it monitors. For instance, some of its ratios for 1,726 lumber and other building materials dealers were:

	CURRENT RATIO (Times)	NET INCOME ON SALES (Percent)	NET INCOME ON STOCK-HOLDERS' EQUITY (Percent)	CURRENT DEBT TO STOCK-HOLDERS' EQUITY (Percent)	TOTAL DEBT TO STOCK-HOLDERS' EQUITY (Percent)	COLLECTION PERIOD (Days)
For 1,726 companies:						
Upper quartile*	4.4	5.3	21.5	22.8	30.1	22.6
Median	2.4	2.5	10.1	53.1	78.0	33.5
Lower quartile	1.5	0.9	3.4	125.4	175.2	48.5

* See pages 737–738 for a description of the quartiles and how the various ratios are compiled.

DIAZ LUMBER
Income Statement
For the Year Ended December 31, 19X2
(in thousands)

Sales, including $188 of cash sales		$900
Cost of goods sold		440
Gross profit (or gross margin)		$460
Operating expenses:		
Wages	$200	
Miscellaneous	189	
Insurance	7	
Depreciation	30	
Total operating expenses		426
Operating income (or operating profit)		$ 34
Other revenue: interest		16
Income before income taxes		$ 50
Income tax expense		20
Net income		$ 30

Required:

1. Present Diaz Lumber's ratios for 19X2 as the final line of the above tabulation of Dun & Bradstreet ratios. Comment on Diaz's ratios in relation to those of similar companies.
2. Compute the following for Diaz:
   a. Inventory turnover
   b. Gross profit percentage of sales.

Add any comments to those made in requirement 1.

DIAZ LUMBER
Statement of Retained Income
For the Year Ended December 31, 19X2

Retained income, December 31, 19X1	$322
Add: Net income for 19X2	30
Total	$352
Deduct: Dividends declared	26
Retained income, December 31, 19X2	$326

DIAZ LUMBER
Balance Sheets

	DECEMBER 31	
ASSETS	19X2	19X1
Current assets:		
Cash	$ 1	$ 21
Accounts receivable	130	100
Note receivable—current portion	100	100
Accrued interest receivable	8	16
Merchandise inventory	240	160
Prepaid fire insurance	32	3
Total current assets	$511	$400
Long-term assets:		
Note receivable—long-term portion	—	100

	DECEMBER 31			
	19X2	19X1		
Equipment, at original cost	$184	$110		
Accumulated depreciation	96	66		
Equipment, net			88	44
Total assets			$599	$544

LIABILITIES AND STOCKHOLDERS' EQUITY

	19X2	19X1
Current liabilities:		
Accounts payable	$110	$ 90
Accrued wages payable	15	8
Accrued income taxes payable	5	4
Dividends payable	26	—
Deferred sales revenue	7	10
Total current liabilities	$163	$112
Stockholders' equity:		
Paid-in capital	$110	$110
Retained income	326	322
Total stockholders' equity	$436	$432
Total liabilities and stockholders' equity	$599	$544

16–36. **TRADING ON THE EQUITY.** Study Appendix 16. Able Company has assets of $250 million, bonds payable of $100 million, and stockholders' equity of $150 million. The bonds bear interest at 10% per annum. Baker Company, which is in the same industry, has assets of $250 million and stockholders' equity of $250 million. Prepare a comparative tabulation of Able Company and Baker Company for each of three years. Show income before interest, interest, net income, return on assets, and return on stockholders' equity. The income before interest for both companies was: Year 1, $25 million; Year 2, $12.5 million; and Year 3, $37.5 million. Ignore income taxes. Show all monetary amounts in millions of dollars. Comment on the results.

16–37. **USING DEBT OR EQUITY.** Study Appendix 16. The Hogan Corporation is trying to decide whether to raise additional capital of $15 million through a new issue of 12% long-term debt or of 9% preferred stock. The income tax rate is 40%. Compute net income less dividends for these alternatives, assuming that income before interest expense is $6 million. Show all dollar amounts in thousands. What is the after-tax cost of capital for debt and for preferred stock expressed in percentages? Comment on the comparison. Compute times interest earned for the first year.

16–38. **COMPUTATION OF FINANCIAL RATIOS.** Study Appendix 16. You are given the financial statements of the Maxim Co.

THE MAXIM CO.
Balance Sheet
(in thousands of dollars)

	DECEMBER 31	
	19X2	19X1
Assets		
Current assets:		
Cash	$ 1,000	$ 1,000
Short-term investments		1,000
Receivables, net	5,000	4,000
Inventories at cost	12,000	9,000
Prepayments	1,000	1,000
Total current assets	$19,000	$16,000
Plant and equipment, net	22,000	23,000
Total assets	$41,000	$39,000
Liabilities and Stockholders' Equity		
Current liabilities:		
Accounts payable	$10,000	$ 6,000
Accrued expenses payable	500	500
Income taxes payable	1,500	1,500
Total current liabilities	$12,000	$ 8,000
8% bonds payable	$10,000	$10,000
Stockholders' equity:		
Preferred stock, 12%, par value $100 per share	$ 5,000	$ 5,000
Common stock, $10 par value	8,000	8,000
Premium on common stock	4,000	4,000
Unappropriated retained earnings	1,000	3,000
Reserve for plant expansion	1,000	1,000
Total stockholders' equity	$19,000	$21,000
Total liab. and stk. eq.	$41,000	$39,000

THE MAXIM CO.
Statement of Income and Reconciliation of Retained Earnings
For the Year Ended December 31, 19X2
(in thousands of dollars)

Sales (all on credit)		$44,000
Cost of goods sold		32,000
Gross profit on sales		$12,000
Other operating expenses:		
Selling expenses	$5,000	
Administrative expenses	2,000	
Depreciation	1,000	8,000
Operating income		$ 4,000
Interest expense		800
Income before income taxes		$ 3,200
Income taxes at 40%		1,280
Net income		$ 1,920
Dividends on preferred stock		600
Net income for common-stock holders		$ 1,320
Dividends on common stock		3,320
Net income retained		$ (2,000)
Unappropriated retained earnings, December 31, 19X1		3,000
Unappropriated retained earnings, December 31, 19X2		$ 1,000

Required:

Compute the following for the 19X2 financial statements:

1. Pretax operating rate of return on total assets.
2. Divide your answer to requirement 1 into two components: operating income percentage of sales and total asset turnover.
3. After-tax rate of return on total assets. Be sure to add the *after-tax* interest expense to net income.
4. Rate of return on total stockholders' equity. Did the preferred and common stockholders benefit from the existence of debt? Explain fully.
5. Rate of return on *common* stockholders' equity. This ratio is the amount of net income available for the common stockholders divided by total stockholders' equity less the par value of preferred stock. Did the common stockholders benefit from the existence of preferred stock? Explain fully.

☐ Understanding Published Financial Reports

16–39. **RECOGNITION CRITERIA.** *Fortune* (July 7, 1986, p. 100) reported on a recent Supreme Court decision related to accrual accounting. The Internal Revenue Service (IRS) and several casinos disagreed on when to recognize revenue and expenses for progressive slot machines. These slot machines have no limit to the payoff. They pay a lucky winner the money others have put into the machine since the last payoff (less the house takeout, of course). The longer since the last win, the larger the jackpot. Progressive slots pay off on average every four and one-half months.

Suppose that on December 31, 1986, Harrah's Casino had a progressive slot machine that had not paid off recently. In fact, $1.2 million had been placed in the machine since its last payoff on February 13, 1986. Assume that the house's takeout is 5%.

The IRS regarded the $1.2 million as revenue but allowed no expense until a payoff occurred. The casinos argued that an expense equal to 95% of the revenue will eventually be incurred, and accrual accounting would require recognition of the expense at the same time as the revenue is recorded.

1. How much revenue should Harrah's recognize in 1986 from the machine? Explain fully.
2. How much expense should Harrah's recognize in 1986 from the machine? Explain fully.
3. The IRS argued that no expense should be recognized until a payoff to the winner had been made. What do you suppose was the basis for their argument?
4. Suppose you are a gambler who uses accrual accounting. How would you account for $100 placed into the progressive slot machine described above? Is this consistent with your answers to requirements 1 and 2? Why or why not?

16–40. **NATURE OF CAPITAL, INCOME, REVENUE** (M. Wolfson, adapted). Here is a letter written by the financial vice-president of Acurex Corporation, a manufacturer of energy, environmental, and agriculture equipment:

Dear Professor:

☐ We are engaged in a somewhat unusual government contract with the Department of Energy as a demonstration, or "showcase," program. We are designing and constructing a fuel delivery system for industrial boilers in which we will cost-share 35% of the total cost with the government. In return, we are awarded immediate title to all the equipment involved, including the government's 65% portion.

☐ It seems to me that there is some real logic in reflecting the government's gift of 65% of total cost in current earnings, subject only to a test of net realizable value. I'd appreciate your thoughts.

Sincerely,

The company's net income the previous year was $1,007,000.

Suppose the cost of the fuel delivery system is $1.2 million. This consists of about $600,000 in "hard assets" (equipment, etc.) and about $600,000 in designing costs. Via journal entries, show at least two ways in which the government contract could be reflected in Acurex's books, assuming the costs are all incurred prior to the end of the year. What is the effect of your two ways on the year's pretax income?

16–41. **INCOME RATIOS AND ASSET TURNOVER.** Color Tile, Inc., is a specialty retailer selling hard surface tiles, paint, and wallpaper through 665 stores. The following items are from the company's 1985 annual report:

Rate of return on stockholders' equity	12.1203%
Operating income percentage on sales	9.5724%
Total asset turnover	1.67886
Average total assets	$206,836,000
Income tax rate	45.1580%
Income tax expense	$10,991,000

1. Complete the following condensed income statment. Round to the nearest thousand.

Sales	$?
Operating expenses	?
Operating income	$?
Interest expense (net)	?
Pretax income	$?
Income tax expense	?
Net income	$?

2. Compute the following:
  a. Pretax operating rate of return on total assets
  b. Rate of return on sales
  c. Average stockholders' equity

16–42. INCOME RATIOS AND ASSET TURNOVER. Dun & Bradstreet Corporation's 1985 annual report to stockholders included the following data:

Net income	$294,708,000
Total assets:	
Beginning of year	2,288,267,000
End of year	2,672,993,000
Net income as a percent of:	
Total revenue	10.6%
Average stockholders' equity	23.0%

Required:

Using only the above data, compute

1. Net income percentage of average assets
2. Total revenues
3. Average stockholders' equity
4. Asset turnover, using two different approaches

16–43. FINANCIAL RATIOS. Skyline Corporation produces manufactured housing and recreational vehicles at thirty-five facilities throughout the United States. The company's income statement and balance sheet for the fiscal year ended May 31, 1985, are shown (slightly condensed) in Exhibit 16–16 on page 764.

Required:

1. Prepare a common-size income statement, that is, one showing component percentages.
2. Compute the following ratios:
  a. Current ratio
  b. Inventory turnover (1984 inventory was $8,002,000)
  c. Total debt to equity
  d. Gross profit rate
  e. Return on stockholders' equity (1984 stockholders' equity was $119,452,000)
  f. Price-earnings ratio (the market price was $14 per share)
  g. Dividend-payout ratio
3. What additional information would help you interpret the percentages and ratios you calculated?

16–44. USING STATEMENTS TO RECONSTRUCT TRANSACTIONS. Pay Less Drug Stores Northwest operates over 150 stores throughout the western United States. The company's balance sheet and statement of changes in financial position are in the financial statements on pages 765 and 766. During the year, Pay Less issued 392,000 common shares to those exercising stock options and 8,831,000 shares as part of a 100% stock dividend.

Required:

Compute the following:

1. Balance, inventories, January 31, 1984.
2. Balance, long-term debt, excluding current maturities, January 31, 1984.
3. Balance, retained earnings, January 31, 1984. Remember the stock dividend.
4. Balance, additional paid-in capital, January 31, 1984.
5. Amortization of goodwill for the year ended January 31, 1984. Pay Less acquired no companies during the fiscal year.
6. Original purchase price of property and equipment disposed of during the fiscal year. Note that property and equipment includes land, buildings, and equipment, leaseholds and leasehold improvements, and leased property under capital leases.

7. Balance, property and equipment, net, January 31, 1984. (*Hint*: Calculate accumulated depreciation and amortization, January 31, 1984. Depreciation and amortization on the changes statement includes both (a) depreciation and amortization of property and equipment and (b) amortization of cost in excess of net assets acquired. It will be important to recognize that the *book value* of property and equipment disposed of is $861,000.)
8. Balance, obligations under capital leases, January 31, 1984.

EXHIBIT 16–16

SKYLINE CORPORATION
Consolidated Statement of Earnings
For the year ended May 31, 1985
(in thousands except per share)

Sales	$327,776
Cost of sales	275,028
Gross profit	52,748
Selling and administrative expenses	47,146
Operating earnings	5,602
Interest income	8,422
Gain on sale of property, plant and equipment	1,014
Earnings before income taxes	15,038
Provision for income taxes	7,120
Net earnings	7,918
Net earnings per share	$ .71
Dividends per share	$ .48

Consolidated Balance Sheet
May 31, 1985
(in thousands)

Assets:	
Current assets:	
Cash	$ 4,577
Treasury bills	88,717
Accounts receivable	17,481
Inventories	7,928
Other	163
Total current assets	118,866
Property, plant and equipment, net	24,412
Other assets	1,278
	$144,556
Liabilities and Shareholders' Equity	
Current liabilities:	
Accounts payable, trade	$ 8,457
Accrued liabilities	14,113
Total current liabilities	22,570
Stockholders' equity:	
Common stock	314
Additional paid-in capital	4,960
Retained earnings	117,268
Less treasury stock	(556)
Total shareholders' equity	121,986
	$144,556

PAY LESS DRUG STORES NORTHWEST
Consolidated Balance Sheets
(in thousands)

	AT JANUARY 31, 1984	AT JANUARY 31, 1983
Assets		
Current assets:		
Cash (note 6)	$ 7,036	$ 5,455
Short-term investments	750	12,500
Receivables, net of $950 allowance for doubtful accounts ($179 in 1983)	?	7,270
Inventories	?	148,885
Prepaid expenses	5,282	4,900
Real properties held for sale, at cost	20,056	13,927
Total current assets	?	192,937
Property and equipment, at cost (notes 2 and 7):		
Land, buildings and equipment	?	92,684
Leaseholds and leasehold improvements	35,482	31,718
Leased property under capital leases	37,707	36,357
Other	699	235
	177,278	160,994
Less accumulated depreciation and amortization	?	39,271
Net property and equipment	?	121,723
Cost in excess of net assets acquired	7,331	7,529
Other assets	1,450	1,638
	?	323,827
Liabilities and Stockholders' Equity		
Current liabilities:		
Notes payable to banks and commercial paper (note 5)	$ 10,700	—
Current maturities of long-term debt (note 7)	10,361	10,039
Current obligations under capital leases (note 2)	?	1,783
Accounts payable (note 6)	56,480	47,758
Accrued expenses and other liabilities	29,555	25,867
Accrued income taxes (note 4)	7,907	8,139
Deferred income taxes, current portion (note 4)	4,805	3,455
Total current liabilities	?	97,041
Deferred income taxes (note 4)	26,813	26,986
Long-term debt, excluding current maturities (note 7)	?	62,940
Obligations under capital leases (note 2)	?	29,787
Stockholders' equity (notes 3, 7 and 10):		
Common stock, $1 par value per share Authorized 40,000,000 shares; issued 18,042,776 shares (8,820,388 shares in 1983)	?	8,820
Preferred stock, $25 par value per share Authorized 2,000,000 shares; no shares issued	—	—
Additional paid-in capital	?	2,526
Retained earnings	?	95,727
Total stockholders' equity	?	107,073
	?	$323,827

Consolidated Statements of Changes in Financial Position
(in thousands)

	YEARS ENDED JANUARY 31,		
	1984	1983	1982
Sources of Working Capital			
Net earnings	$ 24,721	19,375	16,649
Items which do not use working capital:			
Depreciation and amortization	12,097	11,253	10,784
Deferred income taxes	1,859	6,639	11,545
Working capital provided by operations	38,677	37,267	38,978
Disposal of property and equipment	861	379	3,083
Proceeds from issuance of long-term debt	893	1,174	170
Disposal of leased property under capital leases	—	348	351
Additions to obligations under capital leases	1,350	—	—
Proceeds from exercise of employee stock options	2,808	59	156
Other	188	781	139
	44,777	40,008	42,877
Uses of Working Capital			
Additions to property and equipment	17,863	11,042	8,527
Dividends on common stock	4,847	3,879	3,349
Repayments of long-term debt and current maturities	9,899	9,590	5,486
Reductions of obligations under capital leases	1,729	2,187	1,978
Additions to leased property under capital leases	1,350	—	—
Other	2,032	332	974
	37,720	27,030	20,314
Increase in working capital	$ 7,057	12,978	22,563
Changes in Components of Working Capital			
Increase (decrease) in current assets:			
Cash and short-term investments	$(10,169)	9,812	(12,267)
Receivables	(593)	1,674	(1,937)
Inventories	35,923	331	7,108
Prepaid expenses	382	433	(422)
Real properties held for sale, at cost	6,129	6,786	3,427
	31,672	19,036	(4,091)
Increase (decrease) in current liabilities:			
Notes payable to banks and commercial paper	10,700	—	(25,418)
Current maturities of long-term debt	322	4,103	314
Current obligations under capital leases	65	8	(8)
Accounts payable	8,722	(6,691)	(1,305)
Accrued expenses and other liabilities	3,688	2,155	(508)
Accrued income taxes	(232)	7,772	49
Deferred income taxes, current portion	1,350	(1,289)	222
	24,615	6,058	(26,654)
Increase in working capital	$ 7,057	12,978	22,563

See accompanying notes to consolidated financial statements.

16–45. USING STATEMENTS TO RECONSTRUCT TRANSACTIONS. American Software, Inc., develops, markets, and supports business applications software, primarily for IBM mainframe computers. The company's income statement, balance sheet, and statement of changes in financial position (except for the section "Changes in Components of Working Capital") are in the accompanying financial statements. Some items on the statements have question marks. American Software's tax rate for 1985 was 43.4323%, and all assets disposed of had zero book value.

Required:

1. Compute the original purchase price of property and equipment disposed of during fiscal 1985. (*Hint*: Prepare T-accounts for (a) property and equipment, at cost, and (b) accumulated depreciation and amortization. Enter the balances and transaction amounts that are known. A key to computing the unknown entries to the accounts is that all assets disposed of had zero book value.)
2. Fill in the correct amounts for all question marks in the statements. (*Hint*: Begin with either net earnings or earnings before income taxes on the income statement. Also note that property and equipment, at cost, can be computed from the data developed in requirement 1.)
3. A footnote to American Software's financial statements follows:

Revenue Recognition

☐ Upon entering into a licensing agreement for proprietary software, the Company recognizes eighty percent (80%) of the licensing fee upon delivery of the software documentation (system and user manuals), ten percent (10%) upon delivery of the software (computer tapes with source code), and ten percent (10%) upon installation; this is conditioned upon at least fifty percent (50%) of the licensing fee being billable within 45 days and installation contemplated within 180 days of execution of the licensing agreement. Otherwise, the Company recognizes income on proprietary software as billed. Revenue related to custom programming, maintenance, and education is recognized as the related services are performed.

The April 30, 1985, balance sheet shows $2,744,949 of deferred revenue (a better name is *unearned revenue*). What is the most likely explanation for the existence of deferred revenue?

AMERICAN SOFTWARE, INC.
Consolidated Statement of Earnings

Revenues	$?
Cost and expenses:	
Salaries, commissions, and benefits	10,305,926
Other selling, general and administrative	?
Total cost and expenses	22,576,998
Other income:	
Interest income	2,207,924
Other	464,657
Earnings before income taxes	?
Income taxes	4,200,000
Net earnings	$?
Earnings per common share	$?
Weighted average number of shares outstanding	6,374,970

AMERICAN SOFTWARE, INC.
Consolidated Balance Sheets

	APRIL 30,	
	1985	1984
Assets		
Current assets:		
Cash	$ 312,107	$ 370,237
Investments, at cost (approximate market)	18,628,190	22,911,312
Trade accounts receivable, net	?	6,004,691
Other	2,780,410	2,343,134
Total current assets	?	31,629,374
Property and equipment:		
At cost	?	3,996,354
Less accumulated depreciation and amortization	1,720,959	754,447
Net property and equipment	?	3,241,907
Other assets	?	197,275
	?	$35,068,556
Liabilities and Shareholders' Equity		
Current liabilities:		
Accounts payable	$ 687,981	$ 478,992
Deferred income taxes	2,840,760	3,214,760
Deferred revenue	2,744,949	4,830,976
Other current liabilities	1,385,164	800,000
Total current liabilities	7,658,854	9,324,728
Shareholders' equity:		
Common stock, $.10 par value	637,500	637,500
Additional paid-in capital	16,097,729	16,097,729
Retained earnings	14,478,821	9,008,599
Total shareholders' equity	31,214,050	25,743,828
	$38,872,904	$35,068,556

AMERICAN SOFTWARE, INC.
Consolidated Statement of Changes in Financial Position

	YEAR ENDED APRIL 30, 1985
Sources of Working Capital:	
Net earnings	$?
Items which do not use (provide) working capital:	
Depreciation and amortization of property and equipment	1,008,765
Amortization of other assets	30,894
Working capital provided by operations	?
Uses of Working Capital:	
Additions to property and equipment	8,765,874
Increase in other assets	129,531
Total uses of working capital	8,895,405
Decrease in working capital	$?

RECOMMENDED READINGS

The following readings are suggested as an aid to those readers who want to pursue some topics in more depth than is possible in this book. Of course, many of the chapters have footnotes containing suggested readings on a particular topic. Therefore the specific chapters should be consulted for additional references.

There is a hazard in compiling a group of recommended readings. Inevitably, some worthwhile books or periodicals are overlooked. Moreover, such a list cannot include books published subsequent to the compilation here.

Professional journals are typically available in university libraries. The *Journal of Accountancy* emphasizes financial accounting and is directed at the practicing CPA. *Accounting Horizons* stresses current, practice-oriented articles in all areas of accounting. *Management Accounting* and *FE* focus on management accounting. The *Harvard Business Review and Fortune*, which are aimed at general managers, contain many articles on planning and control.

The Accounting Review and the *Journal of Accounting Research* cover all phases of accounting at a more theoretical level than the preceding publications.

The *Opinions* of the Accounting Principles Board are available from the American Institute of CPAs, 1211 Avenue of the Americas, New York, N.Y. 10036. The institute also has a series of research studies on a variety of topics. The pronouncements of the Financial Accounting Standards Board are available from the board's office, High Ridge Park, Stamford, Conn. 06905.

The Financial Executives Institute, 10 Madison Avenue, P.O. Box 1938, Morristown, N.J. 07960, and the National Association of Accountants, 10 Paragon Drive, P.O. Box 433, Montvale, N.J. 07645–0433, have long lists of accounting research publications.

Books on elementary financial accounting are available from almost all major publishers. The next steps in the study of financial accounting are in books entitled *Intermediate Accounting* and then *Advanced Accounting*, which are available from Dryden Press, Richard D. Irwin, Inc., McGraw-Hill Book Co., Prentice-Hall, Inc., South-Western Publishing Co., Wiley-Hamilton, and other publishers.

For the analysis and interpretation of financial statements, especially in relationship to the market prices of stocks and bonds, see W. H. Beaver, *Financial Reporting: An Accounting Revolution*, and G. Foster, *Financial Statement Analysis*, second edition, both published by Prentice-Hall, Inc.

There are many books on elementary management accounting. Also, many books entitled *Cost Accounting* stress a management approach. For examples, see C. T. Horngren and G. L. Sundem, *Introduction to Management Accounting*, the companion to this book. Also see *Cost Accounting: A Managerial Emphasis* by C. T. Horngren and G. Foster. Both are published by Prentice-Hall, Inc.

GLOSSARY

The italicized words within the definitions or explanations are also described in this glossary.

ACCELERATED COST RECOVERY SYSTEM (p. 585). A system of the Internal Revenue Service that requires *depreciation* deductions to be based on arbitrary "recovery periods" instead of useful lives.

ACCELERATED DEPRECIATION (p. 379). Any *depreciation* method that writes off depreciable costs more quickly than the ordinary *straight-line method* based on expected useful life.

ACCOUNT (p. 13). Detailed summary of the changes in a particular *asset*, *liability*, or *owners' equity*.

ACCOUNTANT'S OPINION (p. 7). See *independent opinion*.

ACCOUNT FORM (p. 154). A classified *balance sheet* with the *assets* at the left.

ACCOUNTING CYCLE (p. 155). The various steps in the total processing of accounting data.

ACCOUNTING EVENT (p. 10). See *transaction*.

ACCOUNTING POLICY MAKING (p. 718). Choosing the accounting measurement and disclosure methods to be followed in financial reporting.

ACCOUNTING PRINCIPLES BOARD (APB) (p. 55). The top private-sector regulatory body, which existed from 1959 to 1973, when it was succeeded by the *Financial Accounting Standards Board*.

ACCOUNTING SYSTEM (p. 316). A set of records, procedures, and equipment that routinely deal with the events affecting the financial performance and position of the *entity*.

ACCOUNTING TRANSACTION (p. 10). See *transaction*.

ACCOUNTS PAYABLE (p. 9). The debts shown on the buyer's *balance sheet* when he or she has bought goods or services on *open account*. Usually a *current liability*.

ACCOUNTS RECEIVABLE (p. 218). Amounts owed to an *entity* by customers as a result of delivering goods or services and extending credit in the ordinary course of business.

ACCRUAL BASIS (p. 44). A process whereby *revenue* is recognized as services are rendered and *expenses* are recognized as efforts are expended or services used to obtain the *revenue*, regardless of when cash is received or disbursed.

ACCRUE (p. 118). Accumulation of a receivable or payable during a given period even though no explicit *transaction* occurs.

ACCUMULATED DEPRECIATION (p. 172). The cumulative sum of all *depreciation* recognized since the date of acquisition of the particular *assets* described.

ACRS (p. 585). See *Accelerated Cost Recovery System*.

ADDBACK METHOD (p. 680). The practice of beginning a *statement of changes in financial position* with net income and then adding or deducting *income statement* items not affecting *working capital*.

ADDITIONAL PAID-IN CAPITAL (p. 116). See *paid-in capital in excess of par value*.

ADJUSTING ENTRIES (p. 115). See *adjustments*.

ADJUSTMENTS (p. 115). The key final process (before the computation of ending account *balances*) of assigning the financial effects of *transactions* to the appropriate time periods.

AFFILIATED COMPANY (p. 546). A company that has 20% to 50% of its voting shares owned by another company.

AGING OF ACCOUNTS (p. 237). An analysis of the elements of individual *accounts receivable* according to the time elapsed after the dates of billing.

AICPA (p. 55). American Institute of Certified Public Accountants, the leading organization of the auditors of corporate financial reports.

ALLOWANCE FOR BAD DEBTS (p. 220). See *allowance for uncollectibles*.

ALLOWANCE FOR DEPRECIATION (p. 172). See *accumulated depreciation*.

ALLOWANCE FOR DOUBTFUL ACCOUNTS (p. 220). See *allowance for uncollectibles*.

ALLOWANCE FOR UNCOLLECTIBLES (p. 220). A *contra asset account* that offsets total receivables by an estimated amount that will probably not be collected.

ALLOWANCE METHOD (p. 220). This method of accounting for *bad debt* losses makes use of estimates and the presence of a *contra asset account*, allowance for uncollectible accounts.

AMORTIZATION (p. 373). The systematic reduction of a lump-sum amount.

APB (p. 55). See *Accounting Principles Board*.

APB OPINIONS (p. 55). A series of thirty-one Opinions of the *Accounting Principles Board* issued during 1962–73, many of which are still "the accounting law of the land."

APPROPRIATED RETAINED INCOME (p. 503). Restrictions of *retained income* earmarked on the books of account and in financial statements for some specific or general purpose.

ARREARAGES (p. 485). See *dividend arrearages*.

ASSETS (p. 9). Economic resources that are expected to benefit future cash inflows or help reduce future cash outflows.

ASSET TURNOVER (p. 742). See *total asset turnover*.

AUDIT (p. 7). An examination that is made in accordance with generally accepted auditing standards. Its aim is to give credibility to financial statements.

AUDIT COMMITTEE (p. 319). A committee of the board of directors that oversees the *internal accounting controls*, financial statements, and financial affairs of the corporation.

AUDITOR'S REPORT (p. 7). See *independent opinion*.

AVERAGE COLLECTION PERIOD (p. 238). Average *accounts receivable* divided by sales on account.

BAD DEBT RECOVERIES (p. 223). *Accounts receivable* that were written off as uncollectible but then collected at a later date.

BAD DEBTS (p. 219). Receivables determined to be uncollectible because debtors are unable or unwilling to pay their debts.

BALANCE (p. 78). The difference between the total left-side and right-side amounts in an *account* at any particular time.

BALANCE SHEET (p. 9). A photograph of financial status at an instant of time.

BANK RECONCILIATION (p. 328). An analysis that explains any differences existing between the cash balance shown by the depositor and that shown by the bank.

BASKET PURCHASE (p. 376). The acquisition of two or more types of *assets* for a lump-sum cost.

BEARER INSTRUMENT (p. 434). See *unregistered instrument*.

BENCH MARK (p. 736). General rules of thumb specifying appropriate levels for financial ratios.

BETTERMENT (p. 392). See *improvement*.

BIG EIGHT (p. 8). The eight largest American accounting firms.

BOND (p. 434). A certificate that shows evidence of *long-term debt*. Bonds usually are issued in units of $1,000 of *principal*, with *interest* paid semiannually.

BOOK OF ORIGINAL ENTRY (p. 79). A formal chronological record (usually called a *journal*) of the effects of the *entity's transactions* on the *balances* in pertinent *accounts*.

BOOK VALUE (p. 172). The *balance* of an *account* shown on the books, net of any *contra accounts*. For example, the book value of equipment is its acquisition cost minus *accumulated depreciation*.

BOOK VALUE PER SHARE OF COMMON STOCK (p. 498). *Stockholders' equity* attributable to *common stock* divided by the number of shares outstanding.

CALLABLE BONDS (p. 435). *Bonds* subject to redemption before maturity at the option of the issuer.

CALL PREMIUM (p. 435). A redemption price in excess of *par*.

CAPITAL (p. 16). In accounting, this word is too general by itself. In most cases, capital implies *owner's equity*. However, see *capitalization*. Money generated by *long-term debt* is also often called capital. *Owners' equities* of *proprietorships* and *partnerships* are often identified as capital.

CAPITAL EXPENDITURE (p. 391). An acquisition with long-term effects intended to benefit more than the current *fiscal year*.

CAPITAL IMPROVEMENT (p. 392). See *improvement*.

CAPITALIZATION (p. 748). *Owners' equity* plus *long-term debt*.

CAPITALIZATION STRUCTURE (p. 748). Same as *capitalization*.

CAPITAL LEASE (p. 458). A *lease* that transfers substantially all the risks and benefits of ownership. Leases are equivalent to *installment sales*.

CAPITAL MAINTENANCE (p. 626). See *financial capital maintenance* and *physical capital maintenance*.

CAPITAL STOCK CERTIFICATE (p. 15). See *stock certificate*.

CAPITAL STRUCTURE (p. 748). Same as *capitalization*.

CARRYING AMOUNT (p. 172). Same as *book value*.

CARRYING VALUE (p. 172). Same as *book value*.

CASH BASIS (p. 44). A process of accounting whereby *revenue* and *expense* recognition depend solely on the timing of various cash receipts and disbursements.

CASH DISCOUNTS (p. 215). Reductions of invoice prices awarded for prompt payment.

CASH FLOW (p. 688). An ambiguous term that usually means *cash provided by operations*.

CASH FROM OPERATIONS (p. 688). Same as *cash provided by operations*.

CASH PROVIDED BY OPERATIONS (p. 686). *Working capital* provided by operations plus decreases (and less increases) in noncash working capital. Essentially sales in cash minus all operating *expenses* requiring cash during the current period.

CERTIFICATE (p. 7). See *independent opinion*.

CERTIFICATE OF DEPOSIT (p. 530). Short-term obligations of banks.

CERTIFIED PUBLIC ACCOUNTANT (p. 6). In the U.S., an accountant earns this designation by a combination of education, qualifying experience, and the passing of a three and one-half day written national examination.

CHANGES STATEMENT (p. 672). A *statement of changes in financial position*.

CHARGE (p. 78). A word often used instead of *debit*.

CHART OF ACCOUNTS (p. 82). A list of all *account* titles of an *entity* together with some numbering or coding thereof.

CHECK REGISTER (p. 350). A cash disbursements *journal* used in a *voucher system*. Also is used as a synonym for cash disbursements journal.

CLASSIFIED BALANCE SHEET (p. 126). A *statement of financial position* with its items grouped into various subcategories.

CLOSING (p. 174). See *closing the books*.

CLOSING ENTRIES (p. 174). Entries having the effect of clearing, transferring, or summarizing *revenue* and *expense accounts*. When the closing entries are completed, the current revenue and expense accounts have zero balances.

CLOSING THE BOOKS (p. 174). The final step taken at the end of a given year to facilitate the recording of the next year's *transactions*.

COMMERCIAL PAPER (p. 530). Short-term *notes payable* issued by large *corporations* with top credit ratings.

COMMON-SIZE STATEMENTS (p. 735). Financial statements expressed in *component percentages*.

COMMON STOCK (p. 18). *Stock* representing the class of owners having a "residual" ownership of a *corporation*.

COMPARATIVE BALANCE SHEETS (p. 154). Financial statements that present data for two or more reporting periods. The most recent data are usually shown first, and the columnar format is usually favored.

COMPENSATING BALANCES (p. 326). Required minimum cash *balances* on deposit of the money borrowed from banks.

COMPLETED-CONTRACT METHOD (p. 595). A method that recognizes all *revenues* and costs at the completion of the contract.

COMPONENT PERCENTAGES (p. 738). Analysis and presentation of financial statements in percentage form to aid comparability.

COMPOUND ENTRY (p. 84). A single accounting entry that affects more than two *accounts*.

COMPOUND INTEREST (p. 445). For any period, *interest* rate multiplied by a *principal* amount that is changed each interest period by the previous unpaid interest. The unpaid interest is added to the principal to become the principal for the new period.

COMPREHENSIVE INCOME (p. 723). The change in *owners' equity* (*net assets*) of an enterprise during a period from *transactions* and other events and circumstances from nonowner sources. It includes all changes in *owners' equity* during a period except those resulting from investments by owners in the enterprise and distributions by the enterprise to owners.

CONSERVATISM (p. 278). Selecting the method of measurement that yields the gloomiest immediate financial results.

CONSIGNMENT (p. 342). Goods shipped for future sale, title remaining with the shipper (consignor), for which the receiver (consignee), upon his acceptance, is accountable. The goods are part of the consignor's inventory until sold.

CONSISTENCY (p. 272). Continued uniformity, during a period or from one period to another, in methods of accounting, mainly in valuation bases and methods of *accrual*.

CONSOLIDATED STATEMENTS (p. 537). Combinations of the financial positions and *earnings* reports of the *parent company* with those of various *subsidiaries* into an overall report as a single *entity*.

CONSTANT DOLLARS (p. 627). Those monetary units restated so as to represent the same general purchasing power.

CONTINGENT LIABILITY (p. 431). A potential *liability* that depends on a future event arising out of a past *transaction*.

CONTINUITY CONVENTION (p. 95). The assumption that in all ordinary situations an *entity* persists indefinitely.

CONTRA ACCOUNT (p. 172). A separate but related *account* that offsets a companion account. Examples are *accumulated depreciation* and *allowance for uncollectible accounts*.

CONTRA ASSET (p. 172). A *contra account* that offsets an *asset*.

CONTRACTUAL RATE (p. 434). See *nominal interest rate*.

CONTRIBUTED CAPITAL (p. 16). The total amounts invested by owners at the inception of a business or subsequently. Usually distinguished from *capital* arising from *retained income*.

CONVERTIBLE BONDS (p. 435). *Bonds* that may, at the holder's option, be exchanged for other securities.

COPYRIGHTS (p. 695). Exclusive rights conveyed by federal statute to reproduce and sell a book, design, pamphlet, drawing, or other creations, and to forbid the publication of excerpts or other imitations.

CORPORATE PROXY (p. 481). A written authority granted by individual shareholders to others to cast the shareholders' vote.

CORPORATION (p. 14). An organization that is an "artificial being" created by individual state laws.

COST-BENEFIT CRITERION (p. 96). As a system is changed, its expected additional benefits should exceed its expected additional *costs*.

COST METHOD FOR INVESTMENTS (p. 534). The method whereby the initial investment is recorded at cost and *dividends* received are recorded as *revenues*.

COST OF GOODS SOLD (p. 41). Beginning inventory plus purchases minus ending inventory.

COST OF SALES (p. 41). See *cost of goods sold*.

COST RECOVERY (p. 39). The concept that helps determine whether resources such as *inventories*, prepayments, and equipment should be carried forward to future periods as *assets* or written off to the current period as *expenses*.

COUPON INTEREST RATE (p. 434). See *nominal interest rate*.

COVENANT (p. 434). A provision stated in a *bond*, usually to protect the bondholders' interests.

CREDIT (p. 78). In accounting, this word means one thing and one thing only—"right," as distinguished from "left." It typically refers to an entry in an *account* or the *balance* of an account.

CROSS-SECTIONAL COMPARISON (p. 736). Comparison of a company's financial ratios to the ratios of other companies or to industry averages.

CUMULATIVE DIVIDENDS (p. 484). Undeclared *dividends* on *preferred stock* for a particular period that accumulate as a claim upon past and future *earnings*.

CURRENT ASSETS. (p. 126). Cash plus *assets* that are expected to be converted to cash or sold or consumed during the next twelve months or as a part of the normal *operating cycle*.

CURRENT COST (p. 627). Cost at present-day price levels of some or all of the items making up a *balance sheet* or *income statement*, obtained by applying to historical cost one or more specific index numbers or by substituting for historical prices prevailing prices of equivalent goods and services.

CURRENT COST/CONSTANT DOLLAR METHOD (p. 631). An overall method of accounting that is based on *current costs* and monetary units restated to represent uniform purchasing power.

CURRENT COST/NOMINAL DOLLAR METHOD (p. 629). An overall method of accounting that is based on *current costs* and monetary units not restated for fluctuations in the general purchasing power of the monetary unit.

CURRENT LIABILITIES (p. 126). *Liabilities* that fall due within the coming year or within the normal *operating cycle* if longer than a year.

CURRENT RATIO (p. 127). *Current assets* divided by *current liabilities*.

CURRENT YIELD (p. 434). Usually refers to current *interest* payments divided by the market price of a *bond*. Also see *dividend-yield ratio*.

CUTOFF ERROR (p. 342). Failure to record *transactions* in the correct time period.

DATA PROCESSING (p. 84). The totality of the procedures used to record, analyze, store, and report on chosen activities.

DEBENTURE (p. 433). A *debt* security with a general claim against all *assets* rather than a specific claim against particular assets.

DEBIT (p. 78). In accounting, this word means one thing and one thing only—"left." It typically refers to an entry in an *account* or the *balance* of an account.

DEBT LEVERAGE (p. 748). See *trading on the equity*.

DEBT-TO-ASSETS RATIO (p. 442). Total *liabilities* divided by total *assets*.

DEBT-TO-EQUITY RATIO (p. 442). Total *liabilities* divided by total *stockholders' equity*.

DEDUCTIBLE ITEMS (p. 582). *Expenses* that may be subtracted from *revenues* to determine taxable *income*.

DEFERRAL METHOD (p. 583). A method of accounting for *tax credits* associated with business investments whereby the tax savings are spread over the useful life of the *asset*.

DEFERRED CHARGE (p. 397). An *expenditure* not recognized as a cost of operations of the period in which incurred but carried forward to be written off in one or more future periods.

DEFERRED CREDIT (p. 117). Often used as a synonym for *unearned revenue* or as a description for *deferred income tax*. In its bookkeeping application, the term refers to an amount that is classified as a *liability* that will eventually be transferred as a *credit* to *revenue* or a *credit* to *expense*.

DEFERRED INCOME (p. 118). See *unearned revenue*.

DEFERRED REVENUE (p. 117). See *unearned revenue*.

DEPLETION (p. 394). Gradual exhaustion of the original amounts of natural resources acquired.

DEPRECIABLE VALUE (p. 377). The difference between the total acquisition cost of plant and equipment and the predicted net *disposal value* at the end of useful life.

DEPRECIATION (p. 40). The systematic allocation of the acquisition cost of plant, property, and equipment to the particular periods or products that benefit from the use of the *assets*.

DILUTION (p. 499). Reduction in *stockholders' equity* per share or *earnings per share* that arises from some changes among shareholders' proportional interests.

DISBURSEMENT VOUCHER (p. 350). See *voucher*.

DISCOUNT AMORTIZATION (p. 437). The spreading of *bond discount* over a number of years as *expense*.

DISCOUNT ON BONDS (p. 436). The excess of *face amount* over the proceeds upon issuance.

DISCOUNT RATE (p. 447). The interest rate used in determining *present value*.

DISPOSAL VALUE (p. 170). See *residual value*. This term also has a second, more general, meaning: the expected net cash value from sale of an *asset* at any given date.

DIVIDEND ARREARAGES (p. 485). Accumulated unpaid *dividends* on *preferred stock*.

DIVIDEND-PAYOUT RATIO (p. 61). Common *dividends* per share divided by common *earnings per share*.

DIVIDENDS (p. 49). Distributions of cash (or other *assets*) to stockholders that reduce *retained income*. See also *stock dividend*.

DIVIDEND-YIELD RATIO (p. 60). Common *dividends* per share divided by the market price per share of *common stock*.

DOUBLE-DECLINING-BALANCE DEPRECIATION (DDB) (p. 380). A form of *accelerated depreciation* that results in first-year *depreciation* being twice the amount of *straight-line depreciation* when zero *residual value* is assumed.

DOUBLE-ENTRY SYSTEM (p. 77). The method usually followed for recording *transactions*, whereby at least two *accounts* are always affected by each transaction.

EARNINGS (p. 36). The excess of *revenues* over *expenses*.

EARNINGS COVERAGE (p. 751). See *times interest earned*.

EARNINGS DILUTION (p. 499). See *dilution*.

EARNINGS PER SHARE (EPS) (p. 59). Net income divided by the number of common shares outstanding. However, where *preferred stock* exists, the preferred *dividends* must be deducted in order to compute the net income applicable to *common stock*. See also *primary EPS* and *fully diluted EPS*.

EFFECTIVE INTEREST RATE (p. 436). The market rate on the day of issuance of a *bond*. It is the rate of yield to maturity, as contrasted with the *coupon interest rate*. Thus, if the issuance price is greater than the *face amount* of the bond, the effective rate is lower than the *coupon rate*.

EFFICIENT CAPITAL MARKET (p. 743). One in which market prices "fully reflect" all information available at a given time.

ENTITY (p. 14). A specific area of accountability that is the focus of the accounting process. It may be a single *corporation*, a tax district, a department, a papermaking machine, or a consolidated group of many interrelated corporations.

EQUITY METHOD (p. 535). Accounts for an investment at acquisition cost adjusted for the investor's share of *dividends* and *earnings* or losses of the investee subsequent to the date of investment.

EXPENDITURE (p. 391). Cash or other resources paid, or to be paid, for an *asset* purchased or service acquired.

EXPENSES (p. 36). Generally, a gross decrease in *assets* from delivering goods or services.

EXPLICIT TRANSACTIONS (p. 115). Events such as cash receipts and disbursements that trigger nearly all day-to-day routine entries.

EXTRAORDINARY ITEM (p. 514). An extremely unusual and infrequent *expense* or *revenue* that is shown together with its income tax effects separately from *income* from continuing operations on an *income statement*. Examples are losses from earthquakes and gains or losses on the retirement of *bonds*.

FACE AMOUNT (p. 434). The *principal* as indicated on the certificates of *bonds* or other debt instruments.

FASB (p. 55). *Financial Accounting Standards Board*.

FASB STATEMENTS (p. 55). Official rules and regulations regarding external financial reporting issued in a numbered series by the *Financial Accounting Standards Board*.

FIFO (p. 269). See *first-in, first-out*.

FINANCIAL ACCOUNTING (p. 4). Serves external decision makers, such as stockholders, suppliers, banks, and government agencies. Distinguish from *management accounting*.

FINANCIAL ACCOUNTING STANDARDS BOARD (FASB) (p. 55). The primary regulatory body over accounting principles and practices. It is an independent creature of the private sector.

FINANCIAL CAPITAL MAINTENANCE (p. 626). The quantity of financial resources (usually *historical costs*), as distinguished from physical resources of operating capability, to be recovered before *income* emerges.

FINANCIAL LEVERAGE (p. 748). See *trading on the equity*.

FINANCIAL MANAGEMENT (p. 671). Is mainly concerned with where to get cash and how to use cash for the benefit of the *entity* (that is, obtaining and investing the needed *capital*). Compare with *operating management*.

FIRST-IN, FIRST-OUT (FIFO) (p. 269). This method of accounting for inventory assumes that the units acquired earliest are used or sold first.

FISCAL PERIOD (p. 133). See *fiscal year*.

FISCAL YEAR (p. 133). The year established for accounting purposes for the preparation of annual reports.

FIXED ASSETS (p. 374). Tangible *assets* or physical items that can be seen and touched, often called property, plant, and equipment or plant assets.

FLOW-THROUGH METHOD (p. 583). A method of accounting for tax credits associated with the purchase of business investments whereby the entire tax savings increases the net income for the year of purchase.

F.O.B. (p. 227). "Free on board," meaning the buyer bears the cost of shipping from the F.O.B. point specified by the seller to the receiving point of the buyer.

FOREIGN CORRUPT PRACTICES ACT (p. 318). A federal law that requires adequate *internal controls*, among other requirements.

FRANCHISE (p. 395). A privilege granted by a government, manufacturer, or distributor to sell a product or service in accordance with specific conditions.

FREIGHT IN (p. 228). An additional cost of the goods acquired during the period, which is often shown in the purchases section of an *income statement*.

FREIGHT OUT (p. 228). The transportation costs borne by the seller of merchandise and often shown as a "shipping expense."

FULLY DILUTED EARNINGS PER SHARE (p. 509). An *earnings-per-share* figure on *common stock* that assumes that all outstanding *convertible securities* and *stock options* are exchanged for common stock at the beginning of the period.

FUND (p. 173). A specific amount of cash or investments in securities earmarked for a special purpose.

FUNDS STATEMENT (p. 672). See *statement of changes in financial position*.

GAAP (p. 54). See *generally accepted accounting principles*.

GEARING (p. 749). See *trading on the equity*.

GENERAL JOURNAL (p. 79). A *book of original entry*.

GENERAL LEDGER (p. 90). The record that contains the group of *accounts* that supports the amounts shown in the major financial statement.

GENERALLY ACCEPTED ACCOUNTING PRINCIPLES (GAAP) (p. 54). A technical term including both broad concepts or guidelines and detailed practices. It includes all conventions, rules, and procedures that together make up accepted accounting practice at a given time.

GOING CONCERN CONVENTION (p. 95). See *continuity convention*.

GOODWILL (p. 395). The excess of the cost of an acquired company over the sum of the fair market value of its identifiable individual *assets* less the *liabilities*.

GROSS MARGIN (p. 129). Synonym for *gross profit*.

GROSS MARGIN PERCENTAGE (p. 131). Same as *gross profit percentage*.

GROSS PROFIT (p. 129). The difference between sales *revenue* and the cost of inventories sold.

GROSS PROFIT PERCENTAGE (p. 131). *Gross profit* divided by sales.

GROSS PROFIT TEST (p. 213). The comparing of *gross profit percentages* to detect any phenomenon worth investigating.

HISTORICAL COST (p. 627). The amount originally paid to acquire an asset.

HISTORICAL COST/CONSTANT DOLLAR METHOD (p. 630). An overall method of accounting that is based on *historical costs* restated in monetary units representing uniform purchasing power.

HISTORICAL COST/NOMINAL DOLLAR METHOD (p. 628). An overall method of accounting that is based on *historical costs* not restated for fluctuations in the general purchasing power of the monetary unit.

HOLDING GAINS (OR LOSSES) (p. 629). Increases (or decreases) in the *replacement cost* (or other appropriate measure of current value) of the *assets* held during the current period.

IMPLICIT TRANSACTIONS (p. 115). Events (like the passage of time) that are temporarily ignored in day-to-day recording procedures and are recognized via end-of-period *adjustments*.

IMPREST BASIS (p. 333). A method for accounting for a particular amount of cash, usually petty cash.

IMPROVEMENT (p. 392). A *capital expenditure* that is intended to add to the future benefits from an existing *fixed asset*.

IMPUTATION (p. 456). The process that recognizes a pertinent *expense* or *revenue* that may not be routinely recognized by ordinary accounting procedures.

IMPUTED INTEREST RATE (p. 456). When economic substance prevails over legal form, the *nominal rate* is rejected in favor of the *market rate*. The imputed rate is this resulting interest rate.

INCOME (p. 36). The excess of *revenues* over *expenses*.

INCOME STATEMENT (p. 40). A report of all *revenues* and *expenses* pertaining to a specific time period.

INDENTURE (p. 434). See *trust indenture*.

INDEPENDENT OPINION (p. 7). The accountant's stamp of approval on management's financial statements, based on the findings of an *audit*.

INSTALLMENT METHOD (p. 594). A method that records the *revenue* and associated costs for an installment sale in the years during which the selling price is collected in cash, not necessarily during the year of sale.

INTANGIBLE ASSETS (p. 374). Rights or economic benefits that are not physical in nature. Examples are *franchises*, *patents*, *trademarks*, *copyrights*, and *goodwill*.

INTEREST (p. 433). The cost of using money; the rental charge for cash.

INTEREST COVERAGE (p. 751). See *times interest earned*.

INTERNAL ACCOUNTING CONTROL (p. 317). Methods and procedures that are mainly concerned with the authorization of *transactions*, safeguarding of *assets*, and accuracy of the financial records.

INTERNAL CONTROL (p. 316). See *internal accounting control*.

INTERPERIOD TAX ALLOCATION (p. 590). A method that measures reported income as if it were subject to the full current tax rate even though a more advantageous accounting method was used for tax purposes.

INVENTORY SHRINKAGE (p. 333). Difference between (a) the value of inventory that would occur if there were no pilferage, misclassifications, breakage, and clerical errors and (b) the value of inventory when it is physically counted.

INVENTORY TURNOVER (p. 285). The *cost of goods sold* divided by the average inventory at cost.

INWARD TRANSPORTATION (p. 228). See *freight in*.

JOURNAL ENTRY (p. 79). An analysis in a journal of the effect of a *transaction* on the *accounts*, usually accompanied by an explanation.

KEYING OF ENTRIES (p. 81). The process of numbering or otherwise specifically identifying each *journal entry* and each *posting*.

LAST-IN, FIRST-OUT (LIFO) (p. 270). This inventory method assumes that the units acquired most recently are used or sold first.

LEASE (p. 458). A contract whereby an owner (lessor) grants the use of property to a second party (lessee) for rental payments.

LEASEHOLD (p. 393). The right to use a *fixed asset* for a specified period of time, typically beyond one year.

LEASEHOLD IMPROVEMENTS (p. 393). *Fixed assets* acquired by a lessee, such as installation of new fixtures, panels, and walls that may not be removed from the premises when a lease expires.

LEDGER (p. 76). Group of *accounts* kept up to date in a systematic manner.

LEVERAGING (p. 749). See *trading on the equity*.

LIABILITIES (p. 9). Obligations of the organization to outsiders (nonowners). Probable future sacrifices of economic benefits stemming from present legal, equitable, or constructive obligations of a particular enterprise to transfer *assets* or provide services to other entities in the future as a result of past *transactions* or events affecting the enterprise.

LICENSES (p. 395). Privileges granted by a government, manufacturer, or distributor to sell a product or services in accordance with specified conditions.

LIFO (p. 270). See *last-in, first-out*.

LIFO INCREMENT (p. 276). See *LIFO layer*.

LIFO LAYER (p. 276). A separately identifiable additional segment of *LIFO* inventory.

LIFO POOL (p. 276). See *LIFO layer*.

LIFO RESERVE (p. 290). The difference between a company's inventory valued at *LIFO* and what it would be under *FIFO*.

LIMITED LIABILITY (p. 15). Corporate creditors ordinarily have claims against the corporate *assets* only. Therefore the stockholders as individuals do not have liability beyond their original investment in the *corporation*.

LIQUIDATING VALUE (p. 486). A measure of the preference as to *assets* of various claims against a *corporation* that is facing *liquidation*, that is, the sale of all the *entity's assets*.

LIQUIDATION (p. 52). Payment of a debt, or the conversion of *assets* into cash, or the complete sale of assets and settlement of claims when the *entity* is terminated.

LONG-LIVED ASSETS (p. 373). Resources that are held for an extended time, such as land, buildings, equipment, natural resources, and *patents*.

LONG-TERM DEBT (p. 422). *Liabilities*, usually in the form of some type of loans, that are due beyond the ensuing twelve months.

LONG-TERM DEBT TO EQUITY RATIO (p. 442). Total *long-term debt* divided by total *stockholders' equity*.

LONG-TERM LIABILITIES (p. 422). See *long-term debt*.

LOWER OF COST OR MARKET (p. 279). The superimposition of a market-price test on an inventory cost method.

MANAGEMENT ACCOUNTING (p. 4). Services internal decision makers (i.e., executives and managers within an organization), as distinguished from *financial accounting*.

MANAGEMENT REPORTS (p. 317). Explicit statements in annual reports concerning management's responsibilities for its financial statements.

MARKETABLE SECURITIES (p. 530). Any notes, *bonds*, or stocks that can readily be sold via public markets. The term is often used as a synonym for *short-term investments*.

MARKET INTEREST RATE (p. 436). See *effective interest rate*.

MATCHING (p. 39). The essence of the *accrual basis* whereby *revenue* and *expenses* are assigned to a particular period for which a measurement of *income* is desired.

MATCHING AND COST RECOVERY (p. 39). The procedure of accrual accounting whereby *expenses* either are directly attributed to related *revenues* (*matching*) of a given period or are otherwise regarded as costs that will not be recovered from revenue in future periods. In short, cost recovery is the justification for carrying *unexpired costs* as *assets* rather than writing them off as expenses. Also see *cost recovery* and *matching*.

MATERIALITY (p. 96). See *materiality convention*.

MATERIALITY CONVENTION (p. 96). The characteristic attaching to a statement, fact, or item that, if omitted or misstated, would tend to mislead the user of the financial statements under consideration.

MINORITY INTERESTS (p. 540). The outside shareholders' interests, as opposed to the *parent*'s interests, in a *subsidiary* corporation.

MONETARY ITEMS (p. 640). A claim receivable or payable in a specified number of dollars; the claim remains fixed regardless of changes in either specific or general price levels.

MORTGAGE BOND (p. 433). A form of *long-term debt* that is secured by the pledge of specific property.

MULTIPLE-STEP INCOME STATEMENT (p. 129). An *income statement* that contains one or more subtotals that often highlight significant relationships.

NET ASSETS (p. 155). Total *assets* less total *liabilities*; equal to the total *stockholders' equity*.

NET BOOK VALUE (p. 172). Same as *book value*. Most often, *book value* is used rather than *net book value*.

NET MONETARY POSITION (p. 641). Total monetary *assets* minus total monetary *liabilities*.

NET WORKING CAPITAL (p. 126). See *working capital*.

NET WORTH (p. 10). See *owners' equity*.

NEUTRALITY (p. 721). Choosing accounting policies without attempting to achieve purposes other than measuring economic impact; freedom from bias.

NEXT-IN, FIRST-OUT (NIFO) (p. 277). The *replacement cost* inventory method.

NOMINAL ACCOUNTS (p. 178). Those *accounts* subject to periodic closing, such as *revenues* and *expenses*, frequently called *temporary accounts*.

NOMINAL DOLLARS (p. 626). Those dollars that are not restated for fluctuations in the general purchasing power of the monetary unit.

NOMINAL INTEREST RATE (p. 434). A contractual rate of *interest* paid on *bonds*.

NOTES PAYABLE (p. 9). Promissory notes that are evidence of a debt and state the terms of payment.

OBJECTIVITY (p. 95). Accuracy supported by convincing evidence that can be verified by independent accountants.

OFFSET ACCOUNT (p. 172). See *contra account*.

OPEN ACCOUNT (p. 12). Buying or selling on credit, usually by just an "authorized signature" of the buyer.

OPERATING CYCLE (p. 35). The time span during which cash is used to acquire goods and services, which in turn are sold to customers, who in turn pay for their purchases with cash.

OPERATING INCOME (p. 130). See *operating profit*.

OPERATING INCOME PERCENTAGE ON SALES (p. 742). *Operating income* divided by sales.

OPERATING LEASE (p. 458). A *lease* that should be accounted for by the lessee as ordinary rent *expenses*; no related property or *liabilities* are presented in the body of the lessee's *balance sheet*.

OPERATING MANAGEMENT (p. 671). Is mainly concerned with the major day-to-day activities that generate sales *revenue* (that is, using a given set of resources). Compare with *financial management*.

OPERATING PROFIT (p. 130). *Revenues* from operations minus all operating expenses, including *cost of goods sold*.

OPERATING STATEMENT (p. 40). See *income statement*.

OPINION (p. 7). See *independent opinion*.

OWNERS' EQUITY (p. 10). Residual interest in (that is, remaining claim against) the organization's *assets* after deducting *liabilities*. Obligations of the *entity* to the owners. The interest of stockholders or other owners in the assets of an enterprise; at any time it is the cumulative net result of past *transactions* and other events and circumstances affecting the enterprise.

PAID-IN CAPITAL (p. 16). The *owners' equity* measured by the total amounts invested at the inception of a business and subsequently.

PAID-IN CAPITAL IN EXCESS OF PAR VALUE (p. 16). Amount of *paid-in capital* that is greater than the *par value* of issued shares of stock.

PARENT COMPANY (p. 536). A company owning more than 50% of the voting shares of another company, called the *subsidiary* company.

PARTNERSHIP (p. 14). A special form of organization that joins two or more individuals together as co-owners.

PAR AMOUNT (p. 434). See *par value*.

PAR VALUE (p. 16). The value printed on the face of the security certificate.

PATENTS (p. 395). Grants by the federal government to inventors, giving them the exclusive right to produce and sell their inventions for a period of seventeen years.

PERCENTAGE-OF-COMPLETION METHOD (p. 596). *Revenues* and costs from a contract are allocated to each year based on the percentage of the project's projected total cost that have been expended by the end of the year.

PERIODIC INVENTORY SYSTEM (p. 225). The method used where the *cost of goods sold* is computed periodically by relying solely on physical counts and not keeping day-to-day records of units sold or on hand.

PERMANENT ACCOUNTS (p. 178). See *real accounts*.

PERMANENT DIFFERENCES (p. 602). Differences between *pretax income* as reported to shareholders and taxable income as reported to the government that will not "reverse," or "turn around," in subsequent periods.

PERPETUAL INVENTORY SYSTEM (p. 224). A system that keeps a running, continuous record that tracks inventories and the *cost of goods sold* on a day-to-day basis.

PHYSICAL CAPITAL MAINTENANCE (p. 626). *Income* emerges only after recovering an amount that allows physical operating capability to be maintained.

P. & L. STATEMENT (p. 40). A synonym for *statement of profit and loss*. See *income statement*.

POOLING-OF-INTEREST METHOD (p. 557). A way of accounting for the combination of two *corporations* based on the *book values* of the acquired company's *net assets*, as distinguished from the *purchase method*.

POSTING (p. 81). To record an amount in a *ledger*. The amount is usually transferred from a journal.

PREEMPTIVE RIGHTS (p. 482). The rights to acquire a pro-rata amount of any new issues of capital stock.

PREFERRED STOCK (p. 484). Stock that has some priority over other shares regarding *dividends* or the distribution of *assets* upon *liquidation*.

PREMIUM ON BONDS (p. 436). The excess of the proceeds over the *face amount*.

PRESENT VALUE (p. 447). The value today of a future cash inflow or outflow.

PRETAX INCOME (p. 132). Income reported for accounting purposes before deduction for income tax.

PRETAX OPERATING RATE OF RETURN ON TOTAL ASSETS (p. 741). *Operating income* divided by average total *assets* available.

PRICE-EARNINGS RATIO (p. 59). The market price per share of *common stock* divided by the *earnings per share* of common stock.

PRIMARY EARNINGS PER SHARE (p. 509). EPS calculated as if all *common stock* equivalents that dilute EPS were converted to common stock.

PRINCIPAL (p. 433). The amount invested, borrowed, or used on which *interest* accrues.

PRIVATE ACCOUNTING (p. 5). The fields of accounting where individuals work for businesses and government agencies, including the Internal Revenue Service. Compare with *public accounting*.

PRIVATE PLACEMENT (p. 433). A process whereby notes are issued by *corporations* when money is borrowed from a few sources, not from the general public.

PROFITABILITY EVALUATION (p. 131). The assessment of the likelihood of a particular rate of return on an investment.

PROFITS (p. 36). The excess of *revenues* over *expenses*.

PRO FORMA STATEMENT (p. 736). A carefully formulated expression of predicted results.

PROPRIETORSHIP (p. 14). A separate organization with a single owner.

PROTECTIVE COVENANT (p. 434). See *covenant*.

PUBLIC ACCOUNTING (p. 5). The field of accounting in which practitioners render services to the general public on a fee basis. These accountants are licensed by individual states.

PURCHASE ALLOWANCES (p. 214). The reduction of the selling price received by the buyer; generally, the reduction is below a price previously agreed upon.

PURCHASE METHOD (p. 557). A way of accounting for the acquisition of one company by another; based on the market prices paid for the acquired company's *assets*.

PURCHASE RETURNS (p. 214). See *sales returns*. A customer calls these *purchase returns*.

RATE OF RETURN ON COMMON EQUITY (p. 488). Net income less preferred dividends divided by average common equity.

RATE OF RETURN ON STOCKHOLDERS' EQUITY (p. 748). Net income divided by average *stockholders' equity*.

REAL ACCOUNTS (p. 178). Those *accounts* not subject to periodic *closing*, frequently called *permanent accounts* or *balance sheet* accounts.

REAL INTEREST RATE (p. 436). See *effective interest rate*.

REALIZATION (p. 38). The recognition of *revenue*. Generally three tests must be met. First, the earning process must be virtually complete in that the goods or services must be fully rendered. Second, an exchange of resources evidenced by a market *transaction* must occur. Third, the *asset* received must be cash or convertible into cash with reasonable certainty.

REDEMPTION PRICE (p. 487). The *call price*, which is typically 5% to 10% above the *par value* of the *bond* or *stock*.

REGISTERED INSTRUMENT (p. 434). *Bonds* that require the *interest* and maturity payments to be made to specific owners.

REINVESTED EARNINGS (p. 49). See *retained income*.

RELEVANCE (p. 720). The capability of information to make a difference to the decision maker.

RELIABILITY (p. 720). The quality of information that allows users to depend on it to represent the conditions or events that it purports to represent.

REPLACEMENT COST (p. 277). Cost to replenish a given amount of an *asset*.

REPORT FORM (p. 154). A classified *balance sheet* with the *assets* at the top.

REPRESENTATIONAL FAITHFULNESS (p. 720). The correspondence between the accounting numbers and the resources or events that those numbers purport to represent.

RESERVE (p. 503). Has one of three meanings: (1) a restriction of dividend-declaring power as denoted by a specific subdivision of *retained income*, (2) an *offset* to an *asset*, or (3) an estimate of a definite *liability* of indefinite or uncertain amount.

RESERVE METHOD (p. 221). See *allowance method*.

RESIDUAL VALUE (p. 170). The predicted *disposal value* of a *long-lived asset* at the end of its useful life.

RESTRICTED RETAINED INCOME (p. 503). Any part of *retained income* that may not be reduced by *dividend* declarations.

RESULTS OF OPERATIONS (p. 40). See *income statement*.

RETAIL INVENTORY METHOD (p. 339). A procedure for obtaining an inventory valuation for control and for financial statement purposes.

RETAIL METHOD (p. 339). See *retail inventory method*.

RETAINED EARNINGS (p. 49). See *retained income*.

RETAINED INCOME (p. 38). Additional *owners' equity* generated by *profits*.

RETURN ON SALES (p. 737). Net income divided by sales.

RETURN ON STOCKHOLDERS' EQUITY (p. 748). See *rate of return on stockholders' equity*.

RETURN ON TOTAL ASSETS (p. 748). *Income* before *interest expense* divided by average total *assets*.

REVALUATION EQUITY (p. 629). That portion of *stockholders' equity* that shows all accumulated *holding gains* not otherwise shown in *retained income*.

REVENUE EXPENDITURE (p. 391). One with short-term effects expected to benefit only the current accounting year.

REVENUES (p. 36). Generally, a gross increase in *net assets* from delivering goods or services to customers. More specifically, revenues are inflows or other enhancements of *assets* of an enterprise or settlements of its *liabilities* (or a combination of both) during a period from delivering or producing goods, rendering services, or other activities that constitute the enterprise's ongoing major or central operations.

REVERSING ENTRIES (p. 191). Entries that switch back all *debits* and *credits* made in a related preceding *adjusting entry*.

SALES ALLOWANCE (p. 214). Reductions of the selling price (the original price previously agreed upon).

SALES RETURNS (p. 214). Products returned by the customer.

SALVAGE VALUE (p. 377). See *residual value*.

SCRAP VALUE (p. 377). See *residual value*.

SECURITIES AND EXCHANGE COMMISSION (SEC) (p. 55). The federal agency designated by the U.S. Congress as holding the ultimate responsibility for authorizing the *generally accepted accounting principles* for companies whose stock is held by the general investing public.

SHAREHOLDERS' EQUITY (p. 16). See *stockholders' equity*.

SHORT PRESENTATION (p. 432). An item included in the body of a financial statement, but its amount (if any) is not shown on the face of the *balance sheet*. Used often for *contingent liabilities*.

SHORT-TERM INVESTMENT (p. 530). A temporary investment in *marketable securities* of otherwise idle cash.

SHRINKAGE (p. 333). See *inventory shrinkage*.

SIMPLE ENTRY (p. 84). An accounting entry that affects only two *accounts*. Contrast with *compound entry*.

SIMPLE INTEREST (p. 445). For any period, *interest* rate multiplied by an unchanging *principal* amount. Also see *compound interest*.

SINGLE-STEP INCOME STATEMENT (p. 129). One that groups all *revenue* together (sales plus interest and rent *revenues*) and then lists and deducts all *expenses* together without drawing any intermediate subtotals.

SINKING FUND (p. 435). Cash or securities segregated for meeting obligations on bonded debt.

SINKING FUND BONDS (p. 435). *Bonds* with *indentures* that require the issuer to make annual payments to a *sinking fund*.

SOLVENCY DETERMINATION (p. 127). Assessment of the likelihood of an *entity's* ability to meet its financial obligations as they become due.

SOURCE DOCUMENTS (p. 79). The supporting original records of any *transaction*, internal or external, that occurs in the *entity's* operation. They are memorandums of what happened.

SPECIAL JOURNALS (p. 343). *Journals* used for particular types of voluminous *transactions*. Four widely used special journals are for cash receipts, cash disbursements, credit purchases, and credit sales.

SPECIFIC CHARGE-OFF METHOD (p. 219). See *specific write-off method*.

SPECIFIC IDENTIFICATION (p. 269). This inventory method concentrates on the physical tracing of the particular items sold.

SPECIFIC WRITE-OFF METHOD (p. 219). This method of accounting for *bad debt* losses assumes all sales are fully collectible until proved otherwise.

STATED INTEREST RATE (p. 434). See *nominal interest rate*.

STATED VALUE (p. 16). A nominal value of a *stock certificate* that is usually far below the actual cash invested. See *par value*.

STATEMENT OF CASH FLOWS (p. 672). A *statement of changes in financial position* with a focus on cash. Usually explicitly shows the results of operating, investment, and financing activities.

STATEMENT OF CHANGES IN FINANCIAL POSITION (p. 672). A formal explanation of the sources and uses of resources, either the sources and uses of *working capital* or the sources and uses of cash. The statement summarizes the financing and investing activities of the enterprise.

STATEMENT OF EARNINGS (p. 40). See *income statement*.

STATEMENT OF FINANCIAL CONDITION (p. 9). A synonym for *balance sheet*.

STATE OF FINANCIAL POSITION (p. 9). A substitute term for *balance sheet*.

STATEMENT OF INCOME (p. 40). See *income statement*.

STATEMENT OF OPERATIONS (p. 40). See *income statement*.

STATEMENT OF PROFIT AND LOSS (p. 40). See *income statement*.

STATEMENT OF RETAINED INCOME (p. 49). A statement that lists the beginning *balance* of *retained income*, followed by a description of any changes, and the ending *balance*.

STATEMENT OF REVENUES AND EXPENSES (p. 40). See *income statement*.

STATEMENT OF SOURCES AND APPLICATIONS OF FUNDS (p. 672). See *statement of changes in financial position*.

STOCK CERTIFICATE (p. 15). Formal evidence of ownership shares in a *corporation*.

STOCK DIVIDEND (p. 493). A distribution to stockholders of additional shares of any class of the distributing company's stock, without any payment to the company by the stockholders.

STOCKHOLDERS' EQUITY (p. 16). *Owners' equity* of a *corporation*. The excess of *assets* over *liabilities* of a corporation.

STOCK OPTION (p. 505). Special rights usually granted to executives to purchase a *corporation's* capital stock.

STOCK SPLIT (p. 490). Issuance of additional shares for no payments by stockholders, and under conditions indicating that the objective is to increase the number of outstanding shares for the purpose of reducing the unit market price, in order to bring the stock price down into a more popular range.

STRAIGHTFORWARD METHOD (p. 680). The practice of beginning a changes statement with sales or *revenue* and then deducting only those *income statement* items affecting *working capital*.

STRAIGHT-LINE DEPRECIATION (p. 377). A method of allocating the cost of plant *assets* in equal amounts based on unit of time (years).

SUBORDINATED (p. 433). A creditor claim that is junior to other creditor claims.

SUBORDINATED DEBENTURE (p. 433). *Bonds* that are junior to the other general creditors in the exercise of claims against the total *assets*.

SUBSIDIARY (p. 536). A *corporation* owned or controlled by a parent company, through the ownership of more than 50% of the voting stock.

SUBSIDIARY LEDGER (p. 93). A supporting *ledger* that provides details for a specific *account* in the *general ledger*.

SUM-OF-THE-YEARS'-DIGITS DEPRECIATION (SYD) (p. 379). A popular form of *accelerated depreciation* where the sum of the digits is the total of the numbers representing the years of life.

T-ACCOUNT (p. 76). A *ledger* account that takes the form of the capital letter *T*. It is useful for discussion and learning, but too informal for using in actual books of account.

TANGIBLE ASSETS (p. 374). See *fixed assets*.

TAX ALLOCATION (p. 590). See *interperiod tax allocation*.

TAX CREDIT (p. 582). Direct reductions in a company's income taxes.

TEMPORARY ACCOUNTS (p. 178). See *nominal accounts*.

TERMINAL VALUE (p. 170). See *residual value*.

TIME-SERIES COMPARISONS (p. 736). Comparison of a company's financial ratios with its own historical ratios.

TIMES INTEREST EARNED (p. 751). *Income* before *interest expense* and income taxes divided by interest expense.

TIMING DIFFERENCES (p. 588). Measures of the income tax effect of transactions that affect the computation of *pretax income* reported to shareholders either earlier or later than they affect taxable *income* reported to the income tax authorities.

TOTAL ASSET TURNOVER (p. 742). Sales divided by average total *assets* available.

TRADE DISCOUNTS (p. 215). Those discounts that are based on some larger selling price (list price) and apply a reduction thereto to arrive at the real selling price (invoice price).

TRADEMARKS (p. 395). Distinctive identifications of a manufactured product or of a service taking the form of a name, a sign, a slogan, a logo, or an emblem.

TRADE RECEIVABLES (p. 218). See *accounts receivable*.

TRADING ON THE EQUITY (p. 748). Using borrowed money at fixed *interest* rates with the objective of enhancing the *rate of return on common equity*.

TRANSACTION (p. 10). Any event that affects the financial position of an *entity* and requires recording.

TREASURY STOCK (p. 483). A corporation's issued stock that has subsequently been repurchased by the company and not retired.

TRIAL BALANCE (p. 92). A list of all *accounts* with their *balances*.

TRUE INTEREST RATE (p. 436). See *effective interest rate*.

TRUST INDENTURE (p. 434). A contract whereby the issuing *corporation* of a *bond* promises a trustee that it will abide by stated provisions.

UNDERWRITERS (p. 435). A group of investment bankers that buys an entire *bond* or stock issue from a *corporation* and then sells the bonds to the general investment public.

UNDISTRIBUTED EARNINGS (p. 49). See *retained income*.

UNEARNED INCOME (p. 118). See *unearned revenue*.

UNEARNED REVENUE (p. 117). *Revenue* received or recorded before it is earned.

UNEXPIRED COSTS (p. 43). Any *expenditures* benefiting the future; any *asset*, including prepaid *expenses*, normally appearing on a *balance sheet*.

UNIT DEPRECIATION (p. 378). A method based on units of service when physical wear and tear is the dominating influence on the useful life of the *asset*.

UNLIMITED LIABILITY (p. 486). Legal responsibility not limited by law or contract; personal *assets* can be seized to satisfy corporate debts.

UNREGISTERED INSTRUMENT (p. 434). *Bonds* generally issued by American governmental bodies and requiring interest to be paid to the individual who presents the *interest* coupons attached to the bond.

UNSUBORDINATED DEBENTURES (p. 433). *Bonds* unsecured by the pledge of specific property. The holders of such bonds have the same general priority as ordinary creditors, such as those reflected in *accounts payable*.

VERIFIABILITY (p. 95). See *objectivity*.

VOUCHER (p. 350). A form that verifies a *transaction* and authorizes the writing of a check. Sometimes called a *disbursement voucher*.

VOUCHER REGISTER (p. 350). A *special journal* that is a central part of a *voucher system*.

VOUCHER SYSTEM (p. 350). A system for controlling cash disbursements.

WEIGHTED-AVERAGE COST (p. 270). An average that is affected by the relative number of items and their unit prices rather than just their unit prices alone.

WORKING CAPITAL (p. 126). The excess of *current assets* over *current liabilities*.

WORKING CAPITAL CYCLE (p. 673). The continuous rythmic process of using *working capital* to generate additional working capital. It begins with the purchase of inventory, whether for cash or on *open account*; it ends with a sale, regardless of whether cash is received or a receivable is created.

WORKING CAPITAL FORM (p. 154). A *classified balance sheet* whereby the *current assets* are listed first and the *current liabilities* are deducted, to show *working capital* explicitly.

WORKING CAPITAL RATIO (p. 127). See *current ratio*.

WORKING PAPER (p. 183). See *work sheet*.

WORK SHEET (p. 183). A columnar approach to moving from a *trial balance* to the finished financial statements. Also called *working paper*. In auditing, the term *working papers* has a broader meaning. It refers to all schedules, analyses, memoranda, and so on, prepared by an auditor while making an examination.

YIELD RATE (p. 436). See *effective interest rate*.

INDEX

Current yield, 434
Cutoff errors, 342

D

Datapoint Corporation, 342
Data processing, 94, 188–91, 343
Debentures, 433
Debits, 78–79, 88, 90
Debt:
    vs. equity, 749–51
    reasons for, 747–48
    (*see also* Bonds; Long-term liabilities;
    Notes payable)
Debt leverage, 748–49
Debt-to-equity ratios, 442, 737, 741
Decisions, 2, 4
Deductible items, 582–83
Deferral method, 583–85
Deferred charges, 397
Deferred credit (*see* Unearned revenue)
Deferred income taxes, 587–98, 694
Deferred revenue (*see* Unearned revenue)
Deloitte Haskins & Sells (USA), 607–9
Depletion, 373, 394
Deposits, returnable, 430
Depreciable amount, 389
Depreciable value (*see* Residual value)
Depreciation, 40, 43, 373, 376–86
    accelerated, 379–86, 586–87
    Accelerated Cost Recovery System, 381–
    82, 585–91
    accumulated (*see* Accumulated deprecia-
    tion)
    on balance sheet, 378, 385
    vs. cash generation, 383–86
    declining balance, 379–81, 586
    defined, 377
    estimates, changes in, 388–90
    in general, 376–77
    in general journal, 88, 89, 161, 169, 171,
    173, 177
    in general ledger, 88, 91, 93, 163, 169,
    171, 173, 175, 177
    income measurement methods and,
    638–39
    on income statement, 41, 377, 386
    income taxes and, 382–86, 585–94
    for parts of a year, 390–91
    on statement of changes in financial po-
    sition, 681
    straight-line, 40, 171, 377–86, 586–91
    sum-of-the-years'-digits, 379, 381, 586,
    587
    unit, 378
Digital Equipment Corporation, 442
Dilution, 499
Direct method, 680
Disbursement voucher, 350
Discontinued operations, 515–16
Discount amortization, 436–38
Discounts:
    bond, 435–39, 453–56, 533, 534, 694
    notes payable, 441–42, 456–57
    purchase, 227
    sales, 215–18, 240–42
Disposal value (*see* Residual value)
Dividend arrearages, 485
Dividend-payout ratio, 61, 737
Dividend policy, 52
Dividend ratios, 737

Dividends:
    amount declared, 492
    in balance sheet equation, 48–49
    cash, 52
    common stock vs. preferred stock, 484
    cumulative, 484–86
    declaration of, 491–92
    defined, 49, 491
    in general journal, 161, 168, 178, 492,
    494, 496–98
    in general ledger, 162, 168, 175, 178
    intercorporate investments and, 534–36
    misconceptions about, 52
    noncumulative, 484–85
    steps in paying, 52–53
    stock, 492–96
    stock splits compared with, 495–96
Dividend-yield ratio, 60–61, 737
Documentation, 79
Dollar signs, use of, 50
Double-declining-balance depreciation,
    379–81, 586
Double-entry system, 77–79
Double-underscores, use of, 50
Doubtful accounts (*see* Bad debts)
Dun & Bradstreet, Inc., 738, 740
Duties:
    rotation of, 323
    separation of, 321–22

E

Earnings, 36, 40
    abnormal, 549–51
    retained, reinvested, or undistributed
    (*see* Retained income)
    statement of (*see* Income statement)
    (*see also* Income)
Earnings cycle (*see* Operating cycle)
Earnings multiple (*see* Price-earnings ra-
    tio)
Earnings-per-share (EPS), 58–59, 507–10,
    514, 516, 737
Effective interest rate, 436
Efficient markets, 743–45
Electronic spreadsheets, 179, 187–88
Entity concept, 14–15, 725
Equipment:
    acquisition cost of, 375–76
    on balance sheet, 18–20, 127, 128
    in balance sheet equation, 11, 13
    current-cost disclosure of, 638–39, 649
    depreciation of (*see* Depreciation)
    disposal of, 173
    gains and losses on sale of, 386–89, 694
    in general journal, 83, 84, 88, 89, 161,
    169, 171, 173
    in general ledger, 83, 84, 88, 91, 93, 163,
    169, 171, 173
Equity:
    vs. debt, 749–51
    FASB definition of, 723
    trading on, 748–49
    (*see also* Liabilities; Owner's equity)
Equity method investments, 694–96
Equity securities (*see* Capital stock; Com-
    mon stock; Preferred stock)
Errors:
    control of (*see* Internal accounting con-
    trol)
    inventory, 179–80, 281–83
Exchanges, 503–4

Expenditures, 391–93
Expenses, 35–40
    accrual of unrecorded, 118–22
    bad debts, 220–23, 236–38
    in balance sheet equation, 35–38, 42
    cost of goods sold (*see* Cost of goods sold)
    cost recovery concept and, 39
    deductible, 582–83
    defined, 36
    depreciation (*see* Depreciation)
    FASB definition of, 723
    in general journal, 86–90, 118–20, 160–
    61, 165–70, 176–77, 188–89
    in general ledger, 86–88, 90, 91, 93, 162–
    63, 165–70, 175–77
    on income statement, 41, 43–44, 129,
    130, 132–35
    matching concept and, 39
    rent (*see* Rent expense)
    timing differences and, 601, 602
    wages (*see* Wages)
Expiration of unexpired costs, 43–44, 116,
    121, 122
Explicit transactions, 115
Export disclosures, 552
Extraordinary items, 514–15
Exxon Corporation, 498

F

F.O.B. destination, 227
F.O.B. shipping point, 227
Fair values of individual assets, 549
FASB (*see* Financial Accounting Stan-
    dards Board)
Federal Managers' Financial Integrity Act
    of 1982, 318*n*
FIFO (*see* First-in, first-out inventory
    method)
Financial accounting, 4
Financial Accounting Standards Board
    (FASB), 55–56, 727–28
    on capital maintenance concepts, 626
    Concepts Statement No. 1, 718
    Concepts Statement No. 2, 718–19
    Concepts Statement No. 3, 721–22
    Concepts Statement No. 5, 722–24
    conceptual framework of, 717–30
    Statement No. 2, 396
    Statement No. 3, 438
    Statement No. 13, 458, 459
    Statement No. 14, 551–52
    Statement No. 33, 632–34, 637, 645, 647,
    650–52
    Statement No. 34, 375
    Statement No. 87, 457
    Statement No. 88, 457
    Statement on Objectives, 58–59
Financial capital maintenance, 626
Financial condition, statements of (*see* Bal-
    ance sheet; Statement of changes in fi-
    nancial position)
Financial leverage, 748–49
Financial management, 671, 743
Financial position, statements of (*see* Bal-
    ance sheet; Statement of changes in fi-
    nancial position)
Financial ratios (*see* Ratios)
Financial reporting objectives, 718
Financial statements, 6
    analysis of, 733–45
    audits and, 7